T0180321

Lecture Notes in Computer Science 9914

Commenced Publication in 1973
Founding and Former Series Editors:
Gerhard Goos, Juris Hartmanis, and Jan van Leeuwen

Gang Hua · Hervé Jégou (Eds.)

Computer Vision –
ECCV 2016 Workshops

Amsterdam, The Netherlands, October 8–10 and 15–16, 2016
Proceedings, Part II

 Springer

Editors
Gang Hua
Microsoft Research Asia
Beijing
China

Hervé Jégou
Facebook AI Research (FAIR)
Menlo Park, CA
USA

ISSN 0302-9743   ISSN 1611-3349   (electronic)
Lecture Notes in Computer Science
ISBN 978-3-319-48880-6   ISBN 978-3-319-48881-3   (eBook)
DOI 10.1007/978-3-319-48881-3

Library of Congress Control Number: 2016955507

LNCS Sublibrary: SL6 – Image Processing, Computer Vision, Pattern Recognition, and Graphics

Printed on acid-free paper

This Springer imprint is published by Springer Nature
The registered company is Springer International Publishing AG
The registered company address is: Gewerbestrasse 11, 6330 Cham, Switzerland

Foreword

Welcome to the proceedings of the 2016 edition of the European Conference on Computer Vision held in Amsterdam! It is safe to say that the European Conference on Computer Vision is one of the top conferences in computer vision. It is good to reiterate the history of the conference to see the broad base the conference has built in the 13 editions. First held in 1990 in Antibes (France), it was followed by subsequent conferences in Santa Margherita Ligure (Italy) in 1992, Stockholm (Sweden) in 1994, Cambridge (UK) in 1996, Freiburg (Germany) in 1998, Dublin (Ireland) in 2000, Copenhagen (Denmark) in 2002, Prague (Czech Republic) in 2004, Graz (Austria) in 2006, Marseille (France) in 2008, Heraklion (Greece) in 2010, Florence (Italy) in 2012, and Zürich (Switzerland) in 2014.

For the 14th edition, many people worked hard to provide attendees with a most warm welcome while enjoying the best science. The Program Committee, Bastian Leibe, Jiri Matas, Nicu Sebe, and Max Welling, did an excellent job. Apart from the scientific program, the workshops were selected and handled by Hervé Jégou and Gang Hua, and the tutorials by Jacob Verbeek and Rita Cucchiara. Thanks for the great job. The coordination with the subsequent ACM Multimedia offered an opportunity to expand the tutorials with an additional invited session, offered by the University of Amsterdam and organized together with the help of ACM Multimedia.

Of the many people who worked hard as local organizers, we would like to single out Martine de Wit of the UvA Conference Office, who delicately and efficiently organized the main body. Also the local organizers Hamdi Dibeklioglu, Efstratios Gavves, Jan van Gemert, Thomas Mensink, and Mihir Jain had their hands full. As a venue, we chose the Royal Theatre Carré located on the canals of the Amstel River in downtown Amsterdam. Space in Amsterdam is sparse, so it was a little tighter than usual. The university lent us their downtown campuses for the tutorials and the workshops. A relatively new thing was the industry and the sponsors for which Ronald Poppe and Peter de With did a great job, while Andy Bagdanov and John Schavemaker arranged the demos. Michael Wilkinson took care to make Yom Kippur as comfortable as possible for those for whom it is an important day. We thank Marc Pollefeys, Alberto del Bimbo, and Virginie Mes for their advice and help behind the scenes. We thank all the anonymous volunteers for their hard and precise work. We also thank our generous sponsors. Their support is an essential part of the program. It is good to see such a level of industrial interest in what our community is doing!

Amsterdam does not need any introduction. Please emerge yourself but do not drown in it, have a nice time.

October 2016

Theo Gevers
Arnold Smeulders

Preface

It is our great pleasure to present the workshop proceedings of the 14th European Conference on Computer Vision, which was held during October 8–16, 2016, in Amsterdam, The Netherlands. We were delighted that the main conference of ECCV 2016 was accompanied by 26 workshops. The workshop proceedings are presented in multiple Springer LNCS volumes.

This year, the 2016 ACM International Conference on Multimedia was collocated with ECCV 2016. As a synergistic arrangement, four out of the 26 ECCV workshops, whose topics are of interest to both the computer vision and multimedia communities, were held together with selected 2016 ACM Multimedia workshops.

We received 44 workshop proposals on a broad set of topics related to computer vision. The high quality of the proposals made the selection process rather difficult. Owing to space limitation, 27 proposals were accepted, among which two proposals were merged to form a single workshop due to overlapping themes.

The final 26 workshops complemented the main conference program well. The workshop topics present a good orchestration of new trends and traditional issues, as well as fundamental technologies and novel applications. We would like to thank all the workshop organizers for their unreserved efforts to make the workshop sessions a great success.

October 2016

Hervé Jégou
Gang Hua

Organization

General Chairs

Theo Gevers   University of Amsterdam, The Netherlands
Arnold Smeulders   University of Amsterdam, The Netherlands

Program Committee Co-chairs

Bastian Leibe   RWTH Aachen, Germany
Jiri Matas   Czech Technical University, Czech Republic
Nicu Sebe   University of Trento, Italy
Max Welling   University of Amsterdam, The Netherlands

Honorary Chair

Jan Koenderink   Delft University of Technology, The Netherlands
     and KU Leuven, Belgium

Advisory Program Chair

Luc van Gool   ETH Zurich, Switzerland

Advisory Workshop Chair

Josef Kittler   University of Surrey, UK

Advisory Conference Chair

Alberto del Bimbo   University of Florence, Italy

Local Arrangements Chairs

Hamdi Dibeklioglu   Delft University of Technology, The Netherlands
Efstratios Gavves   University of Amsterdam, The Netherlands
Jan van Gemert   Delft University of Technology, The Netherlands
Thomas Mensink   University of Amsterdam, The Netherlands
Michael Wilkinson   University of Groningen, The Netherlands

Workshop Chairs

Hervé Jégou   Facebook AI Research, USA
Gang Hua   Microsoft Research Asia, China

Tutorial Chairs

Jacob Verbeek   Inria Grenoble, France
Rita Cucchiara   University of Modena and Reggio Emilia, Italy

Poster Chairs

Jasper Uijlings   University of Edinburgh, UK
Roberto Valenti   Sightcorp, The Netherlands

Publication Chairs

Albert Ali Salah   Boğaziçi University, Turkey
Robby T. Tan   Yale-NUS College and National University
                            of Singapore, Singapore

Video Chair

Mihir Jain   University of Amsterdam, The Netherlands

Demo Chairs

John Schavemaker   Twnkls, The Netherlands
Andy Bagdanov   University of Florence, Italy

Social Media Chair

Efstratios Gavves   University of Amsterdam, The Netherlands

Industrial Liaison Chairs

Ronald Poppe   Utrecht University, The Netherlands
Peter de With   Eindhoven University of Technology, The Netherlands

Conference Coordinator, Accommodation, and Finance

Conference Office

Martine de Wit   University of Amsterdam, The Netherlands
Melanie Venverloo   University of Amsterdam, The Netherlands
Niels Klein   University of Amsterdam, The Netherlands

Workshop Organizers

W01 — Datasets and Performance Analysis in Early Vision

Michael Goesele	TU Darmstadt, Germany
Bernd Jähne	Heidelberg University, Germany
Katrin Honauer	Heidelberg University, Germany
Michael Waechter	TU Darmstadt, Germany

W02 — Visual Analysis of Sketches

Yi-Zhe Song	Queen Mary University of London, UK
John Collomosse	University of Surrey, UK
Metin Sezgin	Koç University, Turkey
James Z. Wang	The Pennsylvania State University, USA

W03 — Biological and Artificial Vision

Kandan Ramakrishnan	University of Amsterdam, The Netherlands
Radoslaw M. Cichy	Free University Berlin, Germany
Sennay Ghebreab	University of Amsterdam, The Netherlands
H. Steven Scholte	University of Amsterdam, The Netherlands
Arnold W.M. Smeulders	University of Amsterdam, The Netherlands

W04 — Brave New Ideas For Motion Representations

Efstratios Gavves	University of Amsterdam, The Netherlands
Basura Fernando	The Australian National University, Australia
Jan van Gemert	Delft University of Technology, The Netherlands

W05 — Joint ImageNet and MS COCO Visual Recognition Challenge

Wei Liu	The University of North Carolina at Chapel Hill, USA
Genevieve Patterson	Brown University, USA
M. Ronchi	California Institute of Technology, USA
Yin Cui	Cornell Tech, USA
Tsung-Yi Lin	Cornell Tech, USA
Larry Zitnick	Facebook AI Research, USA
Piotr Dollár	Facebook AI Research, USA
Olga Russakovsky	Carnegie Mellon University, USA
Jia Deng	University of Michigan, USA
Fei–Fei Li	Stanford University, USA
Alexander C. Berg	The University of North Carolina at Chapel Hill, USA

W06 — Geometry Meets Deep Learning

Emanuele Rodolà	Università della Svizzera Italiana, Switzerland
Jonathan Masci	Università della Svizzera Italiana, Switzerland
Pierre Vandergheynst	Ecole Polytechnique Fédérale de Lausanne, Switzerland

Sanja Fidler   University of Toronto, Canada
Xiaowei Zhou   University of Pennsylvania, USA
Kostas Daniilidis   University of Pennsylvania, USA

W07 — Action and Anticipation for Visual Learning

Dinesh Jayaraman   University of Texas at Austin, USA
Kristen Grauman   University of Texas at Austin, USA
Sergey Levine   University of Washington, USA

W08 — Computer Vision for Road Scene Understanding and Autonomous Driving

Jose Alvarez   NICTA, Australia
Mathieu Salzmann   Ecole Polytechnique Fédérale de Lausanne,
                              Switzerland
Lars Petersson   NICTA, Australia
Fredrik Kahl   Chalmers University of Technology, Sweden
Bart Nabbe   Faraday Future, USA

W09 — Challenge on Automatic Personality Analysis

Sergio Escalera   Computer Vision Center (UAB) and University
                              of Barcelona, Spain
Xavier Baró   Universitat Oberta de Catalunya and Computer Vision
                              Center (UAB), Spain
Isabelle Guyon   Université Paris-Saclay, France, and ChaLearn, USA
Hugo Jair Escalante   INAOE, Mexico
Víctor Ponce López   Computer Vision Center (UAB) and University
                              of Barcelona, Spain

W10 — BioImage Computing

Patrick Bouthemy   Inria Research Institute, Switzerland
Fred Hamprecht   Heidelberg University, Germany
Erik Meijering   Erasmus University Medical Center, The Netherlands
Thierry Pécot   Inria, France
Pietro Perona   California Institute of Technology, USA
Carsten Rother   TU Dresden, Germany

W11 — Benchmarking Multi-Target Tracking: MOTChallenge

Laura Leal-Taixé   TU Munich, Germany
Anton Milan   University of Adelaide, Australia
Konrad Schindler   ETH Zürich, Switzerland
Daniel Cremers   TU Munich, Germany
Ian Reid   University of Adelaide, Australia
Stefan Roth   TU Darmstadt, Germany

W12 — Assistive Computer Vision and Robotics

Giovanni Maria Farinella	University of Catania, Italy
Marco Leo	CNR – Institute of Applied Sciences and Intelligent Systems, Italy
Gerard G. Medioni	University of Southern California, USA
Mohan Trivedi	University of California, San Diego, USA

W13 — Transferring and Adapting Source Knowledge in Computer Vision

Wen Li	ETH Zürich, Switzerland
Tatiana Tommasi	University of North Carolina at Chapel Hill, USA
Francesco Orabona	Yahoo Research, NY, USA
David Vázquez	CVC and Universitat Autònoma de Barcelona, Spain
Antonio M. López	CVC and Universitat Autònoma de Barcelona, Spain
Jiaolong Xu	CVC and Universitat Autònoma de Barcelona, Spain
Hugo Larochelle	Twitter Cortex, USA

W14 — Recovering 6D Object Pose

Tae-Kyun Kim	Imperial College London, UK
Jiri Matas	Czech Technical University, Czech Republic
Vincent Lepetit	Technical University Graz, Germany
Carsten Rother	Technical University Dresden, Germany
Ales Leonardis	University of Birmingham, UK
Krzysztof Wallas	Poznan University of Technology, Poland
Carsten Steger	MVTec GmbH, Germany
Rigas Kouskouridas	Imperial College London, UK

W15 — Robust Reading

Dimosthenis Karatzas	CVC and Universitat Autònoma de Barcelona, Spain
Masakazu Iwamura	Osaka Prefecture University, Japan
Jiri Matas	Czech Technical University, Czech Republic
Pramod Sankar Kompalli	Flipkart.com, India
Faisal Shafait	National University of Sciences and Technology, Pakistan

W16 — 3D Face Alignment in the Wild and Challenge

Jeffrey Cohn	Carnegie Mellon University and University of Pittsburgh, USA
Laszlo Jeni	Carnegie Mellon University, USA
Nicu Sebe	University of Trento, Italy
Sergey Tulyakov	University of Trento, Italy
Lijun Yin	Binghamton University, USA

W17 — Egocentric Perception, Interaction, and Computing

Giuseppe Serra	University of Modena and Reggio Emilia, Italy
Rita Cucchiara	University of Modena and Reggio Emilia, Italy
Walterio Mayol-Cuevas	University of Bristol, UK
Andreas Bulling	Max Planck Institute for Informatics, Germany
Dima Damen	University of Bristol, UK

W18 — Local Features: State of the Art, Open Problems, and Performance Evaluation

Jiri Matas	Czech Technical University, Czech Republic
Krystian Mikolajczyk	Imperial College London, UK
Tinne Tuytelaars	KU Leuven, Belgium
Andrea Vedaldi	University of Oxford, UK
Vassileios Balntas	Imperial College London, UK
Karel Lenc	University of Oxford, UK

W19 — Crowd Understanding

François Brémond	Inria Sophia Antipolis, France
Vít Líbal	Honeywell ACS Global Labs Prague, Czech Republic
Andrea Cavallaro	Queen Mary University of London, UK
Tomas Pajdla	Czech Technical University, Czech Republic
Petr Palatka	Neovision, Czech Republic
Jana Trojanova	Honeywell ACS Global Labs Prague, Czech Republic

W20 — Video Segmentation

Thomas Brox	University of Freiburg, Germany
Katerina Fragkiadaki	Google Research, USA
Fabio Galasso	OSRAM GmbH, Germany
Fuxin Li	Oregon State University, USA
James M. Rehg	Georgia Institute of Technology, USA
Bernt Schiele	Max Planck Institute Informatics and Saarland University, Germany
Michael Ying Yang	University of Twente, The Netherlands

W21 — The Visual Object Tracking Challenge Workshop

Matej Kristan	University of Ljubljana, Slovenia
Aleš Leonardis	University of Birmingham, UK
Jiri Matas	Czech Technical University in Prague, Czech Republic
Michael Felsberg	Linköping University, Sweden
Roman Pflugfelder	Austrian Institute of Technology, Austria

W22 — Web-Scale Vision and Social Media

Lamberto Ballan	Stanford University, USA
Marco Bertini	University of Florence, Italy
Thomas Mensink	University of Amsterdam, The Netherlands

W23 — Computer Vision for Audio visual Media

Jean-Charles Bazin	Disney Research, USA
Zhengyou Zhang	Microsoft Research, USA
Wilmot Li	Adobe Research, USA

W24 — Computer Vision for Art Analysis

Joao Paulo Costeira	Instituto Superior Técnico, Portugal
Gustavo Carneiro	University of Adelaide, Australia
Alessio Del Bue	Istituto Italiano di Tecnologia (IIT), Italy
Ahmed Elgammal	Rutgers University, USA
Peter Hall	University of Bath, UK
Ann-Sophie Lehmann	University of Groningen, The Netherlands
Hans Brandhorst	Iconclass and Arkyves, The Netherlands
Emily L. Spratt	Princeton University, USA

W25 — Virtual/Augmented Reality for Visual Artificial Intelligence

Antonio M. López	CVC and Universitat Autònoma de Barcelona, Spain
Adrien Gaidon	Xerox Research Center Europe (XRCE), France
German Ros	CVC and Universitat Autònoma de Barcelona, Spain
Eleonora Vig	German Aerospace Center (DLR), Germany
David Vázquez	CVC and Universitat Autònoma de Barcelona, Spain
Hao Su	Stanford University, USA
Florent Perronnin	Facebook AI Research (FAIR), France

W26 — Joint Workshop on Storytelling with Images and Videos and Large-Scale Movie Description and Understanding Challenge

Gunhee Kim	Seoul National University, South Korea
Leonid Sigal	Disney Research Pittsburgh, USA
Kristen Grauman	University of Texas at Austin, USA
Tamara Berg	University of North Carolina at Chapel Hill, USA
Anna Rohrbach	Max Planck Institute for Informatics, Germany
Atousa Torabi	Disney Research Pittsburgh, USA
Tegan Maharaj	École Polytechnique de Montréal, Canada
Marcus Rohrbach	University of California, Berkeley, USA
Christopher Pal	École Polytechnique de Montréal, Canada
Aaron Courville	Université de Montréal, Canada
Bernt Schiele	Max Planck Institute for Informatics, Germany

Contents – Part II

W19 - Crowd Understanding

W21 - The Visual Object Tracking Challenge Workshop

W08 - Computer Vision for Road Scene Understanding and Autonomous Driving (Continued)

Real-Time Semantic Segmentation with Label Propagation

Rasha Sheikh, Martin Garbade$^{(\boxtimes)}$, and Juergen Gall

Computer Science Institute III, University of Bonn, Bonn, Germany
rasha@uni-bonn.de, {garbade,gall}@iai.uni-bonn.de

Abstract. Despite of the success of convolutional neural networks for semantic image segmentation, CNNs cannot be used for many applications due to limited computational resources. Even efficient approaches based on random forests are not efficient enough for real-time performance in some cases. In this work, we propose an approach based on superpixels and label propagation that reduces the runtime of a random forest approach by factor 192 while increasing the segmentation accuracy.

1 Introduction

Although convolutional neural networks have shown a great success for semantic image segmentation in the last years [1–3], fast inference can only be achieved by massive parallelism as offered by modern GPUs. For many applications like mobile platforms or unmanned aerial vehicles, however, the power consumption matters and GPUs are often not available. A server-client solution is not always an option due to latency and limited bandwidth. There is therefore a need for very efficient approaches that segment images in real-time on single-threaded architectures.

In this work, we analyze in-depth how design choices affect the accuracy and runtime of random forests and propose an efficient superpixel-based approach with label propagation for videos. As illustrated in Fig. 1, we use a very efficient quadtree representation for superpixels. The superpixels are then classified by random forests. For classification, we investigate two methods. For the first method, we use the empirical class distribution and for the second method we model the spatial distributions of class labels by Gaussians. For video data, we propose label propagation to reduce the runtime without substantially decreasing the segmentation accuracy. An additional spatial smoothing even improves the accuracy.

We evaluate our approach on the CamVid dataset [4]. Compared to a standard random forest, we reduce the runtime by factor 192 while increasing the global pixel accuracy by 4 % points. A comparison with state-of-the-art approaches in terms of accuracy shows that the accuracy of our approach is competitive while achieving real-time performance on a single-threaded architecture.

© Springer International Publishing Switzerland 2016
G. Hua and H. Jégou (Eds.): ECCV 2016 Workshops, Part II, LNCS 9914, pp. 3–14, 2016.
DOI: 10.1007/978-3-319-48881-3_1

Fig. 1. For efficient segmentation, we use a quadtree to create superpixels and classify the superpixels by a random forests.

2 Related Work

A popular approach for semantic segmentation uses a variety of features like appearance, depth, or edges and classifies each pixel by a classifier like random forest or boosting [4,5]. Since pixel-wise classification can be very noisy, conditional random fields have been used to model the spatial relations of pixels and obtain a smooth segmentation [6,7]. Conditional random fields, however, are too expensive for many applications. In [8], a structured random forest has been proposed that predicts not a single label per pixel but the labels of the entire neighborhood. Merging the predicted neighborhoods into a single semantic segmentation of an image, however, is also costly. To speed up the segmentation, the learning and prediction of random forests has been also implemented for GPUs [9].

In the last years, convolutional neural networks have become very popular for semantic segmentation [1,2,10]. Recent approaches achieve accurate segmentation results even without CRFs [3]. They, however, require GPUs for fast inference and are too slow for single-threaded architectures. Approaches that combine random forests and neural networks have been proposed as well [8], however, at the cost of increasing the runtime compared to random forests.

Instead of segmenting each frame, segmentation labels can also be propagated to the next frame. Grundmann et al. [11] for example use a hierarchical graph-based algorithm to segment video sequences into spatiotemporal regions. A more advanced approach [12] proposes a label propagation algorithm using a variational EM based inference strategy. More recently, a fast label propagation method based on sparse feature tracking has been proposed [13]. Although our method can be used in combination with any real-time label propagation method like [13], we use a very simple approach that propagates the labels of quadtree superpixels, which have the same location and similar appearance as in the preceding frame.

3   Semantic Segmentation

We briefly describe a standard random forests for semantic image segmentation in Sect. 3.1. In Sect. 3.2, we propose a superpixel approach that can be combined with label propagation in the context of videos.

3.1   Random Forests

Random forests consists of an ensemble of trees [14]. In the context of semantic image segmentation, each tree infers for an image pixel $\mathbf{x}$ the class probability $p(c|\mathbf{x};\theta_t)$ where c is a semantic class and θ_t are the parameters of the tree t. The parameters θ_t are learned in a suboptimal fashion by sampling from the training data and the parameter space Θ. A robust estimator is then obtained by averaging the predictors

$$p(c|\mathbf{x}) = \frac{1}{T} \sum_t p(c|\mathbf{x};\theta_t), \tag{1}$$

where T is the number of trees in the forest. A segmentation of an image can then be obtained by taking the class with highest probability (1) for each pixel.

Learning the parameters θ_t for a tree t is straightforward. First, pixels from the training data are sampled which provide a set of training pairs $\mathcal{S} = \{(\mathbf{x},c)\}$. The tree is then constructed recursively, where at each node n a weak classifier is learned by maximizing the information gain

$$\theta_n = \underset{\theta \in \tilde{\Theta}}{\operatorname{argmax}} \left\{ H(\mathcal{S}_n) - \sum_{i \in \{0,1\}} \frac{|\mathcal{S}_{n,i}|}{|\mathcal{S}_n|} H(\mathcal{S}_{n,i}) \right\}. \tag{2}$$

While $\mathcal{S}_n$ denotes the training data arriving at the node n, $\tilde{\Theta}$ denotes the set of sampled parameters and $H(\mathcal{S}) = -\sum_c p(c;\mathcal{S}) \log p(c;\mathcal{S})$ where $p(c;\mathcal{S})$ is the empirical class distribution in the set $\mathcal{S}$. Each weak classifier $f_\theta(\mathbf{x})$ with parameter θ splits $\mathcal{S}_n$ into the two sets $\mathcal{S}_{n,i} = \{(\mathbf{x},c) \in \mathcal{S}_n : f_\theta(\mathbf{x}) = i\}$ with $i \in \{0,1\}$. After the best weak classifier θ_n is determined, $\mathcal{S}_{n,0}$ and $\mathcal{S}_{n,1}$ is forwarded to the left or right child, respectively. The growing of the tree is terminated when a node becomes pure or $\mathcal{S}_n < 100$ (found using cross-validation). Finally, the empirical class distribution $p(c;\mathcal{S}_l)$ is stored at each leaf node l.

As weak classifiers $f_\theta(\mathbf{x})$, we use four types that were proposed in [5]:

$$R(\mathbf{x} + \mathbf{x}_1, w_1, h_1, k) - R(\mathbf{x} + \mathbf{x}_2, w_2, h_2, k) \leq \tau \tag{3}$$

$$R(\mathbf{x} + \mathbf{x}_1, w_1, h_1, k) + R(\mathbf{x} + \mathbf{x}_2, w_2, h_2, k) \leq \tau \tag{4}$$

$$|R(\mathbf{x} + \mathbf{x}_1, w_1, h_1, k) - R(\mathbf{x} + \mathbf{x}_2, w_2, h_2, k)| \leq \tau \tag{5}$$

$$R(\mathbf{x} + \mathbf{x}_1, w_1, h_1, k) \leq \tau. \tag{6}$$

The term $R(\mathbf{x} + \mathbf{x}_1, w_1, h_1, k)$ denotes the average value of feature channel k in the rectangle region centered at $\mathbf{x} + \mathbf{x}_1$ with $\mathbf{x}_1 \in [-100,\ldots,100]$, width

$w_1 \in [1, \ldots, 24]$, and height $h_1 \in [1, \ldots, 24]$. As feature channels, we use the CIELab color space and the x- and y-gradients extracted by a Sobel filter. To generate $\tilde{\Theta}$, we randomly sample 500 weak classifiers without τ and for each sampled weak classifier we sample τ 20 times, i.e., $\tilde{\Theta}$ consists of 10,000 randomly sampled weak classifiers.

3.2 Superpixels with Label Propagation

A single tree as described in Sect. 3.1 requires on a modern single-threaded architecture 1500 ms for segmenting an image with 960 × 720 resolution. This is insufficient for real-time applications and we therefore propose to classify superpixels. In order to keep the overhead by computing superpixels as small as possible, we use an efficient quadtree structure. As shown in Fig. 1, the regions are not quadratic but have the same aspect ratio as the original image. Up to depth 3, we divide all cells. For deeper quadtrees, we divide a cell into four cells if the variance of the intensity, which is in the range of 0 and 255, within a cell is larger than 49. Instead of classifying each pixel in the image, we classify the center of each superpixel and assign the predicted class to all pixels in the superpixel. For training, we sample 1000 superpixels per training image and assign the class label that occurs most frequently in the superpixel.

While (1) uses the empirical class distribution $p(c; \mathcal{S}_l)$ stored in the leaves for classification, it discards the spatial distribution of the class labels within and between the superpixels ending in a single leaf. Instead of reducing the pixel-wise labels of the training data to a single label per superpixel, we model the spatial distribution by a Gaussian per class. To this end, we use the pixel-wise annotations of the superpixels ending in a leaf denoted by $\mathcal{S}_l = \{(\mathbf{x}_l, c_l)\}$. From all pixels $\mathbf{x}_l$ with class label $c_l = c$, we estimate a spatial Gaussian distribution $\mathcal{N}(\mathbf{y}; \mu_{c,l}, \Sigma_{c,l})$ where $\mathbf{y}$ is a location in the image and $\mu_{c,l}, \Sigma_{c,l}$ are the mean and the covariance of the class specific Gaussian. In our implementation, $\Sigma_{c,l}$ is simplified to a diagonal matrix to reduce runtime.

For inference, we convert a superpixel with width w, height h, and centered at $\mathbf{x}$ also into a Gaussian distribution $\mathcal{N}(\mathbf{y}; \mu_{\mathbf{x}}, \Sigma_{\mathbf{x}})$ where $\mu_{\mathbf{x}} = \mathbf{x}$ and $\Sigma_{\mathbf{x}}$ is a diagonal matrix with diagonal $((\frac{w}{2})^2, (\frac{h}{2})^2)$. The class probability for a single tree and a superpixel ending in leaf l is then given by the integral

$$p(c|\mathbf{x}; \theta_t) = \int \mathcal{N}(\mathbf{y}; \mu_{c,l}, \Sigma_{c,l})\mathcal{N}(\mathbf{y}; \mu_{\mathbf{x}}, \Sigma_{\mathbf{x}})d\mathbf{y} = \mathcal{N}(\mu_{\mathbf{x}}; \mu_{c,l}, \Sigma_{c,l} + \Sigma_{\mathbf{x}}) \quad (7)$$

$$\propto \exp\left(-\frac{1}{2}(\mu_{\mathbf{x}} - \mu_{c,l})^T (\Sigma_{c,l} + \Sigma_{\mathbf{x}})^{-1} (\mu_{\mathbf{x}} - \mu_{c,l})\right). \quad (8)$$

In our implementation, we omit the normalization constant and use (8). Several trees are combined as in (1). Instead of using only one Gaussian per class, a mixture of Gaussians can be used as well.

The accuracy can be further improved by smoothing. Let $N_{\mathbf{x}}$ be the neighboring superpixels of $\mathbf{x}$ including $\mathbf{x}$ itself. The class probability for the superpixel $\mathbf{x}$ is then estimated by

$$p(c|\mathbf{x}) = \frac{1}{|N_\mathbf{x}|} \sum_{\mathbf{y} \in N_\mathbf{x}} p(c|\mathbf{y}). \tag{9}$$

To reduce the runtime for videos, the inferred class for a superpixel can be propagated to the next frame. We propagate the label of a cell in the quadtree to the next frame, if the location and size does not change and if the mean intensity of the pixels in the cell does not change by more than 5. Otherwise, we classify the cell by the random forest.

4 Experiments

For the experimental evaluation, we use the CamVid dataset [4]. The images in this dataset have a resolution of 960 × 720 pixels. The CamVid dataset consists of 468 training images and 233 test images taken from video sequences. There is one sequence where frames are extracted at 15 Hz and 30 Hz and both are included in the training set. Most approaches discard the frames that were extracted at 15 Hz resulting in 367 training images. We report results for both settings. The dataset is annotated by 32 semantic classes, but most works use only 11 classes for evaluation, namely *road, building, sky, tree, sidewalk, car, column pole, fence, pedestrian, bicyclist, sign symbol*. We stick to the 11 class protocol and report the global pixel accuracy and the average class accuracy [3]. The runtime is measured on a CPU with 3.3 GHz single-threaded.

Our implementation is based on the publicly available CURFIL library [9], which provides a GPU and CPU version for random forests. As baseline, we use a random forest as described in Sect. 3.1. In Table 1, we report the accuracy and runtime for a single tree. The baseline denoted by *pixel stride 1* requires around 1500 ms for an image, which is insufficient for real-time applications. The runtime can be reduced by downsampling the image or classifying only a subset of pixels and interpolation. We achieved the best trade-off between accuracy and runtime for a stride of 15 pixels in x and y-direction. The final segmentation is then obtained by nearest-neighbor interpolation. Larger strides decreased the accuracy substantially. While this reduces the runtime by factor 5.6 without reducing the accuracy, the approach requires still 280 ms.

We now evaluate the superpixel based approach proposed in Sect. 3.2. We first evaluate superpixel classification based on the empirical class distribution $p(c; \mathcal{S}_l)$, which is denoted by *sp*. Compared to the baseline the runtime is reduced by factor 56 and compared to interpolation by factor 10 without reducing the accuracy. The proposed approach achieves real-time performance with a runtime of only 27.5 ms. Due to the efficient quadtree structure the computational overhead of computing the superpixels is only 2 ms.

In the following, we evaluate a few design choices. Converting an RGB image into the CIELab color space takes 1 ms. The comparison of *sp* (CIELab) with *sp - RGB* (RGB) in Table 1, however, reveals that the RGB color space degrades the accuracy substantially. We also investigated what happens if the number of parameters of the weak classifiers $f_\theta(\mathbf{x})$ (3)–(6) are reduced by setting $\mathbf{x}_1 = 0$,

Table 1. Results for one tree trained on all 468 training images. The last 4 rows report the results when only the sequences recorded with 30 Hz are used for training (367).

	Global pixel accuracy	Average class accuracy	Average time (ms)
pixel stride 1	63.54	40.61	1549
pixel stride 15	64.92	41.21	277
superpixel (sp)	65.11	41.13	27.50
sp - RGB	62.25	36.42	26.47
sp - fix region (sp-fr)	65.29	42.48	28.11
sp - 1 Gaussian	65.16	41.36	29.64
sp - 2 Gaussians	66.41	42.29	26.58
sp-fr - 2 Gaussians (sp-fr-Gauss2)	67.13	43.19	26.25
sp-fr-Gauss2 + smoothing	75.76	47.93	45.24
sp-fr-Gauss2 + propagate	66.49	42.88	18.24
sp-fr-Gauss2 + sm. + prop.	75.03	47.45	37.10
sp-fr-Gauss2 (367 images)	67.06	43.47	23.26
sp-fr-Gauss2 + smoothing (367 images)	74.80	48.00	41.71
sp-fr-Gauss2 + propagate (367 images)	67.00	43.21	15.89
sp-fr-Gauss2 + sm. + prop. (367 images)	74.67	47.19	34.50

which is denoted by *sp-fr*. It slightly increases the average class accuracy compared to *sp* since one region R is fixed to the pixel location which improves the accuracy for small semantic regions. Small regions, however, have a low impact on the global pixel accuracy. If we use (8) instead of the empirical class distribution to classify a superpixel, denoted by *sp - 1 Gaussian*, the accuracy does not improve but the runtime increases by 2 ms. If we use two Gaussians per class, one for the left side of the image and one for the right side, the accuracy increases slightly. Note that the runtime even decreases since (8) becomes more often zero for *2 Gaussians* than for *1 Gaussian*.

For the further experiments, we use the superpixel classification with fixed region and two Gaussians, denoted by *sp-fr-Gauss2*. As mentioned in Sect. 3.2 the superpixel classification can be improved by spatial smoothing, which is denoted by *smoothing*. This increases the accuracy substantially but also the runtime to 45 ms. The label propagation on the contrary reduces the runtime to 18 ms without a substantial decrease in accuracy. The smoothing can also be combined with label propagation. This gives nearly the same accuracy as *sp-fr-Gauss2 + smoothing*, but the runtime is with 37 ms lower.

If we use only the 367 images sampled at 30 Hz instead of all 468 images for training, the accuracy is the same but the runtime is reduced by around 3 ms. Since the larger set is based on sampling one sequence twice at 15 Hz and 30 Hz, the larger set does not contain additional information and the accuracy therefore remains the same. The additional training data, however, increases the depth of the trees and thus the runtime. The classification without feature computation takes around 4 ms for a tree of depth 20 and 8–10 ms for a tree of depth 100. For 1000 superpixels sampled from each of the 468 training images, the trees can reach a depth of 100.

Table 2. Results for 10 trees trained on all 468 training images. The last 4 rows report the results when only the sequences recorded with 30 Hz are used for training (367).

	Global pixel accuracy	Average class accuracy	Average time (ms)
pixel stride 1	74.60	48.56	11288
pixel stride 15	74.58	48.69	301.7
CCF features	71.68	51.19	28476
sp-fr-Gauss2	77.49	51.29	105.3
sp-fr-Gauss2 + smoothing	79.62	51.77	131.5
sp-fr-Gauss2 + propagate	76.62	49.99	40.19
sp-fr-Gauss2 + sm. + prop.	78.56	50.79	58.75
sp-fr-Gauss2 (367 images)	77.43	51.22	102.5
sp-fr-Gauss2 + smoothing (367 images)	79.99	52.20	111.5
sp-fr-Gauss2 + propagate (367 images)	76.82	50.48	36.48
sp-fr-Gauss2 + sm. + prop. (367 images)	79.30	51.68	55.47

In Table 2, we report the accuracy and runtime for 10 trees. Increasing the number of trees from one to ten increases the global pixel accuracy of the baseline by 11 % points and the average class accuracy by 8 % points. We also evaluated the use of convolutional channel features (CCF) [15] which are obtained by the VGG-16 network [16] trained on the ImageNet (ILSVRC-2012) dataset. As in [17], the features are combined with axis-aligned split functions to build weak classifiers. Without finetuning the features do not perform better on this dataset. The extraction of CCF features is furthermore very expensive without a GPU. Similar to the baseline, the global pixel accuracy and average class accuracy is also increased for *sp-fr-Gauss2* by 10 and 8 percentage points, respectively. Only if spatial smoothing is added the increase is only 4 % points, but it still improves the accuracy. The runtime increases by factor 4, 2.9, 2.2, 1.6 for *sp-fr-Gauss2, sp-fr-Gauss2 + smoothing, sp-fr-Gauss2 + propagate, sp-fr-Gauss2 + sm. + prop.*, respectively. Compared to the baseline *pixel stride 1*, the runtime is reduced by factor 192 while increasing the accuracy if label propagation and smoothing are used. Figure 2 plots the accuracy and runtime of *sp-fr-Gauss2 + propagate* and *sp-fr-Gauss2 + sm. + prop.* while varying the number of trees.

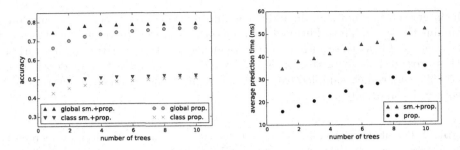

Fig. 2. Accuracy and average prediction time with respect to the number of trees.

The impact of the depth of the quadtree is shown in Fig. 3. The accuracy but also the runtime increases with the depth of the quadtree since the cells get smaller the deeper the trees are. Limiting the depth of the quadtrees to seven gives a good trade-off between accuracy and runtime. This setting is also used in our experiments.

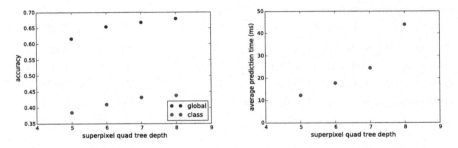

Fig. 3. Accuracy and average prediction time for one tree using different quadtree depths when creating superpixels. The results are reported for *sp-fr-Gauss2*.

We finally compare our approach with the state-of-the-art in terms of accuracy in Table 3. The first part of the table uses all training images for training. Our approach outperforms CURFIL [9] in terms of accuracy and runtime on a single-threaded CPU. Although the approach [18] achieves a higher global pixel accuracy, it is very expensive and requires 16,6 s for an image with resolution of 800 × 600 pixels. Our fastest setting requires only 40 milliseconds.

The second part of the table uses the evaluation protocol with 367 images. The numbers are taken from [3]. The convolutional neural network proposed in [3] achieves the best accuracy and requires around 2 s per image on a GPU. The methods based on CRFs [6] require 30 to 40 s for an image. The method [4] is based on random forests and structure-from-motion. It requires one second per image if the point cloud is already computed by structure-from-motion.

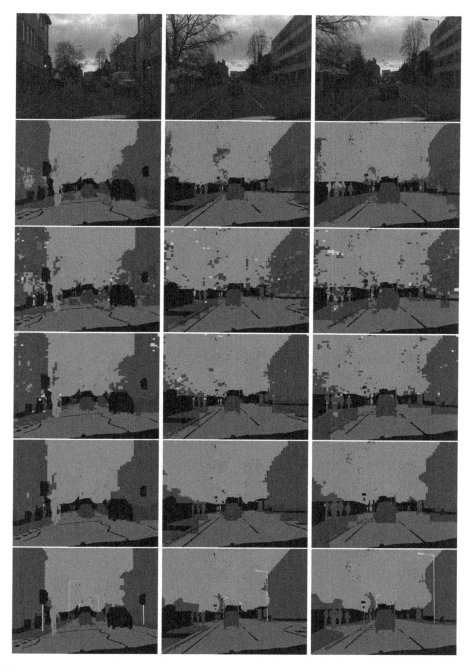

Fig. 4. Examples of segmentation results. First row: original image. Second row: *pixel stride 1*. Third row: *sp-fr*. Fourth row: *sp-fr-Gauss2 + propagate*. Fifth row: *sp-fr-Gauss2 + sm. + prop.* Sixth row: ground truth.

Table 3. Comparison with state-of-the-art approaches. The first six rows shows results for all 468 training images. The lower part report the results when only the sequences recorded with 30 Hz are used for training (367).

	Global pixel accuracy	Average class accuracy	Average time (ms)
Super Parsing [18]	83.3	51.2	
CURFIL [9]	65.9	49.8	34163
sp-fr-Gauss2	77.5	51.3	105.3
sp-fr-Gauss2 + smoothing	79.6	51.8	131.5
sp-fr-Gauss2 + propagate	76.6	50.0	40.2
sp-fr-Gauss2 + sm. + prop.	78.6	50.8	58.8
Appearance [4]	66.5	52.3	
SfM + Appearance [4]	69.1	53.0	
Boosting [6]	76.4	59.8	
Dense Depth Maps [20]	82.1	55.4	
Structured Random Forests [8]	72.5	51.4	
Neural Decision Forests [19]	82.1	56.1	
Local Label Descriptors [21]	73.6	36.3	
SegNet - 4 layer [3]	84.3	62.9	2000
Boosting + pairwise CRF [6]	79.8	59.9	
Boosting + Higher order [6]	83.8	59.2	
Boosting + Detectors + CRF [7]	83.8	62.5	
sp-fr-Gauss2 (367 images)	77.4	51.2	102.5
sp-fr-Gauss2 + smoothing (367 images)	80.0	52.2	111.5
sp-fr-Gauss2 + propagate (367 images)	76.8	50.5	36.5
sp-fr-Gauss2 + sm. + prop. (367 images)	79.3	51.7	55.5

The methods [8,19] are also too slow for real-time applications. In contrast, our approach segments an image not in the order of seconds but milliseconds while still achieving competitive accuracies. A few qualitative results are shown in Fig. 4.

5 Conclusion

In this work, we proposed a real-time approach for semantic segmentation on a single-threaded architecture. Compared to the baseline we reduced the runtime by factor 192 while increasing the accuracy. This has been achieved by combining an efficient superpixel representation based on quadtrees with random forests and combining label propagation with spatial smoothing. Compared to the state-of-the-art in terms of accuracy, our approach achieves competitive results but runs in real-time without the need of a GPU. This make the approach ideal for applications with limited computational resources.

Acknowledgement. The work has been financially supported by the DFG project GA 1927/2-2 as part of the DFG Research Unit FOR 1505 Mapping on Demand (MoD).

References

1. Farabet, C., Couprie, C., Najman, L., LeCun, Y.: Learning hierarchical features for scene labeling. IEEE Trans. Pattern Anal. Mach. Intell. **35**(8), 1915–1929 (2013)
2. Chen, L.C., Papandreou, G., Kokkinos, I., Murphy, K., Yuille, A.: Semantic image segmentation with deep convolutional nets and fully connected CRFs. In: International Conference on Learning Representations (2015)
3. Badrinarayanan, V., Handa, A., Cipolla, R.: Segnet: A deep convolutional encoder-decoder architecture for robust semantic pixel-wise labelling. CoRR abs/1505.07293 (2015)
4. Brostow, G.J., Shotton, J., Fauqueur, J., Cipolla, R.: Segmentation and recognition using structure from motion point clouds. In: Forsyth, D., Torr, P., Zisserman, A. (eds.) ECCV 2008. LNCS, vol. 5302, pp. 44–57. Springer, Heidelberg (2008). doi:10.1007/978-3-540-88682-2_5
5. Shotton, J., Johnson, M., Cipolla, R.: Semantic texton forests for image categorization and segmentation. In: IEEE Computer Vision and Pattern Recognition (2008)
6. Sturgess, P., Alahari, K., Ladicky, L., Torr, P.H.: Combining appearance and structure from motion features for road scene understanding. In: British Machine Vision Conference (2009)
7. Ladický, L., Sturgess, P., Alahari, K., Russell, C., Torr, P.H.S.: What, where and how many? combining object detectors and CRFs. In: Daniilidis, K., Maragos, P., Paragios, N. (eds.) ECCV 2010. LNCS, vol. 6314, pp. 424–437. Springer, Heidelberg (2010). doi:10.1007/978-3-642-15561-1_31
8. Kontschieder, P., Rota Bulò, S., Bischof, H., Pelillo, M.: Structured class-labels in random forests for semantic image labelling. In: IEEE International Conference on Computer Vision, pp. 2190–2197 (2011)
9. Schulz, H., Waldvogel, B., Sheikh, R., Behnke, S.: CURFIL: random forests for image labeling on GPU. In: Proceedings of the International Conference on Computer Vision Theory and Applications (2015)
10. Shelhamer, E., Long, J., Darrell, T.: Fully convolutional networks for semantic segmentation. IEEE Trans. Pattern Anal. Mach. Intell. (2016)
11. Grundmann, M., Kwatra, V., Han, M., Essa, I.: Efficient hierarchical graph-based video segmentation. In: IEEE Computer Vision and Pattern Recognition, pp. 2141–2148 (2010)
12. Budvytis, I., Badrinarayanan, V., Cipolla, R.: Label propagation in complex video sequences using semi-supervised learning. In: British Machine Vision Conference, vol. 2257, pp. 2258–2259 (2010)
13. Reso, M., Jachalsky, J., Rosenhahn, B., Ostermann, J.: Fast label propagation for real-time superpixels for video content. In: IEEE International Conference on Image Processing (2015)

14. Criminisi, A., Shotton, J.: Decision Forests for Computer Vision and Medical Image Analysis. Springer, London (2013)
15. Yang, B., Yan, J., Lei, Z., Li, S.Z.: Convolutional channel features. In: IEEE International Conference on Computer Vision, pp. 82–90 (2015)
16. Simonyan, K., Zisserman, A.: Very deep convolutional networks for large-scale image recognition. CoRR abs/1409.1556 (2014)
17. Iqbal, U., Garbade, M., Gall, J.: Pose for action - action for pose. CoRR abs/1603.04037 (2016)
18. Tighe, J., Lazebnik, S.: Superparsing. Int. J. Comput. Vision **101**(2), 329–349 (2013)
19. Bulo, S., Kontschieder, P.: Neural decision forests for semantic image labelling. In: IEEE Conference on Computer Vision and Pattern Recognition, pp. 81–88 (2014)
20. Zhang, C., Wang, L., Yang, R.: Semantic segmentation of urban scenes using dense depth maps. In: Daniilidis, K., Maragos, P., Paragios, N. (eds.) ECCV 2010. LNCS, vol. 6314, pp. 708–721. Springer, Heidelberg (2010). doi:10.1007/978-3-642-15561-1_51
21. Yang, Y., Li, Z., Zhang, L., Murphy, C., Hoeve, J., Jiang, H.: Local label descriptor for example based semantic image labeling. In: Fitzgibbon, A., Lazebnik, S., Perona, P., Sato, Y., Schmid, C. (eds.) ECCV 2012. LNCS, vol. 7578, pp. 361–375. Springer, Heidelberg (2012). doi:10.1007/978-3-642-33786-4_27

W11 - Benchmarking Multi-target Tracking: MOTChallenge

Performance Measures and a Data Set for Multi-target, Multi-camera Tracking

Ergys Ristani[1(✉)], Francesco Solera[2], Roger Zou[1], Rita Cucchiara[2], and Carlo Tomasi[1]

[1] Computer Science Department, Duke University, Durham, USA
ristani@cs.duke.edu
[2] Department of Engineering, University of Modena and Reggio Emilia, Modena, Italy

Abstract. To help accelerate progress in multi-target, multi-camera tracking systems, we present (i) a new pair of precision-recall measures of performance that treats errors of all types uniformly and emphasizes correct identification over sources of error; (ii) the largest fully-annotated and calibrated data set to date with more than 2 million frames of 1080 p, 60 fps video taken by 8 cameras observing more than 2,700 identities over 85 min; and (iii) a reference software system as a comparison baseline. We show that (i) our measures properly account for bottom-line identity match performance in the multi-camera setting; (ii) our data set poses realistic challenges to current trackers; and (iii) the performance of our system is comparable to the state of the art.

Keywords: Performance evaluation · Multi camera tracking · Identity management · Multi camera data set · Large scale data set

1 Introduction

Multi-Target, Multi-Camera (MTMC) tracking systems automatically track multiple people through a network of cameras. As MTMC methods solve larger and larger problems, it becomes increasingly important (i) to agree on straightforward performance measures that consistently report bottom-line tracker performance, both within and across cameras; (ii) to develop realistically large benchmark data sets for performance evaluation; and (iii) to compare system performance end-to-end. This paper contributes to these aspects.

Performance Measures. Multi-Target Tracking has been traditionally defined as continuously following multiple objects of interest. Because of this, existing performance measures such as CLEAR MOT report how often a tracker makes what types of incorrect decisions. We argue that some system users may instead be more interested in how well they can determine who is where at all times.

This material is based upon work supported by the National Science Foundation under grants CCF-1513816 and IIS-1543720 and by the Army Research Office under grant W911NF-16-1-0392.

© Springer International Publishing Switzerland 2016
G. Hua and H. Jégou (Eds.): ECCV 2016 Workshops, Part II, LNCS 9914, pp. 17–35, 2016.
DOI: 10.1007/978-3-319-48881-3_2

To see this distinction, consider the scenario abstractly depicted in Fig. 1(a) and (c). Airport security is following suspect A spotted in the airport lobby. They need to choose between two trackers, Fig. 1(a) and (c). Both tag the suspect as identity 1 and track him up to the security checkpoint. System Fig. 1(a) makes a single mistake at the checkpoint and henceforth tags the suspect as identity 2, so it loses the suspect at the checkpoint. After the checkpoint, system Fig. 1(c) repeatedly flips the tags for suspect A between 1 and 2, thereby giving police the correct location of the suspect several times also between the checkpoint and the gate, and for a greater overall fraction of the time. Even though system Fig. 1(a) incurs only one ID switch, airport security is likely to prefer system Fig. 1(c), which reports the suspect's position longer—multiple ID switches notwithstanding—and ultimately leads to his arrest at the gate.

We do not claim that one measure is better than the other, but rather that different measures serve different purposes. *Event-based* measures like CLEAR MOT help pinpoint the source of some errors, and are thereby informative for the designer of certain system components. In the interest of users in applications such as sports, security, or surveillance, where preserving identity is crucial, we propose two *identity-based* measures (ID precision and ID recall) that evaluate how well computed identities conform to true identities, while disregarding where or why mistakes occur. Our measures apply both within and across cameras.

Data Set. We make available a new data set that has more than 2 million frames and more than 2,700 identities. It consists of 8 × 85 min of 1080 p video recorded at 60 fps from 8 static cameras deployed on the Duke University campus during periods between lectures, when pedestrian traffic is heavy. Calibration data determines homographies between images and the world ground plane. All trajectories were manually annotated by five people over a year, using an interface we developed to mark trajectory key points and associate identities across cameras. The resulting nearly 100,000 key points were automatically interpolated to single frames, so that every identity comes with single-frame bounding boxes and ground-plane world coordinates across all cameras in which it appears. To our knowledge this is the first dataset of its kind.

Reference System. We provide code for an MTMC tracker that extends a single-camera system that has shown good performance [1] to the multi-camera setting. We hope that the conceptual simplicity of our system will encourage plug-and-play experimentation when new individual components are proposed.

We show that our system does well on a recently published data set [2] when previously used measures are employed to compare our system to the state of the art. This comparison is only circumstantial because most existing results on MTMC tracking report performance using *ground-truth* person detections and *ground-truth* single-camera trajectories as inputs, rather than using the results from *actual* detectors and single-camera trackers. The literature typically justifies this limitation with the desire to measure only what a multi-camera tracker *adds* to a single-camera system. This justification is starting to wane as MTMC tracking systems approach realistically useful performance levels. Accordingly, we evaluate our system end-to-end, and also provide our own measures as a baseline for future research.

2   Related Work

We survey prior work on MTMC performance measures, data sets, and trackers.

Measures. We rephrase existing MTMC performance measures as follows.

- A *fragmentation* occurs in frame t if the tracker switches the identity of a trajectory in that frame, but the corresponding ground-truth identity does not change. The number of fragmentations at frame t is ϕ_t, and $\Phi = \sum_t \phi_t$.
- A *merge* is the reverse of a fragmentation: The tracker merges two different ground truth identities into one between frames t' and t. The number of merges at frame t is γ_t, and $\Gamma = \sum_t \gamma_t$.
- A *mismatch* is either a fragmentation or a merge. We define $\mu_t = \phi_t + \gamma_t$ and $M = \sum_t \mu_t$.

When relevant, each of these error counts is given a superscript w (for "within-camera") when the frames t' and t in question come from the same camera, and a superscript h (for "handover") otherwise.

The number of *false positives* fp_t is the number of times the tracker detects a target in frame t where there is none in the ground truth, the number of *false negatives* fn_t is the number of true targets missed by the tracker in frame t, and tp_t is the number of true positive detections at time t. The capitalized versions TP, FP, FN are the sums of tp_t, fp_t, and fn_t over all frames (and cameras, if more than one), and the superscripts w and h apply here as well if needed.

Precision and *recall* are the usual derived measures, $P = TP/(TP + FP)$ and $R = TP/(TP + FN)$.

Single-camera, multi-object tracking performance is typically measured by the Multiple Object Tracking Accuracy (MOTA):

$$\text{MOTA} = 1 - \frac{FN + FP + \Phi}{T} \qquad (1)$$

and related scores (MOTP, MT, ML, FRG) [3–5]. MOTA penalizes detection errors $(FN + FP)$ and fragmentations (Φ) normalized by the total number T of true detections. If extended to the multi-camera case, MOTA and its companions under-report across-camera errors, because a trajectory that covers n_f frames from n_c cameras has only about n_c across-camera detection links between consecutive frames and about $n_f - n_c$ within camera ones, and $n_c \ll n_f$. To address this limitation handover errors [6] and multi-camera object tracking accuracy (MCTA) [2,7] measures were introduced, which we describe next.

Handover errors focus only on errors across cameras, and distinguish between fragmentations Φ^h and merges Γ^h. Fragmentations and merges are divided further into crossing (Φ^h_X and Γ^h_X) and returning (Φ^h_R and Γ^h_R) errors. These more detailed handover error scores help understand different types of tracker failures, and within-camera errors are quantified separately by standard measures.

MCTA condenses all aspects of system performance into one measure:

$$\text{MCTA} = \underbrace{\frac{2PR}{P+R}}_{F_1} \underbrace{\left(1 - \frac{M^w}{T^w}\right)}_{\text{within camera}} \underbrace{\left(1 - \frac{M^h}{T^h}\right)}_{\text{handover}} . \tag{2}$$

This measure multiplies the F_1 detection score (harmonic mean of precision and recall) by a term that penalizes within-camera identity mismatches (M^w) normalized by true within-camera detections (T^w) and a term that penalizes wrong identity handover mismatches (M^h) normalized by the total number of handovers. Consistent with our notation, T^h is the number of true detections (true positives TP^h plus false negatives FN^h) that occur when consecutive frames come from different cameras.

Comparing to MOTA, MCTA multiplies within-camera and handover mismatches rather than adding them. In addition, false positives and false negatives, accounted for in precision and recall, are also factored into MCTA through a product. This separation brings the measure into the range $[0, 1]$ rather than $[-\infty, 1]$ as for MOTA. However, the reasons for using a product rather than some other form of combination are unclear. In particular, each error in any of the three terms is penalized inconsistently, in that its cost is multiplied by the (variable) product of the other two terms.

Data Sets. Existing multi-camera data sets allow only for limited evaluation of MTMC systems. Some have fully overlapping views and are restricted to short time intervals and controlled conditions [8–10]. Some sports scenarios provide quality video with many cameras [11,12], but their environments are severely constrained and there are no blind spots between cameras. Data sets with disjoint views come either with low resolution video [2,6,13], a small number of cameras placed along a straight path [2,6], or scripted scenarios [2,8–10,13,14]. Most importantly, all existing data sets only have a small number of identities. Table 1 summarizes the parameters of existing data sets. Ours is shown in the last row. It contains more identities than all previous data sets *combined*, and was recorded over the longest time period at the highest temporal resolution (60 fps).

Systems. MTMC trackers rely on pedestrian detection [15] and tracking [16] or assume single-camera trajectories to be given [6,13,17–26]. *Spatial relations between cameras* are either explicitly mapped in 3D [13,19], learned by tracking known identities [25,27,28], or obtained by comparing entry/exit rates across pairs of cameras [6,18,26]. Pre-processing methods may fuse data from partially overlapping views [29], while some systems rely on completely overlapping and unobstructed views [9,17,30–32]. People *entry and exit points* may be explicitly modeled on the ground [6,18,19,26] or image plane [24,27]. *Travel time* is also modeled, either parametrically [13,27] or not [6,19,24–26].

Appearance is captured by color   [6,13,18–21,23–25,27,29] and texture descriptors [6,13,18,20,22,29]. Lighting variations are addressed through color

Table 1. Summary of existing data sets for MTMC tracking. Ours is in the last row.

Dataset	IDs	Duration	Cams	Actors	Overlap	Blind Spots	Calib.	Resolution	FPS	Scene	Year
Laboratory [8]	3	2.5 min	4	Yes	Yes	No	Yes	320x240	25	Indoor	2008
Campus [8]	4	5.5 min	3	Yes	Yes	No	Yes	320x240	25	Outdoor	2008
Terrace [8]	7	3.5 min	4	Yes	Yes	No	Yes	320x240	25	Outdoor	2008
Passageway [9]	4	20 min	4	Yes	Yes	No	Yes	320x240	25	Mixed	2011
Issia Soccer [11]	25	2 min	6	No	Yes	No	Yes	1920x1080	25	Outdoor	2009
Apidis Basket. [12]	12	1 min	7	No	Yes	No	Yes	1600x1200	22	Indoor	2008
PETS2009 [10]	30	1 min	8	Yes	Yes	No	Yes	768x576	7	Outdoor	2009
NLPR MCT 1 [2]	235	20 min	3	No	No	Yes	No	320x240	20	Mixed	2015
NLPR MCT 2 [2]	255	20 min	3	No	No	Yes	No	320x240	20	Mixed	2015
NLPR MCT 3 [2]	14	4 min	4	Yes	Yes	Yes	No	320x240	25	Indoor	2015
NLPR MCT 4 [2]	49	25min	5	Yes	Yes	Yes	No	320x240	25	Mixed	2015
Dana36 [14]	24	N/A	36	Yes	Yes	Yes	No	2048x1536	N/A	Mixed	2012
USC Campus [6]	146	25 min	3	No	No	Yes	No	852x480	30	Outdoor	2010
CamNeT [13]	50	30 min	8	Yes	Yes	Yes	No	640x480	25	Mixed	2015
DukeMTMC (ours)	2834	85 min	8	No	Yes	Yes	Yes	1920x1080	60	Outdoor	2016

normalization [18], exemplar based approaches [20], or brightness transfer functions learned with [23,25] or without supervision [13,19,24,29]. Discriminative power is improved by *saliency* information [33,34] or *learning* features specific to body parts [6,18,20–23,27], either in the image [35–37] or back-projected onto an articulated [38,39] or monolithic [40] 3D body model.

All MTMC trackers employ *optimization* to maximize the coherence of observations for predicted identities. They first summarize spatial, temporal, and appearance information into a graph of *weights* w_{ij} that express the affinity of node observations i and j, and then partition the nodes into identities either greedily through bipartite matching or, more generally, by finding either paths or cliques with maximal internal weights. Some contributions are as follows (Table 2):

Table 2. Optimization techniques employed by MTMC systems.

	Single-camera	Cross-camera	Both
Bipartite	[41–43]	[6,18,20,22]	—
Path	[9,44–46]	[25,27]	[2,29]
Clique	[1,47–55]	[23]	Ours

In this paper, we extend a previous clique method [1] to formulate within- and across-camera tracking in a unified framework, similarly to previous MTMC flow methods [2,29]. In contrast with [23], we handle identities reappearing in the same camera and differently from [8,9] we handle co-occuring observations in overlapping views naturally, with no need for separate data fusion methods.

3 Performance Measures

Current event-based MTMC tracking performance measures count mismatches between ground truth and system output through *changes* of identity over time. The next two Sections show that this can be problematic both within and across cameras. The Section thereafter introduces our proposed measures.

3.1 Within-Camera Issues

With event-based measures, a truly-unique trajectory that switches between two computed identities over n frames can incur penalties that are anywhere between 1, when there is exactly one switch, and $n-1$, in the extreme case of one identity switch per frame. This can yield inconsistencies if correct identities are crucial. For example, in all cases in Fig. 1, the tracker covers a true identity A with computed identities 1 and 2. Current measures would make cases (b) and (c) equally bad, and (a) much better than the other two.

And yet the key mistake made by the tracker is to see two identities where there is one. To quantify the extent of the mistake, we need to decide which of the two computed identities we should match with A for the purpose of performance evaluation. Once that choice is made, every frame in which A is assigned to the wrong computed identity is a frame in which the tracker is in error.

Since the evaluator—and not the tracker—makes this choice, we suggest that it should favor the tracker to the extent possible. If this is done for each tracker under evaluation, the choice is fair. In all cases in Fig. 1, the most favorable choice is to tie A to 1, because this choice explains the largest fraction of A.

Once this choice is made, we measure the number of frames over which the tracker is wrong—in the example, the number of frames of A that are not matched to 1. In Fig. 1, this measure makes (a) and (b) equally good, and (c) better than either. This penalty is consistent because it reflects precisely what the choice made above maximizes, namely, the number of frames over which the tracker is correct about who is where. In (a) and (b), the tracker matches ground truth 67 % of the time, and in (c) it matches it 83 % of the time.

Figure 1 is about fragmentation errors. It can be reinterpreted in terms of merge errors by exchanging the role of thick and thin lines. In this new interpretation, choosing the longest ground-truth trajectory as the correct match for a given computed trajectory explains as much of the tracker's output as possible, rather than as much of the ground truth. In both directions, our *truth-to-result matching* criterion is to let ground truth and tracker output explain as much of each other's data as possible, in a way that will be made quantitative later on.

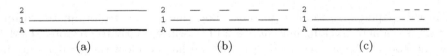

Fig. 1. Where there is one true identity A (thick line, with time in the horizontal direction), a tracker may mistakenly compute identities 1 and 2 (thin lines) broken into two fragments (a) or into eight (b, c). Identity 1 covers 67 % of the true identity's trajectory in (a) and (b), and 83 % of it in (c). Current measures charge one fragmentation error to (a) and 7 to each of (b) and (c). Our proposed measure charges 33 % of the length of A to each of (a) and (b), and 17 % to (c).

3.2   Handover Issues

Event-based measures often evaluate handover errors separately from within-camera errors: Whether a mismatch is within-camera or handover depends on the identities associated to the very last frame in which a trajectory is seen in one camera, and on the very first frame in which it is seen in the next—a rather brittle proposition. In contrast, our measure counts the number of incorrectly matched frames, regardless of other considerations: If only one frame is wrong, the penalty is small. For instance, in the cases shown in Fig. 2, current measures either charge a handover penalty when the handover is essentially correct (a) or fail to charge a handover penalty when the handover is essentially incorrect (b). Our measure charges a one-frame penalty in case (a) and a penalty nearly equal to the trajectory length in camera II in case (b), as appropriate. These cases are not just theoretical. In Sect. 6, we show that 74 % of the 5,549 handovers computed by our tracker in our data set show similar phenomena.

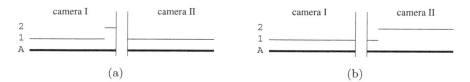

Fig. 2. (a) Ground-truth trajectory A is handed over correctly between cameras, because it is given the same computed identity 1 throughout, except that a short fragment in camera I is mistakenly given identity 2 (red). This counts as a handover error with existing measures. (b) A is handed over incorrectly, but a short fragment in camera II mistakenly given identity 1 (red) makes existing measures *not* count it as a handover error. Existing measures would charge a within-camera fragmentation and an across-camera fragmentation to (a) and one within-camera fragmentation to (b), even if assignment (a) is much better than (b) in terms of target identification. (Color figure online)

These issues are exacerbated in measures, such as MCTA, that combine measures of within-camera mismatches and handover mismatches into a single value by a product (Eq. 2). If one of the anomalies discussed above changes a within-camera error into a handover error or *vice versa*, the corresponding contribution to the performance measure can change drastically, because the penalty moves from one term of the product to another: If the product has the form wh ("within" and "handover"), then a unit contribution to w has value h in the product, and changing that contribution from w to h changes its value to w.

3.3   The Truth-To-Result Match

To address these issues, we propose to measure performance not by *how often* mismatches occur, but by *how long* the tracker correctly identifies targets. To this end, ground-truth identities are first matched to computed ones. More specifically, a bipartite match associates one ground-truth trajectory to exactly one computed trajectory by minimizing the number of mismatched frames over all the available data—true and computed. Standard measures such as precision, recall, and F_1-score are built on top of this truth-to-result match. These scores then measure the number of mismatched or unmatched detection-frames, regardless of where the discrepancies start or end or which cameras are involved.

To compute the optimal truth-to-result match, we construct a bipartite graph $G = (V_T, V_C, E)$ as follows. Vertex set V_T has one "regular" node τ for each true trajectory and one "false positive" node f_γ^+ for each computed trajectory γ. Vertex set V_C has one "regular" node γ for each computed trajectory and one "false negative" node f_τ^-, for each true trajectory τ. Two regular nodes are connected with an edge $e \in E$ if their trajectories overlap in time. Every regular true node τ is also connected to its corresponding f_τ^-, and every regular computed node γ is also connected to its corresponding f_γ^+.

The cost on an edge $(\tau, \gamma) \in E$ tallies the number of false negative and false positive frames that would be incurred if that match were chosen. Specifically, let $\tau(t)$ be the sequence of detections for true trajectory τ, one detection for each frame t in the set $\mathcal{T}_\tau$ over which τ extends, and define $\gamma(t)$ for $t \in \mathcal{T}_\gamma$ similarly for computed trajectories. The two simultaneous detections $\tau(t)$ and $\gamma(t)$ are a *miss* if they do not overlap in space, and we write

$$m(\tau, \gamma, t, \Delta) = 1 . \tag{3}$$

More specifically, when both τ and γ are regular nodes, spatial overlap between two detections can be measured either in the image plane or on the reference ground plane in the world. In the first case, we declare a miss when the area of the intersection of the two detection boxes is less than Δ (with $0 < \Delta < 1$) times the area of the union of the two boxes. On the ground plane, we declare a miss when the positions of the two detections are more than $\Delta = 1$ meter apart. If there is no miss, we write $m(\tau, \gamma, t, \Delta) = 0$. When either τ or γ is an irregular node (f_τ^- or f_γ^+), any detections in the other trajectory are misses. When both τ and γ are irregular, m is undefined. We define costs in terms of binary misses, rather than, say, Euclidean distances, so that a miss between regular positions has the same cost as a miss between a regular position and an irregular one. Matching two irregular trajectories incurs zero cost because they are empty. With this definition, the cost on edge $(\tau, \gamma) \in E$ is defined as follows:

$$c(\tau, \gamma, \Delta) = \underbrace{\sum_{t \in \mathcal{T}_\tau} m(\tau, \gamma, t, \Delta)}_{\text{False Negatives}} + \underbrace{\sum_{t \in \mathcal{T}_\gamma} m(\tau, \gamma, t, \Delta)}_{\text{False Positives}} . \tag{4}$$

A minimum-cost solution to this bipartite matching problem determines a one-to-one matching that minimizes the cumulative false positive and false negative errors, and the overall cost is the number of mis-assigned detections for all types of errors. Every (τ, γ) match is a True Positive ID ($IDTP$). Every (f_γ^+, γ)

match is a False Positive ID ($IDFP$). Every (τ, f_τ^-) match is a False Negative ID ($IDFN$). Every (f_γ^+, f_τ^-) match is a True Negative ID ($IDTN$).

The matches (τ, γ) in $IDTP$ imply a *truth-to-result* match, in that they reveal which computed identity matches which ground-truth identity. In general not every trajectory is matched. The sets

$$MT = \{\tau \mid (\tau, \gamma) \in IDTP\} \quad \text{and} \quad MC = \{\gamma \mid (\tau, \gamma) \in IDTP\} \tag{5}$$

contain the *matched ground-truth trajectories* and *matched computed trajectories*, respectively. The pairs in $IDTP$ can be viewed as a bijection between MT and MC. In other words, the bipartite match implies functions $\gamma = \gamma_m(\tau)$ from MT to MC and $\tau = \tau_m(\gamma)$ from MC to MT.

3.4 Identification Precision, Identification Recall, and F_1 Score

We use the $IDFN$, $IDFP$, $IDTP$ counts to compute identification precision (IDP), identification recall (IDR), and the corresponding F_1 score IDF_1. More specifically,

$$IDFN = \sum_{\tau \in AT} \sum_{t \in T_\tau} m(\tau, \gamma_m(\tau), t, \Delta) \tag{6}$$

$$IDFP = \sum_{\gamma \in AC} \sum_{t \in T_\gamma} m(\tau_m(\gamma), \gamma, t, \Delta) \tag{7}$$

$$IDTP = \sum_{\tau \in AT} \operatorname{len}(\tau) - IDFN = \sum_{\gamma \in AC} \operatorname{len}(\gamma) - IDFP \tag{8}$$

where AT and AC are all true and computed identities in MT and MC.

$$IDP = \frac{IDTP}{IDTP + IDFP} \tag{9}$$

$$IDR = \frac{IDTP}{IDTP + IDFN} \tag{10}$$

$$IDF_1 = \frac{2\,IDTP}{2\,IDTP + IDFP + IDFN} \tag{11}$$

Identification precision (recall) is the fraction of computed (ground truth) detections that are correctly identified. IDF_1 is the ratio of correctly identified detections over the average number of ground-truth and computed detections. ID precision and ID recall shed light on tracking trade-offs, while the IDF_1 score allows ranking all trackers on a single scale that balances identification precision and recall through their harmonic mean.

Our performance evaluation approach based on the truth-to-result match addresses all the weaknesses mentioned earlier in a simple and uniform way, and enjoys the following desirable properties: (1) *Bijectivity:* A correct match (with no fragmentation or merge) between true identities and computed identities is one-to-one. (2) *Optimality:* The truth-to-result matching is the most favorable to the tracker. (3) *Consistency:* Errors of any type are penalized in the same currency, namely, the number of misassigned or unassigned frames. Our approach also handles overlapping and disjoint fields of view in exactly the same way—a feature absent in all previous measures.

3.5   Additional Comparative Remarks

Measures of Handover Difficulty. Handover errors in current measures are meant to account for the additional difficulty of tracking individuals across cameras, compared to tracking them within a single camera's field of view. If a system designer were interested in this aspect of performance, a similar measure could be based on the difference between the total number of errors for the multi-camera solution and the sum of the numbers of single-camera errors:

$$E_M - E_S \quad \text{where} \quad E_M = IDFP_M + IDFN_M \quad \text{and} \quad E_S = IDFP_S + IDFN_S . \tag{12}$$

The two errors can be computed by computing the truth-to-result mapping twice: Once for all the data and once for each camera separately (and then adding the single-camera errors together). The difference above is nonnegative, because the multi-camera solution must account for the additional constraint of consistency across cameras. Similarly, simple manipulation shows that ID precision, ID recall, and IDF_1 score are sorted the other way:

$$IDP_S - IDP_M \geq 0 \quad , \quad IDR_S - IDR_M \geq 0 \quad , \quad F_{1S} - F_{1M} \geq 0$$

and these differences measure how well the overall system can associate across cameras, given within-camera associations.

Comparison with CLEAR MOT. The first step in performance evaluation matches true and computed identities. In CLEAR MOT the event-based matching defines the best mapping sequentially at each frame. It minimizes Euclidean distances (within a threshold Δ) between unmatched detections (true and computed) while matched detections from frame $t-1$ that are still within Δ in t are preserved. Although the per-frame identity mapping is 1-to-1, the mapping for the entire sequence is generally many-to-many.

In our identity-based measures, we define the best mapping as the one which minimizes the total number of mismatched frames between true and computed IDs for the entire sequence. Similar to CLEAR MOT, a match at each frame is enforced by a threshold Δ. In contrast, our reasoning is not frame-by-frame and results in an ID-to-ID mapping that is 1-to-1 for the entire sequence.

The second step evaluates the goodness of the match through a scoring function. This is usually done by aggregating mistakes. MOTA aggregates FP, FN and Φ while we aggregate IDFP and IDFN counts. The notion of fragmentation is not present in our evaluation because the mapping is strictly 1-to-1. In other words our evaluation only checks whether every detection of an identity is explained or not, consistently with our definition of tracking. Also, our aggregated mistakes are binary mismatch counts instead of, say, Euclidean distances.

This is because we want all errors to be penalized in the same currency. If we were to combine the binary IDFP and IDFN counts with Euclidean distances instead of IDTP, the unit of error would be ambiguous: We won't be able to tell whether the tracker under evaluation is good at explaining identities longer or following their trajectories closer.

Comparison with Identity-Aware Tracking. Performance scores similar to ours were recently introduced for this specific task [56]. The problem is defined as computing trajectories for a known set of true identities from a database. This implies that the truth-to-result match is determined during tracking and not evaluation. Instead, our evaluation applies to the more general MTMC setting where the tracker is agnostic to the true identities.

4   Data Set

Another contribution of this work is a new, manually annotated, calibrated, multi-camera data set recorded outdoors on the Duke University campus with 8 synchronized cameras (Fig. 3)[1]. We recorded 6,791 trajectories for *2,834 different identities* (distinct persons) over *1 h and 25 min for each camera*, for a total of more than 10 video hours and more than 2 million frames. There are on average 2.5 single-camera trajectories per identity, and up to 7 in some cases.

Fig. 3. Images and annotations of our DukeMTMC data set for frame 30890.

The cumulative trajectory time is more than 30 h. Individual camera density varies from 0 to 54 people per frame, depending on the camera. There are 4,159 hand-overs and up to 50 people traverse blind spots at the same time. More than 1,800 self-occlusion events happen (with 50 % or more overlap), lasting 60 frames on average. Our videos are recorded at 1080 p resolution and 60 fps to capture spatial and temporal detail. Two camera pairs (2–8 and 3–5) have small overlapping areas, through which about 100 people transit, while the other cameras are disjoint. Full annotations are provided in the form of trajectories of each person's foot contact point with the ground. Image bounding boxes are also available and have been semi-automatically generated. The first 5 min of video

---

[1] http://vision.cs.duke.edu/DukeMTMC.

from all the cameras are set aside for validation or training, and the remaining 80 min per camera are for testing.

Unlike many multi-camera data sets, ours is not scripted and cameras have a wider field of view. Unlike single-camera benchmarks where a tracker is tested on very short videos of different challenging scenarios, our data set is recorded in a fixed environment, and the main challenge is persistent tracking under occlusions and blind spots.

People often carry bags, backpacks, umbrellas, or bicycles. Some people stop for long periods of time in blind spots and the environment rarely constrains their paths. So transition times through blind spots are often but not always informative. 891 people walk in front of only one camera—a challenge for trackers that are prone to false-positive matches across cameras.

Working with this data set requires efficient trackers because of the amount of data to process. To illustrate, it took 6 days on a single computer to generate all the foreground masks with a standard algorithm [57] and 7 days to generate all detections on a cluster of 192 cores using the DPM detector [58]. Computing appearance features for all cameras on a single machine took half a day; computing all tracklets, trajectories, and identities together also took half a day with the proposed system (Sect. 5). People detections and foreground masks are released along with the videos.

Limitations. Our data set covers a single outdoor scene from fixed cameras. Soft lighting from overcast weather could make tracking easier. Views are mostly disjoint, which disadvantages methods that exploit data from overlapping views.

5   Reference System

We provide a reference MTMC tracker that extends to multiple cameras a system that was previously proposed for single camera multi-target tracking [1]. Our system takes target detections from any detection system, aggregates them into tracklets that are short enough to rely on a simple motion model, then aggregates tracklets into single camera trajectories, and finally connects these into multi-camera trajectories which we call *identities*.

In each of these layers, a graph $\mathcal{G} = (V, E)$ has observations (detections, tracklets, or trajectories) for nodes in V, and edges in E connect any pairs of nodes i, j for which *correlations* w_{ij} are provided. These are real values in $[-1, 1]$ that measure evidence for or against i and j having the same identity. Values of $\pm\infty$ are also allowed to represent hard evidence. A Binary Integer Program (BIP) solves the *correlation clustering* problem [59] on $\mathcal{G}$: Partition V so as to maximize the sum of the correlations w_{ij} assigned to edges that connect co-identical observations and the penalties $-w_{ij}$ assigned to edges that straddle identities. Sets of the resulting partition are taken to be the desired aggregates.

Solving this BIP is NP-hard and the problem is also hard to approximate [60], hence the need for our multi-layered solution to keep the problems small. To account for unbounded observation times, solutions are found at all levels over a sliding temporal window, with solutions from previous overlapping windows incorporated into the proper BIP as "extended observations". For additional efficiency, observations in all layers are grouped heuristically into a number of subgroups with roughly consistent appearance and space-time locations.

Our implementation includes default algorithms for the computation of appearance descriptors and correlations in all layers. For appearance, we use the methods from the previous paper [1] in the first layers and simple striped color histograms [61] for the last layer. Correlations are computed from both appearance features and simple temporal reasoning.

6   Experiments

This Section shows that (i) traditional event based measures are not good proxies for a tracker's ID precision or ID recall, defined in Sect. 3; (ii) handover errors, as customarily defined, cause frequent problems in practice; and (iii) the performance of our reference system, when evaluated with existing measures, is comparable to that of other recent MTMC trackers. We also give detailed performance numbers for our system on our data under a variety of performance measures, including ours, to establish a baseline for future comparisons.

ID Recall, ID Precision and Mismatches. Figure 4 shows that fragmentations and merges correlate poorly with ID recall and ID precision, confirming that event- and identity-based measures quantify different aspects of performance.

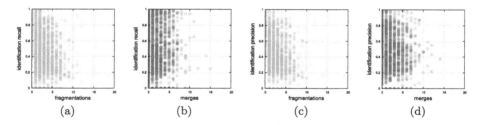

(a)   (b)   (c)   (d)

Fig. 4. Scatter plots of ground-truth trajectory ID recall (a, b) and ID precision (c, d) versus the number of trajectory fragmentations (a, c) and merges (b, d). Correlation coefficients are −0.24, −0.05, −0.38 and −0.41. This confirms that event- and identity-based measures quantify different aspects of tracker performance.

Truth-to-Result Mapping. Section 3 and Fig. 2 describe situations in which traditional, event-based performance measures handle handover errors differently from ours. Figure 5 shows that these discrepancies are frequent in our results.

Traditional System Performance Analysis. Table 3 (top) compares our reference method to existing ones on the NLPR MCT data sets [2] and evaluates performance using the existing MCTA measure. The results are obtained under the commonly used experimental setup where all systems start with the same

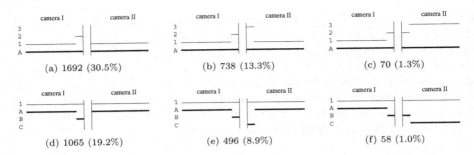

(a) 1692 (30.5%)   (b) 738 (13.3%)   (c) 70 (1.3%)

(d) 1065 (19.2%)   (e) 496 (8.9%)   (f) 58 (1.0%)

Fig. 5. [See Fig. 2 for the interpretation of these diagrams.] In about 74 % (4,119 out of 5,549) of the handovers output by our reference system on our data set, a short trajectory close to the handover causes a marked discrepancy between event-based, traditional performance measures and our identity-based measures. A handover fragmentation error (a, b) or merge error (d, e) is declared where the handover is essentially correct. A handover fragmentation error (c) or merge error (f) is not declared where the handover is essentially incorrect. Each caption shows the number of occurrences and the percentage of the total number of computed handovers.

Table 3. *Top Table:* MCTA score comparison on the existing NLPR data sets, starting from ground truth single camera trajectories. The last column contains the average dataset ranks. *Bottom Table:* Single-camera (white background) and multi-camera (grey background) results on our DukeMTMC data set. For each separate camera we report both standard multi-target tracking measures as well as our new measures.

Systems	NLPR 1	NLPR 2	NLPR 3	NLPR 4	Avg. Rank
USC [18]	**0.9152**	**0.9132**	0.5163	0.7052	2.25
Ours	0.7967	0.7336	0.6543	**0.7616**	2.5
GE [2]	0.8353	0.7034	**0.7417**	0.3845	2.75
hfutdspmct [7]	0.7425	0.6544	0.7368	0.3945	3.5
CRIPAC-MCT [62]	0.6617	0.5907	0.7105	0.5703	4
Adb-Team [7]	0.3204	0.3456	0.1382	0.1563	6

	CLEAR MOT Measures								Our Measures		
Cam	FP↓	FN↓	IDS↓	FRG↓	MOTA↑	MOTP↑	GT	MT↑	ML↓	IDP↑	IDR↑	IDF₁↑
1	9.70	52.90	178	366	37.36	67.57	1175	105	128	79.17	44.97	57.36
2	21.48	29.19	866	1929	49.17	61.70	1106	416	50	69.11	63.78	66.34
3	7.04	39.39	134	336	53.50	63.57	501	229	42	81.46	55.11	65.74
4	10.61	33.42	107	403	55.92	66.51	390	128	21	79.23	61.16	69.03
5	3.48	23.38	162	292	73.09	70.52	644	396	33	84.86	67.97	75.48
6	38.62	48.21	1426	3370	12.94	48.62	1043	207	91	48.35	43.71	45.91
7	8.28	29.57	296	675	62.03	60.73	678	373	53	85.23	67.08	75.07
8	1.29	61.69	270	365	36.98	69.07	1254	369	236	90.54	35.86	51.37
1-8									Upper bound	72.25	50.96	59.77
1-8									Baseline	52.35	36.46	42.98

input of ground-truth single-camera trajectories. On average, our baseline system ranks second out of six by using our simple default appearance features. The highest ranked method [18] uses features based on discriminative learning.

System Performance Details. Table 3 (bottom) shows both traditional and new measures of performance, both single-camera and multi-camera, for our reference system when run on our data set. This table is meant as a baseline against which new methods may be compared.

From the table we see that our IDF_1 score and MOTA do not agree on how they rank the sequence difficulty of cameras 2 and 3. This is primarily because they measure different aspects of the tracker. Also, they are different in the relative value differences. For example, camera 6 appears much more difficult than 7 based on MOTA, but the difference is not as dramatic when results are inspected visually or when IDF_1 differences are considered.

7   Conclusion

We define new measures of MTMC tracking performance that emphasize correct identities over sources of error. We introduce the largest annotated and calibrated data set to date for the comparison of MTMC trackers. We provide a reference tracker that performs comparably to the state of the art by standard measures, and we establish a baseline of performance measures, both traditional and new, for future comparisons. We hope in this way to contribute to accelerating advances in this important and exciting field.

References

1. Ristani, E., Tomasi, C.: Tracking multiple people online and in real time. In: Cremers, D., Reid, I., Saito, H., Yang, M.-H. (eds.) ACCV 2014. LNCS, vol. 9007, pp. 444–459. Springer, Heidelberg (2015)
2. Cao, L., Chen, W., Chen, X., Zheng, S., Huang, K.: An equalised global graphical model-based approach for multi-camera object tracking [cs]. arXiv:11502.03532, February 2015
3. Bernardin, K., Stiefelhagen, R.: Evaluating multiple object tracking performance: the CLEAR MOT metrics. EURASIP J. Image Video Process. **246309**, 1–10 (2008)
4. Wu, B., Nevatia, R.: Tracking of multiple, partially occluded humans based on static body part detection. In: 2006 IEEE Computer Society Conference on Computer Vision and Pattern Recognition, vol. 1, pp. 951–958. IEEE (2006)
5. Milan, A., Schindler, K., Roth, S.: Challenges of ground truth evaluation of multi-target tracking. In: 2013 IEEE Conference on Computer Vision and Pattern Recognition Workshops (CVPRW), pp. 735–742. IEEE (2013)
6. Kuo, C.-H., Huang, C., Nevatia, R.: Inter-camera association of multi-target tracks by on-line learned appearance affinity models. In: Daniilidis, K., Maragos, P., Paragios, N. (eds.) ECCV 2010, Part I. LNCS, vol. 6311, pp. 383–396. Springer, Heidelberg (2010)

7. Multi-camera Object Tracking Challenge: ECCV Workshop on Visual Surveillance and Re-Identification (2014). http://mct.idealtest.org
8. Fleuret, F., Berclaz, J., Lengagne, R., Fua, P.: Multi-camera people tracking with a probabilistic occupancy map. IEEE Trans. Pattern Anal. Mach. Intell. **30**(2), 267–282 (2008)
9. Berclaz, J., Fleuret, F., Türetken, E., Fua, P.: Multiple object tracking using k-shortest paths optimization. IEEE Trans. Pattern Anal. Mach. Intell. **33**(9), 1806–1819 (2011)
10. Ferryman, J., Shahrokni, A.: An overview of the PETS 2009 challenge (2009)
11. D'Orazio, T., Leo, M., Mosca, N., Spagnolo, P., Mazzeo, P.L.: A semi-automatic system for ground truth generation of soccer video sequences. In: Sixth IEEE International Conference on Advanced Video and Signal Based Surveillance, AVSS 2009, pp. 559–564. IEEE (2009)
12. De Vleeschouwer, C., Chen, F., Delannay, D., Parisot, C., Chaudy, C., Martrou, E., Cavallaro, A., et al.: Distributed video acquisition and annotation for sport-event summarization. In: NEM summit 2008: Towards Future Media Internet (2008)
13. Zhang, S., Staudt, E., Faltemier, T., Roy-Chowdhury, A.: A camera network tracking (CamNeT) dataset and performance baseline. In: 2015 IEEE Winter Conference on Applications of Computer Vision (WACV), pp. 365–372, January 2015
14. Per, J., Kenk, V.S., Mandeljc, R., Kristan, M., Kovačič, S.: Dana36: a multi-camera image dataset for object identification in surveillance scenarios. In: 2012 IEEE Ninth International Conference on Advanced Video and Signal-Based Surveillance (AVSS), pp. 64–69. IEEE (2012)
15. Benenson, R., Omran, M., Hosang, J., Schiele, B.: Ten years of pedestrian detection, what have we learned? In: Agapito, L., Bronstein, M.M., Rother, C. (eds.) ECCV 2014 Workshops. LNCS, vol. 8926, pp. 613–627. Springer, Heidelberg (2015)
16. Leal-Taixé, L., Milan, A., Reid, I., Roth, S., Schindler, K.: Motchallenge 2015: towards a benchmark for multi-target tracking. arXiv: 1504.01942, April 2015
17. Bredereck, M., Jiang, X., Korner, M., Denzler, J.: Data association for multi-object Tracking-by-Detection in multi-camera networks. In: 2012 Sixth International Conference on Distributed Smart Cameras (ICDSC), pp. 1–6, October 2012
18. Cai, Y., Medioni, G.: Exploring context information for inter-camera multiple target tracking. In: 2014 IEEE Winter Conference on Applications of Computer Vision (WACV), pp. 761–768, March 2014
19. Chen, K.W., Lai, C.C., Lee, P.J., Chen, C.S., Hung, Y.P.: Adaptive learning for target tracking and true linking discovering across multiple non-overlapping cameras. IEEE Trans. Multimedia **13**(4), 625–638 (2011)
20. Chen, X., An, L., Bhanu, B.: Multitarget tracking in nonoverlapping cameras using a reference set. IEEE Sens. J. **15**(5), 2692–2704 (2015)
21. Chen, X., Huang, K., Tan, T.: Direction-based stochastic matching for pedestrian recognition in non-overlapping cameras. In: 2011 18th IEEE International Conference on Image Processing (ICIP), pp. 2065–2068, September 2011
22. Daliyot, S., Netanyahu, N.S.: A framework for inter-camera association of multi-target trajectories by invariant target models. In: Park, J.-I., Kim, J. (eds.) ACCV Workshops 2012, Part II. LNCS, vol. 7729, pp. 372–386. Springer, Heidelberg (2013)
23. Das, A., Chakraborty, A., Roy-Chowdhury, A.K.: Consistent re-identification in a camera network. In: Fleet, D., Pajdla, T., Schiele, B., Tuytelaars, T. (eds.) ECCV 2014, Part II. LNCS, vol. 8690, pp. 330–345. Springer, Heidelberg (2014)

24. Gilbert, A., Bowden, R.: Tracking objects across cameras by incrementally learning inter-camera colour calibration and patterns of activity. In: Leonardis, A., Bischof, H., Pinz, A. (eds.) ECCV 2006. LNCS, vol. 3952, pp. 125–136. Springer, Heidelberg (2006)
25. Javed, O., Shafique, K., Rasheed, Z., Shah, M.: Modeling inter-camera space time and appearance relationships for tracking across non-overlapping views. Comput. Vis. Image Underst. **109**(2), 146–162 (2008)
26. Makris, D., Ellis, T., Black, J.: Bridging the gaps between cameras. In: Proceedings of the 2004 IEEE Computer Society Conference on Computer Vision and Pattern Recognition, CVPR 2004, vol. 2, June 2004
27. Jiuqing, W., Li, L.: Distributed optimization for global data association in non-overlapping camera networks. In: 2013 Seventh International Conference on Distributed Smart Cameras (ICDSC), pp. 1–7, October 2013
28. Calderara, S., Cucchiara, R., Prati, A.: Bayesian-competitive consistent labeling for people surveillance. IEEE Trans. Pattern Anal. Mach. Intell. **30**(2), 354–360 (2008)
29. Zhang, S., Zhu, Y., Roy-Chowdhury, A.: Tracking multiple interacting targets in a camera network. Comput. Vis. Image Underst. **134**, 64–73 (2015)
30. Ayazoglu, M., Li, B., Dicle, C., Sznaier, M., Camps, O.: Dynamic subspace-based coordinated multicamera tracking. In: 2011 IEEE International Conference on Computer Vision (ICCV), pp. 2462–2469, November 2011
31. Kamal, A., Farrell, J., Roy-Chowdhury, A.: Information consensus for distributed multi-target tracking. In: 2013 IEEE Conference on Computer Vision and Pattern Recognition (CVPR), pp. 2403–2410, June 2013
32. Hamid, R., Kumar, R., Grundmann, M., Kim, K., Essa, I., Hodgins, J.: Player localization using multiple static cameras for sports visualization. In: 2010 IEEE Conference on Computer Vision and Pattern Recognition (CVPR), pp. 731–738, June 2010
33. Martinel, N., Micheloni, C., Foresti, G.L.: Saliency weighted features for person re-identification. In: Agapito, L., Bronstein, M.M., Rother, C. (eds.) ECCV 2014. LNCS, vol. 8927, pp. 191–208. Springer, Heidelberg (2015). doi:10.1007/978-3-319-16199-0_14
34. Zhao, R., Ouyang, W., Wang, X.: Unsupervised salience learning for person re-identification. In: IEEE Conference on Computer Vision and Pattern Recognition (CVPR) (2013)
35. Bedagkar-Gala, A., Shah, S.: Multiple person re-identification using part based spatio-temporal color appearance model. In: 2011 IEEE International Conference on Computer Vision Workshops (ICCV Workshops), pp. 1721–1728, November 2011
36. Bedagkar-Gala, A., Shah, S.K.: Part-based spatio-temporal model for multi-person re-identification. Pattern Recogn. Lett. **33**(14), 1908–1915 (2012). Novel Pattern Recognition-based Methods for Re-identification in Biometric Context
37. Cheng, D., Cristani, M., Stoppa, M., Bazzani, L., Murino, V.: Custom pictorial structures for re-identification. In: Proceedings of the British Machine Vision Conference, pp. 68.1–68.11. BMVA Press (2011). doi:10.5244/C.25.68
38. Baltieri, D., Vezzani, R., Cucchiara, R.: Learning articulated body models for people re-identification. In: Proceedings of the 21st ACM International Conference on Multimedia, MM 2013, pp. 557–560. ACM, New York (2013)

39. Cheng, D., Cristani, M.: Person re-identification by articulated appearance matching. In: Gong, S., Cristani, M., Yan, S., Loy, C.C. (eds.) Person Re-Identification. Advances in Computer Vision and Pattern Recognition, pp. 139–160. Springer, London (2014)
40. Baltieri, D., Vezzani, R., Cucchiara, R.: Mapping appearance descriptors on 3d body models for people re-identification. Int. J. Comput. Vis. **111**(3), 345–364 (2015)
41. Brendel, W., Amer, M., Todorovic, S.: Multiobject tracking as maximum weight independent set. In: 2011 IEEE Conference on Computer Vision and Pattern Recognition (CVPR), pp. 1273–1280. IEEE (2011)
42. Shu, G., Dehghan, A., Oreifej, O., Hand, E., Shah, M.: Part-based multiple-person tracking with partial occlusion handling. In: 2012 IEEE Conference on Computer Vision and Pattern Recognition (CVPR), pp. 1815–1821. IEEE (2012)
43. Wu, B., Nevatia, R.: Detection and tracking of multiple, partially occluded humans by bayesian combination of edgelet based part detectors. Int. J. Comput. Vis. **75**(2), 247–266 (2007)
44. Izadinia, H., Saleemi, I., Li, W., Shah, M.: $(MP)^2T$: multiple people multiple parts tracker. In: Fitzgibbon, A., Lazebnik, S., Perona, P., Sato, Y., Schmid, C. (eds.) ECCV 2012, Part VI. LNCS, vol. 7577, pp. 100–114. Springer, Heidelberg (2012)
45. Pirsiavash, H., Ramanan, D., Fowlkes, C.C.: Globally-optimal greedy algorithms for tracking a variable number of objects. In: 2011 IEEE Conference on Computer Vision and Pattern Recognition (CVPR), pp. 1201–1208. IEEE (2011)
46. Zhang, L., Li, Y., Nevatia, R.: Global data association for multi-object tracking using network flows. In: IEEE Conference on Computer Vision and Pattern Recognition, CVPR 2008, pp. 1–8. IEEE (2008)
47. Butt, A.A., Collins, R.T.: Multiple target tracking using frame triplets. In: Lee, K.M., Matsushita, Y., Rehg, J.M., Hu, Z. (eds.) ACCV 2012, Part III. LNCS, vol. 7726, pp. 163–176. Springer, Heidelberg (2013)
48. Chari, V., Lacoste-Julien, S., Laptev, I., Sivic, J.: On pairwise costs for network flow multi-object tracking. In: Proceedings of the IEEE Conference on Computer Vision and Pattern Recognition, pp. 5537–5545 (2015)
49. Collins, R.T.: Multitarget data association with higher-order motion models. In: 2012 IEEE Conference on Computer Vision and Pattern Recognition (CVPR), pp. 1744–1751. IEEE (2012)
50. Dehghan, A., Assari, S.M., Shah, M.: Gmmcp tracker: globally optimal generalized maximum multi clique problem for multiple object tracking. In: CVPR, vol. 1, p. 2 (2015)
51. Kumar, R., Charpiat, G., Thonnat, M.: Multiple object tracking by efficient graph partitioning. In: Cremers, D., Reid, I., Saito, H., Yang, M.-H. (eds.) ACCV 2014. LNCS, vol. 9006, pp. 445–460. Springer, Heidelberg (2015)
52. Shafique, K., Shah, M.: A noniterative greedy algorithm for multiframe point correspondence. IEEE Trans. Pattern Anal. Mach. Intell. **27**(1), 51–65 (2005)
53. Tang, S., Andres, B., Andriluka, M., Schiele, B.: Subgraph decomposition for multi-target tracking. In: Proceedings of the IEEE Conference on Computer Vision and Pattern Recognition, pp. 5033–5041 (2015)
54. Wen, L., Li, W., Yan, J., Lei, Z., Yi, D., Li, S.Z.: Multiple target tracking based on undirected hierarchical relation hypergraph. In: 2014 IEEE Conference on Computer Vision and Pattern Recognition (CVPR), pp. 1282–1289. IEEE (2014)

55. Roshan Zamir, A., Dehghan, A., Shah, M.: GMCP-tracker: global multi-object tracking using generalized minimum clique graphs. In: Fitzgibbon, A., Lazebnik, S., Perona, P., Sato, Y., Schmid, C. (eds.) ECCV 2012, Part II. LNCS, vol. 7573, pp. 343–356. Springer, Heidelberg (2012)

56. Yu, S.I., Meng, D., Zuo, W., Hauptmann, A.: The solution path algorithm for identity-aware multi-object tracking. In: Proceedings of the IEEE Conference on Computer Vision and Pattern Recognition, pp. 3871–3879 (2016)

57. Yao, J., Odobez, J.M.: Multi-layer background subtraction based on color and texture. In: IEEE Conference on Computer Vision and Pattern Recognition, CVPR 2007, pp. 1–8. IEEE (2007)

58. Felzenszwalb, P., Girshick, R., McAllester, D., Ramanan, D.: Object detection with discriminatively trained part-based models. IEEE Trans. Pattern Anal. Mach. Intell. **32**(9), 1627–1645 (2010)

59. Bansal, N., Blum, A., Chawla, S.: Correlation clustering. In: Foundations of Computer Science (2002)

60. Tan, J.: A note on the inapproximability of correlation clustering (2008)

61. Liu, C., Gong, S., Loy, C.C., Lin, X.: Person re-identification: what features are important? In: Fusiello, A., Murino, V., Cucchiara, R. (eds.) ECCV 2012. LNCS, vol. 7583, pp. 391–401. Springer, Heidelberg (2012). doi:10.1007/978-3-642-33863-2_39

62. Chen, W., Cao, L., Chen, X., Huang, K.: A novel solution for multi-camera object tracking. In: 2014 IEEE International Conference on Image Processing (ICIP), pp. 2329–2333. IEEE (2014)

POI: Multiple Object Tracking with High Performance Detection and Appearance Feature

Fengwei Yu[1,3(✉)], Wenbo Li[2,3], Quanquan Li[3], Yu Liu[3],
Xiaohua Shi[1], and Junjie Yan[3]

[1] Beihang University, Beijing, China
forwil@buaa.edu.cn
[2] University at Albany, SUNY, Albany, USA
[3] Sensetime Group Limited, Beijing, China

Abstract. Detection and learning based appearance feature play the central role in data association based multiple object tracking (MOT), but most recent MOT works usually ignore them and only focus on the hand-crafted feature and association algorithms. In this paper, we explore the high-performance detection and deep learning based appearance feature, and show that they lead to significantly better MOT results in both online and offline setting. We make our detection and appearance feature publicly available (https://drive.google.com/open?id=0B5ACiy41McAHMjczS2p0dFg3emM). In the following part, we first summarize the detection and appearance feature, and then introduce our tracker named Person of Interest (POI), which has both online and offline version (We use POI to denote our online tracker and KDNT to denote our offline tracker in submission.).

1 Detection

In data association based MOT, the tracking performance is heavily affected by the detection results. We implement our detector based on Faster R-CNN [14]. In our implementation, the CNN model is fine-tuned from the VGG-16 on ImageNet. The additional training data includes ETHZ pedestrian dataset [4], Caltech pedestrian dataset [2] and the self-collected surveillance dataset (365653 boxes in 47556 frames). We adopt the multi-scale training strategy by randomly sampling a pyramid scale for each time. However, we only use a single scale and a single model during test. Moreover, we also use skip pooling [1] and multi-region [5] strategies to combine features at different scales and levels.

In considering the definition of MOTA in MOT16 [12], the sum of false negatives (FN) and false positives (FP) poses a large impact on the value of MOTA. In Table 1, we show that our detection optimization strategies lead to the significant decrease in the sum of FP and FN[1].

---

[1] We use detection score threshold 0.3 for Faster R-CNN and -1 for DPMv5, labeling the ID of detection box with incremental integer, and evaluate FP and FN with MOT16 devkit.

© Springer International Publishing Switzerland 2016
G. Hua and H. Jégou (Eds.): ECCV 2016 Workshops, Part II, LNCS 9914, pp. 36–42, 2016.
DOI: 10.1007/978-3-319-48881-3_3

Table 1. Detection performance evaluation (on MOT16 train set)

Strategies	FP	FN	FP + FN
DPMv5	28839	62353	91192
Faster R-CNN baseline	5384	47343	52727
Faster R-CNN + skip pooling	5410	46399	51809
Faster R-CNN + multi-region	4476	46738	51214
Faster R-CNN + both	8722	37865	46587

2 Appearance Feature

The distance between appearance features is used for computing the affinity value in data association. The affinity value based on the ideal appearance feature should be large for persons of the same identity, and be small for persons of different identities. In our implementation, we extract the appearance feature using a network which is similar to GoogLeNet [15]. The input size of our network is 96×96, and the kernel size of *pool5* layer is 3×3 instead of 7×7. The output layer is a fully connected layer which outputs the 128 dimensional feature. In the tracking phase, patches are first cropped according to the detection responses, and then resized to 96×96 for feature extraction. The cosine distance is used for measuring the appearance affinity.

For training, we collect a dataset which contains nearly 119 K patches from 19835 identities. Such a dataset consists of multiple person re-id datasets, including PRW [18], Market-1501 [18], VIPeR [13] and CUHK03 [8]. We use the softmax and triplet loss jointly during training. The softmax loss guarantees the discriminative ability of the appearance feature, while the triplet loss ensures the cosine distance of the appearance features of the same identity to be small.

3 Online Tracker

We implement a simple online tracker, which uses Kalman filter [6] for motion prediction and Kuhn-Munkres algorithm [7] for data association. The overall tracking procedure is described in Algorithm 1.

In the following, we introduce the affinity matrix construction, data association method, threshold value setting and tracking quality metric.

Affinity Matrix Construction. To construct an affinity matrix for the Kuhn-Munkres algorithm, we calculate the affinity between tracklets and detections. We combine motion, shape and appearance affinity as the final affinity. Specifically, the appearance affinity is calculated based on the appearance feature described in Sect. 2. Details of the affinity calculation are given below:

Algorithm 1. Overall Procedure of the Online Tracker

Input: A new frame at the t-th timestep, the detection set D^t, and the tracklet set T^{t-1}
Output: The new tracklet set T^t

1: Calculate the affinity matrix $A^{t-1} = Affinity(T^{t-1}, D^t)$
2: Divide T^{t-1} into high tracking quality set T^{t-1}_{high} and low quality set T^{t-1}_{low} with threshold τ_t
3: Use Kuhn-Munkres algorithm to find the optimal matching between $(T^{t-1}_{high}, T^{t-1}_{low})$ and D^t based on A^{t-1}
4: Use threshold τ_a to decide whether association success or not
5: Obtain association-success set $T^{t-1}_{success_i}$ with matched detection set $D^t_{success_i}$, association-fail tracklet set T^{t-1}_{fail} and unmatched detection set D^t_{fail}
6: Use Kalman filter and feature aggregation to generate new tracklet subset T^t_1 based on association-success set: $T^t_1 = Average(T^{t-1}_{success_i}, D^t_{success_i})$.
7: Use Kalman filter to predict or remove the association-fail tracklets with missing tracklets threshold τ_m: $T^t_2 = Predict\_Or\_Remove(T^{t-1}_{fail}, \tau_m)$.
8: Initialize the unmatched detections as the new tracklets: $T^t_3 = Initialize(D^t_{fail})$.
9: Merge the tracklet subsets to generate new candidate tracklet set : $T^t_{candidate} = T^t_1 \cup T^t_2 \cup T^t_3$.
10: Remove out of image border candidate tracklet set to generate new tracklet set: $T^t = Filter(T^t_{candidate})$

$$aff_{app}(trk_i, det_j) = cosine(feat_{trk_i}, feat_{det_j}) \tag{1}$$

$$aff_{mot}(trk_i, det_j) = e^{-w_1*((\frac{X_{trk_i}-X_{det_j}}{W_{det_j}})^2 + (\frac{Y_{trk_i}-Y_{det_j}}{H_{det_j}})^2)} \tag{2}$$

$$aff_{shp}(trk_i, det_j) = e^{-w_2*(\frac{|H_{trk_i}-H_{det_j}|}{H_{trk_i}+H_{det_j}} + \frac{|W_{trk_i}-W_{det_j}|}{W_{trk_i}+W_{det_j}})} \tag{3}$$

$$affinity(trk_i, det_j) = aff_{app}(trk_i, det_j) * aff_{mot}(trk_i, det_j) * aff_{shp}(trk_i, det_j) \tag{4}$$

aff_{app}, aff_{mot} and aff_{shp} indicate appearance, motion and shape affinity between the detection and tracklet, respectively. We combine these affinities with weights w_1 and w_2 as the final affinity.

Data Association. The tracklets and new detections are associated using the Kuhn-Munkres algorithm. Since the Kuhn-Munkres algorithm attempts to yield the global optimal result, it may fail when some detections are missing. To this end, we use a two-stage matching strategy, which divides T^{t-1} into high tracking quality set T^{t-1}_{high} and low quality set T^{t-1}_{low}. The matching is first performed between T^{t-1}_{high} and D, and then performed between $(T^{t-1}_{high} - T^{t-1}_{success}) \cup T^{t-1}_{low}$ and $D - D_{success}$.

Threshold Value Setting. On line 2 of Algorithm 1, we introduce τ_t to divide T^{t-1} into high and low tracking quality set. The strategy is intuitive: we mark a tracklet with *high* flag whose tracking quality is higher than τ_t, other tracklets will be mark as *low*. On line 4, we use τ_a to mark the association to be success or fail based on the affinity value. On line 7, we use τ_m as a threshold to drop a tracklet which is lost for more than τ_m frames.

Tracking Quality Metric. Tracking quality is designed to measure whether a object is tracking well or not. We use following formula to define tracking quality:

$$Quality(tracklet_i) = \frac{\sum_{k \in couples(tracklet_i)} affinity_k}{length(tracklet_i)} (1 - e^{-w_3 * \sqrt{length(tracklet_i)}})$$

(5)

where $couples(tracklet_i)$, with the form $\{trk_x, det_y\}$, is a set that contains every success association couple in history.

4 Offline Tracker

Our offline tracker an improved version of H^{2}T [16] while based on K-Dense Neighbors [11]. It is more robust and efficient than H^{2}T in handling the complex tracking scenarios. The overall procedure of the tracker is described in Algorithm 2.

Algorithm 2. Overall Procedure of the Offline Tracker

Input: A tracking video and the detections in all frames
Output: The tracking results (trajectories of targets)
  1: Divide the tracking video into multiple disjoint segments in the temporal domain
  2: Use the dense neighbors (DN) search^2 to associate the detection responses into short tracklets
      in each segment
  3: **while** The number of segments is greater than one **do**
  4:    Merge several nearby segments into a longer segment
  5:    Use the DN search in each longer segment to associate existing tracklets into longer tracklets
  6: **end while**

We make the following improvements over H^{2}T [16].

Appearance Representation. To construct the affinity matrix for the dense neighbors (DN) search, we need to calculate three affinities, *i.e*, appearance, motion, and smoothness affinity. Among these three affinities, the appearance affinity is the most important one and we use the CNN based feature described in Sect. 2, instead of the hand-crafted feature in [16].

Big Target. A scenario that H^{2}T [16] does not work well is the mixture of small and big targets. The reason is that the motion and smoothness affinities are unreliable for the big targets. Such unreliability is caused by the unsteady detection responses of the big targets. We introduce two thresholds, τ_s and τ_r, regarding the object scale to deal with this challenge, *i.e*, τ_s for preventing associating detection responses from very different scale, and τ_r for determining whether to reduce the weights of motion and smoothness affinity. Specifically,

---

^{2} The DN search is performed on an affinity matrix which encodes the similarity between two tracklets. Please refer to [3,10,11,16] for details about DN search and its advantages over the GMCP [9,17] as a data association method.

if the ratio of the detection response scale and the target scale is less than τ_s, such a detection response will not be associated with the target. If the ratio of the detection response height and the image height is greater than τ_r, such a detection response will not be associated with the target. Both τ_s and τ_r are set as 0.5.

Algorithm Efficiency. H^2T is slow in handling the long tracking sequence where there exist plenty of targets. Among the steps in the algorithm, the step of DN search is the most time-consuming. To be more specific, the larger an affinity matrix, the longer time it will take to perform the DN search. Thus, we abandon the high-order information [16] when constructing the affinity matrix, which significantly reduces the matrix dimensions and improves the algorithm efficiency.

5   Evaluation

Our online and offline tracker are not learning based algorithm. We only tuning detection score threshold on train set and apply it to its similar scene from test set. For evaluation and submission, 0.1 is set for MOT16-03 and MOT16-04 due to high precision of detection result (03 and 04 are both surveillance scene, which is quite easy while our detector have been trained by self-collected surveillance dataset), and 0.3 is set for other sequences.

For both online[3] and offline tracker, we compare our detector with the official detector, and compare our feature with default CNN feature. The comparison results on MOT16 [12] train set are listed in Tables 2 and 3, respectively. Note that our detector leads to much better results in MT, ML, FP and FN, and our feature helps reduce both IDS and FM.

Table 2. Online tracker result on the train set

Det. and Feat.	MT	ML	FP	FN	IDS	FM	MOTA	MOTP
DPMv5 + Our Feat.	7.54 %	52.42 %	6197	70952	784	2697	29.4	77.2
Our Det. + GoogLeNet Feat.	31.72 %	16.25 %	**3207**	35472	1541	2235	63.6	**82.6**
Our Det. and Feat.	**37.33 %**	**14.70 %**	3497	**34241**	**716**	**1973**	**65.2**	82.4

Table 3. Offline tracker result on the train set

Det. and Feat.	MT	ML	FP	FN	IDS	FM	MOTA	MOTP
DPMv5 + Our Feat.	10.64 %	52.80 %	27238	63443	1540	1853	16.5	77.4
Our Det. + GoogLeNet Feat.	13.93 %	60.93 %	**1258**	58213	1350	2196	44.9	**85.0**
Our Det. and Feat.	**37.52 %**	**17.60 %**	2762	**33327**	**462**	**717**	**66.9**	83.3

---

[3] we use 0.5 for w_1, 1.5 for w_2, 1.2 for w_3, 0.5 for τ_t, 0.4 for τ_a and 100 frames for τ_m.

Table 4. Comparison to the state-of-the-art methods on MOT16 rank list

Tracker	MT	ML	FP	FN	IDS	FM	MOTA	MOTP
KFILDAwSDP (online)	26.9 %	21.6 %	23266	56394	1977	2954	55.2	77.2
MCMOT-HDM (offline)	31.5 %	24.2 %	9855	57257	1394	1318	62.4	78.3
Our online tracker	33.99 %	20.82 %	**5061**	55914	**805**	3093	66.1	**79.5**
Our offline tracker	**40.97**%	**18.97**%	11479	**45605**	933	**1093**	68.2	79.4

6 ECCV 2016 Challenge Results

Our ECCV 2016 Challenge results are listed in Table 4. Obviously, both our online and offline trackers outperform the state-of-the-art approaches by a large margin. Note that our offline tracker achieves the best performance in FN. However, its performance in FP is moderate, due to the interpolation module.

7 Conclusion

In this submission, we take many efforts to get high performance detection and deep learning based appearance feature. We show that they lead to the state-of-the-art multiple object tracking results, even with very simple online tracker. One observation is that with high performance detection and appearance feature, the state-of-the-art offline tracker does not have expected advantages over the much simpler online one. This observation is not reported in many current MOT papers, which often use detections that are not good enough. We make our detections and deep learning based re-ID features on MOT2016 publicly available, and hope that they can help more sophisticated trackers to get better performance.

References

1. Bell, S., Zitnick, C.L., Bala, K., Girshick, R.B.: Inside-outside net: detecting objects in context with skip pooling and recurrent neural networks. CoRR (2015)
2. Dollár, P., Wojek, C., Schiele, B., Perona, P.: Pedestrian detection: a benchmark. In: CVPR (2009)
3. Du, D., Qi, H., Li, W., Wen, L., Huang, Q., Lyu, S.: Online deformable object tracking based on structure-aware hyper-graph. TIP (2016)
4. Ess, A., Leibe, B., Schindler, K., Gool, L.J.V.: A mobile vision system for robust multi-person tracking. In: CVPR (2008)
5. Gidaris, S., Komodakis, N.: Object detection via a multi-region and semantic segmentation-aware CNN model. In: ICCV (2015)
6. Kalman, R.E.: A new approach to linear filtering and prediction problems. J. Basic Eng. **82**, 35–45 (1960)
7. Kuhn, H.W.: The hungarian method for the assignment problem. Naval Res. Logistics Q. **2**, 83–97 (1955)
8. Li, W., Zhao, R., Xiao, T., Wang, X.: Deepreid: deep filter pairing neural network for person re-identification. In: CVPR (2014)

9. Li, W., Wen, L., Chuah, M.C., Lyu, S.: Category-blind human action recognition: a practical recognition system. In: ICCV (2015)
10. Li, W., Wen, L., Chuah, M.C., Zhang, Y., Lei, Z., Li, S.Z.: Online visual tracking using temporally coherent part cluster. In: WACV (2015)
11. Liu, H., Yang, X., Latecki, L.J., Yan, S.: Dense neighborhoods on affinity graph. IJCV **98**(1), 65–82 (2012)
12. Milan, A., Leal-Taixé, L., Reid, I.D., Roth, S., Schindler, K.: MOT16: a benchmark for multi-object tracking. CoRR (2016)
13. Prosser, B., Zheng, W., Gong, S., Xiang, T.: Person re-identification by support vector ranking. In: BMVC (2010)
14. Ren, S., He, K., Girshick, R.B., Sun, J.: Faster R-CNN: towards real-time object detection with region proposal networks. In: NIPS (2015)
15. Szegedy, C., Liu, W., Jia, Y., Sermanet, P., Reed, S.E., Anguelov, D., Erhan, D., Vanhoucke, V., Rabinovich, A.: Going deeper with convolutions. In: CVPR (2015)
16. Wen, L., Li, W., Yan, J., Lei, Z., Yi, D., Li, S.Z.: Multiple target tracking based on undirected hierarchical relation hypergraph. In: CVPR (2014)
17. Roshan Zamir, A., Dehghan, A., Shah, M.: GMCP-tracker: global multi-object tracking using generalized minimum clique graphs. In: Fitzgibbon, A., Lazebnik, S., Perona, P., Sato, Y., Schmid, C. (eds.) ECCV 2012, Part II. LNCS, vol. 7573, pp. 343–356. Springer, Heidelberg (2012)
18. Zheng, L., Zhang, H., Sun, S., Chandraker, M., Tian, Q.: Person re-identification in the wild. CoRR (2016)

Long-Term Time-Sensitive Costs for CRF-Based Tracking by Detection

Nam Le[1,2(✉)], Alexander Heili[1,2], and Jean-Marc Odobez[1,2]

[1] Idiap Research Institute, Martigny, Switzerland
nle@idiap.ch
[2] École Polytechnique Fédéral de Lausanne, Lausanne, Switzerland

Abstract. We present a Conditional Random Field (CRF) approach to tracking-by-detection in which we model pairwise factors linking pairs of detections and their hidden labels, as well as higher order potentials defined in terms of label costs. Our method considers long-term connectivity between pairs of detections and models cue similarities as well as dissimilarities between them using time-interval sensitive models. In addition to position, color, and visual motion cues, we investigate in this paper the use of SURF cue as structure representations. We take advantage of the *MOTChallenge* 2016 to refine our tracking models, evaluate our system, and study the impact of different parameters of our tracking system on performance.

1 Introduction

Automated tracking of multiple people is a fundamental problem in video surveillance, social behavior analysis, or abnormality detection. Nonetheless, multi-person tracking remains a challenging task, especially in single camera settings, notably due to sensor noise, changing backgrounds, high crowding, occlusions, clutter and appearance similarity between individuals. Tracking-by-detection methods aim at automatically associating human detections across frames, such that each set of associated detections univocally belongs to one individual in the scene [2,7]. Compared to background modeling-based approaches, tracking-by-detection is more robust to changing backgrounds and moving cameras.

In this paper, we present our tracking-by-detection approach [5] formulated as a labeling problem in a Conditional Random Field (CRF) framework, where we target the minimization of an energy function defined upon pairs of detections and labels. The specificities of our model is to rely on cue specific and reliability weighted long-term time-sensitive association costs between pairs of detections. This work was original proposed in [4,5], and in this paper, we explored the use of additional cue (SURF) for similarity modeling, and the exploitation of training data to better filter detections or learn the cost models. In the following, we introduce the main modeling elements of the framework, then present the changes more specific to the *MOTChallenge* before presenting the results and analysis of our framework on the *MOTChallenge* data.

G. Hua and H. Jégou (Eds.): ECCV 2016 Workshops, Part II, LNCS 9914, pp. 43–51, 2016.
DOI: 10.1007/978-3-319-48881-3_4

2   CRF Tracking Framework

Our framework is illustrated in Fig. 1. Multi-person tracking is formulated as a labelling problem within a Conditional Random Field (CRF) approach. Given the set of detections $Y = \{y_i\}_{i=1:N_y}$, where N_y is the total number of detections, we search for the set of corresponding labels $L = \{l_i\}_{i=1:N_y}$ such that detections belonging to the same identity are assigned the same label by optimizing the posterior probability $p(L|Y, \lambda)$, where λ denotes the set of model parameters. Alternatively, assuming pairwise factors, this is equivalent to minimizing the following energy potential [5]:

$$U(L) = \left(\sum_{(i,j) \in \mathcal{V}} \sum_{r=1}^{N_s} w_{ij}^r \, \beta_{ij}^r \, \delta(l_i - l_j) \right) + \Lambda(L), \tag{1}$$

with the Potts coefficients defined as

$$\beta_{ij}^r = \log \left[\frac{p(S_r(y_i, y_j)|H_0, \lambda_{\boldsymbol{\Delta}_{ij}}^r)}{p(S_r(y_i, y_j)|H_1, \lambda_{\boldsymbol{\Delta}_{ij}}^r)} \right], \tag{2}$$

and where $\Lambda(L)$ is a label cost preventing creation of termination or trajectories within the image (see [5] for details). The other terms are defined as follows.

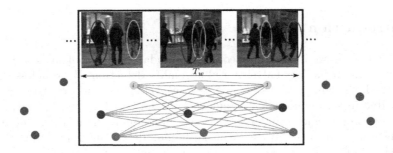

Fig. 1. Tracking as graph clustering task. The detections form the nodes, and a long-term connectivity is used, i.e. all links between pairs of nodes within a temporal window T_w are used to define the cost function. Long-term connectivity combined with time-interval sensitive discriminative pairwise models and visual motion enables dealing with missed detections, e.g. due to occlusion, as well as skipped frames.

First, the energy involves N_s feature functions $S_r(y_i, y_j)$ measuring the similarity between detection pairs as well as confidence weights w_{ij}^r for each detection pair, which mainly depends on overlaps between detection (see [5] for details). Importantly, note that a *long-term connectivity* is exploited, in which the set of valid pairs $\mathcal{V}$ contains *all pairs* whose temporal distance $\boldsymbol{\Delta}_{ij} = |t_j - t_i|$ is lower than T_w, where T_w is usually between 1 and 2 s. This contrasts with most frame-to-frame tracking or path optimization approaches.

Fig. 2. Position models. The different iso-contours of value 0 of the Potts costs for different values of Δ (i.e. location of detections occurring after Δ frames around each shown detection and for which $\beta = 0$), learned from sequences MOT16-01 and MOT16-03. In the region delimited by a curve, association will be favored, whereas outside it will be disfavored. Curves show different moving directions and amplitudes in each sequence.

Secondly, the Potts coefficients themselves are defined as the likelihood ratio of the probability of feature distances under two hypotheses: H_0 if $l_i \neq l_j$ (i.e. detections do not belong to the same face), or H_1 when labels are the same. In practice, this allows to *incorporate discrimination*, by quantifying how much features are similar and dissimilar under the two hypotheses, and not only on how much they are similar for the same identity as done in traditional path optimization of many graph-based tracking methods. Furthermore, note that as these costs depend on the set of parameters $\lambda^r_{\Delta_{ij}}$, they are *time-interval sensitive*, in that they depend on the time difference Δ_{ij} between the detections. This allows a fine modelling of the problem and will be illustrated below.

Finally, in Eq. 1, $\delta(.)$ denotes the Kronecker function ($\delta(a) = 1$ if $a = 0$, $\delta(a) = 0$ otherwise). Therefore, coefficients β^r_{ij} are only counted when the labels are the same. They can thus be considered as costs for associating or not a detection pair in the same track. When $\beta^r_{ij} < 0$, the pair of detections should be associated so as to minimize the energy 1, whereas when $\beta^r_{ij} > 0$, it should not.

2.1 Features and Association Cost Definition

Our approach relies on the unsupervised learning of time sensitive association costs for $N_s = 8$ different features. Below, we briefly motivate and introduce the chosen features and their corresponding distributions. We illustrate them by showing the Potts curves (for their learning see next section), emphasizing the effect of time-interval sensitivity and their easy adaptation to different datasets.

Position. The similarity is the Euclidean distance $S_1(y_i, y_j) = \mathbf{x}_i - \mathbf{x}_j$, with $\mathbf{x}_i$ the image location of the ith detection y_i. The distributions of this feature are modelled as zero mean Gaussians whose covariance Σ^H_Δ depends on the hypothesis (H_0 or H_1) and the time gap Δ between two detections. Figure 2 illustrates the learned models by plotting the zero iso-curves of the resulting β functions. We can notice the non-linearity with respect to increasing time gaps Δ (especially for small Δ increases), and the difference between sequences in viewpoints, moving directions, and amplitudes is captured by the models.

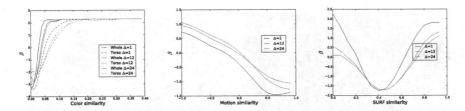

Fig. 3. Automatically learned Potts functions β for the different similarity functions and some values of Δ in sequence MOT16-01. Left: color distances. Middle: motion cue distance. Right: SURF cue distance. (Color figure online)

Motion cues. Motion similarity between detection pairs is assessed by comparing their relative displacement and their visual motion. The similarity is computed as the cosine of the angle between these two vectors. Intuitively, if a person moves in a given direction, the displacement between its detections and their visual motion will be aligned, leading to a motion similarity close to 1. The resulting β curves in the middle plot of Fig. 3 confirm the above intuition, as the β decreases at the cosine value increases.

Appearance (color). Detections are represented by multi-level color histograms in 4 different regions: the whole body and its subparts, the head, torso, and leg regions. The similarity between histograms of the same region of the detections is measured using the Bhattacharyya distance D_h, and the distributions of this distance is modelled using a non-parametric method. Example of Potts curve β are shown in Fig. 3, Left. We can notice here that the statistics associated to each region are relatively different, and although we would not expect so, also varies with the time gap Δ between detections.

Appearance (SURF). Color is sometimes not sufficient to discriminate between people. We thus propose to exploit more structured appearance measures. More precisely, we rely on SURF [1] descriptors computed at interest points detected within the detection bounding box, although better re-identification oriented descriptors could be used. They are invariant to scale, rotation, and illumination changes and are thus suitable for person representation under different lighting conditions or viewpoint changes. As similarity measure, we use the average Euclidean distances between pairs of nearest keypoint descriptors from the two detections. We model the distributions of the similarity measures with a non-parametric approach. As can be seen in the right plot of Fig. 3, the Potts coefficient β is negative for a SURF similarity around 0.4, thus encouraging association for such values. On the other hand, positive coefficients for larger distances - around 0.7 - discourage the association. The β values are surprisingly positive for smaller values, but this can be explained by the fact that small values are very rarely observed, and due to some smoothing applied to probability estimates, β values are either saturated or close to neutral when the distance is small (see [5]).

2.2   MOT-Challenge - Parameter Learning, Optimization

Here we comment on changes and modifications made for the MOT16 benchmark (in addition to evaluating the benefit of SURF features). They relate to detection preprocessing, parameter learning, and optimisation.

Detection filtering. The quality of the detections have a direct impact on the performance of the system. In our work, we rely on the Deformable Part-based Model (DPM) detector [3][1]. In [5], a simple scheme based on size was used to eliminate obvious false detections when calibration was available. Here, we take advantage of the training data to learn simple rules and parameters to increase the precision of the detector according to the following factors.

– Detection size: Because in *MOTChallenge* 2016, training and test sequences are paired with roughly the same viewpoint, the groundtruth (GT) bounding boxes from the training video can be used to filter detections in test sequences. Assuming that the height of one detection linearly relates to its horizontal coordinate, one can estimate the most likely range of height for one detection. Detections that fall out of the range are omitted to remove obvious false alarms and big detections that cover multiple people.

  Concretely, let $[x, y, h]$ be the coordinates and height of on GT bounding boxes. At training time, for each x, one can find h_{min}, h_{max} to be the minimum and maximum height of all boxes with the same horizontal coordinate. The relationship between h_{max}, h_{min} and x and be estimated through linear regression: $h_{min} = a_m \times x + b_m$ and $h_{max} = a_M \times x + b_M$.

  At test time, for one detection $[x_{test}, y_{test}, h_{test}]$, one can find a predictive range $[\bar{h}_{min}, \bar{h}_{max}]$ to accept detections that fall within that range. This constraint helps removing obvious big false alarms or detections covering multiple people. From table Table 1 the filter gives a boost in precision with a small decrease in recall and all tracking metrics are improved.

– Detection score: we can vary the threshold T_{dpm} of the DPM detector to find an appropriate threshold that provides a good compromise between recall and precision.

Parameter learning. Given our non-parametric and time interval sensitive cost model, the number of parameters to learn in λ is quite large. In [5], a two step *unsupervised approach* was used to train the model directly from data. Broadly speaking, a first version of the model is learned for small time interval assuming that closest detections of a given detection in the next frames correspond to the same person. These modes were used to run the tracker a first time. The resulting tracks (usually with high purity) were then used to lean the full model.

  In the context of the MOT challenge, we took advantage of the availability of training data to learn the models from the ground truth (GT), and applied these models to the test data. We also considered relearning the parameters from the

---

[1] Although the detector is the same that produced the public detections, we used our own output to exploit the detected parts for motion estimation.

obtained tracking results before reapplying the model to evaluate the impact of taking into account the noise inherently present in the data.

Optimization. We mainly followed the approach of [5]. For computational efficiency, we used a sliding window algorithm that labels the detections in the current frame as the continuation of a previous track or the creation of a new one, using an optimal Hungarian association algorithm relying on all the pairwise links to the already labelled detections in the past T_w instants. A second step (Block ICM) is then conducted, which accounts for the cost labels and allows the swaping of track fragments at each time instant.

3   Experiments

In [5], the original model was evaluated on the CAVIAR, TUD sequences, PETS-S2L1, TownCenter, and ParkingLot sequences and was providing top results. The new MOT16 benchmark contains 14 sequences with more crowded scenarios, more scene obstacles, different viewpoints and camera motions and weather conditions, making it quite challenging for the method which did not incorporate specific treatments to handle some of these elements (camera motion, scene occluders). The MOT16 challenge thus allows to better evaluate the model under these circumstances.

3.1   Parameter Setting

For each test sequence, there is a training sequence in similar conditions. As explained earlier, we have used the training sequences to learn Potts models, and used them on the test data. Other parameters (e.g. for reliability factors) were set according to [5] and early results on the training data. Unless stated otherwise, the default parameters (used as well on test data) are: $T_w = 24$, $\Delta_{sk} = 3$ (i.e. only frame 1, 4, 7, ... are processed), $d_{\min} = 12$ (short tracks with length below $d_{\min}$ were removed), $T_{dpm} = -0.4$, and linear interpolation between detections were produced to report results.

3.2   Tracking Evaluation

We use the metrics (and evaluation tool) of the MOT challenge. Please refer to [6] for details. In general, except the detection filtering, results (MOTA) were not affected much by parameters changes.

Detection filtering. Table 1 reports the metrics at detection level and tracking level when applying the linear height filtering and with different detection threshold T_{dpm}. The filter gives a boost in precision with a small decrease in recall and all tracking metrics are improved thanks to fewer false alarms. We can also observe that threshold $T_{dpm} = -0.4$ provides an appropriate trade-off between precision and recall and good tracking performance.

Table 1. Detection filtering. Detection precision-recall and tracking performance (note: tracks are not interpolated in results).

	Raw detection	Filtered detection		
	$T_{dpm} = -0.5$	$T_{dpm} = -0.5$	$T_{dpm} = -0.4$	$T_{dpm} = -0.3$
Detection Recall	35.4	35.1	34	32.4
Detection Precision	78.3	86.1	89.9	92.4
MOTA	25.2	29.1	29.8	29.3
MOTP	74.1	74.2	74.3	74.6

Tracking window T_w and step size Δ_{sk}. Different configurations are reported in Table 2. One can observe that with longer tracking context T_w (default $T_w = 24$ vs shorter $T_w = 12$), tracks are more likely to recover from temporary occlusions or missed detections, resulting in higher MT, ML. When detector is applied scarcely (e.g. $\Delta_{sk} = 3$ or 6), we observe a performance decrease (e.g. decrease of MT, increase of ML). Nevertheless, applying the detection every $\Delta_{sk} = 3$ frames reduces the false alarms and improves IDS and FM metrics. Since detection is one of the computation bottlenecks, this provides a good trade-off between performance and speed. When $\Delta_{sk} = 3$, the overall tracking speed also is increased by up to 6 times.

Table 2. Evaluation of our tracking framework with various configurations. Results with the default parameters are shown first, and then performance obtained when varying one of the parameters (provided in first column) are provided.

Parameters	Rec	Pre	FAR	MT	PT	ML	IDS	FM	MOTA	MOTP
Default	38.7	85.9	1.32	49	180	288	211	634	32.1	74.7
$T_w = 12$	35.9	90.5	0.78	39	181	297	275	636	31.9	75.1
$\Delta_{sk} = 1$	40.5	82.8	1.74	52	188	277	273	1199	31.8	73.7
$\Delta_{sk} = 3$	38.7	85.9	1.32	49	180	288	211	634	32.1	74.7
$\Delta_{sk} = 6$	35.5	88.9	0.92	33	177	307	217	459	30.8	75.1
Unsup. models	38.0	86.6	1.22	43	183	291	237	692	31.9	74.7
W/o match. sim.	36.6	89.5	0.89	48	157	312	210	555	32.2	75
With match. sim	37.2	88.8	0.98	49	161	307	203	638	32.3	74.8

Supervised vs unsupervised models. The "Unsup. model's" line in Table 2 provides the results when using association models trained from the raw detection *in an unsupervised fashion as in* [5], which can be compared against of the default ones obtained using tracking models trained from the labeled GT boxes provided in *MOTChallenge* 2016. Interestingly, although the *unsupervised* approach suffer from missing detections and unstable bounding boxes, it performs very close to the supervised models in most tracking metrics.

Matching similarity. Because of the complexity, we used $T_w = 15$ for sequence MOT16-04, the rest use the default parameters. Although SURF matching can be discriminative for objects, it is less effective in human tracking because of clothing similarity, and data resolution where most features are found on human boundaries rather than within. This is reflected in Table 2, where only minor improvement in IDS, ML, MT, and PT are observed. In future work, better tracking oriented cues could be used, such as those developed for re-identification.

3.3   Evaluation on Test Sequences

The results of the method configured with detection filtering and the default parameters for the tracker are reported in Table 3. Overall, the performance are better, showing that the method generalizes well (with its limitation) and qualitative results are aligned with those of the training sequences. The comparison with other trackers can be found in the MOT website[2]. Overall, our tracker achieved fair ranking in comparison to other methods. Considering methods based on the public detections, our tracker exhibit a good precision (rank $5^{th}/20$ on the IDS metric and $8^{th}/20$ on Frag metric) but is penalized by a low recall, resulting on a ranking of $11^{th}/20$ for MOTA. It is important to note that our modeling framework was taken as is from previous paper, and not adapted or over-tuned to the MOT challenge (e.g. for camera motion or viewpoints). In addition, as our framework can leverage any cue in a time-sensitive fashion, other state-of-the-art features like those based on supervised re-identification learning can be exploited and would positively impact performance.

Table 3. Results on the MOT 2016 test data

	FAR	MT	ML	IDS	FM	MOTA	MOTP
LTTSC_CRF	2.0	9.6%	55.2%	481	1012	37.6	75.9

4   Conclusion

We presented a CRF model for detection-based multi-person tracking. Contrarily to other methods, it exploits longer-term connectivities between pairs of detections. Moreover, it relies on pairwise similarity and dissimilarity factors defined at the detection level, based on position, color and also visual motion cues, along with a feature-specific factor weighting scheme that accounts for feature reliability. Experiments on MOTChallenge 2016 validated the different modeling steps, such as the use of a long time horizon T_w with a higher density of connections that better constrains the models and provides more pairwise comparisons to assess the labeling, or an unsupervised learning scheme of time-interval sensitive model parameters. The results also give us hint at future directions such as occlusion and perspective reasoning, handling the high-level of miss-detections, or adapting our framework better to moving platform scenario.

---

[2] https://motchallenge.net/results/MOT16/.

References

1. Bay, H., Tuytelaars, T., Van Gool, L.: SURF: speeded up robust features. In: Leonardis, A., Bischof, H., Pinz, A. (eds.) ECCV 2006, Part I. LNCS, vol. 3951, pp. 404–417. Springer, Heidelberg (2006)
2. Berclaz, J., Fleuret, F., Fua, P.: Multiple object tracking using flow linear programming. In: Winter-PETS, pp. 1–8 (2009). http://fleuret.org/papers/berclaz-et-al-pets2009.pdf
3. Felzenszwalb, P.F., Girshick, R.B., McAllester, D., Ramanan, D.: Object detection with discriminatively trained part-based models. TPAMI **32**(9), 1627–1645 (2010)
4. Heili, A., Chen, C., Odobez, J.M.: Detection-based multi-human tracking using a CRF model. In: IEEE ICCV-VS, International Workshop on Visual Surveillance, Barcelona (2011)
5. Heili, A., Lopez-Mendez, A., Odobez, J.M.: Exploiting long-term connectivity and visual motion in CRF-based multi-person tracking. IEEE Trans. Image Process. **23**(7), 3040–3056 (2014)
6. Milan, A., Leal-Taixe, L., Reid, I., Roth, S., Schindler, K.: Mot16: a benchmark for multi-object tracking. arXiv preprint arXiv:1603.00831 (2016)
7. Yang, B., Nevatia, R.: An online learned CRF model for multi-target tracking. In: CVPR, pp. 2034–2041 (2012). http://dblp.uni-trier.de/db/conf/cvpr/cvpr2012.html

Tracking Multiple Persons Based on a Variational Bayesian Model

Yutong Ban[1], Sileye Ba[2(✉)], Xavier Alameda-Pineda[3], and Radu Horaud[1]

[1] Inria Grenoble Rhône-Alpes, Montbonnot-saint-martin, France
[2] VideoStitch, Paris, France
sileye.ba@video-stitch.com
[3] University of Trento, Trento, Italy

Abstract. Object tracking is an ubiquitous problem in computer vision with many applications in human-machine and human-robot interaction, augmented reality, driving assistance, surveillance, etc. Although thoroughly investigated, tracking multiple persons remains a challenging and an open problem. In this paper, an online variational Bayesian model for multiple-person tracking is proposed. This yields a variational expectation-maximization (VEM) algorithm. The computational efficiency of the proposed method is due to closed-form expressions for both the posterior distributions of the latent variables and for the estimation of the model parameters. A stochastic process that handles person *birth* and person *death* enables the tracker to handle a varying number of persons over long periods of time. The proposed method is benchmarked using the MOT 2016 dataset.

1 Introduction

The problem of object tracking is ubiquitous in computer vision. While many object tracking methods are available, multiple-person tracking remains extremely challenging [1]. In addition to the difficulties related to single-object tracking (occlusions, self-occlusions, visual appearance variability, unpredictable temporal behavior, etc.), tracking a varying and unknown number of objects makes the problem more challenging, for the following reasons: (i) the observations associated with detectors need to be associated to objects being tracked, which includes the process of discarding detection errors, (ii) the number of objects is not known in advance and hence it must be estimated and updated over time, (iii) mutual occlusions (not present in single-tracking scenarios) must be robustly handled, and (iv) the number of objects varies over time and one has to deal with hidden states of varying dimensionality, from zero when there is no visible object, to a large number of detected objects. Note that in this case and if a Bayesian setting is being considered, as is often the case, an exact recursive filtering solution is intractable.

Support from the ERC Advanced Grant VHIA number 340113 and from MIUR Active Aging at Home CTN01 00128 is greatly acknowledged.

© Springer International Publishing Switzerland 2016
G. Hua and H. Jégou (Eds.): ECCV 2016 Workshops, Part II, LNCS 9914, pp. 52–67, 2016.
DOI: 10.1007/978-3-319-48881-3_5

Several multiple-person tracking methods have been proposed within the trans-dimensional Markov chain model [2], where the dimensionality of the state-space is treated as a state variable. This allows to track a variable number of objects by jointly estimating the number of objects and their states. [3–5] exploited this framework for tracking a varying number of objects. The main drawback is that the states are inferred by means of a reversible jump Markov-chain Monte Carlo sampling, which is computationally expensive [6]. The random finite set framework proposed in [7–9] is also very popular, where the targets are modeled as realizations of a random finite set which is composed of an unknown number of elements. Because an exact solution to this model is computationally intensive, an approximation known as the probability hypothesis density (PHD) filter was proposed [10]. Further sampling-based approximations of random-set based filters were subsequently proposed, e.g. [11–13]. These were exploited in [14] for tracking a time-varying number of active speakers using auditory cues and in [15] for multiple-target tracking using visual observations. Recently, conditional random fields have been introduced to address multiple-target tracking [16–18]. In this case, tracking is cast into an energy minimization problem. In radar tracking, popular multiple-target tracking methods are joint probabilistic data association (JPDA), and multiple hypothesis filters [19].

An interesting and less investigated framework for multiple-target tracking is the variational Bayesian class of models for tracking an unknown and varying number of persons. Although variational models are very popular in machine learning, their use for object tracking has been limited to tracking a fixed number of targets [20]. Variational Bayes methods approximate the joint a posteriori distribution of the complete set of latent variables by a separable distribution [21, 22]. In an online tracking scenario, where only past and current observations are available, this leads to approximating the filtering distribution. An interesting aspect of variational methods is that they yield closed-form expressions for the posterior distributions of the hidden variables and for the model parameters, thus enabling an intrinsically efficient filtering procedure implemented via a variational EM (VEM) algorithm. In this paper, we derive a variational Bayesian formulation for multiple-person tracking, and present results on the MOT 2016 challenge dataset [23]. The proposed method extends [24] in many apsects: (i) the assignment variables are included in the filtering equation and therefore the state variables and the assignment variables are jointly inferred, (ii) a temporal window is incorporated in the visibility process, leading to a tracker that is more robust to misdetections, (iii) death process allows to forget about *old* tracks and thus opens the door to large-scale processing, as needed in many realistic situations. Finally, full evaluation of the proposed tracker within the MOT 2016 challenge dataset assesses its performance against other state-of-the-art methods in a principled and systematic way. Examples of results obtained with our method and Matlab code are publicly available.[1]

The remainder of this paper is organized as follows. Section 2 details the proposed Bayesian model and a variational solution is presented in Sect. 3. In Sect. 4,

---

[1] https://team.inria.fr/perception/research/ovbt/.

we depict the birth, visibility and death processes allowing to handle an unknown and varying number of persons. Section 5 presents benchmarking results. Finally, Sect. 6 draws conclusions.

2 Variational Multiple-Person Tracking

We start by introducing our notations. Vectors and matrices are in bold $\mathbf{A}, \mathbf{a}$, scalars are in italic A, a. In general random variables are denoted with upper-case letters, e.g. $\mathbf{A}$ and A, and their realizations with lower-case letters, e.g. $\mathbf{a}$ and a.

Let N be the maximum number of persons. A track $n \leq N$ at time t is associated to the *existence* binary variable e_{tn} taking the value $e_{tn} = 1$ if the person has already been seen and $e_{tn} = 0$ otherwise. The vectorization of the existence variables at time t is denoted by $\mathbf{e}_t = (e_{t1}, ..., e_{tN})$ and their sum, namely the effective number of tracked persons at t, is denoted by $N_t = \sum_{n=1}^{N} e_{tn}$. The existence variables are assumed to be observed in Sects. 3 and 4; Their inference, grounded in a birth stochastic process, is discussed in Sect. 5.

The kinematic state of person n is a random vector $\mathbf{X}_{tn} = (\mathbf{L}_{tn}^\top, \mathbf{U}_{tn}^\top)^\top \in \mathbb{R}^6$, where $\mathbf{L}_{tn} \in \mathbb{R}^4$ is the person location and size, i.e., 2D image position, width and height, and $\mathbf{U}_{tn} \in \mathbb{R}^2$ is the person velocity in the image plane. The multiple-person state random vector is denoted by $\mathbf{X}_t = (\mathbf{X}_{t1}^\top, ..., \mathbf{X}_{tN}^\top)^\top \in \mathbb{R}^{6N}$.

Fig. 1. Examples of detected persons from the MOT 2016 dataset.

We assume the existence of a person detector, providing K_t localization observations at each time t. The k-th localization observation delivered by the detector at time t is denoted by $\mathbf{y}_{tk} \in \mathbb{R}^4$, and represents the location (2D position, width, height) of a person, e.g. Figure 1. The set of observations at time t is denoted by $\mathbf{y}_t = \{\mathbf{y}_{tk}\}_{k=1}^{K_t}$. Associated to $\mathbf{y}_{tk}$, there is a photometric description of the person appearance, denoted by $\mathbf{h}_{tk}$. This photometric observation is extracted from the bounding box of $\mathbf{y}_{tk}$. Altogether, the localization and photometric observations constitute the observations $\mathbf{o}_{tk} = (\mathbf{y}_{tk}, \mathbf{h}_{tk})$ used by our tracker. Definitions analogous to $\mathbf{y}_t$ hold for $\mathbf{h}_t = \{\mathbf{h}_{tk}\}_{k=1}^{K_t}$ and $\mathbf{o}_t = \{\mathbf{o}_{tk}\}_{k=1}^{K_t}$. The probability of a set of random variables is written as $p(\mathbf{o}_t) = p(\mathbf{o}_{t1}, ..., \mathbf{o}_{tK_t})$.

We also define an observation-to-person assignment (hidden) variable Z_{tk}, associated with each observation $\mathbf{o}_{tk}$. $Z_{tk} = n, n \in \{1 \dots N\}$ means that $\mathbf{o}_{tk}$ is associated to person n. It is common that a detection corresponds to some clutter instead of a person. We cope with these false detections by defining a *clutter* target. In practice, the index $n = 0$ is assigned to this clutter target, which is always visible, i.e. $e_{t0} = 1$ for all t. Hence, the set of possible values for Z_{tk} is extended to $\{0\} \cup \{1 \dots N\}$, and $Z_{tk} = 0$ means that observation $\mathbf{o}_{tk}$ has been generated by clutter and not by a person. The practical consequence of adding a clutter track is that the observations assigned to it play no role in the estimation of the parameters of the other tracks, thus leading to an estimation robust to outliers.

2.1   The Online Tracking Model

The online multiple-person tracking problem is cast into the estimation of the filtering distribution of the hidden variables given the causal observations $p(\mathbf{Z}_t, \mathbf{Z}_{t-1}, \mathbf{X}_t, \mathbf{X}_{t-1} | \mathbf{o}_{1:t}, \mathbf{e}_{1:t})$, where $\mathbf{o}_{1:t} = \{\mathbf{o}_1, \dots, \mathbf{o}_t\}$. Importantly, we assume that the observations at time t only depend on the hidden and visibility variables at time t. The filtering distribution can be written as:

$$
\begin{aligned}
&p(\mathbf{Z}_t, \mathbf{Z}_{t-1}, \mathbf{X}_t, \mathbf{X}_{t-1} | \mathbf{o}_{1:t}, \mathbf{e}_{1:t}) = \\
&\frac{p(\mathbf{o}_t | \mathbf{Z}_t, \mathbf{X}_t, \mathbf{e}_t) p(\mathbf{Z}_t, \mathbf{X}_t | \mathbf{Z}_{t-1}, \mathbf{X}_{t-1}, \mathbf{e}_t) p(\mathbf{X}_{t-1}, \mathbf{Z}_{t-1} | \mathbf{o}_{1:t-1}, \mathbf{e}_{1:t})}{p(\mathbf{o}_t | \mathbf{o}_{1:t-1}, \mathbf{e}_{1:t})}.
\end{aligned} \quad (1)
$$

The denominator of (1) only involves observed variables and therefore its evaluation is not necessary as long as one can normalize the expression arising from the numerator. Hence we focus on the two terms of the latter, namely the observation model $p(\mathbf{o}_t | \mathbf{Z}_t, \mathbf{X}_t, \mathbf{e}_t)$ and the dynamic distribution $p(\mathbf{Z}_t, \mathbf{X}_t | \mathbf{Z}_{t-1}, \mathbf{X}_{t-1}, \mathbf{e}_t)$.

The Observation Model. The joint observations are assumed to be independent and identically distributed:

$$
p(\mathbf{o}_t | \mathbf{Z}_t, \mathbf{X}_t, \mathbf{e}_t) = \prod_{k=1}^{K_t} p(\mathbf{o}_{tk} | Z_{tk}, \mathbf{X}_t, \mathbf{e}_t). \quad (2)
$$

In addition, we make the reasonable assumption that, while localization observations depend both on the assignment variable and kinematic state, the appearance observations only depend on the assignment variable, that is the person identity, but not on his/her kinematic state. We also assume the localization and appearance observations to be independent given the hidden variables. Consequently, the observation likelihood of a single joint observation can be factorized as:

$$
\begin{aligned}
p(\mathbf{o}_{tk} | Z_{tk}, \mathbf{X}_t, \mathbf{e}_t) &= p(\mathbf{y}_{tk}, \mathbf{h}_{tk} | Z_{tk}, \mathbf{X}_t, \mathbf{e}_t) \\
&= p(\mathbf{y}_{tk} | Z_{tk}, \mathbf{X}_t, \mathbf{e}_t) p(\mathbf{h}_{tk} | Z_{tk}, \mathbf{e}_t). \quad (3)
\end{aligned}
$$

The localization observation model is defined depending on whether the observation is generated by clutter or by a person:

- If the observation is generated from clutter, namely $Z_{tk} = 0$, the variable $\mathbf{y}_{tk}$ follows an uniform distribution with probability density function $u(\mathbf{y}_{tk})$;
- If the observation is generated by person n, namely $Z_{tk} = n$, the variable $\mathbf{y}_{tk}$ follows a Gaussian distribution with mean $\mathbf{PX}_{tn}$ and covariance $\mathbf{\Sigma}$: $\mathbf{y}_{tk} \sim g(\mathbf{y}_{tk}; \mathbf{PX}_{tn}, \mathbf{\Sigma})$

The linear operator $\mathbf{P}$ maps the kinematic state vectors onto the space of observations. For example, when $\mathbf{X}_{tn}$ represents the full-body kinematic state (full-body localization and velocity) and $\mathbf{y}_{tk}$ represents the full-body localization observation, $\mathbf{P}$ is a projection which, when applied to a state vector, only retains the localization components of the state vector. Finally, the full observation model is compactly defined by the following, where δ_{ij} stands for the Kronecker function:

$$p(\mathbf{y}_{tk}|Z_{tk} = n, \mathbf{X}_t, \mathbf{e}_t) = u(\mathbf{y}_{tk})^{1-e_{tn}} \left(u(\mathbf{y}_{tk})^{\delta_{0n}} g(\mathbf{y}_{tk}; \mathbf{PX}_{tn}, \mathbf{\Sigma})^{1-\delta_{0n}}\right)^{e_{tn}}. \quad (4)$$

The appearance observation model is also defined depending on whether the observations is clutter or not. When the observation is generated by clutter, it follows a uniform distribution with density function $u(\mathbf{h}_{tk})$. When the observation is generated by person n, it follows a Bhattacharya distribution with density defined by

$$b(\mathbf{h}_{tk}; \mathbf{h}_n) = \frac{1}{W_\lambda} \exp(-\lambda d_B(\mathbf{h}_{tk}, \mathbf{h}_n)),$$

where λ is a positive skewness parameter, $d_B(\cdot)$ is the Battacharya distance between histograms, $\mathbf{h}_n$ is the reference appearance model of person n. This gives the following compact appearance observation model:

$$p(\mathbf{h}_{tk}|Z_{tk} = n, \mathbf{X}_t, \mathbf{e}_t) = u(\mathbf{h}_{tk})^{1-e_{tn}} \left(u(\mathbf{h}_{tk})^{\delta_{0n}} b(\mathbf{h}_{tk}; \mathbf{h}_n)^{1-\delta_{0n}}\right)^{e_{tn}}. \quad (5)$$

The Dynamic Distribution. Here we consider two hypotheses, firstly, we assume the at each time instance, assignment variable doesn't depends on the previous assignment. So we can factorize the the dynamic distribution into the observation-to-person prior distribution and the predictive distribution. Secondly, the kinematic state dynamics follow a first-order Markov chain, meaning that the state $\mathbf{X}_t$ only depends on state $\mathbf{X}_{t-1}$.

$$p(\mathbf{Z}_t, \mathbf{X}_t|\mathbf{Z}_{t-1}, \mathbf{X}_{t-1}, \mathbf{e}_t) = p(\mathbf{Z}_t|\mathbf{e}_t)p(\mathbf{X}_t|\mathbf{X}_{t-1}, \mathbf{e}_t). \quad (6)$$

The Observation-to-Person Prior Distribution. The joint distribution of the assignment variables can be factorized as:

$$p(\mathbf{Z}_t|\mathbf{e}_t) = \prod_{k=1}^{K_t} p(Z_{tk}|\mathbf{e}_t). \quad (7)$$

When observations are not yet available, given existence variables $\mathbf{e}_t$, the assignment variables Z_{tk} are assumed to follow multinomial distributions defined as:

$$p(Z_{tk} = n|\mathbf{e}_t) = e_{tn}a_{tn} \quad \text{with} \quad \sum_{n=0}^{N} e_{tn}a_{tn} = 1. \quad (8)$$

Because e_{tn} takes the value 1 only for actual persons, the probability to assign an observation to a non-existing person is null. When person n is visible, a_{tn} represents the probability of observation $\mathbf{y}_{tk}$ to be generated from person n.

The Predictive Distribution. The kinematic state predictive distribution represents the probability distribution of the kinematic state at time t given the observations up to time $t - 1$ and the existence variables $p(\mathbf{X}_t | \mathbf{X}_{t-1}, \mathbf{e}_t)$. The predictive distribution is mainly driven by the dynamics of persons's kinematic states, which are modeled assuming that the person locations do not influence each other's dynamics, meaning that there is one first-order Markov chain for each person. Formally, this can be written as:

$$p(\mathbf{X}_t | \mathbf{X}_{t-1}, \mathbf{e}_t) = \prod_{n=1}^{N} p(\mathbf{X}_{tn} | \mathbf{X}_{t-1n}, e_{tn}). \tag{9}$$

For the model to be complete, $p(\mathbf{X}_{tn} | \mathbf{X}_{t-1,n}, e_{tn})$ needs to be defined. The temporal evolution of the kinematic state $\mathbf{X}_{tn}$ is defined as:

$$p(\mathbf{X}_{tn} = \mathbf{x}_{tn} | \mathbf{X}_{t-1,n} = \mathbf{x}_{t-1,n}, e_{tn}) = u(\mathbf{x}_{tn})^{1-e_{tn}} g(\mathbf{x}_{tn}; \mathbf{Dx}_{t-1,n}, \mathbf{\Lambda}_n)^{e_{tn}}, \tag{10}$$

where $u(\mathbf{x}_{tn})$ is a uniform distribution over the motion state space, g is a Gaussian probability density function, $\mathbf{D}$ represents the dynamics transition operator, and $\mathbf{\Lambda}_n$ is a covariance matrix accounting for uncertainties on the state dynamics. The transition operator is defined as:

$$\mathbf{D} = \begin{pmatrix} \mathbf{I}_{4\times 4} & \begin{matrix} \mathbf{I}_{2\times 2} \\ \mathbf{0}_{2\times 2} \end{matrix} \\ \mathbf{0}_{2\times 4} & \mathbf{I}_{2\times 2} \end{pmatrix}$$

In other words, the dynamics of an existing person n, *either* follows a Gaussian with mean vector $\mathbf{Dx}_{t-1,n}$ and covariance matrix $\mathbf{\Lambda}_n$, *or* a uniform distribution if person n does not exist. The complete set of parameters of the proposed model is denoted with $\mathbf{\Theta} = (\{\mathbf{\Sigma}\}, \{\mathbf{\Lambda}_n\}_{n=1}^{N}, \mathbf{A}_{1:t})$, with $\mathbf{A}_t = \{a_{tn}\}_{n=0}^{N}$.

3   Variational Bayesian Inference

Because of the combinatorial nature of the observation-to-person assignment problem, a direct optimization of the filtering distribution (1) with respect to the hidden variables is intractable. We propose to overcome this problem via a variational Bayesian inference method. The principle of this family of methods is to approximate the intractable filtering distribution $p(\mathbf{Z}_t, \mathbf{Z}_{t-1}, \mathbf{X}_t, \mathbf{X}_{t-1} | \mathbf{o}_{1:t}, \mathbf{e}_{1:t})$ by a separable distribution, e.g. $q(\mathbf{Z}_t) \prod_{n=0}^{N} q(\mathbf{X}_{tn})$. According to the variational Bayesian formulation [21,22], given the observations and the parameters at the previous iteration $\mathbf{\Theta}^{\circ}$, the optimal approximation has the following general expression:

$$\log q(\mathbf{Z}_t) = \mathbf{E}_{q(\mathbf{X}_t)q(\mathbf{X}_{t-1})q(\mathbf{Z}_{t-1})} \left\{ \log \widetilde{P} \right\}, \tag{11}$$

$$\log q(\mathbf{Z}_{t-1}) = \mathbf{E}_{q(\mathbf{X}_t)q(\mathbf{X}_{t-1})q(\mathbf{Z}_t)} \left\{ \log \widetilde{P} \right\}, \tag{12}$$

$$\log q(\mathbf{X}_{tn}) = \mathbf{E}_{q(\mathbf{Z}_t)q(\mathbf{Z}_{t-1})q(\mathbf{X}_{t-1,n}) \prod_{m \neq n} q(\mathbf{X}_{tm})} \left\{ \log \widetilde{P} \right\}, \tag{13}$$

$$\log q(\mathbf{X}_{t-1,n}) = \mathbf{E}_{q(\mathbf{Z}_t)q(\mathbf{Z}_{t-1})q(\mathbf{X}_{t,n}) \prod_{m \neq n} q(\mathbf{X}_{t-1,m})} \left\{ \log \widetilde{P} \right\}, \tag{14}$$

where, for simplicity, we used the notation $\widetilde{P} = p(\mathbf{Z}_t, \mathbf{Z}_{t-1}, \mathbf{X}_t, \mathbf{X}_{t-1}|\mathbf{o}_{1:t}, \mathbf{e}_{1:t}, \mathbf{\Theta}^\circ)$. In our particular case, when these two equations are put together with the probabilistic model defined in (2), (6) and (9), the expression of $q(\mathbf{Z}_t)$ is factorized further into:

$$\log q(Z_{tk}) = \mathbf{E}_{q(\mathbf{X}_t)q(\mathbf{X}_{t-1})q(\mathbf{Z}_{t-1})} \left\{ \log \widetilde{P} \right\}, \tag{15}$$

Note that this equation leads to a finer factorization that the one we initially imposed. This behavior is typical of variational Bayes methods in which a very mild separability assumption can lead to a much finer factorization when combined with priors over hidden states and latent variables, i.e. (2), (6) and (9). The final factorization writes:

$$p(\mathbf{Z}_t, \mathbf{Z}_{t-1}, \mathbf{X}_t, \mathbf{X}_{t-1}|\mathbf{o}_{1:t}, \mathbf{e}_{1:t}) \approx \prod_{k=0}^{K_t} q(Z_{tk}) \prod_{k=0}^{K_{t-1}} q(Z_{t-1,k}) \prod_{n=0}^{N} q(\mathbf{X}_{tn})q(\mathbf{X}_{t-1,n}). \tag{16}$$

Once the posterior distribution over the hidden variables is computed (see below), the optimal parameters are estimated using $\hat{\mathbf{\Theta}} = \arg\max_\mathbf{\Theta} J(\mathbf{\Theta}, \mathbf{\Theta}^\circ)$ with J defined as:

$$J(\mathbf{\Theta}, \mathbf{\Theta}^\circ) = \mathbf{E}_{q(\mathbf{Z},\mathbf{X})} \left\{ \log p(\mathbf{Z}_t, \mathbf{Z}_{t-1}, \mathbf{X}_t, \mathbf{X}_{t-1}, \mathbf{o}_{1:t}|\mathbf{e}_{1:t}, \mathbf{\Theta}, \mathbf{\Theta}^\circ) \right\}. \tag{17}$$

3.1 E-Z-Step

The estimation of $q(Z_{tk})$ is carried out by developing the expectation (15) which yields the following formula:

$$q(Z_{tk} = n) = \alpha_{tkn} = \frac{e_{tn}\epsilon_{tkn}a_{tn}}{\sum_{m=0}^{N} e_{tm}\epsilon_{tkm}a_{tn}}, \tag{18}$$

and ϵ_{tkn} is defined as:

$$\epsilon_{tkn} = \begin{cases} u(\mathbf{y}_{tk})u(\mathbf{h}_{tk}) & n = 0, \\ g(\mathbf{y}_{tk}, \mathbf{P}\boldsymbol{\mu}_{tn}, \mathbf{\Sigma})e^{-\frac{1}{2}\mathrm{Tr}(\mathbf{P}^\top(\mathbf{\Sigma})^{-1}\mathbf{P}\Gamma_{tn})}b(\mathbf{h}_{tk}; \mathbf{h}_n) & n \neq 0, \end{cases} \tag{19}$$

where $\mathrm{Tr}(\cdot)$ is the trace operator and $\boldsymbol{\mu}_{tn}$ and Γ_{tn} are defined by (21) and (22) below. Intuitively, this approximation shows that the assignment of an observation to a person is based on spatial proximity between the observation localization and the person localization, and the similarity between the observation's appearance and the person's reference appearance.

3.2 E-X-Step

The estimation of $q(\mathbf{X}_{tn})$ is derived from (13). Similarly to the previous posterior distribution, which boil down to the following formula:

$$q(\mathbf{X}_{tn}) = u(\mathbf{X}_{tn})^{1-e_{tn}} g(\mathbf{X}_{tn}; \boldsymbol{\mu}_{tn}, \boldsymbol{\Gamma}_{tn})^{e_{tn}}, \tag{20}$$

where the mean vector $\boldsymbol{\mu}_{tn}$ and the covariance matrix $\boldsymbol{\Gamma}_{tn}$ are given by:

$$\boldsymbol{\Gamma}_{tn} = \Big(\sum_{k=0}^{K_t} \alpha_{tkn} \left(\mathbf{P}^\top (\boldsymbol{\Sigma})^{-1} \mathbf{P} \right) + \boldsymbol{\Lambda}_n^{-1} \Big)^{-1}, \tag{21}$$

$$\boldsymbol{\mu}_{tn} = \boldsymbol{\Gamma}_{tn} \Big(\sum_{k=0}^{K_t} \alpha_{tkn} \mathbf{P}^\top (\boldsymbol{\Sigma})^{-1} \mathbf{y}_{tk} + \boldsymbol{\Lambda}_n^{-1} \mathbf{D} \boldsymbol{\mu}_{t-1,n} \Big). \tag{22}$$

Similarly, for the estimation of the distribution

$$q(\mathbf{X}_{t-1,n}) = u(\mathbf{X}_{t-1,n})^{1-e_{tn}} g(\mathbf{X}_{t-1,n}; \widehat{\boldsymbol{\mu}}_{t-1,n}, \widehat{\boldsymbol{\Gamma}}_{t-1,n})^{e_{tn}}, \tag{23}$$

the mean and covariance are:

$$\widehat{\boldsymbol{\Gamma}}_{t-1,n} = \left(\mathbf{D}^\top \boldsymbol{\Lambda}_n^{-1} \mathbf{D} + \boldsymbol{\Gamma}_{t-1,n} \right)^{-1} \tag{24}$$

$$\widehat{\boldsymbol{\mu}}_{t-1,n} = \widehat{\boldsymbol{\Gamma}}_{t-1,n} \left(\mathbf{D}^\top \boldsymbol{\Lambda}_n^{-1} \boldsymbol{\mu}_{t,n} + \boldsymbol{\Gamma}_{t-1,n}^{-1} \boldsymbol{\mu}_{t-1,n} \right). \tag{25}$$

We note that the variational approximation of the kinematic-state distribution reminds the Kalman filter solution of a linear dynamical system with mainly one difference: in our formulation, (21) and (22), the means and covariances are computed by weighting the observations with α_{tkn}, i.e. (21) and (22).

3.3 M-Step

Once the posterior distribution of the hidden variables is estimated, the optimal parameter values can be estimated via maximization of J defined in (17). Concerning the parameters of the a priori observation-to-object assignment $\mathbf{A}_t$ we compute:

$$J(a_{tn}) = \sum_{k=1}^{K_t} e_{tn} \alpha_{tkn} \log(e_{tn} a_{tn}) \quad \text{s.t.} \quad \sum_{n=0}^{N} e_{tn} a_{tn} = 1, \tag{26}$$

and we trivially obtain:

$$a_{tn} = \frac{e_{tn} \sum_{k=1}^{K_t} \alpha_{tkn}}{\sum_{m=0}^{N} e_{tm} \sum_{k=1}^{K_t} \alpha_{tkm}}. \tag{27}$$

The observation covariance $\boldsymbol{\Sigma}$ and the state covariances $\boldsymbol{\Lambda}_n$ can be estimated during the M-step. However, in our current implementation estimates for $\boldsymbol{\Sigma}$ and $\boldsymbol{\Lambda}_n$ are instantaneous, i.e., they are obtained only from the observations at time t (see the experimental section for details).

4 Person-Birth, -Visibility and -Death Processes

Tracking a time-varying number of targets requires procedures to create tracks
when new targets enter the scene and to delete tracks when corresponding targets leave the visual scene. In this paper, we propose a statistical-test based
birth process that creates new tracks and a hidden Markov model (HMM) based
visibility process that handles disappearing targets. Until here, we assumed that
the existence variables e_{tn} were given. In this section we present the inference
model for the existence variable based on the stochastic birth-process.

4.1 Birth Process

The principle of the person birth process is to search for consistent trajectories
in the history of observations associated to clutter. Intuitively, two hypotheses
are confronted, namely: *(i) the considered observation sequence is generated by a
person not being tracked* and *(ii) the considered observation sequence is generated
by clutter.*

The model of *"the considered observation sequence is generated by a person
not being tracked"* hypothesis is based on the observations and dynamic models defined in (4) and (10). If there is a not-yet-tracked person n generating
the considered observation sequence $\{\mathbf{y}_{t-L,k_L}, \ldots, \mathbf{y}_{t,k_0}\}$,[2] then the observation
likelihood is $p(\mathbf{y}_{t-l,k_l}|\mathbf{x}_{t-l,n}) = g(\mathbf{y}_{t-l,k_l}; \mathbf{P}\mathbf{x}_{t-l,n}, \boldsymbol{\Sigma})$ and the person trajectory
is governed by the dynamical model $p(\mathbf{x}_{t,n}|\mathbf{x}_{t-1,n}) = g(\mathbf{x}_{t,n}; \mathbf{D}\mathbf{x}_{t-1,n}, \boldsymbol{\Lambda}_n)$. Since
there is no prior knowledge about the starting point of the track, we assume a
"flat" Gaussian distribution over $\mathbf{x}_{t-L,n}$, namely $p_b(\mathbf{x}_{t-L,n}) = g(\mathbf{x}_{t-L,n}; \mathbf{m}_b, \boldsymbol{\Gamma}_b)$,
which is approximatively equivalent to a uniform distribution over the image.
Consequently, the joint observation distribution writes:

$$\tau_0 = p(\mathbf{y}_{t,k_0}, \ldots, \mathbf{y}_{t-L,k_L})$$
$$= \int p(\mathbf{y}_{t,k_0}, \ldots, \mathbf{y}_{t-L,k_L}, \mathbf{x}_{t:t-L,n}) d\mathbf{x}_{t:t-L,n}$$
$$= \int \prod_{l=0}^{L} p(\mathbf{y}_{t,k_l}|\mathbf{x}_{t-l,n}) \times \prod_{l=0}^{L-1} p(\mathbf{x}_{t-l,n}|\mathbf{x}_{t-l-1,n}) \times p_b(\mathbf{x}_{t-2,n}) d\mathbf{x}_{t:t-L,n}, \quad (28)$$

which can be seen as the marginal of a multivariate Gaussian distribution.
Therefore, the joint observation distribution $p(\mathbf{y}_{t,k_0}, \mathbf{y}_{t-1,k_1}, \ldots, \mathbf{y}_{t-2,k_L})$ is also
Gaussian and can be explicitly computed.

The model of *"the considered observation sequence is generated by clutter"*
hypothesis is based on the observation model given in (4). When the considered
observation sequence $\{\mathbf{y}_{t,k_0}, \ldots, \mathbf{y}_{t-L,k_L}\}$ is generated by clutter, observations
are independent and identically uniformly distributed. In this case, the joint
observation likelihood is

---

[2] In practice we considered $L = 2$, however, derivations are valid for arbitrary values
of L.

$$\tau_1 = p(\mathbf{y}_{t,k_0}, \ldots, \mathbf{y}_{t-L,k_L}) = \prod_{l=0}^{L} u(\mathbf{y}_{t-l,k_l}). \tag{29}$$

Finally, our birth process is as follows: for all $\mathbf{y}_{t,k_0}$ such that $\tau_0 > \tau_1$, a new person is added by setting $e_{tn} = 1$, $q(\mathbf{x}_{t,n}; \boldsymbol{\mu}_{t,n}, \boldsymbol{\Gamma}_{t,n})$ with $\boldsymbol{\mu}_{t,n} = [\mathbf{y}_{t,k_0}^\top, \mathbf{0}_2^\top]^\top$, and $\boldsymbol{\Gamma}_{tn}$ is set to the value of a birth covariance matrix (see (20)). Also, the reference appearance model for the new person is defined as $\mathbf{h}_{t,n} = \mathbf{h}_{t,k_0}$.

4.2   Visibility Process

A tracked person is said to be visible at time t whenever there are observations associated to that person, otherwise the person is considered not visible. Instead of deleting tracks, as classical for death processes, our model labels tracks without associated observations as *sleeping*. In this way, we keep the possibility to awake such sleeping tracks whenever their reference appearance highly matches an observed appearance.

We denote the n-th person visibility (binary) variable by V_{tn}, meaning that the person is visible at time t if $V_{tn} = 1$ and 0 otherwise. We assume the existence of a transition model for the hidden visibility variable V_{tn}. More precisely, the visibility state temporal evolution is governed by the transition matrix, $p(V_{tn} = j|V_{t-1,n} = i) = \pi_v^{\delta_{ij}}(1 - \pi_v)^{1-\delta_{ij}}$, where π_v is the probability to remain in the same state. To enforce temporal smoothness, the probability to remain in the same state is taken higher than the probability to switch to another state.

The goal now is to estimate the visibility of all the persons. For this purpose we define the visibility observations as $\nu_{tn} = e_{tn}a_{tn}$, being 0 when no observation is associated to person n. In practice, we need to filter the visibility state variables V_{tn} using the visibility observations ν_{tn}. In other words, we need to estimate the filtering distribution $p(V_{tn}|\nu_{1:tn}, e_{1:tn})$ which can be written as:

$$p(V_{tn} = v_{tn}|\nu_{1:t}, e_{1:tn}) =$$
$$\frac{p(\nu_{tn}|v_{tn}, e_{tn}) \sum_{v_{t-1,n}} p(v_{tn}|v_{t-1,n}) p(v_{t-1,n}|\nu_{1:t-1,n}, e_{1:t-1})}{p(\nu_{tn}|\nu_{1:t-1,n}, e_{1:t})}, \tag{30}$$

where the denominator corresponds to integrating the numerator over v_{tn}. In order to fully specify the model, we define the visibility observation likelihood as:

$$p(\nu_{tn}|v_{tn}, e_{tn}) = (\exp(-\lambda\nu_{tn}))^{v_{tn}}(1 - \exp(-\lambda\nu_{tn}))^{1-v_{tn}} \tag{31}$$

Intuitively, when ν_{tn} is high, the likelihood is large if $v_{tn} = 1$ (person is visible). The opposite behavior is found when ν_{tn} is small. Importantly, at each frame, because the visibility state is a binary variable, its filtering distribution can be straightforwardly computed. We found this rather intuitive strategy to be somewhat "shaky" over time even taking the Markov dependency into account. This is why we enriched the visibility observations to span over multiple frames $\nu_{tn} = \sum_{l=0}^{L} e_{t+ln}a_{t+ln}$, so that if $v_{tn} = 1$, the likelihood is large when ν_{tn} is high and therefore the target is visible in one or more neighboring frames. This is the equivalent of the hypothesis testing spanning over time associated to the birth process.

4.3   Death Process

The idea of the person-visibility process arises from encouraging track consistency when a target disappears and appears back in the field of view. However, a tracker that remembers *all* the tracks that have been previously seen is hardly scalable. Indeed, the memory resources required by a system that remembers all previous appearance templates grows indefinitely with new appearances. Therefore, one must discard *old* information to facilitate the scalability of the method to large datasets containing sequences with several dozens of different people involved. In addition to alleviating the memory requirements, this also reduces the computational complexity of the tracker. This is the motivation of including a death process into the proposed variational framework. Intuitively one would like to discard those tracks that have not been seen during several frames. In practice, we found that discarding those tracks that are not visible for ten consecutive frames yields a good trade-off between complexity, resource demand and performance. Setting this parameter for a different dataset should not be chimeric, since the precise interpretation of the meaning of it is straightforward.

5   Experiments, Performance Evaluation, and Benchmark

We evaluated the performance of the proposed variational multiple-person tracker on the MOT 2016 dataset challenge [23]. This dataset is composed of seven training videos and seven test videos. Importantly, we use the detections that are provided with the dataset. Because multiple-person tracking intrinsically implies track creation (birth), deletion (death), target identity maintenance, and localization, evaluating multiple-person tracking techniques is a non-trivial task. Many metrics have been proposed, e.g. [25–28].

We adopt the metrics used by the MOT 2016 benchmark, namely [27]. The main tracking measures are: the *multiple-object tracking accuracy* (MOTA), that combines false positives (FP), missed targets (FN), and identity switches (ID); the *multiple-object tracking precision* (MOTP), that measures the alignment of the tracker output bounding box with the ground truth; the false alarm per frame (FAF); the ratio of mostly tracked trajectories (MT); the ratio of mostly lost trajectories (ML) and the number of track fragmentations (Frag).

Figure 2 shows sample images of all test videos: They contain three sequences recorded with static cameras (MOT16-01, MOT16-03 and MOT16-08), which contain very crowded scenes and thus are very challenging, and five sequences with large camera motions, both translations and rotations, which make the data even more difficult to process.

As explained above, we use the public pedestrian detections provided within the MOT16 challenge. These static detections are complemented in two different ways. First, we extract velocity observations by means of a simple optical-flow based algorithm that looks for the most similar region of the next temporal frame within the neighborhood of the original detection. Therefore, the observations operator P is the identity matrix, project the entire state variable into the

(a) MOT16-01   (b) MOT16-03   (c) MOT16-06

(d) MOT16-06   (e) MOT16-07

(f) MOT16-08   (g) MOT16-12   (h) MOT16-14

Fig. 2. Samples images from the MOT 16 test sequences.

observation space. Second, the appearance feature vector is the concatenation of joint color histograms of three regions of the torso in HSV space.

The proposed variational model is governed by several parameters. Aiming at providing an algorithm that is dataset-independent and that features a good trade-off between flexibility and performance, we set the observation covariance matrix Σ and the state covariance matrix Λ_n automatically from the detections. More precisely, both matrices are imposed to be diagonal; for Σ, the variances of the horizontal position, of the width, and of the horizontal speed are $1/3$, $1/3$ and $1/6$ of the detected width. The variances of the vertical quantities are built analogously. The rationale behind this choice is that we consider that the true detection lies, more or less, within the width and height of the detected bounding box. Regarding Λ_n, the diagonal entries are $1, 1$ and $1/2$ of the detected width, and vertical quantities are defined analogously. Furthermore, in order to eliminate arbitrary false detections, we set $L = 5$ in the birth process. Finally, for sequences in which the size of the bounding boxes is roughly constant, we discarded those detections that were too large or too small.

Examples of the tracking results for all the test sequences except MOT16-07 are shown in Fig. 3, while six frames from MOT16-07 are shown in Fig. 4. In all figures, the red boxes represent our tracking result and the numbers within the boxes are the tracking indexes. Generally speaking, on one hand the variational model is crucial to properly associate detections with trajectories. On the other hand, the birth and visibility processes play a role when tracked objects appear and disappear. Regarding Fig. 4, it contains 54 tracks recorded by a moving

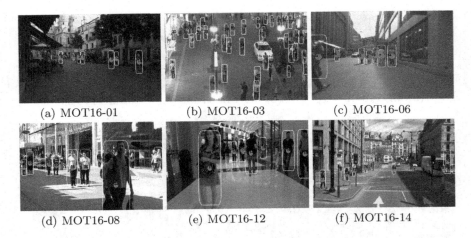

(a) MOT16-01   (b) MOT16-03   (c) MOT16-06

(d) MOT16-08   (e) MOT16-12   (f) MOT16-14

Fig. 3. Sample results on several sequences of MOT16 datasets, red bounding boxes represents the tracking results, and the number inside each box is the track index. (Color figure online)

camera in a sequence of 500 frames. It is a very challenging tracking task, not only because the density of pedestrians is quite high, but also because significant camera motion makes the person trajectories to be both rough and discontinuous. One drawback of the proposed approach is that partially consistent false detections could lead to the creation of a false track, therefore tracking an inexistent pedestrian. On the positive side, the main advantage of the proposed model is that the probabilistic combination of the dynamic and appearance models can decrease the probability of switching the identities of two tracks.

Fig. 4. Sample results on the sequence MOT16-07, encoded as in the previous figure. (Color figure online)

Table 1 reports the performance of the proposed algorithm, which is referred to as OVBT (online variational Bayesian tracker), over the seven test sequences

Table 1. Evaluation of the proposed multiple-person tracking method with different features on the seven sequences of the MOT16 test dataset.

Sequence	MOTA	MOTP	FAF	MT	ML	FP	FN	ID Sw	Frag
MOT16-01	23.9	71.4	1.5	13.0 %	39.1 %	696	4,137	35	89
MOT16-03	46.9	75.7	4.1	17.6 %	20.3 %	6,173	48,631	689	1,184
MOT16-06	32.7	73.2	0.5	3.6 %	58.4 %	562	7,073	124	183
MOT16-07	33.6	73.3	2.2	9.3 %	35.2 %	1,077	9,605	158	272
MOT16-08	24.6	78.4	1.7	3.2 %	41.3 %	1,066	11,402	150	177
MOT16-12	32.8	76.7	0.9	10.5 %	52.3 %	766	4,749	63	80
MOT16-14	18.1	74.5	1.6	2.4 %	61.6 %	1,177	13,866	102	155
Over All	38.4± 8.8	75.4	1.9	7.5 %	47.3 %	11,517	99,463	1,321	2,140

of the MOT 2016 challenge. The results obtained with OVBT are available on the MOT 2016 webpage.[3] One can notice that our method provides high precision (MOTP) but low accuracy (MOTA), meaning that some tracks were missed (mostly due to misetections). This is consistent with a rather low MT measure. This behavior was more extreme when the visibility process did not include any observation aggregation over time. Indeed, we observed that considering multiple observations within the visibility process leads to better performance (for all sequences and almost all measures).

6 Conclusions

We propose a variational Bayesian solution to the multiple-target problem. In the literature, other solutions based on sampling such as MCMC, and random finite set, such as the PHD filter have been proposed to solve the same problem. Comparison with other state of the art methods are available [24].

The main goal of our study was to benchmark the model on MOT Challenge 2016. Implementation issues of the tracker are discussed as well as its strengths and weaknesses regarding the absolute performance on the test sequences and the relative performance when compared with other participants to the MOT Challenges.

The presented model is free from magic parameters, since these are automatically derived from the data. Moreover, the proposed temporal aggregation for the visibility process appears to be an excellent complement to the variational Bayes EM algorithm. In the near future, we plan to derive self-paced learning strategies within this variational framework able to automatically assess which detections must be used for tracking and which should not be utilized.

---

[3] https://motchallenge.net/results/MOT16/.

References

1. Luo, W., Xing, J., Zhang, X., Zhao, W., Kim, T.K.: Multiple object tracking: a review (2015). arXiv:1409.761
2. Green, P.J.: Trans-dimensional Markov chain Monte Carlo. In: Oxford Statistical Science Series, pp. 179–198 (2003)
3. Khan, Z., Balch, T., Dellaert, F.: An MCMC-based particle filter for tracking multiple interacting targets. In: European Conference on Computer Vision, Prague, Czech Republic, pp. 279–290 (2004)
4. Smith, K., Gatica-Perez, D., Odobez, J.M.: Using particles to track varying numbers of interacting people. In: IEEE Computer Vision and Pattern Recognition, San Diego, USA, pp. 962–969 (2005)
5. Yang, M., Liu, Y., Wen, L., You, Z.: A probabilistic framework for multitarget tracking with mutual occlusions. In: IEEE Confenrence on Computer Vision and Pattern Recognition, pp. 1298–1305 (2014)
6. Green, P.J.: Reversible jump Markov chain Monte Carlo computation and Bayesian model determination. Biometrika **82**(4), 711–732 (1995)
7. Mahler, R.P.: Multisource multitarget filtering: a unified approach. In: Aerospace/Defense Sensing and Controls, International Society for Optics and Photonics, pp. 296–307 (1998)
8. Mahler, R.P.S.: Statistics 101 for multisensor, multitarget data fusion. IEEE Aerosp. Electron. Syst. Mag. **19**(1), 53–64 (2004)
9. Mahler, R.P.S.: Statistics 102 for multisensor multitarget data fusion. IEEE Sel. Top. Sign. Proces. **19**(1), 53–64 (2013)
10. Mahler, R.P.S.: A theoretical foundation for the Stein-Winter "probability hypothesis density (PHD)" multitarget tracking approach. Technical report (2000)
11. Sidenbladh, H.: Multi-target particle filtering for the probability hypothesis density. In: IEEE International Conference on Information Fusion, Tokyo, Japan, pp. 800–806 (2003)
12. Clark, D., Bell, J.: Convergence results for the particle PHD filter. IEEE Trans. Sign. Proces. **54**(7), 2652–2661 (2006)
13. Vo, B.N., Singh, S., Doucet, A.: Random finite sets and sequential monte carlo methods in multi-target tracking. In: IEEE International Radar Conference, Huntsville, USA, pp. 486–491 (2003)
14. Ma, W.K., Vo, B.N., Singh, S.S.: Tracking an unknown time-varying number of speakers using TDOA measurements: a random finite set approach. IEEE Trans. Sign. Proces. **54**(9), 3291–3304 (2006)
15. Maggio, E., Taj, M., Cavallaro, A.: Efficient multitarget visual tracking using random finite sets. IEEE Trans. Circ. Syst. Video Technol. **18**(8), 1016–1027 (2008)
16. Yang, B., Nevatia, R.: An online learned CRF model for multi-target tracking. In: IEEE Conference on Computer Vision and Pattern Recognition, Providence, USA, pp. 2034–2041 (2012)
17. Milan, A., Roth, S., Schindler, K.: Continuous energy minimization for multitarget tracking. IEEE Trans. Pattern Anal. Mach. Intell. **36**(1), 58–72 (2014)
18. Heili, A., Lopez-Mendez, A., Odobez, J.M.: Exploiting long-term connectivity and visual motion in CRF-based multi-person tracking. IEEE Trans. Image Process. **23**(7), 3040–3056 (2014)
19. Bar-Shalom, Y., Daum, F., Huang, J.: The probabilistic data association filter: estimation in the presence of measurement origin and uncertainty. IEEE Control Syst. Mag. **29**(6), 82–100 (2009)

20. Vermaak, J., Lawrence, N., Perez, P.: Variational inference for visual tracking. In: IEEE Conference on Computer Vision and Pattern Recognition, Madison, USA, pp. 773–780 (2003)
21. Smidl, V., Quinn, A.: The Variational Bayes Method in Signal Processing. Springer, Heidelberg (2006)
22. Bishop, C.M.: Pattern Recognition and Machine Learning. Information Science and Statistics. Springer, New York (2007)
23. Milan, A., Leal-Taix, L., Reid, I., Roth, S., Schindler, K.: Mot16: A benchmark for multi-object tracking. In: arXiv:1603.00831 [cs] (2016)
24. Ba, S., Alameda-Pineda, X., Xompero, A., Horaud, R.: An on-line variational Bayesian model for multi-person tracking from cluttered scenes. Computer Vision and Image Understanding (2016)
25. Ristic, B., Vo, B.N., Clark, D.: Performance evaluation of multi-target tracking using the OSPA metric. In: IEEE International Conference on Information Fusion, Edinburgh, UK, pp. 1–7 (2010)
26. Smith, K., Gatica-Perez, D., Odobez, J.M., Ba, S.: Evaluating multi-object tracking. In: IEEE CVPR Workshop on Empirical Evaluation Methods in Computer Vision, San Diego, USA, pp. 36–36 (2005)
27. Stiefelhagen, R., Bernardin, K., Bowers, R., Garofolo, J., Mostefa, D., Soundararajan, P.: The CLEAR 2006 evaluation. In: Stiefelhagen, R., Garofolo, J. (eds.) CLEAR 2006. LNCS, vol. 4122, pp. 1–44. Springer, Heidelberg (2007). doi:10.1007/978-3-540-69568-4_1
28. Longyin, W., Du, D., Cai, Z., Lei, Z., Chang, M.C., Qi, H., Lim, J., Yang, M.H., Lyu, S.: DETRAC filter multiple target tracker: a new benchmark and protocol for multi-object tracking, arXiv:1511.04136 (2015)

Multi-class Multi-object Tracking Using Changing Point Detection

Byungjae Lee[1], Enkhbayar Erdenee[1], Songguo Jin[1], Mi Young Nam[2], Young Giu Jung[2], and Phill Kyu Rhee[1(✉)]

[1] Inha University, Incheon, South Korea
pkrhee@inha.ac.kr
[2] NaeulTech, Incheon, South Korea

Abstract. This paper presents a robust multi-class multi-object tracking (MCMOT) formulated by a Bayesian filtering framework. Multi-object tracking for unlimited object classes is conducted by combining detection responses and changing point detection (CPD) algorithm. The CPD model is used to observe abrupt or abnormal changes due to a drift and an occlusion based spatiotemporal characteristics of track states. The ensemble of convolutional neural network (CNN) based object detector and Lucas-Kanede Tracker (KLT) based motion detector is employed to compute the likelihoods of foreground regions as the detection responses of different object classes. Extensive experiments are performed using lately introduced challenging benchmark videos; ImageNet VID and MOT benchmark dataset. The comparison to state-of-the-art video tracking techniques shows very encouraging results.

Keywords: Multi-class and multi-object tracking · Changing point detection · Entity transition · Object detection from video · Convolutional neural network

1 Introduction

Multi-object tracking (MOT) is emerging technology employed in many real-world applications such as video security, gesture recognition, robot vision, and human robot interaction [1–15]. The challenge is drifts of tracking points due to appearance variations caused by noises, illumination, pose, cluttered background, interactions, occlusion, and camera movement. Most MOT methods are suffered from varying numbers of objects, and leading to performance degradation and tracking accuracy impairments in cluttered backgrounds. However, most of them only focus on a limited categories, usually people or vehicle tracking. MOT with unlimited classes of objects has been rarely studied due to very complex and high computation requirements.

The Bayesian filter consists of the motion dynamics and observation models which estimates posterior likelihoods. One of the Bayesian filter based object tracking methods is Markov chain Monte Carlo (MCMC)-based method [2–5],

© Springer International Publishing Switzerland 2016
G. Hua and H. Jégou (Eds.): ECCV 2016 Workshops, Part II, LNCS 9914, pp. 68–83, 2016.
DOI: 10.1007/978-3-319-48881-3_6

which can handle various object moves and interactions of multiple objects. Most MCMC based methods assume that the number of objects would not change over time, which is not acceptable in a real world applications. Reversible jump MCMC (RJMCMC) was proposed by [2,4], where a variable number of objects with different motion changes, such as update, swap, birth, and death moves. They start a new track by initializing a new object or terminates currently tracked object by eliminating the object.

Even MCMC based MOT approaches were successful to some extent, computational overheads are very high due to a high-dimensional state space. The variations in appearances, the interaction and occlusions and changing number of moving objects are challenging, which require high computation overheads. Saka et al. [1] proposes a MCMC sampling with low computation overhead by separating motion dynamics into birth and death moves and the iteration loop of the Markov chain for motion moves of update and swap. If the moves of birth and death are determined inside of the MCMC chain, it requires the dimension changes in the MCMC sampling approaches as [2,3]. Since the Markov chain has no dimension variation in the iteration loop by separating the moves of birth and death, it can reach to stationary states with less computation overhead [1,6]. However, such a simple approach for separating birth and death dynamics cannot deal with complex situations that occur in MOT. Many of them are suffered from track drifts due to appearance variations.

In this paper, we propose a robust multi-class multi-object tracking (MCMOT) that conducts unlimited object classes by combining detection responses and changing point detection (CPD) algorithm. With advances of deep learning based object detection technology such as Faster R-CNN [28], and ResNet [29], it becomes feasible to adopt a detector ensemble with unlimited classes of objects. The detector ensemble combines the model based detector implemented by Faster R-CNN [28] and the motion detector by Lucas-Kanade Tracker (KLT) algorithm [26]. The method separates the motion dynamic model of Bayesian filter into the entity transitions and motion moves. The entity transitions are modeled as the birth and death events. Observation likelihood is calculated by more sophisticated deep learning based data-driven algorithm. Drift problem which is one of the most cumbersome problems in object tracking is attacked by a CPD algorithm similarly to [24]. Assuming the smoothness of motion dynamics, the abrupt changes of the observation are dealt with the CPD algorithm, whereas the abrupt changes are associated illuminations, cluttered backgrounds, poses, and scales. The main contributions of the paper are below:

- MCMOT can track varying number of objects with unlimited classes which is formulated as a way to estimate a likelihood of foreground regions with optimal smoothness. Departing from the likelihood estimation only belong to limited type of objects, such as pedestrian or vehicles, efficient convolutional neural network (CNN) based multi-class object detector is employed to compute the likelihoods of multiple object classes.

- Changing point detection is proposed for a tracking failure assessment by exploiting static observations as well as dynamic ones. Drifts in MCMOT are investigated by detecting such abrupt change points between stationary time series that represent track segment.

This paper is organized as follows. We review related work in Sect. 2. In Sect. 3, the outline of MCMOT is discussed. Section 4 introduces our proposed tracking method. Section 5 describes the experiments, and concluding remarks and future directions are discussed in Sect. 6.

2   Related Work

2.1   Multi Object Tracking

Recent research in MOT has focused on the tracking-by-detection principal to perform data association based on linking object detections through a video sequence. Majority of the batch methods formulates MOT with future frame's information to get better data association via hierarchical tracks association [13], network flows [12], and global trajectory optimization [11]. However, batch methods have higher computational cost relatively. Whereas online methods only consider past and current frame's information to solve the data association problem. Online methods are more suitable for real-time application, but those are likely to drift since objects in a video show significant variations in appearances due to noises, illuminations, poses, viewing angles, occlusions, and shadows, some objects enters or leaves the scene, and sometimes show sharp turns and abrupt stops. Dynamically varying number of objects is difficult to handle, especially when track crowded or high traffic objects in [9,10,14]. Most MOT methods relying on the observation of different features are prone to result in drifts. Against this nonstationarity and nonlinearity, stochastic-based tracking [22–24] appear superior to deterministic based tracking such as Kalman filter [33] or particle filter [2].

2.2   Convolutional Neural Network

In the last few years, considerable improvements have been appeared in the computer vision task using CNN. One of the particularly remarkable studies is R-CNN [34]. They transferred CNN based image classification task to CNN based object detection task using region-based approach. SPPnet [35] and Fast R-CNN [36] extend R-CNN by pooling convolutional features from a shared convolutional feature map. More recently, RPN [28] is suggested to generate region proposals within R-CNN framework using RPN. Those region-based CNN pipelines outperform all the previous works by a significant margin. Despite such great success of CNNs, only a few number of MOT algorithms using the representations from CNNs have been proposed [20–22]. In [20,21], they proposed a CNN based framework with simple object tracking algorithm for MOT task in ImageNet VID. In [22], they used CNN based object detector for MOT Challenge [32]. Our experiment adopts this paradigm of region based CNN to build observation model.

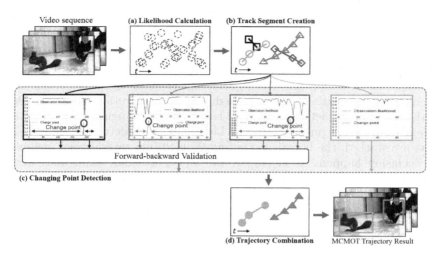

Fig. 1. MCMOT framework has four major steps: (a) Likelihood calculation based on observation models, (b) Track segment creation, (c) Changing point detection, and (d) Trajectory combination. The drifts in segments are effectively controlled by changing point detection algorithm with forward-backward validation.

3   The Outline of MCMOT

We propose an efficient multi-class multi-object tracker, called MCMOT that can deal with object birth, death, occlusion, interaction, and drift efficiently. MCMOT may fail due to the miscalculations of the observation likelihood, interaction model, entry model, and motion model. The objective of MCMOT is to stop the tracking as quick as possible if a drift occurs, recover from the wrong decisions, and to continue tracking. Fig. 1 illustrates the main concept of our framework.

In MCMOT, objects are denoted by bounding boxes which are tracked by a tracking algorithm. In the tracking algorithm, if a possible interaction or occlusion is detected, the trajectory is split into several parts, called track segments. The combination of track segments is controlled by CPD. Considering fallible decision tracker points, CPD monitors a drift due to abnormal events, abrupt changing environments by comparing the localized bounding boxes by the observations within the segment. The motion-based tracking component facilitates KLT [26] adaptive for predicting the region of a next tracking point. The model-based component consists of the global object detector and adaptive local detector. We use a deep feature based multi-class object detector [28] as the global and local object detector. One can notice that the number of object categories can be readily extended depending on object detector capability.

4 Multi-class Multi-object Tracking

MCMOT employs an data-driven approach which investigates the events caused by object-level events, object birth and death, inter-object level events, i.e., interaction and occlusion between objects, and tracking level events, e.g. track birth, update, and death. Possible drifts due to the observation failures are dealt with the abnormality detection method based on the changing point detection.

We define track segments using the birth and death detection. Only visible objects are tracked, the holistic trajectory divided into several track segments, if an occlusion happens as in [16]. If the object becomes ambiguous due to occlusion or noise, the track segment is terminated (associated object death), and the tracker will restart tracking (associated object birth) nearby the terminated tracking point if the same object reoccurs, and the track segment is continuously built, if it is required, or a new track segment is started and merged later.

4.1 Observation Model

We define observation model (observation likelihood) $P(\mathbf{z}_t|\mathbf{x}_t)$ in this section. The observation likelihood for tracked objects need to estimate both the object class and accurate location. MCMOT ensembles object detectors with different characteristics to calculate the observation likelihood accurately. Since the dimensionality of the scene state is allowed to be varied, the measure is defined as the ratio of the likelihoods of the existence and non-existence. As the likelihood of the non-existence set cannot be measured, we adopt a soft max $f(\cdot)$ of the likelihood model, as in [18].

$$\frac{P(\tilde{\mathbf{o}}_t|\mathbf{o}_{id,t})}{P(\tilde{\mathbf{o}}_t|\ \not{o}_{id,t})} = \exp\left(\sum_e f(\lambda_e \log_e(\tilde{\mathbf{o}}_t|\mathbf{o}_{id,t})\right) \tag{1}$$

where $\not{o}_{id,t}$ indicates the non-existence of object id, f soft max function, λ_e the weight of object detector e. The approach is expected to be robust to sporadic noises since each detector has its own pros and cons. We employ ensemble object detectors: deep feature based global object detector (GT), deep feature based local object detector (LT), color detector (CT), and motion detector (MT):

- Global object detector (GT): Deep feature based object detector [28] in terms of hierarchical data model (HDM) [44] is used.
- Local object detector (LT): By fine-tuning deep feature based object detector using confident track segments, issues due to false negatives can be minimized. Deep feature based object detector [28] is used for the local object detector.
- Color detector (CT): Similarity score between the observed appearance model and the reference target is calculated through Bhattacharyya distance [17] using RGB color histogram of the bounding box.
- Motion detector (MT): The presence of an object is checked by using KLT based motion detector [26] which detects the presence of motion in a scene.

4.2 Track Segment Creation

The MCMOT models the tracking problem to determine optimal scene particles in a given video sequence. MCMOT can be thought as reallocation steps of objects from the current scene state to the next scene state repeatedly. First, the birth and death allocations are performed in the entity status transition step. Second, the intermediate track segments are built using the data-driven MCMC sampling step with the assumption that the appearances and positions of track segments change smoothly. In the final step, the detection of a track drift is conducted by a changing point detection algorithm to prevent possible drifts. Change point denotes a time step where the data attributes abruptly change [24] which is expected to be a drift starting point with high probability. We discuss the detail of the data-driven MCMC sampling, and entity status transition in follows.

Date-Driven MCMC Sampling. In a MCMC based sampling, the efficiency of the proposal density function is important since it affects much in constructing a Markov chain with stationary distribution, and thus affects much on tracking performance in practice. The proposal density function should be measurable and can be sampled efficiently from the proposal distribution [2], which is proportional to a desired target distribution. We employ "one object at a time" strategy, whereas one object state is modified at a time, as in [2,7]. Given a particle $\mathbf{x}_t$ at time t, the distribution of current proposal density function $\pi(\mathbf{x}'; \mathbf{x}_t)$ is used to suggest for the next particle. In MCMOT, we assume that the distribution of the proposal density follows the pure motion model for the MCMC sampling, i.e., $\pi(\mathbf{x}'; \mathbf{x}_t) \approx P(\mathbf{x}_{t+1}|\mathbf{x}_t)$, as in [2]. Given a scene particle, i.e., a set of object states $\mathbf{x}_t$, a candidate scene particle $\mathbf{x}'_t$ is suggested by randomly selecting object $\mathbf{o}_{id,t}$, and then determines the proposed state $\mathbf{x}'_t$ relying the object $\mathbf{o}_{id,t}$ with uniform probability assumption. In this paper, a strategy of data-driven proposal density [3] is employed to make the Markov chain has a better acceptance rate. MCMOT proposes a new state $\mathbf{o}'_{id,t}$ according to the informed proposal density with a mixture of the state moves to ensure motion smoothness as in [6]:

$$\pi(\mathbf{o}'_{id,t}; \mathbf{x}_t) = \left[\lambda_1 \frac{1}{N} \sum_s p(\mathbf{o}'_{id,t}|\mathbf{o}^{(s)}_{id,t-1}) + \lambda_2 p(\mathbf{o}'_{id,t}|\mathbf{D}_{id,t}) \right] \qquad (2)$$

where $\lambda_1 + \lambda_2 = 1$. The first term is from the motion model and the second term from the detector ensemble and using the closest result from the all detection of object id.

Remind that the posterior probability for time-step t-1 is assumed to be represented by a set of N samples (scene particles). Given observations from the initial time to the current time t, the calculation of the current posterior is done by MCMC sampling using N samples. We use B samples as burn-in samples [6]. B burn-in samples are used initially and eliminated for the efficient convergence to a stationary state distribution. More details and other practical considerations about MCMC can be found in [42].

Estimation of Entity Status Transition. The entity status is estimated by two binomial probabilities of the birth status and death status according to the entry model at time step t and $t-1$. Let $ES^b_{id,t}(x,y) = \nu$ ($\nu \in \{1, 0\}$) denote the birth status with $\nu = 1$ indicating true, $\nu = 0$ false of an object id in the potion (x,y). Similarly, $ES^d_{id,t}(x,y) = \nu$ denotes death status. The posterior probability of entry status is defined at time t as follows:

$$P_{ES}(\mathbf{o}_{id,t}|\mathbf{o}_{id,t-1}) \approx \begin{cases} P_b = p(ES^b_{id,t}(x,y) = 1|\mathbf{o}_{id,1:t}), & \text{if object } id \text{ exists time } t \text{ and not } t-1 \\ P_d = p(ES^d_{id,t}(x,y) = 1|\mathbf{o}_{id,1:t}), & \text{if object } id \text{ exists at time } t-1 \text{ and not } t \\ P_a = 1 - P_d, & \text{if object } id \text{ exists at time } t-1 \text{ and } t \\ P_\emptyset = 1 - P_b, & \text{if object } id \text{ exists neither time } t \text{ nor } t-1 \end{cases} \quad (3)$$

If a new object id is observed by the observation likelihood mode at time t in position (x,y) which did not exist (detected) in time $t-1$, the birth status of object id $ES^b_{id,t}(x,y)$ is set to 1, otherwise, it is set to 0. If an object id is not observed by the detector ensemble at time t in position (x,y) which existed in time $t-1$, the death status of object id, i.e., $ES^b_{id,t}(x,y)$ is set to 1, otherwise, it is set to 0.

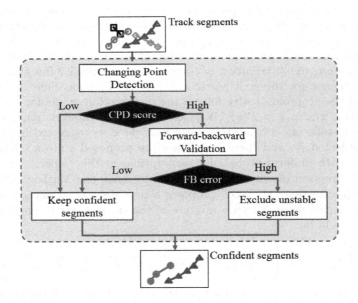

Fig. 2. Illustration of CPD. A change point score is calculated by the changing point detection algorithm. If the high change point score is detected, forward-backward error is checked from the detected change point. FB error checks whether the segment is drifted. A possible track drift is determined effectively by the change point detection method with forward-backward validation.

4.3   Changing Point Detection

MCMOT may fail to track an object if it is occluded or confused by a cluttered background. MCMOT would determine whether or not a track is terminated or continues tracking. Drifts in MCMOT are investigated by detecting such abrupt change points between stationary time series that represent track segment. A higher response indicates a higher uncertainty with high possibility of a drift occurrence [25]. Two-stage time-series learning algorithm is used as in [24], where a possible track drift is determined by a change point detection method [24] as follows. The 2nd level time series is built using the scanned average responses to reduce outliers in the times series. The procedure to prevent drift is illustrated in Fig. 2.

If high CPD response is detected on track segment, the forward-backward error (FB error) validation [7] is defined to estimate the confidence of a track segment by tracking in reverse sequence of the track segments. A given video, the confidence of track segment τ_t is to be estimated. Let τ_t^r denotes the reverse sequential states, i.e., $\mathbf{o}_{id,t:1} = \{\hat{\mathbf{o}}_{id,t}, \ldots, \hat{\mathbf{o}}_{id,1}\}$. The backward track is a random trajectory that is expected to be similar to the correct forward track. The confidence of a track segments is defined as the distance between these two track segments: $\mathrm{Conf}(\tau_t|\tau_t^r) = \mathrm{distance}(\tau_t, \tau_t^r)$. We use the Euclidean distance between the initial point and the end point of the validation trajectory as $\mathrm{distance}(\tau_t, \tau_t^r) = ||\mathbf{o}_{id,1:t} - \mathbf{o}_{id,t:1}||$.

The MCMOT algorithm is summarized in the followings:

Algorithm 1. MCMOT using CPD

Input   : Motion model, entry model
Output: Confident track segments
Step 1. Calculate the posterior $P(\mathbf{x}_t|\mathbf{z}_{1:t}^t)$
Step 2. Generate track segments
Step 3. Detect changing points for all track segments
Step 4. Do forward-backward validation for the track segments with detected changing points
Step 5. Generate resulting trajectories by combining the track segments

---

5   Experiment Results

We describe the details about MCMOT experiment setting, and demonstrate the performance of MCMOT compared to the state-of-the-art methods in challenging video sequences.

5.1   Implementation Details

To build global and local object detector, we use publicly available sixteen-layer VGG-Net [19] and ResNet [29] which are pre-trained on an ImageNet classification dataset. We fine-tune an initial model using ImageNet Challenge Detection dataset (ImageNet DET) with 280 K iterations at a learning rate of 0.001. After 280 K iterations, the learning rate is decreased by a factor of 10 for fine-tuning with 70 K iteration. For region proposal generation, RPN [28] is employed because it is fast and provides accurate region proposals in end-to-end manner by sharing convolutional features. After building initial model, we perform domain-adaptation for each dataset by fine-tuning with similar step described beforehand. Changing point detection algorithms used a two-stage time-series learning algorithm [24] which is computationally effective and achieves high detection accuracy. We consider as change point when change point score is greater than change point threshold. Change point threshold is empirically set as 0.3.

5.2   Dataset

There are a few benchmark datasets available for multi-class multi-object tracking [43]. Since they deal with only two or three classes, we used benchmark datasets, ImageNet VID [31] and MOT 2016 [32], where the former has 30 object classes and the latter is an up-to-date multiple object tracking benchmark. We compare its performance with state-of-the-arts on the ImageNet VID and MOT Benchmark 2016.

ImageNet VID. We demonstrate our proposed algorithm using ImageNet object detection from video (VID) task dataset [31]. ImageNet VID task is originally used to evaluate performance of object detection from video. Nevertheless, this dataset can be used to evaluate MCMOT because this challenging dataset consists of the video sequences recorded with a moving camera in real-world scenes with 30 object categories and the number of targets in the scene is changing over time. Object categories in these scenes take on different viewpoints and are subject to various degrees of occlusions. To ease the comparison with other state-of-the-arts, the performance of MCMOT on this dataset is primarily measured by mean average precision (mAP) which is used in ImageNet VID Challenge [31]. We use the initial release of ImageNet VID dataset, which consists of three splits which are train, validation, and test.

MOT Benchmark 2016. We evaluate our tracking framework on the MOT Benchmark [32]. The MOT Benchmark is an up-to-date multiple object tracking benchmark. The MOT Benchmark collects some new challenging sequences and widely used video sequences in the MOT community. MOT 2016 consists of a total of 14 sequences in unconstrained environments filmed with both static and moving cameras. All the sequences contain only pedestrians. These challenging sequences are composed with various configurations such as different viewpoints, and different weather condition. Therefore, tracking algorithms which are tuned for specific scenario or scene could not perform well. We adopt the CLEAR MOT tracking metrics [23] using MOT Benchmark Development Kit [32] for the evaluation.

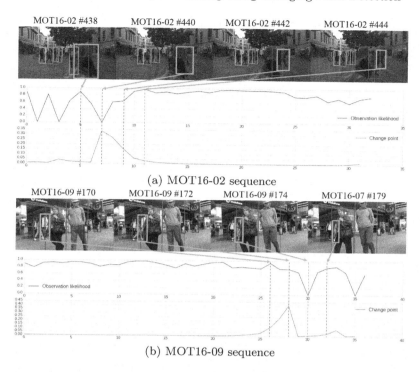

Fig. 3. Change points obtained from the segment in MOT16-02 and MOT16-09 sequence. A higher change point response indicates a higher uncertainty with high possibility of a drift occurrence. Notice that our method can effectively detect drifts in challenging situations.

5.3   MCMOT CPD Analysis

In order to investigate the proposed MCMOT changing point detection component, we select two sequences, MOT16-02 and MOT16-09 from the MOT 2016 training set. For change point detection, we assign a change point if change point score is larger than 0.3. Figure 3 illustrates the observation likelihood and detected change point of the segment. A low likelihood or rapid change in likelihood is an important factor for detecting potential changing point. In the tracking result of MOT16-02 sequence in Fig. 3, unstable likelihood is observed until frame 438, where a motion-blurred half-body person moves. Tracking is drifted because occluded person appears at similar position with previous tracked point at frame 440. After several frames, the target is swapped to another person at frame 444. In this case, bounding boxes within drift area are unstable, which observed strong fluctuation of likelihood. Changing point detection algorithm produces high change point score at frame 440 by detecting this fluctuation. In the tracking result of MOT16-09 sequence in Fig. 3 also illustrates similar

78   B. Lee et al.

Table 1. Effect of different components on the ImageNet VID validation set

	Aero	Antelope	Bear	Bike	Bird	Bus	Car	Cattle	Dog	Cat	Elephant
Detection baseline	84.6	75.8	77.2	57.2	60.8	84.6	62.4	66.3	57.7	62.3	74.0
MCMOT CPD	87.1	81.2	83.2	76.6	64.3	86.1	64.4	79.4	69.4	74.4	77.4
MCMOT CPD FB	86.3	83.4	88.2	78.9	65.9	90.6	66.3	81.5	72.1	76.8	82.4
	Fox	g_panda	Hamster	Horse	Lion	Lizard	Monkey	m-bike	Rabbit	r_panda	Sheep
Detection baseline	79.6	89.9	80.0	58.7	15.5	70.0	45.5	78.1	67.5	51.2	30.7
MCMOT CPD	87.3	90.2	85.3	63.3	31.7	74.8	52.6	86.9	74.7	75.2	30.5
MCMOT CPD FB	88.9	91.3	89.3	66.5	38.0	77.1	57.3	88.8	78.2	77.7	40.6
	Snake	Squirrel	Tiger	Train	Turtle	Boat	Whale	Zebra	Mean AP (%)		
Detection baseline	50.7	29.0	79.5	71.5	68.9	77.0	57.9	77.9	64.7		
MCMOT CPD	43.7	39.0	87.4	75.1	67.0	80.2	59.7	84.1	71.1		
MCMOT CPD FB	50.3	44.3	91.8	78.2	75.1	81.7	63.1	85.2	**74.5**		

Fig. 4. MCMOT tracking results on the validation sequences in the ImageNet VID dataset. Each bounding box is labeled with the identity, the predicted class, and the confidence score of the segment. Viewing digitally with zoom is recommended.

situation explained before. As we can see, a possible track drift is implicitly handled by the change point detection method.

5.4   ImageNet VID Evaluation

Since the official ImageNet Challenge test server is primarily used for annual competition and has limited number of usage, we evaluate the performance of

Table 2. Tracking performance comparison on the ImageNet VID validation set

	Aero	Antelope	Bear	Bike	Bird	Bus	Car	Cattle	Dog	Cat	Elephant
TCN [21]	72.7	75.5	42.2	39.5	25.0	64.1	36.3	51.1	24.4	48.6	65.6
ITLab VID-Inha	78.5	68.5	76.5	61.4	43.1	72.9	61.6	61.1	52.2	56.6	74.0
T-CNN [20]	83.7	85.7	84.4	74.5	73.8	75.7	57.1	58.7	72.3	69.2	80.2
MCMOT (Ours)	86.3	83.4	88.2	78.9	65.9	90.6	66.3	81.5	72.1	76.8	82.4

	Fox	g_panda	Hamster	Horse	Lion	Lizard	Monkey	m-bike	Rabbit	r_panda	Sheep
TCN [21]	73.9	61.7	82.4	30.8	34.4	54.2	1.6	61.0	36.6	19.7	55.0
ITLab VID-Inha	72.5	85.5	67.5	64.7	5.7	54.3	34.7	77.6	53.5	40.8	34.3
T-CNN [20]	83.4	80.5	93.1	84.2	67.8	80.3	54.8	80.6	63.7	85.7	60.5
MCMOT (Ours)	88.9	91.3	89.3	66.5	38.0	77.1	57.3	88.8	78.2	77.7	40.6

	Snake	Squirrel	Tiger	Train	Turtle	Boat	Whale	Zebra	Mean AP (%)
TCN [21]	38.9	2.6	42.8	54.6	66.1	69.2	26.5	68.6	47.5
ITLab VID-Inha	18.1	23.4	69.6	53.4	61.6	78.0	33.2	77.7	57.1
T-CNN [20]	72.9	52.7	89.7	81.3	73.7	69.5	33.5	90.2	73.8
MCMOT (Ours)	50.3	44.3	91.8	78.2	75.1	81.7	63.1	85.2	**74.5**

the proposed method on the validation set instead of the test set as a practical convention [20] for ImageNet VID task. For the ImageNet VID train/validation experiment, all the training and testing images are scaled by 600 pixel to be the length of image's shortest side. This value was selected so that VGG16 or ResNet fits in GPU memory during fine-tuning [28].

Table 1 shows the effect of different components of MCMOT. Each method is distinguished in terms of MCMOT with CPD algorithm (MCMOT CPD), and MCMOT using CPD with forward-backward validation (MCMOT CPD FB). In the following evaluations, we filter out segments that have an average observation score lower than 0.3. As shown in the Table 1, significant improvement can be achieved with 9.8 % from detection baseline by adapting MCMOT CPD, and reached to 71.1 %. After the adaptation of the FB validation, an overall 74.5 % mAP was achieved on the ImageNet VID validation set. Table 2 summarizes the evaluation accuracy of MCMOT and the comparison with the other state-of-the-art algorithms on the whole 281 validation video sequences. Our MCMOT is achieved overall 74.5 % mAP on the ImageNet VID validation set, which is higher than state-of-the-art methods such as T-CNN [20]. This result is mainly due to the MCMOT approach of constructing a highly accurate segments by using CPD. As shown in Fig. 4, unlimited number of classes are successfully tracked with high localization accuracy using MCMOT.

5.5   MOT Benchmark 2016 Evaluation

We evaluate MCMOT on the MOT Challenge 2016 benchmark to compare our approach with other state-of-the-art algorithms. For the MOT 2016 experiment, all the training and testing images are scaled by 800 pixel to be the length of image's shortest side. This larger value is selected because pedestrian bounding box size is smaller than ImageNet VID. In MCMOT, we also implement hierarchical data model (HDM) [44] which is CNN based object detector. The timing excludes detection time.

Table 3 summarizes the evaluation metrics of MCMOT and the other state-of-the-arts on the test video sequences. Figure 5 visualizes examples of MCMOT tracking results on the test sequences. As shown in the Table 3, MCMOT outperforms the previously published state-of-the-art methods on overall performance evaluation metric which is called *multi object tracking accuracy* (MOTA). We also achieved much smaller numbers of *mostly lost targets* (ML) by a significant margin. Even though our method outperforms most of the metrics, *tracker speed in frames per second* (HZ) is faster than other tracking methods. This is thanks to the simple MCMC tracking structure with entity status transition, and selective FB error validation with CPD, which is boosted tracking speed on a multi-object tracking task. However, high *identity switch* (IDS) and high *fragmentation* (FRAG) are observed because of the lack of identity mapping between track segments. More importantly, MCMOT achieves state-of-the-art

Table 3. Tracking performances comparison on the MOT benchmark 2016 (results on 7/14/2016). The symbol ↑ denotes higher scores indicate better performance. The symbol ↓ means lower scores indicate better performance.

Method	MOTA↑	MOTP↑	FAF↓	MT↑	ML↓	FP↓	FN↓	ID Sw↓	Frag↓	Hz↑
GRIM	−14.5%	73.0%	10.0	9.9%	49.5%	59,040	147,908	1,869	2,454	10.0
JPDA_m [41]	26.2%	76.3%	0.6	4.1%	67.5%	3,689	130,549	365	638	22.2
SMOT [40]	29.7%	75.2%	2.9	5.3%	47.7%	17,426	107,552	3,108	4,483	0.2
DP_NMS [39]	32.2%	76.4%	**0.2**	5.4%	62.1%	**1,123**	121,579	972	944	**212.6**
CEM [38]	33.2%	75.8%	1.2	7.8%	54.4%	6,837	114,322	642	731	0.3
TBD [37]	33.7%	76.5%	1.0	7.2%	54.2%	5,804	112,587	2,418	2,252	1.3
LINF1	41.0%	74.8%	1.3	11.6%	51.3%	7,896	99,224	430	963	1.1
olCF	43.2%	74.3%	1.1	11.3%	48.5%	6,651	96,515	381	1,404	0.4
NOMT [22]	46.4%	76.6%	1.6	18.3%	41.4%	9,753	87,565	359	**504**	2.6
AMPL	50.9%	77.0%	0.5	16.7%	40.8%	3,229	86,123	**196**	639	1.5
NOMTw SDP16 [22]	62.2%	**79.6%**	0.9	**32.5%**	31.1%	5,119	63,352	406	642	3.1
MCMOT_ HDM (Ours)	**62.4%**	78.3%	1.7	31.5%	**24.2%**	9,855	**57,257**	1,394	1,318	34.9

Fig. 5. MCMOT tracking results on the test sequences in the MOT Benchmark 2016. Each frame is sampled every 100 frames (these are not curated). The color of the boxes represents the identity of the targets. The figure is best shown in color. (Color figure online)

performance in two different datasets, we demonstrate the general multi-class multi-obejct tracking applicability to any kind of situation with unlimited number of classes.

6 Conclusion

This paper presented a novel multi-class multi-object tracking framework. The framework surpassed the performance of state-of-the-art results on ImageNet VID and MOT benchmark 2016. MCMOT that conducted unlimited object class association based on detection responses. The CPD model was used to observe abrupt or abnormal changes due to a drift. The ensemble of KLT based motion detector and CNN based object detector was employed to compute the likelihoods. A future research direction is to deal with the optimization problem of MCMOT structure and identity mapping problem between track segments.

Acknowledgements. This work was supported by an Inha University research grant. A GPU used in this research was generously donated by NVIDIA Corporation.

References

1. Sakaino, H.: Video-based tracking, learning, and recognition method for multiple moving objects. IEEE Trans. Circuits Syst. Video Technol. **23**, 1661–1674 (2013)
2. Khan, Z., Balch, T., Dellaert, F.: MCMC-based particle filtering for tracking a variable number of interacting targets. TPAMI **27**, 1805–1819 (2005)
3. Zhao, T., Nevatia, R., Wu, B.: Segmentation and tracking of multiple humans in crowded environments. TPAMI **30**, 1198–1211 (2008)
4. Khan, Z., Balch, T., Dellaert, F.: MCMC data association and sparse factorization updating for real time multitarget tracking with merged and multiple measurements. TPAMI **28**, 1960–1972 (2006)
5. Green, P.J.: Trans-dimensional markov chain monte carlo. Oxford Statistical Science Series, pp. 179–198 (2003)
6. Duffner, S., Odobez, J.M.: Track creation and deletion framework for long-term online multiface tracking. IEEE Trans. Image Process. **22**, 272–285 (2013)
7. Kalal, Z., Mikolajczyk, K., Matas, J.: Forward-backward error: automatic detection of tracking failures. In: ICPR (2010)
8. Wang, C., Liu, H., Gao, Y.: Scene-adaptive hierarchical data association for multiple objects tracking. IEEE Signal Process. Lett. **21**, 697–701 (2014)
9. Xing, J., Ai, H., Liu, L., Lao, S.: Multiple player tracking in sports video: a dual-mode two-way Bayesian inference approach with progressive observation modeling. IEEE Trans. Image Process. **20**, 1652–1667 (2011)
10. Berclaz, J., Fleuret, F., Turetken, E., Fua, P.: Multiple object tracking using k-shortest paths optimization. TPAMI **33**, 1806–1819 (2011)
11. Berclaz, J., Fleuret, F., Fua, P.: Robust people tracking with global trajectory optimization. In: CVPR (2006)
12. Zhang, L., Li, Y., Nevatia, R.: Global data association for multi-object tracking using network flows. In: CVPR (2008)
13. Huang, C., Wu, B., Nevatia, R.: Robust object tracking by hierarchical association of detection responses. In: Forsyth, D., Torr, P., Zisserman, A. (eds.) ECCV 2008, Part II. LNCS, vol. 5303, pp. 788–801. Springer, Heidelberg (2008)
14. Breitenstein, M.D., Reichlin, F., Leibe, B., Koller-Meier, E., Van Gool, L.: Online multiperson tracking-by-detection from a single, uncalibrated camera. TPAMI **33**, 1820–1833 (2011)
15. Liu, H., Wang, C.: Hierarchical data association and depth-invariant appearance model for indoor multiple objects tracking. In: ICIP (2013)
16. Xiao, J., Oussalah, M.: Collaborative tracking for multiple objects in the presence of inter-occlusions. IEEE Trans. Circuits Syst. Video Technol. **26**, 304–318 (2016)
17. Bhattacharyya, A.: On a measure of divergence between two multinomial populations. Sankhy: The Indian Journal of Statistics, 401–406 (1946)
18. Choi, W., Pantofaru, C., Savarese, S.: A general framework for tracking multiple people from a moving camera. TPAMI **35**, 1577–1591 (2013)
19. Simonyan, K., Zisserman, A.: Very deep convolutional networks for large-scale image recognition. In: arXiv preprint arXiv:1409.1556 (2014)
20. Kang, K., Li, H., Yan, J., Zeng, X., Yang, B., Xiao, T., Ouyang, W.: T-cnn: Tubelets with convolutional neural networks for object detection from videos. In: arXiv preprint arXiv:1604.02532 (2016)

21. Kang, K., Ouyang, W., Li, H., Wang, X.: Object detection from video tubelets with convolutional neural networks. In: arXiv preprint arXiv:1604.04053 (2016)
22. Choi, W.: Near-online multi-target tracking with aggregated local flow descriptor. In: ICCV(2015)
23. Bernardin, K., Stiefelhagen, R.: Evaluating multiple object tracking performance: the CLEAR MOT metrics. In: EURASIP Journal on Image and Video Processing 2008 (2008)
24. Takeuchi, J.I., Yamanishi, K.: A unifying framework for detecting outliers and change points from time series. IEEE Trans. Knowl. Data Eng. **18**, 482–492 (2006)
25. Akaike, H., Kitagawa, G.: Practices in Time Series Analysis I, II. Asakura Shoten (1995). (in Japanese 1994)
26. Tomasi, C., Kanade, T.: Detection and Tracking of Point Features. School of Computer Science, Carnegie Mellon Univ., Pittsburgh (1991)
27. Gidaris, S., Komodakis, N.: Object detection via a multi-region and semantic segmentation-aware cnn model. In: ICCV (2015)
28. Ren, S., He, K., Girshick, R., Sun, J.: Faster R-CNN: towards real-time object detection with region proposal networks. In: NIPS (2015)
29. He, K., Zhang, X., Ren, S., Sun, J.: Deep residual learning for image recognition. arXiv pre-print arXiv:1512.03385 (2015)
30. Zeiler, M.D., Fergus, R.: Visualizing and understanding convolutional networks. In: Fleet, D., Pajdla, T., Schiele, B., Tuytelaars, T. (eds.) ECCV 2014, Part I. LNCS, vol. 8689, pp. 818–833. Springer, Heidelberg (2014)
31. Russakovsky, O., Deng, J., Su, H., Krause, J., Satheesh, S., Ma, S., Huang, Z., Karpathy, A., Khosla, A., Bernstein, M., Berg, A.C.: Imagenet large scale visual recognition challenge. IJCV **115**, 211–252 (2015)
32. Milan, A., Leal-Taixe, L., Reid, I., Roth, S., Schindler, K.: MOT16: a benchmark for multi-object tracking. arXiv preprint arXiv:1603.00831 (2016)
33. Magee, D.R.: Tracking multiple vehicles using foreground, background and motion models. Image Vis. Comput. **22**, 143–155 (2004)
34. Girshick, R., Donahue, J., Darrell, T., Malik, J.: Rich feature hierarchies for accurate object detection and semantic segmentation. In: CVPR (2014)
35. He, K., Zhang, X., Ren, S., Sun, J.: Spatial pyramid pooling in deep convolutional networks for visual recognition. TPAMI **37**, 1904–1916 (2015)
36. Girshick, R.: Fast R-CNN. In: ICCV (2015)
37. Geiger, A., Lauer, M., Wojek, C., Stiller, C., Urtasun, R.: 3D traffic scene understanding from movable platforms. TPAMI **36**, 1012–1025 (2014)
38. Milan, A., Roth, S., Schindler, K.: Continuous energy minimization for multitarget tracking. TPAMI **36**, 58–72 (2014)
39. Pirsiavash, H., Ramanan, D., Fowlkes, C.C.: Globally-optimal greedy algorithms for tracking a variable number of objects. In: CVPR (2011)
40. Dicle, C., Camps, O.I., Sznaier, M.: The way they move: tracking multiple targets with similar appearance. In: ICCV (2013)
41. Hamid Rezatofighi, S., Milan, A., Zhang, Z., Shi, Q., Dick, A., Reid, I.: Joint probabilistic data association revisited. In: ICCV (2015)
42. Gilks, W.R., Richardson, S., Spiegelhalter, D.J.: Introducing Markov Chain Monte Carlo. Markov chain Monte Carlo in practice 1 (1996)
43. Wang, X., Turetken, E., Fleuret, F., Fua, P.: Tracking interacting objects using intertwined flows. TPAMI **99**, 1–1 (2016)
44. Lee, B., Erdenee, E., Jin, S., Rhee, P.K.: Efficient object detection using convolutional neural network-based hierarchical feature modeling. Sign. Image Video Process. **10**(8), 1503–1510 (2016)

Online Multi-target Tracking
with Strong and Weak Detections

Ricardo Sanchez-Matilla[(⊠)], Fabio Poiesi, and Andrea Cavallaro

Centre for Intelligent Sensing, Queen Mary University of London, London, UK
{ricardo.sanchezmatilla,fabio.poiesi,a.cavallaro}@qmul.ac.uk

Abstract. We propose an online multi-target tracker that exploits both high- and low-confidence target detections in a Probability Hypothesis Density Particle Filter framework. High-confidence (strong) detections are used for label propagation and target initialization. Low-confidence (weak) detections only support the propagation of labels, i.e. tracking existing targets. Moreover, we perform data association just after the prediction stage thus avoiding the need for computationally expensive labeling procedures such as clustering. Finally, we perform sampling by considering the perspective distortion in the target observations. The tracker runs on average at 12 frames per second. Results show that our method outperforms alternative online trackers on the Multiple Object Tracking 2016 and 2015 benchmark datasets in terms tracking accuracy, false negatives and speed.

Keywords: Multi-Target Tracking · Probability Hypothesis Density · Particle Filter

1 Introduction

Multi-target tracking-by-detection performs temporal association of target detections to estimate trajectories, while compensating for miss-detections and rejecting false-positive detections. Trajectories can be generated online [1], offline [2] or with a short latency [3]. *Online trackers* estimate the target state at each time instant as detections are produced. In case of miss-detections, online trackers may rely on predictive models to continue tracking until a matching detection is found [4]. *Offline trackers* use both past and future detections and can therefore better cope with miss-detections using re-identification [5].

An effective filter for online state estimation is the Probability Hypothesis Density (PHD) filter, which can cope with clutter, spatial noise and miss-detections [6,7]. The PHD filter estimates the state of multiple targets by building a positive and integrable function over a multi-dimensional state whose integral approximates the expected number of targets [6,8]. The posterior function can be computed based on a Bayesian recursion that leverages the set of (noisy) detections and it is approximated using Sequential Monte Carlo for computational efficiency via a set of weighted random samples (particles) [8]. This

© Springer International Publishing Switzerland 2016
G. Hua and H. Jégou (Eds.): ECCV 2016 Workshops, Part II, LNCS 9914, pp. 84–99, 2016.
DOI: 10.1007/978-3-319-48881-3_7

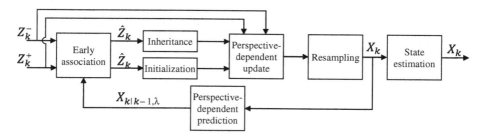

Fig. 1. Block diagram of the proposed multi-target tracking pipeline. At time k, the predicted particles $\mathcal{X}_{k|k-1,\lambda}$ are calculated with a perspective-dependent prediction. Strong Z_k^+ and weak Z_k^- detections are associated to the predicted states calculated from $\mathcal{X}_{k|k-1,\lambda}$. After the early association, two subsets of detections are used for tracking. Detections $\hat{Z}_k$ inherit the identity of the corresponding trajectories and are used for tracking existing states; $\check{Z}_k$ are un-associated strong detections and are used for initializing new states. After the perspective-dependent update, and resampling the particles $\mathcal{X}_k$ are used to estimate the states X_k.

approximation is known as the PHD Particle Filter (PHD-PF) and involves four main steps [6–8]: the *prediction* of particles over time; the *update* of the weights of the particles based on new detections; the *resampling* step to avoid that only few particles monopolize the whole mass; and *state estimation*. A PHD filter needs an additional mechanism to provide target identity information. For example, the particles can be clustered and labeled after resampling to enable the temporal association of the clusters with previous states [7,9,10]. This additional mechanism is computationally expensive and error prone.

In this paper, we formulate an early association strategy between trajectories and detections after the prediction stage, which allows us to perform target estimation and state labeling without any additional mechanisms. Our online multi-target tracker exploits both strong (certain) and weak (uncertain) detections. Strong detections have a higher confidence score and are used for initialization and tracking. Weak detections have a lower confidence score and are used only to support the continuation of an existing track when strong detections are missing. We also introduce a perspective-dependent sampling mechanism to create newborn particles depending on their distance from the camera. Figure 1 shows the block diagram of the proposed online multi-target tracker.

In summary, our contributions include (i) a strategy for the effective exploitation of low-confidence (weak) detections; (ii) a procedure to label states via an early association strategy; (iii) the exploitation of perspective in prediction, update and newborn particle generation. The tracker works on average at 12 frames per second (fps) on an i7 3.40 GHz, 16 GB RAM computer, without any parallelization. We validate our tracking pipeline without using any appearance features and compare our method against state-of-the-art alternatives on the MOT15 and MOT16 benchmark datasets.

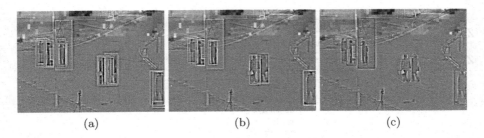

$$\text{(a)} \qquad\qquad\qquad \text{(b)} \qquad\qquad\qquad \text{(c)}$$

Fig. 2. Example of strong and weak detections at frame 43 (crop) in PETS09-S2L1. (a) Initial target detections Z_k^*; (b) combined detections Z_k; (c) strong detections (green) Z_k^+ and weak detections (red) Z_k^- after classification. (Color figure online)

2   Strong and Weak Detections

Let a (large) set of target detections $\mathbf{z}_k^* \in Z_k^*$, ideally without false negatives but potentially with multiple false positives, be generated at each time step k (Fig. 2(a)). These detections can be produced for example by running in parallel multiple detectors, by changing the operational parameters of a detector or with a combination of these two approaches. During this 'over-detection' process a target is likely to generate multiple overlapping detections. Overlapping detections produced by the same target may be combined into a single detection $\mathbf{z}_k \in Z_k$ using, for example, non-maxima suppression [11,12] (Fig. 2(b)) forming the set of combined detections Z_k. Let each combined target detection be defined as

$$\mathbf{z}_k = (x_k, y_k, w_k, h_k)^T, \tag{1}$$

where (x_k, y_k) is the center and (w_k, h_k) are the width and height of the bounding box of the detection on the image plane. Let each $\mathbf{z}_k$ be associated to a detection confidence-score $s_k \in [0, 1]$.

We categorize the set Z_k based on s_k into two subsets: strong (certain) and weak (uncertain) detections (Fig. 2(c)). This categorization can be obtained using the score confidences or via learning certain metrics on a training dataset [13]. *Strong* detections $Z_k^+ = \{\mathbf{z}_k^+ : s_k \geq \tau_s\}$, where τ_s is a confidence threshold, are more likely to be true positives. We will use strong detections for trajectory initialization and for tracking existing targets. *Weak* detections $Z_k^- = \{\mathbf{z}_k^- : s_k < \tau_s\}$ are potential false positives. We will use weak detections for tracking existing targets to shorten the prediction time and to maintain the tracking uncertainty low. The value of τ_s influences the ratio between the false positives and the false negatives, as we discuss in Sect. 6.1.

3   Perspective-Dependent Prediction

Let Λ_k be the set of existing identities at time k whose elements are $\lambda \in \Lambda_k$. Let the state be defined as

$$\mathbf{x}_{k,\lambda} = (x_{k,\lambda}, \dot{x}_{k,\lambda}, y_{k,\lambda}, \dot{y}_{k,\lambda}, w_{k,\lambda}, h_{k,\lambda})^T, \tag{2}$$

where $(x_{k,\lambda}, y_{k,\lambda})$ is the center, $(\dot{x}_{k,\lambda}, \dot{y}_{k,\lambda})$ are the horizontal and vertical components of the velocity, $(w_{k,\lambda}, h_{k,\lambda})$ are the width and height and λ is the identity of the estimated state. Let the set of all estimated states at k be X_k whose elements are $\mathbf{x}_{k,\lambda} \in X_k$. The elements of this set are obtained at each time step from the set of all existing particles $\mathcal{X}_k$ whose elements are $\mathbf{x}_{k,\lambda}^i \in \mathcal{X}_k$, where $\mathbf{x}_{k,\lambda}^i$ is the ith particle.

The prediction step assumes the motion of a target to be independent from the others and propagates each particle $\mathbf{x}_{k-1,\lambda}^i$ as

$$\mathbf{x}_{k,\lambda}^i = G_k \mathbf{x}_{k-1,\lambda}^i + N_k, \tag{3}$$

where G_k is an affine transformation defined as

$$G_k = \begin{pmatrix} A_k & \mathbf{0}_{2\times 2} & \mathbf{0}_{2\times 2} \\ \mathbf{0}_{2\times 2} & B_k & \mathbf{0}_{2\times 2} \\ \mathbf{0}_{2\times 2} & \mathbf{0}_{2\times 2} & \mathbf{I}_{2\times 2} \end{pmatrix}, \tag{4}$$

where $\mathbf{0}$ and $\mathbf{I}$ are the zero and identity matrices, respectively. N_k is an additive Gaussian noise defined as $N_k = \left(n_k^x, n_k^{\dot{x}}, n_k^y, n_k^{\dot{y}}, n_k^w, n_k^h\right)^T$, where each component of N_k is an independent Gaussian variable with zero mean and standard deviation proportional to the bounding box size in the previous frame.

As a target moving at constant velocity produces a smaller apparent displacement on the image plane when it is farther from the camera, we improve the model in Eq. 4 by considering the effect of foreshortening. To this end, we model N_k as a function of the distance from the camera. Specifically, we set the standard deviation of the noise for the horizontal and vertical components to be proportional to the width $w_{k-1,\lambda}$ and height $h_{k-1,\lambda}$ of the state, respectively.

In addition to the above, target acceleration variations, noisy detections and camera motion may generate erroneous predictions. To address these problems, instead of relying only on the previous time step [7], we average the past M states over a longer time interval $[t-M, t-1]$. Therefore, A_k and B_k dynamically update the position and velocity via the average velocity in the previous M frames:

$$A_k = \begin{pmatrix} 1 & \frac{u_{k,\lambda}}{\dot{x}_{k,\lambda}} \\ 0 & \frac{u_{k,\lambda}}{\dot{x}_{k,\lambda}} \end{pmatrix}, \; B_k = \begin{pmatrix} 1 & \frac{v_{k,\lambda}}{\dot{y}_{k,\lambda}} \\ 0 & \frac{v_{k,\lambda}}{\dot{y}_{k,\lambda}} \end{pmatrix}, \tag{5}$$

where $u_{k,\lambda}, v_{k,\lambda}$ are the average horizontal and vertical velocities of the estimated state $\mathbf{x}_{k,\lambda}$, respectively, whose values are computed as

$$(u_{k,\lambda}, v_{k,\lambda}) = \frac{1}{M} \sum_{j=1}^{M} (x_{k-j,\lambda}, y_{k-j,\lambda}), \tag{6}$$

where $M = \min\left(M_{k,\lambda}, M_{max}\right)$, $M_{k,\lambda}$ is the number of time steps since the target $\mathbf{x}_{k,\lambda}$ was initialized and M_{max} the maximum number of time steps.

The weights of the particles, $\pi^i_{k|k-1}$, are not modified during the prediction state, therefore

$$\pi^i_{k|k-1} = \pi^i_{k-1}, \qquad i = 1, ..., L_{k-1}, \tag{7}$$

where L_{k-1} is the number of existing particles at $k - 1$.

4   Labeling

4.1   Early Association (EA)

The PHD-PF estimates the state of each target without labels (i.e. without identity) [9]. Let π^i_{k-1} be the weight associated to particle $\mathbf{x}^i_{k-1,\lambda}$. The PHD-PF posterior $D_{k-1|k-1}(\cdot)$ is approximated as

$$D_{k-1|k-1}\left(\mathbf{x}_{k-1,\lambda}\right) \approx \sum_{i=1}^{L_{k-1}} \pi^i_{k-1}\delta\left(\mathbf{x}_{k-1,\lambda} - \mathbf{x}^i_{k-1,\lambda}\right), \tag{8}$$

where $\delta(\cdot)$ is the Kronecker's delta function. Various works have been published aiming to address the lack of identities in the PHD-PF: (i) clustering after resampling the particles on the right-hand side of Eq. 8 [7], (ii) keeping a separate tracker for each target and then perform 'peak-to-track' association [14], (iii) combining clustering techniques with the introduction of hidden identifiers to the samples of the PHD [8,10,15]. These solutions are computationally expensive and may introduce estimation errors. To avoid these problems, we move the association stage earlier in the pipeline.

We associate the elements of Z^+_k and Z^-_k to the predicted states using the Hungarian algorithm [16]. We refer to this association as *early association* because, unlike [7,8,15], it is performed before the update and resampling stages. The association cost, ω_k, between a detection $\mathbf{z}_k$ and the predicted state $\mathbf{x}_{k|k-1,\lambda}$ is

$$\omega_k = \frac{d_l(\mathbf{z}_k, \mathbf{x}_{k|k-1,\lambda})}{Q_l} \cdot \frac{d_s(\mathbf{z}_k, \mathbf{x}_{k|k-1,\lambda})}{Q_s}, \tag{9}$$

where $d_l(\cdot)$ and $d_s(\cdot)$ are the Euclidean distances between the position and bounding box size elements, respectively. Q_l is the diagonal of the image (i.e. the maximum position variation) and Q_s is the area of the image (i.e. the maximum size variation). Note that we multiply the normalized distances instead of averaging them to penalize when they are dissimilar (e.g. when two targets are far from each other in the scene but appear close to each other on the image plane).

When a trajectory is not associated to any (strong or weak) detections, the state is estimated using existing particles only. When the trajectory is not associated to any detections for a certain temporal interval (V frames, see Sect. 6.1), the state will be discarded before the EA and therefore the weight of its particles will gradually decrease toward zero.

EA enables the tracker to generate newborn particles that inherit the properties of its associated state (*inheritance*) or that produce a new identity (*initialization*).

4.2   Inheritance

Strong detections Z_k^+ generate J_k newborn particles to repopulate the area around existing states. The newborn particles are added to the L_{k-1} existing particles. In [7,8], the newborn particles are created from a newborn importance function $p_k(\cdot)$ [7], which can be independently modeled from the estimated states, as a Gaussian process:

$$\mathbf{x}_{k,\lambda}^i \sim p_k(\mathbf{x}_{k,\lambda}^i|\mathbf{z}_k^+) = \frac{1}{|Z_k^+|} \sum_{\forall \mathbf{z}_k^+ \in Z_k^+} \mathcal{N}(\mathbf{x}_{k,\lambda}^i; \mathbf{z}_k^+, \Sigma), \tag{10}$$

where $|\cdot|$ is the cardinality of a set, $\mathcal{N}(\cdot)$ is a Gaussian distribution and Σ is the covariance matrix. The covariance matrix can be dynamically updated based on parameters as detection size or video frame rate (see Sect. 6.1). Each newborn particle has an associated weight, π_k^i, defined as

$$\pi_k^i = \frac{1}{J_k} \frac{\gamma_k(\mathbf{x}_{k,\lambda}^i)}{p_k(\mathbf{x}_{k,\lambda}^i|\mathbf{z}_k^+)}, \quad i = L_{k-1} + 1, ..., L_{k-1} + J_k, \tag{11}$$

where $\gamma_k(\cdot)$ is the birth intensity, which is assumed to be constant when no prior knowledge about the scene is available [7]. Typically, J_k is chosen to have, on average, ρ particles per newborn target [8]. The process described in Eq. 10 could create newborn particles that are dissimilar from the corresponding state as they are independently created.

Unlike [15,17] that included identities in the state, we consider the identity $\lambda \in \Lambda_k$ as attribute of the state and propagate it over time. Therefore, $|\Lambda_k|$ is the estimated number of targets at time k.

Let $\hat{Z}_k^+$ and $\hat{Z}_k^-$ be the sets that contain, respectively, strong and weak detections that are *associated* to one of the predicted states, i.e. to an existing trajectory. Let $\hat{Z}_k = \hat{Z}_k^+ \cup \hat{Z}_k^-$ be the set of detections that inherit the identity of the corresponding trajectories.

We create newborn particles from $\hat{Z}_k$ and inherit properties from their associated predicted states: the position and bounding box size are created from detections, whereas velocity and identity are inherited from the associated states.

We use a mixture of Gaussians as importance function to sample position and bounding box size elements from the detections as

$$\mathbf{x}_{k,\lambda}^i \sim p_k(\mathbf{x}_{k,\lambda}^i|\hat{\mathbf{z}}_k) = \frac{1}{|\hat{Z}_k|} \sum_{\forall \hat{\mathbf{z}}_k \in \hat{Z}_k} \mathcal{N}(C\mathbf{x}_{k,\lambda}^i; C\hat{\mathbf{z}}_k, C\Sigma_k), \tag{12}$$

where

$$C = \begin{pmatrix} D & 0_{4 \times 2} \\ 0_{2 \times 4} & I_{2 \times 2} \end{pmatrix}, \quad D = \begin{pmatrix} 1 & 0 & 0 & 0 \\ 0 & 0 & 0 & 0 \\ 0 & 0 & 1 & 0 \\ 0 & 0 & 0 & 0 \end{pmatrix}, \tag{13}$$

and

$$\Sigma_k = diag(\sigma_k^x, \sigma_k^{\dot{x}}, \sigma_k^y, \sigma_k^{\dot{y}}, \sigma_k^w, \sigma_k^h)^T, \tag{14}$$

where Σ_k is a time-variant standard deviations matrix that is defined based on the size of the detection bounding box and the weight of the newborn particles is calculated as in Eq. 11. This solution allows us to address the perspective distortion during the generation of newborn particles. The values of these standard deviations are learned from a training dataset (see Sect. 6.1).

The velocities and the identity are inherited from the trajectory as

$$\dot{x}_{k,\lambda}^i = \dot{x}_{k-1,\lambda} + n_k^{\dot{x}},$$
$$\dot{y}_{k,\lambda}^i = \dot{y}_{k-1,\lambda} + n_k^{\dot{y}},$$
$$\lambda_k = \lambda_{k-1}, \tag{15}$$

where $(\dot{x}_{k-1,\lambda}, \dot{y}_{k-1,\lambda})$ are the velocity components of a trajectory X_λ (i.e. each state with identity λ for all k) and $n_k^{\dot{x}}$ and $n_k^{\dot{y}}$ are Gaussian noises that model the velocity variations of a target.

Figure 3 shows the benefit of weak detections. Without weak detections, miss-detections produce false negative trajectories and identity switches (Fig. 3, second row). When weak detections are used the targets are correctly tracked (Fig. 3, third row).

4.3 Initialization

While un-associated *weak* detections are discarded after EA, un-associated *strong* detections form the set $\check{Z}_k = Z_k^+ \backslash \hat{Z}_k^+$ and initialize new target identities. Newborn particles associated to a *new target* are generated in a limited volume of the state space around the un-associated strong detections. The same new identity is assigned to each newborn particle.

We treat spawning targets as new targets. The newborn importance function $p_k(\cdot)$ in Eq. 10 can regulate where targets are likely to spawn or enter in a scene [18]. Each detection in $\check{Z}_k$ initializes a *new trajectory* and generates newborn particles using a mixture of Gaussians as

$$\mathbf{x}_{k,\lambda}^i \sim p_k(\mathbf{x}_{k,\lambda}^i | \check{\mathbf{z}}_k) = \frac{1}{|\check{Z}_k|} \sum_{\forall \check{\mathbf{z}}_k \in \check{Z}_k} \mathcal{N}(\mathbf{x}_{k,\lambda}^i; \check{\mathbf{z}}_k, \Sigma_k), \tag{16}$$

where Σ_k is defined in Eq. 14 and the weights of the particles are calculated as in Eq. 11.

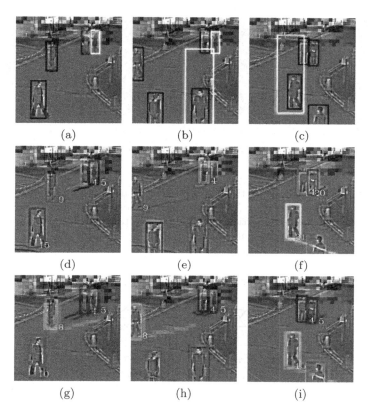

Fig. 3. Examples of tracking at frames 178, 193 and 240 (crops) in PETS09-S2L1 (not) using weak detections. (a), (b), (c) Strong (green) and weak (red) detections. (d), (e), (f) Without using weak detections target 5 is lost and a new trajectory is later initialized with identity 20. (g), (h), (i) Using weak detections target 5 is correctly tracked. (Color figure online)

Figure 4 shows an example of how newborn particles are created. The target on the right is initialized because of the presence of an un-associated strong detection. The target with identity number 2 is localized with a weak detection. The weak detection in this case is a false positive that is discarded because it is not associated with any predicted states.

5 Perspective-Dependent Update, Resampling and State Estimation

Let the set of particles that share the same identity be $\mathcal{X}_{k,\lambda}$ whose elements are $\mathbf{x}_{k,\lambda}^i \in \mathcal{X}_{k,\lambda}$. After new detections are generated, the weights of the particles, π_k^i, are recalculated for allowing the particles to update the estimation [7,9,19].

(a)   (b)

Fig. 4. Example of newborn particles generated at frame 43 (crop) in PETS09-S2L1. (a) Color-coded target identities; (b) existing particles (green dots) and newborn particles (red dots). The newborn particles initialize a new trajectory from an un-associated strong detection. (Color figure online)

The weights at k are *updated* as

$$\pi_k^i = \left[p_M + \sum_{\forall \mathbf{z}_k \in Z_k} \frac{(1 - p_M) g_k(\mathbf{z}_k | \mathbf{x}_{k,\lambda}^i)}{\kappa_k(\mathbf{z}_k) + C_k(\mathbf{z}_k)} \right] \pi_{k|k-1}^i, \tag{17}$$

where p_M is the probability of miss-detection, $\kappa_k(\cdot)$ is the clutter intensity associated to a detection $\mathbf{z}_k$ [7,19], $C_k(\mathbf{z}_k)$ is defined as

$$C_k(\mathbf{z}_k) = \sum_{i=1}^{L_{k-1}+J_k} (1 - p_M) g_k(\mathbf{z}_k | \mathbf{x}_{k,\lambda}^i) \pi_{k|k-1}^i, \tag{18}$$

and $g_k(\mathbf{z}_k | \mathbf{x}_{k,\lambda}^i)$ is the likelihood function defined as

$$g_k(\mathbf{z}_k | \mathbf{x}_{k,\lambda}^i) = \mathcal{N}(C\mathbf{z}_k; C\mathbf{x}_{k,\lambda}^i, C\Sigma_k), \tag{19}$$

where C is defined in Eq. 13. The likelihood function, $g_k(\cdot)$ computes the location and bounding box similarities. Unlike [7,10] where $\Sigma = \Sigma_k$ is fixed, we define Σ_k in Eq. 14 as a time-variant matrix that regulates the location and bounding box similarity between particles and detections (i.e. the particles of an object far from the camera will be less spread than those of a closer object due to the perspective). Figure 5 shows examples of the use of the proposed perspective-dependent approach.

After the update step, *resampling* helps avoiding the degeneracy problem [20]. The standard multinomial resampling [8,20] splits particles proportionally to their weights, frame-by-frame independently. Because newborn particles have in general a lower weight than existing particles, new targets may not be initialized due to repetitive deletion of their particles during resampling. To allow newborn particles to grow over time and reach a comparable weight to that of existing particles, newborn particles are resampled independently from existing

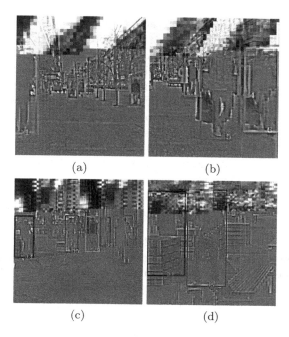

(a)   (b)

(c)   (d)

Fig. 5. Examples of tracking under perspective changes at frames 32 and 102 (crops) in ETH-Bahnhof, and at frames 178 and 375 (crops) in ADL-Rundle-8. Targets 5 and 6 (see (a), (b)) and targets 33 and 35 (see (c), (d)) are correctly tracked despite considerable perspective changes.

particles using a Multi-stage Multinomial Resampling step [7]. Finally, each state $\mathbf{x}_{k,\lambda} \in X_k$ is estimated as the average of all resampled particles sharing the same identity:

$$\mathbf{x}_{k,\lambda} = \frac{1}{|\mathcal{X}_{k,\lambda}|} \sum_{\forall \mathbf{x}_{k,\lambda}^i \in \mathcal{X}_{k,\lambda}} \mathbf{x}_{k,\lambda}^i. \tag{20}$$

6   Results

6.1   Experimental Setup

We validate the proposed tracker[1], the Early Association Probability Hypothesis Density Particle Filter (EA-PHD-PF), and compare it against state-of-the-art online tracking methods on the MOT15 and MOT16 benchmark datasets (motchallenge.net) [21, 22]. We use the *public detections* provided by the MOT benchmark and our *private detections* produced by combining detections from state-of-the-art person detectors. We refer to the tracker using the public detections from MOT benchmark as EA-PHD-PF(Pub) and to the tracker using the private detections as EA-PHD-PF(Priv).

---

[1] Results are available at: http://www.eecs.qmul.ac.uk/~andrea/eamtt.html.

In the specific implementation presented here, the combined detection has position and bounding box size equal to the weighted average of the position and bounding box size of the detections that contributed to the combination. We use detections generated by Discriminatively Trained Deformable Part Models (DTDPM) [12], Scale Dependent Pooling (SDP) [23], Aggregate Channel Features (ACF) [24] trained on INRIA (ACF-I) and Caltech (ACF-C) datasets. We reward detections generated by the combination of a larger number of detectors (possible true positives) and penalize isolated detections (possible false positives). We normalize the confidence score of each detector using the 99th percentile of the detection scores generated by each detector over the training set (and truncating to 1). Then we combine all detections via voting when their overlap area divided by their union area exceeds $\tau_f = 1/3$. Given the normalized detection confidence of each detection, s_j, the confidence score of the combined detection, $s_k \in [0,1]$, is $s_k = \frac{U}{D^2} \sum_{j=1}^{U} s_j$, where U is the number of *contributing* detectors and D is the total number of detectors.

We allow to perform association between detections and predicted states only if their overlap area divided by their union area exceeds $\tau_a = 1/3$. The parameter that controls when a trajectory will not seek for more detections is $V = \lceil f \rceil / 1s$, where f is the frame-rate of the video sequence. The parameter that controls the maximum possible number of frames to consider in the prediction model is $M_{max} = \lceil f/2 \rceil / 1s$.

We train the parameters of our method on the MOT15 and MOT16 training datasets and then use these parameters in MOT15 and MOT16 testing sequences, respectively. For the set of public detections $\tau_s = 0.39$ in MOT15 and $\tau_s = 0.20$ in MOT16. For the set of private detections $\tau_s = 0.35$ in both datasets[2]. The number of particles per target, ρ, is 500. The standard deviation values used for the prediction, update and newborn particle generation are modelled as a function of the bounding box size as

$$\sigma^x = w_{x_k} std \left(\left\{ \frac{1}{w_k^g} \frac{d^2 x_k^g}{dk^2} \right\}_{\forall g} \right), \quad \sigma^y = h_{x_k} std \left(\left\{ \frac{1}{h_k^g} \frac{d^2 y_k^g}{dk^2} \right\}_{\forall g} \right),$$

$$\sigma^{\dot{x}} = w_{x_k} std \left(\left\{ \frac{1}{w_k^g} \frac{d^3 x_k^g}{dk^3} \right\}_{\forall g} \right), \quad \sigma^{\dot{y}} = h_{y_k} std \left(\left\{ \frac{1}{h_k^g} \frac{d^3 y_k^g}{dk^3} \right\}_{\forall g} \right),$$

$$\sigma^w = w_{x_k} std \left(\left\{ \frac{1}{w_k^g} \frac{d^2 w_k^g}{dk^2} \right\}_{\forall g} \right), \quad \sigma^h = h_{x_k} std \left(\left\{ \frac{1}{h_k^g} \frac{d^2 h_k^g}{dk^2} \right\}_{\forall g} \right),$$

where $g \in [1, G]$ indicates a state element of a ground-truth trajectory, $std(\cdot)$ is the standard deviation operation, $\frac{d^2(\cdot)}{dk^2}$ is the second derivative that quantifies the noise in the variation of x, y, w and h over time, and $\frac{d^3(\cdot)}{dk^3}$ is the third derivative that quantifies the noise in the variation of $\dot{x}$ and $\dot{y}$ over time. We use the bounding box size at time k, w_{x_k} and h_{x_k}, in order to adapt the noise to the

---

[2] Larger values of τ_s reduce the number of false positives and lead to a more conservative initialization of the trajectories.

scale of the bounding box. Note that estimated states are used in the prediction step (Sect. 3), whereas detections are used in the generation of newborn particles (Sect. 4) and update step (Sect. 5).

The evaluation measures are Multiple Object Tracking Accuracy (MOTA), Multiple Object Tracking Precision (MOTP) [25], False Alarm per Frame (FAF), Mostly Tracked targets (MT), Mostly Lost targets (ML) [26], Fragmented trajectories (Frag), False Positives (FP), False Negatives (FN), Identity Switches (IDS) and tracker speed in Hz. For a detailed description of each metric, please refer to the MOT website and [21].

6.2 Discussion

Table 1 compares the tracking results of our proposed method using both public and private detections with other online trackers submitted to the MOT15 and MOT16 benchmark[3]. The upper part of the table (MOT15) shows that EA-PHD-PF(Priv) outperforms AMPL, LKDAT_CNN, MDP_SubCNN and *justry*, in terms of MOTA. The number of FN and the ML percentage are overall lower than the other trackers. This is due to the ability of EA-PHD-PF(Priv) to robustly perform state estimation exploiting weak detections without relying on the prediction only when (strong) detections are missing. The higher number of IDS compared to the other methods is due to the fact that we rely only on the position and size of the bounding box inferred from the detections and *we are not using any appearance models* to discriminate nearby targets. Moreover, we do not model spawning targets. Therefore, identity switches are more likely in crowded scenes, as shown in Fig. 6. The bottom part of Table 1 (MOT16) shows that EA-PHD-PF(Priv) outperforms AMPL, olCF and OVBT in terms of MOTA, FN and FP. However, the number of IDS is higher than AMPL and

Table 1. Online tracking results on the MOT15 (TOP-7 trackers) and on the MOT16 (all available trackers) test datasets. Dark gray indicates the best and light gray indicates the second best scores.

Dataset	Tracker	Det	MOTA	MOTP	FAF	MT (%)	ML (%)	FP	FN	IDS	Frag	Hz
	AMPL [21]	Priv	51.9	75.0	1.2	26.4	24.8	6,963	22,225	372	1,130	2.8
	LKDAT_CNN [21]	Priv	49.3	74.5	1.0	20.8	28.4	6,009	24,550	563	1,155	1.2
	MDP_SubCNN [27]	Priv	47.5	74.2	1.5	30.0	18.6	8,631	22,969	628	1,370	2.1
	justry [21]	Priv	45.2	74.7	2.4	40.6	16.0	14,117	18,769	764	1,413	2.6
MOT15	*kalman_mdp* [21]	Pub	37.2	74.5	2.8	38.7	13.3	16,196	20,328	2,065	1,856	21.8
	mLK [21]	Pub	35.1	71.5	1.0	12.3	38.3	5,678	33,815	383	1,175	1.0
	HybridDAT [21]	Pub	35.0	72.6	1.5	11.4	42.2	8,455	31,140	358	1,267	4.6
	EA-PHD-PF	Pub	22.3	70.8	1.4	5.4	52.7	7,924	38,982	833	1,485	12.2
	EA-PHD-PF	Priv	53.0	75.3	1.3	35.9	19.6	7,538	20,590	776	1,269	11.5
	AMPL [22]	Priv	50.9	77.0	0.5	16.7	40.8	3,229	86,123	196	639	1.5
	olCF [22]	Pub	43.2	74.3	1.1	11.3	48.5	6,651	96,515	381	1,404	0.4
MOT16	OVBT [22]	Pub	38.4	75.4	1.9	7.5	47.3	11,517	99,463	1,321	2,140	0.3
	GMPHD_HDA [22]	Pub	30.5	75.4	0.9	4.6	59.7	5,169	120,970	539	731	13.6
	EA-PHD-PF	Pub	38.8	75.1	1.4	7.9	49.1	8,114	102,452	965	1,657	11.8
	EA-PHD-PF	Priv	52.5	78.8	0.7	19.0	34.9	4,407	81,223	910	1,321	12.2

[3] Last accessed on 10th August 2016.

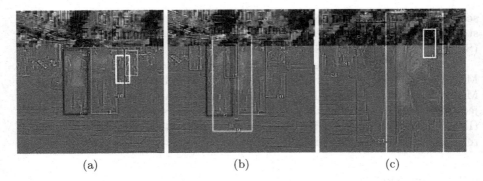

(a)   (b)   (c)

Fig. 6. Examples of tracking under multiple occlusions at frames 22, 97 and 261 (crops) in Venice-1/MOT16-01 using EA-PHD-PF(Priv). (a) Target 6 is correctly tracked while it occludes another target. (b) The occluded target becomes visible and trajectory 6 drifts towards it. Target 6 is reinitialized as target 19 at frame 22. (c) Intermittent detections cause target 6 to be reinitialized as target 29 at frame 97.

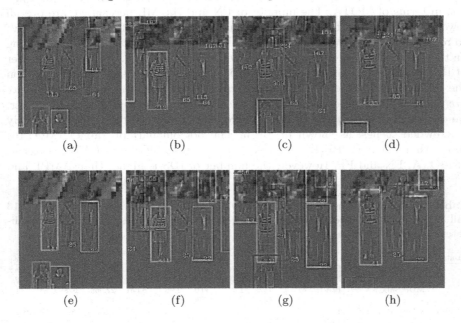

(a)   (b)   (c)   (d)
(e)   (f)   (g)   (h)

Fig. 7. Examples of tracking at frames 240, 461, 645 and 717 (crops) in MOT16-03 using public (first row) and private (second row) detections. (a)–(d) The target identified as 115 is reinitialized multiple times due to occlusions and lack of detections. (e)–(h) The (same) target, identified as 41, is correctly tracked.

olCF, because the features they use are better able to discriminate targets. The results using public detections rank our tracker EA-PHD-PF(Pub) at half-rank overall as it generates a high amount of FN.

Figure 7 compares sample tracking results using public (first row) and private (second row) detections. We can observe along the first row how the target firstly initialized as 115 is then reinitialized, lost and reinitialized again due to the high number of FN in the public dataset. However, the (same) target firstly initialized as 41 in the second row is correctly tracked along the whole sequence. We can observe the presence of false-positive trajectories (i.e. green, purple and red targets in Fig. 7b). These false-positive trajectories are difficult to remove because they are caused by persistent false-positive detections appearing for a few consecutive frames and the confidence scores of those detections are as high as those of true positive detections. With EA-PHD-PF(Priv) these detections are filtered out without adding any false-negative trajectories.

7 Conclusion

We presented an online multi-target tracker that exploits strong and weak detections in a Probability Hypothesis Density Particle Filter framework. Strong detections are used for trajectory initialization and tracking. Weak detections are used for tracking existing targets only to reduce the number of false negatives without increasing the false positives. Moreover, we presented a method to perform early association between trajectories and detections, which eliminates the need for a clustering step for labeling. Finally, we exploited perspective information in prediction, update and newborn particle generation. Results show that our method outperforms alternative online trackers on the Multiple Object Tracking 2016 and 2015 benchmark datasets in terms tracking accuracy, false negatives and speed. The tracker works at an average speed of 12 fps. Future work will involve using appearance features, such as color histograms, to reduce trajectory fragmentation.

Acknowledgements. This work was supported in part by the ARTEMIS JU and the UK Technology Strategy Board (Innovate UK) through the COPCAMS Project, under Grant 332913.

References

1. Solera, F., Calderara, S., Cucchiara, R.: Learning to divide and conquer for online multi-target tracking. In: Proceedings of International Conference on Computer Vision, Santiago, CL, December 2015
2. Wang, B., Wang, G., Chan, K., Wang, L.: Tracklet association with online target-specific metric learning. In: Proceedings of Computer Vision and Pattern Recognition, Columbus, OH, USA, June 2014
3. Poiesi, F., Cavallaro, A.: Tracking multiple high-density homogeneous targets. IEEE Trans. on Circ. Syst. Video Technol. **25**(4), 623–637 (2015)
4. Possegger, H., Mauthner, T., Roth, P., Bischof, H.: Occlusion geodesics for online multi-object tracking. In: Proceedings of Computer Vision and Pattern Recognition, Columbus, OH, USA, June 2014

5. Shu, G., Dehghan, A., Oreifej, O., Hand, E., Shah, M.: Part-based multiple-person tracking with partial occlusion handling. In: Proceedings of Computer Vision and Pattern Recognition, Rhode Island, USA, June 2012
6. Mahler, R.: A theoretical foundation for the Stein-Winter Probability Hypothesis Density (PHD) multitarget tracking approach. In: Proceedings of MSS National Symposium on Sensor and Data Fusion, San Diego, CA, USA, June 2002
7. Maggio, E., Taj, M., Cavallaro, A.: Efficient multitarget visual tracking using random finite sets. IEEE Trans. Circ. Syst. Video Technol. **18**(8), 1016–1027 (2008)
8. Vo, B.N., Singh, S., Doucet, A.: Sequential Monte Carlo implementation of the PHD filter for multi-target tracking. In: Proceedings of Information Fusion, vol. 2, Queensland, AU, July 2003
9. Mahler, R.: PHD filters of higher order in target number. IEEE Aerosp. Electron. Syst. Mag. **43**(4), 1523–1543 (2007)
10. Panta, K., Vo, B., Singh, S.: Improved probability hypothesis density (PHD) filter for multitarget tracking. In: 2005 3rd International Conference on Intelligent Sensing and Information Processing, December 2005
11. Dalal, N., Triggs, B.: Histograms of oriented gradients for human detection. In: Proceedings of Computer Vision and Pattern Recognition, San Diego, CA, USA, June 2005
12. Felzenszwalb, P.F., Girshick, R., Ramanan, D.: Object detection with discriminatively trained part based models. IEEE Trans. Pattern Anal. Mach. Intell. **32**(9), 1627–1645 (2010)
13. Smedt, F.D., Goedeme, T.: Open framework for combinated pedestrian detection. In: Proceedings of Computer Vision, Imaging and Computer Graphics Theory and Applications, Berlin, GE, March 2015
14. Lin, L., Bar-Shalom, Y., Kirubarajan, T.: Data association combined with the Probability Hypothesis Density Filter for multitarget tracking. In: Proceedings of SPIE, August 2004
15. Panta, K., Vo, B.N., Singh, S., Doucet, A.: Probability Hypothesis Density filter versus multiple hypothesis tracking. In: Proceedings of SPIE, August 2004
16. Kuhn, H., Yaw, B.: The Hungarian method for the assignment problem. Naval Res. Logistics Q. **2**, 83–97 (1955)
17. Poiesi, F., Mazzon, R., Cavallaro, A.: Multi-target tracking on confidence maps: an application to people tracking. Comput. Vis. Image Underst. **117**(10), 1257–1272 (2013)
18. Maggio, E., Cavallaro, A.: Learning scene context for multiple object tracking. IEEE Trans. Image Process. **18**(8), 1873–1884 (2009)
19. Vo, B.N., Singh, S., Doucet, A.: Sequential Monte Carlo methods for multitarget filtering with random finite sets. IEEE Aerosp. Electron. Syst. Mag. **41**(4), 1224–1245 (2005)
20. Arulampalam, M., Maskell, S., Gordon, N., Clapp, T.: A tutorial on particle filters for online nonlinear/non-Gaussian Bayesian tracking. IEEE Trans. Sig. Process. **50**(2), 174–188 (2002)
21. Leal-Taixé, L., Milan, A., Reid, I., Roth, S., Schindler, K.: MOTChallenge 2015: towards a benchmark for multi-target tracking, April 2015. arXiv:1504.01942 [cs]
22. Milan, A., Leal-Taixé, L., Reid, I., Roth, S., Schindler, K.: MOT16: a benchmark for multi-object tracking, March 2016. arXiv:1603.00831 [cs]
23. Yang, F., Choi, W., Lin, Y.: Exploit all the layers: fast and accurate CNN object detector with scale dependent pooling and cascaded rejection classifiers. In: Proceedings of Computer Vision and Pattern Recognition, Las Vegas, NV, USA, June 2016

24. Dollar, P., Appel, R., Belongie, S., Perona, P.: Fast feature pyramids for object detection. IEEE Trans. Pattern Anal. Mach. Intell. **36**(8), 1532–1545 (2014)
25. Kasturi, R., Goldgof, D., Soundararajan, P., Manohar, V., Garofolo, J., Bowers, R., Boonstra, M., Korzhova, V., Zhang, J.: Framework for performance evaluation of face, text, and vehicle detection and tracking in video: data, metrics, and protocol. IEEE Trans. Pattern Anal. Mach. Intell. **31**(2), 319–336 (2009)
26. Li, Y., Huang, C., Nevatia, R.: Learning to associate: HybridBoosted multi-target tracker for crowded scene. In: Proceedings of Computer Vision and Pattern Recognition, Miami, FL, USA, June 2009
27. Xiang, Y., Alahi, A., Savarese, S.: Learning to track: online multi-object tracking by decision making. In: Proceedings of International Conference on Computer Vision, Santiago, CL, December 2015

Multi-person Tracking by Multicut and Deep Matching

Siyu Tang$^{(\boxtimes)}$, Bjoern Andres, Mykhaylo Andriluka, and Bernt Schiele

Max Planck Institute for Informatics,
Saarbrücken Informatics Campus, Saarbrücken, Germany
`tang@mpi-inf.mpg.de`

Abstract. In Tang et al. (2015), we proposed a graph-based formulation that links and clusters person hypotheses over time by solving a minimum cost subgraph multicut problem. In this paper, we modify and extend Tang et al. (2015) in three ways: *(1)* We introduce a novel local pairwise feature based on local appearance matching that is robust to partial occlusion and camera motion. *(2)* We perform extensive experiments to compare different pairwise potentials and to analyze the robustness of the tracking formulation. *(3)* We consider a plain multicut problem and remove outlying clusters from its solution. This allows us to employ an efficient primal feasible optimization algorithm that is not applicable to the subgraph multicut problem of Tang et al. (2015). Unlike the branch-and-cut algorithm used there, this efficient algorithm used here is applicable to long videos and many detections. Together with the novel pairwise feature, it eliminates the need for the intermediate tracklet representation of Tang et al. (2015). We demonstrate the effectiveness of our overall approach on the MOT16 benchmark (Milan et al. 2016), achieving state-of-art performance.

1 Introduction

Multi person tracking is a problem studied intensively in computer vision. While continuous progress has been made, false positive detections, long-term occlusions and camera motion remain challenging, especially for people tracking in crowded scenes. Tracking-by-detection is commonly used for multi person tracking where a state-of-the-art person detector is employed to generate detection hypotheses for a video sequence. In this case tracking essentially reduces to an association task between detection hypotheses across video frames. This detection association task is often formulated as an optimization problem with respect to a graph: every detection is represented by a node; edges connect detections across time frames. The most commonly employed algorithms aim to find disjoint paths in such a graph [1–4]. The feasible solutions of such problems are sets of disjoint paths which do not branch or merge. While being intuitive, such formulations cannot handle the multiple plausible detections per person, which are generated from typical person detectors. Therefore, pre- and/or post-processing such as non maximum suppression (NMS) on the detections and/or the final tracks is performed, which often requires careful fine-tuning of parameters.

© Springer International Publishing Switzerland 2016
G. Hua and H. Jégou (Eds.): ECCV 2016 Workshops, Part II, LNCS 9914, pp. 100–111, 2016.
DOI: 10.1007/978-3-319-48881-3_8

The minimum cost subgraph multicut problem proposed in [5] is an abstraction of the tracking problem that differs conceptually from disjoint path methods. It has two main advantages: *(1)* Instead of finding a path for each person in the graph, it links and clusters multiple plausible person hypotheses (detections) jointly over time and space. The feasible solutions of this formulation are components of the graph instead of paths. All detections that correspond to the same person are clustered jointly within and across frames. No NMS is required, neither on the level of detections nor on the level of tracks. *(2)* For the multicut formulation, the costs assigned to edges can be positive, to encourage the incident nodes to be in the same track, or negative, to encourage the incident nodes to be in distinct tracks. Thus, the number and size of tracks does not need to be specified, constrained or penalized and is instead defined by the solution. This is fundamentally different also from distance-based clustering approaches, e.g. [6] where the cost of joining two detections is non-negative and thus, a non-uniform prior on the number or size of tracks is required to avoid a trivial solution. Defining or estimating this prior is a well-known difficulty. We illustrate these advantages in the example depicted in Fig. 1: We build a graph based on the detections on three consecutive frames, where detection hypotheses within and between frames are all connected. The costs assigned to the edges encourage the incident node to be in the same or distinct clusters. For simplicity, we only visualize the graph built on the detections of two persons instead of all. By solving the minimum cost subgraph multicut problem, a multicut of the edges is found (depicted as dotted lines). It partitions the graph into distinct components (depicted in yellow and magenta, resp.), each representing one person's track. Note that multiple plausible detections of the same person are clustered jointly, within and across frames.

The effectiveness of the multicut formulation for the multi person tracking task is driven by different factors: computing reliable affinity measures for pairs of detections; handling noisy input detections and utilizing efficient optimization methods. In this work, we extend [5] on those fronts. First, for a pair of detections, we propose a reliable affinity measure that is based an effective image matching method DeepMatching [7]. As this method matches appearance of local image regions, it is robust to camera motion and partial occlusion. In contrast, the pairwise feature proposed in [5] relies heavily on the spatio-temporal relations of tracklets (a short-term tracklet is used to estimate the speed of a person) which works well only for a static camera and when people walk with constant speed. By introducing the DeepMatching pairwise feature, we make the multicut formulation applicable to more general moving-camera videos with arbitrary motion of persons. Secondly, we eliminate the unary variables which are introduced in [5] to integrate the detection confidence into the multicut formulation. By doing so, we simplify the optimization problem and make it amenable to the fast Kernighan-Lin-type algorithm of [8]. The efficiency of this algorithm eliminates the need for an intermediate tracklet representation, which greatly simplifies the tracking pipeline. Thirdly, we integrate the detection confidence into the pairwise terms such that detections with low confidence simply have a low probability to be clustered with any other detection, most likely ending up as singletons that we remove in a post-processing step. With the above mentioned extensions, we are able to achieve competitive performance on the challenging MOT16 benchmark.

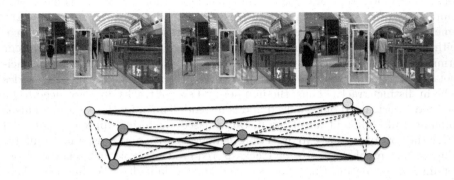

Fig. 1. An example for tracking by multicut. A graph (bottom) is built based on the detections in three frames (top). The connected components that are obtained by solving the multicut problem indicate the number of tracks (there are two tracks, depicted in yellow and magenta respectively) as well as the membership of every detection. (Color figure online)

2   Related Work

Recent work on multi-person tracking primarily focuses on tracking-by-detection. Tracking operates either by directly linking people detections over time [9,10], or by first grouping detections into tracklets and then combining those into tracks [11]. A number of approaches rely on data association methods such as the Hungarian algorithm [12,13], network flow optimization [4,11,14,15], and multiple hypotheses tracking [9], and combine them with novel ways to learn the appearance of tracked targets. [9] proposed to estimate a target-specific appearance model online and used a generic CNN representation to represent person appearance. In [12] it is proposed to formulate tracking as a Markov decision process with a policy estimated on the labeled training data. [16] proposes novel appearance representations that rely on the temporal evolution in appearance of the tracked target. In this paper we propose a pairwise feature that similarly to [10] is based on local image patch matching. Our model is inspired by [7] and it operates on pairs of hypotheses which allows to directly utilize its output as costs of edges on the hypothesis graph. Our pairwise potential is particularly suitable to our tracking formulation that finds tracks by optimizing a global objective function. This is in contrast to target-specific appearance methods that are trained online and require iterative assembly of tracks over time, which precludes globally solving for all trajectories in an image sequence.

Perhaps closest to our work are methods that aim to recover people tracks by optimizing a global objective function [5,14,17]. [17] proposes a continuous formulation that analytically models effects such as mutual occlusions, dynamics and trajectory continuity, but utilizes a simple color appearance model. [14] finds tracks by solving instances of a generalized minimum clique problem, but due to model complexity resorts to a greedy iterative optimization scheme that finds one track at a time whereas we jointly recover solutions for all tracks. We build on the multi-cut formulation proposed in [5] and generalize it to large scale sequences based on the extensions discussed below.

3   Multi-person Tracking as a Multicut Problem

In Sect. 3.1, we recall the minimum cost multicut problem that we employ as a mathematical abstraction for multi person tracking. We emphasize differences compared to the minimum cost subgraph multicut problem proposed in [5]. In Sect. 3.2, we define the novel DeepMatching feature and its incorporation into the objective function. In Sect. 3.3, we present implementation details.

3.1   Minimum Cost Multicut Problem

In this work, multi person tracking is cast as a minimum cost multicut problem [18] w.r.t. a graph $G = (V, E)$ whose node V are a finite set of *detections*, i.e., bounding boxes that possibly identify people in a video sequence. Edges within and across frames connect detections that possibly identify the same person. For every edge $vw \in E$, a cost or reward $c_{vw} \in \mathbb{R}$ is to be payed if and only if the detections v and w are assigned to distinct tracks. Multi person tracking is then cast as a binary linear program

$$\min_{x \in \{0,1\}^E} \quad \sum_{e \in E} c_e x_e \tag{1}$$

$$\text{subject to} \quad \forall C \in \text{cycles}(G) \; \forall e \in C : \; x_e \leq \sum_{e' \in C \setminus \{e\}} x_{e'}. \tag{2}$$

Note that the costs c_e can be both positive or negative. For detections $v, w \in V$ connected by an edge $e = \{v, w\}$, the assignment $x_e = 0$ indicates that v and w belong to the same track. Thus, the constraints (2) can be understood as follows: If, for any neighboring nodes v and w, there exists a path in G from v to w along which all edges are labeled 0 (indicating that v and w belong to the same track), then the edge vw cannot be labeled 1 (which would indicate the opposite). In fact, (2) are generalized transitivity constraints which guarantee that a feasible solution x well-defines a decomposition of the graph G into tracks.

We construct the graph G such that edges connect detections not only between neighboring frames but also across longer distances in time. Such edges $vw \in E$ allow to assign the detections v and w to the same track even if there would otherwise not exist a vw-path of detections, one in each frame. This is essential for tracking people correctly in the presence of occlusion and missing detections.

Differences compared to [5]. The minimum cost multicut problem (1) and (2), we consider here differs from the minimum cost subgraph multicut problem of [5]. In order to handle false positive detections, [5] introduces additional binary variables at the nodes, switching detections on or off. A cost of switching a detection on is defined w.r.t. a confidence score of that detection. Here, we do not consider binary variables at nodes and incorporate a detection confidence into the costs of edges. In order to remove false positive detections, we remove small clusters from the solution in a post-processing step. A major advantage of this modification is that our minimum cost multicut problem (1) and (2), unlike the minimum cost subgraph multicut problem of [5], is amenable to efficient approximate optimization by means of the KLj algorithm [8], without any modification.

This algorithm, unlike the branch-and-cut algorithm of [5], can be applied in practice directly to the graph of detections defined above, thus eliminating the need for the smaller intermediate representation of [5] by tracklets.

Optimization. Here, we solve instances of the minimum cost multicut problem approximatively with the KLj algorithm [8]. This algorithm iteratively updates bipartitions of a subgraph. The worst-case time complexity of any such update is $O(|V||E|)$. The number of updates is not known to be polynomially bounded but is small in practice (less than 30 in our experiments). Moreover, the bound $O(|V||E|)$ is almost never attained in practice, as shown by the more detailed analysis in [8].

3.2   Deep Matching Based Pairwise Costs

In order to specify the costs of the optimization problem introduced above for tracking, we need to define, for any pair of detection bounding boxes, a cost or reward to be payed if these bounding boxes are assigned to the same person. For that, we wish to quantify how likely it is that a pair of bounding boxes identify the same person. In [5], this is done w.r.t. an estimation of velocity that requires an intermediate tracklet representation and is not robust to camera motion. Here, we define these costs exclusively w.r.t. image content. More specifically, we build on the significant improvements in image matching made by DeepMatching [7].

DeepMatching applies a multi-layer deep convolutional architecture to yield possibly non-rigid matchings between a pair of images. Figure 2 shows results of DeepMatching for two pairs of images from the MOT16 sequences[1]. The first pair of images is taken by a moving camera; the second pair of images is taken by a static camera. Between both pairs of images, matched points (blue arrows) relate a person visible in one image to the same person in the second image.

Next, we describe our features defined w.r.t. a matching of points between a pair of detection bounding boxes. Each detection bounding box $v \in V$ has the

---

[1] We use the visualization code provided by the authors of [7].

Fig. 2. Visualization of the DeepMatching results on the MOT16 sequences. (Color figure online)

following properties: its spatio-temporal location (t_v, x_v, y_v), scale h_v, detection confidence ξ_v and, finally, a set of keypoints M_v inside v. Given two detection bounding boxes v and w connected by the edge $\{v, w\} = e \in E$, we define $MU = |M_v \cup M_w|$ and $MI = |M_v \cap M_w|$ and the five features

$$f_1^{(e)} := MI/MU \tag{3}$$

$$f_2^{(e)} := \min\{\xi_v, \xi_w\} \tag{4}$$

$$f_3^{(e)} := f_1^{(e)} f_2^{(e)} \tag{5}$$

$$f_4^{(e)} := (f_1^{(e)})^2 \tag{6}$$

$$f_5^{(e)} := (f_2^{(e)})^2 \tag{7}$$

Given, for any edge $e = \{v, w\} \in E$ between two detection bounding boxes v and w, the feature vector $f^{(e)}$ for this pair, we learn a probability $p_e \in (0, 1)$ of these detection bounding boxes to identify the same person. More specifically, we assume that p_e depends on the features $f^{(e)}$ by a logistic form

$$p_e := \frac{1}{1 + \exp(-\langle \theta, f^{(e)} \rangle)} \tag{8}$$

with parameters θ. We estimate these parameters from training data by means of logistic regression. Finally, we define the cost c_e in the objective function (1) as

$$c_e := \log \frac{p_e}{1 - p_e} = \langle \theta, f^{(e)} \rangle. \tag{9}$$

Two remarks are in order: Firstly, the feature $f_2^{(e)}$ incorporates the detection confidences of v and w that defined unary costs in [5] into the feature $f^{(e)}$ of the pair $\{v, w\}$ here. Consequently, detections with low confidence will be assigned with low probability to any other detection. Secondly, the features $f_3^{(e)}, f_4^{(e)}, f_5^{(e)}$ are to learn a non-linear map from features $f_1^{(e)}, f_2^{(e)}$ to edge probabilities by means of linear logistic regression.

3.3   Implementation Details

Clusters to tracks. The multicut formulation clusters detections jointly over space and time for each target. It is straight-forward to generate tracks from such clusters: In each frame, we obtain a representative location (x, y) and scale h by averaging all detections that belong to the same person (cluster). A smooth track of the person is thus obtained by connecting these averages across all frames. Thanks to the pairwise potential incorporating a detection confidence, low confidence detections typically end up as singletons or in small clusters which are deleted from the final solution. Specifically, we eliminate all clusters of size less than 5 in all experiments.

Maximum temporal connection. Introducing edges that connect detections across longer distance in time is essential to track people in the presence of occlusion. However, with the increase of the distance in time, the pairwise feature becomes less reliable. Thus, when we construct the graph, it is necessary to set a maximum distance in time. In all the experiments, we introduce edges for the detections that are at most 10 frames apart. This parameter is based on the experimental analysis on the training sequences and is explained in more detail in Sect. 4.1.

4   Experiments and Results

We analyze our approach experimentally and compare to prior work on the MOT16 Benchmark [19]. The benchmark includes training and test sets composed of 7 sequences each. We learn the model parameters for the test sequences based on the corresponding training sequences. We first conduct an experimental analysis that validates the effectiveness of the DeepMatching based affinity measure in Sect. 4.1. In Sect. 4.2 we demonstrate that the multicut formulation is robust to detection noise. In Sect. 4.3 we compare our method with the best published results on the MOT16 Benchmark.

4.1   Comparison of Pairwise Potentials

Setup. In this section we compare the DeepMatching (DM) based pairwise potential with a conventional spatio-temporal relation (ST) based pairwise potential.

More concretely, given two detections v and w, each has the following properties: spatio-temporal location (t, x, y), scale h, detection confidence ξ. Based on these properties the following auxiliary variables are introduced to capture geometric relations between the bounding boxes: $\Delta x = \frac{|x_v - x_w|}{h}$, $\Delta y = \frac{|y_v - y_w|}{h}$, $\Delta h = \frac{|h_v - h_w|}{h}$, $y = \frac{|y_v - y_w|}{h}$, $IOU = \frac{|B_v \cap B_w|}{|B_v \cup B_w|}$, $t = t_v - t_w$, where $\bar{h} = \frac{(h_v + h_w)}{2}$, IOU is the intersection over union of the two detection bounding box areas and ξ_{min} is the minimum detection score between ξ_v and ξ_w. The pairwise feature $f^{(e)}$ for the spatio-temporal relations (ST) is then defined as $(\Delta t, \Delta x, \Delta y, \Delta h, IOU, \xi_{min})$. Intuitively, the ST features are able to provide useful information within a short temporal window, because they only model the geometric relations between bounding boxes. DM is built upon matching of local image features that is reliable for camera motion and partial occlusion in longer temporal window.

We collect test examples from the MOT16-09 and MOT16-10 sequences which are recorded with a static camera and a moving camera respectively. The positive (negative) pairs of test examples are the detections that are matched to the same (different) persons' ground truth track over time. The negative pairs also include the false positive detections on the background.

Metric. The metric is the verification accuracy, the accuracy or rate of correctly classified pairs. For a pair of images belong to the same (different) person, if the estimated joint probability is larger (smaller) than 0.5, the estimation is considered as correct. Otherwise, it is a false prediction.

Results. We conduct a comparison between the accuracy of the DM feature and the accuracy of the ST feature as a function of distance in time. It can be seen from Table 1 that the ST feature achieves comparable accuracy only up to 2 frames distance. Its performance deteriorates rapidly for connections at longer time. In contrast, the DM feature is effective and maintains superior accuracy over time. For example on the MOT16-10 sequence which contains rapid camera motion, the DM feature improves over the ST feature by a large margin after 10 frames and it provides stable affinity measure even at 20 frames distance (accuracy $= 0.925$). On the MOT16-09 sequence, the DM feature again shows superior accuracy than the ST feature starting from $\triangle t = 2$. However, the accuracy of the DM feature on the MOT16-09 is worse than the one on MOT16-10, suggesting the quite different statistic among the sequences from the MOT16 benchmark. As discussed in Sect. 3.3, it is necessary to set a maximum distance in time to exclude unreliable pairwise costs. Aiming at a unique setting for all sequences, we introduce edges for the detections that are maximumly 10 frames apart in the rest experiments of this paper.

Table 1. Comparison of tracking results based on the DM and the ST feature. The metic is the accuracy or rate of correctly classified pairs on the MOT16-09 and the MOT16-10 sequences.

MOT16-09: static camera						
Feature	$\triangle t = 1$	$\triangle t = 2$	$\triangle t = 5$	$\triangle t = 10$	$\triangle t = 15$	$\triangle t = 20$
ST	0.972	0.961	0.926	0.856	0.807	0.781
DM	0.970 (-0.2%)	0.963 $(+0.2\%)$	0.946 $(+2\%)$	0.906 $(+5\%)$	0.867 $(+6\%)$	0.820 $(+3.9\%)$
MOT16-10: moving camera						
Feature	$\triangle t = 1$	$\triangle t = 2$	$\triangle t = 5$	$\triangle t = 10$	$\triangle t = 15$	$\triangle t = 20$
ST	0.985	0.977	0.942	0.903	0.872	0.828
DM	0.985	0.984 $(+0.7\%)$	0.975 $(+3.3\%)$	0.957 $(+5.4\%)$	0.939 $(+6.7\%)$	0.925 $(+9.7\%)$

Table 2. Tracking performance on different sets of input detections. $Score_{min}$ indicates the minimum detection score threshold. $|V|$ and $|E|$ are the number of nodes (detections) and edges respectively.

MOT16-09

$Score_{min}$	$-\infty$	-0.3	-0.2	-0.1	0	0.1	1
$|V|$	5377	4636	4320	3985	3658	3405	1713
$|E|$	565979	422725	367998	314320	265174	229845	61440
Run time (s)	30.48	19.28	13.46	11.88	8.39	6.76	1.71
MOTA	37.9	43.1	43.1	44.9	45.8	44.1	34.1

MOT16-10

$Score_{min}$	$-\infty$	-0.3	-0.2	-0.1	0	0.1	1
$|V|$	8769	6959	6299	5710	5221	4823	2349
$|E|$	1190074	755678	621024	511790	427847	365949	88673
Run time (s)	88.34	39.28	30.08	21.99	16.13	13.66	1.94
MOTA	26.8	32.4	34.4	34.5	34.5	33.9	23.3

Table 3. Tracking performance on MOT16.

Method	MOTA	MOTP	FAF	MT	ML	FP	FN	ID Sw	Frag	Hz	Detector
NOMT [10]	46.4	76.6	1.6	18.3%	41.4%	9753	87565	359	504	2.6	Public
MHT [9]	42.8	76.4	1.2	14.6%	49.0%	7278	96607	462	625	0.8	Public
CEM [17]	33.2	75.8	1.2	7.8%	54.4%	6837	114322	642	731	0.3	Public
TBD [21]	33.7	76.5	1.0	7.2%	54.2%	5804	112587	2418	2252	1.3	Public
Ours	46.3	75.7	1.09	15.5%	39.7%	6449	90713	663	1115	0.8	Public

4.2   Robustness to Input Detections

Handling noisy detection is a well-known difficulty for tracking algorithms. To assess the impact of the input detections on the tracking result, we conduct tracking experiments based on different sets of input detections that are obtained by varying a minimum detection score threshold ($Score_{min}$). For example, in Table 2, $Score_{min} = -\infty$ indicates that all the detections are used as tracking input; whereas $Score_{min} = 1$ means that only the detections whose score are equal or larger than 1 are considered. Given the fact that the input detections are obtained from a DPM detector [20], $Score_{min} = -\infty$ and $Score_{min} = 1$ are the two extreme cases, where the recall is maximized for the former one and high precision is obtained for the latter one.

Metric. We evaluate the tracking performance of the multicut model that operates on different sets of input detections. We use the standard CLEAR MOT metrics. For simplicity, in Table 2 we report the Multiple Object Tracking Accuracy (MOTA) that is a cumulative measure that combines the number of False Positives (FP), the number of False Negatives (FN) and the number of ID Switches (IDs).

Results. On the MOT16-09 sequence, when the minimum detection score threshold $(Score_{min})$ is changed from 0.1 to -0.3, the number of detection is largely increased (from 3405 to 4636), however the MOTA is only decreased by 1 percent (from 44.1 % to 43.1 %). Even for the extreme cases, where the detections are either rather noisy $(Score_{min} = -\infty)$ or sparse $(Score_{min} = 1$), the MOTAs are still in the reasonable range. The same results are found on the MOT16-10 sequence as well. Note that, for all the experiments, we use the same parameters, we delete the clusters whose size is smaller than 5 and no further tracks splitting/merging is performed.

These experiments suggest that the multicut formulation is very robust to the noisy detection input. This nice property is driven by the fact that the multicut formulation allows us to jointly cluster multiple plausible detections that belong to the same target over time and space.

We also report run time in Table 2. The KLj multicut solver provides arguably fast solution for our tracking problem. E.g. for the problem with more than one million edges, the solution is obtained in 88.34 s. Detailed run time analysis of the KLj algorithm are shown in [8].

    (a) MOT16-06   (b) MOT16-12   (c) MOT16-03

    (d) MOT16-08   (e) MOT16-07   (f) MOT16-01

(g) MOT16-09 (frame 290) (h) MOT16-09 (frame 360) (i) MOT16-09 (frame 390)

Fig. 3. Qualitative results for all the sequences from the MOT16 Benchmark. The first and second rows are the results from the MOT16-01, MOT16-03, MOT16-06, MOT16-07, MOT16-08 and MOT16-12 sequence. The third row is the result from the MOT16-14 sequence when the camera mounted on a bus is turning fast at a street intersection.

4.3   Results on MOT16

We test our tracking model on all the MOT16 sequences and submitted our results to the ECCV 2016 MOT Challenge [2] for evaluation. The performance is shown in Table 3. The detailed performance and comparison on each sequence will be revealed at the ECCV 2016 MOT Challenge Workshop. We compare our method with the best reported results including NOMT [10], MHT-DAM [9], TBD [21] and CEM [17]. Overall, we achieve the second best performance in terms of MOTA with 0.1 point below the best performed one [10]. We visualize our results in Fig. 3. On the MOT16-12 and MOT16-07 sequences, the camera motion is irregular; whereas on the MOT16-03 and MOT16-08 sequences, scenes are crowded. Despite these challenges, we are still able to link people through occlusions and produce long-lived tracks. The third row of Fig. 3 shows images captured by a fast moving camera mounted on a bus turning at a street intersection. Under such extreme circumstance, our model is able to track people in a stable and persistent way, demonstrating the reliability of the multicut formulation for multi-person tracking task.

5   Conclusion

In this work, we revisit the multi-cut approach for multi-target tracking that is proposed in [5]. We propose a novel pairwise potential that is built based on local image patch appearance matching. We demonstrate extensive experimental analysis and show state-of-art tracking performance on the MOT16 Benchmark. In the future we plan to further develop our approach by incorporating long-range temporal connections in order to deal with longer-term occlusions, and will extend the model with more powerful pairwise terms capable of matching person hypothesis over longer temporal gaps.

Acknowledgements. This work has been supported by the Max Planck Center for Visual Computing and Communication.

References

1. Pirsiavash, H., Ramanan, D., Fowlkes, C.C.: Globally-optimal greedy algorithms for tracking a variable number of objects. In: CVPR (2011)
2. Segal, A.V., Reid, I.: Latent data association: Bayesian model selection for multi-target tracking. In: ICCV (2013)
3. Andriluka, M., Roth, S., Schiele, B.: People-tracking-by-detection and people-detection-by-tracking. In: CVPR (2008)
4. Zhang, L., Li, Y., Nevatia, R.: Global data association for multi-object tracking using network flows. In: CVPR (2008)
5. Tang, S., Andres, B., Andriluka, M., Schiele, B.: Subgraph decomposition for multi-target tracking. In: CVPR (2015)

---

[2] https://motchallenge.net/workshops/bmtt2016/eccvchallenge.html.

6. Wen, L., Li, W., Yan, J., Lei, Z., Yi, D., Li, S.Z.: Multiple target tracking based on undirected hierarchical relation hypergraph. In: CVPR, June 2014
7. Weinzaepfel, P., Revaud, J., Harchaoui, Z., Schmid, C.: DeepFlow: large displacement optical flow with deep matching. In: ICCV (2013)
8. Keuper, M., Levinkov, E., Bonneel, N., Lavoué, G., Brox, T., Andres, B.: Efficient decomposition of image and mesh graphs by lifted multicuts. In: ICCV (2015)
9. Kim, C., Li, F., Ciptadi, A., Rehg, J.M.: Multiple hypothesis tracking revisited. In: ICCV (2015)
10. Choi, W.: Near-online multi-target tracking with aggregated local flow descriptor. In: ICCV (2015)
11. Wang, B., Wang, G., Chan, K.L., Wang, L.: Tracklet association by online target-specific metric learning and coherent dynamics estimation (2015). arXiv:1511.06654
12. Xiang, Y., Alahi, A., Savarese, S.: Learning to track: online multi-object tracking by decision making. In: ICCV (2015)
13. Bewley, A., Ge, Z., Ott, L., Ramos, F., Upcroft, B.: Simple online and realtime tracking (2016). arXiv:1602.00763
14. Roshan Zamir, A., Dehghan, A., Shah, M.: GMCP-tracker: global multi-object tracking using generalized minimum clique graphs. In: Fitzgibbon, A., Lazebnik, S., Perona, P., Sato, Y., Schmid, C. (eds.) ECCV 2012, Part II. LNCS, vol. 7573, pp. 343–356. Springer, Heidelberg (2012)
15. Li, Y., Huang, C., Nevatia, R.: Learning to associate: hybrid boosted multi-target tracker for crowded scene. In: CVPR (2009)
16. Yang, M., Jia, Y.: Temporal dynamic appearance modeling for online multi-person tracking. arXiv preprint (2015). arXiv:1510.02906
17. Milan, A., Roth, S., Schindler, K.: Continuous energy minimization for multitarget tracking. IEEE TPAMI 36(1), 58–72 (2014)
18. Chopra, S., Rao, M.: The partition problem. Math. Program. 59(1–3), 87–115 (1993)
19. Milan, A., Leal-Taixé, L., Reid, I.D., Roth, S., Schindler, K.: MOT16: a benchmark for multi-object tracking (2016). arXiv:1603.00831
20. Felzenszwalb, P.F., Girshick, R.B., McAllester, D., Ramanan, D.: Object detection with discriminatively trained part-based models. IEEE TPAMI 32(9), 1627–1645 (2010)
21. Geiger, A., Lauer, M., Wojek, C., Stiller, C., Urtasun, R.: 3d traffic scene understanding from movable platforms. IEEE TPAMI 36(5), 1012–1025 (2014)

W12 - Assistive Computer Vision and Robotics

Visual and Human-Interpretable Feedback for Assisting Physical Activity

Michel Antunes[(⊠)], Renato Baptista, Girum Demisse, Djamila Aouada, and Björn Ottersten

Interdisciplinary Centre for Security, Reliability and Trust (SnT), University of Luxembourg, Luxembourg, Luxembourg
{michel.antunes,renato.baptista,girum.demisse, djamila.aouada,bjorn.ottersten}@uni.lu

Abstract. Physical activity is essential for stroke survivors for recovering some autonomy in daily life activities. Post-stroke patients are initially subject to physical therapy under the supervision of a health professional, but due to economical aspects, home based rehabilitation is eventually suggested. In order to support the physical activity of stroke patients at home, this paper presents a system for guiding the user in how to properly perform certain actions and movements. This is achieved by presenting feedback in form of visual information and human-interpretable messages. The core of the proposed approach is the analysis of the motion required for aligning body-parts with respect to a template skeleton pose, and how this information can be presented to the user in form of simple recommendations. Experimental results in three datasets show the potential of the proposed framework.

Keywords: Rehabilitation · Stroke · Feedback · Human interpretable

1 Introduction

Physical activity is vital for the general population for maintaining a healthy lifestyle. It is crucial for elderly people in the prevention of diseases, maintenance of independence and improvement of quality of life [17]. For stroke survivors it is critical and essential for recovering some autonomy in daily life activities [8]. Despite the benefits of physical activity, many stroke survivors do not exercise regularly due to many reasons, such as lack of motivation, confidence, and skill levels [13]. Traditionally, the post-stroke patients are initially subject to physical therapy under the supervision of a health professional aimed at restoring and maintaining activities of daily living in rehabilitation centres [20]. The physiotherapist explains the movement to be performed to the patient, and continuously advises her/him how to improve the motion as well as interrupts the exercise in case of health related risk issues. Unfortunately, and due to the high economical burden [1], the *at site* rehabilitation is usually of a short period of time and prescribed treatments and activities for home based rehabilitation are

© Springer International Publishing Switzerland 2016
G. Hua and H. Jégou (Eds.): ECCV 2016 Workshops, Part II, LNCS 9914, pp. 115–129, 2016.
DOI: 10.1007/978-3-319-48881-3_9

usually suggested [9]. Unfortunately, stroke patients, and more frequently older adults, do not appropriately adhere to the recommended treatments, because, among other factors, they do not always understand or remember well enough what and how they are supposed to do the physical treatment.

In order to support the rehabilitation of stroke patients at home, human tracking and gesture therapy systems are being investigated for monitoring and assistance purposes [3,6,12,13,16,25]. These home rehabilitation systems are advantageous not only because they are less costly for the patients and for the health care systems, but also because having it at home and regularly available, the users tend to do more exercise. A well accepted sensing technology for these purposes are RGB-D sensors (e.g. Kinect) that are affordable and versatile, allowing to capture in real-time colour and depth information [3,13].

Existing systems and research either (1) combine exercises with video games as a means to educate and train people, while keeping a high level of motivation [2,7]; or (2) try to emulate a physical therapy session [13,16]. These works usually involve the detection, recognition and analysis of specific motions and actions performed. Very recent works tackle the problem of assessing how well the people perform certain actions [13,14,18,23], which can be used in rehabilitation e.g. to evaluate mobility and measure the risk of relapse. The authors of [14] propose a framework for assessing the quality of actions in videos. Spatio-temporal pose features are extracted and a regression model is estimated that predicts scores of actions from annotated data. Tao et al. [18] also describe an approach for quality assessment of the human motion. The idea is to learn a manifold from normal motion, and then evaluate the deviation from it using specific measures. Wang et al. [23] tackle the problem of automated quantitative evaluation of musculo-skeletal disorders using a 3D sensor. They introduce the Representative Skeletal Action Unit framework from which clinical measurements can be extracted. Very recently, Ofli et al. [13] presented an interactive coaching system using the Kinect. The coaching system guides users through a set of exercises, and the quality of execution of these exercises is assessed based on manually defined pose measurements, such as keeping hands close to each other or maintaining the torso in an upright position.

In this work, we want to go one step further and not only evaluate, but also provide feedback in how people can improve the action being performed. There are two main works that tackle this problem. In the computer vision community, the work of Pirsiavash et al. [14] is the most relevant. After assessing the quality of actions using supervised regression, feedback proposals are obtained by differentiating the scoring with respect to the joint locations, and then selecting the joint and the direction it should move to achieve the largest improvement in the score. In the medical community, Ofli et al. [13] provide assistive feedback during the performance of exercises. For each particular movement, they define constraints such as keeping hands close to each other or maintaining the torso in a upright position. These constraints are constantly measured during the exercise for assessing if the movement is performed correctly and in case pre-defined values for metrics on these constraints are violated, then corrective feedback is provided.

While in [14] the corrective feedback is analysed per joint, which involves a complex set of instructions for suggesting a particular body-part motion (e.g. arm moving up), in [13] the motion constraints are action specific and manually defined.

1.1 Contributions

As discussed previously, the objective of this paper is not only to assess the quality of an action, but also to provide feedback in how to improve the movement being performed. In contrast to previous works, there are three main contributions:

1. We do not compute feedback for single joints, but for body-parts, defined as configurations of skeleton joints that may or may not move rigidly;
2. Feedback proposals are automatically computed by comparing the movement being performed with a template action, without specifying pose constraints of joint configurations;
3. Feedback instructions are not only presented visually, but also human interpretable feedback is proposed from discretized spatial transformations that can be suggest to the user using, for example, audio messages.

1.2 Organization

The article is organized as follows: Sect. 2 introduces the problem that we want to solve, and briefly discusses the pre-processing that is required for spatially and temporarily aligning skeleton sequences. Section 3 presents the body-part representation, the computation of feedback proposals and how they can be translated to human-interpretable messages. Finally, the experimental results are presented in Sect. 4.

2 Problem Definition and Skeleton Processing

This section discusses the problem that we aim to solve, and describes the processing that is performed for spatially and temporally aligning two skeleton sequences.

2.1 Problem Definition

Let $S = [j_1, \ldots, j_n, \ldots, j_N]$ denote a skeleton instance with N joints, where each joint is given by its 3D coordinates $j = [j_x, j_y, j_z]^\mathsf{T}$. Let us define an action or movement as being a skeleton sequence $M = [S_1, \ldots, S_f, \ldots, S_F]$, where F is the number of frames of the sequence. The objective of this paper is to solve the following problem: given a template skeleton sequence $\hat{M}$ and a subject performing a movement M, we want to provide, at each time instant, feedback proposals such that the movement can be iteratively improved to better match $\hat{M}$. As a first step, pre-processing on the input skeleton data is required. Existent approaches were previously introduced in the literature (e.g. [21]), and are adapted for our specific problem.

2.2 Data Normalization

The first requirement for comparing two skeletal sequences is that they need to be spatially registered. This is achieved by transforming the joints of each skeleton S such that the world coordinate system is placed at the hip center, and the projection of the vector from the left hip to the right hip onto the x-y plan is parallel to the x-axis. Then, for achieving invariance to absolute locations, the skeletons in M are normalized such that the body part lengths match the corresponding part lengths of the skeletons in $\hat{M}$. This is performed without modifying the joint angles.

2.3 Temporal Alignment

Different subjects, or the same subject at different times, perform a particular action or movement at different rates. In order to handle rate variations and mitigate the temporal misalignment of time series, Dynamic Time Warping (DTW) is usually employed [15]. In our particular case, we want to align a given sequence M with a template sequence $\hat{M}$. There are two possibilities, we either align M with respect to $\hat{M}$, or vice-versa, $\hat{M}$ with respect to M. We assume the subject is trying to replicate the same action as $\hat{M}$, and given M, we want to provide feedback proposals. Since we want to compute a feedback proposal for each temporal instant of M, it is reasonable to compute the temporal correspondences of $\hat{M}$ with respect to M. Figure 1 shows a temporal alignment example.

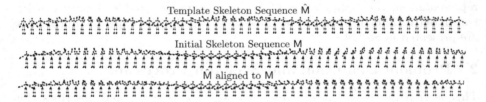

Fig. 1. Temporal alignment of skeleton sequences using DTW. The first row shows the template action $\hat{M}$ (red), the second row shows the skeleton sequence M, and the third row shows $\hat{M}$ aligned with respect to M using DTW. (Color figure online)

3   Human-Interpretable Feedback Proposals

After the spatial and temporal alignment processing described in the previous section, the skeleton instance $\hat{S}_f$ in $\hat{M}$ will be in correspondence with S_f in M. This section explains how to compute the body motion required to align corresponding body-parts of aligned skeletons $\hat{S}$ and S, and proposes a method for extracting human-interpretable feedback from these transformations.

3.1 Body-Part Based Representation

In line with recent research [4,11,19,22], we analyse the human motion using a body-part based representation. A skeleton S can be represented by a set of body-parts $\mathcal{B} = \{b^1, \ldots, b^k, \ldots, b^N\}$. Each body part b^k is composed by n^k joints $b^k = \{b_1^k, \ldots, b_{n^k}^k\}$ and has a local reference system defined by the joint b_r^k. Figure 2 shows the different body-parts defined for the dataset Weight&Balance.

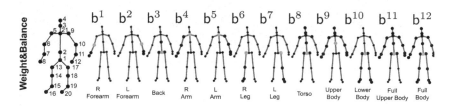

Fig. 2. Proposed body-part representation. The skeleton of the dataset Weight& Balance is composed by 21 joints (left). 12 body-parts were defined. For each body-part, the composing joints were highlighted in green. The red joint corresponds to the local origin b_r^k of a each body-part (R=right, L=left). (Color figure online)

Given the aligned skeletons $\hat{S}$ and S, the objective is to compute the motion that each body-part of S needs to undergo to better match the template skeleton $\hat{S}$. This analysis is performed for each body-part using the corresponding local coordinate system. As a metric for measuring how similar is the pose of corresponding body-parts, we use the Euclidean distance as the scoring function. Following this, the error between b^k and $\hat{b}^k$ is given by:

$$m^k = \sum_{j=1}^{n^k} ||b_j^k - \hat{b}_j^k||^2. \tag{1}$$

Remark that $||b_r^k - \hat{b}_r^k|| = 0$, because the previous computation is performed using the local coordinate systems that are assumed to be in correspondence.

3.2 Feedback Proposals

For providing feedback to the performer of skeleton S on how the movement can be improved to better match $\hat{S}$, we compute the transformation that each body-part b^k needs to undergo for decreasing the scoring function m^k. We anchor the reference joints b_r^k and $\hat{b}_r^k$ (refer to Fig. 2) of the corresponding body-parts. The aim is then to compute the rotation $R^k \in SO(3)$ that minimizes the following error:

$$e^k(R^k) = \sum_{j=1}^{n^k} ||R^k b_j^k - \hat{b}_j^k||^2, \tag{2}$$

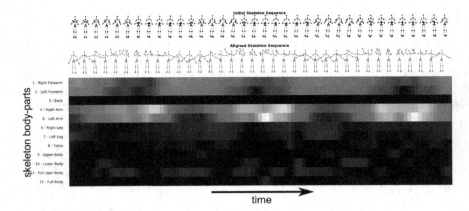

Fig. 3. Intensity of feedback required for each body-part. (Top) Sequence M performing clapping, (middle) target sequence M̂ corresponding to the action waving using two hands after spatial and temporal alignment, and (bottom) the cost c_i^k (refer to Method 1) calculated for each temporal instant independently (the vertical axis corresponds to different body-parts, while the horizontal axis is the temporal dimension.

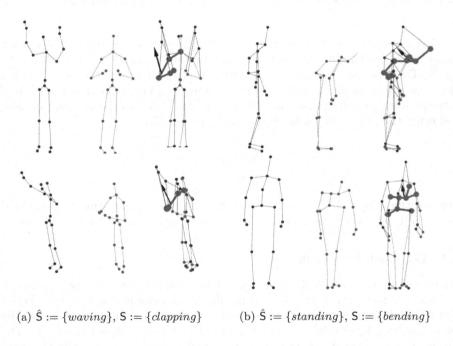

(a) Ŝ := {*waving*}, S := {*clapping*}   (b) Ŝ := {*standing*}, S := {*bending*}

Fig. 4. Two examples for feedback proposals. The target pose Ŝ is shown in blue and the action being performed is shown in red. For each example, the third column shows superimposed the two skeletons, the matching joints (black lines) and the feedback vectors $\mathbf{f}_k$ (black arrows). Only the feedback proposal for R_1 is shown. The different rows present different viewing angles. (Color figure online)

which can be computed in closed form. It is important to refer that since the human motion is articulated, depending on the movement being performed, a given body-part b^k may or may not move rigidly. This is not a critical issue because body-parts that do not moving rigidly have high joint matching error and will be considered not relevant by the method described next. Note that different body-parts b^k can contain subsets of the same joints, which implies that the transformation R^k will also have impact on the location of the other body-parts $b^{l \neq k}$. Taking this into account, we want to compute a sequence of transformations $\mathcal{R} = \{R_1, \dots, R_i, \dots, R_N\}$, one rotation $R_i = R^k$ for each body-part b^k, such that the first rotation R_1 has the highest decrease in the joint location error until R_N, which has the lowest impact in the human pose matching. This sorting is performed maximizing the following cost

$$c_i^k = m^k - e^k(R^k), \tag{3}$$

where in iteration i, the body-parts b^k selected in the previous $i - 1$ iterations are not taken into account. The pseudo-code of the overall scheme is shown in Method 1. Figure 3 show an example of the intensity pattern c_i^k for actions clapping and waving across time.

Input: S, Ŝ, **B**
Output: Sequence of rotations $\mathcal{R}$, list of body-part indexes $\mathcal{K}$
$\mathcal{L} := \mathcal{B}$, $\mathcal{K} = \{\}$, $\mathcal{R} = \{\}$, $i = 1$;
while $\mathcal{L} \neq \{\}$ **do**
    foreach $b^k \in \mathcal{L}$ **do**
        compute R^k that minimizes $e^k(R^k)$ (refer to Equation 2);
        $c_i^k = m^k - e^k(R^k)$ (refer to Equation 3);
    end
    $l := \operatorname*{argmax}_{k} \left(c_i^k \right)$;
    $R_i = R^l$;
    $\mathcal{K} := \mathcal{K} \cup l$, $\mathcal{R} := \mathcal{R} \cup R_i$;
    $\mathcal{L} := \mathcal{L} \setminus b^l$;
    i=i+1;
end

Method 1. Computation of the sequence of body-part transformations that minimizes the skeleton matching error.

The rotations $R_i = R^k$ correspond to the motion required for the best alignment of b^k and $\hat{b}^k$. However, it is difficult to present this rigid-body transformation as feedback proposals on, for example, a screen. For overcoming this, we compute feedback vectors for suggesting improvements on the motion. For each body-part, we pre-calculate the spatial centroid $\mathbf{c}^k$ (note that in case of single limbs, this point is located on the body-part itself). Then, the feedback vector anchored to $\mathbf{c}^k$ is defined as

$$\mathbf{f}^k = R^k \mathbf{c}^k - \mathbf{c}^k. \tag{4}$$

Figure 4 shows feedback vectors for two different pairs of actions being performed.

3.3 Feedback Messages

At this point, we have discussed how to compute the optimal rotation R^k for each body-part b^k, and how this transformation can be presented to a user in form of a feedback vector $\mathbf{f}^k$ anchored to the body-part centroid $\mathbf{c}^k$. Nevertheless, not all the persons have the same spatial awareness to realize how to perform the motion suggested by the feedback vector $\mathbf{f}^k$ (refer to Fig. 4). This difficulty is even more evident in cognitive impaired individuals [5]. In order to support the patient in improving their movements, we introduce in this section a system for presenting simple human-interpretable feedback messages that can be shown or/and spoken to the patient by the computer system.

Let us analyse the case of the body-part b^k that needs to undergo the largest motion $R_1 = R^k$. Initially, to each b^k was assigned a body-part name BN, e.g.

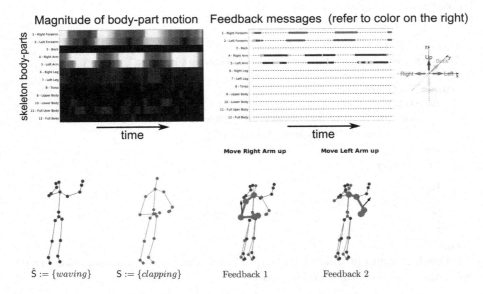

Fig. 5. Feedback message proposals. The target action is waving using two hands and the movement being performed corresponds to clapping. (Top, left) The intensity c_i^k for each body-part b^k; (top, right) the feedback message proposals for the body-parts corresponding to R^1 and R^2. Each point corresponds to a particular message at a given time instant using the body-part name identified on the left and the color coding on the right, e.g. a blue point on the fourth dotted line corresponds to the message *Move Right Arm Up*. (Bottom) a particular instance of the template skeleton $\hat{S}$ (blue), an instance of the skeleton S (red), the feedback vectors for the body-parts corresponding to R^1 and R^2 (black arrows), and the corresponding feedback messages at the top. (Color figure online)

b^1 is the *Right Forearm* and b^8 is the *Torso* (refer to Fig. 2). These labels are used directly for informing the user which body-parts should be moved. Then, the feedback vector $\mathbf{f}^k = [f_x^k, f_y^k, f_z^k]^\mathsf{T}$ is discretized by selecting the dimension d with highest magnitude $|f_d^k|$. The messages regarding the direction of the motion BD are then defined as:

- if $d = x$
  - if $f_x^k < 0$, then $BD = Right$
  - if $f_x^k > 0$, then $BD = Left$
- if $d = y$
  - if $f_y^k < 0$, then $BD = Forth$
  - if $f_y^k > 0$, then $BD = Back$
- if $d = z$
  - if $f_z^k < 0$, then $BD = Down$
  - if $f_z^k > 0$, then $BD = Up$

The feedback proposal messages are represented as the concatenation of strings:

$$\text{Feedback message} := \text{"Move"} + BN + BD. \tag{5}$$

Refer to Fig. 5 for an example of feedback messages, where a color coding is used for identifying the directions BD.

4 Experiments

In this section, we experimentally evaluate the proposed system using three different sets of data. The first is called **ModifyAction**, and we use pairs of

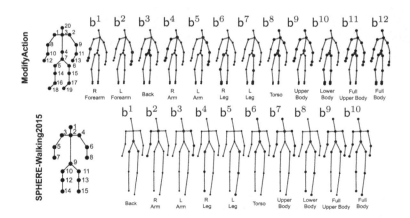

Fig. 6. Proposed body-part representations. Each row shows the skeleton (black) and body-part configurations used for two different datasets. For each body-part, the composing joints were highlighted in green. The red joint corresponds to the local origin b_r of a each body-part. (Color figure online)

actions instances from the datasets *UTKinect* [24] and *MSR-Action3D* [10]. The objective is: given a person performing a particular action M, provide feedback proposals such that the person is able to perform a different action M̂. The skeleton and body-parts used for this dataset are shown in Fig. 6.

The second dataset is **SPHERE-Walking2015** that was introduced in [18]. The skeleton and body-parts used for this dataset are shown in Fig. 6. It contains people walking on a flat surface, and it includes instances of normal walking and subjects simulating the walking of stroke survivors under the guidance of a physiotherapist. The objective in this regard is to analyse the difference in the walking pattern of normal subjects when compared to people with stroke.

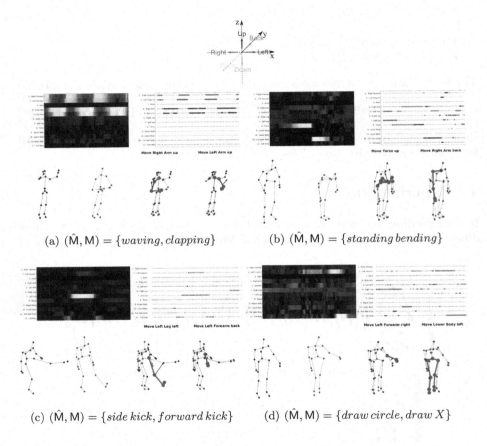

(a) $(\hat{M}, M) = \{waving, clapping\}$ (b) $(\hat{M}, M) = \{standing\, bending\}$

(c) $(\hat{M}, M) = \{side\, kick, forward\, kick\}$ (d) $(\hat{M}, M) = \{draw\, circle, draw\, X\}$

Fig. 7. Four experimental results for the **ModifyAction** dataset are shown. For each example, we show the magnitude of the motion for each body-part (top, left); the feedback messages corresponding to R^1 and R^2 (top, right), refer to the color coding at the top; and the feedback vectors and messages for a particular temporal instant (bottom). (Color figure online)

Finally, the third dataset is new and is called **Weight&Balance**. This data was captured using the Kinect version 2. Refer to Fig. 2 for a detailed description of the body-parts used. The idea is to simulate a person who suffered a stroke (refer to Fig. 10): the *bad arm* issue due to the paralysis of an upper limb is simulated by lifting a kettle-bell using one of the arms, and the *balance* problem is replicated using a balance ball.

Figure 7 shows experimental results of the proposed coaching system for the **ModifyAction** dataset.

4.1   Experiments in SPHERE-Walking2015

In the experiment of Fig. 8, we compared the walking pattern of all the subjects with respect to the walking of healthy people (template action). It shows the intensity profile defined as the sum c_i^k across time for each subject. It is evident that stroke patients have a balance problem, because the body-part corresponding to the torso has high skeleton matching error, while also the stronger paralysis

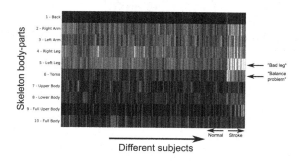

Fig. 8. Motion intensity of different body-parts for different subjects. The subjects on the left of the blue line are healthy people, while the subjects on the right are the (simulated) stroke survivors. (Color figure online)

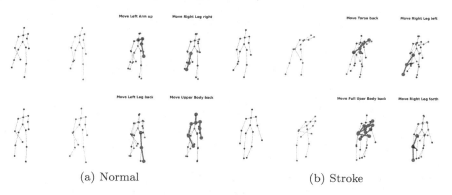

Fig. 9. Feedback proposals. The two subjects on the left are normal people, while the two subjects on the right are stroke survivors

of one of the lower limbs can be identified. Figure 9 shows feedback proposals for normal people and stroke patients.

4.2   Experiments in Weight&Balance

The objective in this section is to simulate a simple physiotherapy session at home, and test if the feedback proposals are able to guide the user. We assume

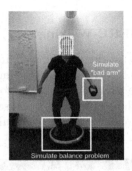

Fig. 10. Weight&Balance dataset. We simulate the motion behaviour of a person who suffered a stroke: the *bad arm* issue due to the paralysis of an upper limb is simulated by lifting a kettle-bell using one of the arms, and the *balance* problem is replicated using a balance ball.

(a) Template $\hat{S}$ (b) S_1 and S_{Best} for Subject 1   (c) S_1 and S_{Best} for Subject 2

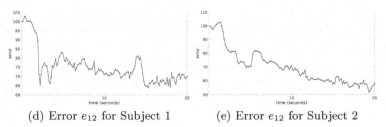

(d) Error e_{12} for Subject 1   (e) Error e_{12} for Subject 2

Fig. 11. Example 1 of **Weight&Balance**. (Top) two views of the template pose $\hat{S}$, and first pose S_1 and best pose S_{Best} for two subjects are shown. The best pose S_{Best} is the one that minimizes the error m^{12}. (Bottom) the relative error (difference between initial and current error divided by the initial error) in % for b^{12} is shown.

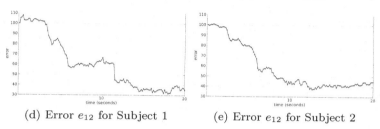

(a) Template $\hat{S}$ (b) S_1 and S_{Best} for Subject 1   (c) S_1 and S_{Best} for Subject 2

(d) Error e_{12} for Subject 1   (e) Error e_{12} for Subject 2

Fig. 12. Example 2 of **Weight&Balance**. (Top) two views of the template pose $\hat{S}$, and first pose S_1 and best pose S_{Best} for two subjects are shown. The best pose S_{Best} is the one that minimizes the error m^{12}. (Bottom) the relative error (difference between initial and current error divided by the initial error) in % for b^{12} is shown.

that a person needs to perform a template human pose $\hat{S}$. The subject puts himself above the balance ball and lifts the kettle-bell. Giving only the guidance of the feedback vectors, body-part motion intensity and feedback messages, the objective is to converge to the template pose without actually seeing it. The exercise lasts for 20 s and feedback proposals are shown at each time instant. The experimental results are shown in Figs. 11 and 12.

5   Conclusions

In this paper, we have introduced a system for guiding a user in correctly performing an action or movement by presenting feedback proposals in form of visual information and human-interpretable feedback. Preliminary experiments show that the provided feedbacks are effective in guiding users towards given human poses. As future work, we intend to incorporate physiotherapy practices in the computation of feedback proposals, and validate the proposed framework using real data.

Acknowledgements. This work has been partially funded by the European Union's Horizon 2020 research and innovation project STARR under grant agreement No.689947. This work was also supported by the National Research Fund (FNR), Luxembourg, under the CORE project C15/IS/10415355/3D-ACT/Björn Ottersten. The authors would like to thank Adeline Paiement and the SPHERE project for sharing the SPHERE-Walking2015 dataset.

References

1. Andlin-Sobocki, P., Jönsson, B., Wittchen, H.U., Olesen, J.: Cost of disorders of the brain in europe. Eur. J. Neurol. (2005)
2. Burke, J.W., McNeill, M., Charles, D., Morrow, P.J., Crosbie, J., McDonough, S.: Serious games for upper limb rehabilitation following stroke. In: Conference on Games and Virtual Worlds for Serious Applications, VS-GAMES 2009. IEEE (2009)
3. Chaaraoui, A.A., Climent-Pérez, P., Flórez-Revuelta, F.: A review on vision techniques applied to human behaviour analysis for ambient-assisted living. Expert Syst. Appl. **39**(12), 10873–10888 (2012)
4. Chaudhry, R., Ofli, F., Kurillo, G., Bajcsy, R., Vidal, R.: Bio-inspired dynamic 3d discriminative skeletal features for human action recognition. In: Proceedings of the IEEE Conference on Computer Vision and Pattern Recognition Workshops (2013)
5. Cicerone, K.D., Langenbahn, D.M., Braden, C., Malec, J.F., Kalmar, K., Fraas, M., Felicetti, T., Laatsch, L., Harley, J.P., Bergquist, T., et al.: Evidence-based cognitive rehabilitation: updated review of the literature from 2003 through 2008. Archives of physical medicine and rehabilitation (2011)
6. Hondori, H.M., Khademi, M., Dodakian, L., Cramer, S.C., Lopes, C.V.: A spatial augmented reality rehab system for post-stroke hand rehabilitation. In: MMVR (2013)
7. Kato, P.M.: Video games in health care: Closing the gap. Rev. Gen. Psychol. (2010)
8. Kwakkel, G., Kollen, B.J., Krebs, H.I.: Effects of robot-assisted therapy on upper limb recovery after stroke: a systematic review. Neurorehabilitation Neural Repair (2007)
9. Langhorne, P., Taylor, G., Murray, G., Dennis, M., Anderson, C., Bautz-Holter, E., Dey, P., Indredavik, B., Mayo, N., Power, M., et al.: Early supported discharge services for stroke patients: a meta-analysis of individual patients' data. The Lancet (2005)
10. Li, W., Zhang, Z., Liu, Z.: Action recognition based on a bag of 3d points. In: Workshop on Human Activity Understanding from 3D Data (2010)
11. Lillo, I., Soto, A., Niebles, J.: Discriminative hierarchical modeling of spatio-temporally composable human activities. In: Proceedings of the IEEE Conference on Computer Vision and Pattern Recognition (2014)
12. Mousavi Hondori, H., Khademi, M.: A review on technical and clinical impact of microsoft kinect on physical therapy and rehabilitation. J. Med. Eng. **2014**, 16 (2014)
13. Ofli, F., Kurillo, G., Obdržálek, S., Bajcsy, R., Jimison, H.B., Pavel, M.: Design and evaluation of an interactive exercise coaching system for older adults: lessons learned. IEEE J. Biomed. Health Inf. **20**(1), 201–212 (2016)
14. Pirsiavash, H., Vondrick, C., Torralba, A.: Assessing the quality of actions. In: Fleet, D., Pajdla, T., Schiele, B., Tuytelaars, T. (eds.) ECCV 2014, Part VI. LNCS, vol. 8694, pp. 556–571. Springer, Heidelberg (2014)
15. Rabiner, L., Juang, B.H.: Fundamentals of speech recognition. Prentice hall (1993)
16. Sucar, L.E., Luis, R., Leder, R., Hernandez, J., Sanchez, I.: Gesture therapy: a vision-based system for upper extremity stroke rehabilitation. In: 2010 Annual International Conference of the IEEE Engineering in Medicine and Biology Society (EMBC) (2010)

17. Sun, F., Norman, I.J., While, A.E.: Physical activity in older people: a systematic review. BMC Public Health (2013)
18. Tao, L., Paiement, A., Aldamen, D., Mirmehdi, M., Hannuna, S., Camplani, M., Burghardt, T., Craddock, I.: A comparative study of pose representation and dynamics modelling for online motion quality assessment. Comput. Vis. Image Underst. **11** (2016)
19. Tao, L., Vidal, R.: Moving poselets: A discriminative and interpretable skeletal motion representation for action recognition. In: ChaLearn Looking at People Workshop. 2015 (2015)
20. Veerbeek, J.M., van Wegen, E., van Peppen, R., van der Wees, P.J., Hendriks, E., Rietberg, M., Kwakkel, G.: What is the evidence for physical therapy poststroke? a systematic review and meta-analysis. PloS one (2014)
21. Vemulapalli, R., Arrate, F., Chellappa, R.: Human action recognition by representing 3d skeletons as points in a lie group. In: Proceedings of the IEEE Conference on Computer Vision and Pattern Recognition (2014)
22. Wang, C., Wang, Y., Yuille, A.: An approach to pose-based action recognition. In: Proceedings of the IEEE Conference on Computer Vision and Pattern Recognition (2013)
23. Wang, R., Medioni, G., Winstein, C., Blanco, C.: Home monitoring musculo-skeletal disorders with a single 3d sensor. In: Proceedings of the IEEE Conference on Computer Vision and Pattern Recognition Workshops (2013)
24. Xia, L., Chen, C.C., Aggarwal, J.K.: View invariant human action recognition using histograms of 3d joints. In: Workshop on Human Activity Understanding from 3D Data (2012)
25. Zhou, H., Hu, H.: Human motion tracking for rehabilitationa survey. Biomed. Signal Process. Control **3**(1), 1–18 (2008)

Mobile Mapping and Visualization of Indoor Structures to Simplify Scene Understanding and Location Awareness

Giovanni Pintore[1(✉)], Fabio Ganovelli[2], Enrico Gobbetti[1],
and Roberto Scopigno[2]

[1] Visual Computing, CRS4, Pula, Italy
{giovanni.pintore,gobbetti}@crs4.it
[2] Visual Computing Group, ISTI-CNR, Pisa, Italy
{ganovelli,scopigno}@isti.cnr.it

Abstract. We present a technology to capture, reconstruct and explore multi-room indoor structures, starting from panorama images generated with the aid of commodity mobile devices. Our approach is motivated by the need for fast and effective systems to simplify indoor data acquisition, as required in many real-world cases where mapping the structure is more important than capturing 3D details, such as the design of smart houses or in the security domain. We combine and extend state-of-the-art results to obtain indoor models scaled to their real-world metric dimension, making them available for online exploration. Moreover, since our target is to assist end-users not necessarily skilled in virtual reality and 3D objects interaction, we introduce a client-server image-based navigation system, exploiting this simplified indoor structure to support a low-degree-of-freedom user interface. We tested our approach in several indoor environments and carried out a preliminary user study to assess the usability of the system by people without a specific technical background.

Keywords: Mobile systems · Scene understanding · Scene reconstruction · Smart environments · Safety and security

1 Introduction

Indoor environments are where humans spend most of their time, and the current evolution towards a digitally assisted society puts them at the center of thriving research and development efforts, aimed at provide a large variety of assistive technologies for improving quality of life. The most direct realization of this trend is the appearance of indoor location based services (Indoor LBS), such as indoor maps or indoor routing [14]. Moreover, recent years have witnessed an increasing interest in *smart homes*, that is, the integration of technology and services through home networking for a better quality of living. The possibility of automatizing the management of a house by introducing sensors and actuators

© Springer International Publishing Switzerland 2016
G. Hua and H. Jégou (Eds.): ECCV 2016 Workshops, Part II, LNCS 9914, pp. 130–145, 2016.
DOI: 10.1007/978-3-319-48881-3_10

handled by AI is now a reality and gave rise to a consistent body of literature and a flourishing industry. Smart homes are not considered just a costly technological gadget anymore, but as a way to make people who are impaired in some way, or exposed to some risk, to be self-sufficient in their home. It is needless to add that, in our aging society, the audience is becoming broader and broader. One obstacle to diffusion of smart homes is the cost to develop them [28]. For this reason several simulators have been proposed to design and test a smart home before putting the hardware into place [1,16,18,20,21]. Such an acquire, simulation, and test approach is used in a variety of other applications, and in particular in the security domain for visually defining and assess concepts and measures for protecting buildings in case of dangerous events [15] (Fig. 1).

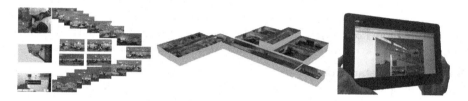

Fig. 1. Our method at a glance: from a set of panoramic photos (left) our system computes a textured 3D model of the indoor boundaries (center) which can be explored with a low-degree-of-freedom web application (right).

One of the major limiting factors in the creation of such simulators, and in creating a large variety of digitally-assisted applications targeting indoor environments, is the lack of suitable 3D mock-ups of the target environment. Since detailed CAD models often do not exist for many buildings, and/or the as-built situation is often very different from the recorded plans, quick and fast ways to create structural and visual information of indoor environments are paramount. Moreover, CAD models alone would not suffice for a variety of needs, such as location awareness, which requires models that are photorealistic enough to recognize real places by just looking at them.

For a widespread use, users should be able to create, access and share digital mock-ups of buildings without requiring the assistance of computer experts to model them. Although devices such as laser scanners often represent the most effective but expensive solution for a dense and accurate acquisition [29], their use is often restricted to specific application domains, such as Cultural Heritage or engineering, as well as this solution requires expensive equipment and very specialized personnel. 3D reconstruction methods based on multiple images have become quite popular and, in certain situations, the accuracy of dense image-based methods is comparable to laser sensor systems at a fraction of the cost [26]. However, they typically require non-negligible acquisition and processing time, and most of these approaches often fail to reconstruct surfaces with poor texture detail. Moreover, the common issue with all these classes of methods is that they require considerable effort to produce structured models of buildings from the high-density data.

Current mobile devices combined with computer vision techniques offer a very attractive platform to overcome these problems. Mobile devices have in-fact become increasingly attractive due to their multi-modal acquisition capabilities and growing processing power, which enables fast digital acquisition, interactive scene understanding, and effective information extraction [8]. Integrating a capture and explore pipeline in a mobile device would boost the development of next-generation, collaborative natural user and visual interfaces for many critical applications, such as the management of building evacuations or real-time security systems [15].

In this work, we propose a novel hybrid approach that uses a cost-effective capture technique based on stitched panoramic images and sensor data acquired with modern mobile devices. The proposed method is capable of extracting a measurable model of room structures, as well as a traversable visual representation, which can be explored with an image-based visual exploration system.

Approach. We start from the assumption that for many typical indoor environments a single equirectangular image of a room can contain enough information to recover the architectural structure. We combine and extend state-of-the-art works to quickly capture indoor environments by acquiring a single equirectangular image per room and a graph of the scene, using panoramic capture tools and instruments commonly available on mobile devices. On the captured scene we perform an automatic reconstruction based on the application of catadioptric theories [2]. Once the multi-room scene has been reconstructed it can be edited and shared and by multiple users, and interactively explored through a platform-independent *WebGL* viewer.

Main contributions. We introduce an integrated system to simplify indoor building capture, mapping and its photorealistic exploration, without actually involving costly and time consuming 3D acquisition pipeline or manual modeling. We combine automated approaches [4,22] with an aided user interface to obtain a 3D textured model in real-world metric dimensions even when automatic tasks fail, such as when the typical assumptions of geometric reasoning [10,17] are not verified (i.e., high piecewise planarity and a large fraction of the room's boundaries unequivocally detectable in the image). Furthermore, since the obtained multi-room environment is already structured and simplified, we exploit an assisted image-based rendering approach to support interactive navigation, instead of using pre-computed video sequences when moving from a room to another one (e.g., [9,25]), thus reducing lag and network bandwidth.

Advantages. The proposed system is targeted to provide a fast and effective method to capture and share real indoor environments to end-users not necessarily skilled in virtual reality and 3D objects interaction. Such a pipeline automatically returns rooms in real-world units only manually entering the height of the observer's eye h_e (such value remains valid for the whole acquisition); moreover it allows the composition of multi-room 3D models with minimal user interaction. In contrast to many of the previous approaches (see Sect. 2), neither further 3D information (e.g., original unstitched images, externally calculated 3D points, MVS data) nor heavy *Manhattan World* [6] assumptions are needed.

Limitations. Relying on a single image per room makes the method sensitive to strong occlusions. Despite these limitations (although common to almost all related approaches), the method is always effective if at least each corner position is visible in the image either on the ceiling or on the floor room's boundaries.

2   Related Work

Reconstruction of indoor scenes. 3D reconstruction of architectural scenes is a challenging problem in both outdoor and indoor environments. Compared to building exteriors, the reconstruction of interiors is complicated by a number of factors. For instance, visibility reasoning is more problematic since a floor plan will in general contain several interconnected rooms. In addition, interiors are often dominated by clutter, surfaces that are barely lit and texture-poor walls. This results in a very challenging reconstruction and in noticeable high frequency rendering artifacts, negatively affecting the quality of visualization. Approaches range from 3D laser scanning [19] to image-based methods [11]. These methods produce high resolution 3D models, which are often an overkill for a large branch of applications, especially those focused on the structure of a building rather than the details of the model.

The use of modern mobile devices has become a promising approach for short-range 3D acquisition and mapping, as witnessed by the well known *Google Project Tango* and *Microsoft Kinect*. However, rooms larger than a few meters, for example a hotel hall, are outside the depth range of these sensors and make the acquisition process more time consuming. Mobile multi-room mapping is useful in many different real-world scenarios, such as smart homes, security management and building protection, etc., mainly to enable non-technical people to create models with enough geometric features for simulations [23] or enough information to support interactive virtual tours [25].

In recent times there has been a renewed interest in omnidirectional images. Applications such as *Android Photo Sphere*, developed by Google, has led to extensive utilization of automatically stitched spherical images in a variety of scenarios. These images are nowadays generated by specific devices, both for entertainment (e.g. *Samsung Gear 360*, *Ricoh Theta S* or general monitoring applications (e.g. fisheye cameras). Cabral et al. [4] extend the work of Furukawa et al. [11] to label indoor structures from omnidirectional images, by exploiting externally calculated depth cues to stereo from the unstitched images. Most of the studies dealing with spherical panoramic images are focused on catadioptric view [2], but many theorems can be applied to all panorama images with practical implications. Following the theories of catadioptric systems [12], Pintore et al. [22] describe a visual model of the scene based on the spherical projection and minimizing geometric constraints. Although their method only acquires the room's footprint and not its entire 3D content, it has the merit of using a single panoramic image per room and no further user interaction, except for handling the capture of multiple rooms. Nevertheless the method is effective only under specific assumptions, such as the presence of large portions of the walls borders easily detectable on the ceiling and the floor.

3D navigation. Navigating a 3D model can be done in several ways. In our case as in many general cases the problem consists in controlling position and orientation of a virtual camera inside a 3D scene, providing the corresponding image. Therefore is broken down to a problem of human machine interaction, as well as a problem of real-time rendering. In classical FPS (first person shooter) videogames [5] the viewer movement is controlled by keys that map to the four main directions (forward, backward, left and right), generally referred as *wasd* mode. Although this interaction paradigm is very effective for a swift control of the viewing parameters in interaction-critical setting, it becomes too much engaging for more generic uses. This is because it requires both hands, and it is simply not doable with modern touch devices, that have neither keyboard nor mouse.

On the other end of the spectrum there are approaches where the view is very constrained and therefore the interaction is minimal. For example there are approaches based on the use of collection of registered images resulting from a SfM reconstruction [27]. In these approaches the views on the 3D scene are those corresponding to the images. The transition between neighbor images can be represented with different strategies. In [27] are rendered by fading between images, or by using partial 3D point cloud reconstruction as outputted by SfM [24]. [3,13] combine the images with a accurate 3D scanning of the location improving them by further processing.

As middle solution between free and constrained navigation are pure image-based techniques that use panoramic images. One well known example is *Google StreetView*, where the viewer can move from on panoramic images to its neighbors by clicking on specific spots. A similar approach is also used in a mobile fashion in [25] for navigating indoor environments. In this case a 360 video panorama for each room is used, in which the user may pan left of right to explore the scene, whereas the transition between panoramas are shown with a video shot while moving from a room to the next. The same combination of panoramas and videos is more generically used in [9] for virtual environments, where both panoramas and videos are obtained by external photorealistic rendering engines. Following the trend of combining mobile and image-based methods we propose the model described in the following sections.

3   System Overview

The proposed pipeline can be outlined as three modules (Fig. 2): **Mobile Capture**, **Scene Analysis** and **Viewer**.

- **Mobile Capture** an interactive mobile application exploiting image and sensor data to:

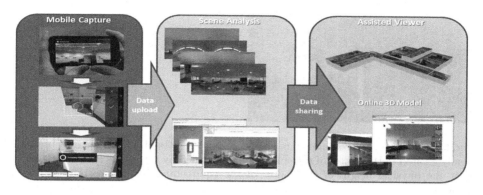

Fig. 2. Mobile Capture module: an interactive mobile application to capture and generate a spherical image for each room, map the multi-room structure by tracking the user movement and recover metric information. **Scene Analysis module:** a scene analysis tool to reconstruct the 3D model and to create a navigable scenegraph. **Assisted Viewer module:** a client/server viewer based on WebGL to navigate inside the 3D model through an assisted navigation interface.

- generate 360 degrees equirectangular images of each indoor environment
- map the multi-room structure by tracking the user movements to generate a navigable scenegraph
- recover the metric information about the structure
- upload the acquired data to the Scene Analysis module
- **Scene Analysis** A scene analysis tool interfaced with a server to:
  - collect the data from the acquisition modules to reconstruct the floor plan structure in real world metric dimensions
  - create the navigable scenegraph for the Viewer's server
- **Viewer** A platform-independent viewer to browse the data on the server and explore the reconstructed scene:
  - based on WebGL and running on standard browsers
  - supporting interactive exploration through a low-DOF navigation interface, suitable for touch interaction on mobile devices

4   Methods

4.1   Scene Capture

Starting from a convenient point of view (from which an observer can see all the room's corners) the user acquires a spheremap of the surrounding environment through the *Mobile Capture* module, generating for each room an *equirectangular* image – i.e., a spherical image which has 360 degrees longitude and 180 degrees latitude field of view (Fig. 3). Equirectangular images are widely used by mobile stitching tools (e.g., *Google Camera with Photo Sphere*), or adopted by systems like Google *Street View*. Moreover these images can be generated

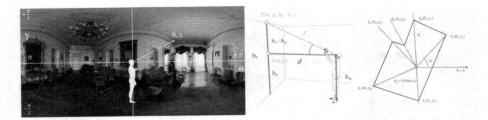

Fig. 3. Left: The equirectangular image represent all possible views for an observer ideally located in the center of the spheremap, identified by the angles θ and γ. Center: h_e is the physical height of the center of the equirectangular image (the ideal eye of the observer) and it is the only value externally entered and not automatically estimated. h_t is the height of the targeted point in respect to the floor plane. Right: The transformation G_h returns real Cartesian coordinates if the height h is known.

by specific hardware, such as compact 360 video cameras (e.g. *Ricoh Theta S*), surveillance circuits, unmanned vehicles instruments. After the acquisition of a room is completed, he/she moves to the next one, tracking the approximative moving direction with respect to the Magnetic North by the aid of the mobile device's IMU. Each spherical image results also spatially referenced, since the equirectangular projection is an angular map and the direction of the image's center is also known through the mobile sensors (w.r.t. the Magnetic North). From these information we easily locate the directions respectively of the exit door from a room and of the entrance door in the next one, and consequently the doors matching between adjacent rooms. At processing time these angular information about doors is thus exploited to recover their local 2D Cartesian coordinates, resulting in a navigable graph of the scene and a spatial mapping of the rooms (see Sect. 4.2).

4.2 Scene Reconstruction

Once the acquired environment has been uploaded to a server we reconstruct the 3D scene starting from the analysis of the single images. Each room is represented by an equirectangular image (see Fig. 3 left), covering every visible point seen by the observer, hence each pixel in the spheremap defines a specific direction of view identified by two angles: θ and γ. The angle θ is the heading of the targeted point respect to the magnetic North, defined as a rotation around the ideal axis between the Sagittal and Coronal planes of the observer. The angle γ (observer tilt) is instead the rotation around the axis between the Coronal and Transverse planes.

Following the basis of the geometric reasoning proposed in [22] we assume that each point in the spheremap can be mapped in 3D space through the following spherical coordinates (see Fig. 3 center):

$$G(r, \theta, \varphi) = \begin{cases} x = r * \sin\varphi * \cos\theta \\ y = r * \sin\varphi * \sin\theta \\ z = r * \cos\varphi \end{cases} \tag{1}$$

We can appropriately convert with respect to the direction of view through the following relations

$$\begin{aligned} \sin\varphi &= \cos\gamma \\ \cos\varphi &= \sin\gamma \\ r &= h/\sin\gamma \end{aligned} \tag{2}$$

substituting for in Eq. 1 we obtain the function:

$$G_h(\theta,\gamma) = \begin{cases} x = h/\tan\gamma * \cos\theta \\ y = h/\tan\gamma * \sin\theta \\ z = h \end{cases} \tag{3}$$

Assuming the walls are vertical G_h maps all the points of the equirectangular image in 3D space as if their height was h:

$$h = \begin{cases} -h_e & floor \\ h_t - h_e & target \end{cases} \tag{4}$$

where h_e is the height of the observer's eye, located in an ideal center of the spheremap, and it is the only value not automatically estimated by our system. Instead h_t is the height of a targeted point (Fig. 3 right) calculated in respect to the floor plane. Since h_e is a constant quantity during the whole acquisition, we obtain the floor plan reconstruction scaled in real-world metric dimensions just entering this value or estimating it with a quick calibration step through the mobile device sensors. Observing Fig. 3-*right* is clear how the shape of the room is known if the angular positions θ_i and γ_i of the *i-corners* (we assume as room's corner position in the image its location on the intersection between wall and ceiling or between wall and floor) are known from the equirectangular map, since the resulting points obtained applying Eq. 3 are actually the Cartesian coordinates of the room.

Although semi-automatic approaches exist to identify the room shape (see Sect. 2), they are hardly practicable in many real-world contexts, since they requires externally calculated 3D data or they work only under certain strictly conditions (i.e., heavy piecewise planarity and walls boundaries easily detectable in the image). After performing a preliminary automatic recognition based on [22], we enable the user to integrate the reconstruction by the interface illustrated in Fig. 4. Through this tool we can easily supervise the automatic reconstruction (Fig. 4 cyan borders) and eventually adjust room's corners, acquire measures (Fig. 4 yellow and red segments) and other features of the room architecture, just establishing a correspondence between picked points (i.e. θ,γ couples) on the screen and geometric points in the indoor scene.

As matter of fact in the spherical panoramic imaging a line in the world is projected onto the unit sphere as an arc segment on a great circle. The arc segment on a great circle forms a curve segment in an omnidirectional image [12]. As practical implication several operation can be performed by the user to integrate the reconstruction or to extract further information. Assuming vertical

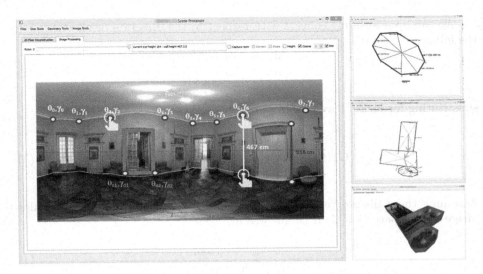

Fig. 4. Server side interface. Left: this tool enables several preliminary scene analysis tasks, like metric measurements on the image (i.e. wall height in yellow, door height in red) and room's corners identification starting from the automatic boundaries detection (i.e. cyan contours). Top right: reconstruction in real-world scale of the analyzed room. Center right: user's path (green) stored during capturing and relative rooms displacement. Bottom right: final 3D textured reconstruction of the acquired floor plan (T2 Table 1). (Color figure online)

walls the distance d from the observer to the wall (Fig. 3 center) is a constant value between the ceiling and the floor boundary. We can automatically calculate this quantity d in respect to the floor combining Eqs. 3 and 4, obtaining the room height (i.e. yellow distance on corner 6 in Fig. 4 left):

$$d = \frac{-h_e}{\tan \gamma_f} \tag{5}$$

where γ_f is the view direction of a targeted point on the intersection between floor and wall planes. If the target point is on the walls ceiling boundary we can estimate the height of the room h_w as:

$$h_w = h_t = d * \tan \gamma_c + h_e \tag{6}$$

where γ_c is the view direction of a targeted point on the intersection between wall and ceiling. Moreover the application of Eq. 3 to $c_1(\theta_1, \gamma_1), \cdots, c_n(\theta_n, \gamma_n)$ returns the positions $p_1, \cdots, p_n \in \mathbb{R}^3$, defining the room's shape (Fig. 3 right). if the automatic reconstruction fails because one or even all corners are not identified the user can recover the task just indicating with a simple click their position in the image click (i.e. yellow circle Fig. 4 left).

In a similar way the positions of the doors are individuated in the image (Fig. 4 green marker), and this information is integrated with the doors matching derived by the acquired user's path (Fig. 4 right center). According with this matching we define a connection between two rooms,e.g. r_j and r_{j+1}, as a couple of doors that fundamentally are the same door expressed in different coordinates. We calculate a transform $M_{j,j+1}$ between r_{j+1} and r_j just comparing the corresponding door extremities. From the rooms connectivity graph we calculate for each room $r_p \in (fr_1 \ldots r_N)$ the path to a global origin room r_0 (usually the first one acquired), as the multiplication of the transforms $\{M_1 \cdots M_p\}$ representing the passages encountered to reach r_0.

As result we obtain a 3D model of the scene ready for the scene exploration (Fig. 5 left). The reconstructed scene is stored on a server as a scene-graph and its relative spheremaps. At run-time, this graph is explored through the system proposed in Sect. 4.3.

4.3   Scene Exploration

In order to browse the scene we adopt an image-based navigation system on a client/server architecture. The server is a standard *http* server (see Sect. 5) hosting the scene-graph and the images, whilst the client is an WebGL-based interactive viewer, implementing an assisted interaction paradigm illustrated in Fig. 5 (center and right). Similarly to other approaches already proven effective such as [9], the viewer operates in two modes: either it shows a panoramic image or it shows the transition from one room to the next. A common way to show equirectangular images consists of first converting the them to cubemaps and then using the cubemap texture capabilities of graphics API to render the image. Instead, we use a simple fragment shader that, for each fragment, takes the direction of the corresponding viewing ray and samples the equirectangular image accordingly. The interaction consists of simply dragging to change view orientation and pinching (or using mouse wheel for non touch screens) to zoom in/out. The right thumbnail bar shows instead all available rooms, and the bottom context-sensitive thumbnail bar shows selected rooms reachable from the current position. Panoramas in the *path bar* correspond to paths leaving the current room (Fig. 5 right, yellow), where the panorama icons are ordered accordingly to the angle between the current view direction and the path direction, so as to always center the rooms bar on the path most aligned with the current view. Such paths are obtained from the reconstruction step as the piecewise line segment connecting two adjacent room centers and passing through the doors. Furthermore a contextual 2D map (Fig. 5 right, green map) of the scene is provided to improve the localization of the viewer in the scene. Unlike in other previous methods [9,25], the transition between panoramas is not a video, that is, our viewer is not purely image based. Instead, thanks to the structured model reconstructed by our system, we create a textured mesh by projecting the panoramas on the 3D model. Since our geometric model only consists of the room's boundary (floor, ceiling and walls) it is clear that projecting the images that also include elements within the room (tables, chairs etc.) creates a model which is only correct when seen from the center of projection while the error become apparent when moving away. However, it must be considered that, during a transition, the viewing direction and the direction of

Fig. 5. Left: top view of the 3D scene reconstructed by our system (T3 Table 1). Center and right: screenshots of interactive browsing of the scene through the Viewer module. The client/server architecture has been defined to achieve a platform independent navigation system running on standard web browsers. (Color figure online)

movement coincide, resulting in a coherent representation. The main advantage of these solutions is that the network bandwidth occupancy is reduced (e.g. with respect to [9,25]), as well as the lag due to video buffering during the movement between rooms, resulting in real-time performance even on low-powered mobile devices or poor network coverage. Summarizing, the tool exploits the specific characteristics of the environment to create a constrained navigation model that does not hinder the possibility of smoothly inspect the scene, providing at the same time an aided user interface that any user can master and so avoiding that the user "feels lost" in the 3D scene.

5   Results and Discussion

To demonstrate the effectiveness of our approach we present its application on real-world cases. As proof-of-concept we employed our method as an assistive technology in the context of security assessment and management of critical buildings. We tested the system with a group of 60 users including different profiles (police, crisis managers and trainers, first responders, fire services), specifically none of them are computer experts, CAD modelers, etc. Such implementation is integrated in to a more general crisis management framework (*reference removed for blind review*) assisting crisis managers and first responders to visually define and assess concepts and measures for protecting buildings.

The *Scene Analysis* module is interconnected with the main *server* by a local area network (Fig. 6), whereas the *Mobile Capture* module and the *Viewer* module are available through a web gateway. The capture tool is implemented as a remote Android application (Android 4.4 or higher compatible) to acquire the indoor environment, the *Scene Analysis* is a stand-alone desktop application to process and upload the data to an *Apache2* web server, and the *Viewer* is a platform independent viewer written in *JavaScript* using *WebGL* and *HTML5*.

The acquisition, reconstruction and visualization tasks were designed in collaboration with real crisis management experts [7], evaluating the system in

Fig. 6. Left: The proposed pipeline is integrated in the main framework through a specialized local area network (illustrated above). Right: Example of a 19-rooms environment (T1 Table 1) employed as training scenario.

terms of usability in a real-world application. The scene acquisition was performed by users (i.e., first responders in our tests) equipped with portable devices, such as touchscreen tablets, and running the *Mobile Capture* module. We asked them to rate the usability of capturing the indoor environment with the provided mobile device (HTC One M8) on a scale from 1 to 5 (very difficult, difficult, moderate, easy, very easy). 60 % of the users found it very easy to capture the indoor environment, whilst 40 % found it to be easy (Fig. 7 left). Managers and trainers instead had access to Scene Server through the *Scene Analysis* module to analyze the reconstructed scene. We asked to rate their satisfaction with the indoor reconstruction system using a scale from 1 to 5 (very dissatisfied, dissatisfied, unsure, satisfied, very satisfied). 35 % end users declared themselves very satisfied with the indoor reconstruction, whilst 65 % of them were satisfied with it (Fig. 7 right).

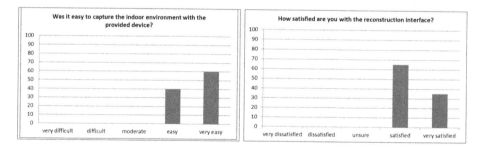

Fig. 7. User score in terms of usability respectively of the capture tool and the reconstruction tool. The system has been tested by a selected end user group of about 60 users. Although a minimal manual interaction was needed in the reconstruction step, the users were very satisfied of the acquisition and reconstruction tools, especially if compared to conventional options (e.g. manual measurements).

In Table 1 we show the capture and reconstruction statistics for several significant scenes, comparing our system to the ground truth. We assume as ground truth blue-prints (when available) and manual measures. The area error is calculated as the ratio of area incorrectly reconstructed to the total ground truth

Table 1. Reconstruction statistics. We indicate the floor area and the number **Rn** of input panorama images/rooms. In the second columns group we show the **maximum** error measured compared to ground truth for the walls length and room height, after both the automatic and interactive editing steps. Finally we show the total capture time, the number **Re** of rooms needing manual intervention after the automatic recognition and the relative editing time.

Scene			Error			Interaction		
Name	Area	Rn	Area	Length	Height	Capture	Re	Editing
T1	$655\,\mathrm{m}^2$	19	2.5 %	11 cm	7 cm	51 m 45 s	3	8 m 25 s
T2	$183\,\mathrm{m}^2$	3	1.1 %	15 cm	5 cm	8 m 20 s	1	3 m 12 s
T3	$64\,\mathrm{m}^2$	7	2.3 %	12 cm	4 cm	18 m 35 s	1	2 m 40 s

area, and the wall length and wall height error are the maximum error measured *after* the manual editing step. This error is not correlated with a specific user behavior (i.e. user interaction for the room's shape recovery consists only in to mark room's corners in the image if automatic detection fails), but it is strictly related to the quality of the images stitching. In the last columns group we show as Capture Time the time needed by an user to acquire a complete stitching of each room and to walk from room to room, finding in every new environment a convenient position to capture the spheremap. **Re** is instead the number of rooms needing manual intervention (Editing time showed in the last column).

As said above the main cause of failure and error in the reconstruction is the quality of the stitching. In the specific case of dataset T1 and T3 the failure cases are corridors, whose stitching is highly distorted. Despite manual intervention a tangible scale error remains. Differently in dataset T2 the automatic recovery didn't really failed in any room, but since the scenario is an ancient building with very highly textured walls, the user had to decide which was the real ceiling level relevant for the reconstruction. In Fig. 6 right we show the reconstruction of the 19 rooms environment, indicated as T1 in Table 1, seen from an above view. The returned model is metrically scaled in real-world dimensions, included the different heights of each room correctly represented. To test the *Viewer module* we asked to a group of end-users NOT involved in the capture and reconstruction tasks, to explore a new acquired environment, employing mobile devices (smartphones and tablet, not only Android) or generic internet browsers (Explorer, Firefox, Chrome) running on commodity PCs and laptops. Users have found the interface comfortable and intuitive, and the first responders category in particular quickly familiarized themselves with the application thanks to the similarity with popular web-based 3D map navigators. We connect the devices through a *wireless-N* local lan and through 3G mobile connection, achieving in all cases a frame rate exceeding 50fps. Differently to approaches based of precomputed video sequences [9], where the frame rate during video transitions drops down to about 20 fps due to video decompression, our system keep the maximum frame rate also during moving between rooms, thanks to the real-time rendering performed on the simplified model. In Fig. 5 we present the 3D model recovered for the T3 dataset (Table 1) and some live screenshots of the interactive browsing through the *Viewer module*. In terms of assistance in designing security, almost all participants stated that the proposed framework adds value to the general process of designing building security, mainly for the capability of being able to visualize a model reconstructed from real data and not replicated by a 3D modeler. More specifically, users are interested in the possibility of designing and testing real path planning and evacuation routes, as well as in being able to simulate the introduction of more sensors in the environment or to incorporate the tools into daily use, integrating it with the CCTV system of a building for example.

6   Conclusions

We presented an image-based system to acquire, reconstruct and explore indoor scenes, starting from data acquired with mobile devices. Combining mobile and web technologies this system can be an effective tool assisting different users to reconstruct and share realistic models of buildings, without the need of any particular 3D expert skill. The resulting model contains enough geometry to support common simulation techniques, and enough visual information to effectively support visual navigation and location recognition. Since the returned scene is already simplified and structured, we exploit such structuring to support a real-time browsing of the acquired scene through a fast interactive WebGL rendering system, running on common mobile devices. For the future we plan to exploit multiple omnidirectional point-of-views, such as the video output of modern mobile 360 camera, to improve scene understanding and/or to support assisted navigation.

Acknowledgements. This work has received funding from the European Union's Seventh Framework Programme for research, technological development and demonstration under grant agreement no 607737 (VASCO). We also acknowledge the contribution of Sardinian Regional Authorities under projects VIGEC and Vis&VideoLab.

References

1. Ariani, A., Redmond, S.J., Chang, D., Lovell, N.H.: Simulation of a smart home environment. In: 2013 3rd International Conference on Instrumentation, Communications, Information Technology, and Biomedical Engineering (ICICI-BME), pp. 27–32, November 2013
2. Bermudez-Cameo, J., Puig, L., Guerrero, J.: Hypercatadioptric line images for 3d orientation and image rectification. Robot. Auton. Syst. **60**(6), 755–768 (2012)
3. Brivio, P., Benedetti, L., Tarini, M., Ponchio, F., Cignoni, P., Scopigno, R.: Photocloud: interactive remote exploration of large 2d–3d datasets. IEEE Comput. Graphics Appl. **33**(2), 86–96 (2013)
4. Cabral, R., Furukawa, Y.: Piecewise planar and compact floorplan reconstruction from images. In: Proceedings of the CVPR, pp. 628–635 (2014)

5. Clarke, D., Duimering, P.R.: How computer gamers experience the game situation: A behavioral study. Comput. Entertain. **4**(3) (2006)
6. Coughlan, J.M., Yuille, A.L.: Manhattan world: Compass direction from a single image by bayesian inference. In: Proceedings of the ICCV, vol. 2, pp. 941–947 (1999)
7. Crisis Plan, B.V.: Crisis management experts. http://www.crisisplan.nl/
8. Dev, K., Lau, M.: Democratizing digital content creation using mobile devices with inbuilt sensors. Comput. Graph. Appl. **35**(1), 84–94 (2015)
9. Di Benedetto, M., Ganovelli, F., Balsa Rodriguez, M., Jaspe Villanueva, A., Scopigno, R., Gobbetti, E.: Exploremaps: Efficient construction and ubiquitous exploration of panoramic view graphs of complex 3d environments. Comput. Graph. Forum **33**(2) (2014). proc. Eurographics 2014
10. Flint, A., Mei, C., Murray, D., Reid, I.: A dynamic programming approach to reconstructing building interiors. In: Daniilidis, K., Maragos, P., Paragios, N. (eds.) ECCV 2010, Part V. LNCS, vol. 6315, pp. 394–407. Springer, Heidelberg (2010)
11. Furukawa, Y., Curless, B., Seitz, S.M., Szeliski, R.: Reconstructing building interiors from images. In: Proceedings of the ICCV (2009)
12. Geyer, C., Daniilidis, K.: A unifying theory for central panoramic systems and practical implications. In: Vernon, D. (ed.) ECCV 2000. LNCS, vol. 1843, pp. 445–461. Springer, Heidelberg (2000)
13. Goesele, M., Ackermann, J., Fuhrmann, S., Haubold, C., Klowsky, R., Steedly, D., Szeliski, R.: Ambient point clouds for view interpolation. ACM Trans. Graph. **29**(4), 95:1–95:6 (2010)
14. Goetz, M., Zipf, A.: Open issues in bringing 3d to location based services (lbs): a review focusing on 3d data streaming and 3d indoor navigation. Remote Sensing and Spatial Information Sciences, pp. 38–4 (2010)
15. Guest, J., Eaglin, T., Subramanian, K., Ribarsky, W.: Interactive analysis and visualization of situationally aware building evacuations. Information Visualization (2014)
16. Helal, S., Mann, W., El-Zabadani, H., King, J., Kaddoura, Y., Jansen, E.: The gator tech smart house: a programmable pervasive space. Computer **38**(3), 50–60 (2005)
17. Hoiem, D., Efros, A.A., Hebert, M.: Geometric context from a single image. In: Proceedings of the ICCV, vol. 1, pp. 654–661. IEEE (2005)
18. Jahromi, Z.F., Rajabzadeh, A., Manashty, A.R.: A multi-purpose scenario-based simulator for smart house environments. (IJCSIS) Int. J. Comput. Sci. Inf. Secur. **9**(1), 13–19 (2011). http://dx.doi.org/10.1007/s00779-014-0813-0
19. Mura, C., Mattausch, O., Gobbetti, A.J.E., Pajarola, R.: Automatic room detection and reconstruction in cluttered indoor environments with complex room layouts. Comput. Graph. **44**, 20–32 (2014)
20. Nguyen, T.V., Kim, J.G., Choi, D.: Iss: The interactive smart home simulator. In: 11th International Conference on Advanced Communication Technology, 2009. ICACT 2009, vol. 03, pp. 1828–1833, February 2009
21. O'Neill, E., Klepal, M., Lewis, D., O'Donnell, T., O'Sullivan, D., Pesch, D.: A testbed for evaluating human interaction with ubiquitous computing environments. In: First International Conference on Testbeds and Research Infrastructures for the Development of Networks and COmmunities. pp. 60–69, February 2005
22. Pintore, G., Garro, V., Ganovelli, F., Agus, M., Gobbetti, E.: Omnidirectional image capture on mobile devices for fast automatic generation of 2.5D indoor maps. In: Proceedings of the IEEE Winter Conference on Applications of Computer Vision (WACV), February 2016

23. Pintore, G., Gobbetti, E.: Effective mobile mapping of multi-room indoor structures. Vis. Comput. **30**, 707–716 (2014). proc. CGI 2014
24. Pintore, G., Gobbetti, E., Ganovelli, F., Brivio, P.: 3dnsite: A networked interactive 3d visualization system to simplify location recognition in crisis management. In: Proceedings of the ACM Web3D International Symposium, pp. 59–67. ACM, New York, August 2012
25. Sankar, A., Seitz, S.: Capturing indoor scenes with smartphones. In: Proceedings of the UIST, pp. 403–412. ACM, New York (2012)
26. Seitz, S.M., Curless, B., Diebel, J., Scharstein, D., Szeliski, R.: A comparison and evaluation of multi-view stereo reconstruction algorithms. In: Proceedings of the CVPR, vol. 1, pp. 519–528 (2006)
27. Snavely, N., Seitz, S.M., Szeliski, R.: Photo tourism: exploring photo collections in 3D. ACM Trans. Graph. **25**(3), 835–846 (2006)
28. Wilson, C., Hargreaves, T., Hauxwell-Baldwin, R.: Smart homes and their users: A systematic analysis and key challenges. Pers. Ubiquit. Comput. **19**(2), 463–476 (2015). http://dx.doi.org/10.1007/s00779-014-0813-0
29. Xiong, X., Adan, A., Akinci, B., Huber, D.: Automatic creation of semantically rich 3D building models from laser scanner data. Autom. Constr. **31**, 325–337 (2013)

Automatic Video Captioning via Multi-channel Sequential Encoding

Chenyang Zhang and Yingli Tian[⊠]

Department of Electrical Engineering,
The City College of New York, New York, NY 10031, USA
czhang10@citymail.cuny.edu, ytian@ccny.cuny.edu

Abstract. In this paper, we propose a novel two-stage video captioning framework composed of (1) a multi-channel video encoder and (2) a sentence-generating language decoder. Both of the encoder and decoder are based on recurrent neural networks with long-short-term-memory cells. Our system can take videos of arbitrary lengths as input. Compared with the previous sequence-to-sequence video captioning frameworks, the proposed model is able to handle multiple channels of video representations and jointly learn how to combine them. The proposed model is evaluated on two large-scale movie datasets (MPII Corpus and Montreal Video Description) and one YouTube dataset (Microsoft Video Description Corpus) and achieves the state-of-the-art performances. Furthermore, we extend the proposed model towards automatic American Sign Language recognition. To evaluate the performance of our model on this novel application, a new dataset for ASL video description is collected based on YouTube videos. Results on this dataset indicate that the proposed framework on ASL recognition is promising and will significantly benefit the independent communication between ASL users and others.

Keywords: Video captioning · Long-short-term-memory · Sequential encoding · American Sign Language

1 Introduction

Automatic visual content understanding and describing have become a fast-growing research area in computer vision for the recent decade. Effective understanding visual medias can significantly improve the performance of computer programs to automatically analyze and organize the online media. With the recent ground-breaking progress in large-scale visual recognition and deep neural networks, an explosive amount of techniques have been proposed in object recognition [1,2], scene understanding [3,4] and action recognition [5,6]. These findings successfully broaden the horizon of visual recognition research. Combining with the rapid progress of natural language processing, visual content describing has drawn more and more attention in the field of computer vision and machine

© Springer International Publishing Switzerland 2016
G. Hua and H. Jégou (Eds.): ECCV 2016 Workshops, Part II, LNCS 9914, pp. 146–161, 2016.
DOI: 10.1007/978-3-319-48881-3_11

learning. How to bridge the gap between visual content and natural human language has become the motivation of many research topics, such as image and video captioning.

Automatic image captioning deals with both images and textual data and generates natural sentences to summarize input image content. Generating descriptive sentences for images requires knowledge from multiple domains such as computer vision, natural language processing, and machine learning. Inspired by the recent renewed interests in deep learning techniques, there are many image captioning frameworks proposed [7–12]. The paradigm for generating captions for images takes two steps: (1) **Encoding stage:** the visual input (an image) is processed by a feature extraction layer (encoder). (2) **Decoding stage:** a language model is applied to decode the input feature encoding to a pre-defined vocabulary. The output sentence is generated based on the probabilistic distribution over the vocabulary using the language model. Recurrent neural network (RNN) has been proven to be an effective choice for the decoder because RNN is capable to address the temporal dynamics in output sentences.

Video captioning is a similar problem with image captioning and the encoder-decoder framework is also applicable for this problem. However, different from static images, videos contain much more semantic information related to temporal dynamics. Therefore, the video captioning framework should be able to model not only the static visual content inside each video frame, but also the temporal order of the frames. To address this problem, researchers have proposed several methods to adapt the encoder-decoder system to handle sequential inputs, such as mean-pooling over frames [13], temporal attention model [14], and directly employing sequence-to-sequence RNNs [15].

In this paper, we propose a novel framework for video captioning task. The main idea is illustrated in Fig. 1. To include more temporal motion-related information from the input video sequences, two channels (motion history images and raw video frames) are employed as video inputs. Our proposed framework integrates three different types of neural networks to perform automatic video captioning: (1) **3D-CNN:** instead of using object-detection-oriented feature extraction networks (such as VGG and AlexNet), we employ 3D convolutional neural networks (3D CNNs) to extract spatial-temporal features from video clips. (2) **RNN Encoder:** since the length of each video is arbitrary, the generated 3D CNN features are also of arbitrary lengths. A recurrent neural network (RNN) with long-short-term-memory (LSTM) cells is employed to map the sequential inputs to a fixed-dimensional encoding space. To jointly learn the encoding from two input channels, one LSTM encoder is assigned to each channel and the two encoders forms a parallel system. The fusion layer is a fully-connected layer which maps the LSTM internal states to the encoding space and the encoded vectors are concatenated. (3) **RNN language model:** the RNN language model defines a probability distribution of the next word in a sequence based on both the context and the current word. In our model, the context encoded in the form of LSTM internal state and initialized by the learned encoding vector.

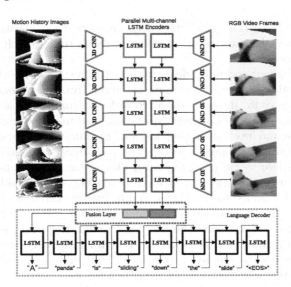

Fig. 1. Illustration of our proposed video captioning framework. Two channels of input frames are utilized: motion history images (MHIs) and RGB video frames. Firstly, raw features are extracted from each input channel frames using 3D convolutional neural networks. The feature extraction phase generates sequential features of arbitrary lengths. Secondly, the sequence of features is encoded using RNNs with LSTM cells for each channel. Then a fusion layer is employed to combine the encoded features from both LSTM encoders. Finally the fused features are fed into a LSTM-based language decoder to be decoded into a sequence of words. "<EOS>" represents the *"end of sentence"* token.

In addition, we also explore the potential utilization of the proposed video captioning framework in automatic video-based American Sign Language (ASL) translation. ASL is a visual gestural language which is used by many people who are deaf or hard-of-hearing. Automatically generating textual descriptions from ASL videos can significantly benefit the ASL-using population to communicate with non-ASL users. To the best of our knowledge, there has been no such effort to link ASL translation with video captioning before. We have collected a large-scale dataset from YouTube uploaded by ASL signers and gained annotations by aligning the video clips with subtitles. The proposed network is able to gain ASL-oriented knowledge from the dataset and to generate meaningful sentences from ASL videos.

The contributions of this work have three aspects:

– A sequential LSTM encoder framework is proposed to learn to embed video sequences addressing both spatial and temporal information.
– Our framework can handle multiple streams of input sequences and automatically learn how to combine.
– We are the first to explore video captioning in the area of ASL translation and provide a novel dataset in this area.

The rest of this paper is organized as the following. Section 2 reviews the related research work. Section 3 elaborates the architecture of the proposed framework. Then the datasets used and proposed by this paper are described in Sect. 4. Section 5 discusses the experiments. Finally the paper is concluded in Sect. 6.

2   Related Work

In this section, we briefly review the related research work in two aspects as below.

Video Captioning. Similar to image captioning, video captioning is also based on building connections between visual signals and textual data. Automatic video captioning is a recent branch of automatic video annotation, which starts with automatic video tagging. In [16], the authors explored to automatically assign conceptual tags to YouTube videos by learning from both visual and audio features. The authors of [17] treated the problem as an activity-recognition problem. They built hierarchical semantic trees to organize detected entities such as actors, actions, and objects. Zero-shot-learning-based language models were applied on the learned hierarchies to assign a short sentence to summary the detected potentials. Similarly, semantic triplets (*subject-verb-object*) were also used in [18] to organize detections of objects and activities for sentence inferencing. Quadruples were utilized in [19] to include more information from the context and scene for more accurate descriptions. Other efforts made to improve the performance of automatic tagging include video tag augmentation [20], video clustering [21], and video re-ranking [22]. Inspired by the successful utilization of LSTM-based RNNs in image captioning, there has been a lot of work using RNNs for video captioning. In [13], Venugopalan *et al.* proposed to apply average pooling over image features extracted from each video frame to obtain a video feature. Then the video feature was encoded to feed into a LSTM-based RNN language model for sentence decoding. To capture more temporal dynamics, attention models were applied in [23] to learn a weighting function over sampled key-frames. In [15], the authors explicitly modeled the sequential input (video) and sequential output (sentence) by exploiting a sequence-to-sequence LSTM architecture. Our work is most related to [15] because we also model the input encoding part with sequential input LSTMs. However, we separate the video encoding and sentence decoding parts to avoid feature entanglement. Additionally, applying such a separate model can enable us to conveniently combine multiple channels of input instead of raw-feature concatenation [23] or late score fusion [15].

American Sign Language Recognition. ASL is used by deaf people across U.S. and Canada. Some researchers have estimated that the population using ASL as a primary language was about $500,000$ [24]. In automatic ASL recognition, early attempts have been made to explore the use of Hidden Markov Models (HMMs) in sequence modeling [25,26]. In [27,28], the authors proposed to track varies facial landmarks for ASL recognition. In recent years, since the progress in commercial multi-modality sensors, researchers have been focusing on exploring the utilizations of multiple sensors. For example, in [29,30], the authors proposed to employ Kinect and Leap Motion sensors, respectively, for real-time hand-gesture-based ASL recognition. In this work, we propose to study ASL recognition from the perspective of data-driven video captioning. To the best of our knowledge, this is the first time ASL recognition is combined with video captioning.

3   Method

The framework of our proposed method is illustrated in Fig. 1. The whole framework is composed of four core modules: (1) 3D CNN-based feature extractor. (2) Sequential feature encoder. (3) Parallel fusion layer. (4) Sentence-generation language module. Both the feature encoder and the language module are based on RNNs with LSTM cells.

3.1   LSTM-based RNNs

Recurrent neural network (RNN) is a category of neural network containing an internal state. RNN is able to encode a dynamic temporal behavior due to its connections between units form directed cycles. The internal state of RNN can be treated as a state of memory, which contains information of both current input and the previous memory. Therefore, RNN has the capability to "remember" the history of both previous inputs and outputs. RNN is widely applied in prediction frameworks which is dependent on context, such as machine-translation [31]. A RNN cell can be formatted as:

$$h_t = \sigma(W_h h_{t-1} + W_x x_t), \tag{1}$$

where h_t and x_t denote the hidden state and input encoding at time step t, respectively; W_h and W_x denote the parameters assigned to each state vector. $\sigma(\cdot)$ denotes the sigmoid function.

However, RNN often suffers from modeling long-term temporal dependencies [32]. A modification called *long-term-short-memory* (LSTM) is proposed for better long-term temporal dependency modeling with more sophisticated internal states and connections. A typical LSTM cell can be formatted as:

$$
\begin{aligned}
i_t &= \sigma(W_i x_t + U_i h_{t-1} + b_i) \\
o_t &= \sigma(W_o x_t + U_o h_{t-1} + b_o) \\
f_t &= \sigma(W_f x_t + U_f h_{t-1} + b_f) \\
\hat{C}_t &= tanh(W_c x_t + U_c h_{t-1} + b_c) \\
C_t &= f_t \odot C_{t-1} + i_t \odot \hat{C}_t \\
h_t &= o_t \odot tanh(C_t),
\end{aligned}
\tag{2}
$$

where $\odot$ is element-wise product; $\sigma(\cdot)$ denotes the sigmoid nonlinearity-introduce function; x_t is the input encoding at each time step t to the LSTM cell; W_i, W_f, W_c, W_o, U_i, U_f, U_c, and U_o are weight matrices assigned to parameters of input gate, forget gate, cell state and output gate, respectively; b_i, b_f, b_c and b_o are bias vectors for corresponding gates and states; i_t, o_t, f_t, C_t and h_t denote the state values of input gate, output gate, forget gate, cell state and hidden state, respectively. $\hat{C}_t$ represents the candidate cell state before combining with the previous cell state (C_{t-1}) and the forget gate.

In our work, the LSTM cells are the building blocks of two types of RNNs: (1) feature encoding RNN and (2) sentence decoding RNN (language model). The illustrations of both RNNs are shown in Fig. 2. The two types of RNN cells are connected as illustrated in Fig. 1. The feature encoding RNN is responsible to encode the sequential inputs from video features; and the sentence decoding RNN is responsible to decode the output from encoding RNN to a sequence of words.

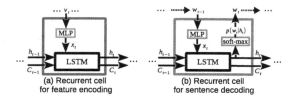

(a) Recurrent cell
for feature encoding   (b) Recurrent cell
for sentence decoding

Fig. 2. Illustration of two types of recurrent cells for feature encoding and sentence decoding, respectively. Both cells contain an internal LSTM cell. At each time step, feature encoding recurrent cell takes an input video feature (v_t) and sentence decoding cell takes an input as the word-prediction (w_t) from the previous time step. Note that the MLPs in both cells act as look-up tables which map the input vector to the internal input vector (x_t).

3.2   Feature Encoder

Suppose the input video sequence $V = \{c_1, c_2, ..., c_T\}$ is composed of T short video clips. Without loss of generality, the length of each video clip $\|c_i\|$ could equal to 1 to represent individual frames. The video sequence can be encoded with a feature extractor ϕ (such as C3D [6] and VGG-net [33]), thus the video can be represented as: $\phi(V) = \{v_1, v_2, ..., v_T\}$, where $v_t = \phi(c_t)$ denotes a video feature vector for a video clip.

Therefore, the input video can be encoded into a sequence of feature vectors $\{v_t\}$. For the feature encoding RNN as illustrated in Fig. 2(a), one video feature v_t is fed into the RNN cell with a multiple-layer-perceptron (MLP). The MLP can represent any multi-layer neural network, and in our case the MLP indicates a fully-connected layer followed by a ReLU layer. Note that the MLP acts like a look-up table, mapping the input feature vector into a continuous RNN embedding space. At each time step t, the RNN cell takes input from both the previous cell and the video sequence; it encodes the input vectors using an internal LSTM cell and output hidden state h_t and cell state C_t to the next cell. The behavior of the internal feature encoding LSTM cell ($LSTM_{FE}$) can be formatted as:

$$[h_t, C_t] = LSTM_{FE}(h_{t-1}, C_{t-1}, MLP(v_t)). \tag{3}$$

Parallel fusion layer. Our framework is designed to handle video encodings from multiple channels of the input video, such as RGB frames and motion history images (MHI) as shown in Fig. 1. Because different channel of video encoding contains different information, each channel should have its own feature encoding so that the intrinsic characteristics can be encoded. In our framework, to connect the output encoding vectors from feature encoding RNNs and the input of sentence decoding RNN, a parallel paradigm to conduct the mapping is employed:

$$ENC(V) = MLP(h_T) \oplus MLP(h_T'), \tag{4}$$

where $ENC(V)$ denotes the final video encoding of the input video V and $\oplus$ denotes vector concatenation; h_T and h_T' denote the final state vector of two streams of RNN encoders. Note that the dimension of $ENC(V)$ matches with the dimension of RNN encoding space in the language model decoder.

3.3 Language Model

A general language model is usually designed to compute the probability of a sequence of words:

$$p(w_1, w_2, ..., w_K) = p(w_K|w_{K-1}, , , w_1) \cdot ... \cdot p(w_2|w_1) \cdot p(w_1), \tag{5}$$

where w_i is the ith word in the output sentence.

In video captioning scenario, the language model is designed to compute the modified probability:

$$p(w_1, w_2, ..., w_K, Y) = p(w_K|w_{K-1}, , , w_1, Y) \cdot ... \cdot p(w_2|w_1, Y) \cdot p(w_1, Y), \tag{6}$$

where $Y = ENC(V)$ represents the encoded video.

In our framework, the language model is implemented with a RNN-based sentence decoder, as shown in Fig. 2(b). More specifically, the RNN decoding cell at each time step computes the probability by providing the previous output words and the video encoding as following:

$$p(w_t|w_{t-1}, , , w_1, Y) = p(w_t|h_t) = SM(h_t)$$
$$[h_t, C_t] = LSTM_{LM}(x_t, h_{t-1}, C_{t-1})$$
$$x_t = \begin{cases} Y, & \text{if } t = 1 \\ MLP(\mathbf{1}(w_{t-1})), & \text{otherwise,} \end{cases} \tag{7}$$

where $SM(\cdot)$ represents a soft-max layer and $\mathbf{1}(\cdot)$ denotes the 1-hot-vector representation of the word index. Note that the MLP learns the mapping from word-index to the RNN internal space. The output word w_t is sampled according to the probability distribution computed by the soft-max layer.

3.4   Video Representation

In this section, the procedure of obtaining video representations, *i.e.* $\phi(V)$, is discussed.

Spatial-temporal feature extraction. In [13], the video representation is obtained from mean-pooling of static image feature vectors of each frame. However, videos are more than combinations of individual frame. Only including static image features can capture the visual appearance such as objects and scenes, but discard the information of temporal motions. For instance, in the example of Fig. 1, information about "panda" could be included in visual appearance features, but information about "sliding" will more likely be included in motion features. To capture sufficient spatial-temporal features, our framework employs two strategies: (1) two channels of raw video representations are included: motion history images and RGB video frames. MHI focus on temporal motions and RGB frames focus on spatial appearances. (2) For each short clips in each channel (16 frames), temporal-spatial features are computed via a 3D convolutional neural network (C3D [6]). The C3D networks are pre-trained on action recognition dataset so that they are capable to capture discriminative spatial-temporal features.

Context embedded video representation. Before feeding the extracted C3D features into video encoding RNNs, an additional pooling layer is added to provide more context information to the video representation:

$$\phi(V) = \{v_0, v_1, ..., v_T\}$$
$$v_t = \begin{cases} max\_pool(v_1, ..., v_T), & \text{if } t = 0 \\ C3D(c_t), & \text{otherwise,} \end{cases} \tag{8}$$

where v_t represents the input for video encoding RNN at each time step t and c_t represents the corresponding video clip.

Therefore, at time step $t = 0$, the encoding RNN will be fed with the "context" vector, which is the max pooling vector over all C3D feature vectors. In this way, the video encoding RNN starts with the holistic knowledge about the whole video before taking the sequential inputs representing each video clip.

4   Datasets

4.1   Microsoft Video Description Corpus

The Microsoft video description (MSVD) corpus is a video snippet-based dataset, which focuses on describing simple interactive events, such as driving, cooking, *etc.* Each video snippet is collected from YouTube. There are about $1,658$ video clips in this corpus which are available by the time of our experiments. Each video snippet lasts from multiple seconds to several minutes. Human annotators were asked to describe the video snippet using one sentence from any language. Since each video snippet was assigned to multiple annotators, there are multiple sentences for one video snippet. Here, our paper only focuses on English descriptions. Among the 1,658 video snippets, 300 are used as testing and the rest are for training.

4.2   Movie Description Datasets

In this paper, two movie description datasets are employed: Max Planck Institute for Informatics Movie Description Dataset (MPII) [34] and Montreal video annotation dataset (MVAD) [35]. Both of the datasets are collected from Hollywood movies. MPII dataset contains over 68,000 video snippets from 94 High-definition movies and MVAD dataset contains 49,000 video snippets from 92 movies. The text annotation from the MVAD dataset is from Descriptive Video Service (DVS), a linguistic description that allows visually impaired people to follow the movie. Besides DVS, the MPII dataset also employs movie scripts to enrich the text annotations. Both datasets are very challenging compared to the MSVD dataset in several aspects: (1) movie videos have more complex scenes and varied backgrounds. (2) The text annotations are sourced from a combined corpus, therefore the linguistic complexity is much higher than well-structured sentences as in the MSVD dataset. The MVAD and the MPII datasets belong to the recent Large Scale Movie Description Challenge (LSMDC). We report evaluation on the public testing set, where the MPII dataset has 3,535 testing video/sentence pairs and the MVAD has 6,518.

4.3   American Sign Language Video Description Corpus

To the best of our knowledge, previous automatic ASL recognition frameworks only focus on hand gesture or facial expression recognition. We further explore the utilization of video captioning framework for ASL recognition. Since there is no proper public dataset for this task, we propose a new dataset, **ASL-TEXT**, collected from YouTube. This proposed dataset is focused on describing videos of ASL signing, and it contains about 20,000 video-sentence pairs. The ASL-TEXT dataset is very challenging in two aspects: (1) the scenes are complex but irrelevant, and the only relevant information is from human facial expressions and body gestures. (2) The sentences are extracted from YouTube subtitles, some of which are generated by automatic voice recognition. Therefore the language complexity and variation are even higher than the previous mentioned movie description datasets.

The resource of ASL on YouTube comes in several categories, such as *ASL lessons, ASL songs,* and *ASL instructions provided by public institutes.* We manually search on YouTube with multiple textual queries such as "ASL", "American Sign Language", and "ASL Lessons", *etc.* The search results are further manually filtered using several criteria: (1) the search results should be correct ASL signing. (2) The subtitles associated with the video snippets should be available. (3) There should be only one frontal-view signer in the video. To further rule out unnecessary background noises, face detection is applied on each video frame and the video frames are then centered and cropped according to the face detection results. Some examples of the dataset are shown in Fig. 3(d).

Following the convention in MPII and MVAD datasets, each video is segmented into several short snippets. Since each video in our dataset has caption (or subtitle) available, we segment the videos so that each video clip corresponds to one sentence in the caption text. As a result, the ASL-TEXT dataset contains 22,527 video/sentence pairs and the average length of video clips is 5.4s. The sizes of vocabularies in the three datasets are comparable but the ASL-TEXT dataset has less words. The ASL-TEXT dataset is more challenging because the averaged word frequency is much lower than in the other two datasets. This dataset will be released to public (Table 1).

Table 1. Comparative statistics of the propose ASL-TEXT dataset with the MSVD and MPII datasets.

	#-sentences	#-words	Vocab. size	Avg. length
MPII	68,375	679,157	21,700	3.9 s
MVAD	56,634	568,408	18,092	6.2 s
ASL-TEXT	22,527	178,637	11,193	5.4 s

5 Experimental Results

5.1 Experimental Setup

Metric. In this paper, we mainly evaluate the proposed framework using the METEOR evaluation metric [36]. Compared to other n-gram-based metrics such as BLEU [37], METEOR is more appropriate to evaluate sequential predictions. METEOR scores the predictions by aligning them to more than one reference sentences, which are based on exact, stem, synonym, and paraphrase matches between words and phrases. Therefore METEOR takes more linguistic and semantic information into consideration.

Loss function. In each iteration during the training process, a batch of images is fed into the neural networks, and the language decoder generates a sequence of probability distributions. A log-likelihood function is applied for each probability vector and corresponding ground-truth vector (1-hot-vector). The losses and gradients are then computed by maximizing the likelihood function. The losses and gradients are averaged and back-propagated to the preceding network modules for parameter updates.

Training and optimization. For computational efficiency, we assign the weights for the C3D networks with a pre-trained network and do not apply fine-tuning. The rest of the modules (LSTM feature encoder, fusion layer, and LSTM language decoder) are trained end-to-end using stochastic gradient descent. The learning rates for all modules are set to 0.0001. Each iteration contains a batch of 16 samples. All RNN sizes are set to 1024. The drop-out rates for both encoder and decoder are set to 0.5. We implement the networks using Torch7 [38] and CuDNN. It takes about 1 to 3 days to converge on the training set using a GeForce TitanX core, depending on the sizes of datasets.

5.2   Video Description Results

MSVD dataset. The comparative METEOR scores of the proposed and other methods are shown in Table 2. The proposed method significantly outperforms the baseline factor graph model (FGM [19]) by 6.3%. Comparing with *mean-pooling* methods [13], the improvements are 1.1%–3.3%, which demonstrate that including more temporal dynamic information is beneficial. Comparing with the current sequential modeling state-of-the-arts, temporal attention (TA) [14] and S2VT [15], our proposed method performs slightly better (30.2% *vs.* 29.0–29.8%). Some qualitative results are shown in Fig. 3(a).

MSVD dataset is more focused on describing static human-object interactions and scenes, such as "someone is doing something in somewhere". Comparing temporal-based methods (the proposed, TA [14] and S2VT [15]) and static-based methods (mean-pooling [13]), there are improvements but limited.

Table 2. METEOR scores on the MSVD dataset.

Method	METEOR (%)
FGM [19]	23.9
AlexNet [13]	26.9
VGG [13]	27.7
AlexNet-COCO [13]	29.1
GoogleNet [14]	28.7
GoogleNet + TA [14]	29.0
GoogleNet + 3D-CNN + TA [14]	29.6
AlexNet(Flow) + S2VT [15]	24.3
AlexNet + S2VT [15]	27.9
VGG + S2VT [15]	29.2
VGG + AlexNet(Flow) + S2VT [15]	29.8
Proposed	**30.2**

MPII and MVAD datasets. To further comparative evaluate our proposed method with the state-of-the-arts on more temporal-focused datasets, two movie-based datasets (MVAD and MPII) are employed for comparison. The proposed framework and other state-of-the-arts are compared in Table 3. Despite the scores

on each of the MPII and MVAD datasets, we also report the overall scores
(weighed by the sizes of testing set). Our result (7.06) outperforms Visual-Labels
(6.55) and VGG (6.31) by 0.51 and 0.75, respectively. It is beneficial to explicitly
model the temporal dynamics of the input videos.

Compared to the previous state-of-the-art sequence-to-sequence model
(S2VT [15]), our framework outperforms by 0.25. The experimental results
demonstrate that our framework can avoid feature entanglement so that it can
better model the temporal structures of videos.

Table 3. METEOR scores (%) on the Movie Description datasets, higher is better.

Method	MPII [34]	MVAD [35]	Overall
SMT [34]	5.6	–	–
Visual-Labels [39]	7.0	6.3	6.55
VGG [13]	6.7	6.1	6.31
Temporal Attention [14]	–	4.3	–
S2VT [15]	7.1	6.7	6.81
Proposed	7.0	7.1	**7.06**

5.3 ASL-TEXT

Since there is no other result available on our ASL-TEXT dataset, we evaluate
the proposed framework on this new dataset comparing among different network
configurations. There are two aspects to be investigated in this comparative
evaluation. Firstly, since our fusion layer can assign different dimensions to each
feature channel, the impact of assigning different portions to RGB and MHI will
be discussed. Secondly, the impact of RNN sizes for both feature encoders and
language decoders will be discussed. $20,527$ training samples and $2,000$ testing
samples from ASL-TEXT are used and the METEOR scores of different configurations are shown in Table 4. In Table 4, $(RGB)\%$ denotes the parameter of how
much percent of the encoding feature dimensions is assigned to RGB channel;
(RNN_{ENC}, RNN_{DEC}) denotes the RNN sizes for encoder and decoder. There
are two observations can be made from Table 4: (1) for each row, the METEOR
score increases as the RNN sizes increases but after an optimal size setting, the
performance starts to decrease. (2) Assigning different dimensions to different
feature channels has little impact on the performance. Observation 1 shows that
the ASL-TEXT dataset is more complex than other datasets because even moderate RNN sizes such as $(512, 512)$ is sufficient to over-fitting. Observation 2
demonstrates that our framework can automatically learn an optimal combination of multiple feature channels. Therefore there is no need to manually tune
the weight of different feature channels.

Table 4. METEOR scores on the ASL-TEXT dataset of different configurations.

		\multicolumn{5}{c}{(RNN_{ENC}, RNN_{DEC})}				
		(128,128)	(256,128)	(256,256)	(512,256)	(512,512)
(RGB)%	10%	3.9	**4.7**	4.3	4.2	3.6
	30%	4.1	3.8	**4.7**	3.5	3.9
	50%	3.7	**4.7**	3.5	3.9	3.9
	90%	3.7	3.7	3.5	**4.5**	4.0

Fig. 3. Qualitative results of the proposed video captioning framework on four datasets: (a) MSVD, (b) MPII, (c) MVAD and (d) ASL-TEXT. The bold sentence under each pair of images is the predicted caption and for ASL-TEXT the ground-truth text is also attached.

Some qualitative results of the proposed framework have been shown in Fig. 3. For simple scenes and interactive actions in Fig. 3(a), our system can accurately generate descriptive sentences. For more complex scenarios as in movies (Fig. 3(b) and (c)), our system can predict well on the main actions (such as "sit", "eat" and "enter") but make errors in objects. For ASL recognition, it is promising to observe that the system has the potential to build relationships between key words (such as "love", "medicare", "WH-sign" and "single/married") and videos. The results demonstrate that exploring temporal structures and combining multiple feature channels are potentially beneficial for video captioning even in complex visual content and sentence structures.

6   Conclusion

In this paper, we have proposed a novel video captioning framework based on a two-stage encoder-decoder system. The encoding part is composed of a multi-channel LSTM-based RNNs which can capture the temporal dynamics in video clips by allowing arbitrary-length input sequences. The decoding part is a LSTM-based language model which can decode the input video feature vector to a sequence of English words. A fusion layer is inserted between the encoder and decoder to automatically learn the optimized combination of multiple channels. To capture spatial-temporal information in the videos, we apply 3D convolutional neural networks pre-trained for action recognition (C3D) to extract features from both MHIs and raw RGB video frames. The whole network can be trained end-to-end using back-propagation. The proposed model is extensively evaluated on three public video description datasets comparing with the state-of-the-art methods and outperforms their performances. Furthermore, we collect an ASL recognition dataset and propose to apply video description framework in the area of automatic ASL recognition.

Acknowledgment. This work was supported in part by NSF grants EFRI-1137172, IIP-1343402, and IIS-1400802.

References

1. Deng, J., Dong, W., Socher, R., Li, L.J., Li, K., Fei-Fei, L.: Imagenet: a large-scale hierarchical image database. In: CVPR, pp. 248–255. IEEE (2009)
2. Sermanet, P., Eigen, D., Zhang, X., Mathieu, M., Fergus, R., LeCun, Y.: Overfeat: integrated recognition, localization and detection using convolutional networks. arXiv preprint arXiv:1312.6229 (2013)
3. Farabet, C., Couprie, C., Najman, L., LeCun, Y.: Learning hierarchical features for scene labeling. IEEE PAMI **35**(8), 1915–1929 (2013)
4. Girshick, R., Donahue, J., Darrell, T., Malik, J.: Rich feature hierarchies for accurate object detection and semantic segmentation. In: CVPR, pp. 580–587 (2014)
5. Le, Q.V., Zou, W.Y., Yeung, S.Y., Ng, A.Y.: Learning hierarchical invariant spatio-temporal features for action recognition with independent subspace analysis. In: CVPR, pp. 3361–3368. IEEE (2011)
6. Tran, D., Bourdev, L., Fergus, R., Torresani, L., Paluri, M.: Learning spatiotemporal features with 3d convolutional networks. In: ICCV, pp. 4489–4497 (2015)
7. Yao, B.Z., Yang, X., Lin, L., Lee, M.W., Zhu, S.C.: I2t: Image parsing to text description. Proc. IEEE **98**(8), 1485–1508 (2010)
8. Chen, X., Fang, H., Lin, T.Y., Vedantam, R., Gupta, S., Dollar, P., Zitnick, C.L.: Microsoft coco captions: data collection and evaluation server. arXiv preprint arXiv:1504.00325 (2015)
9. Mao, J., Xu, W., Yang, Y., Wang, J., Yuille, A.L.: Explain images with multimodal recurrent neural networks. arXiv preprint arXiv:1410.1090 (2014)
10. Karpathy, A., Fei-Fei, L.: Deep visual-semantic alignments for generating image descriptions. arXiv preprint arXiv:1412.2306 (2014)
11. Vinyals, O., Toshev, A., Bengio, S., Erhan, D.: Show and tell: a neural image caption generator. arXiv preprint arXiv:1411.4555 (2014)
12. Chen, X., Zitnick, C.L.: Learning a recurrent visual representation for image caption generation. arXiv preprint arXiv:1411.5654 (2014)
13. Venugopalan, S., Xu, H., Donahue, J., Rohrbach, M., Mooney, R., Saenko, K.: Translating videos to natural language using deep recurrent neural networks. In: NAACL-HLT (2015)

14. Yao, L., Torabi, A., Cho, K., Ballas, N., Pal, C., Larochelle, H., Courville, A.: Describing videos by exploiting temporal structure. In: ICCV, pp. 4507–4515 (2015)
15. Venugopalan, S., Rohrbach, M., Donahue, J., Mooney, R., Darrell, T., Saenko, K.: Sequence to sequence - video to text. In: ICCV (2015)
16. Aradhye, H., Toderici, G., Yagnik, J.: Video2text: learning to annotate video content. In: ICDM Workshop on Internet Multimedia Mining (2009)
17. Guadarrama, S., Krishnamoorthy, N., Malkarnenkar, G., Venugopalan, S., Mooney, R., Darrell, T., Saenko, K.: Youtube2text: recognizing and describing arbitrary activities using semantic hierarchies and zero-shot recognition. In: ICCV, pp. 2712–2719. IEEE (2013)
18. Krishnamoorthy, N., Malkarnenkar, G., Mooney, R., Saenko, K., Guadarrama, S.: Generating natural-language video descriptions using text-mined knowledge. In: NAACL HLT 2013, p. 10 (2013)
19. Thomason, J., Venugopalan, S., Guadarrama, S., Saenko, K., Mooney, R.: Integrating language and vision to generate natural language descriptions of videos in the wild. In: COLING (2014)
20. Morsillo, N., Mann, G., Pal, C.: YouTube scale, large vocabulary video annotation. In: Schonfeld, D., Shan, C., Tao, D., Wang, L. (eds.) Video Search and Mining. SCI, vol. 287, pp. 357–386. Springer, Heidelberg (2010). doi:10.1007/978-3-642-12900-1_14
21. Huang, H., Lu, Y., Zhang, F., Sun, S.: A multi-modal clustering method for web videos. In: Yuan, Y., Wu, X., Lu, Y. (eds.) ISCTCS 2012. CCIS, vol. 320, pp. 163–169. Springer, Heidelberg (2013). doi:10.1007/978-3-642-35795-4_21
22. Wei, S., Zhao, Y., Zhu, Z., Liu, N.: Multimodal fusion for video search reranking. IEEE Trans. Knowl. Data Eng. 22(8), 1191–1199 (2010)
23. Xu, K., Ba, J., Kiros, R., Courville, A., Salakhutdinov, R., Zemel, R., Bengio, Y.: Show, attend and tell: neural image caption generation with visual attention. arXiv preprint arXiv:1502.03044 (2015)
24. Karchmer, M.A., Bachleda, B., Mitchell, R.E., Young, T.A.: How many people use asl in the united states? why estimates need updating. Sign Lang. Stud. 6(3), 306–335 (2006)
25. Vogler, C., Metaxas, D.: Parallel hidden markov models for american sign language recognition. In: ICCV, vol. 1, pp. 116–122. IEEE (1999)
26. Starner, T., Pentland, A.: Real-time american sign language recognition from video using hidden markov models. In: Motion-Based Recognition, pp. 227–243. Springer (1997)
27. Metaxas, D.N., Liu, B., Yang, F., Yang, P., Michael, N., Neidle, C.: Recognition of nonmanual markers in american sign language (asl) using non-parametric adaptive 2d–3d face tracking. In: LREC, pp. 2414–2420. Citeseer (2012)
28. Liu, J., Liu, B., Zhang, S., Yang, F., Yang, P., Metaxas, D.N., Neidle, C.: Recognizing eyebrow and periodic head gestures using crfs for non-manual grammatical marker detection in asl. In: FGR, pp. 1–6. IEEE (2013)
29. Pugeault, N., Bowden, R.: Spelling it out: Real-time asl fingerspelling recognition. In: ICCV Workshops, pp. 1114–1119. IEEE (2011)
30. Fok, K.Y., Ganganath, N., Cheng, C.T., Tse, C.K.: A real-time asl recognition system using leap motion sensors. In: CyberC, pp. 411–414. IEEE (2015)
31. Bahdanau, D., Cho, K., Bengio, Y.: Neural machine translation by jointly learning to align and translate. arXiv preprint arXiv:1409.0473 (2014)
32. Bengio, Y., Simard, P., Frasconi, P.: Learning long-term dependencies with gradient descent is difficult. IEEE Trans. Neural Netw. 5(2), 157–166 (1994)

33. Simonyan, K., Zisserman, A.: Very deep convolutional networks for large-scale image recognition. CoRR abs/1409.1556 (2014)
34. Rohrbach, A., Rohrbach, M., Tandon, N., Schiele, B.: A dataset for movie description. In: CVPR (2015)
35. Torabi, A., Pal, C., Larochelle, H., Courville, A.: Using descriptive video services to create a large data source for video annotation research. arXiv preprint arXiv:1503.01070 (2015)
36. Denkowski, M., Lavie, A.: Meteor universal: language specific translation evaluation for any target language. In: Proceedings of the EACL 2014 Workshop on Statistical Machine Translation, vol. 6 (2014)
37. Papineni, K., Roukos, S., Ward, T., Zhu, W.J.: Bleu: a method for automatic evaluation of machine translation. In: Proceedings of the 40th Annual Meeting on Association for Computational Linguistics, pp. 311–318. Association for Computational Linguistics (2002)
38. Collobert, R., Kavukcuoglu, K., Farabet, C.: Torch7: a matlab-like environment for machine learning. In: BigLearn, NIPS Workshop. Number EPFL-CONF-192376 (2011)
39. Rohrbach, A., Rohrbach, M., Schiele, B.: The long-short story of movie description. In: Gall, J., Gehler, P., Leibe, B. (eds.) GCPR 2015. LNCS, vol. 9358, pp. 209–221. Springer, Heidelberg (2015). doi:10.1007/978-3-319-24947-6_17

Validation of Automated Mobility Assessment Using a Single 3D Sensor

Jiun-Yu Kao[✉], Minh Nguyen, Luciano Nocera, Cyrus Shahabi,
Antonio Ortega, Carolee Winstein, Ibrahim Sorkhoh, Yu-chen Chung,
Yi-an Chen, and Helen Bacon

University of Southern California, Los Angeles, CA, USA
jiunyuka@usc.edu

Abstract. Reliable mobility assessment is essential to diagnose or optimize treatment in persons affected by mobility disorders, e.g., for musculo-skeletal disorders. In this work, we present a system that is able to automatically assess mobility using a single 3D sensor. We validate the system ability to assess mobility and predict the medication state of Parkinson's disease patients while using a relatively small number of motion tasks. One key component of our system is a graph-based feature extraction technique that can capture the dynamic coordination between parts of the body while providing results that are easier to interpret than those obtained with other data-driven approaches. We further discuss the system and the study design, highlighting aspects that provide insights for developing mobility assessment applications in other contexts.

Keywords: Mobility assessment · 3D Sensor · Parkinson's disease · Human performance · Classification

1 Introduction

Observation of a person's movements performing certain tasks is widely used in many contexts, such as early diagnosis and treatment of various diseases, sports and military applications. Example applications include estimating the risk of falls in elderly patients, adjusting medication levels for those being treated for musculo-skeletal disorders or evaluating movement for rehabilitation. It is common practice for physicians to assess mobility, e.g., gait and balance, by direct observation of patients performing standardized tasks. In rare cases highly specialized equipment providing kinematic measurements is used. Clearly, cost as well as personnel/equipment availability make it impossible to provide this kind of assessment more broadly. Thus, while in some situations it would be desirable to assess mobility frequently, and to do so at a patient's home, this is not possible in practice.

Several factors motivate our work aimed at developing an automated mobility assessment systems based on depth sensors. The increased availability of low cost

© Springer International Publishing Switzerland 2016
G. Hua and H. Jégou (Eds.): ECCV 2016 Workshops, Part II, LNCS 9914, pp. 162–177, 2016.
DOI: 10.1007/978-3-319-48881-3_12

wearable sensors and other body sensing technologies provides the opportunity to unobtrusively and continuously sense and assess human mobility. Moreover, harnessing mobility analytics can lead to the development of a broad range of applications. For example, wearable sensors that summarize activity in the field from measurements from various sensors (e.g., acceleration, gyroscope) have already been utilized in various applications [26], 3D sensors (e.g., Microsoft Kinect) have the potential to complement wearable sensor measurements at home or in the clinic providing detailed insights about motion characteristics, while having the advantage of being unobtrusive. In this work, we validate an automated mobility assessment system and provide study design insights in a specific context and highlight design aspects that can be generalized to other applications. For this, we focus on musculo-skeletal disorders as a case study in part because of the existence of abundant literature related to these disorders. Furthermore, there is potential for very significant impact for these automated systems, since common clinical practice already involves mobility assessment protocols carried out on simple activities.

A reliable monitoring system to evaluate musculo-skeletal disorders, e.g., Parkinson's Disease (PD), can be beneficial to both patients and clinicians as the population of patients with these types of disorders is increasing. One example of such a system is introduced in [9] with the $POCM^2$ system, where a single 3D sensor, e.g., Microsoft Kinect, is used to enable frequent mobility assessments from the home. In this work we present a systems to automatically assess mobility. For this, we show that novel preprocessing, feature extraction and classifier selection is required. We present results that demonstrate the effectiveness of the proposed system to predict the medication state of persons with PD. Our proposed system is evaluated based on a real data set collected using MS Kinect camera from a group of subjects with PD.

Gait in persons with PD is characterized by Bradykinesia, instability, episodes of freezing and increased variability, and may be mitigated through medication. Optimized medication and rehabilitation plans require reliable and frequent mobility assessments. In current practice, trained physicians assess the mobility of persons with PD during visits at the clinic by visually observing patients as they perform standardized tasks. In addition to requiring patients to perform these tasks in the controlled environment of the clinic, current practice is limited due to the lack of quantifiable measurements. Current clinical scales, e.g., the Unified Parkinson's Disease Rating Scale (UPDRS), also lack resolution and rely on visual observation.

Our hypothesis is that differences in performance under different medication conditions in subjects with PD can be distinguished from the skeleton data (i.e., joint positions over time) produced by the Kinect sensor. We consider the two medication states in persons with PD, *ON* condition corresponding to a medicated state and *OFF* condition corresponding to a non-medicated state. The *OFF* condition effectively simulates a state in which the medication is no longer effective and mobility may be affected. We further analyze which skeleton data features support classifying the medication state using various machine learning approaches. With our experiments, we focus on *subject-dependent classification* as we are interested in predicting the medication state of specific individuals, however, we provide a comparison with subject-independent classification to show how these results generalize. We further report on performance for different classifiers to determine what approach is most suited for these data.

Results presented are based on a study carried out on 14 PD patients that perform a dual-task walking action, i.e., walking in a figure-of-eight pattern while counting backward, for which the Kinect sensor seems to be the most reliable. The cognitive task further challenges participants, therefore we expect the cognitive task to accentuate the difference between conditions. Previous work [9,25] shows that some gait parameters, e.g., stepping time and step size, are significantly different between PD and non-PD subjects. This paper addresses the more challenging task of distinguishing between different medication levels. We show that more appropriate features (e.g., proposed graph-based features) and system design (e.g., proper normalization and combination of classifiers) are necessary in order to capture the fine movement differences between conditions.

To our knowledge this is the first study to use Kinect skeleton data to discriminate the medication state of persons with PD. Our results show the potential for Kinect type sensors to be used to quantify mobility performance in persons with PD and possibly other mobility related disabilities. The main contributions of this work are: (1) We develop and validate a method to automatically assess mobility using a single 3D sensor that can discriminate the medication state of PD subjects, (2) We propose a novel graph-based feature extraction technique to reveal the dynamic coordination between parts of the body that compared with purely data-driven techniques provide comparable classification performance but is significantly easier to interpret, and (3) We provide study design insights on the proposed system and discuss how they can inform achieve mobility assessment in other contexts.

The remainder of the paper is organized as follows. Section 2 presents a brief review of related work. Section 3 proposes the general methodology and the insight into key factors for deploying a successful automated mobility assessment system. Section 4 describes the features (including the proposed graph-based features) and classification algorithms implemented. Section 5 presents the experimental setup and methods, and experimental results. Finally Sect. 6 concludes the paper and provides future directions.

2   Related Work

New depth sensing technologies [1] capable of providing accurate and reliable measurements of human motion, have prompted researchers to explore how data from these devices can be used to recognize and quantify movement for a wide range of medical applications. One such device, primarily designed for gaming, is Microsoft Kinect, which infers depth information using a stereo sensor and projected structured infrared light. The resulting depth stream at a resolution of 320×240 can be utilized to fit a skeleton of 15 joints at each time frame and in real time [21]. Compared to other motion capture systems, e.g., optical-passive techniques using retro-reflective markers or optical-active LED markers that are tracked by infrared cameras such as the Vicon motion capture system, Kinect offers a passive and non-invasive alternative but at the cost of a lower accuracy [18,22]. Occlusions and self occlusions generate joint coordinate measurement errors that are not filtered out by Kinect as it appears that there is no mechanism to enforce strict rigidity constraints. Thus, developing skeleton features and defining tasks that are robust to noise becomes critical and challenging. In general, gesture recognition remains a difficult problem and for complex tasks the skeleton data is pre-processed so as to segment the movement into simpler repeated movements referred to as skeletal action units (SAU), e.g., in [25] a walking task is segmented into steps and it is shown that these steps can in turn be summarized, thereby reducing noise and providing a representative action unit.

Several previous studies have used Kinect data for action recognition. The approach proposed in [27] extracts the histogram of 3D joint positions in a spherical coordinate system originating at the hip joint. In [16], Sequence of the Most Informative Joints (SMIJ) is proposed by automatically selecting a few skeletal joints at each time stamp that are most informative with respect to the current action according to some interpretable parameters, such as the mean variance of joints angles or the angular velocity of joints. In [28], Yang and Tian develop a representation for actions based on the position differences between joints. They compute the position differences of all pair of joints in one frame, of each joint between two consecutive frames and of joints in any frame and corresponding joints in the initial frame, which captures both spatial and temporal information of the human actions. This study found that the Kinect was good at measuring timing of movements and spatial characteristics of gross movements.

Kinect has previously been used in applications related to PD, primarily as an intervention tool [5,17] where game-play supports motivation and a game score is used as a measure of performance. In [5] a game was developed to train dynamic postural control and the accuracy of Kinect to measure on the spot walking, stepping and reaching. A comparison of the Kinect system against a Vicon motion capture system is presented in [4].

Kinect has also been used to supplement inertial sensor data as part of a home monitoring system for detecting freezing of gait [23]. The $POCM^2$ system [9] used the raw Kinect skeleton data on pilot data to detect pauses and discriminate between a non-PD person and a person with PD using dimensionality reduction techniques. A similar comparison was reported by [14] using a Vicon system and showing a difference between PD patients and healthy controls at similar age both in angle changes and in spatiotemporal parameters of gait.

As the field of signal processing on graphs is emerging, graph-based approaches to represent the motion capture data have been carried out. In [10], spectral graph wavelet transform is applied to a spatial-temporal graph constructed based on the motion data, which provides an over-complete set of features. These features are shown to be good in terms of action recognition accuracy for three state-of-the-art datasets. In [8], graph Fourier transform is applied to a skeletal graph constructed according to the natural connections between human limbs and the generated basis shows the ability to exploit the correlations between body parts.

In this paper, we build on previous work (in particular [9,25]) to tackle the difficult problem of assessing fine changes in mobility induced by medication in PD patients.

3   System Design

In this section, we propose a general methodology for deploying an automated mobility assessment system based on cost-effective 3D sensors. We provide insights into key factors that can lead to the success or failure of the deployment of this type of systems. Key aspects of this methodology will be validated in our evaluation section based on experimental results from our case study.

Hardware and environment: One of the most important factor is the usage and limitation of the 3D sensors in use. Taking Microsoft Kinect sensor as example, its horizontal Field of View has a practical range of 1.2 to 3.5 m while its vertical Field of View has a practical range of 0.8 to 2.5 m. Therefore, when accounting for the environment to deploy the system and the tasks to be performed by the subjects, not to have subjects exceed these ranges is important and critical to the system robustness. For example, an outdoor open environment may not be suitable for deploying this system. Also, requesting the subjects to perform certain tasks such as climbing up stairs or running far away may lead to system failure, as the device Field of View could be exceeded. Furthermore, as the estimation for the 3D positions of skeletal joints with Kinect SDK have much larger estimation errors under certain situations, e.g., walking away from the sensor at the periphery of the Field of View or taking a turn, the environment and task should limit the occurrence of these situations.

Task: The tasks that the subjects are asked to perform should be properly chosen to satisfy the following criteria. First, activities that can fully exploit and examine the mobility of all parts of the body are preferable to those that place explicit constraints on certain parts of body. For example, a task requiring the subject to count silently while walking can be better than a walking task where the subject is required to hold a tray, as the latter activity has less potential to exploit the upper body mobility, while in the former the walking may be more "natural" as the subject has to focus on counting. Secondly, the level of difficulty in performing activities will affect the capability of discriminating subjects' states. An over-simplified task will make it easier for the subjects to control the mobility performance under different states/conditions, which would make it more difficult for the system to distinguish between states/conditions based on the assessed mobility. Finally, it is better to have each task performed repeatedly by each subject in order to improve the robustness of the assessment.

4 Feature Design and Classification

A preliminary statistical analysis on a partial dataset indicated that there were no significant differences between medication states in gait kinematics. Additionally, it appears that when participants performed the task in the OFF state, they took shorter steps and had increased hip flexion, the latter, likely due to increased trunk forward lean. These results prompted us to focus on *subject-dependent classification* and extend the features considered to include angular gait measurements (e.g., angles extracted from the skeleton joints and angular speed) and graph-based features.

Mobility data are often normalized when studied. For example in the context of action recognition [10, 29] proposes a normalization scheme, which is applied first to the captured skeleton data by estimating the expected lengths of skeleton limbs (connections) across subjects from the training data, and then adjusting the locations of joints to achieve the same lengths of limbs, with the limb direction vectors being preserved. We compare the effects of normalization on the subject-independent classification performance in Sect. 5.5.

We provide hereafter details about the features used for classification.

Gait Measurements. To measure the gait statistics, after segmenting the strides we extract a set of spatial-temporal parameters including *step lengths*, *stride time* and *stride width* as suggested in [13]. Since each stride consists two steps, i.e., a left step and a right step, For consistency and across-subjects analysis, we labeled steps based on the most/least affected side (as opposite to using left/right). Consequently, step feature are named as *most-affected-side step length* and *least-affected-side step length*.

Angular Statistics. We extract a set of angular parameters associated with each joint as features, inspired by the SMIJ method [16]. Angles corresponding to each joint at each time stamp are computed by evaluating the dot product of the vectors defined by the limb segments connecting that joint. Assuming the angle corresponding to the dot product is α, we have two possible choices for the joint angle: α and $2\pi - \alpha$. The actual value used is defined by taking into account the type of joint (e.g., elbow or knee) and the direction of motion. We consider 19 angles in total: one angle for elbow, knee, and neck joints and two angles for the hip and shoulder joints. To capture temporal variations we further consider the following five statistics: *average, standard deviation, min, max*, and *angular speed*. The resulting feature vector of angular statistics has a dimension of $19(angles) \cdot 5(statistics) = 95$.

Graph-based Features. In order to extract a set of features which can capture and evaluate more global properties in motions, e.g., the coordination between two body parts, we adopt and modify the graph-based method proposed by Kao et al. [8]. First, the human skeletal structure is modeled as a fixed undirected graph $G = (V, E)$ with the vertex set as $V = \{v_1, v_2, ..., v_{15}\}$ corresponding to the 15 joints detected and estimated by Kinect at each frame. The edge set E consists of the unweighted edges corresponding to the directly connected physical limbs of the human body. Specifically speaking, an edge (i, j) exists in G with its weight set to unity only if there exists a physical limb directly connecting the i-th and j-th joint. Given G decided, the adjacency matrix A and the degree matrix D of G can be computed as well as the normalized Laplacian matrix $\mathcal{L}$ with $\mathcal{L} = I - D^{-1/2}AD^{-1/2}$.

Furthermore, as a graph signal is a function $f : V \rightarrow \mathbb{R}$ that assigns a value to each vertex, which can be represented as a vector $\mathbf{f} \in \mathbb{R}^{|V|}$ lying on the graph, the coordinates of all the joints at each time frame in one SAU can be regarded as a graph signal lying on the above defined skeletal graph G. Specifically speaking, we calculate the difference of 3D position at each joint between two consecutive frames, i.e., $\mathbf{v}_{t,i} = \mathbf{p}_{t,i+1} - \mathbf{p}_{t,i} = [v_{x_i}^{(t)} v_{y_i}^{(t)} v_{z_i}^{(t)}]$, where $i \in \{1, \cdots, 15\}$ and $t \in \{1, \cdots, T-1\}$. By processing each axis of 3D space separately, a graph signal $\mathbf{f}_a^{(t)} \in \mathbb{R}^{15}$ lying on the previously defined G can be defined so that $\mathbf{f}_a^{(t)}(i) = \mathbf{v}_{t,i}(a)$ where $a = \{1, 2, 3\}$ indicating the coordinate axis of choice. According to [2,8], frequency analysis of a graph signal $\mathbf{f}_a^{(t)}(i)$ can be performed by applying the graph Fourier transform (GFT) as $\mathbf{F}_a^{(t)}(i) = U^T \mathbf{f}_a^{(t)}(i)$ where U comes from the eigendecomposition $\mathcal{L} = U \Lambda U^T$. For each frame t, repeating this for three coordinate axis, i.e., $a = \{1, 2, 3\}$, leads to $C^{(t)} = [\mathbf{F}_1^{(t)}, \mathbf{F}_2^{(t)}, \mathbf{F}_3^{(t)}] \in \mathbb{R}^{15 \times 3}$. We vectorize $C^{(t)}$ to a row vector $\mathbf{c}^{(t)}$ with dimension as 45 and concatenate $\mathbf{c}^{(t)}$ from $t = 1$ to $T - 1$, which leads to a matrix $\mathbf{C} \in \mathbb{R}^{(T-1) \times 45}$ with all the transform coefficients.

As illustrated in [8], the GFT basis can capture global motion properties. For example, as shown in Fig. 1, the second basis vector will be able to exploit the coordination between upper and lower body while the third basis vector can help capture and measure the degree of bilateral symmetry which is an important characteristic in walking movement.

Principal component analysis (PCA), whose variants are popular in representing spatial-temporal data such as motion capture data, is one special case of our proposed graph-based feature. Considering a fully connected graph with edge weights set according to the covariance in data, the resulted graph-based basis vectors are exactly the principal components in PCA method. However, constructing the graph without taking data into consideration, as proposed here, can lead to an easier interpretation of the results, as compared to PCA. Figure 1 shows a comparison of the structure of basis vectors obtained using our proposed graph-based features and PCA. We can observe that the component of data that is captured by each PCA basis vector is more difficult to interpret than the GFT basis vectors. For example, the third eigenvector of PCA includes an isolated vertex in the left leg and the component on the fourth eigenvector of PCA is hard to be interpreted as the coordination between upper and lower body. Furthermore, in the evaluation section, our proposed feature shows to be able to achieve comparable performance to PCA does. Finally, our proposed basis is not data-dependent while PCA highly depends on the training dataset. This lack of data-dependence makes it easier to compare results across different subjects, tasks, coordinate systems or datasets.

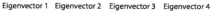

Eigenvector 1   Eigenvector 2   Eigenvector 3   Eigenvector 4

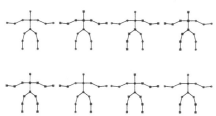

Fig. 1. 15 Kinect skeleton joints. Sign values of graph features basis vectors: blue $(+)$, red $(-)$. *Top:* the proposed graph-based features. Notice that zero-crossings between neighboring vertices increase as the eigenvector corresponds to higher eigenvalue (frequency). *Bottom:* PCA basis constructed with captured data of PD subjects on x-axis. (Color figure online)

To cope with different number of steps in each sequence and to represent the temporal dynamics of the frame-by-frame coefficients, we adopt the temporal pyramid pooling scheme similar to [6,12,24]. We define an average pooling function $\mathcal{F} : \mathbb{R}^{m \times n} \rightarrow \mathbb{R}^{1 \times n}$ such that $\mathbf{z} = \mathcal{F}(\mathbf{B})$ provides column-wise average to a matrix $\mathbf{B}$. Let K denote the maximum number of pyramid levels to be used. Then at level $k \leq K$, we compute the pooled coefficient vector as $\mathbf{z}_k = [\mathcal{F}(\mathbf{B}_1), \cdots, \mathcal{F}(\mathbf{B}_{2^{k-1}})]$, where $\{\mathbf{B}_i\}$ is a set of non-overlapping block matrices uniformly dividing the matrix $\mathbf{C}$ which contains all the transform coefficients as calculated previously. A final feature vector $\mathbf{d}$ is obtained as a concatenation of pooled coefficient vector at each level, i.e., $\mathbf{d} = [\mathbf{z}_1, \mathbf{z}_2, \cdots, \mathbf{z}_K]^T$, with the dimension as $45 \cdot (2^K - 1)$.

Classification Methods. Several classification algorithms were used to categorize the medication state. Extracted features where labeled (with ON and OFF) and used for training. We evaluate our system using Naive Bayes, SVM, k-NN, Decision Tree, and Random Forest classifiers with WEKA [7]. Combining classifiers improves performance as reported in [11,15,19]. We therefore report performance measurements for different combinations of classifiers. We use two ensemble methods: *Average of Probabilities* [3] and *Majority Voting* [20]. The Average of Probabilities fusion method returns the mean value of probabilities of multiple classifiers. The Majority Voting returns the class which gets the most votes among multiple classifiers. In the following Sect. 5, we provide details on the evaluation setup and results.

5   Experiments and Evaluation

5.1   Experimental Methodology

Fourteen adults with PD (9 men, disease duration 8.66 ± 7.48 years, Hoehn and Yahr stage I-III) took part in the pilot study[1]. They each visited a University

---

[1] The retrospective pilot study was approved by the University Institutional Review Board.

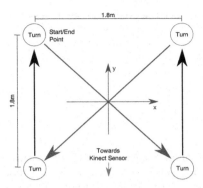

Fig. 2. Walking tasks trajectory used in the experiments. Arrows indicate direction or movement. Only segments shown in red were used to classify the medication state. (Color figure online)

laboratory 4 times. The first and last sessions consisted of qualitative interviews where 2–5 participants were interviewed in focus groups about their expectations and perceptions of the system. The remaining two sessions consisted of quantitative assessments (one each for ON and OFF medication state). Participants performed 7 standardized functional tasks: (1) walking, (2) walking whilst counting, (3) walking whilst carrying a tray, (4) walking around an obstacle, (5) sit-to-stand, (6) lifting a soda can and (7) lifting an object to a shelf. In this paper we focused our analysis on tasks (1) walking, (2) walking whilst counting tasks, and (3) walking whilst carrying a tray. We focused our attention on the walking-based tasks as we found skeleton data had a lower noise/signal ratio compared to other tasks. However, the walking whilst counting task was specifically singled-out because the added cognitive task is known to create an additional challenge in person with PD that we expect to accentuate differences between ON and OFF conditions.

Accelerometer, camcorder video and Kinect where recorded for all tasks, however in this work we consider only Kinect sensor data. Figure 2, shows the trajectories followed for walking-based tasks for which participants walked 5 times in a figure-of-eight pattern and repeated this at least twice.

5.2 Preprocessing and Methods

At each timestamp, we consider a subset of 15 joints (head, neck, torso, shoulders, elbows, hands, hips, knees and feet) in addition to the self-reported most affected side. As shown in the Fig. 2, we exclude segments of the trajectory corresponding to turns and where the sensor did not have a good viewing angle as Kinect skeleton data corresponding to those portions of the trajectory are noticeably noisier. Note that the direction of the trajectory was chosen so that the segments used faced the sensor, to match Kinect's skeleton reconstruction assumption.

Walking sequences were automatically segmented similar to [25] into Skeletal Action Units (SAU) each consisting of two steps and subsequently used to derive linear and angular kinematic measurements. We also limited extracted angles maximum extents to what is bio-mechanically possible (Kinect does not constraint skeleton joins).

We extracted a total of 1521 SAUs. The total number of ON-labeled SAUs is 759 while the total number of OFF-labeled SAUs is 762. These numbers translate to an average of 109 SAUs per subject and 54 SAUs for each condition, ensuring a balanced dataset. Depending on the experiment, feature vectors for each SAU are generated based on the gait, angle and graph features extracted as described in Sect. 4. For the graph-based features (Sect. 4), the maximum number of pyramid levels is set to 3, i.e. $K = 3$. As customary, we further l_2-normalize the feature vector for robustness.

Evaluation results were obtained for Naive Bayes, SVM, k-NN, Decision Tree, and Random Forest primarily for subject-dependent classification. Results for across-subjects classification are also presented to allow comparing both approaches performance.

A 3-fold method is used for training and testing. In the subject-dependent approach, each subject's set of SAUs is uniformly randomly separated into 3 non-intersecting folds; then, two folds are used for the training model and the remaining fold is used to test the trained classifier. In the subject-independent approach, all SAUs of all subjects are combined and then, separated into 3 folds. The 3-fold method steps are used in a similar way for the subject-dependent approach. We also provide the evaluation of combination of multiple classifiers. The performance metrics we report include accuracy, precision, recall and F-measure.

5.3   Feature Performance

The system performance is evaluated based on the walking whilst counting task data and using an SVM classifier trained with separate feature vectors for gait, angle, graph, and for a combination of all of the above. We also include PCA-based feature as a comparison to the proposed graph-based feature. The PCA-based feature is acquired from the training set and followed by exactly the same pyramid pooling scheme as graph-based feature is, which leads to the same dimension of feature vectors for both graph-based method and PCA.

Table 1 provides a summary of results. Our result shows that the combination of three proposed features sets achieve the highest performance metrics. Table 1 shows that the combination of sets in SVM performs the best with 84.79 % of accurate rate, 85.43 % of precision and 83.38 % of recall. When only one type of feature is used the graph-based feature set outperforms the other two choices in terms of all four metrics. Besides, when doing evaluation, we notice that the worst-case accuracy with graph-based features (69.63 %) also highly outperforms the worst-case accuracy with gait (39.53 %) or angular features (53.58 %), which shows that graph-based features are more robust in terms of exploiting the difference in motions between ON and OFF states. The possible reasons include:

Table 1. SVM performance for various features. Accuracy is reported with the format as average accuracy (best accuracy/worst accuracy) across 14 subjects. A: Accuracy, P: Precision, R: Recall and F-M: F-measure. ALL: Gait, Angle, and Graph.

FEATURE	A (%)	P (%)	R (%)	F-M
GAIT	63.58 (88.71/39.53)	57.26	55.40	0.51
ANGLE	75.30 (92.22/53.58)	75.01	74.20	0.74
GRAPH	82.41 (95.68/69.63)	83.04	81.93	0.82
ALL	84.79 (93.95/71.23)	85.43	83.38	0.84
PCA	84.66 (95.32/71.99)	85.30	84.44	0.85

Table 2. Performance of single classifier and multiple classifiers combination. A: Accuracy, P: Precision, R: Recall, F-M: F-measure, AP: Average of Probabilities, MV: Majority Voting, S: SVM, k: k-NN, D: Decision Tree, R: Random Forest.

CLASSIFIER/COMBINATION	A (%)	P (%)	R (%)	F-M
SVM	84.79	85.43	83.38	0.84
RANDOM FOREST	83.09	83.68	83.09	0.83
k-NN	79.24	80.16	79.24	0.79
DECISION TREE	72.66	72.92	72.66	0.73
NAIVE BAYES	71.02	71.64	71.02	0.70
SkR (AP)	87.41	87.61	87.40	0.87
Sk (AP)	87.28	87.49	87.29	0.87
SkR (MV)	85.62	85.79	85.61	0.86
DSk (AP)	85.37	85.61	85.37	0.85
DSk (MV)	85.29	85.51	85.30	0.85

(1) its better ability to capture the characteristics in global coordination among body parts during a motion, and (2) its ability to capture the temporal dynamics/evolution of the frame-based features.

Furthermore, results of PCA-based and graph-based features are comparable. As detailed in Sect. 4, the Graph-based features provide number of advantages including the interpretability of the body coordination, robustness to the noise and selection of the dataset, and comparability between different schemes.

5.4 Classifier Performance

To test the performance for different classifiers we consider the walking whilst counting dataset, a combination of Gait, Angle and Graph features (as we showed it provides the best performance in Sect. 5.3) and the subject-dependent approach. We report performance metrics for Naive Bayes, Decision Tree, k-NN, Random Forest and SVM. Table 2 provides the average performance metrics. According to Table 2, SVM performs the best with 84.79 % of accuracy, 85.43 %

Table 3. Effect of normalization on subject-independent performance. A: Accuracy, P: Precision, R: Recall, F-M: F-measure.

NORMALIZATION	A (%)	P (%)	R (%)	F-M
WITH	72.91	72.32	72.32	0.72
WITHOUT	70.87	71.03	71.03	0.71

of precision, and 83.38 % of recall while Naive Bayes gives the lowest performance rate with 71.02 % - accuracy, 71.64 % - precision, and 71.02 % - recall. Both Random Forest and SVM achieve high accuracy (more than 83 %). We also tested using combination of classifiers with two fusion methods: Average of Probabilities and Majority Voting. Table 2 also presents the performance metrics of five best combinations of classifiers. Comparing to the best of the single classifier, i.e., SVM (Table 2, 84.79 % of accuracy), these results show that combining multiple classifiers can outperform single classifier. The best performance rate is 87.41 % of accuracy (2.62 % better than single SVM), 87.61 % of precision, 87.40 % of recall with combination of SVM, k-NN, and Random Forest using Average of Probabilities fusion method. Overall, the best five combinations have more than 85.00 % of accuracy. It can also be seen that the best five correspond to the combination of the best performing single classifiers: SVM, k-NN, Decision Tree and Random Forest.

5.5   System Performance

We report the system performance using the subject-independent approach. Set-up is similar to the experiments of Sect. 5.4. To assess the effects of normalization we compare results obtained when normalization is applied as suggested in [29] and without normalization using the SVM classifier with graph-based features. Results presented in Table 3 show that normalization does not provide a significant improvement. This counter-intuitive result may be explained by the fact that the effects of PD are highly person-dependent and not correlated to body size.

Table 4 shows the result of classification of five classifiers in this approach: Naive Bayes, Decision Tree, SVM, Random Forest, and k-NN using the combination of feature sets. The accuracy ranges from 60.09 % to 76.86 % while precision is from 60.50 % to 77.10 % and recall ranges from 60.10 % to 76.90 %. k-NN achieves the highest rate (76.86 % of accuracy, 77.10 % of precision, 76.90 % of recall, and 0.77 of F-measure) and Naive Bayes gives the worst value in performance comparing to other classifiers (60.09 % of accuracy, 60.50 % of precision, 60.10 % of recall, and 0.60 of F-measure). Both Random Forest and k-NN has more than 75 % of accuracy.

Possible reasons for the lower performance of subject-independent results include the fact that our model only includes information of most/least affected side. The inclusion of other demographic factors such as age, gender,

Table 4. Subject-independent performance of single classifiers. A: Accuracy, P: Precision, R: Recall, F-M: F-measure.

CLASSIFIER	A (%)	P (%)	R (%)	F-M
NAIVE BAYES	60.09	60.50	60.10	0.60
DECISION TREE	62.98	63.00	63.00	0.63
SVM	67.13	67.10	67.10	0.67
RANDOM FOREST	75.67	75.90	75.70	0.76
K-NN	76.86	77.10	76.90	0.77

Table 5. Subject-independent combination performance. A: Accuracy, P: Precision, R: Recall, F-M: F-measure, AP: Average of Probabilities, MV: Majority Voting, S: SVM, k: k-NN, D: Decision Tree, R: Random Forest.

COMBINATION	A (%)	P (%)	R (%)	F-M
RK (AP)	77.32	77.50	77.30	0.77
SkR (MV)	76.92	77.00	76.90	0.77
RK (MV)	76.59	76.70	76.60	0.77

condition, how long medicated, affected limbs, etc. might improve subject-independent results.

We then test our system using fusion methods, similar to Sect. 5.4. The best three combinations of classifiers' performance metrics are reported in Table 5. Comparing to the best performed single classifier (k-NN with 76.86 % of accuracy), the three combinations reported has comparable result. The best accuracy rate is 77.32 %, which is around 0.5 % higher than that of single classifier, is from combination of Random Forest, and k-NN. It can be seen that the subject-independent approach does not work well in both single classifier and combination of multiple classifiers because each subject has different mobility traits (i.e., most affected side), and differences in mobility for both conditions.

5.6 Impact of Task Difficulty

To evaluate the impact of task difficulty on classification results we compare performance on three tasks: walking whilst counting, walking with holding a tray, and walking only using the same procedures, data size and features than what was used in Sect. 5.3. As summarized in Table 6 we find that the average accuracy of the walking only task is 81.04 %, slightly lower than for the other two dual tasks. Also, the worst accuracy across all subjects is much worse (48.99 %) for the walking only task, compared to 71.23 % with walking whilst counting task. This seems to corroborate the fact that dual tasks add cognitive load and increased coordination that accentuates the motion disabilities between conditions. Furthermore, we can observe that the average accuracy of the walking whilst holding a tray is comparable to that of walking whilst counting, however

Table 6. Performance results for three walking tasks. Accuracy is reported with the format as average accuracy (best accuracy/worst accuracy) across subjects. A, P, R and F-M denote respectively Accuracy, Precision, Recall and F-measure.

Task	A (%)	P (%)	R (%)	F-M
Count	84.79 (93.95/71.23)	85.43	83.38	0.84
Tray	82.04 (94.44/53.63)	82.19	90.00	0.85
Walk	81.04 (96.05/48.99)	81.63	87.75	0.83

the worst accuracy across the subjects is much worse for walking whilst holding a tray. A possible explanation might be that the system is unable to capture changes in mobility between conditions in subjects for which the impairment of movement is mostly affecting the upper-body.

These results show that the task can significantly affect the system performance. Best performance seem to be achieved for tasks: (1) that do not constrain movement, and (2) that are sufficiently challenging.

6   Conclusion and Future Work

Mobility assessment is critical for several applications including rehabilitation, physical therapy, optimizing treatment, or performance in sport and military applications.

In this work, we propose a methodology to develop an automated mobility assessment systems based on motion data captured with a single cost-effective 3D sensor (i.e., Microsoft Kinect). We propose using three types of features that we show are capable to capture fine movement changes. In particular the proposed graph-based features can capture dynamic coordination between the different parts of the body.

We demonstrate the system with a pilot study involving 14 adults with PD (9 men, disease duration 8.66 ± 7.48 years, Hoehn and Yahr stage I-III). Our results support the feasibility of using a Microsoft Kinect to recognize the medication state of persons with PD using a relatively small number of movements in the case of a dual-task, i.e., walking whilst counting. More specifically, we show that for a combination including gait, angle and graph-based features, it is possible to achieve subject-dependent classification performance rates of 87.41 % of accuracy, 87.61 % of precision and 87.40 % of recall with a combination of SVM, k-NN, and Random Forest using and Average of Probabilities fusion method. It appears that among the features proposed, the graph-based features are more robust in terms of exploiting the difference in motions between medication states. Results obtained for subject-independent classification appear significantly worse. We also evaluate how different features, classifiers, approaches and tasks impact the system performance and discuss insights into the key performance factors and failure modes of the proposed system.

Future work will include extending the pilot study to a larger number of subjects to prove the statistical significance of specific features in discriminating between medical states and investigating methods that allow for a more fine grained mobility assessment. Furthermore, extending these results to the new Kinect One system can lead to significant improvements. Complementing the Kinect sensor with data from other wearable sensors could also lead to a boost in performance. Finally, extending the system to be capable of automatically measuring the degree of mobility impairment and deciding the most suitable tasks for subjects to perform can also be beneficial to clinical work.

References

1. Chen, L., Wei, H., Ferryman, J.: A survey of human motion analysis using depth imagery. Pattern Recogn. Lett. **34**(15), 1995–2006 (2013)
2. Shuman, D.I., Narang, S.K., Frossard, P., Ortega, A., Vandergheynst, P.: The emerging field of signal processing on graphs: extending high-dimensional data analysis to networks and other irregular domains. IEEE Sig. Process. Mag. **30**(3), 83–98 (2013)
3. Duin, R.P.W., Tax, D.M.J.: Experiments with classifier combining rules. In: Kittler, J., Roli, F. (eds.) MCS 2000. LNCS, vol. 1857, pp. 16–29. Springer, Heidelberg (2000). doi:10.1007/3-540-45014-9_2
4. Galna, B., Barry, G., Jackson, D., Mhiripiri, D., Olivier, P., Rochester, L.: Accuracy of the microsoft kinect sensor for measuring movement in people with parkinson's disease. Gait Posture **39**(4), 1062–1068 (2014)
5. Galna, B., Jackson, D., Schofield, G., McNaney, R., Webster, M., Barry, G., Mhiripiri, D., Balaam, M., Olivier, P., Rochester, L.: Retraining function in people with parkinson disease using the microsoft kinect: game design and pilot testing. J. Neuroeng. Rehabil. **11**(1), 60 (2014)
6. Gowayyed, M.A., Torki, M., Hussein, M.E., El-Saban, M.: Histogram of oriented displacements (hod): describing trajectories of human joints for action recognition. In: Proceedings of the Twenty-Third International Joint Conference on Artificial Intelligence, pp. 1351–1357 (2013)
7. Hall, M., Frank, E., Holmes, G., Pfahringer, B., Reutemann, P., Witten, I.H.: The weka data mining software: an update. ACM SIGKDD Explor. Newsl. **11**(1), 10–18 (2009)
8. Kao, J.Y., Ortega, A., Narayanan, S.: Graph-based approach for motion capture data representation and analysis. In: 2014 IEEE International Conference on Image Processing (ICIP), pp. 2061–2065, October 2014
9. Kashani, F.B., Medioni, G., Nguyen, K., Nocera, L., Shahabi, C., Wang, R., Blanco, C.E., Chen, Y.A., Chung, Y.C., Fisher, B., et al.: Monitoring mobility disorders at home using 3d visual sensors and mobile sensors. In: Proceedings of the 4th Conference on Wireless Health, p. 9. ACM (2013)
10. Kerola, T., Inoue, N., Shinoda, K.: Spectral graph skeletons for 3D action recognition. In: Cremers, D., Reid, I., Saito, H., Yang, M.-H. (eds.) ACCV 2014. LNCS, vol. 9006, pp. 417–432. Springer, Heidelberg (2015)
11. Kittler, J., Hatef, M., Duin, R.P., Matas, J.: On combining classifiers. IEEE Trans. Pattern Anal. Mach. Intell. **20**(3), 226–239 (1998)
12. Luo, J., Wang, W., Qi, H.: Group sparsity and geometry constrained dictionary learning for action recognition from depth maps. In: 2013 IEEE International Conference on Computer Vision (ICCV), pp. 1809–1816 (2013)

13. McNeely, M.E., Duncan, R.P., Earhart, G.M.: Medication improves balance and complex gait performance in parkinson disease. Gait Posture **36**(1), 144–148 (2012)
14. Mirek, E., Rudzińska, M., Szczudlik, A.: The assessment of gait disorders in patients with parkinson's disease using the three-dimensional motion analysis system vicon. Neurologia i neurochirurgia polska **41**(2), 128–133 (2006)
15. Nguyen, M., Fan, L., Shahabi, C.: Activity recognition using wrist-worn sensors for human performance evaluation. In: The Sixth Workshop on Biological Data Mining and its Applications in Healthcare (2015)
16. Ofli, F., Chaudhry, R., Kurillo, G., Vidal, R., Bajcsy, R.: Sequence of the most informative joints (smij): a new representation for human skeletal action recognition. J. Vis. Commun. Image Represent. **25**(1), 24–38 (2014)
17. Palacios-Navarro, G., García-Magariño, I., Ramos-Lorente, P.: A kinect-based system for lower limb rehabilitation in parkinson's disease patients: a pilot study. J. Med. Syst. **39**(9), 1–10 (2015)
18. Pfister, A., West, A.M., Bronner, S., Noah, J.A.: Comparative abilities of microsoft kinect and vicon 3d motion capture for gait analysis. J. Med. Eng. Technol. **38**(5), 274–280 (2014)
19. Rokach, L.: Ensemble-based classifiers. Artif. Intell. Rev. **33**(1–2), 1–39 (2010)
20. Ruta, D., Gabrys, B.: Classifier selection for majority voting. Inf. Fusion **6**(1), 63–81 (2005)
21. Shotton, J., Sharp, T., Kipman, A., Fitzgibbon, A., Finocchio, M., Blake, A., Cook, M., Moore, R.: Real-time human pose recognition in parts from single depth images. Commun. ACM **56**(1), 116–124 (2013)
22. Stone, E., Skubic, M.: Evaluation of an inexpensive depth camera for in-home gait assessment. J. Ambient Intell. Smart Env. **3**(4), 349–361 (2011)
23. Takač, B., Català, A., Martín, D.R., Van Der Aa, N., Chen, W., Rauterberg, M.: Position and orientation tracking in a ubiquitous monitoring system for parkinson disease patients with freezing of gait symptom. JMIR mHealth and uHealth **1**(2), e14 (2013)
24. Wang, J., Liu, Z., Wu, Y., Yuan, J.: Mining actionlet ensemble for action recognition with depth cameras. In: 2012 IEEE Conference on Computer Vision and Pattern Recognition (CVPR), pp. 1290–1297 (2012)
25. Wang, R., Medioni, G., Winstein, C.J., Blanco, C.: Home monitoring musculoskeletal disorders with a single 3d sensor. In: 2013 IEEE Conference on Computer Vision and Pattern Recognition Workshops (CVPRW), pp. 521–528. IEEE (2013)
26. Weiss, A., Sharifi, S., Plotnik, M., van Vugt, J.P., Giladi, N., Hausdorff, J.M.: Toward automated, at-home assessment of mobility among patients with parkinson disease, using a body-worn accelerometer. Neurorehabilitation Neural Repair **25**(9), 810–818 (2011)
27. Xia, L., Chen, C.C., Aggarwal, J.: View invariant human action recognition using histograms of 3d joints. In: 2012 IEEE Computer Society Conference on Computer Vision and Pattern Recognition Workshops (CVPRW), pp. 20–27. IEEE (2012)
28. Yang, X., Tian, Y.: Eigenjoints-based action recognition using naive-bayes-nearest-neighbor. In: 2012 IEEE Computer Society Conference on Computer Vision and Pattern Recognition Workshops (CVPRW), pp. 14–19. IEEE (2012)
29. Zanfir, M., Leordeanu, M., Sminchisescu, C.: The moving pose: an efficient 3d kinematics descriptor for low-latency action recognition and detection. In: 2013 IEEE International Conference on Computer Vision (ICCV), pp. 2752–2759, December 2013

Deep Eye-CU (DECU): Summarization of Patient Motion in the ICU

Carlos Torres[1](✉), Jeffrey C. Fried[2](✉), Kenneth Rose[1], and B.S. Manjunath[1]

[1] University of California Santa Barbara, Santa Barbara, USA
{carlostorres,rose,manj}@ece.ucsb.edu
[2] Santa Barbara Cottage Hospital, Santa Barbara, USA
jfried@sbch.org

Abstract. Healthcare professionals speculate about the effects of poses and pose manipulation in healthcare. Anecdotal observations indicate that patient poses and motion affect recovery. Motion analysis using human observers puts strain on already taxed healthcare workforce requiring staff to record motion. Automated algorithms and systems are unable to monitor patients in hospital environments without disrupting patients or the existing standards of care. This work introduces the DECU framework, which tackles the problem of autonomous unobtrusive monitoring of patient motion in an Intensive Care Unit (ICU). DECU combines multimodal emissions from Hidden Markov Models (HMMs), key frame extraction from multiple sources, and deep features from multimodal multiview data to monitor patient motion. Performance is evaluated in ideal and non-ideal scenarios at two motion resolutions in both a mock-up and a real ICU.

1 Introduction

The recovery rates of patients admitted to the ICU with similar conditions vary vastly and often inexplicably. ICU patients are continuously monitored; however, patient mobility is not currently recorded and may be a major factor in recovery variability. Clinical observations suggest that adequate patient positioning and controlled motion increase patient recovery, while inadequate poses and uncontrolled motion can aggravate wounds and injuries. Healthcare applications of motion analysis include quantification (rate/range) to aid the analysis and prevention of decubitus ulcers (bed sores) and summarization of pose sequences over extended periods of time to evaluate sleep without intrusive equipment.

Objective motion analysis is needed to produce clinical evidence and to quantify the effects of patient positioning and motion on health. This evidence has the potential to become the basis for the development of new medical therapies and the evaluation of existing therapies that leverage patient pose and motion manipulation. The framework introduced in this study enables the automated collection and analysis of patient motion in healthcare environments. The monitoring system and the analysis algorithm are designed, trained, and tested in a mock-up ICU and tested in a real ICU. Figure 1 shows the major elements of the

© Springer International Publishing Switzerland 2016
G. Hua and H. Jégou (Eds.): ECCV 2016 Workshops, Part II, LNCS 9914, pp. 178–194, 2016.
DOI: 10.1007/978-3-319-48881-3_13

framework (stages A–H). Stage A (top right) contains the references. Stage B (bottom left) shows frames from a sample sequence recorded using multimodal (RGB and Depth) multiview (three cameras) sources. At stage C, the framework selects the summarization resolution and activates the key frame identification stage (if needed). Stage D contains the motion thresholds (dense optic-flow estimated at training) to distinguish between the motion types and account for depth sensor noise. Deep features are extracted at stage E. Stage F shows the key frame computation, which compresses motion and encodes motion segments (encoding of duration of poses and transitions). Stage G shows the multimodal multiview Hidden Markov Model trellis under two scene conditions. Finally, stage H shows the results: pose history and pose transition summarizations.

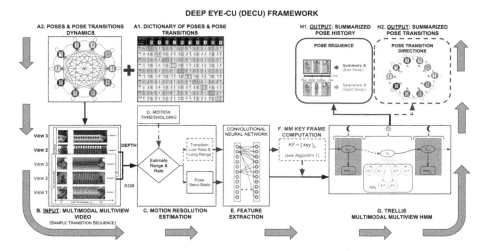

Fig. 1. Diagram explaining the DECU framework, which uses Hidden Markov Modeling and multimodal multiview (MM) data. Stage A provides the references; (A1) a dictionary of poses and pose transitions, and (A2) the illustrative motion dynamics between two poses. Stage B shows the multimodal multiview input video. Stage C selects the summarization resolution and activates key frame identification when required. Stage D integrates the motion thresholds (estimated at training) to account for various levels of motion resolution and sensor noise. Stage F shows the key frame identification process using Algorithm 1. Stage G shows the multimodal multiview HMM trellis, which encodes illumination and occlusion variations. Stage H shows the two possible summarization outputs (H1) pose history and (H2) pose transitions.

Background. Clinical studies covering sleep analysis indicate that sleep hygiene directly impacts healthcare. In addition, quality of sleep and effective patient rest are correlated to shorter hospital stays, increased recovery rates, and decreased mortality rates. Clinical applications that correlate body pose and movement to medical conditions include sleep apnea – where the obstructions of the airway are affected by supine positions [1]. Pregnant women are recommended to sleep on their sides to improve fetal blood flow [2]. The findings of [3–5] correlate sleep positions with quality of sleep and its various effects on patient health. Decubitus ulcers (bed sores) appear on bony areas of the body and are caused by continuous decubitus positions[1]. Although nefarious, bed sores can be prevented by manipulating patient poses over time. Standards of care require that patients be rotated every two hours. However, this protocol has very low compliance and in the U.S., ICU patients have a probability of developing DUs of up to 80 % [6]. There is little understanding about the set of poses and pose durations that cause or prevent DU incidence. Studies that analyze pose durations, rotation frequency, rotation range, and the duration of weight/pressure off-loading are required, as are the non-obtrusive measuring tools to collect and analyze the relevant data. Additional studies analyze pose manipulation effects on treatment of severe acute respiratory failure such as: ARDS (Adult Respiratory Distress Syndrome), pneumonia, and hemodynamics in patients with various forms of shock. These examples highlight the importance of DECU's autonomous patient monitoring and summarization tasks. They accentuate the need and challenges faced by the framework, which must be capable of adapting to hospital environments and supporting existing infrastructure and standards of care.

Related Work. There is a large body of research that focuses on recognizing and tracking human motion. The latest developments in deep features and convolutional neural network architectures achieve impressive performance; however, these require large amounts of data [7–10]. These methods tackle the recognition of actions performed at the center of the camera plane, except for [11], which uses static cameras to analyze actions. Method [11] allows actions to not be centered on the plane; however, it requires scenes with good illumination and no occlusions. At its current stage of development the DECU framework cannot collect the large number of samples necessary to train a deep network without disrupting the hospital.

Multi-sensor and multi-camera systems and methods have been applied to smart environments [12,13]. The systems require alterations to existing infrastructure making their deployment in a hospital logistically impossible. The methods are not designed to account for illumination variations and occlusions and do not account for non-sequential, subtle motion. Therefore, these systems and methods cannot be used to analyze patient motion in a real ICU where patients have limited or constrained mobility and the scenes have random occlusions and unpredictable levels of illumination.

Healthcare applications of pose monitoring include the detection and classification of sleep poses in controlled environments [14]. Static pose classification in a range of simulated healthcare environments is addressed in [15], where the authors use modality trust and RGB, Depth, and Pressure data. In [16], the authors introduce a coupled-constrained optimization technique that allows them to remove the pressure sensor and increase pose classification performance. However, neither method analyzes poses over time or pose transition dynamics.

---

[1] Online Medical Dictionary.

A pose detection and tracking system for rehabilitation is proposed in [17]. The system is developed and tested in ideal scenarios and cannot be used to detect constrained motion. In [18] a controlled study focuses on work flow analysis by observing surgeons in a mock-up operating room. A single depth camera and Radio Frequency Identification Devices (RFIDs) are used in [19] to analyze work flows in a Neo-Natal ICU (NICU) environment. These studies focus on staff actions and disregard patient motion. Literature search indicates that the DECU framework is the first of its kind. It studies patient motion in a mock-up and a real ICU environment. DECU's technical innovation is motivated by the shortcomings of previous studies. It observes the environment from multiple views and modalities, integrates temporal information, and accounts for challenging natural scenes and subtle patient movements using principled statistics.

Proposed Approach. DECU is a new framework to monitor patient motion in ICU environments at two motion resolutions. Its elements include time-series analysis algorithms and a multimodal multiview data collection system. The algorithms analyze poses at two motion resolutions (sequence of poses and pose transition directions). The system is capable of collecting and representing poses from multiview multimodal data. The views and modalities are shown in Fig. 2(a) and (b). A sample motion summary is shown in Fig. 2(c). Patients in the ICU are often bed-ridden or immobilized. Overall, their motion can be unpredictable, heavily constrained, slow and subtle, or aided by caretakers. DECU uses key frames to extract motion cues and temporal motion segments to encode pose and transition durations. The set of poses used to train and test the framework are selected from [15]. DECU uses HMMs to model the time-series multimodal multiview information. The emission probabilities encode view and modality information and the changes in scene conditions are encoded as states. The two resolutions address different medical needs. Pose history summarization is the coarser resolution. It provides a pictorial representation of poses over time (i.e., the history). The applications of the pose history include prevention and analysis of decubitus ulcerations (bed sores) and analysis of sleep-pose effects on quality of sleep. The pose transition summarization is the finer resolution. It looks at the pseudo/transition poses that occur while a patient transitions between two clearly defined sleep poses. Physical therapy evaluation is one application of transition summarization. The pose and transition sets are shown in Fig. 1(A1).

Main Contributions

1. An adaptive framework called DECU that can effectively record and analyze patient motion at various motion resolutions. The algorithms and system detect patient behavior/state and healthy normal motion to summarize the sequence of patient sleep poses and motion between two poses.
2. A system that collects multimodal and multiview video data in healthcare environments. The system is non-disruptive and non-obtrusive. It is robust to natural scenes conditions such as variable illumination and partial occlusions.

3. An algorithm that effectively compresses sleep pose transitions using subset of the most informative and most discriminative frames (i.e., key frames). The algorithm incorporates information from all views and modalities.
4. A fusion technique that incorporates the observations from the multiple modalities and views into emission probabilities to leverage complementary information and estimate intermediate poses and pose transitions over time.

2   System Description

The DECU system is modular and adaptive. It is composed of three nodes and each node has three modalities (RGB, Depth, and Mask). At the heart of each node is a Raspberry Pi3 running Linux Ubuntu, which controls a Carmine RGB-D cameras[2]. The units are synchronized using TCP/IP communication. DECU combines information from multiple views and modalities to overcome scene occlusions and illumination changes.

Multiple Modalities (Multimodal). Multimodal studies use complementary modalities to classify static sleep poses in natural ICU scenes with large variations in illumination and occlusions. DECU uses these findings from [15,16] to justify using multiple views and modalities.

Multiple Views (Multiview). The studies from [16,20] show that analyzing actions from multiple views and multiple orientations greatly improves detection and provides algorithmic view and orientation independence.

Time Analysis (Hidden Semi-Markov Models). ICU patients are often immobilized or recovering. They move subtly and slowly (very different from the walking or running motion). DECU effectively monitors subtle and abrupt patient motion by breaking the motion cues into temporal segments.

3   Data Collection

Pose data is collected in a mock-up ICU with 10 actors and tested in medical ICU with two real patients (two days worth of data). The diagram in Fig. 2(b) shows the top-view of the rigged mock-up ICU room and the camera views. In the mock-up ICU, actors are asked follow the same test sequence of poses. The sequence is set at random using a random number generator. Figure 2(c) shows a sequence of 20 observations, which include ten poses (p_1 to p_{10}) and ten transitions (t_1 to t_{10}) with random transition direction.

All actors in the mock-up ICU are asked to assume and hold each of the poses while data is being recorded from multiple modalities and views. A total of 28 sessions are recorded: 14 under ideal conditions (BC: bright and clear) and 14 under challenging conditions (DO: dark and occluded).

---

[2] Primesense, manufacturer of Carmine sensors, was acquired by Apple Inc. in 2013; however, similar devices can be purchased from structure.io.

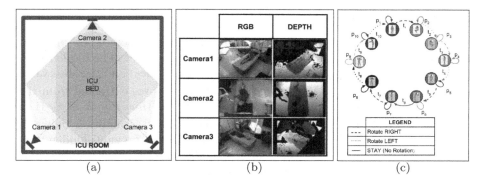

Fig. 2. The transition data is collected in a mock-up ICU and a real ICU: (a) shows the relative position of the cameras with respect to the ICU room and ICU bed; (b) shows a set of randomly selected poses and pose transitions, which are represented by lines (dashed, dotted, and solid lines defined in the legend box); (c) shows the complete set of possible sleep-pose pair combinations.

Pose Data. The actors follow the sequence poses and transitions shown in Stage A from Fig. 1. Each initial pose has 10 possible final poses (inclusive) and each final pose can be arrived to by rotating left or right. The combination of pose pairs and transition directions generates a set of 20 sequences for each initial pose. There are 10 possible initial poses. A recording session of one actor generates 200 sequence pairs. Also, two patients sessions are recorded in the medical ICU for one day each (two-hour long video recordings).

Feature Selection. Previous findings indicate that engineered features such as geometric moments (gMOMs) and histograms of oriented gradients (HOG) are suitable for the classification of sleep poses. However, these features are limited in their ability to represent body configurations in dark and occluded scenarios. The latest developments in deep learning and feature extraction led this study to consider deep features extracted from the VGG [21] and the Inception [22] architectures. Experimental results (see Sect. 5) indicate that Inception features perform better than gMOMs, HOG, and VGG features. Parameters for gMOM and HOG extraction are obtained from [15]. Background subtraction and calibration procedures from [23] are applied prior to feature extraction.

4   Problem Description

Temporal patterns caused by sleep-pose transitions are simulated and analyzed using HSMMs as shown in Sects. 4.1 and 4.2. The interaction between the modalities to accurately represent a pose using different sensor measurements are encoded into the emission probabilities. Scene conditions are encoded into the set of states (i.e., the analysis of two scenes doubles the number of poses).

4.1 Hidden Markov Models (HMMs)

HMMs are a generative approach that models the various poses (pose history) and pseudo-poses (pose transitions summarization) as states. The hidden variable or state at time step k (i.e., $t = k$) is y_k (state$_k$ or pose$_k$) and the observable or measurable variables ($x_{k,m}^{(v)}$, the vector of image features extracted from the k-th frame, the m-th modality, and the v-th view) at time $t = k$ is x_k (i.e., $x_k = x_{k,m}^{(v)} = \{R_k, D_k, ...M_k\}$). The first order Markov assumption indicates that at time t, the hidden variable y_t, depends only on the previous hidden variable y_{t-1}. At time t the observable variable x_t depends on the hidden variable y_t. This information is used to compute the joint probability $P(Y, X)$ via:

$$P(Y_{1:T}, X_{1:T}) = P(y_1) \prod_{t=1}^{T} P(x_t|y_t) \prod_{t=2}^{T} P(y_t|y_{t-1}), \tag{1}$$

where $P(y_1)$ is the initial state probability distribution (π). It represents the probability of sequence starting ($t = 1$) at pose$_i$ (state$_i$). $P(x_t|y_t)$ is the observation or emission probability distribution (**B**) and represents the probability that at time t pose$_i$ (state$_i$) can generate the observable multimodal multiview vector x_t. Finally, $P(y_t|y_{t-1})$ is the transition probability distribution (**A**) and represents the probability of going from pose$_i$ to pose$_o$ (state$_i$ to state$_o$). The HMM has parameters $\mathbf{A} = \{a_{ij}\}$, $\mathbf{B} = \{\mu_{in}\}$, and $\pi = \{\pi_i\}$.

Initial State Probability Distribution (π). The initial pose probabilities are obtained from [4] and adjusted to simulate the two scenes considered in this study. The scene independent initial state probabilities π is shown in Table 1.

State Transition Probability Distribution (A). The transition probabilities are estimated using the transitions from one pose to the next one for Left (L) and Right (R) rotation direction as indicated in the results from Fig. 7.

Emission Probability Distribution (B). The scene information is encoded into the emission probabilities. This information server to model moving from one scene condition to the next shown in Fig. 3. The trellis shows two scenes, which doubles the number of hidden states. The alternating blue and red lines (or solid and dashed lines) indicate transitions from one scene to the next.

One limitation of HMMs is their lack of flexibility to model pose and transition (pseudo-poses) durations. Given an HMM in a known pose or pseudo-pose, the probability that it stays in there for d time slices is: $P_i(d) = (a_{ii})^{d-1}(1 - a_{ii})$, where $P_i(d)$ is the discrete probability density function (PDF) of duration d in pose i and a_{ii} is the self-transition probability of pose i [24].

Table 1. Initial transition probability for each of the 10 poses. Notice that poses facing Up have a higher probability than the poses that face Down, while Left and Right poses are equally probable. Please note that there is a category for poses not covered in this study identifiable by the label Other and the symbol p_{11}. Also, note that one pose can have two states based on the BC and DO scene conditions.

Initial State Probability: $\pi = \{\pi_i\}$						
Pose name	Acronym	Symbol	State - BC	Probability	State - DO	Probability
Soldier up	solU	p1	s_1	0.03	s_{11}	0.02
Fetal right	fetR	p2	s_2	0.145	s_{12}	0.07
Fetal left	fetL	p3	s_3	0.145	s_{13}	0.07
Log right	logR	p4	s_4	0.05	s_{14}	0.03
Soldier down	solD	p5	s_5	0.02	s_{15}	0.01
Yearner left	YeaL	p6	s_6	0.04	s_{16}	0.02
Log left	logL	p7	s_7	0.05	s_{17}	0.03
Faller down	falD	p8	s_8	0.05	s_{18}	0.02
Faller up	falU	p9	s_9	0.05	s_{19}	0.03
Yearner right	yeaR	p10	s_{10}	0.04	s_{20}	0.02
Other	other	p0	s_0	0.036	s_0	0.073

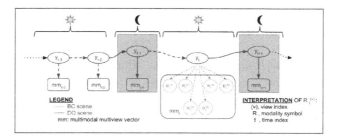

Fig. 3. Multimodal Multiview Hidden Markov Model (mmHMM) trellis. The variation in scene illumination between night and day are examples of scene changes. (Color figure online)

4.2   Hidden Semi-Markov Models (HSMMs)

HSMMs are derived from conventional HMMs to provide state duration flexibility. HSMMs represent hidden variables as segments, which have useful properties. Figure 4 shows the structure of the HSMM and its main components. The sequence of states $y_{1:T}$ is represented by the segments (S). A segment is a sequence of unique, sequentially repeated symbols. The segments contain information to identify when an observation is first detected and its duration based on the number of observed samples. The elements of the j-th segment (S_j) are the indexes (from the original sequence) where the observation (b_j) is detected, the number of sequential observations of the same symbol (d_j), and the state or pose (y_j). For example, the sequence $y_{1:8} = \{1, 1, 1, 2, 2, 1, 2, 2\}$ is represented by the set of segments $S_{1:U}$ with elements $S_{1:J} = \{S_1, S_2, S_3, S_4\} = \{(1,3,1),\ (4,2,2),\ (6,1,1),\ (7,2,2)\}$. The letter J is the total number of segments and the total number of state changes. The elements of the segment $S_1 = (1,3,1)$ are, from left to right: the index of the start of the segment (from the sequence: $y_{1:8}$); the number of times the state is observed; and the symbol.

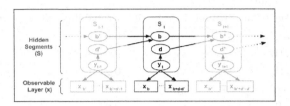

Fig. 4. HSMM diagram indicating the hidden segments S_j indexed by j and their elements $\{b_j, d_j, y_j\}$. The variable b is the first detection in a sequence, y is the hidden layer, (x) is the observable layer containing samples from time b to $b + d - d'$. The variables b and d are the observation's detection (time tick) and duration.

HSMM Elements. The hidden variables are the segments $S_{1:U}$, the observable variables are the features $X_{1:T}$, and the joint probability is given by:

$$P\big(S_{1:U}, X_{1:T}\big) = P\big(Y_{1:U}, b_{1:U}, d_{1:U}, X_{1:T}\big)$$

$$P\big(S_{1:U}, X_{1:T}\big) = P(y_1)P(b_1)P(d_1|y_1) \prod_{t=b_1}^{b_1+d_1+1} P(x_t|y_1) \times$$

$$\prod_{u=2}^{U} P(y_u|y_{u-1})P\big(b_u|b_{u-1}, d_{u-1}\big) \times P(d_u|y_u) \prod_{t=b_u}^{b_1+d_1+1} P(x_t|y_u),$$

$$(2)$$

where U is the sequence of segments such that $S_{1:U} = \{S_1, S_2, ..., S_U\}$ for $S_j = (b_j, d_j, y_j)$ and with b_j as the start position (a bookkeeping variable to track the starting point of a segment), d_j is the duration, and y_j is the hidden state ($\in \{1, ..., Q\}$). The range of time slices starting at b_j and ending at $b_j + d_j$ (exclusively) have state label y_j. All segments have a positive duration and completely cover the time-span $1 : T$ without overlap. Therefore, the constraints $b_1 = 1$, $\sum_{u=1}^{U}$ and $b_{j+1} = b_j + d_j$ hold.

The transition probability $P(y_u|y_{u-1})$, represents the probability of going from one segment to the next via:

$$\mathbf{A} : P\big(y_u = j|y_{t-u} = i\big) \equiv a_{ij} \qquad (3)$$

The first segment (b_u) always starts at 1 ($u = 1$). Consecutive points are calculated deterministically from the previous point via:

$$P\big(b_u = m|b_{u-1} = n, d_{u-1} = l\big) = \delta\big(m, n+l\big) \qquad (4)$$

where $\delta(i,j)$ is the Kroenecker delta function (1, for $i = j$ and 0, else). The duration probability is $P(d_u = l|y_u = i) = P_i(l)$, with $P_i(l) = \mathcal{N}(\mu, \sigma)$.

Parameter Learning. Learning is based on maximum likelihood estimation (mle). The training sequence of key frames is fully annotated, including the exact start and end frames for each segment $X_{1:T}, Y_{1:T}$. To find the parameters that maximize $P(Y_{1:T}, X_{1:T}|\theta)$, one maximes the likelihood parameters of each of the factors in the joint probability. The reader is referred to [25] for more details. In particular, the observation probability $P(x^n|y = i)$, is a Bernoulli distribution whose max likelihood is estimated via:

$$\mu_{n,i} = \frac{\sum_{t=1}^{T} x_t^i \delta(y_t, i)}{\sum_{t=1}^{T} \delta(y_t, i)}, \tag{5}$$

where T is the number of data points, $\delta(i,j)$ is the Kroenecker delta function, and $P(y_t = j|y_{t-1} = i)$ is the multinomial distribution with:

$$a_{ij} = \frac{\sum_{n=2}^{N} \delta(y_n, j) \delta(y_{n-1}, i)}{\sum_{n=2}^{N} \delta(y_{t-1}, j)} \tag{6}$$

4.3   Key Frame (KF) Selection

Data collected from pose transition is very large and often repetitive, since the motion is relatively slow and subtle. The pre-processing stage incorporates a key frame estimation step that integrates multimodal and multiview data. The algorithm used to select a set (KF) of K-transitory frames is shown in Fig. 5 and detailed in Algorithm 1. The size of the key frame set is determined experimentally ($K = 5$) on the feature scape using Inception vectors.

Let $\mathcal{X} = \{x_{m,n}^{(v)}\}_f$ be the set of training features extracted from V views and M modalities over N frames and let P_i and P_o represent the initial and final poses. The transition frames are indexed by n, $1 \leq n \leq |N|$. The views are indexed by v, $1 \leq v \leq |V|$ and the modalities are indexed by m, $1 \leq m \leq |\mathcal{M}|$. Algorithm 1 uses this information to identify key frames. Experimental evaluation of $|KF|$ is shown in Fig. 5. The idea behind key frames selection is to identify informative and discriminative frames using all views and modalities.

5   Experimental Results and Analysis

Static Pose Analysis - Feature Validation. Static sleep-pose analysis is used to compare the DECU method to previous studies. Couple-Constrained Least-Squares (cc-LS) and DECU are tested on the dataset from [16]. Combining the cc-LS method with deep features extracted from two common network architectures improved classification performance over the HOG and gMOM features in dark and occluded (DO) scenes by an average of eight percent with Inception and four percent with Vgg. Deep features matched the performance of cc-LS (with HOG and gMOM) in a bright and clear scenario as shown in Table 2.

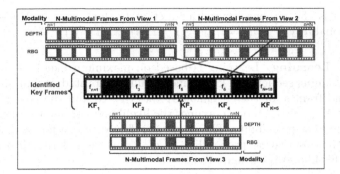

Fig. 5. Selection of transition key frames based on Algorithm 1. This figures shows how the algorithm is used to identify five key frames from three views and two modalities. The first two key frames are extracted from the RGB view 1 video. Subsequent key frames are selected from Depth view 2 and RGB view 3 videos.

Input: $\mathcal{X}$, set of mm features and dissimilarity threshold th;
Result: $KF = \{\text{Key Frames}\}_K$, $K \geq 1$
Initialize: $KF = \{\text{empty}\}_K$, $K \geq 1$ and $count = 0$;
Stage 1: Modality (m) and View (v) Selection;
for $1 < v < V$ *and* $1 < m < M$ **do**
$\quad | \quad D_m^{(v)} = \text{euclid}(x_{mn_i}^{(v)}, x_{mn_o}^{(v)})$, $n_i = 1, n_o = N$;
end
$\hat{v}, \hat{m} = \max D_m^{(v)} > th$;
$\{x_{\hat{m}n_1}^{(\hat{v})}, x_{\hat{m}n_N}^{(\hat{v})}\} \rightarrow FK$;
Stage 2: Find Complementary Frames to KF ;
for $1 < v < V$ *and* $1 < m < M$ *and* $1 < n < N$ **do**
$\quad | \quad D_1 = D_{m,n_1}^{(v)} = \text{euclid}(x_{mn_1}^{(v)}, x_{mn}^{(v)})$;
$\quad | \quad D_2 = D_{m,n_N}^{(v)} = \text{euclid}(x_{mn_N}^{(v)}, x_{mn}^{(v)})$;
end
Sort $D_1 = \{d_1 > d_2 > ... > d_{N-2}\}$ descending;
Sort $D_2 = \{d_1 > d_2 > ... > d_{N-2}\}$ descending;
$d_i \rightarrow KF$ if $\frac{d_i}{d_j} > th$, for $1 < i, j < N - 2$;
Stage 3: Find Center Frame (i.e., Motion Peak);
for KF_2 *and* KF_{K-1} **do**
$\quad | \quad$ Use Stage 2 to compute D_3 and D_4;
$\quad | \quad$ **if** $max(D_3, D_4) > 0)$ **then**
$\quad | \quad | \quad$ max $(D_3, D_4) \rightarrow KF$;
$\quad | \quad$ **end**
end

Algorithm 1. Multimodal multiview key frame selection using euclidean dissimilarity measure. The algorithm is applied at training with labeled frames to estimate the number and indexes of key frames across views and modalities.

Key Frame Performance. The size of the set of key frames that represent a pose transition affects DECU performance. DECU currently uses $|KF| = 5$ and a dissimilarity threshold $th \geq .8$ as shown in Fig. 6.

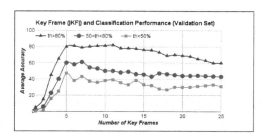

Fig. 6. Performance of the DECU framework for the fine motion summarization based on the number of key frames used to represent transitions and rotations between poses.

Table 2. Evaluation of deep features for sleep-pose recognition tasks using the cc-LS method from [16] in dark and occluded (DO) scenes using. The performance of HOG and gMOM is compared to the performance of the Vgg and Inception features.

Feature Suitability Evaluation with cc-LS [16]			
Scene	HOG + gMOM	Vgg	Inception
BC	100	100	100
DO	65	69 (+4)	73 (+8)

Table 3. Pose history summarization performance (percent accuracy) of the DECU framework in bright and clear (BC) and dark and occluded (DO) scenes. The sequences are composed of 10 poses with durations that range from 10 s to 1 min. The sampling rate is set to once per second.

DECU: Pose History Summarization	
Scene	Average Detection Rate
BC	85
DO	76

Summarization Performance in a Mock-Up ICU Room. The mock-up ICU allows staging the motion and scene condition variations. The sample test sequence is shown in Fig. 2(c).

Pose History Summarization. History summarization requires two parameters: sampling rate and pose duration. The experiments are executed with a sampling rate of one second and an pose duration of 10 s with a minimum average detection of 80 %. A pose is assigned a label if consistently detect 80 % of the time, else they are assigned the label "other". Poses not consistently detected are ignored. The system is tested in the mock-up setting using a randomly selected scene and sequence of poses that can range from two poses to ten poses. The pose durations are also randomly selected with one scene transition (from BC to DO

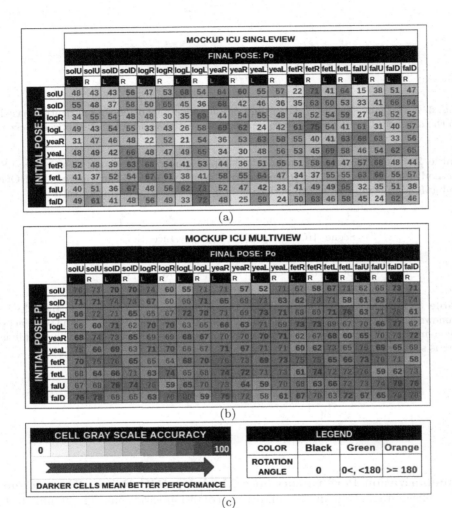

Fig. 7. Performance of DECU in the mock-up ICU under a dark and occluded conditions. Detection results are obtained using (a) single view and (b) multiview data. The cells are gray scaled to indicate detection accuracy. The color coded scale and the legend are shown in (c). Note that overall detection improves with longer rotation angles and worsens when rotations include facing the bed (cameras recording actor backs). (Color figure online)

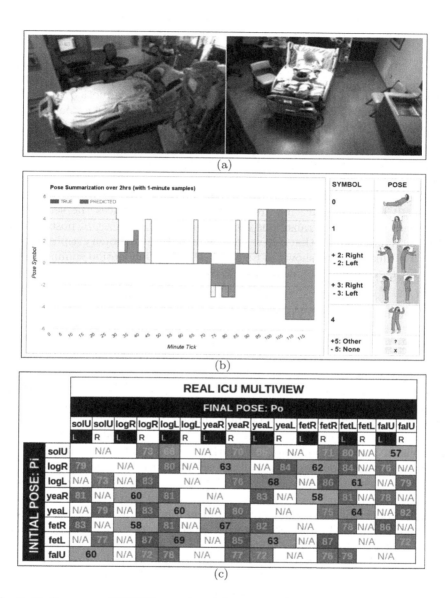

Fig. 8. Performance of DECU pose transition summarization in a real ICU shown in (a) using multimodal data under natural scene conditions. The set of patient poses is reduced and the summarization performance for a two hour session is shown in (b). The detection scores are shown in (c), where the cells are gray scaled to indicate detection accuracy. The font color indicates rotation angle range and N/A indicates the pose is not available (i.e., not possible). The grading color scale is shown in Fig. 7(c). (Color figure online)

or from DO to BC). A sample (long) sequence is shown in Fig. 2(c) and its history summarization performance is shown in Table 3.

Pose Transition Dynamics: Motion Direction. The analysis and pose transitions and rotation directions are important to physical therapy and recovery rate analysis. The performance of DECU summarizing fine motion to describe transitions between poses is shown in Fig. 7. Results for the DO scene with (a) singleview and (b) multiview data. The legend is shown in (c).

Summarization Performance in a Real ICU. The medical ICU environment is shown in Fig. 8(a) and (b). Note that it is logistically impossible to control ICU work flows and to account for unpredictable patient motion. For example, ICU patients are not free to rotate, which reduces the set of pose transitions (unavailable transitions are marked N/A). The set of poses for the history summary require that a new pose be included (pulmonary aspiration). A qualitative illustration is shown in Fig. 8(b). DECU's fine motion summarization results for two patients are shown in Fig. 8(c).

6   Conclusion and Future Work

This work introduced the DECU framework to analyze patient poses in natural healthcare environments at two motion resolutions. Extensive experiments and evaluation of the framework indicate that the detection and quantification of pose dynamics is possible. The DECU system and monitoring algorithms are currently being tested in real ICU environments. The performance results presented in this study support its potential applications and benefits to healthcare analytics. The system is non-disruptive and non-intrusive. It is robust to variations in illumination, view, orientation, and partial occlusions. DECU is non-obtrusive and non-intrusive but not without a cost. The cost is noticed in the most challenging scenario where a blanket and poor illumination block sensor measurements. The performance of DECU to monitor pose transitions in dark and occluded environments is far from perfect; however, most medical applications that analyze motion transitions, such as physical therapy sessions, are carried under less severe conditions.

Future studies will investigate the recognition and analysis of patient motion and interactions in natural hospital scenarios using recurrent neural networks and integrate natural language understating to log ICU actions and events.

Acknowledgements. This research is sponsored in part by the Army Research Laboratory under Cooperative Agreement Number W911NF-09-2-0053 (the ARL Network Science CTA). The views and conclusions contained in this document are those of the authors and should not be interpreted as representing the official policies, either expressed or implied, of the Army Research Laboratory or the U.S. Government. The U.S. Government is authorized to reproduce and distribute reprints for Government purposes notwithstanding any copyright notation here on. The authors thank

Dr. Richard Beswick (Director of Research), Paula Gallucci (Medical ICU Nurse Manager), Mark Mullenary (Director Biomedical-Engineering), and Dr. Leilani Price (IRB Administration) from Santa Barbara Cottage Hospital for their support.

References

1. Sahlin, C., Franklin, K.A., Stenlund, H., Lindberg, E.: Sleep in women: normal values for sleep stages and position and the effect of age, obesity, sleep apnea, smoking, alcohol and hypertension. Sleep Med. **10**, 1025–1030 (2009)
2. Morong, S., Hermsen, B., de Vries, N.: Sleep position and pregnancy. In: de Vries, N., Ravesloot, M., van Maanen, J.P. (eds.) Positional Therapy in Obstructive Sleep Apnea. Springer, Heidelberg (2015)
3. Bihari, S., McEvoy, R.D., Matheson, E., Kim, S., Woodman, R.J., Bersten, A.D.: Factors affecting sleep quality of patients in intensive care unit. J. Clin. Sleep Med. **8**(3), 301–307 (2012)
4. Idzikowski, C.: Sleep position gives personality clue. BBC News, 16 September 2003
5. Weinhouse, G.L., Schwab, R.J.: Sleep in the critically ill patient. Sleep-New York Then Westchester **10**(1), 6–15 (2006)
6. Soban, L., Hempel, S., Ewing, B., Miles, J.N., Rubenstein, L.V.: Preventing pressure ulcers in hospitals. Joint Comm. J. Qual. Patient Saf. **37**(6), 245–252 (2011)
7. Chéron, G., Laptev, I., Schmid, C.: P-cnn: pose-based cnn features for action recognition. In: Proceedings of the IEEE International Conference on Computer Vision, pp. 3218–3226 (2015)
8. Veeriah, V., Zhuang, N., Qi, G.J.: Differential recurrent neural networks for action recognition. In: Proceedings of the IEEE International Conference on Computer Vision, pp. 4041–4049 (2015)
9. Baccouche, M., Mamalet, F., Wolf, C., Garcia, C., Baskurt, A.: Sequential deep learning for human action recognition. In: Salah, A.A., Lepri, B. (eds.) HBU 2011. LNCS, vol. 7065, pp. 29–39. Springer, Heidelberg (2011)
10. Tran, D., Bourdev, L., Fergus, R., Torresani, L., Paluri, M.: Learning spatiotemporal features with 3d convolutional networks. In: 2015 IEEE International Conference on Computer Vision (ICCV), pp. 4489–4497. IEEE (2015)
11. Soran, B., Farhadi, A., Shapiro, L.: Generating notifications for missing actions: don't forget to turn the lights off! In: Proceedings of the IEEE International Conference on Computer Vision, pp. 4669–4677 (2015)
12. Hoque, E., Stankovic, J.: Aalo: activity recognition in smart homes using active learning in the presence of overlapped activities. In: 2012 6th International Conference on Pervasive Computing Technologies for Healthcare (PervasiveHealth) and Workshops, pp. 139–146. IEEE (2012)
13. Wu, C., Khalili, A.H., Aghajan, H.: Multiview activity recognition in smart homes with spatio-temporal features. In: Proceedings of the Fourth ACM/IEEE International Conference on Distributed Smart Cameras, pp. 142–149. ACM (2010)
14. Huang, W., Wai, A.A.P., Foo, S.F., Biswas, J., Hsia, C.C., Liou, K.: Multimodal sleeping posture classification. In: IEEE International Conference on Pattern Recognition (ICPR) (2010)
15. Torres, C., Hammond, S.D., Fried, J.C., Manjunath, B.S.: Multimodal pose recognition in an icu using multimodal data and environmental feedback. In: International Conference on Computer Vision Systems (ICVS). Springer (2015)

16. Torres, C., Fragoso, V., Hammond, S.D., Fried, J.C., Manjunath, B.S.: Eye-cu: sleep pose classification for healthcare using multimodal multiview data. In: Winter Conference on Applications of Computer Vision (WACV). IEEE (2016)

17. Obdržálek, S., Kurillo, G., Han, J., Abresch, T., Bajcsy, R., et al.: Real-time human pose detection and tracking for tele-rehabilitation in virtual reality. Stud. Health Technol. Inform. **173**, 320–324 (2012)

18. Padoy, N., Mateus, D., Weinland, D., Berger, M.O., Navab, N.: Workflow monitoring based on 3d motion features. In: 2009 IEEE 12th International Conference on Computer Vision Workshops (ICCV Workshops), pp. 585–592. IEEE (2009)

19. Lea, C., Facker, J., Hager, G., Taylor, R., Saria, S.: 3d sensing algorithms towards building an intelligent intensive care unit, vol. 2013, p. 136. American Medical Informatics Association (2013)

20. Ramagiri, S., Kavi, R., Kulathumani, V.: Real-time multi-view human action recognition using a wireless camera network. In: ACM/IEEE International Conference on Distributed Smart Cameras (ICDSC) (2011)

21. Simonyan, K., Zisserman, A.: Very deep convolutional networks for large-scale image recognition. arXiv preprint arXiv:1409.1556 (2014)

22. Szegedy, C., Liu, W., Jia, Y., Sermanet, P., Reed, S., Anguelov, D., Erhan, D., Vanhoucke, V., Rabinovich, A.: Going deeper with convolutions. In: Proceedings of the IEEE Conference on Computer Vision and Pattern Recognition, pp. 1–9 (2015)

23. Hartley, R.I., Zisserman, A.: Multiple View Geometry in Computer Vision, 2nd edn. Cambridge University Press, New York (2004)

24. Rabiner, L.R.: A tutorial on hidden markov models and selected applications in speech recognition. Proc. IEEE **77**(2), 257–286 (1989)

25. Van Kasteren, T., Englebienne, G., Kröse, B.J.: Activity recognition using semi-markov models on real world smart home datasets. J. Ambient Intell. Smart Env. **2**(3), 311–325 (2010)

Fall Detection Based on Depth-Data in Practice

Christopher Pramerdorfer[1(✉)], Rainer Planinc[1], Mark Van Loock[2],
David Fankhauser[1], Martin Kampel[1], and Michael Brandstötter[1]

[1] CogVis, Vienna, Austria
pramerdorfer@cogvis.at
[2] Toyota Motor Europe, Brussels, Belgium

Abstract. Falls are a leading cause of accidental deaths among the
elderly population. The aim of fall detection is to ensure quick help
for fall victims by automatically informing caretakers. We present a fall
detection method based on depth-data that is able to detect falls reliably
while having a low false alarm rate – not only under experimental conditions but also in practice. We emphasize person detection and tracking
and utilize features that are invariant with respect to the sensor position,
robust to partial occlusions, and computationally efficient. Our method
operates in real-time on inexpensive hardware and enables fall detection
systems that are unobtrusive, economic, and plug and play. We evaluate
our method on an extensive dataset and demonstrate its capability under
practical conditions in a long-term evaluation.

Keywords: Fall detection · Depth-data · Evaluation · Practice

1 Introduction

Falls are a major public health problem. Between 30 % and 60 % of US citizens
of age 65 or older suffer from falls each year, and 10 % to 20 % of these falls
result in serious injury, hospitalization, or death [1]. In fact, falls are the leading
cause of accidental death in this age group [2]. Immediate help and treatment of
fall-induced injuries is vital for minimizing morbidity and mortality rates [3,4].
However, statistically every other fall victim is unable to get back up without
help [2]. Falls are thus particularly dangerous to older persons that live alone.

To this end, there has been active research in the field of *fall detection*, with
the aim of detecting fall incidents and informing caretakers such as family members or ambulance personnel automatically [4]. One approach to fall detection
is to employ optical sensors and computer vision. For example, several methods
based on video cameras have been proposed [4]. However, camera images convey limited information in terms of scene geometry, reducing the robustness of
such methods. Moreover, cameras do not work in darkness, hence unobtrusive
fall detection during nighttime is not possible. Furthermore, camera-based fall
detection raises privacy concerns [5]. Active depth sensors do not have these
limitations. They work in darkness, measure distances from which scene geometry can be recovered, and are robust to illumination changes and shadows.
A well-known example is the Microsoft Kinect.

© Springer International Publishing Switzerland 2016
G. Hua and H. Jégou (Eds.): ECCV 2016 Workshops, Part II, LNCS 9914, pp. 195–208, 2016.
DOI: 10.1007/978-3-319-48881-3_14

Several fall detection methods using the Kinect sensor have been proposed, most of which utilize background subtraction [6] for person detection and height-based features for fall detection. For instance, [5,7,8] analyze the centroid height of persons, whereas [9] examine head heights. In [10] falls are detected based on the spine height and orientation. Many methods (e.g. [5,11,12]) also incorporate velocities, arguing that the vertical velocity of persons increases significantly during falls. Dubey et al. [13] follow a different approach, extracting HU features [14] from motion history images and using a SVM for classification. All these methods reportedly perform well on simulated falls, but none were evaluated extensively under real-world conditions.

These methods have limitations in practical use, in which falls must be detected regardless of fall speed and ending pose. Under these circumstances, velocity is not a reliable feature for fall detection. Falls may end in a sitting position, but it seems that only [10] take such falls into account. Furthermore, falls might be partially occluded or invisible due to the limited field of view, a challenge that is not addressed by many of these methods. Several methods (e.g. [5,8,9]) do not perform tracking nd thus do not support multiple moving objects.

Some of the discussed methods also lack in terms of practicability. Those presented in [7,13] seem to be too complex for real-time operation on inexpensive hardware such as ARM-based single-board computers, which we consider important to allow for a broad acceptance. The method presented in [9] is able to do so but requires a wearable device, which is intrusive. The features used in [9,13] are not invariant with respect to the sensor position, which restricts the sensor placement and thus complicates the system setup.

In this paper, we present a fall detection method that aims to address these shortcomings. Our method can detect slow and partially occluded falls as well as falls ending in a sitting position. We utilize the available distance information to recover the geometry of objects in an invariant and efficient way, which enables discriminative features for person and fall detection. Automatic calibration enables plug and play operation and flexibility in terms of sensor placement, facilitating the installation. In order to minimize the hardware costs for end users, our method was designed to be efficient enough to run on inexpensive hardware such as the Raspberry Pi 2 or the Odroid C1+. Our method supports various inexpensive off-the-shelf depth sensors including those based on PrimeSense technology (e.g. Kinect 1, Asus Xtion, Orbbec) and Kinect 2.

We evaluate the performance of our fall detection method using a comprehensive test dataset as well as a large publicly available dataset. Furthermore, we present results of a long-term study carried out under real-world conditions. The results show that our method is able to detect even challenging falls reliably while having a low false alarm rate in practice (around one false alarm per week).

This paper is organized as follows. Our fall detection method involves the steps (i) automatic calibration and scene analysis, (ii) motion detection, (iii) person detection and tracking, and (iv) fall detection, which are presented in Sects. 2, 3, 5, and 6, respectively. Experimental results are presented in Sect. 7, and conclusions are drawn in Sect. 8.

2   Automatic Calibration and Scene Analysis

Our fall detection method is flexible in terms of sensor placement in order to facilitate the system setup and support plug-and-play; the only requirement is that a part of the floor must be visible to the sensor. In order to achieve plug-and-play functionality, we perform automatic sensor calibration at system startup in order to estimate the sensor position and orientation. On this basis, we locate areas in which reliable fall detection is possible, and detect scene objects.

2.1   Automatic Calibration

The purpose of automatic calibration is to recover the sensor extrinsics (position and orientation). This is accomplished using ground floor detection. Our algorithm for this purpose is based on filtering using normal vectors followed by iterative RANSAC [15] plane fitting. We found this method to be more reliable than alternatives [16] in case of significant floor occlusions.

Floor detection is accomplished by first converting a depth map $\mathcal{D}$ from the sensor to an organized point cloud $\mathcal{C}$ in camera coordinates (organized means that the structure is preserved, so that $\mathcal{D}(u,v)$ and $\mathcal{C}(u,v)$ correspond). This allows us to estimate normals $\mathcal{N}$ efficiently,

$$\mathcal{N}(u,v) = -\mathbf{n}(u,v)/\|\mathbf{n}(u,v)\|_2$$
$$\mathbf{n}(u,v) = (\mathcal{C}(u+1,v) - \mathcal{C}(u,v)) \times (\mathcal{C}(u,v+1) - \mathcal{C}(u,v)). \tag{1}$$

We then discard all points whose normal vectors do not coincide with the sensor tilt, which is assumed to be between $0°$ and $60°$ downwards. This assumption is general enough to allow for flexible sensor positioning and enables us to discard points that cannot possibly represent the floor. This increases the robustness and efficiency of the subsequent floor detection step.

In order to detect the floor plane reliably in presence of furniture and clutter, we iteratively find the best-fit plane for the remaining points using RANSAC and remove all inliers. This procedure continues until the number of inliers decreases below a threshold. This generally leads to several detected planes. As the sensor is located at the origin of the camera coordinate system, the plane that corresponds to the floor is that with the largest distance to the origin.

The equation of this plane, (a,b,c,d) with $\|(a,b,c)\|_2 = 1$, is then used to recover the extrinsics; the sensor height is d and the orientation corresponds to the rotation that maps $(0,1,0)$ (the normal vector of the floor plane in world coordinates, assuming that the positive Y axis points upwards) to (a,b,c).

2.2   Scene Analysis

Once the extrinsics are estimated, we convert a depth map to a point cloud in world coordinates and detect scene objects via height-based point classification; a point is classified as part of an object if its height is between 30 cm and 90 cm, which includes beds, couches, and other resting accommodations. Object detection is carried out periodically in order to support scene changes at runtime.

Furthermore, we analyze the scene in order to determine which regions qualify for reliable fall detection. This is the case if both fallen and upright persons in a considered region would be in the field of view of the sensor.

The information obtained during scene analysis is utilized for person state prediction (Sect. 6.1), and for visual feedback on the sensor setup (Fig. 1).

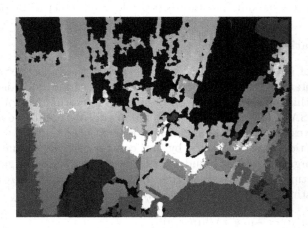

Fig. 1. Scene visualization after automatic calibration and scene analysis. The detected floor is shown in blue, scene objects are yellow, and regions in which reliable fall detection is impossible are shaded (e.g. left side of the image). (Color figure online)

3   Motion Detection

Falls are characterized by motion. For efficiency, we therefore consider only areas in which motion occurs. This is achieved by means of background subtraction, i.e. motion is detected by comparing image frames to a background model that represents the static parts of the scene [17]. Depth maps are well-suited for this purpose as they encode distances and are thus robust to clothing color and illumination changes [18]. On the other hand, this implies that background subtraction must be sensitive in order to reliably capture fallen persons, which are close to the background. To this end, we propose a distance-dependent noise model that ensures that fallen persons are detected reliably.

The noise model described in this section is optimized for PrimeSense sensors, but adaption to other sensors such as Kinect 2 is straightforward.

3.1   Noise Model and Pixel Classification

In [19] it was found that the random measurement errors of the Kinect increase quadratically with distance d, with an RMSE of $e_d \approx 1.425 \cdot 10^{-6} d^2$. We utilize this information to derive a distance-dependent noise model for background subtraction by approximating the noise of the sensor at object distance d as a normal distribution with $\mu = 0$ and $\sigma = e_d$. On this basis, we cast pixel classification as a novelty detection problem; a pixel with value v is classified as foreground if (i) v differs by more than $3e_m$ from the corresponding background model value m, and (ii) if $v - m$ is negative. The second condition encodes the fact that foreground objects must always appear in front of the background. This effectively suppresses ghosts (foreground areas due to background changes [17]).

In order to account for the fact that our noise model is an approximation, as well as increased sensor noise at object borders, we perform morphological erosion with a small structuring element after all pixels are classified.

Our distance-dependent noise model and pixel classification methods ensure a high sensitivity and thus that moving objects are captured reliably throughout the measuring range, while at the same time suppressing noise.

3.2 Background Model

As our noise model is unimodal and depends only on the object distance, we employ a background model in the form of a single matrix that represents the central tendency of the observed measurements in every pixel. This model is simple to process and maintain, which is important considering the limited computational resources available. As the noise model is already known, an initial training phase is not required. In fact, our method only requires a single frame for initialization; the observed pixel values of the first frame constitute the initial values of the background model. Model pixels that are zero (which denotes an unsuccessful measurement) are inpainted.

Under practical conditions, the background might change over time, which must be accounted for by updating the background model. To this end, we periodically compare every pixel value $v \neq 0$ of the current frame with the corresponding background model value m; m is increased if $m < p$ and decreased if $m > p$. This causes m to converge towards the temporal median [20].

Such gradual update strategies entail a compromise in terms of the update rate; high rates cause unmoving foreground objects to disappear quickly (which can hinder fall verification) whereas low rates cause persistent errors in case of background changes. To overcome this problem, we employ a second, complementary means for updating the model; we periodically test for whether $v - m > 3e_m$ and, if so, set $m := v$. This method effectively compensates background changes and allows us to keep the gradual update rate low.

4 Conversion to Plan-View Space

A key characteristic of our fall detection method is that all analysis is done in *plan-view space* [21]. This space, which resembles a synthetic top-view of the scene under orthographic projection, is well-suited for fall detection for two reasons. First, it represents the scene geometry in a concise way, allowing real-time operation on low-end hardware. Second, it is invariant with respect to the

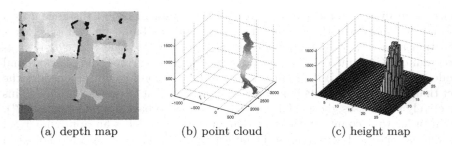

|(a) depth map|(b) point cloud|(c) height map|

Fig. 2. Transformation of foreground pixels (green) to plan-view space. (Color figure online)

sensor position and orientation, enabling invariant features for person and fall detection as well as facilitating the system setup.

Foreground pixels are mapped to plan-view space by first reprojecting them to world coordinates. The resulting points are then downsampled along the X and Z axes (the positive Y axis points upwards) and discretized to obtain plan-view coordinates. In this process, several points may be mapped to the same plan-view coordinates, and different means for consolidating these points to a single scalar result in different scene representations. We employ two kinds of these representations, occupancy maps $\mathcal{O}$ and height maps $\mathcal{H}$ [22]. The former encode the number of points mapped to each plan-view coordinate, whereas the latter store the largest observed Y coordinates [21,22]. Figure 2 illustrates the process of height map generation. After conversion, both maps are smoothed using a Gaussian filter to compensate for rounding effects.

Occupancy and height maps are complementary with regard to person detection. The former are robust to sensor noise but not to occlusions, while the latter are robust to partial occlusions but susceptible to noise. To this end, we set all occupancy and height map pixels whose occupancy is below a threshold to 0, which is a reliable method for noise removal [22,23].

5   Person Detection and Tracking

Our fall detection method includes an effective person detection and tracking stage. This enables reliable analysis even if there are multiple moving objects (e.g. persons or pets) in the scene. This stage entails two steps, the detection of persons in the current frame, and tracking of persons over time.

5.1   Person Detection

We perform person detection on a per-region basis in plan-view space. For this purpose, we find all connected components in the binary height map $\mathcal{H} > 0$, which are then classified as (non-)persons. For classification we use a vector **f** of four features that encode object geometry: (i) occupied area (number of plan-view pixels), (ii) object height (0.95th quantile of height map values), (iii) object density (0.95th quantile of occupancy map values), and (iv) object shape (side ratio of the bounding box). These features have a clear interpretation, are efficient to compute, and robust with respect to person position and orientation.

Classification is performed by a random forest [24] that was trained on about $20,000$ frames depicting persons and other foreground objects such as chairs, rollators, and pets. The frames were extracted from a subset of sequences in our test dataset (Sect. 7.1), and foreground objects were manually segmented to obtain ground-truth data. The frames depict persons performing various activities, including walking, using a wheelchair or rollator, sitting, and lying, in order for the classifier to recognize persons regardless of pose. The frames depict persons at varying levels of occlusions in order to obtain a classifier that is robust in this regard. Random forest hyperparameters were cross-validated.

Random forest classifiers are well-suited for our task because they generalize well [24], are efficient, and predict class-conditional probabilities $\Pr(P|\mathbf{f})$.

5.2   Tracking

The goal of the tracking step is to associate person regions (those for which $\Pr(P = 1|\mathbf{f}) > 0.5$) between frames. For this purpose, we represent each person region R_j by a feature vector $\mathbf{x}_j = (\mathbf{c}_j; \mathbf{f}_j)$, which is utilized for computing association costs. $\mathbf{c}_j = (x_j, z_j)$ is the location (center of mass) of R_j,

$$\mathbf{c}_j = \frac{1}{\sum \mathcal{O}(R_j)} \sum_{\mathbf{p} \in R_j} \mathcal{O}(\mathbf{p})\mathbf{p}. \tag{2}$$

The goal is thus to associate n person regions in the current frame with m regions in the previous frame in a way that minimizes a global association cost. Our per-sample association cost w_{ij} incorporates both proximity and feature similarity of the associated regions R_i and R_j, and is defined as

$$w_{ij} = \begin{cases} \alpha_1 \|\mathbf{c}_i - \mathbf{c}_j\|_2 + \alpha_2 \|\mathbf{f}_i - \mathbf{f}_j\|_2 & \text{if } \|\mathbf{c}_i - \mathbf{c}_j\|_2 < t_c \\ \infty & \text{otherwise.} \end{cases} \tag{3}$$

The factors α_1, α_2 weight the impact of proximity and feature similarity, while t_c accounts for the fact that the velocity of persons is limited.

In order to be able to solve the resulting optimization problem efficiently, we demand that $m = n$ and that each track must be assigned to a different region. This results in a linear assignment problem, which can be solved using the Hungarian algorithm [25]. We ensure that $m = n$ (which is not always the case because persons may enter or leave the view at any time) by introducing dummy regions [26]. Before association, the location of regions of the previous frame are predicted for the current frame using Kalman filters [27].

6   Fall Detection

Fall detection comprises the steps state prediction, event detection, and fall verification. The purpose of the first step is to estimate the state of every person that is being tracked. These state predictions are analyzed over time in order to detect events such as falls. This follows an optional verification step that aims to reduce the false alarm rate via long-term and scene analysis.

State and event detection are carried out in a probabilistic framework. This allows our method to report reliable event confidence scores, enabling caretakers to balance the trade-off between sensitivity and specificity. These scores are also used for automatic event filtering and routing. For instance, our method can be configured to send all fall events with a confidence greater than 0.5 via mail, and additionally send a text message if the confidence is greater than 0.9.

6.1   State Prediction

Persons can be in the following states: (i) Fallen (in a pose typical for fallen persons, such as lying or sitting), (ii) Active (any other pose), and (iii) Resting (being on top of a resting accommodation). State prediction is carried out independently in each frame. For this purpose, we define two binary random variables A and R, with $A = 1$ and $A = 0$ representing the Active and Fallen state, respectively, and R encoding whether the person is resting or not.

To predict $\Pr(A)$, we reuse the feature vector **f**. **f** is discriminative for this purpose as it encodes geometrical properties that change significantly due to falls. For prediction we employ a binary random forest classifier that was trained on a subset of the frames used to train the person classifier (those depicting persons).

$\Pr(R = 1)$ is calculated as the fraction of the area occupied by a person that overlaps with scene objects. In order to ensure that falls beneath such objects (which is possible in case of tables) are correctly detected, person areas must be located above object areas in order to affect $\Pr(R = 1)$.

We are mainly interested in $\Pr(A = 0, R = 0)$, which corresponds to the condition of a person after a fall that should be detected. Assuming that A and R are independent, this joint distribution factorizes to $\Pr(A = 0)\Pr(R = 0)$. Let $\mathcal{P}_A$ and $\mathcal{P}_F$ denote $\Pr(A = 1, R = 0)$ and $\Pr(A = 0, R = 0)$, respectively.

6.2   Event Detection

Falls and other actions performed by humans are temporal in nature. We thus utilize the available tracking information and detect falls and related events via temporal analysis, based on recently observed person states.

Before performing event detection, we integrate state predictions from recent frames in order to increase their reliability. This is motivated by the observation that the state of a person is unlikely to change between frames. For instance, if a person is Active in frame $f - 1$, they are likely to be Active in frame f as well. We considered different temporal models such as Markov chains for modeling this circumstance, but found that simply averaging state probabilities in a short time window leads to comparable results while being more efficient. In mathematical terms, we thus compute e.g.

$$\mathcal{P}_A^{f+} = \frac{1}{\beta} \sum_{t=0}^{\beta-1} \mathcal{P}_A^{f-t}, \tag{4}$$

with with $\mathcal{P}_A^f$ being $\mathcal{P}_A$ in frame f, and $\beta \in \mathbb{N}$ defining the time window.

On this basis, we analyze the temporal evolution of $\mathcal{P}_A^+$ and $\mathcal{P}_F^+$ in order to detect two types of events, falls and recoveries. A fall event is triggered if the maximum over $\mathcal{P}_F^+$ in a time interval around the current frame f exceeds a specified threshold,

$$\mathcal{P}_F^* = \max(\mathcal{P}_F^{f-\gamma+}, \dots, \mathcal{P}_F^{f+}, \dots, \mathcal{P}_F^{f+\gamma+}) > t_{\mathcal{P}_F}. \tag{5}$$

A recovery event signals that a person managed to get back up again after a fall, i.e. if $\mathcal{P}_A^* > t_{\mathcal{P}_A}$ and if a fall event occurred recently for the same person.

We do not analyze the velocity of persons for fall detection, because doing so would prevent us from being able to reliably detect slow falls or falls originating from a position other than upright (e.g. persons rolling out of the bed). In fact, we detect falls solely based on the person pose; if a person lies or sits on the floor for several seconds, a fall event is triggered. This has the advantage that persons that fell outside the field of view can still trigger a fall event (and thus receive help) by crawling into the field of view.

6.3 Fall Verification

The purpose of fall verification is to reduce the false alarm rate. Fall verification consists of three tests that are carried out if a fall event is triggered. All tests can be disabled independently. Test 1 suppresses multiple fall alarms that occur in quick succession for the same person, unless corresponding recovery events occur in between. Test 2 suppresses a fall event if there is another Active person in the scene at the time the event occurs (i.e. if help is already available). Test 3 suppress a fall event if a recovery event is registered for the same person within one minute, i.e. if the person was able to recover on their own.

7 Results and Discussion

We evaluate our fall detection method on an extensive dataset of test sequences and assess its false alarm rate under real-world conditions in a long-term study.

7.1 Performance Under Experimental Conditions

In order to study the fall detection performance, we compiled a dataset of 579 test sequences. These sequences depict persons that simulate different types of falls (following the protocol shown in Table 1) and various activities of daily living (e.g. using a wheelchair or rollator, sitting, cleaning). The sequences were recorded in an attempt to capture as much variability that occurs in practice as possible (e.g. different persons, rooms, and locations; partially visible or occluded actions; interaction with scene objects such as chairs). The dataset includes the CVL dataset [10], which contains 80 fall sequences and 64 sequences with activities of daily living. In total, there are 146 fall incidents in our dataset.

Table 1. Protocol for simulating fall incidents. Our dataset covers all combinations.

Property	Values
Activity prior to fall	Walking, standing, sitting
Fall against	Nothing, wall, unmovable object, movable object
Fall direction	Forward, backward
Partially occluded	No, yes
Walking aid	No, yes

For evaluation, we apply our fall detection method on every test sequence and compare the number of reported fall events to the ground-truth information. On this basis, we compute the precision and recall of our method at varying fall event confidence thresholds $t_{\mathcal{P}_F}$ (between 0.5 and 0.95). The precision is the fraction of triggered fall events that correspond to an actual fall, while the recall is the fraction of falls in the dataset that were detected by our method. We use the same configuration for all sequences and disable fall verification test 3 (Sect. 6.3) as most test sequences are shorter than one minute.

Figure 3 shows the resulting recall vs. precision graph. At $t_{\mathcal{P}_F} = 0.5$, seven of the 146 falls were undetected for the following reasons. In three cases there was significant sensor noise that caused motion detection to fail. This noise occurs only initially and is thus unlikely to affect the fall detection performance in practice. The remaining four falls were particularly challenging because they were from a sitting position, only partially visible, and partially occluded.

18 false alarms were registered at $t_{\mathcal{P}_F} = 0.5$, all of which were due to objects that were left in the scene. In the cases that lead to these false alarms, these objects were considered as persons due to person classification and tracking errors. These errors happened when persons moved large objects such as rollators and chairs while being partially outside the field of view and/or occluded.

Figure 3 illustrates the benefit of the event confidence scores reported by our method: they allow users such as caretakers to balance the trade-off between sensitivity and specificity according to their needs by setting $t_{\mathcal{P}_F}$ accordingly. We note that our method reliably assigns high confidence scores (greater than 0.8) to all but partially invisible or occluded falls. Figure 4 illustrates two challenging test sequences, one that is handled correctly and one that causes a false alarm.

In order to provide a comparison with other fall detection methods, we additionally evaluated our method on the public CVL dataset [10]. To our knowledge,

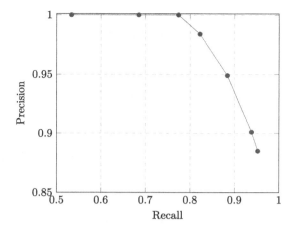

Fig. 3. Recall vs. precision of our fall detection method on the test dataset. The graph was obtained by varying $t_{\mathcal{P}_F} \in \{0.5, 0.6, 0.7, 0.8, 0.85, 0.9, 0.95\}$.

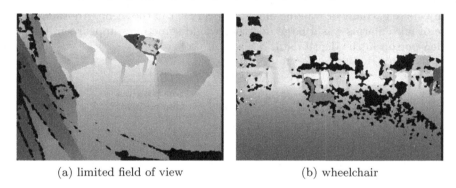

(a) limited field of view   (b) wheelchair

Fig. 4. Challenging test sequences. Left: A fall that is both partially occluded and in a region with limited field of view. Despite these challenging conditions, the fall is detected successfully with a confidence of 58 %. Right: A wheelchair remains at the border of the view, triggering a false alarm with a low confidence. (a) limited field of view (b) wheelchair.

this is the largest public fall dataset available. Our method triggered no false alarms and detected 78 out of 80 falls that occur in this dataset. Both false negatives were caused by the strong sensor noise mentioned before. Method [10] detected all falls, but only half of the CVL dataset was used for evaluation.

7.2   Performance Under Real-World Conditions

At the time of writing, we are performing a long-term evaluation of our fall detection method in nursing and assisted living homes, i.e. under real-world conditions. In this section, we report the results obtained in a period of six months.

During this time, 53 of our fall detection systems were active for 5, 246 full days in total (125, 904 h). To our knowledge, this is the first long-term evaluation of a depth-data-based fall detection method.

For evaluation purposes, we labeled all fall events with a confidence greater than 0.6 in this timeframe as true positives or false positives (false alarms), using event visualizations generated by our method. We labeled 164 fall events as true positives as they were triggered by persons that were lying or sitting on the floor for longer than one minute. No falls were registered by the caretakers in the evaluation period. This means that these events were likely caused by deliberate actions, although it is possible that some were caused by actual falls after which the persons were able to recover on their own. As such, the results reported in this section do not directly correspond to the sensitivity of our method.

Figure 5 summarizes the results, which were obtained by dividing the number of true and false positives by the number of active days. During the considered six-month period, there were 0.14 false alarms with a confidence greater than 0.6 per day on average (i.e. per 24 h of system uptime). This amounts to a single false alarm per week at this confidence threshold. Most false alarms were again caused by objects (e.g. chairs or walking aids) that were left in the scene. Another major cause of false alarms was a large dog that would sometimes appear similarly to a fallen person in the depth data.

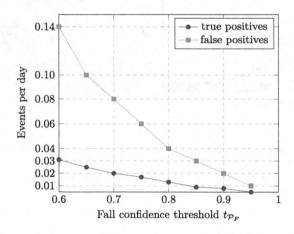

Fig. 5. Average number of true positives and false positives of our fall detection method per day under real-world conditions.

Our fall detection method assigned a low confidence score to a large fraction of these false alarms, so that increasing the threshold to 0.7 almost halves the false alarm rate. Doing so decreases the true positive rate by around one-third in relative terms, affecting mainly falls ending in a sitting position.

Even with conservative confidence thresholds, the false alarm rate is low enough in practice to impose little additional workload for caretakers, and allows a single caretaker to supervise many of our fall detection systems simultaneously.

7.3   Computational Efficiency

Our fall detection method was designed to be efficient enough to run on inexpensive low-end hardware. It achieves more than 30 fps on an Odroid C1+ single board computer, which has a price of only \$32 at the time of writing.

In practice, we limit the sframerate to 15 so that two fall detection instances can run in parallel, enabling simultaneous fall detection in two rooms. This does not decrease the fall detection performance (all results reported in this section were obtained using this framerate).

8   Conclusions

We have presented a fall detection method that analyzes depth data in order to achieve a high sensitivity and specificity under real-world conditions, as verified in a comprehensive performance evaluation. Our method addresses limitations of existing depth-based fall detection methods in terms of sensitivity (inability to detect slow, sitting, or occluded falls) and practicability (high hardware costs, complicated or restrictive system setup), and provides reliable fall confidence scores as additional information for caretakers.

Future work will concentrate on further increasing the fall detection performance of our method. To this end, we are continuing to extend our test dataset in order to obtain more data for classifier training and evaluation. We also plan to improve our algorithms by modeling occlusions explicitly in order to improve person detection and state prediction performance.

References

1. Rubenstein, L.Z.: Falls in older people: epidemiology, risk factors and strategies for prevention. Age Ageing **35**, 1137–1141 (2006)
2. Porter, R.S.: The Merck Manual of Diagnosis and Therapy. Wiley, New York (2011)
3. Noury, N., Rumeau, P., Bourke, A., OLaighin, G., Lundy, J.: A proposal for the classification and evaluation of fall detectors. IRBM **29**(6), 340–349 (2008)
4. Mubashir, M., Shao, L., Seed, L.: A survey on fall detection: principles and approaches. Neurocomputing **100**, 1–9 (2012)
5. Rougier, C., Auvinet, E., Rousseau, J., Mignotte, M., Meunier, J.: Fall detection from depth map video sequences. In: Proceedings of International Conference Smart Homes and Health Telematics, pp. 121–128 (2011)
6. Brutzer, S., Hoferlin, B., Heidemann, G.: Evaluation of background subtraction techniques for video surveillance. In: Proceedings of IEEE Conference on Computer Vision and Pattern Recognition, pp. 1937–1944 (2011)
7. Auvinet, E., Meunier, J.: Head detection using Kinect camera and its application to fall detection. In: Proceedings of International Conference on Information Science, Signal Processing and Their Applications, pp. 164–169 (2012)

8. Dubois, A., Charpillet, F.: Automatic fall detection system with a RGB-D camera using a hidden Markov model. In: Proceedings of International Conference on Smart Homes and Health Telematics, pp. 259–266 (2013)

9. Kepski, M., Kwolek, B.: Fall detection using ceiling-mounted 3D depth camera, pp. 640–647 (2014)

10. Planinc, R., Kampel, M.: Robust fall detection by combining 3D data and fuzzy logic. In: Park, J.-I., Kim, J. (eds.) ACCV Workshops 2012, Part II. LNCS, vol. 7729, pp. 121–132. Springer, Heidelberg (2013)

11. Kumar, D.P., Yun, Y., Gu, I.Y.H.: Fall detection in RGB-D videos by combining shape and motion features. In: Proceedings of International Conference on Acoustics, Speech and Signal Processing, pp. 1337–1341 (2016)

12. Yun, Y., Gu, I.Y.H.: Human fall detection in videos via boosting and fusing statistical features of appearance, shape and motion dynamics on Riemannian manifolds with applications to assisted living. Comput. Vis. Image Underst. **148**, 111–122 (2016)

13. Dubey, R., Ni, B., Moulin, P.: A depth camera based fall recognition system for the elderly. In: Campilho, A., Kamel, M. (eds.) ICIAR 2012, Part II. LNCS, vol. 7325, pp. 106–113. Springer, Heidelberg (2012)

14. Hu, M.K.: Visual pattern recognition by moment invariants. IRE Trans. Inf. Theory **8**(2), 179–187 (1962)

15. Fischler, M.A., Bolles, R.C.: Random sample consensus: a paradigm for model fitting with applications to image analysis and automated cartography. Commun. ACM **24**(6), 381–395 (1981)

16. Labayrade, R., Aubert, D., Tarel, J.P.: Real time obstacle detection in stereovision on non flat road geometry through V-disparity representation. In: IEEE Intelligent Vehicle Symposium, vol. 2, pp. 646–651. IEEE (2002)

17. Toyama, K., Krumm, J., Brumitt, B., Meyers, B.: Wallflower: principles and practice of background maintenance. In: Proceedings of IEEE International Conference on Computer Vision, pp. 255–261 (1999)

18. Pramerdorfer, C.: Evaluation of kinect sensors for fall detection. In: Proceedings of IASTED Conference on Signal Processing, Pattern Recognition and Applications (2013)

19. Khoshelham, K., Elberink, S.: Accuracy and resolution of kinect depth data for indoor mapping applications. Sensors **12**(2), 1437–1454 (2012)

20. McFarlane, N., Schofield, C.: Segmentation and tracking of piglets in images. Mach. Vis. Appl. **8**(3), 187–193 (1995)

21. Beymer, D.: Person counting using stereo. In: Proceedings of Workshop on Human Motion, pp. 127–133 (2000)

22. Harville, M.: Fast, integrated person tracking and activity recognition with plan-view templates from a single stereo camera. In: Proceedings of IEEE Conference on Computer Vision and Pattern Recognition, pp. 398–405 (2004)

23. Muñoz Salinas, R.: A Bayesian plan-view map based approach for multiple-person detection and tracking. Pattern Recogn. **41**(12), 3665–3676 (2008)

24. Breiman, L.: Random forests. Mach. Learn. **45**(1), 5–32 (2001)

25. Kuhn, H.W.: The Hungarian method for the assignment problem. Naval Res. Logistics Q. **2**(1), 83–97 (1955)

26. Papadimitriou, C., Steiglitz, K.: Combinatorial Optimization: Algorithm and Complexity. Prentice Hall, Upper Saddle River (1982)

27. Kalman, R.E.: A new approach to linear filtering and prediction problems. Trans. ASME J. Basic Eng. **82**(D), 35–45 (1960)

A Real-Time Vehicular Vision System to Seamlessly See-Through Cars

Francois Rameau$^{(\boxtimes)}$, Hyowon Ha, Kyungdon Joo, Jinsoo Choi, and InSo Kweon

Electrical Engineering Department, KAIST, Daejeon, South Korea
{frameau,hwha,kdjoo,jschoi,iskweon}@rcv.kaist.ac.kr

Abstract. Overtaking accidents typically occur when the rear car intends to overtake the front car with limited visibility. This lack of visual information is often attributed to the occlusion caused by the front vehicle. Indeed, in many situations the front car hides the presence of obstacles, such as pedestrians or other cars. Nowadays, the generalization of digital camera embedded automotives represents a great potential to reduce the number of these deadly accidents. Thus, we propose a novel collaborative cars method which allows a driver to literally see through the front vehicle to assist in overtaking manoeuvres. In the studied scenario, both cars are equipped with cameras (stereo and monocular cameras for the front and the rear cars, respectively) and share data through an appropriated wireless communication system. Our method generates a seamless transparency effect from the rear car viewpoint using tri-focal tensor image synthesis where the poses of the cameras are estimated using a marker-based pose estimation. In this article, we present an efficient framework designed to reduce the quantity of information to be transferred between the vehicles and to achieve real-time performances (15 fps). Furthermore, our system is assessed through multiple experiments in controlled and real conditions.

Keywords: Augmented reality · Image synthesis · See-through · Marker-based approach · Real-time

1 Introduction

Nearly 1.3 million people die in road crashes each year, while 20 to 50 million people are injured or disabled. According to [1], overtaking contributes to about 1% of all the road accidents but represents a very high percentage of deadly accidents due to frontal impact and high speed - which are typical of overtaking situations. These accidents have multiple causes which are enumerated in [2], where the authors identified the lack of visibility (poor observation) as the major factor in overtaking collisions. These accidents are even more common in low- and middle-income countries due to poor road infrastructures and outdated vehicles. Furthermore, most of these dangerous situations involve large vehicles such as trucks.

© Springer International Publishing Switzerland 2016
G. Hua and H. Jégou (Eds.): ECCV 2016 Workshops, Part II, LNCS 9914, pp. 209–222, 2016.
DOI: 10.1007/978-3-319-48881-3_15

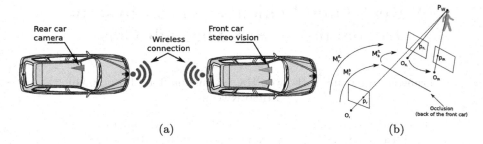

Fig. 1. (a) Main scenario. (b) Model of the problem.

This paper concerns the collaboration between two vehicles equipped with cameras and connected together via a wireless network such that data can be transferred. In real case scenarios, these cars are following each other. As a consequence, the vision of the rear car is occluded by the front car itself, making it impossible to see any hypothetical obstacles - such as pedestrians - (see Fig. 1(a)). Ultimately, the purpose of this work is to overcome this occlusion, in other terms, to see through the front car in order to prevent eventual accidents. Despite the important impact of such technology for automotive safety, this application did not attract much attention yet.

Lately, overtaking accidents have received a renewed interest through the actions of large companies such as Samsung, which installed large LCD screens on the back of their trucks to display the front view of the vehicle[1]. This solution is very practical and efficient but has a very high cost that most of the road transportation companies cannot afford.

A cheaper option is to display the images acquired from the front vehicle directly inside the following cars through an appropriate hardware setup to transfer the data and to visualize it. Olaverri-Monreal *et al.* [3] studied the impact of such technology on drivers' behaviours through simulated experiments. According to their work, such type of system positively impacts the driver's reactions. They also proved the feasibility of the system in real conditions. Therefore, this system is very interesting to provide more information to the drivers thanks to a live video-streaming. Nonetheless, the change of view-point can be confusing to the driver and can cause some miss-interpretation of the scene. For that reason, this work focuses on a more natural way to display the on-coming obstacles occluded by the front vehicle. Indeed, we propose to see-through the front vehicle literally speaking by generating a synthetic non-occluded image using images from both vehicles. Such approaches have been investigated in the past, for instance, in [4,5] the perspective projection is approximated using the distance between cars (obtained with markers) and the size of the front vehicle, however the obtained result is nothing but a rough approximation of the geometry while we aim to see through the vehicle with a seamless transparency effect. In [6], the authors fused a large number of sensors between multiple vehicles,

---

[1] https://www.youtube.com/watch?v=ZetSRWchM4w.

the cars' poses are determined using a laser rangefinder and the synthetic view is generated using ground plane matching, thus only a very small portion of the view is transferred which does not carry relevant information. Finally, the most closely related paper is [7], where the authors propose to use a rough depth map (obtained from a laser scanner on the front vehicle) and a car localization method (based on GPS and laser scanners) to generate a synthetic unoccluded view, while our approach only relies on cameras. Moreover, [7] assumes various hypothesis on the structure of the scene; indeed, the vehicles have to lie on the same plane to be localized efficiently and the approximated depth map generation does not perform well in complex environments. Whereas our approach provides a full transparency effect without geometrical hypothesis on the scene and thus allows a wider number of scenarios (slope, traffic jam, urban canyon, etc.). In fact, in this paper, we describe a versatile framework based on marker-based pose estimation and image synthesis using a tri-focal tensor to see through cars in real-time. It should also be noted that despite the use of markers, the entire method is very generic and the beacons placed on the front car can be replaced by the CAD of the vehicle.

This paper is organised as follows. Section 2 is dedicated to the problem statement and notations, in the Sect. 3 we explain in detail the different steps of our algorithm, while the Sect. 4 provides implementation information necessary to reach real time performances. Our results are available in Sect. 5. Finally this paper ends with a short conclusion.

2   Problem Statement

Given two cars following each other, our goal is to see through the front vehicle from the rear car viewpoint in real time. To this purpose, our system requires three cameras, two are embedded in the front car (to estimate the 3D structure of the scene) and one is mounted on the rear car. With such setup it is clear that the 3D reconstruction from the front car can be reprojected in the rear car image to create an unobstructed picture. This strategy has the great advantage to provide a seamless transparency effect. However, solving this problem is not straightforward.

Figure 1(b) is roughly depicting the scenario we face at time t. In this scheme, $\mathbf{O}_r$ is the camera on the rear car, while $\mathbf{O}_{fL}$ and $\mathbf{O}_{fR}$ are respectively the left and right cameras of the stereo rig mounted on the front car. The occlusion illustrated by a thick line in the figure, is the occlusion generated by the front car. As mentioned previously, the re-projection of the occluded area on the rear camera image is highly dependent upon the 3D geometry of the scene. The front car stereo-vision system is able to provide this very desirable information by triangulating the corresponding image points $\mathbf{p}_{fL}$ and $\mathbf{p}_{fR}$ in order to obtain the 3D point $\mathbf{P}_W$. The problem lies in the re-projection of this 3D point on the rear car camera. If the poses between the front and the rear cameras are known (namely $\mathbf{M}_r^{fL}$), then it is possible to construct a tri-focal tensor. This tri-focal tensor can be further utilized to generate a synthetic image of the occluded region by a point transfer from the front car to the rear car camera. This type of transfer is specific to tri-focal tensor and is called the point-point-point transfer. Note that a dense disparity map is needed in order to generate a proper synthetic image.

Therefore, our method consists of two main steps: the pose estimation of the cameras and the image synthesis. For the pose estimation of the cameras, we propose an appropriate technique to compute the transformation $\mathbf{M}_r^{fL}$. Since it is very challenging to match the images from the rear and the front car (mainly due to the large distance between the cars) we suggest to compute this transformation in two stages. Firstly, a Hand-Eye calibration process is providing the fixed rigid transformation $\mathbf{M}_b^{fL}$. Secondly, for every single time t the pose estimation of the front car $\mathbf{M}_r^b$ is computed thanks to a marker-based approach. Thus, it is obvious that the transformation $\mathbf{M}_r^{fL}$ is nothing but the composition of these two transformations:

$$\mathbf{M}_r^{fL} = \mathbf{M}_b^{fL}\mathbf{M}_r^b. \tag{1}$$

From this pose ($\mathbf{M}_r^{fL}$), the corresponding points, $\mathbf{p}_{fL}$ and $\mathbf{p}_{fR}$, can be transferred in the rear camera image at the pixel coordinates $\mathbf{p}_r$, which, we can call the synthetic image point.

3   Methodology

In this section we present the two main steps of our method, the pose estimation of the cameras (including the calibration of our system) and the generation of a synthetic image using tri-focal tensor.

3.1   Pose Estimation of the Cameras

The previously mentioned point-point-point transfer is possible if and only if the inter-camera poses are known. In our situation it is difficult to estimate the tri-focal tensor using point correspondences between the 3 cameras ($\mathbf{O}_{fL}$, $\mathbf{O}_{fR}$ and $\mathbf{O}_r$) -since the images acquired from the front and rear car can be very dissimilar.

Nonetheless, it is possible to determine the rigid transformation between the back of the front car and its cameras. Then, knowing the pose of the front car with respect to the rear car camera leads to the estimation of the poses of the entire system. In this section we briefly present our solutions to calibrate our system and to estimate the pose of the front car in real time.

Hand-Eye Calibration of the Front Car. A car intrinsically being a rigid structure, it is possible to calibrate the back of the front car with respect to its cameras. It means, solving the rigid transformation $\mathbf{M}_b^{fL}$. This type of problem is tackled under the name of Hand-Eye calibration, it is often solved as a homogeneous matrix equation of the type $\mathbf{AX} = \mathbf{XB}$ [8]. This particular formulation is very interesting since it allows to find the rigid transformation without using any

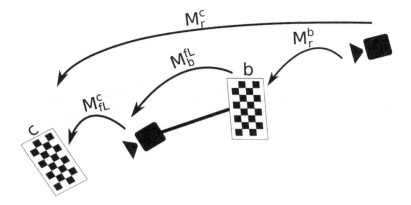

Fig. 2. Hand-Eye calibration scenario (only the left camera has been depicted for the sake of clarity)

inter-camera correspondences [9]. Unfortunately, this solution is very sensitive to degenerated motions. In our case the vehicle usually performs motions on a flat surface which makes it impossible to solve the vertical translation axis. Instead, we developed a more practical approach but where correspondences between the front and rear cameras are necessary.

For our calibration, two checkerboards are needed, one (called b in this paper) is fixed on the back of the front car while the second one c is located in the field of view of the front car camera (see Fig. 2). In case only one set of images is available, solving the desired transformation $\mathbf{M}_b^{fL}$ is straightforward. In fact, as depicted in Fig. 2, the transformations $\mathbf{M}_r^b$ and $\mathbf{M}_{fL}^c$ can be directly computed thanks to the checkerboards. The remaining transformation $\mathbf{M}_r^c$ can be estimated afterwards by removing the vehicle from the field of view of the rear camera. Finally the computation of $\mathbf{M}_b^{fL}$ is found through the following matrix multiplication:

$$\mathbf{M}_b^{fL} = (\mathbf{M}_{fL}^c)^{-1}\mathbf{M}_r^c(\mathbf{M}_r^b)^{-1}. \tag{2}$$

The weakness of the described method lies in the large distance between the front checkerboard and the rear camera which can lead to an inaccurate corner detection. To increase the robustness of the approach, multiple sets of images have to be acquired in order to ensure a good estimation of $\mathbf{M}_b^{fL}$. Hence, a non-linear process minimizing the re-projection error over all the images is applied. In practice, the result from a single set of images is sufficient to initialize the refinement and to ensure a good convergence of the algorithm. In this work, the Levenberg-Marquardt algorithm is utilized to optimize the re-projection error.

Pose Estimation of the Front Car. We propose an efficient marker-based approach to determine, $\mathbf{M}_r^b$, the pose of the front car with respect to the rear car camera.

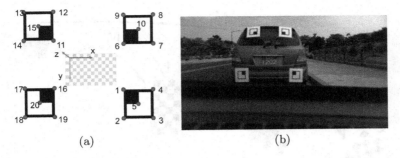

(a)   (b)

Fig. 3. (a) Four markers with 20 corner points used for pose estimation, (b) the markers mounted on the car

The approaches which solve this problem are commonly called "3D model-based pose estimation". A large number of techniques taking advantage of various types of features have already been designed by the community. For instance using points [10], lines [11] or edges [12].

Most of the previously cited approaches are very accurate, however, a complete 3D model of the object of interest is needed in order to estimate its pose. In our case, it is difficult to know the full 3D model of the front car. Thus, we propose to use markers to estimate the pose between cars. The use of markers ensures an accurate, fast and robust localisation of the car, furthermore they are generic and can be setup on various type of vehicles. The markers employed for our pose estimation consist in a white square with thick black margins and containing a black square covering one of its quarters (see Fig. 3). Thus, five corners per marker can be detected and tracked; the four external corners and one in the center of the marker. To ensure a proper pose estimation, four markers are distributed on the back of the front car (see Fig. 3(b)), which represent a total of 20 points to compute the transformation $\mathbf{M}_r^b$. Each of these beacons can be efficiently detected using a basic square detection algorithm [13], while their ID is determined by estimating their orientations (0°, 90°, 180° and 270°). When one marker cannot be detected, its points (from the previous frame) are tracked using the KLT algorithm [14].

Note that in order to compute the pose of the set of markers (the back of the front car), the 3D position of their corners have to be expressed in the same referential coordinate system. In our case, we chose the checkerboard already utilized for the Hand-Eye calibration to be this reference (see Fig. 3). Thus, a camera captures both the checkerboard and the markers simultaneously from various viewpoints. For every single image, an accurate pose estimation of the camera is performed using the checkboard. Therefore the 3D position of the corners can be accurately computed using a bundle adjustment based technique. After the calibration step, the checkboard can be removed from the vehicle. With our experimental setup mounted on a car, 3000 images containing 20 corner points have been acquired. The computed mean reprojection error after optimization is 0.31 pixel.

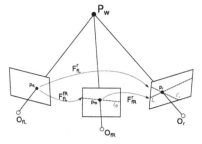

Fig. 4. Epipolar relationships among a tri-focal tensor

Finally, to estimate the transformation $\mathbf{M}_r^b$, we solve a Perspective-n-Point (PnP) problem using the EPnP algorithm described in [15]. Under certain conditions, false detections of the markers can affect the pose estimation. Thus, the robust pose estimation is ensured by a RANSAC process in order to efficiently remove the outlier points. Therefore, this robust estimation is refined by minimizing the re-projection error via a non-linear optimization scheme.

3.2 Image Synthesis Using Tri-Focal Tensor

The geometry of a triplet of images can be modelled using a tri-focal tensor $\mathbf{T}^{i,j,k}$ [16]. $\mathbf{T}^{i,j,k}$ defines the epipolar geometry between the three views indexed i, j, k in a $3 \times 3 \times 3$ cube matrix (see Fig. 4). It is the generalization of the fundamental matrix for a set of 3 views. From this formalism it is possible to transfer lines and points between views. In this section, we explain the computation of such kind of tensor from calibrated cameras, but also the point transfer by $\mathbf{T}^{i,j,k}$ and the image synthesis from a dense disparity map.

Tri-Focal Tensor from Projection Matrices. The trifocal tensor $\mathbf{T}^{fL,fR,r}$ linking the three perspective calibrated views fL, fR and r can be expressed as follow:

$$\mathbf{T}^{fL,fR,r} = [\mathbf{T}_1, \ \mathbf{T}_2, \ \mathbf{T}_3], \tag{3}$$

$$\mathbf{T}_1 = \mathbf{M}_{fL}^{fR}[(^2\mathbf{M}_{fL}^{fL})^T.^3\mathbf{M}_{fL}^{fL} - {}^3\mathbf{M}_{fL}^{fL}.^2\mathbf{M}_{fL}^{fL}]_{[\times]}(\mathbf{M}_{fL}^r)^T, \tag{4}$$

$$\mathbf{T}_2 = \mathbf{M}_{fL}^{fR}[(^3\mathbf{M}_{fL}^{fL})^T.^1\mathbf{M}_{fL}^{fL} - {}^1\mathbf{M}_{fL}^{fL}.^3\mathbf{M}_{fL}^{fL}]_{[\times]}(\mathbf{M}_{fL}^r)^T, \tag{5}$$

$$\mathbf{T}_3 = \mathbf{M}_{fL}^{fR}[(^1\mathbf{M}_{fL}^{fL})^T.^2\mathbf{M}_{fL}^{fL} - {}^2\mathbf{M}_{fL}^{fL}.^1\mathbf{M}_{fL}^{fL}]_{[\times]}(\mathbf{M}_{fL}^r)^T, \tag{6}$$

where $^i\mathbf{M}$ is the ith row of the matrix $\mathbf{M}$ and $\mathbf{X}_{[\times]}$ is the skew-symmetric matrix of the vector $\mathbf{X}$.

Point-Point-Point Transfer. As discussed before, if the tri-focal tensor is known and if a correspondence is found on at least two cameras, then it is possible to re-project this point on the third view of the tensor. A formalism involving two fundamental matrices can be utilized in order to achieve this point transfer in the following manner:

$$\mathbf{p}_r = (\mathbf{F}^r_{fL}\mathbf{p}_{fL}) \times (\mathbf{F}^r_{fR}\mathbf{p}_{fR}), \tag{7}$$

with $\mathbf{F}^r_{fL}$ and $\mathbf{F}^r_{fR}$ respectively the fundamental matrices between the rear camera and the the left and right camera of the stereo-vision system. Nonetheless, this epipolar transfer is subject to many degenerated configurations as defined in [16].

The tri-focal tensor transfer can overcome these cases. Considering that the pose between the two views $\mathbf{O}_{fL}$ and $\mathbf{O}_{fR}$ is known (calibrated stereo-vision system). The point $\mathbf{p}_{fR}$ in the second camera can be expressed with its epipolar line $\mathbf{l}_{fR}$, then the transfer can be simply expressed under the following point-line-point transfer: $\mathbf{p}^k_r = \mathbf{p}^i_{fL}\mathbf{l}^j_{fR}\mathbf{T}^{j,l,k}$. If this expression is used as it is, then, similar degenerated cases occurring with the epipolar transfer are faced. The easiest and more robust way to overcome this, is to use the orthogonal line of $\mathbf{l}_{fR}$ passing by the point $\mathbf{p}_{fR}$. A detailed explanation is provided in [16].

Image Synthesis from Disparity Map. All the pixels composing the images from the stereo rig, can be transferred in order to create a synthetic image from another viewpoint (*i.e.* from the rear car viewpoint). As explained previously, this synthetic image can be obtained only if a dense matching between the two images from the stereo rig is available. Many works have focused on this pixel-to-pixel matching using stereo-vision systems, nonetheless a very few of them allows real time performances. In this paper we use [17], which has the advantage to provide a quasi-dense disparity map in real-time. However, the disparity values for poorly textured surfaces and far away elements are difficult to be estimated. In such scenarios, the very distant objects of the scene (lying at the horizon) as well as the sky, often have no disparity value associated with. This leads to a poor synthetic image quality which is difficultly readable for a human being.

To overcome this problem we propose a simple solution which consists of forcing a very small value to the undetermined disparities. This results in a more realistic synthetic image which is more appropriate for a good scene understanding. Other post-processing algorithms are also applied, such as a simple interpolation of the synthetic image to fulfil the texture-less part of the image and to deal with stereo shadow.

4   Implementation Details

To reach real time performances we designed our algorithm to share the computational cost between both computers embedded in the rear and the front car. The rear car processes are fully dedicated to markers detection, pose estimation and image stitching, while the front car generate the synthetic image accordingly with the information received from the rear car.

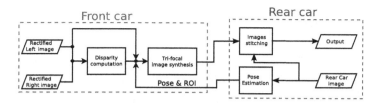

Fig. 5. Algorithm

The particular design of our algorithm also allows to optimize the quantity of data to be transferred between the cars. Indeed, we reached an optimal solution which drastically speed up the data transfer by only transmitting the relevant information. The rear car is simply sending the relative pose between cars and the localization of the ROI (the occlusion) in the image to the front car. These data are analysed to generate a small synthetic image (only covering the occluded region), thereafter this patch is compressed (using jpeg compression) and transferred back to the rear car to be stitched to the current image.

In case of wireless data transfer between moving cars, the distance between the communication platforms reduces the bandwidth, this effect is directly compensated by our solution since the size of the patch is also decreasing with respect to the distance between cars (the apparent size of the front car is shrinking with distance). The Fig. 5 depicts the whole algorithm. This algorithm has been fully developed in C++ and integrated in the middleware Robot Operating System (ROS).

5   Results

In this section, we present a series of experiments with real data emphasizing the efficiency of our method through quantitative and qualitative results. For our experiments, we utilize two cars. The front one is equipped with a *Bumblebee 2* (manufactured by *PointGrey*) in order to acquire well-synchronized stereo images. This sensor provides two $1024 \times 768p$ color images (downscaled to $512 \times 384p$ for speed issue) at 20 frames per second. A low cost USB color camera (Microsoft Lifecam Cinema) with a spatial resolution of $640 \times 360p$ is mounted on the rear vehicle. Since our algorithm does not need high bandwidth network, a standard Wi-Fi 802.11n network is used for our tests in outdoor condition; while most of the multi-vehicle collaboration applications require the use of an expensive Wi-Fi 802.11p network.

5.1   Assessment of Our System with Real Images

To evaluate the accuracy of our method with real images, we propose to estimate the transfer error of the synthetic points through an experimental setup. After the calibration of our system, a checkerboard is installed in front of the car

Fig. 6. (a) Experimental setup to test the accuracy of our point transfer; (b) Reprojection result for the second set of images, the green and red crosses are respectively the ground truth and the transferred points. (Color figure online)

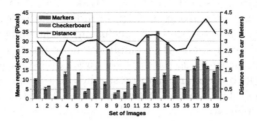

Fig. 7. Mean and standard deviation of the re-projection error of our system for 19 sets of images. The distance between the markers and the rear camera is also available in green (Color figure online)

while a monocular camera is placed behind the vehicle to estimate the pose of the car using the markers (see Fig. 6(a)). Thus, the coordinates of the front checkerboard's corners are transferred to the rear camera image -using a tri-focal tensor. The ground truth is obtained by removing the car from the field of view of the camera. With such setup we evaluate the accuracy of the entire system; the pose estimation and the image synthesis together. An example of transferred points is available in Fig. 6(b).

A series of 19 sets of images have been acquired with different positions of the car, the computed Euclidean re-projection error is available in Fig. 7. We compared the pose estimation obtained using a checkerboard fixed on the back of the car with our markers' based approach. From our results, it is clear that the use of the markers leads to a significantly higher accuracy in the pose estimation of the car. Even with the markers the mean error of the transferred points over all the images is 8.2 pixels. Nonetheless, the standard deviation of this error is very small (under 0.5 pixel) which mean that our synthetic image is coherent but misaligned. This transfer error can be attributed to the noise and the numerical errors accumulated along the different steps of our approach (pose estimation, calibration, stereo matching and tri-focal transfer). In practice, such error in the generation of the synthetic image is acceptable. Indeed, considering the size of the original image used for this test (1280×720 pixels), a misalignment of 8 pixels only represents 0.625 % of the image's width. For the desired application it is enough to generate a realistic seamless transparency effect, as it is emphasized in the next section.

5.2   Results in Real Conditions

For these experiments, two cars are utilized, the front car is equipped with the previously described markers in order to estimate the inter-car poses. The cars have been driven within a speed range of 0 to 40 km/h on a campus. Our algorithm is running at 15 frames per second and all the results presented in this section have been computed on-line. Notice that this frame-rate is significantly higher than existing real-time approaches such as [5] which can only process 5 images per seconds without providing a seamless transparency effect (and using a more cumbersome marker setup).

The Fig. 8 shows a representative set of results, in this figure the yellow bounding box is the ROI to be processed while the red dots are the detected corners utilized for the pose estimation. Overall, we can notice that the images are well aligned and allow the driver to have a good overview over the occluded part. Our algorithm works in many challenging situations such as the downhill case (see Fig. 9(e)), while most of the already existing methods [6,7] cannot deal with such circumstances.

The Fig. 8(f) and (d) show results with far away background and close-by objects. In both cases we are able to obtain an accurate synthetic image of the occluded scene. Other techniques like [6] only work for the ground surface, while [7] relies on a very approximative depth map obtained from a laser range scanner. Therefore they are not able to tackle a large variety of scenarios unlike our method.

During our experiments we also crossed other moving vehicles (see Figs. 8(e) and 9(b)), despite the speed of the cars our algorithm still provides a good image alignment. In the same way, on the Fig. 9(a), our cars are crossing a group of pedestrians.

Even when the vehicles are not aligned, as it is the case in Fig. 9(c) it is still possible to recover a proper image of what is behind the front car. Notice that in some cases the four markers cannot be detected or tracked properly, even in these contexts, the pose estimation remains accurate and efficient. Nonetheless, the proposed approach suffers multiple drawbacks. The main one is probably the limited working distance of the system, indeed, when the cars are spaced by more than 10 m the markers could not be tracked with a sufficient accuracy which leads to a wrong pose estimation. However, this range is usually enough to increase the road safety and to see the dangerous obstacle through the front car. Furthermore, This working distance could be increased with a new design of the markers or by augmenting the resolution or the focal length of the rear car camera.

Note that, the transparency effect cannot be applied on the lower part of the front car since this part is not visible by the stereo-vision system (this is

Fig. 8. Real time results in real condition, (first row) markers detection and pose estimation, (second row) Seeing-through results

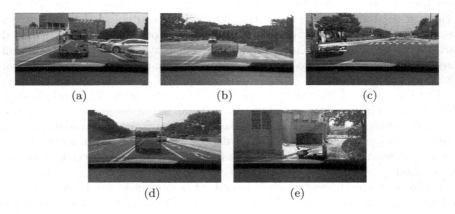

Fig. 9. Sample of results obtained with our approach

actually the part located under the car). This is the reason why this area is not fully recovered in our experiments.

6   Conclusion

In this paper we presented a novel approach to see through the front vehicle in real time using a very low cost setup consisting of only three cameras and a standard Wi-Fi connection. Unlike the already existing methods, our approach provides a seamless transparency effect which respects the geometry of the scene. Furthermore, our algorithm has been designed to reduce the quantity of data to be transferred between the vehicles which allows to process up to 15 frames per second. Moreover, our marker-based approach is very efficient within a range of 1 to 10 m and even when the vehicles are static.

We performed multiple tests with real data which underlines the efficiency of our approach in term of accuracy. Furthermore, a large set of real experiments have been done. In these experiments it is clear that our system is working in practical situations. However, our method can be improved in multiple ways. For instance, the integration of an appropriated display such as a HUD or Google glasses is an interesting direction. For a realistic deployment of this seeing through system, a marker-less approach has to be considered. Our current researches focus on marker-less pose estimation and SLAM-based approach to avoid the use of markers. Finally, our method can easily be declined for night vision by replacing the markers by IR LEDs.

Acknowledgements.. This research was supported by the Shared Sensing for Cooperative Cars Project funded by Bosch (China) Investment Ltd.

The first author was supported by Korea Research Fellowship Program through the National Research Foundation of Korea (NRF) funded by the Ministry of Science, ICT and Future Planning (2015H1D3A1066564).

References

1. Naja, R. (ed.): Wireless Vehicular Networks for Car Collision Avoidance. Springer, New York (2013)
2. Clarke, D., Ward, P., Jones, J.: Overtaking road-accidents: differences in manoeuvre as a function of driver age. Accid. Anal. Prev. **30**(4), 455–467 (1998)
3. Olaverri-Monreal, C., Gomes, P., Fernandes, R., Vieira, F., Ferreira, M.: The see-through system: a VANET-enabled assistant for overtaking maneuvers. In: IV (2010)
4. Gomes, P., Vieira, F., Ferreira, M.: The see-through system: from implementation to test-drive. In: VNC (2012)
5. Gomes, P., Olaverri-Monreal, C., Ferreira, M.: Making vehicles transparent through V2V video streaming. IEEE Trans. Intell. Transp. Syst. **13**(2), 930–938 (2012)
6. Kim, S., Qin, B., Chong, Z., Shen, X., Liu, W., Ang, M.H., Frazzoli, E., Rus, D.: Multivehicle cooperative driving using cooperative perception: design and experimental validation. IEEE Trans. Intell. Transp. Syst. **16**(2), 663–680 (2015)
7. Li, H., Nashashibi, F.: Multi-vehicle cooperative perception and augmented reality for driver assistance: a possibility to see through front vehicle. In: ITSC (2011)
8. Horaud, R., Dornaika, F.: Hand-eye calibration. Int. J. Robot. Res. **14**(3), 195–210 (1995)
9. Lébraly, P., Ait-Aider, O., Royer, E., Dhome, M.: Calibration of non-overlapping cameras-application to vision-based robotics. In: BMVC (2010)
10. Bleser, G., Pastarmov, Y., Stricker, D.: Real-time 3D camera tracking for industrial augmented reality applications (2005)
11. Caron, G., Marchand, E., Mouaddib, E.M.: 3D model based pose estimation for omnidirectional stereovision. In: IROS (2009)
12. Petit, A., Marchand, E., Kanani, K.: Augmenting markerless complex 3D objects by combining geometrical and color edge information. In: ISMAR (2013)
13. Kato, H., Billinghurst, M.: Marker tracking and HMD calibration for a video-based augmented reality conferencing system. In: IWAR (1999)
14. Shi, J., Tomasi, C.: Good features to track. In: CVPR (1994)

15. Lepetit, V., Moreno-Noguer, F., Fua, P.: EPnP: an accurate o(n) solution to the PnP problem. Int. J. Comput. Vision **81**(2), 155–166 (2009)
16. Hartley, R., Zisserman, A.: Multiple View Geometry in Computer Vision. Cambridge Univ Press, New York (2003)
17. Hirschmuller, H.: Stereo processing by semiglobal matching and mutual information. IEEE Trans. Pattern Anal. Mach. Intell. **30**(2), 328–341 (2008)

Solving Rendering Issues in Realistic 3D Immersion for Visual Rehabilitation

Tristan Carrier-Baudouin, Claude Chapdelaine, Marc Lalonde, Philippe Quinn, and Samuel Foucher$^{(\boxtimes)}$

Computer Research Institute of Montréal (CRIM), Montréal, QC, Canada
{tristan.carrier-baudouin,claude.chapdelaine,marc.lalonde,philippe.quinn,
samuel.foucher}@crim.ca

Abstract. When a person becomes visually impaired, intensive rehabilitation is required to learn the skills necessary to accurately interpret the sensory cues. 3D virtual immersion (3D VI) can provide a safe and rich world for rehabilitation by rendering a complex environment. 3D VI can stage challenges that can be faced with less stress than the real outdoor world. In order for 3D VI to be used efficiently, the visual rendering for people with low vision and the audio for both the blind and people with low vision must be as realistic as possible. Building a 3D environment at low cost imposes constraints both on the installation and the technical aspects. This paper describes our current work to solve projections issues for a realistic rendering when images are not aligned and deformed.

Keywords: Visual rehabilitation aid · 3D immersion · Multi-projector calibration

1 Introduction

For people with blindness, knowledge of the environment depends mainly on the interpretation of auditory information available to ensure a safe and efficient travel. Likewise, people with low vision have to learn strategic use of their residual vision while learning how to process appropriate auditory information according to the environment. The research results on the use of 3D VI in visual rehabilitation suggest that the gains made in virtual environments are partly observable in real world settings [1,2]. Blind people gain skills in orientation and mobility (O&M) when they move in 3D VI guided only by auditory cues. This enables them to effectively correct their trajectory in case of deviation and improve their ability to focus on useful cues.

This article presents the constraints related to a low-cost realistic 3D virtual immersion installation that renders a simulation of an urban street designed to assist visual rehabilitation. The fact that the immersion installation is made of a mobile wall that can be rearranged requires a flexible solution with simple equipment and an easy calibration procedure. The paper describes the physical and technical issues that were addressed to solve misalignment and deformation

© Springer International Publishing Switzerland 2016
G. Hua and H. Jégou (Eds.): ECCV 2016 Workshops, Part II, LNCS 9914, pp. 223–237, 2016.
DOI: 10.1007/978-3-319-48881-3_16

problems related to the 3D projection. It details a successful solution based on intra/inter geometric calibrations with a single webcam and discusses future work.

1.1 Description of 3D VI for Vision Rehabilitation

We built a simulated scene (Fig. 1) to assist the learning of how to align to traffic, which is the first step in an O&M outdoor rehabilitation training. This simulation does not cover all aspects of O&M outdoor training but enables four tasks to be mastered indoor before going out into the real world: (1) detecting the direction of incoming/outgoing sounds of vehicles (cars, motorcycles), (2) evaluating the distance between oneself and the vehicles, (3) positioning oneself parallel or perpendicular to traffic and (4) approaching traffic safely.

Fig. 1. Actual urban street simulation for visual rehabilitation in 3D VI

1.2 Challenges and Installed Solutions

Rendering realistic sounds for proper sound interpretation implies taking into account reverberation, distance and direction of objects emitting the sounds [3]. The existing sound databases available for gaming development were not realistic enough since sounds from vehicles are mostly the engine sounds heard from the inside of the vehicle. We needed not only engine sounds from the outside but also the sound of the tires on pavement and the sound of wind on the vehicles body at various speeds. Sound databases used by audiologists are realistic but not in a format that could be fed to a game engine. We recorded the needed sounds with the assistance of an audiologist and our acoustical surrounding sounds were combined in Unity [1] with *Fmod* [2] for a more accurate range of frequencies. But in order to render these sounds accurately in the 3D VI, the loudspeakers had to be placed at ear level (i.e. mid-height of the structure). This added another constraint on the environment since we needed to hide the loudspeakers in order to get a realistic visual rendering.

For rendering realistic and accurate urban settings for people with low vision at the proper scale, we used guidelines that were produced by a group of O&M

---

[1] https://unity3d.com/.
[2] http://www.fmod.org/.

specialists [4]. The perceived length and depth were correctly reproduced and had to be properly projected without deformations or discontinuities. The scene contains a realistic street bordered with trees, houses, commercial buildings and parking lots. The street is approximately one kilometer long. The vehicles can pass by at various realistic speeds, ranging from 35 km/h to 70 km/h. Parked cars can also be added. The user experiences the scene through a first-person view. The person may rotate and take a few steps to align oneself and can also take a few steps to move toward traffic. Furthermore, the simulation can be started from a dozen available points of view.

After visiting and working with specialists in a few Rehabilitation Centers, it became evident that they did not have the space and/or the budget to afford a large and expensive virtual environment. This added the constraint of building the lowest possible cost for 3D environment without jeopardizing efficiency. The lab 3D VI room is a four by three meters with a projection height of 2.44 m in a room of 4 m height. The INLB[3] installation is 4.2 by 4.2 m with a projection height of 2.22 m in a room of 3 m height. It is also equipped with three projectors to cover the left, right and back walls of the room.

The 3D VI consists of a cube-shaped metallic structure assembled from off-the-shelf galvanized steel square tubes and angles screwed together. A white and flexible vinyl fabric is affixed to the four walls of the structure. There is a small entrance and only the middle, eastern and western walls are being projected onto, creating a field of view of approximately 250°. It should be underlined that the projectors are short-throw video projectors fixed to the top of the metal structure. All three projectors are connected to a single computer.

Our first installation with O&M specialists revealed that the visual accuracy was inadequate for the envisioned training with low vision people. Since loud-speakers had to be hidden by curved corners of flexible vinyl sheets to provide the best acoustic possible, it caused deformation to the image projected unto those curved surfaces. Also, the limited height of the room did not allow for optimal installation of the projectors and the projection on the eastern wall had to be tilted, thus creating a deformation at the lower left corner. We saw these constraints as challenges in need of a low-cost solution. This article describes an automatic method capable of successfully calibrating the projectors using a low-cost webcam mounted on a tripod.

1.3   Projections in 3D VI

Unless the projector's axis is perfectly perpendicular to a planar wall, projected images will be distorted in a various ways [5]. Displays are often non-planar, either to improve immersivity [6] or for other reasons such as in our case with the curved corners. Moreover, two projections can be distortion free, but might not be well aligned with each other. In order to avoid black gaps, projectors are usually positioned so that there is a slight overlap between the views. This

---

[3] Institut Nazareth et Louis-Braille.

overlap zone is more luminous and detracts from the rendering quality. Projector calibration aims at correcting these visual issues [7].

Visual correctness of the image is important, because the visually impaired person is expected to take his or her training acquired within the 3D VI to the real world. Being trained with flawed images might reduce the rehabilitation potential of the immersive experience.

Brown et al. [7] describe many approaches that we will review. There are two types of geometric calibrations that need to be performed for each projector: (1) Intra-projector calibration refers to correcting the deformations introduced by non-planar screens or imperfect alignment of the projector with respect to the planar screen [7]; and (2) Inter-projector calibration means adjusting the images of two neighboring projections so they are well aligned with each other (i.e. there are no discontinuities in a line passing through the display [7]). Blending is also part of the calibration process and consists of uniforming the luminosity across the entire projection field [7]. The presented method includes intra and inter geometric calibration, but not blending.

A method capable of calibrating projectors in the context of a low-cost 3D immersion environment is presented. This method relies on a computer vision approach and only needs an inexpensive webcam, even though the field of view of the immersion environment is close to 250°. The method preserves the perspective effect and is based on Alberti's procedure for drawing geometrically correct tiled floors [8].

2   Related Work

The purpose of projector calibration is to obtain a seamless undistorted image with uniform luminosity, regardless of the number of projectors and the shape of the screen surface. A large array of methods are available to obtain such a result. Calibration can be performed through manual adjustments by an expert using special equipment [6]. However, this option is costly because of the regular maintenance, equipment and personnel necessary [7]. It must also be carried out every time the projector or the screen are displaced. In the case of this work, the fact that there is a mobile wall precluded the use of the manual method.

Brown et al. propose another approach based on 3D modeling of the screen including projector positions and parameters [7]. The projection can then be simulated on a computer, with the objective of calculating the appropriate distortion for each projector. This method is convenient when the whole installation is unmovable and the shape of the screen is fixed. Unfortunately, it is not our case.

The third general class of methods consists of using a computer vision approach to calibrate projectors. A grid or a set of features ordered in a rectangular manner are projected on the screen. As explained in Brown et al. [7], the calibration process follows two main steps. During the first step, the camera acquires images of the screen and establishes a correspondence between camera coordinates and projectors coordinates. The second step consists of using this information to warp and blend the images sent to the projectors. Warping means deforming an image in order to obtain spatial continuity between the projections as well as compensating for the curvature of the screen. Blending means adjusting the luminosity in order to make overlaps indistinguishable. Blending typically relies on knowing the correspondence between camera coordinates and projectors coordinates [9]. For the remainder of this section, methods relying on computer vision will be discussed.

In Brown et al., a rectangular array of points is displayed on the screen for each projector [7]. The correspondence between the points viewed by the camera and the projected points is then established. From the camera point of view, the grids are distorted and unaligned with each other. From the projectors point of view, each grid is perfectly square. Both the distorted and undistorted grids are triangulated in order to create a model for texture mapping. The desired image from the simulation is then input to the texture buffer of the distorted grids provided by the camera. Next, a texture mapping between the distorted grids and the undistorted grids given by the simulation is created. The undistorted grids are textured and the result is a warped image that, when projected on the curved display, appears undeformed and well aligned. This method produces excellent results. However, the entirety of the image needs to be visible to the camera, i.e. the camera field of view needs to cover the whole scene. In our case, in order to respect the low-cost constraints, inexpensive cameras were used during this work. Webcams have limited fields of view and a single camera cannot observe the whole immersive environment at the same time. As said earlier, the environment covers an angle of approximately 250°. Moreover, this described method may remove too many deformations depending on the camera location. Only the deformations caused by the curved corners should be removed, not the natural deformations caused by the perspective effect. Let's assume that a person looks at a standard straight corner between two walls. If square grids are superimposed on the walls, the person will observe that the horizontal lines are straight, except in the middle of the corner where there is an abrupt change of direction. Such deformation is caused by perspective and should not be removed.

Garcia-Dorado and Cooperstock make use of homography techniques in order to calibrate projectors [5]. The walls can be planar or curved. If curved, then they must be modeled with OpenGL. The method relies on a motorized pan-tilt camera in order to cover a very wide field of view. Excellent results inside immersive environments can be obtained. In particular, perspective effects are not removed. However, as it was said earlier, the OpenGL modeling of a wall is not very practical when the display undergoes slight modifications from time to time. Moreover, it would be difficult to use this method for an immersive environment when a low-cost webcam is used.

Sajadi and Majumder have designed a method specifically for immersive environments. It assumes that the display is a swept surface and requires the user to input the rotation angle of the profile curve [10]. While this method produces excellent results, a pan-tilt camera is again necessary when the whole screen covers a wide angle. This method cannot be applied to immersive rooms when only a low-cost webcam is provided.

Van Baar et al. have published a method designed for quadric displays [6]. It is capable of calibrating multiple projectors and it can produce distortion free images on curved surfaces, assuming they are quadric. It requires one camera by projector, in other words a standard camera is attached to each projector. This method produces very good results, but the displays are limited to quadric surfaces.

None of the methods described in this section seems to satisfy all the installation and cost constraints mentioned in the Introduction. It has therefore been necessary to develop a new procedure based on computer vision.

3   Requirements and System Design

As shown in Fig. 2, our 3D immersion environment bears certain similarities with classical CAVEs. One difference is the presence of curved sections in the corners.

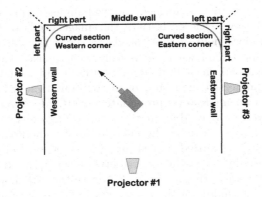

Fig. 2. The 3D immersive environment with the camera aiming at the Western corner

In Fig. 2, projector #2 displays an image on the eastern wall, projector #3 displays an image on the western wall and projector #1 displays an image on the middle wall. The camera can only observe one corner at a time. In order to increase the vertical field of view, the webcam is rotated 90° (portrait mode). The left and right parts of each corner are illuminated by different projectors.

The simulation used to train visually impaired people has been created with the game engine Unity. The Unity code contains three virtual cameras, each one sending the images they acquire to a projector.

Unity can be programmed to correct the distortions caused by the curved corners. The first step consists in accurately modeling the immersive display in 3D. The next step is to render the scene on the 3D model. Three virtual cameras, each one located exactly where there should be a projector in the scaled model, film the modeled display and send what they see to the actual physical projectors. As mentioned in Sect. 2, the main hurdle is the 3D modeling of the display. The display surface may undergo changes and it is flexible. Also, it does not follow any well defined geometrical surface.

Another approach is to model the immersive display without the curved corners. The walls are assumed to be entirely planar. A mesh is applied to each of the three walls. Displacing mesh vertices warps the rendered scene on the wall in a predictable manner. In fact, the scene rendering is used as a texture mapped to the mesh. Unity could then read a file containing the new vertex positions necessary to correct the distortions caused by the curved corners[4]. The scene would appear warped from the projectors' point of view, but undistorted and well-aligned from the user point of view. This approach was implemented and tested. A method capable of creating such a file will be presented.

4   Projector Calibration

In this section, an algorithm capable of aligning the images created by the three projectors in the immersive environment and compensating for the two curved corners is presented. The algorithm currently does not perform blending, i.e. luminosity correction in the overlap regions. However, warping and geometric calibration is an essential step before blending [9].

4.1   Alberti's Method

Alberti's method refers to a very old technique used by painters to create a geometrically correct tiling from a perspective viewpoint [8]. A tiled floor is composed of straight lines. This method relies on the fact that a straight line remains straight regardless of the viewpoint. Of course, two parallel lines may intersect if viewed from elsewhere.

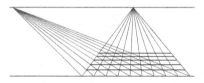

Fig. 3. Alberti's method for tiled floor drawing (Color figure online)

In Fig. 3, the top horizontal line (in green) is the horizon line. The bottom horizontal line is parallel to the first and is divided into equal spacing corresponding to the floor tiles. The blue lines intersect at the vanishing point and the red lines intersect at the secondary vanishing point. The horizontal black lines are the desired floor lines and go through the intersections between the red lines and the blue ones.

---

[4] More specifically, it is the *vertices* property of the Unity *Mesh* that is modified. The three meshes are observed by three Unity *Cameras*.

4.2   Iterative Algorithm

This section discusses intra- and inter-projector calibration. Both consist of iterative processes that use the camera feedback to improve the visual aspect of the projected grids. If some grids can be correctly displayed, then the more complex rendered images of real-world scenes will also be correctly displayed without misalignment and distortion.

Intra-projector Calibration. At the beginning, a grid is projected on one side of the corner, the left or the right. Figure 4(1a) and (1b) show a grid being displayed on the left and right parts of the corner respectively. It is to be noted that they are rendered by two distinct projectors. They are also as wide as the projectors allow. The grid vertices are detected using functions from the OpenCV computer vision library [11]. All the grids used for this work have a size of 11 × 11.

Figure 5 illustrates the perspective correction process. The grid vertices that fall on the planar wall are called unmovable vertices. Those that fall on the curved section are called movable. There are two columns of unmovable vertices and three columns of movable vertices. Both are pale blue in the figure. These numbers are specified by the experimenter based on his or her observations. The camera does not see the entirety of the grid on the left or right side, but this is not an issue as long as there are two columns of unmovable vertices or more.

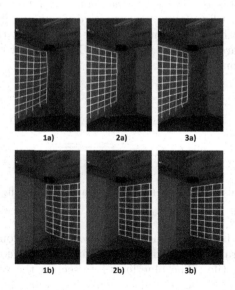

Fig. 4. Grid projected on the left part of the corner, from not corrected (1a) to most corrected (3a). Not optimal iteration in progress (2a) and 2(b). Grid projected on the right part of the corner, from not corrected (1b) to most corrected (3b)

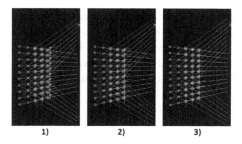

Fig. 5. The iterative process based on Alberti's method, from not corrected (1) to most corrected (3) (Color figure online)

Two points are necessary to determine a line and two columns are necessary to determine the vanishing lines.

The curved sections of the immersive room used at INLB are made of white vinyl. In our lab in order to create a more challenging situation, we used brown paper to mimic the rounded corners. In Fig. 4, one can observe that there are three columns of vertices on the curved section made of brown paper, and two columns of vertices on the planar wall made of white vinyl.

The unmovable vertices are assumed to be correct from a perspective viewpoint. They are used to evaluate where the movable vertices would be if there was no curved section. The goal is to displace the movable vertices at these locations, in order to make the distortion caused by the curved section disappear. As mentioned before, the whole operation is iterative, which implies moving the vertices, detecting them with the use of the camera and computing the new displacements.

Vanishing lines (the red and blue lines in Fig. 3) are retrieved based on the unmovable vertices. These lines are extended into the curved section of the corner and their intersections represent the desired locations of the movable vertices. In Fig. 5, the yellow lines are the vanishing lines from Alberti's method. They are traced based on the two columns of unmovable vertices. Two is the minimum number of columns necessary to determine the vanishing lines, but more can be used if the camera sees them. The yellow points are the intersection points of the vanishing lines. Each column of yellow points should form a perfectly straight line. However, because of the irregularities in the vinyl screen and the imprecision in the OpenCV vertex detection, it is not always the case. Therefore, a least squares method is applied to find the best fit line that goes through each column of yellow points. The big red points are found by intersecting the best fit lines and the horizontal yellow vanishing lines. The red points represent the ideal locations. Movable vertices are iteratively displaced to these locations. The changes are made iteratively because of the non-linearity of the problem. The displacement vectors are transformed from the camera system of coordinates to the projector system of coordinates using a change of basis matrix based on the local vertical and horizontal segments of a grid cell. These segments are green in

Fig. 5. There is a relaxation factor of 0.5. In other words, a vertex is not moved to the ideal location, but halfway of it. The intent is to facilitate convergence.

Figure 4(2a) and (2b) show the resulting grids after 2 iterations. Figure 4(3a) and (3b) show the resulting grids after 6 iterations. Three iterations are sufficient, because they will be repeated many times during the inter-projector calibration process.

Inter-projector Calibration. The intra-projector calibration is embedded in the inter-projector calibration and the whole process must be repeated several times. The left and right sides of the corner are corrected in alternation. After three iterations on each side, the grids on the left and right are moved either closer together or farther from each other depending on whether there is a gap or an overlap. For example, 5 cycles were necessary to produce the results presented later in this article. Each cycle is composed of 3 Alberti's iterations for the left side (intra), 3 Alberti's iterations for the right side (intra) and one step of moving the whole grids (inter). These numbers were found by trial and error to give visually acceptable results. The whole process hopefully converge toward an acceptable solution. After a certain number of iterations and cycles, improvements become non-existent. At this point, grid vertices only oscillate around a certain position. More iterations would only consume more time.

Figure 6(1) shows a case where there is gap instead of an overlap. The gap is reduced until the two grids collide, as illustrated in Fig. 6(3).

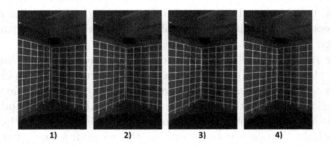

Fig. 6. Inter-projector calibration process, from the beginning (1) to the end (4)

The camera coordinates of the left and right border vertices that should coincide are known. It is therefore possible to compute the inter-projector calibration with the middle ground between these two locations. The middle point minus the actual location of the border vertex forms the displacement vector in camera coordinates. The displacement vector in projector coordinates can be computed for each of the border vertices using a change of basis. These displacement vectors are then averaged. The whole grids are moved according to these average displacement vectors until they collide without overlapping. In an attempt to improve convergence, a relaxation factor of 0.9 is used, i.e. the displacement

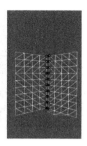

Fig. 7. The left and right grids in the process of being connected together

vector in projector coordinates is multiplied by 0.9. Figure 7 shows the left and right border vertices along with the middle points.

Because the border vertices of the left and right grids may not form perfectly parallel lines, the final step consists in connecting the corresponding border vertices two by two, ignoring perspective which needs to be repeated three times. Distortion files are written immediately after. This step makes any gap disappear even though the perspective may be slightly inexact, as shown in Fig. 6(4).

Each of the two corners is corrected separately, creating four distortion files to be read by the Unity simulation. The distortion files for the right part of the western corner (WR) and the left part of the eastern corner (EL) both describe how to warp the image of the middle projector. They contain the new locations of the grid vertices in the projector coordinate system. The two files are therefore merged together. Some grid cells from the planar section may need to be stretched, especially if the two grids have been moved toward the corners, but the visual impact is not very noticeable. Also, the grids projected on the middle wall are never moved vertically during the correction process. Only the grids on the eastern and western walls move vertically. This is necessary in order to be able to connect the grid from the WR file with the one from the EL file.

In the event that a projector is tilted, an additional parameter can be introduced to rotate the grid by a certain amount of degrees. The parameter is chosen by the user. The rotation origin is the upper left vertex for a grid displayed on the right part of the corner, and the upper right vertex for a grid displayed on the left. In the current implementation, upper vertices should always be visible, because they are used to determine the left and right neighbors of each vertex in the grid. In return, knowing the right and left neighbor of each vertex allows the program to draw the vanishing lines of Alberti's method.

4.3   Implementation Details

Figure 8(1) shows the detected grid vertices. Each vertex is a corner created by the intersection of a vertical and horizontal grid segment of non-zero width. The OpenCV method *goodFeaturestotrack* was used to detect these intersections. In Fig. 8(2), the points are aggregated in order to have only one vertex by intersection. In Fig. 8(3), the vertices are triangulated following Delaunay's method. For

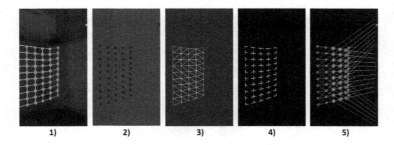

Fig. 8. Detected features (1), vertices after aggregation (2), triangulation (3), graph of neighbors (4), Alberti's method (5)

each vertex, the top, bottom, left and right neighbors are identified in Fig. 8(4). Alberti's method is displayed in Fig. 8(5).

The calibration algorithm was implemented in C++ and uses the FreeGlut graphical library for displaying the grids [12]. Calibration time is approximately 7 min per corner. The camera does not need to be calibrated, but should at best be level with the floor.

5   Experiments and Results

Distortion files for the 3D immersion environment were created by the implementation discussed in this article. In this section, screen captures of the scene generated by the Unity simulation after correction are shown in Fig. 9. Corrected and uncorrected versions of the same point of view are displayed side by side in order to facilitate comparison. As seen in Fig. 9(1B) and (2B), uncorrected images are afflicted by excessive overlap, misalignment of the left and right parts as well as distortions induced by the screen curvature. A slight rotation of the projection on the right part of the corner is also visible. On the contrary, Fig. 9(1A) and (2A) contain minimal overlap. The alignment was also restored. While the distortion created by the screen curvature was reduced, smaller distortions generated by the wobbliness of the paper were not eliminated. This mishap could possibly be due to the coarseness of the 11 × 11 grid.

The luminosity on the darker paper is much lower than on the white vinyl. Such an issue is not present in the actual immersive environment used for rehabilitation. Five cycles of 6 iterations (3 left and 3 right) were necessary in order to obtain these images.

Figure 10 shows two plots of the error as a function of the number of iterations/cycles. For intra-projector calibration, error is defined as the sum of the squared vertex displacements required to comply with the perspective retrieved by Alberti's method. For inter-projector calibration, the error is defined as the sum of the squared vertex displacements necessary to avoid an overlap or a gap between the left and right grids. As seen from the plots, both the intra- and inter-projector calibration processes converge. Three iterations for the left and right sides were performed for 5 cycles, which means 15 iterations, in addition to three final cycles that join the border vertices together while ignoring perspective.

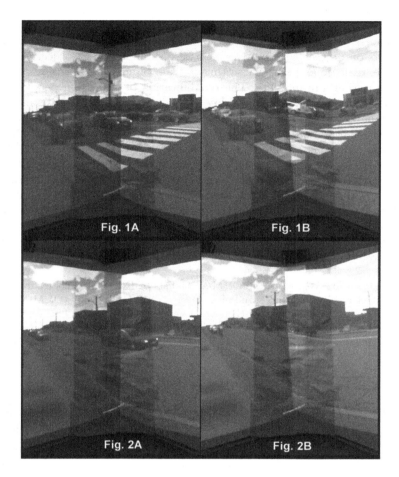

Fig. 9. Two corrected (1A, 2A) and uncorrected views (1B, 2B) of the Unity scene

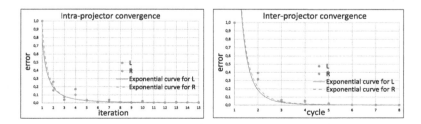

Fig. 10. Convergence plots: Normalized error as a function of the number of iterations (left) and cycles (right)

6   Conclusions

A 3D immersive environment has been presented. Both the visual and the audio components of a street with moving cars were simulated. The objective was to offer a safe, realistic and efficient setting to train blind and low-vision people in urban orientation and mobility. The rehabilitation of low-vision people can be maximized if the projected image is free from distortions and misalignments. A method capable of calibrating projectors while respecting cost constraints was devised. This method uses camera feedback to correct projected grids iteratively. The desired positions of the grid vertices are given by Alberti's perspective technique. The warping used to obtain visually correct grids is applied to the simulation, thus yielding an accurate representation of a street with traffic.

The current method has some limitations. In particular, the luminosity is not entirely uniform, especially in the thin overlapping regions. Blending would be part of a future work and would consist in attenuating the zones of higher luminosity. Additional tests in other immersive rooms would also be welcome in order to evaluate the robustness of the algorithm.

Acknowledgment. We thank the O&M specialists of INLB for their feedback. Our gratitude to Dr. Tony Leroux (audiologist), Pr. Agathe Ratelle (O&M specialist trainer) and Dany Vaillancourt for their creative and helpful skills. This work is supported by CRIM, ISED (Innovation, Science and Economic Development Canada), and le MESI (Ministère de l'Économie, de la Science et de l'Innovation du Québec).

References

1. Merabet, L., Sánchez, J.: Audio-based navigation using virtual environments: combining technology and neuroscience. AER J. Res. Pract. Vis. Impairment Blindness **2**(3), 128–137 (2009)
2. Sánchez, J., Saenz, M., Garrido, J.M.: Usability of a multimodal video game to improve the navigational skills for blind children. ACM Trans. Accessible Comput. **3**(2), 7 (2010)
3. LaGrow, S.J.: Improving perception for orientation and mobility. In: Wiener, W.R., Welsh, R.L., Blasch, B.B. (eds.) Foundations of Orientation and Mobility, vol. 2, 3rd edn, pp. 3–26. AFB Press, New York (2010)
4. Couturier, J., Ratelle, A.: Manuel d'Intervention en Orientation et Mobilité. Université de Montréal and INLB, Québec, Canada. Course Notes (2012)
5. Garcia-Dorado, I., Cooperstock, J.R.: Fully automatic multi-projector calibration with an uncalibrated camera. In: Proceedings of the Computer Vision and Pattern Recognition Workshops, Colorado Springs, pp. 29–36. IEEE, June 2011
6. Baar, J.V., Willwacher, T., Rao, S., Raskar, R.: Seamless multi-projector display on curved screens. In: Proceedings of the Workshop on Virtual Environments, Zurich, pp. 281–286. ACM (2003)
7. Brown, M., Majumder, A., Yang, R.: Camera-based calibration techniques for seamless multiprojector displays. IEEE Trans. Visual Comput. Graphics **11**(2), 193–206 (2005)
8. Stillwell, J.: Mathematics and its History. Springer, New York (2010)

9. May, B.B., Cahill, N.D., Rosen, M.R.: Calibration of a multi-projector system for display on a cylindrical surface. In: Proceedings of the Image Processing Workshop, Rochester, New York, pp. 6–9. IEEE (2010)
10. Sajadi, B., Majumder, A.: Auto-calibration of multi-projector cave-like immersive environments. IEEE Trans. Visual Comput. Graphics **18**(3), 381–393 (2011)
11. Bradski, G.: The opencv library. Dr. Dobb's Journal of Software Tools (2000)
12. Olszta, P.W., Umbach, A., Baker, S., Fay, J.: The freeglut library (version 3.0.0). (2015). freeglut.sourceforge.net

Human-Drone-Interaction: A Case Study to Investigate the Relation Between Autonomy and User Experience

Patrick Ferdinand Christ[1,3(✉)], Florian Lachner[2,3], Axel Hösl[3], Bjoern Menze[1], Klaus Diepold[4], and Andreas Butz[2]

[1] Image-based Biomedical Modeling Group,
Technical University of Munich (TUM), Munich, Germany
{patrick.christ,bjoern.menze}@tum.de
[2] Chair for Human-Computer-Interaction, University of Munich (LMU),
Munich, Germany
{florian.lachner,butz}@ifi.lmu.de
[3] Center for Digital and Technology Management, TUM and LMU,
Munich, Germany
axel.hoesl@ifi.lmu.de, {christ,lachner}@cdtm.de
[4] Department Electrical and Computer Engineering,
Technical University of Munich (TUM), Munich, Germany
kldi@tum.de

Abstract. Autonomous robots effectively support the human workforce in a variety of industries such as logistics or health care. With an increasing level of system autonomy humans normally have to give up control and rely on the system to react appropriately. We wanted to investigate the effects of different levels of autonomy on the User Experience (UX) and ran a case study involving autonomous flying drones. In a student competition, four teams developed four drone prototypes with varying levels of autonomy. We evaluated the resulting UX in 24 semi-structured interviews in a setting with high perceived workload (competition, autonomous vs. manual) and a non-competition setting (autonomous). The case study showed that the level of autonomy has various influences on UX, particularly in situations with high perceived workload. Based on our findings, we derive recommendations for the UX-oriented development of autonomous drones.

Keywords: Human-robot interaction · Drones · Assistive technologies · User experience

1 Introduction

With an increasing technical reliability of autonomous systems, more and more human responsibilities are carried out by machines. The increasing level of autonomy shall increase the efficiency and the safety and shall simultaneously decrease

---

P.F. Christ and F. Lachner contributed equally.

© Springer International Publishing Switzerland 2016
G. Hua and H. Jégou (Eds.): ECCV 2016 Workshops, Part II, LNCS 9914, pp. 238–253, 2016.
DOI: 10.1007/978-3-319-48881-3_17

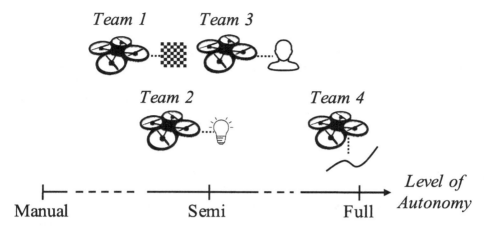

Fig. 1. Levels of autonomy of the team's drone prototypes using a checkerboard (1), a light source (2), a human face (3), and a floor marking (4) as control unit.

the human workload [1]. Traditionally, the design of autonomous systems focuses on the technical implementation aspects, especially technology-heavy disciplines such as computer vision and robotics, ranging from the system's functionality to associated sensors and software [2]. Previous research in the field of human-robot interaction, such as [3–6], already intensively analyzes the utility of computer vision technology for autonomous drones. However, these projects do not focus on the experience of interacting with vision-based drones.

In this paper, we want to take this thought further and investigate the relation between autonomy and User Experience (UX) under different levels of perceived workload. We see this consideration as a key issue in the success of future assistive technologies. To create different levels of perceived workload, we chose to conduct a case study with four teams in competitive settings using (semi-)autonomously flying drones as exemplary systems. The teams used four different control mechanisms based on state-of-the art computer vision algorithms (see Fig. 1). Hence, the research question of this study can be summarized as follows:

RQ: *"How does the user's experience when interacting with flying robots differ in situations with different perceived workload?"*

This study provides two main contributions: First, based on the analysis of four different drone prototypes, each based on an individual (semi-)autonomous interaction design, we investigated the relation between autonomy level and UX. Second, we propose concrete design recommendations for the UX-oriented design of future (semi-)autonomous flying robots.

The goal of this paper is to foster the discussion of experiences with flying robots in the computer vision community and to encourage researchers and practitioners to consider both technical and UX-related attributes when building next generation of assistive flying robots.

2 Background

The term UX is an established concept in a variety of different disciplines, ranging from ergonomics to human factors and human-computer interaction. An established approach to consolidate the variety of different perspectives is the breakdown of UX into pragmatic and hedonic product attributes [7]. However, pragmatic product attributes (i.e., the usability) of technological tools is more and more taken for granted [8]. With an increasing technological maturity researchers should put more emphasis on hedonic product attributes in order to ensure the quality of everyday actions - particularly when designing assistive technologies.

As found by Fitts [9], machines perform better than human operators in certain aspects, such as precision and efficiency, in ensuring consistent quality in repetitive tasks, or in moving heavy loads smoothly. In other aspects humans outperform machines, e.g., in improvising and using flexible procedures, in identifying visual patterns, in reasoning or in exercising judgement. Consequently, when done properly, exploiting machine benefits generally leads to a reduction of workload for users and decreased stress, fatigue, or human error. To make these benefits accessible to users, interaction with systems is necessary, yet at the same time systems need to be able to execute tasks or subtasks on their own. How independently a system can operate is generally referred to as its autonomy. The term itself, as coined in research on human-robot interaction [10], has multiple definitions in the literature [11–14] with varying characterizations. Sheridan and Verplank [14] characterized it by distinguishing ten *levels of autonomy* (LOA) ranging from 'Human does it all (1)' to'Computer acts entirely autonomously (10)' with increasing autonomy for each level. How autonomously a system can operate is determined by its design (e.g.,'Computer executes alternative if human approves (5)'). In some use cases a more or respectively less autonomous design is desirable. Therefore, flexible or adaptive autonomy approaches with a dynamically changing level of autonomy were proposed e.g., by Miller and Parasuraman [15]. Looking at the consequences for users and results when interacting with such systems, they describe an *inevitable trade-off between workload and unpredictability*: The more autonomously systems operate, the more workload[1] is taken off the user's shoulders. In consequence, however, the unpredictability of the results increases as users are no longer in control of the execution details. The more users need or want to be in control of the execution details on the other hand, the more their workload increases in turn.

Drones can serve well as a practical example in applying Sheridan and Verplanks LOA as they incorporate multiple at once. One reason for their popularity is their ease of control compared to remote controlled helicopters, for instance. This is due to their four (or more) rotor design leading to easier in-air stabilization. The stabilization is done fully autonomously by a built-in control unit (10).

---

[1] Hart 1988 introduced in his work NASA TLX the concept of perceived workload as a combination of mental, physical, and temporal demand as well as performance, effort, and frustration [16].

The different LOA can be used depending on usage contexts such as manual control for recording landscape or semi-autonomous tracking of and circling around a protagonist as in action sports.

3   Related Work

A range of prior work investigated interactions between humans and autonomously controlled systems (i.e., ground and aerial robots) in a variety of different settings.

With an increasing interest in the interaction between humans and autonomous systems, researchers move away from a pure analysis of input devices towards the investigation of more natural control gestures. Ende et al. [17] thereby focus on co-working tasks of technical robots, whereas Nagi et al. [18] analyze the interplay of gesture and facial recognition. Based on the analysis of human-drone interaction, Cauchard et al. [19] illustrate that natural gesture control generally lead to more personal relations to autonomous systems. The work of Ng and Sharlin [20] that examines body controls of drones inspired by falconeering gestures supports this view on natural human-drone interaction. Furthermore, Cid et al. [21], Heenan et al. [22], and Szafir et al. [23] highlight that visual feedback increases the level of empathy of human-robot interaction.

Against the background of these studies, we want to investigate how different levels of autonomy of an autonomous drone influence the interaction with the associated UX. First attempts to analyze the perception of different levels of autonomy are mentioned by Rödel et al. [24] and Hassenzahl and Klapprich [1]. These studies, however, do not comprehensively analyze the complexity of autonomous system but remain on a higher level of automation tasks (see [1]) or focus on the indication of the presumable UX of future autonomous cars (see [24]).

Based on the NASA TLX, researchers have already shown that with an increasing level of system autonomy the perceived workload decreases [16,25]. The challenge of analyzing the interaction with autonomous systems is based on the subjective interpretation of each facet of the experienced interaction, ranging from usability over workload to experience. For the course of this study we want to investigate existing measurement tools in order to derive an interview guideline that is applicable for our particular research question. The interview guideline is comprehensively explained in the next section *Methodology*.

4   Methodology

As the implementation of autonomous flying robots is still on the rise, we decided to organize a student competition in order to develop various prototypes. We chose a a Parrot AR Drone 2.0 with the goal to implement different interaction designs.

The student competition was conducted in the form of a case study. First, students from our research institution were able to sign up for a drone course.

Within this course, the students developed different prototypes. Second, the course ended in a competition, where the prototypes were put into practice. Third, we conducted interviews with the participants in order to analyze their experiences of the interaction with the drone.

4.1 Development of Prototypes

The case study was announced as a one-week student competition at our research institution[2]. The course itself consisted of two steps: Initially, the registered students were coupled in teams and had one week the develop a drone prototype. After one week, the student teams put their work into practice in three different settings, as described below.

Participants, Setting, and Task: In total, eight participants from different academic backgrounds (6x Computer Science, 1x Electrical Engineering, and 1x Communication Studies) and ages ($22\,\text{to}\,26\,\mu = 24$) signed up for the one-week student competition without a financial reward. At the beginning of the competition, the students were randomly coupled in four teams of two. Over the course of the initial development phase, the participants were trained in python programming, image processing, computer vision, feedback control theory, state estimation, and autonomous navigation by academic and industry experts to ensure an equally distributed level of knowledge regarding the design of autonomous systems.

In the first phase of the case study the teams had to program a Parrat AR Drone 2.0 (52,5 cm x 51,5 cm), a quadcopter with an integrated HD camera, using a open-source python API[3]. The student teams were asked to process the video stream of the drone in real-time in order to fly and compete autonomously in a race at the end of the course. However, the teams were not dictated an obligatory interaction design. All four teams were told to individually develop a prototype with a desired level of autonomy at their own discretion. In the final race, each drone prototype had to pass the same predetermined track consisting of three hockey goals that were positioned in a L-shaped track. Figure 3 shows an impression of the drone race.

Prototypes: The four student teams programmed and implemented four unique types of drone interactions that cover different levels of autonomy. For the analysis in this paper, we were able to distinguish two types of autonomous interaction designs: *"Semi-autonomous"* when the drone "executes an alternative if the human approves" and *"full-autonomous"* when "the drone decides everything" - related to the LOA according to Sheridan and Verplank [14]. Figure 1 illustrates the four different drone prototypes and the associated interaction design whereas algorithm 1 exemplarily for all four teams demonstrates the algorithm of team 1 as described below.

---

[2] Course Information can be found at http://drones.cdtm.de.

[3] Source-code can be found at https://github.com/CDTM/Autonomous-Drones.

Team 1: Recognition of a printed checkerboard. Team 1 implemented an algorithm based on Rufli et al. [26] that enabled the drone's front camera to detect and follow the movements of a checkerboard that was printed on a piece of paper. Based on the known geometry the center of the checkerboard is found using corner and edge detection. The drone is steered and controlled as it tries to keep the centroid in the center of the image frame. Furthermore, through the identification of the outer-most square it is possible to push and pull the drone forward and backward. In order to avoid oscillation, a PID controller is used to improve the magnitude of the movement speeds. This interaction is semi-autonomous.

```
Data: Drone front camera stream
Result: Drone movement
while drone not landed do
    read current frame;
    if frame is valid then
        recognize Checkerboard;
        if Checkerboard is recognized then
            Find center of Checkerboard;
            Calculate offset of checkerboard center to camera center;
            Calculate and apply steering commands to PID Controller;
            Move Drone;
        else
            break
        end
        Drone hover;
    end
end
```

Algorithm 1. Exemplary algorithm for semi-autonomous drone interaction using a checkerboard recognition by Rufli et al. [26].

Team 2: Recognition of a color/light source. Team 2 employed an algorithm based on Comaniciu et al. [27] that allowed the drone's front camera to detect a homogeneously colored object or a light source. This mechanism had a setup phase, in which the algorithm was trained to recognize either a colored object or a light source. In the final competition, the team used a light source to control the drone. After the setup phase the drone tried to center the light-source in the image frame and follow the track of the light-source. This interaction is semi-autonomous.

Team 3: Recognition of a human face. Team 3 programmed a face detection algorithm based on Viola and Jones [28] that recognizes a human face from the drone's front camera. In this approach the drone tried to center a human face in the image frame and therefore follow the track and movements of the respective human. Furthermore, an additionally implemented emergency mode allowed the drone to keep its position through "hovering" as soon as the face recognition is interrupted. This interaction is semi-autonomous.

Team 4: Recognition of a floor marking. Team 4 implemented an algorithm based on Hart [29] that can detect and follow a colored line on the ground using the drone's bottom camera as an input device. Thereby, the drone is positioned at a certain height above the particular line. In the final race at the end of the student competition, the team used a red tape to mark the respective line on the ground. The algorithm recognized the line (i.e., the tape) and constantly tried to keep this line in the center of the bottom camera frame. As soon as the line is not centered anymore the correct angle to approach the line again is calculated. This interaction is full-autonomous.

4.2 Competition, Data Collection, and Analysis

In order to analyze the experience of interacting with flying robots in situations with differently perceived workloads we identified four suitable settings for the final race. We distinguished different perceived workloads through the setting dimensions *"Competition vs. No Competition"* and *"Manual Control vs. Autonomous Control"*. As Cauchard et al. [19] already conducted an elaborate study on manually controlled human-drone interactions in a setting without competition we concentrated on (1) *Competition/Autonomous*, (2) *No Competition/Autonomous*, and (3) *Competition/Manual Control* as described below and illustrated in Fig. 2. In all three settings, both participants of the four teams had three attempts to finish the track. As the best run of each participant counted we ended up with 24 eligible runs in total.

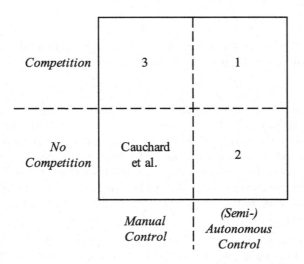

Fig. 2. Allocation of the three analyzed settings. (1) Competition/Autonomous, (2) No Competition/Autonomous and (3) Competition/Manual Control.

1. Competition/Autonomous: In the Competition/Autonomous setting the student teams had to compete in the race using the autonomous control algorithm of their drone prototype. A manual interaction would disqualify them for the current run. The best student team was rewarded with a gift.

2. No Competition/Autonomous: In the No Competition/Autonomous setting the student teams where asked to autonomously direct their drone prototype through the track. However, no time was tracked in this setting.

3. Competition/Manual Control: In the Competition/Manual Control setting the student teams had to use the official Parrot App for Smartphones to steer the drone manually through the track. The autonomous control mechanisms were deactivated in this setting. The best student team was rewarded with a gift.

After all three attempts per setting we conducted interviews with all eight participants (in total 24 interviews, each between 15 and 20 min) to analyze experience-related aspects of the interaction with the drone prototypes. Our interviews were semi-structured and audio-recorded for post-hoc analysis.

In order to meet the requirements of our research question we developed an interview guideline that served as a basis for the semi-structured interviews (see Table 1). Inspired by related work in the fields of UX, usability, and workload evaluation (as indicated in Table 1), relevant experience- and workload-related categories (e.g., "User" and "Environment") and dimensions (e.g., "Mental Demand" and "Frustration Level") and associated interview questions were developed by the first and the second author.

Post-hoc coding was conducted according to Mayring and Fenzl [30] by the second author, who has a broad experience in open-coding of interview data. Interview statements were therefore clustered according to the questions' categories (see table 1). The objective was to identify key issues across the study settings and to derive design recommendations that strengthen the linkage of computer vision and robotics and the interaction of technological tools with people.

5 Results

The next sections represent the results of our case study. First, we demonstrate the outcome of our interviews with regards to the three study settings. Thereby, we focus on the perceived workload (based on the dimension *"Competition vs. No Competition"*) as well as the participants' experiences with autonomous and manual control mechanisms (based on the dimension *"Manual Control vs. Autonomous Control"*). Second, based on these outcomes we derive design recommendations for (semi-)autonomous flying robots.

5.1 Interview Outcomes

To analyze the relation between autonomy and UX (i.e., the associated perceived workload) of vision-based drones we consolidated key findings of our interviews. These key findings allow the consequent derivation of design recommendations to understand the interaction of people with flying robots.

Table 1. Semi-structured interview guideline.

Dimension	Scale (qualitative)	Related Work
Mental Demand	Can you describe a situation that was mentally demanding for you?	
Physical Demand	Can you describe a situation that was physically demanding for you?	
Autonomy / Independence	Can you describe a situation where you had the feeling that you directly control the drone?	[31–34]
	Can you describe a situation where you had the feeling that you were not in full control over the drone?	
Competence	At what point of the course did you feel confident in performing the task?	
Enjoyment, Pleasure	Can you describe the most enjoyable aspect of performing the task?	
Frustration Level	Can you describe the most frustrating aspect of performing the task?	[31–33,35,36]
	Can you describe the most stressful aspect of performing the task?	
Perceived Ease of Use	Which part of your interaction/solution would you describe as easy to use?	
	Which part of your interaction/solution would you describe as difficult to use?	
Personal Attachment	In which way did you build a relationship to your drone?	[37]
	How did the relationship to your drone influence how you interacted with the drone?	
Performance/Outcome Satisfaction	How would you describe your performance?	
	If you could optimize one thing next time, what would it be?	[31,32,38]
Unpredictability/Error-handling	What kind of problems did you have to overcome?	
	What went differently than expected and how did you handle these situations?	[31,32,35,36,38]
Temporal Demand (hurried or rushed)	At what time of the course did you feel being rushed or hurried?	

System Feedback Enhances the Experience of interactions: All participants enjoyed interacting with their drones regardless of the respective level of autonomy. Having established a feeling of control, directing the (semi-)autonomously controlled drone was considered as very enjoyable (setting 1 and 2). The pleasure of being in control arose either through feedback from the (semi-autonomous) drone, a tangible input device (semi-autonomous) or through a reduced workload (autonomous drone). A student from team 1 (semi-autonomous drone) mentioned: *"I think it was very enjoyable [...] that we could take very direct influence on the drone using the checkerboard. It kind of was like in the circus, where you have a tiger and you say 'jump over this' [...] and we basically made the same thing with the drone navigating it through the obstacle course"* [P1]. The instant feedback from the prototype facilitated the development of a feeling of being in control. However, external factors as well as latency reduced the feeling of being in control: *"When the drone reacted to my input or my actions without much of a delay I felt confident. For example, when moving the light [source] to left or right [and] the drone also directly rotated to the left or the right, I had the feeling of complete control. So I think it is also a matter of latency"* [P3]. The team that used the autonomously controlled drone (team 4), however, described the decreased workload as enjoyable, *"[The] most enjoyable moment in the race was, when the drone surprisingly went along the path without any [manual] corrections"* [P7].

Direct feedback mechanisms also positively influenced the ease of use of the prototypes: *" [The interaction] did not really need a lot of time to explain someone who has never seen this specific drone and implementation or control. You just say 'here is the checkerboard'. And even with small movements you [realize] how the drone moves and it is very easy to keep the drone on track"* [P2]. However, participants from team 2 (recognition of color/light source) and team 3 (recognition of a human face) mentioned difficulties regarding the ease of use due to a lack of robustness of the associated algorithms. External factors such as different lighting, fast movements of the tracked object, and a lack of control mechanisms (e.g., a PID controller) led to difficulties in the interaction with the drone. The participants highlighted that they had difficulties *"If the background is too bright, it [did not] work [recognition of a light source]"* [P4]. and while *"Holding it stable, while moving, shaking it not too much, was difficult"* [P3].

Environment Perception Influences the Feeling of control: Environmental factors played an important role in the autonomous setting with competition (setting 1). Unexpected environmental conditions, bystanders, and the orientation of the drone in space were the most prominent environmental factors as, for example, *"this direct sunlight completely misguided the drone. [...] We did not anticipate that problem"* [P2]. Furthermore, *"There were a lot of faces in the room [...] and also different parts of walls were recognized as faces"* [P6]. For others it was *"hard to locate where the obstacle is, relatively to the drone, because [the student] was looking at the drone and then while flying fast [one] can not really see if the path [the drone is] taking will work out or if [the drone will] touch something"* [P8]. All in all, these unexpected environmental factors lowered the perceived feeling of control. In the manual setting (setting 3), the participants were less bothered by external influences. The possibility to use an additional

Fig. 3. Impressions from the autonomous drone race competition. Four student teams had to program a Parrot AR Drone 2.0 in order to fly autonomously in a drone race. In this picture a semi-autonomous interaction using face recognition is depicted.

input device even increased one student's risk tolerance: *"I would try to check whether you can even increase the speed in the setting, lower the limitations of the drone. So basically taking away safety features" [P3].*

5.2   Design Recommendations

Based on the investigation of the three different perceived workload settings, we derived three design recommendations for autonomous flying robots. The goal of these recommendations is to support a user-centered design of future autonomous flying robots and to carry on the concept of UX in the field of computer vision and robotics.

Maneuvering in 3D Space: Autonomous systems such as naval or aerial drones move in 3D space. We observed that maneuvering and interacting with a flying drone in 3D Space was mentally demanding for all participants, particularly at the beginning of each race. Adding an additional degree of freedom led to a high cognitive load, since the participants were accustomed to 2D movements, such as walking or driving a car.

Experiences from the case study: In the manual controlled setting, the participants needed a certain amount of time to familiarize themselves with the control mechanism in a 3D space. *"I think it's getting better and better the more I try. So it's really something which is dependent on my skills" [P2].* In the autonomous controlled setting, the participants reduced the complexity of the (semi-)autonomously controlled drone in 3D space by reducing the numbers of allowed movement directions. Team 2, for example, disabled the backward pitch movement of their drone to overcome the obstacles. Team 1 restricted the drone to a fixed altitude to simplify the semi-autonomous interaction. *"We lacked the controls to move the drone up and downwards. We just thought the drone will fit through the gates in the end" [P1].*

Recommendation: With an increasing number of degrees of freedom, familiarization with the control of a system becomes more time consuming. For manual and autonomous interactions, we recommend to restrict the number of possible movements to the movements that are necessary in the respective use case. For example, one can fix or autonomously adjust the altitude of an autonomous system (e.g., of a surveillance drone) or restrict the system to one type of movement at a time. Consequently, (semi-)autonomous control mechanisms can support the handling in complex situations.

Precision, Feedback, and Latency: The interaction with autonomous systems requires a precise, direct, and instant feedback to foster the feeling of control. Latency in performing an interaction or the lack of feedback can substantially reduce the perceived feeling of control.

Experiences from the case study: We observed that for both systems, semi-autonomous and autonomous, a precise and direct feedback of the system led to a high feeling of control and consequently a positive UX. *"It was a great feeling, [...] I could feel [...] the small changes and when I changed the position of the paper [i.e., the checkerboard] it was following it" [P3].* In contrast, latency within the interaction with the drone harmed the feeling of control, although it was regained again afterwards. *"I thought it actually lost [the detection of] my face but it didn't. So again the [latency] problem solved itself by being a little bit more patient" [P7].*

Recommendation: As a conclusion, we suggest to design direct feedback mechanisms, as similarly mentioned by Cauchard et al. [19]. Moreover, the implementation of advanced and precise control procedures, such as a PID Controller, and the reduction of latency through a stable interaction design can promote a higher feeling of control and consequently a better UX.

Natural Emergency Procedures: Dealing with emergency situations is one of the key issues in designing autonomous flying robots for assistive purposes. Emergency situations are unforeseen and potentially harm people or the environment. Thus, the interaction with autonomous flying robots in an emergency situation is generally demanding. The challenge in emergency situations is based on the loss of control of the user and the consequential requirement of a suitable emergency procedure. In our case study four emergency actions were possible: direct control, immediate stop, immediate landing, and hovering (i.e., constant positioning in 3D space).

Experiences from the case study: In manual interactions we observed that in emergency situations the participants automatically used the immediate stop mechanism or the landing function. *"In the second run [of the manual competition] I first anticipated the drone's path [...] when I lost control I tried to to regain control, but then I emergency landed it" [P3].* In autonomous interactions we observed that participants resolved emergency situations initially using the hovering mechanism and later using immediate landing. *"I bumped into the goal [i.e., one of the obstacles], which was not a big problem because [...] you could just wait a few seconds, the drone hovered and you could just start again" [P1].*

Recommendation: With an increasing level of autonomy the importance of emergency considerations increases as users have to rely on the system to function correctly. Therefore, we suggest to design natural emergency handling schemes (i.e., hovering for drones) according to the level of autonomy in order to assist the user in potential breakdowns. Natural emergency procedures allow the user to realize and understand the need to interfere. Thus, a positive UX can be ensured.

6   Limitations and Future Work

This study aims to foster an multilateral discourse about autonomous systems. However, experiences and associated evaluations are subjective in nature, thus complicating generalization. Extensive and diverse studies are required to comprehensively understand users' feelings and emotions. For our case study we were able to count eight registered participants from our research institution. We asked the participants to develop an individual interaction design for a aerial robot (i.e., a flying drone) in teams of two. Thus, we ended up with four different drone prototypes, whereas the analysis of more interaction designs as well as different levels of autonomy can lead to further and more profound insights. Nevertheless, we were able to derive reasonable insights and design recommendation across all prototypes. Here, the study can serve as a basis and provide comparative data for future research.

To ensure the comparability of the experienced interactions of all participants we chose drones as the development object for all teams. As a consequence, we focused on merely one specific aspect (i.e., the relation between autonomy and UX) in our case study and neglected further peculiarities of drones, such as noise generation of the rotor blades or specific flight characteristics. Moreover, the particular study setting (i.e., participants developed the interaction design themselves) may have resulted in a higher personal attachment compared to just using the system. We therefore want to motivate other researchers to take the concept of UX-oriented, autonomous systems further to additional application domains, such as ground or naval robots.

7   Conclusion

The central issue of this study was to analyze the relation between different levels of autonomy and the associated UX. To investigate this relation, we implemented a case study in the form of a student competition and selected flying drones as exemplary autonomous systems. In the end, we were able to contrast four different human-drone interactions based on semi-structured interviews with all participants. Altogether, we derive two main contributions from this study. First, we found autonomy-specific insights on the UX of human-drone interaction. Second, we presented three design recommendations for the future design of autonomous flying robots.

In summary, we see our work as a step towards the design of UX-sensitive autonomous flying robots. We want to highlight the consideration of UX as a crucial factor and foster an ongoing discussion in the field of computer vision and robotics research.

References

1. Hassenzahl, M., Klapperich, H.: Convenient, Clean, and efficient? The experiential costs of everyday automation. In: Proceeding of NordiCHI 2014, pp. 21–30. ACM (2014)
2. Parasuraman, R., Sheridan, T.B., Wickens, C.D.: A model for types and levels of human interaction with automation. Syst. Man Cybern. Part A Syst. Hum. **30**(3), 286–297 (2000)
3. Layne, R., Hospedales, T.M., Gong, S.: Investigating open-world person re-identification using a drone. In: Agapito, L., Bronstein, M.M., Rother, C. (eds.) ECCV 2014. LNCS, vol. 8927, pp. 225–240. Springer, Heidelberg (2015). doi:10.1007/978-3-319-16199-0_16
4. Gemert, J.C., Verschoor, C.R., Mettes, P., Epema, K., Koh, L.P., Wich, S.: Nature conservation drones for automatic localization and counting of animals. In: Agapito, L., Bronstein, M.M., Rother, C. (eds.) ECCV 2014. LNCS, vol. 8925, pp. 255–270. Springer, Heidelberg (2015). doi:10.1007/978-3-319-16178-5_17
5. Dotenco, S., Gallwitz, F., Angelopoulou, E.: Autonomous approach and landing for a low-cost quadrotor using monocular cameras. In: Agapito, L., Bronstein, M.M., Rother, C. (eds.) ECCV 2014. LNCS, vol. 8925, pp. 209–222. Springer, Heidelberg (2015). doi:10.1007/978-3-319-16178-5_14
6. Kim, J., Lee, Y.S., Han, S.S., Kim, S.H., Lee, G.H., Ji, H.J., Choi, H.J., Choi, K.N.: Autonomous flight system using marker recognition on drone. In: 21st Korea-Japan Joint Workshop on Frontiers of Computer Vision (FCV), pp. 1–4. IEEE (2015)
7. Hassenzahl, M.: User experience (UX): towards an experiential perspective on product quality. In: Proceeding of IHM 2008, pp. 11–15 (2008)
8. Pine, J., Gilmore, J.H.: Welcome to the experience economy. Harvard Bus. Rev. **76**(4), 97–105 (1998)
9. Fitts, P.M.: Human Engineering for an Effective Air-Navigation and Traffic-Control System. National Research Council, Division of Anthropology and Psychology, Committee on Aviation Psychology (1951)
10. Goodrich, M.A., Schultz, A.C.: Human-robot interaction: a survey. Foundations Trends Hum. Comput. Interact. **1**(3), 203–275 (2007)
11. Albus, J.S.: Outline for a theory of intelligence. IEEE Trans. Syst. Man Cybern. **21**(3), 473–509 (1991)
12. Beavers, G., Hexmoor, H.: Types and limits of agent autonomy. In: Nickles, M., Rovatsos, M., Weiss, G. (eds.) AUTONOMY 2003. LNCS (LNAI), vol. 2969, pp. 95–102. Springer, Heidelberg (2004). doi:10.1007/978-3-540-25928-2_8
13. Crandall, J.W., Goodrich, M., Olsen Jr., D.R., Nielsen, C.W., et al.: Validating human-robot interaction schemes in multitasking environments. IEEE Trans. Syst. Man Cybern. **35**(4), 438–449 (2005). others:
14. Sheridan, T.B., Verplank, W.L.: Human and Computer Control of Undersea Tele-operators. Technical report, DTIC Document (1978)
15. Miller, C.A., Parasuraman, R.: Designing for flexible interaction between humans and automation: delegation interfaces for supervisory control. Hum. Factors **49**(1), 57–75 (2007)

16. Hart, S.G., Staveland, L.E.: Development of NASA-TLX (Task Load Index): results of empirical and theoretical research. Adv. Psychol. **52**, 139–183 (1988)
17. Ende, T., Haddadin, S., Parusel, S., Wüsthoff, T., Hassenzahl, M., Albu-Schäffer, A.: A human-centered approach to robot gesture based communication within collaborative working processes. In: Proceeding of IROS 2011, pp. 3367–3374 (2011)
18. Nagi, J., Giusti, A., Di Caro, G.A., Gambardella, L.M.: Human control of UAVs using face pose estimates and hand gestures. In: Proceeding of HRI 2014, pp. 1–2. ACM (2014)
19. Cauchard, J.R., Jane, L.E., Zhai, K.Y., Landay, J.A.: Drone and me: an exploration into natural human-drone interaction. In: Proceeding UbiComp 2015, pp. 361–365. ACM (2015)
20. Ng, W.S., Sharlin, E.: Collocated interaction with flying robots. In: Proceeding IEEE RO-MAN 2011, pp. 143–149 (2011)
21. Cid, F., Manso, L.J., Calderita, L.V., Sánchez, A., Nuñez, P.: Engaging human-to-robot attention using conversational gestures and lip-synchronization. J. Phys. Agents **6**(1), 3–10 (2012)
22. Heenan, B., Greenberg, S., Manesh, S.A., Sharlin, E.: Designing social greetings in human robot interaction. In: Proceeding DIS 2014, pp. 855–864. ACM (2014)
23. Szafir, D., Mutlu, B., Fong, T.: Communicating directionality in flying robots. In: Proceeding HRI 2015, vol. 2, pp. 19–26 (2015)
24. Rödel, C., Stadler, S., Meschtscherjakov, A., Tscheligi, M.: Towards Autonomous Cars: the effect of autonomy levels on acceptance and user experience. In: Proceeding AutoUI 2014, Seattle, WA, USA, pp. 1–8. ACM (2014)
25. Steinfeld, A., Fong, T., Kaber, D., Lewis, M., Scholtz, J., Schultz, A., Goodrich, M.: Common metrics for human-robot interaction. In: Proceedings of the 1st ACM/IEEE International Conference on Human-Robot Interaction, pp. 33–40. ACM (2006)
26. Rufli, M., Scaramuzza, D., Siegwart, R.: Automatic detection of checkerboards on blurred and distorted images. In: Proceeding IROS 2008, pp. 3121–3126 (2008)
27. Comaniciu, D., Ramesh, V., Meer, P.: Real-time tracking of non-rigid objects using mean shift. IEEE Conf. Comput. Vis. Pattern Recogn. **2**(7), 142–149 (2000)
28. Viola, P., Jones, M.: Rapid object detection using a boosted cascade of simple features. In: Conference on Computer Vision and Pattern Recognition (CVPR) (2001)
29. Hart, P.E.: Use of the hough transformtion to detect lines. Commun. ACM **15**, 11–15 (1972)
30. Mayring, P., Fenzl, T.: Qualitative Inhaltsanalyse. Springer, Wiesbaden (2014)
31. Hart, S.G.: Nasa-Task Load Index (NASA-TLX); 20 Years Later. In: Proceedings of the Human Factors and Ergonomics Society Annual Meeting, vol. 50(9) (2006)
32. Reid, G.B., Potter, S.S., Bressler, J.R.: Subjective Workload Assessment Technique (SWAT): A User's Guide. Technical report (1989)
33. Sheldon, K.M., Elliot, A.J., Kim, Y., Kasser, T.: What is satisfying about satisfying events? Testing 10 candidate psychological needs. J. Personal. Soc. Psychol. **80**(2), 325–339 (2001)
34. Brooke, J.: SUS - a quick and dirty usability scale. Usability Eval. Ind. **189**(195), 4–7 (1996)
35. Laugwitz, B., Held, T., Schrepp, M.: Construction and evaluation of a user experience questionnaire. In: Holzinger, A. (ed.) USAB 2008. LNCS, vol. 5298, pp. 63–76. Springer, Heidelberg (2008)
36. Lund, A.M.: Measuring usability with the USE questionnaire. Usability Interface **8**(2), 3–6 (2001)

37. Madsen, M., Gregor, S.: Measuring human-computer trust. In: Proceeding ACIS 2000, pp. 6–8 (2000)
38. Lewis, J.: IBM computer usability satisfaction questionnaires: psychometric evaluation and instructions for use. Int. J. Hum.-Comput. Interact. **7**(1), 57–78 (1995)

Feasibility Analysis of Eye Typing with a Standard Webcam

Yi Liu[1,2(✉)], Bu Sung Lee[2], Andrzej Sluzek[3], Deepu Rajan[2], and Martin Mckeown[4]

[1] Nanyang Institute of Technology in Health and Medicine, Singapore, Singapore
yliu028@e.ntu.edu.sg
[2] SCSE, Nanyang Technological University, Singapore, Singapore
[3] Khalifa University, Abu Dhabi, United Arab Emirates
[4] University of British Columbia, Vancouver, BC, Canada

Abstract. With the development of assistive technology, eye typing has become an alternative form of text entry for physically challenged people with severe motor disabilities. However, additional eye-tracking devices need to be used to track eye movements which is inconvenient in some cases. In this paper, we propose an appearance-based method to estimate the person's gaze point using a webcam, and also investigate some practical issues of the method. The experimental results demonstrate the feasibility of eye typing using the proposed method.

Keywords: Assistive technology · Eye typing · Gaze estimation · Appearance-based method

1 Introduction

In modern society, being healthy means more than just not being sick. To maintain good health, it is necessary to not only take care of the physical aspect but also the emotional one, with engagement with the community. Communication is an important tool to staying engaged. However, physically challenged people with motor disabilities have difficulty in communicating. About 120,000 cases of motor neuro disease (MND) are diagnosed worldwide every year [16]. People with these conditions may not be able to use speech, and movement of the eyes might be the only means by which they communicate.

In daily life, more than eighty percent of all information received comes from the eyes. Eyes and their movements play an important role in expressing human being's desires, cognitive processes, emotion states, and interpersonal relations. With advances in both eye-tracking technology and computer systems, eye-tracking research has gradually focused on human-computer interaction rather than just cognitive analysis. Eye-tracking devices has helped, in limited manner, some disable people to enter text into their computer via eye typing system [15, 21, 25, 30], which provides an effective method of communication. However, early dwell-based eye-typing systems were limited in terms of the

© Springer International Publishing Switzerland 2016
G. Hua and H. Jégou (Eds.): ECCV 2016 Workshops, Part II, LNCS 9914, pp. 254–268, 2016.
DOI: 10.1007/978-3-319-48881-3_18

speed of text entry due to large dwell time [4,8,14,19]. In order to increase the speed, dwell-free eye-typing systems were proposed [9,17,18], but they are error-prone and cannot handle some common typing errors in practice [11]. Recently, Liu [10,31] proposed a robust recognition method to address these challenging issues, even under low-accuracy eye tracker and low-quality calibration. However, the additional eye-tracking device (i.e. eye tracker) still needs to be used which is somehow burdensome. As the webcam is becoming a standard component in computers, especially in mobile devices, replacing the eye tracker with a webcam would simplify the setup of eye-typing equipment, and also facilitate the prevalence of eye-tracking applications.

Therefore, in this paper we investigated the feasibility of the development of eye typing system using a webcam as the input device. We showed that appearance-based method is an effective method for gaze estimation. During the course of our research we have improved the performance in terms of accuracy of gaze estimation by applying the average filter to the images. In addition, we investigated the effective eye areas that contribute the eye-appearance variance and finally determine the gaze estimation. According to the effective area analysis, the dimensionality of the eye-image feature can be reduced to achieve lower computational complexity. Finally performance evaluation indicates that the proposed method is sufficient to achieve a practical eye typing system using the standard system.

The reminder of the paper is organized as follows. Section 2 reviews related work. Section 3 describes the appearance-based method. Section 4 presents the results of the experiments followed by conclusion.

2   Related Work

Early research work on eye tracking with the standard webcam is mainly focusing on *eye detection/localization* [3,6]. Eye detection deals with detecting the presence of eyes, accurately interpreting eye positions in the images, or tracking the eyes from frame to frame for video images, while eye localization refers to individual eye areas, i.e. to localize eyebrows, eyelids, eye corners, sclera, iris, and pupils. Various established techniques [7,23,26,29,33,34] have been proposed to detect/localize eyes, in which most of them are robust in both indoor and outdoor environment, under different eye poses, and even with some degree of occlusion. More recently, the detected eyes in images or videos are used to estimate and track what a person is looking at, and this process is called *gaze estimation* [5]. Gaze estimation can be either a gaze direction in the 3D space, or a gaze point which is the intersection of gaze direction and a 2D plane.

In general, a person's gaze is determined by head pose and eyeball orientation as shown in Fig. 1. Usually head movement and eyeball rotation occur simultaneously, in which the person moves the head to a comfortable position before rotating the eyeball. Therefore, both head pose and pupil position need to be modelled for gaze estimation, which is very challenging. Currently most of research work on gaze estimation makes an assumption that the head pose

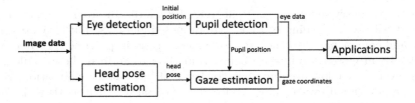

Fig. 1. Gaze determination with pupil position and head pose

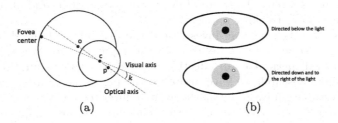

(a)   (b)

Fig. 2. The 3D-mode-based and feature-based approaches. (a) shows the 3D eye structure. The optical axis is connecting the pupil center, cornea center, and the eyeball center. The visual axis is connecting fovea center and cornea center, which is the true gaze direction. The angular offset between visual axis and optical axis is called *kappa* (k), which is a person-dependent constant. (b) shows the relation between pupil center and the cornea reflection

is fixed, and only considers the eye area [12,13,24]. Thus the main task of gaze estimation is modelling the relation between the image data of eye areas and the gaze direction/point. Similarly, we have adopted this same assumption in our gaze estimation study. Basically there are three types of approaches on gaze estimation [5], 3D-model-based, feature-based and appearance-based approaches.

The 3D-model-based approaches [2,27,28] try to explicitly model the visual dynamics of the eyeball, and a simplified structure of the eyeball is shown in Fig. 2a. Although the visual axis is the actual gaze direction, the optical axis is usually determined instead, because the eyeball center and pupil center are relatively easier to estimate, and the angle between visual axis and optical axis is constant to each person. In order to avoid explicitly calculating the intersection of gaze direction and the 2D plane, the feature-based methods assume the underlying mapping from the eye features (e.g. pupil, iris, eye corners) to the gaze coordinates. Pupil center-cornea reflection vector [1] is the most common method to estimate the gaze point shown as Fig. 2b. Due to the limitation of the infrared light, some research work also suggests that the pupil center-eye corners vector can be an alternative which has the acceptable accuracy [22].

However, the 3D-model-based and feature-based approaches require highly-accurate feature detection, and are prone to errors. In addition, they usually need a high-resolution camera and infrared light. Unlike the above two approaches, appearance-based approaches use the whole image content as an input that maps to gaze coordinates without the explicit local feature extraction [12,13,24]. In addition, the setup is more flexible, and the single webcam with relative low resolution is sufficient. Thus the appearance-based method is becoming promising gaze estimation technique for gaze estimation.

In the paper, we further investigated the performance of approach-based method in gaze estimation. We also discussed some practical issues of the method. Finally we investigated the feasibility of eye typing using the method. Although the accuracy is still less than the commercial eye tracker, it demonstrates the potential of eye typing using a standard webcam.

3   Appearance-Based Method

Instead of extracting local features of eyes, appearance-based methods use an entire image of the eye as a high-dimensional input. The image is described as a feature vector in a high-dimensional space. A number of feature vectors will constitute a manifold which has an approximately 2D surface, because the eyeball movement has only 2° of freedom. Assuming locally linear combination existing in the manifold, the 2D gaze points are estimated with the same locally linear mapping.

3.1   Eye-Appearance Feature Vector

The first task in an appearance-based approach is to crop the whole image and extract eye images (containing the eye area) as shown in Fig. 3. The RGB images are first converted to gray-scale images. Haar-cascade classifier is used to extract the rough eye regions in the image. The extracted images usually contain the eyebrow, which is removed using simple integrated projection technique. The eyebrow removal technique basically integrate the intensity values across a row of pixels. This will generate two global peaks (darkest parts), and using a threshold to eliminate the area around the upper peak. Canny edge filter is used to detect the inner and outer corners [12]. The eye image is cropped with a fixed size (Fig. 3a) in terms of the corners. We initially set the aspect ration to 60×36 pixels as suggested in [32]. Finally the feature vector of the eye appearance is generated by raster scan of the eye intensity images (Fig. 3b), and each pixel in the original image corresponds to an element in the vector. The eye-appearance image can be regarded as a point in a high dimensional space (i.e. the 2160-dimensional space). A set of these points will constitute a manifold in the high dimensional space, called eye-appearance manifold.

3.2   Eye-Appearance Manifold

Although the eye-appearance manifold is being in a high dimensional space, it has an approximately 2D surface [12], because the eyeball rotates in the 3D space. Therefore, when a person looks at different keys on an on-screen virtual keyboard, the eyeball rotations are different, and thus the corresponding eye-appearance points are differentiable in the manifold. To verify this, we conducted

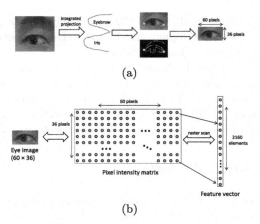

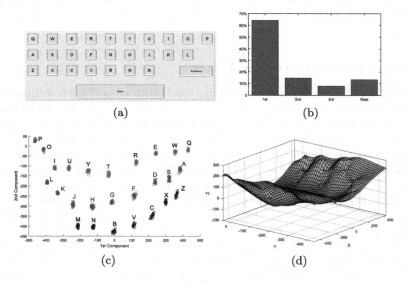

Fig. 3. Eye-appearance feature generation. (a) shows the procedures of cropping eye image. (b) illustrates the feature vector generation from the cropped eye image.

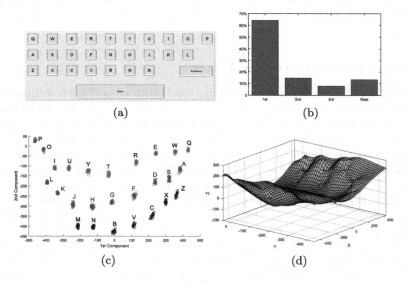

Fig. 4. The PCA projection. (a) shows the 26-letter keyboard layout used as the reference points. (b) shows the percentage of eigenvalues. (c) shows the first two principal components transformed by PCA into 2D space with the corresponding key labels. (d) illustrates the first three principal component forming the 2D surface which is the eye-appearance manifold in 3D space.

a preliminary experiment. A person sat in front of a monitor with a webcam, and he was asked to look at each character key in order on the virtual keyboard (Fig. 4a) which was used in [10,31]. When he looked at a key, fifty consecutive images of his frontal face were captured by the camera. After generating the eye-appearance feature vectors, we use PCA transformation to project these eye-appearance points into 2D/3D space as shown in Fig. 4.

There are some interesting observations: (1). The first three components contain most of the information (around 90 % of accumulated eigenvalues), which is consistent with the observation in [12]. (2). The eye-appearance points can be clearly separated in 2D space. In another view, we can regard this as a classification of the 26 keys into 26 classes. (3). The relative positions of gaze points in 2D coordinate are maintained in the eye-appearance manifold. (4). The eye-appearance manifold is approximately a 2D surface embedded in a high dimensional space, and then it is possible to be modelled as a regression problem.

These observations help us understand the intuition of the appearance-based method, and how the eye appearance in high dimensional space changes with various gaze points in 2D space. Although the appearance-based methods do not estimate explicit parameters, (e.g. the eyeball centre, pupil centre and kappa in 3D-model-based methods, and pupil center-cornea reflection vector in feature-based methods), some underlying key parameters that determine the mapping relation between the eye appearance points and gaze points could be obtained implicitly.

3.3   Locally Linear Embedding

In order to maintain the relative positions of gaze points in the eye-appearance manifold, the interpolation-based method with locally linear embedding [20,24] is used to find the mapping relation. The method finds locally linear mapping instead of global mapping directly from high-dimensional data to low-dimensional data. The basic idea is estimating the mapping parameters (weights) of a new high-dimensional data point from its neighbouring data, and assuming the low-dimensional space also shares the same locally linear mapping, and then applying the same parameters to the corresponding low-dimensional data points to obtain the new low-dimensional data point (Eq. 1).

$$
\begin{aligned}
Xw &= \widehat{x} \\
Pw &= \widehat{p}
\end{aligned}
\tag{1}
$$

where X is a matrix consisting of eye-appearance feature vector, P is the matrix consisting of corresponding gaze points, and w is the parameter that needs to be estimated. We do not estimate the mapping parameters between X and P. Given a new eye-image data point $\widehat{x}$, we find the local mapping parameter w among its neighbors, and then estimate the gaze point $\widehat{p}$, by assuming it shares the same neighboring mapping with the new eye-image data. However, it contains errors between the locally linear combination Xw and the new eye-image point $\widehat{x}$, because the equation is overdetermined. The objective is to minimize the error by tuning parameter w. Therefore, we have the gaze estimation function with optimization constrains in Eq. 2

$$\widetilde{w} = \arg\min \left| \widehat{x} - \sum_{i}^{k} w_i x_i \right|, s.t. \sum_{i}^{k} w_i = 1$$

$$\widehat{p} = \sum_{i}^{k} w_i p_i \tag{2}$$

where $\widetilde{w}$ is optimal weight vector formed by the scalars w_i. $p_1...p_k$ are the corresponding gaze points in 2D space. Once the optimal weights $\widetilde{w}$ are obtained, the gaze point $\widehat{p}$ is estimated using the same weights.

4   Experiments

To further verify our observation and deepen our understanding of eye gaze estimation, we designed a more in-depth experiment. Other related work [12,13] has already investigated the effect of the different number of reference points. In our experiments, our objectives were two fold: (1). improving the estimation of gaze position by having better calibration reference points. (2). determining the important features of image of the eye in determining the gaze point. This is done by reducing the size of the image and thus reducing the dimension size and complexity. In addition, we carried out some initial comparative study of eye typing using the appearance-based method and using the eye-tracker system.

4.1   Data Collection

We developed the system on a desktop computer with a 23-inch LED-lit monitor attaching an off-the-shelf webcam (30fps) as shown in Fig. 5a. The eye tracker (TheEyeTribe, 30 Hz) was placed under the monitor. The chin rest, placed 50 cm in front of the monitor, is used to minimize the head movement of the participants. The experiment procedure is as follows: the participants first did the nine-point calibration with the eye tracker. Thirty-five cross-hair markers are individually displayed on the screen and the participants are asked to look at the central of the marker, and the participants were asked to look at the marker centre. To help the participants fixate at the centre, they were instructed to move the mouse cursor to align with the marker, and shape of the mouse cursor is the same as the marker [24]. When the mouse cursor overlaps with the marker, the participants are required to click on the mouse key. The webcam will simultaneously capture 10 images of the participants. Both the marker's position and the gaze coordinate estimation of the eye tracker are also recorded. Three volunteers (3 male, 25–33 years) from the local university participated in the experiment. All of them had normal vision. One of the participants had prior experience with the use of eye tracking input software/devices while the remaining two volunteers are novice.

The leave-one-out cross validation is employed in which one eye image is used as the test image and the rest for training. To measure the accuracy, the mean estimated angular error is calculated as Eq. 3:

$$error = \frac{1}{n} \sum_{i=1}^{n} \arctan\left(\frac{\|\widehat{p}_i - p_i\|_2}{d}\right) \tag{3}$$

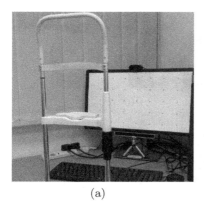
(a)

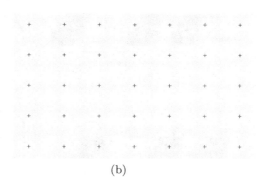
(b)

Fig. 5. Experiment setup. (a) shows the placement of the monitor, webcam, eye tracker, chin rest. (b) shows the layout of reference points

where $\|\widehat{p}_i - p_i\|$ is the Euclidean distance between estimated gaze position $\widehat{p}_i$ and actual gaze position p_i. d is the distance between participant's eyes and the screen. We assume that the line of sight of the participant is perpendicular to the screen when the participant fixates at the centre.

4.2 Artifacts Elimination

In this experiment, we investigate the effect of image bias caused by artifacts using the appearance-based method. Since the reference points are very important for estimating the new gaze point, small bias of the reference points might result in large error in subsequent gaze estimation. In the experiment of previous work [12,24], only one image of the participant's appearance was captured while doing the calibration. However, although the experiment is in a well controlled laboratory, some uncontrollable factors could affect the captured image, such as fine motion of eyeball, instant illumination variance. These artifacts will cause some bias of eye-appearance images even though the person is fixating at the same point on the screen, resulting in large error of gaze estimation. Therefore, it is necessary to eliminate or at least reduce/minimize its effect during eye gaze calibration period.

In our experiment, multiple images (10 images) were captured once the participant clicked the reference point while doing the calibration. Since 35 reference points are used for calibration, there are 35 sets of images where each set contains 10 images (Fig. 6a). If we use only one image from each set of images, there are 10^{35} images combinations, and we randomly selected only 10,000 combinations, i.e. randomly selected one image from each group respectively (Fig. 6b), and repeated ten thousand times. For minimizing the effect of artifacts, we used an average filter to 10 images of each group (Fig. 6c). Figure 6d shows the result of the comparison. There are three groups of bars indicating three participants. In each group, the first bar is the average error of using individual image (average

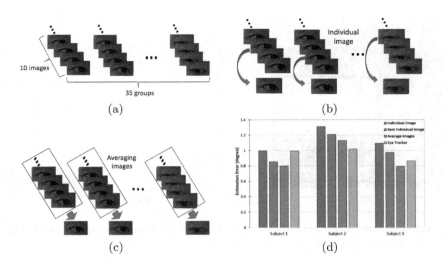

Fig. 6. Comparison of selecting individual image and averaging images

error of 10,000 combinations), and the second bar is the minimum error of using individual image (minimum error of 10,000 combinations). The third bar is the error using the proposed average filter. The fourth bar is gaze estimation error of the eye tracker. From Fig. 6d, the gaze estimation errors using the proposed average filter is 0.2° less than using individual images (average of 10,000 images), and 0.1° when compared with the minimum error when using individual image.

The results confirm our initial observation that artifacts of images captured in the calibration process could greatly affect the gaze estimation, and our proposed average filter is a good method to reduce the error. We plot the respective manifolds into 3D space by PCA transformation for visualization. Figure 7a shows the projection of all eye-image points, and Fig. 7b shows the projection of average eye-image points. As we can see, the manifold using the average filter has a much smoother surface, and thus it has a better locally linear mapping to estimate the gaze point.

4.3   Effective Area Detection

In this experiment, we investigate the effect of the size of the eye area on gaze estimation. First we define three cropping operations, horizontal cropping, vertical cropping, and full cropping (Fig. 8a). A single horizontal cropping operation is cropping a row of both top and bottom pixels of the eye image. A single vertical cropping operation is cropping one column of both right and left pixels. A single full cropping operation is a combination of horizontal and vertical cropping. The original size of the eye image is 60 × 36 pixels. Figure 8b, c and d show the results of the three cropping operations, where the x-axis is the number of times that the image is cropped, and the y-axis denotes the estimated angular

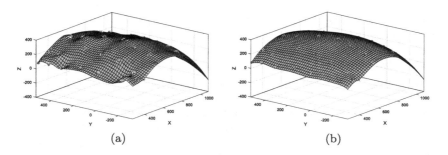

Fig. 7. Eye-appearance manifolds in 3D space. (a) shows the manifold consisting of all individual images. (b) shows the manifold consisting of the average images.

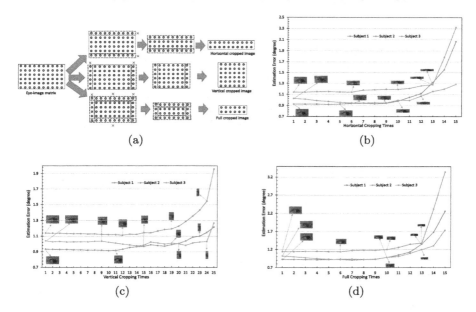

Fig. 8. Cropping operations. (a) shows the process of two-time horizontal, vertical, and full cropping operations, respectively. (b)(c) and (d) show the error of horizontal, vertical, and full cropping operations in different cropping times. Different lines indicate different participants.

error. There are two observations: (1). the estimation errors remain almost constant as the image is cropped horizontally until the "knee" point, above which the estimating error increases drastically. It was observed that the "knee" point occurs when the upper eyelid is cropped; (2). the effect of vertical cropping is less than horizontal cropping. Although both outer and inner eye corners are cropped, the error does not increase drastically. This suggests that eye corners as used in feature based methods are less critical. If the image can contain the whole iris, the gaze estimation error does not increase drastically.

These observations help us understand which parts of the eye in the image that contribute more to eye-appearance variance. Besides the iris part, we find the upper eyelid has large impact on the gaze estimation which is not the case for 3D-model-based and feature-based methods. In 3D-model-based and feature-based methods, they focus mainly on the movement of iris or pupil part. In appearance-based method, although the degree of eyelid openness does not determine the gaze direction, it changes the eye appearance of the person and then affect the gaze estimation. Meanwhile, these observations also help us to reduce the dimensionality of eye-appearance feature vector. For example, as shown in Fig. 8d, if we do 10-time full cropping, the performance is almost same as the using the original image, but the size is reduced from 60×36 pixels to 40×16 pixels, and the 2160 dimension is reduced to 640 dimension, which is much more efficient in time and computing complexity.

4.4   Eye-Typing Experiment

In this experiment, we investigate the feasibility of eye typing using webcam. The setup of the monitor, webcam, eye tracker and chin rest is the same as our previous experiments. The reference points used in the calibration are the 26-letter keys. After calibration with the 26-letter keys, the subject was asked to type ten random words by gazing at letters of the words sequentially. The random-word selection refers to [10]. To help mark typing duration of each word, the participant clicked the mouse key alternatively (the first click for starting, the next click for stopping). The webcam recorded the video clips with 30fps, and estimated gaze points from the eye tracker (30fps, the same frequency with the webcam) were also recorded. All corresponding gaze points of these video clips were estimated using the proposed appearance-based method. In order to evaluate the performance of the method and the eye tracker, we used the recognition algorithm, LCSMapping, of the eye-typing system [10]. The LCSMapping algorithm will recommend top five words ranked by the probability based on the estimated gaze points, and if the intended word is listed in the top-5 words, it is regarded as a correct recommendation.

Figure 9 shows the gaze points on the keyboard coordinate estimated by the appearance-based method (blue dots) and the eye tracker (red dots) while typing the ten words respectively, and also shows the top-5 words by LCSMapping using estimated points of the appearance-based method (the upper right box) and the eye tracker (the lower right box). There are several observations, (1). The estimated points of eye tracker looks fewer, because eye tracker is more stable, and multiple estimated points have the same coordinates. These estimated points of eye tracker are more clustered together and accurate than the appearance-based method using the webcam, and the intended words are always listed at the top-1 position; (2). although our appearance-based method is less accurate and there are small position shift, most of words are recognized and listed at top-1 position as shown in Fig. 9a–f; (3). some words are still accurately recognized even though there is a large shift as shown in Fig. 9g-h; (4). if the large shift

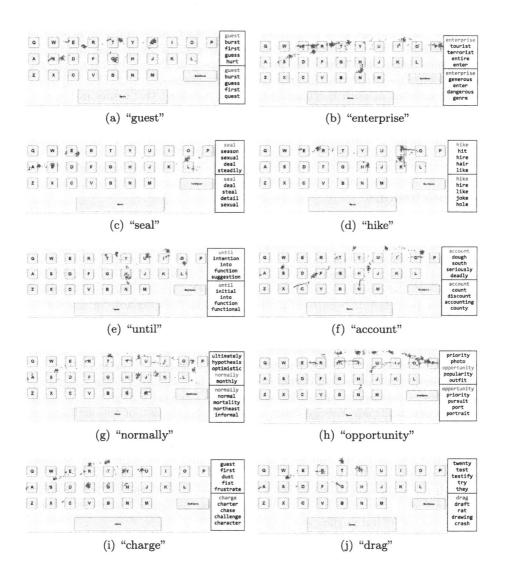

Fig. 9. Estimated gaze points of appearance-based method and eye tracker. They show the estimated points of typing ten words, "guest", "enterprise", "seal", "hike", "until", "account", "normally", "opportunity", "charge", "drag". The blue dots denote points estimated by the appearance-based method, and the red dots denote points by eye tracker. The upper right box shows top-5 words recommended using estimated points of the method, and the lower right box shows top-5 words using points of the eye tracker. (Color figure online)

causes the pattern of other words, the intended word cannot be recognized as shown in Fig. 9i-j.

These observations help us understand the practical issues of appearance-based method. The calibration shift is the most critical factor that affects our appearance-based algorithm. The probable causes of the calibration shift are fine/small motion of the head and the degree of openness of eyelid. This will cause a higher number of both neighbour-letter and missing-letter errors in the eye-typing system [10]. The LCSMapping recognition algorithm can overcome some of these defects, however as the number of letter errors increase, the recognition algorithm begins to deteriorate. Therefore, it is feasible to achieve the eye typing using the webcam even with some degree of shift.

5   Conclusions

In order to improve the communication ability of people with motor disabilities, eye-based typing systems have been proposed. However, most typing systems require an external eye-tracking device. Recently, some eye-tracking research has been working on gaze estimation using the normal webcam. Compared with 3D-model-based and feature-based gaze estimation, the appearance-based method has higher potential of been used in the eye-typing area because of the simple setup without the high-resolution camera.

In the paper, we investigated whether the appearance-based method is able to differentiate eye-appearance points clearly while looking at different keys on the virtual keyboard, i.e. if it is feasible to classify the letter typed by eye movement. Our investigation found that the image bias caused by the uncontrollable artifacts existing in calibration would cause large error of gaze estimation. We proposed using an average filter to reduce the impact of the artifacts on gaze estimation. Another investigation is the determination of the effective area determining the gaze direction, it is possible to reduce the dimensionality of eye-appearance feature vector and decrease the time and space complexity. We also investigated the feasibility of eye typing using a webcam, in which we found that although the estimated points of the appearance-based method is less accurate than the eye tracker, the intended words can be recognized using the robust recognition algorithm in the eye-typing system.

In the future work, we will further investigate the impact of eyelid openness using the appearance-based method. The eyelid does not determine gaze direction, but it will affect gaze estimation. If we can find some specific patterns of eyelid and even reduce the impact, the accuracy of gaze estimation would improve. We will also integrate the appearance-based method with the robust eye-typing system, and more eye-typing experiments will be designed for investigation of practical issues of the method.

Acknowledgments. This work is a collaboration with the Joint NTU-UBC Research Centre of Excellence in Active Living for the Elderly (LILY).

References

1. Cerrolaza, J.J., Villanueva, A., Cabeza, R.: Taxonomic study of polynomial regressions applied to the calibration of video-oculographic systems. In: Proceedings of the 2008 Symposium on Eye Tracking Research & Applications, pp. 259–266. ACM (2008)
2. Chen, J., Ji, Q.: Probabilistic gaze estimation without active personal calibration. In: 2011 IEEE Conference on Computer Vision and Pattern Recognition (CVPR), pp. 609–616. IEEE (2011)
3. Feng, G.C., Yuen, P.C.: Multi-cues eye detection on gray intensity image. Pattern Recogn. **34**(5), 1033–1046 (2001)
4. Hansen, D.W., Hansen, J.P., Nielsen, M., Johansen, A.S., Stegmann, M.B.: Eye typing using markov and active appearance models. In: Proceedings of the Sixth IEEE Workshop on Applications of Computer Vision (WACV 2002), pp. 132–136. IEEE (2002)
5. Hansen, D.W., Ji, Q.: In the eye of the beholder: a survey of models for eyes and gaze. IEEE Trans. Pattern Anal. Mach. Intell. **32**(3), 478–500 (2010)
6. Hansen, D.W., Pece, A.E.: Eye tracking in the wild. Comput. Vis. Image Underst. **98**(1), 155–181 (2005)
7. Kim, S.T., Choi, K.A., Shin, Y.G., Ko, S.J.: A novel iris center localization based on circle fitting using radially sampled features. In: 2015 IEEE International Symposium on Consumer Electronics (ISCE), pp. 1–2. IEEE (2015)
8. Kotani, K., Yamaguchi, Y., Asao, T., Horii, K.: Design of eye-typing interface using saccadic latency of eye movement. Int. J. Hum. Comput. Interact. **26**(4), 361–376 (2010)
9. Kristensson, P.O., Vertanen, K.: The potential of dwell-free eye-typing for fast assistive gaze communication. In: Proceedings of the Symposium on Eye Tracking Research and Applications, pp. 241–244. ACM (2012)
10. Liu, Y., Lee, B.S., McKeown, M.J.: Robust eye-based dwell-free typing. Int. J. Hum. Comput. Interact. **32**(9), 682–694 (2016)
11. Liu, Y., Zhang, C., Lee, C., Lee, B.S., Chen, A.Q.: Gazetry: swipe text typing using gaze. In: Proceedings of the Annual Meeting of the Australian Special Interest Group for Computer Human Interaction, pp. 192–196. ACM (2015)
12. Lu, F., Sugano, Y., Okabe, T., Sato, Y.: Inferring human gaze from appearance via adaptive linear regression. In: 2011 IEEE International Conference on Computer Vision (ICCV), pp. 153–160. IEEE (2011)
13. Lu, F., Sugano, Y., Okabe, T., Sato, Y.: Adaptive linear regression for appearance-based gaze estimation. IEEE Trans. Pattern Anal. Mach. Intell. **36**(10), 2033–2046 (2014)
14. MacKenzie, I.S., Zhang, X.: Eye typing using word and letter prediction and a fixation algorithm. In: Proceedings of the 2008 Symposium on Eye Tracking Research & Applications, pp. 55–58. ACM (2008)
15. Majaranta, P., Ahola, U.K., Špakov, O.: Fast gaze typing with an adjustable dwell time. In: Proceedings of the SIGCHI Conference on Human Factors in Computing Systems, pp. 357–360. ACM (2009)
16. Majaranta, P., Aoki, H., Donegan, M., Hansen, D.W., Hansen, J.P.: Gaze Interaction and Applications of Eye Tracking: Advances in Assistive Technologies, 1st edn. Information Science Reference - Imprint of: IGI Publishing, Hershey (2011)
17. Pedrosa, D., Pimentel, M.d.G., Truong, K.N.: Filteryedping: a dwell-free eye typing technique. In: Proceedings of the 33rd Annual ACM Conference Extended Abstracts on Human Factors in Computing Systems, pp. 303–306. ACM (2015)

18. Pedrosa, D., Pimentel, M.D.G., Wright, A., Truong, K.N.: Filteryedping: design challenges and user performance of dwell-free eye typing. ACM Trans. Accessible Comput. (TACCESS) **6**(1), 3 (2015)

19. Räihä, K.J., Ovaska, S.: An exploratory study of eye typing fundamentals: dwell time, text entry rate, errors, and workload. In: Proceedings of the SIGCHI Conference on Human Factors in Computing Systems, pp. 3001–3010. ACM (2012)

20. Roweis, S.T., Saul, L.K.: Nonlinear dimensionality reduction by locally linear embedding. Science **290**(5500), 2323–2326 (2000)

21. Sarcar, S., Panwar, P., Chakraborty, T.: Eyek: an efficient dwell-free eye gaze-based text entry system. In: Proceedings of the 11th Asia Pacific Conference on Computer Human Interaction, pp. 215–220. ACM (2013)

22. Sesma, L., Villanueva, A., Cabeza, R.: Evaluation of pupil center-eye corner vector for gaze estimation using a web cam. In: Proceedings of the Symposium on Eye Tracking Research and Applications, ETRA 2012, pp. 217–220. ACM, New York (2012). http://doi.acm.org/10.1145/2168556.2168598

23. Skodras, E., Fakotakis, N.: Precise localization of eye centers in low resolution color images. Image Vis. Comput. **36**, 51–60 (2015)

24. Tan, K.H., Kriegman, D.J., Ahuja, N.: Appearance-based eye gaze estimation. In: Proceedings of the Sixth IEEE Workshop on Applications of Computer Vision (WACV 2002), pp. 191–195. IEEE (2002)

25. Urbina, M.H., Huckauf, A.: Alternatives to single character entry and dwell time selection on eye typing. In: Proceedings of the 2010 Symposium on Eye-Tracking Research & Applications, pp. 315–322. ACM (2010)

26. Valenti, R., Gevers, T.: Accurate eye center location through invariant isocentric patterns. IEEE Trans. Pattern Anal. Mach. Intell. **34**(9), 1785–1798 (2012)

27. Villanueva, A., Cabeza, R., Porta, S.: Gaze tracking system model based on physical parameters. Int. J. Pattern Recogn. Artif. Intell. **21**(05), 855–877 (2007)

28. Wang, J.G., Sung, E., Venkateswarlu, R.: Estimating the eye gaze from one eye. Comput. Vis. Image Underst. **98**(1), 83–103 (2005)

29. Wang, P., Green, M.B., Ji, Q., Wayman, J.: Automatic eye detection and its validation. In: IEEE Computer Society Conference on Computer Vision and Pattern Recognition-Workshops, CVPR Workshops, pp. 164–164. IEEE (2005)

30. Ward, D.J., MacKay, D.J.: Artificial intelligence: fast hands-free writing by gaze direction. Nature **418**, 838 (2002)

31. Liu, Y., Bu-Sung Lee, M.M., Lee, C.: A robust recognition approach in eye-based dwell-free typing. In: Proceedings of 2015 International Conference on Progress in Informatics and Computing, pp. 5–9. IEEE (2015)

32. Zhang, X., Sugano, Y., Fritz, M., Bulling, A.: Appearance-based gaze estimation in the wild. In: Proceedings of the IEEE Conference on Computer Vision and Pattern Recognition, pp. 4511–4520 (2015)

33. Zhou, Z.H., Geng, X.: Projection functions for eye detection. Pattern Recogn. **37**(5), 1049–1056 (2004)

34. Zhu, Z., Ji, Q.: Robust real-time eye detection and tracking under variable lighting conditions and various face orientations. Comput. Vis. Image Underst. **98**(1), 124–154 (2005)

A Technological Framework to Support Standardized Protocols for the Diagnosis and Assessment of ASD

Marco Leo$^{(\boxtimes)}$, Marco Del Coco, Pierluigi Carcagnì, Pier Luigi Mazzeo, Paolo Spagnolo, and Cosimo Distante

CNR-ISASI, Lecce, Italy
{marco.leo,marcodel.coco,pierluigi.carcagni,pierluigi.mazzeo,
paolo.spagnolo,cosimo.distante}@isasi.cnr.it

Abstract. In this work a first attempt to undertake the difficult challenge of embedding a technological level into a standardized protocol for Autism spectrum disorders (ASD) diagnose and assessment is introduced. In particular the Autism Diagnostic Observation Schedule (ADOS-2) is taken under consideration and a technological framework is introduced to compute, in an objective and automatic way, the evaluation scores for some of the involved tasks. The proposed technological framework makes use of a hidden RGB-D device for scene acquisition. Acquired data then feed a cascade of algorithmic steps by which people and objects are detected and temporally tracked and then extracted information is exploited by fitting a spatial and temporal model described by means of an ontology-based approach. The ontology metadata are finally processed to find a mapping between them and the behavioral tasks described in the protocol.

Keywords: Autism spectrum disorders · ADOS · RGB-D device · People and object tracking · Ontology

1 Introduction

Autism spectrum disorders affect three different areas of a child's life: Social interaction, Communication (both verbal and nonverbal) and Behaviors and interests. Diagnosis and assessment of ASD can be difficult since children with ASD vary considerably in their individual strengths and difficulties. Detailed assessment of communication, neuropsychological functioning, motor and sensory skills, and adaptive functioning has to be carried out and to do that different scheduled methods have been introduced. These methods provide standard contexts to elicit relevant social and communicative behaviours. Healthcare professionals should directly observe and assess the child or young persons social and communication skills and behaviour. ICT applications, already in use to deliver educational and behavioral services to individuals with ASD [1], have

© Springer International Publishing Switzerland 2016
G. Hua and H. Jégou (Eds.): ECCV 2016 Workshops, Part II, LNCS 9914, pp. 269–284, 2016.
DOI: 10.1007/978-3-319-48881-3_19

been recently also exploited to develop advanced tools that allow an early identification and assessment of the disorder during its evolution. In particular technologies have enabled the introduction of interactive and virtual environments [2,3], serious games [4] and telerehabilitation [5]. The crucial point is that the technological trend in place requires the abandonment of standardized traditional protocols to allow the introduction of new ones built around the available technologies. However, many improvements are still needed to attain significant success in treating individuals with autism using ICT: in particular practical and clinical issues have yet to be addressed [6]. From the practical perspective, the adoption of ICT based protocols requires the medical staff training (which in turn can be successful only if there is a caregivers' strong willingness and conviction), acceptance by parents and an evaluation phase on the individual child to check his inclination towards new diagnostic methods and therapies that use technologies. Besides, many of the existing technologies have limited capabilities in their performance and this limit the success in the therapeutic approach of children with ASD. Clinically, most of the ICT proposals have not been validated outside the context of proof of concept studies [7]. As a consequence more studies should be performed to assess whether ICT architectures and devices are clinically relevant. It's clear that the development of ICT based protocols have to be more and more investigated and this process it is not straightforward since it necessitates a multidisciplinary collaborative effort between engineers, psychologists, neuropsychiatrics and cognitive scientists. A different way to exploit the proliferation of inexpensive technology also for diagnose and assessment of ASD, could be to hold standardized protocols and to embed in them a technological level (that the subject under evaluation does not perceive) which support the care-givers by the mining of objective evaluation scores from the observation of the subject during scheduled sessions. The main advantage of this approach is its peculiarity to work without any intervention in the standardized assessment protocols and in the environment (preserving ecological validity). This makes it very attracting for caregivers but, unfortunately, it requires additional efforts from the technological side since involved algorithms have to deal with unconstrained environments and non-collaborative subjects. Most likely, these are the reasons why there are no work in the literature for this applicative context. To partially fill this gap, in this work a first attempt to undertake this difficult challenge is introduced: in particular the standardized Autism Diagnostic Observation Schedule (ADOS-2) is taken under consideration and a technological framework is introduced to compute, in an objective and automatic way, numerical information that can be used by the therapist in order to assign the scores for some of the involved tasks. In particular the module 1 of the protocol (see Sect. 2 for details) has been explored and the 4 tasks involved in the phase 1 (free play) have been analyzed by the proposed technological framework that makes use of an RGB-D device for scene acquisition. Acquired data then feed a cascade of algorithmic steps by which people and objects are detected and temporally tracked and then extracted information is exploited by fitting a spatial and temporal model described by means of an ontology approach. The ontology metadata are finally processed to find a mapping between them and the behavioral tasks described in the protocol. The validity of the proposed approach was proved during preliminary experiments carried out in the lab and by the exploitation of the framework during two actual ASD assessment sessions. In the rest of the paper Sect. 2 gives a short overview of the ADOS-2 protocol, Sect. 3 describes the technological component of the proposed framework and, finally, Sect. 4 reports experimental outcomes. Section 5 will conclude the paper.

2 Autism Diagnostic Observation Schedule (ADOS-2)

The Autism Diagnostic Observation Schedule (ADOS-2) [8] is one of the few standardized diagnostic and assessment measures that involves scoring direct observations of the childs communication, social interaction, play, and restricted and repetitive behaviours. The ADOS-2 includes five modules, each requiring just 40 to 60 min to administer. The individual being evaluated is given only one module, selected on the basis of his or her expressive language level and chronological age:

1. Toddler Module: For children between 12 and 30 months of age who do not consistently use phrase speech
2. Module 1: For children 31 months and older who do not consistently use phrase speech
3. Module 2: For children of any age who use phrase speech but are not verbally fluent
4. Module 3: For verbally fluent children and young adolescents
5. Module 4: For verbally fluent older adolescents and adults

Each module engages the individual in a series of activities involving interactive stimulus materials. In particular Module 1 (on which this paper focuses) includes ten activities (Free Play, Response to Name, Response to Joint Attention, Bubble Play, Anticipation of a Routine With Objects, Responsive Social Smile, Anticipation of Social Routine, Functional and Symbolic Imitation, Birthday Party, Snack) that are appropriate for children who have an expressive language level of less than three years of age. Activities within this module focus on a childs ability to interact playfully with toys and other items appropriate for use with very young children. The technological framework presented in this paper maps into objective numerical data the behavioral observations carried out during the free play activity. In particular behavioral observations focus on the propensity of the child to parental/caregiver involvement, child's way to explore materials (both symbolic and functional), dwell time (time performing the same activity) and interactions that display affection.

3   The Proposed Technological Framework

The proposed framework, schematized in Fig. 1, is composed by an RGB-D acquisition device and a cascade of algorithmic steps by which objective numerical outcomes are extracted and linked to some of the behavioral tasks described in the ADOS-2 protocol.

The algorithmic core consists of three processing modules: the first one performs the *Detection, Localization and Tracking of People and Objects* in the scene; the second one combines the extracted spatial information and then, through an *Ontology*, it maps them into different semantic states; the last step processes the temporal sequences of semantic states in order to get numerical scores associated to each behavioral tasks (*Behavioral Scoring*).

In the following the aforementioned modules will be detailed.

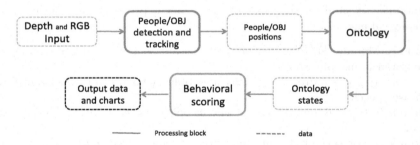

Fig. 1. Pipeline of the framework: RGBD input data are processed in order to track people and objects in the scene and successively work out them through an ontological approach and a behavioral module. (Color figure online)

3.1   Detection, Localization and Tracking of People and Objects

This module is mainly aimed to compute, frame by frame, the positions of both people and toys of interest by means of an algorithmic scheme, illustrated in Fig. 2, exploiting a joint analysis of RGB and depth data. As shown in the scheme, two different approaches have been used for people and toys respectively. This choice came from the consideration that the clinical protocol indicates a finite number of items to be used during diagnostic and therapeutic sessions and then the relative patterns can be preventively learned and stored in a repository. In other words, the system continuously searches in the RGB images the textural patterns of expected items and, once it detects one of the known items, it tracks its position in the image plane. The detection and tracking is based on a framework designed for long-term tracking proposed in [9]. The components of the framework are: (1) the *Tracker* that estimates the objects motion between consecutive frames, (2) the *Detector* that treats every frame as independent and performs full scanning of the image to localize all appearances that have been observed and learned in the past and (3) the *Learning* that observes performance of tracker and detector and it estimates detectors errors and generates training examples to avoid these errors in the future. The 2D object coordinates are finally mapped into the 3D point cloud coordinate system.

On the other side, detection, localization and tracking of people has to be treated differently since no a-priori appearance information is available. In this case the detection and localization are performed by an advanced background subtraction approach that exploits multiple noise modeling in order to make the background subtraction available beyond the limit of 4, 5 m (constraint of the standard Kinect SDK) relaxing the environmental constraints [10]. Background subtraction is performed in the depth image to identify foreground region that contains both moving objects and potential noise. These foreground pixels are then clustered into objects based on their depth values and neighborhood information. Among these objects, people are detected using a head and shoulder detector and tracking information about previously detected people. Detected persons are tracked by an algorithm which uses a feature pool to compute the matching score [11]. This feature pool includes 2D, 3D displacement distances, 2D sizes, color histogram, histogram of oriented gradient (HOG), color covariance and dominant color. At this point, the available positions of objects and people in the scene are expressed into the 3-dimensional reference system of the acquisition device. Since, as will be detailed in the next session, the proposed ontology defines semantic occupancy areas then the positions of objects and people onto the floor plain have to be recovered. To do that the floor plane has to be preventively estimated and this is done by an evolution of the classical RANSAC ("RANdom SAmple Consensus") algorithm that searches the best model that fits a 3D point cloud, avoiding the influence of possible outliers. The original algorithm was introduced by Fischler [12]. However, RANSAC requires to select some tuning coefficients such as the error tolerance which is unknown in advance in many real world problems. The performance of standard RANSAC were successively improved by modifying its cost function using an M-Estimator Sample and Consensus (MSAC) [13] approach, but this also requires a user-specified error tolerance, i.e. the process is terminated when the probability of finding a better model becomes lower than a user-specified probability. To overcome this problem in this paper the recently proposed RANSAC-LEL technique is exploited [14] where LEL stands for Least Entropy-Like. The key to robustness with respect to outliers is related to the fact that the devised penalty function does not directly measure the (weighted) mean square error (that as known tends to level out or low pass residuals), but only the distribution of the relative squared errors. Once the plane coordinates are available the positions onto

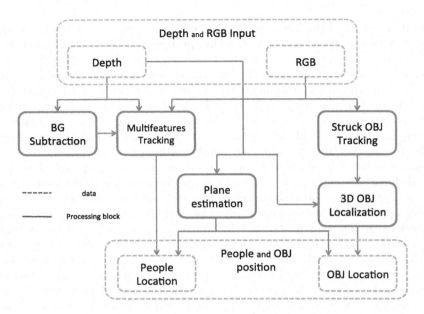

Fig. 2. People and object tracking scheme: the data provided by the RGB-D sensor are exploited by two separate tracking algorithms for people and objects respectively; the 3D positions are finally mapped in a common 2D plane (floor) reference system previously estimated. (Color figure online)

the floor plain of objects and people can be computed by projection. In particular this allows the systems to match (in an unsupervised manner) the generic labels used by the tracker with the semantic entities given by the ontology (child, caregiver and parents). This is done by counting the occurrences of a given label into a specific semantic area.

3.2   Ontology

In computer science, an ontology is a formal naming and definition of the types, properties, and interrelationships of entities of a specific context. In other words, an ontology models a set of rules defining semantic states and events that represent a generic baseline for a subsequent processing.

The proposed ontology is inspired by the structure proposed in [15], a declarative constraint based ontology that defines state/event models based on *prior* knowledge about the context, the scene and the real-world objects involved. A state/event model can be composite of three main key elements:

- Physical objects refer to real-world objects involved in the realization of the event (e.g., person, toys, areas).
- Components refer to sub-events of which the model is composed of.
- Constraints are conditions that the physical objects and/or the components should satisfy.

Going into detail three kinds of physical objects have been considered in this work: person, toy and area. Person is a class of physical object characterized by two main properties: the people role (child, caregiver, parent) and the position (coordinate on the floor coordinate system). Toy represents a class that has properties similar to the previous one. It is characterized by an ID (opportunely mapped on a known repository) and a position on the floor coordinate system. Area represents a specific space zone of the scene (as showed in Fig. 3) that is aimed to a specific purpose characterized in a semantic way (i.e. *play area* is the area where the child is free to play and to move, *parental area* is aimed to host the parents and *caregiver area* is the area where the caregiver use to stay). Constraints are defined in terms of space location of a subject/toy (relation with an area), temporal persistence of a specific state or as the simultaneous occur of two states/events. Given the elements cited above, state and events hierarchy can be defined as:

- Primitive State models a value of property of a physical object constant in a time interval.
- Composite State refers to a composition of two or more primitive states.
- Primitive Event models a change in value of a physical objects property (e.g., posture), and
- Composite Event defines a temporal relationship between two sub-events (components).

Following the above mentioned structure, a specific ontology has been defined. More specifically each state/event (primitive or composite) is made up by the involved physical objects (PsyOby), the components representing the state or event (if necessary), of the same hierarchy level or lower, involved in the definition (Comp) and the constraints defining the condition that physical objects or components must respect (Const). Moreover, in order to simplify the ontology managing, two assumptions have been made: both the caregiver and the parents have to stay in their respective areas.

Let CH be the child, PA the parents, CG the caregiver, A_{PY}, A_{PA}, A_{CG} respectively the play area, the parents area and the caregiver area and TYi the i-th toys.

Concerning the **primitive states** the following cases have been defined:

$$PS1 : \begin{cases} \text{PsyOby} = \text{CH}, \text{A}_{PY} \\ \text{Const} = \text{CH} \to \text{pos} \in \text{A}_{PY} \\ \text{Child is in play area} \end{cases}$$

$$PS2 : \begin{cases} \text{PsyOby} = \text{CH}, \text{A}_{PA} \\ \text{Const} = \text{CH} \to \text{pos} \in \text{A}_{PA} \\ \text{Child is in parental area} \end{cases}$$

$$PS3 : \begin{cases} \text{PsyOby} = \text{CH}, \text{A}_{CG} \\ \text{Const} = \text{CH} \to \text{pos} \in \text{A}_{CG} \\ \text{Child is in caregiver area} \end{cases} \tag{1}$$

$$PS4_i : \begin{cases} \text{PsyOby} = \text{CH}, \text{TY}_i \\ \text{Const} = \sum_{t=t}^{t-T_w} \text{TY}_i \to \text{pos}_t - \text{TY}_i \to \text{pos}_{t-1} > \text{THM} \\ \text{Toy } i \text{ is moving} \end{cases}$$

$$PS5 : \begin{cases} \text{PsyOby} = \text{CH}, \text{PA} \\ \text{Const} = \text{CH} \to \text{pos} - \text{PA} \to \text{pos} < \text{TH} \\ \text{Child is close to parents} \end{cases}$$

$$PS6 : \begin{cases} \text{PsyOby} = \text{CH}, \text{CG} \\ \text{Const} = \text{CH} \to \text{pos} - \text{CG} \to \text{pos} < \text{TH} \\ \text{Child is close to caregiver} \end{cases}$$

where t is the current frame, T_w is the windows size, pos is the position property (x, y coordinates on the floor plane) of the physical object, TH a proximity threshold, THM a movement threshold and the minus is referred to euclidean distance.

Concerning the **Composite states** the following cases have been defined

$$CS1_i : \begin{cases} \text{PsyOby} = \text{CH}, \text{TY}_i \\ \text{Comp} = PS4_i \\ \text{Const} = \text{CH} \to \text{pos} - \text{TY}_i \to \text{pos} < TH_{TC} \\ \text{Child is playing with object i} \end{cases}$$

$$CS2_i : \begin{cases} \text{PsyOby} = \text{CH}, \text{TY}_i \text{A}_{PA} \\ \text{Comp} = CS1_i, PS2 \\ \text{Const} = CS1_i \text{ and }, PS2 \\ \text{Child is interacting with object i and parents} \end{cases}$$

$$CS3_i : \begin{cases} \text{PsyOby} = \text{CH}, \text{TY}_i \text{A}_{CG} \\ \text{Comp} = CS1_i, PS3 \\ \text{Const} = CS1_i \text{ and } PS3 \\ \text{Child is interacting with object i and caregiver} \end{cases} \tag{2}$$

Concerning the **primitive events** the following cases have been defined

$$PE1_i : \begin{cases} \texttt{PsyOby} = \texttt{TY}_i \\ \texttt{Const} = \begin{cases} \sum_{t=t}^{t-T_w} \texttt{TY}_i \to \texttt{pos}_t - \texttt{TY}_i \to \texttt{pos}_{t-1} > \texttt{THM} \\ \sum_{t=t-T_w-2}^{t-2T_w} \texttt{TY}_i \to \texttt{pos}_t - \texttt{TY}_i \to \texttt{pos}_{t-1} < \texttt{THM} \end{cases} \\ \texttt{Toy i starts moving} \end{cases} \quad (3)$$

Concerning the **Composite events** the following cases have been defined

$$CE1_i : \begin{cases} \texttt{PsyOby} = \texttt{TY}_i, \texttt{CH} \\ \texttt{Comp} = PE1_i \texttt{Const} = CHP - TYiP < TH_{TC} \\ \texttt{Child starts interacting with toy i} \end{cases}$$

$$CE2 : \begin{cases} \texttt{PsyOby} = \texttt{CH}, \texttt{A}_{PA} \\ \texttt{Comp} = PS2 \\ \texttt{Const} = PS2 > \texttt{3sec} \\ \texttt{Child starts interacting with parents} \end{cases}$$

$$CE3 : \begin{cases} \texttt{PsyOby} = \texttt{CH}, \texttt{A}_{CG} \\ \texttt{Comp} = PS3 \\ \texttt{Const} = PS3 > \texttt{3sec} \\ \texttt{Child starts interacting with caregiver} \end{cases}$$

$$CE4_i : \begin{cases} \texttt{PsyOby} = \texttt{TY}_i, \texttt{CH}, \texttt{A}_{PA} \\ \texttt{Comp} = PE1_i, PS2 \\ \texttt{Const} = \texttt{CH} \to \texttt{pos} - \texttt{TY}_i \to \texttt{pos} < THP, PE1_i \text{ and } PS2 \\ \texttt{Child starts interacting with parents with toy i} \end{cases}$$

$$CE5_i : \begin{cases} \texttt{PsyOby} = \texttt{TY}_i, \texttt{CH}, \texttt{A}_{CG} \\ \texttt{Comp} = PE1_i, PS3 \\ \texttt{Const} = \texttt{CH} \to \texttt{pos} - \texttt{TY}_i \to \texttt{pos} < TH_{TC}, PE1_i \text{ and } PS3 \\ \texttt{Child starts interacting with caregiver with toy i} \end{cases}$$

$$CE7 : \begin{cases} \texttt{PsyOby} = \texttt{CH}, \texttt{PA} \\ \texttt{Comp} = PS5 \\ \texttt{Const} = PS5 > \texttt{3sec} \\ \texttt{Child shows affect for parents} \end{cases}$$

$$CE8 : \begin{cases} \texttt{PsyOby} = \texttt{CH}, \texttt{CG} \\ \texttt{Comp} = PS6 \\ \texttt{Const} = PS6 > \texttt{3sec} \\ \texttt{Child shows affect for caregiver} \end{cases} \quad (4)$$

where THP is the proximity threshold.

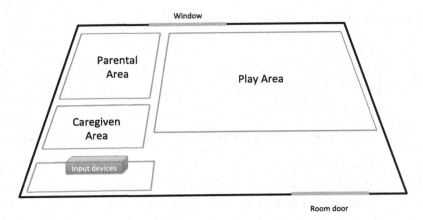

Fig. 3. Semantic areas in the therapy room: The room is virtually divided in semantic areas related to different kind of activities. The scene is monitored by the RGB-D device positioned in an upper corner of the room.

3.3   Behavioral Scoring

Once the ontology states (i.e. active states at each sample time) are available, the information useful to the therapist can be obtained. In this work, the attention has been focused on the *free play* phase of the second module of ADOS 2 evaluation protocol. It considers some aspects, some of which are most oriented to a subjective evaluation, whereas, others, would be widely treated by means of a numerical evaluation. This phase of the protocol tries to understand fundamental child behaviors in some specific scenarios, some of these have been here accounted, whereas others have been scheduled as future works. More precisely the knowledge of the approach adopted by the child in order to interact with other people when objects (toys) are available is observed. Some points of the protocol can be summarized in the following questions: Does the child use the object in the room as an iteraction instrument? Does the child focus his attention on a single toy or does he move his attention among toys quickly? Does the child expresse love?

As first aspect, the way the child use to interact with parents and caregiver (by means of the toys or just look for affection interactions) is treated. The proposed ontology makes the answer quite easy; two possible situation have been considered:

TI *Time spent interacting by means toys*: the child use the toys available in the room during the communication with parents or caregiver; this time is computed counting the consecutive occurrences of $CS2_i$ and $CS3_i$ ($\forall i$) respectively triggered by the composite events $CE4_i$ and $CE5_i$.

FI *Time spent on free interaction*: the child interacts with parents or caregiver overlooking the toys; this time is computed counting the consecutive occurrences of $PS2_i$ and $PS3_i$ ($\forall i$) respectively triggered by the composite events $CE2_i$ and $CE3_i$.

It is important to stress as the use of events (including temporal restriction to the event recognition) as a trigger for counting the consecutive occurrences of a specific state allows to avoid the counting of spurious state occurrences. It is straightforward as the a comparison between the total time under the condition TI and the total time under the condition FI represents a quantitative answer to the protocol question. This first case is sufficient to highlight as the availability of a precise numerical quantification of these temporal scoring to track the evolution of the child throughout sessions.

A second aspect of interest is about the approach of the child toward the toys. More precisely the protocol asks how much quickly the child moves his attention from an object to another one. Moreover, a meeting with the staff of the NPO *Amici di Nico* has brought out as the selection of a favorite toy would be useful. With this in mind the following parameters have modeled and computed.

Let I be the number of object under exam, T_{i_s} the duration of the s-th interaction of child with the i-th object computed as the number of consecutive occurrences of the composite state $CS1_i$ between the s-th composite event $CE1_i$ and the next one whereas S_i is the number of interaction of the child with the i-th object computed as the number of occurrence of composite event $CE1_i$,

The total number of times that the child move his attention among different object is defined as

$$T_C = \sum_{i=1}^{I} S_i \tag{5}$$

The total time spent playing with object i is:

$$T_i = \sum_{s=1}^{S_i} T_{i_s} \tag{6}$$

The total time spent playing with objects is:

$$T_{CO} = \sum_{i=1}^{I} \sum_{s=1}^{S_i} T_{i_s} \tag{7}$$

The variance of the usage time of the object i is defined as

$$V_i = \frac{1}{S_i} \sum_{s=1}^{S_i} [T_{i_s} - \overline{T_i}]^2 \tag{8}$$

where $\overline{T_i}$ is the average time spent on the object i.

As a last aspect an evaluation of the display of affection has been studied. In this case the specific kind of interaction with the parents and the caregiver has been evaluated. To this aim the following definitions are mandatory

T_{AP} : it is time spent on affection interaction with parents; it is computed counting the number of consecutive occurrences of the state $PS5$ triggered by the event $CE7$

T_{AT} : it is time spent on affection interaction with therapist; it is computed counting the number of consecutive occurrences of the state $PS6$ triggered by the event $CE8$

T_P : it is time spent on the s-th interaction with parents; it is computed counting the number of consecutive occurrences of the state $PS2$ triggered by the event $CE3$

T_T : it is time spent on the s-th interaction with therapist; it is computed counting the number of consecutive occurrences of the state $PS3$ triggered by the event $CE4$

S_{AP} : is the number of affection interaction with the parents, corresponding to the occurrences of the event $CE7$

S_{AT} : is the number of affection interaction with the therapist, corresponding to the occurrences of the event $CE8$

S_P : is the number of interaction with the parents, corresponding to the occurrences of the event $CE3$

S_T : is the number of interaction with the therapist, corresponding to the occurrences of the event $CE4$

4   Experimental Outcomes

The validity of the proposed framework was proved by two different experimental phases performed by placing the acquisition device on a closet (to make it invisible for children). The first experimental phase, performed in the ISASI-CNR Computer Vision Lab, was aimed to set some system parameters (e.g., proximity and motion thresholds, TH, THP, THM in Sect. 3.2) and, at the same time, to give a qualitative evaluation of the reliability of algorithmic steps. In particular, this was carried out by reproducing in the lab a typical therapeutic room (with the play, parental and caregiver area) and then running the algorithms on the data acquired while two adults and a child (without ASD) moved in the scene performing a specific list of activities (walking around, taking and leaving a specific toy, carrying the toy to the caregiver or the parents and so on). At the end of this phase the predefined list of activities was compared with the list of those automatically estimated by the cascade of involved algorithms. In Fig. 5 a graphical comparison between actual (leftmost) and estimated (rightmost) activities is reported. In particular Y-axis represents the floor area in which the child was detected (0 for play area, 1 for parental area e 2 for caregiver area) whereas line colours are associated to the manipulated object (black for no object, red blue and green for object 1 2 and 3 i.e. doll, puppet and toy car). Finally, the marker'x' is associated to affective occurrences, i.e. when the distance between the child and the adults was under the proximity thresholds. The similarity between the two plots indicates that persons and objects were properly detected and tracked and then the ontology was successfully applied to determine the semantic states that are the input of the subsequent behavioral scoring phase. For a better comprehension, one of the frame acquired during

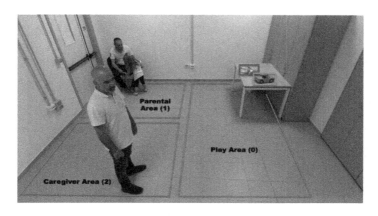

Fig. 4. One frame extracted from the preliminary experimental phase carried out in the ISASI-CNR Computer Vision Lab.

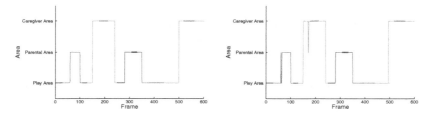

Fig. 5. Comparison between actual (leftmost) and estimated (rightmost) activity states during preliminary experimental sessions performed in our lab

this phase is reported in Fig. 4. The figure contains the superimposed information about floor areas (with relative identification number) as well as the colour assigned to the object manipulated by the child.

The second experimental phase was carried out at the NPO "Amici di Nico" by acquiring two ADOS-2 sessions. The first session was scheduled to asses a 5 years old child with ASD whereas the second one was scheduled for diagnosing if the language delay of a 3 year old child was associated to ASD (fortunately it was not).

In Table 1 the outcomes of the proposed framework at the end of the sessions are reported. In particular, according to Subsect. 3.3 the following behavioral scores were extracted: TI = Time of interaction by means toys, FI = Time of free interaction, T_CO = The total time spent playing with objects, T_C = Toys changes, T_i = The total time spent playing with object i, S_i = Number of interaction with the i-th toy, V_i = variance on the time of interaction with the i-th toy through sessions, T_{AP} =, Total time on affection interaction with parents, T_{AT} =, Total time on affection interaction with therapist, T_P = Total time on interaction with parents, T_T = Total time on interaction with therapist, TT = total session time. The clinical evaluation of the data is out of the scope of this

Fig. 6. One frame extracted from the experimental phase carried out at the NPO "Amici di Nico" by acquiring two ADOS-2 sessions.

paper. However what we think is important to highlight here is the capability of the framework to provide the caregiver with objective data extracted from the scene allowing him to achieve a fair assessment of the child.

Both reports are divided in 3 part corresponding to the three aspects/questions described in Subsect. 3.3 respectively. As widely discussed, these results

Table 1. Statistics carried out for the two children under exam: the two tables show the results for Child 1 and child 2 respectively. Each report is divided in 3 parts referred to different focuses of the ADOS 2 protocol.

Child 1		Child 2	
Part 1		Part 1	
TI	21 min	TI	26 min
FI	24 min	FI	14 min
Part 2		Part 2	
T_{CO}	37 min	T_{CO}	42 min
T_C	12	T_C	7
T_i	(1) 7 min; (2) 18 min; (3) 12 min;	T_i	(1) 21 min; (2) 10 min; (3) 11 min;
S_i	(1) 4; (2) 2; (3) 6;	S_i	(1) 2; (2) 2; (3) 3;
V_i	(1) 0.92; (2) 32; (3) 0.8;	V_i	(1) 40; (2) 2; (3) 1.3;
Part 3		Part 3	
T_{AP}	5 min	T_{AP}	6 min
T_{AT}	1 min	T_{AT}	3 min
T_P	27 min	T_P	26 min
T_T	12 min	T_T	5 min
TT	63 min	TT	54 min

would be highly useful in the diagnosis process. As an instance, looking to the part 1 it is clear that the child 2 is more oriented to an interaction via toys compared with the child 1 that shows a more balanced attitude for both toys/non toys interaction. Concerning the second part many information about the attitude to play with object are provided. More precisely it would be interesting to observe as the second child is highly interested in objects and that he is capable to pay more attention in each of them avoiding frequent changes. Moreover S_i and V_i are useful data in order to take awareness of a preference on a specific toys or how the child rise out an interest for one of them. The last part highlight the time spent with parents or therapist and if this interaction is oriented to a affection interaction or a most standard interaction.

5   Conclusions and Future Works

In this work a first attempt to undertake the difficult challenge of embedding a technological level into a standardized protocol for ASD diagnose and assessment has been introduced. Experimental proofs demonstrated the huge potentiality of this research trend since, by this technological tools, objective data can be provided to the caregivers in order to get a more accurate diagnose and assessment of ASD. In this work only the module 1 of the ADOS-2 protocol has been explored and the 4 tasks involved in the phase 1 (free play) have been analyzed by the proposed technological framework. Future works will deal with the extension of the framework to other phases and modules of the ADOS-2 protocol: this will be done by including new functionalities facing emotions recognition, gesture analysis for symbolic and functional manipulation of objects and a deeper analysis of interactions between children and adults.

References

1. Lofland, K.B.: The use of technology in the treatment of autism. In: Technology and the Treatment of Children with Autism Spectrum Disorder, pp. 27–35. Springer International Publishing, Cham (2016)
2. Warren, Z., Zheng, Z., Das, S., Young, E.M., Swanson, A., Weitlauf, A., Sarkar, N.: Brief report: development of a robotic intervention platform for young children with asd. J. Autism Dev. Disord. **45**(12), 3870–3876 (2015)
3. Cheung, S.C.S.: Integrating multimedia into autism intervention. IEEE MultiMedia **22**, 4–10 (2015)
4. Bernardini, S., Porayska-Pomsta, K., Smith, T.J.: Echoes: an intelligent serious game for fostering social communication in children with autism. Inf. Sci. **264**, 41–60 (2014). Serious Games
5. Shamsuddin, S., Yussof, H., Mohamed, S., Hanapiah, F.A., Ainudin, H.A.: Telerehabilitation service with a robot for autism intervention. Procedia Comput. Sci. **76**, 349–354 (2015). IEEE International Symposium on Robotics and Intelligent Sensors (IEEE IRIS 2015) (2015)
6. Boucenna, S., Narzisi, A., Tilmont, E., Muratori, F., Pioggia, G., Cohen, D., Chetouani, M.: Interactive technologies for autistic children: a review. Cogn. Comput. **6**(4), 722–740 (2014)

7. Crippa, A., Salvatore, C., Perego, P., Forti, S., Nobile, M., Molteni, M., Castiglioni, I.: Use of machine learning to identify children with autism and their motor abnormalities. J. Autism Dev. Disord. **45**(7), 2146–2156 (2015)
8. Lord, C., Rutter, M., DiLavore, P.C., Risi, S., Gotham, K., Bishop, S.: Autism diagnostic observation schedule: ADOS-2. Western Psychological Services Los Angeles, CA (2012)
9. Kalal, Z., Mikolajczyk, K., Matas, J.: Tracking-learning-detection. IEEE Trans. Pattern Anal. Mach. Intell. **34**(7), 1409–1422 (2012)
10. Nghiem, A.T., Bremond, F.: Background subtraction in people detection framework for rgb-d cameras. In: 2014 11th IEEE International Conference on Advanced Video and Signal Based Surveillance (AVSS), pp. 241–246, August 2014
11. Chau, D.P., Bremond, F., Thonnat, M.: A multi-feature tracking algorithm enabling adaptation to context variations. In: 4th International Conference on Imaging for Crime Detection and Prevention 2011 (ICDP 2011), pp. 1–6, November 2011
12. Fischler, M.A., Bolles, R.C.: Random sample consensus: a paradigm for model fitting with applications to image analysis and automated cartography. Commun. ACM **24**(6), 381–395 (1981)
13. Torr, P.H., Zisserman, A.: Mlesac: a new robust estimator with application to estimating image geometry. Comput. Vis. Image Underst. **78**(1), 138–156 (2000)
14. Distante, C., Indiveri, G.: Ransac-lel: an optimized version with least entropy like estimators. In: 2011 18th IEEE International Conference on Image Processing, pp. 1425–1428, September 2011
15. Crispim, C.F., Bathrinarayanan, V., Fosty, B., Konig, A., Romdhane, R., Thonnat, M., Bremond, F.: Evaluation of a monitoring system for event recognition of older people. In: 2013 10th IEEE International Conference on Advanced Video and Signal Based Surveillance (AVSS), pp. 165–170, August 2013

Combining Human Body Shape and Pose Estimation for Robust Upper Body Tracking Using a Depth Sensor

Thomas Probst[✉], Andrea Fossati, and Luc Van Gool

Computer Vision Lab, ETH Zurich, Zürich, Switzerland
{probstt,fossati,vangool}@vision.ee.ethz.ch

Abstract. Rapid and accurate estimation of a person's upper body shape and real-time tracking of the pose in the presence of occlusions is crucial for many future assistive technologies, health care applications and telemedicine systems. We propose to tackle this challenging problem by combining data-driven and generative methods for both body shape and pose estimation. Our strategy comprises a subspace-based method to predict body shape directly from a single depth map input, and a random forest regression approach to obtain a sound initialization for pose estimation of the upper body. We propose a model-fitting strategy in order to refine the estimated body shape and to exploit body shape information for improving pose accuracy. During tracking, we feed refinement results back into the forest-based joint position regressor to stabilize and accelerate pose estimation over time. Our tracking framework is designed to cope with viewpoint limitations and occlusions due to dynamic objects.

Keywords: Human pose estimation · Human body shape · Pose tracking · Model fitting · Real-time · Occlusion handling · Random forest · Subspace

1 Introduction

Automatic perception of human subjects will play a key role in assistive technology and medical applications. For instance, systems for medical imaging, treatment planning, radiation therapy, interventional imaging and virtual reality benefit from a precise recognition of the patient in his/her distinct pose [1]. In general, potential advantages are more accurate interactions, compliant systems, alleviation for users and reduced costs. Future applications of computer-assisted surgery and telemedicine will provide even physical interaction with the patient by means of teleoperation techniques, and therefore rely crucially on a good localization and tracking of the subject.

Since the availability of low-cost depth sensors, real-time pose estimation has advanced fast and is present in many commercial videogame consoles [2]. However, the requirements regarding body poses, occlusions, field of view, body

© Springer International Publishing Switzerland 2016
G. Hua and H. Jégou (Eds.): ECCV 2016 Workshops, Part II, LNCS 9914, pp. 285–301, 2016.
DOI: 10.1007/978-3-319-48881-3_20

shape fidelity and accuracy are quite different compared to professional and medical applications. In our work we investigate depth-based sensors in the scenario of tracking the torso of a person in lie-down poses. Our goal is to accurately estimate the upper body pose and surface of the subject in the presence of severe occlusions due to viewpoint limitations and potential occluding objects in front of the sensor.

In particular, we are involved in the *ReMeDi* research project that aims to develop a telediagnosis system: This will allow doctors to remotely perform physical and ultrasonography examinations by teleoperating a multifunctional robotic device at the patient side. Potential advantages are the provision of sparsely populated areas, enhanced availability of expert knowledge, more beneficial time schedules and reduced health care costs. In excess of teleconferencing, haptic interfaces, force-feedback and multisensory data representing the remote environment provide proactive support for the doctor. One goal of the project is to mimic the real examination process for the doctor as close as possible. In order to provide an intuitive and safe way of interaction with the patient, the robotic device has to perform certain tasks autonomously. Computer Vision methods serve the critical need of perceiving the patient in his/her distinct pose in order to estimate the position of the end effector with respect to the body. A Kinect sensor mounted on the robot's head is providing real-time depth data during the examination, while the patient is lying on a bed and the robot arm moving in front of the sensor. Our focus therefore is to accurately estimate the surface of the patient's upper body in order to determine the position of the examination probe relative to the torso. This knowledge can subsequently be used to map probe measurements to a human body model, providing an intuitive way of storing, visualizing and comparing examination results. The efficiency and usability of the teleoperation system directly depends on the speed and accuracy of this estimation process.

In general, there are discriminative (fast, lower accuracy) and generative (expensive, higher accuracy, but prone to local minima) approaches to both body shape and pose estimation problems. While we extend well known random forests for pose estimation [2–4], we propose to tackle prediction of body shape parameters from a single depth image by means of a linear subspace representation. To improve tracking accuracy and exploit shape information on top of our discriminative approach, we combine the two paradigms by subsequently performing additional model-fitting based refinement iterations.

The remainder of the paper is organized as follows: We provide an overview of the related work in Sect. 2. In Sect. 3, we present our framework for body shape estimation and pose tracking. Then we report quantitative and qualitative results of the proposed methods in Sect. 4, and conclude by discussing limitations and future work in Sect. 5.

2   Related Work

In is this section we relate our method to body shape and pose estimation approaches that have been proposed in the literature.

Body Shape Estimation from Depth. Body shape estimation work is dominated by generative model-fitting approaches. Fitting a human body model to the observed depth data is very robust to noise. In this context, the SCAPE model [5] is the most popular one, but other models [6–9] have been investigated, or could potentially be used for this purpose. For instance, [10,11] follow a procedure based on the Iterative Closest Point (ICP) algorithm to fit a SCAPE model to observed point clouds. In [12,13], the SCAPE model is employed to obtain the human body shape under the garments worn by the subject. Weiss et al. [14] optimize the SCAPE parameters to jointly maximize the overlap of the projected model with the RGB-silhouette and minimize the distance between corresponding points on the model and on an input range image. Bogo et al. [15] propose a coarse-to-fine model fitting strategy.

Among the model-free approaches, methods similar to KinectFusion [16,17] perform 3D body reconstructions from RGB-D sequences or multiple views [11, 18–21].

By contrast, we obtain an initial estimate of low dimensional body shape parameters (using a variant of the SCAPE body model) from a *single frame*. To this end, we propose to exploit depth image subspace features by training a regression forest to predict body shape parameters. Then we apply an ICP-based model fitting algorithm to refine the estimation and improve accuracy.

Human Pose Estimation from Depth. In general, generative models attempt to fit an articulated body model to the observed data by finding 3D-contour- or silhouette-based correspondences with an ICP-like approach [14,22–24]. Discriminative methods however try to directly infer pose information in a data-driven manner. Depth difference features as introduced by [2] enable training of random forest models that are capable of real-time inference [3,4,25]. Many hybrid approaches were proposed to combine the benefits of both worlds [10,26–28] by using database look-up to obtain a good initialization. In the same sense, [29,30] employ random forests to predict dense correspondences for a subsequent iterative model fitting procedure. Our work specializes the approach of [3] by improving the accuracy of the joint position estimation for upper body joints using a global forest refinement strategy. We further improve the upper body localization by fitting the estimated body shape to the observed data. We assume the torso shape to change rigidly with pose and therefore use an efficient rigid ICP-based alignment. To improve stability and robustness over time, the refined joint positions are fed back to the joint position estimation.

3   Method

We now introduce our framework for human body shape estimation and upper body tracking. We first propose to make use of a subspace representation of canonical depth maps to predict a set of human body shape parameters. Second, we extend the random forest framework by Girshick et al. [3] to accurately estimate upper body joint positions. We then compute a coarse alignment using

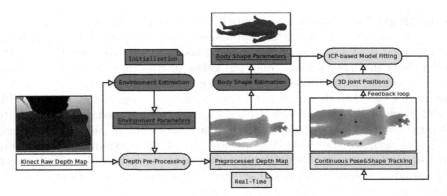

Fig. 1. Pipeline overview: At the initialization stage (orange) we estimate the environment and the patient's body shape. During the real-time phase (blue), we track the patient using the previously estimated parameters. To this end, we perform discriminative body pose estimation in combination with a model fitting procedure and introduce robustness and temporal consistency by a feedback loop. (Color figure online)

the predicted joint positions and initialize a model-fitting based refinement with our estimated upper body shape model. The whole pipeline is illustrated in Fig. 1.

3.1 Preprocessing

As a first step, we estimate the 3D environment of the scene. In our medical scenario, we estimate the ground plane and the position and height of the patient's bed to define a volume of interest. This enables efficient pre-processing (planar clipping) of the depth images during the real-time phase. During the initialization phase, we require the patient to lie on the bed and the scene to be free of external objects.

3.2 Body Shape Estimation via Subspace Regression

The motivation for our approach is the observation that model-fitting procedures require a good initialization in order to converge to the correct minimum. As we show in our experiments, this is a serious disadvantage in terms of accuracy and run time. Therefore we propose a method to obtain a sound data-driven initialization to jump-start the model-fitting and to guide the algorithm towards the correct solution.

Our approach to rapidly obtaining an estimate of the body shape from a single frame is partly inspired by [27]. First, a normalized view of the subject is created by means of discriminative pose estimation. Then we compute a linear subspace of all canonical depth images to reduce complexity. The subspace coefficients ultimately serve as features for a random regression forest to predict a set of body shape parameters.

Body Shape Model. In particular, we employ the MPII Human Shape model [7]. The shape parameters **s** of this statistical shape model represent a small number of directions with high variance from the mean body shape (principal components). They have been estimated using principal component analysis (PCA) on a varied dataset of aligned 3D scans of the human body. Figure 2 visualizes the variations captured by the first 5 shape parameters. For instance, the first component captures variations due to body height, while the second component $\mathbf{s}^1$ is dominantly influenced by the torso shape. This model allows to compactly represent body shapes and to generate corresponding mesh models for fitting purposes.

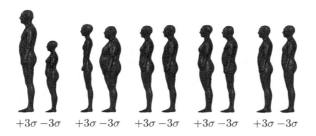

$+3\sigma\ -3\sigma \qquad +3\sigma\ -3\sigma \qquad +3\sigma\ -3\sigma \qquad +3\sigma\ -3\sigma \qquad +3\sigma\ -3\sigma$

Fig. 2. Body shape variations captured by the first 5 PCA coefficients (from [7]). The renderings depict the deviation from the mean body shape resulting from setting each of the coefficients to $\pm 3\sigma$.

Canonical View. The goal of this step is to normalize the depth camera's point of view w.r.t. the subject. To this end, we predict the joint positions of the subject using the method described in Sect. 3.3. We define a coordinate frame by a subset of the upper body joints, and define a canonical viewpoint as a rigid transformation originating from this frame. In particular, we choose to center the hip in the image and set the viewpoint 2 m in front of it. Choosing the distance is a trade-off between effective resolution, field-of-view size and robustness towards misalignment. Then we project the point cloud onto a virtual camera in this canonical pose. By contrast, the authors of [27] use the centroid and the principal directions of the point cloud to perform normalization, which is very problematic in the presence of (self-)occlusions.

We assume the point cloud data to be dense, and the range of rotation angles to be limited to roughly frontal/side views. The transformation to the canonical view can therefore be approximated with efficient point-wise rigid transformations and projections into the 2D virtual camera frame, without reconstructing the 3D surface. After applying the normalization, we obtain a training set of canonical depth images, showing different subjects in various poses from the same viewpoint and distance.

Learning. Intuitively, the appearance of the canonical depth images contains information about the body shape. To reduce complexity and exploit correlations between pixel locations, we compute a linear subspace using principal component analysis. To efficiently handle a big set of image data with high dimensionality, we use an approximation based on randomized projections.[1] We keep the N_d orthonormal directions (eigen-images) that contain the most variance in the data (highest eigenvalues). This yields a low-dimensional subspace representation of a depth image, denoted as a coefficient vector $\mathbf{c}$. Figure 3 visualizes the variances captured by the first three eigen-images. Note that variations are not only caused by shape, but also pose and misalignment noise are captured by the subspace coefficients. We therefore assume the relationship between the image subspace and the shape parameters to be nonlinear in general. Learning a dictionary like Ye et al. [27] resulted in bad generalization in our case. In order to learn which combination of coefficients is correlated with body shape, we employ a random forest model. We train an ensemble of regression forests to predict each of the body shape parameters in $\mathbf{s}$, using $\mathbf{c}$ as features. Note that we perform the PCA on rendered canonical images (without normalization artifacts), whereas normalized depth images are projected to the subspace (see next paragraph) and serve as input to the forest training.

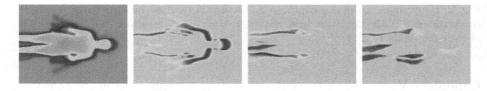

Fig. 3. Visualization of the mean canonical depth image and the first three eigen-images obtained by PCA. Note that the first eigen-image is sensitive to the global body size while the second dominantly captures variances in the lower body width. The third principal direction however seems to be mostly related to pose differences.

Inference for a New Image. At test time, we first estimate the set of 3D upper body joint positions (see Sect. 3.3) necessary to generate the canonical view. The task now is to find the most plausible subspace coefficients $\mathbf{c} \in \mathbb{R}^{N_d}$ explaining the observed canonical depth image. Due to the presence of occlusions and artifacts introduced by our normalization, considering all pixels would deteriorate the results. Instead of projecting the canonical depth map by performing the inner products with the eigen-images $P \in \mathbb{R}^{N_{\text{pixels}} \times N_d}$, we propose to minimize the squared reconstruction error only on visible points:

$$E(\mathbf{c}|I) = \frac{1}{2}(I_{\text{visible}} - \Pi(P\mathbf{c}))^2 . \tag{1}$$

---

[1] RedSVD implementation. https://code.google.com/archive/p/redsvd/.

$I_{\text{visible}} \in \mathbb{R}^{N_v}$ denotes the stacked intensity (depth) vector of all N_v visible pixels and $\mathbf{c}$ is the vector of subspace coefficients, while $\Pi(\cdot)$ selects and orders the reconstructed pixels according to the order in I_{visible}. We solve this convex minimization by performing gradient descent.[2] Using the optimal subspace coefficients $\mathbf{c}$ as features, the body shape parameters are finally predicted by the trained regression forest.

3.3   Joint Position Estimation

Our work on discriminative pose estimation is based on the efficient method by Girshick et al. [3]. The idea is to directly regress votes for predicting 3D joint positions from the depth map. First, a set of points is randomly sampled from the image. Then a random forest is trained using local depth features around each sample point. The regression target value is a 3D offset vector pointing from a sample point to the position of the body joint. The employed depth-difference features are invariant to translation and depth of the visible subject. We account for different viewpoint angles and body shapes by using high variety training data.

Girshick et al. [3] (re-)use the same forest structure (trained originally for body part classification) by dropping down samples and computing leaf statistics for the different joints using mean-shift. Similar to tree growing, this procedure follows a rather greedy strategy and does not obey a global cost function.

Multipurpose Forest Refinement. We therefore extend the forest refinement strategy by Ren et al. [31] to serve two goals: First, we aim to improve joint prediction accuracy for upper body joints by redistributing the prediction errors more favorably. Second, we exploit the refinement to make the forest structure reusable for multiple joints.

In the following formulation, every dimension of the 3D output vector is treated independently. Formally, let $\mathcal{P}_I = \{(\mathbf{x}_i^I, y_i^I)\}$ represent the set of samples belonging to image I, where y_i^I denotes one dimension of the target 3D offset. We model the refinement process as that of learning leaf weights $\mathbf{w}$ generating a per-sample offset prediction of the form

$$\hat{y}_i^I(\mathbf{w}|\mathbf{x}_i^I) = \mathbf{w}^T \phi(\mathbf{x}_i^I) . \tag{2}$$

By $\phi(\mathbf{x}_i)$ we denote the binary vector whose j^{th} position $\phi_j(\mathbf{x}_i)$ has value 1 if the local sample i has reached the corresponding leaf in the forest, and 0 otherwise[3]. Our goal of learning the optimal prediction value of each leaf can be thought of as a linear regression problem on the leaf weights $\mathbf{w}$, using the leaf indices corresponding to each sample as categorical features.

---

[2] Note that solving for $\mathbf{c}$ in equation $I(\mathbf{c}) = \Pi(P\mathbf{c})$ is overdetermined as long as there are more than N_d visible points/pixels. If all pixels are taken into account, the result of the optimization equals projecting the canonical depth map on the eigenimages.

[3] Note that this vector concatenates the leaves of all the trees in the forest.

However, we found that directly applying the method of [31] worsens the overall results. This stems from the fact that the predictions are treated independently for each sample: the optimization overfits to sets of samples from images that are easy to predict, ignoring those samples which would improve prediction on difficult images.

Hence we extend the approach of [31], and account for combined predictions of the entire image, by defining an image-level prediction as the mean of all votes for the absolute joint position:

$$\bar{y}^I(\mathbf{w}) = \frac{1}{N_s} \sum_{\{\mathbf{x}_i^I\}} \left(p_i^I + \hat{y}_i^I(\mathbf{w}|\mathbf{x}_i^I)\right) \ , \tag{3}$$

where N_s is the number of sample points i in image I, and p_i^I the position of the sample point.

To account for the global image prediction in our refinement procedure, we therefore introduce an energy of the form

$$E(\mathbf{w}) = \frac{1}{2}\|\mathbf{w}\|_2^2 + \frac{1}{2}\frac{\lambda_1}{|\mathcal{I}|}\sum_{I \in \mathcal{I}}(y^I - \bar{y}^I(\mathbf{w}))^2 + \frac{1}{2}\frac{\lambda_2}{|\{\mathbf{x}_i\}|}\sum_{\{\mathbf{x}_i\}}(y_i - \hat{y}_i(\mathbf{w}|\mathbf{x}_i))^2 \ , \tag{4}$$

where the first term regularizes the leaf weights, the second term optimizes for the combined votes on a *per image* base and the third one further regularizes the weights by minimizing the error of the offset predictions *per sample point*. We solve this sparse linear regression problem using stochastic gradient descent with momentum and a lazy update strategy for the L2 regularization. We report the hyper-parameters in Table 1.

Inference for a New Image. Following [3], we evaluate our forest at randomly sampled center pixels according to Eq. 2. Then we generate the votes for each of the 3 dimensions by

$$v_i = p_i^I + \hat{y}_i^I(\mathbf{w}|\mathbf{x}_i^I) \ , \tag{5}$$

and propose a vote weight of the form

$$u_i = \mathbf{v}^T\phi(\mathbf{x}_i^I) \ \text{with} \ \mathbf{v}_l = e^{-E_l^2} \tag{6}$$

Each element $\mathbf{v}_l$ of the leaf confidence vector $\mathbf{v}$ depends on the average error E_l produced by the associated leaf l at training time.

Finally, we combine all 3D votes using a weighted mean-shift strategy. To exploit temporal consistency, we add a 3D Gaussian prior on the joint position of either the last time step or from the model fitting component feedback (see Sect. 3.4) to the mean shift weights. This smooths the tracking and introduces additional robustness towards occlusions.

3.4   Model Fitting and Tracking

For many professional applications, the coarse accuracy of discriminative methods is a significant drawback. We propose to combine our data-driven shape and pose estimation by means of a model-fitting strategy: by taking both the predicted body shape and the coarse alignment provided by the joint positions into account, we improve the accuracy of shape and pose estimation.

Body Shape Refinement. Starting from our subspace-based estimates for the body shape coefficients, we now add a refinement step to further improve the torso shape and surface estimation accuracy. We propose a model fitting procedure with two alternating ICP-based methods. One iteration starts by correcting for the misalignment of the model with the observed data using standard rigid registration. Then the body shape is adapted by performing gradient descent on model parameters to fit corresponding points as closely as possible. This two-step process is repeated until convergence. Note that we already have coarse initializations for both the alignment and the shape parameters. We assume the upper body pose to change rigidly with pose and therefore use rigid (non-articulated) ICP on points associated with the upper body.

We then formulate the shape fitting as an energy minimization problem on the body shape coefficients $\mathbf{s}$:

$$E(\mathbf{s}|C, s_0) = \frac{\lambda}{2}\|\mathbf{s}\|_2^2 + \frac{1}{2}(\mathbf{s} - s_0)^T \Lambda(\mathbf{s} - s_0) + \frac{1}{2}\frac{1}{N_p}\|(C - (M + V\mathbf{s}))\|_2 . \quad (7)$$

Given the observed points $C \in \mathbb{R}^{3N_p}$ corresponding to the N_p model points, we minimize the squared error to the model, which is computed as the mean shape $M \in \mathbb{R}^{3N_p}$ plus the shape variations $V \in \mathbb{R}^{3N_p \times 20}$ according to the current shape coefficients $\mathbf{s}$. The first term penalizes the distance from the mean shape to avoid unlikely shapes. If prior information about the shape s_0 is available, we incorporate it using a diagonal regularization matrix Λ. In doing so, we are able to control which parameters of $\mathbf{s}$ should be primarily refined by the process, given that some parameters of the prior s_0 are already estimated with high confidence and should not be affected during optimization. Both regularizations effectively serve as (anisotropic) Gaussian priors. This convex optimization problem can be solved efficiently via gradient descent techniques.

Model-Based Surface Tracking and Feedback. Fitting the refined body model to the observed data is a straight-forward and effective way to exploit body shape information for tracking. In every new frame, we make use of our discriminative 3D joint position estimates and initialize an ICP-based rigid alignment to improve accuracy.

The refined joint positions are then fed back to serve as a prior for the mean-shift procedure in Sect. 3.3. Only a few ICP iterations are enough to improve accuracy, since the initialization can be assumed to already be reasonably good, especially once the feedback loop is closed. This approach is very robust towards dynamic occlusions and enables efficient model-based tracking of the upper body surface.

Table 1. Hyperparameters for our 3D body joint estimation algorithm

Tree training		Refinement	
Sample points	512 per image	Method	SGD+Momentum
Trees	3	Initial LR	1
Tree depth	24	λ_1	10^{-3}
		λ_2	10^{-4}
Decision Functions		Momentum	0.8
Probe offset range	+-50px	Epochs	48
Threshold range	+-5cm	Batch size	1
Candidates	128 per split	LR decay	0.9
min. #Samples	50 to split		

4   Experiments

4.1   Dataset

To evaluate our methods on a large set of different body shapes and poses, we use the *HumanVP* dataset created from synthetically generated mesh data. The motivation behind this is that it allows us to easily annotate the ground-truth shape parameters and joint positions, and carefully evaluate the behavior of our methods under different conditions, such as different body shapes, different poses, and different levels of occlusions.

In particular, we employed the MPII Human Shape Model [7]. This rigged statistical shape model was created from the CAESAR dataset [32], which contains a wide variety of body shapes represented as 3D meshes. These meshes are in vertex correspondence, and annotations for body parts and joint positions are provided. The depth data was obtained by sampling from the 4000 CAESAR-fitted body meshes of [7]. We randomly assigned a pose combination chosen from a set of 750 sub-poses of upper body (bending, torsion), arm (straight, angled, supporting head, ...) and leg (straight, angled) to each one of these meshes. Two example meshes are shown in Fig. 4a. We rendered depth images from 12 different viewpoints (random rotations around 2 rotation axes) using OpenGL. To this end, we employed a virtual camera that mimics the projection properties

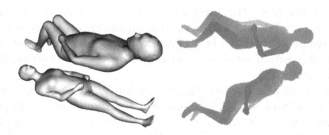

Fig. 4. Example posed body meshes from the MPII Human Shape Model [7] and rendered synthetic depth images from our *HumanVP* dataset.

(FoV angles, resolution, aspect ratio) of the Kinect sensor. We further used the noise model of [33], which has been shown to yield synthetic depth maps that are very similar to real ones. This resulted in a total of about 50 000 images. Figure 4b shows some example images. In our experiments, we partitioned these images into training and test sets based on the 4000 mesh models, and thus divided the images created from the models accordingly. We used 70 % of the models for training and 30 % for testing.

4.2 Body Shape Estimation from a Single Frame

We compare our subspace-based shape estimation method on the *HumanVP* dataset with plain model-fitting and their combination. To this end, we report estimation errors on the first 5 shape coefficients. Since these coefficients represent a body shape in a linear subspace of a high-dimensional statistical shape model, the prediction errors can be seen as a proxy for the average per-vertex error between the reconstructed body model and the ground truth model. The second shape parameter $\mathbf{s}^1$ mainly captures the belly/upper body shape (see Fig. 2) and is therefore the most interesting in this context. All methods are provided with the same initial 3D joint positions. Our reported values are normalized by the respective PCA standard deviation (see Sect. 3.2).

We learn $N_d = 20$ eigen-images for our subspace representation of the canonical images (640×480 px) and train a forest of 16 trees to predict the body shape coefficients using the MATLAB TreeBagger implementation. For the model fitting (see Eq. 7), we chose $\lambda = 0.1$ and the maximum correspondence distance for ICP to 0.1 m.

Subspace Regression vs. Model Fitting. To enable a fair comparison and to avoid distortion of the results due to local minima during model fitting, we take the following measures: We start from a set of initial shapes and select the best fitting solution. Also, we reject unlikely shape results, if at least one predicted shape parameter exceeds the $\pm 3\sigma$ threshold. We therefore discarded about 17 % of test images for the model fitting results.

Figure 5 shows the resulting RSME (b) and error standard deviation (c) for the first 5 shape coefficients. Our subspace-based regression method consistently provides lowest errors on all shape parameters and poses a very reasonable initialization. We can see that on the most important coefficient $\mathbf{s}^1$, the methods perform on a similar level, model fitting however induces slightly less RSME and less error deviation. Due to the fact that we only fit to the upper body, model fitting alone is not able to recover shape parameters that are less related to the torso shape. Also, the higher order coefficients capture smaller shape details which tend to result in more noisy estimates. While the baseline needs about 12 s per frame, our subspace-based method runs significantly faster, demanding less than 2 s on average.[4]

---

[4] Evaluation hardware: Intel Core i7-4790K CPU 4.00 GHz, 16 Gb RAM.

Combining Subspace Regression and Model Fitting. Following our paradigm of combining discriminative and generative methods, we investigated the benefits of using our subspace-based method to initialize the model fitting procedure. We set $\Lambda_{i \neq 1} = \mathrm{diag}(1)$, $\Lambda_1 = 10^{-3}$ to focus on refining the torso shape while keeping the other coefficients close to the initial estimate (see Eq. 7). Our results show that our refinement strategy significantly improves the accuracy of the torso shape coefficient s^1 compared to the initial shape provided by our subspace regression method. As desired, prediction errors of other parameters change only marginally. Due to the effective regularization, the refinement converges after about 6 s on average.

Shape Estimation Efficiency. To gauge the dense surface accuracy of the estimated upper body shape, we evaluated the 3D displacement error per model vertex and the error standard deviation. Note that we consider the complete set of vertices of the full upper body model. Since a significant portion of points is not visible in a single image, this measure is a very interesting accuracy benchmark and shows the strength of model-based approaches. Our combined approach achieves an average error of approximately 9 mm ($\sigma = 6$ mm) per model vertex, compared to 12 mm ($\sigma = 9$ mm) without model-fitting. Since the data-driven subspace method does not consider the domain shift from synthetic data, it is however safe to assume that this difference will increase when dealing with real data. We can therefore conclude that our approach yields upper body shape estimates of reasonable accuracy.

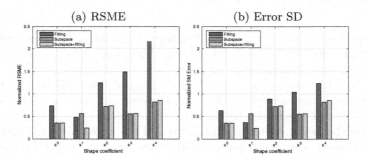

Fig. 5. Body shape estimation: (a) normalized RSME and (b) standard deviation (SD) of our subspace method, model-fitting, and their combination on *HumanVP*.

4.3   Joint Position Estimation from a Single Frame

To evaluate the accuracy of the predicted 3D salient point positions, we report both the joint detection rate (true positive, if the prediction is within 3 cm from the GT) and the RSME across 6 upper body joints/salient points. As our method extends the one proposed by Girshick et al. [3], it is a natural choice to compare the two methods on our *HumanVP* dataset. We use the same hyper-parameters for both methods and optimize the mean-shift procedure to the upper body joints. In order to better handle occlusions, we reduced the range of probing offsets to 50 px (see Table 1), without noticeable loss in prediction accuracy for upper body joints. The results in Fig. 6 show that our forest refinement strategy consistently improves prediction accuracy on all upper body joints but the belly reference point. This could indicate an upper bound on the attainable accuracy with this random forest model, since the belly point predictions are the most accurate among all predicted points. Figure 7 depicts some qualitative results on real Kinect data. Combining discriminative pose estimation with ICP-based refinement using our estimated body model (Fig. 6b) significantly boosts localization accuracy.

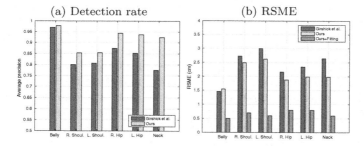

Fig. 6. 3D Joint position estimation: Comparison of our methods with [3] on our *HumanVP* dataset. (a) Detection rate (3 cm threshold) (b) Localization error

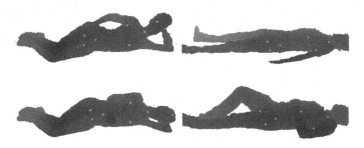

Fig. 7. Visualization of discriminative joint position estimates on real data, showing different exemplary subjects and poses. They provide a sound initialization for subsequent model fitting.

4.4   Robust Upper Body Tracking Framework

We now give a preliminary qualitative impression of our complete tracking framework, combining shape and pose information with temporal feedback. We visualize results on real data, since we do not have annotated depth sequences for evaluations yet. Our data originates from a mobile robot platform that features a 7 DoF robotic arm used for performing remote-controlled ultrasonography examinations within the *ReMeDi* project. Our task is to localize the end-effector w.r.t. the patient under severe occlusions due to viewpoint limitations and the robot arm moving in front of the sensor. We implemented our method as three processing nodes (shape estimation, pose estimation and model-fitting) within the ROS[5] framework. Without further optimization, the tracking update frequency is about 10 Hz on a conventional laptop[6]. The Kinect coordinate frame has been calibrated to the robot base frame to enable transformations between the 3D data and the robot arm. Looking at the random forest estimates for the joint position in Fig. 7 reveals that they pose a sound initialization for the subsequent model fitting. Figure 8a visualizes the localization of the patient w.r.t. to the robotic platform while the robotic arm is partly occluding the subject.

Hands-on experiments showed that for typically slow upper body motions of the patient, our approach yields practical results for online mapping of probe measurements to a position on the 3D body model during examination (see Fig. 8b). In contrast, using only discriminative pose estimation produces qualitatively more unstable and inaccurate results on the body surface. This confirms our results on the synthetic data (Fig. 6b). ICP-based refinement with an adequate body model is able to correct for surface misalignment and introduces significant robustness towards occlusions and missing body parts.

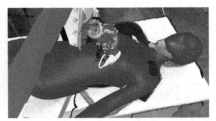   

(a) Overlaying the estimated body model   (b) Online probe mapping (red dot)
with the synchronous Kinect RGB-D stream.   and tracking history (green)

Fig. 8. Visualization of the estimated localized patient w.r.t. the robot platform. (a) During examination, the robotic arm is partly occluding the subject. Note that we only fit to the torso of the patient. (b) Estimated probe position w.r.t to mannequin upper body. Our approach remains robust towards occluded/missing body parts. (Color figure online)

---

[5] Robot Operating System (ROS). http://www.ros.org/.
[6] Hardware: Intel Core i7-4510U 2.0 Ghz, 8 Gb RAM.

5   Conclusion and Future Work

We have proposed a hybrid approach towards rapid shape estimation and real-time pose tracking of the human upper body. We employ fast data-driven methods in combination with a model fitting-based refinement strategy to exploit body shape for accurate torso tracking in real-time.

We introduced a subspace-based algorithm to estimate body shape parameters directly from a single depth image and showed that it provides a sound initialization for model fitting methods. Our second contribution is the development of a suitable random forest refinement strategy for the well known body joint position estimation framework by Girshick et al. [3]. Our experiments show that the prediction error is distributed advantageously across training images and the method therefore generalizes better on upper body joints.

Moreover, we provided our tracking framework with an ICP-based refinement for both upper body shape and pose, and presented qualitative results on real data. To encourage temporal consistency and induce robustness towards occlusions due to dynamic objects in the scene, we proposed a feedback mechanism that improves the interplay between data-driven and model-based torso tracking.

For future work, we plan to evaluate our tracking method on depth image sequences in a more quantitative manner. We also intend to tackle the problem of non-rigid shape changes induced by bending and torsion poses and aim to investigate novel methods for predicting body shape directly from depth data.

Acknowledgment. This work is funded by the EU Framework Seven project *ReMeDi* (grant 610902).

References

1. Bauer, S., Seitel, A., Hofmann, H., Blum, T., Wasza, J., Balda, M., Meinzer, H.-P., Navab, N., Hornegger, J., Maier-Hein, L.: Real-time range imaging in health care: a survey. In: Grzegorzek, M., Theobalt, C., Koch, R., Kolb, A. (eds.) Time-of-Flight and Depth Imaging. LNCS, vol. 8200, pp. 228–254. Springer, Heidelberg (2013). doi:10.1007/978-3-642-44964-2_11
2. Shotton, J., Fitzgibbon, A., Cook, M., Sharp, T., Finocchio, M., Moore, R., Kipman, A., Blake, A.: Real-time human pose recognition in parts from single depth images. In: Cipolla, R., Battiato, S., Farinella, G.M. (eds.) Machine Learning for Computer Vision. SCI, pp. 119–135. Springer, Heidelberg (2013). doi:10.1007/978-3-642-28661-2_5
3. Girshick, R., Shotton, J., Kohli, P., Criminisi, A., Fitzgibbon, A.: Efficient regression of general-activity human poses from depth images. In: Proceedings of the IEEE International Conference on Computer Vision, pp. 415–422 (2011)
4. Jung, H.Y., Lee, S., Comp, D., Eng, E.S.: Random tree walk toward instantaneous 3D human pose estimation. In: Proceedings of the IEEE Computer Society Conference on Computer Vision and Pattern Recognition (2015)
5. Anguelov, D., Srinivasan, P., Thrun, S., Daphne, K., Davis, J., Rodgers, J.: SCAPE: shape completion and animation of people, LNCS (PART 2) vol. 7729, pp. 133–147 (2013)

6. Hasler, N., Stoll, C.: A statistical model of human pose and body shape. Eurographics **28**(2), 1–10 (2009)
7. Pishchulin, L., Wuhrer, S., Helten, T., Theobalt, C., Schiele, B.: Building statistical shape spaces for 3D human modeling. arXiv (2015)
8. Zuffi, S., Black, M.J.: The stitched puppet: a graphical model of 3D human shape and pose. In: The IEEE Conference on Computer Vision and Pattern Recognition (CVPR) (2015)
9. Loper, M., Mahmood, N., Romero, J., Pons-Moll, G., Black, M.J.: SMPL: a skinned multi-person linear model. ACM Trans. Graph. (Proc. SIGGRAPH Asia) **34**(6), 248:1–248:16 (2015)
10. Helten, T., Baak, A., Bharaj, G., Muller, M., Seidel, H.P., Theobalt, C.: Personalization and evaluation of a real-time depth-based full body tracker. In: International Conference on 3D Vision (3DV) (2013)
11. Zhang, Q., Fu, B., Ye, M.: Quality dynamic human body modeling using a single low-cost depth camera. In: The IEEE Conference on Computer Vision and Pattern Recognition (CVPR) (2014)
12. Xu, H., Yu, Y., Zhou, Y., Li, Y., Du, S.: Measuring accurate body parameters of dressed humans with large-scale motion using a Kinect sensor. Sensors **13**(9), 11362–11384 (2013)
13. Perbet, F., Johnson, S., Pham, M.T., Stenger, B.: Human body shape estimation using a multi-resolution manifold forest. In: The IEEE Conference on Computer Vision and Pattern Recognition (CVPR) (2014)
14. Weiss, A., Hirshberg, D., Black, M.J.: Home 3D body scans from noisy image and range data. In: International Conference on Computer Vision (ICCV) (2011)
15. Bogo, F., Black, M.J., Loper, M., Romero, J.: Detailed full-body reconstructions of moving people from monocular RGB-D sequences. In: ICCV (2015)
16. Newcombe, R.A., Fox, D., Seitz, S.M.: DynamicFusion: reconstruction and tracking of non-rigid scenes in real-time. In: The IEEE Conference on Computer Vision and Pattern Recognition (CVPR) (2015)
17. Newcombe, R.A., Molyneaux, D., Kim, D., Davison, A.J., Shotton, J., Hodges, S., Fitzgibbon, A.: KinectFusion: real-time dense surface mapping and tracking. In: Proceedings of the 24th Annual ACM Symposium on User Interface Software and Technology (2011)
18. Cui, Y., Chang, W., Tobias, N.: KinectAvatar: fully automatic body capture using a single kinect. In: ACCV Workshop on Color Depth Fusion in Computer Vision (2012)
19. Zeng, M., Zheng, J., Cheng, X., Liu, X.: Templateless quasi-rigid shape modeling with implicit loop-closure. In: 2013 IEEE Conference on Computer Vision and Pattern Recognition, pp. 145–152 (2013)
20. Tong, J., Zhou, J., Liu, L., Pan, Z., Yan, H.: Scanning 3D full human bodies using kinects. IEEE Trans. Vis. Comput. Graph. **18**, 643–650 (2012)
21. Li, H., Vouga, E., Gudym, A., Luo, L., Barron, J.T., Gusev, G.: 3D Self-Portraits
22. Ganapathi, V., Plagemann, C., Koller, D., Thrun, S.: Real-time human pose tracking from range data. In: Fitzgibbon, A., Lazebnik, S., Perona, P., Sato, Y., Schmid, C. (eds.) ECCV 2012, Part VI. LNCS, vol. 7577, pp. 738–751. Springer, Heidelberg (2012). doi:10.1007/978-3-642-33783-3_53
23. Gall, J., Stoll, C., De Aguiar, E., Theobalt, C., Rosenhahn, B., Seidel, H.P.: Motion capture using joint skeleton tracking and surface estimation. In: 2009 IEEE Computer Society Conference on Computer Vision and Pattern Recognition Workshops, CVPR Workshops 2009, pp. 1746–1753 (2009)

24. Grest, D., Krüger, V., Koch, R.: Single view motion tracking by depth and silhouette information. In: Ersbøll, B.K., Pedersen, K.S. (eds.) SCIA 2007. LNCS, vol. 4522, pp. 719–729. Springer, Heidelberg (2007). doi:10.1007/978-3-540-73040-8_73

25. Sun, M., Kohli, P., Shotton, J.: Conditional regression forests for human pose estimation. In: Proceedings of the IEEE Computer Society Conference on Computer Vision and Pattern Recognition, pp. 3394–3401 (2012)

26. Baak, A., Muller, M., Bharaj, G., Seidel, H.P., Theobalt, C.: A data-driven approach for real-time full body pose reconstruction from a depth camera. In: Proceedings of the IEEE International Conference on Computer Vision, pp. 1092–1099 (2011)

27. Ye, M., Yang, R., Pollefeys, M.: Accurate 3D pose estimation from a single depth image. In: 2011 International Conference on Computer Vision, pp. 731–738 (2011)

28. Ganapathi, V., Plagemann, C., Koller, D., Thrun, S.: Real time motion capture using a single time-of-flight camera. In: 2010 IEEE Computer Society Conference on Computer Vision and Pattern Recognition (CVPR 2010), pp. 755–762 (2010)

29. Pons-Moll, G., Javier, R., Mahmood, N., Black, M.J.: Dyna: a model of dynamic human shape in motion. ACM Trans. Graph. 34, 1–14 (2015)

30. Taylor, J., Shotton, J., Sharp, T., Fitzgibbon, A.: The Vitruvian manifold: inferring dense correspondences for one-shot human pose estimation. In: The IEEE Conference on Computer Vision and Pattern Recognition (CVPR), pp. 103–110 (2012)

31. Ren, S., Cao, X., Wei, Y., Sun, J.: Global refinement of random forest. In: The IEEE Conference on Computer Vision and Pattern Recognition (CVPR) (2015)

32. Robinette, K.M., Daanen, H., Paquet, E.: The CAESAR project: a 3-D surface anthropometry survey. In: International Conference on 3-D Digital Imaging and Modeling (1999)

33. Nguyen, C.V., Izadi, S., Lovell, D.: Modeling kinect sensor noise for improved 3D reconstruction and tracking. In: International Conference on 3D Imaging, Modeling, Processing, Visualization and Transmission (3DIMPVT) (2012)

Multi-level Net: A Visual Saliency Prediction Model

Marcella Cornia[✉], Lorenzo Baraldi, Giuseppe Serra, and Rita Cucchiara

Department of Engineering "Enzo Ferrari",
University of Modena and Reggio Emilia, Modena, Italy
{marcella.cornia,lorenzo.baraldi,
giuseppe.serra,rita.cucchiara}@unimore.it

Abstract. State of the art approaches for saliency prediction are based on Fully Convolutional Networks, in which saliency maps are built using the last layer. In contrast, we here present a novel model that predicts saliency maps exploiting a non-linear combination of features coming from different layers of the network. We also present a new loss function to deal with the imbalance issue on saliency masks. Extensive results on three public datasets demonstrate the robustness of our solution. Our model outperforms the state of the art on SALICON, which is the largest and unconstrained dataset available, and obtains competitive results on MIT300 and CAT2000 benchmarks.

Keywords: Visual saliency · Saliency prediction · Convolutional neural network · Deep learning

1 Introduction

For many applications in image and video compression, video re-targeting and object segmentation, estimating where humans look in a scene is an essential step [6,9,22]. Neuroscientists [2], and more recently computer vision researches [13], have proposed computational saliency models to predict eye fixations over images.

Most traditional approaches typically cope with this task by defining hand-crafted and multi-scale features that capture a large spectrum of stimuli: lower-level features (color, texture, contrast) [11] or higher-level concepts (faces, people, text, horizon) [5]. In addition, since there is a strong tendency to look more frequently around the center of the scene than around the periphery [33], some techniques incorporate hand-crafted priors into saliency maps [19,20,35,36]. Unfortunately, eye fixation can depend on several aspects and this makes it difficult to design properly hand-crafted features.

Deep learning techniques, with their ability to automatically learn appropriate features from massive annotated data, have shown impressive results in several vision applications such as image classification [18] and semantic segmentation [24]. First attempts to define saliency models with the usage of deep

© Springer International Publishing Switzerland 2016
G. Hua and H. Jégou (Eds.): ECCV 2016 Workshops, Part II, LNCS 9914, pp. 302–315, 2016.
DOI: 10.1007/978-3-319-48881-3_21

convolutional networks have recently been presented [20, 35]. However, due to the small amount of training data in this scenario, researchers have presented networks with few layers or pretrained in other contexts. By publishing the large dataset SALICON [12], collected thanks to crowd-sourcing techniques, researches have then increased the number of convolutional layers reducing the overfitting risk [19, 25].

In this paper we present a general deep learning framework to predict saliency maps, called ML-Net. Differently from the previous deep learning approaches, that build saliency images based on the last convolutional layer, we propose a network that is able to combine multiple features coming from different layers of the network. The proposed solution is also able to learn its own prior from the training data, avoiding an hand-crafted definition. Finally, a new loss function is presented to tackle the imbalance problem of saliency maps, in which salient pixels are usually a minor percentage. Experimental results on three public datasets validate our solution.

2   Related Works

Early works on saliency detection were concerned with defining biologically-plausible architecture inspired by the human visual attention system. Koch, Ullman [17] and Itti et al. [13] were among the earliest ones. In particular, they proposed to extract multi-scale image features based on color, intensity and orientation, mimicking the properties of primate early vision. More recently, Hou and Zange [11] presented a technique based on log spectral representations of images, which extracted the spectral residual of an image, thus simulating the behavior of pre-attentive visual search. Differently, Torralba et al. [34] showed how the human visual system makes extensive use of contextual information in natural scenes. Similarly, Goferman et al. [8] proposed an approach that detects salient regions which are distinctive with respect to both their local and global surroundings. Judd et al. [16] and Cerf et al. [5] presented two techniques based on the combination of low-level features (color, orientation and intensity) and high-level semantic information (i.e. the location of faces, cars and text) and showed that this strategy significantly improves saliency prediction. However, all these methods employed hand-tuned features or trained specific higher-level classifiers.

Recently, Deep Convolutional Networks (DCNs) were used by several authors and appear much more appropriate to support saliency detection. Indeed, DCNs have been proved to be able to build descriptive features. Vig et al. [35] presented Ensembles of Deep Networks (eDN), a convolutional neural network with three layers. Since the annotated data available at that time to learn saliency was limited, their architecture could not outperform the current state-of-the art. To overcome this problem, Kümmerer et al. [20] suggest to reuse existing neural networks trained for object recognition and propose Deep Gaze, a neural network based on the AlexNet [18] architecture. Similarly, Huang et al. [12] present a DCN architecture for saliceny prediction that combines multiple DCNs pretrained for object recognition (AlexNet [18], VGG-16 [30] and GoogLeNet [32]).

The fine-tuning procedure of this architecture is performed using an objective function based on saliency evaluation metrics, such as the Normalized Scanpath Saliency, Similarity and KL-Divergence.

Liu *et al.* [23] present a multi-resolution Convolutional Neural Network which is trained from image regions centered on fixation and non-fixation locations over multiple resolutions. Srinivas *et al.* [19] propose a network, called DeepFix, that includes Location Biased Convolution filters able to identify location dependent patterns. Pan *et al.* [25] show how two different architectures, a shallow convent trained from scratch and a deep convent that uses parameters previous learned on the ILSVRC-12 dataset [29], can achieve state of the art results.

3   Our Approach

We argue that saliency prediction can benefit from both low level and high level features. For this reason, we build a saliency prediction model which combines features extracted at multiple levels from a Fully Convolutional Neural Network (FCN). Since the role of this network in our model is that of extracting features, instead of predicting a saliency map, we call this component *Feature extraction network*. An *Encoding network* is then designed to weight and combine feature maps extracted from the FCN, and training is performed by means of a loss function which tackles the problem of imbalance on saliency maps. An overview of our architecture, which we call ML-Net, is presented in Fig. 1.

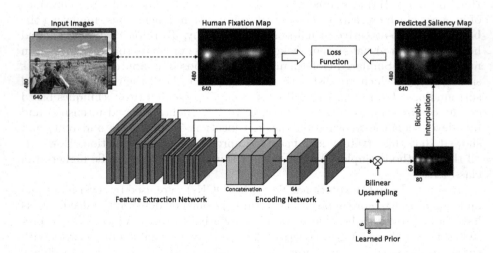

Fig. 1. Architecture of ML-Net.

Table 1. Output size of each layer of the FCN models used in our architecture. First column is the model inspired by VGG-16, second column is the one inspired by VGG-19 and the last one is inspired by AlexNet.

VGG-16 inspired model:

Input	$3 \times 480 \times 640$
conv1-1	$64 \times 480 \times 640$
conv1-2	$64 \times 480 \times 640$
maxpool1	$64 \times 240 \times 320$
conv2-1	$128 \times 240 \times 320$
conv2-2	$128 \times 240 \times 320$
maxpool2	$128 \times 120 \times 160$
conv3-1	$256 \times 120 \times 160$
conv3-2	$256 \times 120 \times 160$
conv3-3	$256 \times 120 \times 160$
maxpool3	$256 \times 60 \times 80$
conv4-1	$512 \times 60 \times 80$
conv4-2	$512 \times 60 \times 80$
conv4-3	$512 \times 60 \times 80$
maxpool4	$512 \times 60 \times 80$
conv5-1	$512 \times 60 \times 80$
conv5-2	$512 \times 60 \times 80$
conv5-3	$512 \times 60 \times 80$

VGG-19 inspired model:

Input	$3 \times 480 \times 640$
conv1-1	$64 \times 480 \times 640$
conv1-2	$64 \times 480 \times 640$
maxpool1	$64 \times 240 \times 320$
conv2-1	$128 \times 240 \times 320$
conv2-2	$128 \times 240 \times 320$
maxpool2	$128 \times 120 \times 160$
conv3-1	$256 \times 120 \times 160$
conv3-2	$256 \times 120 \times 160$
conv3-3	$256 \times 120 \times 160$
conv3-4	$256 \times 120 \times 160$
maxpool3	$256 \times 60 \times 80$
conv4-1	$512 \times 60 \times 80$
conv4-2	$512 \times 60 \times 80$
conv4-3	$512 \times 60 \times 80$
conv4-4	$512 \times 60 \times 80$
maxpool4	$512 \times 60 \times 80$
conv5-1	$512 \times 60 \times 80$
conv5-2	$512 \times 60 \times 80$
conv5-3	$512 \times 60 \times 80$
conv5-4	$512 \times 60 \times 80$

AlexNet inspired model:

Input	$3 \times 480 \times 640$
conv1	$96 \times 118 \times 158$
maxpool1	$96 \times 58 \times 78$
conv2	$256 \times 58 \times 78$
maxpool2	$256 \times 56 \times 76$
conv3	$384 \times 56 \times 76$
conv4	$384 \times 56 \times 76$
conv5	$256 \times 56 \times 76$

3.1 Feature Extraction Network

Current Fully Convolutional models can be described as sequences of convolutional and max-pooling layers, which process an input tensor to produce activation maps. Due to the presence of spatial pooling layers, convolutional layers with stride greater than one, or border effects, activation maps are usually smaller than input images.

The spatial resolution of an intermediate activation map, with respect to the input of the layer, can be written as $\left(\lfloor \frac{H+2p-k}{s} \rfloor + 1 \right) \times \left(\lfloor \frac{W+2p-k}{s} \rfloor + 1 \right)$, where $H \times W$ is the spatial resolution of the input, s is the stride, p is the padding and k is the kernel size. For instance, the AlexNet model [18] by Krizhevsky *et al.* uses different values of s, p and k across different layers ($s = 4$, $p = 0$ and $k = 11$ in the first convolutional layer, $s = 1, p = 1, k = 3$ for the last convolutional layer), while VGG-16 and VGG-19 models [31] use $s = 1$, $p = 1$ and $k = 3$ for convolutional layers and $s = 2, p = 0, k = 2$ for max-pooling layers.

To combine low level and high level features extracted from a FCN model, one could in principle reduce activation maps to a common spatial resolution, through downsampling or upsampling operations, and then concatenate them to form a single feature tensor. In contrast to this approach, which would imply a loss of information, in the case of downsampling, or a non-exact reconstruction of missing information, in the case of upsampling, we modify the stride of some layers in order to maintain the same spatial resolution across different layers. We apply this technique to three popular CNN models: VGG-16, VGG-19 and AlexNet.

In the case of the VGG-16 model, we set the stride on layer `maxpool4` to one, so to have activation maps from layers `conv5-3`, `maxpool4` and `maxpool3` with the same spatial size. We do the same in the VGG-19 model, again by setting the stride of `maxpool4` to one and considering feature maps from layers `conv5-4`, `maxpool4` and `maxpool3`. Finally, for the AlexNet model, we set the stride of layer `maxpool2` equal to one, to have the output of layers `maxpool1`, `maxpool2` and `conv5` having almost the same spatial support. These activation maps are then zero-padded to bring them to the same spatial resolution. All three models, as well as the output size of each of their layers, are reported in Table 1 for reference.

3.2   Encoding Network

Since feature maps extracted from the FCN model have the same spatial resolution, it is reasonable to concatenate them to form a single feature tensor. It is worth mentioning that the resulting tensor encodes features extracted from different levels of a FCN, and thus it is far more informative than the activation tensor coming from the last convolutional layer, which is usually employed to predict fixation maps. Beside containing high level features, like the responses to object detectors and part of object detectors, indeed, it contains responses to middle level features, like textures.

To combine features maps coming from different levels, and in order to form the final saliency map, we build an encoding network, whose aim is to weight low level, middle level and high level features to produce a provisional saliency prediction. The encoding network is composed of two convolutional layers, the first one having kernel size 3×3 and 64 feature maps, and the last one having a 1×1 kernel and a single feature map. Being the two convolutional layers separated by a ReLU activation stage, the provisional prediction can be a non-linear combination of input activation maps.

3.3   Prior Learning

The combination of a FCN model with the previously defined encoding network lets the network learn more robust saliency features, thus increasing the accuracy of predicted saliency maps. However, what the encoding network can not deal with is the role of the relative and absolute position of salient areas in the image. Indeed, the center of an image is well known to be more salient than the periphery, and this notion is usually incorporated in saliency models by means of a prior. Instead of using an hand-crafted prior, as done in the past, we let the network learn its own prior.

In particular, we learn a coarse $w' \times h'$ mask, which is upsampled and applied to the predicted saliency map with pixel-wise multiplication. The mask is initialized to one, so that the network can learn a prior by reducing excessive values.

Given the learned prior U with shape $w' \times h'$, we interpolate the pixels of U to produce an output prior map V of size $w \times h$, being w and h respectively the width and height of the predicted saliency map. We compute a sampling grid G of shape $w' \times h'$ associating each element of U with real-valued coordinates into V. If $G_{i,j} = (x_{i,j}, y_{i,j})$ then $U_{i,j}$ should be equal to V at $(x_{i,j}, y_{i,j})$; however since $(x_{i,j}, y_{i,j})$ are real-valued, we convolve with a sampling kernel and set

$$V_{x,y} = \sum_{i=1}^{w'} \sum_{j=1}^{h'} U_{i,j} k_x(x - x_{i,j}) k_y(y - y_{i,j}) \tag{1}$$

where $k_x(\cdot)$ and $k_y(\cdot)$ are bilinear kernels, corresponding to $k_x(d) = \max\left(0, \frac{w}{w'} - |d|\right)$ and $k_y(d) = \max\left(0, \frac{h}{h'} - |d|\right)$. w' and h' were set to $\lfloor w/10 \rfloor$ and $\lfloor h/10 \rfloor$ in all our tests.

3.4 Training

For training, we randomly sample a minibatch containing N training saliency maps, and encourage the network to minimize a loss function through Stochastic Gradient Descent. While the majority of saliency prediction models employ a MSE or a KL-Divergence loss, we build a custom loss function which tackles the problem of imbalance in saliency maps.

Our loss function is motivated by three observations: first of all, predictions should be pixelwise similar to ground truth maps, therefore a square error loss $\|\phi(\mathbf{x}_i) - \mathbf{y}_i\|^2$, between the predicted saliency map $\phi(\mathbf{x}_i)$ and the ground-truth map $\mathbf{y}_i$, is a reasonable starting model. Secondly, predicted maps should be invariant to their maximum, and there is no point in forcing the network to produce values in a given numerical range, so predictions are normalized by their maximum. Third, the loss should give the same importance to high and low ground truth values, even though the majority of ground truth pixels are close to zero. For this reason, the deviation between predicted and ground-truth values is weighted by a linear function $\alpha - \mathbf{y}_i$, which tends to give more importance to pixels with high ground-truth fixation probability.

The overall loss function is thus

$$L(\mathbf{w}) = \frac{1}{N} \sum_{i=1}^{N} \left\| \frac{\frac{\phi(\mathbf{x}_i)}{\max \phi(\mathbf{x}_i)} - \mathbf{y}_i}{\alpha - \mathbf{y}_i} \right\|^2 + \lambda \|\mathbf{1} - U\|^2 \tag{2}$$

where a L_2 regularization term is added to penalize the deviation of the prior mask U from its initial value, thus encouraging the network to adapt to ground truth maps by changing convolutional weights rather than modifying the prior.

4 Experimental Evaluation

4.1 Datasets

For training and evaluation we employ the following datasets: SALICON [14], MIT1003 [16], MIT300 [15] and CAT2000 [1].

SALICON contains 20,000 images taken from the Microsoft CoCo dataset [21] and divided in 10,000 training images, 5,000 validation images and 5,000 testing images. It is currently the largest public dataset available for saliency prediction though its saliency maps were not collected with eye-tracking systems as in classical datasets for saliency prediction. Saliency maps were indeed generated by collecting mouse movements, and authors showed, both qualitatively and quantitatively, an high degree of similarity between their maps and those created from eye-tracking data.

MIT1003 includes 1003 random images taken from Flickr and LabelMe. Its saliency maps were generated using eye-tracking data from fifteen participants. MIT300 contains 300 natural images from both indoor and outdoor scenarios. Despite its limited size, it is the one of the most commonly used datasets for saliency prediction. Its saliency maps, that have been created from eye-tracking data of 39 observers, are not public available. To evaluate the effectiveness of our model on this dataset, we submitted our predictions to the MIT saliency benchmark [3].

CAT2000 is a collection of 4,000 images divided in 20 different categories such as *Cartoons, Art, Satellite, Low resolution images, Indoor, Outdoor, Line drawings*, ect. and each category contains 200 images. Saliency maps of this dataset have been created using eye-tracking data from 24 users. Images are divided in training set and test set where each of them consists of 2,000 images. Saliency maps of the test set are held-out and also in this case we submitted our predictions to the MIT saliency benchmark to evaluate performances of our model.

4.2 Evaluation Metrics

Several evaluation metrics have been proposed for saliency predictions: Normalized Scanpath Saliency (NSS), Earth Mover's Distance (EMD), Linear Correlation Coefficient (CC), Similarity, AUC Judd, AUC Borji and AUC shuffled (sAUC). Some of these metrics consider saliency at discrete fixation locations, while others treat both predicted saliency maps and ground truth maps, generated from fixation points, as distributions [4,27].

The Normalized Scanpath Saliency (NSS) metric was introduced specifically for the evaluation of saliency models [26]. The idea is to quantify the saliency map values at the eye fixation locations and to normalize it whit the saliency map variance

$$NSS(p) = \frac{SM(p) - \mu_{SM}}{\sigma_{SM}} \tag{3}$$

where p is the location of one fixation and SM is the saliency map which is normalized to have a zero mean and unit standard deviation. The final NSS score is the average of $NSS(p)$ for all fixations

$$NSS = \frac{1}{N} \sum_{p=1}^{N} NSS(p) \tag{4}$$

where N is the total number of eye fixations.

Earth Mover's Distance (EMD) represents the minimal cost to transform the probability distribution of the saliency map SM into the one of the human eye fixations FM. Therefore, a larger EMD indicates a larger difference between the two maps.

The Linear Correlation Coefficient (CC) instead is the Pearson's linear coefficient between SM and FM and is computed as

$$CC = \frac{conv(SM, FM)}{\sigma_{SM} * \sigma_{FM}} \tag{5}$$

It ranges between -1 and 1, and a score close to -1 or 1 indicates a perfect linear relationship between the two maps.

The Similarity metric [15] is computed as the sum of pixel-wise minimums between the predicted saliency map SM and the human eye fixation map FM, after normalizing the two maps

$$S = \sum_{x=1}^{X} min(SM(x), FM(x)) \tag{6}$$

where SM and FM are supposed to be probability distributions and sum up to one. A similarity score of one indicates that the predicted map is identical to the ground truth one.

Finally, the Area Under the ROC curve (AUC) is one of the most widely used metrics for the evaluation of maps predicted from saliency models. The saliency map is treated as a binary classifier of fixations at various threshold values, and a ROC curve can be drawn by measuring the true and false positive rates under each binary classifier. There are several different implementations of this metric which differ in how true and false positives are calculated. In our experiments we use AUC Judd, AUC Borji and shuffled AUC. The AUC Judd and the AUC Borji choose non-fixation points with a uniform distribution, otherwise shuffled AUC uses human fixations of other images in the dataset as non-fixation distribution. In that way, centered distribution of human fixations of the dataset is taken into account.

4.3   Implementation Details

Using the three feature extraction networks described in Sect. 3.1 (inspired by AlexNet, VGG-16 and VGG-19), we build three different variations of our

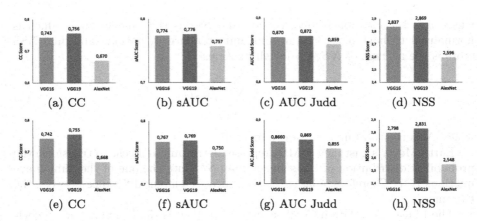

Fig. 2. Comparison between our three ML-Nets on SALICON dataset [14]. Each plot corresponds to a different evaluation metric (i.e. CC, sAUC, AUC Judd and NSS). Plots a-d correspond to the results on SALICON validation set, while plots e-h correspond to the results on SALICON test set.

saliency prediction model. Weights of all feature extraction networks are initialized to those of pre-trained models on the ILSVRC-12 dataset [29], while weights of the encoding networks are initialized according to [7], and biases are initialized to zero. SGD is applied with Nesterov momentum 0.9, weight decay 0.0005 and learning rate 10^{-3}. Parameters α and λ are respectively set to 1.1 and $1/(w' \cdot h')$ in all our experiments. Finally, the batch size N is set to 10.

We evaluate on the SALICON, on the MIT300 and on the CAT2000 datasets. First of all, we train our network on SALICON training set using the 5,000 images of SALICON validation set to validate the model. Secondly, we finetune our architecture on the MIT1003 dataset and on the CAT2000 training set to evaluate our model also on MIT300 dataset and CAT2000 testing set, respectively. In particular, we randomly split images of MIT1003 in 900 training images and 103 validation images and, after the training, we test our model on MIT300. For the CAT2000 instead, we randomly choose 200 images of training set (10 images for each category) as validation and we finetune the network on remaining images. Finally we test our network on the CAT2000 testing set.

Images from all datasets were resized to 640 × 480. In particular, images of MIT1003 and MIT300 datasets were zero-padded to fit a 4 : 3 aspect ratio and then resized to 640 × 480, while images from CAT2000 dataset were resized and then cropped to have a dimension of 640 × 480. Predicted saliency maps are upsampled with bicubic interpolation to the original image size before evaluation.

4.4   Quantitative Results

To investigate the performance of our solution, we first conduct a series of experiments on the SALICON dataset using the three different feature extraction networks. Figure 2 reports the results of our architecture when using the three FCN

Table 2. Comparison results on the SALICON test set [14].

	CC	sAUC	AUC Judd
ML-Net (VGG-19)	**0.7562**	**0.7782**	**0.8721**
Pan *et al.* [25] - Deep	0.6220	0.7240	0.8580
Pan *et al.* [25] - Shallow	0.5957	0.6698	0.8364
WHU IIP	0.4569	0.6064	0.7923
Rare 2012 Improved [28]	0.5108	0.6644	0.8148
Xidian	0.4811	0.6809	0.8051
Baseline: BMS [37]	0.4268	0.6935	0.7899
Baseline: GBVS [10]	0.4212	0.6303	0.7899
Baseline: Itti [13]	0.2046	0.6101	0.6669

Table 3. Comparison results on the MIT300 dataset [15].

	Sim	CC	sAUC	AUC Borji	AUC Judd	NSS	EMD
Infinite humans	1.00	1.00	0.80	0.87	0.91	3.18	0.00
DeepFix [19]	0.67	0.78	0.71	0.80	0.87	2.26	2.04
SALICON [12]	0.60	0.74	0.74	0.85	0.87	2.12	2.62
ML-Net (VGG-19)	**0.60**	**0.69**	**0.70**	**0.77**	**0.85**	**2.06**	**2.45**
Pan *et al.* - Deep [25]	0.52	0.58	0.69	0.82	0.83	1.51	3.31
BMS [37]	0.51	0.55	0.65	0.82	0.83	1.41	3.35
Deep Gaze 2 [20]	0.46	0.51	0.76	0.86	0.87	1.29	4.00
Mr-CNN [23]	0.48	0.48	0.69	0.75	0.79	1.37	3.71
Pan *et al.* - Shallow [25]	0.46	0.53	0.64	0.78	0.80	1.47	3.99
GBVS [10]	0.48	0.48	0.63	0.80	0.81	1.24	3.51
Rare 2012 Improved [28]	0.46	0.42	0.67	0.75	0.77	1.34	3.74
Judd [16]	0.42	0.47	0.60	0.80	0.81	1.18	4.45
eDN [35]	0.41	0.45	0.62	0.81	0.82	1.14	4.56

in terms of CC, AUC shuffled, AUC Judd and NSS. VGG-16 and VGG-19 can clearly extract better features than the AlexNet model, and VGG-19 achieves the best performance according to all performances measures.

In Table 2 we then compare the performance of our model on the SALICON test set with respect to the current state of the art, in terms of CC, AUC shuffled and AUC Judd. As it can be noticed, our solution outperforms all other approaches by a significant margin on all evaluation metrics.

We also evaluate our model on two others publicly available saliency benchmarks, MIT300 and CAT2000. Table 3 compares the results of our approach to the top performers of MIT300, while Table 4 reports performances on the CAT2000 benchmark. Our method outperforms the majority of the solutions in

Table 4. Comparison results on the CAT2000 test set [1].

	Sim	CC	sAUC	AUC Borji	AUC Judd	NSS	EMD
Infinite humans	1.00	1.00	0.62	0.84	0.90	2.85	0.00
DeepFix [19]	0.74	0.87	0.58	0.81	0.87	2.28	1.15
ML-Net (VGG-19)	**0.68**	**0.78**	**0.58**	**0.81**	**0.86**	**2.00**	**1.16**
BMS [37]	0.61	0.67	0.59	0.84	0.85	1.67	1.95
eDN [35]	0.52	0.54	0.55	0.84	0.85	1.30	2.64
Rare 2012 Improved [28]	0.54	0.57	0.59	0.81	0.82	1.44	2.72
GBVS [10]	0.51	0.50	0.63	0.79	0.80	1.23	2.99
Judd [16]	0.46	0.54	0.56	0.84	0.84	1.30	3.61

both leaderboards, and achieves competitive results when compared to the top ranked approaches.

4.5   Qualitative Results

Figures 3 and 4 present instead a qualitative comparison showing ten randomly chosen input images from SALICON and MIT1003 datasets, their corresponding ground truth annotations and predicted saliency maps. These examples show

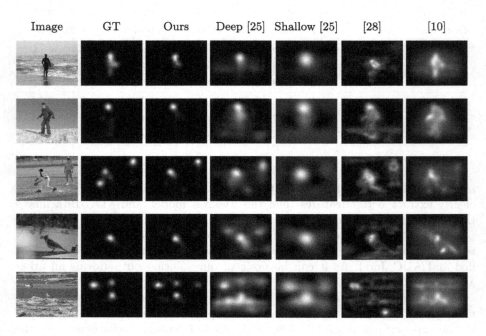

Fig. 3. Qualitative results on validation images from SALICON dataset [14].

Image	GT	Ours	[35]	[10]	[23]	[28]

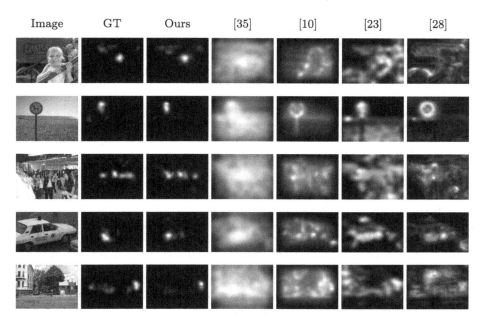

Fig. 4. Qualitative results on validation images from MIT1003 dataset [16].

how our approach is able to predict saliency maps that are very similar to the ground truth, while saliency maps generated by other methods are far less consistent with the ground truth.

5 Conclusions

In this paper we presented a new end-to-end trainable network for saliency prediction called ML-Net. Our solution learns a non-linear combination of multi-level features extracted from different layer of the CNN and a prior map. Qualitative and quantitative results on three public benchmarks show the validity of our proposal.

References

1. Borji, A., Itti, L.: Cat 2000: A large scale fixation dataset for boosting saliency research. In: CVPR 2015 Workshop on "Future of Datasets", arXiv preprint arXiv:1505.03581 (2015)
2. Buswell, G.T.: How people look at pictures: a study of the psychology and perception in art (1935)
3. Bylinskii, Z., Judd, T., Borji, A., Itti, L., Durand, F., Oliva, A., Torralba, A.: Mit saliency benchmark. http://saliency.mit.edu/

4. Bylinskii, Z., Judd, T., Oliva, A., Torralba, A., Durand, F.: What do different evaluation metrics tell us about saliency models? arXiv preprint arXiv:1604.03605 (2016)
5. Cerf, M., Frady, E.P., Koch, C.: Faces and text attract gaze independent of the task: experimental data and computer model. J. Vis. **9**(12), 10–10 (2009)
6. Gao, D., Vasconcelos, N.: Discriminant saliency for visual recognition from cluttered scenes. In: ANIPS (2004)
7. Glorot, X., Bengio, Y.: Understanding the difficulty of training deep feedforward neural networks. In: International Conference on Artificial Intelligence and Statistics, pp. 249–256 (2010)
8. Goferman, S., Zelnik-Manor, L., Tal, A.: Context-aware saliency detection. IEEE TPAMI **34**(10), 1915–1926 (2012)
9. Hadizadeh, H., Bajic, I.V.: Saliency-aware video compression. IEEE Trans. Image Process. **23**(1), 19–33 (2014)
10. Harel, J., Koch, C., Perona, P.: Graph-based visual saliency. In: ANIPS, pp. 545–552 (2006)
11. Hou, X., Zhang, L.: Saliency detection: a spectral residual approach. In: IEEE International Conference on Computer Vision and Pattern Recognition (2007)
12. Huang, X., Shen, C., Boix, X., Zhao, Q.: SALICON: reducing the semantic gap in saliency prediction by adapting deep neural networks. In: IEEE International Conference on Computer Vision, pp. 262–270 (2015)
13. Itti, L., Koch, C., Niebur, E.: A model of saliency-based visual attention for rapid scene analysis. IEEE TPAMI **11**, 1254–1259 (1998)
14. Jiang, M., Huang, S., Duan, J., Zhao, Q.: Salicon: saliency in context. In: IEEE International Conference on Computer Vision and Pattern Recognition, pp. 1072–1080. IEEE (2015)
15. Judd, T., Durand, F., Torralba, A.: A benchmark of computational models of saliency to predict human fixations (2012)
16. Judd, T., Ehinger, K., Durand, F., Torralba, A.: Learning to predict where humans look. In: IEEE International Conference on Computer Vision (2009)
17. Koch, C., Ullman, S.: Shifts in selective visual attention: towards the underlying neural circuitry. In: Matters of Intelligence, pp. 115–141. Springer, Netherlands (1987)
18. Krizhevsky, A., Sutskever, I., Hinton, G.E.: Imagenet classification with deep convolutional neural networks. In: ANIPS, pp. 1097–1105 (2012)
19. Kruthiventi, S.S., Ayush, K., Babu, R.V.: DeepFix: A Fully Convolutional Neural Network for predicting Human Eye Fixations. arXiv preprint arXiv:1510.02927 (2015)
20. Kümmerer, M., Theis, L., Bethge, M.: Deep Gaze I: Boosting saliency prediction with feature maps trained on ImageNet. arXiv preprint arXiv:1411.1045 (2014)
21. Lin, T.-Y., Maire, M., Belongie, S., Hays, J., Perona, P., Ramanan, D., Dollár, P., Zitnick, C.L.: Microsoft COCO: common objects in context. In: Fleet, D., Pajdla, T., Schiele, B., Tuytelaars, T. (eds.) ECCV 2014. LNCS, vol. 8693, pp. 740–755. Springer, Heidelberg (2014). doi:10.1007/978-3-319-10602-1_48
22. Liu, F., Gleicher, M.: Video retargeting: automating pan and scan. In: ACM International Conference on Multimedia (2006)
23. Liu, N., Han, J., Zhang, D., Wen, S., Liu, T.: Predicting eye fixations using convolutional neural networks. In: IEEE International Conference on Computer Vision and Pattern Recognition (2015)

24. Long, J., Shelhamer, E., Darrell, T.: Fully convolutional networks for semantic segmentation. In: IEEE International Conference on Computer Vision and Pattern Recognition (2015)
25. Pan, J., McGuinness, K., E., S., O'Connor, N., Giró-i Nieto, X.: Shallow and deep convolutional networks for saliency prediction. In: IEEE International Conference on Computer Vision and Pattern Recognition (2016)
26. Peters, R.J., Iyer, A., Itti, L., Koch, C.: Components of bottom-up gaze allocation in natural images. Vis. Res. **45**(18), 2397–2416 (2005)
27. Riche, N., Duvinage, M., Mancas, M., Gosselin, B., Dutoit, T.: Saliency and human fixations: state-of-the-art and study of comparison metrics. In: IEEE International Conference on Computer Vision, pp. 1153–1160 (2013)
28. Riche, N., Mancas, M., Duvinage, M., Mibulumukini, M., Gosselin, B., Dutoit, T.: Rare 2012: a multi-scale rarity-based saliency detection with its comparative statistical analysis. Sig. Process. Image Commun. **28**(6), 642–658 (2013)
29. Russakovsky, O., Deng, J., Su, H., Krause, J., Satheesh, S., Ma, S., Huang, Z., Karpathy, A., Khosla, A., Bernstein, M., et al.: Imagenet large scale visual recognition challenge. Int. J. Comput. Vision **115**(3), 211–252 (2015)
30. Simonyan, K., Zisserman, A.: Very deep convolutional networks for large-scale image recognition. CoRR abs/1409.1556 (2014)
31. Simonyan, K., Zisserman, A.: Very Deep Convolutional Networks for Large-Scale Image Recognition. CoRR abs/1409.1556 (2014). http://arxiv.org/abs/1409.1556
32. Szegedy, C., Liu, W., Jia, Y., Sermanet, P., Reed, S., Anguelov, D., Erhan, D., Vanhoucke, V., Rabinovich, A.: Going deeper with convolutions. In: IEEE International Conference on Computer Vision and Pattern Recognition (2015)
33. Tatler, B.W.: The central fixation bias in scene viewing: selecting an optimal viewing position independently of motor biases and image feature distributions. J. Vis. **7**(14), 4–4 (2007)
34. Torralba, A., Oliva, A., Castelhano, M.S., Henderson, J.M.: Contextual guidance of eye movements and attention in real-world scenes: the role of global features in object search. Psychol. Rev. **113**(4), 766 (2006)
35. Vig, E., Dorr, M., Cox, D.: Large-scale optimization of hierarchical features for saliency prediction in natural images. In: IEEE International Conference on Computer Vision and Pattern Recognition (2014)
36. Yang, Y., Song, M., Li, N., Bu, J., Chen, C.: What Is the Chance of Happening: A New Way to Predict Where People Look. In: Daniilidis, K., Maragos, P., Paragios, N. (eds.) ECCV 2010. LNCS, vol. 6315, pp. 631–643. Springer, Heidelberg (2010). doi:10.1007/978-3-642-15555-0_46
37. Zhang, J., Sclaroff, S.: Saliency detection: A boolean map approach. In: IEEE International Conference on Computer Vision, pp. 153–160 (2013)

Learning and Detecting Objects with a Mobile Robot to Assist Older Adults in Their Homes

Markus Vincze$^{(\boxtimes)}$, Markus Bajones, Markus Suchi, Daniel Wolf,
Astrid Weiss, David Fischinger, and Paloma da la Puente

Technische Universität Wien, Vienna, Austria
`vincze@tuwien.ac.at`

Abstract. Older adults reported that a robot in their homes would be of great help if it could find objects that users regularly search for. We propose an interactive method to learn objects directly with the user and the robot and then use the RGB-D model to search for the object in the scene. The robot presents a turntable to the user for rotating the part in front of its camera and obtain a full 3D model. The user is asked to turn the object upside down and the two half-models are merged. The model is then used at predefined search locations for detecting the object on tables or other horizontal surfaces. Experiments in three environments, up to 14 objects and a total of 1080 scenes indicate that present detection methods need to be considerably improved to provide a good service to users. We analyse the results and contribute to the discussion on how to overcome limited image quality and resolution by exploiting the robotic system.

Keywords: Robot object learning · 3D object modelling · RGB-D model · Object detection in clutter

1 Introduction

Recently several vision methods have been used on mobile assistive or companion robots. These can be summarised to fall into three groups [1]: face, gesture and posture recognition methods for interacting with the user, navigation methods beyond using laser but rather RGB-D sensors to cope with the truly 3D environment, and methods to recognise objects.

It is interesting to note that most of the robots operate in care facilities. First robots have been operated either locally or remotely and did not possess autonomous navigation capabilities. Only recently a few robots moved out into the homes of users, e.g. [2,3]. The big step forward in recent work is that the robot should be at least partially autonomous in the user's home. So far robots have been operated remotely or only for very few tasks in a home during limited time of user trials, for example in [4–6]. It was pointed out by the researchers that the autonomous navigation capability would be of high importance.

Autonomous navigation in user homes enlarges the possible set of assistive functions. Experience has shown and user studies have confirmed that a modular

© Springer International Publishing Switzerland 2016
G. Hua and H. Jégou (Eds.): ECCV 2016 Workshops, Part II, LNCS 9914, pp. 316–330, 2016.
DOI: 10.1007/978-3-319-48881-3_22

approach with customisable features would most suitably satisfy the heterogeneous group of older people who could benefit from the use of a mobile robot in their homes. Example functions that could use computer vision methods are detecting emergencies, adaptive robot behaviour depending on user behaviour, picking up objects from the floor or other locations, or the detection of objects.

In workshops with older adults, users indicated that it would be a very useful function if the robot could find and detect objects. They reported to search relatively often for a few typical objects such as handbag or mug.

To realise this demand, we developed a procedure to detect objects that are of interest to users. This demand generalises to object search and delivery scenarios. To implement such an assistive function for robots needs three basic robot and vision capabilities.

1. Learn about the object of interest that the user wants to be detected and create a model for later usage.
2. Detect the object using the learned model.
3. Grasp the object and deliver it to the user either in the gripper or in a storage tray on the robot.

In this paper we report on the first two capabilities. Object grasping has been shown elsewhere already and object learning and detection are the core abilities for a robot in an object search and deliver scenario. For object learning and detection in a home setting there are two specific challenges that need to be tackled.

1. *Autonomous object learning:* The objects of interest will vary for every user. Hence, it is necessary to learn these objects. In a beginning phase an adviser or care person could assist, but assuming a wide use of service robots, this would not be feasible. Consequently, a method is needed that allows the user herself to teach the robot which objects are of her interest and need to be detected.
2. *Variety of home settings:* the detection procedure needs to be able to cope with detecting everyday objects that have very different types and it needs to find them under the largely varying conditions in a home environment. This conditions include but are not limited to the ambient illumination situation and that objects are typically not standing alone but rather found in cluttered scenes.

Further requirements such as detecting good search positions in the first places or an autonomous detection of such search location are beyond the scope of this work. We will focus on these two functions that are challenging in themselves.

The contribution of this paper is an approach that first lets the user model an object together with the robot and that then uses the learned model for detecting the object at specified search locations. To the best of our knowledge this is the first time that a user will trigger the learning procedure and conduct the procedure to acquire a full 3D model of the object of interest. Figure 1 shows the robot with the turntable that is used for object learning. The detection procedure itself capitalises on a mix of well established methods to combine colour and depth information of the learned models for object detection. The method of acquiring the model of a specific object will be made available open source.

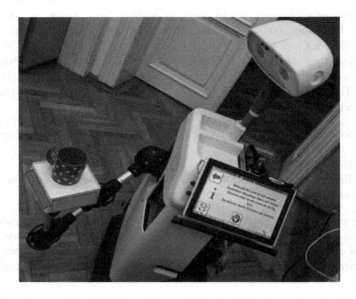

Fig. 1. The robot used for learning object models and then using the models for object detection. The robot is shown during the acquisition of the model of an object of interest. It uses an active robot head to direct an RGB-D camera towards the object. The object is placed on a turntable including natural script on its side walls (masked for reasons of anonymity). The user initiates the robot learning procedure and then the robot guides the user through the necessary modelling steps. The processing steps are executed autonomously.

The second contribution of the paper is to evaluate the learning and object recognition method in a robotic use case and scenario. We evaluated the method by presenting the robot with real-world scenes in three different environments. This includes that the robot autonomously navigated to the target locations. The intention is to learn the difficulties in real-world settings and to propose further work to render vision methods for assistive robots more and more robust.

The paper is structured as follows. After reviewing related work on model learning, we introduce the robot system approach to learning an object model and recognising the models in Sect. 2. Section 3 describes how the learned model is used in the robotic search procedure to detect the object. And Sect. 4 summarises the results of the experiments, analyses the problematic cases and discusses possibly improvements.

1.1 Related Work

Object modelling typically involves steps to accurately track the moving camera, segment the object from the background, and post-processing such as global camera pose optimisation and surface refinement. Approaches to learn models of objects either use distinctive features or the shape of the object in an iterative optimisation approach.

Regarding distinctive features, the most well-known methods are the Scale Invariant Feature Transform (SIFT) [7]. The feature points are used to find correspondences of object points in image pairs. This enables the registration of RGB-D images for modelling an object or scene in general. For example, in [8] the authors developed a Visual SLAM (Simultaneous Localisation and Mapping) approach that tracks the camera pose and registers point clouds in large environments. Distinctive points can also be used to directly reconstruct models for object recognition. For example, Collet et al. [9] register a set of images and compute a spare recognition model using a Structure from Motion approach.

Another type of method to acquire a model of an object from multiple images is based on the well established Iterative Closest Point (ICP) algorithm. For example, Huber et al. [10] as well as Fantoni et al. [11] focus on the registration of unordered sets of range images, while Weise et al. [12] track range images and propose an online loop closing approach.

Objects are typically learnt by using a turntable, e.g., [13]. There are also a few works that model objects in the hand of a robot. In [14] the authors propose a robotic object modelling approach where the object and the robotic arm are tracked with a variation of the articulated ICP approach. [15] tracks the target object including a loop closure for adjusting the model points after a full 360 degrees rotation. And the authors in [16] proposed an efficient SLAM-based registration method. Object models are built by selecting a volume of interest, defined by a user as an input mask in one image, plus the height above the support plane.

We extend these methods by allowing the user to handle and drive the modelling steps. With this we make sure that constraints due to the modelling methods are handled by the robot system rather than an expert user as in the works above. There is no need to select an object region or other expert input. It is also not necessary to control the distance of the object to the camera, to segment objects from the background, and tracking uses fiducial markers. Furthermore, we directly link the learned model to the object detection step. Regarding object detection, methods are numerous and a full review goes beyond the scope of this workshop paper. Existing object detection methods consider the case where a database of trained objects is used to match it with sensor data. Typically, the systems focus on individual algorithms that only work on objects with specific object characteristics, e.g., point features for 3D opaque objects [17], visual keypoint descriptor based systems like MOPED [9] for textured or [18] for translucent objects. Users neither nor not want to know about object features or characteristics. Hence, we will use a method that combines known detection methods for object detection.

2 Learning and Detecting Objects of Users

In the spirit of an assistive robot, learning of objects must be interactive. We implemented this on our robot depicted in Fig. 1. To overcome practical issues of object learning as indicated above, we devised a turntable that is mounted within the robot body and that the robot can extract for this purpose. Earlier trials with asking the user to put the turntable into the hand of the robot failed since it is then difficult to obtain a repeatable location of the turntable in the robot hand. In the following we outline the learning procedure.

First, the user has to call the robot to bring it in a position close to the user. The user initiates the task of learning an object either by pressing the button on the touch screen or a verbal command. The robot moves slightly from the user using the depth image from the head to have sufficient clear space to be able to extend its arm. It then grasps the turntable located on its body and presents the turntable to the user in a position such that it can be reached conveniently.

In the next phase, the robot guides the user through the steps of learning the object model. First, the robot asks the user to place the object on the turntable. It then rotates executes a full rotation with the turntable while acquiring images from its head RGB-D sensor. The robot then asks the user to turn the object upside down and repeats the procedure. Finally the robot asks the use to take the object from the turntable and it restores the turn table into the robot body. This procedure takes about three minutes with the robot, where the arms moves particularly slowly when it is retrieved and restored to make sure the arm moves safely and will not hit the user or the environment.

As Fig. 1 shows, we designed a squared turntable which enables robust and accurate camera pose tracking relative to the turntable. Hence, any kind of object regardless of its texture or shape can be learned. Next, we summarise the model learning method using the acquired images.

2.1 Learning Object Models on a Turntable of the Robot

Given the positions of the turntable from tracking its pose, object learning is based on RTM - Toolbox for Recognition, Tracking and Modelling of Objects presented in [19] and available on-line (http://www.acin.tuwien.ac.at/?id=450). It operate as follows. First RGB-D images are captured and the camera pose is tracked with respect to the region of interest (ROI) covering the object and the squared turn table. Since the robot pose is known this ROI can be easily set using a depth segmentation around the known pose of the turntable.

Two algorithms, namely an image key point based pose tracking pipeline and an Iterative Closest Point (ICP) approach are implemented to estimate the camera motion. Both algorithms are state of the art and allow robust camera pose tracking. Additionally, we implemented the non-linear pose optimization proposed by Fantoni et al. [11], which compensates the drift. A final filtering step using a weighted voxel grid inspired by KinectFusion [20] is used to sub-sample and smooth the reconstructed object point cloud. Results of learned RGB-D models are shown in Fig. 2. It shows rendering of eight objects from the textured 3D model.

Fig. 2. Examples of models obtained from a set of images when rotating the object. The models are stored as textured 3D point clouds.

The RTM toolbox for object modelling and recognition [19] works best with object distances of about 80 to 160 cm using the standard Kinect. It can also be used with other RGBD sensors. Since resolution drops significantly at larger distances, models will then not be as accurate but modelling is possible.

2.2 Detecting Objects Using the Learned Object Model

For object detection we adopt a method that recently solved several databases for 3D object recognition [21]. We select this method since it combines in an optimisation framework the advantages of local and global methods of object recognition and proved to be effective by fully solving several challenges in databases for the first time. This serves the purpose of handling methods that can detect different types of objects with different characteristics such as with and without texture as outlined above.

The method is based on a combination of different recognition pipelines, each exploiting the data in a different manner and generating object hypotheses that are later fused in a Hypothesis Verification stage [22] that globally enforces geometric consistency between model hypotheses and the scene. Such a scheme boosts the overall recognition performance as it enhances the strength of the different recognition pipelines while diminishing the impact of their specific weaknesses. Specifically, the currently implemented pipelines take advantage of the multi-modality of the RGB-D data:

- A semi-global 3D descriptor representing an extension of CVFH approach [23] based on the colour, shape and object size cues. Regarding the segmentation stage required by the semi-global pipeline, we adopted the standard plane segmentation methods as available in the Point Cloud Library [24].
- A 2D local descriptor, SIFT [7], which is able to generate object hypotheses with associated 6 DOF (Degrees of Freedom) pose by back-projection of the 2D keypoint locations into the 3D space.
- A 3D local descriptor, SHOT [25] aimed at establishing correspondences between model and scene surface patches.

Given the object models as learned above, also detection works best in distances up to two metres. As will be explained in the procedure below, we used the proper distance to define appropriate search locations. The view angle is given due to the fixed height of the robot and a good angle down onto the table. Note, that object orientation can still be random since the full viewing sphere od the object has been model. An evaluation of object detection over distances is part of future work.

3   Procedure for Robotic Object Detection

Ideally the robot is able to search for the object of interest in any environment. However this would mean to autonomously create a sequence of view points that cover the full 3D environment. Such methods are not yet available [26]. Using the human model, the search should also take into account previously seen object locations and rooms, semantic information on where typically a specific object is located, or contextual information from the room structure that may bais the object search.

The actual robot implementation used a simple search procedure, based on the optimization of a cost function. As a prerequisite, several "search locations" per room have to be defined in the map during the initialization phase. These search locations are defined with the users and comprise tables and shelves where to detect the objects of interest. This may seems as a restriction at first, but be aware that algorithmic solutions are difficult [26] and would still need to capture the semantics of rooms and objects, both open research topics. Hence, in a first practical approach to evaluate real-world object detection, this seems a fair approach until more advanced methods become available. What comes close to include these semantics is the approach taken in [27], where the labels of items in the rooms [28] are taken to generate search locations on the fly.

If an object has to be searched for, the cost function is evaluated for every search location. The locations are then sorted according to their corresponding cost, which yields the optimized search procedure for the object. The cost function takes several aspects into account, such that a good trade-off between the probability of the object being found at a search location and the time it takes to get there can be found. While the different locations are searched by the robot one-by-one, the probabilities of the object being there are permanently updated depending if the object has been found or not.

Moreover, a penalty term is added to locations which are in the same room as the user, as we assume that the object is most likely located in a different room which should therefore be searched first. If a room cannot be reached because the path is blocked, the costs for all search locations in that room are increased such that these locations are considered last during the search procedure.

This comes close to using a semantic scene segmentation algorithm. The purpose of such an approach is to generate a segmentation of the scene, visible by the head Kinect, into semantically meaningful parts, like floor, wall, table, shelf, etc., e.g., [29]. Using the additional knowledge of the semantic segmentation result, the search procedure for objects could be further automated and optimized, without the need of specifically labelled search locations. Instead, the robot figures out itself, where possible object locations might be (objects are most likely located on tables, shelves...) and where it has to navigate to in order to be able to detect them. The knowledge could be exploited even further, to generate complete semantic maps of the environment, allowing the user to send the robot to automatically detected places like the table in the living room.

The proposed method uses this knowledge only insofar as it fits planes as part of the fitting procedure. The selection is given by the pre-set search locations. This is also necessary to obtain an evaluation of the detection methods and not mix detection with semantic labelling or view point selection.

The scenario we evaluate is the request of a user to detect a specific object. An example is given in Fig. 3. The evaluation procedure takes the image and detection is run versus all stored object models using the global hypothesis verification framework [21]. In a last step it uses the generated object detection hypothesis in a verification step, where the model is fit to the data. If this fit gives a confidence above 95 percent, the detection is reported as successful. Other detections with lower probabilities are not considered since most of the time found to be not correct. A thorough evaluation of this initial procedure is future work. In the following we describe the experiments conducted in more detail.

Fig. 3. Example of a search procedure. The task is to search for the red mug. When entering the room, two other locations are closer and searched first. Other known objects are found and their location is stored for future search operations.

4   Experiments

The tests for the object detection scenario were conducted in three environments that were built and furnished to resemble home settings. Systematic tests in a user home could not yet be made, since permitted time at the user sites was too short. The three test environments have been an office setting, where objects of daily use have been arranged in typically cluttered scenes (Env1), an ambient assisted living (AAL) laboratory that has been built with the purpose to resemble an older user home (Env2), and a living room setting specifically designed for testing assistive robot capabilities (Env3).

When conducting user trials with older adults, we defined search positions related to tables or boards where the users would typically place objects (anonymous, paper submitted). We replicated this procedure by defining four search positions in each of the three environments.

During the experiments for object detection the robot will navigate to the position that has the highest probability to find the object. This will use the knowledge of where the object has been seen before respectively knowledge about the typical rooms where a certain object is found. The robot will plan the shortest path to the selected search position to reduce unnecessary power usage.

The tests in user homes also indicated that objects are often found in clutter rather in the first test scenes such as Fig. 3. For our test we set up each scene with clutter. We also place one or multiple known objects on the table to check if more than one known object can be detected. We count objects only if they are within the robot's field of view at the search position. When the robot arrives at the search positions, it starts the recognition and records, which objects were recognized, which object were not recognized, and where an object was falsely reported (false positives). We conducted 10 trials for each search place. Figure 4 gives four examples scenes indicating the typical clutter, object occlusions, background illumination, and other effects that render object detection difficult in a natural environment.

We used 12 respectively 14 different objects in the three scenarios. For three environments this results in a total of 1080 trials where the robot autonomously navigated to one of the search locations and initiated the detection of all of the learned objects.

Table 1 summarises the results for the objects, the three environments and gives a summary. There have been no false positives–the method was tuned to not falsely report object detections. On the other hand, this leads to more objects going undetected. In the tables we report the number of successful detection out of the multiples of 10 trials each (different for each object between 10 and 50 trials). We report only positive detections, since the procedure as outlined above uses a verifications step that is very confident to select the correct object given the viewing of an object is satisfactory. An extension to work with less likely hypothesis is a good extension as indicated by the reviewers.

On first view the overall result of 52 % detection rate is not satisfactory. On the other hand, the task is indeed challenging and individual methods would rank much lower since specialised on one type and characteristics of objects

Fig. 4. Four example images showing the objects and the scenes with clutter. Note that objects can have very different viewpoints and scenes include cases with strong background that render detections difficult to infeasible.

only. A comparison to other methods is not directly feasible. As of today, there is no other modelling tool available that would allow a robot to obtain an object model and move in the environment to detect the object. A similar attempt has been made by learning objects from the robot in [30], but the robot navigates around objects rather than moves it with the robot arm and only a partial viewing sphere is captured.

Table 2 summarises results for the three different environments. Performance is similar. While the detection results of slightly more than half the objects are not impressive, this result was expected and reflects the present state-of-the-art in object detection methods when applied to the wild and in realistic settings. Furthermore, we know from the detection methods that feature-less objects such as toilet paper and water boiler are difficult to distinguish from the background. Similar difficulties give handbags if they are rather feature-less like the one used. On the other hand, larger objects with clear texture such as the ketchup, Mueller bottles, and tea box exhibit the expected satisfactory to good results.

Table 1. Summary of detection rate for each object and environment (Env# where # is 1 to 3; EnvAll refers to the sum of all three Environments). The numbers in the table give the successful detections of the target objects out of the 10 to 50 trials. In total 1080 object detections would have been possible.

Object	Env1		Env2		Env3		EnvAll		Rate
Asus Xtion box	0	10	20	20	12	40	32	70	0,46
Cisco telephone	20	40	21	40	30	40	71	120	0,59
Cleaning agent bottle	11	30	20	30	28	30	59	90	0,66
Felix ketchup bottle	10	10	17	20			27	30	0,9
Handbag	1	10	0	40	16	50	17	100	0,17
Muellermilch bottle banana	20	30	1	20	30	30	51	80	0,64
Muellermilch bottle choco	20	40	20	20	30	30	70	90	0,78
OpenCV book	25	30	13	40	1	10	39	80	0,49
Red mug with white dots	33	40	11	40	0	10	44	90	0,49
Strands mounting unit	10	20	1	20	0	10	11	50	0,22
Tea box	9	20	34	40	24	40	67	100	0,67
Toilet paper roll	0	30			0	30	0	60	0
Water boiler	0	10					0	10	0
Yellow toy car	29	40	20	30	21	40	70	110	0,64
Total	188	360	178	360	192	360	558	1080	0,52

Table 2. Summary of detection rate for the three environments.

Environment	# of different objects	# of trials	Detection rate
1	14	360	52,2
2	12	360	49,4
3	12	360	53,3
Total	14	1080	51,7

4.1 Discussion

When analysing the results, there are several factors that explain the many cases where objects are not detected.

- Limited dynamic range of the camera: often the robot enters a room and on the other side is a table. Looking against windows introduces highlights and reflections and renders objects dark. For robot navigation purposes we used high dynamic range cameras that improve but not resolve this case. Similarly, object detection methods need a mechanism to evaluate if the image in itself has feasible dynamic range and in principle allows to detect an object.

- Specific limits of sensitivity: sunlight through the window renders the depth image void. Similar to above, detecting these cases and reverting to methods that rely on other modalities will be the better robot system approach. Even better cameras and sensor will have specific characteristics that are better handled from a system perspective.
- Limited resolution of depth camera: non-textured objects are detected using the depth image. The resolution of the depth channel of present range cameras is much smaller than of colour images. Particularly with increasing distance, and this may well be the far end of the table, detection results deteriorate quickly. This cries for alternative sensors or using other approaches to overcome this issue.

For all the cases above, assistive vision approaches may profit most if the robot system exploits its mobility to select better view points and uses all its contextual knowledge about the environment for pruning hypothesis. The robot could exploit far and close range methods and purposively combine weak hypotheses by getting closer. It could detect other objects and use priors. And certainly, the robot will also profit from more advanced methods of reliably detecting objects in images, in particular objects of very different characteristics such as with and without texture, simple and complex shapes, or single and many colours.

Finally, the steady advance in camera technology brought us already to the level where we are right now. Hence, we can expect more and more advances and improvements in the near future from this side alone. Still, camera technology alone will not solve the case. The complementarity of methods and the exploitation of the robot system and the knowledge about the environment it has needs to be exploited in a much more rigorous fashion.

5   Conclusions

In this paper we investigated the scenario of assisting older adults with a method to learn their favourite objects and to detect the learned objects in a home environment. To this end we adapted a method to learn the object autonomously from the robot using a turntable and a clear procedure to guide the user through the learning method. We then spent considerable effort to run the robot autonomously to 1080 locations and view a given setting with small navigation uncertainties. Navigation in itself was fond to be accurate within a few centimetre and less than one degree. What we tested was the detection of up to 14 target objects using a set of four pre-set search locations with the small navigation uncertainties in three different environments.

We challenged the system by using target objects that had different characteristics with and without texture, single and multiple colours, and basic and more elaborate shapes. Adapting a method that globally optimises over multiple hypothesis we combines three detection methods to cope with these different object characteristics.

The results show that even a combination of methods achieves hardly satisfactory results. The analysis of the results indicates that camera properties are not sufficient: both dynamic range and resolution are the main reasons for missed detections in a non optimal setting. Having control over object size, setting and image quality would render result much better. However these factors are difficult to control in an open home setting.

On the contrary, on of the intansion of this workshop paper is to contribute to the discussion on how vision methods that are typically trained on an image database can be made more suitable to the open settings on robots. The study indicates that present object detection methods are getting useful for assistive robots in a home setting but further work is needed.

Future work should have a look at the practical challenges posed in actual home settings. One such challenge is to locate objects that are visible but in the image the resolution, illumination situation or clutter do not allow present methods to detect the object. Following an idea presented already a decade ago in [31] we might use the cognitive power of humans to aid in detecting the target objects and learn from these detections. While in itself a cumbersome approach that will need a lot of user interaction, older adults indicated that they would be interested to help the robot. An ease-to-use interface with potentially indicated object hypotheses may be one option. We could here use less likely detections that may also include false positives, but users would be very quick to select the correct object. In this way the robot would learn both correct and false detections and could improve its object detection capability.

We see this only as starting a deeper discussion of the discrepancy between databse driven research and the open settings a robot would approach in homes. There is the need to make explicit the type of objects that can be handled by a certain method, discuss methods that integrate other methods, and—we think most of all—how to better exploit the contextual knowledge a robot has about a scene to improve detection results. Given a robot system it seems much more obvious to detect and exploit scene context rather than detecting it in an image alone.

Acknowledgements. The research leading to these results has received funding from the European Communitys Seventh Framework Programme FP7/2007-2013 under grant agreement No. 600623, STRANDS and No. 610532, SQUIRREL as well as No. 288146, HOBBIT.

References

1. Kragic, D., Vincze, M.: Vision for robotics. Foundations Trends Robot. **1**(1), 1–78 (2010)
2. Fazekas, G., Tth, A., Rumeau, P., Zsiga, K., Pilissy, T., Dupourque, V.: Cognitive-care robot for elderly assistance: preliminary results of tests with users in their homes. In: AAL Forum, Netherlands (2012)
3. Panek, P., Beck, C., Edelmayer, G., Mayer, P., Rauhala, M., Zagler, W.L.: Connecting AAL devices and systems to improve service delivery. In: AAL Forum: Broader, p. 2014. Romania, Bigger, Better - AAL solutions for Europe, Palace of Parliament, Bucharest (2014)

4. Bedaf, S., Gelderblom, G.J., de Witte, L., Syrdal, D., Lehnmann, H., Amirabdol-lahian, F., Dautenhahn, K.: Selecting services for a service robot - evaluating the problematic activities threatening the independence of elderly persons. In: ICORR (2013)
5. Ullberg, J., Loutfi, A., Pecora, F.: A customizable approach for monitoring activities of elderly users in their homes. In: Mazzeo, P.L., Spagnolo, P., Moeslund, T.B. (eds.) AMMDS 2014. LNCS, vol. 8703, pp. 13–25. Springer, Heidelberg (2014)
6. Glende, S., Conrad, I., Krezdorn, L., Klemcke, S., Krtzel, C.: Increasing acceptance of assistive robotics for older people through marketing strategies based on stakeholder needs. Int. J. Soc. Robot. **8**, 355–369 (2016)
7. Lowe, D.G.: Distinctive image features from scale-invariant keypoints. Int. J. Comput. Vis. **60**(2), 91–110 (2004)
8. Endres, F., Hess, J., Sturm, J., Cremers, D., Burgard, W.: 3-D mapping with an RGB-D camera. IEEE Trans. Robot. **30**(1), 177–187 (2014)
9. Collet, A., Martinez, M., Srinivasa, S.S.: The moped framework: object recognition and pose estimation for manipulation. Int. J. Rob. Res. **30**(10), 1284–1306 (2011)
10. Huber, D.F., Hebert, M.: Fully automatic registration of multiple 3D data sets. Image Vis. Comput. **21**(7), 637–650 (2003)
11. Fantoni, S., Castellani, U., Fusiello, A.: Accurate and automatic alignment of range surfaces. In: Second International Conference on 3D Imaging, Modeling, Processing, Visualization and Transmission (3DIMPVT), pp. 73–80 (2012)
12. Weise, T., Wismer, T., Leibe, B., Gool, L.V.: Online loop closure for real-time interactive 3D scanning. Comput. Vis. Image Underst. **115**(5), 635–648 (2011)
13. Dimashova, M., Lysenkov, I., Rabaud, V., Eruhimov, V.: Tabletop object scanning with an RGB-D sensor. In: SPME (2013)
14. Krainin, M., Curless, B., Fox, D.: Autonomous generation of complete 3D object models using next best view manipulation planning. In: IEEE International Conference on Robotics and Automation (ICRA), pp. 5031–5037, May 2011
15. Weise, T., Wismer, T., Leibe, B., Gool, L.V.: In-hand scanning with online loop closure. In: IEEE ICCV Workshop (2009)
16. Stueckler, J., Behnke, S.: Multi-resolution surfel maps for efficient dense 3D modeling and tracking. J. Vis. Commun. Image Represent. **25**(1), 137–147 (2014)
17. Aldoma, A., Marton, Z.C., Tombari, F., Wohlkinger, W., Potthast, C., Zeisl, B., Rusu, R.B., Gedikli, S.: Using the point cloud library for 3D object recognition and 6dof pose estimation. IEEE Robot. Autom. Mag. **9**, 80–91 (2012)
18. Lysenkov, I., Eruhimov, V., Bradski, G.: Recognition and pose estimation of rigid transparent objects with a kinect sensor. In: Proceedings of Robotics: Science and Systems, Sydney, Australia, July 2012
19. Prankl, J., Aldoma, A., Svejda, A., Vincze, M.: RGB-D object modelling for object recognition and tracking. In: IEEE/RSJ International Conference on Intelligent Robots and Systems (IROS), pp. 96–103, September 2015
20. Newcombe, R.A., Izadi, S., Hilliges, O., Molyneaux, D., Kim, D., Davison, A.J., Kohli, P., Shotton, J., Hodges, S., Fitzgibbon, A.: Kinectfusion: Real-time dense surface mapping and tracking. In: Proceedings of the 2011 10th IEEE International Symposium on Mixed and Augmented Reality, ISMAR 2011, pp. 127–136. IEEE Computer Society (2011)
21. Aldoma, A., Tombari, F., Stefano, L.D., Vincze, M.: A global hypothesis verification framework for 3D object recognition in clutter. IEEE Trans. Pattern Anal. Mach. Intell. **PP**(99), 1 (2015)

22. Aldoma, A., Tombari, F., Di Stefano, L., Vincze, M.: A global hypotheses verification method for 3D object recognition. In: Fitzgibbon, A., Lazebnik, S., Perona, P., Sato, Y., Schmid, C. (eds.) ECCV 2012, Part III. LNCS, vol. 7574, pp. 511–524. Springer, Heidelberg (2012)

23. Aldoma, A., Tombari, F., Rusu, R.B., Vincze, M.: OUR-CVFH – oriented, unique and repeatable clustered viewpoint feature histogram for object recognition and 6DOF pose estimation. In: Pinz, A., Pock, T., Bischof, H., Leberl, F. (eds.) DAGM and OAGM 2012. LNCS, vol. 7476, pp. 113–122. Springer, Heidelberg (2012)

24. Rusu, R.B., Cousins, S.: 3D is here: point cloud library (PCL). In: IEEE International Conference on Robotics and Automation (ICRA), Shanghai, China, pp. 1–4, 9–13 May 2011

25. Tombari, F., Salti, S., Stefano, L.: Unique signatures of histograms for local surface description. In: Daniilidis, K., Maragos, P., Paragios, N. (eds.) ECCV 2010. LNCS, vol. 6313, pp. 356–369. Springer, Heidelberg (2010). doi:10.1007/978-3-642-15558-1_26

26. Andreopoulos, A., Hasler, S., Wersing, H., Janssen, H., Tsotsos, J., Korner, E.: Active 3D object localization using a humanoid robot. IEEE Trans. Rob. **27**(1), 47–64 (2011)

27. Bajones, M., Wolf, D., Prankl, J., Vincze, M.: Where to look first? Behaviour control for fetch-and-carry missions of service robots. In: Austrian Robotics Workshop(2014)

28. Wolf, D., Prankl, J., Vincze, M.: Enhancing semantic segmentation for robotics: the power of 3-D entangled forests. IEEE Robot. Autom. Lett. **1**(1), 49–56 (2016)

29. Silberman, N., Hoiem, D., Kohli, P., Fergus, R.: Indoor segmentation and support inference from RGBD images. In: Fitzgibbon, A., Lazebnik, S., Perona, P., Sato, Y., Schmid, C. (eds.) ECCV 2012, Part V. LNCS, vol. 7576, pp. 746–760. Springer, Heidelberg (2012)

30. Fäulhammer, T., Ambrus, R., Burbridge, C., Zillich, M., Folkesson, J., Hawes, N., Jensfelt, P., Vincze, M.: Autonomous learning of object models on a mobile robot. IEEE Robot. Autom. Lett. **2**(1), 26–33 (2016)

31. Makihara, Y., Takizawa, M., Shirai, Y., Miura, J., Shimada, N.: Object recognition supported by user interaction for service robots. In: 16th International Conference on Pattern Recognition, Proceedings, vol. 3, pp. 561–564 (2002)

An Interactive Multimedia System for Treating Autism Spectrum Disorder

Massimo Magrini[1,2(✉)], Ovidio Salvetti[1,2], Andrea Carboni[1,2],
and Olivia Curzio[1,2]

[1] ISTI-CNR, Pisa, Italy
{Massimo.Magrini,Ovidio.Salvetti,
Andrea.Carboni}@isti.cnr.it,
[2] IFC-CNR, Pisa, Italy
Olivia.Curzio@ifc.cnr.it

Abstract. A system for real-time gesture tracking is presented, used in active well-being self-assessment activities and in particular applied to medical coaching and music-therapy. The system is composed of a gestural interface and a computer running own (custom) developed software. During the test sessions a person freely moves his body inside a specifically designed room. The algorithms detect and extrapolate features from the human figure, such us spatial position, arms and legs angles, etc. An operator can link these features to sounds synthesized in real time, following a predefined schema. The augmented interaction with the environment helps to improve the contact with reality in subjects having autism spectrum disorders (ASD). The system has been tested on a set of young subjects and a team of psychologists has analyzed the results of this experimentation. Moreover, we started to work on graphical feedback in order to realize a multichannel system.

1 Introduction

In recent years specific activity has been carried out for developing sensor-based interactive systems capable to help the treatment of learning difficulties and disabilities in children [1–3]. These systems generally consist of sensors connected to a computer, programmed with special software that reacts to the sensor data with multimedia stimuli. The general philosophy of these systems is based on the idea that even profoundly physically or learning impaired individuals can become expressive and communicative using music and sound [4]. The sense of control which these systems provide can be a powerful motivator for subjects with limited interaction with reality.

While a great part of systems, like SoundBeam (www.soundbeam.co.uk), totally rely on ultrasonic sensors, our approach is mostly based on real-time video processing techniques; moreover, our solution makes also it possible to easily use additional sets of sensors (e.g., infrared or ultrasonic) in the same scene. The use of video-processing techniques adds more parameters suitable to localize exactly and detail all the human gestures we want detect and recognize. By using a custom software interface, the operator can link the extracted video features to sounds synthesized in real time, following a predefined schema.

© Springer International Publishing Switzerland 2016
G. Hua and H. Jégou (Eds.): ECCV 2016 Workshops, Part II, LNCS 9914, pp. 331–342, 2016.
DOI: 10.1007/978-3-319-48881-3_23

The developed system has been experimented in a test campaign on a set of young patients affected by Low-Functioning Autism (autism spectrum disorder, ASD), in order to provide a personal increased interaction over the operational environment and to reduce pathological isolation [5]. Results were very positive and encouraging, as confirmed by both clinical psychologist and parents of the kids. In particular, the therapists reported a positive outcome from the assisted coaching therapies. Indeed, this positive evolution was crucial to improve the motivation and curiosity for a full communication interaction in the external environment, thus affecting subjects' well-being.

In order to maintain the obtained benefits, we developed a simplified version of the system, based on Kinect, to be used at home by the parents and children. The present project program trains parents of children with autistic spectrum disorders using the DIR/Floortime model of Stanley Greenspan MD. Parents were encouraged to deliver 15 h per week of 1:1 interaction. Pilot studies [6, 7] suggested that this kind of models have potential to be a cost-effective intervention for young children with autism.

2 Autism

ASD is a neurodevelopmental disorder characterized by impaired social interaction and communication. It is a pervasive developmental disorder, characterized by a triad of impairments: social communication problems, difficulties with reciprocal social interactions, and unusual patterns of repetitive behavior [8]. Leo Kanner, a child psychiatrist [8], described it for the first time in 1943. An exhaustive description of this disorder in medical terms is beyond the scope of this paper.

Unfortunately, no medications can cure autism or treat its core symptoms, but rather can help some people affected feel better. A large part of the interventions focuses on behavioral approaches, of which the best known is the ABA (Applied Behavior Analysis) method [10], based on repetitive patterns and reinforcements. Other approaches follow instead the Developmental Individual Difference Relationship (DIR) model [11]. DIR acts at various levels of involvement, attempting a containing action against the central symptoms of autism according to the following guidelines: (1) involvement against isolation (2) communication and flexibility versus rigidity and persistence (3) gestures against stereotypies and aggressive behaviors. In the design of our system we were inspired, even not strictly, by the DIR model.

3 The System

The system was developed in two different steps, using different technologies. The first version is based over video capture and processing, where all the body recognition routines are software-based. This system needed a controlled environment and the presence of a technician during each session. The second version relies on the use of Kinect v2, which solved some of the problems of the previous version. This version allows the tracking of full body movements in 3D space, has the peculiarity of being designed to be installed in the user's home, and provides an intuitive interface, to be easily used by the children's families.

3.1 Camera Based Version

The first version of the system has been based on real-time video processing. The software has been developed in C++ on an Apple Macintosh computer running the latest version of Mac OS X. A video camera is connected through a Firewire digitizer, the Imaging Source DFG1394, a very fast digitizer that allows a latency of only one frame in the video processing path. As output audio card we use the Macintosh internal one, sufficient for our purposes. A couple of TASCAM amplified loudspeakers completes the basic system.

We used the Mac OS platform for its reliability in real time multimedia applications, thanks to its very robust frameworks: Core Audio and Core Image libraries permit very fast elaboration without glitches and underruns.

Finally, the system is installed in a special empty room, with most of the surfaces (walls, floor) covered by wood. The goal is to build a warm space which, in some way, recalls the prenatal ambient. All system parts, such as cables, plugs, and so on are carefully hidden as they could be potential elements of distraction. The ambient light is gentle and indirect, thus avoiding shadows that could also affect the precision of motion detection. Nevertheless, large changes in the environment light may affect the system's setup, so that the software needs some recalibration.

System Architecture. The implemented system (Fig. 1) is organized in several specialized coordinated modules. The core of the software is composed by the Sequence grabber, which manages the stream of video frames coming from the video digitizer, the Video processor, which performs realtime image elaborations, the Skeleton reconstructor, which analyses the frames and extrapolates gesture parameters, the Data mapper, responsible for transforming the detected gesture parameters into sounds parameters and finally the Sound synthesizer.

The biggest problem regarding the gesture control of sounds is latency, which is the delay between the gesture and the correspondent effect on the generated sound.

Our approach guarantees the minimum latency for the adopted frame rate, which is 40 ms at 25 FPS or 33.3 ms at 30 FPS.

Processing algorithm. In the first step of the algorithm each grayscale frame grabbed in real time from the video camera is smoothed with a Gaussian filter (fast computed using the CoreImage library). The output is then processed in one of two alternative operating modes: area-based or edge-based. In the area-based modality, the segmentation is performed considering the entire envelope (area) of the figure of the subject examined. In the edge-based modality, instead, an edge detection filter is applied to the image. The next step consists in a background subtraction technique computed to isolate the human figure from the ambient. In order to fulfill this task, each time the background changes, it has to be stored, area or edge based, with no human subject in front of the camera. If this background exists it is used in the following iterations of the algorithm and compared with the incoming frames containing the human figure using a dynamic threshold, obtaining a binary matrix. The average threshold used in this operation can be tuned by the operator in real time. It is not necessary to set again this sensitivity if the ambient light does not change. Finally, we apply an algorithm for removing unconnected small areas from the matrix, usually generated by image noise.

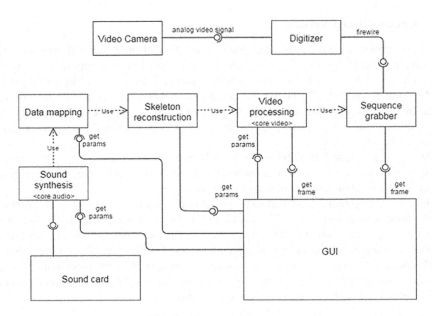

Fig. 1. System architecture.

The final binary image is then ready to be processed by the gesture tracking algorithm. The frame resolution is 320 × 240 pixels, full frame rate (e.g. 25 FPS) can be achieved because all the image filters are executed by the GPU. Starting from the binary raster matrix we apply an algorithm to detect a set of gesture parameters. This heuristic algorithm supposes that the segmented image obtained by the image elaboration process is a human figure, extracting data from it. This process starts searching a simplified model of the human figure, shown in the GUI (Fig. 3). Additional models for detailed parts of the body (face, hands) are currently under development, so that they can be used for more "zoomed" versions of the system. Starting from time dependent position of detected body joints we decided to compute the following parameters: *Arm angles and speed (left/right), Leg angles and speed (left/right), Torso angle, Barycenter coordinates, Distance from camera.*

The distance from the camera actually is just an index related to the real distance: it is simply computed as a ratio between the frame height and the detected figure maximum height. The leg speed is computed analyzing the last couple of received frames; it is useful for triggering sounds with "kick-like" movements. We also compute these two additional parameters: global activity, crest factor (Fig. 2).

The first is an indicator of overall quantity of movement (0.0 if the subject is standing still with no moments), while the second one is an indication of the concavity of the posture: (0.0 means that the subject is in standing position with arms kept along the body). Few optimizations are performed starting the frame analysis from an area centered in the last detected barycenter. Generally speaking, we tried to implement the detection algorithms in a very optimized way in order to maintain the target frame rate (25 FPS), minimizing the latency between gestures and sounds.

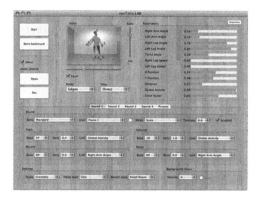

Fig. 2. Graphical User Interface

Sound Generation. The sound generation is based on the Mac OS CoreAudio library.

The mapper module translates the detected features into MIDI commands for the musical synthesizers. There are four independent synthesizers: for each of them the sound's parameters (pitch, volume, etc.) can be easily linked to the detected gesture parameters using the GUI. For example, we can link the Global Activity to the pitch: the faster you move the higher pitched notes you play. The synthesized MIDI notes are chosen from a user selectable scale: there's a large variety of them, ranging from the simplest ones (e.g. major and minor) to the more exotic ones. As an alternative, it is possible to select continuous pitch, instead of discrete notes: in this way the linked detected features controls the pitch in a "glissando" way. Sound can be triggered in a "Drum mode" way, too: the MIDI note C played when the linked parameters reach a selected threshold. All these links settings can be stored in presets, easily selectable from the operators.

3.2   Kinect Based Version

The experimentation has proven the positive effects so, in order to maintain its benefits, we developed a more user-friendly version to be used at home, avoiding the need of specialized personnel.

The user interface of this home version is greatly simplified compared to the video camera one and simply presents a series of easily selectable, not editable, presets. The body detection algorithm benefits from the use of Microsoft Kinect v2 SDK, which not requires the critical camera settings of the first version.

Microsoft Kinect. The Microsoft Kinect is a line of well-known motion sensing input devices originally created for Xbox 360 and Xbox One video game consoles and then Windows PCs. This device enables users to control and interact with their console/ computer without the need for a game controller, through a natural user inter-face using gestures. The first Kinect version was using a structured infrared light approach while V2 (the version we used) is based on the Time-of-Flight (ToF) principle. Using these technologies, the device can compute a depth map of the environment. The Microsoft

Kinect SDK libraries can process this depth map and extract the tridimensional coordinates of (up to) 26 joints of the human skeleton. Up to 6 skeletons can be tracked in real time. While Kinect V1 (which was considered during the development of the camera version) still suffered from large latency, the V2 partially solved this issue so that we finally decided to use it in the home version.

Software. This architecture of the SW, compared to the one described in Sect. 3.1, has the three modules Sequence Grabber Video Processor and Skeleton Reconstruction, replaced by routines developed with the Kinect SDK. Since this SDK provides only the spatial coordinates of the joints, we included a module for performing geometrical transformations on them, computing a set of features, basically the angles between body parts, that are invariant in relation to the body position and rotation. These features are then aggregated and mapped to sound with the same algorithm used in the camera based version.

Instead of supplying a rather complex GUI in which the user can create and customize presets (each one describing the relationship between motion and sounds) in this home version we include a set of predefined presets, easily accessible from a drop-down list. With this set we tried to cover a broad range of interaction modalities/gestures (arm motion, kicks, jumps etc.).

We included two special modes, designed for improving motor coordination. In the first one different movements trigger playbacks of a sampled voice pronouncing

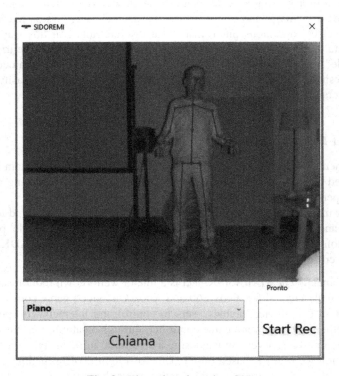

Fig. 3. Kinect based version GUI

numbers: the subject has to sequence movements according to numbers order (randomly shuffled at each program launch). The second one is similar but we use fragments of sentences instead of numbers: here the user has to sequence these fragments to reconstruct a story.

This home version is intended to be used by the children's parents, not necessarily skilled. For this reason, they could eventually need a remote assistance. In order to provide a simple way to provide assistance we included a video chat mechanism in the software: the user, simply pressing a "call" button can make a video call to our technical staff.

Movement Recordings. We included a "record" button: pressing it all the child movements are recorded on disk for off-line analysis (for diagnostic purposes). The psychologist team that support the project suggested to analyze movements of the subject during the various sessions in order to objectively evaluate the effects of systems. We basically extract these features, as a function of time:

Average of movements amount (whole body, upper, lower), Variance of movements amount (whole body, upper, lower), Average of movement speed (whole body, upper, lower), Variance of movements speed (whole body, upper, lower), Coordination (correlation between movements of different part of the body).

Since the concept of imitation is very important in the evaluation of autism spectrum disorder, we included an algorithm for computing cross-correlation of movements of two different bodies (the subject's one and the parent's one): this similarity index is strongly related to evidence of imitation (Fig. 4).

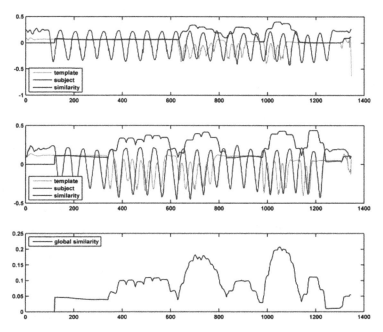

Fig. 4. Elbow movements in the two arms (upper graphs), for the subject and for his parent and (below) the resulting similarity index.

4 Experimentation

The experimentation [12] was performed in the school environment on 4 subjects (5–7 years, all males) diagnosed with Low-Functioning Autism (autism spectrum disorder, ASD). The weekly intervention lasted about 30 min. The children involved in the experimentation were evaluated in a cross sectional and follow up pilot study. Clinical features evaluated by mental health centers and information from the "Questionnaire on motor control and sensory elaboration" [13], compiled by parents, and from the "Short Sensory Profile" [14] filled up by the teachers were analyzed at baseline. Three clinical psychologists, not previously involved in the experimentation, analyzed the first eight videos of the intervention, completing an observation grid for every session. The grid was structured ad hoc by the research team on the basis of the DIR Floortime model and technique in relation to the benchmarks of the main sensory profiles. This grid was partially taken from the questionnaire of Politi and colleagues [15] aimed at assessing the sensitivity of music in children affected by autism spectrum disorder. The instrument is made up of nineteen items relating to the child's behavior during the sessions and measured the characteristics of each sensory profile in terms of the "four A": Arousal, Attention, Affection and Action [16].

In this experimentation to consider the sensory profile of the infant that undergoes the sound stimulation and interaction was crucial. The choice of sound stimuli related to the movement has been made individually for each child during the first sessions through broad-spectrum stimuli. All the interventions were calibrated on the basis of the observations drawn from the video of the previous meeting, viewed by the reference clinician, a child neuropsychiatrist. It is important to highlight that the clinical reference as well as the operator who conducted the interventions with children had formal training in DIR Floortime method (Fig. 5).

5 Results

The concordance rate between the three psychologists' behavioral observation grid was calculated with the interclass correlation coefficient. Moderate to good inter-rater agreement [interclass correlation coefficient (ICC) comprised between 0.596 (95 %CI 0.41–0.853) and 0.799 (95 %CI 0.489–0.933)] were found. A repeated measures design was performed to evaluate change over time for each child for the first eight sessions (T1–T8). The analysis of variance was performed to assess if there has been an improvement in specific symptomatic areas. The repeated measures analysis of variance indicated an overall increase of the scores drawn up by psychologists (T1–T8; $p < 0.05$) (Fig. 6).

Concerning statistical indexes our study highlights that participants had improved several skills. These variations in behavioral expressions reflect a relational evolution indicating the beginning of an opening attempt to someone no longer perceived as a threat but as someone from which to draw contentment, through playful interaction with the sounds. This pilot study demonstrates positive results: children developed skills in establishing joint attention, imitation of caregivers, communicating with gesture and symbols (Fig. 7).

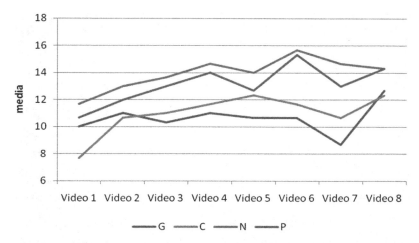

Fig. 5. Mean total scores of the behavior observation grid to assess change over time for each child (T1–T8).

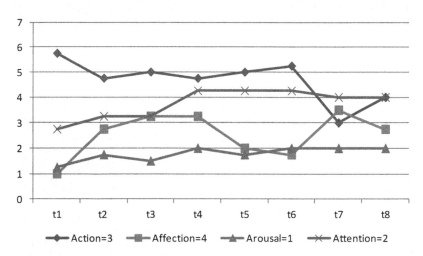

Fig. 6. Children's behavior (first eight videos) - Characteristics of each sensory profile in terms of Arousal, Attention, Affection and Action - From the observation grid of the first psychologist.

6   Further Development

The presented systems are audio feedback based, our goal is to provide multichannel feedback adding video interaction to the current system. We are testing different approaches, using Unity and Processing frameworks to enhance the visual experience. Three main demos are under testing: in the first one the subject movements are replicated by a 3D avatar (Fig. 8), both the avatar and the scenario can be customized and provide a great sense of immersion in an imaginary world. The second one is based

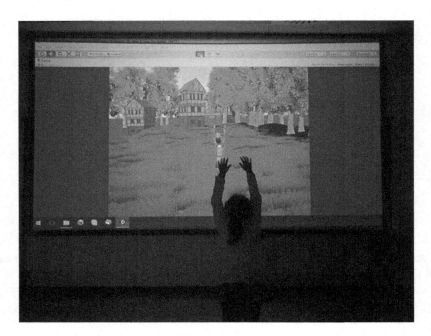

Fig. 7. Kinect controlled avatar

Fig. 8. Aerial painting system

on imitation, a video shows a trainer doing some move or postures and the subject have to correctly replicate the same movements. At the end of the exercise an algorithm assigns a score to the execution. The last demo is about aerial painting, the subject waves his hands in the air and those movements are mapped to brush strokes on a virtual canvas (Fig. 9). The next step of our work consists in the integration of these new activities in the current system and, in strict collaboration with the medical stuff, in the creation of new multichannel feedback based exercises to be tested in the next experimentation session.

7 Conclusions

We described an interactive, computer based system based on real-time image processing, which reacts to movements of a human body playing sounds. The map-ping between body motion and produced sounds is easily customizable with a graphical user interface. This system has been used for testing an innovative music-therapy technique for treating autistic children. The experimentation with real cases demonstrated several benefits from the application of the proposed system. These have been confirmed both by the team of clinical psychologists (using a validation protocol) and by the parents of the young patients. The most interesting outcome of the experimentation was the relational improvement. This promises to transfer the behavior shown in the setting to the external environment, increasing communication and interaction in the real world. We are continuing our experiments using Microsoft Kinect v.2. Our future approach will combine the Kinect's proprietary technology with the image processing techniques used in the camera based version.

The project addressed many challenges. Each autistic child is unique in the sense that improvements in abilities are very subjective and some study limitations have to be mentioned: first of all, the small size and the non-homogeneity of the sample; this is due to the difficulty of enrolling Low-Functioning Autism children with similar profiles. Participation is self-selected and sample bias cannot be excluded. A more rigorous assessment and selection of participants and the selection of a matched control group will guarantee results of higher value. Moreover, progress trends could depend upon external factors such as family involvement and health/treatment conditions. The outcome measurement also presented some limitations: our main measurement was the observational grid that is not a standardized instrument; moreover, information on important outcomes was not measured, such as cognitive skills and school perfor-mance. These data would be extremely interesting for creating the bases for using accessible technology-enhanced environments.

References

1. Magrini, M., Carboni, A., Salvetti, O., Curzio, O.: An auditory feedback based system for treating autism spectrum disorder. In: REHAB 2015 Proceedings of the 3rd 2015 Workshop on ICTs for Improving Patients Rehabilitation Research Techniques, pp. 30–33. ACM, New York (2015)

2. Ould Mohamed, A., Courbulay, V.: Attention analysis in interactive software for children with autism. In: Proceedings of the 8th International ACM SIGACCESS Conference on Computers and Accessibility, Portland, Oregon, USA (2006)
3. Kozima, H., Nakagawa, C., Yasuda, Y.: Interactive robots for communication-care: a case-study in autism therapy. In: International IEEE Workshop on Robot and Human Interactive Communication (2005)
4. Villafuerte, L., Markova, M., Jorda, S.: Acquisition of social abilities through musical tangible user interface: children with autism spectrum condition and the reactable. In: Proceedings of CHI EA 2012–CHI 2012 Extended Abstracts on Human Factors in Computing Systems, pp. 745–760. ACM, New York (2012)
5. Riva, D., Bulgheroni, S., Zappella, M.: Neurobiology, Diagnosis & Treatment in Autism: An Update, John Libbey Eurotex (2013)
6. Pajareya, K., Nopmaneejumruslers, K.: A pilot randomized controlled trial of DIR/Floortime™ parent training intervention for pre-school children with autistic spectrum disorders. Autism 15(5), 563–577 (2011)
7. Solomon, R., et al.: Pilot study of a parent training program for young children with autism The PLAY Project Home Consultation program. Autism 11(3), 205–224 (2007)
8. Wing, L., Gould, J.: Severe impairments of social interaction and associated abnormalities in children: epidemiology and classification. J. Autism Dev. Disord. 9, 11–29 (1979)
9. Vismara, L.A., Rogers, S.J.: behavioral treatments in autism spectrum disorder: what do we know? Annu. Rev. Clin. Psychol. 6, 447–468 (2010)
10. Kanner, L.: Autistic disturbances of affective contact. Nervous Child 2, 217–250 (1943)
11. Greenspan, S., Wieder, S.: The Child with Special Needs. Perseus. Pub., New York (1998)
12. Magrini, M., et al.: Progetto "SI RE MI" Sistema di Rieducazione Espressiva del Movimento e dell'Interazione. Autismo e disturbi dello sviluppo, Erickson (2015)
13. De Gangi, G., Berck, R.: DeGangi-Berck: Test of Sensory Integration. Western Psychological Services. Los Angeles (1983)
14. Dunn, W.: Sensory Profile-School Companion Manual. Psychological Corporation, San Antonio (2006)
15. Politi, P., Emanuele E. e Grassi, M.: The Invisible Orchestra Project. Development of the "Playing-in-Touch" (PiT) questionnaire. Neuroendocrinol. Lett. 33(5), 552–558 (2012)
16. Meini, C., Guiot, G., Maria Teresa Sindelar, M.T.: Autismo e musica. Il modello Floortime nei disturbi della comunicazione e della relazione, Erickson

Vision-Based SLAM Navigation for Vibro-Tactile Human-Centered Indoor Guidance

Thomas Gulde[1(✉)], Silke Kärcher[2], and Cristóbal Curio[1]

[1] Cognitive Systems, School of Informatics,
Reutlingen University, Reutlingen, Germany
`thomas.gulde@reutlingen-university.de`
[2] Institute of Cognitive Science, University of Osnabrück, Osnabrück, Germany

Abstract. Based on well-established robotic concepts of autonomous localization and navigation we present a system prototype to assist camera-based indoor navigation for human utilization implemented in the Robot Operating System (ROS). Our prototype takes advantage of state-of-the-art computer vision and robotic methods. Our system is designed for assistive indoor guidance. We employ a vibro-tactile belt to serve as a guiding device to render derived motion suggestions to the user via vibration patterns. We evaluated the effectiveness of a variety of vibro-tactile feedback patterns for guidance of blindfolded users. Our prototype demonstrates that a vision-based system can support human navigation, and may also assist the visually impaired in a human-centered way.

Keywords: Mobility aids · Navigation systems · Applications for the visually impaired · Mobile and wearable systems

1 Introduction

As humans have become accustomed to a variety of outdoor navigation solutions in their daily lives, we are recognizing an increase in indoor navigation needs as well. People want to find specific rooms, meeting places or other target locations in unknown buildings, e.g. airports or stations, which confront them with the risk of getting lost or wasting time while searching for the right path to their destination. The *Global Positioning System* (GPS) network conventionally performs a localization task in outdoor environments and is not suitable for direct use in indoor scenarios and nor it is able to provide reliable information regarding the user's orientation. By virtue of a construction-related low signal quality and multipath propagation as well as poor satellite positions, GPS can not provide an indoor localization accurate enough to justify its adoption for navigation within typical indoor scenarios [1]. To achieve the ability to navigate inside buildings, we need to find a substitute for such a localization system

© Springer International Publishing Switzerland 2016
G. Hua and H. Jégou (Eds.): ECCV 2016 Workshops, Part II, LNCS 9914, pp. 343–359, 2016.
DOI: 10.1007/978-3-319-48881-3_24

and provide the needed information with technologies well-suited to meet the requirements of indoor fields of operation.

There is vast research on mobile robot navigation and localization where the key problem that is solved is simultaneous localization and mapping (SLAM). SLAM approaches attempt to create a map of unknown areas while simultaneously tracking the current position or pose of the considered system relative to the permanently extended and updated map [2]. To solve this problem a wide range of different sensor technologies like laser [3], sonar [4], radar [5,6] or a variety of cameras [7,8] can be used to acquire the required features of the confronted environment. Especially for camera-based technologies, various methods, algorithms and frameworks to perform visual SLAM (VSLAM) have started to become available and are used extensively in a wide range of robotic applications [9]. VSLAM and related technologies therefore represent a way to realize the needed localization in the targeted areas combined with the generation of usable maps with a suitable level of detail. In contrast to other common signal-based indoor positioning methods [10], most VSLAM approaches are able to estimate poses with six degrees of freedom (6DoF), i.e. position and orientation in 3D space. This knowledge and additionally movement can be used to solve even more accurately positioning tasks. Thus this allows for navigating the user not only to the dedicated position, but also a targeted orientation, if required. With the availability of digital maps and localization methods, VSLAM systems provide the opportunity to derive conceivable paths or trajectories to accomplish a multitude of different navigation tasks. In addition to SLAM-technologies, the robotics community offers many different approaches to solve the challenge of such a final path and motion planning step [11]. In order to create an entire navigation system for human utilization, a proper interface is needed. We would like to expand the target audience of our system, with a specific emphasis on including users with visual impairments. People with partial or complete vision loss rely on versatile assistive technologies like the blind cane or electronic devices [12] to support their daily lives. In order to provide a navigation system for the visually impaired, custom solutions specific to their special needs are needed. Challenges arise primarily in the two-way communication interface between the visually impaired user and the technical system. Due to the deficit in visual perception, well-known and easy-to-use interfaces like touchscreens may be difficult to use in such scenarios. As such, there is a necessity to use alternative interface technologies to offer a meaningful user experience. These circumstances lead to a rethinking of the information processing modality and presentation. One example is guidance by non-intrusive, intuitively understandable tactile signals. In our case, we employ a belt with 32 vibromotors placed equidistantly around the waist. Previous research has shown that tactile direction signals provided around the waist in a 360 degree manner can instantly be integrated in behavior and may even circumvent the bottleneck of attention [13–16]. Our research work aims to ensure the basic applicability of a VSLAM based navigation system prototype to a spectrum of users ranging from those with normal vision to those with complete visual impairment by using an alternate information interface.

2   Related Work

The here presented project is firmly based on basic approaches and methods of mapping, navigation and VSLAM used by mobile robots. It is beyond the scope of this paper to grant a wide and comprehensive overview on this spacious matter and the breadth of basic technologies that it encompasses. We thereby refer the interested reader to available survey publications on this topic [9,17–19].

A focused survey on implemented navigation systems reveals present works bearing similarities to our proposal. Shoval *et al.* presented a waist-worn belt called *Navbelt*, which was also based on robotic concepts and is intended to be used as a computerized travel aid [20]. However, in contrast to our project, the belt does not serve as a feedback element, but rather relies on an ultrasonic sensory system to acquire the real world data and mainly uses auditory feedback to display information regarding the surroundings.

Wachaja *et al.* mounted two laser scanners on a walking frame and also use a vibro-tactile belt with angularly-aligned actuators [21]. Like Zöllner *et al.* [22] or Cardin *et al.* [23], they used the belt to encode distances to detected obstacles rather than for navigation purposes, which clearly makes it different from our work.

Borenstein and Ulrich developed an active blind cane [24] based on multiple sonar sensors. The sensory systems have been placed inside a cane construction with a set of tires which is controllable via servo drives. Thus, the cane also offers active feedback to lead the user through the environment and avoid obstacles which is the system's major task.

Schwarze *et al.* [25] presented a stereo vision-based navigation system with head-mounted image sensors combined with an inertial measurement unit (IMU) and acoustic feedback. The system has been developed for outdoor environments and also concentrates on direct obstacle detection rather than navigation but also builds a global environment model by using the camera's odometry. Schwarze *et al.* solely integrated acoustic feedback by placing virtual sound sources inside the derived global representation.

Lee and Medioni [26] also presented a vision-based and head-mounted system for indoor environments with integrated IMU sensory. They also use vibro-tactile feedback which is similar to our approach but with far fewer actuators. A relatively smaller number of vibration modules does not allow for rendering of fine direction differences. Lee and Medioni also use feature-based visual odometry as well as 2D mapping and path planning methods to generate the system's feedback.

The system presented by Nguyen *et al.* [27] is also based on image sensors and a localization method like FAB-MAP [28] and is targeted for use in indoor environments. Nguyen's work focuses on a SLAM system to provide maps and localization information but does not include feedback systems nor path planning component.

3   The System Concept

To provide maximal interoperability for research and development purposes we define the main building blocks and their relationships within our navigation-assistance system as shown in Fig. 1.

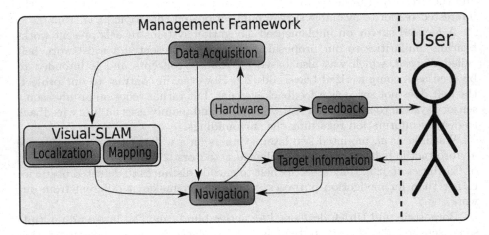

Fig. 1. Proposed system architecture based on individual and independent subsystems.

As is the case with any technical system, a suitable *Hardware* setup forms the foundation. In this case, suitable hardware entails a proper camera system, the hardware requirements for the chosen method of information display discussed earlier and a computing unit with sufficient processing power to run the VSLAM algorithm, perform camera depth calculations, and solve other highly computationally expensive tasks. Furthermore, adequate open interfaces are needed for the hardware integration itself.

The *Image Capturing* software module is essentially responsible for acquiring images from the camera system and passes the potentially processed data to the *Visual-SLAM* and *Navigation* modules in a format that is compatible with the rest of the system. Thus, the *Data Acquisition* module serves as an interface between these modules and should be responsible for the calculation of depth information, in case the SLAM system or camera is not capable to perform this on their on. This allows for flexibility in exchanging the camera sensors that are used in mono-, multi-view- or active-stereo systems while still being able to use the same software components.

Based on the acquired data, the selected *Visual-SLAM* framework provides the estimated pose as well as the generated map data primarily used by the *Navigation* module. The *Navigation* module is responsible for the interpretation of the obtained map, the computation of the path or motion plan based on the defined navigation target (*Target Information*) and for the consideration of current sensor data for several purposes including, e.g., collision avoidance, as discussed in [29]. Finally, the *Navigation* module's planning results are passed to the *Feedback* element, which can process the data and convert the information to a format that can be sent to the *Hardware* element. To merge all software components together, we strongly recommend using an adequate modular *Management Framework* to encapsulate all elements.

We propose that the sensing camera system should be mounted on the user's chest area (Fig. 2). In contrast to head-mounted approaches (cf. Sect. 2), this camera placement allows us to directly make use of the estimated ego-motion, provided by the SLAM system for navigation purposes, because the obtained pose points straight towards the major body direction and not to the user's line of sight.

Fig. 2. Proposed camera mounting position at the user's chest area.

As the system's main assistance element, we suggest a vibro-tactile belt. This element should ideally be placed on the waist area as shown in Fig. 3. The multiple vibration modules with defined, equidistant inter-element distances render signals at different angles around the user's body. As the relative position of both camera and belt can assumed to be fixed, we obtain a joint reference system for the generation of vibro-tactile feedback signals. This allows for direct generation of motion signals based on the current SLAM pose without the need to pay attention to other parts of the body or the user's current line of sight.

In addition to the vibro-tactile interface, the presented concept framework can be extended to include extra feedback elements. Elements that would allow the system to cater to a visually-impaired target audience include auditory, haptic [30], or any other modality that can be interpreted by users with visual deficits.

When targeting visually-impaired users, another challenge besides appropriately providing feedback is the interpretation of information given as input by system users. In the framework of a navigation system, we primarily consider

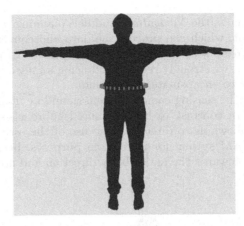

Fig. 3. Proposed placement of the vibro-tactile belt.

discrete *Target Information* as possible input data. As this information can easily be provided by human voice, we propose a speech recognition system as a solution to the input problem. Such systems are able to extract spoken information, like for requesting destinations and, combined with the already mentioned auditory interface, they can offer map-related target proposals and provide a dialog-based system interface, as proposed in [31].

4   The Final System Setup

For the implementation of the system conceptualized in the previous section, we rely on the open source meta operation system ROS [32]. ROS provides the required modular architecture and offers a huge community that provides many open source implementations of robotic and automotive applications and methods. ROS also allows the use of all relevant data types, messages to communicate between various packages, and common system drivers, which allows for seamless integration of any chosen hardware elements. For the image sensor we used common RGB-D camera models, such as the *Kinect* or the *Asus Xtion Pro Live*, mounted on the user's chest or on a small cart for mapping purposes. Once the needed sensor characteristics have been obtained using established calibration methods like those provided by *OpenCV* [33], the rectified RGB image and the corresponding depth information can be passed to the VSLAM system using ROS's messaging system.

The centerpiece of the software composition forms the VSLAM system which is responsible for providing the maps and localization information used from the navigation. For our project, we decided to use the *Real-Time Appearance-Based Mapping* (RTabMap) framework, developed by Labbé *et al.* [34]. Their appearance-based approach considers not just single image features but rather a combination of several feature vectors called *visual words* (VW). Managed within an incrementally built up vocabulary, these VWs can be used for image alignment, odometry derivation and for recognition of already-visited areas. Combined with a special memory management solution [35], Labbé and colleagues were able to achieve real-time performance for large scale maps with integrated online loop closure detection [36] based on RGB-D data. The use of this approach provides global map data in the form of a composite point cloud and a projected 2D *occupancy grid* [37]. It also grants access to the estimated 6DoF SLAM pose as it relates to the created map.

All of this information and data is used as input for the common ROS navigation stack [38]. A rough 2D footprint (see Fig. 4) is used to calculate the cost of every single element of the matrix-based occupancy grid. The resulting *costmap* is used as the configuration space for an $A*$ algorithm originally presented in [39]. This global planner supplies our navigation system with the global path, starting at a current 2D pose estimated by the VSLAM and ending at a set target. The global path, combined with the current data from the vision sensor, is then used by the *dynamic window approach* introduced by Fox *et al.* [40] to compute local guidance paths. The resulting local plan provides local path information in the form of circular trajectories, as shown in Fig. 4. Such a path leads to the global path and is used to derive the feedback signal. We use the absolute angle difference between the current SLAM orientation and the latest available point of the computed local path. This navigation angle is directly passed to the vibro-tactile, waist-mounted feedback element. Its integration is further explained in Sect. 5. All of the aforementioned techniques related to navigation in ROS, are described in detail in [41].

A speech synthesis module based on the free software *Festival* [42] was also integrated into our system. This additional feedback source is primarily used to

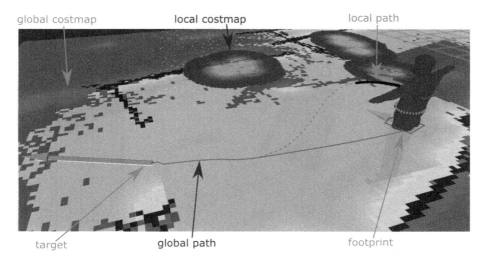

Fig. 4. Visualization of a current system state using *RViz*. Showing the estimated SLAM pose, derived global and local 2D maps and paths, rough footprint as well as the feedback and user visualization.

indicate reached targets but can be easily extended for use in passing all kinds of information related to the navigation task as well as the sensed environment.

To provide a sufficient representation of the system state, for research and development purposes, we decided to create a visualization based on ROS's *RViz*. We display the derived global and local maps and paths, estimated poses and the feedback that is sent to the *Feedback* element. An example visualization of the displayed information is shown in Fig. 4.

All software components run on a Linux-based laptop computer, which can be carried inside a backpack.

For the current version of our project, we decided not to implement the complete user interface that was detailed in the system conceptualization section above. At present, we have provided functionalities to set goals within the recorded maps by a third party member. However, this way to set the navigation goals can not be used by the blind or visually impaired. The implementation of a suitable user interface will be within the scope of further work.

5   Information Display and Vibro-Tactile Patterns

To implement the vibro-tactile information display concept (Sect. 3), we used a prototype of a vibro-tactile belt developed and provided by the University of Osnabrück [14]. Figure 5 shows an overview of the belt system.

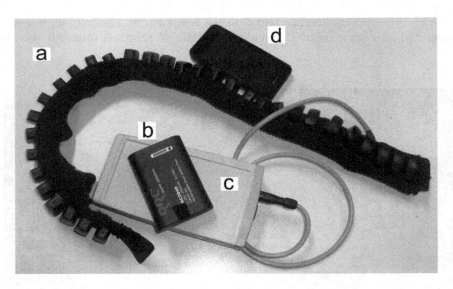

Fig. 5. Prototype of a vibro-tactile belt. (a) Belt with vibration modules, (b) external battery, (c) battery box with belt-controller, (d) mobile phone for interaction.

The belt can be worn on the waist and provides 32 vibration modules (Fig. 5a) spread equidistantly along its length, thereby providing an absolute angle resolution of $\frac{360°}{32} = 11,25°$. A Python interface allowed seamless integration of the belt component into our ROS environment without taking a detour via a mobile phone (Fig. 5d). Note that for later user application packages, smartphones might replace the current computing solution to make the navigation solution more portable. According to the given hardware constraints of the prototype, the defined ROS-packages offer the possibility for simultaneous direct control of up to two vibro-tactile modules and send final commands to the hardware via the belt's wireless *Bluetooth* interface placed inside the controller box (Fig. 5c), which also holds the battery (Fig. 5b). Due to the belt's hardware design, we are not able to control the tactile intensity of the vibration modules in this version and are therefore restricted to a predefined intensity.

We defined several vibro-tactile patterns to provide a variety of different interpretable signals for the user, as described in Sect. 4. Another prime goal of our project is to determine which of the introduced signal patterns are most suitable for fulfilling a guidance task. A thorough evaluation of the signal patterns follows in Sect. 6. Figure 6 illustrates and defines the parameters of our guidance controller.

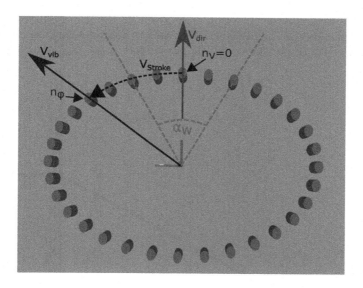

Fig. 6. Overview of the guidance controller reference parameters. V_{dir} denotes estimated SLAM pose, V_{vib} the direction for navigation signal, $\Delta\phi$ the absolute signal-angle sent to the belt, V_{Stroke} the direction for stroke signal, α_W the tolerance window, n the specific vibration element.

The frontal vibration element ($n_v = 0$) is defined to be the element which points in the direction of the estimated SLAM pose V_{dir} (given by the transformation constraints explained in Sect. 3). The controller tries to minimize the difference angle (n_ϕ) between V_{dir} and V_{vib}. V_{vib} refers to the current local path information provided by the *Navigation* component described in Sect. 4. The final piece of information sent to the belt is $\Delta\phi$, which indicates the absolute position of element n_ϕ and can be directly derived from vector V_{vib}.

Based on these reference values we can define the following patterns:

Direct vibration. Single vibration of one element in one direction
Stroke vibration. Create a stroke signal in the direction of V_{Stroke}, that sequentially triggers all elements from $n_v = 0$ to n_ϕ for a given span of time

To extend the range of possible feedback patterns that can be provided by the belt we implemented a tolerance window, defined here as a linearly increasing angular aperture α_W, which depends on the absolute two-dimensional Euclidean distance d between the current user position and the global navigation target. If the proposed V_{vib} lies within this window, a vibrational feedback signal will not be rendered to the user. This strategy was primarily introduced to avoid a sensory overload of the human tactile sensing system due to excessive vibration as discussed in [43]. We want to make sure α_W will not get too generous (i.e. $\alpha_{max} \,\hat{=}\,$ maximal angular aperture), and ensure that its max value will be cut off at a maximum, small enough to offer a proper final destination target. For this we defined a domain-based function $A(d)$ given by Eq. 1 and illustrated by the normalized plot in Fig. 7. This function is used to compute the absolute angular aperture α_W with respect to the static parameters d_{max}, d_{min} and α_{max}.

$$A(d) = \begin{cases} 0 & , d < d_{min} \\ \frac{\alpha_{max}}{d_{max}} \, d & , d_{min} \le d \le d_{max} \\ \alpha_{max} & , d > d_{max} \end{cases} \tag{1}$$

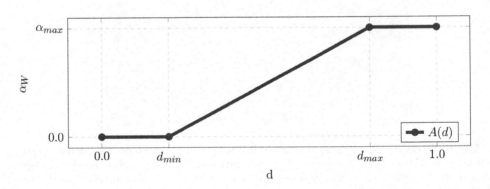

Fig. 7. Plot of the domain-defined function $A(d)$ formulated in Eq. 1.

The different combinations of all the aforementioned operation modes can be summarized by the following six feedback pattern variants (Table 1).

The evaluation of the described patterns, based on a user test, is detailed in the following section.

Table 1. Summary of the designed vibro-tactile feedback patterns.

1	**D**irect (**D**): Direct vibration of one single element
2	**S**troke (**S**): Stroke from $\mathbf{n_v} = \mathbf{0}$ to n_φ in direction of $\mathbf{V_{stroke}}$
3	**S**troke + **W**indow (**S + W**): Mode 2 combined with the tolerance window
4	**S**troke + Di**R**ection (**S + R**): Stroke from $\mathbf{n_v} = \mathbf{0}$ to n_φ with constant vibration of the element in final direction
5	**S**troke + Di**R**ection + **W**indow (**S + R + W**): Mode 4 combined with the tolerance window
6	**D**irect + **W**indow (**D + W**): Mode 1 combined with the tolerance window

6 Evaluation

For the evaluation of the navigation system and especially the different vibro-tactile stimulation patterns introduced in Sect. 5 we set up a small testing area. The area and the resultant map are shown in the form of a point cloud generated by the VSLAM system, as seen in Fig. 8, and a derived 2D costmap in Fig. 9, respectively.

Fig. 8. 3D point cloud provided by the VSLAM system.

The coordinates of both navigation goals, indicated in Fig. 9, have been preset and held constant across all trials to ensure the same target positions for all given navigation tasks. The predefined goals, together with the fixed environment and illumination, ensure equal conditions for all test runs. We tested each pattern in a random order with six participants (all with no actual visual impairments, but blindfolded) and set both navigation targets one after the other. We returned the participants back to a fixed starting position after each trial. We formulated the following three statements, which the participants had to subjectively rate on a given scale each time they reach both goals of a feedback pattern. The

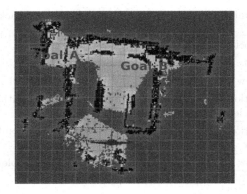

Fig. 9. Derived 2D navigation costmap of the test area.

scale-based answers were designed to provide indications of possible weaknesses and limitations of each feedback pattern.

- **A: I have always been able to identify the displayed direction correctly.** *[Scale: 0–10]*
  This statement is used to rate the overall *identifiability* of the signals.
- **B: I have always been able to transfer the given signals into my movements.** *[Scale: 0–10]*
  This statement is used to rate how *intuitively* each signal can be transferred into movements.
- **C: The number of signals received have been too little/too much.** *[Scale: −3–+3]*
  This statement evaluates the number of vibro-tactile feedback signals and allows for drawing conclusions as to a possible lack or overload of the discrete signals.

The user tests revealed significant differences between the individual feedback patterns. The graphs shown in Fig. 10 display the arithmetic mean values ($\bar{x}$, blue), the medians ($\tilde{x}$, orange) and the occurred variances (σ^2, green) for the ratings of each feedback method, grouped by the individual types. While mean or median allows a direct judgment of a pattern, the variance can be considered as an indicator of the conformity or lack thereof in participant feedback.

If we consider the identifiability and intuitiveness (highest values are best) of the patterns we find that the best ratings are those for modes one and six. Together with the best quantity ratings (zero is best) and the low variances in all evaluation criteria, we conclude that for a majority of users the single vibration mode is the best choice for fulfilling a given navigation task. All modes based on stroke signals show higher variances and lower ratings of the identifiability, when compared to the single signal feedback patterns. This leads us to presume that the stroke signals are harder to perceive and that the perception of strongly dynamic signals differs from person to person. The same judgments are revealed

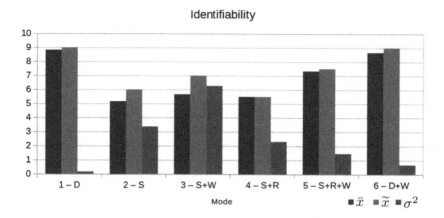

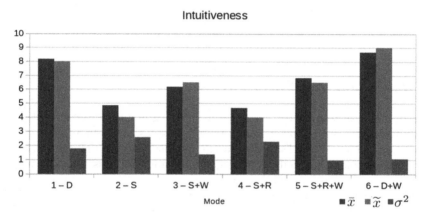

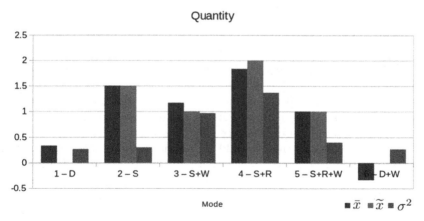

Fig. 10. Summarized results of the user survey. Mean, median and between subject variances are rendered by $\bar{x}$, $\tilde{x}$, σ^2, respectively. (Color figure online)

by considering the intuitiveness of the stroke patterns with the only difference being that the user evaluation we received had slightly lower variances.

All users noted that the integrated tolerance window and thus, the corresponding lack of vibro-tactile feedback, was interpreted as an indicator for a correct heading direction and provides better signal interpretation, as indicated by the ratings, especially in relation to the rated intuitiveness.

Our evaluation reveals that the developed prototype, i.e. the computer-vision based navigation planner combined with the vibro-tactile interface, is able to guide a person through a mapped environment, regardless of the ultimately chosen vibro-tactile pattern. The evaluation confirms the general functionality of the prototype and demonstrates that the computational methods we transferred from the robotics domain, can indeed be exploited for assistive human navigation. The user test also revealed advantages and disadvantages of the different feedback patterns and that simple, steady and easily perceivable patterns are preferred over rapidly changing or very dynamic signals, when designing an information display. These preferences are in line with the finding of Nagel et al. [13], where participants stated that two simultaneously vibrating motors are more distracting than helpful.

7   Conclusion and Future Work

We presented a system prototype which is able to guide blindfolded (potentially visually impaired) individuals through unknown areas based on a body-mounted vision-sensor combined with a vibro-tactile feedback system. The proposed system concept implements well-known algorithms and methods typically used for autonomous navigation of mobile robots and transfers the obtained information to the end user via vibro-tactile motion cues. We thereby demonstrated that such robotic concepts can also be used to guide human subjects. The modularity of the system we developed allows for an easy exchange of the hardware and software subsystem components and for a straightforward expansion of the general system by new modules, thus opening a window to future research.

One of our future goals is to provide novel path- and motion-planning solutions based on additional data acquired from the user. For example, we expect that more detailed knowledge derived from articulated body pose or specific dynamic states can be used to influence the planning results of the system and help to develop even more human-centered approaches. Our prototype will be extended with a proper user-interface. Namely, to provide a fully functional user interface, the system user should be provided the option and capability to set targets and control the system's functionality themselves. These requirements demand the development of methods and algorithms for map-analysis, map-labeling and map-interpretation as well as the integration of additional hardware elements, if necessary, to allow for a natural user interface compatible with visually-impaired users. Additionally, a user friendly solution for the computation device (e.g. a smartphone app) could be developed to further the application potential for daily living.

Another advancement our system would include the use of 3D maps. An additional height dimension would allow for more reliable local obstacle avoidance when taking into account the user's height relative to hanging or other roof-mounted objects.

References

1. Kjærgaard, M.B., Blunck, H., Godsk, T., Toftkjær, T., Christensen, D.L., Grønbæk, K.: Indoor positioning using GPS revisited. In: Floréen, P., Krüger, A., Spasojevic, M. (eds.) Pervasive 2010. LNCS, vol. 6030, pp. 38–56. Springer, Heidelberg (2010)
2. Thrun, S., Leonard, J.J.: Simultaneous localization and mapping. In: Springer Handbook of Robotics, pp. 871–889. Springer, Heidelberg (2008)
3. Cole, D.M., Newman, P.M.: Using laser range data for 3d slam in outdoor environments. In: Proceedings International Conference on Robotics and Automation, ICRA 2006, pp. 1556–1563 (2006)
4. Leonard, J.J., Durrant-Whyte, H.F.: Directed sonar sensing for mobile robot navigation, vol. 175. Springer Science & Business Media (2012)
5. Schuster, F., Keller, C.G., Rapp, M., Haueis, M., Curio, C.: Landmark based radar slam using graph optimization. In: 19th IEEE Intelligent Transportation Systems Conference (2016)
6. Schuster, F., Wörner, M., Keller, C., Haueis, M., Curio, C.: Robust localization based on radar signal clustering. In: IEEE 19th Symposium on Intelligent Vehicles (2016)
7. Engel, J., Schöps, T., Cremers, D.: LSD-SLAM: large-scale direct monocular SLAM. In: Fleet, D., Pajdla, T., Schiele, B., Tuytelaars, T. (eds.) ECCV 2014. LNCS, vol. 8690, pp. 834–849. Springer, Heidelberg (2014). doi:10.1007/978-3-319-10605-2_54
8. Paz, L.M., Piniés, P., Tardós, J.D., Neira, J.: Large-scale 6-DOF SLAM with stereo-in-hand. IEEE Trans. Robot. 24(5), 946–957 (2008)
9. Bonin-Font, F., Ortiz, A., Oliver, G.: Visual navigation for mobile robots: a survey. J. Intell. Robotics Syst. 253(3), 263–296 (2008)
10. Liu, H., Darabi, H., Banerjee, P., Liu, J.: Survey of wireless indoor positioning techniques and systems. IEEE Trans. Syst. Man Cybern. Part C Appl. Rev. 37(6), 1067–1080 (2007)
11. Latombe, J.C.: Robot motion planning, vol. 124. Springer Science & Business Media (2012)
12. Dakopoulos, D., Bourbakis, N.G.: Wearable obstacle avoidance electronic travel aids for blind: a survey. IEEE Trans. Syst. Man Cybern. Part C Appl. Rev. 40(1), 25–35 (2010)
13. Nagel, S.K., Carl, C., Kringe, T., Märtin, R., König, P.: Beyond sensory substitution-learning the sixth sense. J. Neural Eng. 2(4), R13 (2005)
14. Kärcher, S.M., Fenzlaff, S., Hartmann, D., Nagel, S.K., König, P.: Sensory augmentation for the blind. Front. Hum. Neurosci. 6, 37 (2012)
15. König, S.U., Schumann, F., Keyser, J., Goeke, C., Krause, C., Wache, S., Lytochkin, A., Ebert, M., Brunsch, V., Wahn, B., Kaspar, K., Nagel, S.K., Meilinger, T., Bülthoff, H., Wolbers, T., Büchel, C., König, P.: Learning new sensorimotor contingencies: Effects of long-term use of sensory augmentation on brain plasticity and conscious perception. (forthcoming)

16. Kaspar, K., König, S., Schwandt, J., König, P.: The experience of new sensorimotor contingencies by sensory augmentation. Conscious. Cogn. **28**, 47–63 (2014)
17. Thrun, S., et al.: Robotic mapping: a survey. Exploring Artif. Intell. New Millennium **1**, 1–35 (2002)
18. DeSouza, G.N., Kak, A.C.: Vision for mobile robot navigation: a survey. Pattern Anal. Mach. Intell. **24**(2), 237–267 (2002)
19. Carlone, L., Tron, R., Daniilidis, K., Dellaert, F.: Initialization techniques for 3d slam: a survey on rotation estimation and its use in pose graph optimization. In: IEEE International Conference on Robotics and Automation (ICRA), pp. 4597–4604 (2015)
20. Shoval, S., Borenstein, J., Koren, Y.: Auditory guidance with the navbelt-a computerized travel aid for the blind. IEEE Trans. Syst. Man Cybern. Part C Appl. Rev. **28**(3), 459–467 (1998)
21. Wachaja, A., Agarwal, P., Adame, M.R., Möller, K., Burgard, W.: A navigation aid for blind people with walking disabilities. In: IROS Workshop on Rehabilitation and Assistive Robotics, Chicago, USA (2014)
22. Zöllner, M., Huber, S., Jetter, H.-C., Reiterer, H.: NAVI – a proof-of-concept of a mobile navigational aid for visually impaired based on the microsoft kinect. In: Campos, P., Graham, N., Jorge, J., Nunes, N., Palanque, P., Winckler, M. (eds.) INTERACT 2011. LNCS, vol. 6949, pp. 584–587. Springer, Heidelberg (2011). doi:10.1007/978-3-642-23768-3_88
23. Cardin, S., Thalmann, D., Vexo, F.: A wearable system for mobility improvement of visually impaired people. Vis. Comput. **23**(2), 109–118 (2007)
24. Borenstein, J., Ulrich, L.: The guidecane-a computerized travel aid for the active guidance of blind pedestrians. In: Proceedings International Conference on Robotics and Automation, vol. 2, pp. 1283–1288. IEEE (1997)
25. Schwarze, T., Lauer, M., Schwaab, M., Romanovas, M., Bohm, S., Jurgensohn, T.: An intuitive mobility aid for visually impaired people based on stereo vision. In: Proceedings of the IEEE International Conference on Computer Vision Workshops, pp. 17–25 (2015)
26. Lee, Y.H., Medioni, G.: Wearable RGBD indoor navigation system for the blind. In: Agapito, L., et al. (eds.) ECCV 2014 Workshops. LNCS, vol. 8927, pp. 493–508. Springer, Heidelberg (2014)
27. Nguyen, Q.H., Vu, H., Tran, T.H., Van Hamme, D., Veelaert, P., Philips, W., Nguyen, Q.H.: A visual slam system on mobile robot supporting localization services to visually impaired people. In: Agapito, L., et al. (eds.) ECCV 2014 Workshops. LNCS, vol. 8927, pp. 716–729. Springer, Heidelberg (2014)
28. Cummins, M., Newman, P.: Fab-map: Probabilistic localization and mapping in the space of appearance. Int. J. Robot. Res. **27**(6), 647–665 (2008)
29. Hakobyan, L., Lumsden, J., O'Sullivan, D., Bartlett, H.: Mobile assistive technologies for the visually impaired. Survey Ophthalmol. **58**(6), 513–528 (2013)
30. Sjöström, C.: Using haptics in computer interfaces for blind people. In: CHI 2001 Extended Abstracts on Human Factors in Computing Systems, pp. 245–246. ACM (2001)
31. Helander, M.G.: Handbook of human-computer interaction. Elsevier (2014)
32. Quigley, M., Conley, K., Gerkey, B.P., Faust, J., Foote, T., Leibs, J., Wheeler, R., Ng, A.Y.: ROS: an open-source Robot Operating System. In: ICRA Workshop on Open Source Software (2009)
33. Bradski, G., et al.: The opencv library. Doctor Dobbs J. **25**(11), 120–126 (2000)
34. Labbe, M., Michaud, F.: Appearance-based loop closure detection for online large-scale and long-term operation. IEEE Trans. Robot. **29**(3), 734–745 (2013)

35. Labbé, M., Michaud, F.: Memory management for real-time appearance-based loop closure detection. In: IEEE/RSJ International Conference on Intelligent Robots and Systems (IROS), pp. 1271–1276 (2011)
36. Labbe, M., Michaud, F.: Online global loop closure detection for large-scale multi-session graph-based slam. In: IEEE/RSJ International Conference on Intelligent Robots and Systems (IROS), pp. 2661–2666 (2014)
37. Elfes, A.: Using occupancy grids for mobile robot perception and navigation. Computer **22**(6), 46–57 (1989)
38. Marder-Eppstein, E., Berger, E., Foote, T., Gerkey, B., Konolige, K.: The office marathon (2010)
39. Hart, P.E., Nilsson, N.J., Raphael, B.: A formal basis for the heuristic determination of minimum cost paths. IEEE Trans. Syst. Sci. Cybern. **4**(2), 100–107 (1968)
40. Fox, D., Burgard, W., Thrun, S.: The dynamic window approach to collision avoidance. IEEE Robot. Autom. Mag. **4**(1), 23–33 (1997)
41. Guimarães, R.L., de Oliveira, A.S., Fabro, J.A., Becker, T., Brenner, V.A.: Ros navigation: Concepts and tutorial. In: Koubaa, A. (ed.) Robot Operating System (ROS). SCI, vol. 625, pp. 121–160. Springer, Switzerland (2016)
42. Black, A., Taylor, P., Caley, R., Clark, R., Richmond, K., King, S., Strom, V., Zen, H.: The festival speech synthesis system, version 1.4. 2. Unpublished document available via (2001). http://www.cstr.ed.ac.uk/projects/festival.html
43. Van Erp, J.B.: Guidelines for the use of vibro-tactile displays in human computer interaction. In: Proceedings of Eurohaptics, vol. 2002, pp. 18–22 (2002)

Perfect Accuracy with Human-in-the-Loop Object Detection

Rorry Brenner$^{(\boxtimes)}$, Jay Priyadarshi, and Laurent Itti

Computer Science and Neuroscience,
University of Southern California, Los Angeles, USA
{rorry.brenner,jpriyada,itti}@usc.edu

Abstract. Modern state-of-the-art computer vision systems still perform imperfectly in many benchmark object recognition tasks. This hinders their application to real-time tasks where even a low but non-zero probability of error in analyzing every frame from a camera quickly accumulates to unacceptable performance for end users. Here we consider a visual aid to guide blind or visually-impaired persons in finding items in grocery stores using a head-mounted camera. The system uses a human-in-the-decision-loop approach to instruct the user how to turn or move when an object is detected with low confidence, to improve the object's view captured by the camera, until computer vision confidence is higher than the highest mistaken confidence observed during algorithm training. In experiments with 42 blindfolded participants reaching for 25 different objects randomly arranged on shelves 15 times, our system was able to achieve 100 % accuracy, with all participants selecting the goal object in all trials.

Keywords: Scene understanding · Quality of life technologies · Sensory substitution · Mobile and wearable systems · Applications for the visually impaired · Egocentric and first-person vision · Computer vision · Object detection

1 Introduction and Background

People who are blind have more difficulty navigating the world than those with sight, even in places they have been before [8,23]. This is a condition that affects 39 million people worldwide [32]. Much progress has been achieved in developing electronic travel aids to assist them as technology has advanced. One method is to convert images to soundscapes which some subjects can learn to interpret well enough to differentiate places, and to identify and locate some objects [27]. Others include localization in an environment using stereo cameras, accelerometers, and even wifi access points [6,13]. Advances have also been made to traditional aids such as canes, by developing electronic replacements using, e.g., sonar to increase their warning range or grant the same feedback but without a physical cane [20,31], and replacing guide dogs with robots [16]. Among these devices

© Springer International Publishing Switzerland 2016
G. Hua and H. Jégou (Eds.): ECCV 2016 Workshops, Part II, LNCS 9914, pp. 360–374, 2016.
DOI: 10.1007/978-3-319-48881-3_25

many utilize computer vision to help with navigation, text reading, and object recognition. [1, 18–20, 29].

Many advances have been made in computer vision, yet, even state of the art algorithms have not yet been able to achieve perfect accuracy on standard datasets [7, 12, 28]. Our algorithm's success is founded in the areas of dynamic thresholding and active vision [2]. Active vision is the process of changing views to better identify what is being looked at. This can be through changing the pose of the camera or choosing a region of interest with a larger field of view and then attempting identification within that region using a zoomed-in image [3, 5, 11, 30]. Dynamic thresholding is any recognition system which has a decision threshold more complicated than a single number. For example, some methods include different thresholds for parts vs. whole object detection [9], adaptive local thresholding [14, 33], and connectivity based thresholding [22].

Despite the discussed advances in assistance for the blind, shopping can still be a nearly impossible task. Many boxed and canned items have identical shapes, which means without one of these aids, or normal vision, help from a person with vision is required for selecting the correct item [17]. Even successful devices such as OrCam [19] require the user to point at the desired object to be identified. This is great for people with poor vision, but not helpful for the fully blind. To address this, systems have been proposed that read barcodes [21] or identify items on the shelves using computer vision algorithms [18, 29]. On the one hand, barcode scanners never make mistakes, although they can be tedious to use when looking for a specific item in a large grocery store (as shown in our own results, see below). On the other hand, a serious problem with using a computer vision system for this application is that if they make too many mistakes, users will likely stop using them [10, 24]. An acceptable system cannot ever tell the user to select an item they do not want.

2   Motivation

In a typical object detection computer vision system each input image requires the system to determine a confidence for how likely it is that any items trained for are currently in that image. If the confidence is high enough it will tell the user it has found the item. However, no matter where the confidence threshold is set, for most objects and algorithms there will be some range of values where the system will make mistakes [18], either false alarms or misses. If the threshold is set too high the system can decide it has not found the item when it was present (miss), and if the threshold is set too low and the system can decide it has found the item when the item was not present (false alarm). This problem happens with almost every system with a confidence threshold for detection because there often are some images without a particular item where the confidence may be higher than for some images with the item.

To show this point using the set of 25 objects used in our experiments below (Fig. 1), a dataset of pictures was collected in our simulated grocery store setting. A camera was placed in a fixed position and objects were arranged in front of

Fig. 1. Template images for objects in database by row, left to right. 1, Cereal: PEB, CP, HNC, LUC, MGC. 2, Snacks: SR, HBN, OCP, PS, NB. 3, Pasta: HH, KRA, PR, MAC, VEL. 4, Tea: SM, LIP, FTS, FR, STA. 5, Candy: NRD, HT, GNP, MD, JM.

it with their centers two feet away from the camera. Objects were then rotated vertically and horizontally at 15° degree intervals for each picture from negative 45° to positive 45° offset giving a total of 1225 images. Images in which the object pose (homography, discussed in the following section) could not be recovered by our algorithm were not included because the system would not be able to guide the user from those images. Removing these images left a total of 1112 usable images or 44.5 images on average per item. Figure 2-A shows receiver operating characteristic (ROC) curves for recognizing each of the objects in the dataset individually and Fig. 2-B shows one ROC curve over all objects. Confidences were calculated using the SURF [4] algorithm. Some objects had less of a problem than others, with a smaller portion of overlap between the highest confidence without the object and the lowest confidence with the object. Only 2 objects had no overlap at all. This means just these 2 objects of 25, with the images collected, would yield no mistakes with a fixed threshold. The ROC curves for some of the other items are quite good as well; however, even an error rate of only 1 %, might cause an error every 25 s in our system that runs in real time at approximately 4 frames per second. In the discussion section we will detail why every mistake is a large issue for the user. The only way to solve this problem is to not have a yes/no threshold, and instead allow the system to output that it is unsure within this range of values where there will be uncertainty.

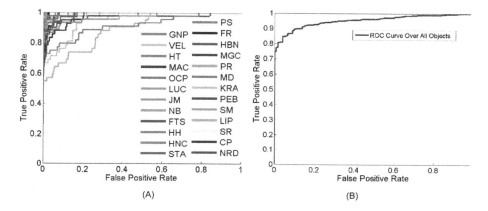

Fig. 2. (A) ROC curves of confidence values over all images and all objects collected. PEB and HNC are the only ones where all confidences for images of other objects are lower than all confidences for images of themselves. (B) ROC curve for correctness with a single fixed threshold over all objects being tested on.

3   Proposed System

The proposed system consists of a camera mounted on a pair of glasses, which captures images in real time. Users can provide instructions as to which object they want to reach for next (in experiments, that was controlled by the experimenter). Camera images are then analyzed as the user moves through the environment until at least some weak evidence for the presence of the object is determined by the vision algorithm. If there is evidence that the object may be present, but the system is uncertain (as further detailed below), the user is not yet told that the object has been found. Instead the user is instructed to turn, move, strafe, or crouch in a way that will decrease the difference in object pose between the current camera view and the system's template image for that object. Template images for the objects are front and centered. As the viewpoint changes and provides increasingly more front and centered views of the object, confidence of the vision algorithm is expected to increase. When confidence exceeds the threshold necessary to ensure no mistake, the object is declared found. The user may still be further guided so that the object becomes centered in the camera's field of view. At this point the user is informed that the

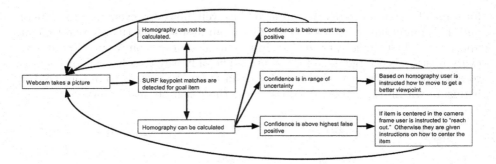

Fig. 3. Flow diagram of choices algorithm makes.

object is straight in front of their face and that they should reach out to grasp it. A simple flow diagram of this process is shown in Fig. 3.

Thus, our approach uses the cognitive abilities of the users (to understand instructions) and their mobility (to execute the suggested moves) to improve the quality of the view of an object as captured by the head mounted camera. Because our main application is for blind users, the system never needs to rely on any human visual ability.

Training is performed to find confidence thresholds for the top and bottom of the uncertainty range for each item. This range is defined as the values between the lowest true positive threshold, and the highest false positive threshold. The lowest true positive is the smallest confidence score ever given to an image that an item is present where the item being trained for was actually in the image. The highest false positive is the largest confidence ever given that an item was in a training image when it was not present. Training and testing incorporate the use of homography matrixes. A homography matrix is a representation of where the camera is relative to a set of points in space that all lie on the same plane. Homographies are calculated based on the relative positions of a set of points in relation to each other in a template image compared to their relative positions in a camera image. For example, if the points are all proportionally closer, the homography would show the camera is further away from the object than where it was when the template image was taken. Another example can be seen in Fig. 4. In our case, the template points are from the goal object for which the system is currently training. Because the points must be on the same plane, in the current instantiation of the system objects being found must be in boxes, as opposed to cans or other objects without a flat front surface. To calculate a homography a keypoint matching algorithm is required. These algorithms calculate feature descriptors in images and finds matches between similar descriptors in other images. Matches will include a match confidence as well as the pixel positions in both images, as needed for the homography calculation. We chose SURF [4], as opposed to others such as SFIT [15], because of it's speed. In the end system, homography matrices are the method used to give instructions. To train the lowest true positive threshold, objects are displayed to the camera and rotated

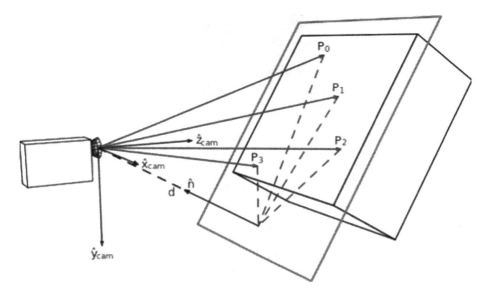

Fig. 4. Visual representation of Homography calculation [26]. In this case the points will be proportionally closer in the y-axis, while in the x-axis they will closer at the top and further apart at the bottom. The calculated homography would describe a position where the camera is looking up at the object from below.

in all directions and moved closer and farther away. The lowest true positive value is determined to be the lowest confidence value seen where a homography is still able to be calculated. If a homography cannot be calculated these confidences are not used because we would not be able to direct the user from those images. The highest false positive value is trained at the same time. While training the lowest true positive for one object, confidences are recorded for every other object in the database. The strongest confidence ever seen for each object, while actually looking at other objects, sets the thresholds for the highest false positives. To be safe, we additionally add 15 % of the range between thresholds to this value as a buffer. An example of scores relative to these thresholds is shown in Fig. 5.

During a run, if the confidence is within the uncertainty range the system outputs that it doesn't know the answer. However, it uses the information it has to arrive at a better decision later. If the confidence is between these thresholds, and a homography can be calculated, the system will know where the camera is relative to the points on the object used in the homography calculation. It can then pass on this information to the component that moves the camera. In our application that component is the human user. Using audio feedback our system tells the user how to move in order to guide the camera to a better viewing angle. If homographies continue to be calculated, eventually an ideal, front and centered, viewpoint can be achieved. Images from this camera angle generate the most similar keypoints to the template's keypoints, giving the highest confidences. If the confidence of an image

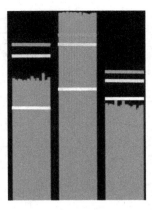

Fig. 5. Confidence threshold display for three items. Bars represent confidence values over last 20 frames. No units are shown because display confidences for each are relative percentage between max and min ever seen by the system when searching for each item. Middle threshold is the highest false positive. Bottom threshold is the lowest true positive. Top threshold is the extra buffer, 15 % above of the range above the highest false positive. Left confidence is in the range of uncertainty, if this was the item being searched for directions would be given. Middle confidence is above the max false positive value meaning this item is actually in the camera frame. Right confidence is below the lowest true positive so this item is certain to not have enough keypoint matches in the image to recover a homography.

surpasses the highest false positive value for the goal object correctness is certain. If, with an ideal viewpoint, the item is still not above this threshold the user knows to move on. This will happen when items have enough keypoints in common that a homography for the goal item is still able to be calculated from keypoints found on the alternate item. Most frequently this is seen between objects which share brand logos or other portions of similar visuals.

The physical system consists of three components. The first is the headset, created by attaching a webcam to a pair of glasses. The camera is attached directly in the middle to best capture images replicating where a person would be looking. The next is a pair of headphones to allow the user to hear the audio feedback. The last is the computer which performs SURF template matching, checks confidences, and gives instructions. We have used a GigaByte Brix which is able to be placed in a backpack and powered with a battery while the user is performing the task. These components are all controlled via SSH by a Samsung tablet.

4   Experiment Setup

For real world applications a computer vision system must be flawless, or close to flawless in identifying what it is being used for. A system saying it has found what it is looking for when it has not could range from catastrophic to just inconvenient, but in any case it would not be widely used with more than a minute allowance for mistakes. The goal of our system is to show that this method of thresholding can achieve perfect accuracy. Blind grocery shopping tests this goal. The visually impaired user is able to use human decision making and movement for all parts of the task other than the actual vision. Grocery shopping is also a task where a system telling the user to purchase the wrong item even once would be considered a serious mistake.

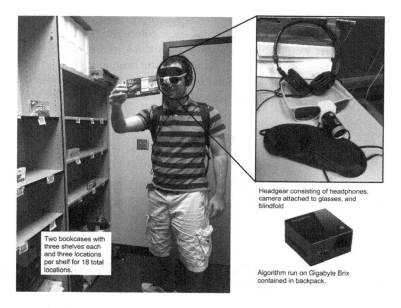

Fig. 6. Experiment setup. Shown is a user confirming a selected item in the simulated grocery store.

4.1 Environment and Instructions

Our experiment took place in a simulated grocery store aisle using blindfolded participants as shown in Fig. 6. Subjects were 42 students. We arranged two bookshelves next to each other where our grocery store items could be placed. Each bookshelf has three shelves and we allowed items to be placed in three locations per shelf making 18 total locations items could be placed. During any given run five items would be out on the shelves at a time. These items came from one of five categories; cereal, snacks, pasta, tea, and candy. The five items arranged together during each trial would be from the same category. Users all performed 1 trial from each category with the same locations, and 2 trials from each category with randomized positions which were unique, for a total of 15 trials per subject. To begin each trial, the user would stand against the back wall of the room facing the items. At this point the system would be turned on with the goal item selected. The user was instructed to move slowly around the room, while facing the shelves, until an initial movement command was given by the system. This would occur when SURF matches were made in arrangements where homographies could be calculated and the confidence was above the lower worst true positive threshold. Once an instruction was received the user was to follow the instructions which would guide them to be centered in front of the item. Instructions included "Left," "Right," "Up," "Down," "Left Up," "Left Down," "Right Up," "Right Down," "Strafe Left," "Strafe Right," "Strafe Up," "Strafe Down," "Step Forward," "Step Back," and "Reach Out." Examples of images which would elicit direction commands can be seen in Fig. 7. Direction commands were to move in those directions, strafe commands were to move in that direction but rotate the opposite direction, and Reach Out was the command which was only given when the object was directly centered and the confidence was above the worst false positive confidence plus buffer threshold.

Fig. 7. Instructions correspond to camera's position based on homography calculation. User is guided to make camera point directly at center of object. Center image shows a strafe command where user would be instructed to rotate in addition to move.

When the "Reach Out" command was given users were to reach out, from the camera, and pick up the item in front of them. Once this item was grasped they turned 90°, to be sure no other items from the shelves were in the background, and confirm the item by receiving a second "Reach Out" command. This would be done by holding the item up to the camera and moving the item based on the audio feedback, rather than moving themselves as was done with the item on the shelf. Sometimes users would be guided towards incorrect items when two items had similar enough features that confidence would be high when looking at the wrong item and points matched in such a way that homographies could still be calculated. However, when centered on the incorrect item the worst false positive threshold would not be surpassed, and hence no "Reach Out" command would be issued. It would be up to the participant to decide to move on to other locations in the occasions where they had centered onto an object but were not being instructed to reach out.

4.2 Training

Each participant was first briefly trained on how to use the system. Training started with all 25 items out on the shelves. This would be more difficult than during non-training trials, where the items would be less crowded. Participants ran the experiment three times without a blindfold, and then three times with a blindfold to get a feel for the system. At that time the participant continued training until they successfully performed three trials in a row without making a mistake. Mistakes are defined in two ways. One was if they picked up the wrong item. Users knew not to pick anything up until they received the "Reach Out" command, but actually reaching out towards the location directly in front of the camera's center of field proved to not be an inherently easy function to perform. Some users reached slightly to the left or right, or even too high or too low to a different shelf. The second predetermined mistake to avoid was "losing" the item once tracking had begun. When the system was initially turned on, instructions typically were not received as the item to be searched for was either not in the camera frame, or far away and therefore too small in the image to get enough keypoint matches to calculate a homography. This was the "no instruction" condition. In this case the user was to scan the shelves without instructions until a first instruction was given. At this point the user followed instructions which would guide the object to the center of the camera frame. If the user moved in such a way that the object was lost from the camera frame and they were relapsed to the "no instruction" condition that would be considered a failure during training. During the actual experiment, trials would not be aborted whenever the subject "lost" an item, and users had to recover from it on their own. Likewise, if the user picked up an item but could not confirm it and decided they had reached incorrectly, the item would be returned to the shelf and the trial would continue. Failures during the experiment could hence occur if users both picked up and confirmed the wrong item, or if they gave up on a given trial (which never happened).

4.3 Control Experiment

Our control experiment was performed in a similar manner using a barcode scanner. This was chosen, rather than another computer vision system, because we were confident we could achieve perfect accuracy and wanted to test against a second option which would have perfect accuracy [21]. The barcode scanner used was an Amazon Dash. Experimental setup for these trials was kept as parallel as possible to a grocery store setup. The same two bookshelves were used, again with 18 possible locations. As in modern grocery stores the barcodes were placed directly on the front face of the shelf. In these trials one barcode was selected at random as the goal. Users scanned every barcode in any order they chose until the correct one was scanned. No mistake conditions were defined for these trials. Training simply consisted of giving the user the scanner and a blindfold and they were allowed to practice indefinitely until they felt confident.

5   Experimental Results

Experiments were run as described on 42 participants. For all trials with all participants the correct item was always correctly obtained by the participant. Barcode scanning trials also were always successful. In each trial three time points were collected. The first was the time at which the first instruction was received. This cutoff was included because in some trials participants would take the majority of their total time moving blindly before receiving any instructions. With the barcode scanner, subjects would start trials with the scanner already held to the first barcode. The first scan would regularly take less than a second, so we wanted to have a cutoff for the first piece of feedback for our system. The second time recorded was the time of the first "Reach Out" command. At this point the system was 100 % sure the user has found the item they are looking for and it was directly in front of them. The final time recorded was the additional time needed for the user to actually pick up and confirm the item, a final step not taken during the barcode scanning trials.

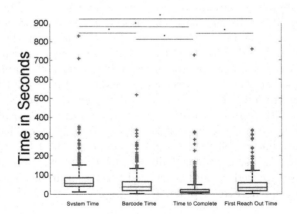

Fig. 8. Boxplots for total time taken for runs of the system and the barcode scanner, "time to complete" times for the system, and first "Reach Out" times for the system. Wilcoxon Rank Sum Tests were run on each pair to test if they could have come from continuous distributions with equal medians. All but Barcode Time vs First Reach Out Time had significant p-values: System Time vs Barcode Time: 1.5e-24, System Time vs Time to Complete: 6.2e-118, Barcode Time vs Time to Complete: 2.4e-46, System Time vs First Reach Out Time: 1.2e-34, First Reach Out Time vs Time to Complete: 7.4e-46, and Barcode Time vs First Reach Out Time: 0.18.

Mean total time for our system was 73.1 s per trial. Mean Barcode scanner time was 49.4 s. Using total time, this would mean the barcode scanner was distinctly faster. However, mean for first instruction time with our system was 23.7 s and for first "Reach Out" command was 46.5 s. This gives a mean "time to complete" with our system, time between first instruction and first "Reach Out" command, a mean time of only 18.1 s. We believe this is the time that should be compared, as further discussed in the next section. These results are shown in Fig. 8.

Surveyed participants were asked to assign a value 1–10 to their preference of systems with 10 being completely preferred our system, and 1 being completely preferred the barcode scanner. Mean score was 7.8 with only 2 participants reporting that they preferred the barcode scanner. Many reported their preference came from our system being able to provide more continuous feedback than a barcode scanner as guidance to the goal object. Of course, there could be some response bias of the subjects wanting to be "friendly" participants.

6 Discussion

The strongest algorithm from the most recent ImageNet Challenge [25] was developed by MSRA [12]. They achieved an accuracy rate of 62.07 % (as reported by [25]) over all object categories in the dataset, with a range of 95.93 % for the most accurate category and only 19.41 % for the weakest. This is still an outstanding result with the complexity of the ImageNet dataset, and impressive work with deep residual neural networks to achieve it. However, this rate of accuracy would be far too low for any real world applications where mistakes are costly. In situations such as assistance to blind grocery shoppers it is essential to not make mistakes. In earlier instantiations of our algorithm "Wrong Item" was also an instruction. It was given when an object was centered but the worst false positive threshold was not surpassed. The intention was to inform users they had centered on an item with similar enough keypoints to calculate homographies for the goal item, even though it was not the goal item itself. However, in the cases when this happened when they were actually looking at the goal item, only because one frame didn't calculate good keypoints, users would typically move away immediately. This choice sometimes added minutes more to their time before coming back to the correct item. This is why we decided to instead give no instruction when the item was centered but the threshold was not surpassed, and rely on the participant to decide on their own when they had centered on an incorrect item. As seen in the ROC curves earlier, with a fixed threshold a SURF based algorithm could perform with reasonable error rates on all of the items in our dataset. However, when even a single bad instruction from a single frame can increase your time significantly, and the algorithm is running at many frames per second, perfect accuracy is necessary for an algorithm to be optimal. Our experiment has shown that using this human-in-the-loop system 100 % accuracy is, in fact, possible with a computer vision based system in a real life application. Using a human's mobility and decision making allows the algorithm to not have a fixed threshold and instead postpone decisions when uncertain. Without forcing answers from uncertain conditions the algorithm is able to never make mistakes.

Time for the barcode scanner was stopped when the user scanned the correct barcode. These trials did not require the user to pick up an actual item or confirm it. Removing the time to pick up and confirm with our system makes the two more equivalent. The time before first command is also not parallel for the barcode scanner. In barcode scanning trials the subjects were allowed to start with the scanner already held up to the first barcode of their choice. This often meant the first piece of feedback would be immediate. In trials for our system the time taken before the first command was received was regularly a large majority of the total time taken. A major cause of this was the choice of webcam for our original system. With a low definition webcam, the smaller items would sometimes require users to have to get within a couple feet from the item before they took up a large enough portion of the image to detect any keypoints. This meant the subject might have to blindly scan all 18 positions before getting any feedback whatsoever. Sometimes they would even have to do this more than once if they did not scan correctly the first time. With an HD webcam the user should be able to scan all 18 positions on both bookshelves at once from the starting position at the back wall. This would eliminate all time taken before first command.

As evidence for this, for the larger items in the cereal category this was already the case. With such large items initial instructions were often heard immediately. Considering only this category, mean total time was 57.1 s. However, for cereals first instruction time had a mean of 9.1 s compared to 27.5 for the other categories. With a mean time of 34.6 s to pick up and confirm an item after receiving the first "Reach Out" command this gave cereals a mean "time to complete" time of only 13.5 s and a mean time from start to the first "Reach Out" command of 22.5 s. Either of these times are more comparable to the barcode scanner times, since barcode trials did not require confirmation and started feedback immediately, and both are faster.

Compared to a barcode scanner the total times for our system were slower. However, when only considering "time to complete," the time needed for the subject to center the correct item in the camera frame after receiving their first instruction, our system was faster. Also considering only time to first "Reach Out" command, ignoring time taken to grasp and confirm the item not necessary in barcode scanner trials, times did not show significant difference. Importantly, surveyed participants reported they preferred the constant guided feedback of our system against the yes/no feedback the barcode scanner could provide, even in our reduced store with only two shelves. We hence conclude that this study has successfully demonstrated a user-in-the-loop machine vision algorithm that made no mistakes and could be an interesting basis for a new generation of visual aids.

Acknowledgment. This work was supported by the National Science Foundation (grant numbers CCF-1317433 and CNS-1545089), and the Office of Naval Research (N00014-13-1-0563). The authors affirm that the views expressed herein are solely their own, and do not represent the views of the United States government or any agency thereof.

References

1. Adebiyi, A., Mante, N., Zhang, C., Sahin, F.E., Medioni, G.G., Tanguay, A.R., Weiland, J.D.: Evaluation of feedback mechanisms for wearable visual aids. In: 2013 IEEE International Conference on Multimedia and Expo Workshops (ICMEW), pp. 1–6. IEEE (2013)
2. Aloimonos, J., Weiss, I., Bandyopadhyay, A.: Active vision. Int. J. Comput. Vis. **1**(4), 333–356 (1988)
3. Bagdanov, A.D., Del Bimbo, A., Nunziati, W.: Improving evidential quality of surveillance imagery through active face tracking. In: 18th International Conference on Pattern Recognition (ICPR 2006), vol. 3, pp. 1200–1203. IEEE (2006)
4. Bay, H., Tuytelaars, T., Gool, L.: SURF: speeded up robust features. In: Leonardis, A., Bischof, H., Pinz, A. (eds.) ECCV 2006. LNCS, vol. 3951, pp. 404–417. Springer, Heidelberg (2006). doi:10.1007/11744023_32
5. Bjorkman, M., Eklundh, J.O.: Vision in the real world: finding, attending and recognizing objects. Int. J. Imaging Syst. Technol. **16**(5), 189–208 (2006)
6. Bowen III, C.L., Buennemeyer, T.K., Burbey, I., Joshi, V.: Using wireless networks to assist navigation for individuals with disabilities. In: California State University, Northridge Center on Disabilities' 21st Annual International Technology and Persons with Disabilities Conference (2006)
7. Ciregan, D., Meier, U., Schmidhuber, J.: Multi-column deep neural networks for image classification. In: 2012 IEEE Conference on Computer Vision and Pattern Recognition (CVPR), pp. 3642–3649. IEEE (2012)
8. Dramas, F., Thorpe, S.J., Jouffrais, C.: Artificial vision for the blind: a bio-inspired algorithm for objects and obstacles detection. Int. J. Image Graph. **10**(04), 531–544 (2010)
9. Felzenszwalb, P.F., Girshick, R.B., McAllester, D.: Cascade object detection with deformable part models. In: 2010 IEEE Conference on Computer Vision and Pattern Recognition (CVPR), pp. 2241–2248. IEEE (2010)
10. Fok, D., Polgar, J.M., Shaw, L., Jutai, J.W.: Low vision assistive technology device usage and importance in daily occupations. Work **39**(1), 37–48 (2011)
11. Gratal, X., Romero, J., Bohg, J., Kragic, D.: Visual servoing on unknown objects. Mechatronics **22**(4), 423–435 (2012)
12. He, K., Zhang, X., Ren, S., Sun, J.: Deep residual learning for image recognition. arXiv preprint arXiv:1512.03385 (2015)
13. Hub, A., Hartter, T., Ertl, T.: Interactive tracking of movable objects for the blind on the basis of environment models and perception-oriented object recognition methods. In: Proceedings of the 8th International ACM SIGACCESS Conference on Computers and Accessibility, pp. 111–118. ACM (2006)
14. Jiang, X., Mojon, D.: Adaptive local thresholding by verification-based multi-threshold probing with application to vessel detection in retinal images. IEEE Trans. Pattern Anal. Mach. Intell. **25**(1), 131–137 (2003)
15. Ke, Y., Sukthankar, R.: Pca-sift: a more distinctive representation for local image descriptors. In: Proceedings of the 2004 IEEE Computer Society Conference on Computer Vision and Pattern Recognition, CVPR 2004, vol. 2, p. II-506. IEEE (2004)

16. Kulykukin, V., Gharpure, C., DeGraw, N.: Human-robot interaction in a robotic guide for the visually impaired. In: AAAI Spring Symposium, pp. 158–164 (2004)
17. Kulyukin, V., Gharpure, C., Nicholson, J.: Robocart: toward robot-assisted navigation of grocery stores by the visually impaired. In: 2005 IEEE/RSJ International Conference on Intelligent Robots and Systems, pp. 2845–2850. IEEE (2005)
18. Merler, M., Galleguillos, C., Belongie, S.: Recognizing groceries in situ using in vitro training data. In: 2007 IEEE Conference on Computer Vision and Pattern Recognition, pp. 1–8. IEEE (2007)
19. Na'aman, E., Shashua, A., Wexler, Y.: User wearable visual assistance system, 23 August 2012, uS Patent Ap. 13/397,919
20. Nanayakkara, S., Shilkrot, R., Maes, P.: Eyering: a finger-worn assistant. In: CHI 2012 Extended Abstracts on Human Factors in Computing Systems, pp. 1961–1966. ACM (2012)
21. Nicholson, J., Kulyukin, V., Coster, D.: Shoptalk: independent blind shopping through verbal route directions and barcode scans. Open Rehabil. J. **2**(1), 11–23 (2009)
22. O'Gorman, L.: Binarization and multithresholding of document images using connectivity. CVGIP. Graph. Models Image Process. **56**(6), 494–506 (1994)
23. Passini, R., Proulx, G.: Wayfinding without vision an experiment with congenitally totally blind people. Environ. Beh. **20**(2), 227–252 (1988)
24. Phillips, B., Zhao, H.: Predictors of assistive technology abandonment. Assistive Technol. **5**(1), 36–45 (1993)
25. Russakovsky, O., Deng, J., Su, H., Krause, J., Satheesh, S., Ma, S., Huang, Z., Karpathy, A., Khosla, A., Bernstein, M., et al.: Imagenet large scale visual recognition challenge. Int. J. Comput. Vis. **115**(3), 211–252 (2015)
26. Scientist 47: Homography-transl. In: Wikimedia.org (2008)
27. Striem-Amit, E., Guendelman, M., Amedi, A.: 'Visual' acuity of the congenitally blind using visual-to-auditory sensory substitution. PloS One **7**(3), e33136 (2012)
28. Szegedy, C., Liu, W., Jia, Y., Sermanet, P., Reed, S., Anguelov, D., Erhan, D., Vanhoucke, V., Rabinovich, A.: Going deeper with convolutions. In: Proceedings of the IEEE Conference on Computer Vision and Pattern Recognition, pp. 1–9 (2015)
29. Thakoor, K.A., Marat, S., Nasiatka, P.J., McIntosh, B.P., Sahin, F.E., Tanguay, A.R., Weiland, J.D., Itti, L.: Attention biased speeded up robust features (ab-surf): a neurally-inspired object recognition algorithm for a wearable aid for the visually-impaired. In: 2013 IEEE International Conference on Multimedia and Expo Workshops (ICMEW), pp. 1–6. IEEE (2013)
30. Ude, A., Gaskett, C., Cheng, G.: Foveated vision systems with two cameras per eye. In: Proceedings 2006 IEEE International Conference on Robotics and Automation, ICRA 2006, pp. 3457–3462. IEEE (2006)
31. Ultracane: Ultracane: Putting the world at your fingertips (2016). http://www.ultracane.com/about_the_ultracane
32. WHO: World health organization fact sheet. WHO N°282 (2014)
33. Zhao, X., Ong, S.: Adaptive local thresholding with fuzzy-validity-guided spatial partitioning. In: Proceedings of the Fourteenth International Conference on Pattern Recognition, vol. 2, pp. 988–990. IEEE (1998)

Using Computer Vision to See

Bogdan Mocanu[1,2], Ruxandra Tapu[1,2(✉)], and Titus Zaharia[2]

[1] Telecommunication Department, Faculty of ETTI,
University "Politehnica" of Bucharest, Bucharest, Romania
[2] ARTEMIS Department, Institut Mines-Telecom/Telecom SudParis,
UMR CNRS MAP5 8145, Evry, France
{bogdan.mocanu,ruxandra.tapu,titus.zaharia}@telecom-sudparis.eu

Abstract. In this paper we propose a navigation assistant for visually impaired people, which uses computer vision techniques and is integrated on a wearable device. The system makes it possible to detect and recognize, in real-time, both static and dynamic objects existent in outdoor urban scenes without any a priori knowledge about the obstruction type or location. The detection system is based on relevant interest point extraction and tracking, background/camera motion estimation and foreground object identification through motion vectors clustering. The classification method receives as input image patches extracted by the detection module, performs global image representation using binary VLAD and prediction based on SVM. The feedback of our system is transmitted to visually impaired users through bone-conduction headphones as a set of audio warning messages. The entire system is fully integrated on a regular smartphone. The experimental evaluation performed on a set of 20 videos acquired with the help of VI users, demonstrates the pertinence of the proposed methodology.

Keywords: Assistive wearable device · Obstacle localization and recognition · Acoustic feedback · Visually impaired users

1 Introduction

For people suffering of visual impairment, common daily activities such as the autonomous navigation to a desired destination, familiar face recognition or independent buying of specific products can represent an important challenge. The safety displacement in outdoor scenario is very difficult because of VI people reduced capacity to understand and perceive the environment, the continuous change of the scene [1] or possible collision with moving objects (e.g. pedestrians, cars, bicycles or animals) or static obstructions (e.g. traffic signs, waste containers, fences, trees, etc.). If for a common setting the position of static hazards can be learned, the location estimation of dynamic obstacles is particularly difficult.

In an unknown setting most VI users relay on assistive devices such as the white canes or guiding dogs to acquire additional information about the potential obstructions. The white cane is effective in detecting objects situated directly in

© Springer International Publishing Switzerland 2016
G. Hua and H. Jégou (Eds.): ECCV 2016 Workshops, Part II, LNCS 9914, pp. 375–390, 2016.
DOI: 10.1007/978-3-319-48881-3_26

front of the person and it requires an actual physical contact with obstruction. However, even though the white cane is largely accessible to anyone, it shows quickly its limitations when confronted with real life situations (i.e. it cannot identify further away or overhanging objects, it cannot offer additional information about the type of obstruction and its degree of danger)[2]. Even though the trained dogs help reducing some of the above shortcoming they are highly expensive, have reduce operational time and require an extensive training phase.

In this context, the present paper introduces a complete navigation assistance system that facilitates the safe displacement of visually impaired (VI) people in urban areas. The proposed solution aims at improving the life quality of VI users by increasing their mobility and willingness to travel. At the hardware level our solution is based on a regular smartphone device, bone conduction headphones and chest mounted harness. The core of our framework is represented by the smartphone used both as an acquisition system (i.e. the video camera and the gyroscope sensor) and as a processing unit. The proposed technology is low-cost because it does not require any dedicated hardware architecture but regular components accessible on the market. The modules are lightweight making the systems wearable and portable, satisfying the hands-free and ears-free requirements imposed by VI users. At the software level the major contribution of the paper is the introduction of a method, based on computer vision and machine learning techniques that works in real time, returning warning messages fast enough so that the user could walk normally. The algorithms were carefully designed and optimized in order to work efficiently on a low processing unit.

The rest of the paper is structured as follows. In Sect. 2 we review the state of the art in the domain of assistive technologies. The focus is put on wearable devices that use computer vision techniques. In Sect. 3 we describe in details the proposed obstacles recognition methodology (Sect. 3.1. obstacle detection and Sect. 3.2. object classification). Section 4 presents the experimental evaluation of the proposed framework. For testing we used actual VI users in real life situations with: various moving objects, irregular camera displacement, abrupt changes in the illumination conditions. In Sect. 5 we conclude our work and open some perspectives of future work.

2   Related Work

In the last couple of years various navigation assistance systems were introduced, designed to create a digital enhancement to the white cane. In this chapter we briefly describe and analyze the technical literature focusing on the main strengths and limitation of each framework.

One of the first methods introduced in the state of the art [3] offers obstacle detection and guided navigation functionalities by using commercial available hardware components. The system is difficult to carry, is invasive and cannot identify overhead obstacles. In [4], in order to differentiate between foreground and background obstructions a fuzzy neural network is employed. In [5], a CCD camera system that transforms the information from an obstacle detection module to a voice message system is proposed. An indoor and outdoor navigation assistant called SmartVision is proposed in [6]. The system is highly depended on the quality of the GPS (Global Positioning System) signal acquired and on the initial position estimation.

In [7], the authors propose to mount the video camera on the VI user waist. The method is highly sensitive on the camera position and has never been tested on real life scenarios. Recently, with the development of the smartphone industry various authors proposed transforming the assistant into an Android application. In [8], the indoor obstacles, situated at arbitrary heights, are identified with high confidence scores. However, the system violates the hand-free conditions imposed by the VI user [9] and is not able to differentiate between obstacles. The authors of [10] introduce a novel obstacle recognition method that performs both detection and classification.

In [11], a navigation assistant based on depth map estimation is proposed. The system is designed to detect obstacles situated at arbitrary levels of heights. A wearable device that facilitates the safe indoor displacement is presented in [12]. The information about possible obstructions is stored as a metric map that is very difficult to exploit by VI users. In order to develop an object detection and localization method, the authors in [13] use 3D object reconstruction, while in [14], an overhead obstacle detection system is introduced based on 3D map and motion estimation using 6DOF. Recently, in [15], an indoor and outdoor navigation system has been proposed based on conditional random fields and depth maps.

The KinDetect system introduced in [16] is designed as an obstacle detection method that combines information coming from Kinect and depth sensors. A different method able to recognize various types of obstacles using a Kinect sensor is proposed in [17]. In [18], nearby structure information is converted into acoustic maps. Both systems [17] and [18] can perform the detection and recognition in real-time by using a powerful backpack processing unit. Recently in [19] an object detection and tracking together with a 3D map construction is introduced, while the authors in [20] develop a 3D face recognition method designed to help VI users identify familiar faces.

After analyzing the state of the art we can conclude that every method has its own advantages and limitations over the others, but no one can offer, in a satisfactory degree, all necessary features for the autonomous navigation of VI users in an unknown setting. Under this perspective, the proposed solution is designed not to replace the cane but to complete it with additional functionalities (e.g. guidance information, obstacle recognition capabilities and object degree of danger estimation).

The main contributions of the present paper concern: (1) an obstacle detection system based on relevant interest points extraction and tracking, camera motion estimation using multiple homographies per frame. By analyzing the motion information we estimate the location of various objects and their degree of danger relative to the VI user. (2) an obstacle recognition method using relevant interest points, global image representation using VLAD and SVM classification using one versus all strategy. (3) an acoustic feedback system that uses bone conduction headphones and stereo principles.

All the methods were designed and tuned to achieve real-time capabilities on light processing units as smartphone devices.

3 Proposed Approach

The autonomous navigation in outdoor environments can be facilitated by a system able to recognize obstructions (i.e. static and dynamic) and transmit alert messages. Our framework is designed to detect and semantically understand, in real time, potential dangerous situation and to warn VI users about various obstructions encountered along the walking path.

3.1 Obstacle Detection and Localization

Relevant Interest Point Extraction. The method starts by extracting interest points using the pyramidal FAST algorithm [21]. We have empirically observed that regular FAST method returns a high number of interest points even for low resolution images/videos. Moreover, the descriptor is focused on highly textured regions situated in most of the cases in the background while for foreground objects little or no information is extracted. Because our application is designed to work in real-time on a low processing device we decided to privilege a semi-dense sampling approach that reduces the total number of interest points. We overlap a regular grid over the first frame and we determine for each cell the associated interest points. Then, we propose to retain for each cell only one point, the most relevant, i.e. the one with the highest value of the Harris-Laplacian operator [22]. Different from other filtering strategies [23] that retain the best top-k points based on their magnitude value without considering any information about the spatial location our method insures that the points are better distributed within the image. Our strategy is able to capture more informational content of the image, while avoiding accumulation of points in certain textured areas. Figure 1 illustrates three different extraction strategies: Fig. 1a presents the interest points retained using the traditional FAST method; Fig. 1b shows the set of points obtained after applying the method introduced in [23], while Fig. 1c presents the results obtained with the above-described strategy. Let us underline that the examples illustrated in Fig. 1b and c contain the same number of interest points.

The performance of the approach and also the computational burden is controlled by the grid size defined as: $G_{size} = (W * H)/N_{points}$, where W and H are the width and height of the image, N_{points} is the maximum number of interest points we retain (e.g. for a video stream with the resolution of 320×240 pixels we fixed N_{points} to 1000 points).

Interest Point Tracking. The selected interest points are tracked between successive frames using the multiscale Lucas-Kanade (LK) algorithm [24]. Even though the LK tracking method proves to be sensitive to light variation and is inconsistent in estimating the motion vectors, we adopted LK algorithm

a.   b.   c.

Fig. 1. Relevant interest point extraction using: (a) the traditional FAST method; (b) the strategy introduced in [23]; (c) our method based on regular grid filtering

because it offers the best compromise between the quality of the motion flow and the processing time. The LK method is initialized with the set of interest points extracted using the regular grid strategy. Then, the points are tracked within the video stream. However, for low textured zones within the image or for regions depicting objects disappearing or that reenter the scene, it is necessary to reinitialize the tracker. In such specific areas we locally apply as input to the LK algorithm the relevant set of points obtained (*cf.* grid strategy described in Sect. 3.1). If we denote one interest point within the reference image as: $p_{1m}(x_{1m}, y_{1m})$ then the correspondent one in the successive image, established using the tracking algorithm is denoted by $p_{2m}(x_{2m}, y_{2m})$. The associated motion vector $v_m(v_{mx}, v_{my})$ magnitude and orientation can be determined as:

$$D_{12} = \sqrt{v_{mx}^2, v_{my}^2} \quad ; \quad \theta_{12} = arctg\frac{v_{my}}{v_{mx}} + k\pi \tag{1}$$

Camera Motion Estimation. For the global motion model we have adopted the RANSAC algorithm [25] that estimates the optimal homographic matrix (H) between successive frames. For any point expressed in homogenous coordinates $p_{1m}(x_{1m}, y_{1m}, 1)^T$ we can determine its novel position ($p_{2m}^{est}(x_{2m}, y_{2m}, 1)^T$) in the adjacent frame by multiplying p_{1m} with H. Then, we can determine the prediction error (Er) by computing the Euclidian distance ($L_2norm\| \cdot \|$) between the current point position (establish using the tracking algorithm) and its predicted location:

$$E_r(p_{2m}) = \|p_{2m}^{est} - p_{2m}\| \tag{2}$$

In the ideal case the prediction error is equal to zero. However, for real-life application we need to compare Er to a pre-established threshold (Th_1) in order to determine the set of inliers/outlier. The interest points belonging to the inliers class satisfy the transformation and belong to camera or background motion. The outlier class contains all other types of motion present in the scene.

Foreground Object Detection. We focus next in identifying different classes of motion existent in the scene. Due to the foreground apparent motion even static object (situated in the foreground) act like moving objects relatively to the global background displacement. A clustering analysis is performed on the outlier set of interest points, by taking into account both the motion vector magnitude and orientation. However, a direct clustering within the polar coordinates domain is not feasible. Typically, the motion vectors angle have a circular range between 0 and 2π, so a clustering algorithm based on the L_2 distance, such as k-means, which assume that the input data is distributed in the Cartesian space is inappropriate (since 0 and 2π should be interpreted as equivalent values). We propose performing a non-linear transformation from the polar coordinates to the 2D Cartesian domain using the following trigonometric relations:

$$v^*_{mx} = r \times \cos\theta_{12} \quad ; \quad v^*_{my} = r \times \sin\theta_{12} \tag{3}$$

where r represents the radial coordinate, that incorporates the magnitude information. The value of r is computed as: $r = 1 + D_{12}/D_{Max}$, with D_{Max} the maximum displacement of a motion vector. In this way we impose all points to lay on an annulus with the two radiuses equal to 1 and 2, respectively. Moreover, diametrically opposite points will not be cluster together. In Fig. 2 we give a graphical representation of the interest points distribution in the Cartesian domain by using motion vectors magnitude and orientations.

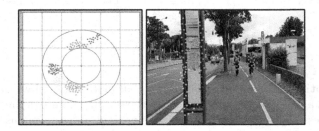

Fig. 2. Relevant interest point annular representation using motion vectors magnitude and orientations

The motion classes are determined after applying the k-means clustering algorithm [26], within the considered representation space:

$$\arg min_{\{\alpha_1,...,\alpha_k\}} = \sum_{i=1}^{k} \sum_{v^*_m \in \Xi} \|v^*_m - \alpha_i\|^2 \tag{4}$$

where v^*_m is the novel motion vector $v^*_m(v^*_{mx}, v^*_{my})$ associated to an interest point, α_i is the cluster centroid by averaging all interest points included in a class Ξ, k is the total number of clusters in k-means. The value of k is set to 5 in our experiments. Finally, we verify the clusters consistency by analyzing the interest

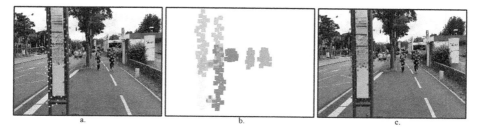

Fig. 3. Motion classes estimation: (a) the interest points clustered using k-means; (b) binary masks associated to each cluster; (c) clusters grouping/division based on spatial principles

points spatial variance within the image. It can be observed that various moving objects existent in the scene can be characterized by the same motion patterns (Fig. 3a). In order to distinguish between dynamic objects with similar motion features (*e.g.* two vehicles approaching or two pedestrians walking in the same direction) we propose to verify the spatial distribution of points within a group. For each cluster we construct a binary mask using the interest points location and its associated region (p_{area}) defined as twice the area of the grid cell used for relevant interest point extraction (Fig. 3b). Clusters satisfying the spatial consistency will contain only interest points that define connected image areas. However, if a cluster forms multiple independent regions it is divided into small classes one for each independent area (Fig. 3c). On the contrary, if two clusters share in common more than 10 % of the total region areas the classes are merged together (Fig. 3c). Finally we assign to the background small clusters with less than ten interest points.

Object Degree of Danger Estimation. After objects are identified we need to determine their degree of danger relative to a VI and to classify them. We observed that not all detected obstacles represent a potential risk (*e.g.* far away objects). In this context, we propose defining two areas of proximity, both with a trapezoidal shape, in the near surrounding of a user: one situated on the walking path and the other on the head level (Fig. 4). An obstacle will be considered as having a high degree of danger if it's situated in one of the proximity areas, otherwise it will be marked as non-relevant for the navigation. The size of the proximity areas is depended on the smartphone angle of view (θ) and elevation (E).

If the smartphone has a field of view of 69°, is attached at an elevation of 1.3 m and the trapezium height is a third of the image height we can determine the distance from the user and the upper pixel of the trapezium as:

$$D_{object} = 3 \cdot \frac{E}{\tan(\frac{\theta}{2})} = 5.5\,\text{m} \tag{5}$$

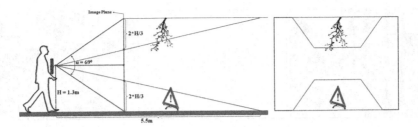

Fig. 4. Obstacles degree of danger estimation based on user proximity areas

The use of the proximity areas prevents our system to continuous launch warning messages for any type of object existent in the outdoor environment. However, the sizes of the trapeziums can be accidentally modified during navigation. In order to prevent accidental errors caused by the device position variation we use the accelerometer sensors existent on the smartphone to determine the device tilt angle. If the tilt angle varies between 60 and 90° the system is considered to function normally. After we established the object location and its degree of danger we need to capture its semantic nature that will helps differentiate between various obstructions situated in the user proximity area. It is important to transmit first an acoustic warning about a vehicle that is approaching VI people rather than an alarm about the presence of a static obstruction such as fence or a garbage can. So, we introduce next a classification framework that will help us better understand the scene and prioritize the set of warnings.

3.2 Obstacle Classification

In order to capture the semantic meaning of all objects existent in the scene, we start the classification framework by constructing offline a training dataset. The training database is divided in four major categories based on their relevance to a VI user as follows: vehicles, bicycles, pedestrians and static objects. In the static obstruction class we included a high variability of instances as: trees, bushes, fences, garbage cans, pylons, traffic signs and lights, mail boxes, stairs. We selected to use only four major categories because our major concern was to develop an efficient classification application that function in real time on a low processing unit. The entire training set is composed of 10000 images selected from the PASCAL repository [27]. We decided to have an equal number of images for each category in order not to advantage a class.

Relevant Interest Point Extraction. Every image patch extracted with the previously described obstacle detection method (Sect. 3.1) is resized so that includes a maximum number of 12 k pixels, while preserving the original aspect ratio. For every patch, we extract interest points using pyramidal FAST [21] algorithm that are further described with BRIEF descriptors [28]. The output of the BRIEF algorithm is a binary vector where each bit is obtained as the result of intensity test between two adjacent pixels. We could have selected a more powerful interest point descriptor as SIFT [29] or SURF [30], but they prove to be highly expensive in terms of computational time. The main advantage of BRIEF is given by the fact that the descriptor is very fast to compute and compare. Because, the descriptor is a binary vector, the Hamming distance can be here exploited, which is much faster to compute than Euclidian distances between SURF/SIFT descriptors.

Global Image Representation. In order to describe the informational content of an extracted image patch, we propose to develop a global image representation using the VLAD (*Vector of Locally Aggregated Descriptors*) approach [31]. We start with an offline process by constructing a visual codebook $C = \{c_1, c_2, \ldots, c_k\} \in \Re^{d \times k}$ using the training dataset and the k-means clustering method. We set k to 256 words. Then, for each detected obstacle we extract low level features $D_i = \{d_{i1}, d_{i2}, \ldots, d_{in}\} \in \Re^{d \times n}$ and we assign every local descriptor to its closest visual word from the vocabulary c_i. The residual r_i for a visual word is computed by accumulating all differences between the local descriptor $d \in D$ and the associated centroid (word in the vocabulary c_i):

$$r_i = \sum_{d \in D; d \cong c_i} d - c_i; \quad i \in 1, \ldots, k \qquad (6)$$

In order to reduce the influence of frequently occurring components, we applied the power low normalization on the residual vectors: $r'_{i,j} = r^{\alpha}_{i,j}$. Where $r_{i,j}$ represents the jth element of the residual vector associated to a codebook word c_i. In the experimental evaluation we observed that the optimal value for the α parameter is 0.8. Furthermore, because we want to balance the local descriptors contribution, we apply the residual normalization [32] as follows:

$$r''_i = \frac{r'_i}{\|r'_i\|}; \quad i \in 1, \ldots, k \qquad (7)$$

The image patch representation using VLAD is obtained as the direct concatenation of all residual vectors (r''_i): $v = [r''_1, r''_2, \ldots, r''_k]$. The dimension of a VLAD vector is $p \times k$, where k is the size of the vocabulary and p is the dimension of the binary descriptor. We set the size of BRIEF descriptor to 256. Finally, the vector v is normalized to unit length, which corresponds to:

$$\bar{v} = \frac{v}{\|v\|} = \frac{v}{\sqrt{k}} \qquad (8)$$

In order to further reduce the memory requirements we applied the PCA [33] transformation on VLAD vectors. The PCA alleviated the influence of correlated patterns between BRIEF binary components. Hence, we observed that the first 128 components include all the essential information about the feature descriptor, so we performed a dimensionality reduction over VLAD. Finally, the zero-centered vector is binarized to the final vector V by thresholding.

Image Classification. The image classification process can be divided into two parts: an offline process (*i.e.* SVM training) and an online process (*i.e.* SVM prediction). For the SVM training we used the proposed image dataset for which we aimed to determine the optimal decision function that finds a separation hyperplane, between two classes by maximizing the margin:

$$f(V) = \sum_{i=1}^{n} y_i \cdot \alpha_i \cdot \kappa(V, V_i) + b \tag{9}$$

where $\{(\alpha_i, y_i)\}_{i=1}^{n}$ is the training set with $y_i \in \{-1, +1\}$, b is the hyperplane free term, α_i is a parameter dependent on the kernel type, while $\kappa(\cdot, \cdot)$ is the selected kernel. In theory $\kappa(\cdot, \cdot)$ can be any reasonable Mercer function, but we observed from our experiments that the chi-square kernel is the most suitable when representing images based on global binary descriptors. The SVM training represents the final step of our offline process. In the online process, for each image patch extracted using the obstacle detection method introduced in Sect. 3.1 we start developing a global representation using the binary VLAD. Then the vector is applied as input to the SVM machine. If $f(V) > 0$ then the example is classified as positive, otherwise it passes to the next SVM machine corresponding to the following category. In order to speed up the decision process the entire online classification method is parallelized on multiple threads, depending on the total number of obstacles present in the analyzed scene.

3.3   Acoustic Feedback

The acoustic feedback improves VI user cognition over the surrounding environment by transmitting warning messages regarding different types of obstacles existent in the scene. In the case of the proposed framework and after discussion with two blind and visually impaired associations, we decided to use the bone conduction headphones technology that satisfies the ears-free constraint and is easy to wear. Moreover, the transmitted sound patterns are carefully designed in order to keep the system intuitive to users without any training phase. The sound patterns are selected not to interfere with other natural environmental sounds. The warning messages are encoded and transmitted in stereo based on the location of a detected obstacle: if the obstruction is situated on the left side of the user the alert message is transmitted on the left helmet and vice-versa for obstruction situated on the right side. For objects positioned on the walking path the VI user will receive the warning message in both helmets.

A final step is represented by the selection of relevant messages to be transmitted depending on the user current situation. In on outdoor navigation scenario, in real urban environments, more potential dangerous objects can be encountered in the near vicinity of a person. To keep the acoustic feedback intuitive and useful we propose to prioritize the warning messages depending on the object type and its distance from the current walking direction of user. The following set off alarms can be generated: "vehicle", "bicycle", "pedestrian" and "obstruction". In order not to confuse the user we decided to launch warning messages with a frequency rate inferior to two seconds, regardless of the scene dynamics.

4   Experimental Evaluation

4.1   Objective Evaluation

The evaluation of the proposed framework is performed on a database with 20 videos, filmed in real life outdoor environments, with the help of visually impaired people. Each video has an average duration of 10 min, is processed at a resolution of 320×240 pixels and include multiple obstructions either static or dynamic. In addition, because the acquisition process is performed using the video camera embedded on a regular smartphone, attached to the VI user with the help of a chest mounted harness all videos are characterized by various type of background/camera motion, include abrupt changes in the light intensity, are trembled or cluttered. Each frame of the video stream was annotated by a set of human observers. Once the ground truth dataset is available the performances of the detection and the classification modules can be globally estimated using two error parameter, denoted $M_{D/C}$ and $F_{D/C}$ representing the number of missed detected/classified obstacles and the number of false alarms (false detected/classified obstructions). Finally, $N_{D/C}$ represents the total number of dynamic/static objects correctly detected/classified by our module. In order to determine globally the performances of each module we used for evaluation the traditional metrics as precision (P), recall (R) and $F - score$ defined as:

$$R = \frac{N_{D/C}}{N_{D/C} + M_{D/C}}; P = \frac{N_{D/C}}{N_{D/C} + F_{D/C}}; F - score = \frac{2 \cdot P \cdot R}{R + P} \qquad (10)$$

Table 1 presents the experimental results obtained for the obstacle identification module. As it can be observed, the average $F - score$ for all types of obstacles is 85 %. Particularly better results are obtained for vehicles due to the distinctiveness of the motion vector magnitudes. In Table 2 we present the performance of the classification module in terms of precision, recall and $F - score$ when applying as input the image patches extracted by detection system. The experimental results validate our approach, with recognition scores superior to 82 % for every category. In particular, the lowest results are obtained for the Bicycles category because when we trained the SVM most of the bikes were static without any human hiding them. In our case the detection module, returns as input to the classification system a patch containing both the bikes and the human.

In Fig. 5 we give a graphical representation of the experimental results obtained by our obstacle detection and classification modules. In all cases, the video camera is characterized by an important variation caused by the subject displacement. We marked the detected objects with rectangles of different colors in order to differentiate between various elements existent in the scene. Our system is able to detect static hazards such as: road signs, pylons or bushes

Table 1. Experimental results of the obstacle localization module

	Ground truth	N_D	M_D	F_D	Recall	Precision	$F - score$
Vehicle	568	505	63	42	0.89	0.92	0.9
Pedestrians	448	381	67	58	0.85	0.86	0.85
Bicycles	210	175	35	24	0.83	0.87	0.85
Obstructions	402	344	58	41	0.85	0.89	0.87

Table 2. Experimental results of the obstacle classification module

	Ground truth	N_C	M_C	F_C	Recall	Precision	$F - score$
Vehicle	505	464	41	24	0.91	0.95	0.93
Pedestrians	381	351	30	27	0.92	0.92	0.92
Bicycles	175	144	31	8	0.82	0.94	0.88
Obstructions	344	308	36	22	0.89	0.93	0.91

based situated on head or foot level using only the camera apparent motion. However, the method will not identify all static obstacles existent in the scene, but just the one situated on the VI user walking path. This behavior does not penalize the performance of the application since users are not interest in any type of obstruction present in an outdoor scenario, but only about objects that could affect the safety navigation. Regarding the dynamic obstacles, they can be identified at larger distances from the subject (superior to ten meters) due to the more important magnitude of the associated motion vectors. The method is able to correctly classify pedestrians, bikes or vehicles with high $F - score$ rates. However, in the case of pedestrians, which are non-rigid objects, characterized by various types of motions, in some situations the object is divided into multiple unconnected parts (Fig. 5). In this case, the classification method will receive as input only parts of the subject and may return incorrect results. In terms of the computational time, when implementing the entire framework on a regular smartphone device (Samsung S7) running Android as an operating system we obtain an average processing speed of 100 ms per image for both the obstacle detection and classification modules. In this context the processing speed is around 10 fps.

4.2   Subjective Evaluation

In the following part of the experimental evaluation we were focused on determining the VI users' degree of satisfaction after using the proposed system prototype. The main objective of the testing phase was to determine if the users can: start the application, walk safe in an outdoor environment, avoid collision and acquire sufficient additional knowledge over the environment. The participant was asked to complete a pre-established route in two scenarios: the first

Fig. 5. Experimental results of the combined framework: obstacle detection and classification (Color figure online)

one assumes navigating using only the white cane and the second when combining the white cane with our system as an assistive device. After the task was finished, an observer conducted an interview and each participant was asked a set of questions about their impressions over the device.

The following conclusions can be highlighted: (1) some users, because of their resilience and mistrust of new technologies felt insecure to use electronic assistive devices. In their opinion it is important to develop a system designed not to replace the cane, but to complement it with additional functionalities. (2) The users considered the system very useful and easy to worn and understand, but an initial training phase is required in order to understand all functionalities. However, VI users already manipulating smartphone devices expressed strong interest on this type of application. (3) The acoustic feedback is transmitted fast enough in order to avoid dangerous situations. The VI considered that bone-conduction headphone is appropriate to wear because it does not impede the ambient sound cues.

5   Conclusions and Perspectives

In this paper we introduced a blind and visually impaired navigational assistant, designed to detect and recognize both static and dynamic obstacles encountered by visually impaired users during outdoor navigation. In contrast to prior state of the art methods, our technique does not require any information about the obstacle type and position and was designed to achieve real-time capabilities on a smartphone device. The output of the recognition module is transformed into set of warning messages transmitted to the VI users through acoustic feedback.

The evaluation of our framework was performed on a video corpus, with 20 elements, acquired with the help of VI users and depicting urban outdoor environments. The system proves to be robust to important camera/background motion or to changes in the illumination. The video stream is processed with an average speed of 10 fps (on a Samsung S7 device), while the warning messages are transmitted fast enough so that user walks normally. In addition, we introduced a subjective evaluation over the system by presenting the VI people degree of satisfaction and comments after using our prototype.

For further work and implementation we proposed integrating in our framework additional functionalities, such as: guided navigation, face recognition capabilities and a shopping assistance in supermarkets. Moreover, with the development of the smartphone industry, the 3D video cameras will be available shortly on commercial devices (e.g. Lenovo Phab 2 Pro). In this context we envisage better estimating the distances between obstacles and VI people by using depth information.

Acknowledgement. This work was supported by a grant of the Romanian National Authority for Scientific Research and Innovation, CNCS - UEFISCDI, project number: PN-II-RU-TE-2014-4-0202.

References

1. Blasch, B.B., Wiener, W.R., Welsh, R.L.: Foundations of Orientation and Mobility, 2nd edn. American Foundation for the Blind, New York (1997)
2. Golledge, R.G., Marston, J.R., Costanzo, C.M.: Attitudes of visually impaired persons towards the use of public transportation. J. Vis. Impairment Blindness **90**, 446–459 (1997)
3. Johnson, L.A., Higgins, C.M.: A navigation aid for the blind using tactile-visual sensory substitution. In: 28th Annual International Conference of the IEEE Engineering in Medicine and Biology Society, pp. 6289–6292 (2006)
4. Sainarayanan, G., Nagarajan, R., Yaacob, S.: Fuzzy image processing scheme for autonomous navigation of human blind. Appl. Soft Comput. **7**(1), 257–264 (2007)
5. Yu, J., Chung, H.I., Hahn, H.: Walking assistance system for sight impaired people based on a multimodal information transformation technique. In: ICCAS-SICE, pp. 1639–1643 (2009)
6. José, J., Farrajota, M., Rodrigues, J., Buf, J.D.: The smart vision local navigation aid for blind and visually impaired persons. Int. J. Digital Content Technol. Appl. **5**, 362–375 (2011)
7. Lin, Q., Hahn, H., Han, Y.: Top-view based guidance for blind people using directional ellipse model. Int. J. Adv. Robot. Syst. **1**, 1–10 (2013)
8. Peng, E., Peursum, P., Li, L., Venkatesh, S.: A smartphone-based obstacle sensor for the visually impaired. In: Yu, Z., Liscano, R., Chen, G., Zhang, D., Zhou, X. (eds.) UIC 2010. LNCS, vol. 6406, pp. 590–604. Springer, Heidelberg (2010)
9. Manduchi, R.: Mobile vision as assistive technology for the blind: an experimental study. In: Miesenberger, K., Karshmer, A., Penaz, P., Zagler, W. (eds.) ICCHP 2012, Part II. LNCS, vol. 7383, pp. 9–16. Springer, Heidelberg (2012)

10. Tapu, R., Mocanu, B., Bursuc, A., Zaharia, T.: A smartphone-based obstacle detection and classification system for assisting visually impaired people. In: IEEE International Conference on Computer Vision Workshops (ICCVW), pp. 444–451 (2013)
11. Dakopoulos, D., Bourbakis, N.: Preserving visual information in low resolution images during navigation of visually impaired. In: Proceedings of the 1st International Conference on PErvasive Technologies Related to Assistive Environments, pp. 1–27 (2008)
12. Saez, J.M., Escolano, F., Penalver, A.: First steps towards stereo-based 6DoF SLAM for the visually impaired. In: IEEE Computer Society Conference on Computer Vision and Pattern Recognition (CVPR), p. 23 (2005)
13. Pradeep, V., Medioni, G., Weiland, J.: Robot vision for the visually impaired. In: IEEE Computer Society Conference on Computer Vision and Pattern Recognition, pp. 15–22 (2010)
14. Saez, J.M., Escolano, F.: Stereo-based aerial obstacle detection for the visually impaired. In: Workshop on Computer Vision Applications for the Visually Impaired (2008)
15. Schauerte, B., Koester, D., Martinez, M., Stiefelhagen, R.: Way to go! detecting open areas ahead of a walking person. In: Agapito, L., Bronstein, M.M., Rother, C. (eds.) ECCV 2014 Workshops. LNCS, vol. 8927, pp. 349–360. Springer, Heidelberg (2015)
16. Khan, A., Moideen, F., Lopez, J., Khoo, W.L., Zhu, Z.: KinDectect: kinect detecting objects. In: Miesenberger, K., Karshmer, A., Penaz, P., Zagler, W. (eds.) ICCHP 2012. LNCS, vol. 7383, pp. 588–595. Springer, Heidelberg (2012). doi:10. 1007/978-3-642-31534-3_86
17. Takizawa, H., Yamaguchi, S., Aoyagi, M., Ezaki, N., Mizuno, S.: Kinect cane: an assistive system for the visually impaired based on three-dimensional object recognition. In: IEEE/SICE International Symposium on System Integration (SII), pp. 740–745 (2012)
18. Brock, M., Kristensson, P.: Supporting blind navigation using depth sensing and sonification. In: Proceedings of the ACM Conference on Pervasive and Ubiquitous Computing Adjunct Publication, pp. 255–258 (2013)
19. Panteleris, P., Argyros, A.A.: Vision-based SLAM and moving objects tracking for the perceptual support of a smart walker platform. In: Agapito, L., Bronstein, M.M., Rother, C. (eds.) ECCV 2014. LNCS, vol. 8927, pp. 407–423. Springer, Heidelberg (2015). doi:10.1007/978-3-319-16199-0_29
20. Li, W., Li, X., Goldberg, M., Zhu, Z.: Face recognition by 3D registration for the visually impaired using a RGB-D sensor. In: Agapito, L., Bronstein, M.M., Rother, C. (eds.) ECCV 2014. LNCS, vol. 8927, pp. 763–777. Springer, Heidelberg (2015). doi:10.1007/978-3-319-16199-0_53
21. Tuzel, O., Porikli, F., Meer, P.: Region covariance: a fast descriptor for detection and classification. In: Leonardis, A., Bischof, H., Pinz, A. (eds.) ECCV 2006. LNCS, vol. 3952, pp. 589–600. Springer, Heidelberg (2006)
22. Harris, C., Stephens, M.: A combined corner and edge detector. In: Proceedings of Fourth Alvey Vision Conference, pp. 147–151 (1988)
23. Mikolajczyk, K., Schmid, C.: Scale and affine invariant interest point detectors. Int. J. Comput. Vis. 60, 63–86 (2004). Ubiquitous Intelligence and Computing SE - 45
24. Lucas, B., Kanade, T.: An iterative image registration technique with an application to stereo vision. In: Proceedings of the 7th International Joint Conference on Artificial Intelligence, vol. 2, pp. 674–679 (1981)

25. Lee, J., Kim, G.: Robust estimation of camera homography using fuzzy RANSAC. In: Gervasi, O., Gavrilova, M.L. (eds.) ICCSA 2007. LNCS, vol. 4705, pp. 992–1002. Springer, Heidelberg (2007). doi:10.1007/978-3-540-74472-6_81

26. Hamerly, G., Elkan, C.: Learning the k in k-means. In: Neural Information Processing Systems (2003)

27. Everingham, M., Gool, L., Williams, C.K., Winn, J., Zisserman, A.: The pascal visual object classes (voc) challenge. Int. J. Comput. Vis. **88**, 303–338 (2010)

28. Calonder, M., Lepetit, V., Strecha, C., Fua, P.: BRIEF: binary robust independent elementary features. In: Daniilidis, K., Maragos, P., Paragios, N. (eds.) ECCV 2010, Part IV. LNCS, vol. 6314, pp. 778–792. Springer, Heidelberg (2010)

29. Lowe, D.: Distinctive image features from scale-invariant keypoints. Int. J. Comput. Vis. **60**, 91–110 (2004)

30. Bay, H., Ess, A., Tuytelaars, T., Gool, L.V.: Speeded-up robust features (SURF). Comput. Vis. Image Underst. **110**(3), 346–359 (2008)

31. Jegou, H., Douze, M., Schmid, C.: Product quantization for nearest neighbor search. IEEE Trans. Pattern Anal. Mach. Intell. **33**(1), 117–128 (2011)

32. Delhumeau, J., Gosselin, P.H., Jegou, H., Perez, P.: Revisiting the VLAD image representation. In: Proceedings of the 21st ACM International Conference on Multimedia, pp. 653–656 (2013)

33. Zou, H., Hastie, T., Tibshirani, R.: Sparse principal component analysis. J. Comput. Graph. Stat. **15**(2), 265–286 (2006)

Brazilian Sign Language Recognition Using Kinect

José Elías Yauri Vidalón and José Mario De Martino[✉]

School of Electrical and Computer Engineering,
University of Campinas, Campinas, SP, Brazil
{elias,martino}@dca.fee.unicamp.br

Abstract. The simultaneous-sequential nature of sign language production, which employs hand gestures and body motions combined with facial expressions, still challenges sign language recognition algorithms. This paper presents a method to recognize Brazilian Sign Language (Libras) using Kinect. Skeleton information is used to segment sign gestures from a continuous stream, while depth information is used to provide distinctive features. The method was assessed in a new data-set of 107 medical signs selected from common dialogues in health-care centers. The dynamic time warping–nearest neighbor (DTW-kNN) classifier using the leave-one-out cross-validation strategy reported outstanding results.

Keywords: Sign language · Isolated sign language recognition · Brazilian Sign Language · Libras · Dynamic time warping · k–Nearest Neighbor

1 Introduction

In daily life, deaf and hearing impaired people use sign language as a communication system [1]. Sign language combines hand gestures, body postures, and facial expressions to convey meaning. The richness of sign language lexicon allows, as any other language, the expression of concepts, ideas, feelings, mood, or thoughts. Contrary to popular belief, sign language is not a universal language. There are many different sign languages around the world, for instance, the American Sign Language (ASL) in United States, British Sign Language (BSL) in England, Brazilian Sign Language (Libras) in Brazil. Furthermore, different countries that have the same spoken language may have their own sign language, e.g., although United States and England share the English as common oral language, ASL differs from BSL.

Despite sign language capabilities to communicate messages, there is a strong barrier between deaf and hearing people. This language barrier arises because deaf people usually do not master spoken and written language and only few hearing people can communicate using sign language. Aiming to reduce this language barrier, research efforts have been conducted in sign language recognition (SLR) [2–4]. Automatic SLR systems translate sign language into text and

© Springer International Publishing Switzerland 2016
G. Hua and H. Jégou (Eds.): ECCV 2016 Workshops, Part II, LNCS 9914, pp. 391–402, 2016.
DOI: 10.1007/978-3-319-48881-3_27

can improve the interaction between deaf and hearing people. Critical situations where the communication is decisive, such as the access to emergency health services, may greatly benefit from automatic sign language technologies.

Currently, powered by new sensing technologies, new promising SLR approaches are being developed. The advent of depth cameras [5], also known as RGB-D cameras, has been an important milestone in the computer vision community because they can provide multimodal data, such as RGB or color images, depth range images, body skeleton, and user silhouettes, that can help to overcome the traditional restrictions of illumination changes and cluttered background of SLR systems based on traditional imaging systems.

Despite great progress in the last years, the building of robust and reliable SLR systems is still in its infancy. The high variability both in appearance and motion of signs, the signer dependence, the size of the vocabulary, the signing environment and imaging conditions still challenge any SLR algorithms.

This paper presents a method to recognize isolated signs of the Brazilian Sign Language (Libras) using Microsoft Kinect. First, motion analysis of the body skeleton allows for both segmenting signs from a continuous stream and categorizing them as either one-handed or two-handed. Next, the histogram of direction cosines (HDC) [6] are computed from the depth images of the segmented sign. To evaluate performance of the solution, a data-set of 107 medical signs were recorded. Our approach, based on dynamic time warping nearest neighbor classification strategy, reached an accuracy over 98.69% on the data-set.

The remainder of this paper is organized as follows. Section 2 presents the related work in SRL. Section 3 explains the proposed method. Section 4 details the experimental results. Finally, Sect. 5 exposes conclusions and future work.

2   Sign Language Recognition

Sign language is a visual-spatial language that uses hands, body, head, and facial expressions to convey meaning [1,7]. In sign language, the meaningful unit is the sign. To be analyzed, a sign can be decomposed into manual and non-manual parameters. The manual parameters relate to the shape, location, movement, and orientation of the hands, while the facial expressions and body postures are the non-manual parameters. The manual component of the signs usually carries the most of the meaning, however the presence of non-manual components may change or modulate the meaning.

Automatic sign language recognition (SLR) aims to recognize and translate sign language into text [2]. To face the challenge, SLR methods focus either on recognizing isolated signs or recognizing continuous sentences. Methods for isolated sign recognition usually assume that the boundaries of signs are easy to estimate, so they are most focused on the recognition task. On the other hand, because the boundaries of signs in sentences are unclear, methods for continuous sign recognition are more complex because they have to estimate the start and end frames of signs before performing recognition tasks. Although isolated sign recognition is more simpler than the continuous case, it provides an important learning stage before going to develop continuous sign recognizers.

According to the sensor being used for capturing sign language, SLR methods can be categorized into wearable sensor based or vision based. Wearable sensors combine data-gloves and body markers to track the hands and the body motion. On the other hand, vision based methods use cameras that mimic the human vision for imaging the scene. Although color cameras allow approaches to detect and track the hands, body, and facial characteristics, they are sensible to changes in illumination and background conditions. The advent of depth sensors offers new forms of deal with images [5]. Geometric information contained in depth images has become an essential tool to improve approaches only based on color images, as well as a new source for new discriminative features [8].

Recent SLR methods seek to take advantage of the multimodal data provided by depth sensors. Usually, color and depth images are used to extract shape features of the hands, body, and facial expressions, while skeletons are used to provide motion features of body parts. To perform recognition, machine learning approaches are mostly used [9]. In this context, signs can be modeled either as time-series or as a single feature vector that assumes that all signs have the same length. Dynamic time warping (DTW), hidden Markov models (HMM), and lately conditional random field (CRF) algorithms are suitable for the former, while support vector machine (SVM), random forest (RF), neural network (NN), and deep learning methods are applicable for the latter.

In the following paragraphs, we highlight some recent proposed approaches that use the Kinect depth sensor for SRL. Nonetheless, a extensive thorough review of SLR methods can be found in [2–4].

Escobedo-Cardenas and Camara-Chavez [10] used SIFT features extracted from intensity and depth images in a bag-of-words combined with the upper body skeleton positions to recognize 20 signs of the Italian Sign Language (ISL). They assumed that all signs have N key-frames (N = 10) for removing their temporal variation. Performance evaluation reported 88.39 % of average recognition using SVM classifier.

Pigou et al. [11] presented a method for feature learning based on 2D convolutional neural network (CNN). The CNN processes N key-frames (N=32) from both intensity and depth images for feature extraction. Performance evaluation in 20 sign of ISL achieved 95.68 % of average recognition using ANN classifier.

Conly et al. [12] proposed a method to retrieve the most similar signs to a given one. Based on the movement trajectories of the hands, DTW computes similarities between signs and returns a list of the top-k most close signs. Performance evaluation in a data-set of 1113 ASL signs shows that in 62.00 % of cases the sign being queried is found in the top 20 list.

Hanjie et al. [13] used HOG and body skeleton features to recognize Chinese Sign Language (CSL). To reduce the HMM recognition time, a low-rank approximation of feature vectors furnishes both the key-frames of signs and the presumable number of hidden states of the model. Hence, the HMM speeds-up to three times the recognition time. Performance evaluation on data-sets of

370 and 1000 CSL signs reported 94.00 % and 84.00 % of average recognition, respectively.

The recognition of Brazilian Sign Language (Libras) was also addressed by some researches. Anjo et al. [14] had a 100 % of success in recognized 10 static poses of the manual alphabet using Kinect and ANN. Souza and Pizzolato [15] used Kinect to recognize both finger-spelled words and isolated signs using SVM and CRF, respectively. Later, Moreira et al. [16] used a fingertip detector and tracker sensor to recognize 26 letters of the manual alphabet. They achieved 61.53 % of average recognition using ANN. Recently, Bastos et al. [17] used HOG and Zernike moments to recognize 40 predefined static signs. They reported 96.77 % of average recognition using ANN.

Despite the progress, automatic recognition of sign language is still in its infancy and Kinect has not been fully explored to develop applications that might benefit to deaf and hearing impaired people.

This paper presents a method to recognize isolated signs of the Brazilian Sign Language using Kinect. Instead of dealing with multiple data sources, we propose to use the only depth image to extract discriminative features. In our approach, the signer performs signs continuously following the *stop–motion* strategy (i.e., the hands are down and stopped before and after a sign is performed). Accordingly, signs are segmented in time by a simple motion analysis of the hands. Motion analysis also allows for labeling the signs as either one-handed or two-handed to reduce the searching space during the classification stage. Finally, signs are modeled as time-series which are classified using the dynamic time warping–nearest neighbor (DTW-kNN) algorithm.

3   Proposed Method

Figure 1 illustrates the proposed framework for sign language recognition. In short, the framework uses both the depth image and the skeleton data provided by Kinect [18]. To segment signs from a continuous stream, the system detects stop–motion patterns based on the skeleton information and also determines the hand dominance (i.e., one-handed or two-handed). Once identified the start and end of a sign, the histogram of direction cosines [6] features is computed for the depth images. During training, feature descriptors together with the hand dominance labels are stored in a database of sign models. During testing, the unknown sign is recognized via dynamic time warping–nearest neighbor classifier.

Next, we describe the main stages of the framework:

3.1   Sign Segmentation

To be more closer to real-life situations where a speaker produces sequence of words, our system allows the subjects to sign constantly following a stop–motion scheme. Our stop–motion scheme establishes that the hands are down and stopped before and after a sign is performed, so patters of "silence" (stop) and "activity" (motion) are easily detected in the continuous stream of signs.

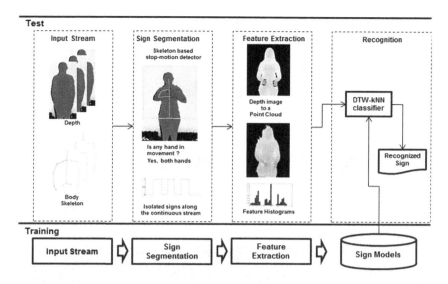

Fig. 1. Framework for sign language recognition.

A stop state indicates a non-sign segment, whereas a motion state indicates a sign segment.

In order to detect stop–motion segments, the system uses the 3D skeleton data provided by Kinect. The user usually shrinks the arms when he/she is signing, therefore the angle ω between the forearm and arm in the 3D space gives a clue whether a stop state or a moving state is happening in the stream. For each frame over time t, angles are evaluated according to:

$$S(t) = \begin{cases} 1, & \omega < Th_{angle} \\ 0, & otherwise \end{cases} \tag{1}$$

resulting in a sequence $S(t)$ of 0s and 1s, for each arm. Usually, a transition from zero to one indicates the start of the sign, whereas the transition from one to zero means the end of the sign. Measurement of 1s in $S(t)$ also allows to determine the dominant hand. Figure 2 presents examples of stop and motion frames of a sign.

3.2 Depth Image Preprocessing

Once identified the boundaries of signs, their depth images are processed as follows:

Step 1: Defining the region of interest. Since the subject usually occupies a small region of the image and the signing occurs in the upper region of the body, the system defines a region of interest (ROI) in the first depth frame.

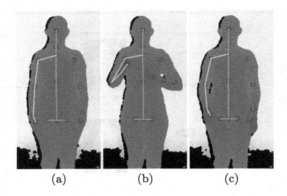

Fig. 2. Skeleton based stop–motion detection. (a) Stop, (b) Motion, and (c) Stop frames.

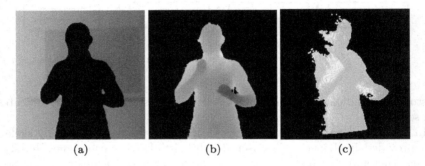

Fig. 3. Depth image preprocessing: (a) After Cropping with a ROI, (b) After depth thresholding, and (c) After mapping to a point cloud.

The ROI is specified around the Head, Spine-Base, Shoulder-Left, and Shoulder-Right joints of the 2D skeleton given by Kinect. The skeleton keeps the aspect ratio of the user, so the ROI is robust against changes in both the user size and location.

Using the ROI, all the depth images of a sign are cropped. An illustration of the cropping result is shown in Fig. 3a.

Step 2: Removing the background. To segment the body of the user, we perform segmentation along the depth axis. Depth values beyond a threshold are zeroed in the image. The system uses the threshold

$$Th_{depth} = Head_{depth} + \Delta \tag{2}$$

the depth value of the Head position plus an additional depth value Δ. An illustration of the segmentation result is shown in Fig. 3b.

Step 3: Mapping to a point cloud: Segmented depth images are mapped to point clouds using the intrinsic camera parameters of Kinect. A point cloud is a set of spatially organized points along the X, Y, Z coordinates of the camera. An illustration of the point cloud of a depth image is shown in Fig. 3c.

3.3   Feature Extraction

As a feature descriptor, we use the histogram of direction cosines (HDC). The HDC was successfully used to classify static hand postures of ASL [6], however in this work we extend it to classify isolated signs.

Direction cosines are the cosine angles between a vector and the Cartesian axes, and a HDC histogram accumulates direction angles in the same way as to histogram of oriented gradients [19].

For a vector $v = a\hat{i} + b\hat{j} + c\hat{k}$ in the 3D Cartesian coordinates, the direction cosines are:

$$p = \cos\alpha = \frac{a}{a^2 + b^2 + c^2}$$

$$q = \cos\beta = \frac{b}{a^2 + b^2 + c^2} \tag{3}$$

$$r = \cos\theta = \frac{c}{a^2 + b^2 + c^2}$$

where $p^2 + q^2 + r^2 = 1$. The angles α, β, and θ can be obtained by inverting the function.

Geometrically, direction cosines characterize a vector using its orientation relative to the Cartesian axes. For a set of vectors, direction cosines portrays the surface encompassed by the vectors.

To increase the distinctiveness of the original HDC, we propose a slight modification in the weighted vote on each bin of the histogram. Steps to compute HDC from a point cloud PC are:

1. Determine the central point p_c of PC.
2. Generate the directional vectors for all points p_i of PC.

$$v_{p_i} = \{p_c - p_i | \forall p_i \in PC\} \tag{4}$$

3. For each v_{p_i} estimates its direction cosines (according Eq. 3) to obtain the orientation angles α, β, and θ as well as the magnitude $\| v_{p_i} \|$.
4. Calculate the histogram of cumulative magnitudes for each coordinate axis. Each histogram encompasses 9-bins from 0 to 180°. Each vector v_{p_i} casts an orientation-based vote in which its magnitude is weighted and distributed to three histograms. The closer the vector is to an axis, the greater the weight is to the respective histogram.
5. The final feature vector FV consists of the concatenation of the three cumulative histograms. Finally, FV is normalized scaling to unit length.

$$FV = \{h_x, h_y, h_z\} \tag{5}$$

For a depth image, the HDC gives a 27-dimensional feature vector, i.e., 3 histograms $\times$ 9 bins = 27.

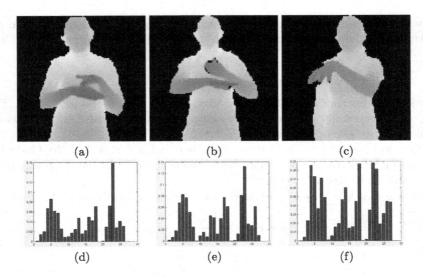

Fig. 4. Different depth images (a), (b), (c) and their HDC features (d), (e), (f), respectively.

Figure 4 illustrates the HDC features calculated from three different depth images. Visually, the two images have very similar postures, varying slightly in the hand shape, whereas the posture in the third image is quite different of them. In order to figure out the degree of closeness of the images, we measured the Euclidean distance between histogram H_i : $distance(\mathbf{H_1}, \mathbf{H_2}) = 0.0458, distance(\mathbf{H_1}, \mathbf{H_3}) = 0.0883$, and $distance(\mathbf{H_2}, \mathbf{H_3}) = 0.0851$. Accordingly, the two first images are similar, but slightly different from the third.

3.4 DTW-Based Recognition

Subjects sign in different ways –e.g., different impetus, speed, and style– so the same sign can change in time even for the same user. Therefore, the time-series model of signs have different lengths, which should be identified in order to recognize the signs.

Because its simplicity and flexibility to compare two different time-series which are similar but locally out of phase, we propose to use the dynamic time warping (DTW) technique. DTW allows for a non linear mapping of one time-series to another by minimizing the distance between them [20].

The proposed system recognizes signs in two steps:

1. Measuring the DTW distance between the queried time-series against the time-series stored in a pre-built database.
2. Classifying the queried time-series using the k-Nearest Neighbor algorithm based on DTW measurements.

4   Experimental Results

We have collected a new data-set using Kinect v2 [18]. The vocabulary consists of 107 medical signs of the Brazilian Sign Language (Libras)–65 one-handed and 42 two-handed signs. Signs were recorded in continuous streams following the stop–motion scheme. A deaf informant performed each sign 5 times. The distance between the sensor and user is between 1.5–2.0 m. An outline of the vocabulary is exposed in Table 1.

Table 1. Medical sign vocabulary in Libras

Sicken, Medical scheduling, Now, Severe, Needle, Allergy, Tomorrow, Tonsillitis, Year, Anxiety, Appendicitis, Heart attack, Well, Bronchitis, Head, Mumps, Surgery, Pill, Medical consultation, Contusion, Chronic, To heal, His, Delirium, Insanity, Dengue, Tooth, Depression, Brain stroke, Dehydration, Diabetes, Disease, To ache, Headache, Electrocardiogram, He, Address, Nursing, Sprain, Poisoning, Stable, Stethoscope, Stomach, I, Medical exam, Fever, Fracture, Future, Flu, Bleeding, Hepatitis, Hypertension, Today, Hospital, Age, Unstable, Respiratory infection, Injection, Intoxication, To go, Laceration, Injury, Knife injury, Gun injury, Slight, Hurt, Doctor, My, Die, Very/Too, To cannot, To want not, To have not, Nausea, Name, Yesterday, Hearing people, Past, Kidney stone, Chest, To can, A few, Need, Clinic history, Psychosis, Lung, Burs, To want, X-rays, Medical prescription, Remedy, Medical risk, Bad, Salmonella, Healthy, To feel, Your, Yes, Deaf people, To have, Dizziness, Cough, Vaccine, To come, You, Vomit

We used the following parameters in our experiment:

- Angle threshold $\omega = 130$ between the arm and forearm for temporal segmentation of signs.
- Region of interest (ROI) around the Head, Spine-base, Shoulder-left, and Shoulder-right for cropping depth images.
- Depth value $\Delta = 200$ mm as a step value for background subtraction behind the user.
- Median mask 3×3 for filtering noise in depth images.
- Mapping depth images to point clouds (PC) for computing their histogram of direction cosines (HDC) features.
- DTW–Nearest Neighbor classifier.
- Leave-one-out cross-validation (LOOCV) for performance evaluations [9].

The data-set contains $\Sigma = 107 \times 5 = 535$ signs. To evaluate the classification performance we use the LOOCV because the signs contain few examples. In this way, there are $n = 535$ cases to be evaluated, so the case i is tested against the training set which consists of all cases except i.

Table 2. Classification performance result

Average accuracy	Average precision	Average recall
98.69	98.88	98.69

After experimenting, we achieved an average accuracy of 98.88 %. The result was promising, however, we perceived that the computational complexity of feature extraction is highly correlated with the size of the images. Such computational cost can be reduced by processing the depth image pixels at a given offset. An offset = 2 reduces the computation time up to a quarter, without affecting performance (average accuracy of 98.69 %). Nonetheless, offsets greater than 2 steps diminish the discriminative power of feature vectors due to the loss of fine details in the image (average accuracy lower than 90 %). Table 2 shows in details the classification performance of the DTW–nearest neighbor classifier.

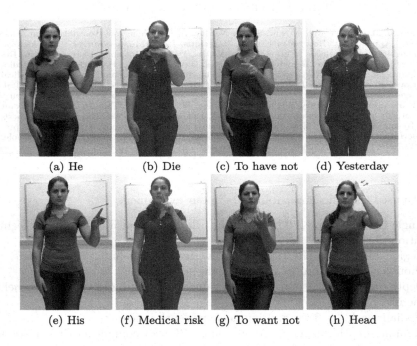

(a) He   (b) Die   (c) To have not   (d) Yesterday

(e) His   (f) Medical risk   (g) To want not   (h) Head

Fig. 5. Screen-shot of some misclassified signs

The results evidence the discriminative power of depth based features and the feasibility to use for isolated sign recognition. However, it is worth remarking that several signs were misclassified. For instance, the system fails in differentiation the signs He and His, Die and Medical risk, To have not and To want not, and Yesterday and Head. Screen-shots of some misclassified signs are shown in Fig. 5.

It seems that signs that are misclassified are those that differ in one or two characteristics, usually named minimal pairs [1,7]. For instance, the signs He–His and To have not–To want not differ only in the hand configuration, whereas the signs Die–Medical risk and Yesterday–Head differ both in configuration and subtle movements of the hands. Moreover, these signs are hardly distinguishable since the arm poses are similar and only vary in either the hand shape or the hand movement beyond the wrist. A dedicated recognizer of the hands may help to detect and disambiguate signs that have slight differences between them.

5   Conclusions and Future Work

This paper presented a method to recognize 107 medical signs of the Brazilian Sign Language (Libras) using Kinect. The method takes advantage of the geometric information contained in depth images to compute a high discriminative spatial-appearance feature. Classification experiments using DTW-kNN reported an striking result of 98.69 % in a single signer-dependent data-set. No tracking, no locations, and no region cropped of the hands were required. Furthermore, aiming to work in real-life scenarios, a skeleton based stop–motion detector was introduced to segment signs performed continuously. In order to improve the robustness of the proposed approach, skeleton and hand shape features will be added, the vocabulary will be extended with signs recorded from different users, and distance metric learning strategies will be explored in a future work.

Acknowledgment. The authors would like to thank the Brazilian agency CAPES for its financial support.

We also thank the anonymous reviewers for their valuable criticism and suggestion which have greatly contributed to the final version of the manuscript.

References

1. Valli, C.: Linguistics of American Sign Language: An Introduction. Gallaudet University Press, Washington, DC (2000)
2. Cooper, H., Holt, B., Bowden, R.: Sign language recognition. In: Moeslund, T.B., Hilton, A., Krüger, V., Sigal, L. (eds.) Visual Analysis of Humans: Looking at People, pp. 539–562. Springer, London (2011)
3. Sahoo, A.K., Mishra, G.S., Ravulakollu, K.K.: Sign language recognition: state of the art. ARPN J. Eng. Appl. Sci. **9**, 116–134 (2014)
4. Classification, V.-B.S.L., Joudaki, S., bin Mohamad, D., Saba, T., Rehman, A., Al-Rodhaan, M., Al-Dhelaan, A.: Vision-based sign language classiffication: a directional review. IETE Tech. Rev. **31**, 383–391 (2014)
5. Lefloch, D., Nair, R., Lenzen, F., Schäfer, H., Streeter, L., Cree, M.J., Koch, R., Kolb, A.: Technical foundation and calibration methods for time-of-flight cameras. In: Grzegorzek, M., Theobalt, C., Koch, R., Kolb, A. (eds.) Time-of-Flight and Depth Imaging. Sensors, Algorithms, and Applications. LNCS, vol. 8200, pp. 3–24. Springer, Heidelberg (2013). doi:10.1007/978-3-642-44964-2_1
6. Escobedo Cardenas, E., Camara Chavez, G.: Finger spelling recognition from depth data using direction cosines and histogram of cumulative magnitudes. In: 2015 28th SIBGRAPI Conference on Graphics, Patterns and Images (SIBGRAPI), pp. 173–179 (2015)
7. de Quadros, R.M., Karnopp, L.B.: Língua de Sinais Brasileira - Estudos Linguísticos. Artmed, Porto Alegre (2004)
8. Suarez, J., Murphy, R.: Hand gesture recognition with depth images: a review. In: RO-MAN 2012, pp. 411–417. IEEE (2012)

9. Murphy, K.P.: Machine Learning: A Probabilistic Perspective. The MIT Press, Cambridge (2012)
10. Escobedo-Cardenas, E., Camara-Chavez, G.: A robust gesture recognition using hand local data and skeleton trajectory. In: 2015 IEEE International Conference on Image Processing (ICIP), pp. 1240–1244 (2015)
11. Pigou, L., Dieleman, S., Kindermans, P.-J., Schrauwen, B.: Sign language recognition using convolutional neural networks. In: Agapito, L., Bronstein, M.M., Rother, C. (eds.) ECCV 2014 Workshops. LNCS, vol. 8925, pp. 572–578. Springer, Heidelberg (2015)
12. Conly, C., Zhang, Z., Athitsos, V.: An integrated RGB-D system for looking up the meaning of signs. In: Proceedings of the 8th ACM International Conference on PErvasive Technologies Related to Assistive Environments (PETRA 2015), pp. 24: 1–24: 8. ACM, New York (2015)
13. Wang, H., Chai, X., Zhou, Y., Xilin, C.: Fast sign language recognition benefited from low rank approximation. In: 2015 11th IEEE International Conference and Workshops on Automatic Face and Gesture Recognition (FG), vol. 1, pp. 1–6. IEEE (2015)
14. Anjo, M.D.S., Pizzolato, E.B., Feuerstack, S.: A real-time system to recognize static gestures of Brazilian sign language (Libras) alphabet using kinect. In: Proceedings of the 11th Brazilian Symposium on Human Factors in Computing Systems (IHC 2012), Porto Alegre, Brazil, pp. 259–268. Brazilian Computer Society (2012)
15. de Souza, C.R., Pizzolato, E.B.: Sign language recognition with support vector machines and hidden conditional random fields: going from finger spelling to natural articulated words. In: Perner, P. (ed.) MLDM 2013. LNCS, vol. 7988, pp. 84–98. Springer, Heidelberg (2013)
16. Matuck, G.R., Moreira, G.S.P., Saotome, O., da Cunha, A.M.: Recognizing the Brazilian signs language alphabet with neural networks over visual 3d data sensor. In: Bazzan, A.L.C., Pichara, K. (eds.) IBERAMIA 2014. LNCS, vol. 8864, pp. 637–648. Springer, Heidelberg (2014)
17. Bastos, I.L.O., Angelo, M.F., Loula, A.C.: Recognition of static gestures applied to Brazilian sign language (Libras). In: Proceedings of the 2015 International Conference on Image Processing, Computer Vision, and Pattern Recognition (IPCV 2015) (2015)
18. Microsoft Inc. Kinect for Windows SDK 2.0. (2014). https://developer.microsoft.com/en-us/windows/kinect/develop. Accessed 19 Aug 2016
19. Dalal, N., Triggs, B.: Histograms of oriented gradients for human detection. In: IEEE Computer Society Conference on Computer Vision and Pattern Recognition (CVPR 2005), vol. 1, pp. 886–893 (2005)
20. Müller, M.: Information Retrieval for Music and Motion. Springer, Heidelberg (2007)

Human Interaction Prediction Using Deep Temporal Features

Qiuhong Ke[1(✉)], Mohammed Bennamoun[1], Senjian An[1], Farid Boussaid[2], and Ferdous Sohel[3]

[1] School of Computer Science and Software Engineering,
The University of Western Australia, Crawley, Australia
qiuhong.ke@research.uwa.edu.au,
{mohammed.bennamoun,senjian.an,farid.boussaid}@uwa.edu.au
[2] School of Electrical, Electronic and Computer Engineering,
The University of Western Australia, Crawley, Australia
[3] School of Engineering and Information Technology,
Murdoch University, Murdoch, Australia
F.Sohel@murdoch.edu.au

Abstract. Interaction prediction has a wide range of applications such as robot controlling and prevention of dangerous events. In this paper, we introduce a new method to capture deep temporal information in videos for human interaction prediction. We propose to use flow coding images to represent the low-level motion information in videos and extract deep temporal features using a deep convolutional neural network architecture. We tested our method on the UT-Interaction dataset and the challenging TV human interaction dataset, and demonstrated the advantages of the proposed deep temporal features based on flow coding images. The proposed method, though using only the temporal information, outperforms the state of the art methods for human interaction prediction.

Keywords: Interaction prediction · CNN · Temporal convolution

1 Introduction

Interaction prediction, or early event recognition, aims to infer an interaction at its early stage [1]. It can help in preventing harmful events (*e.g.*, fighting) in a surveillance scenario. It is also essential to robot-human interaction (*e.g.*, when a human lifts his/her hand or opens his/her arms, the robot could then respond accordingly).

Unlike interaction recognition, interaction prediction requires the inference of the action before it occurs. This requires the prediction of any potential future action, using the frames captured prior to the action. We can see from Fig. 1 that it is difficult to infer the action class from a single frame. The temporal information and the combination of several frames, on the other hand, provide more information about the future action class. In this paper, we focus on the

© Springer International Publishing Switzerland 2016
G. Hua and H. Jégou (Eds.): ECCV 2016 Workshops, Part II, LNCS 9914, pp. 403–414, 2016.
DOI: 10.1007/978-3-319-48881-3_28

Fig. 1. Human interaction prediction. The goal is to predict the interaction class before it happens, which is difficult to achieve from a single frame.

temporal information of video sequences and introduce a new deep temporal feature for human interaction prediction.

Existing interaction prediction methods mainly use spatial features (*e.g.*, bag-of-words) [1], or combine spatial and temporal features (*e.g.*, histogram of oriented optical flow) [2] to represent the video frames. These hand-crafted features are, however, not powerful enough to capture the salient motion information for interaction prediction due to their loss of the global structure in the data [3]. Recent works in large-scale recognition tasks [4,5] show that deep learned representations perform better than the traditional hand-crafted features. The generic features extracted with the pre-trained convolutional neural networks (CNN) are very powerful for image classification and object detection tasks [6–9]. In this paper, we show that the same pre-trained CNN model can also be used to extract deep temporal features. This is possible since a deep neural network can learn transferable features for a wide variety of vision tasks [9]. The CNN models are trained with natural images, so in order to extract effective representations, the key step is to represent the temporal information (optical flow) in a manner that is compatible with natural images. We propose to use the flow coding images as a low-level temporal information and extract deep temporal features from them using a CNN model. We show that the proposed deep temporal features outperform the methods which combine low-level spatial and temporal representations. In addition, we propose to learn convolutional filters to combine consecutive video frames. Specifically, we investigate two learning convolution methods: simultaneous convolution and separate convolution. We show (Sect. 3) that the learning convolutional filters further improves the accuracy compared to a simple average pooling.

The main contributions of this paper include: **(1)** the introduction of flow coding images to represent the low-level temporal information of a video sequence; **(2)** the extraction of deep temporal features using a pre-trained CNN model from ImageNet [10] and the learning of temporal convolution across frames; **(3)** extensive experiments show that the proposed method, though using only the temporal information, outperforms the state of the art methods which combine spatial and temporal features [2].

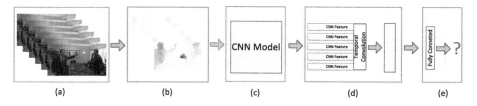

Fig. 2. Outline of our approach. (a) Sample frames from the TV human interaction dataset [11]. (b) The flow coding images computed from the input frames are normalized by cropping the human regions. (c) Deep temporal CNN feature extraction. The publicly available pre-trained CNN-M-2048 model [12] is used to extract CNN features. (d) Temporal convolution learning. The CNN features are concatenated to learn the temporal convolution. (e) Fully connected feedforward neural network, including a hidden layer to reduce the feature dimension and a softmax layer to output the interaction class.

2 Proposed Approach

A work flow of our method is shown in Fig. 2. It includes four parts. **First**, flow coding images are computed from consecutive video frames. **Second**, a deep CNN network is used to extract deep temporal features from flow coding images. **Then**, the output features of several frames are concatenated together to learn the temporal convolution. **Finally**, a fully connected feedforward neural network, including a hidden layer and a softmax layer, is used for classification. Next, we describe the details of these four steps.

2.1 Flow Coding Image

In this paper, we use the optical flow between two consecutive frames to represent the motion information. The most widely used techniques for optical flow computation are differential methods [14]. These algorithms are based on the assumptions of constancy of the intensity (i.e., the grey values of two consecutive frames do not change over time) and the smoothness of flow field (i.e., the total variation of the flow field should not be too large) [15].

Let v_x and v_y be the x and y components of the optical flow at a pixel, respectively. The flow coding image is obtained as follows [16,17]. First, the magnitude r and the angle θ of the velocity are computed:

$$r = \sqrt{v_x^2 + v_y^2})\tag{1}$$

$$\theta = \arctan 2\left(\frac{v_y}{v_x}\right) + \pi\tag{2}$$

The next step computes the color for each velocity according to the magnitude and angle of the velocity. The idea is based on the color wheel [18]. As shown in Fig. 3, different hues are assigned to different orientations, varying from

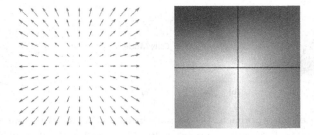

Fig. 3. Color coding of flow vector. Each flow vector is assigned a color according to the orientation and magnitude of the vector. The hue of the color represents the orientation while the saturation represents the magnitude. (Color figure online)

Fig. 4. Flow coding image. (a) and (c) are video frames from the UT-Interaction dataset Set 1 and Set 2 [13]. The arrows show the overall motion directions of the humans. (b) and (d) are the corresponding flow coding images. The orientations and magnitudes of the flow vectors are mapped to the corresponding hues and saturations of colors. (Color figure online)

red, yellow, green, cyan, blue to magenta. As the magnitude becomes larger, the saturation increases. Two examples of flow coding images are shown in Fig. 4. Compared with the raw video frames, the flow coding images retain the human motion in a more explicit way. It can be seen that the humans with different directions of motions are assigned different colors, with variant saturation corresponding to different magnitudes of the motions. In addition, the flow coding images assign the white color to the background as there is no motion and the magnitude is zero. Therefore, the flow coding images do not contain complex (*e.g.*, textured) backgrounds, especially when the video is captured with a static camera.

2.2 Deep Temporal CNN Feature

CNN Model. Once the flow coding images are obtained from the optical flow, they are fed into the pre-trained CNN-M-2048 model [12] to extract deep temporal features. The network was learnt on ILSVRC-2012 [10]. The architecture is shown in Fig. 5. It is similar to the one used by Zeiler and Fergus [8]. In the convolutional layers, there are 96 to 1024 kernels with size varying from 3×3 to 7×7. The rectification (ReLU) [19] is used as a nonlinear activation function. For robustness to intra-class deformations, max pooling kernels of size 3×3 with stride 2 are used at different layers. In all experiments, the output of the first fully connected layer (layer 19) of the network is used as the feature vector.

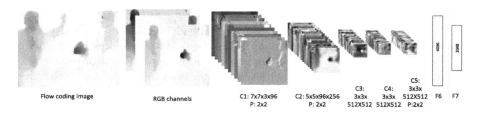

Fig. 5. Single CNN feature extraction. The input is the flow coding image (i.e., a single frame). The architecture is based on CNN-M-2048 model. "C", "P" and "F" denote "convolution", "max pooling" and "fully connected", respectively. The output of "F7" is used as the temporal feature vector.

Region of Interest. Human interaction like handshake or kicking involves the stretching of hands or legs. These body parts are important for accurate interaction prediction. However, the bounding boxes of humans do not include all of the body parts. In this case, the region of interest (ROI) is selected by merging the bounding boxes of the two humans. Each flow coding image is then normalized by cropping the ROI. As shown in Fig. 6, for the TV human interaction dataset, the given upper body annotations are used to select the left, right and upper bound of the ROI. The lower bound is chosen as the height of the frame. For the UT-Interaction dataset, the tracking algorithm [20] is applied to detect humans. The ROI is selected as the region $[x_{min} : x_{max}, y_{min} : y_{max}]$, where $x_{min}, x_{max}, y_{min}, y_{min}$ denote the minimum and maximum x and y coordinates of the human bounding boxes, respectively.

2.3   Learning Temporal Convolution & Classification

As shown in Fig. 6, our ROI covers the two interacting humans. We investigate two different methods to extract CNN features and learn the temporal convolution using the ROI:

(1) **Simultaneous convolution:** the ROI is fed into the deep model as a whole image to extract CNN features. For each frame, the dimension of the output feature vector is 2048. This method tries to learn the temporal convolution for two humans simultaneously.

(2) **Separate convolution:** the ROI is divided into two equal sized images: the left and the right half images. The CNN features are extracted separately from these half images. They are then concatenated as a large feature vector. As a result, the dimension of the output feature vector is 4096 for each flow coding image. This method separates the two interacting humans and learns the convolution for each of them separately.

The output deep temporal features of several consecutive frames are concatenated in the temporal dimension to form a *temporal image* (as shown in Fig. 2(c)). A fully temporal convolution is applied to combine several consecutive frames. This fully temporal convolution is used to compute the weights of the consecutive frames. Given a *temporal image* generated from a sequence of several frames, a 1D temporal convolutional filter is learned. The size of the filter is the same as the number of frames. The vector can be treated as the weighted sum feature vector of these features, as shown in Eq. (3).

$$\mathbf{x_i} = \begin{bmatrix} \mathbf{v}_{i-k+1} & \mathbf{v}_{i-k+2} & \cdots & \mathbf{v}_i \end{bmatrix} \begin{bmatrix} \alpha_1 \\ \alpha_2 \\ \vdots \\ \alpha_k \end{bmatrix} \tag{3}$$

where $\alpha = [\alpha_1, \alpha_2, \cdots, \alpha_k]^T$ denotes the learning convolutional filter. $\mathbf{v}_j$ denotes the CNN feature at frame j. k is the number of concatenated frames. $\mathbf{x}_i$ denotes the output feature vector after convolution, which is fed to a "ReLU" transform function. The output is further reduced dimension with a full connected (FC) layer:

$$\mathbf{z} = f(W_1^T f(\mathbf{x}) + \mathbf{b_1}) \tag{4}$$

where $\mathbf{z}$ is the output of the first hidden layer, W_1 and $\mathbf{b_1}$ are the weight matrix and the bias of the first hidden layer, respectively. $f(\cdot)$ is the "ReLU" activation function given by:

$$f(\mathbf{x}) = \max(0, \mathbf{x}) \tag{5}$$

$\mathbf{z}$ is fed to another FC layer with a softmax activation function to output the final probability distribution of classes (i.e., y):

$$\mathbf{y} = g(W_2^T \mathbf{z} + \mathbf{b_2}) \tag{6}$$

where W_2 and $\mathbf{b_2}$ are the model weight and the bias of the output layer, respectively. $g(\cdot)$ is the softmax operation function given by:

$$g(\mathbf{z}) = [g_1(\mathbf{z}), g_2(\mathbf{z}), \cdots, g_d(\mathbf{z})]$$
$$g(z_j) = \frac{e^{z_j}}{\sum_{i=1}^{d} e^{z_i}}, \quad j = 1, \cdots, d \tag{7}$$

where $\mathbf{z} = [z_1, z_2, \cdots, z_d]$, d is the dimension of z. In this case, d is the number of action classes. $\mathbf{y}$ is the probability distribution of classes. The loss function between the probability distribution and the ground-truth class label is computed as follows:

$$L = -\frac{1}{N} \sum_{i=1}^{N} \log\left(\mathbf{y}\left(c_i\right)\right) \tag{8}$$

where N is the number of training samples, c_i is the class of the ith data. The model parameters are updated using the mini-batch stochastic gradient descent algorithm [21].

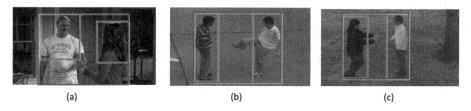

| (a) | (b) | (c) |

Fig. 6. Region of interest (ROI). (a) Video frame from the TV human interaction dataset. The green box is the provided upper body annotation. The red box is the selected ROI. (b) and (c) are video frames from the UT-Interaction dataset Set 1 and Set 2, respectively. The green box is the detected human bounding box. The red box is the selected ROI. Each flow coding image is cropped into the ROI before feeding it to the CNN model. (Color figure online)

3 Experiments

We tested our method on the TV human interaction dataset [11] and the UT-Interaction dataset [13]. The network weights were learnt using the mini-batch stochastic gradient descent with a batch size of 100. Each 100 training data was uniformly sampled across the class. Based on empirical test, the optimal number of nodes in the hidden layer was set to 512. The momentum was set to 0.9.

3.1   TV Human Interaction Dataset

This dataset consists of 300 video clips collected from more than 20 different TV shows. It contains 5 interaction classes: hand shake, high five, hug, kiss and a "none" class that dose not contain any of the interactions above, such as talking and walking. The dataset also provides annotations for each frame of the video, including the bounding boxes of the upper human bodies, action labels for each person and whether there is interaction or not. As mentioned in Sect. 2.2, in each frame, we used the provided bounding boxes of humans in actions to extract the ROI.

We used the training/testing split provided along with the dataset and we trained all of the frames from the training videos. The training epoch was set to 30. The learning rate was initialized to 10^{-3}, and was decreased to 10^{-4} after 30 epochs.

The testing protocols in [2] were adopted. The prediction accuracy was tested on 5 different temporal stages (i.e., distance between the testing frame and the starting frame of the interaction, measured in the number of frames), from –20 to 0, with a step size of 5. "–20" denotes that the temporal distance between the testing frame and the starting frame of the interaction is within 20 frames. "0" means that the testing frames are within 5 frames after the interaction happened. We tested the accuracies of learning simultaneous convolution and separate convolution with a convolution filter size of 3 and 7. The comparison results are shown in Fig. 7. Our simultaneous convolution learning method outperforms the state of the art. The accuracy is about 5 % better in the "–10" temporal stage, and it is 15 % better in the final temporal stage. The results show that our deep temporal features are much more powerful in capturing the motion information

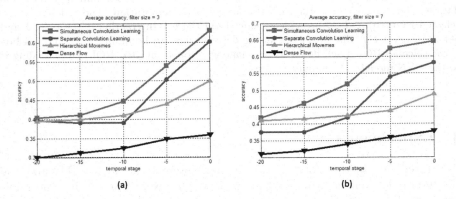

(a)   (b)

Fig. 7. Early interaction prediction accuracies on the TV human interaction dataset. (a) and (b) show comparisons of our two convolution learning methods and comparisons with other methods, including the "hierarchical movemes" and dense flow [2] on the TV human interaction dataset. Our simultaneous convolution learning method outperforms the state of the art.

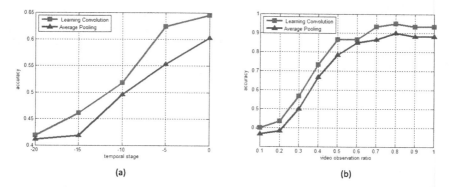

Fig. 8. Performance comparison of the learning convolution and the average pooling method: (a) TV human interaction dataset; (b) UT-interaction dataset.

in the video sequences and perform better than the combination of low-level spatial and temporal hand-crafted features.

For the TV interaction dataset, the simultaneous convolution performs better than the separate convolution. This is because the TV show dataset comes from movies and contains a lot of shots from different viewpoints with moving cameras and various viewpoints. Some frames include only one person. Learning the convolution simultaneously is more robust than separating the frames into two halves.

We also compared the performances of learning simultaneous convolution and the average pooling given the CNN deep features extracted from the flow coding images of 7 frames. Both methods output one feature vector which is fed into neural network for classification. The results are shown in Fig. 8(a). The learning temporal convolution performs better than the simple average pooling. The accuracy is about 8 % better in the "−5" temporal stage. The results show that using learning convolution to produce the weighted sum of consecutive frames captures more salient motion information in the video sequence than a simple average pooling.

3.2   UT-Interaction Dataset

This dataset includes two sets. In Set 1 the background is simpler and mostly static. In contrast, in Set 2 the background is complex and slightly moving. Each set includes 10 sequences. Each sequence is segmented into 6 classes of videos, i.e., handshake, hug, pointing, kick, push and punch.

There are no training/testing splits provided with this dataset. The performance is measured using leave-one-sequence-out cross validation, i.e., for each set, 9 sequences of segmented videos (54) are used for training and the remaining 6 videos are used for testing. The learning rate was set to 10^{-3}, and the training stopped after 30 epochs.

Table 1. Recognition performance with respect to the first half length of the videos. The accuracy of most previous methods drops dramatically on Set 2 where the background is more complicated and the set is more challenging compared to Set 1. Our method achieves state-of-the-art recognition performance when only half of the videos are available, and outperforms the current best result [2] by about 12 % on Set 2.

Methods	Accuracy wrt. half videos (Set 1)	Accuracy wrt. half videos (Set 2)
Our Method	**88.3 %**	**81.7 %**
hierarchical movemes [2]	83.1 %	69.0 %
Dynamic BoW [1]	70.0 %	54.0 %
Integral BoW [1]	61.8 %	49.4 %
Cuboid + Bayesian [1]	30.0 %	28.0 %
Cuboid + SVMs [1]	31.7 %	35.0 %
BP + SVM [22]	65.0 %	54.0 %

We learned the separate convolution with a filter size of 5 to recognize 50 % of videos (i.e., given a video of d frames, using the sequence of $[1, round(0.5 * d)]$ to predict the action class). The results are shown in Table 1. Our method outperforms the state of the art. The accuracy of most previous methods drops significantly on Set 2 where, again, the background is more complicated and challenging. Our method achieves state-of-the-art prediction when only the half of the video is available, and outperforms the current best result [2] by about 5 % when tested on Set 1 and about 12 % when tested on Set 2.

Figure 9 illustrates the details of interaction prediction when tested on Set 2. Each video was tested with 10 different observation ratios from 0.1 to 1, with a step of 0.1, *e.g.*, given the video length d, the observation ratio 0.3 means that the sequence of $[1, round(0.3 * d)]$ is provided for testing. We tested our method with learning simultaneous convolution and separate convolution with a convolution filter size k of 3 and 7. Given a test video of n frames, we derive $d - k + 1$ predicting classes. The prediction of the video is given by the max voting strategy, i.e., the number of each class is calculated in the $d - k + 1$ classes and the maximum number of class is chosen as the interaction class of the video. We can see that our separate convolution learning method outperforms the state of the art. It improves the accuracy by roughly 9 % when only the first 10 % of the length of each video is provided. When the full length of the videos is provided, the improvement is about 10 %. It shows that the proposed method is valuable for both prediction and recognition. The separate convolution is seen to perform better than the simultaneous convolution. For the UT-Interaction dataset, given that the actions are captured with a static view point, the separate convolution can learn specific and detailed temporal information for each of the two humans.

Figure 8(b) compares the learning of the separate convolution and the average pooling given the deep temporal features extracted from flow coding images of 7 frames. We can see that learning temporal convolution performs better than the average pooling method.

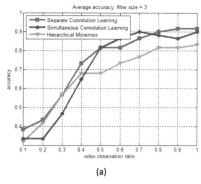

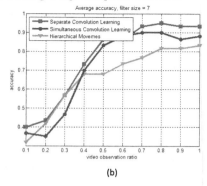

(a)   (b)

Fig. 9. Early interaction prediction accuracies on the UT-Interaction dataset. The comparisons of our two convolution learning methods and the "hierarchical movemes" approach [2] on the UT-Interaction dataset. The video observation ratio denotes the given testing sequence length, *e.g.*, "0.3" means that the testing sequence consists of the first 30 % of the video frame. Our separate convolution learning method performs better than the "hierarchical movemes" approach under different observation ratios.

4   Conclusion

In this paper, we have proposed a learning method to exploit the deep temporal features of video frames for human interaction prediction. We tested our method on the UT-Interaction dataset and the challenging TV human interaction dataset. Although our method only uses temporal information, it still outperforms the state of the art when tested on challenging datasets. The experimental results clearly illustrate that the proposed learning method enables an early recognition of human interaction.

Acknowledgement. This work was partially supported by Australian Research Council grants DP150100294, DP110103336, and DE120102960.

References

1. Ryoo, M.: Human activity prediction: Early recognition of ongoing activities from streaming videos. In: 2011 IEEE International Conference on Computer Vision (ICCV), pp. 1036–1043. IEEE (2011)
2. Lan, T., Chen, T.-C., Savarese, S.: A hierarchical representation for future action prediction. In: Fleet, D., Pajdla, T., Schiele, B., Tuytelaars, T. (eds.) ECCV 2014, Part III. LNCS, vol. 8691, pp. 689–704. Springer, Heidelberg (2014)
3. Acar, E., Hopfgartner, F., Albayrak, S.: Understanding affective content of music videos through learned representations. In: Gurrin, C., Hopfgartner, F., Hurst, W., Johansen, H., Lee, H., O'Connor, N. (eds.) MMM 2014, Part I. LNCS, vol. 8325, pp. 303–314. Springer, Heidelberg (2014)
4. Le, Q.V., Zou, W.Y., Yeung, S.Y., Ng, A.Y.: Learning hierarchical invariant spatio-temporal features for action recognition with independent subspace analysis. In: 2011 IEEE Conference on Computer Vision and Pattern Recognition (CVPR), pp. 3361–3368. IEEE (2011)

5. Ren, X., Ramanan, D.: Histograms of sparse codes for object detection. In: 2013 IEEE Conference on Computer Vision and Pattern Recognition (CVPR), pp. 3246–3253. IEEE (2013)
6. Donahue, J., Jia, Y., Vinyals, O., Hoffman, J., Zhang, N., Tzeng, E., Darrell, T.: Decaf: A deep convolutional activation feature for generic visual recognition. arXiv preprint arXiv:1310.1531 (2013)
7. Oquab, M., Bottou, L., Laptev, I., Sivic, J.: Learning and transferring mid-level image representations using convolutional neural networks. In: 2014 IEEE Conference on Computer Vision and Pattern Recognition (CVPR), pp. 1717–1724. IEEE (2014)
8. Zeiler, M.D., Fergus, R.: Visualizing and understanding convolutional networks. In: Fleet, D., Pajdla, T., Schiele, B., Tuytelaars, T. (eds.) ECCV 2014, Part I. LNCS, vol. 8689, pp. 818–833. Springer, Heidelberg (2014)
9. Razavian, A.S., Azizpour, H., Sullivan, J., Carlsson, S.: Cnn features off-the-shelf: an astounding baseline for recognition. In: 2014 IEEE Conference on Computer Vision and Pattern Recognition Workshops (CVPRW), pp. 512–519. IEEE (2014)
10. Russakovsky, O., Deng, J., Su, H., Krause, J., Satheesh, S., Ma, S., Huang, Z., Karpathy, A., Khosla, A., Bernstein, M., et al.: Imagenet large scale visual recognition challenge. Int. J. Comput. Vis., 1–42 (2014)
11. Patron-Perez, A., Marszalek, M., Zisserman, A., Reid, I.D.: High five: Recognising human interactions in tv shows. In: BMVC, vol. 1, p. 2, Citeseer (2010)
12. Chatfield, K., Simonyan, K., Vedaldi, A., Zisserman, A.: Return of the devil in the details: Delving deep into convolutional nets. arXiv preprint arXiv:1405.3531 (2014)
13. Ryoo, M.S., Aggarwal, J.K.: Spatio-temporal relationship match: Video structure comparison for recognition of complex human activities. In: 2009 IEEE 12th International Conference on Computer vision, pp. 1593–1600. IEEE (2009)
14. Bruhn, A., Weickert, J., Schnörr, C.: Lucas/kanade meets horn/schunck: Combining local and global optic flow methods. Int. J. Comput. Vision 61(3), 211–231 (2005)
15. Brox, T., Bruhn, A., Papenberg, N., Weickert, J.: High accuracy optical flow estimation based on a theory for warping. In: Pajdla, T., Matas, J.G. (eds.) ECCV 2004. LNCS, vol. 3024, pp. 25–36. Springer, Heidelberg (2004)
16. Baker, S., Scharstein, D., Lewis, J., Roth, S., Black, M.J., Szeliski, R.: A database and evaluation methodology for optical flow. Int. J. Comput. Vision 92(1), 1–31 (2011)
17. Liu, C.: Beyond pixels: exploring new representations and applications for motion analysis. Ph.D. thesis, Citeseer (2009)
18. http://members.shaw.ca/quadibloc/other/colint.htm. Accessed 15 June 2015
19. Nair, V., Hinton, G.E.: Rectified linear units improve restricted boltzmann machines. In: Proceedings of the 27th International Conference on Machine Learning (ICML-10), pp. 807–814 (2010)
20. Ess, A., Leibe, B., Schindler, K., Gool, L.V.: A mobile vision system for robust multi-person tracking. In: IEEE Conference on Computer Vision and Pattern Recognition, CVPR 2008. pp. 1–8. IEEE (2008)
21. Bottou, L.: Large-scale machine learning with stochastic gradient descent. In: Proceedings of COMPSTAT 2010, pp. 177–186 (2010)
22. Laviers, K., Sukthankar, G., Aha, D.W., Molineaux, M., Darken, C., et al.: Improving offensive performance through opponent modeling. In: AIIDE (2009)

Human Joint Angle Estimation and Gesture Recognition for Assistive Robotic Vision

Alp Guler[1], Nikolaos Kardaris[2], Siddhartha Chandra[1(✉)], Vassilis Pitsikalis[2], Christian Werner[3], Klaus Hauer[3], Costas Tzafestas[2], Petros Maragos[2], and Iasonas Kokkinos[1]

[1] Inria GALEN & Centrale Supélec Paris, Châtenay-Malabry, France
siddhartha.chandra@inria.fr
[2] National Technical University of Athens, Athens, Greece
[3] University of Heidelberg, Heidelberg, Germany

Abstract. We explore new directions for automatic human gesture recognition and human joint angle estimation as applied for human-robot interaction in the context of an actual challenging task of assistive living for real-life elderly subjects. Our contributions include state-of-the-art approaches for both low- and mid-level vision, as well as for higher level action and gesture recognition. The first direction investigates a deep learning based framework for the challenging task of human joint angle estimation on noisy real world RGB-D images. The second direction includes the employment of dense trajectory features for online processing of videos for automatic gesture recognition with real-time performance. Our approaches are evaluated both qualitative and quantitatively on a newly acquired dataset that is constructed on a challenging real-life scenario on assistive living for elderly subjects.

1 Introduction

The increase in elderly population is a fact worldwide [1]. In this context computer vision and machine learning research applied on human-robot-interaction from the perspective of assistive living has both scientific interest and social benefits. In this work we focus on two prominent directions and apply the respective methods in the context of a challenging assistive living human-robot interaction scenario. This involves a robotic rollator that interacts with the elderly subjects using visual sensors, assisting them in every-day activities. These directions involve the use of state of the art deep learning based approaches for human joint angle estimation for the future goal of subject stability estimation, as well as the application of action recognition methods to enable elderly subjects interact with the robot by means of manual gestures. Herein we focus on the visual processing pipelines of this interface, and show a variety of rich applications and experiments.

There has been a furore of activity on the pose estimation front in recent years. Pose estimation usually involves inferring the locations of landmarks or body parts and the quality of the prediction is measured by metrics that involve

© Springer International Publishing Switzerland 2016
G. Hua and H. Jégou (Eds.): ECCV 2016 Workshops, Part II, LNCS 9914, pp. 415–431, 2016.
DOI: 10.1007/978-3-319-48881-3_29

comparing the predicted and the ground truth locations in the image plane. In this work we address the problem of estimating human joint angles. The joint angle estimation task involves estimating the angles made by segments of the human body at the joint landmarks in world coordinates. More specifically, we are interested in estimating (a) the knee angles, that is, the angles between by the thigh and the shank segments of the left and right legs, and (b) the hip angles, or the angles made by the torso and thigh segments. These angles will later be used to determine if the user's pose is unstable. In case of instability, the robot can assist the user achieve a stable position by exerting a physical force of the optimal magnitude in the optimal direction.

Human action recognition is a very active research area with a multitude of applications, such as video retrieval, health monitoring as well as human-computer interaction for assistive robotics. Proposed approaches on action recognition span several directions, such as deep architectures [2] and local spatio-temporal features with the popular Bag-of-Visual-Words (BoVW) paradigm [3–5], as well as one of the top performing approaches, the dense trajectories [6,7]. Application on human-robot interaction [8] has received relatively little attention mainly due to the increased computational requirements of most action recognition systems, which prevents them from performing in real-time. We target the rocognition of elderly subjects' gestural commands by employing dense trajectories and exploring alternative encoding methods. We have implemented a real-time version of our gesture recognition system that uses an activity detector and is currently integrated in the robotic platform.

In this work we present our contributions on applying these approaches on data containing actual elderly subjects. We are guided by a vision whereby assistive human-robot interaction is advanced by state-of-the-art results in mid and higher level vision applications. The assistive scenario involves a robotic rollator equiped with multiple sensors, as shown in Fig. 2, that is capable of estimating the pose and the joint angles, as well as recognizing manual gestures using the proposed approaches. We utilize a deep learning based 2D joint localization approach fused with 3D information acquired from RGB-D sensors to localize joints in 3D and estimate the angles between line segments(see Sect. 3). Moreover, we apply our action-gesture recognition approach based on the recent dense trajectories features [6], employing a variety of encoding schemes. We also feed mid-level vision information [9] to the higher level of action-gesture recognition. All cases are evaluated on rich scenarios of a new dataset and task with elderly subjects showing promising results. Finally, we examine practical issues concerning an online version of the system that is integrated in the robotic platform and has close-to-real-time performance.

2   The Human-Robot Interaction Assistive Dataset

The experimental prototype used for data acquisition [10] consists of a robotic rollator equipped with sensors such as laser range sensors that scan the walking area for environment mapping, obstacle detection and lower limbs movement

Fig. 1. Sample gestures from Task-6a and illustration of the visual processing with dense trajectories for gesture recognition (Sect. 4). First row: "Come here". Second row: "I want to stand up".

detection, force/torque handle sensors and visual sensors: an HD camera to record patient's upper body movements and two Kinect sensors. The first Kinect captures the torso, waist and hips and the second faces downwards towards the lower limbs. The recording process involved acquiring RGB-D videos using the open-source Robotics Operating System (ROS) software capturing human subjects in a set of predefined use-cases and scenarios.

The dataset we use for estimating joint angles (Fig. 2) consists of (a) colour and depth images captured by the ROS-Kinect system, and (b) human-joint landmark point trajectories captured by a *Qualisys* motion capture (*MoCap*) system. This dataset has $9K$ images coming from 27 video recordings.

The data acquired for gesture recognition ("Task-6a") comprises recordings of the patient sitting in front of the rollator, which is placed at a distance of 2.5 meters. Task-6a includes 19 different gestural and verbal commands. Each command is performed by the 13 patients, 3−6 times. Sample gestures are depicted in Fig. 1. The task is challenging, as mobility disabilities seriously impede the performance ability of a verbal and/or gestural command. Moreover, due to the cognitive disabilities of some users, in some cases we observe different pronunciations of a command even among multiple performances of the same user. In essence, we miss the consistency that is sometimes assumed in other datasets [11]. In addition, background noise and other people moving in the scene make the recognition task even harder.

3   Human Joint Angle Estimation from Kinect RGB-D Images

Our first contribution is a deep learning framework for human pose estimation. More precisely, we are interested in estimating the hip and the knee angles. We define (a) the hip angle as the angle made at the hip joint by the shoulders and the knees, and (b) the knee angle as the angle made at the knee by the hips and the ankles. These angles give a fair indication of the human pose, and can be exploited to determine if the user's pose is unstable.

3.1 Pose Estimation Dataset

Our objective is to use the RGB-D images to estimate the joint-angles in the world coordinate system, and evaluate them against the angles computed from the point-trajectories. We assume that any deviation between the actual joint angles and those computed from the point-trajectories, due to an offset between the motion capture markers and the human body, is neglegible. Our dataset suffers from several severe limitations. Firstly, the upper, lower kinect and MoCap systems are not aligned in time. Secondly, the upper and lower kinect sensors look at parts of the human body individually, and do not see the entire context. Finally, the depth images from the kinect are sparse and noisy (Fig. 2). We alleviate the first two limitations by using preprocessing procedures described in the rest of this section. To cope with noisy depth estimates, we use a sparse coding based strategy to denoise the predictions. This is described in Sect. 3.6.

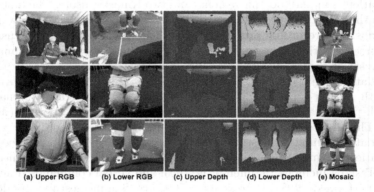

(a) Upper RGB   (b) Lower RGB   (c) Upper Depth   (d) Lower Depth   (e) Mosaic

Fig. 2. Example images from our dataset. Notice the scale changes, and noise in the depth images. Our dataset also suffers from occlusion and truncation of body parts. We also have multiple people in the videos.

Data Alignment. As mentioned, our input data and our ground truth are recorded by two different systems, and are not aligned. To evaluate the accuracy of our predictions, we require that the images are aligned-in-time with the joint-angle trajectories. More specifically, we need to know which image-frame corresponds to which time-stamp in the MoCap trajectory. This alignment problem is non-trivial due to several factors.

Firstly, the two recording systems do not start at the same time. Secondly, the two systems capture data at different frequencies. Besides, while the MoCap system has a constant frequency, the frequency of the ROS-kinect system varies with the system load. Due to this, the upper-body frames and lower-body frames coming from the two kinect sensors are not aligned. To fix the variable frame rate issue, we re-sample the kinect captured videos at 10 *fps* via nearest neighbour interpolation. To align the upper and lower body frames, we only use images from the time-stamps when both upper and lower frames are available, discarding the remaining frames. Finally, to align the MoCap trajectories with the kinect frames, we design an optimization framework. More specifically, we define variation-functions for the images and trajectories. The variation functions can be understood as how the data changes over time. Once we define these functions, we can align the data by ensuring that these variations are correlated in time, since each variation results from the same cause, namely the human subject moving.

We denote by $f_x(t)$ the variation function of the point trajectories. $f_x(t)$ is defined to be simply the L_2 norm of the position of center of the human body at each timestamp t in the point trajectories,

$$f_x(t) = ||b(t)||_2^2, \tag{1}$$

where $b(t)$ denotes the center of the body (the pelvis). We define, $f_y(t)$, the variation function of the images I as the L_2 distance, in the HOG feature space, of an image at timestamp t from the first image $(t = 0)$ in the sequence.

$$f_y(t) = ||I_t^{hog} - I_0^{hog}||_2^2 \tag{2}$$

The alignment problem can now be solved by aligning the f_x and f_y signals. To achieve this, we minimize the cross-correlation between them by exhaustively sampling a *delay* parameter between them. The exhaustive search takes less than 2–3 min per video. Figure 3 shows the variation functions as the result of our alignment procedure for two different videos.

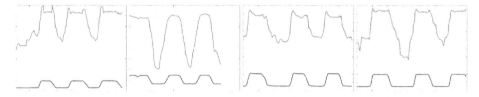

Fig. 3. Results of our alignment procedure for 4 videos. The green curve shows the image variation function $f_x(t)$, the red curve shows the trajectory variation function $f_x(t)$. The human subjects in these videos performed the sit-stand exercise 3 times. (Color figure online)

Image Stitching. In our experiments, we observed that images containing only the lower or the upper body are very hard samples for pose estimation methods because these lack a lot of informative context about the pose. To cope with this issue, we stitch the images from the lower and upper kinect to obtain a single image containing the full human body. This stitching is done by estimating a planar homography transformation between manually selected keypoints. Using this geometric transformation we overlay the upper and lower sensor images to get the *mosaic* image. However, the mosaic images look unrealistic due to perspective distortion. We fix this by performing perspective correction on the mosaic image by estimating the necessary affine transformation. Since the kinect sensors are stationary, this procedure is done only once, we use the same transformation matrices for all images in our dataset. Results of image stitching can be seen in Fig. 2. In the following sections, we describe our approach.

3.2   Related Work

In the recent years, deep learning has emerged as the gold standard of machine learning on nearly all benchmarks, including the task of human pose estimation. A number of deep learning methods solve the pose estimation problem by first estimating the spatial locations of interesting landmarks, and then inferring the pose from these landmark locations. In a broad sense, these approaches can be classified into two categories. The first category consists of methods that directly recover spatial locations of interesting landmarks via regression. Inspired by the deep convolutional cascaded network of Sun et al. [12], the *Deep Pose* approach by Toshev et al. [13] treats pose estimation as a regression task, refining the predictions iteratively via a cascaded network architecture. The second class of methods estimate probability distributions of the presence of these landmarks, which can then be treated as unaries in an inference procedure that enforces spatial constraints to recover the likelihoods of these landmarks [14–18]. These approaches typically use fully convolutional neural networks to estimate a per pixel likelihood of joint locations. A number of these approaches [19,20] employ *iterative error feedback*, that is, a cascaded system to repeatedly refine the per pixel likelihoods, similar to recurrent networks. The *DeeperCut* approach [21] exploits a very deep residual neural network and achieves promising results without using a sequential refinement scheme. More recently, Haque et al. [18] proposed a viewpoint invariant pose estimation framework for RGB-D images that utilizes Long Short Term Memory (LSTM) [22] to incorporate the idea of error feedback.

3.3   Joint Angle Estimation from RGB-D Images

The joint angle estimation task can be addressed by either (a) directly regressing the angles from the images, or (b) first estimating the spatial locations of the human parts, and then estimating the joint angles using geometry. As described in Sect. 3.2, we have two broad classes of methods that address the problem of spatial localization of landmarks. An advantage of methods that directly regress landmark locations from the image data is that they can learn pairwise interactions in a fully connected graph efficiently via fully connected layers, thereby exploiting the holistic context in the image. However, these methods typically use an object detector at the testing stage [13] and then regress from the detected bounding boxes to the landmark locations. Object detection is necessary to prevent noise in the context around the object of interest from corrupting the features. While this is a reasonable strategy, this two step procedure can be undesirable for datasets containing low resolution images, or images captured in the wild where object detection can be inaccurate. Methods that estimate the probability distributions can work around this requirement by estimating the probability distributions over the entire image, and then inferring the landmark locations by enforcing spatial constraints. Our dataset has noisy, low resolution images, with significant occlusion, and dramatic scale changes. This motivates us to employ a fully convolutional network to estimate the spatial locations of the human parts in the image plane.

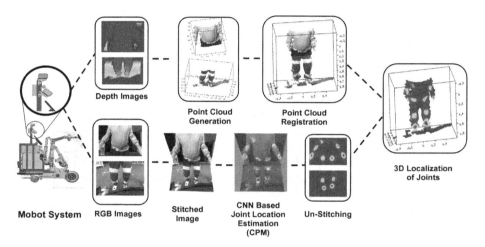

Fig. 4. A schematic representation of our joint angle estimation pipeline. We have two stationary RGBD sensors (shown in the circle in the first column) on a moving rollator. We stitch the upper and lower RGB images, and perform part localization on the mosaic image using Convolutional Pose Machines. The mosaic image is then unstitched and the part beliefs are transferred to the registered point cloud. This gives us the spatial locations of the body parts in the world space. Given these part locations, we estimate the joint angles using vector algebra.

For our task of 3D localization of the human parts, it is natural to use the depth cues from the depth images. The depth field of view of the Microsoft Kinect sensor ranges from 25 centimeters to a few meters. This leads to a noisy and sparse reconstruction of the depth field in cases where the object of interest is close to the sensor. Our dataset has numerous instances where the human is too close to the kinect sensor. Consequently, the depth information is unreliable (or absent) in these cases. The RGB sensors do not suffer from this limitation. This motivates the usage of the clean RGB image for the estimation of joint locations, later to be combined with the depth information to reconstruct the 3d joint locations. We therefore, first estimate the part positions from the RGB images, then use the depth images to reconstruct the part positions in the world system, and finally estimate the joint angles via geometry. Our pipeline is described in Fig. 4. For estimating the part positions in 2D, we use the *Convolutional*

Pose Machines[15] approach which achieves the state of the art results on the challenging MPII dataset [23]. This approach was trained using thirty thousand images from the MPII and Leeds Sports [23,24] datasets.

3.4   Convolutional Pose Machines

As mentioned in Sect. 3.3, our method is based on the *convolutional pose machines* [15] approach, that uses sequential prediction convolutional blocks that operate on image and intermediate belief maps and learn implicit image-dependent spatial models of the relationships between parts. We now briefly describe the prediction strategy.

The human part localization task is done in several stages. The first stage of the method predicts part beliefs from local image evidence via a fully convolutional network. The network has seven convolutional layers, trained to minimize the L_2 distance between the predicted beliefs and the ground truth beliefs. The ground truth beliefs are synthesized by putting Gaussian peaks at ground truth locations of parts. The second stage learns convolutional features from the image, and combines them with the beliefs from the first stage (via concatenation), and again learns a classifier to predict part beliefs from this combination of features and beliefs using the L_2 loss. The third stage predicts the part beliefs by combining features and the beliefs from the second stage and so on. While the network in [15] uses six stages, our network uses a cascade of four stages. The network is designed to learn interactions within increasingly larger neighbourhoods by repeatedly increasing the receptive fields of the convolutions in each subsequent stage of the cascade. Larger receptive fields are able to model long-range spatial interactions between the landmarks, and help impose geometrical constraints on the locations of the body parts, such as the knee, the hip, the shoulder, etc. The cascaded network predicts the per-pixel beliefs for fourteen landmarks, namely the neck, head, and the left and right ankle, knee, hip, wrist, elbow, shoulder and wrist.

3.5   Joint Angles from Part Locations

The method described in Sect. 3.4 predicts human part locations in the image plane. However, our objective is to estimate joint angles in the world space. After the part beliefs are estimated in the mosaic image, we unstitch the mosaic image, and transfer the part beliefs to the upper and lower images. We then construct the 3D point cloud using the depth images and the intrinsic parameters of the kinect sensors, and transfer the part beliefs to the point clouds. This is followed by registering the point clouds of the upper and lower kinect sensors so that they are in the same space, and transferring the part beliefs to the common system. For each part, we choose the location to be the point with the maximum belief. If the maximum belief for a part is below a threshold ϵ, we conclude that this part is either occluded or truncated. This gives us 3D spatial locations of the body parts. Given the part locations in the world coordinate system, we compute the joint angles using vector algebra.

3.6   Denoising via Sparse Coding

As described in Sect. 3.3, our dataset suffers from drastic scale changes causing the depth to be sparse and noisy. This causes the angle estimates to be noisy. To overcome this difficulty, we pose reconstruction of our predictions as a classic sparse coding based denoising approach. We estimate a dictionary $\mathcal{D}$ of codewords from the ground truth angles $\hat{x}$ by solving the following optimization

$$\mathcal{D}^* = \operatorname*{argmin}_{\mathcal{D},w} ||\hat{x} - \mathcal{D}w||_2^2 + \lambda_1 ||w||_1 + \lambda_2 ||w||_2^2. \tag{3}$$

The reconstruction of noisy predictions x is done by estimating a sparse linear combination w^* of the dictionary as

$$w^* = \operatorname*{argmin}_{w} ||x - \mathcal{D}^*w||_2^2 + \lambda_1 ||w||_1 + \lambda_2 ||w||_2^2$$
$$y = \mathcal{D}^*w^* \tag{4}$$

This reconstruction suggests that the predictions can be represented sparsely over the dictionary, and helps tilt the distribution of the predicted angles towards the ground truth angles. We use this technique to denoise our hip angle predictions. We report results of denoising in Sect. 3.7.

3.7   Experiments and Discussions

In this section we report empirical results for the estimation of hip, and knee angles. As described in Sect. 3.1, our dataset has 27 videos, containing about $9K$ image frames. We use the point trajectories of the shoulders, hips, knees and angles from the MoCap data to compute the ground truth angles. Our prediction pipeline is described in Sect. 3.4. Our networks are trained on $30K$ images from the *MPII* and *Leeds Action Dataset*, as mentioned in Sect. 3.4, and are the state of the art on these challenging datasets. The evaluation criterion is the Root Mean Square Error (RMSE) in degrees between the predicted angles and the ground truth angles. We also report the detection rate for each angle. An angle is said to be *detected* if the locations of all three parts constructing the angle are available. The detection rate for an angle is defined to be the ratio of frames in which the angle is detected.

We first study the effect of changing the threshold ϵ described in Sect. 3.5. This threshold is applied to the maximum beliefs of parts, and introduces a measure of confidence in the part localization. If the maximum belief of a part is below ϵ we conclude that the part is absent. This absence occurs because of occlusion or truncation of parts of interest. Figure 5 shows the variation of RMSE and detection rate for different values of ϵ. As the minimum accepted confidence ϵ increases, RMSE decreases substantially and naturally the detection rate drops due to increasing number of rejected angles. High confidence in part locations, which mainly depends on visibility of parts, leads to better estimates of joint angles. This increase in performance with large ϵ is observed despite the remaining erroneous joint locations, which would have been corrected if more context (and in many cases joints themselves) were visible. This provides evidence that a better placement of the cameras such that full body context is provided to the algorithm would lead to an increase in the performance of the algorithm. To further emphasize this, we exemplify estimated angles and groundtruth angles as a function of time for the same subject and same task under two different camera configurations in Fig. 6. In the configuration where the patient is closer to the sensors and the ankles and shoulders are occluded the algorithm is not able to estimate the angles, whereas in the setting where the subject is distanced from the sensor, the angle estimation is more accurate.

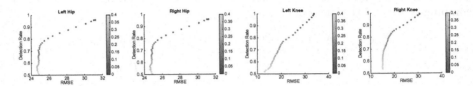

Fig. 5. Variation of *Root Mean Square Error* in degrees and detection rate with confidence threshold ϵ. As the confidence threshold increases (as the colours become hotter), the detection rate and the angle estimation errors decrease.

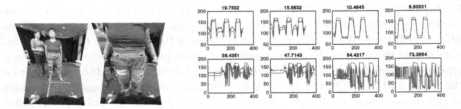

Fig. 6. Angle estimation on same subject and same task(sitting - standing) under different camera configurations. The left image corresponds to a time instance in the top row time series and the right image corresponds to an instance in the bottom row time series: Estimated (red) and the groundtruth angle (blue). The columns portray Left Hips, Right Hips, Left Knee and Right Knee angles respectively. Corresponding RMSE values are displayed on top of each time series. (Color figure online)

For our quantitative results, we choose $\epsilon = 0.2$, which gives a detection rate of 0.75 (Fig. 5). Our results are reported in Table 1. We report the RMSE values for the estimation of the left and right knee and hip angles, averaged over the entire dataset. It can be seen that the errors in estimation of the hip angles are higher than those corresponding to the knee angles. This is due to two factors: (a) the shoulders are truncated when the human subject to too close to the camera (Fig. 2, row 3), and (b) the hip joints are occluded by the elbows and hands (Fig. 2, row 1). Table 1 also reports the estimation errors after the denoising

Table 1. Quantitative results of our Convolutional Pose Machines pipeline for the estimation of joint angles. The evaluation metric is the Root Mean Square Error in degrees. Denoising using a sparse coding strategy improves average performance by 5.4 degrees.

Method	Left knee	Right knee	Left hip	Right hip	Average
CPM	16.16	15.24	24.51	25.27	20.29
CPM + Denoising	13.66	14.23	15.06	16.48	14.86

process described in Sect. 3.6. To estimate the dictionary (Eq. 3), we use a leave-one-out strategy. The dictionary for denoising of a video is constructed using the dataset, leaving out this particular video. The parameters for the dictionary learning procedure are as follows: $\lambda_1 = 10$, $\lambda_2 = 0.001$, and the size of the codebook $K = 200$. We see an improvement in estimation of both the knee and hip angles after denoising, however the improvement in case of the hip angles is more prominent.

4 Dense Trajectories for Gesture Recognition

Gesture recognition allows the interaction of the elderly subjects with the robotic platform through a predefined set of gestural commands. Our gesture classification pipeline, depicted in Fig. 7, employs Dense Trajectories features along with the Bag-of-Visual-Words framework. We briefly describe the individual steps involved and present our experimental results on Task-6a. Dense trajectories [25] consists in sampling feature points from each video frame on a regular grid and tracking them through time based on optical flow. Different descriptors are computed within space-time volumes along each trajectory. Descriptors are: the Trajectory descriptor, HOG [26], HOF [27] and MBH [26].

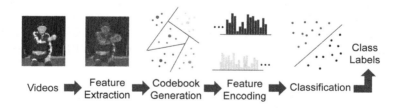

Fig. 7. Gesture classification pipeline.

Features are encoded using BoVW, VLAD or Fisher vector to form a video representation. BoVW uses a codebook which is constructed by clustering a subset of randomly selected training features into $K = 4000$ clusters. Each trajectory is assigned to its closest visual word and a histogram of visual word occurrences is computed, yielding a sparse K-dimensional representation. VLAD encodes first order statistics among features by computing differences between extracted features and the visual words. Fisher vector encodes first and second order statistics using a Gaussian Mixture Model (GMM) with $K = 256$ gaussians. To compensate for the high dimensionality of FV, we reduce the descriptors' dimensionality by a factor of 2 using Principal Component Analysis.

Videos encoded with VLAD or Fisher vector are classified using linear support vector machines (SVMs). Different descriptors are combined by concatenating their respective VLAD or FV vectors. In the BoVW case, videos are classified using SVMs with the χ^2 [26] kernel. Different descriptors are combined in a multichannel approach, by computing distances between BoVW histograms as:

$$K\left(\mathbf{h}_i, \mathbf{h}_j\right) = \exp\left(-\sum_c \frac{1}{A_c} D\left(\mathbf{h}_i^c, \mathbf{h}_j^c\right)\right), \tag{5}$$

where c is the c-th channel, i.e. $\mathbf{h}_i^c$ is the BoVW representation of the i-th video, computed for the c-th descriptor, and A_c is the mean value of χ^2 distances $D\left(\mathbf{h}_i^c, \mathbf{h}_j^c\right)$ between all pairs of training samples. Since we face multiclass classification problems, we follow the one-against-all approach and select the class with the highest score.

Experiments. Gesture classification is carried out on a subset of the Task-6a dataset comprising 8 subjects and 8 gestures[1], without limiting the generality of results. Results are shown in Table 2. It is evident that the large variability of the gesture performance among patients has a great impact on performance. The combined descriptor performs consistently better, since it encodes complementary information extracted from the RGB channel. VLAD and Fisher vector further improve performance, since they encode rich information about the visual words' distribution. Figure 8 depicts the mean confusion matrix over all patients computed for BoVW and the MBH descriptor. Naturally, gestures that are more easily confused by the elderly subjects are harder to classify correctly, e.g. "Help" and "PerformTask" both consist of a similar horizontal movement but in different height.

To demonstrate the difficulty of the task, we use the same gesture classification pipeline on the dataset acquired in [28]. It includes 13 young subjects (Fig. 9) that perform the same 19 gestures as the ones in Task-6a under similar conditions. Training and testing is carried out with the same settings using BoW encoding. Mean classification over all subjects is reported. Comparative results shown in Table 3 illustrate that variability in the execution of the gestures among healthy and cognitively intact subjects is effectively handled by our pipeline. This highlights the challenge that the development of a gestural communication interface for elderly people presents.

---

[1] The 8 selected gestures are: "Help", "WantStandUp", "PerformTask", "WantSitDown", "ComeCloser", "ComeHere", "LetsGo", "Park".

Table 2. Classification accuracy (%) per patient on a subset of the Task-6a dataset that contains 8 gestures performed by 8 subjects. Results for different encoding methods are shown; "avg." stands for average accuracy over all patients.

	BoW									VLAD	Fisher
	p1	p4	p7	p8	p9	p11	p12	p13	Avg.	Avg.	Avg.
Traject	50.0	24.0	35.3	30.3	20.8	43.8	37.5	68.8	38.8	37.0	45.0
HOG	56.3	28.0	38.2	48.5	25.0	62.5	37.5	71.9	46.0	56.6	48.0
HOF	62.5	36.0	32.4	45.5	54.2	46.9	62.5	71.9	51.5	54.9	51.7
MBH	62.5	56.0	44.1	51.5	58.3	56.3	45.8	81.3	57.0	69.9	66.3
Combined	75.0	52.0	52.9	57.6	58.3	65.6	62.5	75.0	**62.4**	**67.6**	**68.1**

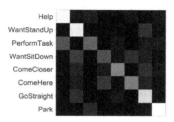

Fig. 8. Mean confusion matrix over all subjects of the Task-6a dataset. The results are obtained with the MBH descriptor and BoW encoding (6th row of Table 2).

Fig. 9. Sample frames from the gesture dataset acquired in [28].

Table 3. Comparative results on Task-6a and the dataset acquired in [28]. Mean classification accuracy (%) over all subjects is reported.

	Task-6a	Dataset from [28]
Traject	38.8	74.0
HOG	46.0	53.8
HOF	51.5	77.3
MBH	57.0	82.5
Combined	62.4	84.8

4.1 Filtering Background Trajectories

To further improve our gesture recognition results, we have worked towards the integration of the body part segmentation method introduced in [9] into our gesture recognition pipeline. Specifically, we use the subject's bounding box to reject noisy background trajectories (see Fig. 10). We compute a separate BoVW histogram that corresponds to the area enclosed by the bounding box, which is used to augment the original BoVW vector. The mask shown in the Fig. 10 is the output of the semantic segmentation algorithm introduced in [9]

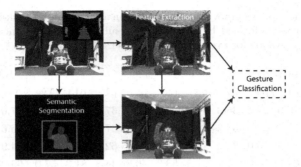

Fig. 10. Combining semantic segmentation with feature extraction for gesture classification on the Task-6a. A separate BoVW histogram is computed for the whole frame and the area enclosed by the bounding box. The two vectors are combined into a single video representation.

and applied on Task-6a data. Following the same experimental protocol as in the rest of the experiments described in this section, we obtained additional improvements on the related Task-6.a scenario, as shown in Table 4 below. Given the simplicity of the employed approach, results show remarkable improvement. A holistic approach for gesture recognition, such as dense trajectories, can greatly benefit from exploiting mid-level information to remove background noise. Our current research plans include more efficient exploitation of the rich information contained in the output of the semantic segmentation pipeline.

Table 4. Average classification accuracy (%) over all 8 patients using our baseline method (first column) and employing the foreground-background mask (second column). Results show a consistent improvement (third column) over multiple feature descriptors. Results are obtained using the BoW encoding.

Feat. Descr.	GR	SS+GR	Impr. (%)
Traject	38.8	42.1	8.59
HOG	46.0	46.7	1.47
HOF	51.5	56.3	9.33
MBH	57.0	63.9	12.18
Combined	62.4	65.6	5.22

4.2   On-Line Processing

Towards the realisation of a user interface that enables elderly subjects interact with the robotic platform, we have implemented an on-line version of our system that performs continuous gesture recognition. ROS is employed to provide the main software layer for interprocess communication.

Our overall system comprises two separate sub-systems: (a) the activity detector (*AD node*) that performs temporal localization of segments that contain visual activity and (b) the gesture classifier (*GC node*) that assigns each detected activity segment into a class. The AD node processes the RGB stream in a frame-by-frame basis and determines whether there is any visual activity in the scene, based on an activity "score", whose value is thresholded. The GC node is appropriately signaled at the beginning and the end of the activity segments. Small segments of activity are rejected to ensure that small spontaneous movements of the user are not processed.

The Gesture Classifier node processes video segments and assigns them to one of the pre-defined categories using the classification pipeline described previously. To reduce the total processing time we downsample RGB frames both in space and time by a factor of 2. The GC node caches input frames from the camera. When the appropriate signal is received, feature extraction begins immediately, starting from the indicated frame's timestamp. When the activity segment ends features are extracted from the remaining frames of the activity segment, the classification pipeline continues. The robot reacts to the recognized gestural command by either providing audio responses or moving in order to assist the elderly user. The system has been integrated in the robotic platform and used by actual elderly patients. It operates approximately at 20 fps on an Intel i7 CPU.

5   Conclusions

In this work we have examined multiple directions on an assistive human-robot interaction task, from the visual processing point of view. We have provided rich algorithmic and experimental evidence on how one may estimate joint angles of the elderly subjects with the given challenging setup and have signified the importance of the sensor localization that includes a full view of the subject. Additionally, we have shown that the adopted sparse coding based denoising approach increases performance. Another application concerns the automatic recognition of gesture commands, as well as a practical integrated system that online processes streaming video data, and accurately recognizes the commands with real-time performance. The systems are currently under validation studies conducted with elderly subjects in geriatric clinics, opening new perspectives in the field of robotic vision for assistive living. Ongoing and future plans involve the more deep integration of the multiple directions presented in this paper, by incorporating the information of the estimated pose and joint angles for gesture recognition, as well as the integration of gesture recognition in an overall network that jointly estimates the pose, and the higher level gesture concepts. Finally, further exploiting the computer vision interface applications with geriatric clinician experts can lead to a deeper understanding on how we should advance and jointly experiment with our approaches so that it would be for the best interest of the interdisciplinary research communities and above all for the benefit of the elderly population.

References

1. OECD: Elderly population (indicator) (2016)
2. Simonyan, K., Zisserman, A.: Two-stream convolutional networks for action recognition in videos. In: Advances in Neural Information Processing Systems, pp. 568–576 (2014)
3. Niebles, J.C., Fei-Fei, L.: A hierarchical model of shape and appearance for human action classification. In: IEEE Conference on Computer Vision and Pattern Recognition, 2007, CVPR 2007, pp. 1–8. IEEE (2007)
4. Niebles, J.C., Wang, H., Fei-Fei, L.: Unsupervised learning of human action categories using spatial-temporal words. Int. J. Comput. Vis. **79**(3), 299–318 (2008)
5. Marszalek, M., Laptev, I., Schmid, C.: Actions in context. In: IEEE Conference on Computer Vision and Pattern Recognition (CVPR 2009), pp. 2929–2936. IEEE (2009)
6. Wang, H., Klaser, A., Schmid, C., Liu, C.L.: Action recognition by dense trajectories. In: 2011 IEEE Conference on Computer Vision and Pattern Recognition (CVPR), pp. 3169–3176. IEEE (2011)
7. Wang, H., Schmid, C.: Action recognition with improved trajectories. In: 2013 IEEE International Conference on Computer Vision (ICCV), pp. 3551–3558. IEEE (2013)
8. Fanello, S.R., Gori, I., Metta, G., Odone, F.: Keep it simple and sparse: Real-time action recognition. J. Mach. Learn. Res. **14**, 2617–2640 (2013)
9. Chandra, S., Tsogkas, S., Kokkinos, I.: Accurate human-limb segmentation in rgb-d images for intelligent mobility assistance robots. In: Proceedings of the IEEE International Conference on Computer Vision Workshops, pp. 44–50 (2015)
10. Fotinea, E.S., Efthimiou, E., Dimou, A.L., Goulas, T., Karioris, P., Peer, A., Maragos, P., Tzafestas, C., Kokkinos, I., Hauer, K., et al.: Data acquisition towards defining a multimodal interaction model for human-assistive robot communication. In: Stephanidis, C., Antona, M. (eds.) UAHCI/HCII 2014. LNCS, vol. 8515, pp. 613–624. Springer, Heidelberg (2014)
11. Escalera, S., Gonzàlez, J., Baró, X., Reyes, M., Guyon, I., Athitsos, V., Escalante, H., Sigal, L., Argyros, A., Sminchisescu, C., Bowden, R., Sclaroff, S.: Chalearn multi-modal gesture recognition 2013: grand challenge and workshop summary. In: Proceedings of the 15th ACM on International Conference on Multimodal Interaction, pp. 365–368. ACM (2013)
12. Sun, Y., Wang, X., Tang, X.: Deep convolutional network cascade for facial point detection. In: Proceedings of the IEEE Conference on Computer Vision and Pattern Recognition, pp. 3476–3483 (2013)
13. Toshev, A., Szegedy, C.: Deeppose: Human pose estimation via deep neural networks. In: Proceedings of the IEEE Conference on Computer Vision and Pattern Recognition, pp. 1653–1660 (2014)
14. Tompson, J., Jain, A., LeCun, Y., Bregler, C.: Joint Training of a convolutional network and a graphical model for human pose estimation. In: NIPS (2014)
15. Wei, S.E., Ramakrishna, V., Kanade, T., Sheikh, Y.: Convolutional pose machines. arXiv preprint arXiv:1602.00134 (2016)
16. Belagiannis, V., Zisserman, A.: Recurrent human pose estimation. arXiv preprint arXiv:1605.02914 (2016)
17. Lifshitz, I., Fetaya, E., Ullman, S.: Human pose estimation using deep consensus voting. arXiv preprint arXiv:1603.08212 (2016)

18. Haque, A., Peng, B., Luo, Z., Alahi, A., Yeung, S., Fei-Fei, L.: Viewpoint invariant 3d human pose estimation with recurrent error feedback. arXiv preprint arXiv:1603.07076 (2016)
19. Ramakrishna, Varun, Munoz, Daniel, Hebert, Martial, Andrew Bagnell, James, Sheikh, Yaser: Pose machines: articulated pose estimation via inference machines. In: Fleet, David, Pajdla, Tomas, Schiele, Bernt, Tuytelaars, Tinne (eds.) ECCV 2014. LNCS, vol. 8690, pp. 33–47. Springer, Heidelberg (2014). doi:10.1007/978-3-319-10605-2_3
20. Carreira, J., Agrawal, P., Fragkiadaki, K., Malik, J.: Human pose estimation with iterative error feedback. arXiv preprint arXiv:1507.06550 (2015)
21. Insafutdinov, E., Pishchulin, L., Andres, B., Andriluka, M., Schiele, B.: Deepercut: A deeper, stronger, and faster multi-person pose estimation model. arXiv preprint arXiv:1605.03170 (2016)
22. Hochreiter, S., Schmidhuber, J.: Long short-term memory. Neural Comput. 9(8), 1735–1780 (1997)
23. Andriluka, M., Pishchulin, L., Gehler, P., Schiele, B.: 2d human pose estimation: New benchmark and state of the art analysis. In: IEEE Conference on Computer Vision and Pattern Recognition (CVPR), June 2014
24. Johnson, S., Everingham, M.: Clustered pose and nonlinear appearance models for human pose estimation. In: Proceedings of the British Machine Vision Conference (2010). doi:10.5244/C.24.12
25. Wang, H., Klaser, A., Schmid, C., Liu, C.L.: Action recognition by dense trajectories. In: 2011 IEEE Conference on Computer Vision and Pattern Recognition (CVPR), pp. 3169–3176, June 2011
26. Wang, H., Ullah, M.M., Klser, A., Laptev, I., Schmid, C.: Evaluation of local spatio-temporal features for action recognition. In: University of Central Florida, U.S.A. (2009)
27. Laptev, I., Marszalek, M., Schmid, C., Rozenfeld, B.: Learning realistic human actions from movies. In: IEEE Conference on Computer Vision and Pattern Recognition, CVPR 2008, pp. 1–8, June 2008
28. Rodomagoulakis, I., Kardaris, N., Pitsikalis, V., Arvanitakis, A., Maragos, P.: A multimedia gesture dataset for human-robot communication: acquisition, tools and recognition results. In: IEEE International Conference on Image Processing (ICIP 2016), September 2016

A 3D Human Posture Approach for Activity Recognition Based on Depth Camera

Alessandro Manzi$^{(\boxtimes)}$, Filippo Cavallo, and Paolo Dario

The BioRobotics Institute, Scuola Superiore Sant'Anna, Pisa, Italy
{a.manzi,f.cavallo,p.dario}@sssup.it

Abstract. Human activity recognition plays an important role in the context of Ambient Assisted Living (AAL), providing useful tools to improve people quality of life. This work presents an activity recognition algorithm based on the extraction of skeleton joints from a depth camera. The system describes an activity using a set of few and basic postures extracted by means of the X-means clustering algorithm. A multi-class Support Vector Machine, trained with the Sequential Minimal Optimization is employed to perform the classification. The system is evaluated on two public datasets for activity recognition which have different skeleton models, the CAD-60 with 15 joints and the TST with 25 joints. The proposed approach achieves precision/recall performances of 99.8 % on CAD-60 and 97.2 %/91.7 % on TST. The results are promising for an applied use in the context of AAL.

Keywords: Activity monitoring systems · Human activity recognition · Depth camera · RGB-D camera · Ambient Assisted Living · Assistive technologies

1 Introduction

Human activity recognition is one of the most important areas of computer vision research today. It can be described as the spatiotemporal evolutions of different body postures and its main goal is to automatically detect human activities analyzing data from various types of devices (e.g. color cameras or range sensors). Regarding the assistive technologies, the possibility of application is really wide, in particular, they can include surveillance and monitoring systems, and a large range of applications involving human-machine interactions [1]. Although the recognition of human actions is very important for many real applications, it is still a challenging problem. In the past, the research has mainly focused on recognizing activities from video sequences by means of color cameras. However, capturing articulated human motion from monocular video sensors results in a considerable loss of information [2]. These solutions are often constrained in terms of computational efficiency and robustness to illumination changes [3]. Another approach is to use 3D data from marker-based motion capture or stereo camera systems, i.e. capturing 2D image sequences from multiple views to reconstruct 3D information [4]. Nowadays, the use of depth cameras has become very

© Springer International Publishing Switzerland 2016
G. Hua and H. Jégou (Eds.): ECCV 2016 Workshops, Part II, LNCS 9914, pp. 432–447, 2016.
DOI: 10.1007/978-3-319-48881-3_30

popular, because the technological progress has made available devices that are cost effective providing also 3D data at suitable resolution rate. Recently, this kind of sensors has led several new works on activity recognition from depth data [5,6]. These inexpensive devices, such as Microsoft Kinect or Asus Xtion, allow capturing both color and depth information. Moreover, specific tracker software can efficiently detect the human skeleton directly from the depth maps [7]. These features can be exploited in order to develop effective solutions for Ambient Assistive Living applications, simplify the problem of human detection and segmentation. In particular, the depth maps are not affected by environment light variations and, at the same time, they guarantee the user privacy more than the color information [8]. Although there are several types of research on this topic, challenges still remain on how to process these kinds of data to effectively detect actions in real world scenarios.

The present work describes a human activity recognition system based on skeleton data extracted from a depth camera. The activity is represented with few and basic postures obtained with the X-means clustering algorithm. The Sequential Minimal Optimization (SMO) is used to train a multiclass SVM in order to classify the different activities. The system is trained on two publicly available datasets, the CAD-60, widely used for activity recognition and the TST, a dataset created for assistive technologies. The performances outperform the state-of-the-art on these datasets making the system suitable for Ambient Assistive Living real applications.

The remainder of the paper is organized as follows. Section 2 summarizes activity recognition methods, while the Sect. 3 details the developed system. The experimental results are presented in the Sect. 4 and Sect. 5 concludes the paper.

2   Related Works

In the past, human activities recognition methods have been focused on the processing of color images from traditional cameras. Some authors focus on the extraction of the human silhouettes from images using HMMs [9,10] or SVMs [11] to classify different postures. The drawbacks of these methods are low robustness in the case of complex environments and light variations. Other approaches are based on the detection of scale-invariant spatiotemporal features [12]. These features are convenient to detect moving objects, but problems arise in the presence of multiple persons and dynamic background. Wearable sensors are another alternative for activity recognition [13,14]. Usually, they provide more accurate information, but they are too intrusive for most people.

Recently, depth cameras are become very popular on the activity recognition topic, because they offer several advantages over traditional video cameras. First of all, they are inexpensive devices able to work also in poor light conditions. In addition, the RGB-D cameras provide human skeleton information that can significantly simplify the task of human detection. Wang et al. [15] introduce the concept of actionlet, which is a particular sequence of features, so-called local occupancy features. An activity is described as a combination of actionlet. In [16], action recognition is performed extracting human postures. The postures are represented as a bag of 3D points and the actions are modeled as a graph, whose nodes are the extracted postures. Sung et al. [17] represent an activity as a set of subactivities, which is modeled using more than 700 features computing the Histogram of Oriented Gradient both on color images and on depth maps. A hierarchical maximum entropy Markov model is used to associate sub-activities with an high-level activity. Other authors focus on the use of multimodal features, i.e. combining color and depth information [18,19]. Space-Time Occupancy Patterns is proposed in [20] that divides space and time axes in multiple segments in order to embed a depth map sequence in multiple 4D grids. In [21] the EigenJoints feature descriptor is proposed, combining static posture, motion property and dynamics. They use motion energy to select the informative frame and use a Naive-Bayes-Nearest-Neighbor classifier for classification. Koppula et al. [22] use also object affordances and a Markov Random Field to represent their relationship with sub-activities. Zhu et al. [23] employ several spatio-temporal interest point features extracted from depth maps in combination of skeleton joints to classify actions with an SVM. These methods can reach good results, but usually, their performances depend on the complexity of the background scene and on the noise present on the depth data.

Other approaches use only the 3D human skeleton model to extract informative features to classify. Several joints representations have been proposed, Gan and Chen [24] propose the APJ3D representation computing the relative positions and local spherical angles from the skeleton joints. The HOJ3D, presented in [25], associates each joint to a particular area using a Gaussian weight function. The temporal evolution of the postures is modeled with a discrete Hidden Markov Model. Gaglio et al. [26] estimate the postures using a multiclass SVM and create an activity model using discrete HMM. Other works consider also trajectories of joints [27]. Some researchers focus on the selection of the most informative joints to improve the classification results [28,29]. In [30] a clustering method is applied to extract relevant features and a multiclass SVM is used for classification.

Looking at the aforementioned works, it is possible to understand that some authors try to extrapolate relevant features from multimodal data, while others exclusively rely on the human skeleton obtained from tracker software. Using more data not always yields better results, and sometimes simple solutions are preferable. The present work belongs to the latter case and it is based on the concept of informative postures known as "key poses". This concept has been introduced in [31] and extensively used in the literature [32,33]. Some authors identify key poses calculating the kinetic energy [34,35] to segment an activity in static and dynamic poses. But not all the activities can be represented by alternating static and dynamic motions. Our approach is similar to [30], which uses clustering techniques to extrapolate the key poses, but conversely, our method represents an activity with a set of features based on few and basic informative postures.

3   Activity Recognition System

The aim of the implemented system is to infer the user activity using a combination of machine learning techniques. As already said in Sect. 1, we develop a system based only on the 3D skeleton data in order to deal with less number of features compared to color images. Moreover, using only skeleton data allows having much high privacy for the user. The idea is to describe an activity with a sequence of few and informative basic postures.

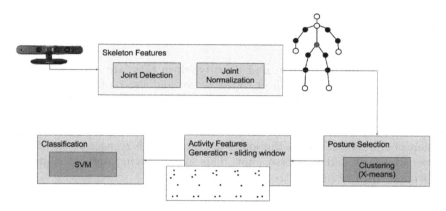

Fig. 1. The system is composed of 4 steps. The skeleton data are obtained from the sensor, and the posture features are processed. Informative postures are extracted from the sequence. Then, the activity features are generated from the basic postures. Finally, a classifier is applied.

The system is composed of four main steps (see Fig. 1). First of all, the relevant skeleton features (i.e. spatial joints) are extracted from the RGB-D device. Then, the basic and informative postures are selected using a clustering method. Afterwards, a new sequence of cluster centroids is built to have a temporal sequence of cluster transitions and an activity window is applied in order to create the activity feature. Finally, a classifier is trained to perform the recognition of the activity.

3.1   Posture Features

The coordinates of the human skeleton are extracted from the depth maps captured by the RGB-D sensor [7]. A human pose is represented by a number of joints that varies depending on the skeleton model of the software tracker (usually it can be 15, 20, or 25). The Fig. 2(a) shows a skeleton made of 15 joints. Each joint is described with three-dimensional Euclidean coordinates with respect to the sensor. The posture features are extracted directly from this skeleton model.

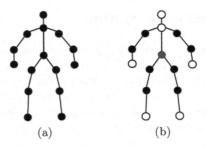

Fig. 2. Representation of the human skeleton: (a) Original 15 joints (b) Subset of joints for the posture feature (white), and the reference joint (torso) is in gray.

These raw data cannot be used directly, since they are dependent on the position of the human with respect to the sensor and also on the subject dimension, such as height and limb length. Therefore, the skeleton data are normalized following a widely used method [26, 30, 34]. The reference system is changed from the camera to the torso joint, in order to have data that are independent of the position of the sensor. Then, the joints are scaled with respect to the distance between the neck and the torso joint. This allows having data that are more independent with respect to the person specific size.

Formally, considering a skeleton with N joints, the skeleton feature vector $\mathbf{f}$ is defined as:

$$\mathbf{f} = [\, \mathbf{j}_1, \mathbf{j}_2, \ldots, \mathbf{j}_{N-1} \,] \tag{1}$$

where each $\mathbf{j}_i$ is the vector containing the 3-D normalized coordinates of the ith joint $\mathbf{J}_i$ detected by the sensor. Therefore, $\mathbf{j}_i$ is defined as

$$\mathbf{j}_i = \frac{\mathbf{J}_i - \mathbf{J}_0}{\|\mathbf{J}_1 - \mathbf{J}_0\|}, \quad i = 1, 2, ..., N - 1 \tag{2}$$

where $\mathbf{J}_0$ and $\mathbf{J}_1$ are the coordinates of the torso and the neck joint respectively. These normalized skeleton features can be seen as a set of distance vectors with respect to the torso joint and the number of attributes of the feature vector $\mathbf{f}$ in (1) is $3(N-1)$. Many works use a reduced set of joints since not all of them are really informative for the recognition of an activity. Moreover, using all the joints leads an increase of the complexity of the problem affecting the performances of the recognition phase. In Sect. 4, we will show results using different subsets of joints. However, our best results are obtained using a feature vector with $N = 7$, namely the head, the neck, the hands, and the feet (see Fig. 2(b)) and the torso as a reference. It is worth to note that we have tested our system on two datasets containing a different representation of the skeleton (15 and 25 joints) and we obtained our best performances with the same value of N. This restricted set of joints has shown to be the most discriminative for activity recognition, allowing also to reduce the complexity of the further steps of computation. As a consequence, in this case, a posture feature is made by

18 attributes. The next section describes how the most informative postures are selected from the all activity sequence.

3.2 Selection of Postures

The aim of the system is to represent an activity as multiple sequences of few and basic postures, i.e. key poses. This phase is in charge of select general and informative postures for each activity. Some authors [23,34] identify key poses calculating their kinetic energy and then considering a template of static and dynamic postures. This approach can be successfully used to discriminate some kinds of actions, but it is not necessarily the most suitable for others. In fact, some action samples may not have identifiable poses with zero kinetic energy, as also pointed out in [34]. Conversely, our approach aims to extrapolate few postures that are able to describe a specific activity by means of a clustering technique. One of the most used algorithms is the K-means, introduced in [36] and developed in many variations [37,38]. However, one of the main issues of this method is that the number of desired K clusters needs to be known a priori. Another possible approach is to run the K-means algorithm repeatedly for different values of K. However, this method is time consuming. As an alternative, we adopt the X-means algorithm [39], which is an optimized version of the previous one. It attempts to split the centers into regions and to select the number of clusters using a probabilistic scheme called Bayes Information Criterion. The X-means is much faster that run repeatedly K-means with a different number of clusters and it has proved to be less prone to local minima than its counterpart. In addition, it automatically finds the optimal number of clusters [40].

For each activity, the X-means is applied using the Euclidean distance function as a metric. In detail, given an activity composed by M posture features $[\mathbf{f}_1, \mathbf{f}_2, \ldots, \mathbf{f}_M]$, the X-means gives k clusters $[\mathbf{C}_1, \mathbf{C}_2, \ldots, \mathbf{C}_k]$, so as to minimize the intra-cluster sum of squares

$$\arg\min_{\mathbf{C}} \sum_{j=1}^{k} \sum_{\mathbf{f}_i \in C_j} \|\mathbf{f}_i - \mu_j\|^2 \tag{3}$$

where μ_j is the mean value of the cluster $\mathbf{C}_j$. At this stage, the set of posture features $\mathbf{f}_i$ representing an activity sequence is replaced with the centroid that the posture feature belongs, hence the centroids can be seen as the key poses of the activity.

3.3 Activity Features Generation

The aim of this step is to generate suitable features able to encode an activity. At this stage, the activity is composed of a set of centroids representing the most important postures for the sequence aligned in temporal order. The cardinality of this set is equal to the number of frames constituting the original action data. The features computed in the Sect. 3.2 need to be reduced in order to lower the complexity and increase the generality of the representation. An important aspect to take into account is also the speed invariance of the feature since different person performs activities at different speed. In other words, this step considers only the transitions between key poses, i.e. transitions between centroids. For this reason, the temporal sequence obtained in Sect. 3.2 is now simplified in order to include only the transitions between clusters. This means that all the equal centroids that are consecutive in temporal order are discarded. This new compressed sequence allows to have a more compact representation of the activity and it is also speed invariant. At the end of the process, an action sequence is encoded in a temporally ordered sequence of centroids transitions. In order to be as general as possible, our aim is to characterize an activity defining several n-tuples composed of n poses. Therefore, the problem is to segment the obtained sequence. But, what exactly characterize an activity? Let consider a person who is drinking a glass of water. Does the action start when he is actually drinking? Or does it start when he begin to move his hand close to the mouth? And also, a person can drink in one or several gulps. To obtain our n-tuples, we adopt a sliding window on the sequence and we generate a set of new instances to represent the whole activity sequence. Consequently, the new instances are composed of a set of features with a size of $3L(N-1)$, where L is the length of the sliding window and N is the number of the selected skeleton joints.

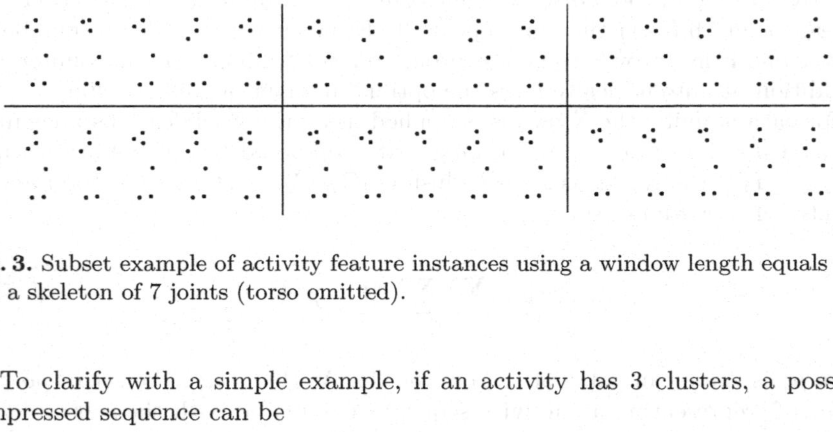

Fig. 3. Subset example of activity feature instances using a window length equals to 5 and a skeleton of 7 joints (torso omitted).

To clarify with a simple example, if an activity has 3 clusters, a possible compressed sequence can be

$$\mathbf{A} = [\mathbf{C}_1, \mathbf{C}_3, \mathbf{C}_2, \mathbf{C}_3, \mathbf{C}_2, \mathbf{C}_3, \mathbf{C}_2, \mathbf{C}_3, \mathbf{C}_2] \tag{4}$$

if the length of the sliding window is $L = 5$, the cardinality of the activity feature instances is 3:

$$\begin{aligned}
\mathbf{A}_1 &= [\mathbf{C}_1, \mathbf{C}_3, \mathbf{C}_2, \mathbf{C}_3, \mathbf{C}_2] \\
\mathbf{A}_2 &= [\mathbf{C}_3, \mathbf{C}_2, \mathbf{C}_3, \mathbf{C}_2, \mathbf{C}_3] \\
\mathbf{A}_3 &= [\mathbf{C}_2, \mathbf{C}_3, \mathbf{C}_2, \mathbf{C}_3, \mathbf{C}_2]
\end{aligned} \tag{5}$$

The cardinality of the instances is related to the number of different transitions between different key poses. This means that actions which are repetitive during the time will have fewer features instances than the ones with more variability between key poses. However, the newly generated instances are directly proportional to the window size in most of the cases. Figure 3 shows some activity feature instances of the drinking action using $L = 5$ and $N = 7$ (torso is omitted). For the training phase of the classifier, a dataset of activity feature instances has been built. The weight of the instances is increased if the same tuple appears in the sequence.

3.4 Activity Recognition

The activity recognition step involves the use of a classifier to associate the features created in the Sect. 3.3. Usually, machine learning techniques are applied to accomplish this task. In this work, we adopt the Sequential Minimal Optimization (SMO) [41] to train a multiclass Support Vector Machine (SVM) [42]. SVMs are supervised learning models used for binary classification calculating the optimal hyperplane that separates two classes in the feature space, while SMO makes use of improved internal structures and linear kernels in order to optimize the training phase. The multiclass SVM version is implemented by combining several binary SVMs using, in our case, a one-versus-one strategy [43].

4 Experimental Results

The system is implemented in Java using the Weka library [44], which is an open source software containing a collection of machine learning algorithms for data mining tasks. We have tested our system on two publicly available datasets, the first one is the well-known Cornell Activity Dataset (CAD-60) [17], widely used in activity recognition, while the second one is the fairly new TST dataset [45], specifically created for Activities of Daily Living (ADL). The skeleton model of these datasets are quite different, the first one represents it with 15 joints, while the second one uses 25 joints.

4.1 CAD-60 Dataset

The dataset focuses on realistic actions from daily life. It has been collected using a depth camera and contains actions performed by four different human subjects, two males, and two females. Three of the subjects use the right hand to perform actions, while one of them uses the left hand. There are 12 types of actions in the dataset, which are: "talking on the phone", "writing on whiteboard", "drinking water", "rinsing mouth with water", "brushing teeth", "wearing contact lenses", "talking on couch", "relaxing on couch", "cooking (chopping)", "cooking (stirring)", "opening pill container", and "working on computer". The dataset contains RGB, depth, and skeleton data, with 15 joints available. Each subject performs the activity twice, so one sample contains two occurrences of the same activity.

Table 1. Overall precision and Recall (%) values using 4 clusters and different window activity sizes on CAD-60.

Window size	"new person"	
	Precision	Recall
5	98.5	98.4
6	98.9	98.6
7	99.4	99.4
8	99.2	99.2
9	99.5	99.5
10	99.6	99.5
11	99.8	99.8
12	99.8	99.8

To be able to compare the results, we employ the same experimental settings of [17]. It consists of two cases: the "have seen" and "new person" setting. In the first case, the classification is done with the data of all the four persons, splitting the data in half. The latter uses a leave-one-out cross-validation approach for testing. This means that the classifier is trained on three of the four people and tested on the fourth. Since one person is left-handed, all the skeleton data are mirrored with respect to the sagittal plane of the skeleton. Conversely from [34], in which the right and left-handed samples are trained and tested separately, our samples contains both original and mirrored data. As for the other works on the CAD dataset, the performance is reported in terms of the average precision and recall among all the activities according to the "new person" test case.

At the beginning, the posture features are extracted as explained in the Sect. 3.1. After extensive tests, we have found that the most informative joints for our system are the head, the neck, hands and feet ($N = 7$). The output of the X-means algorithm (Sect. 3.2) gives 4 clusters as results for the majority of the activities. The activity features are generated following the procedure detailed in the Sect. 3.3. The last parameter that needs to be find is the size of the sliding window. We trained our classifier using different window size, ranging from 5 to 12. Therefore, the length of activity features has a minimum value of 90 and a maximum of 216, according to the window size.

In the "have seen" setting, the overall precision/recall reach always the 100 % for all the values of the clusters and the window size. This is coherent with the other works on the same dataset, in which most of them reaches the same result. More interesting is the outcome of the "new person" test case. The precision and recall values for all the tested window size are reported in Table 1. All of them produce high values in terms of precision and recall. Considering that the number of generated activity instances increases with the size of the window, we decided to select $N = 11$ to minimize the number of instances and maximize the performance. In this case, the total number of activity features is 199, i.e.

Table 2. Precision and Recall values for each activity, using 4 clusters and a window size of 11 elements on CAD-60.

Activity	"new person"	
	Precision	Recall
talking on the phone	1.0	1.0
writing on whiteboard	1.0	1.0
drinking water	1.0	1.0
rinsing mouth with water	1.0	1.0
brushing teeth	1.0	1.0
wearing contact lenses	1.0	1.0
talking on couch	1.0	1.0
relaxing on couch	1.0	1.0
cooking (chopping)	1.0	.977
cooking (stirring)	.969	1.0
opening pill container	1.0	1.0
working on computer	1.0	1.0
Overall	**.998**	**.998**

Table 3. The confusion matrix of the "new person" test case using $K = 4$ clusters and $N = 11$ window activity size on CAD-60.

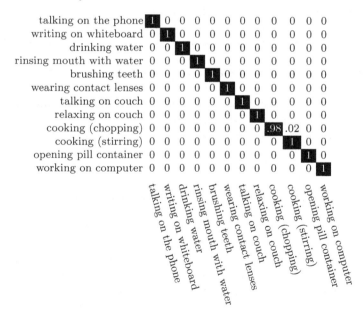

Table 4. Precision and Recall values for different joint configuration on CAD-60.

Joints	"new person"	
	Precision	Recall
15	0.826	0.851
11	0.816	0.823
7	0.998	0.998

Table 5. State of the art precision and recall values (%) on CAD-60 dataset.

	Precision	Recall
Zhu et al. [23]	93.2	84.6
Faria et al. [46]	91.1	91.9
Shan et al. [34]	93.8	94.5
Parisi et al. [47]	91.9	90.2
Cippitelli et al. [30]	93.9	93.5
Our method	99.8	99.8

size of the window equals to 11, and 7 joints, plus the activity attribute. The Table 2 shows the precision and recall values according to each activity using $K = 4$ clusters and $N = 11$ window activity size for the "new person" test case as usually reported for the CAD-60 dataset, while Table 3 shows the relative confusion matrix. The "cooking (chopping)" activity has been misclassified with the "cooking (stirring)" in only a few instances, indeed these activities are very similar. The algorithms have been run on a machine with a 2.4 GHz quad-core i7 processor and 8 Gb RAM. The activity features extraction took 70 milliseconds per activity. In the "new person" test case, the time to train the classifier was 1.24 s on 3564 instances. The time took for the test phase was 0.13 s on 920 instances. We have also conducted additional tests using different joint configuration: all 15 skeleton joints and 11 joints (excluding only shoulder and hip joints). Results prove that adding more joints does not improve the classification rate (see Table 4). The overall precision and recall value is 0.998 and this result outperforms the other works on the CAD-60 dataset. In the Table 5 is reported the current 5 best results of the CAD-60 dataset.

4.2 TST Dataset

We have tested our system also on the fairly new TST Fall detection database (version 2) [45]. The dataset has been collected using Microsoft Kinect v2 and IMU (Inertial Measurement Unit). It is composed of ADL and fall actions simulated by 11 volunteers. The people involved in the test are aged between 22 and 39, with different height (1.62–1.97 m) and sizes. The actions performed by a single person are separated into two main groups: ADL and Fall. Each activity is repeated three

Table 6. Overall precision and Recall values using 4 clusters and different window activity sizes on TST dataset.

Window size	"new person"			
	ADL		Fall	
	Precision	Recall	Precision	Recall
5	1	1	.960	.955
6	.962	.958	.955	.947
7	.951	.944	.95	.938
8	.940	.929	.946	.929
9	.938	.923	.942	.923
10	.938	.917	.938	.917
11	.938	.917	.938	.917
12	.938	.917	.938	.917

Table 7. Precision and Recall values for each activity, using 4 clusters and a window size of 5 elements on TST Dataset.

	"new person"		
	Activity	Precision	Recall
ADL	sit on chair	1.0	1.0
	walk and grasp	1.0	1.0
	walk back and forth	1.0	1.0
	lie down	1.0	1.0
Overall		**1**	**1**
Fall	frontal fall	1.0	.667
	backward fall	.889	1.0
	side fall	1.0	1.0
	backward fall and sit	1.0	1.0
Overall		**.972**	**.917**

times by each subject involved. The database contains 264 different actions for a total of 46k skeleton samples and 230 k acceleration values. Each person performs the following movements: "sit on chair", "walk and grasp an object", "walk back and forth", "lie down", "frontal fall and lying", "backward fall and lying", "side fall and lying", "fall backward and sit". Also for this dataset, we obtain the best performances using $N = 7$ joints. Applying the X-means algorithm we have an average number of clusters of $K = 4$ as for the CAD-60 dataset. We employ the same experimental settings as before, testing the classifier with the "new person" configuration. The Table 6 reports the overall precision and recall values of the ADL and Fall samples. In this case, the best window size is 5. This is coherent with the fact that each sample of the TST dataset contains a subject that performs the action only once, while the subjects of the CAD-60 dataset perform the actions twice. We report in Table 7 the precision and recall values for each activity using 4 clusters and a window size of 5 elements. Only few frontal fall samples are misclassified with a backward falling, while the other samples are correctly classified.

5   Conclusion

This paper describes an activity recognition system using skeleton data obtained from an RGB-D sensor. The developed system is based on the idea of representing an activity with few and basic key poses, i.e. informative skeleton postures. The key poses are extracted using the X-means algorithm, and the activity features are built considering the centroid transition during the action. A multiclass SVM, trained with the SOM optimization, is used for the classification step. The system is tested on two publicly available datasets, the CAD-60 and the TST (version 2). The first is a well-known and widely used dataset for activity recognition. The results outperform the state-of-the-art, achieving an overall precision and recall of 0.998. The TST is a new dataset more close to the assistive technologies containing ADL and also Fall samples. The system does not misclassify sample of ADL case, and the overall precision and recall for the falling samples are 0.97 and 0.92 respectively. In particular, the misclassification happens with the frontal fall detected as backward fall. It does not represent a real issue from the perspective of a monitoring application for the ambient assistive living since these actions are essentially the same. It is also worth to note that the most informative skeleton joints are the same for both datasets, despite the fact that the original model is different, 15 against 25 joints.

These encouraging results make it feasible to use the presented system for assistive application and it will concern our future works. Anyway, one of the main drawbacks of the adopted classifier is that it is not able to handle unknown classes. In fact, it will always return one of the classes that better adapts to the observed one. Further study will be conducted in order to develop a real-time system for assistive scenarios exploiting the presented system.

References

1. Poppe, R.: A survey on vision-based human action recognition. Image Vis. Comput. **28**(6), 976–990 (2010)
2. Aggarwal, J.K., Ryoo, M.S.: Human activity analysis: a review. ACM Comput. Surv. (CSUR) **43**(3), 16 (2011)
3. Weinland, D., Ronfard, R., Boyer, E.: A survey of vision-based methods for action representation, segmentation and recognition. Comput. Vis. Image Underst. **115**(2), 224–241 (2011)
4. Argyriou, V., Petrou, M., Barsky, S.: Photometric stereo with an arbitrary number of illuminants. Comput. Vis. Image Underst. **114**(8), 887–900 (2010)
5. Aggarwal, J.K., Xia, L.: Human activity recognition from 3d data: a review. Pattern Recogn. Lett. **48**, 70–80 (2014)

6. Han, J., Shao, L., Xu, D., Shotton, J.: Enhanced computer vision with microsoft kinect sensor: a review. IEEE Trans. Cybern. **43**(5), 1318–1334 (2013)
7. Shotton, J., Sharp, T., Kipman, A., Fitzgibbon, A., Finocchio, M., Blake, A., Cook, M., Moore, R.: Real-time human pose recognition in parts from single depth images. Commun. ACM **56**(1), 116–124 (2013)
8. Padilla-López, J.R., Chaaraoui, A.A., Gu, F., Flórez-Revuelta, F.: Visual privacy by context: proposal and evaluation of a level-based visualisation scheme. Sensors **15**(6), 12959–12982 (2015)
9. Yamato, J., Ohya, J., Ishii, K.: Recognizing human action in time-sequential images using hidden markov model. In: 1992 IEEE Computer Society Conference on Computer Vision and Pattern Recognition, 1992. Proceedings CVPR 1992, pp. 379–385. IEEE (1992)
10. Kellokumpu, V., Pietikäinen, M., Heikkilä, J.: Human activity recognition using sequences of postures. In: MVA, pp. 570–573 (2005)
11. Scholkopf, B., Smola, A.J.: Learning with kernels: support vector machines, regularization, optimization, and beyond. MIT press (2001)
12. Willems, G., Tuytelaars, T., Van Gool, L.: An efficient dense and scale-invariant spatio-temporal interest point detector. In: Forsyth, D., et al. (eds.) ECCV 2008. LNCS, vol. 5303, pp. 650–663. Springer, Heidelberg (2008)
13. Preece, S.J., Goulermas, J.Y., Kenney, L.P., Howard, D., Meijer, K., Crompton, R.: Activity identification using body-mounted sensorsa review of classification techniques. Physiol. Meas. **30**(4), R1 (2009)
14. Bao, L., Intille, S.S.: Activity recognition from user-annotated acceleration data. In: Ferscha, A., Mattern, F. (eds.) PERVASIVE 2004. LNCS, vol. 3001, pp. 1–17. Springer, Heidelberg (2004)
15. Wang, J., Liu, Z., Wu, Y.: Learning actionlet ensemble for 3d human action recognition. In: Human Action Recognition with Depth Cameras, pp. 11–40. Springer, Heidelberg (2014)
16. Li, W., Zhang, Z., Liu, Z.: Action recognition based on a bag of 3d points. In: 2010 IEEE Computer Society Conference on Computer Vision and Pattern Recognition-Workshops, pp. 9–14. IEEE (2010)
17. Sung, J., Ponce, C., Selman, B., Saxena, A.: Unstructured human activity detection from rgbd images. In: 2012 IEEE International Conference on Robotics and Automation (ICRA), pp. 842–849. IEEE (2012)
18. Ni, B., Pei, Y., Moulin, P., Yan, S.: Multilevel depth and image fusion for human activity detection. IEEE Trans. Cybern. **43**(5), 1383–1394 (2013)
19. Ni, B., Wang, G., Moulin, P.: Rgbd-hudaact: a color-depth video database for human daily activity recognition. In: Fossati, A., et al. (eds.) Consumer Depth Cameras for Computer Vision, pp. 193–208. Springer, London (2013)
20. Vieira, A.W., Nascimento, E.R., Oliveira, G.L., Liu, Z., Campos, M.F.: Stop: Space-time occupancy patterns for 3d action recognition from depth map sequences. In: Alvarez, L., et al. (eds.) CIARP 2012. LNCS, vol. 7441, pp. 252–259. Springer, Heidelberg (2012)
21. Yang, X., Tian, Y.: Effective 3d action recognition using eigenjoints. J. Vis. Commun. Image Represent. **25**(1), 2–11 (2014)
22. Koppula, H.S., Gupta, R., Saxena, A.: Learning human activities and object affordances from rgb-d videos. Int. J. Robot. Res. **32**(8), 951–970 (2013)
23. Zhu, Y., Chen, W., Guo, G.: Evaluating spatiotemporal interest point features for depth-based action recognition. Image Vis. Comput. **32**(8), 453–464 (2014)
24. Gan, L., Chen, F.: Human action recognition using apj3d and random forests. J. Softw. **8**(9), 2238–2245 (2013)

25. Xia, L., Chen, C.C., Aggarwal, J.: View invariant human action recognition using histograms of 3d joints. In: 2012 IEEE Computer Society Conference on Computer Vision and Pattern Recognition Workshops, pp. 20–27. IEEE (2012)
26. Gaglio, S., Re, G.L., Morana, M.: Human activity recognition process using 3-d posture data. IEEE Trans. Hum. Mach. Syst. 45(5), 586–597 (2015)
27. Ding, W., Liu, K., Cheng, F., Zhang, J.: Stfc: spatio-temporal feature chain for skeleton-based human action recognition. J. Vis. Commun. Image Represent. 26, 329–337 (2015)
28. Jiang, M., Kong, J., Bebis, G., Huo, H.: Informative joints based human action recognition using skeleton contexts. Sig. Process. Image Commun. 33, 29–40 (2015)
29. Chaaraoui, A.A., Padilla-López, J.R., Climent-Pérez, P., Flórez-Revuelta, F.: Evolutionary joint selection to improve human action recognition with rgb-d devices. Expert Syst. Appl. 41(3), 786–794 (2014)
30. Cippitelli, E., Gasparrini, S., Gambi, E., Spinsante, S.: A human activity recognition system using skeleton data from rgbd sensors. Comput. Intell. Neurosci. 2016, 14 (2016)
31. Baysal, S., Kurt, M.C., Duygulu, P.: Recognizing human actions using key poses. In: 2010 20th International Conference on Pattern Recognition (ICPR), pp. 1727–1730. IEEE (2010)
32. Ballan, L., Bertini, M., Bimbo, A.D., Seidenari, L., Serra, G.: Effective codebooks for human action categorization. In: IEEE 12th International Conference on Computer Vision Workshops (ICCV Workshops), pp. 506–513, September 2009
33. Raptis, M., Sigal, L.: Poselet key-framing: a model for human activity recognition. In: Proceedings of the 2013 IEEE Conference on Computer Vision and Pattern Recognition, CVPR 2013, pp. 2650–2657. IEEE Computer Society, Washington, DC (2013)
34. Shan, J., Akella, S.: 3d human action segmentation and recognition using pose kinetic energy. In: IEEE International Workshop on Advanced Robotics and its Social Impacts, pp. 69–75. IEEE (2014)
35. Zhu, G., Zhang, L., Shen, P., Song, J., Zhi, L., Yi, K.: Human action recognition using key poses and atomic motions. In: 2015 IEEE International Conference on Robotics and Biomimetics (ROBIO), pp. 1209–1214, December 2015
36. MacQueen, J.: Some methods for classification and analysis of multivariate observations. In: Proceedings of the Fifth Berkeley Symposium on Mathematical Statistics and Probability, vol. 1: Statistics, Berkeley, Calif., pp. 281–297. University of California Press (1967)
37. Kanungo, T., Mount, D.M., Netanyahu, N.S., Piatko, C.D., Silverman, R., Wu, A.Y.: An efficient k-means clustering algorithm: analysis and implementation. IEEE Trans. Pattern Anal. Mach. Intell. 24(7), 881–892 (2002)
38. Arthur, D., Vassilvitskii, S.: k-means++: the advantages of carefull seeding. In: Proceedings of the Eighteenth Annual ACM-SIAM Symposium on Discrete Algorithms, pp. 1027–1035 (2007)
39. Pelleg, D., Moore, A.W.: X-means: Extending k-means with efficient estimation of the number of clusters. In: Seventeenth International Conference on Machine Learning, pp. 727–734. Morgan Kaufmann (2000)
40. Witten, I.H., Frank, E., Hall, M.A.: Data Mining: Practical Machine Learning Tools and Techniques, 3rd edn. Morgan Kaufmann Publishers Inc., San Francisco (2011)
41. Platt, J.: Fast training of support vector machines using sequential minimal optimization. In: Schoelkopf, B., Burges, C., Smola, A. (eds.) Advances in Kernel Methods - Support Vector Learning. MIT Press (1998)

42. Chang, C.C., Lin, C.J.: LIBSVM: a library for support vector machines. ACM Trans. Intell. Syst. Technol. 2 (2011) 27: 1–27: 27 Software available at. http://www.csie.ntu.edu.tw/cjlin/libsvm

43. Hastie, T., Tibshirani, R.: Classification by pairwise coupling. In: Jordan, M.I., Kearns, M.J., Solla, S.A. (eds.) Advances in Neural Information Processing Systems, vol. 10, MIT Press (1998)

44. Hall, M., Frank, E., Holmes, G., Pfahringer, B., Reutemann, P., Witten, I.H.: The weka data mining software: an update. SIGKDD Explor. Newsl. **11**(1), 10–18 (2009)

45. Gasparrini, S., Cippitelli, E., Gambi, E., Spinsante, S., Wåhslén, J., Orhan, I., Lindh, T.: Proposal and experimental evaluation of fall detection solution based on wearable and depth data fusion. In: Loshkovska, S., Koceski, S. (eds.) ICT Innovations 2015. AISC, vol. 399, pp. 99–108. Springer, Heidelberg (2016)

46. Faria, D.R., Premebida, C., Nunes, U.: A probabilistic approach for human everyday activities recognition using body motion from rgb-d images. In: The 23rd IEEE International Symposium on Robot and Human Interactive Communication, pp. 732–737, August 2014

47. Parisi, G.I., Weber, C., Wermter, S.: Self-organizing neural integration of pose-motion features for human action recognition. Front. Neurorobotics **9**(3) (2015)

ISANA: Wearable Context-Aware Indoor Assistive Navigation with Obstacle Avoidance for the Blind

Bing Li[1], J. Pablo Muñoz[2], Xuejian Rong[1], Jizhong Xiao[1,2(✉)], Yingli Tian[1,2], and Aries Arditi[3]

[1] The City College, City University of New York, New York, NY, USA
{bli,xrong,jxiao,ytian}@ccny.cuny.edu
[2] Graduate Center, City University of New York, New York, NY, USA
jmunoz2@gradcenter.cuny.edu
[3] Visibility Metrics LLC, Chappaqua, NY, USA
arditi@visibilitymetrics.com

Abstract. This paper presents a novel mobile wearable context-aware indoor maps and navigation system with obstacle avoidance for the blind. The system includes an indoor map editor and an App on Tango devices with multiple modules. The indoor map editor parses spatial semantic information from a building architectural model, and represents it as a high-level semantic map to support context awareness. An obstacle avoidance module detects objects in front using a depth sensor. Based on the ego-motion tracking within the Tango, localization alignment on the semantic map, and obstacle detection, the system automatically generates a safe path to a desired destination. A speech-audio interface delivers user input, guidance and alert cues in real-time using a priority-based mechanism to reduce the user's cognitive load. Field tests involving blindfolded and blind subjects demonstrate that the proposed prototype performs context-aware and safety indoor assistive navigation effectively.

Keywords: Indoor assistive navigation · Context-aware · Semantic map · Obstacle avoidance · Tango device

1 Introduction

In recent decades, numerous indoor assistive navigation systems have been explored to augment the navigation capabilities of people with mobility impairments, especially the blind and the visually impaired. According to the fact sheet of Visual Impairment and Blindness from World Health Organization as of August 2014, 285 million people are estimated to be visually impaired worldwide, among which 39 million are blind and 246 million have low vision [1]. In addition, according to statistics data from the National Eye Institute, cases of blindness in the United States have increased from 0.9 million in 2000 to 1.3 million in 2010, showing that the number of people living with blindness is increasing [2].

© Springer International Publishing Switzerland 2016
G. Hua and H. Jégou (Eds.): ECCV 2016 Workshops, Part II, LNCS 9914, pp. 448–462, 2016.
DOI: 10.1007/978-3-319-48881-3_31

Indoor assistive navigation has been an important research focus in the robotics community, especially addressing the following multiple challenges: (1) Indoor localization where GPS fails; (2) Obstacle avoidance for safe travel in dynamic environments; (3) High-level indoor spatial-temporal modeling to support semantic context awareness; (4) System integration to produce a compact and wearable device. Various proprioceptive and exteroceptive sensors have been applied to indoor autonomous robots, such as inertial measurement units (IMU), magnetometers, wireless models, infrared, sonar, laser scanners, and vision (RGB or/and Depth) cameras. Recently, compact mobile devices have emerged with real-time 3D vision computational capabilities, including embedded graphics processing units. The availability of visual-inertial odometry (VIO) algorithms on these platforms (such as Google Tango or Structure IO) provides the potential to support portable real-time indoor assistive and safe navigation.

Based on our previous research on visual SLAM-based assistive navigation and obstacle avoidance [3–6], in this paper, we present the Intelligent Situation Awareness and Navigation Aid (ISANA) system for the blind. Its functions include indoor assistive navigation with context-aware indoor maps, navigation guidance, obstacle avoidance and user-friendly speech-audio human machine interaction (HMI) [7]. We developed the ISANA system based on the Google Tango device[1], an RGB-Depth camera integrated mobile Android tablet, with the capabilities of six degree-of-freedom (6-DOF) ego-motion VIO tracking and feature-based localization.

The main contributions of this research are as follows:

(1) Novel semantic maps to support high-level semantic localization, navigation and context awareness, through alignment of the semantic map with feature-based localization maps from Tango device. We developed an indoor map editor to parse semantic and topological information from the building architectural model files, and alignment algorithm to bridge the localization among semantic map and 6-DOF pose from the device.
(2) An efficient and real-time obstacle detection and avoidance approach was designed based on the 2D projection and analysis from the point cloud detection. Obstacles are tracked using a connected component labeling algorithm.
(3) Our implementation of the ISANA prototype in field tests with blindfolded and blind subjects demonstrates the effectiveness of the system in aiding the blind safely with indoor independent navigation.

The remainder of this paper is organized as follows. In Sect. 2, several recent vision-based indoor assistive navigation systems for the visually impaired are reviewed. Subsequently, an overview of our system is presented in Sect. 3. In Sects. 4 and 5, we explain our approaches to how the semantic map, semantic localization, navigation with obstacle avoidance, and speech-audio user interaction all work together. In Sect. 6, the experimental obstacle detection and avoidance, and system evaluation are described. Finally Sect. 7 presents conclusion and discusses directions of future research.

---

[1] https://developers.google.com/tango/.

2   Related Work

In this section, various vision-based portable/wearable assistive navigation systems are reviewed. Because vision cameras can be context-rich, low cost, low-power consumption and light weight, they have been utilized for real-time assistive navigation systems in several variants, such as monocular cameras [8–11], stereo cameras [12–14], fisheye cameras [15], omnidirectional camera [16], and RGB-D cameras [17–20].

The University of Southern California stereo system [13] is known as an early complete wearable navigation prototype which applied a head-mounted vision sensor and a tactile feedback actuator. Stereo visual odometry (VO) is estimated by matching features across two stereo views, then simultaneous localization and mapping (SLAM) is performed. Obstacle detection is obtained from stereo point cloud processing and represented in the traversability map. Finally, the system alerts the subject for the existence of the obstacles. However, the system still lacks obstacle modeling in a global map representation for navigation with obstacle avoidance.

RGB-D camera-based indoor assistive navigation systems have been also explored by researchers in recent years. The release of affordable commercial RGB-D cameras (such as Microsoft Kinect, Asus Xtion Pro Live) has attracted a great deal of attention among researchers and produced a surge in 3D SLAM research. It has been utilized effectively to acquire 3-Depth information, along with RGB images to augment indoor assistive navigation [17,18,20–22]. In the system of [20], the fast odometry from vision (FOVIS) algorithm is designed to perform real-time VO using RGB and depth images. Then a traversability 2D grid map is built for path planning. Obstacle avoidance is performed locally in real time. Finally, a tactile feedback system generates cues to guide the user (visually impaired) along the computed path and alerts obstacle existence. The mobility experiment shows the efficiency of the system. However, it relies on heavy and complex handhold devices, which limits its portability and feasibility for daily use.

The notion of "context-aware computing" was first advanced in the early 90's [23]. It was gradually integrated into assistive navigation systems [24–29]. However, this early research was more from a spatial-temporal knowledge modeling and management perspective, rather than being adopted into an assistive navigation prototype.

By integrating cutting-edge techniques and taking advantage of the feature-based localization on the Tango platform, the proposed system aims at providing a complete indoor assistive navigation prototype for the blind, with indoor semantic maps to support context awareness and real-time obstacle alert and avoidance for safety.

3   System Overview

Our platform is running on a portable Tango Android tablet mobile device, which has builtin functionalities of area description file (ADF, a feature map of the environment) and VIO. The VIO and loop closure with ADF provide the localization/re-localization capabilities for the device. The functionalities of ISANA include:

(1) An indoor map editor parses semantic information from architectural CAD models;
(2) Localization alignment on the semantic indoor maps based on the ADF and VIO;
(3) A path planner and waypoint algorithm design [5];
(4) Obstacle avoidance and alert, for both in-front and head-height obstacles;
(5) Assistive text and sign reading [30];
(6) Speech-audio HMI [7].

The physical configuration of ISANA is shown in Fig. 1, which shows a Tango device, a holder, and a white cane.

Fig. 1. ISANA system configuration on a blind subject (photo courtesy)

ISANA provides blind users with high-level context awareness based on semantic indoor maps and navigation with obstacle avoidance functionalities, along with user-friendly speech-audio interaction. The system architecture of ISANA is illustrated in Fig. 2. Indoor maps provide spatial models of the environment as well as user profiling (such as stride length). The RGB-D camera supports scene recognition and obstacle detection. Assistive navigation generates the route and interacts with the user by speech-audio interface. The blind user is the final decision maker, since ISANA will respond to the user's motion, rather than controlling it. In addition, the blind user still can, as usual, use a white cane to gain tactile feedback for the safety zone in front.

There are two distinct applications in our system. The ISANA indoor map editor performs offline semantic map construction by parsing architectural model files. The ISANA App performs the functionalities of semantic localization on the semantic map, navigation guidance, obstacle avoidance and alert, and speech-audio HMI for the user.

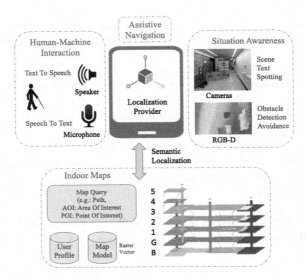

Fig. 2. ISANA navigation system overview

4   Indoor Semantic Maps and Localization

Computer-aided design (CAD) files are the most commonly used models for building architectural drawings. They oftern contain raw geometric information about the building, such as door sectors, room text labels, fire exit labels, wall.

4.1   Semantic Map Analysis

We have automated the semantic map generation process by developing our indoor map editor which converts raw building drawing exchange format (DXF) files of architectural floor plans into spatial semantic information maps. Then, based on region segmentation analysis and the dimensional information for all regions, our indoor map editor recognizes hallways, and topographic relationships between room and labels of corresponding doors are further retrieved (although with some failures, shown as red area) in Fig. 3.

4.2   Alignment for Semantic Localization

By parsing the CAD file of an architectural floor, we acquire an indoor semantic map of the floor with semantic information marking the locations of rooms and doors. Then, using the indoor map editor, necessary semantic landmarks such as elevators, stairs, and labeling information for each room are added into the semantic map.

ISANA provides semantic localization on top of the ADF map. The ADF map is created by the Tango device, containing the visual features of keyframes

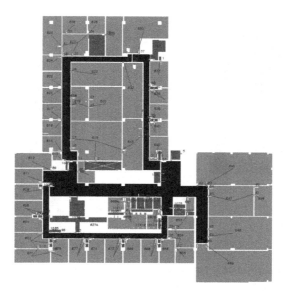

Fig. 3. The semantic and topology information retrieving (with room labels, doors, topologies, hallways, etc. Red areas are regions fail to find topological connections to doors.) (Color figure online)

from camera images. Figure 4 illustrates the concepts of maps alignment for localization on the semantic map.

The procedure of map alignment is:

(1) ISANA starts and localizes itself within the ADF map, based on the loop closure of the Tango VO.
(2) The user walks around the environment and stops by several doors. The user may request ISANA's scene text recognition module [30] to acquire door label text. In the case where no text regions can be found, control points will be set in the semantic map for the alignment, using screen tactile input during walking.
(3) Pairs of door locations on the semantic map and corresponding locations in ADF are recorded.
(4) Using singular value decomposition (SVD) algorithm, calculate the affine transformation alignment matrix between ADF and the indoor semantic map.

5   Navigation in Dynamic Environments

In this section, we elaborate the design of the navigation functionalities of ISANA in dynamic environments. With the semantic map and alignment localization, a quick-response obstacle detection approach is performed in real-time to update

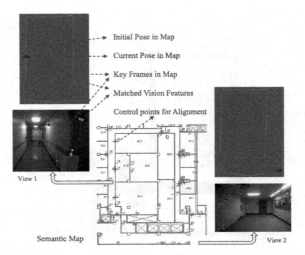

Fig. 4. Indoor semantic and ADF maps alignment (The middle is the semantic map with POIs, and control point are shown as the stars which are detected by text recognition. The side figures show the ADF features in keyframes.)

the global traversability 2D grid map and provide safety alerts, with head-height obstacle detection as well. Then the path planner [5,31] generates a safe route based on the updated map information. Finally, a priority-based speech-audio HMI provides interaction guidance and alert cues for the user.

5.1 Obstacle Detection

For the safety of blind users, we designed a quick-response obstacle detection procedure using the 5HZ Infrared (IR) depth camera to run in real-time on the Tango device. This operates efficiently without model retrieving of 3D point cloud. A novel two 2D depth projection approach provides both obstacle updates for the navigation map (by horizontal projection), and front obstacle alert (by vertical projection). We improved computational efficiency by handling the data processing with linear complexity regarding point number in the detected range, comparing with our previous result [6] using random sample consensus (RANSAC) segmentation. As shown in the left part of Fig. 5, first a noise filter is performed to remove the stand-alone points, and then based on the pitch angle of the current pose information, a de-skewing process is performed to align the 3D point cloud with the horizontal floor plane. The local 2D grid map is acquired by the 3D to 2D projections, in both horizontal and vertical directions.

Then in the right of Fig. 5, the depth data is updated for the 2D grid maps in the local and global world frame, for purpose of obstacle detection. A connected component labeling algorithm [32] (or [33]) is applied to cluster the connected objects in the grid maps.

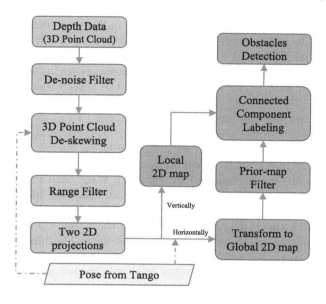

Fig. 5. Obstacle detection process flowchart

5.2 Navigation with Obstacle Avoidance

Based on the semantic map and localization, A^* [5,31] algorithm is applied in ISANA as the path planner to find the route to a desired destination. Meanwhile, we perform obstacle avoidance for safety route as a safety measure.

Obstacle avoidance is supported both locally and globally. For the non-navigation model (which the user has not set his/her destination), local obstacle avoidance provides the user with obstacle-free direction guidance when there are obstacles detected based on the vertical projection. During the navigation process, global obstacle avoidance is performed by updating the global 2D grid map based on the horizontal projection. Then, ISANA generates a new path and gives the user new guidance direction information. The procedure for obstacle avoidance during navigation is as following:

(1) Obstacle detection using a connected component labeling algorithm.
(2) Update occupancy information of obstacles into grid map.
(3) Use A^* to compute a new guidance route on the gird map.
(4) Deliver audio guidance on user direction, incorporating updated path information.

5.3 Navigation Guidance HMI

Speech-audio HMI is an important and challenging part for any assistive navigation system. Traditionally, many assistive navigation systems have used other HMI modes, such as tactile feedback, limited audio feedback, or a keyboard to minimize cognitive interference with the user's auditory environment. However, in order to provide rich and effective semantic and guidance information, ISANA uses speech-audio HMI, and delivers safety alerts to the user using a priority-based mechanism. This allows high priority messages to be delivered in real-time to the user, with permission to overwrite the current occupied delivering message.

Specifically, we use the Android Text-to-Speech (TTS) module[2] to convey obstacle detection results and other environmental information to the user, including HMI command feedback, real-time guidance, current location, etc.

As for system input, many previous assistive navigation systems rely on a physical button or touchscreen devices. However, these tend to be inconvenient for a blind user since they require the use of at least one hand. Instead, we implemented a Speech-to-Text (STT) module [7] based voice input to help the user interact with the ISANA system. We use the CMU PocketSphinx[3] STT engine to receive the voice commands from the user. The blind user can also query his/her real-time location based on the semantic localization. A specific acoustic model is also trained to further improve the recognition accuracy and decrease the influence of the environmental noise. We also built a keyword list and grammar to narrow down the search space of the speech recognition module and improve the performance of the statistical language model. The effectiveness of the TTS and STT modules has been validated in our experiments, and holds promise for significantly enhancing the practicability of our proposed algorithm and system.

6   Experiment

We tested the ISANA system using blindfolded and blind subjects, for its qualitative effectiveness in guiding users to their destinations. By defining the graph connections between different floors through connectors such as stairs, elevators or escalators, multi-floor navigation is supported as well.

6.1   Obstacle Detection

Figure 6 shows a final visualization of detected obstacles in a hallway on the ISANA graphic user interface (GUI), with wall filtering based on the semantic map and localization. Different objects are shown as different bounding boxes in front of the user.

A more detailed evaluation of the obstacle detection including walls was performed in a hallway, where both the user and a cart are moving. The horizontal 2D projection and its histogram analysis are shown in Fig. 7, and the vertical 2D projection and its histogram analysis in Fig. 8.

Figure 7 (left) shows the 2D projection to floor plane. Walls are shown on the two sides of the figure, and we compute the closest obstacle point (shown as red

---

[2] http://tinyurl.com/Android-TTS.
[3] http://cmusphinx.sourceforge.net.

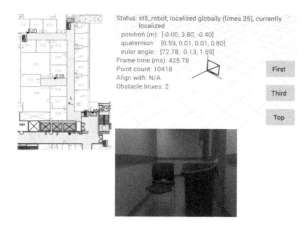

Fig. 6. Obstacle detection results from depth detection projection (The two objects in-front are projected from the 3D point cloud horizontal projection, and are detected and tracked by the connected component labeling algorithm.)

"x" in front). Figure 7 (right) is the weighted histogram of the floor plane projection to show the obstacle-free path direction based on vector field histogram (VFH) [34] approach.

To handle head-height obstacles, we performed a vertical plane 2D projection, as shown in Fig. 8 (left). The red "x" shows the obstacle height (relative to the Tango device) as the closest obstacle detected by the vertical floor projection. Figure 8 (right) shows the front obstacle-free VFH histogram of vertical plane projection with respect to the front direction in degree.

6.2   Navigation with Obstacle Avoidance

After we acquire the detected obstacle boxes and points in the global world frame, obstacle avoidance is performed based on the path planner of A^* algorithm. Figure 9(1) shows the path when there are no obstacles. Then when ISANA detects obstacles in front, a new route will be generated as shown in Fig. 9(2), and as the obstacles move, routes will be updated according to the obstacle detection, as shown in Fig. 9(3).

6.3   System Evaluation

An ISANA single floor navigation screenshot on the Tango device is shown in Fig. 10. Semantic maps with grid maps are processed by the indoor map editor. The online and dynamic path to a desired destination is updated by the path planner based on obstacle detection, with multiple waypoints on the path for guidance. Obstacles are detected using the RGB-D sensor and point cloud is projected in 2D horizontally and vertically. To make alerts more relevant, existing walls and objects whose height is within the white cane's sensing range do not

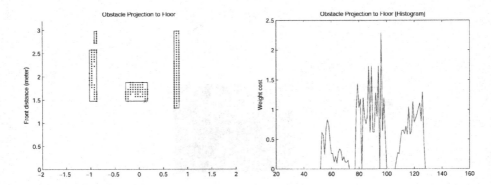

Fig. 7. Left: Obstacle detection floor plane projection, red "x" is the closest point, the horizontal axis is the left to right direction in meter, and the vertical axis represents the forward direction in meter. Right: Obstacle histogram, the horizontal axis is the angular directon of obstacle in degree, and the vertical axis represents the weighted cost of obstacle points with related to their distance in horizontal plane to the user. (Color figure online)

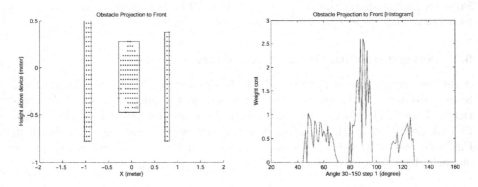

Fig. 8. Left: Obstacle detection vertical plane projection, red "x" is the closest point, the horizontal axis is the left to right direction in meter, and the vertical axis represents the upward direction in meter. Right: Obstacle histogram, the horizontal axis is the angular direction of obstacle in degree, and the vertical axis represents the weighted cost of obstacle points with related to their distance in vetical plane to the user. (Color figure online)

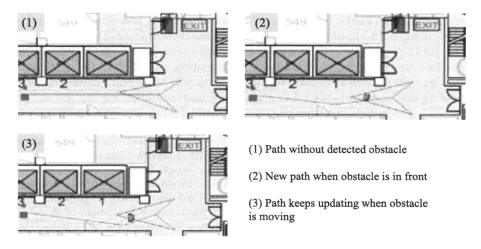

(1) Path without detected obstacle

(2) New path when obstacle is in front

(3) Path keeps updating when obstacle is moving

Fig. 9. Obstacle avoidance

elicit alerts from ISANA. As shown in Fig. 10, the yellow safety fence is detected as an front-left obstacle and alert is issued to the user. A beeping alert sound is also conveyed to the user, with distance to the obstacle signaled by beep frequency.

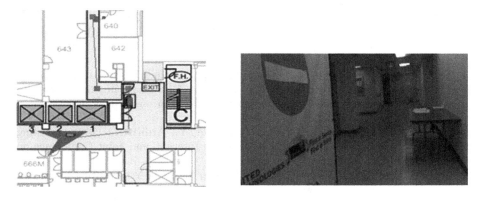

Fig. 10. ISANA App GUI with camera view

7 Conclusions and Future Work

In this research, we have proposed and designed a mobile wearable context-aware Intelligent Situation Awareness and Navigation Aid (ISANA) prototype system as an aid to the blind people for indoor assistive traveling. Our experimental demo with blindfolded and blind subjects demonstrates the effectiveness of our ISANA prototype in providing the blind community with an aiding tool for indoor traveling, context awareness and situation awareness of the user's surrounding cyber-physical world. Our future work will focus on dynamic obstacle modeling and prediction, and on environment understanding.

Acknowledgements. This work was supported in part by U.S. Federal Highway Administration (FHWA) grant DTFH 61-12-H-00002, National Science Foundation (NSF) grants CBET-1160046, EFRI-1137172 and IIP-1343402, National Institutes of Health (NIH) grant EY023483. Dr. J. Xiao thanks Google Project Tango for providing a grant to CCNY Robotics Lab as well as free Tango devices and technical support. Dr. J. Xiao thanks the Alexander von Humboldt Foundation for providing the Humboldt Research Fellowship for experienced researchers and Prof. Jianwei Zhang at University of Hamburg for hosting the research stay in summers of 2013–2015. The authors acknowledge Ms. Barbara Campbell for her valuable feedback and suggestion for ISANA. The authors would like to thank Dr. Ivan Dryanovsky, Dr. Chucai Yi, Dr. Samleo L. Joseph, Xiaochen Zhang, Mohammed Amin, Patrick Centeno, Luciano C. Albuquerque, Norbu Tsering for their contributions to this research.

References

1. World Health Organization: Towards universal eye health: a global action plan 2014 to 2019 report (2013)
2. United States National Eye Institute: United states prevalent cases of blindness (in thousands): Changes of cases between 2000 and 2010 (2010)
3. Xiao, J., Joseph, S.L., Zhang, X., Li, B., Li, X., Zhang, J.: An assistive navigation framework for the visually impaired. IEEE Trans. Hum.-Mach. Syst. **45**(5), 635–640 (2015)
4. Zhang, X., Li, B., Joseph, S.L., Xiao, J., Sun, Y., Tian, Y., Muñoz, J.P., Yi, C.: A slam based semantic indoor navigation system for visually impaired users. In: 2015 IEEE International Conference on Systems, Man, and Cybernetics (SMC), pp. 1458–1463. IEEE (2015)
5. Muñoz, J.P., Li, B., Rong, X., Xiao, J., Tian, Y., Arditi, A.: Demo: assisting visually impaired people navigate indoors. In: International Joint Conference on Artificial Intelligence (2016)
6. Li, B., Zhang, X., Muñoz, J.P., Xiao, J., Rong, X., Tian, Y.: Assisting blind people to avoid obstacles: a wearable obstacle stereo feedback system based on 3d detection. In: 2015 IEEE International Conference on Robotics and Biomimetics (ROBIO), pp. 2307–2311. IEEE (2015)
7. Munoz, R., Rong, X., Tian, Y.: Depth-aware indoor staircase detection and recognition for the visually impaired. In: IEEE ICME Workshop on Mobile Multimedia Computing (MMC) (2016)
8. Jia, B., Liu, R., Zhu, M.: Real-time obstacle detection with motion features using monocular vision. Vis. Comput. **31**(3), 281–293 (2015)
9. He, H., Li, Y., Guan, Y., Tan, J.: Wearable ego-motion tracking for blind navigation in indoor environments. IEEE Trans. Autom. Sci. Eng. **12**(4), 1181–1190 (2015)

10. Apostolopoulos, I., Fallah, N., Folmer, E., Bekris, K.E.: Integrated online localization and navigation for people with visual impairments using smart phones. ACM Trans. Interact. Intell. Syst. (TiiS) **3**(4), 21 (2014)
11. Mattoccia, S., Macrı, P.: 3D glasses as mobility aid for visually impaired people. In: Agapito, L., Bronstein, M.M., Rother, C. (eds.) ECCV 2014. LNCS, vol. 8927, pp. 539–554. Springer, Heidelberg (2015). doi:10.1007/978-3-319-16199-0_38
12. Howard, A.: Real-time stereo visual odometry for autonomous ground vehicles. In: IEEE/RSJ International Conference on Intelligent Robots and Systems, IROS 2008, pp. 3946–3952. IEEE (2008)
13. Pradeep, V., Medioni, G., Weiland, J.: Robot vision for the visually impaired. In: 2010 IEEE Computer Society Conference on Computer Vision and Pattern Recognition Workshops (CVPRW), pp. 15–22. IEEE (2010)
14. Schwarze, T., Lauer, M., Schwaab, M., Romanovas, M., Böhm, S., Jürgensohn, T.: A camera-based mobility aid for visually impaired people. KI-Künstliche Intelligenz **30**(1), 29–36 (2016)
15. Courbon, J., Mezouar, Y., Eck, L., Martinet, P.: A generic fisheye camera model for robotic applications. In: IEEE/RSJ International Conference on Intelligent Robots and Systems, IROS 2007, pp. 1683–1688. IEEE (2007)
16. Terashima, K., Watanabe, K., Ueno, Y., Masui, Y.: Auto-tuning control of power assist system based on the estimation of operator's skill level for forward and backward driving of omni-directional wheelchair. In: 2010 IEEE/RSJ International Conference on Intelligent Robots and Systems (IROS), pp. 6046–6051. IEEE (2010)
17. Lee, Y.H., Medioni, G.: A rgb-d camera based navigation for the visually impaired. In: RSS 2011 RGBD: Advanced Reasoning with Depth Camera Workshop, pp. 1–6 (2011)
18. Lee, Y.H., Medioni, G.: Wearable RGBD indoor navigation system for the blind. In: Agapito, L., Bronstein, M.M., Rother, C. (eds.) ECCV 2014. LNCS, vol. 8927, pp. 493–508. Springer, Heidelberg (2015). doi:10.1007/978-3-319-16199-0_35
19. Milotta, F.L.M., Allegra, D., Stanco, F., Farinella, G.M.: An electronic travel aid to assist blind and visually impaired people to avoid obstacles. In: Azzopardi, G., Petkov, N. (eds.) CAIP 2015. LNCS, vol. 9257, pp. 604–615. Springer, Heidelberg (2015). doi:10.1007/978-3-319-23117-4_52
20. Lee, Y.H., Medioni, G.: Rgb-d camera based wearable navigation system for the visually impaired. Comput. Vis. Image Underst. **149**, 3–20 (2016)
21. Zöllner, M., Huber, S., Jetter, H.-C., Reiterer, H.: NAVI – a proof-of-concept of a mobile navigational aid for visually impaired based on the microsoft kinect. In: Campos, P., Graham, N., Jorge, J., Nunes, N., Palanque, P., Winckler, M. (eds.) INTERACT 2011. LNCS, vol. 6949, pp. 584–587. Springer, Heidelberg (2011). doi:10.1007/978-3-642-23768-3_88
22. Brock, M., Kristensson, P.O.: Supporting blind navigation using depth sensing and sonification. In: Proceedings of the 2013 ACM Conference on Pervasive and Ubiquitous Computing Adjunct Publication, pp. 255–258. ACM (2013)
23. Schilit, B., Adams, N., Want, R.: Context-aware computing applications. In: First Workshop on Mobile Computing Systems and Applications, WMCSA 1994, pp. 85–90. IEEE (1994)
24. Gribble, W.S., Browning, R.L., Hewett, M., Remolina, E., Kuipers, B.J.: Integrating vision and spatial reasoning for assistive navigation. In: Mittal, V.O., Yanco, H.A., Aronis, J., Simpson, R. (eds.) Assistive Technology and Artificial Intelligence. LNCS, vol. 1458, pp. 179–193. Springer, Heidelberg (1998). doi:10.1007/BFb0055978

25. Lyardet, F., Grimmer, J., Muhlhauser, M.: Coins: context sensitive indoor navigation system. In: Eighth IEEE International Symposium on Multimedia, ISM 2006, pp. 209–218. IEEE (2006)

26. Lyardet, F., Szeto, D.W., Aitenbichler, E.: Context-aware indoor navigation. In: Aarts, E., Crowley, J.L., de Ruyter, B., Gerhäuser, H., Pflaum, A., Schmidt, J., Wichert, R. (eds.) AmI 2008. LNCS, vol. 5355, pp. 290–307. Springer, Heidelberg (2008)

27. Ferraiolo, D., Kuhn, D.R., Chandramouli, R.: Role-Based Access Control. Artech House, Boston (2003)

28. Afyouni, I., Cyril, R., Christophe, C.: Spatial models for context-aware indoor navigation systems: a survey. J. Spat. Inf. Sci. 1(4), 85–123 (2012)

29. Afyouni, I.: Knowledge Representation and Management in Indoor Mobile Environments. Ph.D. thesis, Université de Bretagne occidentale-Brest (2013)

30. Rong, X., Yi, C., Tian, Y.: Recognizing text-based traffic guide panels with cascaded localization network. In: Hua, G., Jégou, H. (eds.) ECCV 2016 Workshops. LNCS, vol. 9913, pp. 109–121. Springer, Heidelberg (2016). doi:10.1007/978-3-319-46604-0_8

31. Hart, P.E., Nilsson, N.J., Raphael, B.: A formal basis for the heuristic determination of minimum cost paths. IEEE Trans. Syst. Sci. Cybern. 4(2), 100–107 (1968)

32. Rosenfeld, A., Pfaltz, J.L.: Sequential operations in digital picture processing. J. ACM (JACM) 13(4), 471–494 (1966)

33. Cabaret, L., Lacassagne, L.: What is the world's fastest connected component labeling algorithm? In: SiPS: IEEE International Workshop on Signal Processing Systems, p. 6. IEEE (2014)

34. Borenstein, J., Koren, Y.: Histogramic in-motion mapping for mobile robot obstacle avoidance. IEEE Trans. Robot. Autom. 7(4), 535–539 (1991)

An Integrated Framework for 24-hours Fire Detection

Jongwon Choi and Jin Young Choi[✉]

ASRI, Department of Electrical and Computer Engineering,
Seoul National University, Seoul, South Korea
jwchoi.pil@gmail.com, jychoi@snu.ac.kr

Abstract. In this paper, the integrated framework for 24-hours fire detection with a camera is proposed. The framework consists of four novel modules: an integration module, a flame detector with a visible-light camera, a flame detector with an infrared-ray camera, and a smoke detector. According to the state decided by the integration module, different detectors are selected to find fires. The flame detector with a visible-light camera determines flame patches from candidates through the cascaded classifiers, based on the color, shape, and randomness of flames. The flame detector with an infrared-ray camera finds flames, using the random movement of blob candidates. The smoke detector recognizes the smoke regions by utilizing the colors and the transparent property of smoke. The three detectors and the integrated framework are tested with numerous videos, which validates the generality and the robustness of the proposed framework.

Keywords: Integrated framework · Fire detection · Flame detection · Smoke detection · 24 hours

1 Introduction

According to the reports from National Fire Protection Association [1], 15 % of home fire victims have been caused by the physical disability, which ranked second among the fatal factors of home fires. Most of the victims could not avoid the death because of delayed escapes from a fire. However, because conventional fire warning systems, such as a water sprinkler and a manual warning lever, are operated only by strong fires, it becomes too late for the physically disabled people to escape from the fire.

Therefore, the fire warning system for all day is essential for the physically disabled people. Among the various fire warning systems, the systems based on a vision sensor have been spotlighted due to its low price and easy installation. Therefore, there has been various research for the early fire detection with cameras.

The most general fire detection algorithm is a flame detection based on a visible light (VL) camera, which can be categorized into three types: pixel-level,

© Springer International Publishing Switzerland 2016
G. Hua and H. Jégou (Eds.): ECCV 2016 Workshops, Part II, LNCS 9914, pp. 463–479, 2016.
DOI: 10.1007/978-3-319-48881-3_32

(a) Flame and smoke by visible light cameras   **(b)** Flame by infrared-ray cameras

Fig. 1. Various Images of Fire. The shapes of fire are various according to scenes and material. (a) shows the fire images captured by visible light cameras. (b) shows the fire images captured by infrared ray cameras.

blob-level, and patch-level algorithms. The pixel-level algorithms find flames by utilizing pixel-wise features including colors and flickers [2,3]. The pixel-level algorithms work very fast, but they show low performance because the shape of flame cannot be considered and the classifiers with the simple pixel-wise features can be easily biased by training data. The blob-level algorithms detect flames by extracting features from blob-level candidates [4,5,7]. The blob-level algorithms show better performance than the pixel-level algorithms, but their classifiers are hard to be trained due to the various shapes of flame blobs as shown in Fig. 1(a). For complementing the limitations of the pixel-level and blob-level algorithms, the patch-level algorithm is developed recently [6]. The patch-level algorithm showed good performance by considering local appearance, but the algorithm gave too many outliers yet to be applied in real scenes.

Furthermore, there have been flame detection algorithms based on an infrared-ray (IR) camera to detect fires at night [8–11]. The algorithms utilized the properties of flame captured by IR camera, including high intensities and frequent flickers. However, as shown in Fig. 1(b), because the flames from IR cameras have no color information and no distinctive appearance shape, the algorithms show unsatisfactory performances.

Smoke detection algorithms also have been developed [12–15]. Because smoke appears before the flame becomes strong, the algorithms work as an important role for the fire warning. However, due to the less visual distinctiveness of smokes than flames, the methods issued many outliers and the performance can be easily biased by training samples. The previous works are described in detail in Sect. 2.

In addition to the limitations of the individual algorithms, the algorithms are improper for 24-hours surveillance environments because general surveillance cameras selectively use a VL camera and an IR camera. The two cameras are alternatively utilized according to the current visual state such as daytime and nighttime. As shown in Fig. 1, the visual characteristics of flames are very different between VL and IR camera images, which makes it inefficient to detect the flame by a single algorithm.

To solve the problems, we propose novel algorithms for fire detection and an integrated framework of the algorithms working for all day. The proposed framework consists of four modules: integration module, VL flame detector, smoke detector, and IR flame detector. The integration logic controls and optimizes the operation of the detectors by automatically recognizing the current state of the camera. The VL flame detector works by the patch-level flame detection scheme, showing higher performance with fewer parameters to be set than the previous method. The IR flame detector considers the temporal randomness of a flame region, which is defined as an irregular shape change of blobs. The smoke detector works based on the transparent property of smoke, meaning that the background appearance becomes dim but remains in smoke regions. The detectors and the integrated framework are validated by numerous videos including generally used videos [16] and newly captured videos, and the results verify the robustness and the generality of the proposed framework.

2   Related Works

For the pixel-level flame detection algorithms based on a VL camera, Phillips *et al.* [2] proposed a framework to detect flames by the colors and the temporal variation of candidate pixels. In addition, Chenebert *et al.* [3] utilized color values in HSV domain and the texture features.

Most flame detection algorithms with a VL camera are based on blob-level classifiers. Toreyin *et al.* [4] analyzed the flickering property of flames and the irregularity of flame boundary. Ham *et al.* [5] utilized fuzzy finite automation to classify the irregular patterns of candidate blobs. Morerio *et al.* [7] obtained the color information, motion models, and temporal dynamics of the blobs in parallel to detect flames.

Choi *et al.* [6] proposed the patch-level VL flame detection algorithm which extracts candidate patches from an input image and classifies the patches as a flame by their appearance and randomness.

For detecting flames with an IR camera, Maoult *et al.* [8] analyzed the property of flames with various gas types and materials, which was utilized to reject flame-like objects captured by IR cameras. Owrutskya *et al.* [9] combined the images captured by a VL camera and the ones by an IR camera to obtain high performance of the flame detector. Even though Tasdemir *et al.* [10] used a VL camera, they tried to use the properties of night flames such as a slow movement, high intensity, periodic motion, and a self-motion. Toreyin *et al.* [11] detected flames with an IR camera by utilizing the spatial and temporal changes of the wavelet information on flame boundaries.

To detect smoke, Ho [13] tried to fuse the spectral, spatial, and temporal probability densities on candidate regions. Kim and Wang [14] focused on the smoke captured in outdoor and utilized the temporal information of colors and shapes extracted from the smoke. Chen *et al.* [15] proposed a smoke detector working with two rules of a chromaticity-based static decision and a diffusion-based dynamic characteristic decision. Toreyin *et al.* [12] classified blob-level candidates by recognizing a decrease in the energy content of edges and analyzing the blob boundaries. The algorithm showed good performance by utilizing the transparent property of smoke as the proposed algorithm. However, the algorithm estimated the transparency just by comparing the energy content of edges,

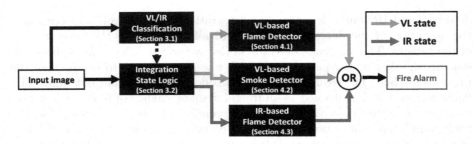

Fig. 2. Integrated Framework. In the integrated framework, there are four modules: an integration logic, a VL flame detector, a smoke detector, and an IR flame detector. The final fire alarm is given with any alarm from the detectors.

while the proposed algorithm represents the transparency robustly by comparing the normalized gradients of a background and a smoked region.

3   Integrated Framework

The integration module recognizes the current state of a camera and selectively executes the detectors which are proper to the state, as described in Fig. 2.

3.1   VL/IR Classification

From some cameras, the state between VL and IR camera can be obtained by a switching signal. However, for the other cameras not sending the switching signal, it is necessary to recognize the state from input frames. In this paper, the state is recognized by estimating the difference among R, G, B channel images represented by $\mathbf{F}_r$, $\mathbf{F}_g$, and $\mathbf{F}_b$, respectively. For IR cameras, R, G, B channel values of each pixel should be equivalent. Therefore, the current state is classified as IR state when

$$
\begin{aligned}
(1/WH) \sum_{x,y=1}^{W,H} \|\mathbf{F}_r^{(x,y)} - \mathbf{F}_g^{(x,y)}\|_2 < \epsilon_{sw}, \\
(1/WH) \sum_{x,y=1}^{W,H} \|\mathbf{F}_r^{(x,y)} - \mathbf{F}_b^{(x,y)}\|_2 < \epsilon_{sw}, \\
(1/WH) \sum_{x,y=1}^{W,H} \|\mathbf{F}_g^{(x,y)} - \mathbf{F}_b^{(x,y)}\|_2 < \epsilon_{sw}
\end{aligned}
\tag{1}
$$

are all satisfied where $W \times H$ is the image size. If one or more conditions are not satisfied, the current state is classified as VL state. The predefined threshold θ_{sw} is used to consider the noise of input frames.

When the state is switched right after satisfying the condition, the state switching can recur at evening due to the ambiguous brightness at that time. For overcoming the problem, the state is switched after a different state is continuously detected during 1000 frames.

3.2   Integration Logic

When the three detectors operate simultaneously, a significant computational resource is needed and many outliers can be issued. Therefore, only the detectors proper to the current state are selected to detect fire. When the camera state is VL state, the VL flame detector and smoke detector work. The alarms of the two detectors are integrated by OR operation. On the other hand, when the camera state is IR state, the IR flame detector runs.

When a fire occurs in the nighttime, the state can be changed to VL state by the bright fire. Then, the VL flame detector works even with the flame which is easy to be detected by the IR flame detector. For overcoming the problem, working detectors run continuously even with the state switching if one or more maximum scores of the detectors are larger than a predefined threshold ϵ_{ct}. At that time, the other detectors do not start working to conserve the computational load.

4   Individual Detectors

4.1   VL Flame Detector

The VL flame detector is improved from Choi *et al.* [6] which shows the state-of-the-art performance. As shown in Fig. 3, the VL flame detector works with three subsequent steps: a candidate extraction, an appearance classifier, and a randomness classifier. After extracting the patch candidates from a fire-like probability map, the candidates are classified by the two classifiers in a cascade scheme. A detection map is obtained from the candidates classified as flames, and the fire alarm is determined after the spatiotemporal association of the consecutive detection maps.

Candidate Extraction: At first, the temporal change is estimated for every pixel to consider the temporal movement of flames. The moving pixel is determined by

$$\sum_{c=r,g,b} \|\mathbf{F}_c^{(x,y,t)} - \mathbf{F}_c^{(x,y,t-1)}\|_1 > \epsilon_{vl}, \tag{2}$$

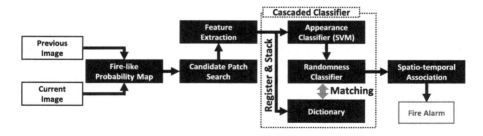

Fig. 3. Framework of VL flame detector. The detector extracts the patch-level candidates from an input image. Then, the candidates are classified as a flame by cascaded classifiers checking their shapes and randomnesses. After the spatiotemporal association of the results, a fire alarm is decided.

where ϵ_{vl} is a predefined threshold. For the moving pixels, the fire-like probability is estimated by using pixel-wise features, while the probability is set to 0 for the remaining static pixels. In the input frame of time t, a pixel at (x, y) has six pixel-wise features $\mathbf{Z}^{(x,y,t)} = \{\mathbf{F}_r^{(x,y,t)}, \mathbf{F}_g^{(x,y,t)}, \mathbf{F}_b^{(x,y,t)}, \Delta_1\mathbf{F}_r^{(x,y,t)}, \Delta_1\mathbf{F}_g^{(x,y,t)}, \Delta_1\mathbf{F}_b^{(x,y,t)}\}$, which are the RGB values and the magnitude of derivative for each of RGB channels, respectively. The magnitude of derivative for each channel is estimated as

$$\Delta_1\mathbf{F}_c^{(x,y,t)} = \|\mathbf{F}_c^{(x-1,y,t)} - \mathbf{F}_c^{(x+1,y,t)}\|_1 + \|\mathbf{F}_c^{(x,y-1,t)} - \mathbf{F}_c^{(x,y+1,t)}\|_1, \quad (3)$$

where $c \in \{r, g, b\}$. The estimation is based on 1-norm for a low computational load.

From, the pixel-wise features, the fire-like probability is calculated by

$$\mathbf{P}^{(x,y)} = \mathbf{W}^T\mathbf{F}^{(x,y)}, \quad (4)$$

where $\mathbf{W} \in I\!R^6$. The fire-like probability is built to be high on the boundary of a flame because the pixels on the boundary move actively and the patches on the boundary have more distinctive appearance than the ones inside the flame. Contrary to Choi et al. [6] setting the weights manually, the weight vector $\mathbf{W}$ is trained by linear regression algorithm [19]. The ground truth of the probability map for the regression is obtained by blurring the binary map with Gaussian kernel, which is set to 1 on the boundary of flame.

From the estimated probability map, the local maximums are extracted as the center points of patch candidates. The local maximums are used to reduce the computational load by rejecting the neighboring patches analogous to each other. Also, to reject the outliers with the colors far from flames, the detector chooses only the candidates where the probability is above the predefined threshold θ_{pr}. When the number of the selected candidates is over N_c, only the candidates with top N_c probability values are used to limit the computational load.

Appearance classifier: The patch-level features are obtained by concatenating three SURF features [20] each extracted from the candidate in one of RGB channels. Contrary to Choi et al. [6] which extracts the features only in R channel, the distinctiveness of appearance feature would be improved by utilizing all the RGB channels.

To handle the non-linearity of classification problem, the dimension of the patch-level features are expanded by a Chi-squared kernel, following Vedaldi and Zisserman [21]. With the expanded features, the classifier is trained by linear SVM. For the training, the positive samples are extracted from the patches where the ground truth probability is above 0.8, while the negative samples are obtained randomly from the outside of flame. In the test sequence, the appearance classifier determines the candidate as a flame if the SVM margin is over 0.

Randomness classifier: Because the shape of a flame changes randomly by air convection, the candidates can be rejected by classifying the randomness of the shape. The method to detect the randomness is same as Choi et al. [6], but the used feature is different because the patch-level feature is extracted from three channels in the proposed detector. The detail description of the randomness classifier can be referred by [6].

Temporal association: A current likelihood map $\mathbf{L}_{vl}$ has the same size of the input image, and all the pixels located in the detected fire parts are set to one, while the other pixels are set to zero. In order to reject remaining outliers, consecutive $\mathbf{L}_{vl}$ are temporally associated. Therefore, the final detection map $\mathbf{D}_{vl}$ with the same size of $\mathbf{L}_{vl}$ is estimated by

$$\mathbf{D}_{vl}^{(x,y,t)} = \alpha \mathbf{D}_{vl}^{(x,y,t-1)} + (1-\alpha)\mathbf{L}_{vl}^{(x,y)}, \tag{5}$$

where $\mathbf{D}_{vl}^{(x,y,0)} = 0$. When the maximum value of $\mathbf{D}_{vl}$ becomes over a predefined threshold ζ_{vl}, the fire alarm is given.

Fig. 4. Framework of Smoke Detector. After extracting the pixel-wise features from candidate blobs, the blob-level features are obtained from the distribution of the pixel-wise features and classified by SVM. A fire alarm is decided after the temporal association of the classification results.

4.2 Smoke Detector

The proposed smoke detector determines blob-level candidates as a smoke by utilizing the transparency property of smoke in addition to the general color and shape features of smoke. The transparency property means that the background is dimmed but remains at the region of smoke. Figure 4 describes the entire framework of the proposed smoke detector. At first, the blob candidates are extracted by background subtraction. Then, the pixel-wise features are extracted from the pixels of one blob candidate, which include colors, shapes, and transparency features. The blob-level feature is obtained from the distribution of the pixel-wise features, which is used for the smoke classification. Finally, the fire alarm resulted from the temporal association of the smoke regions.

Candidate Blob Search: Because the transparency property is weak on thick smoke, we should find candidate blobs where the smoke just expands to use the transparency property efficiently. The expanded region can be easily found by a temporal difference image. To consider the variety of expanding speed of smoke, the difference image is obtained between a current image and a previous image before N_s frames as

$$\mathbf{B}_s^{(x,y,t)} = \sum_{c \in \{r,g,b\}} \|\mathbf{F}_c^{(x,y,t)} - \mathbf{F}_c^{(x,y,t-N_s)}\|_2. \tag{6}$$

From the binary image obtained by thresholding B_s by ϵ_{sm}, blob candidates are extracted by connected component algorithm [22]. To limit the computational load, only top three candidates are chosen in order of volume.

Feature Extraction: There are three types of pixel-wise features: colors, shapes, and transparency features. The color feature consists of six channel including L, a, b in Lab color space and R, G, B in RGB domain. The magnitude of the derivative on each of RGB channels is used as the shape feature. The magnitude is estimated by

$$\Delta_2 \mathbf{F}_c = \|(\Delta_x \mathbf{F}_c, \Delta_y \mathbf{F}_c)\|_2, \quad c \in \{r, g, b\}, \tag{7}$$

where $\Delta_x \mathbf{F}_c$ and $\Delta_y \mathbf{F}_c$ are obtained by filtering $\mathbf{F}_c$ with x-directed and y-directed Sobel window [23], respectively.

The transparency feature is obtained by two channels: a gradient correlation and a dark channel difference. The gradient correlation is based on the characteristic of the transparency where the shape of the background remains under smoke. The gradient correlation is estimated by the difference between the normalized derivative vectors on the current and previous images as

$$\mathbf{F}_{gc}^{(x,y,t)} = \sqrt{\sum_{c=\{r,g,b\}} \left[\left(\frac{\Delta_x \mathbf{F}_c^{(x,y,t)}}{\Delta_2 \mathbf{F}_c^{(x,y,t)}} - \frac{\Delta_x \mathbf{F}_c^{(x,y,t-N_s)}}{\Delta_2 \mathbf{F}_c^{(x,y,t-N_s)}} \right)^2 + \left(\frac{\Delta_y \mathbf{F}_c^{(x,y,t)}}{\Delta_2 \mathbf{F}_c^{(x,y,t)}} - \frac{\Delta_y \mathbf{F}_c^{(x,y,t-N_s)}}{\Delta_2 \mathbf{F}_c^{(x,y,t-N_s)}} \right)^2 \right]}. \tag{8}$$

Therefore, F_{gc} becomes small for the smoke because the normalized gradients of the background should be preserved through the transparent smoke.

The dark channel difference is based on dark channel prior [25]. Following the dark channel prior, air lights diffused by fog or smoke are colorless, so the minimum value of R, G, B channels becomes high on smoke regions. Following the property, the dark channel difference is estimated by

$$F_{dc}^{(x,y,t)} = \min_{c \in \{r,g,b\}} \left(F_c^{(x,y,t)} \right) - \min_{c \in \{r,g,b\}} \left(F_c^{(x,y,t-N_s)} \right). \tag{9}$$

Then, the pixel-wise features are obtained for every pixel contained in a target blob candidate. However, because the numbers of pixels in blob candidates are various, the distribution of the pixel-wise features is utilized as a blob-wise feature to represent blobs in the same dimension. The distribution is represented by a covariance matrix and a mean vector of the whole pixel-wise features contained in the target blob. Therefore, 72 channel vector composed of 64 values from the covariance matrix and 8 values from the mean vector is used as the blob-level feature.

Classification: The classification method is same as the method used for the VL flame detector, which utilizes the homogeneous kernel mapping [21] and linear SVM. Contrary to the previous smoke detectors [12–15] which need the labeled region of smoke to train their classifiers, the proposed algorithm do not need the labeled region if only smoke is moving in the training video. When only the smoke moves in the training video, positive samples can be obtained by applying the two previous steps including the candidate search and feature extraction on the video. Negative samples are obtained from non-smoke videos by the same method. In the test sequence, a blob candidate is classified as smoke if its SVM margin is over 0.

Temporal Association: After the classification step, for a binary detection map $\mathbf{L}_{sm}$, the pixels of the blobs classified as smoke are set to one and the other pixels are zero. To remove remaining outliers, the consecutive detection maps are temporally associated as

$$\mathbf{D}_{sm}^{(x,y,t)} = \alpha \mathbf{D}_{sm}^{(x,y,t-1)} + (1-\alpha)\mathbf{L}_{sm}^{(x,y)}, \tag{10}$$

where $\mathbf{D}_{sm}^{(x,y,0)} = 0$. Then, the values of $\mathbf{D}_{sm}$ are between 0 and 1, and the detector gives a fire alarm when the maximum value of $\mathbf{D}_{sm}$ is over a predefined threshold ζ_{sm}.

4.3   IR Flame Detector

When the signal can be represented by a repeat of basic signal, the signal shows weak randomness so that the blob would be a fire-like outlier such as a turn signal and a neon sign. Therefore, the randomness of a signal can be defined as the absence of repeated basic signal in the signal, which is utilized in the proposed IR flame detector.

The entire framework of the IR flame detector is described in Fig. 5. At first, blob candidates are extracted by grouping bright pixels. Then, blob-wise shape features are estimated from the shapes of the blobs. After tracking the blobs temporally, the temporal shape change of a blob is expressed by a blob shape signal obtained by stacking the shape features of the tracked blobs. Based on the randomness of the signal, a classifier determines the candidate blobs as a flame. Finally, the classified flame blobs are temporally associated, and a fire alarm is given according to the temporally associated result.

Candidate Blob Search: Because the IR flame detector works on an IR camera, the input image is transformed to a gray image $\mathbf{I}$ by averaging the whole

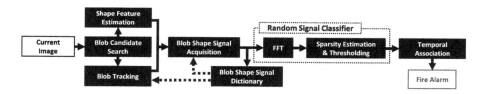

Fig. 5. Framework of IR Flame Detector. After extracting the bright regions as candidate blobs, a shape feature is obtained for each blob. The candidate blobs are tracked continuously, and the shape features are stacked to acquire a blob shape signal. By testing the randomness of the shape signal, the flame candidate is determined. After the temporal association of the flame candidates, a fire alarm is given.

channels. In order to regard the brightness of flames in an IR camera, a binary map $\mathbf{B}_{ir}$ is estimated by thresholding $\mathbf{I}$ as

$$\mathbf{B}_{ir}^{(x,y)} = \begin{cases} 1 & \text{if } \mathbf{I}^{(x,y)} > \epsilon_{ir} \\ 0 & \text{otherwise,} \end{cases} \tag{11}$$

where ϵ_{ir} is a predefined threshold. After applying a denoising sequence with dilation and erosion filters, the blob candidates are obtained by connected component algorithm [22]. Among all the blobs, the small blobs are rejected, which contain fewer pixels than a predefined number N_{sb}.

Shape Feature Estimation: From l-th blob candidate, a shape feature V^l is estimated by summing the variances of x and y positions of the containing pixels as

$$\begin{aligned} V^l &= \sum_{i=1}^{N^l}(x_i^l - m_x^l)^2 + (y_i^l - m_y^l)^2, \\ \mathbf{m}^l &= (m_x^l, m_y^l) = (\sum_{i=1}^{N^l} x_i^l/N^l, \sum_{i=1}^{N} y_i^l/N^l), \\ \mathbf{X}^l &= \{(x_1^l, y_1^l), ..., (x_{N^l}^l, y_{N^l}^l)\}, \end{aligned} \tag{12}$$

where $\mathbf{X}^l$ is a position set of pixels labeled as l-th blob and N^l is the number of the pixels.

Blob Shape Signal Acquisition: For tracking the blobs on consecutive frames, a tracking algorithm based on the distances among the blobs is used. A previous blob at time $(t-1)$ is connected to a current blob at time (t) if the current blob is closest to the previous blob and the distance between the center points of the two blobs is less than a predefined threshold ϵ_{di}. When the previous blob has no connection, the previous blob becomes a finished blob. On the other hand, the current blob becomes an initial blob when the blob is not connected to any previous blob.

For the connected blobs, the shape features are stacked temporally to build the blob shape signal. The size of the blob shape signal for one blob is limited by N_M, and the oldest blob value is removed in a first-in-first-out scheme when the size goes over the limitation. Algorithm 1 describes the method acquiring the blob shape signal in detail.

$\mathbf{M}$ is a set of blob center points, $\mathbf{S}$ is a set of blob shape signals, $\mathbf{V}$ is a set of shape features, and K and L are the number of candidate blobs at $(t-1)$ and (t), respectively.

Classification: The blobs tracked over N_M frames are applied to the classification. For verifying the absence of a repeated basic signal, the sparsity of the signal in Fourier domain is estimated. When the entire signal $\mathbf{s}(t)$ with length T is repeated N-times by a basic signal $\mathbf{s}^o(t)$, the signal in time domain can be simplified as $\mathbf{s}(t) = \mathbf{s}^o(t) * \sum_{k=0}^{N-1} \delta\left(t - \frac{kT}{N}\right)$, which can be represented in Fourier domain as

$$\mathcal{F}(\mathbf{s}(t)) = \mathcal{F}(\mathbf{s}^o(t)) \sum_{k=-\infty}^{\infty} \delta\left(w - k\frac{2\pi N}{T}\right), \tag{13}$$

Algorithm 1. Blob Shape Signal Acquisition

$\mathbf{M}^{(0)} = \emptyset,\ \mathbf{S}^{(0)} = \emptyset,$
$\mathbf{M}^{(t-1)} = \{\mathbf{m}^{1,(t-1)}, ..., \mathbf{m}^{K,(t-1)}\},\ \mathbf{S}^{(t-1)} = \{\mathbf{S}^{1,(t-1)}, ..., \mathbf{S}^{K,(t-1)}\}$
$\mathbf{M}^{(t)} = \{\mathbf{m}^{1,(t)}, ..., \mathbf{m}^{L,(t)}\},\ \mathbf{V}^{(t)} = \{V^{1,(t)}, ..., V^{L,(t)}\}$
for $l = 1...L$ **do**
    $r = arg_k \min_{k \in \{1,...,K\}} (\|\mathbf{m}^{l,(t)} - \mathbf{m}^{k,(t-1)}\|_2)$
    if $\|\mathbf{m}^{l,(t)} - \mathbf{m}^{r,(t-1)}\|_2 < \theta_d$ **then**
        $\mathbf{S}^{l,(t)} = [\mathbf{S}^{r,(t-1)}, V^{l,(t)}]$
        if $length\left(\mathbf{S}^{l,(t)}\right) > N_M$ **then**
            $\mathbf{S}^{l,(t)} = \mathbf{S}^{l,(t)}(2:end)$
        end
    else
        $\mathbf{S}^{l,(t)} = [V^{l,(t)}]$
    end
end

where $\mathcal{F}(\bullet)$ returns a magnitude of an input signal in Fourier domain. Therefore, the signal in Fourier domain becomes sparse due to the multiplication of delta functions. On the contrary, a random signal has no sparse element in Fourier domain because the entire frequency elements are necessary for representing the random signal [24].

According to the property, the temporal randomness of a blob candidate is measured by the sparsity of the blob shape signal in Fourier domain. The sparsity of l-th blob F_{sp}^l is estimated by

$$F_{sp}^l = \left\| scad\left(\mathcal{F}\left(\mathbf{S}^{l,(t)}\right)\right) \right\|_1 \tag{14}$$

In the equation, the scad function [26] approximates the sparsity when the input signal contains noises. Finally, the l-th candidate blob is determined as a flame if F_{sp}^l is larger than a predefined threshold θ_{sp}.

Temporal Association: A binary detection map $\mathbf{L}_{ir}$ is obtained by setting one for the pixels on the flame blobs and zero for the other pixels. The detection map $\mathbf{D}_{ir}$ is temporally associated to remove remaining outliers as

$$\mathbf{D}_{ir}^{(x,y,t)} = \alpha \mathbf{D}_{ir}^{(x,y,t-1)} + (1-\alpha)\mathbf{L}_{ir}^{(x,y)}, \tag{15}$$

where $\mathbf{D}_{ir}^{(x,y,0)} = 0$. Finally, when the maximum value of $\mathbf{D}_{ir}$ is over a predefined threshold ζ_{ir}, the fire alarm is decided to result.

5   Experiments

5.1   Implementation

The used parameters are represented in Table 1 and decided experimentally. The size of SURF used for the VL flame detector was 32×32. The orders of

Table 1. Summary of parameters

	Parameter	Value	Description
Integration module	ϵ_{sw}	0.002	Threshold to decide VL/IR state
	ϵ_{ct}	0.05	Min. detector score to stop switching the state
VL flame detector	ϵ_{vl}	0.3	Threshold for moving pixels
	θ_{pr}	0.5	Threshold for color classifier
	N_c	20	Max. number of candidates
	N_d	10000	Max. size of dictionary
Smoke detector	N_s	30	Frame gap for a difference image
	ϵ_{sm}	0.2	Threshold for candidate extraction
IR flame detector	ϵ_{ir}	0.98	Threshold for candidate pixels
	N_{sb}	800	Min. size of blobs
	ϵ_{di}	300	Min. distance for blob tracking
	N_M	100	Max. length of shape signal
	θ_{sp}	0.005	Threshold for classification
Etc.	α	0.99	Weight for temporal association

homogeneous kernel mapping were set to 3 for VL flame detector and 5 for VL smoke detector.

The entire framework was implemented in C++ with OpenCV and VLFeat library. With one core of 3.40 GHz CPU and 16 GB memory, the computational speed was 35.71 fps in VL state and 47.62 fps in IR state for 1280 × 720 videos, so that the proposed framework worked in real-time.

5.2 Experimental Details

The experiments were executed by three datasets of which all the positive videos are different. The first dataset is 'General Dataset' consisting of 41 fire videos and 54 fire-like outlier videos, which were gathered from previous papers [16] and other uploaded datasets [17,18]. The videos were captured only by VL camera in various environments including indoor and outdoor scenes. The second dataset is 'Indoor Dataset' consisting of 99 fire videos and 141 fire-like outlier videos, which were newly captured indoor. Among the fire videos, 54 videos were captured by VL cameras and the other videos were by IR cameras to confirm the 24-hours performance of the proposed framework. Among the fire-like outlier videos, 102 videos were captured by VL cameras and the other 39 videos were by IR cameras. For verifying the robustness, the videos were captured in numerous environments, such as a house, a storehouse, and an office. The third dataset is 'Smoke Dataset' consisting of 60 smoke videos, which were captured by ourselves with the various environment. In all the videos of the dataset, smoke occurs to test the performance of the proposed smoke detector, because smoke

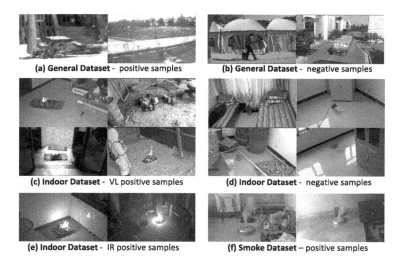

Fig. 6. Sample images of used datasets. We used three datasets: (a-b) General Dataset, (c-e) Indoor Dataset, and (f) Smoke Dataset.

is not shown in many fire videos of the other two datasets. The fire-like out-lier videos captured by a VL camera among Indoor Dataset were used as the negative videos of Smoke Dataset (Fig, 6).

General Dataset videos are utilized as training samples for the experiments using Indoor Dataset. On the other hand, the framework is trained by General Dataset for the experiments of General Dataset.

The performances of algorithms are estimated by two measures: detection ratio and false positive ratio. The detection ratio is obtained by dividing the number of correctly detected fire videos by the number of the tested fire videos. The detection of a video is determined when one or more fire alarms are detected from the fire video. The false positive ratio is evaluated by dividing the number of wrongly detected negative videos by the number of the tested negative videos. Because a negative video becomes a wrongly detected negative video even with one false alarm, the measure is very challenging for fire detection frameworks. As the algorithm shows high detection ratio with a low false positive ratio, the performance of the algorithm becomes good. With a ROC curve of detection ratio and false positive ratio, the performances of algorithms can be compared by the area under the curve. In the following experiments, the ROC curves were obtained by varying the thresholds $(\zeta_{vl}, \zeta_{sm}, \zeta_{ir})$ which determine the fire alarm from the temporally associated detection maps.

5.3   Self-comparison

Effectiveness of Sparsity Estimation in IR Flame Detector. To show the effectiveness of sparsity estimation used in the IR flame detector, we compared the distributions of the sparsity values estimated from flame videos and

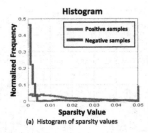
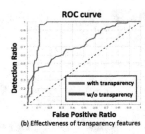

(a) Histogram of sparsity values   (b) Effectiveness of transparency features

Fig. 7. Results of self-comparison experiments. (a) shows the difference in the distribution of the sparsity values from IR flames and the ones of flame-like objects. (b) presents the effectiveness of the proposed transparency features in the smoke detector.

flame-like outlier videos. A flame histogram was built from the sparsity values of all the blob candidates extracted from the flame videos captured by IR cameras among Indoor Dataset. An outlier histogram was obtained by the sparsity values estimated from the negative videos captured by IR cameras among Indoor Dataset.

The flame histogram and outlier histogram are compared in Fig. 7(a). As shown in the histograms, about 80 % of sparsity values from outliers were located in 0–0.005 region, while about 90 % of sparsity values from flames were distributed out of the region. Therefore, as suggested in this paper, most of the flame-like outliers with IR cameras can be rejected by the sparsity of a shape signals in Fourier domain.

Effectiveness of Transparency Features in Smoke Detector. For validating the effectiveness of transparency features used for the smoke detector, we compared the proposed detector with a naive detector which utilizes same features excepting for the two transparency features. Smoke Dataset was used as a test set, and the two detectors were trained by five positive videos with smoke and all the negative videos of General Dataset.

The experimental results are shown in Fig. 7(b). As shown in the results, the proposed detector utilizing the transparency features showed much better performance than the naive detector. From the results, the proposed transparency features can be verified as robust features to distinguish smokes from outliers.

5.4   Performance

General Dataset. General Dataset was used to show the improvement of the VL flame detector from the previous flame detection algorithms. The flame detector was compared with Choi et al. [6], which has shown the state-of-the-art performance. The performance comparison is shown in Fig. 8(a), verifying that the proposed detector shows better performance than the state-of-the-art algorithm in general environments.

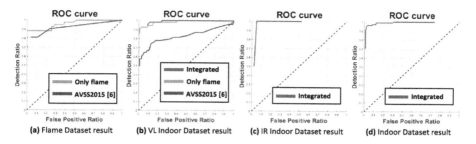

Fig. 8. Performance Evaluation. (a) shows the performance of VL flame detector with General Dataset. (b) presents the performance of integrated framework with the VL videos of Indoor Dataset. (c) is the results of integrated framework with the IR videos of Indoor Dataset. (d) shows the performance of integrated framework with the entire videos of Indoor Dataset.

Indoor Dataset. Indoor Dataset can be divided by VL Indoor Dataset and IR Indoor Dataset according to the used camera. The performance estimated by VL Indoor Dataset and IR Indoor Dataset shows the respective performance of the proposed framework for each state.

In the experiment using VL Indoor Dataset, we compared three algorithms including Choi *et al.* [6], the VL flame detector, and the integrated framework, as shown in Fig. 8(b). The ROC curve of the integrated framework was obtained by changing ζ_{vl}, while ζ_{ir} and ζ_{sm} were fixed by 0.9 and 0.6, respectively. The proposed algorithm shows better performance than Choi *et al.* [6]. Also, it can be confirmed that the proposed algorithm shows much better performance in indoor scenes than in general scenes by comparing the performance gap between [6] and the proposed framework. When the performances of the VL flame detector and the integrated framework are compared, it can be checked that the smoke detector is helpful for fire detection.

Only the proposed algorithm was tested for IR Indoor Dataset, and the results are shown in Fig. 8(c). In the experiment, IR flame detector wrongly detects outliers from only two of 39 negative videos, while all the positive videos are correctly detected.

By testing the integrated framework for Indoor Dataset, the 24-hour performance of the framework was evaluated as shown in Fig. 8(d). Because the switching signal from a camera cannot be used in the experiment, the proposed VL/IR classification method was applied to recognize the current camera state. Following the results, the proposed integrated framework showed good performance in various indoor scenes.

6   Conclusion

In this paper, we proposed the framework for 24-hours fire detection, including the integration module and the three novel fire detectors of VL flame detector, smoke detector, and IR flame detector. The integration module selectively operates the detectors proper to the current state of VL/IR cameras. The VL flame detector was improved from the previous patch-level flame detector, showing higher performance than the previous one. The smoke detector was newly developed, which considered the transparency property of smoke by gradient correlations and dark channel differences. Also, the IR flame detector was built to find flames with an IR camera by testing the randomness in the temporal changes of a blob shape. The three detectors and the integrated framework were tested by three datasets consisting of numerous videos, showing satisfactory performances to be applied to real scenes even in real-time.

Acknowledgment. This work was partly supported by the ICT RD program of MSIP/IITP[B0101-15-0552, Development of Predictive Visual Intelligence Technology], the Brain Korea 21 Plus Project, and EU FP7 project WYSIWYD under Grant 612139.

References

1. Ahrens, M.: Characteristics of home fire victims. National Fire Protection Association (2014). http://www.nfpa.org/
2. Phillips III, W., Shah, M., Lobo, N.V.: Flame recognition in video. PRL **23**, 319–327 (2002)
3. Chenebert, A., Breckon, T.P., Gaszczak, A.: A non-temporal texture driven approach to real-time fire detection. In: ICIP (2011)
4. Toreyin, B.U., Dedeoglu, Y., Gudukbay, U., Cetin, A.E.: Computer vision based method for real-time fire and flame detection. PRL **27**, 49–58 (2006)
5. Ham, S., Ko, B., Nam, J.: Fire-flame detection based on fuzzy finite automation. In: ICPR (2010)
6. Choi, J., Choi, J.Y.: Patch-based fire detection with online outlier learning. In: AVSS (2015)
7. Morerio, P., Marcenaro, L., Regazzoni, C.S., Gera, G.: Early fire and smoke detection based on colour features and motion analysis. In: ICIP (2012)
8. Maoult, Y.L., Sentenac, T., Orteu, J.J., Arcens, J.P.: Fire detection, a new approach based on a low-cost CCD camera in the near infrared. Process Saf. Environ. Prot. **85**, 193–206 (2007)
9. Owrutsky, J.C., Steinhurst, D.A., Minor, C.P., Rose-Pehrsson, S.L., Williams, F.W., Gottuk, D.T.: Long wavelength video detection of fire in ship compartments. Fire Saf. J. **41**, 315–320 (2006)
10. Tasdemir, K., Gunay, O., Toreyin, B.U., Cetin, A.E.: Video based wildfire detection at night. In: Signal Processing and Communications Applications Conference (2009)
11. Toreyin, B.U., Cinbis, R.G., Dedeoglu, Y., Cetin, A.E.: Fire detection in infrared video using wavelet analysis. Opt. Eng. **46**, 067204 (2007)
12. Toreyin, B.U., Dedeoglu, Y., Cetin, A.E.: Contour based smoke detection in video using wavelets. In: European Signal Processing Conference (2006)
13. Ho, C.: Machine vision-based real-time early flame and smoke detection. Meas. Sci. Technol. **20**, 045502 (2009)
14. Kim, D., Wang, Y.: Smoke detection in video. In: World Congress on Computer Science and Information Engineering (2009)

15. Chen, T., Yin, Y., Huang, S., Ye, Y.: The smoke detection for early fire-alarming system base on video processing. In: International Conference on Intelligent Information Hiding and Multimedia Signal Processing (2006)
16. Ko, B., Ham, S., Nam, J.: Modeling and formalization of fuzzy finite automata for detection of irregular fire flames. Trans. Circuits Syst. Video Technol. **21**, 1903–1912 (2011)
17. Foggia, P., Saggese, A., Vento, M.: Real-time fire detection for video surveillance applications using a combination of experts based on color, shape and motion. Trans. Circuits Syst. Video Technol. (2015)
18. Lascio, R.D., Greco, A., Saggese, A., Vento, M.: Improving fire detection reliability by a combination of videoanalytics. In: International Conference on Image Analysis and Recognition (2014)
19. Hoerl, A.E., Kennard, R.W.: Ridge regression: biased estimation for nonorthogonal problems. Technometrics **12**, 55–67 (1970)
20. Bay, H., Ess, A., Tuytelaars, T., Gool, L.V.: Speeded-up robust features (SURF). CVIU **110**, 356–359 (2008)
21. Vedaldi, A., Zisserman, A.: Efficient additive kernels via explicit feature maps. TPAMI **34**, 480–492 (2012)
22. Samet, H., Tamminen, M.: Efficient component labeling of images of arbitrary dimension represented by linear bintrees. TPAMI **10**, 579–586 (1988)
23. Sobel, I.: History and Definition of the Sobel Operator, Report (2014)
24. Oppenheim, A.V., Schafer, R.W.: Discrete-Time Signal Processing, 3rd edn. Pearson, Upper Saddle River (2010)
25. He, K., Sun, J., Tang, X.: Single image haze removal using dark channel prior. TPAMI **33**(12), 2341–2353 (2011)
26. Fan, J., Li, R.: Variable selection via nonconcave penalized likelihood and its oracle properties. J. Am. Stat. Assoc. **96**, 1348–1360 (2001)

Smart Toothbrushes: Inertial Measurement Sensors Fusion with Visual Tracking

Marco Marcon(✉), Augusto Sarti, and Stefano Tubaro

Dipartimento di Elettronica, Informazione e Bioingegneria, Politecnico di Milano,
Piazza Leonardo da Vinci, 32, 20133 Milano, Italy
{marco.marcon,augusto.sarti,stefano.tubaro}@polimi.it

Abstract. A proper toothbrushing is a crucial aspect to preserve person's dental health. Furthermore different brushing techniques have been defined for kids, adults and people with different dental appliances, prostheses, partial dentures or oral pathologies. In order to provide a real-time feedback to the user there are, mainly, two approaches: the first one is based on intelligent toothbrushes (called smart toothbrushes) where Inertial Measurement Units, bristles pressure sensor, and also cameras are placed on the toothbrush; data acquired is then transmitted and processed on a smartphone or tablet that monitor the user's habit and provide him/her with brushing statistics together with suggestions to tune brushing timing and technique. The second approach simplifies the toothbrush device transferring the computational efforts to the hand-held device: from the onboard camera it has to track both user's face and toothbrush in order to extract brushing parameters. In this paper we compare the two approaches concluding that only a fusion of their data can produce an all-around exhaustive analysis of the tooth brushing technique.

Keywords: Dental care · Target tracking · Toothbrushing analysis

1 Introduction

Intelligent Toothbrush systems, or, as the are commonly called, Smart Toothbrushes (ST) represent a novel technology in the Cyber Physical Systems context for human healthcare. ST can be equipped with a wide variety of sensors, from IMU [12], to bristles pressure detectors [2], from timers [20] to cameras for teeth analysis [18]. Lot of companies are investing in advanced ST technologies and apps in order to improve toothbrushing habits of everyone; e.g. in order to make the procedure more attractive for kids, usually gamification techniques are adopted: [4,11,17]. A different approach is presented in [5,7] and in our previous work [13] where the toothbrush motion analysis is performed through the camera available on the smartphone or tablet. In this last case a target, that can be easily recognized and tracked, is applied on the toothbrush, and, usually, the face and the facial parts of the used are also tracked. In this paper we compare the two approaches in order to find advantages and disadvantages and to

© Springer International Publishing Switzerland 2016
G. Hua and H. Jégou (Eds.): ECCV 2016 Workshops, Part II, LNCS 9914, pp. 480–494, 2016.
DOI: 10.1007/978-3-319-48881-3_33

cross-check their accuracy and reliability. We want to underline that the aim of this work is not to compare the manual toothbrush with the electric one but to assert how oral care for kids, adults and people with dental diseases can take great advantage from the next generation of STs.

2 Experimental Setup

We equipped a manual toothbrush with a coloured target, according to [13] and with a battery powered G-Module from ST Microelectronics. A picture of the adopted setup is visible in Fig. 1. The G-Module and the Li-ion battery can be easily placed inside the toothbrush handle; The adopted G-Module uses a LSM6DS3 iNEMO inertial SiP (System-in-packages) accelerometer and gyroscope (6DoF) and a LIS3MDLTR magnetometer (3DoF) providing a total of 9 axes solution. The set of these two sensors constitute what is commonly called an Attitude and Heading Reference System (AHRS); on the same PCB there is also a BlueNRG: a Bluetooth Low Energy (4.0) network processor to transfer data to a PC and a STM32F411CEY ARM Cortex-M4 core with DSP and FPU capabilities. Further details can be found in [19].

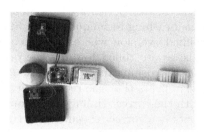

Fig. 1. The ST Microelectronics G-Module and the coloured target integrated into a toothbrush. The usb port and the on/off switch are connected just during recharge phase. Both the G-Module and the Battery are hosted inside the toothbrush handle.

3 Toothbrushing Analysis

The toothbrushing analysis aims at evaluating the following parameters:

- The proper brushing of each portion of the dental arches.
- The timing dedicated to each portion.
- The correctness of the adopted brushing technique.

All the three mentioned parameters, as mentioned in [13], are crucial for a proper brushing technique, furthermore, for people with particular dental pathologies, different techniques can be prescribed by the dentist (see, e.g. [16]) in order to tackle specific criticalities. For example, people with fixed orthodontic appliances should use the Bass/Sulcular technique that is much more

Fig. 2. One of the most effective toothbrushing technique for the Orthodontic Gingival index is the Bass technique: keeping the bristles at 45° a rotational movement is applied on dental vestibular surface

effective on the reduction of Plaque index and Gingival index with respect to Scrubbing or Stillman technique, that, on the contrary, are more adequate for gingivitis. The Bass technique, however, is quite complex to be properly performed since the bristles must be kept with an angle of 45° with respect to the tooth vertical direction (see Fig. 2). For kids and for most of adult users the Bass technique could result a bit too complex, so the main goal in toothbrush analysis is to prevent wrong motions like horizontal Scrub method where the bristles are activated following an horizontal scrubbing method on the vestibular dental surface. Such a motion can easily induce Tooth Cervical Abrasion. Furthermore, for other periodontal diseases, like patients with damages at the gingival sulcus, the three most famous brushing techniques (Bass, Stillman's and Charter's) are suggested in a "Modified" version where, at the end of each technique on a dental portion, the bristles are rolled towards the occlusal surface. Further details about different tooth brushing techniques can be found in [3]. From the aforementioned aspects it appears that the recognition of a proper toothbrushing execution together with the correct timing is a complex task. The presented approach can assist patients in a correct execution. In the following we compare two possible techniques based on visual tracking and on the data analysis from the inertial Measurement Unit (IMU).

4   IMU Data Analysis

In order to analyze data from ST IMU we adopted an approach similar to [10]; we sampled the toothbrush motion at 12 Hz since the dominant brushing frequency, related to the main hand oscillations, in all the analyzed cases, ranges from 3.5 to 4.8 Hz. Our aim, as depicted in Sect. 3, is to recognize the toothbrush motion with respect to the reference system on the user's mouth. In particular, analysing the behaviour of a set of users, the following assumptions can be done:

- Until one is brushing the same dental portion the bristles movement is periodic.
- Apart from some specific techniques (usually called "Modified", e.g. modified Bass, modified Stillman, modified etc. etc. where rolling is present) the toothbrush motion in most of practical cases, is always planar in a plane orthogonal to the bristles direction (brushing plane).
- The z axis of the toothbrush (along its handle) always belongs to the plane described in the previous item.

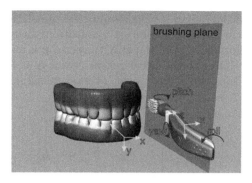

Fig. 3. The axes orientation in the mouth reference frame, and in the toothbrush reference frame (x and z axes belong to the brushing plane). The three possible rotation angles are also represented.

- Pitch (rotation in the bristles direction) is never present.
- Yaw is usually small and is related to a residual wrist rotation performed during brushing.

Refer to Fig. 3 for the aforementioned orientations. These hypotheses allow us to simplify the toothbrushing analysis however a crucial aspect is related to the knowledge of the mouth position and, consequently, to the local reference system that, obviously, cannot be detected from the ST IMU. This aspect will be analyzed in Sect. 5.

4.1   Toothbrush Orientation and Brushing Analysis

The conventional algorithm for orientation estimation involves using estimates of the Earth gravity vector and the Earth magnetic field reference. Naturally, the horizontal component of the Earth ambient magnetic field originates from the magnetic south pole and points towards the magnetic North pole. Magnetic field strength measurements, relative to previously measured calibration values, from the magnetometer are used to calculate the heading of the AHRS (IMU). The direction of gravity is calculated using the accelerometer readings. However, under external magnetic field disturbances, for example when the IMU is close to a ferrous or magnetic object, the estimated heading is incorrect, and so, the orientation estimates are inaccurate. However we do not need an absolute orientation with respect to the North pole but just a relative orientation to estimate horizontal rotations (in the plane orthogonal to the gravity vector). Since, as previously stated, most of the analyzed motions are just translational in the brushing plane (see Fig. 3) the orientation of the gravity vector with respect to the brushing plane remains almost constant until the toothbrush is moved to another dental part. This means that the projection of the gravity vector on each axis of the 3D accelerometer stays constant for a pure translational motion and represents the continuous component (DC) of the sensor reading on each axis;

on the contrary the variable part (AC) contains the translational details on each axis. In Fig. 5 we show the accelerometer acquisitions brushing the maxillary occlusal surface. The orientation of the gravity vector **g** is extracted applying an average (rectangular) filter to the acceleration vector **a** at least two seconds of samples (in order to take the average over, at least 20 samples):

$$g_{x,y,z}(n) = \frac{1}{L} w_L(n) * a_{x,y,z}(n) \tag{1}$$

where:

$$w_L(n) = \begin{cases} 1 & for \ \ 0 \le n < L \\ 0 & otherwise \end{cases} \tag{2}$$

in the following we will call $\bar{\mathbf{a}}(n) = \mathbf{a}(n) - \mathbf{g}(n)$ the normalized acceleration where the average gravity component (DC) has been removed.

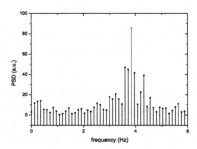

Fig. 4. The Power Spectrum Density estimated by the Periodogram from 100 samples; The representation, from 0 Hz to the Nyquist frequency, shows the dominant peak at 3.84 Hz (in red) indicating the average brushing frequency. (Color figure online)

Some relevant information can be obtained analyzing $\bar{\mathbf{a}}(n)$; in particular the dominant frequency in its Power Spectral Density, obtained, e.g. using the periodogram [6], indicates the brushing period. As an example, assuming that the acceleration direction with the maximum spread is z we can evaluate:

$$brushing frequency = \max_f \frac{\Delta t}{N} \left| \sum_{n=0}^{L-1} \bar{a}_z(n) e^{-i2\pi n \Delta t f} \right|^2 \ \ with \ 0 < f \le \frac{1}{2\Delta t}. \tag{3}$$

In Fig. 4 there is a representation of the periodogram with the dominant brushing frequency.

Another relevant analysis is based on the covariance matrix of $\bar{\mathbf{a}}(n)$:

$$\Sigma = \mathrm{E}\left[(\bar{\mathbf{a}} - \mathrm{E}[\bar{\mathbf{a}}]) (\bar{\mathbf{a}} - \mathrm{E}[\bar{\mathbf{a}}])^\top \right] \tag{4}$$

where $\bar{\mathbf{a}}$ is a column vector of 3 elements, the expected value is commonly estimated over 2–3 s and its value is usually very close to zero during a periodic brushing action since the gravity component has already been removed.

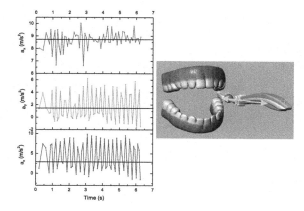

Fig. 5. In this figure we present the acceleration components along the three tooth-brush axes (represented in Fig. 3. The straight lines represent the average value (i.e. the gravity components: $g_x = 8.71, g_y = 1.69, g_z = 4.21$)). As can be seen the component with the widest spread is a_z indicating that the motion is a translational along the toothbrush handle. The dominant component of g_x indicates that the bristles are oriented vertically insisting on the maxillary dental arch.

Analyzing the eigenvalues of Σ when the user is insisting on the same dental portion we found that an eigenvalue, λ_1 is usually much smaller with respect to the other two (more than one order of magnitude) indicating that the brushing action is performed moving cyclically the toothbrush in the same plane (the brushing plane), furthermore the normal to the brushing plane (in the toothbrush coordinate system) is the eigenvector $\mathbf{v}_1$ associated to that eigenvalue. Analyzing the remaining two eigenvalues we can classify the movement: in particular if their values are very similar it means that the motion is uniformly distributed in the brushing plane and, for the tooth brushing procedures, this usually means an almost circular motion in the brushing plane. While if $\lambda_2 \ll \lambda_3$ the motion is pure translational. In Fig. 6 we show what is going on with a circular motion in the brushing plane: in the bottom part of the figure there is the projection of the $\bar{\mathbf{a}}(n)$ on the second and third eigenvector (v_2 and v_3) associated to the second and third eigenvalue of the covariance matrix. It is clear that analyzing the eigenvalues of the covariance matrix and the position of the gravity vector we can easily discriminate between different brushing techniques.

4.2   Gyroscope Analysis

In all the examined cases from different users, for all the brushing techniques that do not explicitly requires a rotation of the brushing plane, all the actions, included the ones requiring a circular motion like the Bass technique (see, e.g. the top left part of Fig. 6) the angular velocities measured by the gyroscope are lower than $1 rad/s$ indicating that there is just a minimum yaw rotation in the brushing plane. In particular this is related to the small usage of wrist rotations

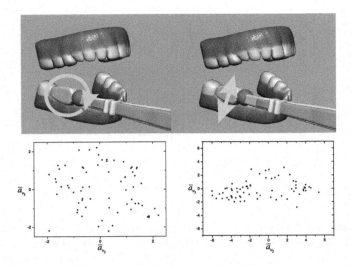

Fig. 6. On top left a circular bristles motion brushing the vestibular surface while on top right a vertical oscillatory motion of the bristles. On bottom we report the reprojection of the samples of the normalized acceleration vector $\bar{\mathbf{a}}(n)$ on the second and third eigenvectors of the covariance matrix (associated to the two largest eigenvalues).

during toothbrushing that would result in a quite uncomfortable and fatiguing gesture. In Fig. 7 we show the angular velocities for rotation along the roll axis; it can be seen that, since such a rotation of the toothbrush handle involves both the forearm and the wrist, the angular velocity vector ω is not exactly aligned with the toothbrush $z - axis$ but a yaw component and a small pitch component are also present. However, such a particular gesture is required only in some specific brushing techniques (like "Modified Bass" and "Modified Stillman") that will help patients with gingival problems clearing out the debris and biofilm out of Embrasures; in particular the Rolling motion avoids damaging the base of the gingival sulcus.

4.3   Toothbrushing Action Segmentation

Thanks to the periodicity and to the permanence of the motion vector in the same brushing plane for every specific toothbrushing action, an automatic segmentation of different actions (i.e. when the bristles are moved to a different dental arch portion) can be easily performed simply applying a threshold in the orientation variations of the brushing plane orientation. As a rule of thumb, inspecting a series of toothbrushing actions, we saw that a threshold of 25° between two orientations of the toothbrush plane can be adopted as a criterion to properly segment most of sequences.

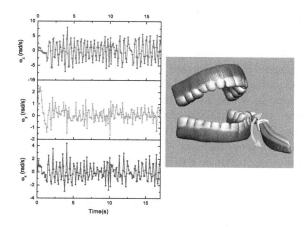

Fig. 7. The three angular velocities are represented for a rotational periodic movement. It is clear that, due to the involvement of the forearm and the wrist in this specific gesture, the rotation axis is not exactly along the toothbrush handle but presents a combination of roll and yaw rotations while the pitch (ω_y) is usually lower.

5   Visual Tracking Analysis

The toothbrushing analysis based on the ST IMU appears to be an effective and reliable tool to accurately analyse the brushing habit of the user; in particular, as described in Sect. 7, a Radial Basis Function Neural Network together with some handmade conditions can provide us with a satisfying classification engine. However, analyzing in deeper detail the brushing habits of our volunteers we found some aspects that cannot be simply handled just using IMU data. The first complex aspect is to distinguish if the bristles are insisting on the left or on the right side the mouth. As described in Sect. 4.1, we can get an absolute reference vector, invariant under toothbrush motion, that, even if could deviate a lot from the real North Pole direction, provides us with a fixed direction. However this does not allow us to simply distinguish between left, right or central dental arch portions where toothbrush is insisting: tracking, for example, the $z - axis$ of the toothbrush we need to get samples from both left and right mouth parts in order to estimate a possible central orientation aligned with the $z - axis$ of the mouth reference system.

Another drawback is the fact that users, when changing the brushed zone usually rotate their head, this aspect if further emphasised if they need to look at the smartphone or tablet placed in front of them during toothbrushing. The bathroom furniture also affects the toothbrushing styles, in particular, since people usually look at themselves during this procedure, if there is a high wall mirror usually people keep their head horizontal while, if the bottom of the mirror is close to the sink and the smartphone device is placed on the sink itself people tilt their head forward. All the aforementioned issues introduce a large variability in the orientation of the mouth reference system, which is reflected in the uncertainty in the relative orientation of the toothbrush axes with respect to the mouth one. This effect partially invalidate the accurate brushing analysis described in the previous sections. To overcome this problem, we fused ST IMU data with information from face and toothbrush tracking [13]. Unfortunately most of the tested android phones did not provide an accurate value for the focal length of their cameras while we need at least a rough estimation of its value in order to etimate the orientation of the mouth reference system with respect to the camera one. We then evaluate the camera internal parameters using 3DF Lapyx, a free software from 3DFlow [1]. For example, using a Samsung Galaxy SII we got the following intrinsic calibration matrix [8]:

$$\mathbf{K} = \begin{bmatrix} f_x & s & p_x \\ 0 & f_y & p_y \\ 0 & 0 & 1 \end{bmatrix} = \begin{bmatrix} 2889.83 & 0 & 1600.14 \\ 0 & 2892.84 & 1193.29 \\ 0 & 0 & 1 \end{bmatrix} \tag{5}$$

and

$$\mathbf{K}^{-1} = \begin{bmatrix} 1/f_x & 0 & -p_x/f_x \\ 0 & 1/f_y & -p_y/f_y \\ 0 & 0 & 1 \end{bmatrix} \tag{6}$$

Where all parameters are expressed in pixels. Assuming that the user is looking at the mobile device, once the face and the mouth is localized in the image, the mouth direction from the camera center (i.e. the orientation of the $z - axis$ of the mouth reference system) can be obtained, with reference to Fig. 8, using the following formula ([8] p. 82):

$$\cos \theta = \frac{(\mathbf{d}^\top \mathbf{p}_{axis})}{\sqrt{\mathbf{d}^\top \mathbf{d}} \sqrt{\mathbf{p}_{axis}^\top \mathbf{p}_{axis}}} \tag{7}$$

where $\mathbf{p}_{axis} = \begin{bmatrix} 0 & 0 & 1 \end{bmatrix}^\top$ represents the Principal axis direction. We are only interested in the elevation angle of the vector $\mathbf{d}$ since the Azimuth of the mouth is not relevant for our purpose of correcting the toothbrush accelerations according to the head forward tilt. If $\mathbf{x_m}$ is the mouth center reprojected on the image plane, we force its horizontal component to p_x so the angle evaluated by Eq. 8 will be exactly the mouth elevation angle θ_{elev}. The Eq. 7 becomes:

$$\cos \theta_{elev} = \frac{\left(\mathbf{K}^{-1}\bar{\mathbf{x}}_m\right)^\top \begin{bmatrix} 0 & 0 & 1 \end{bmatrix}^\top}{|\mathbf{K}^{-1}\bar{\mathbf{x}}_m|} \tag{8}$$

where $\bar{\mathbf{x}}_m$ is equal to $\mathbf{x}_m$ but with the first component equal to p_x. The previous equation becomes:

$$\cos \theta_{elev} = \left(\sqrt{\left(\frac{x_{my} - p_y}{f_y}\right)^2 + 1} \right)^{-1} \tag{9}$$

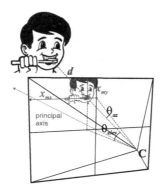

Fig. 8. The center of the mouth is reprojected on the mobile phone camera image plane through the ray whose direction is **d** (in *green*). The intersection is at coordinates x_{mx} and x_{my} (in *blue*) in the image plane coordinate system. The mouth orientation with respect to the camera principal axis is represented by θ_{elev} for the elevation and θ_{az} for the azimuth. (Color figure online)

where x_{my} is the vertical coordinate of the mouth in the image plane (see Fig. 8). Obviously the same can also be applied to the azimuth angle:

$$\cos\theta_{az} = \left(\sqrt{\left(\frac{x_{mx} - p_x}{f_x}\right)^2 + 1}\right)^{-1}. \tag{10}$$

6   Target Tracking

As described in Sect. 2, we adopted a similar target tracking procedure as described in [13]. It is based on a multi-coloured spherical target placed on the tail of the toothbrush: we are, in particular, interested in recognizing target position and orientation in the inversion points during pure translation motions; inversion motion points represent target positions where velocity is minimal, and blurring effects are minimized. However is some specific lighting conditions the mobile camera could automatically tune its exposure parameters on some background objects resulting in underexposed or overexposed target image; in Fig. 9 a target acquired in an unfavourable lighting condition presents an inaccurate segmentation in the HSV space. In order to improve accuracy in target orientation we fitted a circle around the segmented blob. This approach will allow us to know the exact size of the target (in terms of pixels) in the acquired image: we can, then, normalize the 6-bins histogram of the six hue values (Red, Green, Blue, Cyan, Magenta, Yellow) to the total number of pixels of the target circle instead of considering only the blob pixels. Combining IMU and visual tracking data, most of brushing information can be retrieved in a deterministic way and we adopted a Radial Basis Function Neural Network (RBFNN) (see Sect. 7) to extract the detailed motion of specific brushing techniques.

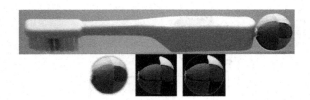

Fig. 9. A target acquired in an unfavourable lighting condition: After the saturation segmentation some target portions disappear as can be seen in the central image on the bottom. On the right a circle is fitted to the target to improve toothbrush orientation estimation

7   Toothbrushing Classification Results

Before applying a classifier to IMU and Visual tracking data some aspects must be considered since both of them, singularly adopted, do not allow an exhaustive toothbrushing analysis. The IMU allows an accurate analysis of the toothbrush motion but some major weaknesses are present:

– It is impossible to distinguish between brushing left, right or frontal mouth parts, i.e. a vestibular left brushing is very similar to an oral right brushing or to a vestibular frontal brushing: the orientation provided by the IMU is usually useless since it is a common habit of users to rotate their head when changing the brushed zone in order to see it better in the mirror.
– Different bathroom furniture could require different smartphone placements and the head forward inclination could change for the same brushing gesture: this could result in a rotation of the brushing plane and a consequent relative rotation of the gravity vector **g** for the same brushing gesture.
– Without a visual control there is no way to check if the user is keeping the toothbrush in the mouth or is just swinging it around: we noticed this behaviour in kids trying to cheating the system.

The visual tracking of the face and of the coloured target offers the following advantages:

– It allows to estimate the toothbrush position with respect to the mouth (if the target is found on the left of the facial sagittal plane the bristles will be on the right and vice versa).
– Once the brushed mouth side is defined it is possible to estimate the brushing plane and, once the head inclination is evaluated (according to Eq. 9) we can rotate the **g** vector accordingly. This allows us to normalize all the IMU data to an horizontal head orientation.

However the visual target tracking presents also other drawbacks:

– The accuracy in the orientation estimation depends from many factors: environmental lighting, self-shadows, mobile camera position (glares and overexposed conditions could occur) and resolution (usually the frontal camera, the one used in our application, has lower resolution and quality with respect to the rear one).

- Some in-plane circular movements, like, e.g. the Bass method, due to the small target displacement and to the absence of target rotation, can hardly be recognized.

We have to underline that all the described procedures allow an accurate analysis of the tootbrushing procedure, however no one of the examined techniques is able to distinguish on vertical dental surfaces between maxillary and mandibular parts since both IMU and visual tracking data are very similar for both parts.

7.1 The Classification Procedure

Considering the aforementioned advantages and disadvantages of the two methods, we decided to fuse their information in order to get a more robust classifier. Our classifier can be subdivided into two parts the first one is more "deterministic" while the second uses a Radial Basis Function Neural Network [9] as the final classifier. The first part follows this sequence:

1. Get at least 20 samples for the G-Module and extract the gravity vector orientation and the $\bar{a}(n)$ values.
2. Check the variance in the gravity vector orientation within the set of the previous 20 values. If the value is above a predefined threshold it could be that the user is changing the brushing part or a "modified" technique is applied involving rolling along the toothbrush handle. As described in Sect. 4.2, in order to distinguish these two possible cases we check the amount of pitch rotation (ω_y) with respect to the other two components of ω.
3. If the user is not changing the brushed dental portion the classification process goes on. We then analyze the mouth and toothbrush target position into the acquired frames. To minimize the processed frames and the risk of blurred target images we just analyze frames corresponding to highest acceleration values (since in a periodic motion the acceleration is highest in the motion inversion points, i.e. where the velocity is minimal).
4. The target color analysis is particularly relevant in order to estimate the dental portion on which the user is insisting. As can be seen in Fig. 10, this analysis allows to estimate accurately the dental portion on which the user is insisting, furthermore it allows to define the brushing plane orientation with respect to the mouth reference system.
5. Assuming that the user is looking at the mobile phone device, from Eq. 9, since we know from the previous step, the orientation of the brushing plane with respect to the mouth reference system, we can rotate the $\mathbf{g}$ vector in order to normalize the accelerometer data as if the mouth would be horizontal.

Fig. 10. Different sides of the target seen by the camera during vestibular brushing on different dental arch portions

7.2   The Radial Basis Function Neural Network Classifier

In order to properly classify the brushing action we adopted a Radial Basis Function Neural Network. We chose such a classifier since the acquired data from the IMU is quite noisy and this kind of Neural Networks has less training problems with respect to feedforward networks, in particular when a large amount of training data are available like in this case. Furthermore we need that the chosen classifier is able to interpolate and generalise the brushing habit to unknown users. Since the bristles orientation is known from the IMU data, we are interested in understanding the brushing motion: in particular it could be:

1. (A) "horizontal scrubbing" along the toothbrush handle,
2. (B) "vertical scrubbing" along the toothbrush $y - axis$,
3. (C) "circular scrubbing" or "Fones' technique" [15] just rotating bristles on the teeth surface following large, sweeping circles,
4. (D) "Roll Stroke" rotating the bristles along the toothbrush handle axis.

These 4 motions represent the basic bricks for all the tooth brushing techniques and in some practical applications, due to poor lighting conditions, blurring due to fast toothbrush oscillations and inaccurate background segmentation, can be confused with each other adopting just the visual approach described in [13]. Obviously, as described in Sect. 4.2, since these movements also interest the forearm and the wrist, different people perform them in different ways, with different accelerations and angular velocities: this is the main reason for which we need a classifier able to generalize classification to different users. We feed the RBF network with a vector containing 7 elements: the average magnitudes of the three components of $\bar{a}$ ($\frac{1}{L} \sum_{n=0}^{L-1} |a_{x,y,z}(n)|$), the three components of ω ($\frac{1}{L} \sum_{n=0}^{L-1} |\omega_{x,y,z}(n)|$) and the ratio between the two largest eigenvalues of the covariance matrix of $\bar{a}$ (see Sect. 4.1) (L is usually chosen in order to average the samples over a couple of seconds). We used a two-layer network using the MATLAB *newrbe* function [14]. We acquired 18 sequences from 9 volunteers, we segmented by hand those sequences and labeled them according to the previous 4 classes: "horizontal scrubbing" corresponds to a training output vector $[1\,0\,0\,0]$, while, e.g. "Roll Stroke" corresponds to a vector $[0\,0\,0\,1]$. Comparing results using 12 randomly chosen sequences for training and the remaining 6 for testing we got the results of Table 1.

Table 1. The Confusion Matrix representing classification results

	Predicted values			
	A	B	C	D
A	0.98	0	0.02	0
B	0	0.92	0.03	0.05
C	0.05	0.04	0.90	0.01
D	0	0.08	0.03	0.89

8   Conclusions

In this paper we presented a combined approach to improve effectiveness and usefulness of Smart Toothbrushes. Using a manual toothbrush equipped with an IMU unit and a color target, we analyzed information obtained from an IMU and from a visual target analysis approach. Both of these approaches present strengths and weaknesses and we showed that only combining information from both of them we are able to compensate head motion, and other difficulties arising from a simple visual approach. We also shown that we can recognize the exact dental portion brushed. Thanks to the IMU information we are also able to distinguish different toothbrush motions that could be used to asses the correct execution of a brushing procedure. The data fusion from IMU and visual tracking can then be considered as a promising technique to get an exhaustive toothbrushing analysis.

Acknowledgements. The research for this paper was financially supported by the Horizon 2020 European Project COSSIM (id: 644042-H2020-ICT-2014-1).

References

1. 3DFlow: Lapyx, a free software that extracts the typical intrinsics camera parameters. http://www.3dflow.net/technology/
2. Allen, C., Hunsley, N., Macgregor, I.: An instrument for measuring toothbrushing force using PIC microcontroller technology, pp. 861–866 (1995)
3. Asadoorian, J.: CDHA position paper on tooth brushing. Can. J. Dent. Hyg. **40**(5), 232–248 (2006)
4. Beam: Beam technologies inc. (2016). https://beam.dental/tech/
5. Chang, Y.C., Lo, J.L., Huan, C.J., Hsu, N.Y., Chu, H.H., Wang, H.Y., Pei-Yu, C., Hsieh, Y.L.: Playful toothbrush: ubicomp technology for teaching tooth brushing to kindergarten children. In: ACM CHI, pp. 363–372. ACM (2008)
6. Diniz, P., da Silva, E., Netto, S.: Digital Signal Processing: System Analysis and Design. Cambridge University Press, Cambridge (2010)
7. Flagg, A., Boger, J., Mihaidilis, A.: An intelligent toothbrush: machines for smart brushing. In: Proceedings of RESNA/ICTA (2011)
8. Hartley, R.I., Zisserman, A.: Multiple View Geometry in Computer Vision, 2nd edn. Cambridge University Press (2004). ISBN: 0521540518

9. Haykin, S.: Neural Networks and Learning Machines, vol. 10. Prentice Hall, New York (2009)
10. Kim, K.S., Yoon, T.H., Lee, J.W., Kim, D.J.: Interactive toothbrushing education by a smart toothbrush system via 3D visualization. Comput. Meth. Programs Biomed. **96**(2), 125–132 (2009)
11. Kolibree: Kolibree toothbrush (2014). http://kolibree.com/en/
12. Lee, Y.J., Lee, P.J., Kim, K.S., Park, W., Kim, K.D., Hwang, D., Lee, J.W.: Toothbrushing region detection using three-axis accelerometer and magnetic sensor. IEEE Trans. Biomed. Eng. **59**(3), 872–881 (2012)
13. Marcon, M., Sarti, A., Tubaro, S.: Toothbrush motion analysis to help children learn proper tooth brushing. Comput. Vis. Image Underst. **148**, 34–45 (2016). http://dx.doi.org/10.1016/j.cviu.2016.03.009
14. MATLAB: Neural network toolbox release 2016a, the mathworks, inc., natick, massachusetts, united states
15. Mosby, A.D.: Mosby's Medical Dictionary. 9th edn. Elsevier, Maryland Heights (2009)
16. Nassar, P.O., Bombardelli, C.G., Walker, C.S., Neves, K.V., Tonet, K., Nishi, R.N., Bombonatti, R., Nassar, C.A.: Periodontal evaluation of different toothbrushing techniques in patients with fixed orthodontic appliances. Dent. Press J. Orthod. **18**(1), 76–80 (2013)
17. Oral-B: Oral-b pro 5000 smartseries with bluetooth connectivity (2014). http://www.oralb.com/products/pro-5000-electric-toothbrush-with-smartguide-bluetooth/
18. Prophix: Prohix smart toothbrush by onvi, llc. (2016). https://www.getprophix.com/
19. STMicroelectronics: G-module, an inertial and environmental sensor module for iot. http://www.st.com/
20. TAOClean: Aura clean system - sonic toothbrush & cleaning station. http://www.taoclean.com/

Evaluation of Infants with Spinal Muscular Atrophy Type-I Using Convolutional Neural Networks

Bilge Soran[1](✉), Linda Lowes[2], and Katherine M. Steele[1]

[1] Mechanical Engineering Department, University of Washington, Seattle, USA
bilge@cs.washington.edu, kmsteele@uw.edu
[2] Clinical Therapies Department, Nationwide Children's Hospital, Columbus, USA
linda.lowes@nationwidechildrens.org

Abstract. Spinal Muscular Atrophy is the most common genetic cause of infant death. Due to its severity, there is a need for methods for automated estimation of disease progression. In this paper we propose a Convolutional-Neural-Network (CNN) model to estimate disease progression during infants' natural behavior. With the proposed methodology, we were able to predict each child's score on current behavior-based clinical exams with an average per-subject error of 6.96 out of 72 points ($<10\%$ difference), using 30-second videos in leave-one-subject-out-cross-validation setting. When simple statistics were used over 30-second video-segments to estimate a score for longer videos, we obtained an average error of 5.95 ($\sim 8\%$ error rate). By showing promising results on a small dataset (N = 70, 2-minute samples, which were handled as 1487, 30-second video segments), our methodology demonstrates that it is possible to benefit from CNNs on small datasets by proper design and data handling choices.

Keywords: Spinal muscular atrophy · Longitudinal anlaysis · Microsoft kinect · Convolutional neural networks · Regression

1 Introduction

Spinal Muscular Atrophy (SMA) is a neuromuscular disorder caused by a genetic defect in the SMN1 gene which affects the motor nerve cells in the spinal cord leading to progressive weakness. The incidence of SMA, which can be diagnosed with DNA tests, is approximately 14 out of every 100,000 live-born infants [10]. There is no cure for SMA and current treatments focus on supportive care, not an improvement in the disease.

There are four different types of SMA [35], which are classified genetically by the copy number of the SMN2 gene or clinically based on motor function capability and age of diagnosis [25]. SMA type-I is the most severe form and presents in infants younger than 6 months of age leading to severe muscle weakness, progressive respiratory insufficiency and typically death before the age of 2 years. Due to

© Springer International Publishing Switzerland 2016
G. Hua and H. Jégou (Eds.): ECCV 2016 Workshops, Part II, LNCS 9914, pp. 495–507, 2016.
DOI: 10.1007/978-3-319-48881-3_34

the severity and rapid progression of this disorder, there is a need for new tools to track its progression. In this paper, we propose a method to evaluate infant movements in order to estimate disease progression in infants with SMA type-I. It is well known that clinical trials for infants with SMA type-I pose unique challenges due to the profound weakness, respiratory insufficiency and vulnerability to complications related to participation in trials, such as travel [31]. Clinical trials could be advanced by an outcome measure that is relevant to families and the FDA, reliably quantifies small changes, and minimizes stress on fragile infants with SMA and their families [6].

Until recently, disease progression in SMA was quantified by time until death or the need for 16 h of ventilator support. The current standard clinical evaluation is done based on the Children's Hospital of Philadelphia Infant Test of Neuromuscular Disorders (CHOP INTEND) score, which was developed to evaluate motor function in infants with a variety of neuromuscular disorders. It evaluates a child's ability to move his/her extremities, head and trunk by rating performance over 16 items using a 4-point scale [10]. A trained evaluator elicits movement from the child through a series of items such as encouraging the child to roll onto their stomach by pulling on the arm or leg. Additional items include supporting the child in sitting or in prone with the neck flexed and observing if the infant will attempt to lift their head. Unfortunately, these activities can be extremely taxing on fragile infants with compromised respiratory systems. The CHOP INTEND has been shown to track the decline in motor function over time in infants with SMA and is related to other electro-physiological indicators [4,7,8]; however, this evaluation is subjective and requires extensive training to be performed reliably. An affordable, easy-to-use, and accurate system for evaluating infant movement, assessing risk, and tracking disease progression would be a welcome addition to enhance patient care.

In this paper, we are proposing method pipelines for the automatic evaluation of infants with SMA, the most common genetic cause of infant death, using depth camera technology. We used 2-minute-long videos of awake supine infants to demonstrate that motion of the arms and legs can be used to longitudinally track disease progression of infants with SMA with comparison to current clinical standard, the CHOP INTEND. The proposed pipelines could also be applied to analysis of other pediatric neuromuscular disorders, such as cerebral palsy. *Note that we are estimating CHOP INTEND extremity scores from videos of infants during natural behavior, however the groundtruth CHOP INTEND extremity scores are given by functional assessments.* This distinction increases the challenge in estimating disease progression and comparing novel methods to current clinical standards, which are limited by dependence on the subjective opinion of the assessor [4], and are fatiguing to the infant as they require the child to attempt activities and be placed in positions (head lifting, prone suspension) that can increase the work of breathing.

2   Related Work

Prechtl *et al.* described a type of spontaneous movements in infants 10–15 weeks of age, called fidgety or general movements [23], and characterized by small amplitude circular movements of the neck, trunk and limbs. General Movement Assessments (GMA) involves observing and rating these movements in infants [13], which is a reliable, non-invasive predictor of neurological problems. Compared to traditional methods GMA is a cost-effective technique for prediction and analysis of neurological impairments, including cerebral palsy and autism [2,22]. On individuals with impaired nervous systems, general movements lack complex patterns seen in typically-developing infants. GMA has been shown to predict neurological outcome at 2 years more precisely than standard neurological examination [5]. Based on this work, we expect movements of the limbs during early infancy to be important predictors and hypothesize that analyzing infants while they are lying awake on their back will enable us to quantify motor abilities.

Although promising, adoption of GMA in standard practice has been extremely slow. The methodology is qualitative and classifications are made based on subjective judgments. Costly professional training by the General Movements Trust is required to implement this assessment and enrollment is very limited with roughly 6 courses worldwide each year allowing around 50 people each. This is yet another indication that a low-cost alternative would be extremely useful. Although there exists previous work on analysis of other neurological disorders from videos of infants (e.g [24,30]), to the best of our knowledge there exists *no* research on automated evaluation of patients with SMA.

Depth cameras and depth estimation methods has been used for analysis and prediction of movement disorders caused by other neurological impairments. A Kinect based upper extremity motion analysis system was used to determine the spectrum of reachable workspace in facioscapulohumeral muscular dystrophy [14] and in byamyotrophic lateral sclerosis [21]. A Parkinson patient's movements was automatically analyzed by [27,28] showed a system that could reliably detect voice, postural and Parkinson's tremors. A vision system for physical rehabilitation at home was proposed by [3]. Illness stage of patients with Alzheimer's disease were determined in [16]. A system for cognitive assessment and rehabilitation of individuals with body scheme dysfunctions and left-right confusion was proposed by [12]. Disease progression in MS patients by analyzing selected movements performed by patients was measured by [17]. For a detailed review on the impact of Kinect for understanding neurological impairments please see [15].

For many years, traditional features have been widely used in all different types of vision problems. However, manually-designing those features required a lot of engineering effort and many times the designed features may not represent the problem domain properly especially for complex domains. Convolutional Neural Networks (CNNs) have the ability to learn the features (both low level and high level) directly from input data, which has been successfully used to address many computer vision problems, with state-of-the-art results (e.g., [18, 34]). Especially large problems that require intensive processing power to train models have benefited from GPU technology and their success (e.g., [26,32]) spread the use of CNNs.

Despite the successful applications of CNNs to many computer vision tasks, the application of CNNs to regression problems are limited compared to recognition/detection/classification problems. One of the problems that CNNs successfully employed for regression analysis is age estimation. For example, [20] designed the problem as ordinal regression, [33] trained a complete multi-scale-network that can estimate age from pixels. Additionally, [9,19] handled age estimation as a classification problem by discretizing the scores and handling each one as a separate class. However, when handled as a classification problem, different classes have implicitly assumed to be independent from each other and the closeness of two class labels has no meaning to the model, which is actually informative. Therefore, we approached the score estimation task as a regression problem.

3   Dataset

Fig. 1. Camera setting used for data collection with Kinect

In this research, we used a dataset of the Microsoft Kinect V2, 70 two-minute recordings of the natural movements of 15 infants with SMA type-I between the ages 0–790 days. During the recordings infants wore colored coflex tape on their hands and feet (which were later used as color markers for limb tracking), and were positioned supine on a neutral-colored sheet. The camera was positioned above the infant centered over the sheet, which can be seen in Fig. 1. To confirm the movement quality output derived by our analysis we compared our generated motor score to the CHOP INTEND score obtained on the same day. As the CHOP INTEND has items evaluating head control, trunk control, and extremity movement and our generated motor score only includes the extremities, we separated out only those CHOP items pertaining to extremity movement and call this the CHOP INTEND extremity score. This included 9 items that were scored for both the left and right side on a 0–4 scale [10], resulting in a maximum score of 72 points for the self-described "extremities" subset of the test, which was composed of items such as spontaneous arm movement, spontaneous leg movement, hand grip, hip strength, shoulder movement, reaching, kicking, leg movement and arm pulling.

4   Method

The main goal of this research is to make an assessment method for the progression of SMA type-I on infants using convolutional-neural-networks. We will describe a possible network architecture, together with the parameters used for training.

We propose a system that is capable of analyzing infant movements from videos recorded by a depth camera for disease progression assessment. A color tracker system is used to track each limb over time. For training, we use the current clinical standard, the CHOP INTEND scores for each limb assigned by trained physical therapists to evaluate neuromuscular function.

4.1   Data Preparation

For estimating a score, we used the tracking data of four limbs available for each recording. We employed a simple color tracking technique to track limbs' x, y, z positions over time. For this, markers were manually selected by clicking to the corresponding color locations in the beginning of each video and the center of the blobs with similar hue value in proximity to the clicked location was tracked throughout the video. The output of the tracking module was the x, y, z coordinates of each limb, namely left arm, left foot, right arm and right foot for each unit time $(1/30\,\mathrm{s})$. The x axis corresponds to a line that would run vertically from head to toe on the child, the y axis corresponds to movement across the body or side-to-side and the z axis corresponds to movement up off the surface toward the Kinect camera. We ignore frames when tracking of one of the limbs fails, such as when an infant's hand moves behind his/her head.

4.2   Regression Using Convolutional Neural Networks

Since we have recordings of infants over time and the corresponding CHOP INTEND extremity scores from the same day, we compare the predicted scores with the groundtruth. We evaluate the performance of the proposed system by calculating the average error in the predicted scores over-time in leave-one-infant-out-cross-validation, which involves using one subject's data as the test set and the remaining subjects' data as the training set. Our primary measure is the average error, calculated over the data of all infants when training and testing is repeated for each infant separately.

Since our purpose is to estimate a score per sample we used an Euclidean loss $(\frac{1}{2N} \sum_{n=1}^{N} \|\hat{y}_n - y_n\|_2^2)$ layer in the final layer. However, it is more difficult to optimize for Euclidean loss compared to Softmax, which is more stable. Euclidean loss is required to output exactly one correct value for each input while, for example, in Softmax the magnitude of the score is more important instead of the exact value. Also the effect of outliers are more important because of the squared-term [1]. For these reasons, the parameter selections were more critical in our case, compared to more stable loss functions.

The number of recordings in our dataset is very limited (N = 70) to train a robust convolutional neural network if tracking data for each recording is used as one sample. For this reason, we used a sliding window approach to sample the data used in both training and testing, which reduces the problem to score estimation using only K frames (instead of M frames of approximately $120\,s * 30$ fps = 3600). The sliding amount S effects the number of samples obtained from one recording as $((M - K)/S) + 1$. In our experiments, we used a window size of 900 frames ($\approx 30\,s$ of video in 30 fps) and a sliding amount of $S = 50$ frames. Therefore each sample used had 12×900 dimensions to be inputted to our network. Our dataset contains many samples, where the tracking of one or more limb is lost for a period of time (e.g. an infant might place his/her hand under his/her head) besides dropping frames. In order to overcome the inconsistencies between different trackings we ignored the potions of data when the tracking of all four limbs are not available, or the difference of timestamps between two frames is bigger than a preset threshold. Figure 2 represents the described sampling process.

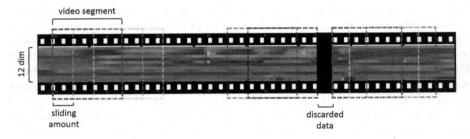

Fig. 2. The sampling process of tracking data. Our data has 12 dimensions per frame; each three consecutive component of which represent the $x - y - z$ coordinates of one particular limb: right hand, left hand, right foot and left foot.

Before sliding window sampling, we standardized each recording to zero-mean and one standard deviation for each tracking feature separately. Since the infants in our dataset are pose normalized before tracking, the positions of the limbs of infants are similar between infants. Therefore, we did not apply a standardization among different recordings. Considering the outliers might dominate the optimization when $L2$ loss is used, we tried normalizing the regression labels but that did not produce any better results on our dataset.

Our network consists of three convolutional layers, each followed by an activation layer and a pooling layer. Rectified Linear Units (ReLU) is used for the activation layers. We have two fully connected layers connecting the convolutional layers to the loss layer. Between these two fully connected layers, our network has another activation layer followed by a dropout layer to avoid overfitting [29]. Table 1 summarizes the network architecture we used.

The fully connected layers are prone to over-fitting more than other layers, because of the large number of parameters. Therefore we introduced an increased

Table 1. Convolutional Neural Network architecture.

Layer	Type	Top shape	Filter size	Stride	Padding
0	Input	$1 \times 1 \times 12 \times 900$	–	–	–
1	Convolutional	$1 \times 48 \times 4 \times 300$	3×3	3×3	0
2	ReLU	$1 \times 48 \times 4 \times 300$	–	–	–
3	Max-pooling	$1 \times 48 \times 4 \times 150$	1×3	1×2	0
4	Convolutional	$1 \times 128 \times 4 \times 150$	3×3	1×1	1
5	ReLU	$1 \times 128 \times 4 \times 150$	–	–	–
6	Max-pooling	$1 \times 128 \times 4 \times 75$	1×3	1×2	0
7	Convolutional	$1 \times 256 \times 4 \times 69$	1×7	1×1	0
8	ReLU	$1 \times 256 \times 4 \times 69$	–	–	–
9	Max-pooling	$1 \times 256 \times 4 \times 34$	1×3	1×2	0
10	Fully-connected	1×1024	–	–	–
11	ReLU	1×1024	–	–	–
12	Drop-out	1×1024	–	–	–
13	Fully-connected	1×1	–	–	–
14	L2 Loss	–	–	–	–

weight-decay while learning the fully connected layers. We initialized all convolutional and fully-connected layers randomly as suggested by [11] and used a
constant bias. In our final model, all of our pooling layers perform max-pooling
operation. We experimented with different batch sizes, and decided to use 400
samples for estimating stochastic gradients on our dataset. At each iteration
we shuffled the samples since our dataset is not large enough for compensating
sequential data access. We used a fixed learning-rate of 10^{-4} throughout the
iterations. To avoid local-minimum we used a momentum of 0.95 and to avoid
over-fitting we used $L2$ regularization with a factor of 0.9. We trained our model
for 1000 iterations (approximately 286 epochs).

5 Results

5.1 Score Estimation for Extremities Using 30 s Videos

Using CNNs we could estimate the CHOP INTEND extremity scores (0–72
points) with an average error of less than 7 points per sliding window of length
900 frames. That means we could estimate the severity of SMA type-I condition on an infant with an average of less than 10 % error rate using 30-seconds
video recorded while the infant is behaving naturally. Note that, the ground-
truth CHOP INTEND scores are assigned through a medical evaluation using
distractors and response measures to these distractors. We postulate an automated solution to evaluation of severity of SMA type-I on infants while the infant

is acting naturally, which otherwise requires intensive expertise and interaction with fragile infants.

We shuffle the data at every iteration and use a batch size of 400 samples. Considering average training set size is about 1388 samples, (15 folds, leave-one-subject-out cross validation, dataset size is 1487, 30-second video-segments) we reach an epoch in approximately 3.5 iterations. Since we don't have a validation set for each fold, we observed the error on a random subset of training set.

Table 2 shows the results of score estimation experiments and standard baselines. As standard baselines we use linear regression and L2 regularized form of it: LASSO. As infants with SMA show decreased motor ability [10], we expect the correlation of different limb movements to be an indicator of severity of the disease. Therefore, for the other regression models, we used average correlation between coordinates of limb positions in each x, y, and z domain separately as our feature representation. For the LASSO regression, we used a geometric sequence of regularization coefficients, and used the largest coefficient that gives the non-null model.

Table 2. Average errors for 30-second tracking data, obtained from CNN, Linear Regression and LASSO

Method	Average error per subject (Fold)	Overall average error
Proposed CNN model	6.9645	8.1287
Linear regression	17.6026	15.7261
LASSO	18.3830	14.8281

Note that, we do not incorporate the time dimension during the score estimation. Therefore, the score of each 30-second video segment (sliding window) is estimated individually, in leave-one-subject-out-cross-validation setting, which during training requires not including any video of the test subject. Average error and average per subject (fold) error differs as the number of 30-second samples in each fold are not equal. Figure 3 shows the error in score estimation per 30-second video-segment using Convolutional Neural Networks.

5.2   Score Estimation for the Whole Video

Although our intention was to predict the CHOP INTEND extremity scores from limb-tracking data of a short video (which is 30 s in our case), we also estimated a final score per 2-minute recoding using different simple statistics. Note that, in our dataset every video recording has an assigned score, but during regression we sample each video to video-segments using the sliding-window approach and therefore, every video-segment coming from the same video recording share the same ground-truth label.

In order to estimate a score per video recording, first we took the average of estimated scores of all 30-second video-segments of the corresponding video.

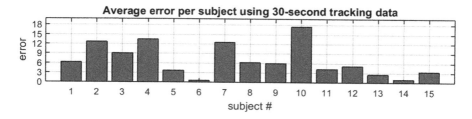

Fig. 3. Error in CHOP INTEND extremity score estimation for each 30-second video-segment sampled from 2-minute videos, which recorded over multiple visits, for each infant.

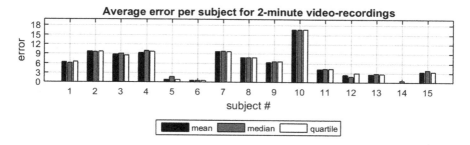

Fig. 4. Average errors per subject using mean, median and quartile analysis over video-segments of the corresponding 2-minute videos.

As a second method, we assigned the final score per video as the median of all estimated scores of related video-segments. Finally, we used quartile analysis for estimating a score per recording. For this, first we calculated the outliers from score estimations of 30-second video-segments per corresponding 2-minute video. We used interpolation to find upper and lower quartiles. Then, for calculating a score per 2-minute video out of the estimated scores of related video-segments, we used the average of the predictions between lower and upper fence defined as $Q1 - 1.5*IQR$ and $Q3 + 1.5*IQR$, respectively, where $Q1$ and $Q3$ represent the lower and upper quartiles and IQR represents the inter-quartile range defined as the difference between upper and lower quartiles.

Table 3. Average errors for 2 min videos, obtained from mean, median and quartile analysis.

Method	Average of average error per subject	Overall average error
Mean	7.9648	5.9495
Median	8.0499	6.1175
Quartile analysis	8.0066	6.0291

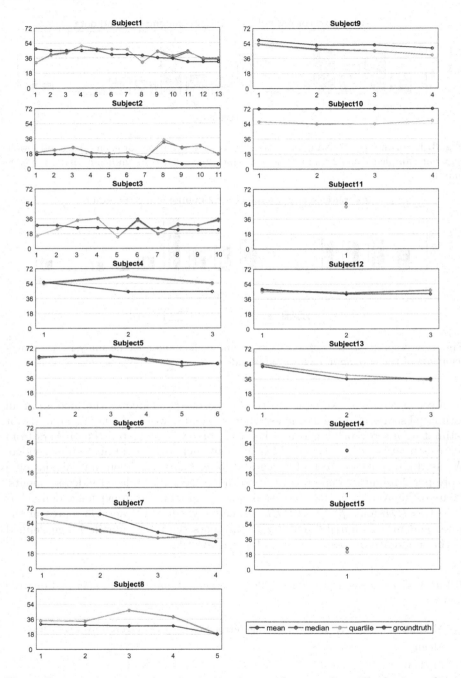

Fig. 5. Estimated regression scores per 2-minute video-recording. The horizontal axis shows 2-minute video-recording number for each infant, and the vertical axis shows the scores obtained using mean, median and quartile analysis over 30-second video segments of the corresponding 2-minute video.

Figure 4 shows the average error in the estimation of CHOP INTEND extremity scores per subject using mean, median and quartile analysis over video-segments of the corresponding 2-minute videos of each subject. The average errors of using these statistics for the whole 2-minute video dataset is given in Table 3. The lowest overall average error was 5.94 points, obtained by assigning a score for each 2-minute video as the mean of its video-segments' scores. The average of average error per subject differs from overall average error since the number of samples for each subject are not equal.

Figure 5 shows CHOP INTEND extremity score estimation for each 2-minute video of all subjects, obtained by using mean, median and quartile analysis over the 30-second video segments of the corresponding 2-minute video together with the related groundtruth scores.

6   Conclusions and Future Work

In this paper we proposed a model for the problem of estimating the progression of SMA on naturally behaving infants. This is a very important problem due to the severity and rapid progression of the disease. CHOP INTEND is the current gold standard for evaluating SMA, which requires a lot of time for assessment, extensive clinician training, and requires interaction with the fragile infant using distractors. Our model relies on the tracking data, and does not make any domain related assumptions, therefore can be applied to progression estimation of other neuromuscular disorders.

Our experiments show that it is possible to evaluate the severity of SMA during infants' natural behavior using automated analysis of limb tracking data obtained from very short videos recorded by Kinect V2. The average per-subject error we got is < 7 out of 72 points metric in leave-one-subject-out cross-validation setting for 30-second videos. When the scores estimated from 30-second video-segments of a longer video is averaged to produce a final score, we got an average error of 5.95 points.

Future work includes applying ordinal-regression that can benefit from the order of the recordings and their corresponding scores. Our results suggest that it is possible to benefit from CNNs even when the dataset size is small with the proper design and parameter selection. However, the data collection for the dataset used in this paper is still in progress. With the addition of more data, deeper and wider networks can be trained. Finally in order to estimate a score for a longer video from its segments we used simple statistical methods like mean, median, quartile analysis over the estimated scores of the shorter video-segments. As a next step, with the help of a second layer model, the estimated scores of video-segments can be combined more intelligently to produce a score for the corresponding longer video.

References

1. http://cs231n.github.io/neural-networks 2. Accessed 25 June 2016
2. Adde, L., et al.: General movement assessment: predicting cerebral palsy in clinical practise. Early Hum. Dev. **83**(1), 13–18 (2007)
3. Benettazzo, F., Iarlori, S., Ferracuti, F., Giantomassi, A., Ortenzi, D., Freddi, A., Monteriù, A., Innocenzi, S., Capecci, M., Ceravolo, M.G., Longhi, S.: Low cost RGB-D vision based system to support motor disabilities rehabilitation at home. In: Andó, B., Siciliano, P., Marletta, V., Monteriú, A. (eds.) Ambient Assisted Living. Biosystems & Biorobotics, pp. 449–461. Springer, Cham (2015)
4. Cano, S., et al.: Rasch analysis of clinical outcome measures in spinal muscular atrophy. Muscle Nerve **49**(3), 422–430 (2014)
5. Cioni, G., et al.: Which better predicts later outcome in fullterm infants: quality of general movements or neurological examination? Early Hum. Dev. **50**(1), 71–85 (1997)
6. Crawford, T.: Concerns about the design of clinical trials for spinal muscular atrophy. Neuromuscul. Disord. **14**(8), 456–460 (2004)
7. Finkel, R.: Electrophysiological and motor function scale association in a presymptomatic infant with spinal muscular atrophy type I. Neuromuscul. Disord. **23**(2), 112–115 (2013)
8. Finkel, R., et al.: Observational study of spinal muscular atrophy type I and implications for clinical trials. Neurology **83**(9), 810–817 (2014)
9. Geng, X., et al.: Automatic age estimation based on facial aging patterns. PAMI **29**(12), 2234–2240 (2007)
10. Glanzman, A., et al.: The Children's hospital of philadelphia infant test of neuromuscular disorders (CHOP INTEND): test development and reliability. Neuromuscul. Disord. **20**(3), 155–161 (2010)
11. Glorot, X., Bengio, Y.: Understanding the difficulty of training deep feedforward neural networks. In: AISTATS (2010)
12. González-Ortega, D., et al.: A kinect-based system for cognitive rehabilitation exercises monitoring. Comput. Methods Programs Biomed. **113**(2), 620–631 (2014)
13. Hadders-Algra, M.: Evaluation of motor function in young infants by means of the assessment of general movements: a review. Ped. Phys. Ther. **13**(1), 27–36 (2001)
14. Han, J., et al.: Reachable workspace in facioscapulohumeral muscular dystrophy (FSHD) by kinect. Muscle Nerve **51**(2), 168–175 (2015)
15. Hondori, H., et al.: A review on technical and clinical impact of microsoft kinect on physical therapy and rehabilitation. J. Med. Eng. (2014)
16. Iarlori, S., et al.: RGBD camera monitoring system for alzheimers disease assessment using recurrent neural networks with parametric bias action recognition. In: ICCHP (2014)
17. Kontschieder, P., et al.: Quantifying progression of multiple sclerosis via classification of depth videos. In: Golland, P., Hata, N., Barillot, C., Hornegger, J., Howe, R. (eds.) MICCAI 2014, Part II. LNCS, vol. 8674, pp. 429–437. Springer, Heidelberg (2014)
18. Krizhevsky, A., Sutskever, I., Hinton, G.E.: Imagenet classification with deep convolutional neural networks. In: NIPS (2012)
19. Mu, G., et al.: Human age estimation using bio-inspired features. In: CVPR (2009)
20. Niu, Z., et al.: Ordinal regression with multiple output CNN for age estimation. In: CVPR (2016)

21. Oskarsson, B., et al.: Upper extremity 3-dimensional reachable workspace assessment in amyotrophic lateral sclerosis by kinect sensor. Muscle Nerve **53**(2), 234–241 (2016)
22. Phagava, H., et al.: General movements in infants with autism spectrum disorders. In: Georgian Medical News (2008)
23. Prechtl, H., Hopkins, B.: Developmental transformations of spontaneous movements in early infancy. Early Hum. Dev. **14**(3), 233–238 (1986)
24. Rahmati, H., et al.: Frequency-based features for early cerebral palsy prediction. In: EMBC (2015)
25. Russman, B.S.: Spinal muscular atrophy: clinical classification and disease heterogeneity. J. Child Neurol. **22**(8), 946–951 (2007)
26. Simonyan, K., Zisserman, A.: Very deep convolutional networks for large-scale image recognition. CoRR (2014)
27. Sooklal, S., et al.: Using the kinect for detecting tremors: challenges and opportunities. In: BHI (2014)
28. Spasojević, S., et al.: A vision-based system for movement analysis in medical applications: the example of parkinson disease. In: Computer Vision Systems (2015)
29. Srivastava, N., et al.: Dropout: a simple way to prevent neural networks from overfitting. J. Mach. Learn. Res. **15**(1), 1929–1958 (2014)
30. Stahl, A., et al.: An optical flow-based method to predict infantile cerebral palsy. Neural Syst. Rehabil. Eng. **20**(4), 605–614 (2012)
31. Swoboda, K.J., et al.: Perspectives on clinical trials in spinal muscular atrophy. J. Child Neurol. **22**(8), 957–966 (2007)
32. Szegedy, C., et al.: Going deeper with convolutions. In: CVPR (2015)
33. Yi, D., Lei, Z., Li, S.Z.: Age estimation by multi-scale convolutional network. In: Cremers, D., Reid, I., Saito, H., Yang, M.-H. (eds.) ACCV 2014. LNCS, vol. 9005, pp. 144–158. Springer, Heidelberg (2015)
34. Zeiler, M.D., Fergus, R.: Visualizing and understanding convolutional networks. In: Fleet, D., Pajdla, T., Schiele, B., Tuytelaars, T. (eds.) ECCV 2014, Part I. LNCS, vol. 8689, pp. 818–833. Springer, Heidelberg (2014)
35. Zerres, K., Rudnik-Schoneborn, S.: Natural history in proximal spinal muscular atrophy: clinical analysis of 445 patients and suggestions for a modification of existing classifications. Arch. Neurol. **52**(5), 518–523 (1995)

W16 - 3D Face Alignment in the Wild and Challenge

The First 3D Face Alignment in the Wild (3DFAW) Challenge

László A. Jeni[1(✉)], Sergey Tulyakov[2], Lijun Yin[3], Nicu Sebe[2],
and Jeffrey F. Cohn[1,4]

[1] Robotics Institute, Carnegie Mellon University, Pittsburgh, PA, USA
laszlojeni@cmu.edu
[2] DISI, University of Trento, Trento, Italy
[3] Department of Computer Science, State University of New York at Binghamton,
Binghamton, USA
[4] Department of Psychology, The University of Pittsburgh, Pittsburgh, PA, USA

Abstract. 2D alignment of face images works well provided images are
frontal or nearly so and pitch and yaw remain modest. In spontaneous
facial behavior, these constraints often are violated by moderate to large
head rotation. 3D alignment from 2D video has been proposed as a
solution. A number of approaches have been explored, but comparisons
among them have been hampered by the lack of common test data. To
enable comparisons among alternative methods, The 3D Face Alignment
in the Wild (3DFAW) Challenge, presented for the first time, created an
annotated corpus of over 23,000 multi-view images from four sources
together with 3D annotation, made training and validation sets available to investigators, and invited them to test their algorithms on an
independent test-set. Eight teams accepted the challenge and submitted
test results. We report results for four that provided necessary technical
descriptions of their methods. The leading approach achieved prediction
consistency error of 3.48 %. Corresponding result for the lowest ranked
approach was 5.9 %. The results suggest that 3D alignment from 2D
video is feasible on a wide range of face orientations. Differences among
methods are considered and suggest directions for further research.

Keywords: 3D alignment from 2D video · Head rotation · Prediction
consistency error · Faces in-the-wild

1 Introduction

Face alignment – the problem of automatically locating detailed facial landmarks
across different subjects, illuminations, and viewpoints – is critical to face analysis applications, such as identification, facial expression analysis, robot-human
interaction, affective computing, and multimedia.

Previous methods can be divided into two broad categories: 2D approaches
and 3D approaches. 2D approaches treat the face as a 2D object. This assumption holds as long as the face is frontal and planar. As face orientation varies

© Springer International Publishing Switzerland 2016
G. Hua and H. Jégou (Eds.): ECCV 2016 Workshops, Part II, LNCS 9914, pp. 511–520, 2016.
DOI: 10.1007/978-3-319-48881-3_35

from frontal, 2D annotated points lose correspondence. Pose variation results in self-occlusion that confounds landmark annotation. 2D approaches include Active Appearance Models [5,16], Constrained Local Models [6,21] and shape-regression-based methods [4,8,18,24]). These approaches train a set of 2D models, each of which is intended to cope with shape or appearance variation within a small range of viewpoints.

3D approaches have strong advantages over 2D with respect to representational power and robustness to illumination and pose. 3D approaches [2,7,12,27] accommodate a wide range of views. Depending on the 3D model, they easily can accommodate a full range of head rotation. Disadvantages are the need for 3D images and controlled illumination, as well as the need for special sensors or synchronized cameras in data acquisition.

Because these requirement often are difficult to meet, 3D alignment from 2D video or images has been proposed as a potential solution. A number of research groups have made advances in 3D alignment from 2D video [15,17,19, 20,22]. How these various methods compare is relatively unknown. No commonly accepted evaluation protocol exists with which to compare them.

To enable comparisons among alternative methods of 3D alignment from 2D video, we created an annotated corpus of multi-view face images, partitioned training and hold-out test sets, and invited investigators to enter competition. The corpus includes images obtained under a range of conditions from highly controlled to in-the-wild. The resulting challenge provides a benchmark with which to evaluate 3D face alignment methods and enable researchers to identify new goals, challenges, and targets. This paper describes the 3D Face Alignment in the Wild Challenge and presents an overview of the results. The Challenge was held in conjunction with the 14th European Conference on Computer Vision.

2   Dataset

Four databases were used for the Challenge. They were the BU-4DFE [25], BP4D-Spontaneous [26], MultiPIE [11], and time-sliced videos from the internet. All four databases were annotated in a consistent way using a model-based structure-from-motion technique [14]. To increase variability in head rotation, we synthesized images across a range of pitch and yaw orientations as explained below.

2.1   BU-4DFE and BP-4D Spontaneous

BU-4DFE consists of approximately 60,600 3D frame models from 101 subjects (56 % female, 44 % male). Subjects ranged in age from 18 to 70 years and were ethnically and racially diverse (European-American, African-American, East-Asian, Middle-Eastern, Asian, Indian, and Hispanic Latino). Subjects were imaged individually using a Di3D (Dimensional Imaging[1]) dynamic face capturing system while posing six prototypic emotion expressions (anger, disgust,

---

[1] http://www.di3d.com.

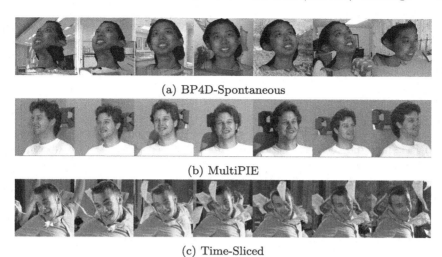

(a) BP4D-Spontaneous

(b) MultiPIE

(c) Time-Sliced

Fig. 1. Selected examples from the benchmark datasets. Selected views from the BP4D-Spontaneous (a), MultiPIE (b), and Time-Sliced (c) dataset. The contours of key facial parts are highlighted in blue for display purpose. (Color figure online)

happiness, fear, sadness, and surprise). The Di3D system consisted of two stereo cameras and a texture video camera arranged vertically. Both 3D model and 2D texture videos were obtained for each prototypic expression and subject. Given the arrangement of the stereo cameras, frontal looking faces have the most complete 3D information and smallest amount of texture distortion.

BP-4D-Spontaneous dataset [26] consists of over 300,000 frame models from 41 subjects (56 % female, 48.7 % European-American, average age 20.2 years) of similarly diverse backgrounds to BU-4DFE. Subjects were imaged using the same Di3D system while responding to a varied series of 8 emotion inductions; these were intended to elicite spontaneous facial expressions of amusement, surprise, fear, anxiety, embarrassment, pain, anger, and disgust. The 3D models range in resolution between 30,000 and 50,000 vertices. For each sequence, manual FACS coding [9] by highly experienced and reliable certified coders was obtained.

In BP-4DFE, 1365 uniformly distributed frames were sampled. In BP4D-Spontaneous, 930 frames were sampled based on FACS (Facial Action Coding System [9]) annotation to include a wide range of expressions.

The selected 3D meshes were manually annotated with 66 landmarks, referred to as facial fiducial points. The annotations were independently cross-checked by another annotator. Since the annotation was 3D, we can identify the self-occluded landmarks from every pose.

For each of the final 2295 annotated meshes, we synthesized 7 different views using a weak perspective camera model. These views span the range of $[-45,45]$ degrees of yaw rotations in 15 degrees increments. The pitch rotation was randomly selected for each view from the range of $[-30, 30]$ degrees. Figure 1 shows selected examples. In total 16,065 frames were synthesized. For each view we calculated the corresponding rotated 3D landmarks and their 2D projections with self-occlusion information. Since the 3D meshes lacked backgrounds, we added randomly selected non-face backgrounds from the SUN2012 dataset [23] in the final 2D images.

2.2 MultiPIE

Multi-PIE face database [11] contains images from 337 subjects acquired in a wide range of pose, illumination, and expression conditions. Images were captured in rapid order in a multi-camera, multi-flash recording. For the current database, we sampled 7000 frames from 336 subjects. For each frame, the visible portion of the face was annotated with 66 2D landmarks. Self-occluded landmarks were marked and excluded from the annotation.

2.3 Time-Sliced Videos

The above datasets were recorded in a laboratory under controlled conditions. To include uncontrolled (in-the-wild) images in the challenge, we collected time-sliced videos from the internet. In these videos subjects were surrounded by an array of still cameras. During the recording, the subjects displayed various expressions while the cameras fired simultaneously. Single frames from each camera were arranged consecutively to produce an orbiting viewpoint of the subject frozen in time.

We sampled 541 frames that correspond to several viewpoints from different subjects and expressions. Due to the unconstrained setting, the number of viewpoints per subjects varied between 3 and 7 views. For each frame, the visible portion of the face was annotated with 66 2D landmarks. Self-occluded landmarks were marked and excluded from the annotation.

2.4 Consistent 3D Landmark Annotation

Providing consistent 3D landmark annotation across viewpoints and across datasets was paramount for the challenge. In the case of BU4D and BP4D-Spontaneous data, we had 3D landmark annotation that is consistent across synthesized views of the same face. To provide the same consistency for the other two datasets, we employed a two-step procedure. First we built a deformable 3D face model from the annotated 3D meshes of BU4D and BP4D-Spontaneous. Second, we used a model-based structure-from-motion technique on the multi-view images [14].

Linear Face Models. A shape model is defined by a 3D mesh and, in particular, by the 3D vertex locations of the mesh, called landmark points. Consider the 3D shape as the coordinates of 3D vertices that make up the mesh:

$$\mathbf{x} = [x_1; y_1; z_1; \ldots; x_M; y_M; z_M], \tag{1}$$

or, $\mathbf{x} = [\mathbf{x}_1; \ldots; \mathbf{x}_M]$, where $\mathbf{x}_i = [x_i; y_i; z_i]$.

The 3D point distribution model (PDM) describes non-rigid shape variations linearly and composes it with a global rigid transformation, placing the shape in the image frame:

$$\mathbf{x}_i = \mathbf{x}_i(\mathbf{p}, \mathbf{q}) = s\mathbf{R}(\bar{\mathbf{x}}_i + \boldsymbol{\Phi}_i \mathbf{q}) + \mathbf{t} \quad (i = 1, \ldots, M), \tag{2}$$

where $\mathbf{x}_i(\mathbf{p}, \mathbf{q})$ denotes the 3D location of the ith landmark and $\mathbf{p} = \{s, \alpha, \beta, \gamma, \mathbf{t}\}$ denotes the rigid parameters of the model, which consist of a global scaling s, angles of rotation in three dimensions ($\mathbf{R} = \mathbf{R}_1(\alpha)\mathbf{R}_2(\beta)\mathbf{R}_3(\gamma)$), a translation $\mathbf{t}$. The non-rigid transformation is denoted with $\mathbf{q}$. Here $\bar{\mathbf{x}}_i$ denotes the mean location of the ith landmark (i.e. $\bar{\mathbf{x}}_i = [\bar{x}_i; \bar{y}_i; \bar{z}_i]$ and $\bar{\mathbf{x}} = [\bar{\mathbf{x}}_1; \ldots; \bar{\mathbf{x}}_M]$). The d pieces of $3M$ dimensional basis vectors are denoted with $\boldsymbol{\Phi} = [\boldsymbol{\Phi}_1; \ldots; \boldsymbol{\Phi}_M] \in \mathbb{R}^{3M \times d}$. Vector $\mathbf{q}$ represents the 3D distortion of the face in the $3M \times d$ dimensional linear subspace.

To build this model we used the 3D annotation from the selected BU-4DFE [25] and BP4D-Spontaneous [26] frames.

3D Model Fitting. To reconstruct the 3D shape from the annotated 2D shapes ($\mathbf{z}$) we need to minimize the reconstruction error using Eq. (2):

$$\arg\min_{\mathbf{p}, \mathbf{q}} \sum_{i=1}^{M} \|\mathbf{P}\mathbf{x}_i(\mathbf{p}, \mathbf{q}) - \mathbf{z}_i\|_2^2 \tag{3}$$

Here $\mathbf{P}$ denotes the projection matrix to 2D, and $\mathbf{z}$ is the target 2D shape. An iterative method can be used to register 3D model on the 2D landmarks [12]. The algorithm iteratively refines the 3D shape and 3D pose until convergence, and estimates the rigid ($\mathbf{p} = \{s, \alpha, \beta, \gamma, \mathbf{t}\}$) and non-rigid transformations ($\mathbf{q}$).

Applying Eq. (3) on a single image frame from a monocular camera has a drawback of simply "hallucinating" a 3D representation from 2D. From a single viewpoint there are multiple solutions that satisfy Eq. (3). To avoid the problem of single frame 2D-3D hallucination we apply the method simultaneously across multiple image-frames of the same subject. Furthermore, we have partial landmark annotation in the MultiPIE and TimeSliced data due to self-occlusion. We can incorporate the visibility information of the landmarks in Eq. (3), by constraining the process to the visible landmarks.

Let $\mathbf{z}^{(1)}, \ldots, \mathbf{z}^{(C)}$ denote the C number of 2D measurements from the different viewpoints of the same subject. The exact camera locations and camera calibration matrices are unknown. In this case all C measurements represent the same 3D face, but from a different point of view. We can extend Eq. (3) to this scenario by constraining the reconstruction to all the measurements:

$$\arg\min_{\mathbf{p}^{(1)}, \ldots, \mathbf{p}^{(C)}, \mathbf{q}} \sum_{k=1}^{C} \sum_{i \in \boldsymbol{\xi}^{(k)}} \left\|\mathbf{P}\mathbf{x}_i(\mathbf{p}^{(k)}, \mathbf{q}) - \mathbf{z}_i^{(k)}\right\|_2^2 \tag{4}$$

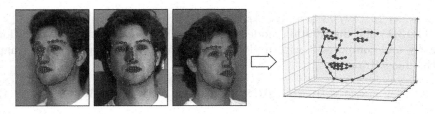

Fig. 2. The 3D shapes from the different views from the same subject and expression are consistent, they can be superimposed on each other in a canonical space.

where superscripts (k) denote the kth measurement, with a visibility set of $\boldsymbol{\xi}^{(k)}$. Minimizing Eq. (4) can be done by iteratively refining the 3D shape and 3D pose until convergence. For more details see [13,14] (Fig. 2).

3   Evaluation Results

3.1   Data Distribution

Data were sorted into three subsets (training, validation, and test sets) and distributed in two phases using the CodaLab platform[2]. In Phase-I, participants were granted access to the complete training set of images, ground truth 3D landmarks, and face bounding boxes and the validation set images and their bounding boxes. Participants became acquainted with the data and could train and perform initial evaluations of their algorithms. In Phase-II, they were granted access to the ground truth landmarks of the validation set and images and bounding boxes from the final test set. See Table 1 for more details.

3.2   Performance Measures

For comparative evaluation in the Challenge, we used the widely accepted evaluation matrices Ground Truth Error (GTE) and Cross View Ground Truth Consistency Error (CVGTCE). GTE is the average point-to-point Euclidean error

Table 1. Distribution of the different sets.

	Training	Validation	Test	Total
BP-4DFE	5677	1960	1918	9555
BP-4D-Spontaneous	3794	1365	1351	6510
MultiPIE	4200	1400	1400	7000
TimeSliced	298		243	541

---

[2] https://competitions.codalab.org/.

normalized by the outer corners of the eyes (inter-ocular). It is computed as:

$$GTE(\mathbf{x}^{pre}, \mathbf{x}^{gt}) = \frac{1}{M} \sum_{k=1}^{M} \frac{\|\mathbf{x}_k - \mathbf{y}_k\|_2}{d_i} \tag{5}$$

where M is the number of points, $\mathbf{x}^{gt}$ is the ground truth 3D shape, $\mathbf{x}^{pre}$ is the predicted shape and d_i is the inter-ocular distance for the i-th image.

CVGTCE evaluates cross-view consistency of the predicted landmarks from the 3D model. It is computed as:

$$CVGTCE(\mathbf{x}^{pre}, \mathbf{x}^{gt}, \mathbf{p}) = \frac{1}{M} \sum_{k=1}^{M} \frac{\|(s\mathbf{R}\mathbf{x}_k^{pre} + \mathbf{t}) - \mathbf{x}_k^{gt}\|_2}{d_i} \tag{6}$$

where the rigid transformation parameters $\mathbf{p} = \{s, \mathbf{R}, \mathbf{t}\}$ can be obtained in a similar fashion as in Eq. (3).

3.3   Participation

Eight teams submitted results. Of these, four completed the challenge by submitting a technical description of their methods. In the following we briefly describe their methods. More detail is provided in the respective papers. The final scores for all methods are available on the competition website[3].

Zavan et al. [1] proposed a method that requires only the nose region for assessing the orientation of the face and the position of the landmarks. First, a Faster R-CNN was trained on the images to detect the nose. Second, a CNN variant was trained to categorize the face into several discretized head-pose categories. In the final step, the system imposes the average face landmarks onto the image using the previously estimated transformation parameters.

Zhao et al. [28] used a deep convolutional network based solution that maps the 2D image of a face to its 3D shape. They defined two criteria for the optimization: (i) learn facial landmark locations in 2D (ii) and then estimate the depth of the landmarks. Furthermore, a data augmentation approach was used to aid the learning. The latter involved applying 2D affine transformations to the training set and generating random occluding boxes to improve robustness to partial occlusion.

Gou et al. [10] utilized a regression-based 3D face alignment method that first estimates the location of a set of landmarks and then recovers 3D face shape by fitting a 3D morphable model. An alternative optimization method was employed for the 3D morphable model fitting to recover the depth information. The method incorporates shape and local appearance information in a cascade regression framework to capture the correspondence between pairs of points for 3D face alignment.

Bulat and Tzimiropoulos [3] proposed a two-stage alignment method. At the first stage, the method calculates heat-maps of 2D landmarks using convolutional

---

[3] https://competitions.codalab.org/competitions/10261.

part heat-map regression. In the second stage, these heat-maps along with the original RGB image were used as an input to a very deep residual network to regress the depth information.

3.4 Results

Table 2 shows the Prediction Consistency Errors (CVGTCE) and Standard Errors (GTE) of the different methods on the final test set. Figure 3 shows the cumulative error distribution curves (CED) of the different methods.

Table 2. Prediction Consistency Error (CVGTCE) and Standard Error (GTE) of the different methods on the Test set.

Rank	Team	CVGTCE %	GTE %
1	Bulat and Tzimiropoulos [3]	3.4767	4.5623
2	Zhao et al. [28]	3.9700	5.8835
3	Gou et al. [10]	4.9488	6.2071
4	Zavan et al. [1]	5.9093	10.8001

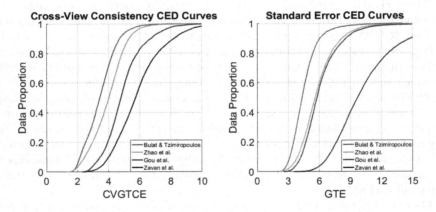

Fig. 3. Cumulative error distribution curves (CED) of the different methods for Cross-View Consistency (left) and Standard Error (right).

4 Conclusion

This paper describes the First 3D Face Alignment in the Wild (3DFAW) Challenge held in conjunction with the 14th European Conference on Computer

Vision 2016, Amsterdam. The main challenge of the competition was to estimate a set of 3D facial landmarks from still images. The corpus includes images
obtained under a range of conditions from highly controlled to in-the-wild. All
image sources have been annotated in a consistent way, the depth information has been recovered using a model-based Structure from Motion technique.
The resulting challenge provides a benchmark with which to evaluate 3D face
alignment methods and enable researchers to identify new goals, challenges, and
targets.

Acknowledgements. This work was supported in part by US National Institutes of
Health grant MH096951 to the University of Pittsburgh and by US National Science
Foundation grants CNS-1205664 and CNS-1205195 to the University of Pittsburgh and
the University of Binghamton. Neither agency was involved in the planning or writing
of the work.

References

1. de B. Zavan, F.H., Nascimento, A.C.P., e Silva, L.P., Bellon, O.R.P., Silva, L.:
   3d face alignment in the wild: A landmark-free, nose-based approach. In: 2016
   European Conference on Computer Vision Workshops (ECCVW) (2016)
2. Blanz, V., Vetter, T.: A morphable model for the synthesis of 3d faces. In: Proceedings of the 26th Annual Conference on Computer Graphics and Interactive
   Techniques, pp. 187–194. SIGGRAPH (1999). http://dx.doi.org/10.1145/311535.
   311556
3. Bulat, A., Tzimiropoulos, G.: Two-stage convolutional part heatmap regression for
   the 1st 3d face alignment in the wild (3DFAW) challenge. In: European Conference
   on Computer Vision Workshops (ECCVW) (2016)
4. Cao, X., Wei, Y., Wen, F., Sun, J.: Face alignment by explicit shape regression.
   In: IEEE Conference on Computer Vision and Pattern Recognition (CVPR), pp.
   2887–2894, June 2012
5. Cootes, T., Edwards, G., Taylor, C.: Active appearance models. IEEE Trans. Pattern Anal. Mach. Intell. **23**(6), 681–685 (2001)
6. Cristinacce, D., Cootes, T.: Automatic feature localisation with constrained
   local models. Pattern Recogn. **41**(10), 3054–3067 (2008). http://dx.doi.org/10.
   1016/j.patcog.2008.01.024
7. Dimitrijevic, M., Ilic, S., Fua, P.: Accurate face models from uncalibrated and ill-lit
   video sequences. In: IEEE Conference on Computer Vision and Pattern Recognition (CVPR). vol. 2, pp. II-1034-II-1041, June 2004
8. Dollar, P., Welinder, P., Perona, P.: Cascaded pose regression. In: IEEE Conference
   on Computer Vision and Pattern Recognition (CVPR), pp. 1078–1085, June 2010
9. Ekman, P., Friesen, W., Hager, J.: Facial Action Coding System (FACS): Manual.
   A Human Face, Salt Lake City (2002)
10. Gou, C., Wu, Y., Wang, F.Y., Ji, Q.: Shape augmented regression for 3d face align-
    ment. In: 2016 European Conference on Computer Vision Workshops (ECCVW)
    (2016)
11. Gross, R., Matthews, I., Cohn, J., Kanade, T., Baker, S.: Multi-pie. Image Vis.
    Comput. **28**(5), 807–813 (2010)
12. Gu, L., Kanade, T.: 3d alignment of face in a single image. IEEE Comput. Soc.
    Conf. Comput. Vis. Pattern Recogn. (CVPR) **1**, 1305–1312 (2006)

13. Jeni, L.A., Cohn, J.F., Kanade, T.: Dense 3d face alignment from 2d videos in real-time. In: 2015 11th IEEE International Conference and Workshops on Automatic Face and Gesture Recognition (FG) (2015). http://zface.org
14. Jeni, L.A., Cohn, J.F., Kanade, T.: Dense 3d face alignment from 2d video for real-time use. Image Vis. Comput. **28**(5), 807–813 (2016)
15. Jourabloo, A., Liu, X.: Large-pose face alignment via cnn-based dense 3d model fitting. In: CVPR (2016)
16. Matthews, I., Baker, S.: Active appearance models revisited. Int. J. Comput. Vis. **60**(2), 135–164 (2004)
17. Piotraschke, M., Blanz, V.: Automated 3d face reconstruction from multiple images using quality measures. In: Proceedings of the IEEE Conference on Computer Vision and Pattern Recognition, pp. 3418–3427 (2016)
18. Ren, S., Cao, X., Wei, Y., Sun, J.: Face alignment at 3000 fps via regressing local binary features. In: IEEE Conference on Computer Vision and Pattern Recognition (CVPR), pp. 1685–1692, June (2014)
19. Roth, J., Tong, Y., Liu, X.: Adaptive 3d face reconstruction from unconstrained photo collections. In: CVPR (2016)
20. Sánchez-Escobedo, D., Castelán, M., Smith, W.A.: Statistical 3d face shape estimation from occluding contours. Comput. Vis. Image Underst. **142**, 111–124 (2016)
21. Saragih, J.M., Lucey, S., Cohn, J.F.: Deformable model fitting by regularized landmark mean-shift. Int. J. Comput. Vis. **91**(2), 200–215 (2011). http://dx.doi.org/10.1007/s11263-010-0380-4
22. Tulyakov, S., Sebe, N.: Regressing a 3d face shape from a single image. In: IEEE International Conference on Computer Vision (ICCV), pp. 3748–3755. IEEE (2015)
23. Xiao, J., Hays, J., Ehinger, K.A., Oliva, A., Torralba, A.: Sun database: Large-scale scene recognition from abbey to zoo. In: 2010 IEEE Conference on Computer Vision and Pattern Recognition (CVPR), pp. 3485–3492. IEEE (2010)
24. Xiong, X., De la Torre, F.: Supervised descent method and its applications to face alignment. In: IEEE Conference on Computer Vision and Pattern Recognition (CVPR), pp. 532–539, June (2013)
25. Yin, L., Chen, X., Sun, Y., Worm, T., Reale, M.: A high-resolution 3d dynamic facial expression database. In: 8th IEEE International Conference on Automatic Face Gesture Recognition, 2008. FG 2008, pp. 1–6, Sept 2008
26. Zhang, X., Yin, L., Cohn, J.F., Canavan, S., Reale, M., Horowitz, A., Liu, P., Girard, J.M.: Bp. 4d-spontaneous: a high-resolution spontaneous 3d dynamic facial expression database. Image Vis. Comput. **32**(10), 692–706 (2014). best of Automatic Face and Gesture Recognition 2013
27. Zhang, Z., Liu, Z., Adler, D., Cohen, M.F., Hanson, E., Shan, Y.: Robust and rapid generation of animated faces from video images: A model-based modeling approach. Int. J. Comput. Vis. **58**(2), 93–119 (2004). http://dx.doi.org/10.1023/B:VISI.0000015915.50080.85
28. Zhao, R., Wang, Y., Benitez-Quiroz, C.F., Liu, Y., Martinez, A.M.: Fast & precise face alignment and 3d shape recovery from a single image. In: 2016 European Conference on Computer Vision Workshops (ECCVW) (2016)

3D Face Alignment Without Correspondences

Zsolt Sánta and Zoltan Kato$^{(\boxtimes)}$

Institute of Informatics, University of Szeged, PO. Box 652, Szeged 6701, Hungary
{santazs,kato}@inf.u-szeged.hu

Abstract. A novel correspondence-less approach is proposed to find a thin plate spline map between a pair of 3D human faces represented by triangular surface meshes. The proposed method works without landmark extraction and feature correspondences. The aligning transformation is simply found by solving a system of nonlinear equations. Each equation is generated by integrating a non-linear function over the surfaces represented as fuzzy sets of triangles. We derive approximating formulas for the efficient computation of these integrals. Based on a series of comparative tests on a standard 3D face dataset, our triangular mesh-based algorithm outperforms state of the art methods in terms of computing time while maintaining accuracy.

Keywords: 3D face · Alignment · Thin plate spline · Correspondence-less

1 Introduction

The analysis of 3D faces is an important task in many applications, like face comparison, face motion capture, facial expression recognition [5], biometric identification [16] as well as several medical related problems, *e.g.* surgical planning [8,26] and craniofacial dysmorphology [29]. A core component of many 3D face analysis tasks is the geometric alignment of faces. Most of the alignment algorithms are relying on the extraction of well-defined feature points or landmarks. Detection of face landmarks in 2D images has a long research track in the literature [4,10]. With new 3D image acquisition devices and technologies, 3D face scans are becoming widespread [6,14,16,20,29]. One of the main advantage of the 3D scans over 2D images is that they are not affected by viewpoints and lighting conditions. Unfortunately, landmark localization in 3D data is a hard task even by user interaction. Current methods are relying on either geometric (*e.g.* curvature of the face surface) or color information only. For example, nose tip is usually detected as peak in the curve of the face [14,19,29], while color-based features are typically extracted by adopting 2D feature point detector and descriptor techniques such as SIFT [16]. Training-free landmark localization methods are using carefully designed rules [29]. However, these rules are usually not independent from each other, where estimation errors are propagated to subsequent stages [29]. On the contrary, training-based methods are more flexible but require a sufficiently large training dataset [29]. These type of methods

© Springer International Publishing Switzerland 2016
G. Hua and H. Jégou (Eds.): ECCV 2016 Workshops, Part II, LNCS 9914, pp. 521–535, 2016.
DOI: 10.1007/978-3-319-48881-3_36

are built upon *e.g.* statistical models [19] or techniques originated from machine learning [6,29].

In this paper, we propose a different strategy for 3D face alignment, which works without point correspondences. Given a pair of *template* and *observation* 3D face scans, we trace back the alignment to the solution of a system of non-linear equations, which directly provides the parameters of the aligning transformation. What kind of transformation should we consider? Obviously, face alignment requires a generic elastic transformation. The most generic mapping between the faces could be given as a vector field $\phi : \mathbb{R}^3 \rightarrow \mathbb{R}^3$, but such a transformation has too many degree of freedom, which makes its estimation difficult. Therefore, to reduce the complexity of the problem, the general mapping is often replaced by a parametric deformation model. Following [9] and [28], the deformation models could be organized into three main groups: physical model based, models derived from interpolation and approximation theory, and knowledge-based geometric transformations. In our approach, we propose to model the deformation by thin plate splines (TPS) [3,31,32]. TPS models are often used whenever a parametric free-form registration is required but the underlying physical model of the object deformation is unknown or too complex.

Observing the possible deformations in face alignment task, we can either consider intra- or inter-person registration [30]. In the former case we register different scans from the same person, therefore the deformation usually caused by various facial expressions. In the latter case scans from different people are registered, thus we have to deal with large non-rigid deformations caused by the variation of faces in size and shape from one person to another. Moreover, in intra-person registration the deformation is acting more locally with respect to the inter-person case, hence it is easier to find similar areas to restrict the space of possible deformations. In the current proposal, our aim is to solve the inter-person registration problem.

From a methodological point of view, registration methods can be classified into two main groups: geometric (or landmark-based) methods and iconic (or area-based) approaches [28]. The fundamental difference is that geometric methods rely on extracted landmarks placed in salient image locations while iconic methods are using the whole image domain to determine the transformation. Geometric methods are challenged by the correspondence problem, which is particularly difficult to solve in the case of non-linear deformations. Iconic approaches are typically relying on the availability of rich radiometric information which is used to construct a similarity measure based on some kind of intensity correlations. The aligning transformation is then found by maximizing similarity between the objects, which usually yields a complex non-linear optimization procedure. Hybrid methods are also available, combining the bests properties of both worlds [28]. Unfortunately, non of these methods are well adapted to 3D face registration problems, as radiometric information is either missing or low quality.

In practice, 3D surfaces are given as triangular surface meshes. Current methods are either using the whole triangular surface [24] or focusing on registering the vertex set only [11,18]. In the latter case, a popular way to deal with unstructured point sets is to represent each set by a suitable, problem specific model (*e.g.* Gaussian mixtures): In [18], a probabilistic model is proposed where a Gaussian mixture with centroids corresponding to the *template* set is fit to the *observation* set by maximizing the likelihood. Thus, an energy function composed of the negative log-likelihood and an additional regularization term is minimized using the Expectation Maximization algorithm. The transformation is represented by parametric radial basis functions using a Gaussian kernel. In [11], both point sets are represented as a Gaussian Mixture Model and then the L2 distance of the two mixtures is minimized. The authors use a closed-form expression to calculate the distance between the Gaussian mixtures efficiently. The underlying deformation is modeled using thin plate splines. Both approaches reported to be robust against occlusions, however they are inefficient for large point sets, due to the computational cost.

In this paper, a TPS-based method is proposed for aligning triangulated facial 3D scans based on a recent registration framework [7,24]. The method relies on geometric information only and the parameters of the TPS is obtained directly as a solution of a properly generated system of equations. The main idea behind the generation is to integrate a set of non-linear functions over the domains of the input data in order to eliminate the need for individual point correspondences. Unlike [24], which works only for closed surfaces (*i.e.* volumetric objects) and [7], which works only for 2D planar regions, the proposed approach is specifically developed for open 3D surfaces. The performance of the algorithm is evaluated on a subset of the Bosphorus Dataset [25]. We remark, that by aligning 3D face scans, one can transfer landmarks from one scan to the other. Although this is not a usual way to solve landmark extraction, similar approaches could be found in the literature. For example, a training-free method is proposed in [14], where the initial landmark estimation is refined by a deformable registration approach [1], using a few extracted landmark location as constraints on the final result.

2   3D Face Alignment

The proposed method has a very limited assumption about the input: faces are represented as triangulated surface meshes without any radiometric data. Obviously, the spatial resolution of the input mesh determines the possible alignment precision, hence good quality input is critical for precise alignment. Let us now consider two faces represented as 3D surfaces: one is called the *template* and the other one is called the *observation*, denoted by $\mathcal{F}_t \subset \mathbb{R}^3$ and $\mathcal{F}_o \subset \mathbb{R}^3$, respectively. We are looking for the aligning transformation $\varphi : \mathbb{R}^3 \to \mathbb{R}^3$ such that for all $\mathbf{x} \in \mathcal{F}_t$ there exists a $\mathbf{y} \in \mathcal{F}_o$ satisfying the so called *identity relation*

$$\varphi(\mathbf{x}) = \mathbf{y} \qquad (1)$$

In classical landmark based approaches, a large number of corresponding landmarks are extracted from $\mathcal{F}_t$ and $\mathcal{F}_o$, giving sufficiently many constraints through

Eq. (1) to find the parameters of the transformation. An alternative solution has been proposed in [7,24], which relies on segmented regions instead of point correspondences: The idea is to integrate out individual point pairs in Eq. (1) over the the foreground domains of the objects yielding the following equation:

$$\int_{\mathcal{F}_o} \mathbf{y} \, d\mathbf{y} = \int_{\varphi(\mathcal{F}_t)} \mathbf{z} \, d\mathbf{z}. \tag{2}$$

While in landmark-based approaches each point correspondence will generate a new equation of the form Eq. (1); Eq. (2) provides only three equations ($\mathbf{y}, \mathbf{z} \in \mathbb{R}^3$)! As a consequence, Eq. (2) alone is not enough to solve for the transformation parameters. In order to generate more equations, observe that Eq. (1) (hence Eq. (2)) remains valid when a non-linear $\omega : \mathbb{R}^3 \to \mathbb{R}$ function is acting on both sides [7,24]. Thus applying a set of independent non-linear functions $\{\omega_i\}_{i=1}^{\ell}$ yields a system of ℓ equations [24]:

$$\int_{\mathcal{F}_o} \omega_i(\mathbf{y}) \, d\mathbf{y} = \int_{\varphi(\mathcal{F}_t)} \omega_i(\mathbf{z}) \, d\mathbf{z} \qquad i = 1, \ldots, \ell. \tag{3}$$

Since the *template* and *observation* surfaces are represented by their triangular surface meshes, let us denote them by $T_\triangle$ and $O_\triangle \subset \mathbb{R}^3 \times \mathbb{R}^3 \times \mathbb{R}^3$, respectively. They are a piecewise linear approximation of the true surfaces $\mathcal{F}_t$ and $\mathcal{F}_o$, hence

$$T_\triangle \approx \mathcal{F}_t$$
$$O_\triangle \approx \mathcal{F}_o$$
$$\varphi(T_\triangle) \approx \varphi(\mathcal{F}_t) \tag{4}$$

and thus the integrals over the triangular surfaces will be approximations of the integrals over the true surfaces as well. The integrals over the triangular surfaces can be expressed as sums of integrals over the triangles of each mesh:

$$\sum_{o \in O_\triangle} \int_o \omega_i(\mathbf{y}) \, d\mathbf{y} \approx \sum_{\pi \in \varphi(T_\triangle)} \int_\pi \omega_i(\mathbf{z}) \, d\mathbf{z}. \tag{5}$$

Theoretically, any integrable $\{\omega_i\}_{i=1}^{\ell}$ function set could be used, but for computational efficiency we will use low-order power functions

$$\omega_i(\mathbf{x}) = x_1^{n_i} x_2^{m_i} x_3^{o_i}, \tag{6}$$

where $\{(n_i, m_i, o_i)\}_{i=1}^{\ell} = \{(a, b, c) \mid a + b + c = O\}$ and $O \in \{0, \ldots, M\}$. The M value corresponds to the maximal degree of the polynomial set and it is chosen to provide the necessary amount of functions to determine the parameters of the transformation. Note that, using these ω_i functions the integrands will be various geometric moments of each triangle, which can be efficiently computed by making use of the methods proposed in [13,22].

2.1 Determining the Integration Domains

One can consider Eq. (5) as an object level *identity relation*, because here we only require, that the object domains $\mathcal{F}_t$ and $\mathcal{F}_o$ be in correspondence as a whole. How to ensure this region-level correspondence for 3D faces? This is by far not a trivial question, because facial scans typically focus on the frontal face, but depending on the actual setting, other parts of the head are also visible. Therefore the scanned surfaces will not match as a whole! Moreover, the exact segmentation of corresponding parts is a rather complex problem as there are no clearly defined borders of a face in a 3D scan. Instead of solving a hard 3D face segmentation problem, let us define the integration domains in Eq. (5) as fuzzy sets [33] with a $W_{\lambda_1\lambda_2} : (\boldsymbol{A}, \boldsymbol{B}, \boldsymbol{C}) \rightarrow [0,1]$ membership function giving the weight of each triangle in the integrals of Eq. (5):

$$\sum_{o \in N_o(O_\triangle)} W_{\lambda_1\lambda_2}(o) \int_o \omega_i(\mathbf{y})\, d\mathbf{y} \approx \sum_{\pi \in \varphi(N_t(T_\triangle))} W_{\lambda_1\lambda_2}(\pi) \int_\pi \omega_i(\mathbf{z})\, d\mathbf{z}, \qquad (7)$$

The membership function $W_{\lambda_1\lambda_2}$ is governed by three parameters:

1. λ_1 is the upper threshold of the inner parts (where $W_{\lambda_1\lambda_2} = 1$)
2. λ_2 is the lower threshold of the outer parts (where $W_{\lambda_1\lambda_2} = 0$)
3. the interpolation method for the area between λ_1 and λ_2, which is either a linear or a step function. For the *step* method, $W_{\lambda_1\lambda_2} = 0.5$ between λ_1 and λ_2, while the *linear* method sets $W_{\lambda_1\lambda_2}$ between 0 and 1 proportionally to the distance.

The thresholds λ_1 and λ_2 are determined based on geodesic distances and by making use of a training set with ground truth landmark locations. First, we choose an origin point on the surface for the geodesic distance calculation. This point should be easy and stable to detect, therefore we recommend to use the nose tip. Moreover, this point is approximately at the middle of all important facial landmarks. Next, we determine the maximal geodesic distance with respect to the nose tip. We tried two different maximal values: (1) the true maximal geodesic distance as well as (2) the mean of the top 5 % geodesic distances from the nose tip. In the next step, we calculate the geodesic distance to each ground truth landmark location and normalize the calculated distances with the previously determined maximal value in order to achieve head size invariance. In our experiments, we observed that taking the mean of the normalized distances on all training data will give an area containing most of the landmarks. Therefore, we define λ_1 as this mean value. Similarly, for λ_2 we simply add the standard deviation of the normalized distances to λ_1. Thus the thresholds are expressed as the percentage of the maximal geodesic distance within the face. An example is shown in Fig. 1.

The main advantage of this fuzzy representation is that we can focus the equations on the more stable, inner parts of faces without the need of a high precision segmentation of the 3D meshes.

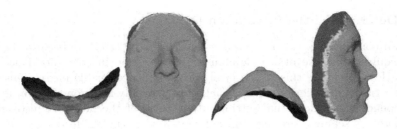

Fig. 1. An example for the membership functions. The green area denotes the inner parts having a membership value of 1, while the yellow and red regions denote the areas between λ_1 and λ_2, and the areas above λ_2, respectively. (Color figure online)

2.2 Computing the Integrals over Triangular Meshes

Now, we will derive an efficient numerical schemes for the calculation of the integrals, which uses a linear approximation of the ω_i functions yielding a fast algorithm. Following [22], we will use barycentric parametrization of the triangles. Considering an arbitrary triangle $o = (A, B, C)$, every p point of the triangle can be expressed as a weighted sum of the vertices:

$$p = uA + vB + wC, \tag{8}$$

with $u, v, w \geq 0$ and $u + v + w = 1$. Thus the above formula has two free parameters as one weight can be expressed by the other two, *e.g.* $w = 1 - u - v$. Since we apply the above transformation, the area changes $\|(A - C) \times (B - C)\| = 2\,\mathrm{area}(o)$ induced by this reparametrization has to be taken into account in the integrals over a triangle o. Thus the first integral in Eq. (7) becomes

$$\sum_{o \in O_\triangle} W_{\lambda_1 \lambda_2}(o) \int_o \omega_i(\mathbf{y})\, d\mathbf{y} \quad =$$

$$\sum_{o \in O_\triangle} 2\,\mathrm{area}(o) W_{\lambda_1 \lambda_2}(o) \int_0^1 \int_0^{1-u} \omega_i(uA + vB + wC)\, dv\, du, \tag{9}$$

where $i = 1, \ldots, \ell$ and $w = 1 - u - v$. A similar formula can be derived for the other integral in Eq. (7). Considering the $\{\omega_i\}$ set from Eq. (6) and the barycentric parameterization from Eq. (8), we can linearly interpolate the $\{\omega_i\}$ functions using the vertices of each triangle $o = (A, B, C)$ as

$$\omega_i(\mathbf{p}) \approx u\omega_i(A) + v\omega_i(B) + w\omega_i(C) \quad i = 1, \ldots, \ell. \tag{10}$$

Substituting the above approximation into Eq. (9), we get the following approximation for the integral:

$$\sum_{o \in O_\triangle} W_{\lambda_1 \lambda_2}(o) \int_o \omega_i(\hat{\mathbf{y}})\, d\hat{\mathbf{y}} \approx$$

$$\sum_{o \in O_\triangle} 2\,\mathrm{area}(o) W_{\lambda_1 \lambda_2}(o) \int_0^1 \int_0^{1-u} u\omega_i(A) + v\omega_i(B) + w\omega_i(C)\, dv\, du, \tag{11}$$

where $w = 1 - u - v$ and $i = 1, \ldots, \ell$. Since ω_i is independent from the integration variables, we get the closed form expression

$$\int_o \omega_i(\mathbf{y}) \, d\mathbf{y} \approx \text{area}(o) \frac{\omega_i(\mathbf{A}) + \omega_i(\mathbf{B}) + \omega_i(\mathbf{C})}{3}, \tag{12}$$

which is simply the mean of the function values in the vertices weighted by the area of the triangle. Note that this formula will be exact for every linear functions, thus the precision of the approximation depends on the local linearity of the function and the size of the triangle. The complexity of this algorithm is $\mathcal{O}(M^3)$, where M is the maximal order of the ω_i functions.

2.3   Transformation Model

While the proposed method works with almost any parametric transformation model ϕ, what is the optimal choice for 3D face alignment? Obviously, we need an elastic transformation to warp faces between different persons. From a computation point of view, the transformation should have a minimal number of parameters, because the number of equations in Eq. (12) directly depends on this number. Thin plate splines (TPS) [3,31,32] are broadly used for such alignment problems.

In 3D, a TPS transformation $\varphi : \mathbb{R}^3 \rightarrow \mathbb{R}^3$ can be decomposed as three coordinate functions $\varphi(\mathbf{x}) = [\varphi_1(\mathbf{x}), \varphi_2(\mathbf{x}), \varphi_3(\mathbf{x})]^T$, $\forall \varphi_i(\mathbf{x}) : \mathbb{R}^3 \rightarrow \mathbb{R}$. Given a set of control points $c_k \in \mathbb{R}^3$ and associated mapping coefficients $a_{ij}, w_{ki} \in \mathbb{R}$ with $i = 1, \ldots, 3$, $j = 1, \ldots, 4$ and $k = 1, \ldots, K$, the TPS functions are

$$\varphi_i(\mathbf{x}) = a_{i1}x_1 + a_{i2}x_2 + a_{i3}x_3 + a_{i4} + \sum_{k=1}^{K} w_{ki}U(\|c_k - \mathbf{x}\|), \tag{13}$$

where $U(r) = -r$ [31] is called radial basis function. The transformation has $N = 3(K + 4)$ parameters: 12 affine parameters a_{ij} and 3 local coefficients w_{ki} for each control point c_k satisfying the following additional constraints [31,32], which ensure that the TPS at infinity behaves according to its affine term:

$$\sum_{k=1}^{K} w_{ki} = 0 \quad \text{and} \quad \sum_{k=1}^{K} c_{k_j} w_{ki} = 0 \qquad i, j = 1, 2, 3. \tag{14}$$

When correspondences are available, the exact mapping of the control points are also known which, using Eq. (13), provides constraints on the unknown parameters. Thus in classical correspondence based approaches, control points are placed at extracted point matches, and the deformation at other positions is interpolated by the TPS. Therefore in such cases, a TPS can be regarded as an optimal *interpolating* function whose parameters are usually recovered via a complex optimization procedure [3,32]. However, in the current approach, TPS is used as a parametric model to *approximate* the true deformation [7]. How to place the control points in such cases? A trivial way, also explored in [7], is to have them equally sampled over the whole surface. However, this leads to a high number of parameters, which increases computational complexity. This has been pointed out in [17], where application-specific control point locations have been derived. In the same spirit, we propose to pick control points using the *Farthest Point Sampling* method [21], which uniformly samples the *template* surface maximizing the geodesic distance between the closest points. Note that, this approach also guarantees that control points are placed on the surface only.

3   Experimental Results

In this section we summarize our experimental results obtained on the Bosphorus Dataset [25]. This dataset consists of 4666 face scans with 2D color images and 3D surface points. The ground truth landmark locations are also marked in at most 24 points, giving the opportunity to evaluate our approach using ground truth data. The tests have been made on a randomly generated subset containing 153 pairs of faces with neutral facial expression from different people (*i.e.* we performed *inter-person* registration).

The triangular surface meshes have been created from the Bosphorus 3D point cloud using the *Poisson algorithm* [12] implemented using the CGAL Library [2]. The library implements a *Delaunay refinement* algorithm, allowing to construct meshes at different resolutions [23,27]. In our tests, we controlled the resolution of the triangular meshes by the maximal radius r of the corresponding Delaunay sphere for each triangle. For the TPS model, we used 64 control points placed on the surface using the *Farthest Point Sampling* strategy. This model has 204 parameters, therefore we constructed a system of 220 equations by choosing M, the maximal order of polynomials, to be 9 for the function set from Eq. (6). Note that, since we have an overdetermined system, it is solved in the least squares sense by the *Levenberg-Marquardt* algorithm. The solver has been initialized by the identity transformation and the integrals have been normalized according to the algorithm described in [24].

The algorithm have been implemented in C++ using the *Levenberg-Marquardt* implementation `levmar` of Lourakis [15]. All tests have been ran on a laptop with Core i5 3.1 GHz architecture.

The results have been quantitatively evaluated based on the average landmark distances between the transformed and the ground truth locations:

$$D_{GT} = \frac{1}{N} \sum_{i=1}^{N} \|\mathbf{x}_i - \hat{\mathbf{x}}_i\|, \qquad (15)$$

where N is the number of available landmarks for a pair of scans, $\mathbf{x}_i \in O_\triangle$ is the ground truth and $\hat{\mathbf{x}}_i = \varphi(\mathbf{z}_i), \mathbf{z}_i \in T_\triangle$ is the transformed landmark position of the ith landmark using the estimated aligning transformation φ. The overall surface alignment accuracy has been also characterized by the maximal root mean square (RMS) error between the closest points of the triangular meshes:

$$D_{RMS} = \max\{RMS(O_\triangle, \varphi(T_\triangle)), RMS(\varphi(T_\triangle), O_\triangle)\}, \qquad (16)$$

where

$$RMS(S_1, S_2) = \sqrt{\frac{1}{|V(S_1)|} \sum_{\boldsymbol{p} \in V(S_1)} \inf_{\boldsymbol{q} \in S_2} \|\boldsymbol{p} - \boldsymbol{q}\|^2},$$

and S_1, S_2 are the corresponding surfaces, while $V(S_1)$ denotes the set of all vertices of S_1. The RMS function basically estimates the distance between each vertex of the first triangular surface and the closest (not necessarily vertex) point of the second triangular surface. This measure is more accurate than the simple vertex-wise distances and by taking the maximum of the values computed with swapped arguments leads to a symmetric measure between the surfaces. Note that, this value is only determined for the inner parts of the membership functions. In our first experiment, we tried each membership function with meshes generated by $r = 10$ as maximal radius of the enclosing Delaunay sphere. Note that each membership function depends on two parameters: the value of the thresholds (λ_1 and λ_2) and the interpolation method for the areas between the thresholds. For the possible combinations, see Table 1. As we mentioned in Sect. 2.1, the geodesic distance computation needs a specific origin point, which is the nose tip. The coordinate system of the scans in the Bosphorus dataset is established such a way, that the point having the maximal value on the Z axis is a good estimate for the nose tip, thus we used this point in the geodesic distance calculations. The results of this test is shown in Fig. 2. According to the D_{GT} error metric in Eq. (15), the best alignment is provided by using the thresholds from the top 5 % distances. Moreover, we have noticed that the interpolation method has no strong influence on the outcome of the algorithm, therefore we recommend to use the step interpolation.

Table 1. The weight functions used for our experiments

Test Case	Interpolation	λ_1	λ_2
top	linear, step	74.84 %	80.95 %
top 5 %	linear, step	71.07 %	75.82 %

For our next experiments we tried several triangular surface resolutions with $r \in \{2, 3, 5\}$ as maximal radius for the enclosing Delaunay sphere of each triangle. This is necessary because the triangulation will eventually reduce the resolution of the input data by removing points and smoothing the surface. An approximation for the loss in the resolution can be found in Table 2. In this table, we measured the average distance for each neighborhood containing 6 points. The resolution loss effect could be reduced by extracting a more detailed mesh from the input, but this will increase the amount of input data and lead to higher running times. The aim of the current experiment is to find the best runtime over quality ratio. The outline of this test is shown in Fig. 3. We achieved the best results on the $r = 3$ case, with respect to the D_{GT} metric and the runtime of the algorithm. The average D_{GT} error for the test dataset is $6.71mm$

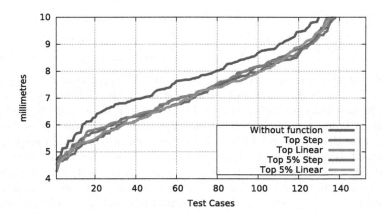

Fig. 2. The average landmark localization error in the first experiment. Each plot shows results with different weight functions. We achieved the best outcome using the thresholds defined by top 5 % distances.

with average running time of 16.4 seconds. Some results are presented in Fig. 5. For the surface alignment accuracy we got $D_{RMS} = 1.76mm$ (see Fig. 4 for an example). From the results we conclude that the algorithm achieves good results near the areas with significant curvature changes (*e.g.* nose and mouth), however performs poorly near the noisy eyebrows.

Table 2. The resolutions of the input sets expressed as the average Euclidean-distance between the 5 closest points in millimeters.

Point Cloud [25]	$r = 10$	$r = 5$	$r = 3$	$r = 2$
0.78	3.48	3.73	3.10	2.17

In the last experiment, we have compared our results to the point-based registration frameworks in [11] (GMMREG) and [18] (CPD). We used the C++ implementation of these methods available from http://code.google.com/p/gmmreg and set the parameters to their default values (within the given Matlab framework). Since the runtime of these algorithms are enormously high for the full original point sets (the average is around 7–8 h for one pair of faces), we ran the experiments using the vertices of the same surface meshes as we used for our algorithm. The results can be found in Fig. 6. We used the `top 5%` thresholds with the `step` interpolation method for this test. The GMMREG algorithm has achieved very good results, slightly outperforming our method and the CPD algorithm on the D_{GT} error, but CPD gives inferior alignment compared to our approach. However, the proposed approach achieved the lowest running time.

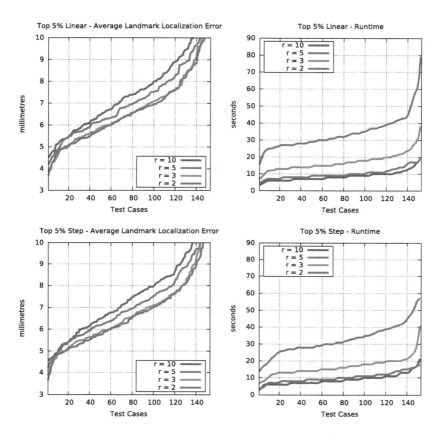

Fig. 3. Average landmark localization errors and running times for each resolutions of $r \in \{2, 3, 5, 10\}$ using the **top 5 %** thresholds. The localization error determined as the Euclidean distance of the transformed and the ground truth landmark locations. In the first line corresponds to the step, the second line to the linear interpolation method.

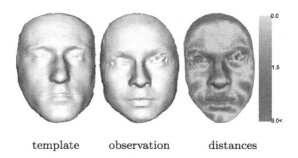

template   observation   distances

Fig. 4. Example alignment on the Bosphorus dataset. The $D_{RMS} = 1.17mm$ and the $D_{GT} = 5.4mm$.

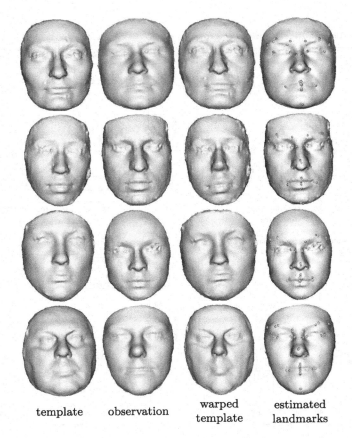

template   observation   warped   estimated
                              template   landmarks

Fig. 5. Landmark detection results on the Bosphorus dataset. In each row we show the *template*, the *observation*, the warped *template* and the localization results, respectively. In the last column green denotes the ground truth position and red is the estimated location. While the proposed approach achieved good results near nose and mouth areas, the highest errors are near the eyebrows. (Color figure online)

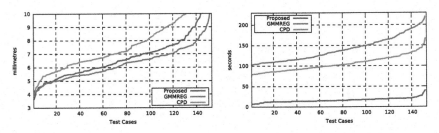

Fig. 6. Comparison between the proposed, the GMMREG and the CPD algorithms. On the left diagram the D_{GT} metric is presented, while on the right we show the running times of each algorithm. The GMMREG slightly outperformed the proposed approach and the CPD algorithm in the landmark localization error, but the proposed approach has the best running time

4   Conclusion

We proposed a novel deformable registration algorithm for aligning human faces. The algorithm is motivated by a recent approach proposed in [7,24]. The physical deformation is approximated by a parametric TPS model and the parameters are directly obtained as a solution of a system of nonlinear equations. Experimental results on the Bosphorus dataset [25] confirmed the state of the art capabilities of the proposed approach. Furthermore, in terms of computational complexity, our method compares favorably to two recent state-of-the-art methods published in [11] and [18]. While the achieved results are promising, further research aims to enhance the accuracy of the method by introducing face specific priors into the system. Moreover, since the proposed algorithm has many independent components, the running time could be drastically reduced through parallelization on a GPU.

Acknowledgment. The face scans have been obtain from Bosphorus Dataset [25]. We would like to thank the authors of [11] and [18] for providing their implementations for our experiments.

References

1. Allen, B., Curless, B., Popović, Z.: The space of human body shapes: Reconstruction and parameterization from range scans. ACM Trans. Graph. **22**(3), 587–594 (2003)
2. Alliez, P., Saboret, L., Guennebaud, G.: Surface reconstruction from point sets. In: CGAL User and Reference Manual. CGAL Editorial Board, 4.4 edn. (2000). http://doc.cgal.org/4.4/Surface_reconstruction_points_3/index.html#Chapter_Surface_Reconstruction_from_Point_Sets
3. Bookstein, F.L.: Principal warps: Thin-plate splines and the decomposition of deformations. IEEE Trans. Pattern Anal. Mach. Intell. **11**(6), 567–585 (1989)
4. Cao, X., Wei, Y., Wen, F., Sun, J.: Face alignment by explicit shape regression. Int. J. Comput. Vis. **107**(2), 177–190 (2014)
5. Corneanu, C.A., Simn, M.O., Cohn, J.F., Guerrero, S.E.: Survey on rgb, 3d, thermal, and multimodal approaches for facial expression recognition: History, trends, and affect-related applications. IEEE Trans. Pattern Anal. Mach. Intell. **38**(8), 1548–1568 (2016)
6. Creusot, C., Pears, N., Austin, J.: A machine-learning approach to keypoint detection and landmarking on 3D meshes. Int. J. Comput. Vis. **102**(1–3), 146–179 (2013)
7. Domokos, C., Nemeth, J., Kato, Z.: Nonlinear shape registration without correspondences. IEEE Trans. Pattern Anal. Mach. Intell. **34**(5), 943–958 (2012)
8. Heike, C.L., Cunningham, M.L., Hing, A.V., Stuhaug, E., Starr, J.R.: Picture perfect?: Reliability of craniofacial anthropometry using three-dimensional digital stereophotogrammetry. Plast. Reconstr. Surg. **124**(4), 1261–1272 (2009)
9. Holden, M.: A review of geometric transformations for nonrigid body registration. IEEE Trans. Med. Imaging **27**(1), 111–128 (2008)
10. Jeni, L.A., Cohn, J.F., Kanade, T.: Dense 3d face alignment from 2d videos in real-time. Proc. IEEE Int. Conf. Workshops Autom. Face Gesture Recogn. **1**, 1–8 (2015)

11. Jian, B., Vemuri, B.: Robust point set registration using Gaussian mixture models. IEEE Trans. Pattern Anal. Mach. Intell. **33**(8), 1633–1645 (2011)

12. Kazhdan, M., Bolitho, M., Hoppe, H.: Poisson surface reconstruction. In: Proceedings of the Fourth Eurographics Symposium on Geometry Processing, pp. 61–70. SGP 2006, Eurographics Association, Aire-la-Ville, Switzerland, Switzerland (2006)

13. Koehl, P.: Fast recursive computation of 3D geometric moments from surface meshes. IEEE Trans. Pattern Anal. Mach. Intell. **34**(11), 2158–2163 (2012)

14. Liang, S., Wu, J., Weinberg, S.M., Shapiro, L.G.: Improved detection of landmarks on 3d human face data. In: Proceedings of 2013 35th Annual International Conference of the IEEE Engineering in Medicine and Biology Society (EMBC), pp. 6482–6485, Jul 2013

15. Lourakis, M.: levmar: Levenberg-marquardt nonlinear least squares algorithms in C/C++. http://www.ics.forth.gr/~lourakis/levmar/

16. Mian, A., Bennamoun, M., Owens, R.: An efficient multimodal 2d–3d hybrid approach to automatic face recognition. IEEE Trans. Pattern Anal. Mach. Intell. **29**(11), 1927–1943 (2007)

17. Mitra, J., Kato, Z., Marti, R., Oliver, A., Llado, X., Sidibe, D., Ghose, S., Vilanova, J.C., Comet, J., Meriaudeau, F.: A spline-based non-linear diffeomorphism for multimodal prostate registration. Med. Image Anal. **16**(6), 1259–1279 (2012)

18. Myronenko, A., Song, X.B., Carreira-Perpiñán, M.Á.: Non-rigid point set registration: Coherent point drift. In: Schölkopf, B., Platt, J.C., Hoffman, T. (eds.) Proceedings of the Advances in Neural Information Processing Systems, pp. 1009–1016. MIT Press, Vancouver, British Columbia, Canada, Dec 2006

19. Nair, P., Cavallaro, A.: 3D face detection, landmark localization, and registration using a point distribution model. IEEE Trans. Multimedia **11**(4), 611–623 (2009)

20. Perakis, P., Passalis, G., Theoharis, T., Kakadiaris, I.A.: 3D facial landmark detection & face registration. Technical report TP-2010-01, CGL Technical Report (2010)

21. Peyré, G., Cohen, L.: Geodesic methods for shape and surface processing. In: Tavares, J.M.R.S., Jorge, R.M.N. (eds.) Advances in Computational Vision and Medical Image Processing. Computational Methods in Applied Sciences, vol. 13, pp. 29–56. Springer, Netherlands (2009)

22. Pozo, J.M., Villa-Uriol, M.C., Frangi, A.F.: Efficient 3D geometric and Zernike moments computation from unstructured surface meshes. IEEE Trans. Pattern Anal. Mach. Intell. **33**(3), 471–484 (2011)

23. Rineau, L., Yvinec, M.: A generic software design for Delaunay refinement meshing. Comput. Geom. **38**(12), 100–110 (2007)

24. Sánta, Z., Kato, Z.: Correspondence-less non-rigid registration of triangular surface meshes. In: Proceedings of IEEE Conference on Computer Vision and Pattern Recognition, pp. 2275–2282. IEEE, Portland, Oregon, June 2013

25. Savran, A., Alyüz, N., Dibeklioğlu, H., Çeliktutan, O., Gökberk, B., Sankur, B., Akarun, L.: Bosphorus database for 3D face analysis. In: Schouten, B., Juul, N.C., Drygajlo, A., Tistarelli, M. (eds.) BIOID 2008. LNCS, vol. 5372, pp. 47–56. Springer, Heidelberg (2008)

26. Sharifi, A., Jones, R., Ayoub, A., Moos, K., Walker, F., Khambay, B., McHugh, S.: How accurate is model planning for orthognathic surgery? Int. J. Oral Maxillofac. Surg. **37**(12), 1089–1093 (2008)

27. Shewchuk, J.R.: Delaunay refinement algorithms for triangular mesh generation. Comput. Geom. **22**(13), 21–74 (2002). 16th ACM Symposium on Computational Geometry

28. Sotiras, A., Davatzikos, C., Paragios, N.: Deformable medical image registration: A survey. IEEE Trans. Med. Imaging **32**(7), 1153–1190 (2013)
29. Sukno, F.M., Waddington, J.L., Whelan, P.F.: 3-d facial landmark localization with asymmetry patterns and shape regression from incomplete local features. IEEE Trans. Cybern. **45**(9), 1717–1730 (2015)
30. Unzueta, L., Pimenta, W., Goenetxea, J., Santos, L.P., Dornaika, F.: Efficient generic face model fitting to images and videos. Image Vis. Comput. **32**(5), 321–334 (2014)
31. Wahba, G.: Spline models for observational data. Soc. Ind. Appl. Math. (1990)
32. Zagorchev, L., Goshtasby, A.: A comparative study of transformation functions for nonrigid image registration. IEEE Trans. Image Process. **15**(3), 529–538 (2006)
33. Zimmermann, H.J.: Fuzzy Set Theory - and Its Applications. Springer, Heidelberg (2001)

Bi-Level Multi-column Convolutional Neural Networks for Facial Landmark Point Detection

Yanyu Xu$^{(\boxtimes)}$ and Shenghua Gao

School of Information Science and Technology,
ShanghaiTech University, Shanghai, China
{xuyy2,gaoshh}@shanghaitech.edu.cn

Abstract. We propose a bi-level Multi-column Convolutional Neural Networks (MCNNs) framework for face alignment. Global CNNs are used to roughly estimate the coordinates of all landmark points, and Local CNNs take patches sampled from the landmarks predicted by Global CNNs as input to predict the displacement between the ground truth and the landmark predicted by Global CNNs. The multi-column architecture leverages the findings that the optimal resolutions for different points are different. Further, the coordinates of all landmark and their displacement are simultaneously estimated in Global and Local CNNs, hence global shape constraints are naturally and implicitly imposed to make it very robust to significant variations in pose, expression, occlusion, and illumination. Extensive experiments demonstrate our method achieves state of the art performance for both image and video based face alignment on many publicly available datasets.

Keywords: Bi-Level Multi-column CNNs · Facial landmark points detection · Global CNNs · Local CNNs

1 Introduction

Facial landmark points detection, also known as face alignment, is an important component for many face based applications, for example, face recognition/verification [9], face animation [6], expression recognition [2], *etc.* Thus it has been extensively studied [1, 4, 7, 15, 16, 22, 23, 28, 35, 36, 38, 41, 43]. However, diverse and severe changes in poses, occlusion, and illumination make facial landmark point detection remain an extremely challenging task in practice.

The existing facial landmark point detection methods can be roughly categorized as detection-based methods and regression-based methods. Detection-based methods depend on the detection of each landmark point, which may encounter difficulty when multiple candidates (false positive) or no candidates (occlusion) present. Then global shape constraints are imposed to find an optimal configuration; In contrast, regression-based methods directly estimate the coordinates of all the facial points, and they can be further divided into two subcategories: initial shape based methods [23, 28], and no initial shape based on methods [31, 41].

© Springer International Publishing Switzerland 2016
G. Hua and H. Jégou (Eds.): ECCV 2016 Workshops, Part II, LNCS 9914, pp. 536–551, 2016.
DOI: 10.1007/978-3-319-48881-3_37

In initial shape based methods, a mean shape which is obtained from the training set is used as the initialization, and then it is gradually updated based on the shape constraints and local context information. Thanks to advances in Deep Neural Networks (DNNs), people have started to use DNNs to map an input face image to the coordinates of landmark points with an end-to-end framework, and mean shape is not needed any more. Such methods have achieved state-of-the-art performance.

Motivated by the successes of DNNs based facial landmark point detection, in this paper, we propose a Bi-Level strategy for facial landmark point detection. Specifically, the first level Convolutional Neural Networks (CNNs), which are termed as Global CNNs, leverage the whole faces to predict all landmarks points simultaneously. Based on the prediction from the first level CNNs, we sample patches around the predicted points, and use the second level CNNs to learn the mapping between these patches and the remaining displacement between the ground truth landmarks and those predicted by the Global CNNs. Since the local information is used for the second level CNNs, we term the second level CNNs as Local CNNs. Moreover, as Fig. 1 shows, we found through experiments that using face images at different scales helps the prediction of different facial points. The detection accuracy of a given landmark point is related to whether a node in the last layer corresponds to a semantic meaningful region in the raw image for inferring the location of this point. Different points have different optimal resolutions. For the given kernel size and network depth in our implementation, the 96 × 96 resolution is close to be optimal for most points. While for other points, say point 59–61, 128 × 128 is better. For point 9, 78 × 78 is better. We hence propose to combine multiple CNNs for faces of different resolutions within a Multi-column CNNs (MCNNs) framework. Such a framework is applied for both Global CNNs and Local CNNs.

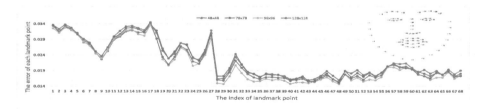

Fig. 1. Performance comparisons of CNNs for faces at different resolutions (marked with different colors). Different landmark points clearly have different sensitivity to change in face resolution. The error for each landmark point is calculated as the distance between the ground truth and the predicted coordinates, normalized by the width of image.

The contributions of our framework can be summarized as follows: (i) Our work shows that optimal resolutions of different points are different, thus we propose a multi-columns CNNs architecture to leverage faces of multiple resolutions for face alignment. (ii) Our bi-level architecture leverages a coarse-to-fine strategy for face alignment, i.e., we use global CNNs to roughly estimate all points and use local CNNs to fine-tune the coordinates of all landmark points. (iii) We propose to predict the coordinates of all points simultaneously in local CNNs, which encodes the shape constraints of all facial points, thus further boosts the face alignment accuracy.

2   Related Work

Among many of the models proposed for facial landmark points detection, Active Appearance Models (AAM) based methods [12,24] are very representative. AAM-like methods [12,24] used Principle Component Analysis (PCA) to model the facial shape and texture. But the effectiveness of such global appearance models can be affected by severe pose variations as well as occlusion. Then local models, including Active Shape Model (ASM) [13,16,25], Constrained Local Model (CLM) [14] are proposed to remedy the situation. These models use local features extracted from patches around estimated landmark points to refine the estimates, together with certain global shape constraint imposed. Such methods can effectively handle local occlusion, but their accuracy can be effected by certain non-discriminative local patches/regions. Within the CLM framework, Saragih et al. [27] has proposed to use better optimization method to optimize the problem in CLM, and their method achieves better performance compared to CLM. In [3], a discriminative response map fitting with constrained local model (DRMF) [3] is proposed to learn probability response maps dictionaries and use linear regression, and such method further improved CLM. Moreover, Xiong et al. [38] has proposed a supervised descent method (SDM) to solve the non-linear least square optimization problem in facial landmark point detection. It is also worth noting that all these local models depend on the initial shape, so they may get trapped in a local minimum. To resolve this issue, Cao et al. [6] has proposed to use multiple initializations, Burgos-Artizzu et al. [5] has proposed to adopt a restart strategy, and Zhu et al. [42] has proposed to use a coarse-to-fine shape searching over a shape space. These methods further boost the performance of facial landmark point detection.

Recently, deep learning has demonstrated successes in many computer vision tasks, including image classification [20], face recognition [29,32,33], as well as facial landmark point detection [31,41]. In [31], Sun et al. has proposed to use Deep Convolutional Neural Networks (DCNNs) to predict the five landmark points. Then multiple CNNs are trained to further refine the coordinates of each point. But in the second stage, since they refine each point separately, global shape constraints among all the landmarks are not considered. Zhang et al. have proposed to use coarse-to-fine auto-encoder networks (CFAN) for facial landmark point detection. They use the auto-encoder to predict the landmark points on a low-resolution face first, then they use features extracted from all landmark points to further refine the their coordinates. But their method uses hand-crafted features, which may not be the best for the prediction of landmark points.

3   Our Method

We here propose a Bi-Level MCNNs framework for facial landmark point detection, in which the Global CNNs are used to estimate approximate locations of all the landmark points, and then Local CNNs are used to correct the errors in the predicted landmark points with the help from local information.

3.1   Global Convolutional Neural Networks

Given an image $x \in \mathbb{R}^{m \times n}$, we denote the coordinates of p landmark points as $S_g(x) \in \mathbb{R}^{2p}$, then DNNs based facial landmark point detection aims at learning a nonlinear function F that maps x to $S_g(x)$, i.e., $F : x \mapsto F(x) \approx S_g(x)$. To learn F, we need to solve the following problems:

$$F^* = \arg\min_{F} \|S_g(x) - F(x)\|. \tag{1}$$

In this work, we adopt CNNs to model F in view of the following good properties of CNNs for facial landmark point detection. (i) In practice, faces come along with different illumination, poses, expression, even occlusion. Therefore the capacity of F should be high. Multi-layer nonlinearity in CNNs satisfies such requirements. (ii) In CNNs, each filter works as a detector, which makes CNNs be able to localize the landmark points. (iii) In a CNNs framework, all points are predicted simultaneously and that allows the model to implicitly learn and enforce certain global shape constraints. Therefore, such a model is able to handle difficult situations such as with missing points caused by occlusion or pose variation. (iv) Compared with Auto-encoders based models [41], CNNs share the filters over the whole image, so both the model's complexity and computational complexity are significantly reduced.

On one hand, to learn the global shape of a face, it is desirable that a node in a top layer would be able to correspond to semantically meaningful part of faces, say an eye, or nose. So the size of the region that such a node corresponds to should not be too large. On the other hand, to precisely locate the coordinates of all facial landmark points, we need filters that can represent fine details around each point. So the receptive fields of such filters cannot be too large and higher resolution faces are preferred. To resolve this dilemma for facial landmark point detection, we therefore propose to use multiple CNNs whose inputs are the face image resized to different resolutions (from the full resolution to several downsized ones). We combine their output features (FC1 features in Fig. 2-(a)) to estimate the landmark points with a fully connected layer. We term such a framework as Multi-column CNNs (MCNNs) based facial landmark point detection.

The overall structure of the proposed MCNNs is shown in Fig. 2-(a) and it consists of four columns. The CNN in each column contains 4 convolutional layers, 3 max pooling layers, and one fully connected layer in the end. For each column, the sizes of filters and the number of features maps are all the same and specified in Fig. 2-(b). Motivated by the success of pretraining in RBM model [18], we also

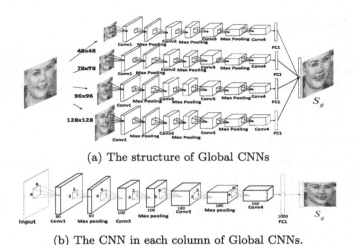

(a) The structure of Global CNNs

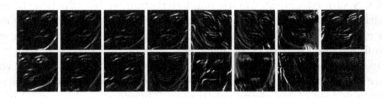

(b) The CNN in each column of Global CNNs.

Fig. 2. The architecture of Global CNNs. Dash line indicates the pretraining procedure.

Fig. 3. Some feature maps in Conv1 layer of Global CNNs. Images are from the LFPW dataset

pre-train CNN in each column by mapping its $FC1$ features to the ground-truth coordinates of landmark points. Such pretraining is necessary because it helps find a good initialization of parameters and avoids the effect of gradient vanishing phenomenon in training deep neural networks (Please refer to Fig. 5-(e) to find out the effect of pretraining.). We also show some feature maps in the first convolutional layers $Conv1$ in Fig. 3. This figure shows that these the face shape has larger responses.

Remarks on MCNNs: The concept of Multi-column CNNs is proposed by Ciresan *et al.* in [11]. In [11], the CNNs in different columns have exactly the same architectures, while in this paper, CNNs in different columns use faces with different resolutions as inputs. Further, in [11], the outputs of CNNs in different columns are averaged, while we use one fully connected layer to connect all features to estimate the coordinates of landmark points in Global CNNs, or to estimate the displacement between the ground truth and the estimation of Global CNNs and Local CNNs. As shown in Fig. 5-(d) that such fully connected layer does improve the facial landmark detection accuracy, which demonstrates the effectiveness of our network architecture.

3.2   Local Convolutional Neural Networks

Global CNNs take a whole image as the input, and obtain an approximate estimation of all landmark points. After the Global CNNs, we use local information around each facial landmark to further predict the displacement between the ground truth S_g and current prediction S_1. We denote such displacement as $\Delta S \doteq S_g - S_1$. One possible choice for Local CNNs is that we design a different CNN for each of the different landmark points [31]. But such a strategy is not scalable because there will be too many networks to be optimized if we have many landmark points (typical standard is 68 landmark points). Moreover, the separate landmark points prediction based on such CNNs may not work well for those missing/occluded facial landmarks because no global shape constraints are imposed.

In this paper, we propose to model and train the Local CNNs for all points simultaneously. For each facial point, we take an $l \times l$ patch around the prediction of Global CNNs S_1. Then we stack all p patches and get an $l \times l \times p$ cuboid. We use this cuboid as the input of the Local CNNs. However, the best patch sizes for predicting the displacement between the ground truth and the previous prediction can be different for different landmark points. For example, for landmark points with larger displacement, larger patch size should be used; and for landmark points with smaller displacement, smaller patches would be enough. To deal with such variability, similar to Global CNNs, we also adopt an MCNNs architecture for the Local CNNs. The overall structure of Local CNNs is shown in Fig. 4-(a). Specifically, we sample the aforementioned patch cuboids with the same sizes for faces with different resolutions based on the results of Global CNNs. Then we use these cuboids as the input to different CNNs in the Local MCNNs. In Local CNNs, the architecture of CNN in each column contains only two convolutional layers, one max pooling layer and one fully connected layer in the end, as shown in Fig. 4-(b). Local CNNs in each column of the Local MCNNs are also pretrained in a similar manner as in the global case. Then we concatenate the output $FC1$ features and map them to ΔS [1]. We denote the mapping function learned by the Local CNNs as $f_L(*)$, and denote the patch cuboids for face x_i as P_{x_i}. Combining the results of Global MCNNs and Local MCNNs, the final coordinates of facial landmarks can be calculated as: $S_2(x_i) = S_1(x_i) + f_L(P_{x_i})$.

3.3   Comparison with Other Approaches

Our work is different from the existing DNN based facial landmark point detection frameworks, including CFAN [41] and DCNN [31], as well as Cascaded Regression methods with Multi-scale feature extraction and concatenation like SDM [38], in the following aspects.

---

[1] In our experiments, ΔS is calculated based on faces with the largest resolution, i.e., 140×140. We find that empirically there is little difference in the results based on Δ calculated with other resolutions.

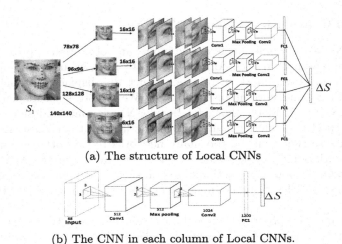

(a) The structure of Local CNNs

(b) The CNN in each column of Local CNNs.

Fig. 4. The architecture of Local CNNs. Dash line indicates the pretraining procedure.

Comparison with CFAN. The coarse-to-fine prediction strategy is commonly used in facial landmark point detection methods, including CFAN, but our method differs from CFAN in the following aspects: (i) Our framework is based on CNNs while CFAN is based on auto-encoder. (ii) Our Local CNNs use local patches as input to further improve the accuracy while CFAN use hand-crafted features as input in the last few levels. (iii) Our local networks only contain two levels while CFAN contains multiple layers. (vi) CFAN employs multi-scale process in a serial way, and each phase only uses face with one resolution. However, our method uses multi-scale process in parallel way, and each level uses faces with several different resolutions. Such multi-column strategy takes full advantage of our findings that different landmark points have different optimal resolutions.

Comparison with DCNN. (i) We propose to use MCNNs to take advantage of faces in multiple resolutions for facial landmark point detection, while Sun *et al.* [31] only use faces of one resolution for alignment. (ii) DCNNs use separate CNNs to refine separate points, but such a strategy is not scalable to facial landmark point detection with multiple points, say 68 points. Meanwhile such a strategy may distort the overall face shape without considering the global shape constraints of all facial points. We propose to use the same CNNs for all points, which implicitly models, learns and encodes the constrains among all points, and also makes our method more scalable to facial landmark point detection with many landmark points.

Comparison with SDM. (i) Non-deep methods like SDM employ the linear regression to learn the mapping from face images to facial landmarks, while deep model uses nonlinear function to regress the facial landmarks with lower error rate. (ii) Mean shape is used as initialization, which is far away from the ground truth. It is worth noting that even our Global CNNs already achieves almost the same performance with SDM on LFPW, as shown in Figs. 5-(c) and 7-(b).

4   Experiments

The implementation of our method is based on CAFFE framework developed by Jia et. al. [19]. We augment the training data through translation, rotation and scaling operations to greatly enlarge the size of training sets. Such data augmentation strategy helps avoid over-fitting and make trained model more robust to pose and scale variations in practical face images. We keep the same data augmentation strategy with [41], and generate 19 images for each face by using random translation, rotation and scaling parameters within the given range. So the whole training set is enlarged by 20 folds for all datasets.

4.1   Evaluation Protocol

We first use 5 commonly used image based facial landmark points detection datasets for evaluation, including XM2VTS [24], LFPW [4], HELEN [21], AFW [43], and iBug [26]. Images in LFPW, HELEN, AFW, and iBug are collected under uncontrolled scenarios, while images in the XM2VTS dataset are collected under a lab environment. Then we evaluate our method with a recently proposed video based facial landmark points detection dataset–the 300-VW [30] dataset.

For image based facial landmark points detection, we directly use the bounding box of faces provided by iBug website [2], the ground truth annotations of 68 landmark points are provided in [26].

We compare our method with the following baseline methods (1) DRMF [3], (2) SDM [38], (3) the work of Zhu et al. [43], (4) the work of Yu et al. [40], (5) CFAN [41], and (6) DCNN [31]. In these baselines, CFAN and DCNN use DNNs for facial landmark point detection and achieve state-of-art performance for facial landmark point detection. By following the work of [3,41], we train the model with 68 landmark points, and evaluate the model with 66 landmark points (The inner corners of mouth are not used in evaluation stage.). The reason for this may be that the relative positions of inner and outer corners of mouth are stable, thus we can predict the coordinates of inner corners based on that of outer corners. The 68 landmark points are shown in Fig. 1. It is worth noting that the comparisons between our method with DRMF, SDM, the work of Zhu et al. , the work of Yu et al. , CFAN are based on 66 points, but our comparisons with DCNN are based on 5 points (two eye centers, two outer mouth corners, and nose tip) because DCNN is not scalable to multiple points.[3]

---

[2] http://ibug.doc.ic.ac.uk/resources/300-VW/.

[3] Multiple CNNs are trained for each point, there would a large amount of CNNs to be trained for multiple landmark points detection in DCNN, which cannot be done. Therefore DCNN is not scalable to the number of landmark points.

As for the evaluation metric, we utilize the commonly used normalized root mean squared error (NRMSE) to measure the errors between the predicted landmark points and the ground truth. For the ith ($\imath = 1, \ldots, p$) landmark point whose ground truth coordinates are (x_g^i, y_g^i) and predicted coordinates are (x_p^i, y_p^i), if the distance between two eye centers as d, then NRMSE can be calculated as follows $\text{NRMSE} = \frac{1}{p} \sum_{i=1}^{p} \frac{\sqrt{(x_g^i - x_p^i)^2 + (y_g^i - y_p^i)^2}}{d}$.

Here d is used to get rid of the effect of different image sizes in the comparison of different methods. Then a cumulative distribution function (CDF) of NRMSE is used for the evaluation of different methods.

4.2   Evaluation of Different Components in Bi-Level MCNNs

The following experiment is designed to measure the functions of different components in our bi-level MCNNs framework. We follow the commonly used experimental setup in LFPW [41] to conduct the model evaluation experiments. Specifically, the training set includes the LFPW training set [4], HELEN [21] and AFW [43], and the test set is the test set of LFPW [4]. All the following experiments follow the same setting unless a different setting is specified.

Single Column CNNs vs. MCNNs. We show the performance difference between single column CNNs and MCNNs for both Global CNNs and Local CNNs in Fig. 5-(a) and (b). It is clear to see that the single column CNN performs worse than MCNNs for both Global CNNs and Local CNNs, because MCNNs leverages the advantages of faces with different resolutions for global face estimation in Global CNNs, and MCNNs leverage the patches sampled at different scales for the displacement prediction of all landmark points in Local CNNs. The detection accuracy improvement of MCNNs over best single column CNN is about 8.7 % when NRMSE is 0.05 in Global CNNs, which is already very significant for facial landmark point detection.

Global MCNNs vs. Local MCNNs. The performance of Global CNNs and Local CNNs is shown in Fig. 5-(c). This figure clearly shows that Local CNNs improve upon the performance of Global CNNs because the local information is used to correct the prediction errors of the Global CNNs. Further, as we can see from the results, the CDF of Global CNNs is 0.45 when NRMSE is 0.1, which is significantly better than mean shape, and such a performance is already very close to the cumulative error distribution curve of SDM [38] on LFPW (Please refer to Fig. 7-(a)). This further demonstrates the effectiveness of MCNNs.

Averaging vs. FC layer. We also compare the effect of averaging strategy and fully connected layer(FC) after multicolumn CNN on LFPW, and the results are shown in Fig. 5-(d). It clearly shows that our strategy achieves better accuracy than the averaging strategy in MDNN [11], which demonstrates the effectiveness our network architecture.

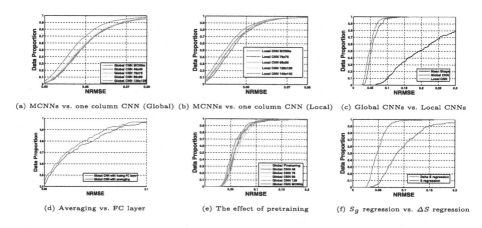

(a) MCNNs vs. one column CNN (Global) (b) MCNNs vs. one column CNN (Local) (c) Global CNNs vs. Local CNNs

(d) Averaging vs. FC layer   (e) The effect of pretraining   (f) S_g regression vs. ΔS regression

Fig. 5. The effect of different components in our MCNNs, evaluated on LFPW. (Best viewed in color)

Importance of Pretraining for MCNNs. Figure 5-(e) shows the results of MCNNs with pretraining and MCNNs without pretraining. As there are too many parameters in MCNNs, if MCNNs are trained without pretraining, its performance is even worse than that of each single column CNN in MCNNs. The reason for this phenomenon may be that if there are too many parameters to be optimized in MCNNs, the deep architecture will cause the effect of gradient vanishing. Thus parameter optimization may easily get stuck in some poor local minimum. Similar to the pretraining in deep belief network [18], the preptraining in MCNNs may help MCNNs to start with a good initialization which makes the whole network converge to a good solution, hence helps the facial landmark point detection.

ΔS regression vs. S_g regression in Local CNNs. In our Local CNNs, we use MCNNs to map the raw patches to the displacement (ΔS) between the ground truth and current estimation of Global CNNs. Besides the ΔS regression, we also try to use patches to directly estimate S_g. We show results of these two different strategies in Fig. 5-(f). We can see that the ΔS regression achieves higher accuracy. Since each patch does not contain any global information any more, it would be quite difficult to predict the absolute coordinates of the landmark points in the whole image by using local patches only. Therefore the displacement regression would be a better choice for local refinement.

Bi-Level is sufficient. We show the NRMSE on the training set for both Global CNNs and Local CNNs in Fig. 6 on the LFPW dataset. We can see that the training NRMSE for Global CNNs is not so good on training data, so the performance can be further improved by refinement. However, with the help of Local CNNs, the training NRMSE is significantly reduced and there is almost no space left to further improve the NRMSE. So this suggests Bi-Level MCNNs structure

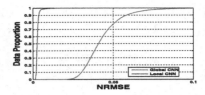

Fig. 6. The cumulative error distribution curves of our method on the training set of LFPW.

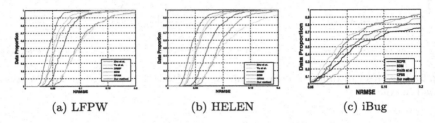

(a) LFPW   (b) HELEN   (c) iBug

Fig. 7. Performance comparison of different different methods on LFPW, HELEN, and iBug with 68 landmark points. (Best viewed in color)

already has enough modeling capacity to fit the training data, and no deeper architectures are needed. [4]

Time costs. We test the running time of our method on LFPW. Our algorithm is implemented with Spyder(Python 2.7) on the NVIDIA GeForce GTX 980 GPU platform. We run our program 22 times and obtain the average running time for each image. More precisely, the average running time of Global CNNs is 3.15ms, while the running time of Local CNNs is 1.24ms. The time cost of Global and Local CNNs is 9.51ms and 11.09ms, respectively on a CPU. Following the work Ref [17], on LFPW, the time reported doesnt include cropping and scaling time on LFPW (The time cost for cropping and scaling is about 0.7ms and 0.9ms, respectively).

4.3   Performance Comparison on Image Based Landmark Point Detection Datasets

The dateset introduction and experimental setup on LFPW, HELEN, and iBug are listed as follows: (i) Labeled Face Parts in the Wild (LFPW) dataset [4] consists of 1432 face images taken from wild condition. These faces are further

---

[4] It is also worth noting that our Bi-Level MCNNs architecture leverages the idea of error correction with deep structure which is also used in the work of CFAN [41], deep residual network [17], and pose estimation [8]. The number of levels (the depth of error correction components) should be determined by a specific task. Empirically we found that bi-level is enough for face alignment by using our method.

divided into 1132 training images and 300 test images. The faces in this dataset show large variations in pose, illumination, expression and partial occlusion, which is aimed to test facial point detection under uncontrolled conditions. [4] provides only image URLs and some image links are not available any more. Therefore, by following the work of [41], we use the 811 training samples and 224 test samples provided on iBug website for training and testing. The DRMF method uses the tree-based face detector to arrive more accurate face detection. (ii) Helen dataset [21] is collected under wild conditions. There are 2330 images with large variations in pose, lighting, occlusion and expression. By following the evaluation convention on this dataset [41], the images from Helen training set, LFPW training set and AFW are used to train our models. The 330 images from Helen test set are used to evaluate all methods. (iii) The iBug dataset is recently released, and it is used for facial landmark detection challenge. This dataset contains 135 images. By following the work of [42], we use the images from Helen training set, LFPW training set and AFW as training set.

The performance of different methods on these datasets is shown in Fig. 7. We can see that our method achieves the best performance on LFPW, HELEN. On the very challenging iBug, our method achieves comparable accuracy with Coarse-to-Fine Shape Searching [42] which is a non-CNN based method, but with less running time (4.39ms vs 28ms). Specifically, on LFPW dataset, our method has the best performance on this dataset, even better than SDM, which benefitted from its supervised descent solution. Furthermore, by comparing this figure with Fig. 5-(a), we can see that the predictions of the Global CNNs already have the almost same performance as the final results of CFAN. In this experiment, testing data is collected in the lab and has similar pose, expression and illumination, while training data has significant variation in pose, expression and illumination. The distributions of training and test data are very different, but our method still achieves very good performance, which indicates our method is robust to the out-of-database challenge. On LPFW, our method achieves a better prediction accuracy with an improvement up to about 20 % than CFAN when NRMSE is smaller than 0.05, and such an improvement is rather significant. On HELEN, CFAN performs the best among all existing methods, whereas our method outperforms CFAN and achieves the best performance among all, which further demonstrates the effectiveness of our method.

We show the average error (%) of all points for Coarse to fine shape matching (CFSS) [42] and project out cascaded regression (POCR) [34] and our work under the following two commonly used settings in Tables 1 and 2. We can see that our

Table 1. 49 points

Dataset	CFSS	POCR	Ours
LFPW	3.80	4.08	3.65
HELEN	3.50	3.90	3.49

Table 2. 68 points

Dataset	CFSS	Ours
LFPW	4.90	4.60
HELEN	4.72	4.66

method outperforms CFSS and POCR which demonstrates the effectiveness of our method.

Moreover, we also show the detected landmark points for some representative images in LFPW in Fig. 8. We can see that our model is robust to the variances in occlusion, expression, as well as pose.

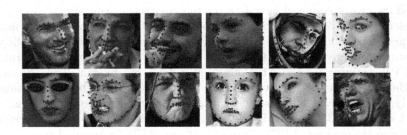

Fig. 8. Some facial landmark point detection results on LFPW, HELEN, and iBug.

4.4   Comparisons on 300-VW Video Based Landmark Points Detection Challenge

We also evaluate our method with the ICCV'2015 300 Videos in the Wild (300-VW) Challenge [10,30,34] to show our method's extension ability. This competition aims at evaluating the ability of different systems for fitting unseen persons with different poses, expressions, illuminations, occlusions, and image quality. The videos are further separated into three different categories: (i) Category one contains faces recorded with well lighting condition but with various head poses and occlusions; (ii) Category two contains faces captured with different illuminations and expressions; (iii) Category three contains videos captured under arbitrary conditions, including the change in illumination, occlusion, expression, pose, *etc.* We treat each frame as one image without taking advantage of the relationships of frames between consecutive frames.[5] By following the setup of 300-VW, we train one single model with all training data and test on different testing categories. The complete 300-VW dataset has been released[6]. We requested the training/test split used in the 300-VW challenge from the competition organizers. Therefore the comparisons between the performance of our method and results reported in the competition is fair.

The performance of different methods is shown in Fig. 9. In category one, our method achieves comparable accuracy with the work of Yang *et al.* [39] which

---

[5] As our method can process each 1280×720 frame in about 0.011 secs, which satisfies the requirements that the submitted trackers should track with a speed of at least 2 secs/frame in 300-VW challenge. 300VW competition requires the participants to report the total time costs including that of cropping and scaling, thus the time is different from that reported on LFPW.

[6] http://ibug.doc.ic.ac.uk/download/300VW_Dataset_2015_12_14.zip/.

achieved the best accuracy in category one in this challenge. In category two, our work still achieves similar performance with that of Yang *et al.* [39], but is less accurate than the work of Xiao *et al.* [37], which achieved the highest accuracy in category two in this challenge. It is worth noting that in category two, [37] uses temporal information to track the landmark points. By considering the relationships between facial landmark points in neighbouring frames, the performance of our method is likely to be further boosted. Even though temporal information is not used in our work in category three where videos are recorded under arbitrary condition, such as videos with occlusions, large pose variations, and sudden changes in expressions, our method greatly outperforms the work of Yang *et al.* [39] and that of Xiao *et al.* [37], and achieves the highest accuracy. The performance of our method on 300-VW further demonstrates the effectiveness of our method for facial landmark points detection.

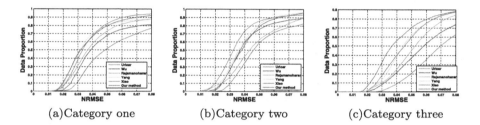

(a)Category one   (b)Category two   (c)Category three

Fig. 9. Performance comparisons of different methods on 300-VW challenge (Best viewed in color)

5   Conclusion

We propose a multi-columns coarse-to-fine CNN framework for facial landmark points detection, and such strategy demonstrates good performance on publicly available datasets. In future, we will apply the proposed method for video based face alignment, i.e., use the output of previous frame as a rough estimation of next frame, and use local CNNs to fine-tune the landmark points. Further, the proposed framework can also be applied for pose estimation.

References

1. Amberg, B., Vetter, T.: Optimal landmark detection using shape models and branch and bound. In: ICCV, pp. 455–462. IEEE (2011)
2. Ashraf, A.B., Lucey, S., Cohn, J.F., Chen, T., Ambadar, Z., Prkachin, K.M., Solomon, P.E.: The painful face-pain expression recognition using active appearance models. Image Vis. Comput. **27**(12), 1788–1796 (2009)
3. Asthana, A., Zafeiriou, S., Cheng, S., Pantic, M.: Robust discriminative response map fitting with constrained local models. In: CVPR, pp. 3444–3451. IEEE (2013)

4. Belhumeur, P.N., Jacobs, D.W., Kriegman, D.J., Kumar, N.: Localizing parts of faces using a consensus of exemplars. Pattern Anal. Mach. Intell. IEEE Trans. **35**(12), 2930–2940 (2013)
5. Burgos-Artizzu, X.P., Perona, P.: Dollár, P.: Robust face landmark estimation under occlusion. In: ICCV, pp. 1513–1520. IEEE (2013)
6. Cao, C., Hou, Q., Zhou, K.: Displaced dynamic expression regression for real-time facial tracking and animation. ACM Trans. Graph. (TOG) **33**(4), 43 (2014)
7. Cao, X., Wei, Y., Wen, F., Sun, J.: Face alignment by explicit shape regression (Dec 27 2012), uS Patent Ap. 13/728,584
8. Carreira, J., Agrawal, P., Fragkiadaki, K., Malik, J.: Human pose estimation with iterative error feedback. arXiv preprint (2015). arXiv:1507.06550
9. Chen, C., Dantcheva, A., Ross, A.: Automatic facial makeup detection with application in face recognition. In: Biometrics (ICB), pp. 1–8. IEEE (2013)
10. Chrysos, G., Antonakos, E., Zafeiriou, S., Snape, P.: Offline deformable face tracking in arbitrary videos. In: ICCVW, pp. 1–9 (2015)
11. Ciresan, D., Meier, U., Schmidhuber, J.: Multi-column deep neural networks for image classification. In: CVPR, pp. 3642–3649. IEEE (2012)
12. Cootes, T.F., Edwards, G.J., Taylor, C.J.: Active appearance models. IEEE Trans. Pattern Anal. Mach. Intell. **6**, 681–685 (2001)
13. Cootes, T.F., Taylor, C.J., Cooper, D.H., Graham, J.: Active shape models-their training and application. Comput. Vis. Image Underst. **61**(1), 38–59 (1995)
14. Cristinacce, D., Cootes, T.F.: Feature detection and tracking with constrained local models. In: BMVC. vol. 1, p. 3. Citeseer (2006)
15. Dantone, M., Gall, J., Fanelli, G., Van Gool, L.: Real-time facial feature detection using conditional regression forests. In: CVPR, pp. 2578–2585. IEEE (2012)
16. Gu, L., Kanade, T.: A generative shape regularization model for robust face alignment. In: Forsyth, D., Torr, P., Zisserman, A. (eds.) ECCV 2008, Part I. LNCS, vol. 5302, pp. 413–426. Springer, Heidelberg (2008)
17. He, K., Zhang, X., Ren, S., Sun, J.: Deep residual learning for image recognition. arXiv preprint (2015). arXiv:1512.03385
18. Hinton, G.E., Osindero, S., Teh, Y.W.: A fast learning algorithm for deep belief nets. Neural Comput. **18**(7), 1527–1554 (2006)
19. Jia, Y., Shelhamer, E., Donahue, J., Karayev, S., Long, J., Girshick, R., Guadarrama, S., Darrell, T.: Caffe: Convolutional architecture for fast feature embedding. arXiv preprint (2014). arXiv:1408.5093
20. Krizhevsky, A., Sutskever, I., Hinton, G.E.: Imagenet classification with deep convolutional neural networks. In: Advances in Neural Information Processing Systems, pp. 1097–1105 (2012)
21. Le, V., Brandt, J., Lin, Z., Bourdev, L., Huang, T.S.: Interactive facial feature localization. In: Fitzgibbon, A., Lazebnik, S., Perona, P., Sato, Y., Schmid, C. (eds.) ECCV 2012, Part III. LNCS, vol. 7574, pp. 679–692. Springer, Heidelberg (2012)
22. Liang, L., Xiao, R., Wen, F., Sun, J.: Face alignment via component-based discriminative search. In: Forsyth, D., Torr, P., Zisserman, A. (eds.) ECCV 2008, Part II. LNCS, vol. 5303, pp. 72–85. Springer, Heidelberg (2008)
23. Liu, X.: Generic face alignment using boosted appearance model. In: CVPR, pp. 1–8. IEEE (2007)
24. Messer, K., Matas, J., Kittler, J., Luettin, J., Maitre, G.: Xm2vtsdb: The extended m2vts database. In: Second international conference on audio and video-based biometric person authentication. vol. 964, pp. 965–966. Citeseer (1999)

25. Milborrow, S., Nicolls, F.: Locating facial features with an extended active shape model. In: Forsyth, D., Torr, P., Zisserman, A. (eds.) ECCV 2008, Part IV. LNCS, vol. 5305, pp. 504–513. Springer, Heidelberg (2008)
26. Sagonas, C., Tzimiropoulos, G., Zafeiriou, S., Pantic, M.: A semi-automatic methodology for facial landmark annotation. In: CVPRW, pp. 896–903. IEEE (2013)
27. Saragih, J.M., Lucey, S., Cohn, J.F.: Face alignment through subspace constrained mean-shifts. In: ICCV, pp. 1034–1041. IEEE (2009)
28. Sauer, P., Cootes, T.F., Taylor, C.J.: Accurate regression procedures for active appearance models. In: BMVC, pp. 1–11 (2011)
29. Schroff, F., Kalenichenko, D., Philbin, J.: Facenet: A unified embedding for face recognition and clustering. arXiv preprint (2015). arXiv:1503.03832
30. Shen, J., Zafeiriou, S., Chrysos, G.G., Kossaifi, J., Tzimiropoulos, G., Pantic, M.: The first facial landmark tracking in-the-wild challenge: Benchmark and results. In: Proceedings of the IEEE International Conference on Computer Vision Workshops, pp. 50–58 (2015)
31. Sun, Y., Wang, X., Tang, X.: Deep convolutional network cascade for facial point detection. In: CVPR, pp. 3476–3483. IEEE (2013)
32. Sun, Y., Wang, X., Tang, X.: Deep learning face representation from predicting 10,000 classes. In: CVPR, pp. 1891–1898. IEEE (2014)
33. Taigman, Y., Yang, M., Ranzato, M., Wolf, L.: Deepface: Closing the gap to human-level performance in face verification. In: CVPR, pp. 1701–1708. IEEE (2014)
34. Tzimiropoulos, G.: Project-out cascaded regression with an application to face alignment. In: CVPR, pp. 3659–3667. IEEE (2015)
35. Valstar, M., Martinez, B., Binefa, X., Pantic, M.: Facial point detection using boosted regression and graph models. In: CVPR, pp. 2729–2736. IEEE (2010)
36. Wu, H., Liu, X., Doretto, G.: Face alignment via boosted ranking model. In: CVPR, pp. 1–8. IEEE (2008)
37. Xiao, S., Yan, S., Kassim, A.: Facial landmark detection via progressive initialization. In: ICCVW, pp. 33–40 (2015)
38. Xiong, X., De la Torre, F.: Supervised descent method and its applications to face alignment. In: CVPR, pp. 532–539. IEEE (2013)
39. Yang, J., Deng, J., Zhang, K., Liu, Q.: Facial shape tracking via spatio-temporal cascade shape regression. In: ICCVW, pp. 41–49 (2015)
40. Yu, X., Huang, J., Zhang, S., Yan, W., Metaxas, D.N.: Pose-free facial landmark fitting via optimized part mixtures and cascaded deformable shape model. In: ICCV, pp. 1944–1951. IEEE (2013)
41. Zhang, J., Shan, S., Kan, M., Chen, X.: Coarse-to-fine auto-encoder networks (CFAN) for real-time face alignment. In: Fleet, D., Pajdla, T., Schiele, B., Tuytelaars, T. (eds.) ECCV 2014, Part II. LNCS, vol. 8690, pp. 1–16. Springer, Heidelberg (2014)
42. Zhu, S., Li, C., Loy, C.C., Tang, X.: Face alignment by coarse-to-fine shape searching. In: Proceedings of the IEEE Conference on Computer Vision and Pattern Recognition, pp. 4998–5006 (2015)
43. Zhu, X., Ramanan, D.: Face detection, pose estimation, and landmark localization in the wild. In: CVPR, pp. 2879–2886. IEEE (2012)

Fully Automated and Highly Accurate Dense Correspondence for Facial Surfaces

Carl Martin Grewe$^{(\boxtimes)}$ and Stefan Zachow

Mathematics for Life and Materials Sciences, Zuse Institute Berlin, Berlin, Germany
{grewe,zachow}@zib.de

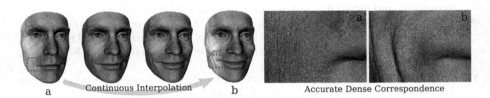

Fig. 1. Two facial expressions (a,b) from our database set into dense correspondence using the proposed framework. High geometric and photometric details are accurately morphed between both expressions via a dense corresponding mesh.

Abstract. We present a novel framework for fully automated and highly accurate determination of facial landmarks and dense correspondence, *e.g.* a topologically identical mesh of arbitrary resolution, across the entire surface of 3D face models. For robustness and reliability of the proposed approach, we are combining 2D landmark detectors and 3D statistical shape priors with a variational matching method. Instead of matching faces in the spatial domain only, we employ image registration to align the 2D parametrization of the facial surface to a planar template we call the *Unified Facial Parameter Domain* (UFPD). This allows us to simultaneously match salient photometric and geometric facial features using robust image similarity measures while reasonably constraining geometric distortion in regions with less significant features. We demonstrate the accuracy of the dense correspondence established by our framework on the BU3DFE database with 2500 facial surfaces and show, that our framework outperforms current state-of-the-art methods with respect to the fully automated location of facial landmarks.

Keywords: Dense face matching · Face shape and appearance models · Markerless motion capture

Electronic supplementary material The online version of this chapter (doi:10.1007/978-3-319-48881-3_38) contains supplementary material, which is available to authorized users.

G. Hua and H. Jégou (Eds.): ECCV 2016 Workshops, Part II, LNCS 9914, pp. 552–568, 2016.
DOI: 10.1007/978-3-319-48881-3_38

1   Introduction

The fully automated matching of sparse or dense facial landmarks in unconstrained 2D or 3D measurement data, *e.g.* the semantic annotation of facial images captured *in the wild*, is of great interest in various fields, ranging from entertainment to affective computing. When dealing with conventional cameras, the loss of information due to the perspective projection requires sophisticated techniques for robust estimation of pose or facial landmarks. Even more demanding is the ill-posed inverse problem of estimating the 3D shape from 2D images. Knowledge about plausible variations in facial shape and appearance as well as their correlation are learned from training samples and used to constrain results to desired solutions especially in unconstrained environments. Similarly, for the semantic annotation and tracking of facial features from 3D data, statistical shape and appearance models (SSAM) of faces improve the reliability and robustness of automated approaches as has been shown recently [1].

Facial morphology varies between individuals due to factors like sex, age, or ethnicity, while significant intra-individual changes are caused by facial expressions. Although 3D databases including a wide variety of both, inter- and intra-individual factors, are publicly available (*e.g.* [2,3]), the training samples used to construct statistical face models are restricted to face scans in neutral position (see [4,5]). Only few models include expressions, for instance the work published by Brunton, Bolkart, and Wuhrer in [6] or Cao *et al.* [7]. Unfortunately, these models do not include appearance and solely capture 3D shape variation. They are thus limited for applications in computer vision.

A reason for the rare availability of statistical models of facial shape and appearance lies in the challenging problem of dense correspondence estimation for faces. Many generic shape matching methods as well as approaches specifically tuned to estimate dense correspondence for faces have been proposed, but they either lack accuracy, robustness or automation. Nevertheless, approaches satisfying all these characteristics are needed to establish the next generation of 3D face models, and in order to handle improved geometric and photometric resolution of new scanning devices, growing 3D databases, and applications requiring highly accurate semantic annotation of faces in raw measurement data.

With applications for fully automated processing of large-scale databases in mind, we propose a new framework for dense 3D face matching (see Fig. 2). To ensure robustness of the automated processing, we extract reliable prior knowledge on facial shape and appearance from the input data using 2D facial landmark detectors and non-rigid fitting of 3D face models. Highly-accurate dense correspondence, even for fine facial structures (see Fig. 1), is obtained by combining the prior knowledge with a variational approach for the matching of geometric and photometric facial features. We evaluate and compare the performance of our method in localizing facial landmarks on 2500 scans of the publicly available BU3DFE dataset [2] as well as on 400 high-resolution 3D face models acquired using our own prototypic stereophotogrammetric setup. The accuracy of the dense correspondence established by our method can not only be used to improve various applications such as the retargeting of facial shape and texture

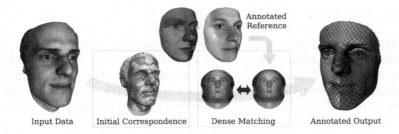

Fig. 2. The proposed framework includes two stages for initialization and dense match-ing of accurate correspondence. The matching allows to transfer semantic annotations and a reference mesh to the input data.

or the detection of facial expressions. By providing the basis for fully automated computation of individual blendshape rigs as well as large-scale statistical face models, our framework opens up new directions for computer vision tasks, par-ticularly in the emerging field of consumer devices equipped with 3D sensors.

2   Related Work

Semantic face annotation has been subject of active research in different com-munities during the last twenty years. The general problem can be stated as the definition of inter-individually corresponding facial landmarks, ranging from few landmarks at clear anatomical structures to an arbitrary number of points covering the entire face, and their identification in raw measurement data. How-ever, the measurement device and its sensor characteristics affect how accurately significant features can be located and distinguished from other landmarks as well as from surrounding facial and non-facial parts.

In the case of 2D images taken with conventional cameras, a great variety of algorithms exist for the detection of sparse facial landmarks [8]. Usually, locally significant, intensity-based features around landmark points are extracted from facial images contained in a database and used to train landmark predictors. Current methods are able to locate the silhouette of a face, as well as a number of sparse landmarks reliably from the frontal view in presence of a wide range of inter- and intra-individual variation even in unconstrained situations [9–12]. Sim-ilarly, for the detection of sparse landmarks on 3D measurement data, knowledge about characteristic geometric properties is gathered from an annotated data-base. For instance, in [13–15] local quantities like geodesic length, surface area or curvature measures are employed to learn the relevant features of distinct facial landmarks for later prediction.

More challenging is the problem of establishing dense correspondence across the entire face where landmarks cannot be clearly defined by local photographic or geometric features. Instead, correspondence estimation in regions like the cheeks or the forehead is usually constrained by means of mathematical objec-tives. In the case of 2D warping techniques, the topological subdivision of the facial region into geometric primitives allows the definition of dense correspondence. For example in [16,17], triangular patches covering the facial region are established and affinely warped to match new landmark positions. These approaches yield continuous correspondence mappings for the entire face varying inter- and intra-individually, but suffer from the strong assumption of affine warps.

Recent methods that directly operate in the 3D domain take advantage of the ability to measure distortion of the surface or the embedding space when deforming a shape into an other. In the computer graphics community, general non-rigid shape matching approaches have been developed that are based, for instance, on the *as-isometric-as-possible* assumption or by measuring the deformation energy (*e.g.* [18–22] for a comprehensive survey). A common strategy often adopted in computer vision tasks is to use spatial warping techniques, like non-linear variants of the well-known Iterative Closest Point algorithm (ICP) [23], that deform a template surface into the target *e.g.* by locally constraining coherent deformation of the surface (see *Coherent Point Drift* for a general technique [24], and [4,5] particularly for faces).

When matching objects of a specific type, like human faces, methods significantly benefit from additional prior knowledge that is incorporated into the matching process. For instance in [7,14], a 3D statistical shape model (SSM) of the face is fitted to the target. Non-linear ICP is then used to warp the template to the target in order to project dense correspondence. Similarly in [15], Gilani, Shafait, and Ajmal combined feature detectors based on geodesic curves with the fitting of a deformable model to assign dense corresponding points to unseen faces. The advantages of these methods are their reliability and robustness, which make them ideally suited for the automated processing of large databases. However, the accuracy of the established correspondence is limited, mainly because of two reasons: (1) The constraints derived from the prior knowledge are not flexible enough to match individual features, and (2) most approaches only use the facial geometry for matching.

Alternatively, the problem of face matching can be casted into an image registration task. Using the continuous parametrization of the target and the template surfaces, their features can be commonly mapped into the plane (see Fig. 3). In [25], annotated surface patches were matched to a template by mapping both to the unit circle. Via the common parametrization, dense correspondence was established to build a statistical shape model of anatomical structures that was successfully applied in medical image processing [26,27]. Additionally, methods like Optical Flow can be used to improve dense correspondence between the flattened photographic textures. As appearance varies heavily between individuals, the method of [28,29] applied a smoothing filter to the estimated flow field to obtain valid correspondences. By exploiting the temporal dependency between successive scans recorded with professional 3D video setups, recent work has shown that highly accurate dense correspondence can be established over entire facial performances of an actor [30–32]. Kaiser *et al.* [33] as well as Savran and Sankur [34] proposed variational registration methods employing robust similar-

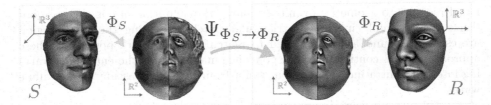

Fig. 3. Matching of a facial surface S to the reference R: Parametrizations Φ_S and Φ_R are computed and photometric as well as geometric features are mapped to the plane. The dense correspondence mapping $\Psi_{\Phi_S \to \Phi_R}$ accurately registers photographic and geometric features from S and R.

ity measures on photographic and geometric features. They showed that image registration methods can be used to successfully establish accurate dense correspondence between individuals. However, variational approaches are typically prone to converge to undesired local minima or require additional user interaction, which prevents them from being used in a fully automated processing of large-scale face databases.

3   Challenges and Overview

The estimation of dense correspondences on human faces is particularly challenging, mainly due to the following reasons: (1) global facial morphology significantly varies between individuals, (2) facial expressions cause large intra-individual changes in shape and appearance, and (3) large regions like the cheeks or the forehead provide little information on correspondence between individuals.

To build a fully automated method for accurate dense correspondence estimation on human faces, we propose a novel pipeline that addresses these challenges by combining the reliability of methods using prior knowledge with the accuracy of variational matching based on image registration (see Fig. 2). Our key contribution can be divided into two subsequent processing stages:

1. Given a photographically textured raw 3D surface S, we estimate reliable initial correspondence using 2D facial landmark detectors and non-rigid fitting of a 3D SSAM to S. The initial correspondence estimates are used to compute a parametrization for the surface $\Phi_S : S \subset \mathbb{R}^3 \mapsto \mathbb{R}^2$ that maps features into the plane as reliable initial values for variational correspondence matching.
2. We employ an image registration approach to estimate a mapping $\Psi_{\Phi_S \to \Phi_R} : \mathbb{R}^2 \mapsto \mathbb{R}^2$ that optimizes dense correspondence accurately by matching individual photographic and geometric features from Φ_S to a reference template Φ_R which we call *Unified Facial Parameter Domain* (UFPD) (see Fig. 3).

By using prior information to compute Φ_S, our framework accounts for challenges (1) and (2). The combination of photometric and geometric features with reasonable constraints which penalize non-isometric deformations during image

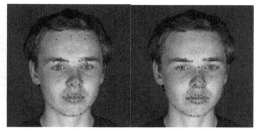

Fig. 4. Left: Our prototypical stereophotogrammetric setup. Right: Facial landmarks detected in a frontal view using implementations of [35] and [11]. The set of landmarks used for SSAM fitting and parametrization are marked in green. (Color figure online)

registration further helps to define correspondence according to (3) and to accurately match intra- and inter-individual features that have roughly been aligned in the first stage.

A central concept of our approach is the definition of the planar UFPD $\subset$ $[0,1]^2$ (see Subsect. 4.1). We propose the UFPD as the reference template domain Φ_R aggregating all relevant information for robust and reliable optimization of the dense correspondence mapping $\Psi_{\Phi_S \to \Phi_R}$. Similar to the template provided by face SSMs, we learn significant geometric and photometric features in the UFPD from our high-resolution face database, that serves as the reference during the variational matching stage. Using the inverse of $\Psi_{\Phi_S \to \Phi_R}$, we are able to transfer a dense corresponding mesh to the surface S via $\Phi_S^{-1} \circ \Psi_{\Phi_S \to \Phi_R}^{-1} \circ \Phi_R$.

4 Method

This section describes the main parts of our matching framework. The data is acquired with our prototypical stereophotogrammetric setup using eight DSLR cameras (six Nikon D800E, two Nikon D810, 36 MP each) in four stereo-pairs, and two flashes (Elinchrom 1000) arranged in a semicircular arc around a common focal point. We employed the method of Beeler *et al.* [36] for stereo-matching and *Poisson surface reconstruction* [37] to obtain detailed facial surfaces. High-resolution photographic textures are seamlessly composed by *Poisson image editing* [38]. Before describing the processing stages for new facial surfaces in detail, we define the UFPD as follows.

4.1 The Unified Facial Parameter Domain

A key strategy of our framework is a *Unified Facial Parameter Domain* (UFPD), that serves as a flattened facial template during variational matching similar to [28]. As the UFPD $\subset [0,1]^2$ represents inter- and intra-individually varying faces, we propose to learn significant photometric and geometric facial features from a representative database.

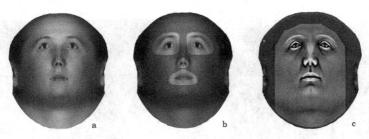

Fig. 5. The *unified facial parameter domain*: average photographic texture with the set of sparse landmarks (a), the same texture overlayed with its corresponding weight map (b) and the curvature where values are mapped to a normalized gray scale ranging from black (min) to white (max) (c).

Initially, a reference parametrization Φ_R of the average face of the *Basel Face Model* (BFM, see [4]) has been computed employing the *QuadCover* method presented in [39] as it minimizes isometric distortion. Using Φ_R, the set of sparse facial landmarks provided by the 2D landmark detectors as described in Subsect. 4.2 is marked on the average face and mapped to the UFPD accordingly. As the BFM only provides low-resolution vertex colors, we have computed an average photographic texture (16 MP resolution) from the high-resolution face database acquired with our own setup by projecting the initial parametrization of the fitted BFM to the facial surfaces (see Subsect. 4.2). The rendered textures were then median-averaged to retain sharp edges and salient features around anatomical structures like the eyes. We use mean curvature as the geometric feature of each surface during surface matching. To avoid unwanted influence of non-corresponding high-frequency features like facial hair or small wrinkles, all surfaces were filtered using Laplacian surface smoothing. According to the generation of the photographic texture, the averaged mean curvature images were mapped to the UFPD (see Fig. 5).

To account for the specific value of the photometric and geometric features in various facial regions during dense correspondence optimization, we have defined weight maps in the UFPD. The photometric texture is particularly informative in the regions around the eyes, eye-brows, and mouth because they clearly separate skin from other anatomical structures. Similarly, the color of the nostrils is highly valuable for matching due to its high contrast to the skin tone. The geometric features are matched on the entire facial surface except the outer hairline, because this region varies heavily between individuals and disrupts the matching procedure.

Together the set of sparse landmarks, the textures and the weight maps define the UFPD as shown in Fig. 5. Note that the particular definition of UFPD is done once in advance and is independent of the proposed approach. In principle, the parametrization of the UFPD is extensible and can simply be adopted to different scenarios. Additional features or weight maps used for dense matching can easily be integrated.

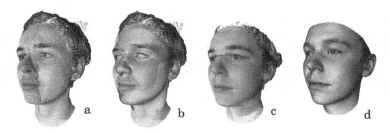

Fig. 6. For model fitting to (a), the SSAM is first rigidly aligned using 3D landmarks (b) and fitted to the data (c). The resulting SSAM instance as shown in (d) roughly matches the facial features (mouth, nose or eyes).

4.2   Initial Estimation of Facial Landmarks

The detection of sparse facial landmarks is done on the frontal view of a face using two state-of-the-art algorithms (see Fig. 4). The method of Kazemi and Sullivan [11] employs cascades of weak learners, which showed to be more accurate in detecting landmarks with respect to individual morphological features and facial expressions. STASM provided by Milborrow and Nicolls [35] fits a statistical shape and appearance model to the image data and appeared to be more robust. Both methods detect 68 and 77 facial landmarks in frontal faces, respectively. We combined a set of well-defined landmarks faithfully predicted by both approaches for further processing (Exo- and Endocanthion, Pronasale, and Cheilion).

Dense correspondence is further estimated using an SSAM fitted to the raw 3D data similar to [7] (see Fig. 6). Since we desire a combination of shape and color information for better alignment of significant structures like the eyes or mouth, we implemented a fitting routine using the BFM. The sparse facial landmarks are used to estimate the initial parameters of the similarity transform aligning the SSAM with the raw data by performing a single ICP step [23]. Starting with the average face of the BFM, new shape and intensity parameters $P = (P_S \in \mathbb{R}^m, P_I \in \mathbb{R}^n)$ are obtained as the maximum-aposteriori estimates employing a centered isotropic Gaussian prior with hyper-parameter $\sigma = (\sigma_S, \sigma_I)$ according to

$$p(P|C) \sim p(C|P)\, p(P|0, \sigma), \tag{1}$$

where $C \subset \mathbb{N} \times \mathbb{N} \times \mathbb{R}$ is our set of robust landmarks between the SSAM and the point cloud with an additional weight assigned. For color estimation, correspondence is established by nearest-neighbour lookup, while for shape estimation, points are also matched by similar colors. Data likelihoods $p(C|P)$ are defined as isotropic Gaussians according to their Euclidean distance by

$$p(C|P) = \prod_{(i,j,\beta) \in C} \mathcal{N}(x_i | m_j, \beta), \tag{2}$$

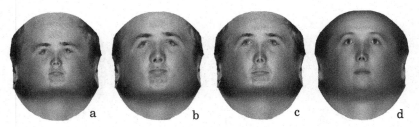

a   b   c   d

Fig. 7. Initial parametrizations Φ_S for a sad expression computed without any soft-constraints (a), with constraints for the inner vertices V° (b), and additionally combined with facial landmarks L (c). Note that the latter already aligns features to the UFPD nicely (d).

where x_i are positions or colors of the point cloud and m_j of model vertices. Varying point density in both, the BFM as well as the target, introduces a bias into the data likelihood $p(C|P)$ (*e.g.* high vertex density around the cheeks in the BFM). We therefore determined the correspondence weights β to be the inverse sum of both frequencies, in which each point occurs in the set of correspondences. Correspondences are determined in each optimization step and new parameters for shape and intensity are estimated using the solution of the system of linear equations with Tikhonov regularization (see [40]) equivalent to Eq. 1.

4.3   Computation of the Initial Parametrization Φ_S

Because variational methods are prone to convergence to local minima, we propose a method to estimate the initial parametrization Φ_S, such that it roughly aligns with features of the UFPD. We constrain the computation of Φ_S using the sparse facial landmarks and the reference parametrization Φ_R projected from the fitted SSAM.

The set of sparse facial landmarks on S is used to match the corresponding positions x_i as defined in the UFPD. Nearest vertices on the surface mesh $S = (V, E)$ are determined and a set of labeled correspondences $L = \{(v_i, x_i) \mid v_i \in V, \ x_i \in \text{UFPD}\}$ is assembled. Using the projected reference parametrization Φ_R, the facial region on S is segmented and non-facial parts that map outside the UFPD are discarded. We fix the boundary of the facial region as defined by Φ_R to its corresponding position in the UFPD. Similarly, the inner vertices are soft-constrained to their positions as defined by Φ_R. Two separate sets are determined by $K^\partial = \{(v_i, y_i) \mid v_i \in V^\partial, \ y_i \in \text{UFPD}\}$ for the boundary vertices V^∂ of S and K° for the inner vertices $V^\circ = V \backslash V^\partial$.

To compute Φ_S while accounting for the soft constraints defined by the landmarks L and the inner vertices K° as well as the fixed boundary K^∂ of the facial surface, we adopt the approach of convex-combination maps [41]. Here, the mapping of vertices is expressed as a weighted sum of its 1-ring neighbors:

$$u(v_i) = \sum_{j \in N_1(v_i)} \lambda_{ij} u(v_j). \tag{3}$$

To keep geometric distortion minimal, λ_{ij} is calculated as the mean value weight defined in [42] while the boundary vertices are constrained according to K^∂. By rewriting Eq. 3 as a linear least squares problem in the mapped coordinates of the inner vertices $u(V^\circ)$, the soft constraints

$$\frac{\alpha}{|L|} \sum_{(v_i, x_i) \in L} \|u(v_i) - x_i\|^2 + \frac{\beta}{|K^\circ|} \sum_{(v_i, y_i) \in K^\circ} \|u(v_i) - y_i\|^2 \tag{4}$$

can conveniently be added, where α, β are weighting factors accounting for the influence of the soft constraints. The solution of the equivalent sparse system of linear equations in V° gives the desired mapping Φ_S (see Fig. 7).

4.4 Variational Matching for Accurate Dense Correspondence

Dense correspondence of S is improved using a variational approach for surface matching inspired by the work presented in [18,33,34]. The initial surface parametrization Φ_S allows us to map arbitrary features of S into the plane. We can then use off-the-shelf image registration frameworks that allow us to combine robust similarity measures with reasonable regularization terms into a common objective for optimization of the correspondence mapping $\Psi_{\Phi_S \to \Phi_R}$.

To measure the similarity between photographic and geometric features, we use two data terms accordingly defined to the weight maps in the UFPD (see Fig. 5b and c). Several image metrics have been investigated (*e.g.* sum of squared differences, flavors of mutual information, gradient metrics) and we found an advanced version of Normalized Cross Correlation (NCC, see [43]) to be well suited for our purpose. As a correlation measure, the advantage of NCC is its robustness to changes *e.g.* in lightning or exposure as well as individual facial characteristics like skin tone that vary significantly with respect to the UFPD.

To regularize the correspondence mapping $\Psi_{\Phi_S \to \Phi_R}$ in regions with less significant facial features, we use a regularization term similar to [34]. This term, called orthonormality criterion P_{oc} as defined by Eq. (7) in [44], employs the Green-Lagrange strain to measure isometric distortion. Additionally, local foldings of $\Psi_{\Phi_S \to \Phi_R}$ are avoided by the bending energy P_{be} as defined by Klein and Staring [43].

We discretized the correspondence mapping $\Psi_{\Phi_S \to \Phi_R} \in F$, where F is the space of cubic B-spline transformations with 128^2 basis functions located on a uniform regular grid covering the UFPD. The objective used to solve the image registration therefore becomes:

$$O(u) = \int_{\text{UFPD}} w_{be} P_{be}(u, x) + w_{oc} P_{oc}(u, x) dx$$

$$+ \int_{\text{UFPD}} m_P(x) NCC(P_S(u(x)), P_R(x)) dx \tag{5}$$

$$+ \int_{\text{UFPD}} m_G(x) NCC(G_S(u(x)), G_R(x)) dx,$$

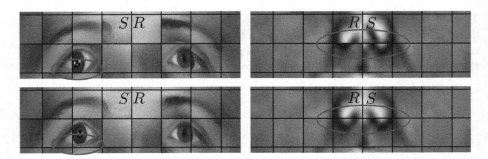

Fig. 8. Close-up of the photometric (eyes) as well as the geometric features (nose area) before (upper row), and after (lower row) dense correspondence has been optimized. UFPD and the individual features are overlayed using a chessboard pattern as indicated by S, R. Note the accurate correspondence between characteristic morphological structures.

where $m_P(x), m_G(x)$ are weight maps of the photometric (P_S, P_R) and the geometric (G_S, G_R) features from S and the UFPD. The optimization of Eq. 5 was implemented using *elastix*, a framework for rigid and non-rigid image registration [45]. A multi-scale approach for both, the discretization of the correspondence mapping and image resolution is used during optimization. We employ quasi-Newton L-BFGS optimizer including line-search for faster convergence.

5   Experiments and Results

We built a database consisting of 400 facial surfaces aquired with our stereophotogrammetric setup as described in the beginning of Sect. 4. We tested the proposed framework on our database because it contains highly detailed reconstructions including high-resolution photographic textures comparable to 3D models acquired with state-of-the-art stereophotogrammetric devices. We refer the reader to the supplementary material provided with this paper for a collection of representative surfaces from our database.

We also run extensive experiments on all 2500 cases of the BU3DFE database [2]. This database contains 3D models of 100 persons varying in sex, age and ethnicity. The faces are captured in neutral position as well as 6 basic emotions of the *Facial Action Coding System* [46] in 4 levels of intensity. An initial surface reconstruction using [37] was done to close holes or remove meshing artifacts frequently contained in the raw data (*e.g.* below the chin). All data was processed in a fully automatic fashion.

During initial correspondence estimation in the first stage of our framework, sparse facial landmarks were reliably located at the expected positions in the 2D images. In some cases, especially in presence of extreme expressions or when the camera perspective significantly differs from the frontal view, facial landmark detection was less accurate. However, the combination of landmarks

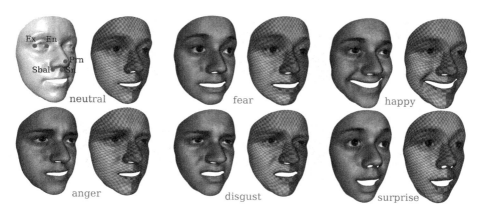

Fig. 9. Results for several expressions from the BU3DFE. Note the accurate dense correspondence established over the entire surface. The red dots indicate the location of landmarks used for quantitative evaluation. (Color figure online)

from both detectors is generally reliable and serves as valuable information in further processing. During fitting of the SSAM, the incorporation of color information improves the registration to structures like the mouth, eyes, and eyebrows where geometric information is less significant. Unfortunately, the BFM is build from a dataset containing neutral expressions only and it fails to adapt to strong variations in shape of the mouth or the eyes. To avoid implausible results in case of expressions, we gave high weight to the prior distribution in shape space and chose $\sigma = (10, 1)$ in Eq. 1.

For the same reason, the initial surface parametrization Φ_S was computed with higher weight given to the set of landmarks L than to the inner vertices V° with $\alpha = 1, \beta = 0.001$. Theoretically, the constraints that we have added to Eq. 4 might lead to non-injective parametrizations (see [41] for a discussion). In practice, we did not find any cases were this occurred. The initial parametrizations obtained are roughly aligned with the UFPD and served as suitable starting values for the optimization of dense correspondence (see Fig. 7).

The dense correspondence mapping accurately registers photographic and geometric features with the UFPD (see Fig. 8). We fixed weights $w_{be} = 150$ and $w_{oc} = 2$ to ensure bijectivity of $\Psi_{\Phi_S \to \Phi_R}$ and to reasonably constrain matching in regions with less significant features. To quantitatively evaluate our approach, we measured the deviation of landmarks distributed with the BU3DFE. Corresponding landmarks were defined in the UFPD and identified accordingly on the original surfaces after matching. Landmark-wise Euclidean distance was computed and averaged (see Table 1). Using the proposed framework, we were able to predict the landmarks with higher accuracy than previous approaches (except Pronasale in [13] where about 200 cases have been discarded). Moreover as depicted by the standard deviations, the prediction-uncertainty has been significantly reduced.

Table 1. Localization error on the BU3DFE database (for landmarks see Fig. 9). The improvement with respect to the best result from previous work is reported in the last column.

	Segundo et al. [13]		Salazar et al. [14]		Gilani et al. [15]		This paper		
	Mean	SD	Mean	SD	Mean	SD	Mean	SD	impr.
Ex(L)	-	-	9.63	6.12	4.42	2.74	2.95	1.93	33.3%
En(L)	6.33	4.82	6.75	4.54	4.75	2.64	3.04	1.75	36%
Ex(R)	-	-	8.49	5.82	4.35	2.70	3.22	2.18	26.0%
En(R)	6.33	5.04	6.14	4.21	3.29	2.67	3.23	1.86	1.80%
Sn	-	-	-	-	3.90	3.26	1.97	1.06	49.49%
Prn	1.87	1.12	5.87	2.70	2.91	2.03	2.05	1.21	-9.63%
Sbal(L)	-	-	-	-	4.86	2.80	2.37	1.37	51.23%
Sbal(R)	-	-	-	-	3.57	2.59	2.47	1.29	30.81%

In fact, using the surface mapping established with our approach, we are able to predict any number of landmarks or mesh vertices that are identified in the UFPD. Here, we used a low-level reference mesh of about 15k vertices as it is sufficient for the resolution available in BU3DFE. We have segmented facial regions in the UFPD and generated a color-coded texture overlayed with a chessboard pattern. The result for several facial expression scans of a single individual is shown in Fig. 9.

Finally, the reference mesh was transferred to all surfaces of the BU3DFE. To demonstrate the suitability of our approach for morphological analysis and generation of statistical face models, we have build two SSAMs using Principal Component Analysis (PCA) on the vertex positions and the photographic textures of the 3D face models. The first SSAM contains the geometric variation related to the inter-individual morphology using the neutral scans only. The second model captures the intra-individual variations due to facial expressions. We have simply computed displacement vector fields for the expressions with respect to the neutral scan of each subject and applied it to the average face of the first SSAM using vertex correspondence. Note the morphological variation captured by the shape parameters in Fig. 10. The chessboard pattern is accurately morphed when the shape varies.

6   Limitations and Future Work

In some rare cases of extreme expressions, we found that matching in the mouth and the forehead region is disturbed by folds, e.g. by matching them to other features like the eyebrows. Special detectors could be used to remove these features from textures. Similar strategies could be integrated to handle severe changes in surface area/topology by an open mouth or closed eyes. In the future, we will use the BU3DFE-SSAM instead of the BFM because it already contains several expressions and thus better adapts to an individual morphology. A Riemannian variant of the BU3DFE-SSAM will be established, as non-linear shape

Fig. 10. The BU3DFE-SSM. Left: the face shape according to $\pm 2SD$ of the first three shape parameters of the neutral model. Middle: The average neutral face. Right: The first three shape parameters ($\pm 2SD$) of the expression model.

spaces have been shown to be superior to PCA based models *e.g.* for learning relationships between shape and expressions.

The variational matching in the plane comes at the cost of geometric distortions introduced by the parametrization. As the proposed framework is independent of the actual UFPD, improved definitions will be investigated in further experiments. Similarly, we aim in learning the parameters used in our framework from an annotated ground truth database to further improve accuracy and robustness of automated data processing. The run time of the framework highly depends on the resolution of the input data. In our experiments, we measured times between 0.5 and 3 min on a standard workstation without optimizing our code. We believe that the computation time could be significantly reduced if certain routines are implemented more efficiently and by employing computational parallelism.

7   Conclusions

We have presented a framework for the fully automated determination of highly-accurate dense correspondence for facial surfaces. We showed that the proposed approach works well on a wide range of textured 3D face models varying inter- and intra-individually. Our approach outperforms state-of-the-art methods as confirmed by our experiments. To the best of our knowledge, no SSAM of faces based on a variety of facial expressions with dense correspondence has been released to the research community yet. We are aiming to publish the BU3DFE-SSAM and believe, that this model including geometric as well as photometric variation will help researchers to understand the complex nature of facial morphology. The proposed framework will help to build the next generation of highly-detailed 3D face models on a large scale basis and thus opens up new directions for applications in computer vision and computer graphics.

Acknowledgments. Special thanks go to Olaf Hellwich, Gabriel Le Roux, The Anh Pham, Sven-Kristofer Pilz, Honglei Wang, and Martin Zänker for their valuable contribution and support. Our research is funded by the *Image Knowledge Gestaltung. Cluster of Excellence at the Humboldt-Universität zu Berlin*, with financial support from the German Research Foundation as a part of the Excellence Initiative.

References

1. Brunton, A., Salazar, A., Bolkart, T., Wuhrer, S.: Review of statistical shape spaces for 3D data with comparative analysis for human faces. Comput. Vis. Image Underst. **128**, 1–17 (2014). Elsevier
2. Yin, L., Wei, X., Sun, Y., Wang, J., Rosato, M.J.: A 3D facial expression database for facial behavior research. In: IEEE International Conference Automatic Face and Gesture Recognition (FGR), pp. 211–216 (2006)
3. Savran, A., Alyüz, N., Dibeklioğlu, H., Çeliktutan, O., Gökberk, B., Sankur, B., Akarun, L.: Bosphorus database for 3D face analysis. In: Schouten, B., Juul, N.C., Drygajlo, A., Tistarelli, M. (eds.) BIOID 2008. LNCS, vol. 5372, pp. 47–56. Springer, Heidelberg (2008)
4. Paysan, P., Knothe, R., Amberg, B., Romdhani, S., Vetter, T.: A 3D face model for pose and illumination invariant face recognition. In: IEEE International Conference On Advanced Video and Signal Based Surveillance (AVSS), pp. 296–301. IEEE (2009)
5. Booth, J., Roussos, A., Zafeiriou, S., Ponniah, A., Dunaway, D.: A 3D morphable model learnt from 10,000 faces. In: IEEE Conference on Computer Vision and Pattern Recognition (CVPR) (2016)
6. Brunton, A., Bolkart, T., Wuhrer, S.: Multilinear wavelets: a statistical shape space for human faces. In: Fleet, D., Pajdla, T., Schiele, B., Tuytelaars, T. (eds.) ECCV 2014, Part I. LNCS, vol. 8689, pp. 297–312. Springer, Heidelberg (2014)
7. Cao, C., Weng, Y., Zhou, S., Tong, Y., Zhou, K.: Facewarehouse: a 3D facial expression database for visual computing. IEEE Trans. Vis. Comput. Graph. **20**, 413–425 (2014). IEEE
8. Zafeiriou, S., Zhang, C., Zhang, Z.: A survey on face detection in the wild: past, present and future. Comput. Vis. Image Underst. **138**, 1–24 (2015)
9. Cootes, T.F., Ionita, M.C., Lindner, C., Sauer, P.: Robust and accurate shape model fitting using random forest regression voting. In: Fitzgibbon, A., Lazebnik, S., Perona, P., Sato, Y., Schmid, C. (eds.) ECCV 2012, Part VII. LNCS, vol. 7578, pp. 278–291. Springer, Heidelberg (2012)
10. Ren, S., Cao, X., Wei, Y., Sun, J.: Face alignment at 3000 fps via regressing local binary features. In: IEEE Conference on Computer Vision and Pattern Recognition (CVPR), pp. 1685–1692 (2014)
11. Kazemi, V., Sullivan, J.: One millisecond face alignment with an ensemble of regression trees. In: IEEE Conference on Computer Vision and Pattern Recognition (CVPR), pp. 1867–1874 (2014)
12. de la Torre, F., Chu, W.S., Xiong, X., Vicente, F., Ding, X., Cohn, J.: Intraface. In: IEEE International Conference Automatic Face and Gesture Recognition (FGR), vol. 1, pp. 1–8. IEEE (2015)
13. Segundo, M.P., Silva, L., Bellon, O.R.P., Queirolo, C.: Automatic face segmentation and facial landmark detection in range images. IEEE Trans. Syst. Man Cybern. B: Cybern. **40**, 1319–1330 (2010). IEEE

14. Salazar, A., Wuhrer, S., Shu, C., Prieto, F.: Fully automatic expression-invariant face correspondence. Mach. Vis. Appl. **25**, 859–879 (2014). Springer
15. Gilani, Z.S., Shafait, F., Mian, A.: Shape-based automatic detection of a large number of 3D facial landmarks. In: IEEE Conference on Computer Vision and Pattern Recognition (CVPR), pp. 4639–4648 (2015)
16. Matthews, I., Baker, S.: Active appearance models revisited. Int. J. Comput. Vis. **60**(2), 135–164 (2004)
17. Theobald, B.J., Matthews, I., Mangini, M., Spies, J.R., Brick, T.R., Cohn, J.F., Boker, S.M.: Mapping and manipulating facial expression. Lang. Speech **52**(2–3), 369–386 (2009)
18. Litke, N., Droske, M., Rumpf, M., Schröder, P.: An image processing approach to surface matching. Symp. Geom. Process. (SGP) **255**, 207–216 (2005)
19. Bronstein, A.M., Bronstein, M.M., Kimmel, R.: Generalized multidimensional scaling: a framework for isometry-invariant partial surface matching. Proc. Natl Acad. Sci. **103**, 1168–1172 (2006)
20. Windheuser, T., Schlickewei, U., Schmidt, F.R., Cremers, D.: Geometrically consistent elastic matching of 3D shapes: a linear programming solution. In: 2011 International Conference on Computer Vision (ICCV), pp. 2134–2141. IEEE (2011)
21. Dubrovina, A., Kimmel, R.: Approximately isometric shape correspondence by matching pointwise spectral features and global geodesic structures. In: Advances in Adaptive Data Analysis, vol. 3, pp. 203–228. World Scientific (2011)
22. Van Kaick, O., Zhang, H., Hamarneh, G., Cohen-Or, D.: A survey on shape correspondence. Comput. Graph. Forum **30**(6), 1681–1707 (2011)
23. Besl, P.J., McKay, N.D.: Method for registration of 3-D shapes. In: Robotics-DL tentative, International Society for Optics and Photonics, pp. 586–606 (1992)
24. Myronenko, A., Song, X.: Point set registration: coherent point drift. IEEE Trans. Pattern Anal. Mach. Intell. **32**, 2262–2275 (2010)
25. Lamecker, H., Seeba, M., Hege, H.C., Deuhard, P.: A 3D statistical shape model of the pelvic bone for segmentation. In: Proceedings SPIE Medical Imaging, vol. 5370, pp. 1341–1351 (2004)
26. Duy, N.T., Lamecker, H., Kainmueller, D., Zachow, S.: Automatic detection and classification of teeth in CT data. In: Ayache, N., Delingette, H., Golland, P., Mori, K. (eds.) MICCAI 2012. LNCS, vol. 7510, pp. 609–616. Springer, Heidelberg (2012). doi:10.1007/978-3-642-33415-3_75
27. Ehlke, M., Ramm, H., Lamecker, H., Hege, H.C., Zachow, S.: Fast generation of virtual x-ray images for reconstruction of 3D anatomy. IEEE Trans. Vis. Comput. Graph. **19**(12), 2673–2682 (2013)
28. Blanz, V., Vetter, T.: Face recognition based on fitting a 3D morphable model. IEEE Trans. Pattern Anal. Mach. Intell. **25**, 1063–1074 (2003). IEEE
29. Blanz, V., Vetter, T.: A morphable model for the synthesis of 3D faces. In: Proceedings of the Annual Conference on Computer Graphics and Interactive Techniques, pp. 187–194. ACM Press/Addison-Wesley Publishing Co. (1999)
30. Bradley, D., Heidrich, W., Popa, T., Sheffer, A.: High resolution passive facial performance capture. ACM Trans. Graph. (TOG) **29**, 1–10 (2010). ACM
31. Beeler, T., Hahn, F., Bradley, D., Bickel, B., Beardsley, P., Gotsman, C., Sumner, R.W., Gross, M.: High-quality passive facial performance capture using anchor frames. ACM Trans. Graph. (TOG) **30**, 75–85 (2011). ACM
32. Fyffe, G., Jones, A., Alexander, O., Ichikari, R., Debevec, P.: Driving high-resolution facial scans with video performance capture. ACM Trans. Graph. (TOG) **34**, 8 (2014). ACM

33. Kaiser, M., Störmer, A., Arsić, D., Rigoll, G.: Non-rigid registration of 3D facial surfaces with robust outlier detection. In: IEEE Winter Conference on Applications of Computer Vision (WACV), pp. 1–6 (2009)
34. Savran, A., Sankur, B.: Non-rigid registration of 3D surfaces by deformable 2D triangular meshes. In: IEEE Computer Society Conference on Computer Vision and Pattern Recognition Workshops (CVPRW), pp. 1–6 (2008)
35. Milborrow, S., Nicolls, F.: Active shape models with SIFT descriptors and MARS. In: International Joint Conference on Computer Vision, Imaging and Computer Graphics Theory and Applications (VISAPP), pp. 380–387 (2014)
36. Beeler, T., Bickel, B., Beardsley, P., Sumner, B., Gross, M.: High-quality single-shot capture of facial geometry. ACM Trans. Graph. (TOG) **29**, 41–50 (2010). ACM
37. Kazhdan, M., Bolitho, M., Hoppe, H.: Poisson surface reconstruction. In: Proceedings of the Fourth Eurographics Symposium on Geometry Processing, vol. 7, pp. 61–70 (2006)
38. Pérez, P., Gangnet, M., Blake, A.: Poisson image editing. ACM Trans. Graph. (TOG) **22**, 313–318 (2003). ACM
39. Kälberer, F., Nieser, M., Polthier, K.: Quadcover-surface parameterization using branched coverings. Comput. Graph. Forum **26**, 375–384 (2007). Wiley
40. Bishop, C.M.: Pattern Recognition and Machine Learning. Springer, New York (2006)
41. Floater, M.S.: Parametrization and smooth approximation of surface triangulations. Comput. Aided Geom. Des. **14**, 231–250 (1997). Elsevier
42. Floater, M.S.: Mean value coordinates. Comput. Aided Geom. Des. **20**, 19–27 (2003). Elsevier
43. Klein, S., Staring, M.: elastix the manual v4.7. Technical report, Image Sciences Institute, University Medical Center, Utrecht (2014)
44. Staring, M., Klein, S., Pluim, J.P.: A rigidity penalty term for nonrigid registration. In: Medical Physics, vol. 34, pp. 4098–4108. American Association of Physicists in Medicine (2007)
45. Klein, S., Staring, M., Murphy, K., Viergever, M., Pluim, J.P., et al.: elastix: a toolbox for intensity-based medical image registration. IEEE Trans. Med. Imaging **29**, 196–205 (2010). IEEE
46. Ekman, P., Friesen, W.V.: Unmasking the face: a guide to recognizing emotions from facial clues (2003)

Joint Face Detection and Alignment
with a Deformable Hough Transform Model

John McDonagh and Georgios Tzimiropoulos[⊠]

Computer Vision Laboratory, University of Nottingham, Nottingham, UK
yorgos.tzimiropoulos@nottingham.ac.uk

Abstract. We propose a method for joint face detection and alignment in unconstrained images and videos. Historically, these problems have been addressed disjointly in literature with the overall performance of the whole pipeline having been scantily assessed. We show that a pipeline built by combining state-of-the-art methods for both tasks produces unsatisfactory overall performance. To address this limitation, we propose an approach that addresses both tasks, which we call Deformable Hough Transform Model (DHTM). In particular, we make the following contributions: (a) Rather than scanning the image with discriminatively trained filters, we propose to employ cascaded regression in a *sliding window* fashion to fit a facial deformable model over the whole image/video. (b) We propose to capitalize on the large basin of attraction of cascaded regression to set up a Hough-Transform voting scheme for detecting faces and filtering out irrelevant background. (c) We report state-of-the-art performance on the most challenging and widely-used data sets for face detection, alignment and tracking.

Keywords: Face detection · Alignment · Tracking · Cascaded regression · Hough Transform

1 Introduction

From Viola and Jones [1] to Deformable Part Models [2–4] and from Active Appearance Models [5] to Cascaded Regression [6–9], face detection, alignment and tracking have all witnessed tremendous progress over the last years. Besides new methodologies, another notable development in the field has been the collection and annotation of large facial data sets captured in-the-wild [3,10–13], for which a number of newly developed methods have been shown to produce remarkable results.

Despite the progress in the field, the majority of prior work has disjointly considered the two problems: there is a large number of papers on face detection and perhaps even a larger number of papers on face alignment and tracking, but to the best of our knowledge there are only two papers [3,14] that study the combined problem of detection and alignment and no method that addresses and evaluates all three tasks jointly. However, for many subsequent, higher level

© Springer International Publishing Switzerland 2016
G. Hua and H. Jégou (Eds.): ECCV 2016 Workshops, Part II, LNCS 9914, pp. 569–580, 2016.
DOI: 10.1007/978-3-319-48881-3_39

tasks, like face recognition, facial expression and attribute analysis, what matters is the *overall performance* in terms of accuracy in landmark localization. Notably, recent state-of-the-art methods for such tasks heavily rely on the accurate detection of landmarks (see for example [15,16]).

As we show hereafter, the overall performance in landmark localization accuracy might be unsatisfactory even by putting two recently proposed state-of-the-art methods (we used [4] for face detection and [9] for landmark localization) together. The reason for this is that face detection follows object detection in terms of measuring performance and, in particular, it uses the PASCAL VOC precision-recall protocol for object detection, thus requiring 50 % overlap between the ground truth and detected bounding boxes. As our results have shown, this accuracy is insufficient for initializing current landmark localization algorithms, even state-of-the-art methods like the one of [9] which is robust to poor initialization.

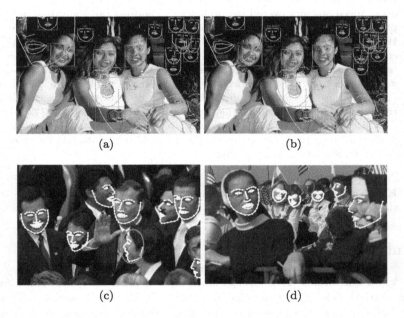

Fig. 1. (a), (b): Overview of DHTM. Our system scans an image in a sliding window fashion and for each candidate location fits a facial deformable model using PO-CR. Image locations that converge to the same location cast votes for that location in a Hough Transform fashion. Thresholding the voting surface and performing NMS results in a few candidate locations for which SVM scores are calculated by extracting SIFT and colour features. (a) System responses that received the highest number of votes. (b) Scores after applying SVM. (c, d) Output of our system on two challenging images from FDDB. The green ellipse shows a face that is not annotated. The red ellipse shows a missed face. (Color figure online)

1.1 Contributions

To address the aforementioned problem, we propose Deformable Hough Transform Model (DHTM). DHTM is largely motivated by the efficiency and robustness of cascaded regression methods for facial landmark localization. Essentially, rather than using a face detector to initialize them, we instead propose to employ them in order to jointly detect and track the location of faces and facial features in images/videos, too. Overall, our model jointly addresses face detection, alignment and tracking via scanning the image with Project-Out Cascaded Regression (PO-CR) [9] and aggregating the fitting results using a Hough-Transform (HT) voting scheme. In particular, we make the following contributions:

- Rather than exhaustively evaluating multiple templates as in [3,4] in order to cope with pose or other deformations, we propose to employ cascaded regression [6] in a *sliding window* fashion in order to evaluate the score of a *single* deformable template over a grid of image locations. For a deformable template, we choose one based on a parametric, densely connected shape model and an appearance model built from SIFT features. We fit this model using PO-CR [9], the complexity of which is only $O(nN)$ per iteration, where N is the number of features in the appearance model, and n is the number of parameters in the shape model.
- We propose to capitalize on the large basin of attraction of PO-CR and formulate a Hough-Transform voting scheme that filters out irrelevant objects and background areas, while at the same time "rewards" candidate image locations for which PO-CR converges to similar solutions. The main idea is that if the algorithm converges to the same solution for multiple initializations, then the converged solution "must" be a face.
- We report state-of-the-art results on challenging data sets for all 3 tasks: For face detection, DHTM is among the top performing methods on FDDB [10] and AFW [3] using the discrete score and sets a new state-of-the-art for the continuous score on FDDB. For face alignment, DHTM achieves state-of-the-art performance on the most challenging COFW [17] in terms of landmark localization error. For face tracking, DHTM achieves state-of-the-art performance on the 300-VW data set [18] in terms of landmark localization error.

2 Related Work

In this section, we review related work on face detection, alignment and performance measures.

Face detection. Face detection is one of the most popular and well-studied problems in computer vision with a multitude of approaches proposed over the last years reporting varying degrees of success. A comprehensive review of the topic is beyond the scope of this section, and we refer the reader to [4] for a recent survey. Interestingly, in the same paper, it is reported that a multi-channel, multi-view version of the Viola-Jones detector performs comparably with a properly tuned vanilla Deformable Part Models (DPM) face detector, and that they both produce state-of-the-art performance on FDDB [10] and AFW [3] data sets. Hence, it is argued that part-based approaches are not always advantageous over standard approaches based on multi-view rigid templates, especially when a large amount of training data is available. A part-based approach to face detection is advocated in [3] and more recently in [14]. The Tree-Structure Model of [3] proposes a supervised way to train a DPM face detector based on manual annotations of parts, and a tree-based shape model that allows for a globally optimized model. An interesting extension of [3] that deals better with occlusion is described in [19]. The joint cascade detection and alignment algorithm of [14] proposes to use shape-indexed features for classification. [14] and [4] along with the more recent deep architectures of [20–22] are the state-of-the-art in face detection. Our work is similar to [3,14] in a sense that it produces the location of landmarks along with that of the face. However, both [3,14] are based on classification. In contrast, the main scoring scheme in the proposed DHTM is a novel voting scheme based on the large basin of attraction of cascaded regression that is used to cast votes for the location of candidate faces. A voting scheme for detecting faces is proposed in [23], however the voting is not based on deformable model fitting (as in our work), but on rigid image retrieval and is fundamentally different from the method presented herein. Finally, we note that although our method achieves state-of-the-art performance using standard SIFT and colour features, it could further benefit from region proposals and deep features as in [20–22].

Facial landmark localization. DHTM uses cascaded regression to fit a deformable template to each sub-window of a given image. Cascaded regression [6] is an iterative regression method in which the output of regression at iteration $k - 1$ is used as input for iteration k, and each regressor uses image features that depend on the current pose estimate. DHTM is somewhat related to a number of regression-based face alignment methods [7–9,24–27] that have recently emerged as the state-of-the-art. Consensus methods for face alignment have been proposed in [17,28,29]. However, the aim of our work is not face alignment *given* a face detection initialization (as in all aforementioned algorithms) but joint face and facial landmark detection.

Performance measures. In face detection, performance is measured using the PASCAL VOC precision-recall protocol, requiring 50 % overlap between the ground truth and detected bounding boxes. In the FDDB benchmark, this is called "discrete" measure. FDDB also describes a "continuous" measure in which the detection score is weighted by the corresponding overlapping ratio. The continuous measure is thus more appropriate to reflect on the accuracy of the detected bounding box. The proposed DHTM has performance comparable to state-of-the-art when the discrete measure is considered and establishes a new state-of-the-art for the case of the continuous measure. In face alignment and tracking, performance is measured using the average normalized point-to-point (pt-pt) error between ground truth and detected landmarks. Performance strongly depends on the quality of initialization. DHTM produces state-of-the-art results when the joint problem of face and facial landmark detection is considered, and performance is measured using the pt-pt error: DHTM largely outperforms the combination of [4] (for face detection) and [9] (for landmark localization).

3   Deformable Hough Transform Model

Our system scans an image in a sliding window fashion and for each candidate location $\mathbf{x}$, it fits a generative facial deformable model using PO-CR [9]. Image locations that converge to the same location cast votes for that location in a fashion similar to Hough Transform. Thresholding the surface of votes, obtained by our voting scheme, and performing non-maximal suppression, we end up with a few candidate locations per image. For these locations, multiple initializations are combined by taking the median and finally, SVM scores are calculated by extracting SIFT and colour features around the landmarks of each of the fitted shapes. Figure 1 aims to provide an overview of our system. The main components of the proposed Deformable Hough Transform Model (DHTM) are analyzed as follows.

3.1   Shape Model and Appearance

Shape model. DHTM uses cascaded regression to fit a deformable template to each sub-window of a given image. Our cascaded regression method of choice for this purpose is the recently proposed PO-CR [9] which has been shown to produce good fitting results for faces with large pose and expression variation. PO-CR uses parametric shape and appearance models both learned with PCA. Let us assume that we are given a set of training facial images $\mathbf{I}_i$ annotated with u fiducial points. For each image, the set of all points defines a vector $\in \mathcal{R}^{2u \times 1}$. The annotated shapes are firstly normalized by removing similarity transformations using Procrustes Analysis and the shape model is obtained by applying PCA on the normalized shapes. The model is defined by the mean shape $\mathbf{s}_0$ and n shape eigenvectors $\mathbf{s}_i$ represented as columns in $\mathbf{S} \in \mathcal{R}^{2u \times n}$. Finally, to model similarity transforms, $\mathbf{S}$ is appended with 4 additional bases [30]. Using this model a shape can be instantiated by:

$$\mathbf{s}(\mathbf{p}) = \mathbf{s}_0 + \mathbf{S}\mathbf{p}, \tag{1}$$

where $\mathbf{p} \in \mathcal{R}^{n \times 1}$ is the vector of the shape parameters.

Appearance. To represent appearance in facial images, an image is firstly warped to a reference frame so that similarity transformations are removed. Then, the local appearance around each landmark is encoded using SIFT [31] and all descriptors are stacked in a vector $\in \mathcal{R}^{N \times 1}$ which defines the part-based facial appearance. Finally, PCA is applied on all training facial images to obtain the appearance model defined by the mean appearance $\mathbf{A}_0$ and m appearance eigenvectors $\mathbf{A}_i$ represented as columns in $\mathbf{A} \in \mathcal{R}^{N \times m}$. Using this model a part-based facial representation can be instantiated by:

$$\mathbf{A}(\mathbf{c}) = \mathbf{A}_0 + \mathbf{A}\mathbf{c}, \tag{2}$$

where $\mathbf{c} \in \mathcal{R}^{m \times 1}$ is the vector of the appearance parameters.

3.2 Deformable Model Fitting with PO-CR

We assume that a sub-window of our original image contains a facial image. We also denote by $\mathbf{I}(\mathbf{s}(\mathbf{p})) \in \mathcal{R}^{N \times 1}$ the vector obtained by generating u landmarks from a shape instance $\mathbf{s}(\mathbf{p})$ and concatenating the SIFT descriptors for all landmarks. To localize the landmarks in the given sub-window, we fit the shape and appearance models (described in the previous section) by solving the following optimization problem:

$$\arg\min_{\mathbf{p},\mathbf{c}} ||\mathbf{I}(\mathbf{s}(\mathbf{p})) - \mathbf{A}(\mathbf{c})||^2. \tag{3}$$

As Eq. (3) is non-convex, a locally optimal solution can be readily provided in an iterative fashion using the Lucas-Kanade algorithm [30,32].

In particular, given an estimate of $\mathbf{p}$ and $\mathbf{c}$ at iteration k, linearisation of Eq. (3) is performed and updates, $\Delta\mathbf{p}, \Delta\mathbf{c}$ can be obtained in closed form. Notably, one can by-pass the calculation of $\Delta\mathbf{c}$ (for more details see [33]) by solving

$$\arg\min_{\Delta\mathbf{p}} ||\mathbf{I}(\mathbf{s}(\mathbf{p})) + \mathbf{J}_I \Delta\mathbf{p} - \mathbf{A}_0||^2_{\mathbf{P}}, \tag{4}$$

where $||\mathbf{x}||^2_{\mathbf{P}} = \mathbf{x}^T \mathbf{P} \mathbf{x}$ is the weighted ℓ_2-norm of a vector $\mathbf{x}$. The solution to the above problem is readily given by

$$\Delta\mathbf{p} = -\mathbf{H}_P^{-1}\mathbf{J}_P^T(\mathbf{I}(\mathbf{s}(\mathbf{p})) - \mathbf{A}_0), \tag{5}$$

where $\mathbf{J}_P = \mathbf{P}\mathbf{J}_I$ and $\mathbf{H}_P = \mathbf{J}_P^T\mathbf{J}_P$, $\mathbf{P} = \mathbf{E} - \mathbf{A}\mathbf{A}^T$ is a projection operator that projects out appearance variation from the image Jacobian $\mathbf{J}_I$, and $\mathbf{E}$ is the identity matrix.

Note that the above algorithm can be implemented in real-time for a single fitting, yet it is too slow to be employed for all sub-windows of a given image as the Jacobian, the Hessian and its inverse need to be re-computed per iteration. PO-CR by passes this computational burden by pre-computing a sequence of averaged projected-out Jacobians and Hessians (one per iteration) using regression. In particular, for iteration k, PO-CR pre-computes "averaged" matrices $\widehat{\mathbf{J}}_P(k)$, $\widehat{\mathbf{H}}_P(k) = \widehat{\mathbf{J}}_P(k)^T\widehat{\mathbf{J}}_P(k)$ and finally $\mathbf{R}(k) = \widehat{\mathbf{H}}_P(k)^{-1}\widehat{\mathbf{J}}_P(k)^T$. During testing, an update for iteration k can be obtained from $\Delta\mathbf{p}(k) = \mathbf{R}(k)(\mathbf{I}(\mathbf{s}(\mathbf{p}(k))) - \mathbf{A}_0)$ with cost $O(nN)$, only. Hence, fitting in PO-CR is very fast, with our parallel implementation running in a few thousand frames per second (one initialisation per frame).

3.3 Hough-Transform Voting

The proposed DHTM detects faces via a Hough-Transform voting scheme by capitalizing on the properties of the iterative optimization procedure employed by PO-CR. In particular, our system scans an image in a sliding window fashion and for each location $\mathbf{x}$ (we used a grid of equally spaced points, see Sect. 3.5), it fits our facial deformable model using the PO-CR described in the previous section. Voting in the proposed system is performed in a straightforward fashion. We simply extract the translational component from **p** which represents the location of the fitted shape in the image. Then, for that location we cast a vote.

As with standard gradient descent fitting (PO-CR is a regression-based solution to Gauss-Newton optimization), we posit that when initialized in locations where no faces are present, PO-CR will converge to random locations/solutions. Examples of such cases are illustrated in Fig. 1 (a) as cyan "faces"'. The numbers in boxes indicate the number of times that the algorithm has converged to the nearby locations. As we may observe there are no more than 80 times that the algorithm converged to a similar solution. On the contrary, when initialized close to a face, because of the large basin of attraction of regression-based approaches, PO-CR is very likely to accurately recover both the face and its parts. Two examples of this idea are illustrated in Fig. 1(a) as red faces, with the numbers indicating that more than 150 times for both faces PO-CR has converged to the same solution. Thresholding the surface of votes, obtained by our voting scheme, and performing non-maximal suppression, our system removes most of the background clutter ending up with a few candidate locations per image. Finally, as our system is based on aggregating votes from different initializations, it comes naturally to consider how these initializations can be combined to produce a single fitting. We address this by simply taking the median of all fitted shapes that cast votes for the same peak in Hough space.

3.4   Final Re-scoring

Once the final fitted shape has been obtained, we perform re-scoring of the candidate face by evaluating an SVM trained on SIFT and colour features [4]. The overall detection process in DHTM is illustrated in Fig. 1(b).

3.5   Complexity and Implementation

Complexity. Assume that the PO-CR model has K levels of cascade. For each level, a regression matrix $\mathbf{R}(k)$ is learned having n regressors with N features each (columns of $\mathbf{R}(k)$). Recall that n is the number of parameters in our shape model. Hence, the complexity of fitting per sub-window is $O(K(nN))$. Because of the large basin of attraction of PO-CR, we perform fitting only on a grid of equally spaced points using a stride of 10 pixels. If there are L locations per image to perform fitting, the total complexity is $O(LK(nN))$ for a single level of the image pyramid. By making an analogy between the regressors in $\mathbf{R}(k)$ and the number of mixtures in [3] (the number of regressors ($n = 15 - 20$) is indeed similar to the number of mixtures in [3]), and assuming that [3] is also evaluated on L locations, we conclude that our model is slower than [3] only by a factor of K. However, L is smaller in DHTM because PO-CR optimizes for translation too, having very large basin of attraction. Additionally, by optimizing at the first level of the cascade only for scale, rotation and translation, and then casting votes in Hough space (as explained in the previous section), our method largely filters out most of the irrelevant background in the image leaving very few locations to evaluate in the subsequent levels of the cascade. Hence, in practice, the total complexity is $O(LK(nN))$ with $K = 1$ and $n = 4$. For a VGA image, our parallel, but not entirely optimized implementation, runs at 1–2 Hz [1]. Note that we can readily attain much higher speeds, by applying any object/face proposal techniques to reduce the number of evaluations per image.

Training. Training in DHTM is very simple and includes learning $\mathbf{R}(k)$ as described in Sect. 3.2, and learning the SVM model for face re-scoring as described in Sect. 3.4. To learn $\mathbf{R}(k)$, we used the available landmark annotations of the 300-W challenge [13]. Our PO-CR model built from this data set is able to fit images with large yaw variation ($\pm 60°$) but not entirely profile images (yaw $\approx 90°$). Hence, we annotated more than 1000 profile images from the ALFW dataset and the internet, which we will make publicly available. For training the SVM model, we fitted our PO-CR approach to our training sets and used the fitted shapes as positive examples. This resulted in more realistic positive examples than using the ground truth shapes. Finally, negative examples were obtained by scanning background images and then recording all locations for which the number of votes obtained by HT voting was greater than 40.

4   Results

We report results on three tasks namely face detection, face detection followed by face alignment and face tracking.

4.1   Face Detection Experiments

To evaluate the performance of our method on face detection, two of the most popular in-the-wild datasets were used, namely AFW [3] and FDDB [10]. AFW is built from Flickr images. It consists of 205 images with a total of 474 annotated faces [4]. The images within this dataset tend to contain cluttered background and faces with large variations in both viewpoint and appearance. FDDB consists of 2845 images, with a total of 5171 ellipse face annotations. This dataset includes very challenging low resolution, out of focus and occluded faces. To report face detection performance, we generated the familiar precision-recall curve using the standard PASCAL protocol. In particular, faces are only considered detected if the intersection-over-union (IoU) ratio between the ground truth and the detected bounding box exceeds 50 %. For FDDB, we also report the value of IoU, known as "continuous score". In addition to the performance of DHTM, we report the performance of the top performing methods for each dataset.

Figure 2 summarizes our results on AFW. We compare with the methods recently reported in [4]. When the IoU overlap is set to 50 %, our detector is

---

[1] All tests were done using a NVIDIA GeForce GTX 980 GPU and an Intel I7–4790 k CPU, on a PC running Windows 8.1 64-bit with 16 GB of RAM. The proposed system was compiled for GPU devices of compute capability 3.5 and above, using the CUDA 7.0 development toolkit.

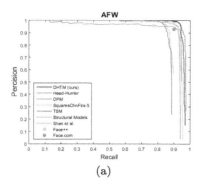 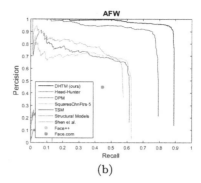

(a)   (b)

Fig. 2. Precision recall for AFW. (a) IoU ratio is set to the standard 50 %. (b) IoU ratio is set to 75 %.

comparable to both current commercial and published state-of-the-art methods. To further show the accuracy of our proposed detector, we increased the IoU overlap to 75 %, and as can be seen in Fig. 2(b), our detector clearly outperforms all commercial and published methods by a margin of over 10 % in detection accuracy.

Figure 3 summarizes our results on FDDB. We compare the performance of our proposed detector against the currently published state-of-the-art methods of [3,4,14,20–22,34,35]. For discrete scores, as shown in Fig. 3(a), our system is one of the top performing methods being outperformed only by [20–22]. All three methods are based on deep learning features. We have found that although PO-CR can fit some very difficult faces, the weakest component of our system is the SVM based on SIFT/colour features which for such faces yields low scores. Hence by incorporating deep learning features into our system, one can expect much better performance (this is left for future work). Notably, our system is the top performing method when using the continuous score, outperforming all [20–22] by a large margin.

4.2 Face Alignment and Tracking Experiments

For this experiment, we show localization performance of the *complete* DHTM system including face detection followed by facial feature localization. To measure landmark localization performance, we used the point-to-point Euclidean distance (pt-pt error) normalized by face size and report the cumulative curve corresponding to the fraction of images for which the error was less than a specific value [3]. We report performance on two very challenging datasets.

The first data set is COFW [17]. We chose this data set as it contains images with large amounts of occlusion. This not only affects face detection performance but also precise face localization which in turn affects facial feature localization accuracy. For comparison, we also report the performance of the combined system HeadHunter [4] followed by PO-CR. Figure 4(a) shows our results. Clearly, DHTM outperforms HeadHunter plus PO-CR by a large margin.

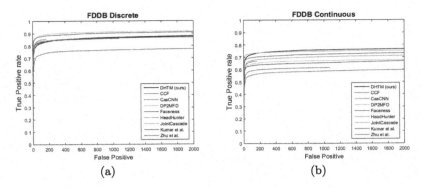

Fig. 3. Performance curves for FDDB. (a) Discrete score. (b) Continuous score.

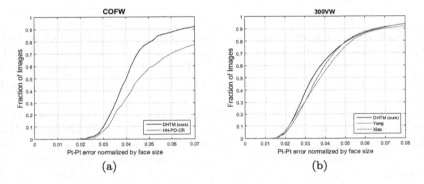

Fig. 4. Point-to-point error, relative to face size, for (a) COFW data set and (b) 300-VW (Category C) data set.

The second data set is the 300 videos in-the-wild (300-VW) data set recently released in [18]. We chose category C to report performance on as it is the most difficult category. This category contains 14 videos and more than 20,000 frames, therefore this is a very large scale experiment. Face localization in video is considered easier than in still images as one can exploit temporal coherency to improve performance, and indeed the top performing methods [22,36] do so. Instead, we considered each frame as a separate image and run our system to simultaneously detect the face and localize the landmarks. As Fig. 4(b) shows, even this case our system is outperforming the winners of the 300-VW competition.

5   Conclusions

We proposed a novel approach to face detection and landmark localization which we call Deformable Hough-Transform Model (DHTM). Our approach is largely motivated by the efficiency and robustness of recent cascaded regression approaches to facial landmark localization; essentially, rather than using a face detector to initialize them, we instead propose to employ them in order to detect the location of faces in an image too. Rather than scanning the image with discriminatively trained filters, we propose to employ the PO-CR algorithm in a *sliding window* fashion to fit a facial deformable model and capitalize on the large basin of attraction of PO-CR to set up a Hough-Transform voting scheme. We report comparable performance to that of state-of-the-art face detection algorithms and significant improvement over the standard face detection/landmark localization pipeline when performance is measured in terms of landmark localization.

References

1. Viola, P., Jones, M.: Rapid object detection using a boosted cascade of simple features. In: CVPR (2001)
2. Felzenszwalb, P.F., Girshick, R.B., McAllester, D., Ramanan, D.: Object detection with discriminatively trained part-based models. IEEE TPAMI 32(9), 1627–1645 (2010)
3. Zhu, X., Ramanan, D.: Face detection, pose estimation, and landmark estimation in the wild. In: CVPR (2012)
4. Mathias, M., Benenson, R., Pedersoli, M., Van Gool, L.: Face detection without bells and whistles. In: Fleet, D., Pajdla, T., Schiele, B., Tuytelaars, T. (eds.) ECCV 2014, Part IV. LNCS, vol. 8692, pp. 720–735. Springer, Heidelberg (2014)
5. Cootes, T., Edwards, G., Taylor, C.: Active appearance models. TPAMI 23(6), 681–685 (2001)
6. Dollár, P., Welinder, P., Perona, P.: Cascaded pose regression. In: CVPR (2010)
7. Cao, X., Wei, Y., Wen, F., Sun, J.: Face alignment by explicit shape regression. In: CVPR (2012)
8. Xiong, X., De la Torre, F.: Supervised descent method and its applications to face alignment. In: CVPR (2013)
9. Tzimiropoulos, G.: Project-out cascaded regression with an application to face alignment. In: CVPR (2015)
10. Jain, V., Learned-Miller, E.G.: FDDB: a benchmark for face detection in unconstrained settings. UMass Amherst Technical Report (2010)
11. Belhumeur, P., Jacobs, D., Kriegman, D., Kumar, N.: Localizing parts of faces using a consensus of exemplars. In: CVPR (2011)
12. Le, V., Brandt, J., Lin, Z., Bourdev, L., Huang, T.S.: Interactive facial feature localization. In: Fitzgibbon, A., Lazebnik, S., Perona, P., Sato, Y., Schmid, C. (eds.) ECCV 2012, Part III. LNCS, vol. 7574, pp. 679–692. Springer, Heidelberg (2012)
13. Sagonas, C., Tzimiropoulos, G., Zafeiriou, S., Pantic, M.: A semi-automatic methodology for facial landmark annotation. In: CVPR-W (2013)
14. Chen, D., Ren, S., Wei, Y., Cao, X., Sun, J.: Joint cascade face detection and alignment. In: Fleet, D., Pajdla, T., Schiele, B., Tuytelaars, T. (eds.) ECCV 2014, Part VI. LNCS, vol. 8694, pp. 109–122. Springer, Heidelberg (2014)
15. Chen, D., Cao, X., Wen, F., Sun, J.: Blessing of dimensionality: high-dimensional feature and its efficient compression for face verification. In: CVPR (2013)
16. Chew, S.W., Lucey, P., Lucey, S., Saragih, J., Cohn, J.F., Matthews, I., Sridharan, S.: In the pursuit of effective affective computing: the relationship between features and registration. IEEE SMC-B 42(4), 1006–1016 (2012)

17. Burgos-Artizzu, X.P., Perona, P., Dollár, P.: Robust face landmark estimation under occlusion. In: ICCV (2013)
18. Shen, J., Zafeiriou, S., Chrysos, G., Kossaifi, J., Tzimiropoulos, G., Pantic, M.: The first facial landmark tracking in-the-wild challenge: benchmark and results. In: ICCV-W (2015)
19. Ghiasi, G., Fowlkes, C.C.: Occlusion coherence: detecting and localizing occluded faces. In: CVPR (2014)
20. Li, H., Lin, Z., Shen, X., Brandt, J., Hua, G.: A convolutional neural network cascade for face detection. In: CVPR (2015)
21. Ranjan, R., Patel, V.M., Chellappa, R.: A deep pyramid deformable part model for face detection. arXiv preprint (2015). arXiv:1508.04389
22. Yang, S., Luo, P., Loy, C.C., Tang, X.: From facial parts responses to face detection: a deep learning approach. In: ICCV (2015)
23. Shen, X., Lin, Z., Brandt, J., Wu, Y.: Detecting and aligning faces by image retrieval. In: CVPR (2013)
24. Sun, Y., Wang, X., Tang, X.: Deep convolutional network cascade for facial point detection. In: CVPR (2013)
25. Ren, S., Cao, X., Wei, Y., Sun, J.: Face alignment at 3000 FPS via regressing local binary features. In: CVPR (2014)
26. Asthana, A., Zafeiriou, S., Cheng, S., Pantic, M.: Incremental face alignment in the wild. In: CVPR (2014)
27. Kazemi, V., Josephine, S.: One millisecond face alignment with an ensemble of regression trees. In: CVPR (2014)
28. Cootes, T.F., Ionita, M.C., Lindner, C., Sauer, P.: Robust and accurate shape model fitting using random forest regression voting. In: Fitzgibbon, A., Lazebnik, S., Perona, P., Sato, Y., Schmid, C. (eds.) ECCV 2012, Part VII. LNCS, vol. 7578, pp. 278–291. Springer, Heidelberg (2012)
29. Yu, X., Lin, Z., Brandt, J., Metaxas, D.N.: Consensus of regression for occlusion-robust facial feature localization. In: Fleet, D., Pajdla, T., Schiele, B., Tuytelaars, T. (eds.) ECCV 2014, Part IV. LNCS, vol. 8692, pp. 105–118. Springer, Heidelberg (2014)
30. Matthews, I., Baker, S.: Active appearance models revisited. IJCV 60(2), 135–164 (2004)
31. Lowe, D.G.: Distinctive image features from scale-invariant keypoints. IJCV 60(2), 91–110 (2004)
32. Baker, S., Matthews, I.: Lucas-kanade 20 years on: a unifying framework. IJCV 56(3), 221–255 (2004)
33. Tzimiropoulos, G., Pantic, M.: Gauss-Newton deformable part models for face alignment in-the-wild. In: CVPR (2014)
34. Yang, B., Yan, J., Lei, Z., Li, S.Z.: Convolutional channel features. In: ICCV (2015)
35. Kumar, V., Namboodiri, A., Jawahar, C.: Visual phrases for exemplar face detection. In: ICCV (2015)
36. Xiao, S., Yan, S., Kassim, A.: Facial landmark detection via progressive initialization. In: ICCV-W (2015)

3D Face Alignment in the Wild: A Landmark-Free, Nose-Based Approach

Flávio H. de Bittencourt Zavan$^{(\boxtimes)}$, Antônio C.P. Nascimento, Luan P. e Silva, Olga R.P. Bellon, and Luciano Silva

Departmento de Informática, Universidade Federal do Paraná, Curitiba, Brazil
{flavio,antonio.paes,luan.porfirio,olga,luciano}@ufpr.br

Abstract. We present a methodology for 3D face alignment in the wild, such that only the nose is required as input for assessing the position of the landmarks. Our approach works by first detecting the nose region, which is used for estimating the head pose. After that, a generic face landmark model, obtained by averaging all training images, is rotated, translated and scaled based on the size and localization of the nose. Because little information is needed and there are no refinement steps, our method is able to find suitable landmarks even in challenging poses. While not taking into account facial expressions and specific facial traits, our algorithm achieved competitive scores on the 3D Face Alignment in the Wild (3DFAW) challenge. The obtained results have the potential to be used as rough estimation of the position of the 3D face landmarks in the wild images, which can be further refined by specially designed algorithms.

Keywords: 3D face alignment · Head pose estimation · Faces in the wild

1 Introduction

Face alignment is defined as determining the position of a set of known facial points across different subjects, illuminations, expressions and poses [4]. 3D face alignment in the wild is defined as determining the position of these landmarks in the 3D space given only a 2D image acquired in unconstrained environments. This information can be used for several computer vision applications, such as face recognition [11], pose estimation [7], face tracking [14,15], 3D face reconstruction [1] and expression transfer [12,13].

Recent face alignment work can be subdivided into 2D and 3D methods. Zhu and Ramanan [19] use mixtures of trees with a shared pool of parts for sparsely aligning faces even in profile head poses, successfully calculating the position of the 2D landmarks. Ren *et al.* [8] uses regression local binary features to perform 2D sparse face landmark estimation at 3000 frames per second. Jeni *et al.* [4] is able achieve state-of-the-art real-time 3D dense face alignment by fitting a 3D model on images acquired in controlled environments. The use of cascaded

© Springer International Publishing Switzerland 2016
G. Hua and H. Jégou (Eds.): ECCV 2016 Workshops, Part II, LNCS 9914, pp. 581–589, 2016.
DOI: 10.1007/978-3-319-48881-3_40

coupled-regressors, by integrating a 3D point distribution model was proposed by Jourabloo and Liu [5] for estimating sparse 3D face landmarks in extreme poses.

In this paper, we present our entry for the 3D Facial Alignment in the Wild (3DFAW) challenge. Our approach is landmark-free in the sense that it does not need any specific face information, only a detected nose region that is used to estimate the head pose. A generic face landmark model is rotated based on the head pose, translated and scaled to fit the detected nose. We choose to use the nose as basis of our work as it has been shown efficient for head pose estimation, does not deform easily when facial expressions are present, is not easily occluded by accessories and is visible even in extreme profile head poses [17]. Our method does not make use of any facial trait specific to the subject and does not take facial expression into account, yet it achieves competitive results. Our approach works well as an initial estimation for the position of the landmarks, since it only needs the nose region, which can be easily obtained with existing detection methods even in challenging environments.

The 3DFAW challenge presents a set of images and annotations for evaluating the performance of in the wild 3D sparse face alignment methods. Part of the data is from the MultiPIE dataset [2] or from images and videos collected on the internet, having its depth information been recovered through a dense 3D from 2D videos alignment method [4]. The rest of the data was synthetically generated by rendering the 3D models present in the BU-4DFE [16] and BP4D-Spontaneous [18] databases onto different backgrounds. The training data includes the face bounding box and the 3D coordinates of 66 facial landmarks, while the testing data only includes the face bounding box.

The results obtained on the challenge's dataset are evaluated using two different metrics: Ground Truth Error (GTE) (Eq. 1) and Cross View Ground Truth Consistency Error (CVGTCE) (Eq. 2), such that X is the prediction, Y is the ground-truth, d_i is the Euclidean distance between the corner of the eyes for the i-th image [10] and P is obtained using Eq. 3.

$$E(X,Y) = \frac{1}{N} \sum_{k=1}^{N} \frac{\|x_k - y_k\|_2}{d_i} \tag{1}$$

$$E_{vc}(X,Y,P) = \frac{1}{N} \sum_{k=1}^{N} \frac{\|(sRx_k + t) - y_k\|_2}{d_i} \tag{2}$$

$$P = \{s, R, t\} = \operatorname*{argmin}_{s,R,t} \sum_{k=1}^{N} \|y_k - (sRx_k + t)\|_2^2 \tag{3}$$

This paper is structured as follows: Sect. 2 explains our method in detail, with attention to each step; Sect. 3 presents and explains our results on the 3DFAW challenge; and Sect. 4 includes final remarks.

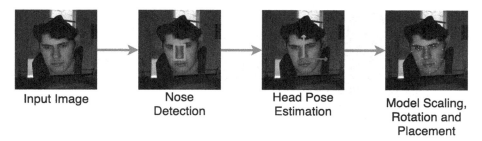

| Input Image | Nose Detection | Head Pose Estimation | Model Scaling, Rotation and Placement |

Fig. 1. Overview of our method

2 Our Approach

Our method is composed of seven steps, four offline and three online: 1. A nose detector is trained; 2. An average face model is generated to be used as template and for calibrating the pose; 3. Ground-truth head poses are extracted; 4. A head pose estimator is trained; 5. Nose detection is performed; 6. The detected region is used for estimating the head pose; 7. The face model is adjusted to the pose and fitted using the nose for alignment. The simplicity of the online steps is outlined in Fig. 1.

2.1 Landmark Model and Head Pose Ground-Truth Generation

A near frontal image (0° head yaw, pitch and roll) from the training subset was chosen to be used for calibrating all other images (Fig. 2(a)), it is defined as not having any rotation on any of the three axes.

For generating the ground-truth head pose, an affine transformation is applied to the landmarks belonging to all images in the training subsets relative to the landmarks in the calibration image (Fig. 2(b)), such that a transformation matrix including translation, scale and rotation is generated. The Euler angles are extracted from this matrix and defined as the ground-truth head yaw, pitch and roll.

The landmark model (Fig. 2(c)) is generated by applying the aforementioned transformation to the training data, normalizing the scale based on the distance of landmarks number 32 and 36 on the base of the nose and averaging the position of each landmark. The resulting model roughly represents the average face with a neutral expression in the dataset.

2.2 Nose Detection

Ground-truth nose regions are extracted by cropping the training images around the nose landmarks. Faster R-CNN [9] is trained with all training images in the 3DFAW dataset and used for detection. The Faster R-CNN introduces the novel concept and use of a Region Proposal Network, that generates both candidate bounding-boxes and detection confidence scores.

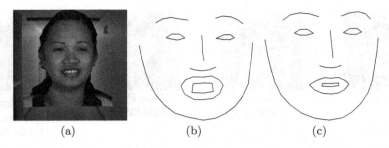

(a)	(b)	(c)

Fig. 2. (a) Calibration image; (b) Calibration landmarks; (c) Landmark model viewed with the calibration pose

When processing the testing images, the detected region with the highest confidence score is selected. If Faster R-CNN yields no candidates, a region at the center of the image is selected.

2.3   Head Pose Estimation

For performing head pose estimation, the CNN variant of NosePose [17] is applied. It uses a network similar to those crafted for face recognition [3,6], but modified to be trained with a smaller number of images and to support the smaller nose regions.

Training was performed using all images in all training subsets. The ground-truth head pose was discretized for both yaw and pitch in steps of 7.5°, the yaw ranges from −60 to 60 and the pitch, from −52.5 to 52.5°, relative to the calibration image. The roll is not estimated as only small variations are present in the dataset. These values were all empirically determined and a single network is trained for estimating both the yaw and the pitch simultaneously.

2.4   Model Fitting

Given the detected nose region, an optional face bounding box and the estimated head pose, the landmark model, explained in Sect. 2.1, is fitted on the face according to Algorithm 1. While having the face bounding box allows the method to perform a slightly more precise scaling of the model, it is not required as it is possible to infer the size of the face from the size of the nose.

Figure 3 contains examples of this process, including the detected nose region and face bounding-box. If the face bounding box is given, when scaling the model, three constants for minimizing the error are used, one for each axis. The best position used for aligning the model with the nose region and the factor used when scaling according to it were also determined in a similar fashion.

3   Experimental Results

In order to assess the performance of our nose detection step, manual verification of the results was performed on all 4,912 images in the testing subset. Only

Algorithm 1. Model Fitting Algorithm

function FITMODEL($model, noseBB, headPose, faceBB$)

　　$modelNoseBase \leftarrow average(model.noseBaseLeft, model.noseBaseRight)$

　　$rotate(model, modelNoseBase, headPose)$

　　if $isDefined(faceBB)$ **then**

　　　　$xScale \leftarrow .975 * faceBB.width/model.width$

　　　　$yScale \leftarrow .975 * faceBB.height/model.height$

　　　　$zScale \leftarrow (xScale + yScale)/2 * .95$

　　　　$scale(model, xScale, yScale, zScale)$

　　else

　　　　$modelNoseWidth \leftarrow l2Norm(model.noseBaseLeft, model.noseBaseRight)$

　　　　$scale(model, .6 * nose.width/modelNoseWidth)$

　　end if

　　$noseBase \leftarrow \{nose.x + nose.width * .5, nose.y + nose.height * .9, 0\}$

　　$translate(model, modelNoseBase - noseBase)$

　　$translate(model, \{0, 0, -average(model).z\})$

　　return model

end function

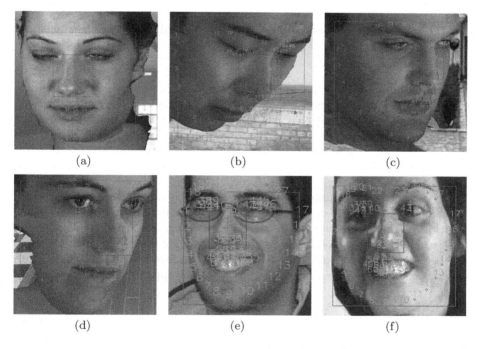

Fig. 3. Example results of the model fitting stage, showing the face bounding-box in red, the detected nose region in blue and the estimated position of the landmarks in green. (a) Near frontal good fit; (b) Bad fit caused by bad head pitch estimation; (c) and (d) Half-profile good fit; (e) Good fit in an image sourced from the MultiPIE dataset; (f) Modest fit in one of the most challenging images in the dataset (Color figure online)

nine images failed to yield detections, however, the wrong region was detected in four images and the nose belonging to the wrong subject was detected in one. The detection was accurate in 99.71 % of the images. This high rate is expected as a state-of-the-art detection method was used and all images are high resolution with very few of them including blur and variations in lighting. Figure 4 illustrates three cases where the detector failed.

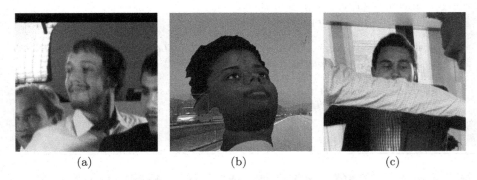

(a)   (b)   (c)

Fig. 4. Images where the nose detection (blue box) failed: (a) Wrong nose detected; (b) False positive; (c) No detection (Color figure online)

Isolating and assessing the head pose estimation performance is not possible as the ground-truth landmarks were not made available and visually verifying the correctness of the head pose is a difficult problem for humans [17]. Its performance, however, reflects on the final landmark estimation score, which was calculated by the challenge's web system. Our method achieved 5.9093 CVGTCE and 10.8001 GTE when scaling the model according to the size of the face bounding box.

Due to the limited number of allowed submissions to the web system and not being able to locally assess our method's performance, we do not present a quantitative evaluation when the size of the nose region is used to infer the size of the face. However, we performed visual inspection of the results and concluded they are consistent with those obtained using the face bounding box. Figure 5 presents examples of our results using both scaling approaches, for comparison.

4   Final Remarks

We presented a nose region based approach for in the wild 3D landmark estimation, our entry for the 3D Face Alignment in the Wild Challenge. A generic face landmark model is generated using the information present in the training subset of the challenge. A high-performance, state-of-the-art nose detector and head pose estimator are trained using the nose regions extracted from the landmark annotations. The detected nose is used for estimating the head pose and

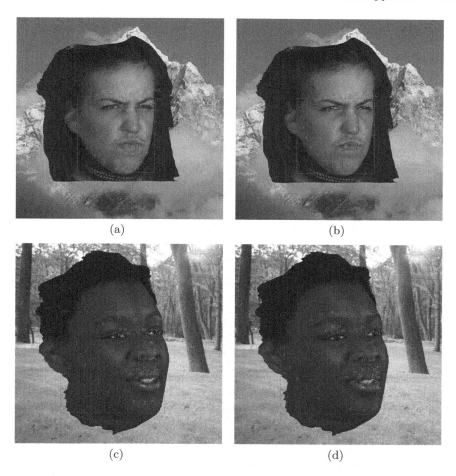

Fig. 5. Visual comparison between the two different model scaling methods. The results obtained using the detected nose region are on the left and the ones obtained with the face bounding box are on the right. (a) and (b) the model fitted with the nose is noticeably larger; (c) and (d) using the nose yielded better results

projecting the rotated landmark model according to the size of the face, either inferred from the size of the nose or from the available face bounding-box. Competitive results were achieved while taking neither facial expressions nor facial traits into account. Because only the nose region is needed for performing our estimation, it has the potential to be used for calculating useful initial landmark positions that can be refined for finer face alignment.

Acknowledgment. The authors would like to thank CNPq and CAPES for supporting this research.

References

1. Blanz, V., Vetter, T.: A morphable model for the synthesis of 3d faces. In: Proceedings of the 26th Annual Conference on Computer Graphics and Interactive Techniques (SIGGRAPH 1999), pp. 187–194. ACM Press/Addison-Wesley Publishing Co., New York (1999). http://dx.doi.org/10.1145/311535.311556
2. Gross, R., Matthews, I., Cohn, J., Kanade, T., Baker, S.: Multi-pie. In: 8th IEEE International Conference on Automatic Face Gesture Recognition (FG 2008), pp. 1–8 (2008)
3. Hu, G., Yang, Y., Yi, D., Kittler, J., Christmas, W., Li, S., Hospedales, T.: When face recognition meets with deep learning: an evaluation of convolutional neural networks for face recognition. In: IEEE International Conference on Computer Vision Workshops (ICCVW), pp. 142–150 (2015)
4. Jeni, L.A., Cohn, J.F., Kanade, T.: Dense 3D face alignment from 2D video for real-time use. In: Image and Vision Computing (2016). http://www.sciencedirect.com/science/article/pii/S0262885616300877
5. Jourabloo, A., Liu, X.: Pose-invariant 3D face alignment. In: The IEEE International Conference on Computer Vision (ICCV) (2015)
6. Krizhevsky, A., Sutskever, I., Hinton, G.E.: Imagenet classification with deep convolutional neural networks. In: Advances in Neural Information Processing Systems (NIPS), pp. 1097–1105 (2012)
7. Murphy-Chutorian, E., Trivedi, M.M.: Head pose estimation in computer vision: a survey. IEEE Trans. Pattern Anal. Mach. Intell. **31**(4), 607–626 (2009)
8. Ren, S., Cao, X., Wei, Y., Sun, J.: Face alignment via regressing local binary features. IEEE Trans. Image Process. **25**(3), 1233–1245 (2016)
9. Ren, S., He, K., Girshick, R., Sun, J.: Faster R-CNN: towards real-time object detection with region proposal networks. In: Cortes, C., Lawrence, N.D., Lee, D.D., Sugiyama, M., Garnett, R. (eds.) Advances in Neural Information Processing Systems, pp. 91–99. Curran Associates, Inc., Red Hook (2015). http://papers.nips.cc/paper/5638-faster-r-cnn-towards-real-time-object-detection-with-region-proposal-networks.pdf
10. Sagonas, C., Antonakos, E., Tzimiropoulos, G., Zafeiriou, S., Pantic, M.: 300 faces in-the-wild challenge: database and results. Image Vis. Comput. 47, 3–18 (2016), 300-W, The First Automatic Facial Landmark Detection in-the-Wild Challenge. http://www.sciencedirect.com/science/article/pii/S0262885616000147
11. Taigman, Y., Yang, M., Ranzato, M., Wolf, L.: Deepface: closing the gap to human-level performance in face verification. In: 2014 IEEE Conference on Computer Vision and Pattern Recognition, pp. 1701–1708 (2014)
12. Thies, J., Zollhöfer, M., Nießner, M., Valgaerts, L., Stamminger, M., Theobalt, C.: Real-time expression transfer for facial reenactment. ACM Trans. Graph. (TOG) **34**(6), 183 (2015)
13. Thies, J., Zollhöfer, M., Stamminger, M., Theobalt, C., Nießner, M.: Face2face: real-time face capture and reenactment of RGB videos. In: Proceedings of Computer Vision and Pattern Recognition (CVPR). IEEE (2016)
14. la Torre, F.D., Chu, W.S., Xiong, X., Vicente, F., Ding, X., Cohn, J.: Intraface. In: 2015 11th IEEE International Conference and Workshops on Automatic Face and Gesture Recognition (FG), vol. 1, pp. 1–8 (2015)
15. Yang, J., Deng, J., Zhang, K., Liu, Q.: Facial shape tracking via spatio-temporal cascade shape regression. In: 2015 IEEE International Conference on Computer Vision Workshop (ICCVW), pp. 994–1002 (2015)

16. Yin, L., Chen, X., Sun, Y., Worm, T., Reale, M.: A high-resolution 3D dynamic facial expression database. In: 8th IEEE International Conference on Automatic Face Gesture Recognition (FG 2008), pp. 1–6 (2008)
17. Zavan, F.H.B., Nascimento, A.C.P., Bellon, O.R.P., Silva, L.: Nosepose: a competitive, landmark-free methodology for head pose estimation in-the-wild (2016)
18. Zhang, X., Yin, L., Cohn, J.F., Canavan, S., Reale, M., Horowitz, A., Liu, P., Girard, J.M.: BP-4D-spontaneous: a high-resolution spontaneous 3D dynamic facial expression database. Image Vis. Comput. 32(10), 692–706 (2014), Best of Automatic Face and Gesture Recognition 2013. http://www.sciencedirect.com/science/article/pii/S0262885614001012
19. Zhu, X., Ramanan, D.: Face detection, pose estimation, and landmark localization in the wild. In: 2012 IEEE Conference on Computer Vision and Pattern Recognition (CVPR), pp. 2879–2886 (2012)

Fast and Precise Face Alignment and 3D Shape Reconstruction from a Single 2D Image

Ruiqi Zhao, Yan Wang, C. Fabian Benitez-Quiroz, Yaojie Liu,
and Aleix M. Martinez[✉]

The Ohio State University, Columbus, USA
{zhao.823,wang.9021,benitez-quiroz.1,liu.4002,martinez.158}@osu.edu

Abstract. Many face recognition applications require a precise 3D reconstruction of the shape of the face, even when only a single 2D image is available. We present a novel regression approach that learns to detect facial landmark points and estimate their 3D shape rapidly and accurately from a single face image. The main idea is to regress a function $f(.)$ that maps 2D images of faces to their corresponding 3D shape from a large number of sample face images under varying pose, illumination, identity and expression. To model the non-linearity of this function, we use a deep neural network and demonstrate how it can be efficiently trained using a large number of samples. During testing, our algorithm runs at more than 30 frames/s on an i7 desktop. This algorithm was the top 2 performer in the 3DFAW Challenge.

Keywords: 3D modeling and reconstruction of faces · Fine-grained detection · 3D shape from a single 2D image · Precise and detailed detections

1 Introduction

Humans can readily and accurately estimate the 3D shape of a face by simply observing a single 2D image example of it. Recent results demonstrate that humans use this shape information to infer identity, expression, facial actions and other properties from such 3D reconstructions [1]. Several computer vision approaches have been developed over the years that attempt to replicate this outstanding ability, e.g., [2–6] provide 3D shape estimates of a set of 2D landmark points on a single image, [7,8] use 2D landmark points over several images, and [9–11] provide 3D shape reconstructions from 2D images. Unfortunately, the results of these algorithms are not yet comparable to those of humans [12].

The present paper describes a novel algorithm that provides a fast and precise estimation of the 3D shape of a face from a single 2D image. The major idea of the paper is to define a mapping function $f(.)$ that identifies the 3D shape of a face from the shading patterns observed in a 2D image. This is illustrated in Fig. 1. As seen in this image, the goal is to define a function $\mathbf{s} = f(\mathbf{a})$ that, given an image $\mathbf{a} \in \mathbb{R}^p$ (p the number of pixels), yields the 3D coordinates of the l landmark points defining the shape of the face, $\mathbf{s} \in \mathbb{R}^{3l}$.

© Springer International Publishing Switzerland 2016
G. Hua and H. Jégou (Eds.): ECCV 2016 Workshops, Part II, LNCS 9914, pp. 590–603, 2016.
DOI: 10.1007/978-3-319-48881-3_41

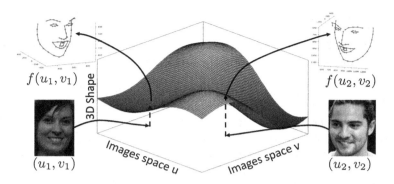

Fig. 1. Conceptual illustration of the proposed approach. The u and v axes correspond to the face image space (pixel values), while the z axis corresponds to the 3D shape. A finite set of face image samples and their associated 2D shape landmarks are used to estimate the parameters of a deep network. This network defines a mapping $f(.)$ from a face image sample to its associated 3D shape.

Given the large number of possible identities, illuminations, poses and expressions, this functional mapping $f(.)$ is difficult to estimate. To resolve this problem, we use a deep neural network. A deep neural network is a regression approach to estimate non-linear mappings of the form $\mathbf{s} = f(\mathbf{a})$, where $\mathbf{a}$ is the input and $\mathbf{s}$ is the output. This means that the network must have p input and $3l$ output nodes. The number of hidden layers and non-linear functions between layers are what allow us to learn the complex 2D image to 3D shape mapping. This is in sharp contrast to linear regression methods attempted before [2–6] as well as non-linear attempts to model 2D shape from a single image [13–15] or 3D shape from multiple images [6, 16].

Compared to previous approaches, our algorithm is also able to learn from a small and large number of 3D sample shapes. A small number of samples might not seem sufficient to learn our regressor, but we define data augmentation methods that allow us to circumvent this problem. This is done by using a camera model to generate multiple views of the same 3D shape and the matching 2D landmark point on the original sample image. We demonstrate how this approach is able to successfully and accurately recover the 3D shape of faces from a single view.

We submitted the results of the herein defined algorithm to the 3D Face Alignment in the Wild (3DFAW) challenge. Our algorithm yielded an accuracy of 3.97 %. This was the second best result (with the top algorithm only slightly better at 3.47 % accuracy). We provide additional comparative results with the other 3DFAW participants and algorithms defined in the literature.

It is also important to mention that our derived multilayer neural network can be trained very quickly and testing runs faster than real-time (> 30 frames/s).

2 Related Work

Three-dimensional (3D) reconstruction from a single face image can be roughly divided into two approaches: dense 3D estimation using synthesis and 3D landmark estimation.

With respect to dense 3D face modeling, the main challenge is locating a dense set of corresponding face features in a variety of face images [9]. A parametric morphable face model is generally used to generate arbitrary synthetic images under different poses and illumination, using a 3D Point Distribution Model (PDM) on the morphing function to constrain the face space [9]. Basel Face Model (BFM) [10] improves the texture accuracy while reducing correspondence artifacts by improving the scanning methodology and the registration model. To learn a model from a set of 3D scans of faces, an automatic framework was designed to estimate 3D face shape and texture of faces under varying pose and illumination [16]. In [17], a 3D morphable model was constructed from > 9,000 3D facial scans, by using a novel and almost fully automated construction pipeline. And, in [18], a single template face is used as a reference prior to reconstruct the 3D surface of test faces using a shape-from-shading algorithm. Other approaches are designed to combine 2D and 3D Active Appearance Models (AAM) by constraining a 2D AAM with the equivalent 3D shape modes, which has advantages in both fitting speed and ease of model construction [19,20]. In [11] a monocular face shape reconstruction is formulated as a 2-fold Coupled Structure Learning process, which consists of the regression between two subspaces spanned by 3D and 2D sparse landmarks, and a coupled dictionary of 3D dense and sparse shapes. These models tend to be computational expensive and their model complexity typically yields subpar alignments and reconstructions.

The alternative approach is 3D landmark estimation where we use an image to infer a set of points describing the contour of a set of facial features, e.g., eyes, eyebrows, nose, mouth, etc. These methods are directly related with our proposed algorithm. In [21], a fully automatic method to estimate 3D face shape from a single image is proposed without resorting to manual annotations. This is done by first computing gradient features to get a rough initial estimate of the 2D landmarks. These initial positions are iteratively refined by estimating the 3D shape and pose using an EM-like algorithm. Recently, Cascaded Regression Approach (CRA) has been employed to detect 3D face landmarks from a single image [22,23]. The general idea of CRA is to start from an initial estimate and then learn a sequence of regressors to gradually reduce the distance between this estimate and the actual ground-truth. Specifically, in [22] the authors assume that 3D face shapes can be modeled using PDM. In [23], a direct 3D landmark detection approach is proposed. Here, from an initial set of 3D landmark points, tree-based regressors are used to improve the estimate of the 3D shape of the face. The authors argue that a two steps approaches, i.e., 2D landmark detection and 3D estimation, is generally computationally expensive and needs to be avoided. We prove otherwise. A contribution of our work is to demonstrate that the step of *upgrading* from 2D to 3D landmark points is computationally efficient (running at > 1,000 images/s) and yields better accuracies than previous algorithms.

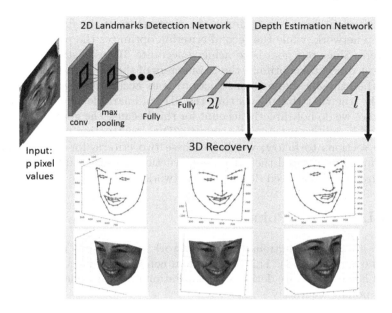

Fig. 2. Proposed network architecture. The face is detected using a standard face detector. The first layers of the network detect the 2D coordinates of l landmarks, x and y coordinates of the landmark points. The latter layers of our network then add the depth information to these 2D landmark points, z values.

3   Method Overview

Our proposed method is illustrated in Fig. 1. As described earlier, our goal is to learn (regress) the non-linear mapping function $\mathbf{s} = f(\mathbf{a})$ from an image $\mathbf{a}$ to a set of 3D landmark points $\mathbf{s}$ defining the 3D shape of the face.

We derive a deep neural network to regress this function $f(.)$. Deep neural networks allow us to model complex, non-linear functions from large numbers of samples. Our samples include 2D images of faces $\mathbf{a}_i$, $i = 1, \ldots, n$, and $n = n_1 + n_2$, with the first n_1 images with their corresponding 2D and 3D shapes, $\mathbf{s}_i$, and the second n_2 images with just 2D shapes. Our proposed network architecture is illustrated in Fig. 2. As can be seen in this figure, we have p entry nodes, representing the p image pixels of the face, and $3l$ output nodes, defining the 3D shape of the face. To facilitate the learning of the function $f(.)$, the entry p nodes must only define the face and, hence, this needs to be aligned. To this end, we use [24] to detect the face, so that the bounding box is resized to have p pixels.

Next, we need to define the optimization criteria of our neural network. The proposed approach requires us to define two optimization criteria. First, we need to derive a criterion for the accurate detection of the 2D landmark points on the aligned image. Second, we must define a criterion for converting these 2D landmark points to 3D. These two criteria are illustrated in Fig. 2. Note that the first criterion is used to optimize the parameters of the first several layers of our deep network, while the second criterion optimizes the parameters of the latter layers. Since our goal is to achieve accurate 3D reconstructions, we will use gradient descent to optimize the parameters of the network until the second criterion (i.e., the 3D shape reconstruction) is as accurate as possible. While it is generally true that this means that the 2D landmark detections needs to be accurate too, we do not directly account for this because the goal of the 3DFAW competition is only to provide an accurate 3D reconstruction of the face.

In the sections to follow, we derive these two criteria for the detection of the 2D fiducial points and their 3D reconstruction and define the details of the architecture of the proposed deep neural network.

4   2D Landmark Points

We define a deep convolutional neural network with p input nodes, $2l$ output nodes and 6 layers (Fig. 2). This includes four convolutional layers and two fully-connected layers. Next, we derive an optimization criterion to learn to detect 2D landmark points accurately.

4.1   Optimization Criterion

Let us define the image samples and their corresponding 2D output variable (i.e., 2D landmark points) as the set $\{(\mathbf{a}_1, \mathbf{o}_1), \ldots, (\mathbf{a}_n, \mathbf{o}_n)\}$, where $\mathbf{o}_i$ is the true (desirable) location of the 2D landmark points of the face. Note that $\mathbf{o}_i$ is a vector of $2l$ image coordinates, $\mathbf{o}_i = (u_{i1}, v_{i1}, \ldots, u_{il}, v_{il})^T$, where $(u_{ij}, v_{ij})^T$ is the jth landmark point.

The goal of a computer vision system is to identify the vector of mapping functions $\mathbf{f}(\mathbf{a}_i, \mathbf{w}) = (f_1(\mathbf{a}_i, w_1), \ldots, f_r(\mathbf{a}_i, w_l))^T$ that converts the input image $\mathbf{a}_i$ to an output vector $\mathbf{o}_i$ of detections, and $\mathbf{w} = (w_1, \ldots, w_l)^T$ is the vector of parameters of these mapping functions. Hence, $f_j(\mathbf{a}_i, w_j) = (\hat{u}_{ij}, \hat{v}_{ij})^T$ are the estimates of the 2D image coordinates u_{ij} and v_{ij}, and w_j are the parameters of the function f_j.

For a fixed mapping function $\mathbf{f}(\mathbf{a}_i, \mathbf{w})$ (e.g., a ConvNet), the goal is to optimize $\mathbf{w}$; formally,

$$\mathcal{J}(\widetilde{\mathbf{w}}) = \min_{\mathbf{w}} \mathcal{L}_{\text{local}}(\mathbf{f}(\mathbf{a}_i, \mathbf{w}), \mathbf{o}_i), \tag{1}$$

where $\mathcal{L}_{\text{local}}(.)$ denotes the loss function. Specifically, we use the L^2-loss defined as,

$$\mathcal{L}_{\text{local}}(\mathbf{f}(\mathbf{a}_i, \mathbf{w}), \mathbf{o}_i) = l^{-1} \sum_{j=1}^{l} (f_j(\mathbf{a}_i, w_j) - \mathbf{o}_{ij})^2, \tag{2}$$

where $\mathbf{o}_{ij}$ is the jth element of $\mathbf{o}_i$, i.e., $\mathbf{o}_{ij} \in \mathbb{R}^2$.

Without loss of generality, and to simplify notation, we will use $\mathbf{f}_i$ in lieu of $\mathbf{f}(\mathbf{a}_i, \mathbf{w})$ and f_{ij} instead of $f_j(\mathbf{a}_i, w_j)$. Note that the functions f_{ij} are the same for all i, but may be different for distinct values of j.

The above derivations correspond to a *local* fit. That is, (1) and (2) attempt to optimize the fit of each one of the outputs *independently* and then take the average fit over all outputs. This approach has several solutions, even for a fixed fitting error. For example, the error can be equally distributed across *all* outputs $\|f_{ij} - \mathbf{o}_{ij}\|_2 \approx \|f_{ik} - \mathbf{o}_{ik}\|_2$, $\forall j, k$, where $\|.\|_2$ is the 2-norm of a vector. Or, most of the error is in one (or a few) of the estimates: $\|f_{ij} - \mathbf{o}_{ij}\|_2 >> \|f_{ik} - \mathbf{o}_{ik}\|_2$ and $\|f_{ik} - \mathbf{o}_{ik}\|_2 \approx 0$, $\forall k \neq j$. In general, for a fixed fitting error, the latter example is less preferable, because it leads to large errors in one of the output variables. When this happens we say that the algorithm did not converge as expected.

One solution to this problem is to add an additional constraint to minimize

$$\frac{2}{r(r+1)} \sum_{1 \leq j < k \leq r} |(f_{ij} - \mathbf{o}_{ij}) - (f_{ik} - \mathbf{o}_{ik})|^c , \tag{3}$$

with $c \geq 1$. However, this typically results in very slow training, limiting the amount of training data that can be efficiently used. By reducing the number of training samples, we generalize worse and typically obtain less accurate detections [25]. Another typical problem of this equation is that it sometime leads to non-convergence (or convergence with very large fitting error), because the constraint is not flexible enough for current optimization algorithms. We solve these problems by adding a *global* fitting criterion that instead of slowing or halting desirable convergences, it speeds them up.

To do this, it is key to note that the constraint in (2) is local because it measures the fit of each element of $\mathbf{o}_i$ (i.e., $\mathbf{o}_{ij}$) independently. By *local*, we mean that we only care about that one local result. The same criterion can nonetheless be used to measure the fit of pairs of points; formally,

$$\mathcal{L}_{\text{pairs}}(\mathbf{f}_i, \mathbf{o}_i) = \frac{2}{l(l+1)} \sum_{1 \leq j < k \leq l} \left(g\left(f_{ij}, f_{ik}\right) - g\left(\mathbf{o}_{ij}, \mathbf{o}_{ik}\right)\right)^2 , \tag{4}$$

where $g(\mathbf{d}, \mathbf{e}) = \|\mathbf{d} - \mathbf{e}\|_b$ is the *b*-norm of $\mathbf{d} - \mathbf{e}$ (e.g., the 2-norm, $g(\mathbf{d}, \mathbf{be}) = \sqrt{(\mathbf{d} - \mathbf{e})^T (\mathbf{d} - \mathbf{e})}$).

Key to these derivations is to realize that (4) is no longer local, since it takes into account the *global* structure of each pair of elements. This resolves the problems of (2) enumerated above, yielding accurate detections of landmark points and fast training.

4.2   Implementation Details

We set $l = 66$ and use $n_1 + n_2 = 18600$ samples. As mentioned above, we use four convolutional layers, two max pooling layers and two fully connected layers. Following [26], we apply normalization, dropout, and rectified linear units (ReLU) at the end of each convolutional layer. One advantage of our proposed algorithm is that learning can be efficiently performed with very large datasets. Since we wish to have a landmark detector invariant to any affine transformation and partial occlusions, we also use a data augmentation approach. Specifically, we generated an additional $80,000$ images by applying two-dimensional affine transformations to the existing training set, i.e., scale, reflection, translation and rotation; scale was between 2 and .5, rotation was $-10°$ to $10°$, and translation and reflection were randomly generated. To make the network more robust to partial occlusions, we added random occluding boxes of $d \times d$ pixels as in [27], with d between .2 and .4 times the inter-eye distance; 25 % of our training images have partial occlusions.

5   3D Shape

Next, we describe how to recover the 3D information (i.e., the depth value) of the 2D landmark points detected above. We start by writing the n 2D landmark points on the ith image in matrix from as

$$\mathbf{U}_i = \begin{pmatrix} u_{i1} & u_{i2} & \cdots & u_{in} \\ v_{i1} & v_{i2} & \cdots & v_{in} \end{pmatrix} \in \mathbb{R}^{2 \times n}. \tag{5}$$

Our goal is to recover the 3D coordinates of these 2D landmark points,

$$\mathbf{S}_i = \begin{pmatrix} x_{i1} & x_{i2} & \cdots & x_{in} \\ y_{i1} & y_{i2} & \cdots & y_{in} \\ z_{i1} & z_{i2} & \cdots & z_{in} \end{pmatrix} \in \mathbb{R}^{3 \times n}, \tag{6}$$

where $(x_{ij}, y_{ij}, z_{ij})^T$ are the 3D coordinates of the jth face landmark.

Assuming a weak-perspective camera model, with calibrated camera matrix $\mathcal{M} = \begin{pmatrix} \lambda & 0 & 0 \\ 0 & \lambda & 0 \end{pmatrix}$, the weak-perspective projection of the face 3D landmark points is given by

$$\mathbf{U}_i = \mathcal{M}\mathbf{S}_i. \tag{7}$$

This result is of course defined up to scale, since $\boldsymbol{u}_i = \lambda \boldsymbol{x}_i$ and $\boldsymbol{v}_i = \lambda \boldsymbol{y}_i$, where $\mathbf{x}_i^T = (x_{i1}, x_{i2}, ..., x_{in})$, $\mathbf{y}_i^T = (y_{i1}, y_{i2}, ..., y_{in})$, $\mathbf{z}_i^T = (z_{i1}, z_{i2}, ..., z_{in})$, $\mathbf{u}_i^T = (u_{i1}, u_{i2}, ..., u_{in})$ and $\mathbf{v}_i^T = (v_{i1}, v_{i2}, ..., v_{in})$. This will require that we standardize our variables when deriving our algorithm.

5.1   Deep 3D Shape Reconstruction from 2D Landmarks

Proposed Neural Network. Given a training set with l 3D landmark points $\{\mathbf{S}_i\}_{i=1}^l$, we aim to learn the function $f : \mathbb{R}^{2l} \to \mathbb{R}^n$, that is,

$$\widehat{\mathbf{z}}_i = f(\widehat{\mathbf{x}}_i, \widehat{\mathbf{y}}_i), \tag{8}$$

where $\widehat{\mathbf{x}}_i$, $\widehat{\mathbf{y}}_i$ and $\widehat{\mathbf{z}}_i$ are obtained by standardizing $\mathbf{x}_i$, $\mathbf{y}_i$ and $\mathbf{z}_i$ as follows,

$$\begin{aligned} \widehat{x}_{ij} &= \frac{x_{ij} - \overline{\mathbf{x}}_i}{(\sigma(\mathbf{x}_i) + \sigma(\mathbf{y}_i))/2}, \\ \widehat{y}_{ij} &= \frac{y_{ij} - \overline{\mathbf{y}}_i}{(\sigma(\mathbf{x}_i) + \sigma(\mathbf{y}_i))/2}, \\ \widehat{z}_{ij} &= \frac{z_{ij} - \overline{\mathbf{z}}_i}{(\sigma(\mathbf{x}_i) + \sigma(\mathbf{y}_i))/2}, \end{aligned} \tag{9}$$

where $\overline{\mathbf{x}}_i$, $\overline{\mathbf{y}}_i$ and $\overline{\mathbf{z}}_i$ are mean values, and $\sigma(\mathbf{x}_i)$, $\sigma(\mathbf{y}_i)$ and $\sigma(\mathbf{z}_i)$ are the standard deviation of the elements in $\mathbf{x}_i$, $\mathbf{y}_i$ and $\mathbf{z}_i$, respectively.

We standardize $\mathbf{x}_i$, $\mathbf{y}_i$ and $\mathbf{z}_i$ to eliminate the effect of scaling and translation of the 3D face, as noted above. Herein, we model the function $f(.)$ using a multilayer neural network.

Figure 2 depicts the overall architecture of our neural network. It contains M layers. The mth layer is defined by,

$$a^{(m+1)} = \tanh\left(\Omega^{(m)}a^{(m)} + b^{(m)}\right),\tag{10}$$

where $a^{(m)} \in \mathbb{R}^d$ is an input vector, $a^{(m+1)} \in \mathbb{R}^r$ is the output vector, d and r specify the number of input and output nodes, respectively, and $\Omega \in \mathbb{R}^{r \times d}$ and $b \in \mathbb{R}^r$ are network parameters, with the former a weighting matrix and the latter a basis vector. Our neural network uses a Hyperbolic Tangent function, $\tanh(.)$.

Our objective is to minimize the sum of the Euclidean distances between the predicted depth location $a_i^{(m)}$ and the ground-truth $\widehat{z}_i$ of our l 3D landmark points, formally,

$$\min \sum_{i=1}^{l} \|\widehat{z}_i - a_i^{(m)}\|_2,\tag{11}$$

with $\|.\|_2$ the Euclidean distance of two vectors. We utilize the RMSProp algorithm [28] to optimize our model parameters.

Testing. When testing on the tth face, we have $\mathbf{u}_t$ and $\mathbf{v}_t$, and want to estimate $\mathbf{x}_t$, $\mathbf{y}_t$ and $\mathbf{z}_t$. From Eq. (7) we have $u_t = \lambda x_t$ and $v_t = \lambda y_t$. Thus, we first standardize the data,

$$\begin{aligned}\widehat{u}_{tj} &= \frac{u_{tj} - \overline{u}_t}{(\sigma(u_t) + \sigma(v_t))/2}, \\ \widehat{v}_{tj} &= \frac{v_{tj} - \overline{v}_t}{(\sigma(u_t) + \sigma(v_t))/2}.\end{aligned}\tag{12}$$

This yields $\widehat{x}_t = \widehat{u}_t$ and $\widehat{y}_t = \widehat{v}_t$. Therefore, we can directly feed $(\widehat{u}_t, \widehat{v}_t)$ into the trained neural network to obtain its depth $\widehat{z}_t$. Then, the 3D shape of the face can be recovered as $(\widehat{u}_t^T, \widehat{v}_t^T, \widehat{z}_t^T)^T$, a result that is defined up to scale.

Implementation Details. Our feed-forward neural network contains six layers. The number of nodes in each layer is $2n$, $2n$, $2n$, $2n$, $2n$, and n. We divide our training data into a training and a validation set. In each of these two sets, we perform data augmentation. Specifically, we use the weak-perspective camera model defined above to generate new 2D views of the 3D landmark points given in the training set. This process helps the algorithm learn how each 3D shape is seen from a large variety of 2D views (translation, rotation, scale). We use Keras library [29] on top of Theano [30] to develop our multilayer neural network. Early stopping is enabled to prevent overfitting and accelerate the training process.

We stop the training process if the validation error does not decrease after 10 iterations. We set the learning rate at .01.

6   Experimental Results

We report the result of our experiment on the data of the 3D Face Alignment in the Wild Challenge (3DFAW). Three of the four datasets in the challenge are subsets of MultiPIE [31], BU-4DFE [32] and BP4D-Spontaneous [33] databases respectively. Another dataset TimeSlice3D that contains annotated 2D images are extracted from online videos. The depth has been recovered using a model-based Structure from Motion technique [34]. In total, there are 18, 694 training images. Each image has 66 labeled 3D fiducial points and a face bounding box centered around the mean 2D projection of the landmarks. The 2D to 3D correspondence assumes a weak-perspective projection. The depth values have been normalized to have zero mean. Another 4, 912 images are used for testing. Participants in the challenging only had access to the testing images and their bounding box, but not the 3D landmarks.

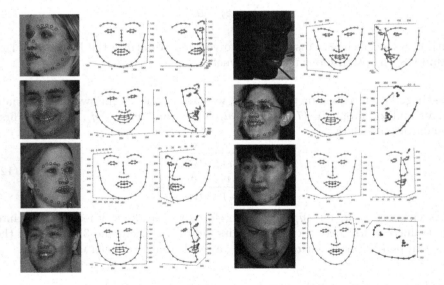

Fig. 3. Qualitative results on the testing set of the challenge. Our approach can detect 3D landmarks of face with large head pose precisely.

Detection error is evaluated using Ground Truth Error (GTE) and Cross View Ground Truth Consistency Error (CVGTCE). GTE is the average point-to-point Euclidean error between prediction and ground truth normalized by the Euclidean distance between the outer corners of the eyes. Formally,

$$E_{gte}(\mathbf{S}, \widetilde{\mathbf{S}}) = \frac{1}{n} \sum_{k=1}^{n} \frac{\|\mathbf{s}_k - \widetilde{\mathbf{s}}_k\|}{d}, \tag{13}$$

where $\|.\|$ is the L_2-norm, $\mathbf{S}$ and $\widetilde{\mathbf{S}}$ are the 3D prediction and ground truth, $\mathbf{s}_k$ and $\widetilde{\mathbf{s}}_k$ are the kth 3D point of $\mathbf{S}$ and $\widetilde{\mathbf{S}}$ respectively, and d is the Euclidean distance between the outer corners of the eyes.

CVGTCE is a measurement that evaluates cross-view consistency of the predicted landmarks by comparing the prediction and ground truth from a different view of the same target. Formally,

$$E_{cvgtce}(\mathbf{S}, \widetilde{\mathbf{S}}, P) = \frac{1}{n} \sum_{k=1}^{n} \frac{\|(c\mathbf{R}\mathbf{s}_k + \mathbf{t}) - \widetilde{\mathbf{s}}_k\|}{d}, \tag{14}$$

where $P = \{c, \mathbf{R}, \mathbf{t}\}$ encodes the rigid transformation, i.e., scale (c), rotation ($\mathbf{R}$), and translation ($\mathbf{t}$) between $\mathbf{S}$ and $\widetilde{\mathbf{S}}$. These can be obtained by optimizing the following:

$$\{c, \mathbf{R}, \mathbf{t}\} = \underset{c, \mathbf{R}, \mathbf{t}}{\operatorname{argmin}} \sum_{k=1}^{n} \|\widetilde{\mathbf{s}}_k - (c\mathbf{R}\mathbf{s}_k + \mathbf{t})\|$$

Our GTE and CVGTCE for testing images are 5.88% and 3.97%, respectively. Figure 3 shows the qualitative results on the testing set of the challenge. Additionally, we performed another test on the training set of the challenge. We randomly select 13,694 images from training set to train the multi-layer neural network for 3D shape estimation from 2D landmarks. We test on the other 5,000 images in the training set with ground truth 2D face landmarks. The GTE is 2.00%. Comparison of our method with other top ranked methods on 3DFAW challenge dataset is shown in Table 1.

6.1 Across Database Testing

To compare with the state-of-the-art method, we performed another experiment on the images of the BP4D-S database [33]. Note that we tested the proposed approach using the pre-trained model on the 3DFAW dataset of the previous section. That is, no images or 3D data from BP4D-S are used as part of our

Table 1. Comparisons of the GTE and CVGTCE on 3DFAW challenge dataset.

Participant	CVGTCE	GTE
psxab5	3.4767	4.5623
Ours	3.9700	5.8835
rpiisl	4.9488	6.2071
trigeorgis	5.4595	7.6403
olgabellon	5.9093	10.8001

training procedures, i.e., *the experiment is across datasets*. For fair comparison, we followed the procedure in [22]. We randomly selected 100 images with yaw angle between 0° and 10°, 500 images with yaw angle between 10° and 20° and other 500 images with yaw angle between 20° and 30° for a total of 1100 images. Since the landmarks in BP4D-S database are different from the challenge database, we selected the 45 overlapping landmarks to test our algorithm. The reported error in [22] was calculated using the average of point-wise estimation error (APE) as follows:

$$E_{ape}(\mathbf{S}, \widetilde{\mathbf{S}}) = \frac{1}{n} \sum_{k=1}^{n} \|\mathbf{s}_k - \widetilde{\mathbf{s}}_k\| \tag{15}$$

As shown in Table 2, our pre-trained model achieves the smallest APE compared with [22] and the baseline (i.e., using the 3D mean face of the samples in [33]). Figure 4 shows the qualitative results of the proposed approach on samples from BP4D-S.

Table 2. Comparisons of the APE on BP4D-S database.

Ours	PIFA [22]	Baseline
4.14	4.75	5.02

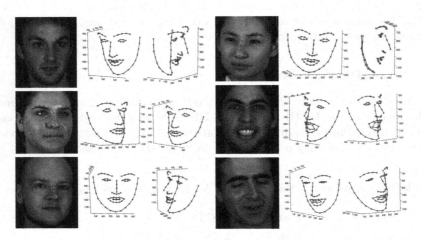

Fig. 4. Qualitative results on the BP4D-S database. Our pre-train model can detect 3D landmarks of face with large head pose and facial expressions precisely.

7 Conclusions

We have presented an algorithm for the reconstruction of the 3D shape of a face from a single 2D image. The proposed algorithm yields very low reconstruction errors and was the top 2 in the 3DFAW competition. Our approach is based on the idea of learning a mapping function from an image of a face to its 3D shape. Herein, we proposed to use a feed-forward neural network to learn this mapping. We defined two criteria, one to learn to detect important shape landmark points on the image and another to recover their depth information. We also presented a data augmentation approach that utilizes camera models to aid the learning of this complex, non-linear mapping function. The derived deep architecture and optimization criteria can be efficiently learned using a large number of samples and testing runs at > 30 frames/s on an i7 desktop.

Acknowledgements. Supported by the National Institutes of Health, grants R01-EY-020834 and R01-DC-014498, and a Google Faculty Research Award.

References

1. Martinez, A., Du, S.: A model of the perception of facial expressions of emotion by humans: research overview and perspectives. J. Mach. Learn. Res. **13**(1), 1589–1608 (2012)
2. Zhou, X., Leonardos, S., Hu, X., Daniilidis, K.: 3D shape estimation from 2D landmarks: a convex relaxation approach. In: The IEEE Conference on Computer Vision and Pattern Recognition (CVPR), pp. 4447–4455 (2015)
3. Ramakrishna, V., Kanade, T., Sheikh, Y.: Reconstructing 3D human pose from 2D image landmarks. In: Fitzgibbon, A., Lazebnik, S., Perona, P., Sato, Y., Schmid, C. (eds.) ECCV 2012, Part IV. LNCS, vol. 7575, pp. 573–586. Springer, Heidelberg (2012)
4. Lin, Y.-L., Morariu, V.I., Hsu, W., Davis, L.S.: Jointly optimizing 3D model fitting and fine-grained classification. In: Fleet, D., Pajdla, T., Schiele, B., Tuytelaars, T. (eds.) ECCV 2014, Part IV. LNCS, vol. 8692, pp. 466–480. Springer, Heidelberg (2014)
5. Kar, A., Tulsiani, S., Carreira, J., Malik, J.: Category-specific object reconstruction from a single image. In: The IEEE Conference on Computer Vision and Pattern Recognition (CVPR), pp. 1966–1974 (2015)
6. Hamsici, O.C., Gotardo, P.F.U., Martinez, A.M.: Learning spatially-smooth mappings in non-rigid structure from motion. In: Fitzgibbon, A., Lazebnik, S., Perona, P., Sato, Y., Schmid, C. (eds.) ECCV 2012, Part IV. LNCS, vol. 7575, pp. 260–273. Springer, Heidelberg (2012)
7. Fayad, J., Russell, C., Agapito, L.: Automated articulated structure and 3D shape recovery from point correspondences. In: The IEEE International Conference on Computer Vision (ICCV), pp. 431–438 (2011)
8. Gotardo, P.F.U., Martinez, A.M.: Kernel non-rigid structure from motion. In: IEEE International Conference on Computer Vision (ICCV), pp. 802–809 (2011)
9. Blanz, V., Vetter, T.: A morphable model for the synthesis of 3D faces. In: 26th Annual Conference on Computer Graphics and Interactive Techniques (SIGGRAPH), pp. 187–194 (1999)

10. Paysan, P., Knothe, R., Amberg, B., Romdhani, S., Vetter, T.: A 3D face model for pose and illumination invariant face recognition. In: Sixth IEEE International Conference on Advanced Video and Signal Based Surveillance (AVSS), pp. 296–301 (2009)

11. Dou, P., Wu, Y., Shah, S., Kakadiaris, I.: Robust 3D face shape reconstruction from single images via two-fold coupled structure learning and off-the-shelf landmark detectors. In: the British Machine Vision Conference, BMVA Press (2014)

12. Ding, L., Martinez, A.: Features versus context: an approach for precise and detailed detection and delineation of faces and facial features. IEEE Trans. Pattern Anal. Mach. Intell. **28**(8), 1274–1286 (2006)

13. Rivera, S., Martinez, A.M.: Learning deformable shape manifolds. Pattern Recogn. **45**(4), 1792–1801 (2012)

14. Xiong, X., De la Torre, F.: Supervised descent method and its applications to face alignment. In: IEEE Conference on Computer Vision and Pattern Recognition (CVPR) (2013)

15. Xiong, X., la Torre, F.D.: Global supervised descent method. In: Conference on Computer Vision and Pattern Recognition (CVPR) (2015)

16. Blanz, V., Vetter, T.: Face recognition based on fitting a 3D morphable model. IEEE Trans. Pattern Anal. Mach. Intell. **25**(9), 1063–1074 (2003)

17. Booth, J., Roussos, A., Zafeiriou, S., Ponniah, A., Dunaway, D.: A 3D morphable model learnt from 10,000 faces. In: The IEEE Conference on Computer Vision and Pattern Recognition (CVPR), June 2016

18. Kemelmacher-Shlizerman, I., Basri, R.: 3D face reconstruction from a single image using a single reference face shape. IEEE Trans. Pattern Anal. Mach. Intell. **33**(2), 394–405 (2011)

19. Hamsici, O.C., Martinez, A.M.: Active appearance models with rotation invariant kernels. In: 12th International Conference on Computer Vision (ICCV), pp. 1003–1009 (2009)

20. Xiao, J., Baker, S., Matthews, I., Kanade, T.: Real-time combined 2D+3D active appearance models. In: The IEEE Computer Society Conference on Computer Vision and Pattern Recognition (CVPR), pp. 535–542 (2004)

21. Gu, L., Kanade, T.: 3D alignment of face in a single image. In: The IEEE Computer Society Conference on Computer Vision and Pattern Recognition (CVPR), pp. 1305–1312 (2006)

22. Jourabloo, A., Liu, X.: Pose-invariant 3D face alignment. In: The International Conference on Computer Vision (ICCV) (2015)

23. Tulyakov, S., Sebe, N.: Regressing a 3D face shape from a single image. In: The International Conference on Computer Vision (ICCV) (2015)

24. Viola, P., Jones, M.: Rapid object detection using a boosted cascade of simple features. In: IEEE Computer Society Conference on Computer Vision and Pattern Recognition (CVPR) (2001)

25. Martínez, A.M., Kak, A.C.: PCA versus LDA. IEEE Trans. Pattern Anal. Mach. Intell. **23**(2), 228–233 (2001)

26. Krizhevsky, A., Sutskever, I., Hinton, G.E.: Imagenet classification with deep convolutional neural networks. In: Advances in Neural Information Processing Systems (2012)

27. Martínez, A.M.: Recognizing imprecisely localized, partially occluded, and expression variant faces from a single sample per class. IEEE Trans. Pattern Anal. Mach. Intell. **24**(6), 748–763 (2002)

28. Tieleman, T., Hinton, G.: Lecture 6.5-RmsProp: Divide the gradient by a running average of its recent magnitude. In: COURSERA: Neural Networks for Machine Learning (2012)
29. Chollet, F.: keras (2015). https://github.com/fchollet/keras
30. Bastien, F., Lamblin, P., Pascanu, R., Bergstra, J., Goodfellow, I., Bergeron, A., Bouchard, N., Warde-Farley, D., Bengio, Y.: Theano: new features and speed improvements. arXiv preprint arXiv:1211.5590 (2012)
31. Gross, R., Matthews, I., Cohn, J., Kanade, T., Baker, S.: Multi-pie. Image Vis. Comput. **28**(5), 807–813 (2010)
32. Yin, L., Chen, X., Sun, Y., Worm, T., Reale, M.: A high-resolution 3D dynamic facial expression database. In: 8th IEEE International Conference On Automatic Face & Gesture Recognition, FG 2008, pp. 1–6. IEEE (2008)
33. Zhang, X., Yin, L., Cohn, J.F., Canavan, S., Reale, M., Horowitz, A., Liu, P., Girard, J.M.: BP4D-spontaneous: a high-resolution spontaneous 3D dynamic facial expression database. Image Vis. Comput. **32**(10), 692–706 (2014)
34. Jeni, L.A., Cohn, J.F., Kanade, T.: Dense 3D face alignment from 2D video for real-time use. Image and Vision Computing (2016)

Shape Augmented Regression
for 3D Face Alignment

Chao Gou[1,3(✉)], Yue Wu[2], Fei-Yue Wang[1,3], and Qiang Ji[2]

[1] Institute of Automation, Chinese Academy of Sciences, Beijing, China
{gouchao2012,feiyue.wang}@ia.ac.cn
[2] ECSE, Rensselaer Polytechnic Institute, Troy, USA
{wuy9,jiq}@rpi.edu
[3] Qingdao Academy of Intelligent Industries, Qingdao, China

Abstract. 2D face alignment has been an active topic and is becoming mature for real applications. However, when large head pose exists, 2D annotated points lose geometric correspondence with respect to actual 3D location. In addition, local appearance varies more dramatically when subjects are with large pose or under various illuminations. 3D face alignment from 2D images is a promising solution to tackle this problem. 3D face alignment aims to estimate the 3D face shape which is consistent across all poses. In this paper, we propose a novel 3D face alignment method. This method consists of two steps. First, we perform 2D landmark detection based on the shape augmented regression. Second, we estimate the 3D shape using the detected 2D landmarks and 3D deformable model. Experimental results on benchmark database demonstrate its preferable performances.

Keywords: Shape augmented regression · 3D face alignment

1 Introduction

Face alignment aims to estimate the locations of semantic facial landmarks such as eye corners, mouth corners and nose tip in a given image. 2D facial landmark detection has been an important research topic due to its wide applications such as facial action unit recognition [1], face recognition [2], head pose estimation [3] and 3D face reconstruction [4]. Recently, cascade regression framework has shown good performances for 2D facial landmark detection [5–7]. It begins with an initial guess about the facial landmark locations and it iteratively updates the landmark locations based on the local appearance features. Different regression models for each cascade level are applied to map the local appearance features to shape updates. Cascade regression framework is promising because iteratively updating through a supervised scheme is more efficient than solving an optimization problem for each image.

One limitation of 2D face alignment is that it can not capture the actual 3D shape correspondence especially if the face is with large poses. As shown in Fig. 1,

© Springer International Publishing Switzerland 2016
G. Hua and H. Jégou (Eds.): ECCV 2016 Workshops, Part II, LNCS 9914, pp. 604–615, 2016.
DOI: 10.1007/978-3-319-48881-3_42

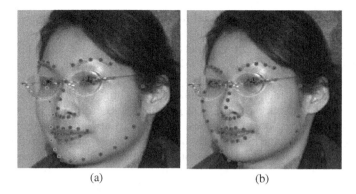

Fig. 1. 3D face alginment are more consistent than 2D face alignment across different poses. Landmarks on cheek occluded by head pose are marked green for better view. (a) 3D face alignment. (b) 2D face alginment. (Color figure online)

different from 2D face alignment which estimates the 2D landmark locations in the image plane, 3D face alignment aims to estimate the 3D landmark locations corresponding to the real 3D information of face. Recently, 3D face alignment from a 2D image is becoming an active research topic due to its robustness to pose and strong representational power. There are two major paradigms for 3D face alignment: one is first 2D landmark detection followed by fitting a 3D face model to estimate a 3D face shape, and another is directly estimating 3D deformable parameters and 3D shape based on discriminate features. It is worth nothing that, direct estimating the 3D shape in one step needs large number of 3D annotation data for training to cover the various 3D texture and shape while the two-step based methods need a few 3D data to train the 3D deformable shape model. Hence, in this paper, we follow the first paradigm. We detect 2D landmark based on cascade regression framework first, followed by fitting a off-line trained 3D deformable model to estimate 3D shape. Different from 2D face alignment task, the shape information is more important for 3D face alignment because it can capture the actual correspondence of 3D shape. For 2D landmark detection, we incorporate the shape and appearance information in a cascade regression framework. Then we combine the detected 2D landmarks and 3D morphable model to estimate the 3D shape.

In the rest of this paper, we first review the related works of 2D and 3D face alignment in Sect. 2. Our proposed approach is described in Sect. 3. Section 4 reports the experimental results with discussions. Section 5 concludes the paper.

2   Related Work

Face alignment can be classified into 2D face alignment and 3D face alignment. The goal of 2D face alignment is predicting locations of semantic facial landmarks in a given image with limited head pose. 3D face alignment is an extension of 2D face alignment and estimate 3D facial landmarks w.r.t a pre-defined coordinate system (eg. camera coordinate system).

In particular, 2D face alignment methods can be classified into holistic methods [8–10], Constrained Local Model (CLM) [11–13] and regression based [5, 6]. Holistic method learns models that can capture the global appearance and face shape information. It focuses on designing algorithms that minimize the difference between the current estimate of appearance and ground truth. CLM learns a set of local appearance models and a global shape models. For inference, it estimates each landmark locations based on local searching region features and global shape constraints. Regression based methods estimate the landmark locations or displacements through local appearance features using the off-line trained regression models. Cascade regression framework has been successfully applied to facial landmark detection and achieves state-of-the-art performance recently [5]. In this paper, we also utilize the cascade regression framework. Different from conventional cascade regression framework that the regression parameters are constant for each iteration, we propose shape augmented regression to adjust the parameters iteratively based on the current estimated shape and corresponding local appearance features.

Many works are done on 3D face shape estimation from a single image [7, 14–20]. The related works can be classified into two types: (I)two-step based methods that perform 2D landmark detection first followed by fitting 3D model to estimate the 3D shape, (II)one-step based methods that directly estimate the 3D shape based on discriminative shape invariant features. For the two-step based methods, Gu and Kanade [15] align 3D morphable model to a single image based on local patches related to a set of sparse 3D points. Cao et al. [17] propose to recover face pose and facial expression by fitting a user-specific blendshape model for landmark detection in 2D video frames. In [16] and [21], the authors propose to estimate the locations of landmarks and related visibility. They then recover the 3D shape by fitting a part-based 3D model. For the one-step based methods, Tulyakov and Sebe [7] estimate the 3D shape from a single image based on cascade regression framework using the shape invariant features. Jourabloo and Liu [18] present a cascaded coupled-regressor to jointly update the projection matrix and 3D deformable parameters for 3D landmark locations based on local appearance features. In [19], they further extend it to combine the 3DMM and cascaded CNN regressor for 3D face shape estimation. Zhu et al. [20] consider a dense 3DMM and the projection matrix as a representation of 2D face image. They propose to use CNN as the regressor in the cascaded framework to learn the mapping between the 2D face image and 3DMM with projection matrix.

3   Approach

Our overall framework is illustrated in Fig. 2. We perform two steps for 3D face alignment. The 2D landmarks are detected first, followed by 3D morphable fitting with off-line trained deformable model. Then we can estimate the 3D

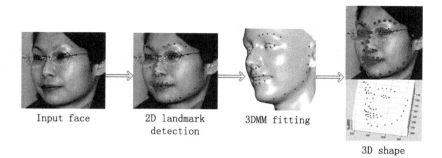

Input face   2D landmark   3DMM fitting

detection

3D shape

Fig. 2. Overall framework of our proposed method. It performs 2D landmark detection based on shape augmented regression method. It then fits the 3D demorphable model to estimate the 3D shape.

Algorithm 1. General cascaded regression framework.

Input: Facial landmark locations $\mathbf{x}^0$ are initialized by mean face.

Do cascade regression:

   for t=1,2,...,T **do**

      Update the key point locations $\mathbf{x}^t$ given the current key point locations $\mathbf{x}^{t-1}$ and image $\mathbf{I}$.

$$f_t : \mathbf{I}, \mathbf{x}^{t-1} \rightarrow \Delta\mathbf{x}^t$$
$$\mathbf{x}^t = \mathbf{x}^{t-1} + \Delta\mathbf{x}^t$$

   end for

Output:

   Landmark locations $\mathbf{x}^T$.

---

facial shape. In the following, we firstly describe the general cascaded regression framework for 2D landmark detection. Then we discuss the shape augmented method for 2D landmark detection. Finally we introduce the method that fits the 3D deformable model based on 2D landmark for 3D shape estimation.

3.1 General Cascaded Framework

General cascaded framework approximately solves the optimization problem by learning several sequential regressors based on the local appearance. The Supervised Decent Method (SDM) [5] is one popular cascade framework as shown in Algorithm 1. The facial landmark locations are denoted as $\mathbf{x}^t = \{x_1^t, x_2^t, ..., x_D^t\}$, where D denotes the number of landmarks and t denotes the iteration in cascaded regression framework. At iteration t, given the image $\mathbf{I}$, it uses the linear regression function f_t to map the high dimension features (eg. SIFT [22]) around the landmarks to the updates $\Delta\mathbf{x}^t$ of landmark locations. $\mathbf{x}^0$ is usually initialized as the mean face.

3.2 Shape Augmented Cascaded Regression

For 3D face alignment, it is critical to capture the shape correspondence when 3D face is projected onto image plane. To incorporate the shape information, we utilize the shape augmented regression method [6] to adjust the regression parameters iteratively according to the current estimated shape and related local appearance. The overall framework is shown in Algorithm 2. In this paper, given the image $\mathbf{I}$, 2D face alignment objective function can be formulated as Eq. 1:

$$f(\mathbf{x}) = \frac{1}{2}||\Phi(\mathbf{x}, \mathbf{I}) - \Phi(\mathbf{x}^*, \mathbf{I})||^2 + \frac{1}{2}||\Psi(\mathbf{x}) - \Psi(\mathbf{x}^*)||^2, \qquad (1)$$

where $\mathbf{x}$ are the landmark locations, $\mathbf{x}^*$ are the ground truth locations, $\Phi(\mathbf{x}, \mathbf{I})$ are the local SIFT features around the current landmark locations, and $\Psi(\mathbf{x})$ are the shape features which are the difference among pairs of landmarks. Hence, landmark locations can be estimated by solving the optimization problem $\tilde{\mathbf{x}} = arg\min_{\mathbf{x}} f(\mathbf{x})$. We further apply a second order Taylor expansion on Eq. 1:

$$f(\mathbf{x}) = f(\mathbf{x}^0 + \Delta\mathbf{x}) \approx f(\mathbf{x}^0) + J_f(\mathbf{x}^0)^T \Delta\mathbf{x} + \frac{1}{2}\Delta\mathbf{x}^T H_f(\mathbf{x}^0)\Delta\mathbf{x}, \qquad (2)$$

where $J_f(\mathbf{x}^0)$ and $H_f(\mathbf{x}^0)$ are the Jacobian and Hessian matrices of function $f(\cdot)$ evaluated at the current location $\mathbf{x}^0$, respectively. After taking the derivation of $f(\mathbf{x})$ in Eq. 2 and set it to zero, we can get the update for landmark locations as shown in Eq. 3.

$$
\begin{aligned}
\Delta\mathbf{x} = &- H_f(\mathbf{x}^0)^{-1} J_f(\mathbf{x}^0) \\
= &- H_f(\mathbf{x}^0)^{-1}[J_\Phi(\mathbf{x}^0)(\Phi(\mathbf{x}^0, \mathbf{I}) - \Phi(\mathbf{x}^*, \mathbf{I})) + J_\Psi(\mathbf{x}^0)(\Psi(\mathbf{x}^0) - \Psi(\mathbf{x}^*))] \\
= &- H_f(\mathbf{x}^0)^{-1} J_\Phi(\mathbf{x}^0)\Phi(\mathbf{x}^0, \mathbf{I}) - H_f(\mathbf{x}^0)^{-1} J_\Psi(\mathbf{x}^0)\Psi(\mathbf{x}^0) \\
&+ H_f(\mathbf{x}^0)^{-1}(J_\Phi(\mathbf{x}^0)\Phi(\mathbf{x}^*, \mathbf{I}) + J_\Psi(\mathbf{x}^0)\Psi(\mathbf{x}^*))
\end{aligned}
\qquad (3)
$$

It is computationally expensive to estimate Hessian and its inverse. In addition, the ground truth landmark locations $\mathbf{x}^*$ are unknown but fixed as constant during inference. Similar to SDM, we introduce the related parameters as below:

$$
\begin{aligned}
\mathbf{P} &= -H_f(\mathbf{x}^0)^{-1} J_\Phi(\mathbf{x}^0) \\
\mathbf{Q} &= -H_f(\mathbf{x}^0)^{-1} J_\Psi(\mathbf{x}^0) \\
\mathbf{b} &= H_f(\mathbf{x}^0)^{-1}(J_\Phi(\mathbf{x}^0)\Phi(\mathbf{x}^*, \mathbf{I}) + J_\Psi(\mathbf{x}^0)\Psi(\mathbf{x}^*))
\end{aligned}
\qquad (4)
$$

At iteration t for cascade regression, we can rewrite Eq. 3 as Eq. 5 to estimate the updates of landmark locations:

$$\Delta\mathbf{x}^t = \mathbf{P}^t\Phi(\mathbf{x}^{t-1}, \mathbf{I}) + \mathbf{Q}^t\Psi(\mathbf{x}^{t-1}) + \mathbf{b}^t \qquad (5)$$

Hence, we need to learn the parameters in Eq. 4 for cascade regression. Given the i-th face image $\mathbf{I}_i$ with estimated landmark locations $\mathbf{x}_i^{t-1}$, the local appearance features $\Phi(\mathbf{x}^{t-1}, \mathbf{I})$ and shape features $\Psi(\mathbf{x}^{t-1})$ of i-th image can be calculated. For iteration t, the updates $\Delta\mathbf{x}_i^t$ of landmark locations can be acquired by

Algorithm 2. Shape augmented regression framework.

Input: Facial landmark locations $\mathbf{x}^0$ are initialized by mean face.
Do cascade regression:
   for t=1,2,...,T **do**
      Given the current key point locations $\mathbf{x}^{t-1}$ and image $\mathbf{I}$, estimate the update of
      landmarks through Eq. 5.
         $\varDelta\mathbf{x}^t = \mathbf{P}^t\varPhi(\mathbf{x}^{t-1}, \mathbf{I}) + \mathbf{Q}^t\varPsi(\mathbf{x}^{t-1}) + \mathbf{b}^t$
      Update the key point locations $\mathbf{x}^t$
         $\mathbf{x}^t = \mathbf{x}^{t-1} + \varDelta\mathbf{x}^t$
   end for
Output:
   Landmark locations $\mathbf{x}^T$.

subtracting the current locations $\mathbf{x}_i^{t-1}$ from the ground truth locations $\mathbf{x}_i^*$. The initialization of landmark locations are mean face denoted by $\mathbf{x}_i^0$. The learning of $\mathbf{P}^t$, $\mathbf{Q}^t$ and bias $\mathbf{b}^t$ can be formulated as a standard least-squares formulation with closed form solution:

$$\mathbf{P}^{t^*}, \mathbf{Q}^{t^*}, \mathbf{b}^{t^*} = arg\min_{\mathbf{P}^t, \mathbf{Q}^t, \mathbf{b}^t} \sum_{i=1}^{K} \parallel \varDelta\mathbf{x}_i^t - \mathbf{P}^t\varPhi(I_i, \mathbf{x}_i^{t-1}) - \mathbf{Q}^t\varPsi(I_i, \mathbf{x}_i^{t-1}) - \mathbf{b}^t \parallel^2$$

(6)

where K is the number of training samples.

For testing, given the face image $\mathbf{I}$ and current key point locations $\mathbf{x}^{t-1}$ at iteration t, we can estimate the update locations $\varDelta\mathbf{x}^t$ by learned parameters $\mathbf{P}^t$, $\mathbf{Q}^t$ and bias $\mathbf{b}^t$. Then the landmark locations can be acquired through $\mathbf{x}^t = \mathbf{x}^{t-1} + \varDelta\mathbf{x}^t$.

3.3 3D Morphable Model Fitting

Given the detected 2D landmark locations on the testing image and a 3D morphable model [14], we can recover 3D face by estimating the 3D pose and non-rigid deformation via the fitting process. 3DMM is defined as a shape model with dense mesh. In particular, it can be simplified by the 3D vertex locations(landmark points) of the related dense mesh. Hence, it can describe 3D face nonrigid shape variations with mean 3D shape and PCA space linearly as below:

$$\mathbf{s} = \bar{\mathbf{s}} + \mathbf{Bq}$$

(7)

Here, $\mathbf{s}$ is the 3D shape of N landmarks in head coordinate system denoted by $\mathbf{s} = \{x_1, y_1, z_1, ..., x_N, y_N, z_N\}$, $\bar{\mathbf{s}}$ is the mean 3D shape, $\mathbf{B}$ represents the learned orthonormal bases, and $\mathbf{q}$ denotes the nonrigid shape variation parameters. We learn the mean 3D shape $\bar{\mathbf{s}}$ and PCA bases $\mathbf{B}$ of 3D model in Eq. 7 from the annotations provided in [7].

Assuming 3D face is projected onto the image plane with weak perspective projection, the k-th landmark location in image plane can be calculated by:

$$\begin{bmatrix} u_k \\ v_k \end{bmatrix} = \mathbf{M}\mathbf{s} + \mathbf{t} = \begin{bmatrix} \dfrac{1}{\bar{z}_c} f s_x \mathbf{r}_1 \\ \dfrac{1}{\bar{z}_c} f s_y \mathbf{r}_2 \end{bmatrix} \begin{bmatrix} x_k \\ y_k \\ z_k \end{bmatrix} + \mathbf{t}, \tag{8}$$

where $\bar{z}_c$ is the mean depth in camera coordinate, f is the focal length, s_x and s_y are the sampling frequency in rows and columns (also known as scaling factors), $\mathbf{r}_i = (r_{i1}, r_{i2}, r_{i3})$ is the i-th row of 3 by 3 rotation matrix $\mathbf{R}$ which is encoded by three head poses(pitch α, yaw β, roll γ), and $\mathbf{t} = (t_1, t_2)^T$ is the 2D translation vector. Since f, s_x and s_y are intrinsic parameters and $\bar{z}_c$ is constant, we set $\dfrac{1}{\bar{z}_c} f s_x = \lambda_1$ and $\dfrac{1}{\bar{z}_c} f s_y = \lambda_2$ as two unknown parameters for simplicity. As a result, we can rewrite Eq. 8 as below:

$$\begin{bmatrix} u_k \\ v_k \end{bmatrix} = \mathbf{x}_{2d}(\mathbf{p}) = \begin{bmatrix} \lambda_1 & 0 \\ 0 & \lambda_2 \end{bmatrix} \mathbf{R}_{2\times3}(\bar{\mathbf{s}}_k + \mathbf{B}_k\mathbf{q}) + \mathbf{t} \tag{9}$$

where $\mathbf{x}_{2d}$ is landmark location in image plane, $\mathbf{R}_{2\times3} = \begin{bmatrix} \mathbf{r}_1 \\ \mathbf{r}_2 \end{bmatrix}$ is the first two rows of rotation matrix $\mathbf{R}$ and $\mathbf{p} = \{\lambda_1, \lambda_2, \alpha, \beta, \gamma, t_1, t_2, \mathbf{q}\}$ denotes the parameters of the model.

Given the pre-trained 3D model and 2D landmark locations $\mathbf{x}$, we can estimate the model parameters by minimizing the misalignment error of projected locations $\mathbf{x}_{2d}$ and detected 2D landmark locations $\mathbf{x}$ for all landmark points:

$$\begin{aligned} \mathbf{p} &= arg\min_{\mathbf{P}} \sum_{k=1}^{K} \| \mathbf{x}_k - \mathbf{x}_{2d,k} \|^2 \\ &= arg\min_{\mathbf{P}} \sum_{k=1}^{K} \| \mathbf{x}_k - (\begin{bmatrix} \lambda_1 & 0 \\ 0 & \lambda_2 \end{bmatrix} \mathbf{R}_{2\times3}(\bar{\mathbf{s}}_k + \mathbf{B}_k\mathbf{q}) + \mathbf{t}) \|^2 \end{aligned} \tag{10}$$

where $\mathbf{p} = \{\mathbf{h}, \mathbf{q}\} = \{\lambda_1, \lambda_2, \alpha, \beta, \gamma, t_1, t_2, \mathbf{q}\}$ denotes the model parameters. To solve this optimization problem, we alternatively update the transformation parameters $\mathbf{h} = \{\lambda_1, \lambda_2, , \alpha, \beta, \gamma, t_1, t_2\}$ and deformable parameters $\mathbf{q}$ until it converges. We first initialize the deformable parameters $\mathbf{q}$ as zeros and we can get the 3D locations in head coordinate systems. Then we solve the linear optimization problem of Eq. 10 to get the parameters of $\mathbf{h}$. After estimating $\mathbf{h}$, we feed it into Eq. 10 and estimate the deformable parameters $\mathbf{q}$. We repeat until the max update of pose parameters (α, β, γ) is less than 0.1 in degree.

After estimating parameters $\mathbf{p}$, we can calculate the 3D shape as follows (according to the definition of the 3DFAW challenge and [16,21]):

$$\mathbf{x}_{3d} = \lambda \mathbf{R}\mathbf{s} + \mathbf{T} = \lambda \mathbf{R}(\bar{\mathbf{s}} + \mathbf{B}\mathbf{q}) + \mathbf{T} \tag{11}$$

where $\mathbf{x}_{3d}$ denotes the 3D landmark locations, λ is the scale factor, $\mathbf{R}$ is a 3 by 3 rotation matrix, $\mathbf{T} = (t_1, t_2, t_3)^T$ is the 3D translation vector. In this paper, we approximate the scale factor by $\lambda = \dfrac{\lambda_1 + \lambda_2}{2}$, t_1, t_2 are the same as Eq. 8, t_3 is set to zero and $\mathbf{r}_3$ is the cross product of $\mathbf{r}_1$ and $\mathbf{r}_2$. After calculating the 3D shape, we normalize the depth to zero mean.

4   Experiments

In this section, we first describe the implementation details. Then, we conduct experiments and comparisons.

4.1   Database

The experimental dataset is from ECCV2016 workshop on 3D face alignment in the wild (3DFAW) challenge. It consists of MultiPIE [23], BU-4DFE [24], BP4D-Spontaneous [25] and some image frames of videos collected from web. The landmark annotations consist 23606 images of 66 3D points and the depth information is recovered using a model-based structure from motion technique [16,21]. It is divided into four sub-datasets: 13671 images for training, 4725 images for validation, 4912 for testing and 298 images for extra training.

The facial images are normalized to 200 pixels in width. Mean face shape are calculated on all normalized facial images. Similar to [6] during training, we generate multiple initial face shapes by rotating, scaling and shifting the mean face shape to improve the robustness. For cascade regression, the number of iteration is 4. We use the detected 2D landmarks as the estimated locations of 3D shape.

4.2   Evaluation Criteria

For fair comparisons, we use the widely accepted evaluation matrices named Ground Truth Error (GTE) and Cross View Ground Truth Consistency Error (CVGTCE). GTE is the average point-to-point Euclidean error normalized by the outer corners of the eyes (inter-ocular) formulated as below:

$$GTE(\mathbf{x}_{gt}, \mathbf{x}_{pre}) = \frac{1}{K} \sum_{k=1}^{K} \frac{||\mathbf{x}_{gt}^k - \mathbf{x}_{pre}^k||_2}{d_i} \tag{12}$$

where K is the number of points, $\mathbf{x}_{gt}$ is the ground truth 3D shape, $\mathbf{x}_{pre}$ is the prediction and d_i is the inter-ocular distance for the i-th image. CVGTCE is used to evaluate cross-view consistency of the predicted landmarks from 3D model. It is computed as below:

$$CVGTCE(\mathbf{x}_{gt}, \mathbf{s}, \mathbf{p}) = \frac{1}{K} \sum_{k=1}^{K} \frac{||\mathbf{x}_{gt}^k - (f\mathbf{P}\mathbf{s}^k + \mathbf{t})||_2}{d_i} \tag{13}$$

where $\tilde{\mathbf{x}}_{pre} = f\mathbf{P}\mathbf{s} + \mathbf{t}$ is the predicted 3D shape for another view of the subject, $\mathbf{p} = \{f, \mathbf{P}, \mathbf{t}\}$ is the model parameters, f is the scale factor and $\mathbf{P}$ is the rotation matrix.

4.3   Experimental Results

We first train shape augmented cascade regression models for 2D landmark detection on training dataset. We conduct comparisons with SDM [5] which follows the same procedure and retrain on the same database. After detecting the 2D landmark, we use the same 3D deformable model fitting process to estimate the 3D shape. The 3D face shape detection experimental results on validation dataset are shown in Table 1. Some qualitative results are shown in Fig. 3 and inaccurate results are shown in Fig. 4. From Table 1, incorporating the shape information help improve the results especially for the 3D face alignment. As we discussed before, 3D face alignment is more consistent with respect to large pose. Shape information between pair of points is very important when 3D shape are projected onto image plane. As shown in Fig. 4 for the inaccurate detection results, it fails when the subjects are with extreme head pose and the appearance is very ambiguous. For our proposed method, it is important to predict 2D landmarks which are used to estimate the 3D model parameters.

Table 1. 3D landmark detection comparison on validation dataset

Mehtod	GTE(%)
SDM [5]+3DMM	6.34
Ours	**5.90**

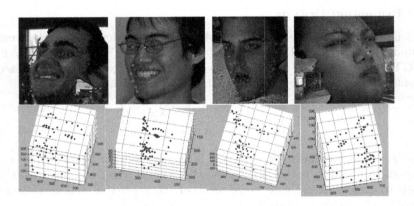

Fig. 3. Qualitative 3D face alginment results on validation dataset. Landmarks on cheek occluded by head pose are marked green for better view. (Color figure online)

We further train our model on training, extra training and validation dataset and test on testing dataset. Experimental results are shown in Table 2 and Fig. 5. The performance of our method are preferable on challenging testing dataset.

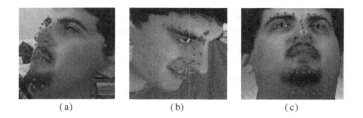

(a)   (b)   (c)

Fig. 4. Inaccurate detection results on validation dataset. The calcuated GTE for (a), (b), (c) are 16.18, 23.05, 13.87, respectively.

Table 2. 3D landmark detection results on testing dataset

CVGTCE(%)	GTE(%)
6.21	4.95

Fig. 5. Qualitative 3D face alginment resutls on testing data. Landmarks on cheek occluded by head pose are marked green for better view. (Color figure online)

As shown in Table 2, we can achieve 4.95 of GTE on all the testing dataset. In addition, we also get 6.21 of CVGTCE which demonstrates that our method is cross-view consistent for 3D face alignment. As shown in Fig. 5, our method is robust to illuminations and can achieve reasonable detection results when subjects are with extreme head pose.

5   Conclusions

In this paper, we propose to firstly estimate the location of a set of landmarks based on shape augmented regression framework, then recover the 3D face shape by fitting a 3D morphable model. By incorporating the shape and local appearance information in the cascade regression framework, our proposed method can capture the geometric correspondence between pair of points for 3D face alignment. An alternative optimizing method for estimating 3D morphable model parameters is adopted to estimate the 3D shape including the depth information. Experimental results on large scale of testing dataset validate the robustness and effectiveness of proposed method.

The appearance of occluded landmarks is not reliable for the prediction of location. Future work will focus on inferring the visibility of landmarks which can be used to weight the related appearance. In addition, we will iteratively update the 2D landmark location and corresponding 3D morphable model parameters during a unified cascade regression framework based on the local appearance.

Acknowledgments. This work was completed when the first author visited Rensselaer Polytechnic Institute (RPI), supported by a scholarship from University of Chinese Academy of Sciences (UCAS). The authors would like to acknowledge support from UCAS and RPI. This work was also supported in part by National Science Foundation under the grant 1145152 and by the National Natural Science Foundation of China under Grant 61304200 and 61533019.

References

1. Wu, Y., Ji, Q.: Constrained joint cascade regression framework for simultaneous facial action unit recognition and facial landmark detection. In: Proceedings of the IEEE Conference on Computer Vision and Pattern Recognition, CVPR (2016)
2. Wagner, A., Wright, J., Ganesh, A., Zhou, Z., Mobahi, H., Ma, Y.: Toward a practical face recognition system: robust alignment and illumination by sparse representation. IEEE Trans. Pattern Anal. Mach. Intell. **34**(2), 372–386 (2012)
3. Narayanan, A., Kaimal, R.M., Bijlani, K.: Estimation of driver head yaw angle using a generic geometric model. IEEE Trans. Intell. Transp. Syst. **PP**(99), 1–15 (2016)
4. Roth, J., Tong, Y., Liu, X.: Adaptive 3D face reconstruction from unconstrained photo collections. In: Proceedings of the IEEE Conference on Computer Vision and Pattern Recognition, CVPR (2016)
5. Xiong, X., De la Torre, F.: Supervised descent method and its applications to face alignment. In: IEEE Conference on Computer Vision and Pattern Recognition (CVPR), pp. 532–539. IEEE (2013)
6. Wu, Y., Ji, Q.: Shape augmented regression method for face alignment. In: Proceedings of the IEEE International Conference on Computer Vision Workshops, pp. 26–32 (2015)
7. Tulyakov, S., Sebe, N.: Regressing a 3D face shape from a single image. In: 2015 IEEE International Conference on Computer Vision (ICCV), pp. 3748–3755. IEEE (2015)
8. Cootes, T.F., Edwards, G.J., Taylor, C.J.: Active appearance models. IEEE Trans. Pattern Anal. Mach. Intell. **6**, 681–685 (2001)
9. Matthews, I., Baker, S.: Active appearance models revisited. Int. J. Comput. Vis. **60**(2), 135–164 (2004)
10. Lucey, S., Navarathna, R., Ashraf, A.B., Sridharan, S.: Fourier lucas-kanade algorithm. IEEE Trans. Pattern Anal. Mach. Intell. **35**(6), 1383–1396 (2013)

11. Saragih, J.M., Lucey, S., Cohn, J.F.: Face alignment through subspace constrained mean-shifts. In: 2009 IEEE 12th International Conference on Computer Vision, pp. 1034–1041. IEEE (2009)
12. Cristinacce, D., Cootes, T.F.: Feature detection and tracking with constrained local models. 1(2), 3 (2006)
13. Lindner, C., Bromiley, P.A., Ionita, M.C., Cootes, T.F.: Robust and accurate shape model matching using random forest regression-voting. IEEE Trans. Pattern Anal. Mach. Intell. 37(9), 1862–1874 (2015)
14. Blanz, V., Vetter, T.: A morphable model for the synthesis of 3D faces. In: Proceedings of the 26th Annual Conference on Computer Graphics and Interactive Techniques, pp. 187–194. ACM Press/Addison-Wesley Publishing Co. (1999)
15. Gu, L., Kanade, T.: 3D alignment of face in a single image. In: 2006 IEEE Computer Society Conference on Computer Vision and Pattern Recognition (CVPR 2006), vol. 1, pp. 1305–1312. IEEE (2006)
16. Jeni, L.A., Cohn, J.F., Kanade, T.: Dense 3D face alignment from 2D videos in real-time. In: 11th IEEE International Conference and Workshops on Automatic Face and Gesture Recognition (FG), vol. 1, pp. 1–8. IEEE (2015)
17. Cao, C., Weng, Y., Lin, S., Zhou, K.: 3D shape regression for real-time facial animation. ACM Trans. Graph. (TOG) 32(4), 41 (2013)
18. Jourabloo, A., Liu, X.: Pose-invariant 3D face alignment. In: Proceedings of the IEEE International Conference on Computer Vision, pp. 3694–3702 (2015)
19. Jourabloo, A., Liu, X.: Large-pose face alignment via CNN-based dense 3D model fitting. In: Proceedings of the IEEE Conference on Computer Vision and Pattern Recognition, CVPR (2016)
20. Zhu, X., Lei, Z., Liu, X., Shi, H., Li, S.Z.: Face alignment across large poses: a 3D solution. In: Proceedings of the IEEE Conference on Computer Vision and Pattern Recognition, CVPR (2016)
21. Jeni, L.A., Cohn, J.F., Kanade, T.: Dense 3D face alignment from 2D video for real-time use. Image and Vision Computing (2016)
22. Lowe, D.G.: Distinctive image features from scale-invariant keypoints. Int. J. Comput. Vis. 60(2), 91–110 (2004)
23. Gross, R., Matthews, I., Cohn, J., Kanade, T., Baker, S.: Multi-pie. Image Vis. Comput. 28(5), 807–813 (2010)
24. Yin, L., Chen, X., Sun, Y., Worm, T., Reale, M.: A high-resolution 3D dynamic facial expression database. In: 8th IEEE International Conference on Automatic Face & Gesture Recognition, FG 2008, pp. 1–6. IEEE (2008)
25. Zhang, X., Yin, L., Cohn, J.F., Canavan, S., Reale, M., Horowitz, A., Liu, P., Girard, J.M.: BP4D-spontaneous: a high-resolution spontaneous 3D dynamic facial expression database. Image Vis. Comput. 32(10), 692–706 (2014)

Two-Stage Convolutional Part Heatmap Regression for the 1st 3D Face Alignment in the Wild (3DFAW) Challenge

Adrian Bulat$^{(\boxtimes)}$ and Georgios Tzimiropoulos

Computer Vision Laboratory, University of Nottingham, Nottingham, UK
{adrian.bulat,yorgos.tzimiropoulos}@nottingham.ac.uk

Abstract. This paper describes our submission to the 1st 3D Face Alignment in the Wild (3DFAW) Challenge. Our method builds upon the idea of convolutional part heatmap regression (Bulat and Tzimiropoulos, 2016), extending it for 3D face alignment. Our method decomposes the problem into two parts: (a) X,Y (2D) estimation and (b) Z (depth) estimation. At the first stage, our method estimates the X,Y coordinates of the facial landmarks by producing a set of 2D heatmaps, one for each landmark, using convolutional part heatmap regression. Then, these heatmaps, alongside the input RGB image, are used as input to a very deep subnetwork trained via residual learning for regressing the Z coordinate. Our method ranked 1st in the 3DFAW Challenge, surpassing the second best result by more than 22 %. Code can be found at http://www.cs.nott.ac.uk/~psxab5/.

Keywords: 3D face alignment · Convolutional Neural Networks · Convolutional part heatmap regression

1 Introduction

Face alignment is the problem of localizing a set of facial landmarks in 2D images. It is a well-studied problem in Computer Vision research, yet most of prior work [1,2], datasets [3,4] and challenges [4,5] have focused on frontal images. However, under a totally unconstrained scenario, faces might be in arbitrary poses. To address this limitation of prior work, recently, a few methods have been proposed for large pose face alignment [6–9]. 3D face alignment goes one step further by treating the face as a full 3D object and attempting to localize the facial landmarks in 3D space. To boost research in 3D face alignment, the 1st Workshop on 3D Face Alignment in the Wild (3DFAW) & Challenge is organized in conjunction with ECCV 2016 [10]. In this paper, we describe a Convolutional Neural Network (CNN) architecture for 3D face alignment, that ranked 1st in the 3DFAW Challenge, surpassing the second best result by more than 22 %.

Our method is a CNN cascade consisting of three connected subnetworks, all learned via residual learning [11,12]. See Fig. 1. The first two subnetworks perform residual part heatmap regression [13] for estimating the X,Y coordinates of

© Springer International Publishing Switzerland 2016
G. Hua and H. Jégou (Eds.): ECCV 2016 Workshops, Part II, LNCS 9914, pp. 616–624, 2016.
DOI: 10.1007/978-3-319-48881-3_43

the facial landmarks. As in [13], the first subnetwork is a part detection network trained to detect the individual facial landmarks using a per-pixel softmax loss. The output of this subnetwork is a set of N landmark detection heatmaps. The second subnetwork is a regression subnetwork that jointly regresses the landmark detection heatmaps stacked with image features to confidence maps representing the location of the landmarks. Then, on top of the first two subnetworks, we added a third very deep subnetwork that estimates the Z coordinate of each fiducial point. The newly introduced network is guided by the heatmaps produced by the 2D regression subnetwork and subsequently learns where to "look" by explicitly exploiting information about the 2D location of the landmarks. We show that the proposed method produces remarkable fitting results for both X,Y and Z coordinates, securing the first place on the 3DFAW Challenge.

This paper is organized as follows: Sect. 2 describes our system in detail. Section 3 describes the experiments performed and our results on the 3DFAW dataset. Finally, Sect. 4 summarizes our contributions and concludes the paper.

2   Method

The proposed method adopts a *divide et impera* technique, splitting the 3D facial landmark estimation problem into two tasks as follows: The first task estimates the X,Y coordinates of the facial landmarks and produces a series of N regression heatmaps, one for each landmark, using the network described in Sect. 2.1. The second task, described in Sect. 2.2, predicts the Z coordinate (i.e. the depth of each landmark), using as input the stacked heatmaps produced by the first task, alongside the input RGB image. The overall architecture is illustrated in Fig. 1.

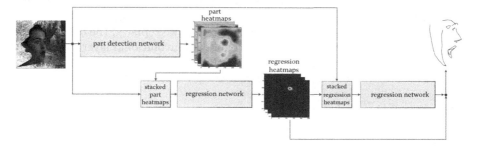

Fig. 1. The system submitted to the 3DFAW Challenge. The part detection and regression subnetworks implement convolutional part heatmap regression, as described in [13], and produce a series of N heatmaps, one for the X,Y location of each landmark. They are both very deep networks trained via residual learning [12]. The produced heatmaps are then stacked alongside the input RGB image, and used as input to the Z regressor which regresses the depth of each point. The architecture for the Z regressor is based on ResNet [12], as described in Sect. 2.2.

2.1   2D (X,Y) Landmark Heatmap Regression

The first part of our system estimates the X,Y coordinates of each facial landmark using part heatmap regression [13]. The network consists of two connected subnetworks, the first of which performs landmark detection while the second one refines the initial estimation of the landmarks' location via regression. Both networks are very deep been trained via residual learning [11,12]. In the following, we briefly describe the two subnetworks; the exact network architecture and layer specification for each of them are described in detail in [13].

Landmark detection subnetwork. The architecture of the landmark detection network is based on a ResNet-152 model [11]. The network was adapted for landmark localization by: (1) removing the fully connected layer alongside the preceding average pooling layer, (2) changing the stride of the 5th block from 2 to 1 pixels, and (3) adding at the end a deconvolution [14] followed by a fully convolutional layer. These changes convert the model to a fully convolutional network, recovering to some extent the lost spatial resolution. The ground truth was encoded as a set of N binary maps (one for each landmark), where the values located within the radius of the provided ground truth landmark are set to 1, while the rest to 0. The radius defining the "correct location" was empirically set to 7 pixels, for a face with a bounding box height equal to approximately 220 pixels. The network was trained using the pixel wise sigmoid cross entropy loss function.

Landmark regression subnetwork. As in [13], the regression subnetwork plays the role of a graphical model aiming to refine the initial prediction of the landmark detection network. It is based on a modified version of the "hourglass network" [15]. The hourglass network starts from the idea presented in [16], improving a few important concepts: (1) it updates the model using residual learning [11,12], and (2) introduces an efficient way to analyze and recombine features at different resolutions. Finally, as in [13], we replaced the original nearest neighbour upsampling of [15] by learnable deconvolutional layers, and added another deconvolutional layer in the end that brings the output to the input resolution. The network was then trained using a pixel wise L2 loss function.

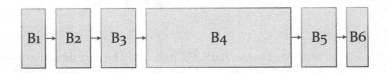

Fig. 2. The architecture of the Z regression subnetwork. The network is based on ResNet-200 (with preactivation) and its composing blocks. The blocks B1–B6 are defined in Table 1. See also text.

Table 1. Block specification for the Z regression network. Torch notations (channels, kernel, stride) and (kernel, stride) are used to define the conv and pooling layers. The bottleneck modules are defined as in [12].

B1	B2	B3	B4	B5	B6
1x conv layer (64,7 × 7,2 × 2) 1x pooling (3 × 3, 2 × 2)	3x bottleneck modules [(64,1 × 1), (64,3 × 3), (256,1 × 1)]	24x bottleneck modules [(128,1 × 1), (128,3 × 3), (512,1 × 1)]	38x bottleneck modules [(256,1 × 1), (256,3 × 3), (1024,1 × 1)]	3x bottleneck modules [(512,1 × 1), (512,3 × 3), (2048,1 × 1)]	1x fully connected layer (66)

2.2 Z Regression

In this section, we introduce a third subnetwork for estimating the Z coordinate i.e. the depth of each landmark. As with the X,Y coordinates, the estimation of the Z coordinate is performed jointly for all landmarks. The input to the Z regressor subnetwork is the stacked regression heatmaps produced by the regression subnetwork alongside the input RGB image. The use of the stacked heatmaps is a key feature of the subnetwork as they provide pose-related information (encoded by the X,Y location of all the landmarks) and guide the network where to "look", explicitly showing where the depth should be estimated.

We encode each landmark as a heatmap using a 2D Gaussian with std = 6 pixels centered at the X,Y coordinates of that landmark. The proposed Z regression network is based on the latest ResNet-200 network with preactivation modules [12] modified as follows: in order to adapt the model for 1D regression, we replaced the last fully connected layer (used for classification) with one that has N output channels, one for each landmark. Additionally, the first convolutional layer of the network was modified to accommodate 3+N input channels. The network is described in detail in Fig. 2 and Table 1. All newly introduced filters were initialized randomly using a Gaussian distribution. Finally, the network was trained using the L2 loss:

$$l_2 = \frac{1}{N} \sum_{n=1}^{N} (\widetilde{z}_n - z_n)^2, \tag{1}$$

where $\widetilde{z}_n$ and z_n are the predicted and ground truth Z values (in pixels) for the nth landmark.

2.3 Training

For training, all images were cropped around an extended (by 20–25 %) bounding box, and then resized so that the final cropped image had a resolution of 384 × 384 pixels. While batch normalization is known to prevent overfitting to some extent, we additionally augmented the data with a set of image transformations applied randomly: flipping, in-plane rotation (between -35° and 35°), scaling (between 0.85 and 1.15) and colour jittering. While the entire system, shown in Fig. 1, can be trained jointly from the beginning, in order to accelerate convergence we trained each task independently.

For 2D (X,Y) landmark heatmap regression, the network was fine-tuned from a pretrained model on the large ImageNet [17] dataset, with the newly introduced layers initialized with zeros. The detection component was then trained for 30 epochs with a learning rate progressively decreasing from $1e-3$ to $2.5e-5$. The regression subnetwork, based on the "hourglass" architecture was trained for 30 epochs using a learning rate that varied from $1e-4$ to $2.5e-5$. During this, the learning rate for the detection subnetwork was frozen. All the newly introduced deconvolutional layers were initialised using the bilinear upsampling filters. Finally, the subnetworks were trained jointly for 30 more epochs.

For Z regression, we again fine-tuned from a model previously trained on ImageNet [17]; this time we used a ResNet-200 network [12]. The newly introduced filters in the first convolutional layer were initialized from a Gaussian distribution with std = 0.01. The same applied for the fully connected layer added at the end of the network. During training, we used as input to the Z regression network both the heatmaps generated from the ground truth landmark locations and the ones estimated by the first task. We trained the subnetwork for about 100 epochs with a learning rate varying from $1e-2$ to $2.5e-4$.

The network was implemented and trained using Torch7 [18] on two Titan X 12Gb GPUs using a batch of 8 and 16 images for X,Y landmark heatmap regression and Z regression, respectively.

3   Experimental Results

In this section, we present the performance of our system on the 3DFAW dataset.

Dataset. We trained and tested our model on the 3D Face Alignment in the Wild (3DFAW) dataset. [19–22] The dataset contains images from a wide range of conditions, captured in both controlled and in-the-wild settings. The dataset includes images from MultiPIE [19] and BP4D [21] as well as images collected from the Internet. All images were annotated in a consistent way with 66 3D fiducial points. The final model was trained on the training set (13672 images) and the validation set (4725 images), and tested on the test set containing 4912 images. We also report results on the validation set with a model trained on the training set, only.

Metrics. Evaluation was performed using two different metrics: Ground Truth Error(GTE) and Cross View Ground Truth Consistency Error(CVGTCE).

GTE measures the average point-to-point Euclidean error normalized by the inter-ocular distance, as in [4]. GTE is calculated as follows:

$$E(\mathbf{X}, \mathbf{Y}) = \frac{1}{N} \sum_{n=1}^{N} \frac{\|\mathbf{x}_n - \mathbf{y}_n\|_2}{d_i}, \tag{2}$$

where $\mathbf{X}$ is the predicted set of points, $\mathbf{Y}$ is their corresponding ground truth and d_i denotes the interocular distance for the ith image.

Table 2. Performance on the 3DFAW test set.

Method	GTE (%)	CVGTCE (%)
Ours	**4.5623**	**3.4767**
Second best	5.8835	3.9700

CVGTCE evaluates the cross-view consistency of the predicted landmarks of the same subject and is defined as follows:

$$E_{vc}(\mathbf{X}, \mathbf{Y}, T) = \frac{1}{N} \sum_{n=1}^{N} \frac{\|s\mathbf{R}\mathbf{x}_n - \mathbf{y}_n\|_2}{d_i}, \tag{3}$$

where $P = \{s, \mathbf{R}, \mathbf{t}\}$ denotes scale, rotation and translation, respectively. CVGTCE is computed as follows:

$$\{s, \mathbf{R}, \mathbf{t}\} = \underset{s, \mathbf{R}, \mathbf{t}}{\operatorname{argmin}} \sum_{n=1}^{N} \|\mathbf{y}_k - (s\mathbf{R}\mathbf{x}_k + \mathbf{t})\|_2^2. \tag{4}$$

Results. Table 2 shows the performance of our system on the 3DFAW test set, as provided by the 3DFAW Challenge team. As it can be observed, our system outperforms the second best method (the result is taken from the 3DFAW Challenge website) in terms of GTE by more than 22 %.

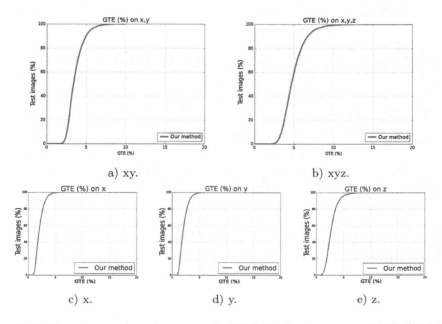

a) xy.

b) xyz.

c) x.

d) y.

e) z.

Fig. 3. GTE vs fraction of test images on the 3DFAW validation set, on (X,Y), (X,Y,Z), X alone, Y alone and Z alone.

Table 3. Performance on the 3DFAW validation set, on (X,Y), (X,Y,Z), X alone, Y alone and Z alone.

Axes	GTE (%)
xy	3.6263
xyz	4.9408
x	2.12
y	2.48
z	2.77

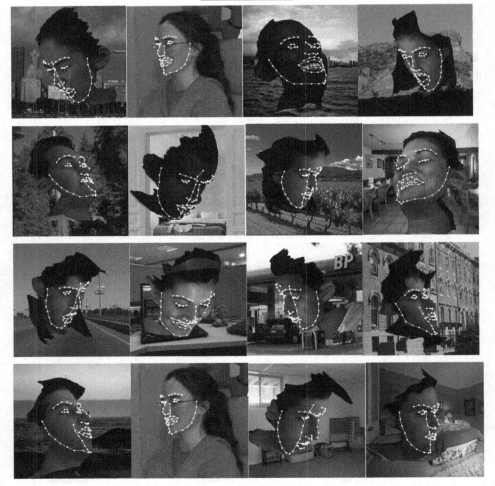

Fig. 4. Fitting results produced by our system on the 3DFAW test set. Observe that our method copes well with a large variety of poses and facial expressions on both controlled and in-the-wild images. Best viewed in colour. (Color figure online)

In order to better understand the performance of our system, we also report results on the validation set using a model trained on the training set, only. To measure performance, we used the Ground Truth Error measured on (X,Y), (X,Y,Z), X alone, Y alone and Z alone, and report the cumulative curve corresponding to the fraction of images for which the error was less than a specific value. Results are reported in Fig. 3 and Table 3. It can be observed that our system performs better on predicting the X and Y coordinates (compared to Z), but this difference is quite small and, to some extent, expected as Z is estimated at a later stage of the cascade. Finally, Fig. 4 shows a few fitting results produced by our system.

4   Conclusions

In this paper, we proposed a two-stage CNN cascade for 3D face alignment. The method is based on the idea of splitting the 3D alignment task into two separate subtasks: 2D landmark estimation and 1D (depth) estimation, where the first one guides the second. Our system secured the first place in the 1st 3D Face Alignment in the Wild (3DFAW) Challenge.

Acknowledgments. This work was supported in part by the EPSRC project EP/M02153X/1 Facial Deformable Models of Animals.

References

1. Cao, X., Wei, Y., Wen, F., Sun, J.: Face alignment by explicit shape regression. In: CVPR (2012)
2. Xiong, X., De la Torre, F.: Supervised descent method and its applications to face alignment. In: CVPR, pp. 532–539(2013)
3. Sagonas, C., Tzimiropoulos, G., Zafeiriou, S., Pantic, M.: A semi-automatic methodology for facial landmark annotation. In: CVPR-W (2013)
4. Sagonas, C., Tzimiropoulos, G., Zafeiriou, S., Pantic, M.: 300 faces in-the-wild challenge: the first facial landmark localization challenge. In: CVPR, pp. 397–403 (2013)
5. Shen, J., Zafeiriou, S., Chrysos, G., Kossaifi, J., Tzimiropoulos, G., Pantic, M.: The first facial landmark tracking in-the-wild challenge: benchmark and results. In: ICCV-W (2015)
6. Jourabloo, A., Liu, X.: Pose-invariant 3D face alignment. In: CVPR, pp. 3694–3702 (2015)
7. Jourabloo, A., Liu, X.: Large-pose face alignment via CNN-based dense 3D model fitting. In: CVPR (2016)
8. Zhu, S., Li, C., Change Loy, C., Tang, X.: Face alignment by coarse-to-fine shape searching. In: CVPR, pp. 4998–5006 (2015)
9. Bulat, A., Tzimiropoulos, G.: Convolutional aggregation of local evidence for large pose face alignment. In: BMVC (2016)
10. 1st Workshop on 3D Face Alignment in the Wild (3DFAW) & Challenge. http://mhug.disi.unitn.it/workshop/3dfaw/. Accessed 30 Aug 2016

11. He, K., Zhang, X., Ren, S., Sun, J.: Deep residual learning for image recognition. arXiv preprint arXiv:1512.03385 (2015)
12. He, K., Zhang, X., Ren, S., Sun, J.: Identity mappings in deep residual networks. arXiv preprint arXiv:1603.05027 (2016)
13. Bulat, A., Tzimiropoulos, G.: Human pose estimation via convolutional part heatmap regression. In: ECCV (2016)
14. Zeiler, M.D., Taylor, G.W., Fergus, R.: Adaptive deconvolutional networks for mid and high level feature learning. In: ICCV, pp. 2018–2025. IEEE (2011)
15. Newell, A., Yang, K., Deng, J.: Stacked hourglass networks for human pose estimation. arXiv preprint arXiv:1603.06937 (2016)
16. Long, J., Shelhamer, E., Darrell, T.: Fully convolutional networks for semantic segmentation. In: CVPR, pp. 3431–3440 (2015)
17. Deng, J., Dong, W., Socher, R., Li, L.J., Li, K., Fei-Fei, L.: Imagenet: A large-scale hierarchical image database. In: CVPR, pp. 248–255. IEEE (2009)
18. Collobert, R., Kavukcuoglu, K., Farabet, C.: Torch7: A matlab-like environment for machine learning. In: NIPS-W. Number EPFL-CONF-192376 (2011)
19. Gross, R., Matthews, I., Cohn, J., Kanade, T., Baker, S.: Multi-pie. Image Vis. Comput. 28(5), 807–813 (2010)
20. Yin, L., Chen, X., Sun, Y., Worm, T., Reale, M.: A high-resolution 3D dynamic facial expression database. In: 8th IEEE International Conference on Automatic Face & Gesture Recognition, FG 2008, pp. 1–6. IEEE (2008)
21. Zhang, X., Yin, L., Cohn, J.F., Canavan, S., Reale, M., Horowitz, A., Liu, P., Girard, J.M.: BP4D-spontaneous: a high-resolution spontaneous 3D dynamic facial expression database. Image Vis. Comput. 32(10), 692–706 (2014)
22. Jeni, L.A., Cohn, J.F., Kanade, T.: Dense 3D face alignment from 2D video for real-time use. Image and Vision Computing (2016)

W19 - Crowd Understanding

Multi-person Pose Estimation with Local Joint-to-Person Associations

Umar Iqbal[✉] and Juergen Gall

Computer Vision Group, University of Bonn, Bonn, Germany
{uiqbal,gall}@iai.uni-bonn.de

Abstract. Despite of the recent success of neural networks for human pose estimation, current approaches are limited to pose estimation of a single person and cannot handle humans in groups or crowds. In this work, we propose a method that estimates the poses of multiple persons in an image in which a person can be occluded by another person or might be truncated. To this end, we consider multi-person pose estimation as a joint-to-person association problem. We construct a fully connected graph from a set of detected joint candidates in an image and resolve the joint-to-person association and outlier detection using integer linear programming. Since solving joint-to-person association jointly for all persons in an image is an NP-hard problem and even approximations are expensive, we solve the problem locally for each person. On the challenging MPII Human Pose Dataset for multiple persons, our approach achieves the accuracy of a state-of-the-art method, but it is 6,000 to 19,000 times faster.

1 Introduction

Single person pose estimation has made a remarkable progress over the past few years. This is mainly due to the availability of deep learning based methods for detecting joints [1–5]. While earlier approaches in this direction [4,6,7] combine the body part detectors with tree structured graphical models, more recent methods [1–3,8–10] demonstrate that spatial relations between joints can be directly learned by a neural network without the need of an additional graphical model. These approaches, however, assume that only a single person is visible in the image and the location of the person is known a-priori. Moreover, the number of parts are defined by the network, *e.g.*, full body or upper body, and cannot be changed. For realistic scenarios such assumptions are too strong and the methods cannot be applied to images that contain a number of overlapping and truncated persons. An example of such a scenario is shown in Fig. 1.

In comparison to single person human pose estimation benchmarks, multi-person pose estimation introduces new challenges. The number of persons in an image is unknown and needs to be correctly estimated, the persons occlude each other and might be truncated, and the joints need to be associated to the correct person. The simplest approach to tackle this problem is to first use a person detector and then estimate the pose for each detection independently [11–13].

© Springer International Publishing Switzerland 2016
G. Hua and H. Jégou (Eds.): ECCV 2016 Workshops, Part II, LNCS 9914, pp. 627–642, 2016.
DOI: 10.1007/978-3-319-48881-3_44

Fig. 1. Example image from the multi-person subset of the MPII Pose Dataset [16].

This, however, does not resolve the joint association problem of two persons next to each other or truncations. Other approaches estimate the pose of all detected persons jointly [14,15]. In [2] a person detector is not required. Instead body part proposals are generated and connected in a large graph. The approach then solves the labeling problem, the joint-to-person association problem and non-maximum suppression jointly. While the model proposed in [2] can be solved by integer linear programming and achieves state-of-the-art results on a very small subset of the MPII Human Pose Dataset, the complexity makes it infeasible for a practical application. As reported in [5], the processing of a single image takes about 72 h.

In this work, we address the joint-to-person association problem using a densely connected graphical model as in [2], but propose to solve it only locally. To this end, we first use a person detector and crop image regions as illustrated in Fig. 1. Each of the regions contains sufficient context, but only the joints of persons that are very close. We then solve the joint-to-person association for the person in the center of each region by integer linear programming (ILP). The labeling of the joints and non-maxima suppression are directly performed by a convolutional neural network. We evaluate our approach on the MPII Human Pose Dataset for multiple persons where we slightly improve the accuracy of [2] while reducing the runtime by a factor between 6,000 and 19,000.

2   Related Work

Human pose estimation has generally been addressed under the assumption that only a single person is visible. For this, earlier approaches formulate the problem in a graphical model where interactions between body parts are modelled in a tree structure combined with local observations obtained from discriminatively trained part detectors [17–23]. While the tree-structured models provide efficient inference, they struggle to model long-range characteristics of the human body. With the progress in convolutional neural network architectures, more recent works adopt CNNs to obtain stronger part detectors but still use graphical models to obtain coherent pose estimates [4,6,7].

The state-of-the-art approaches, however, demonstrate that graphical models are of little importance in the presence of strong part detectors since the long-range relationships of the body parts can be directly incorporated in the part detectors [1–3,5,8–10]. In [3,8,9] multi-staged CNN architectures are proposed where each stage of the network takes as input the score maps of all parts from its preceding stage. This provides additional information about the interdependence, co-occurrence, and context of parts to each stage, and thereby allows the network to implicitly learn image dependent spatial relationships between parts. Similarly, instead of a multi-staged architecture, [5] proposes to use a very deep network that inherently results in large receptive fields and therefore allows to use contextual information around the parts. All of these methods report impressive results for single person pose estimation without an additional graphical model for refinement.

In contrast to the single person pose estimation, multi-person pose estimation poses a significantly more complex problem, and only a few works have focused in this direction [2,5,11–14,22,24–26]. [22,24] perform non-maximum suppression on the marginals obtained using a graphical model to generate multiple pose hypotheses in an image. The approaches, however, can only work in scenarios where persons are significantly distant from each other and consider only the fully visible persons. The methods in [11–13] first detect the persons in an image using a person detector and then estimate the body pose for each person independently. [24] employs a similar approach for 3D pose estimation of multiple persons in a calibrated multi-camera scenario. The approach first obtains the number of persons using a person detector and then samples the 3D poses for each person from the marginals of a 3D pictorial structure model. For every detected person, [13] explores a range of tree structured models each containing only a subset of upper-body parts, and selects the best model based on a cost function that penalizes a model containing occluded parts. Since the search space of the models increases exponentially with the number of body parts, the approach is very expensive for full body skeletons. [14,15] define a joint pose estimation model for all detected persons, and utilize several occlusion clues to model interactions between people. All these approaches rely on a standard pictorial structure model with tree structures and cannot incorporate dependencies beyond adjacent joints.

More recently, [2] proposed a joint objective function to solve multi-person pose estimation. The approach does not require a separate person detector or any prior information about the number of persons. Unlike earlier works it can tackle any type of occlusion or truncation. It starts by generating a set of class independent part proposals and constructs a densely connected graph from the proposals. It uses integer linear programming to label each proposal by a certain body part and assigns them to unique individuals. The optimization problem proposed in [2] is theoretically well founded, but is an NP-Hard problem to solve and prohibitively expensive for realistic scenarios. Therefore, it limits the number of part proposals to 100. This means that the approach can estimate the poses of at most 7 fully visible persons with 14 body parts per person. Despite the restriction, the inference takes roughly 72 h for a single image [5]. In [5], the authors build upon the same model and propose to use stronger part detectors and image dependent spatial models along with an incremental optimization approach that significantly reduces the optimization time of [2]. The approach, however, is still too slow for practical applications since it requires 8 min per image and still limits the number of proposals to a maximum of 150.

3   Overview

Our method solves the problem of joint-to-person association locally for each person in the image. To this end, we first detect the persons using a person detector [27]. For each detected person, we generate a set of joint candidates using a single person pose estimation model (Sect. 4). The candidates are prone to errors since the single person models do not take into account occlusion or truncation. In order to associate each joint to the correct person and also to remove the erroneous candidates, we perform inference locally on a fully connected graph for each person using integer linear programming (Sect. 5). Figure 2 shows an overview of the proposed approach.

Fig. 2. Overview of the proposed method. We detect persons in an image using a person detector (a). A set of joint candidates is generated for each detected person (b). The candidates build a fully connected graph (c) and the final pose estimates are obtained by integer linear programming (d). (best viewed in color) (Color figure online)

4   Convolutional Pose Machines

Given a person in an image $\mathbf{I}$, we define its pose as a set $\mathcal{X} = \{\mathbf{x}_j\}_j = 1 \ldots J$ of $J = 14$ body joints, where the vector $\mathbf{x_j} \in \mathcal{X}$ represents the 2D location

(u, v) of the jth joint in the image. The convolutional pose machines consist of a multi-staged CNN architecture with $t \in \{1 \dots T\}$ stages, where each stage is a multi-label classifier $\phi_t(\mathbf{x})$ that is trained to provide confidence maps $s_t^j \in \mathbb{R}^{w \times h}$ for each joint $j = 1 \dots J$ and the background, where w and h are the width and the height of the image, respectively.

The first stage of the architecture uses only the local image evidence and provides the confidence scores

$$\phi_{t=1}(\mathbf{x}|\mathbf{I}) \rightarrow \{\mathbf{s}_1^{\mathbf{j}}(\mathbf{x_j} = \mathbf{x})\}_{\mathbf{j}=1\dots\mathbf{J}+1}. \tag{1}$$

whereas, in addition to the local image evidence, all subsequent stages also utilize the contextual information from the preceding stages to produce confidence score maps

$$\phi_{t>1}(\mathbf{x}|\mathbf{I}, \psi(\mathbf{x}, \mathbf{s_{t-1}})) \rightarrow \{\mathbf{s}_{\mathbf{t}}^{\mathbf{j}}(\mathbf{x_j} = \mathbf{x})\}_{\mathbf{j}=1\dots\mathbf{J}+1}, \tag{2}$$

where $\mathbf{s_t} \in \mathbb{R}^{\mathbf{w} \times \mathbf{h} \times (\mathbf{J}+1)}$ corresponds to the score maps of all body joints and the background at stage t, and $\psi(\mathbf{x}, \mathbf{s_{t-1}})$ indicates the mapping from the scores $\mathbf{s_{t-1}}$ to the context features for location $\mathbf{x}$. The receptive field of the subsequent stages is increased to the extent that the context of the complete person is available. This allows to model complex long-range spatial relationships between joints, and to leverage the context around the person. The CPM architecture is completely differentiable and allows end-to-end training of all stages. Due to the multi-stage nature of CPM, the overall CNN architecture consists of many layers and is therefore prone to the problem of vanishing gradients [3,28,29]. In order to solve this problem, [3] uses intermediate supervision by adding a loss function at each stage t. The CNN architecture used for each stage can be seen in Fig. 3. In this paper we exploit the intermediate supervision of the stages during training for multi-person human pose estimation as we will discuss in the next section.

4.1   Training for Multi-person Pose Estimation

Each stage of the CPM is trained to produce confidence score maps for all body joints, and the loss function at the end of every stage computes the l_2 distance between the predicted confidence scores and the target score maps. The target score maps are modeled as Gaussian distributions centered at the ground-truth locations of the joints. For multi-person pose estimation, the aim of the training is to focus only on the body joints of the detected person, while suppressing joints of all other overlapping persons. We do this by creating two types of target score maps. For the first stage, we model the target score maps by a sum of Gaussian distributions for the body joints of all persons appearing in the bounding box enclosing the primary person that appears roughly in the center of the bounding box. For the subsequent stages, we model only the joints of the primary person. An example of target score maps for different stages can be seen in Fig. 4.

Figure 5 shows some examples how the inferred score maps evolve as the number of stages increases. In [3], the pose of the person is obtained by taking the maximum of the inferred score maps, $i.e.$, $\mathbf{x_j} = \text{argmax}_{\mathbf{x}} \mathbf{s}_{\mathbf{T}}^{\mathbf{j}}(\mathbf{x})$.

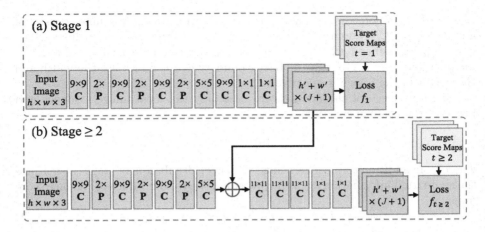

Fig. 3. CPM architecture proposed in [3]. The first stage (a) utilizes only the local image evidence whereas all subsequent stages (b) also utilize the output of preceding stages to exploit the spatial context between joints. The receptive field of stages $t \geq 2$ is increased by having multiple convolutional layers at the 8 times down-sampled score maps. All stages are locally supervised and a separate loss is computed for each stage. We provide multi-person target score maps to stage 1, and single-person score maps to all subsequent stages.

Fig. 4. Example of target score maps for the head, neck and left shoulder. The target score maps for the first stage include the joints of all persons (left). The target score maps for all subsequent stages only include the joints of the primary person.

This, however, assumes that all joints are visible in the image and results in erroneous estimates for invisible joints and can wrongly associate joints of other nearby persons to the primary person. Instead of taking the maximum, we sample N candidates from each inferred score map s_T^j and resolve the joint-to-person association and outlier removal by integer linear programming.

5   Joint-to-Person Association

We solve the joint-to-person association using a densely connected graphical model as in [2]. The model proposed in [2], however, aims to resolve joint-to-person associations together with proposal labeling globally for all persons, which makes it very expensive to solve. In contrast, we propose to solve this problem locally for each person. We first briefly summarize the DeepCut method [2] in Sect. 5.1, and then describe the proposed local joint-to-person association model in Sect. 5.2.

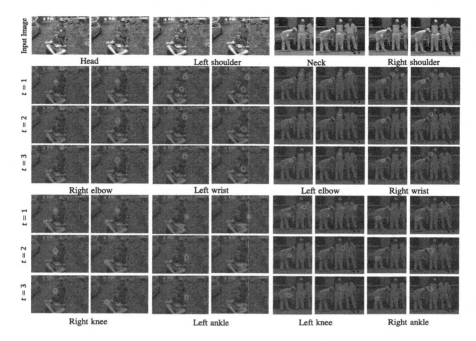

Fig. 5. Examples of score maps provided by different stages of the CPM. The first stage of CPM uses only local image evidence and therefore provides high confidence scores for the joints of all persons in the image. Whereas all subsequent stages are trained to provide high confidence scores only for the joints of the primary person while suppressing the joints of other persons. The primary person is highlighted by a yellow dot in the first row. (best viewed in color) (Color figure online)

5.1 DeepCut

DeepCut aims to solve the problem of multi-person human pose estimation by jointly modeling the poses of all persons appearing in an image. Given an image, it starts by generating a set D of joint proposals, where $\mathbf{x_d} \in \mathbb{Z}^\mathbf{2}$ denotes the 2D location of the dth proposal. The proposals are then used to formulate a graph optimization problem that aims to select a subset of proposals while suppressing the incompatible proposals, label each selected proposal with a joint type $j \in 1 \ldots J$, and associate them to unique individuals.

The problem can be solved by integer linear programming (ILP), optimizing over the binary variables $x \in \{0,1\}^{D \times J}$, $y \in \{0,1\}^{\binom{D}{2}}$, and $z \in \{0,1\}^{\binom{D}{2} \times J^2}$. For every proposal d, a set of variables $\{x_{dj}\}_{j=1\ldots J}$ is defined where $x_{dj} = 1$ indicates that the proposal d is of body joint type j. For every pair of proposals dd', the variable $y_{dd'}$ indicates that the proposals d and d' belong to the same person. The variable $z_{dd'jj'} = 1$ indicates that the proposal d is of joint type j, the proposal d' is of joint type j', and both proposals belong to the same person ($y_{dd'} = 1$). The variable $z_{dd'jj'}$ is constrained such that $z_{dd'jj'} = x_{dj}x_{d'j'}y_{dd'}$. The solution of the ILP problem is obtained by optimizing the following objective function:

$$\min_{(x,y,z)\in X_D} \langle \alpha, x \rangle + \langle \beta, z \rangle \tag{3}$$

subject to

$$\forall d \in D \; \forall jj' \in \binom{J}{2} : \quad x_{dj} + x_{dj'} \leq 1 \tag{4}$$

$$\forall dd' \in \binom{D}{2} : \quad y_{dd'} \leq \sum_{j\in J} x_{dj}, \quad y_{dd'} \leq \sum_{j\in J} x_{d'j} \tag{5}$$

$$\forall dd'd'' \in \binom{D}{3} : \quad y_{dd'} + y_{d'd''} - 1 \leq y_{dd''} \tag{6}$$

$$\forall dd' \in \binom{D}{2} \; \forall jj' \in J^2 : \quad x_{dj} + x_{d'j'} + y_{dd'} - 2 \leq z_{dd'jj'}$$

$$z_{dd'jj'} \leq min(x_{dj}, x_{d'j'}, y_{dd'}) \tag{7}$$

and, optionally,

$$\forall dd' \in \binom{D}{2} \; \forall jj' \in J^2 : \quad x_{dj} + x_{d'j'} - 1 \leq y_{dd'} \tag{8}$$

where

$$\alpha_{dj} = \log \frac{1 - p_{dj}}{p_{dj}} \tag{9}$$

$$\beta_{dd'jj'} = \log \frac{1 - p_{dd'jj'}}{p_{dd'jj'}} \tag{10}$$

$$\langle \alpha, x \rangle = \sum_{d\in D} \sum_{j\in J} \alpha_{dj} x_{dj} \tag{11}$$

$$\langle \beta, z \rangle = \sum_{dd'\in\binom{D}{2}} \sum_{j,j'\in J} \beta_{dd'jj'} z_{dd'jj'}. \tag{12}$$

The constraints (4)–(7) enforce that optimizing (3) results in valid body pose configurations for one or more persons. The constraints (4) ensure that a proposal d can be labeled with only one joint type, while the constraints (5) guarantee that any pair of proposals dd' can belong to the same person only if both are not suppressed, i.e., $x_{dj} = 1$ and $x_{d'j'} = 1$. The constraints (6) are transitivity constraints and enforce for any three proposals $dd'd'' \in \binom{D}{3}$ that if d and d' belong to the same person, and d' and d'' also belong to the same person, then the proposals d and d'' must also belong to the same person. The constraints (7) enforce that for any $dd' \in \binom{D}{2}$ and $jj' \in J^2$, $z_{dd'jj'} = x_{dj} x_{d'j'} y_{dd'}$. The constraints (8) are only applicable for single-person human pose estimation, as they enforce that two proposals dd' that are not suppressed must be grouped together. In (9), $p_{dj} \in (0,1)$ are the body joint unaries and correspond to the probability of any proposal d being of joint type j. While in (10), $p_{dd'jj'}$ correspond to the conditional probability that a pair of proposals dd' belongs to the same person, given that d and d' are of joint type j and j', respectively. In [2] this ILP formulation is referred as *Subset Partitioning and Labelling Problem*, as it partitions the initial pool of proposal candidates to unique individuals, labels each proposal with a joint type j, and inherently suppresses the incompatible candidates.

5.2   Local Joint-to-Person Association

In contrast to [2], we solve the joint-to-person association problem locally for each person. We also do not label generic proposals as part of the ILP formulation since we use a neural network to obtain detections for each joint as described in Sect. 4. We therefore start with a set of joint detections D_J, where every detection d_j at location $\mathbf{x_{d_j}} \in \mathbb{Z}^2$ has a known joint type $j \in 1 \dots J$. Our model requires only two types of binary random variables $x \in \{0,1\}^{D_J}$ and $y \in \{0,1\}^{\binom{D_J}{2}}$. Here, $x_{d_j} = 1$ indicates that the detection d_j of part type j is not suppressed, and $y_{d_j d'_{j'}} = 1$ indicates that the detection d_j of type j, and the detection $d'_{j'}$ of type j' belong to the same person. The objective function for local joint-to-person association takes the form:

$$\min_{(x,y)\in X_{D_J}} \langle \alpha, x \rangle + \langle \beta, y \rangle \tag{13}$$

subject to

$$\forall d_j d'_{j'} \in \binom{D_J}{2} : \quad y_{d_j d'_{j'}} \leq x_{d_j}, \quad y_{d_j d'_{j'}} \leq x_{d'_{j'}} \tag{14}$$

$$\forall d_j d'_{j'} d''_{j''} \in \binom{D_J}{3} : \quad y_{d_j d'_{j'}} + y_{d'_{j'} d''_{j''}} - 1 \leq y_{d_j d''_{j''}} \tag{15}$$

$$\forall d_j d'_{j'} \in \binom{D_J}{2} : \quad x_{d_j} + x_{d'_{j'}} - 1 \leq y_{d_j d'_{j'}} \tag{16}$$

where

$$\alpha_{d_j} = \log \frac{1 - p_{d_j}}{p_{d_j}} \tag{17}$$

$$\beta_{d_j d'_{j'}} = \log \frac{1 - p_{d_j d'_{j'}}}{p_{d_j d'_{j'}}} \tag{18}$$

$$\langle \alpha, x \rangle = \sum_{d_j \in D_J} \alpha_{d_j} x_{d_j} \tag{19}$$

$$\langle \beta, y \rangle = \sum_{d_j d'_{j'} \in \binom{D_J}{2}} \beta_{d_j d'_{j'}} y_{d_j d'_{j'}}. \tag{20}$$

The constraints (14) enforce that detection d_j and $d'_{j'}$ are connected ($y_{d_j d'_{j'}} = 1$) only if both are not suppressed, *i.e.*, $x_{d_j} = 1$ and $x_{d'_{j'}} = 1$. The constraints (15) are transitivity constraints as before and the constraints (16) guarantee that all detections that are not suppressed belong to the primary person. We can see from (3)–(8) and (13)–(16), that the number of variables are reduced from $(D \times J + \binom{D}{2} + \binom{D}{2} \times J^2)$ to $(DJ + \binom{DJ}{2})$. Similarly, the number of constraints is also drastically reduced.

In (17), $p_{d_j} \in (0,1)$ is the confidence of the joint detection d_j as probability. We obtain this directly from the score maps inferred by the CPM as $p_{d_j} = f_\tau(s_T^j(\mathbf{x_{d_j}}))$, where

$$f_\tau(s) = \begin{cases} s & \text{if } s \geq \tau \\ 0 & \text{otherwise,} \end{cases} \tag{21}$$

and τ is a threshold that suppresses detections with a low confidence score.

In (18), $p_{d_j d'_{j'}} \in (0,1)$ corresponds to the conditional probability that the detection d_j of joint type j and the detection $d'_{j'}$ of joint type j' belong to the same person. For $j = j'$, it is the probability that both detections d_j and $d'_{j'}$ belong to the same body joint. For $j \neq j'$, it measures the compatibility between two detection candidates of different joint types. Similar to [2], we obtain these probabilities by learning discriminative models based on appearance and spatial features of the detection candidates. For $j = j'$, we define a feature vector

$$f_{d_j d'_{j'}} = \{\triangle\mathbf{x}, \exp(\triangle\mathbf{x}), (\triangle\mathbf{x})^\mathbf{2}\}, \tag{22}$$

where $\triangle\mathbf{x} = (\triangle\mathbf{u}, \triangle\mathbf{v})$ is the 2D offset between the locations $\mathbf{x_{d_j}}$ and $\mathbf{x_{d'_{j'}}}$. For $j \neq j'$, we define a separate feature vector based on the spatial locations as well as the appearance features obtained from the joint detectors as

$$f_{d_j d'_{j'}} = \{\triangle\mathbf{x}, \|\triangle\mathbf{x}\|, \arctan\left(\frac{\triangle\mathbf{v}}{\triangle\mathbf{u}}\right), \mathbf{s_T}(\mathbf{x_{d_j}}), \mathbf{s_T}(\mathbf{x_{d'_{j'}}})\}, \tag{23}$$

where $\mathbf{s_T}(\mathbf{x})$ is a vector containing the confidences of all joints and the background at location $\mathbf{x}$. For both cases, we gather positive and negative samples from the annotated poses in the training data and train an SVM with RBF kernel using LibSVM [30] for each pair $jj' \in \binom{J}{2}$. In order to obtain the probabilities $p_{d_j d'_{j'}} \in (0,1)$ we use Platt scaling [31] to normalize the output of the SVMs to probabilities. After optimizing (13), the pose of the primary person is given by the detections with $x_{d_j} = 1$.

6   Experiments

We evaluate the proposed approach on the Multi-Person subset of the MPII Human Pose Dataset [16] and follow the evaluation protocol proposed in [2]. The dataset consists of 3844 training and 1758 testing images with multiple persons. The persons appear in highly articulated poses with a large amount of occlusions and truncations. Since the original test data of the dataset is withheld, we perform all intermediate experiments on a validation set of 1200 images.

The validation set is sampled according to the split proposed in [4] for the single person setup, *i.e.*, we chose all multi-person images that are part of the validation test set proposed in [4] and use all other images for training. In addition we compare the proposed method with the state-of-the-art approach [2] on their selected subset of 288 images, and also compare with [5] on the complete test set. The accuracy is measured by average precision (AP) for each joint using the scripts provided by [2].

6.1 Implementation Details

In order to localize the persons, we use the person detector proposed in [27]. The detector is trained on the Pascal VOC dataset [32]. For the quantitative evaluation, we discard detected persons with a bounding box area less equal to 80×80 pixels since small persons are not annotated in the MPII Human Pose Dataset. For the qualitative results shown in Fig. 7, we do not discard the small detections. For the CPM [3], we use the publicly available source code and train it on the Multi-Person subset of the MPII Human Pose Dataset as described in Sect. 4. As in [3], we add images from the Leeds Sports Dataset [33] during training, and use a 6 stage $(T = 6)$ CPM architecture. For solving (13), we use the Gurobi Optimizer.

6.2 Results

We first evaluate the impact of the parameter τ in $f_\tau(s)$ (21) on the pose estimation accuracy measured as mean AP on the validation set containing 1200 images. Figure 6 shows that the function f_τ improves the accuracy when τ is increased until $\tau = 0.3$. For $\tau > 0.4$, the accuracy drops since a high value discards correct detections. For the following experiments, we use $\tau = 0.2$.

Table 1 reports the pose estimation results under different settings of the proposed approach on the validation set. We also report the median run-time

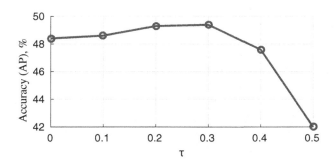

Fig. 6. Impact of the parameter τ in (21) on the pose estimation accuracy.

Table 1. Pose estimation results (AP) on the validation test set (1200 images) of the MPII Multi-Person Pose Dataset.

Setting	Head	Shoulder	Elbow	Wrist	Hip	Knee	Ankle	Total	time (s)
CPM only	56.5	55.2	47.6	39.1	48.1	39.6	30.3	45.2	2
CPM + L − JPA (N = 1)	59.9	57.5	50.5	41.8	49.8	45.5	39.5	49.2	3
CPM + L − JPA (N = 3)	59.9	57.4	50.7	42.1	50.0	45.5	39.5	49.3	8
CPM + L − JPA (N = 5)	60.0	57.5	50.7	42.1	50.1	45.5	39.4	49.3	10
CPM + L − JPA (N = 5) + GT Torso	92.9	91.3	78.4	61.8	81.0	71.4	61.8	76.9	10

Table 2. Comparison of pose estimation results (AP) with state-of-the-art approaches on 288 images [2].

Setting	Head	Shoulder	Elbow	Wrist	Hip	Knee	Ankle	Total	time (s)
Ours	70.0	65.2	56.4	46.1	52.7	47.9	44.5	54.7	10
DeepCut [2]	73.1	71.7	58.0	39.9	56.1	43.5	31.9	53.5	57995
DeeperCut [5]	87.9	84.0	71.9	63.9	68.8	63.8	58.1	71.2	230
Ours GT ROI	87.7	81.6	68.9	56.1	66.4	59.4	54.0	67.7	10
DeepCut GT ROI [2]	78.1	74.1	62.2	52.0	56.9	48.7	46.1	60.2	-
Chen et al., GT ROI [6]	65.0	34.2	22.0	15.7	19.2	15.8	14.2	27.1	-

Table 3. Pose estimation results (AP) on the withheld test set of the MPII Multi-Person Pose Dataset.

Setting	Head	Shoulder	Elbow	Wrist	Hip	Knee	Ankle	Total	time (s)
Ours	58.4	53.9	44.5	35.0	42.2	36.7	31.1	43.1	10
DeeperCut [5]	78.4	72.5	60.2	51.0	57.2	52.0	45.4	59.5	485
Using GT ROIs									
Ours + GT Torso	85.6	79.4	62.9	48.9	62.6	51.9	43.9	62.2	10

required by each setting[1]. Using only the CPM to estimate the pose of each detected person achieves 45.2 % mAP and takes only 2 s per image. Using the proposed Local Joint-to-Person Association (L-JPA) model with 1 detection candidate per joint ($N = 1$) to suppress the incompatible detections improves the performance from 45.2 % to 49.2 % with a very slight increase in run-time. Increasing the number of candidates per joint increases the accuracy only slightly. For the following experiments, we use $N = 5$. When we compare the numbers with Fig. 6, we observe that CPM + L − JPA outperforms CPM for any $0 \leq \tau \leq 0.4$.

The accuracy also depends on the used person detector. We use an off-the-shelf person detector without any fine-tuning on the MPII dataset. In order to evaluate the impact of the person detector accuracy, we also estimate poses when the person detections are given by the ground-truth torso (GT Torso) locations of the persons provided with the dataset. This results in a significant improvement

---

[1] Measured on a 2 GHz Intel(R) Xeon(R) CPU with a single core and NVidia Geforce GTX Titan-X GPU.

Fig. 7. Some qualitative results for the MPII Multi-person Pose Dataset.

in accuracy from 49.3 % to 76.9 % mAP, showing that a better person detector would improve the results further.

Table 2 compares the proposed approach with other approaches on a selected subset of 288 test images used in [2]. Our approach outperforms the state-of-the-art method DeepCut [2] (54.7 % vs. 53.5 %) while being significantly faster

(10 s vs. 57995 s). If we use $N = 1$, our approach requires only 3 s per image with a minimal loss of accuracy as shown in Table 1, *i.e.*, our approach is more than 19,000 times faster than [2]. We also compare with a concurrent work [5]. While the approach [5] achieves a higher accuracy than our method, our method is significantly faster (10 s vs. 230 s). In contrast to [5], we do not perform fine-tuning of the person detector on the MPII Multi-Person Pose Dataset and envision that doing this will lead to further improvements. We therefore compare with two additional approaches [2,6] when using GT bounding boxes of the persons. The results for [6] are taken from [2]. Our approach outperforms both methods by a large margin.

Finally in Table 3, we report our results on all test images of the MPII Multi-Person Pose Dataset. Our method achieves 43.1 % mAP. While the approach [2] cannot be evaluated on all test images due to the high computational complexity of the model, [5] reports a higher accuracy than our model. However, if we compare the run-times in Tables 2 and 3, we observe that the run-time of [5] doubles on the more challenging test set (485 s per image). Our approach on the other hand requires only 10 s in all evaluation settings and is around 50 times faster. If we use $N = 1$, our approach is 160 times faster than [5]. Using the torso annotation (GT Torso) as person detections results again in a significant improvement of the accuracy (62.2 % vs. 43.1 % mAP). Some qualitative results can be seen in Fig. 7.

7   Conclusion

In this work we have presented an approach for multi-person pose estimation under occlusions and truncations. Since the global modeling of poses for all persons is impractical, we demonstrated that the problem can be formulated by a set of independent local joint-to-person association problems. Compared to global modeling, these problems can be solved efficiently while still being effective for handling severe occlusions or truncations. Although the accuracy can be further improved by using a better person detector, the proposed method already achieves the accuracy of a state-of-the-art method, while being 6,000 to 19,000 times faster.

Acknowledgements. The work was partially supported by the ERC Starting Grant ARCA (677650).

References

1. Carreira, J., Agrawal, P., Fragkiadaki, K., Malik, J.: Human pose estimation with iterative error feedback. In: CVPR (2016)
2. Pishchulin, L., Insafutdinov, E., Tang, S., Andres, B., Andriluka, M., Gehler, P., Schiele, B.: Deepcut: Joint subset partition and labeling for multi person pose estimation. In: CVPR (2016)
3. Wei, S.E., Ramakrishna, V., Kanade, T., Sheikh, Y.: Convolutional pose machines. In: CVPR (2016)

4. Tompson, J., Goroshin, R., Jain, A., LeCun, Y., Bregler, C.: Efficient object localization using convolutional networks. In: CVPR (2015)
5. Insafutdinov, E., Pishchulin, L., Andres, B., Andriluka, M., Schiele, B.: DeeperCut: a deeper, stronger, and faster multi-person pose estimation model. In: Leibe, B., Matas, J., Sebe, N., Welling, M., Travkin, O. (eds.) ECCV 2016. LNCS, vol. 9910, pp. 34–50. Springer, Heidelberg (2016). doi:10.1007/978-3-319-46466-4_3
6. Chen, X., Yuille, A.L.: Articulated pose estimation by a graphical model with image dependent pairwise relations. In: NIPS (2014)
7. Tompson, J., Jain, A., LeCun, Y., Bregler, C.: Joint training of a convolutional network and a graphical model for human pose estimation. In: NIPS (2014)
8. Newell, A., Yang, K., Deng, J.: Stacked hourglass networks for human pose estimation. In: Leibe, B., Matas, J., Sebe, N., Welling, M., Chang, L. (eds.) ECCV 2016. LNCS, vol. 9912, pp. 483–499. Springer, Heidelberg (2016). doi:10.1007/978-3-319-46484-8_29
9. Bulat, A., Tzimiropoulos, G.: Human pose estimation via convolutional part heatmap regression. In: ECCV (2016)
10. Rafi, U., Kostrikov, I., Gall, J., Leibe, B.: An efficient convolutional network for human pose estimation. In: BMVC (2016)
11. Pishchulin, L., Jain, A., Andriluka, M., Thormählen, T., Schiele, B.: Articulated people detection and pose estimation: Reshaping the future. In: CVPR (2012)
12. Gkioxari, G., Hariharan, B., Girshick, R., Malik, J.: Using k-poselets for detecting people and localizing their keypoints. In: CVPR (2014)
13. Chen, X., Yuille, A.L.: Parsing occluded people by flexible compositions. In: CVPR (2015)
14. Eichner, M., Ferrari, V.: We Are Family: joint pose estimation of multiple persons. In: Daniilidis, K., Maragos, P., Paragios, N. (eds.) ECCV 2010, Part I. LNCS, vol. 6311, pp. 228–242. Springer, Heidelberg (2010)
15. Ladicky, L., Torr, P.H., Zisserman, A.: Human pose estimation using a joint pixelwise and part-wise formulation. In: CVPR (2013)
16. Andriluka, M., Pishchulin, L., Gehler, P., Schiele, B.: 2D human pose estimation: new benchmark and state of the art analysis. In: CVPR (2014)
17. Felzenszwalb, P.F., Huttenlocher, D.P.: Pictorial structures for object recognition. IJCV 61(1), 55–79 (2005)
18. Tran, D., Forsyth, D.: Improved human parsing with a full relational model. In: Daniilidis, K., Maragos, P., Paragios, N. (eds.) ECCV 2010, Part IV. LNCS, vol. 6314, pp. 227–240. Springer, Heidelberg (2010)
19. Andriluka, M., Roth, S., Schiele, B.: Discriminative appearance models for pictorial structures. IJCV 99(3), 259–280 (2012)
20. Pishchulin, L., Andriluka, M., Gehler, P., Schiele, B.: Poselet conditioned pictorial structures. In: CVPR (2013)
21. Wang, F., Li, Y.: Beyond physical connections: tree models in human pose estimation. In: CVPR (2013)
22. Yang, Y., Ramanan, D.: Articulated human detection with flexible mixtures of parts. TPAMI 35(12), 2878–2890 (2013)
23. Dantone, M., Leistner, C., Gall, J., Van Gool, L.: Body parts dependent joint regressors for human pose estimation in still images. TPAMI 36(11), 2131–2143 (2014)
24. Sun, M., Savarese, S.: Articulated part-based model for joint object detection and pose estimation. In: ICCV (2011)
25. Ladicky, L., Torr, P., Zisserman, A.: Human pose estimation using a joint pixel-wise and part-wise formulation. In: CVPR (2013)

26. Belagiannis, V., Amin, S., Andriluka, M., Schiele, B., Navab, N., Ilic, S.: 3D pictorial structures revisited: Multiple human pose estimation. TPAMI (2015)
27. Ren, S., He, K., Girshick, R., Sun, J.: Faster R-CNN: Towards real-time object detection with region proposal networks. In: NIPS (2015)
28. Bengio, Y., Simard, P., Frasconi, P.: Learning long-term dependencies with gradient descent is difficult. TNN (1994)
29. Glorot, X., Bengio, Y.: Understanding the difficulty of training deep feedforward neural networks. In: AISTATS (2010)
30. Chang, C.C., Lin, C.J.: LIBSVM: A library for support vector machines. ACM TIST (2011)
31. Platt, J.C.: Probabilistic outputs for support vector machines and comparisons to regularized likelihood methods. In: Advances in Large Margin Classifiers (1999)
32. Everingham, M., Eslami, S.M.A., Van Gool, L., Williams, C.K.I., Winn, J., Zisserman, A.: The PASCAL visual object classes challenge: a retrospective. IJCV (2015)
33. Johnson, S., Everingham, M.: Clustered pose and nonlinear appearance models for human pose estimation. In: BMVC. (2010)

Density-Aware Pedestrian Proposal Networks for Robust People Detection in Crowded Scenes

Sangdoo Yun, Kimin Yun, Jongwon Choi, and Jin Young Choi[(⊠)]

ASRI, Department of Electrical and Computer Engineering,
Seoul National University, Seoul, South Korea
{yunsd101,ykmwww,jychoi}@snu.ac.kr, jwchoi.pil@gmail.com

Abstract. In this paper, we propose a density-aware pedestrian proposal network (DAPPN) for robust people detection in crowded scenes. Conventional pedestrian detectors and object proposal algorithms easily fail to find people in crowded scenes because of severe occlusions among people. Our method utilizes a crowd density map to resolve the occlusion problem. The proposed network is composed of two networks: the proposal network and the selection network. First, the proposal network predicts the initial pedestrian detection proposals and the crowd density map. After that, the selection network selectively picks the final proposals by considering the initial proposals and the crowd density. To validate the performance of the proposed method, experiments are conducted on crowd-scene datasets: WorldExpo10 and PETS2009. The experimental results show that our method outperforms the conventional method and achieves near real-time speed on a GPU (25 fps).

1 Introduction

1.1 Motivations and Objectives

Pedestrian detection is one of the most important tasks in computer vision. Recently, deep convolutional neural network (DCNN) based pedestrian detectors [7,10,14,18] have achieved state-of-the-art performance. DCNN-based detection systems mainly have two stages: First, numerous object candidates, often called "proposals," are extracted as preprocessing through regression on possible locations of pedestrians. Second, DCNN-based detector classifies the proposals and determines the final detections. Since regions except the proposals in image are ignored, high-quality proposals could improve detection performance by rejecting false positives and make whole detection speed faster than using the traditional *sliding window* methods. Therefore, generation of high-quality proposals is essential for fast and accurate object detection.

In this work, we focus on the challenging crowded scene as shown in Fig. 1. Our goal is to find high-quality pedestrian proposals in highly crowded scenes. The main difficulty of generating pedestrian proposals in a crowded scene is caused by severe occlusions among people. Commonly used pedestrian proposal methods, such as LDCF [11] or ACF [4] detectors, are known to show a weak

© Springer International Publishing Switzerland 2016
G. Hua and H. Jégou (Eds.): ECCV 2016 Workshops, Part II, LNCS 9914, pp. 643–654, 2016.
DOI: 10.1007/978-3-319-48881-3_45

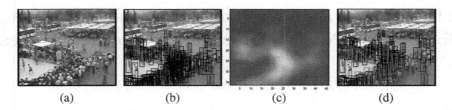

Fig. 1. (a) An example of a crowded scene. (b) The results of the LDCF detector [11]. The black boxes are missed pedestrians, and the red boxes are the correctly detected pedestrians (IoU > 0.5). (c) The crowd density map of the scene. (d) The results of the proposed methods. (Color figure online)

performance in a crowded scene with severe occlusions as shown in Fig. 1, which results in slow speed compared with other fast proposal algorithms [14, 21]. However, these methods [14, 21] do not consider the occlusion and just try to detect each pedestrian independently. Therefore, understanding the occlusion patterns in the whole scene is the key factor to solve this crowded-scene pedestrian proposal problem.

In this paper, we propose a density-aware pedestrian proposal network (DAPPN) to solve the occlusion problem in a crowded scene. We observe that there exists an intimate relationship between crowd density and people detections. For example, a high-density region is more likely to have occlusions of people than a lower-density region. Following this observation, we propose a pedestrian proposal network that considers crowd density in a global view. The proposed DAPPN is composed of two networks: the *proposal network* and the *selection network*. The *proposal network* predicts a density map in a crowded-scene image in addition to rough pedestrian proposals as bounding boxes by RPN [14]. The coarse proposals from RPN [14] are quite useful but not enough to handle the severe occlusion case. In order to obtain high-quality pedestrian proposals in a crowded scene, we introduce a density-aware selection network. The *selection network* selectively picks the final pedestrian proposals by considering both the coarse proposals and the crowd density from the *proposal network*. Since the structure of the proposed network still forms a feed-forward network, the forward pass takes only 40 ms on a GPU.

In experiments, we evaluate the *recall* performance of our method in the popular crowded-scene datasets: *WorldExpo10* [20] and *PETS2009* [1]. The experiments show that the proposed method outperforms the conventional proposal generation algorithms.

1.2   Related Works

Pedestrian Detection. Traditional pedestrian detectors such as DPM [6], ACF [4], and LDCF [11] utilize low-level features to recognize people in images. As a result of their simple and efficient structure, they have demonstrated promising detection quality with acceptable speed using only CPUs. In recent

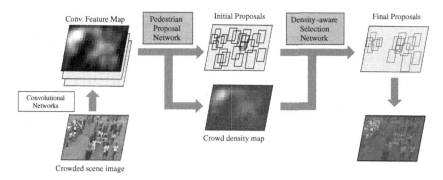

Fig. 2. The framework of the proposed system.

years, DCNN-based detectors [7–9,17] have achieved excellent performance in object classification and detection challenges such as PASCAL VOC [5] and ILSVRC [15]. These DCNN-based detectors strongly require high-quality object proposals as preprocessing. In a crowded scene, Ouyang *et al.* proposed pedestrian detectors handling occlusions by modeling the visibility of individual pedestrian [13] and training occlusion patterns of two coupled people [12]. However, they had difficulty in handling the global occlusion patterns in a crowded scene since they only regard partial occlusions in a local perspective.

Object Proposal. Using the object region proposals in images, object detection algorithms can be faster with significantly reduced search space than using the *sliding-window*-based searching strategy. Also, one can expect a better precision performance by rejecting false positives during the object proposal process than using the sliding window method. There is a wide literature on object proposal methods based on a segmentation approach [2,3,16] and low-level features [21]. The segmentation-based methods promise high-quality object proposals; however, they have a computational bottleneck in object detection because of their time-consuming procedure. EdgeBoxes [21] utilizes edges to provide reasonable proposal quality and fast speed within 1 second. Ren *et al.* proposed a DCNN-based object proposal algorithm, Region Proposal Network(RPN) [14]. It achieved a high detection rate and near real-time speed with the help of GPU computing. However, the above mentioned proposal methods do not consider the severe occlusions in image; therefore, they have difficulty dealing with a crowded scene.

2 Density-Aware Pedestrian Proposal Networks

The overall framework of the proposed system is illustrated in Fig. 2. The proposed system is composed of two networks: the pedestrian proposal network (PPN) and the density-aware selection network (DASN). The convolutional feature map is extracted from the pre-trained convolutional network. The PPN

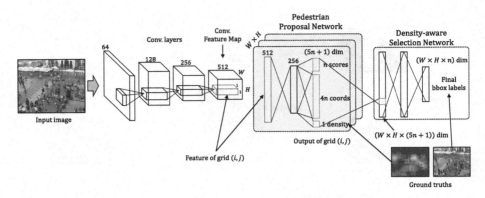

Fig. 3. The proposed density-aware pedestrian proposal network. The network is composed of mainly two parts: pedestrian proposal network, and density-aware selection network. Details of the network are described in Sect. 2.

predicts the initial proposals and the crowd density map. Since the initial proposals from the PPN are independently predicted in local view, the occlusion patterns are not considered. For the global view, the DASN selects the final pedestrian proposals from the initial proposals and the crowd density map. The detailed network structure of the proposed density-aware pedestrian proposal network (DAPPN), is illustrated in Fig. 3.

In Sect. 2.1, we describe the structure of the pedestrian proposal network and the designed multi-task loss function to jointly predict proposals and the density map. In Sect. 2.2, we introduce the density-aware selection network which decides the final pedestrian proposals considering overall scene occlusions.

2.1 Pedestrian Proposal Networks

For the convolutional feature map, we use the 13 layers of VGG-16 model [17] which is pre-trained on ImageNet Dataset [15]. The convolutional feature map has the size $W \times H$ and each cell has 512-dimensional depths. The feature vector of each grid ($1 \times 1 \times 512$) is fed into the fully connected module to predict n proposals and the crowd density of the grid location (n=24 in our experiments). The fully connected module has an intermediate layer to encode features into 256-dimensional vectors. The encoded features are passed through three type of output layers: classification layer to determine the confidence of the proposal, regression layer to localize the proposal's bounding box(bbox), and density regression layer. The classification, bbox regression, and density regression layers output n classification scores, $4n$ bbox coordinates $[x, y, w, h]$, and the scalar value of crowd density at the grid location respectively. Over all the grid locations, the network outputs ($W \times H \times n$) bounding boxes with scores and crowd density map whose size of ($W \times H$). The fully connected layers are shared for the features of every grid positions. The shared network reduces a risk of overfitting problem [14].

Anchors. We follow [14] to simultaneously predict multiple pedestrian proposals at each feature location. To regress n bounding boxes at each grid location, each grid has n *anchors* as the reference of proposal bounding boxes. An anchor is represented by the related location (a_x, a_y) from grid center and its size (a_w, a_h). To train the network stably, the anchors should have similar sizes and positions with the true bounding boxes. In order to train anchors, the bounding boxes of training data are grouped into k clusters with their sizes (w, h). In our experiments, we used K-means clustering algorithm ($k = 6$). And also each feature grid is divided into 4 sub-regions, having k anchors in each sub-region. Therefore, the number of predicted bboxes at each grid becomes 24 ($n = 4k$).

Multi-task Loss Function. To train the pedestrian proposal network, we first assign the binary labels (true or false) to the predicted bboxes. For each ground truth box, we select a the predicted box with the highest Intersection-over-Union(IoU) ratio. The selected boxes mean positive samples and the labels are assigned as true. The predicted bboxes who are not selected as corresponding to a ground truth are assigned as negative samples and the labels are assigned as false. If IoU ratio of the selected box is below than 0.5, which means the selected box is not matched well with the ground truth box, then the selected box is treated as negative labels.

Using the assigned labels, we optimize the objective function in order to jointly predict the bounding boxes of proposals and the crowd density map. We formulate the multi-task loss function inspired by the loss function of Fast R-CNN [7]. Letting optimization variables c_i and b_i be the confidence score and bounding box representation for the i-th anchor, and additional variable $\mathbf{d}$ be the vectorized density map, the loss function is defined as follows,

$$Loss(\{c_i\}, \{b_i\}, \mathbf{d}) = \frac{\lambda_c}{N_p} \sum_i L_{conf}(c_i, c_i^*) + \frac{\lambda_b}{N_p} \sum_i c_i^* L_{reg}(b_i, b_i^*) + \lambda_d L_{den}(\mathbf{d}, \mathbf{d}^*),$$
$$L_{conf}(c_i, c_i^*) = c_i^* \log \sigma(c_i) + (1 - c_i^*) \log(1 - \sigma(c_i)),$$
$$L_{reg}(b_i, b_i^*) = \|b_i - b_i^*\|_1,$$
$$L_{den}(\mathbf{d}, \mathbf{d}^*) = \|\mathbf{d} - \mathbf{d}^*\|_2, \tag{1}$$

where $(\cdot)^*$ indicates the ground truth of $(\cdot)$, L_{conf}, L_{reg}, and L_{den} denote the confidence score loss, bbox regression loss, and density estimation loss respectively. The loss terms are weighted by the parameters λ_c, λ_b, and λ_d, and the number of samples N_p. In the confidence score loss, $\sigma(\cdot)$ denotes the sigmoid function and we use the sigmoid cross entropy loss for binary classification. The bounding box representation (b_i and b_i^*) is expressed by the parameterized coordinates [7]. The regression loss is given by L_1 norm and triggered only for the positive samples ($c_i^* = 1$). The density estimation loss is given by L_2 norm.

2.2   Density-Aware Selection Network

The pedestrian proposals from pedestrian proposal network, called initial proposals, are independently generated from each grid of the convolutional feature map. Therefore, since they are not considering the whole scene, the initial proposals may contain redundant proposals or miss pedestrians in the occlusion situation. We address this problem by considering the crowd density map. For example, high-density regions have high probability of occlusion, therefore the abundant proposals are needed. Conversely, in low-density area, since the proposals are likely to be false positives, a small number of proposals are necessary.

The proposed density-aware selection network (DASN) generates the final proposals from the initial proposals by awaring the crowd density map. As shown in Fig. 3, the DASN consists of two fully connected layers. The total output of the proposal network for all grids ($W \times H$) are aggregated and vectorized into ($W \times H \times (5n + 1)$) dimensional vector. This vector, which contains the entire proposals (bboxes and scores) and the density map, is fed into the selection network as input. Through the 1024-dim intermediate layer, the output layer predicts ($W \times H \times n$)-dim final bbox confidence scores.

The objective of the selection network is to re-score the confidence scores of proposals in global view. Similarly to the PPN, we assign the positive label ($s_i^* = 1$) to i-th proposal bbox when the proposal is matched with ground truth bbox (IoU > 0.5), otherwise, negative label ($s_i^* = 0$) is assigned. The loss function of DASN is defined as follows,

$$Loss(\{s_i\}) = \frac{1}{N_s} \sum_i \|s_i - s_i^*\|_2, \tag{2}$$

where s_i is the predicted score of i-th proposal and s_i^* is the ground truth label. We empirically select L_2 norm to optimize the selection network.

3   Experiments

In the experiments, we used intel $i5$-2500 CPU, 16 GB RAM, and NVIDIA GTX970 GPU. The implementation of the proposed system was based on **matConvNet** library [19] and the experiments were performed using **MATLAB 2015B**.

3.1   Implementation Details

The image size was set to 576×720 in both training and testing procedures and the convolutional feature map was designed to have ($18 \times 23 \times 512$) dimensions. All the convolutional layers from VGG-16 [17] were initialized by the pre-trained model for ImageNet classification [15]. The fully-connected layers in both PPN and DASN were initialized with a zero-mean Gaussian distribution with standard deviation 0.01.

The proposed network was trained on *WorldExpo* dataset containing 3374 training images. The parameter settings are illustrated in Table 1. The learning rate η to 10^{-6} for the first 20 epochs of the training data whereas to 10^{-7} for next 40 epochs. The training parameters for our network were determinded by

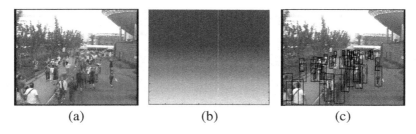

(a)   (b)   (c)

Fig. 4. An example of generating bounding boxes using annotated head positions and perspective map of *WorldExpo'10 dataset* [20]. **(a)** the annotated head positions of pedestrians. **(b)** the given perspective map. **(c)** the estimated bounding boxes.

referring to the settings of Faster R-CNN [14]. The weight parameters of the multi-task loss function in (1) were introduced to adjust the relative importance of each loss term. Total $18 \times 23 \times 24 = 9936$ predicted proposals were extracted per image but the number of true pedestrians were hundreds at most. Therefore, the negative samples became dominant and this would lead to biased training results. To avoid the bias, we randomply sampled equal number of positive proposals and negative proposals (128 each) as for the training samples.

3.2   Experiments on WorldExpo'10 Dataset

We developed two-step training scheme to train the proposed network. We first trained PPN and the convolutional networks by back-propagation and stochastic gradient descent (SGD) with the ground truth bboxes and density map. In this step, the PPN is trained to produce initial proposals and crowd density map. After the training the PPN, then we trained the DASN using the ground truth bboxes to suggest the final proposal scores. In this step, the PPN was fixed and only the two fully-connected layers of the DASN were trained by back-propagation and SGD.

Table 1. Parameter Settings

Symbol	Definition	Values
λ_c	Weight of the confidence score loss	1
λ_b	Weight of the regression loss	1
λ_d	Weight of the density estimation loss	$\frac{1}{128}$
N_p	Number of samples (proposal network)	256
N_s	Number of samples (selection network)	256
η	Learning rate	10^{-6} to 10^{-7}
γ	Weight decay	0.0005
μ	Momentum	0.9

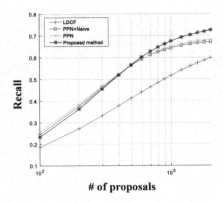

# of proposals

Fig. 5. Comparison of different methods in pedestrian proposal on *WorldExpo'10* dataset.

The Ground Truths. The *WorldExpo'10 dataset* [20] is a crowd counting dataset including 3875 images from 108 scenes, which provides the annotated head positions of people and the perspective map of scenes. Although this dataset is an excellent large-scale dataset for crowd counting, it has no annotated bounding boxes which is essential for the purpose of pedestrian detection. Therefore, we estimate bounding boxes using the given head position and perspective maps of the dataset and use the boxes as the ground truth. As shown in Fig. 4, the locations and sizes of the crowd people are easily estimated by predicting the size of pedestrian using the perspective map. We assumed the aspect ratio of pedestrian should be consistent and fixed by 3 (width/height). In addition, since the proposed method utilizes the crowded density map, the ground truths of the crowd density should be constructed. The density map of an image has 18×23 cells and each cell counts the number of ground truth bboxes of the image whose center is inside the cell.

Processing Times. One strong point of our method is the speed much faster than that of LDCF [11] or EdgeBoxes [21]. Since the proposed network forms a feed-forward network, the forward pass for a test image (576×720) takes about 40 ms on a GPU (25 fps).

Evaluation. We used 3376 images for training the proposed network and 599 images for testing in the same setting of [20]. The trained DAPPN was also used for the crowd-scene dataset *PETS2009* [1]. To evaluate the effectiveness of our algorithm, we compared various methods such as LDCF, PPN, PPN+Naive, and DAPPN (the proposed method). We trained the LDCF detector using training images of *WorldExpo'10*. Since the performance of LDCF is affected by the size of test images, we empirically resized the test images two times to achieve the best performance of LDCF. In order to validate the pedestrian proposal networks (PPN) in Sect. 2.1, the initial proposals from PPN were evaluated. In addition, we developed a naive approach (PPN+Naive) which re-weights the confidence scores of PPN by multiplying their density values.

The quantitative results are shown in Fig. 5, where the recall performance (IOU > 0.5) is depicted versus the number of proposals per image. As shown in the Fig. 5, PPN, PPN+Naive, and the proposed method outperformed LDCF detector. PPN and PPN+Naive show almost the same results even though PPN+Naive approach re-weights the confidence scores of PPN using the crowd density. The reason is that since the ground truths of crowd density are provided into PPN in training phase, the trained PPN contains enough crowd density information. Figure 7 shows the qualitative comparisons of LDCF and the proposed method. The black boxes mean the missed pedestrians and the red boxes represent the correctly detected pedestrians. The top-300 scored pedestrian proposals are illustrated in Fig. 7. The proposed method shows the better proposal performance than LDCF in the crowded region. On the contrary, LDCF has an advantage to detect the isolated pedestrians in non-crowded region. Since the proposed method depend on the crowd density, the confidence scores of the proposals in low density region are tend to be low.

3.3 Experiments on PETS2009 Dataset

The purpose of *PETS2009* [1] dataset is to provide crowded scenes and people annotations to analyze the behaviors of the occluded people. We performed experiments in S2L2 and S2L3 scenes with 656 images. In these scenes, more than 20 people are walking around with heavy occlusions. The test images were resized to 576×720 to fit the proposed network input size. The qualitative and quantitative results are shown in Figs. 6 and 8 respectively. The test settings for LDCF detector and the proposed method were the same as Sect. 3.2. The recall performance of the proposed method outperformed PPN and LDCF [11]. As shown in Fig. 8, our method successfully localized the pedestrians in the situation of severe occlusions while LDCF failed to find the occluded people.

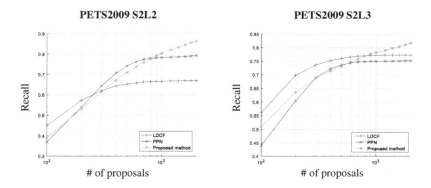

Fig. 6. Comparison of different methods in pedestrian proposal on *PETS2009* dataset.

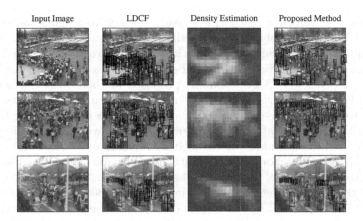

Fig. 7. Examples of the qualitative results on *WorldExpo'10* dataset. The black colored bounding boxes denote the missed ground truths and the red boxes mean the true positives. (Color figure online)

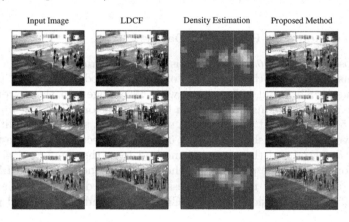

Fig. 8. Examples of the qualitative results on *PETS2009* dataset.

4   Conclusion

In this paper, we proposed a density-aware pedestrian proposal network to solve the occlusion problems in crowded scenes. Since the traditional pedestrian detectors [6, 11] or object proposal methods [14, 21] try to find pedestrians in a crowded scene without considering the occlusions, performance degradation often occurs. The proposed method utilizes a crowd density map in order to generate pedestrian proposals robust against severe occlusions. We have designed the proposal network to produce initial proposals and the selection network to determine the final proposals using crowd density. We have evaluated the proposed method on *WorldExpo10* [20] and *PETS2009* [1] datasets. The experiments verified the effectiveness of the proposed method by comparing it with the conventional method LDCF [11].

References

1. http://www.cvg.reading.ac.uk/PETS2009/a.html (2009)
2. Arbeláez, P., Pont-Tuset, J., Barron, J., Marques, F., Malik, J.: Multiscale combinatorial grouping. In: Proceedings of the IEEE Conference on Computer Vision and Pattern Recognition, pp. 328–335 (2014)
3. Carreira, J., Sminchisescu, C.: CPMC: automatic object segmentation using constrained parametric min-cuts. IEEE Trans. Pattern Anal. Mach. Intell. **34**(7), 1312–1328 (2012)
4. Dollár, P., Appel, R., Belongie, S., Perona, P.: Fast feature pyramids for object detection. IEEE Trans. Pattern Anal. Mach. Intell. **36**(8), 1532–1545 (2014)
5. Everingham, M., Van Gool, L., Williams, C.K.I., Winn, J., Zisserman, A.: The PASCAL visual object classes challenge 2012 (VOC2012) results. http://www.pascal-network.org/challenges/VOC/voc2012/workshop/index.html
6. Felzenszwalb, P., McAllester, D., Ramanan, D.: A discriminatively trained, multiscale, deformable part model. In: IEEE Conference on Computer Vision and Pattern Recognition (CVPR 2008), pp. 1–8. IEEE (2008)
7. Girshick, R.: Fast R-CNN. In: Proceedings of the IEEE International Conference on Computer Vision, pp. 1440–1448 (2015)
8. Girshick, R., Donahue, J., Darrell, T., Malik, J.: Rich feature hierarchies for accurate object detection and semantic segmentation. In: Proceedings of the IEEE Conference on Computer Vision and Pattern Recognition, pp. 580–587 (2014)
9. Krizhevsky, A., Sutskever, I., Hinton, G.E.: Imagenet classification with deep convolutional neural networks. In: Advances in Neural Information Processing Systems, pp. 1097–1105 (2012)
10. Li, J., Liang, X., Shen, S., Xu, T., Yan, S.: Scale-aware fast R-CNN for pedestrian detection. arXiv preprint (2015). arXiv:1510.08160
11. Nam, W., Dollár, P., Han, J.H.: Local decorrelation for improved pedestrian detection. In: Advances in Neural Information Processing Systems, pp. 424–432 (2014)
12. Ouyang, W., Wang, X.: Single-pedestrian detection aided by multi-pedestrian detection. In: Proceedings of the IEEE Conference on Computer Vision and Pattern Recognition, pp. 3198–3205 (2013)
13. Ouyang, W., Zeng, X., Wang, X.: Modeling mutual visibility relationship in pedestrian detection. In: Proceedings of the IEEE Conference on Computer Vision and Pattern Recognition, pp. 3222–3229 (2013)
14. Ren, S., He, K., Girshick, R., Sun, J.: Faster R-CNN: towards real-time object detection with region proposal networks. In: Advances in Neural Information Processing Systems, pp. 91–99 (2015)
15. Russakovsky, O., Deng, J., Su, H., Krause, J., Satheesh, S., Ma, S., Huang, Z., Karpathy, A., Khosla, A., Bernstein, M., Berg, A.C., Fei-Fei, L.: ImageNet large scale visual recognition challenge. Int. J. Comput. Vis. (IJCV) **115**(3), 211–252 (2015)
16. Van de Sande, K.E., Uijlings, J.R., Gevers, T., Smeulders, A.W.: Segmentation as selective search for object recognition. In: 2011 IEEE International Conference on Computer Vision (ICCV), pp. 1879–1886. IEEE (2011)

17. Simonyan, K., Zisserman, A.: Very deep convolutional networks for large-scale image recognition. arXiv preprint (2014). arXiv:1409.1556
18. Tian, Y., Luo, P., Wang, X., Tang, X.: Deep learning strong parts for pedestrian detection. In: Proceedings of the IEEE International Conference on Computer Vision, pp. 1904–1912 (2015)
19. Vedaldi, A., Lenc, K.: Matconvnet - convolutional neural networks for matlab (2015)
20. Zhang, C., Li, H., Wang, X., Yang, X.: Cross-scene crowd counting via deep convolutional neural networks. In: Proceedings of the IEEE Conference on Computer Vision and Pattern Recognition, pp. 833–841 (2015)
21. Zitnick, C.L., Dollár, P.: Edge boxes: locating object proposals from edges. In: Fleet, D., Pajdla, T., Schiele, B., Tuytelaars, T. (eds.) ECCV 2014, Part V. LNCS, vol. 8693, pp. 391–405. Springer, Heidelberg (2014)

People Counting in Videos by Fusing Temporal Cues from Spatial Context-Aware Convolutional Neural Networks

Panos Sourtzinos[1], Sergio A. Velastin[2(✉)], Miguel Jara[3],
Pablo Zegers[4], and Dimitrios Makris[1]

[1] School of Computer Science and Mathematics,
Kingston University, Kingston, UK
psourt@gmail.com, d.makris@kingston.ac.uk
[2] Department of Computer Science,
Universidad Carlos III de Madrid, Getafe, Spain
sergio.velastin@ieee.org
[3] Departmento de Informática,
Universidad de Santiago de Chile, Santiago, Chile
miguel.jara.rodriguez@gmail.com
[4] Faculty of Engineering and Applied Sciences,
Universidad de los Andes, Santiago, Chile
pablozegers@gmail.com

Abstract. We present an efficient method for people counting in video sequences from fixed cameras by utilising the responses of spatially context-aware convolutional neural networks (CNN) in the temporal domain. For stationary cameras, the background information remains fairly static, while foreground characteristics, such as size and orientation may depend on their image location, thus the use of whole frames for training a CNN improves the differentiation between background and foreground pixels. Foreground density representing the presence of people in the environment can then be associated with people counts. Moreover the fusion, of the responses of count estimations, in the temporal domain, can further enhance the accuracy of the final count. Our methodology was tested using the publicly available Mall dataset and achieved a mean deviation error of 0.091.

Keywords: People counting · Convolutional neural networks · Video analysis

1 Introduction

Counting people can provide useful information for monitoring purposes in public areas, assist urban planners in designing more efficient environments, provide cues for situations that might endanger the safety of civilians, and also be used by shopping mall and retail store managers for evaluating their business practices. In principle, such knowledge can be obtained by analysing image and video footage from location specific cameras with the goal to measure the number of people in them. For this reason in this work we present an efficient method for counting people in images and video

© Springer International Publishing Switzerland 2016
G. Hua and H. Jégou (Eds.): ECCV 2016 Workshops, Part II, LNCS 9914, pp. 655–667, 2016.
DOI: 10.1007/978-3-319-48881-3_46

sequences, from fixed cameras which incorporates the fusion of context aware cues from CNN in the temporal domain.

People counting is a very challenging problem, and although commercial solutions exist, these focus mainly in top-view cameras, where occlusions between people are minimal. An effective approach is to detect the heads of the pedestrians present in an image, since they are less prone to disappear in the image through occlusions, and then sum the head detections to measure the total count. Such an approach seems consistent to how humans would approach the problem, as implied by expressions such as 'headcount'. Furthermore since our interest is in measuring the count of people using stationary cameras, where background is assumed fairly static, a local context-aware detector that is spatially tuned to distinguish foreground objects (e.g. heads) from the background scene is more promising than a general-purpose detector.

The main contribution of this work is the proposal of a convolutional neural network (CNN) that uses global image information, rather than cropped images, for people counting and the use of temporal coherence for enhancing the precision in the obtained results. Feeding the CNN with whole images allows modelling of the local context, i.e. the expected local appearance (e.g. size, orientation) of the foreground pedestrian heads and the spatial distribution of pixel luminance in the background. The output of the CNN for each frame is an intermediate density map and head counts are estimated using regression. Temporal coherence is exploited by refined regression of count estimations from multiple frames. In Sect. 2 a background study on the methods for people counting is presented, while in Sect. 3 the methodology of our approach is described. Finally in Sect. 4 the results and a critical discussion of our methodology are given followed by the concluding section in Sect. 5.

2   Previous Work

Counting methods can be mainly categorised into two groups. Counting by detection and counting by regression. In the former case, human shape models are used to localise people on the image plane, while the latter is based on the relationship between a distribution of low level features in the whole image and the number of people in it. Hybrid methods combine these two approaches, i.e. a person detector is used to create a footprint on a distribution describing the whole image, which then is used to infer the number of people in it. The use of CNNs for the task of people counting is by its nature such an approach. In the following sections we identify some methods, but as the literature on the topic is extensive, space limitations prevent us from giving a fuller review.

In counting by detection [16] the idea is to detect the presence of people in an image and then sum the detections to produce the final count. People detections is achieved by object detectors (whole or part-based), based on learned models that use features such as histogram of oriented gradients (HOG), poselets, edgelets and others which describe a shape model of a human body using pixel information. Traditionally, a location invariant object detector is applied using a sliding window technique followed by non-maximal suppression to localise the objects of interest.

In [16] a HOG detector is used to create a probability distribution over the image. To deal with occlusions, the HOG detector is trained to learn only the upper part of the human body. Next the optical flow between two consecutive frames is computed. Assuming that the upper human body exhibits a uniform motion in contrast with the motion generated from the limbs, a mask resembling the shape of upper human body, is scanned through the optical flow response and a probability distribution of uniform motion is computed. The probability distributions learned from the shape model and the uniform motion model are then combined and the fused probability distribution is searched, using Mean Shift Mode Estimation to localise head detections.

A pitfall of using counting by detection techniques is that they do not perform well in images with low resolution, since objects, in these, appear small and they do not generate enough information in order to be detected. Moreover, since most of these approaches use a sliding window to scan the whole image multiple times in different scales, they are computational heavy and thus slow.

In counting by regression [1, 11, 13], a mapping from some low level image characteristics, like edges or corners, to the number of objects is estimated using machine learning methods. Although this approach avoids the hard task of object detection, ambiguities may arise from the presence of objects of other classes that may also generate responses. Furthermore since some of these methods are location-invariant,, the training phase requires large amount of data, in order to cover all the possible perspective nonlinearities of the image plane. On the other hand, annotating the ground truth data is simpler as it only involves manual counting.

In [13] the main idea is that integrals of density functions over pixel grids should match the object counts in an image. It is assumed that each pixel is characterised by a discretized feature vector and the training data are dot annotated (e.g. torso). Each annotated pixel is then characterised, using a randomised tree approach, by a feature descriptor combining the modalities of the actual image, the difference image and the foreground image. For each pixel, a linear transformation of its feature descriptor is learned, using a random forest to match the ground truth density function.

In [11] a mixture of Gaussians is initially applied to extract foreground information. Histograms of the area of the foreground blobs and edge orientation are then used as features to describe the image. Finally a feed forward back propagation neural network is used with the histograms of the normalised features as inputs, learning the number of pedestrians in the image.

In [1] a method for counting people using the Harris corner detector is presented. Motion vectors are used to differentiate between static and moving corners. Assuming that each person in the image generates the same amount of moving corners, the number of people in a frame is therefore computed based on the ratio of the moving corners detected over the average number of corners per person. As a consequence, this approach fails to recognise static people. Also the camera perspective effect is not taken into consideration which could invalidate the regression assumption.

A drawback of all regression approaches is that they cannot discriminate well between intra class variations (i.e. differences in human sizes, humans carrying objects, humans with bicycles etc.) and since they lack learning object shape models, they are unable to differentiate between interclass (e.g. animals) differences. Thus their application is mostly location specific.

Hybrid methods [7, 10, 17, 20] aim to combine the benefits of both approaches by fusing their techniques. For instance, in [17] combines a density image is computed where each pixel value defines the confidence output of the person detector used in [13]. This value is then discretized and represented by a binary feature vector. SIFT features are extracted from the image in order to compute another binary feature vector. The concatenation of the two binary feature vectors is then used to describe each pixel, and by minimizing the regularised MESA distance, the weight of each discretized feature is learned. The density of each pixel is thus calculated by multiplying its feature descriptor with the learned weight vector, and the count of people in the image is then estimated by the integral of the density of the image.

Another example of a hybrid approach is presented in [10] that copes with crowded situations. A Gaussian mixture model is initially applied on a grayscale video sequence to obtain the foreground information. After perspective correction this is further processed using a closing operation. Counting then becomes a problem of finding a relationship between the number of foreground pixels and the number of humans present in the image, a relationship which is learned using a neural network.

Finally two hybrid approaches [7, 20] are the only ones, as far as we know, that use CNN purely for people counting. Both attempt to exploit the CNN characteristic of the spatial invariance in the detection of patterns, and thus the networks described are trained as human detectors by using spatial crops from whole images for training. In [7] a CNN learns to estimate the density of people in an image by using cropped images from the full resolution training dataset. The trained network is then applied to the whole image information to produce a density map of human presence and moreover its parameters are transferred to two similar networks that are applied on different resolutions of the global image. The response from the three networks is then averaged to produce a final density map. To count the number of people in the density image, each point of the density estimated is fed to a linear regression node. The weights then of the node are learned independently for the density estimation. In [20] cropped images are also used for training, however the learning of the density and the total count is not sequential, but takes place in parallel. Both the density map and the linear regression node are connected to the same CNN and learning takes place by altering the cost function between the one used for the density estimation and the one used for count estimation.

3   Method

Deep learning machines have addressed many problems that were deemed as unsolvable in a surprisingly easy way. However, most of the research has focused on the use of static architectures ignoring relevant dynamics aspects of some of the problems. This is especially true in video analytics, where analysis is mainly frame-based, and traditionally the information obtained from each of them has been integrated using some heuristic-based algorithm. This has been recognized by many in the field and many recent publications extended and complemented the convolutional neural network (CNN) architecture into the time domain achieving good results (e.g. [4, 8, 9, 19]). Our work explores how to use time cues in an efficient manner, therefore we avoided recurrent neural networks or other time domain architectures. Specifically, three replicated CNNs are used to process consecutive time frames and their combined output is fed into a final layer to produce the final estimate. Our approach, following the methodology proposed in [7], first generates a density map to indicate the presence of humans in the image followed by learning the regression relationship between the distribution of activations and the actual count number. The proposed architecture is shown in Fig. 1 and it uses the outcomes of three different instants in time learning the relationship between them to produce the desired results. This is a generalization of averaging the three results. The pipelines are identical in their parameters settings and only one is needed to be trained to reproduce the others. For more information on convolutional layers and their structure the reader is referred to [15].

The performance of a supervised neural network is dependent mainly on three factors: (a) the input data, (b) the network's architecture and its parameters and (c) the ground truth data. Appropriate representation of the input can lead to better and faster learning of the network [15]. In our case the input layer of a single pipeline is an RGB image of size 240×320 pixels. Every frame, is pre-processed by initially calculating the mean in all training images and subtracting it from all the pixels, before entering the network. Then data is centred around zero in all dimensions and scaling in values between -1 and 1 is performed applying Eq. 1 on each pixel:

$$p_{x,y,c,s} = 2 \cdot \frac{p_{x,y,c,m} - \min(f_t)}{\max(f_t) - min(f_t)} - 1 \qquad (1)$$

where $p_{x,y,c,m}$ is the pixel value of frame f_t at location x,y of channel c, after the mean subtraction and $p_{x,y,c,s}$ is the pixel value after the scaling which we will refer as $p_{x,y,c}$. The data is zero centred to facilitate learning of the network and specifically for the gradient descent algorithm to avoid zigzagging while minimising the cost of the network.

3.1 Density Estimation

The density learning pipeline (Fig. 1) is comprised of four convolutional layers followed by a fully connected one. For the convolutional part of the density estimation pipeline, C_1 has 15 features of size 316×236, C_2 has 10 features of size 154×114, C_3 has 20 features of size 73×53 and finally C_4 has 10 features of size 33×23. The detection kernel of all convolutional layers is 5×5 with a stride of 1 and the feature activations, except from those of C_4, are max pooled with a kernel of shape 2×2 and stride of 2; thus halving each dimensionality of a feature before feeding it as an input to a subsequent convolutional layer.

In contrast to [7], where all activations in a feature share the same bias, in our case each feature activation is characterised from its own bias. Since the input is the whole image, the network is allowed to further tune the importance of a feature to a spatial location. Following the notation of Eq. 1 the activation function applied for a neuron belonging to a feature f in the proposed CNN is the hyperbolic tangent given by

$$a_{f,j,k} = \frac{1 - e^{-2 \cdot z}}{1 + e^{-2 \cdot z}} \qquad (2)$$

$$where z = b_{f,j,k} + \sum_{f_{-1}} \sum_{l=0}^{4} \sum_{m=0}^{4} v_{f,l,m} \cdot a_{f-1,j+l,k+m} \qquad (3)$$

where the leftmost summation sums over all the features present in the previous layer (as mentioned before, in the case where the previous layer is the input image, each channel of the image represents one feature). The last layer of the density estimation pipeline is a fully connected one (F_1 in Eq. 1) and has as many neurons as there are present in one feature of the previous layer (i.e. C_4). Each neuron in F_1 is connected to all the neurons present in C_4 and thus the weight vector v_i of each neuron i has 7590 ($33 \times 23 \times 10$) dimensions. The activation function used for each neuron of this layer is the sigmoid thus Eqs. (4) and (5) apply.

$$a_i = \frac{1}{1 + e^z} \qquad (4)$$

$$z = b_i + \sum_{f=1}^{10} \sum_{l=1}^{33} \sum_{m=1}^{23} v_{i,r} \cdot a_{f,l,m}, r = 759 \cdot (f - 1) + 23 \cdot (l - 1) + m \qquad (5)$$

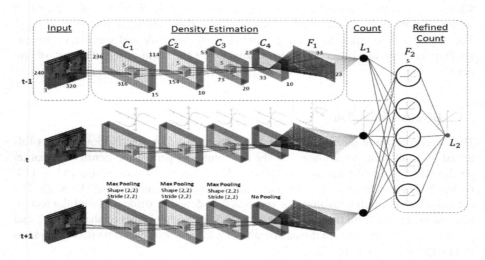

Fig. 1. The proposed architecture for pedestrian counting. In the left we can see the temporal data input in a form of consecutive in time RGB frames, while for the density estimation a pipeline with 4 convolutional layers followed by a full connected sigmoid layer having the task to produce the density images. For the count of a single pipeline a linear regression unit combines the 759 inputs to produce a final result. Finally by combining the results from the counts of 3 pipelines in full connected rectifier layer we feed a node to perform linear regression and produce the final result.

F_1 is the last layer in our density estimation pipeline and the 33×23 responses a_i of the layer are compared against the equivalent y_i of a ground truth density of same dimensionality to measure the error that will be back propagated for the learning. The cost function we use for the comparison is the Kullback–Leibler divergence shown in Eq. 6, and the error produced is the mean cost across all the examples seen.

$$KL(y_i \| a_i) = y_i \cdot log \frac{y_i}{a_i} + (1 - y_i) \cdot log \frac{1 - y_i}{1 - a_i} \qquad (6)$$

3.2   Counting

The final layer of each pipeline is dedicated to estimate the relationship between this density and the actual count of people. So, a single linear neuron (L_1 in Fig. 1) is fully connected with the sigmoid neurons of F_1. Learning is performed by linear regression using the mean square error across a number of examples as cost function. Thus if a_i denotes the ith activation from layer F_1 and v_i the entry in the weight vector of L_1 associated with a_i, and b_c the bias and a_c activation value of L_1 then,

$$a_c = b_c + \sum_i v_i \cdot a_i \qquad (7)$$

and the cost for a single example, when y is the ground truth count, is given by $(a_c - y)^2$.

3.3   Refined Counting

The accuracy of people counting, is further improved by fusing measurements from networks operating on subsequent frames along the temporal dimension. Hence, three pipelines operating on frames with timestamps $t - 1$, t and $t + 1$ are fully connected to a vector of five rectified linear units. Each rectified neuron has as activation function similar to Eq. 7 with the only difference that negative values, produced by the summation of the weighted input with the bias, produce a zero output. Finally, all five outputs from the rectified linear units are connected to the linear neuron L_2 for the refined count. The only difference in the linear regression performed in this neuron compared to the one in L_1 is the cost function, since for this we use the absolute difference of the estimated count against the ground truth.

4   Results

The network described earlier was implemented using Python and the pylearn2 and theano machine learning libraries [2, 3]. For our experiments we used the publicly available Mall crowd counting dataset [5, 6, 14], of which a couple of illustrative frames are shown in Fig. 2(a)-(b).

Fig. 2. By measuring the size of people in different time frames (a), (b), the perspective map denoting the relative scale of pixels in the real word dimension.

The dataset consists of 2000 time consecutive frames recorded by a fixed camera in an indoor shopping mall in 640×480 resolution with a frame rate around 2 Hz. Over 60.000 pedestrians are annotated, with a point indicating their head location. It is a challenging dataset with constant movement, where pedestrians wander freely, alone or in groups, forming a cluttered environment with many occlusions. Moreover, reflections occur in both the shop windows and the floor, the lighting conditions change, and the viewing angle of the camera causes pedestrians to vary in scale.

We also implemented the only two other methods, that to our knowledge, [7, 20] perform people counting using CNNs. As in our case, the three main pipelines of the architecture in [7] are identical in their configuration and in their parameter settings. However they apply each pipeline at different scales of the images in order to infuse scale invariance in their network. To train a single pipeline they use cropped images thus aiming to get a location invariant person detector, which is then applied to the whole image for density estimation. Since the scale of the input images in the pipelines is different, they use one bias per feature in contrast to our approach where every node in a feature is associated with a single bias. Each pipeline estimates a human density and their average merge layer merges the three different density estimations into one followed by a linear regression node for the count estimation.

The second method we implemented is the one presented in [20]. In this approach, similarly to [7], cropped images are used for training, however the learned network is applied on the whole image in a sliding window fashion, where each detection window generates a local density. The density estimate for the whole image is calculated by creating a mosaic from the local ones. Instead of learning a density and then performing a linear regression to estimate the count, the training of the density and the counting takes place in an alternate way. The layers are alternated until neither cost is further improved. To learn the density estimation, the ground truth consists of a density image created from the responses of a Gaussian distribution, centred at the head of a person, and a bivariate normal distribution, placed at the body of the person. The combined distributions describing a person are then normalised to add up to one. Then, counting is just a summation of the entries in the ground truth density image.

The head regions were represented by squares centred at the annotation points and size consistent to the perspective map of the scene. Pixels that belong to head regions have a value of 1, while all other pixels have a value of 0. Since the density estimation resolution in our pipeline is 33 × 23, the generated binary images of 640 × 480 were scaled down and each image was normalised to have values in the range between zero and one. For [7], the ground truth was based on cropped images of size 320 × 240 from the original 640 × 480 binary images created in the previous step, scaled to a resolution of 33 × 23 and normalised with values between 0 and 1. For [20] the ground truth density images were generated using a Gaussian kernel summing to one, centred at each annotation point and with a standard deviation based on the values of the perspective map of the dataset. Crops of size 72 × 72 from the 640 × 480 density images were then extracted and scaled down to size 18 × 18. Figure 3 shows some examples.

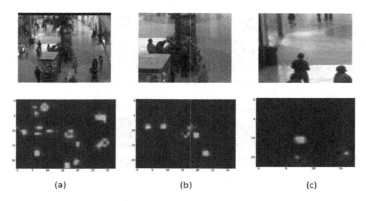

(a)   (b)   (c)

Fig. 3. Examples of training input images (upper row) generated from the same frame, to the three different networks and their associated ground truth (lower row) for density estimation. (a) resample whole frame 320 × 240 used by our approach, (b) cropped images 320 × 240 used by [7], (c) cropped images 72 × 72 used by [20]

From the 2000 frames of the dataset, 1000 were used for training 250 for validation and 750 for testing. For [7] we used 5 cropped images (size 320 × 240) per training whole image (640 × 480), while for [20] we extracted 50 cropped images. The input image resolution we used to test out methodology is 320 × 240.

Training a CNN requires fine tuning of various parameters. However some of the training parameters were kept constant through all the experiments. The dropout rate was fixed to 0.5 for all layers. This means that during training each node has 50 % chance to be activated, and its parameters to get updated, which assists for regularisation and thus avoiding overfitting the network parameters to the training dataset. Another parameter we kept constant was pooling, by always using the same pooling kernel with same stride. Also all weights were initialised using a uniform distribution and with range (−0.05, 0.05). Other parameters however, such as the learning rate, the use of momentum, the maximum norm of the weight vectors were selected separately for each experiment by testing their impact on the learning behaviour of a network on small subset of the training dataset. The algorithm used for the training was stochastic gradient descent with mini batches. Thus the update of the network parameters occurred regularly and not at the end of each epoch (i.e. estimating the cost after seeing all training data once).

Figure 4 shows density estimation results from the different methods. Our approach manages to describe the distribution of the pedestrians quite well. In contrast, the responses from [7] are not descriptive, since it appears that although there is a change in the density estimation from frame to frame it follows a general pattern, and it seems that the network failed to learn the people's density. Also the density results derived by [20], although more descriptive regarding the presence and the position of the pedestrians in the space than [7], still generates many false positives.

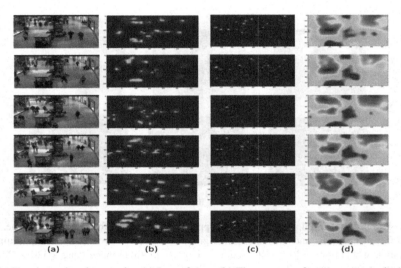

Fig. 4. Density estimation results. (a) Input frame, (b) The response from our approach, (c) The response from [20], (d) The response from [7]

Let's consider the number of parameters in the configuration of each network. The total number of free parameters for learning in the network of [6] is 14,930. While for the one in [20] the number of parameters that are available for learning is 21,373,532. In our proposed network the number of parameters is 5,871,954. Finally the difference between our approach and the other two is that we use for training input whole images while they use cropped images.

Based on the information provided above, our assumption is that the method of [7], not only has too few parameters to offer a reliable solution to the problem, but also because it lacks any fully connected layer, no information is exchanged between the nodes that can result to a combination of features detected. On the other hand the approach in [20], has a plethora of parameters to adjust and to solve the problem of detecting people in an image, and furthermore they exchange node information by using fully connected layers. However by using cropped images as input it does not provide any spatial localised information that would facilitate learning the presence of the background in the whole image.

Our proposed network, with almost a quarter of parameters compared to [20], assumes whole input images, combines the information from the various nodes of the detectors and therefore it can learn localised background/foreground information. In other words, if our task was to find a fly on a wall, the approach in [7] scans the wall to find the fly with a lens that makes things to appear very blurry and the presence of the fly is diffused on the wall, while the one in [20] scans the wall with a lens that can see every little detail, thus some irrelevant complex patterns of the wall may confuse it. In contrast to the other two methods, our approach instead of scanning the wall, it just subtracts it and observes the difference.

After the density is estimated, the next step is to perform the counting. The mean deviation error (MDE) ε of the counting step,

$$\varepsilon = \frac{1}{N} \cdot \sum_N \frac{|y - \bar{y}|}{y} \tag{8}$$

where y is the ground truth, $\bar{y}$ is the estimated count and N the number of images in the test dataset, is shown on Table 1.

As expected from the resulting density images, the error of the two competitive methods is relatively high. For [7] the linear regression is unable to learn the proper relationship between density and the count number. Even the approach in [20], which estimates the count by summing up all the responses from the density map, the counting error is significant. The counting error can further be reduced, by combining temporal information to remove noise from the measurements. Specifically, the combination of three pipelines with input frames at $t - 1$, t and $t + 1$ in order to estimate the count of frame t generates a mean relative error of 0.091. Table 2 presents results obtained by combining information from varying number of frames (one pipeline per frame is used) using the MDE and the Mean Squared Error (MSE) and the Mean Absolute Error (MAE). Considering the frame rate of the MALL dataset (2fps), optimal coherence is achieved in a temporal window of 1 s, i.e. using 3 consecutive frames. For videos with higher frame rate, optimal performance would be achieved by using more frames.

Table 3 compares our method with other non-CNN approaches for people counting performed in the MALL dataset. Our approach seems to perform similarly with other people counting methods.

Table 1. Mean Deviation Error for Counting.

Approach	MDE
Ours	0.094
Method presented in [20]	0.770
Method presented in [7]	0.230

Table 2. Comparison of varying number of pipelines, where one pipeline per frame is used.

Number of pipelines	MAE	MSE	MDE
1	3.15	16.9	0.093
3	**3.00**	**15.7**	**0.091**
5	3.77	23.8	0.109
7	5.91	46.6	0.200

Table 3. Comparison with other non-CNN methods in the Mall dataset

Method	MAE	MSE	MDE
CHEN_1 [6]	3.59	19.0	0.110
CHEN_2 [5]	3.43	17.7	0.105
LOY [14]	–	17.8	–
ZHANG [21]	2.69	12.1	0.082
KUMAGAI [12]	2.89	13.4	0.091
PHAM [18]	**2.50**	**10.0**	**0.080**
OURS	3.00	15.7	0.091

5   Conclusion

In this work a methodology using CNN was presented for people counting. We have demonstrated that using the whole image information as training input instead of using cropped images, performs better as the network is able to learn how to distinguish between the foreground and the background. Furthermore by fusing the count estimate in the temporal domain, count estimations are further improved. To the best to our knowledge, our method is the first to propose the application of a CNN on the whole image for the task of people counting and furthermore to use temporal information for the same task. Possible future lines of research may include to minimise the information theoretical measure instead of the Euclidean error in order to take into account the probabilistic nature of the problem. Moreover network architectures that utilise recurrent nodes can be used to take advantage of their application in the temporal domain, but also the use of other CNN architectures which incorporate temporal features, such as optical flow, can be investigated.

References

1. Albiol, A., Silla, M.J., Albiol, A., Mossi, J.E.M.: Video analysis using corner motion statistics. In: IEEE International Workshop on Performance Evaluation of Tracking and Surveillance, pp. 31–38 (2009)
2. Bastien, F., Lamblin, P., Pascanu, R., Bergstra, J., Goodfellow, I., Bergeron, A., Bouchard, N., Warde-Farley, D., Bengio, Y.: Theano: new features and speed improvements. arXiv preprint arXiv:1211.5590 (2012)

3. Bergstra, J., Breuleux, O., Bastien, F., Lamblin, P., Pascanu, R., Desjardins, G., Turian, J., Warde-Farley, D., Bengio, Y.: Theano: a CPU and GPU math expression compiler. In: Proceedings of the Python for scientific computing conference (SciPy), vol. 4, p. 3 (2010)
4. Byeon, W., Breuel, T. M., Raue, F., Liwicki, M.: Scene labeling with lstm recurrent neural networks. In: Proceedings of the IEEE Conference on Computer Vision and Pattern Recognition, pp. 3547–3555 (2015)
5. Chen, K., Gong, S., Xiang, T., Change Loy, C.: Cumulative attribute space for age and crowd density estimation. In: Proceedings of the IEEE Conference on Computer Vision and Pattern Recognition, pp. 2467–2474 (2013)
6. Chen, K., Loy, C.C., Gong, S., Xiang, T.: Feature Mining for Localised Crowd Counting. In: BMVC, vol. 1, no. 2, p. 3 (2012)
7. Conti, F., Pullini, A., Benini, L.: Brain-inspired classroom occupancy monitoring on a low-power mobile platform. In: IEEE Conference on Computer Vision and Pattern Recognition Workshops (CVPRW), 2014, pp. 624–629. IEEE (2014)
8. Gkioxari, G., Malik, J.: Finding action tubes. In: Proceedings of the IEEE Conference on Computer Vision and Pattern Recognition, pp. 759–768 (2015)
9. Hosang, J., Omran, M., Benenson, R., Schiele, B.: Taking a deeper look at pedestrians. In: Proceedings of the IEEE Conference on Computer Vision and Pattern Recognition, pp. 4073–4082 (2015)
10. Hou, Y.-L., Pang, G.K.: People counting and human detection in a challenging situation. IEEE Trans. Syst. Man Cybern. Part A Syst. Hum. 41(1), 24–33 (2011)
11. Kong, D., Gray, D., Tao, H.: A viewpoint invariant approach for crowd counting. In: 18th International Conference on Pattern Recognition, ICPR 2006, vol. 3, pp. 1187–1190. IEEE (2006)
12. Kumagai, S., Hotta, K.: LAC between Cells of HOG Feature for Crowd Counting. In: Advances in Visual Computing, pp. 688–697. Springer International Publishing, Switzerland (2014)
13. Lempitsky, V., Zisserman, A.: Learning to count objects in images (2010)
14. Change Loy, C., Gong, S., Xiang, T.: From semi-supervised to transfer counting of crowds. In: IEEE International Conference on Computer Vision (ICCV), pp. 2256–2263. IEEE (2013)
15. Nielsen, M.: Neural Networks and Deep Learning. Determination Press 1 (2014)
16. Patzold, M., Evangelio, R.H., Sikora, T.: Counting people in crowded environments by fusion of shape and motion information. In: Seventh IEEE International Conference on Advanced Video and Signal Based Surveillance (AVSS), pp. 157–164. IEEE (2010)
17. Perko, R., Schnabel, T., Fritz, G., Almer, A., Paletta, L.: Counting people from above: Airborne video based crowd analysis. arXiv preprint arXiv:1304.6213 (2013)
18. Pham, V.Q., Kozakaya, T., Yamaguchi, O., Okada, R.: COUNT Forest: CO-voting uncertain number of targets using random forest for crowd density estimation. In: Proceedings of the IEEE International Conference on Computer Vision, pp. 3253–3261 (2015)
19. Vu, T.H., Osokin, A., Laptev, I.: Context-aware CNNs for person head detection. In: Proceedings of the IEEE International Conference on Computer Vision, pp. 2893–2901 (2015)
20. Zhang, C., Li, H., Wang, X., Yang, X.: Cross-scene crowd counting via deep convolutional neural networks. In: Proceeding CVPR (2015)
21. Zhang, Z., Wang, M., Geng, X.: Crowd counting in public video surveillance by label distribution learning. Neurocomputing 166, 151–163 (2015)

Abnormal Crowd Behavior Detection Based on Gaussian Mixture Model

Oscar Ernesto Rojas$^{(\boxtimes)}$ and Clesio Luis Tozzi

School of Electrical and Computer Engineering, UNICAMP,
Av. Albert Einstein, 400, Campinas, SP, Brazil
oscar.rojas87@gmail.com, clesio@dca.fee.unicamp.br

Abstract. Many of the state-of-the-art approaches for automatic abnormal behavior detection in crowded scenes are based on complex models which require high processing time and several parameters to be adjusted. This paper presents a simple new approach that uses background subtraction algorithm and optical flow to encode the normal behavior pattern through a Gaussian Mixture Model (GMM). Abnormal behavior is detected comparing new samples against the mixture model. Experimental results on standards anomaly detection and localization benchmarks are presented and compared to other algorithms considering detection rate and processing time.

Keywords: Anomaly behavior detection · Optical flow · Crowded scenes analysis · Anomaly localization

1 Introduction

Abnormal behavior analysis on crowded scenes is an important and growing research field. Video cameras, given their ease installation and low cost, have been widely used for monitoring internal and external areas such as buildings, parks, stadiums etc. Algorithms for pose detection and action recognition for single or, in some cases, very low density groups of people are extensively treated in the pattern recognition community. Nevertheless, many of these algorithms need to segment each person which is impractical in crowded scenes due to high levels of occlusion.

Abnormal behavior situations are always associated with the scene context, a behavior considered as normal in a scene may be considered abnormal in other. These specific conditions increase the difficulties for automatic analysis and require specific modeling of the abnormal behavior for each particular scene.

In order to build such models many algorithms have been proposed. In [7] optical flow is used to compute interaction forces between adjacent pixels and a bag of words approach is used to classify frames as normal or abnormal. In [6] dynamic textures (DT) are used to model the appearance and dynamics of normal behavior, samples with low probabilities in the model are labeled as abnormal. In [8] entropy and energetic concepts are used as features to model

© Springer International Publishing Switzerland 2016
G. Hua and H. Jégou (Eds.): ECCV 2016 Workshops, Part II, LNCS 9914, pp. 668–675, 2016.
DOI: 10.1007/978-3-319-48881-3_47

the probability of finding abnormal behavior in the scene. Natural language processing is used in [11] as a classification algorithm for features recognition based on viscous fluid field concepts.

Many algorithms employ machine learning techniques for classification. Support Vector Machine (SVM) is used in [9,12] to classify histograms of the orientation of optical flow. Multilayer Perceptron Neural Network is used in [14]. k-Nearest Neighbors is used in [1] to classify outlier observed trajectories as abnormal behavior. Finally, Fuzzy C-Means are used in [3,4] to derive an unsupervised model for the crowd trajectory patterns.

Most of the recent algorithms employ supervised or unsupervised machine learning techniques. Supervised techniques are employed when all possible abnormal situations are well known and there are a sufficient number of video samples with both normal and abnormal situations. In most of the cases supervised techniques present very limited results since it is difficult to obtain the information of all the possible abnormal situations and the number of samples with this type of behavior is usually very low. The detection of abnormal behavior using unsupervised algorithms can be seen as a problem of outlier detection. A model is constructed using only samples of normal behaviors and in the test phase each sample that does not fit the model is labeled as abnormal.

In general, to construct the feature vector used in many of the algorithms described above, a set of parameters must be correctly defined in order to achieve the performance reported by the authors. Some of the state-of-the-art methods are based in complex probabilistic models which leads to high processing time. Despite being the processing time per frame reported only for very few papers, it is in general high. For example, in [6] the authors reported a test time of 25 s per frame for 160×240 pixel images and in [13] the reported test time per frame is 5 s in videos with 320×240 pixel resolution.

The main contribution of this paper is a simple but efficient method for abnormal crowd behavior detection that reduces the processing time per frames allowing practical use.

The rest of this paper is organized as follows. Section 2 describes the proposed approach. Section 3 presents the experimental results. Section 4 presents the conclusions.

2   Proposed Method

2.1   Pre-processing

The dense optical flow for each input frame is obtained using the algorithm presented in [2]. The optical flow information $F(x, y) = (v_x(x, y), v_y(x, y))$ can be expressed as a vector of horizontal $v_x(x, y)$ and vertical $v_y(x, y)$ velocity components for each image pixel (x, y). The magnitude and direction of each optical flow vector is obtained using Eqs. 1 and 2 respectively.

$$m(x,y) = \sqrt{v_x(x,y)^2 + v_y(x,y)^2} \, , \tag{1}$$

$$\alpha(x,y) = arctan\left(\frac{v_y(x,y)}{v_x(x,y)}\right). \tag{2}$$

In parallel with the optical flow computation, the background segmentation algorithm presented in [10] is used to obtain a foreground binary mask I_f. The foreground information will be used to reduce the number of optical flow vectors processed as shown in the next section.

2.2 Normal Behavior Model

The normal behavior model is obtained from a sequence of N frames containing only normal behavior samples. First, each input frame is divided into smaller regions R_i of fixed size $\widehat{w} \times \widehat{h}$. The regions are overlapped in the x and y direction by $\widehat{w}/2$ and $\widehat{h}/2$ respectively. Consequently, a total T regions are obtained, where T is computed using

$$T = \left(\frac{h}{\widehat{h}} * 2 - 1\right) * \left(\frac{w}{\widehat{w}} * 2 - 1\right) , \tag{3}$$

where w and h are the width and the height of the input frame respectively.

A matrix $\boldsymbol{\mathcal{X}}_i$, shown in Eq. 4, is used to store the magnitude and direction values of the optical flow vectors for all the training frames within the region R_i.

$$\boldsymbol{\mathcal{X}}_i = \begin{bmatrix} \alpha_1^j & m_1^j \\ \alpha_2^j & m_2^j \\ \vdots & \vdots \\ \alpha_N^j & m_N^j \end{bmatrix} . \tag{4}$$

where the column vector α_i^j will contain the direction values and the column vector m_i^j their corresponding magnitude within the i-th region of the j-th frame according to Eqs. 5 and 6 respectively.

$$\alpha_i^j = \{\alpha(x,y) \mid I_f(x,y) \neq 0, (x,y) \in R_i\} \; \forall \; j \in [1,N] , \tag{5}$$

$$m_i^j = \{m(x,y) \mid I_f(x,y) \neq 0, (x,y) \in R_i\} \; \forall \; j \in [1,N] , \tag{6}$$

where $I_f(x,y)$ is the foreground image obtained as described in the previous section.

Assuming that all the magnitude and direction values of a specific (x,y) point through the training video can be modeled as a mixture of M 2D Gaussian distributions, the probability of a particular pair $\boldsymbol{x} = (\alpha(x,y), m(x,y))$ being part of the Gaussian Mixture distribution is given by

$$P\left(\boldsymbol{x}|\boldsymbol{\Theta_i}\right) = \sum_{k=1}^{M} \lambda_k^i \, \mathcal{N}\left(\boldsymbol{x}|\boldsymbol{\mu}_k^i, \boldsymbol{\Sigma}_k^i\right) , \tag{7}$$

where $\boldsymbol{\Theta}_{\mathbf{i}} = \{\lambda_1^i, \ldots, \lambda_M^i, \boldsymbol{\mu}_1^i, \ldots, \boldsymbol{\mu}_M^i, \boldsymbol{\Sigma}_1^i, \ldots, \boldsymbol{\Sigma}_M^i\}$ are the model parameter vectors, λ_k^i are the mixing coefficients, $\boldsymbol{\mu}_k^i$ and $\boldsymbol{\Sigma}_k^i$ are the mean vector and the covariance matrix of $\boldsymbol{\mathcal{X}}_i$ respectively and $\mathcal{N}$ is the Multivariate Gaussian distribution given by

$$\mathcal{N}\left(\boldsymbol{x}|\boldsymbol{\mu}_k^i, \boldsymbol{\Sigma}_k^i\right) = \frac{1}{(2\pi)^{\frac{n}{2}} \mid \boldsymbol{\Sigma}_k^i \mid} exp\left(-\frac{1}{2}\left(\boldsymbol{x} - \boldsymbol{\mu}_k^i\right)^T \left(\boldsymbol{\Sigma}_k^i\right)^{-1}\left(\boldsymbol{x} - \boldsymbol{\mu}_k^i\right)\right). \quad (8)$$

The mixture parameter vectors $\boldsymbol{\Theta}_{\mathbf{i}}$ are obtained through the Expectation-Maximization (EM) algorithm.

Figure 1 shows an example region (in red), the $\boldsymbol{\mathcal{X}}_i$ matrix formation and the contour map of the Gaussian Distribution obtained from $\boldsymbol{\mathcal{X}}_i$, with $i = 22$. From the Gaussian Distribution it is observed that, in the example region, the main displacement directions are approximately $10°$, $180°$ and $360°$ and the main magnitude value is approximately 0.8.

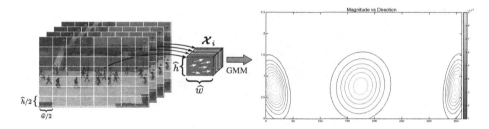

Fig. 1. Gaussian Distributions contours plot obtained from the region marked in red using all the training videos. (Color figure online)

2.3   Abnormal Detection

In the test phase a binary image I_b is obtained for each input frame. The I_b image has the same size as the input frames and its values are computed as is shown in Eq. 9.

$$I_b(x, y) = \begin{cases} 1, & \text{if } P(\boldsymbol{x}|\boldsymbol{\Theta}_{\mathbf{i}}) < T_h \\ 0, & \text{otherwise} \end{cases}, \quad (9)$$

where $\boldsymbol{x} = (\alpha(x,y), m(x,y))$ is the optical flow direction and magnitude at point (x, y), $\boldsymbol{\Theta}_{\mathbf{i}}$ is the parameter vector for the Gaussian Mixture Model at the region R_i and T_h is a threshold that specify the probability limit where the pixel (x, y) is marked as normal (0) or abnormal (1).

In order to improve the algorithm's performance a FIFO type list with fixed size S is defined and filled up with the latest S binary images $I_b(x, y)$. A connected component analysis is performed on each new image $I_b(x, y)$. If any pixel within a blob appears as abnormal in at least W images within the list, where

$W < S$, then the whole blob is marked as abnormal. The list size S and the number W are user controlled parameters and can be used for sensitivity adjustment, since a higher value of W means a higher alarm delay time.

3   Results and Comparisons

The proposed algorithm was implemented in Qt/C++ using OpenCV 3.0 on a 2.7 GHz Intel Core i7 PC with 16 GB of RAM. The parameters of the model were fixed to $M = 5$ (number of Gaussian in the mixture), $S = 3$, $W = 2$. All frames, regardless the dataset, were divided into $T = 35$ regions, that means that the $\widehat{w}$ and $\widehat{h}$ values will depend on the input frame size. The presented method was tested in two publicly available anomaly detection datasets: UMN[1] and UCSD[2]. Figure 2 shows a normal frame for each scenarios in the UMN dataset, the abnormality detected by the proposed approach and the performance comparison against the ground truth.

Fig. 2. Abnormal behavior detection: normal (*top*) and detected abnormal (*bottom*) situations in UMN dataset.

The Fig. 3 shows six examples frames with abnormal behavior detection from the UCSD dataset.

The proposed method was compared with similar state-of-the-art algorithms including Mixture Dynamic Texture (MDT) [6], Mixture of Optical Flow (MPPCA) [5], Social Force [7], Social Force with MPPCA [5] and the Hierarchical Activity Approach [13]. Figure 4 shows the Receiver Operation Characteristic (ROC) curves for the proposed method and the comparative algorithms, taken from [13]. Table 1 shows the Area Under the ROC curve (AUC) for the five comparative methods and the proposed one. Finally, Fig. 5 shows the processing time per frame for some state-of-the-art algorithms and the proposed in this paper.

---

[1] http://mha.cs.umn.edu/proj events.shtml.
[2] http://www.svcl.ucsd.edu/projects/anomaly/dataset.htm.

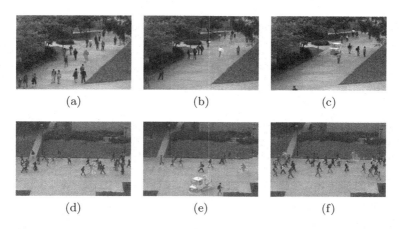

(a)   (b)   (c)

(d)   (e)   (f)

Fig. 3. Example of abnormal behavior detection in the UCSD dataset. UCSDped1 (*top*) and UCSDped2 (*bottom*).

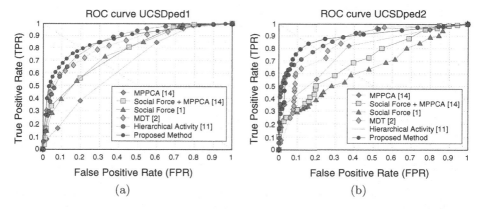

(a)   (b)

Fig. 4. Quantitative comparison of abnormal behavior detection in (a) UCSDped1 and (b) UCSDped2 against state-of-the-art algorithms.

Table 1. Area Under Curve of the proposed method compared with the others algorithms

Algorithm	Area Under Curve (AUC)	
	UCSDped1	UCSDped2
MPPCA [14]	0.59	0.693
Social Force [1]	0.675	0.556
Social Force + MPPCA [14]	0.668	0.613
MDT [2]	0.818	0.829
Hierarchical Activity [11]	0.854	0.882
Proposed Method	**0.8641**	**0.903**

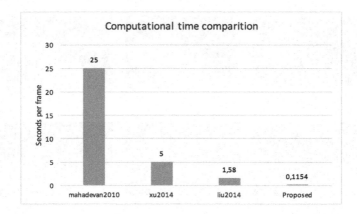

Fig. 5. Comparison of consumed time per frame with others state-of-the-art algorithms. Showed time is for the test phase in UCSDped1.

4   Conclusions

This paper presents a new method for abnormal behavior detection. It is based on optical flow and Mixture of Gaussians Model. The experimental results show that the proposed method presents a better performance in both detection rate and time processing per frame compared to other state-of-the-art algorithms.

Acknowledgments. The authors wish to thank Conselho Nacional de Desenvolvimento Científico (CNPq), Brazilian Research Support Foundations, for sponsoring this work.

References

1. Alvar, M., Torsello, A., Sanchez-Miralles, A., Armingol, J.M.: Abnormal behavior detection using dominant sets. Mach. Vis. Appl. **25**(5), 1351–1368 (2014)
2. Brox, T., Bruhn, A., Papenberg, N., Weickert, J.: High accuracy optical flow estimation based on a theory for warping. In: Pajdla, T., et al. (eds.) ECCV 2004, vol. 3024, pp. 25–36. Springer, Heidelberg (2004)
3. Chen, Z., Tian, Y., Wei Zeng, T.H.: Detecting abnormal behaviors in surveillance videos based on fuzzy clustering and multiplr auto-encoders. In: IEEE International Conference on Multimedia and Expo, pp. 1–6 (2015)
4. Cui, J., Liu, W., Xing, W.: Crowd behaviors analysis and abnormal detection based on surveillance data (2014)
5. Kim, J., Grauman, K.: Observe locally, infer globally: a space-time mrf for detecting abnormal activities with incremental updates. In: Proceedings of the International Conference on Computer Vision and Pattern Recognition (CVPR) (2009)
6. Mahadevan, V., Li, W., Bhalodia, V., Vasconcelos, N.: Anomaly detection in crowded scenes. In: IEEE Conference on Computer Vision and Pattern Recognition, pp. 1975–1981 (2010)
7. Mehran, R., Oyama, A., Shah, M.: Abnormal crowd behavior detection using social force model. In: IEEE Conference on Computer Vision and Pattern Recognition, vol. 2, pp. 935–942 (2009)

8. Ren, W.Y., Ll, G.H., Chen, J., Liang, H.Z.: Abnormal crowd beravior detection using beravior entropy model. In: International Conference on Wavelet Analysis and Pattern Recognition, pp. 212–221 (2012)
9. Snoussi, H., Wang, T.: Detection of abnormal visual events via global optical flow orientation histogram. IEEE Trans. Inf. Forensics Secur. **9**(6), 988–998 (2014)
10. Stauffer, C., Grimson, W.: Adaptive background mixture models for real-time tracking. In: Proceedings in IEEE Computer Society Conference on Computer Vision and Pattern Recognition 2 (1999)
11. Su, H., Yang, H., Zheng, S., Fan, Y., Wei, S.: Crowd event perception based on spatio-temporal viscous fluid field. In: IEEE Ninth International Conference on Advanced Video and Signal-Based Surveillance, pp. 458–463 (2012)
12. Wang, T., Snoussi, H.: Histograms of optical flow orientation for visual abnormal events detection. In: IEEE Ninth International Conference on Advanced Video and Signal-Based Surveillance (AVSS), pp. 13–18 (2012)
13. Xu, D., Song, R., Wu, X., Li, N., Feng, W., Qian, H.: Video anomaly detection based on a hierarchical activity discovery within spatio-temporal contexts. Neurocomputing **143**, 144–152 (2014)
14. Zhang, D., Peng, H., Haibin, Y., Lu, Y.: Crowd abnormal behavior detection based on machine learning. Inf. Technol. J. **12**, 1199–1205 (2013)

Unsupervised Deep Domain Adaptation for Pedestrian Detection

Lihang Liu[1], Weiyao Lin[1(✉)], Lisheng Wu[1], Yong Yu[1], and Michael Ying Yang[2]

[1] Shanghai Jiao Tong University, Shanghai, China
wylin@sjtu.edu.cn
[2] ITC-EOS, University of Twente, Enschede, The Netherlands

Abstract. This paper addresses the problem of unsupervised domain adaptation on the task of pedestrian detection in crowded scenes. First, we utilize an iterative algorithm to iteratively select and auto-annotate positive pedestrian samples with high confidence as the training samples for the target domain. Meanwhile, we also reuse negative samples from the source domain to compensate for the imbalance between the amount of positive samples and negative samples. Second, based on the deep network we also design an unsupervised regularizer to mitigate influence from data noise. More specifically, we transform the last fully connected layer into two sub-layers — an element-wise multiply layer and a sum layer, and add the unsupervised regularizer to further improve the domain adaptation accuracy. In experiments for pedestrian detection, the proposed method boosts the recall value by nearly 30 % while the precision stays almost the same. Furthermore, we perform our method on standard domain adaptation benchmarks on both supervised and unsupervised settings and also achieve state-of-the-art results.

Keywords: Unsupervised domain adaptation · Unsupervised regularizer · Deep neural network · People detection

1 Introduction

Deep neural networks have shown great power on traditional computer vision tasks, however, the labelled dataset should be large enough to train a reliable deep model. The annotation process for the task of pedestrian detection in crowded scenes is even more resource consuming, because we need to label concrete locations of pedestrian instances. In modern society, there are over millions of cameras deployed for surveillance. However, these surveillance situations vary in lights, background, viewpoints, camera resolutions and so on. Directly utilizing models trained on old scenes will result in poor performance on new situations due to data distribution changes. It is also unpractical to annotate pedestrian instances for every surveillance situation.

When there are few or no labelled data in the target domain, domain adaptation helps to reduce the amount of labelled data needed. Basically, unsupervised domain adaptation aims to shift the model trained from the source domain to

© Springer International Publishing Switzerland 2016
G. Hua and H. Jégou (Eds.): ECCV 2016 Workshops, Part II, LNCS 9914, pp. 676–691, 2016.
DOI: 10.1007/978-3-319-48881-3_48

the target domain for which only unlabelled data are provided. Most traditional works [1–5] either learn a shared representation between the source and target domain, or project features into a common subspace. Recently, there are also works [6–8] proposed to learn a scene-specific detector by deep architectures. However, heuristic methods are needed either for constructing feature space or re-weighting samples. Our motivation of developing a domain adaptation architecture is to reduce heuristic methods required during the adaptation process.

In this paper, we propose a new approach for unsupervised deep domain adaptation for pedestrian detection. First, we utilize an iterative algorithm to iteratively auto-annotate target examples with high confidence as positive pedestrian instances on the target domain. During each iteration, these auto-annotated data are regarded as the training set to update the target model. However, these auto-annotated samples still have the limitations of lack of negative samples and existence of false positive samples, which will no doubt lead to exploration of predictions on non-pedestrian instances. Therefore, in order to compensate for the quantitative imbalance between positive and negative samples, we randomly sample negative instances from the source domain and mix into training set. Second, based on deep network, we further design an unsupervised regularizer to mitigate influence from data noise and avoid overfitting. More specifically, in order to have a better regularization effect during the adaptation process, we propose to transform the last fully connected layer of the deep model into two sub-layers, an element-wise multiply layer and a sum layer. Thus, the unsupervised regularizer can be added on the element-wise multiply layer to adjust all weights in the deep network and gain better performance.

The contributions of our work are three folds.

– We propose an adaptation framework to learn scene-specific deep detectors for target domains by unsupervised methodologies, which adaptively selects positive instances with high confidence. This can be easily deployed to various surveillance situations without any additional annotations.
– Under this framework, we combine both supervised term and unsupervised regularizer into our loss function. The unsupervised regularizer helps to reduce influence from data noise in the auto-annotated data.
– More importantly, for better performance of the unsupervised regularizer we propose to transform the last fully connected layer of the deep network into two sub-layers, an element-wise multiply layer and a sum layer. Thus, all weights contained in the deep network can be adjusted under the unsupervised regularizer. To the best of our knowledge, this is the first attempt to transform fully connected layers for the purpose of domain adaptation.

The remainder of this paper is organized as follows. Section 2 reviews related works. Section 3 presents the details of our approach. Experimental results are shown in Sect. 4. Section 5 concludes the paper.

2   Related Work

In many detection works, the generic model trained from large amount of samples on the source domain is directly utilized to detect on the target domain. They assume that samples on the target domain are subsets of the source domain. However, when the distribution of data on the target and source domain vary largely, the performance will drop significantly. Domain adaptation aims to reduce the amount of data needed for the target domain.

Many domain adaptation works try to learn a common representation space shared between the source and target domain. Saenko et al. [1,2] propose both linear-transform-based techniques and kernel-transform-based techniques to minimize domain changes. Gopalan et al. [3] project features into Grassmann manifold instead of operating on features of raw data. Alternatively, Mesnil et al. [9] use transfer learning to obtain good representations. However, these methods have limitations since scene-specific features are not learned to boost accuracy.

Another group of works [4,5,10,11] on domain adaptation is to make the distribution of the source and target domain more similar. Among these works, Maximum Mean Discrepancy (MMD) [12] is used to as a metric to reselect samples from the source domain in order to have similar distribution as target samples. In [13], MMD is added on the last feature vector of the network as a regularization. Different from these methods, our work transforms the last fully connected layer into two sub-layers, an element-wise multiply layer and a sum layer. As the element-wise multiply layer is the last layer that contains weights before output layers, our unsupervised regularizer on the element-wise multiply layer can adjust all weights of the deep network during training.

There are also works on deep adaptation to construct scene-specific detectors. Wang et al. [6] explore context cues to compute confidence, [7] learn distributions of target samples and propose a cluster layer for scene-specific visual patterns. These works re-weight auto-annotated samples for their final object function and additional context cues are needed for reliable performance. However, heuristic methods are required to select reliable samples. Alternately, Hattori et al. [8] learn scene-specific detector by generating a spatially-varying pedestrian appearance model. And Pishchulin et al. [14] use 3D shape models to generate training data. However, synthesis for domain adaptation is also costly. Compared with these methods, our approach does not include the heuristic pre-processing steps. Thus, the performances of our approach are not affected by the pre-processing steps.

3   Our Approach

In this section, we introduce our unsupervised domain adaptation architecture on the task of pedestrian detection in crowded scenes. Unsupervised domain adaptation aims to shift the model trained from the source domain to the target domain for which only unlabelled data are provided. Under the unsupervised setting, we use an iterative algorithm to iteratively auto-annotate target samples and update the target model. As the auto-annotated samples may contain noises, the performances may be affected by the wrongly annotated samples. Therefore, an unsupervised regularizer is introduced to mitigate the influence from data noise on the target model. More specifically, based on the assumption that the source domain and the target domain should share the same feature space after feature extraction layers, we encode the unsupervised regularizer to make a constraint that the distribution of data representation on the element-wise multiply layer should be similar between the source domain and the target domain.

The adaptation architecture of our approach consists of three parts – the source stream, the target stream and an unsupervised regularizer, as shown in Fig. 1. The source stream takes samples from the source domain as input, while the target stream is trained from auto-annotated positive samples from the target domain and negative samples from the source domain. These two streams can utilize any deep detection network as their basic model, as well as their detection loss function as supervised loss functions of two streams. In our experiments, we use the detection network mentioned in Sect. 4.1 as the basic model. The unsupervised regularizer is integrated into the loss function of the target stream.

In the following, we will first describe our iterative algorithm which iteratively selects samples from the target domain, and updates the target model accordingly (Sect. 3.1). Then, we will introduce the loss function we designed for updating the target model (Sect. 3.2), as well as the proposed unsupervised regularizer for improving the domain adaptation performance (Sect. 3.3).

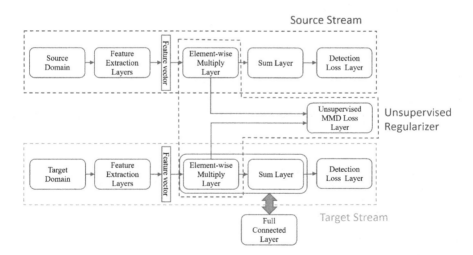

Fig. 1. The adaptation architecture consists of three parts, the source stream, the target stream and an unsupervised regularizer. The last fully connected layers of both source and the target stream are transformed into element-wise layer and sum layer for the purpose of the unsupervised regularizer. Best view in colors.

3.1 Iterative Algorithm

In this section, we introduce the iterative algorithm which is the training method of the target stream of our adaptation architecture. There are two reasons to employ the iterative algorithm. First, auto-annotated data on the target domain vary for every adaptation iteration and new positive samples will be auto-annotated as training set. Compared to methods without the iterative algorithm, it helps to avoid overfitting caused by lack of data. Second, unsupervised regularizer performs better with more training data as it's a distribution based regularizer.

There are two stages for the iterative algorithm. The source stream and the target stream are separately trained at different stages. At initialization stage, the source model of the source stream are trained under a supervised loss function with abundant labelled data, $(\mathbf{X}^S, \mathbf{Y}^S)$, from the source domain. After its convergence, the weights of the source model θ^S are taken to initialize the target stream. At adaptation stage, the target model is trained from auto-annotated positive samples $(\mathbf{X}^{T,n}, \mathbf{Y}^{T,n})$ from the target domain and randomly-selected negative samples $(\mathbf{X}^{S,n}, \mathbf{Y}^{S,n})$ from the source domain under both supervised loss function and unsupervised regularizer. Since auto-annotated data are all regarded as positive samples, negative samples from the source domain are randomly selected to compensate for lack of negative instances, which are human annotated and can thus provide true negative samples. Note that we do not jointly train two streams at adaptation stage and the weights of the source model stay static which serves as a distribution reference for the unsupervised regularizer at the adaptation stage. The complete adaptation process is illustrated in Algorithm 1. After a predetermined iteration limit N^I is reached, we obtain our final detection model on the target domain.

Algorithm 1. Deep domain adaptation algorithm

1: **procedure** DEEP DOMAIN ADAPTATION
2: Train the source model M^S on the source stream with abundant annotated data $(\mathbf{X}^S, \mathbf{Y}^S)$
3: Use M^S to initialize the target model on the target stream as M_0
4:     **for** i = 0:N^I **do**
5:         M_i generate auto-annotated positive samples $(\mathbf{X}^{T,n}, \mathbf{Y}^{T,n})$ of the target domain
6:         Randomly sampled negative instances $(\mathbf{X}^{S,n}, \mathbf{Y}^{S,n})$ from the source domain
7:         $\mathbf{X}^n = \{\mathbf{X}^{T,n}, \mathbf{X}^{S,n}\}$
8:         $\mathbf{Y}^n = \{\mathbf{Y}^{T,n}, \mathbf{Y}^{S,n}\}$
9:         Take $(\mathbf{X}^n, \mathbf{Y}^n)$ as training data to upgrade M_i into M_{i+1}
10:     **end for**
11: M_{N^I}: final model.
12: **end procedure**

3.2 Loss Function for the Target Stream

In this section, we introduce our loss function on the target stream of our adaptation architecture, which is composed of a supervised loss and an unsupervised regularizer. The supervised loss is to learn the scene-specific bias for the target domain, while the unsupervised regularizer introduced in Sect. 3.3 plays an important part in reducing influence from data noise as well as avoiding overfitting.

We denote training samples from the source domain as $\mathbf{X}^S = \{x_i^S\}_{i=1}^{N^S}$. For training samples on the source domain, we have corresponding annotations $\mathbf{Y}^S = \{y_i^S\}_{i=1}^{N^S}$ with $y_i^S = (b_i^S, l_i^S)$, where $b_i^S = (x, y, w, h) \in R^4$ is the bounding box location and $l_i^S \in \{0, 1\}$ is the label indicating whether x_i^S is a pedestrian instance. At the nth adaptation iteration, we have two set of training samples, $N^{T,n}$ auto-annotated positive samples from the target domain $\mathbf{X}^{T,n} = \{x_j^{T,n}\}_{j=1}^{N^{T,n}}$ and $N^{T,n}$ negative samples from the source domain $\mathbf{X}^{S,n} = \{x_k^{S,n}\}_{k=1}^{N^{T,n}}$. Their corresponding annotations can be denoted as $\mathbf{Y}^{T,n} = \{y_j^{T,n}\}_{j=1}^{N^{T,n}}$ and $\mathbf{Y}^{S,n} = \{y_k^{S,n}\}_{k=1}^{N^{T,n}}$ with $y_j^{T,n} = (b_j^{T,n}, l_j^{T,n} \equiv 1, c_j^{T,n})$, and $y_k^{S,n} = (b_k^{S,n}, l_k^{S,n} \equiv 0)$, respectively. $c_*^{T,n}$ is the confidence given by the auto-annotation tool and N^I is the maximum number of adaptation iterations. Now we can formulate the combination of supervised loss and unsupervised regularizer as follows:

$$L(\theta^{T,n}|\mathbf{X}^{T,n}, \mathbf{Y}^{T,n}, \mathbf{X}^{S,n}, \mathbf{Y}^{S,n}, \mathbf{X}^S, \theta^S) = L_S + \alpha * L_U$$

$$L_S = \sum_{j=1}^{N^{T,n}} H(c_j^{T,n}) * (R(\theta^{T,n}|x_j^{T,n}, b_j^{T,n}) + C(\theta^{T,n}|x_j^{T,n}, l_j^{T,n})) \tag{1}$$

$$+ \sum_{k=1}^{N^{T,n}} (R(\theta^{T,n}|x_k^{S,n}, b_k^{S,n}) + C(\theta^{T,n}|x_k^{S,n}, l_k^{S,n})) \tag{2}$$

$$L_U = L_{EWM}(\theta^{T,n}|\mathbf{X}^T, \mathbf{X}^S, \theta^S) \tag{3}$$

where L_S is the supervised loss to learn scene-specific detectors and L_U is the unsupervised regularizer part. $\alpha = 0.8$ is the coefficient balancing the effect of supervised and unsupervised loss. $\theta^{T,n}$ denote the coefficients of the network in the target stream at n^{th} adaption and θ^S denote the coefficients of the network in the source stream. $H(\cdot)$ is a step function in order to select positive samples with high confidence among auto-annotated data on the target domain. $R(\cdot)$ is a regression loss for bounding box locations, such as norm-1 loss, and $C(\cdot)$ is a classification loss for bounding box confidence, such as cross-entropy loss. And $L_{EWM}(\cdot)$, to be introduced in Sect. 3.3, is a MMD-based loss added on the element-wise multiply layer for unsupervised regularization.

3.3   Unsupervised Weights Regularizer on Element-Wise Multiply Layer

As mentioned before, the unsupervised regularizer plays an important role in reducing influence from data noise and avoiding overfitting. In this paper, we propose to transform the last fully connected layer in order to have better effect on unsupervised regularization.

Element-Wise Multiply Layer. In deep neural network, the data of the last feature vector layer is taken as an important data representation of input images. However, in this paper, we take one step further to focus on the last fully connected layer which serves as an decoder to decode rich information of the last feature vector into final outputs. As the source model is trained with abundant labelled data on the source domain, the weights of the last fully connected layer are also well converged. A regularizer on the last fully connected layer can adjust all weights of the network compared with that on the last feature vector layer. Denote the last feature vector, the weights of the last fully connected layer and the final outputs as $\boldsymbol{f}_{(1 \times N^D)}$, $\mathbf{C}_{(N^D \times N^O)}$ and $\boldsymbol{p}_{(1 \times N^O)}$. N^D, N^O are the dimension of feature vector and the dimension of output layer, respectively. Thus the operation of the fully connected layer can be formulated as matrix multiply:

$$\boldsymbol{p} = \boldsymbol{f} * \mathbf{C} \qquad (4)$$

where

$$p_o = \sum_d f_d * C_{d,o} \qquad (5)$$

Inspired by this form, we separate the above formula into two sub-operations – the element-wise multiply operation and the sum operation, which can be formulated as:

$$m_o = [f_d * C_{d,o}]_{d=1}^{N^D} \qquad (6)$$

$$p_o = \boldsymbol{m}_o * \overrightarrow{\mathbf{1}} \qquad (7)$$

where $\mathbf{M}_{(N^O \times N^D)} = [\boldsymbol{m}_o]$ is the intermediate results of the element-wise multiply operation. $\boldsymbol{m}_o$ is a vector with N^D dimensions, which will be the object of the unsupervised regularizer. Finally, we can equivalent-transform the last fully connected layer into an element-wise multiply layer and a sum layer. The transformed element-wise multiply layer is thus the last layer with weights before output layers. Figure 2 illustrates the transformation.

Unsupervised Regularizer on Element-Wise Multiply Layer. This section introduces our unsupervised regularizer. As stated in Sect. 3.1, there are false positive samples among auto-annotated data, which will mislead the network and result in worse performance. Thus, we designed an unsupervised

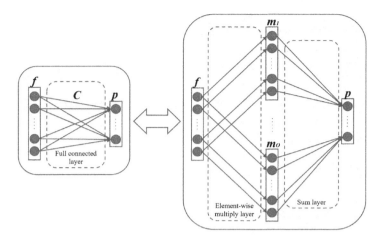

Fig. 2. Illustration of transformation of the fully connected layer $\mathbf{C}$ into element-wise multiply layer and sum layer. After the transformation, the element-wise layer become the last layer which contains weights before output layer p. Thus, an unsupervised regularizer can be added on m_o.

regularizer to mitigate the influence. We have the assumption that the weights of the element-wise multiply layer of the last fully connected layer have well converged under the training of abundant source samples. Thus, when tasks are similar, the distribution of data representations of the element-wise multiply layer on the source domain and the target domain should also be similar. While false samples are easier to mutate the distribution of data representations. This observation can be illustrated in Fig. 3, where the center of m_o of true target samples is far closer to the center of source samples, compared to that of false target samples. Confining that the distribution of data representations between the source and target domain to be similar helps to reduce the influence caused by data noise to some extent.

To encode this similarity, we utilize MMD (maximum mean discrepancy) [12] to compute distance between distributions of the element-wise multiply layers of the source domain and the target domain:

$$L_{EWM}(\theta^{T,n}|\mathbf{X}^S, \mathbf{X}^{T,n}, \theta^S) = \frac{1}{N^O} \sum_{o=1}^{N^O} \| \frac{\sum_{j=1}^{N^{T,n}} (m_o^{T,n}|x_j^{T,n})}{N^{T,n}} - \frac{\sum_{i=1}^{N^S} (m_o^S|x_i^S)}{N^S} \|^2$$

(8)

which can also interpreted as the Euclidean distance between the center of $m_o^{T,n}$ and m_o^S across all output dimensions. As a comparison, the MMD regularizer on feature vector layer can be formulated as:

$$L_{FV}(\theta^{T,n}|\mathbf{X}^S, \mathbf{X}^{T,n}, \theta^S) = \| \frac{\sum_{j=1}^{N^{T,n}} (f^{T,n}|x_j^{T,n})}{N^{T,n}} - \frac{\sum_{i=1}^{N^S} (f^S|x_i^S)}{N^S} \|^2$$

(9)

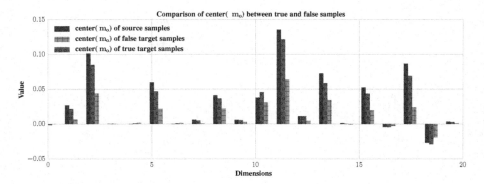

Fig. 3. Comparison of the center of m_o between true and false samples on the first 20 dimensions. The center of m_o of true target samples is far closer to the center of source samples, compared to that of false target samples. This observation supports our assumption that false instances among auto-annotated target samples tend to mutate the distribution of data representations on the element-wise multiply layer.

where f is data of the feature vector layer in Eq. 4 and m_o is the data of the element-wise multiply layer in Eq. 6.

Since it's unpractical to get the distribution of the whole training set, while too few images cannot obtain a stable distribution for regularization. In our experiments, the $L_{EWM}(\cdot)$ loss is calculated for every batch. An example comparison of centers of m_o^S of different batches are shown in Fig. 4.

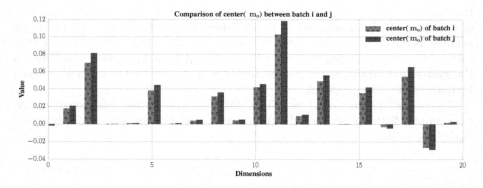

Fig. 4. Comparison of the center of m_o between two different batches on the first 20 dimensions. These two centers are close to each other, which supports our assumption that data distributions on the element-wise multiply layer between the source and target domain should be similar.

4 Experiment Results

In this section, we introduce our experiment results on both surveillance applications and the standard domain adaptation dataset. We firstly evaluate our approach on video surveillance. Then we employ our approach to standard domain adaptation benchmarks on both supervised and unsupervised settings to demonstrate the effectiveness of our method.

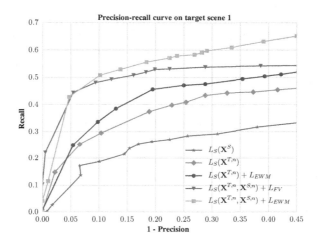

Fig. 5. Precision-recall curve of 5 comparison methods on target scene 1.

4.1 Domain Adaptation on Crowd Dataset

Dataset and Evaluation Metrics. To show the effectiveness of our domain adaptation approach for pedestrian detection, we collected a dataset[1] consisting of 3 target scenes for the target domain. These three scenes contain 1308, 1213 and 331 unlabelled images, respectively. For each scene, 100 images are annotated for evaluation. Instead of labelling the whole body of a person, we label the head of a person as bounding box during training. The motivation for labelling only pedestrian heads comes from detection of indoor pedestrian or in crowded scenes, where the body of a person may be invisible. The dataset for the source domain are Brainwash Dataset [15].

Our evaluation metrics for detection uses the protocol defined in PASCAL VOC [16]. To judge a predicted bounding box whether correctly matches a ground truth bounding box, their intersection over their union must exceed 50 %. And Multiple detections of the same ground truth bounding box are regarded as one correct prediction. For overall performance evaluation, the F1 score $F1 = 2 * precision * recall/(precision + recall)$ [17] are utilized. Higher F1 score means better performance. At the same time, the precision-recall curves are also plotted.

---

[1] Our dataset will be made available on http://wylin2.drivehq.com/.

Experimental Settings. Our generic detection model of adaptation architecture can be implemented by many deep detection models. In our experiment, we use the model proposed by Stewart et al. [15], which is an end to end detection network without any precomputed region proposals needed. For each iteration, 100 auto-annotated images from the target domain and 1000 annotated images from the source domain are alternatively used for training. The outputs of our detection network include bounding box locations and corresponding confidences, thus there are two fully connected layers between the last feature vector layer and the final outputs. In our experiments, when an unsupervised regularizer on the element-wise multiply layer predicting box confidence is added already, the unsupervised regularizer on the element-wise multiply layer predicting bounding box locations have little performance improvement. Experiments on 3 target scenes are executed separately.

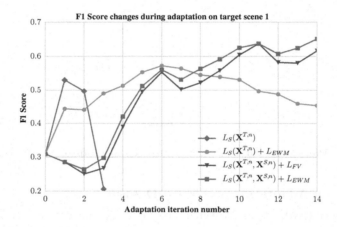

Fig. 6. F1 score changes of 5 comparison methods during adaptation on target scene 1

Comparison with Different Methods. To demonstrate the effectiveness of our approach, 5 methods are compared among which method $L_S(\mathbf{X}^{T,n}, \mathbf{X}^{S,n}) + L_{EWM}$ is our final approach:

$L_S(\mathbf{X}^S)$ Source model only trained from the source domain.

$L_S(\mathbf{X}^{T,n})$ Only auto-labeled samples on the target domain are used for training, and without any unsupervised regularizer.

$L_S(\mathbf{X}^{T,n}) + L_{EWM}$ Only auto-labeled samples on the target domain are used for training, with an unsupervised MMD regularizer added on the last element-wise multiply layer.

$L_S(\mathbf{X}^{T,n}, \mathbf{X}^{S,n}) + L_{FV}$ Both auto-labeled images from the target domain and labeled images from the source domain are alternately sampled for training, with an unsupervised MMD regularizer [13] added on the last feature vector layer.

Table 1. Detection results of 5 compared methods on 3 target scenes

	Scene 1			Scene 2			Scene 3		
	1-Pr	Re	F1	1-Pr	Re	F1	1-Pr	Re	F1
$L_S(\mathbf{X}^S)$	0.101	0.187	0.309	0.015	0.683	0.807	0.035	0.412	0.577
$L_S(\mathbf{X}^{T,n})$	0.245	0.408	0.530	0.632	0.905	0.524	0.176	0.778	0.800
$L_S(\mathbf{X}^{T,n}) + L_{EWM}$	0.284	0.476	0.572	0.012	0.837	**0.906**	0.078	0.653	0.764
$L_S(\mathbf{X}^{T,n}, \mathbf{X}^{S,n}) + L_{FV}$	0.109	0.496	0.637	0.002	0.721	0.838	0.044	0.611	0.746
$L_S(\mathbf{X}^{T,n}, \mathbf{X}^{S,n}) + L_{EWM}$	0.140	0.530	**0.656**	0.006	0.811	0.893	0.097	0.778	**0.836**

$L_S(\mathbf{X}^{T,n}, \mathbf{X}^{S,n}) + L_{EWM}$ Both auto-labeled images from the target domain and labeled images from the source domain are alternately sampled for training, with an unsupervised MMD regularizer added on the last element-wise multiply layer.

Figure 5 plots the precision-recall curves of the above comparison methods in target scene 1. Also, the changes of F1 score of every adaptation iteration are also depicted in Fig. 6. Table 1 gives concrete precision and recall value of the 5 comparison methods on three target scenes when the F1 scores are at their highest. Examples of adaptation results are shown in Fig. 7.

Performance Evaluation. From the Table 1, we have the following observations:

- Compared to method $L_S(\mathbf{X}^S)$, the recall values of other methods, which all utilize iterative algorithm for training, are explicitly larger. This implies the effectiveness of our iterative algorithm on boosting recall.
- The average F1 score of $L_S(\mathbf{X}^{T,n}) + L_{EWM}$ are larger than that of method $L_S(\mathbf{X}^{T,n})$. Also, the average (1-precision) value of $L_S(\mathbf{X}^{T,n}) + L_{EWM}$ is far smaller. Their difference in whether the unsupervised regularizer is added into loss function demonstrates that our unsupervised regularizer can mitigate the influence of data noise and thus boost F1 score.
- Compared to method $L_S(\mathbf{X}^{T,n}) + L_{EWM}$, the average F1 score of method $L_S(\mathbf{X}^{T,n}, \mathbf{X}^{S,n}) + L_{EWM}$ is higher. This demonstrate the effectiveness of negative source samples added into the training set during adaptation process.
- Compared to method $L_S(\mathbf{X}^{T,n}, \mathbf{X}^{S,n}) + L_{FV}$, the recall values of method $L_S(\mathbf{X}^{T,n}, \mathbf{X}^{S,n}) + L_{EWM}$ are further increased. This shows that unsupervised regularizer added on the element-wise layer will provide better regularizer effect compared to that on the feature vector layer.
- Our final method $L_S(\mathbf{X}^{T,n}, \mathbf{X}^{S,n}) + L_{EWM}$ achieves best results on target scene 1 and target scene 3. The performance on target scene 2 is rather close to the best result, which may result from large discrepancy of background between the source and target domain.

Fig. 7. Example results of 5 comparison methods on 3 target scenes.

Fig. 8. Example images on Office dataset.

4.2   Domain Adaptation on Standard Classification Benchmark

In order to further demonstrate the effectiveness and generalization of our adaptation architecture, we test our method on the standard domain adaptation benchmark Office dataset [1].

Office Dataset and Experimental Settings. The Office dataset comprises 31 categories of objects from 3 domains (Amazon, DSLR, Webcam). Example images are depicted in Fig. 8. We take Amazon domain as the source domain and Webcam domain as the target domain. We follow the standard protocol for both supervised and unsupervised settings. We reused the architecture in pedestrian detection and utilize AlexNet [18] as the generic model of both streams.

Performance Evaluation. In Table 2, we compare our approach with other seven recently published works in both supervised and unsupervised settings. The outstanding performance on both settings confirms the effectiveness of our iterative algorithm and MMD regularizer on the element-wise multiply layer.

Table 2. Multi-class accuracy evaluation on Office dataset with supervised and unsupervised settings

	A → W	
	Supervised	Unsupervised
GFK (PLS, PCA) [19]	46.4	15.0
SA [20]	45.0	15.3
DA-NBNN [21]	52.8	23.3
DLID [22]	51.9	26.1
DeCAF$_6$S [23]	80.7	52.2
DaNN [11]	53.6	35.0
DDC [13]	84.1	59.4
Ours	**85.4**	**69.3**

5   Conclusions

In this paper, we introduce an adaptation architecture to learn scene-specific deep detectors for the target domains. Firstly, an iterative algorithm is utilized to iteratively auto-annotate target samples and update the target model. As auto-annotated data are lack of negative samples and contain data noise, we randomly sample negative instances from the source domain. At the same time, an unsupervised regularizer is also designed to mitigate influence from data noise. More importantly, we propose to transform the last fully connected layer into an element-wise multiply layer and a sum layer for better regularizer effect.

Acknowledgments. The work is partially funded by the following grants: DFG (German Research Foundation) YA 351/2-1, NSFC 61471235, Microsoft Research Asia Collaborative Research Award. The authors gratefully acknowledge the support.

References

1. Saenko, K., Kulis, B., Fritz, M., Darrell, T.: Adapting visual category models to new domains. In: Daniilidis, K., Maragos, P., Paragios, N. (eds.) ECCV 2010, Part IV. LNCS, vol. 6314, pp. 213–226. Springer, Heidelberg (2010)
2. Kulis, B., Saenko, K., Darrell, T.: What you saw is not what you get: domain adaptation using asymmetric kernel transforms. In: IEEE Conference on Computer Vision and Pattern Recognition (CVPR), pp. 1785–1792 (2011)
3. Gopalan, R., Li, R., Chellappa, R.: Domain adaptation for object recognition: an unsupervised approach. In: IEEE International Conference on Computer Vision (ICCV), pp. 999–1006 (2011)
4. Huang, J., Gretton, A., Borgwardt, K.M., Schölkopf, B., Smola, A.J.: Correcting sample selection bias by unlabeled data. In: Advances in Neural Information Processing Systems (NIPS), pp. 601–608 (2006)
5. Gretton, A., Smola, A., Huang, J., Schmittfull, M., Borgwardt, K., Schölkopf, B.: Covariate shift by kernel mean matching. Dataset Shift Mach. Learn. **3**(4), 5 (2009)
6. Wang, X., Wang, M., Li, W.: Scene-specific pedestrian detection for static video surveillance. IEEE Trans. Pattern Anal. Mach. Intell. **36**(2), 361–374 (2014)
7. Zeng, X., Ouyang, W., Wang, M., Wang, X.: Deep learning of scene-specific classifier for pedestrian detection. In: Fleet, D., Pajdla, T., Schiele, B., Tuytelaars, T. (eds.) ECCV 2014, Part III. LNCS, vol. 8691, pp. 472–487. Springer, Heidelberg (2014)
8. Hattori, H., Naresh Boddeti, V., Kitani, K.M., Kanade, T.: Learning scene-specific pedestrian detectors without real data. In: IEEE Conference on Computer Vision and Pattern Recognition (CVPR), pp. 3819–3827 (2015)
9. Mesnil, G., Dauphin, Y., Glorot, X., Rifai, S., Bengio, Y., Goodfellow, I.J., Lavoie, E., Muller, X., Desjardins, G., Warde-Farley, D., et al.: Unsupervised and transfer learning challenge: a deep learning approach. In: ICML Unsupervised and Transfer Learning Workshop, vol. 27, pp. 97–110 (2012)
10. Gong, B., Grauman, K., Sha, F.: Connecting the dots with landmarks: discriminatively learning domain-invariant features for unsupervised domain adaptation. In: International Conference on Machine Learning (ICML), pp. 222–230 (2013)
11. Ghifary, M., Kleijn, W.B., Zhang, M.: Domain adaptive neural networks for object recognition. In: Pham, D.-N., Park, S.-B. (eds.) PRICAI 2014. LNCS, vol. 8862, pp. 898–904. Springer, Heidelberg (2014)
12. Gretton, A., Borgwardt, K.M., Rasch, M., Schölkopf, B., Smola, A.J.: A kernel method for the two-sample-problem. In: Advances in Neural Information Processing Systems, pp. 513–520 (2006)
13. Tzeng, E., Hoffman, J., Zhang, N., Saenko, K., Darrell, T.: Deep domain confusion: Maximizing for domain invariance. arXiv preprint arXiv:1412.3474 (2014)
14. Pishchulin, L., Jain, A., Wojek, C., Andriluka, M., Thormählen, T., Schiele, B.: Learning people detection models from few training samples. In: IEEE Conference on Computer Vision and Pattern Recognition (CVPR), pp. 1473–1480 (2011)
15. Stewart, R., Andriluka, M., Ng, A.: End to end people detection in crowded scenes. In: IEEE Conference on Computer Vision and Pattern Recognition (CVPR) (2016)

16. Everingham, M., Eslami, S.A., Van Gool, L., Williams, C.K., Winn, J., Zisserman, A.: The pascal visual object classes challenge: a retrospective. Int. J. Comput. Vision **111**(1), 98–136 (2015)
17. Powers, D.M.: Evaluation: from precision, recall and f-measure to roc, informedness, markedness and correlation (2011)
18. Krizhevsky, A., Sutskever, I., Hinton, G.E.: Imagenet classification with deep convolutional neural networks. In: Advances in Neural Information Processing Systems (NIPS), pp. 1097–1105 (2012)
19. Gong, B., Shi, Y., Sha, F., Grauman, K.: Geodesic flow kernel for unsupervised domain adaptation. In: IEEE Conference on Computer Vision and Pattern Recognition (CVPR), pp. 2066–2073 (2012)
20. Fernando, B., Habrard, A., Sebban, M., Tuytelaars, T.: Unsupervised visual domain adaptation using subspace alignment. In: IEEE Conference on Computer Vision and Pattern Recognition (CVPR), pp. 2960–2967 (2013)
21. Tommasi, T., Caputo, B.: Frustratingly easy nbnn domain adaptation. In: IEEE Conference on Computer Vision and Pattern Recognition (CVPR), pp. 897–904 (2013)
22. Chopra, S., Balakrishnan, S., Gopalan, R.: Dlid: deep learning for domain adaptation by interpolating between domains. In: ICML Workshop on Challenges in Representation Learning, vol. 2 (2013)
23. Donahue, J., Jia, Y., Vinyals, O., Hoffman, J., Zhang, N., Tzeng, E., Darrell, T.: Decaf: A deep convolutional activation feature for generic visual recognition. arXiv preprint arXiv:1310.1531 (2013)

Pixel Level Tracking of Multiple Targets in Crowded Environments

Mohammadreza Babaee$^{(\boxtimes)}$, Yue You, and Gerhard Rigoll

Institute for Human-Machine Communication,
Technical University of Munich, Munich, Germany
{reza.babaee,yue.you,rigoll}@tum.de

Abstract. Tracking of multiple targets in a crowded environment using tracking by detection algorithms has been investigated thoroughly. Although these techniques are quite successful, they suffer from the loss of much detailed information about targets in detection boxes, which is highly desirable in many applications like activity recognition. To address this problem, we propose an approach that tracks superpixels instead of detection boxes in multi-view video sequences. Specifically, we first extract superpixels from detection boxes and then associate them within each detection box, over several views and time steps that lead to a combined segmentation, reconstruction, and tracking of superpixels. We construct a flow graph and incorporate both visual and geometric cues in a global optimization framework to minimize its cost. Hence, we simultaneously achieve segmentation, reconstruction and tracking of targets in video. Experimental results confirm that the proposed approach outperforms state-of-the-art techniques for tracking while achieving comparable results in segmentation.

Keywords: Superpixels · Segmentation · Reconstruction · Tracking · Hypergraph

1 Introduction

Tracking of multiple targets in a crowded and unconstrained environment has many applications in video surveillance and security systems. This is a challenging problem due to the high amount of noise in the measured data, occlusion among targets, and interaction of targets with themselves or with other objects. Currently, tracking-by-detection is considered as the most successful solution for this problem [4,26,27,29,33]. However, tracking of detection boxes is not enough for many real applications such as human activity recognition and analysis.

In this work, we propose an approach to track segmented targets instead of their corresponding detection boxes in multi-view video sequences. We extract superpixels from detection boxes in all images and associate them over different views and time steps. Association of several superpixels in a detection box results in a segmentation. Moreover, association of several segmentations from

© Springer International Publishing Switzerland 2016
G. Hua and H. Jégou (Eds.): ECCV 2016 Workshops, Part II, LNCS 9914, pp. 692–708, 2016.
DOI: 10.1007/978-3-319-48881-3_49

different views results in a 3D reconstruction. Finally, association of segmentations or reconstructions over time (i.e., temporal association) results in tracking of segmented targets in video sequences. In other words, we address the problem of segmentation, reconstruction and tracking of multiple targets in multi-view video sequences.

In contrast to previous works, we aim to assign a unique target ID not only to each individual detection, but to every superpixel in the entire multi-view video sequence. In common with some other approaches [14,18], the problem is first formulated as a maximum a-priori problem and then mapped into a constraint flow graph, which can be efficiently solved by available off-the-shelf binary linear programming solvers. This work is an extension of the work of [18] which has considered reconstruction in tracking and is inspired by the work of [25] that addresses both video segmentation and tracking. Our main contributions are (1) combined segmentation, reconstruction and tracking of unknown number of targets in multi-view video sequences; (2) a new constrained flow graph that takes multi-view couplings and low-level superpixel information into account. Experimental result on standard, publicly available datasets show that the method can outperform many other methods with tracking performance while achieving comparable segmentation performance.

2   Related Work

Tracking-by-detection is the most successful strategy that has been explored intensively by many researchers [1,20,23,31,33]. Here, first a set of detections is obtained by applying object detection algorithms on all images and then is fed into a data association algorithm to track the targets (i.e., finding the identities of targets) in the sequence of frames such that the trajectories of targets are smooth. The main challenge is the data association problem, where the number of possible association of targets over the time frames increases exponentially with the number of targets. To address this problem, modern approaches cast this problem in different ways such as a graph optimization whose solution can be obtained using Integer Linear Programming [5,6], a network flow [31,34], continuous or discrete-continuous energy minimization [3,26], and generalized clique graphs [12,33]. In order to make the problem tractable, some researchers apply some restrictions, such as reducing the targets' state to the observations in the optimization problem [6,21,34] or sting measurements [10,21,22,34]. However, these techniques are only able to track a set of bounding boxes containing the objects. Evidently in many applications finer tracking of the targets is highly desirable.

In order to have finer tracking of objects, video segmentation techniques [8,9,16] are used to assign semantic labels to the pixels in a sequence of frames such that pixels belonging to the same target should preserve their label throughout the entire video sequence. For instance, the authors in [19,28] use video segmentation for pedestrian tracking. Fragkiadaki and Shi [14] cast the problem of multi-target tracking as clustering of low-level trajectories in order to enhance the tracking results in cluttered situations. Milan et al. [25] aim to track superpixels over the frame sequence by casting the superpixel tracking as a multi-label

optimization problem. They define several types of cost functions in their graphical model (i.e., Conditional Random Field (CRF)). The solution of optimization
leads to a joint segmentation and tracking of targets. However, their approach
is based on a single view.

Here, we use integer linear programming for joint segmentation, reconstruction and tracking of multiple targets observed by multiple cameras. The proposed approach performs data association among extracted superpixels in each
view and also among several views. In our approach, we aim to simultaneously
segment, reconstruct, and track targets in a multi-view setup.

3   Approach

A 2D image detection is defined by a tuple $\mathcal{D}_i = (x_i, s_i, c_i, t_i)$, where x_i is the
position, s_i the size of the detection, c_i the camera and t_i the time. A superpixel
sp_j is a group of image pixels in one frame that have similar color and each
detection $\mathcal{D}_i$ can be split into several superpixels. A segmentation $\mathcal{S}_i = \{sp_j\}$ of
a detection $\mathcal{D}_i$ is then a set of at least one superpixel which represent a target
(e.g., human body).

$$\mathcal{S}_i \subseteq \{sp | \forall sp_j, sp_k \in \mathcal{S}_i, j \neq k : c_{sp_j} = c_{sp_k} \wedge t_{sp_j} = t_{sp_k}\}. \tag{1}$$

where c_{sp_j} is the camera and t_{sp_j} is the time of superpixel sp_j. The set of all
feasible segmentations is $\mathcal{S} = \{\mathcal{S}_i\}$. A 3D reconstruction $\mathcal{R}_k$ is a set of segmentations from different views. We denote the number of segmentations within one
reconstruction as its cardinality $|\mathcal{R}_k|$. Every reconstruction must have at least
two coupled segmentations, i.e., $|\mathcal{R}_k| \geq 2$. The set of all reconstructions is $\mathcal{R}$.
Ideally, one reconstruction corresponds to one real world target. Thus, from each
camera at most one segmentation can be included in one $\mathcal{R}_k$:

$$\mathcal{R}_k \subseteq \{\mathcal{S} | \forall \mathcal{S}_i, \mathcal{S}_j \in \mathcal{R}_k, i \neq j : c_i \neq c_j \wedge t_i = t_j\}. \tag{2}$$

where c_i is the camera and t_i the time of segmentation $\mathcal{S}_i$. The set of the union
of segmentations and reconstructions is denoted as $V = \mathcal{S} \cup \mathcal{R}$. A trajectory
hypothesis is defined as $\mathcal{T}_u = \{V_{u_1}, V_{u_2}, ..., V_{u_n}\}$, which means each node in
a trajectory can be either a segmentation or a reconstruction. The complete
association hypothesis $\mathcal{T}$ is a set of trajectory hypotheses, i.e., $\mathcal{T} = \{\mathcal{T}_u\}$. Given
a set of segmentations $\mathcal{S}$ and a set of reconstructions $\mathcal{R}$, the tracking task is
achieved by finding an optimal set of tracks $\mathcal{T}^*$, which has the Maximum a-
Posteriori (MAP) probability:

$$
\begin{aligned}
\mathcal{T}^* &= \operatorname*{argmax}_{\mathcal{T}} P(\mathcal{T} | \mathcal{R}, \mathcal{S}) \\
&= \operatorname*{argmax}_{\mathcal{T}} P(\mathcal{R}, \mathcal{S} | \mathcal{T}) P(\mathcal{T}) \\
&= \operatorname*{argmax}_{\mathcal{T}} P(\mathcal{R} | \mathcal{T}) P(\mathcal{S} | \mathcal{R}, \mathcal{T}) P(\mathcal{T}) \\
&= \operatorname*{argmax}_{\mathcal{T}} P(\mathcal{S} | \mathcal{T}) P(\mathcal{R} | \mathcal{T}) P(\mathcal{T})
\end{aligned}
\tag{3}
$$

Using Bayes rule, the posterior probability can be written as the multiplication of the likelihood and prior probabilities. The likelihood term can be further decomposed since segmentation $\mathcal{S}$ and reconstruction $\mathcal{R}$ are conditionally independent. Next we introduce two constraints: two different segmentations $\mathcal{S}_i$ and $\mathcal{S}_j$ cannot share the same superpixel, and two different reconstructions $\mathcal{R}_k$ and $\mathcal{R}_l$ cannot share the same segmentation:

$$\mathcal{S}_i \cap \mathcal{S}_j = \emptyset, \ \forall i \neq j, \ \forall \mathcal{S}_i, \mathcal{S}_j \in \mathcal{T}$$
$$\mathcal{R}_k \cap \mathcal{R}_l = \emptyset, \ \forall k \neq l, \ \forall \mathcal{R}_k, \mathcal{R}_l \in \mathcal{T} \tag{4}$$

We further assume non-overlapping trajectories, i.e., one segmentation $\mathcal{S}_i$ or one reconstruction $\mathcal{R}_k$ can only be part of at most one trajectory:

$$\mathcal{T}_u \cap \mathcal{T}_v = \emptyset, \ \forall u \neq v \tag{5}$$

With these non-overlapping assumptions, the individual segmentation likelihood probabilities $P(\mathcal{S}_i|\mathcal{T})$ are conditionally independent and so are the individual reconstruction likelihood probabilities $P(\mathcal{R}_k|\mathcal{T})$. Moreover, the individual prior probabilities $P(\mathcal{T}_u)$ are independent as well. So the MAP formulation can be factorized as:

$$\mathcal{T}^* = \underset{\mathcal{T}}{\mathrm{argmax}} \prod_{\mathcal{S}_i \in \mathcal{S}} P(\mathcal{S}_i|\mathcal{T}) \prod_{\mathcal{R}_k \in \mathcal{R}} P(\mathcal{R}_k|\mathcal{T}) \prod_{\mathcal{T}_u \in \mathcal{T}} P(\mathcal{T}_u)$$
$$s.t. \mathcal{S}_i \cap \mathcal{S}_j = \emptyset, \ \forall i \neq j, \ \forall \mathcal{S}_i, \mathcal{S}_j \in \mathcal{T}$$
$$\mathcal{R}_k \cap \mathcal{R}_l = \emptyset, \ \forall k \neq l, \ \forall \mathcal{R}_k, \mathcal{R}_l \in \mathcal{T}$$
$$\mathcal{T}_u \cap \mathcal{T}_v = \emptyset, \ \forall u \neq v \tag{6}$$

Here, the segmentation likelihood $P(\mathcal{S}_i|\mathcal{T})$ and the reconstruction likelihood $P(\mathcal{R}_k|\mathcal{T})$ measure the quality of the segmentation and reconstruction, respectively. They are precisely defined in Sect. 5.

The nodes (which are either segmentations or reconstructions) in a trajectory hypothesis $\mathcal{T}_u$ form a Markov chain. Hence, the a priori probability of a single trajectory $P(\mathcal{T}_u)$ is defined as:

$$P(\mathcal{T}_u) = P(\{V_{u_1}, V_{u_2}, ..., V_{u_n}\})$$
$$= P_{en}(V_{u_1}) P_{link}(V_{u_2}|V_{u_1})...P_{ex}(V_{u_n}) \tag{7}$$

where $P_{en}(V_{u_i})$ and $P_{ex}(V_{u_i})$ are the probabilities of a trajectory to start or terminate at node V_{u_i}, respectively. $P_{link}(V_{u_j}|V_{u_i})$ defines the transition probability from V_{u_j} to V_{u_i}. By solving the optimization problem of Eq. (3), which corresponds to a hypergraph like the one in Fig. 1, we are able to track, segment, and reconstruct all the objects simultaneously. The final MAP formulation can be solved by K-shortest path [6], Dynamic Programming [34] or Binary Integer Programming (BIP) [17,18]. In this work, we reformulate it into as a constrained cost-flow graph and solve it using Binary Integer Programming.

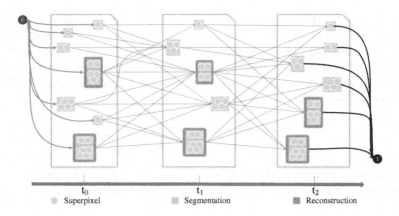

Fig. 1. An example of the proposed flow graph for three time steps ($t_0 - t_2$). One to several superpixels can be associated to build a segmentation node. Several segmentation nodes can be associated to build a reconstruction node. The association of all nodes over time leads to target tracking. E indicates source node and T indicates sink node.

4   Min-Cost Flow Graph

A hypergraph G is defined as the set of vertices and edges $G = \{\mathcal{V}, \mathcal{E}\}$. The set of all vertices is the union of segmentations and reconstructions, as well as additional source and sink nodes E (start of a trajectory) and T (end of a trajectory), i.e. $\mathcal{V} = \mathcal{S} \cup \mathcal{R} \cup \{E, T\}$. The edges $\mathcal{E}$ consist of hyperedges $\mathcal{S}_i$ and $\mathcal{R}_k$, corresponding to 2D segmentations, and 3D reconstructions, respectively, as well as the temporal edges $\mathcal{E}_{k,l} = (\mathcal{V}_k, \mathcal{V}_l)$, which connect two nodes between frames. In addition, we connect each reconstruction to a source node E via a source edge and a sink node T via a sink edge. The introduction of source and sink nodes enables the hypergraph to solve the problem even when the number of trajectories (targets) is not known as a prior.

As a flow graph, each edge is able to carry a certain amount of flow f with a unit cost c per flow. More specifically, the segmentation hyperedge $\mathcal{S}_k$ has a flow $f_{\mathcal{S}_k}$ with cost $C_{\mathcal{S}_k}$, the reconstruction hyperedge $\mathcal{R}_k$ has a flow $f_{\mathcal{R}_k}$ with cost $C_{\mathcal{R}_k}$ and a temporal edge $\mathcal{E}_{k,l}$ has a flow $f_{k,l}$ with cost $C_{k,l}$. Analogously, the source and sink edges have flow of $f_{en,k}$ and $f_{ex,k}$ with cost $C_{en,k}$ and $C_{ex,k}$ respectively.

Due to the trajectory non-overlapping constraint in Eq. (5), each flow path through the graph corresponds to a trajectory, thus the total number of trajectories exactly corresponds to the amount of flows from E to T. The maximum allowed flow through an edge is set to be 1, as one object can only belong to one trajectory and vice versa. A flow of $f = 0$ means the corresponding edge is not chosen and a flow of $f = 1$ implies the edge is part of the trajectory.

The constraint defined in Eq. (5) is reformulated as the flow conservation constraint, i.e., the sum of the outgoing flows of one node equals the sum of the incoming flows:

$$f_{en,i} + \sum_j f_{j,i} = f_{S_i} = \sum_j f_{i,j} + f_{ex,i}$$

$$f_{en,k} + \sum_l f_{l,k} = f_{R_k} = \sum_l f_{k,l} + f_{ex,k} \tag{8}$$

In Eq. (4) we also introduce constraints of non-overlapping segmentations and reconstructions. This coupling constraint can be reformulated to the flow graph representation as:

$$\sum_{S_i \in Q_j} f_{S_i} \le 1, \quad \forall j, Q_j = \{i | sp_j \in S_i\}$$

$$\sum_{R_k \in O_l} f_{R_k} \le 1, \quad \forall l, O_l = \{k | S_l \in R_k\} \tag{9}$$

These constraints mean, for all segmentations S_i and S_j, which have the same superpixel, i.e. $S_i \cap S_i \ne \emptyset$, the sum of the corresponding flows f_{S_i} and f_{S_j} must be less or equal to 1; analogously, for all reconstructions R_k and R_l, which share the same segmentation, the sum of the corresponding flows f_{R_k} and f_{R_l} must be either 0 or 1.

Next, we reformulate the problem of maximizing the probabilities of the assignment hypothesis T as the problem of finding the best flow through the whole graph with minimum overall cost. The flow costs can be related to the probabilities after taking the negative logarithm on the MAP formulation:

$$
\begin{aligned}
T^* &= \underset{T}{\text{argmax}} \sum_{S_i \in T_u} - \log(P(S_i|T)) + \sum_{R_k \in T_u} - \log(P(R_k|T)) + \sum_{T_u \in T} - \log(P(T_u)) \\
&= \underset{T}{\text{argmax}} \sum_{S_i \in T_u} - \log(P(S_i|T)) + \sum_{R_k \in T_u} - \log(P(R_k|T)) \\
&\quad + \sum_{T_u \in T} (- \log P_{en}(V_{u_1}) + \sum_j - \log P_{link}(V_{u_{j+1}}|V_{u_j}) - \log P_{ex}(V_{u_n})) \\
&= \underset{T}{\text{argmax}} \sum_i C_{S_i} f_{S_i} + \sum_k C_{R_k} f_{R_k} \\
&\quad + \sum_k C_{en,k} f_{en,k} + \sum_{k,l} C_{k,l} f_{k,l} + \sum_k C_{ex,k} f_{ex,k}
\end{aligned}
\tag{10}
$$

Obviously, we get the costs C from the MAP formulation:

$$
\begin{aligned}
C_{S_i} &= - \log P(S_i|T) \\
C_{R_k} &= - \log P(R_k|T) \\
C_{en,k} &= - \log P_{en}(V_k) \\
C_{k,l} &= - \log P_{link}(V_l|V_k) \\
C_{ex,k} &= - \log P_{ex}(V_k)
\end{aligned}
\tag{11}
$$

In this way, the tracking, segmentation and reconstruction problem is modeled as a BIP problem. The above presented BIP is solvable using cutting-plane methods, branch and cut or branch and price methods. In our implementation we use CPLEX integer programming solver.

5   Definitions of Probabilities

In order to formulate the problem, we must define all the probabilities presented in the model. They are precisely defined in this section.

5.1   Segmentation Likelihood $P(\mathcal{S}_i|\mathcal{T})$

The segmentation likelihood $P(\mathcal{S}_i|\mathcal{T})$ defines the quality of a segmentation given a set of trajectories $\mathcal{T}$. It depends on the position and appearance of the super-pixels inside the detection box, as well as the configuration of the overall segmentation (union of the superpixels).

$$P(\mathcal{S}_i|\mathcal{T}) = P_{pos}(\mathcal{S}_i|\mathcal{T})P_{app}(\mathcal{S}_i|\mathcal{T})P_{conf}(\mathcal{S}_i|\mathcal{T}) \tag{12}$$

The position of segmentation likelihood term $P_{pos}(\mathcal{S}_i|\mathcal{T})$ is defined as:

$$P_{pos}(\mathcal{S}_i|\mathcal{T}) = \begin{cases} P_{pos}(\mathcal{S}_i), & \mathcal{S}_i \in \mathcal{T} \\ 1 - P_{seg}(\mathcal{S}_i), & \text{otherwise} \end{cases} \tag{13}$$

where $P_{pos}(\mathcal{S}_i)$ is the a priori position of segmentation probability. Analogously, $P_{app}(\mathcal{S}_i|\mathcal{T})$ and $P_{conf}(\mathcal{S}_i|\mathcal{T})$ are defined by the a priori probability $P_{app}(\mathcal{S}_i)$ and $P_{conf}(\mathcal{S}_i)$, respectively. Next we present these a priori probabilities precisely.

Each superpixel in the detection box has a prior probability of being part of the segmentation $I_{\mathcal{M}}(\boldsymbol{x}(sp_j))$, where $I_{\mathcal{M}}(\cdot)$ is intensity of an object shape mask $\mathcal{M}$ [25] and $\boldsymbol{x}(sp_j)$ is the center point of the superpixel. The probability $P_{pos}(\mathcal{S}_i)$ measures the probability that all the superpixels within $\mathcal{S}_i$ form a feasible segmentation. The a priori position probability is then modeled as:

$$p(sp_j) = I_{\mathcal{M}}(\boldsymbol{x}(sp_j))$$
$$P_{pos}(\mathcal{S}_i) = P_{pos}\Big(\bigcap_{sp_j \in \mathcal{S}_i} sp_j \Big)$$
$$= \prod_{sp_j \in \mathcal{S}_i} p(sp_j) \tag{14}$$

where, we assume that the events of a superpixel being part of a segmentation are independent from each other. Therefore, the probability of the intersection of the events equals to the multiplication of all the individual probabilities.

The a priori appearance probability takes the similarity of superpixels within one segmentation into account. It depends on the mean color difference of the superpixels:

$$P_{app}(\mathcal{S}_i) = \frac{1}{\text{Pair}(|\mathcal{S}_i|)} \sum_{\substack{sp_j, sp_k \in \mathcal{S}_i \\ i \neq j}} \mathcal{F}(1 + ||Lab(sp_j) - Lab(sp_k)||, 0, \varepsilon_{Lab}) \tag{15}$$

where $\mathrm{Pair}(|\mathcal{S}_i|)$ is the number of pairs of superpixels within segmentation $\mathcal{S}_i$, $Lab(sp_j)$ is the average color of superpixel sp_j in LAB color space, cardinality $|\mathcal{S}_i|$ is the number of superpixels within the segmentation, and ε_{Lab} is the maximum allowed color deviation in LAB color space. Large color deviation is penalized since at our datasets, we observed that the objects contain only 1–3 colors each. To this end, we introduce the decreasing function $\mathcal{F}$ and use it to map the error to probability:

$$\mathcal{F}(d, d_{min}, d_{max}) = \frac{1}{2}\mathrm{erfc}(4\frac{d - d_{min}}{d_{max} - d_{min}} - 2) \qquad (16)$$

The a priori configuration probability models the quality of overall shape of the segmentation. A segmentation is expected to cover α percent area of the detection box, to be connected and to have a certain width/height ratio as it represents a shape of a human. This term is defined as:

$$P_{conf}(\mathcal{S}_i) = \frac{1}{\mathrm{CN}(\mathcal{S}_i)} \exp(-||\rho - \alpha|| - \left|\left| \frac{w(\mathcal{S}_i)}{h(\mathcal{S}_i)} - \frac{w_i}{h_i} \right|\right|) \qquad (17)$$

where ρ is the ratio that the segmentation covers the detection box, α is the expected ratio of segmentation, $w(\mathcal{S}_i)$ and $h(\mathcal{S}_i)$ are the width and the height of segmentation $\mathcal{S}_i$, respectively, w_i and h_i are the width and the height of corresponding detection $\mathcal{D}_i$, respectively. $\mathrm{CN}(\mathcal{S}_i)$ is the number of connected components of the segmentation $\mathcal{S}_i$. To compute this value, we label all the superpixels and assign the same label to the connected superpixels. The number of unique labels is $\mathrm{CN}(\mathcal{S}_i)$. Note that, a segmentation with too less superpixels ($\rho \ll \alpha$) or an unexpected shape (segmentation width/height ratio does not equal detection ratio) will be penalized.

5.2 Reconstruction Likelihood $P(\mathcal{R}_k|\mathcal{T})$

The probability $P(\mathcal{R}_k|\mathcal{T})$ measures the likelihood of a 3D reconstruction $\mathcal{R}_k$ given a set of trajectories $\mathcal{T}$. This probability depends on (1) the geometric positions, (2) appearance similarity and (3) qualities of the 2D segmentations $\mathcal{S}_j$ within reconstruction $\mathcal{R}_k$.

$$P(\mathcal{R}_k|\mathcal{T}) = P_d(\mathcal{R}_k|\mathcal{T})P_c(\mathcal{R}_k|\mathcal{T})P_s(\mathcal{R}_k|\mathcal{T}) \qquad (18)$$

Similar to Eq. 13, the geometric and appearance likelihoods in Eq. (18) is defined by the corresponding a priori probabilities $P_d(\mathcal{R}_k)$ and $P_c(\mathcal{R}_k)$. Quality likelihood term can be further decomposed. We precisely define these terms in the following.

Geometric Probability. Ideally, all the segmentations in a reconstruction should project to the same position in the world coordinate system. However, due to the calibration error and the imprecise segmentations, the world positions of the 2D segmentations are unlikely to match up exactly. In this situation, high deviations are penalized.

The geometric reconstruction error ε_k is defined as the root mean square deviation of the segmentations in $\mathcal{R}_k$ from their mean position in world coordinate system:

$$\varepsilon_k = \sqrt{\frac{1}{|\mathcal{R}_k|} \sum_{S_i \in R_k} |\phi^c(S_i) - \bar{x}_k|^2}$$

$$\bar{x}_k = \frac{1}{|\mathcal{R}_k|} \sum_{S_i \in R_k} \phi^c(S_i) \tag{19}$$

here, $|R_k|$ is the number of segmentations with the reconstruction. $\phi^c(S_i)$ transforms the position of the segmentation to world coordinate system for camera c.

Using the decreasing function $\mathcal{F}$, the geometric reconstruction probability $P_d(\mathcal{R}_k)$ is defined as:

$$P_d(\mathcal{R}_k) = \mathcal{F}(\varepsilon_k, 0, \varepsilon_{max}(\mathcal{R}_k)) \tag{20}$$

where $\varepsilon_{max}(\mathcal{R}_k)$ is the maximum allowed reconstruction error. This value depends on the detector inaccuracies (error in 2D image) as well as on the error of camera calibration (error in 3D ground plane) and varies for every position. Thus, $\varepsilon_{max}(\mathcal{R}_k)$ is defined as:

$$\varepsilon_{max}(\mathcal{R}_k) = \varepsilon_{det} \sum_{S_j \in \mathcal{R}_k} ||\Theta^c(S_j)|| + \varepsilon_{cal} \tag{21}$$

here, ε_{cal} is the calibration error of the cameras and is set to be a constant. ε_{det} is the detection error resulted from the inaccuracies of the detection bounding boxes. Due to the distortion of the camera calibration, the influence of the detection error ε_{det} largely depends on the object location. In order to model this part, we first compute the sensitivity of the world coordinate projection function $\phi^c(\boldsymbol{x})$ at each image position. This sensitivity depends on the Jacobian matrix of $\phi^c(\boldsymbol{x})$ [18]:

$$\frac{\partial}{\partial \boldsymbol{x}} \phi^c(\boldsymbol{x}) = J^c(\boldsymbol{x}) = \begin{pmatrix} \frac{\partial \phi^c_{x_\omega}}{\partial x} & \frac{\partial \phi^c_{x_\omega}}{\partial y} \\ \frac{\partial \phi^c_{y_\omega}}{\partial x} & \frac{\partial \phi^c_{y_\omega}}{\partial y} \end{pmatrix} \tag{22}$$

The sensitivity of the projection function is then defined as the lengths of the gradients of both x_ω and y_ω components:

$$\Theta^c(\boldsymbol{x}) = \begin{pmatrix} ||\nabla_{x_\omega} \phi^c(\boldsymbol{x})|| \\ ||\nabla_{y_\omega} \phi^c(\boldsymbol{x})|| \end{pmatrix} \tag{23}$$

In Eq. (21), the detection error ε_{det} acts as a weight factor of the sum of projection sensitivities of all cameras that are involved in reconstruction $\mathcal{R}_k$.

Appearance Similarity. The segmentations within one reconstruction represent the same target viewed by different cameras, thus they have the similar appearance. The appearance similarity $P_c(\mathcal{R}_k)$ depends on the average color of the segmentations from different views:

$$P_c(\mathcal{R}_k) = \frac{1}{\mathrm{Pair}(|\mathcal{R}_k|)} \sum_{\substack{\mathcal{S}_i,\mathcal{S}_j \in \mathcal{R}_k \\ i \neq j}} \mathcal{F}(1 + ||Lab(\mathcal{S}_i) - Lab(\mathcal{S}_j)||, 0, \varepsilon_{Lab}) \qquad (24)$$

where $\mathrm{Pair}(|\mathcal{R}_k|)$ is the number of pairs of segmentations within reconstruction $\mathcal{R}_k$.

Quality of the involved segmentations. $P_s(\mathcal{R}_k|\mathcal{T})$ defines the overall quality of the segmentations within the reconstruction $\mathcal{R}_k$. A reconstruction that contains good segmentations has a higher probability and vice versa. It is defined as the multiplication of the segmentation likelihoods of all the segmentations within $\mathcal{R}_k$:

$$P_s(\mathcal{R}_k|\mathcal{T}) = \prod_{\mathcal{S}_i \in R_k} P(\mathcal{S}_i|\mathcal{T}) \qquad (25)$$

where the definition of segmentation likelihood $P(\mathcal{S}_i|\mathcal{T})$ is same as Eq. 12.

5.3   Transition Probability P_{link}

For two nodes V_l, V_k, the transition probability $P_{link}(V_l|V_k)$ defines the probability of the reconstructions to be in the same trajectory. Here V_l and V_k can be both segmentations, both reconstructions, or one segmentation and one reconstruction. This probability consists of three terms: (1) the spatial and (2) the temporal distance probability between the two nodes, as well as (3) the super-pixel linking probability:

$$P_{link}(V_l|V_k) = P(\bar{x}_l|\bar{x}_k, \Delta\tau)P(\Delta\tau)P_t(V_l|V_k) \qquad (26)$$

Spatial Distance Probability. The spatial term is defined by the distance probability function:

$$P(\bar{x}_l|\bar{x}_k, \Delta\tau) = \mathcal{F}(||\bar{x}_l - \bar{x}_k||, 0, \frac{v_{max}}{f}\Delta\tau)$$
$$\Delta\tau = \tau_l - \tau_k \qquad (27)$$

where v_{max} is the maximum velocity of the target, f is the frame rate and $\Delta\tau$ is the frame gap.

Temporal Distance probability. Like in [21], the temporal term is defined with a exponential model:

$$P(\Delta\tau) = \gamma^{n(\tau-1)} \qquad (28)$$

where γ is the false negative rate of the detector and n is the number of cameras that should generate observations of the targets in the frame gap.

Superpixel Linking Probability. In oder to generate the temporal links between the superpixels, we first run the temporal superpixel (TSP) algorithm of Chang *et al.* [11]. Then the superpixel linking probability depends on the number of the superpixels that have same ID in the two reconstructions:

$$P_t(\mathcal{V}_l|\mathcal{V}_k) = \frac{1}{\min(N_l, N_k)} \sum_{\substack{sp_i \in \mathcal{V}_l \\ sp_j \in \mathcal{V}_k}} [TSP(sp_i) = TSP(sp_j)] \qquad (29)$$

where $[\cdot]$ is the indicator function and N_k is the number of superpixels within the node V_k (which can be either segmentation or reconstruction). This term prefers keeping the superpixels that have same ID in the whole trajectory.

5.4 Entrance and Exit Probabilities P_{en} and P_{ex}

The entrance and exit probabilities of one node (segmentation or reconstruction) measure the probability of a trajectory to start and terminate at this node. Similar to [18], we assume these probabilities are positive when (1) the position of the node is close enough to the image border, (2) the size of the node is about the minimum detection size of the object detector and (3) all nodes in the first frame and the last frame have a high entrance probability and exit probability, respectively. Otherwise the entrance and exit probabilities are 0.

6 Experiments

6.1 Tracking

Dataset. For the evaluation of tracking performance, we test our algorithm on the widely used PETS 2010 Benchmark [13] including S2L1, S2L2, S2L3, S1L2. The sequences in benchmark show variable pedestrian densities and dynamic behaviors. Many inter-object and long term occlusions exist in the dataset, which makes it very challenging for detection and multiple targets tracking. Moreover, the frame rate of PETS 2010 is only 7 frames per second, this means far object movement between two consecutive frames, making precise tracking even more challenging.

Evaluation Metrics. We use the same detection result as in [18] and the public available ground truth in [2,18]. As in [26,32], the Hungarian algorithm is employed to assign tracking output to the ground truth. For tracking precision and recall, we report the frequently used CLEAR MOT metrics in [7], including Multiple Object Tracking Accuracy (MOTA) and Multiple Object Tracking Precision (MOTP). We also quote three popular metrics proposed in [24]: mostly tracked (MT, > 80 % overlap), mostly lost (ML, < 20 % overlap), partly tracked (PT). These metrics show the temporal coverage of truth trajectories by the algorithm.

Settings. Although our algorithm supports arbitrary number of views, we report our results for using one to three views for every video sequence. We also employ

Table 1. Quantitative tracking results on PETS 2010 dataset. Evaluations are compared to cl2 [15], DP [31], DCO [27], SegTrack [25].

Sequence	Method	Camera IDs	MOTA(%)	MOTP(%)	MT(%)	PT(%)	ML(%)
PETS S2L1	cl2	1	52.6	72.8	31.6	63.2	5.2
	DP	1	79.9	74.6	89.5	10.5	**0.0**
	DCO	1	90.3	74.2	**94.7**	**5.3**	**0.0**
	SegTrack	1	85.8	75.5	**94.7**	**5.3**	**0.0**
	our	1	**99.0**	**80.4**	83.3	16.7	**0.0**
	our	1+3	98.0	79.2	83.3	16.7	**0.0**
	our	1+3+4	98.0	78.6	83.3	16.7	**0.0**
PETS S2L2	cl2	1	20.5	68.6	0.0	58.1	41.9
	DP	1	34.5	61.3	0.0	**76.7**	23.3
	DCO	1	58.2	59.8	25.6	72.1	2.3
	SegTrack	1	63.3	58.0	51.2	48.8	**0.0**
	our	1	70.6	68.5	68.6	28.6	2.8
	our	1+2	**81.7**	68.7	**77.1**	20.0	2.9
	our	1+2+3	75.6	**68.9**	62.9	34.3	2.8
PETS S2L3	cl2	1	21.8	68.9	4.5	43.2	52.3
	DP	1	31.3	64.9	15.9	36.4	47.7
	DCO	1	40.1	65.3	18.2	38.6	43.2
	SegTrack	1	50.0	62.3	29.5	38.6	31.9
	our	1	60.5	70.9	50.0	40.9	**9.1**
	our	1+2	**69.0**	**71.6**	**56.8**	22.7	20.5
	our	1+2+4	65.1	71.2	43.2	**40.9**	15.9
PETS S1L2	cl2	1	27.1	59.5	4.8	**47.6**	47.6
	DP	1	19.9	64.2	4.8	38.1	57.1
	DCO	1	29.6	58.8	4.8	45.2	50.0
	SegTrack	1	36.9	54.5	21.4	45.2	33.4
	our	1	**66.7**	64.9	**50.0**	16.7	33.3
	our	1+2	46.8	**67.9**	33.3	41.7	**25.0**

the sliding window, which is the commonly used methodology to process video sequences with arbitrary length. In our experiments, we use a sliding window of 50 frames, with an overlap of 9 frames. The result of the whole sequence is obtained by Hungarian algorithm [30], matching trajectories between adjacent windows.

Next we set the parameters that are required by the model for all the scenarios. These parameters are intuitive and we report the set of parameters which has best performance in our experiments.

The average detection box inaccuracy ε_{det} is set to be 4px and the expected calibration error ε_{cal} is 0.5 m. We choose false negative rate $\gamma = 0.3$ to cope with different densities of scenarios. The maximum color deviation in LAB color space is set to $\varepsilon_{Lab} = 50$. The expected segmentation ratio α is 0.8.

The maximal walking speed of a person is limited to $v_{max} = 5\,\mathrm{m/s}$, making it possible to track a running person. The maximum frame gap is set to $\delta\tau_{max} = 9$. A higher frame gap results to more transition connections in the graph and higher computational cost, a lower frame gap reduces performance.

The boundary of the scene is set to $d_{b,max} = 1$. For all enter and exit probabilities, we set the maximum value to $P_{en,max} = P_{ex,max} = 0.1$.

6.2 Segmentation

We evaluate the segmentation performance on PETS-S2L2 sequence. This scenario has a medium person density and contains many target occlusions, which makes it very challenging for object segmentation. We report the following error metrics: the clustering error (percentage of misclassified pixels, abbreviated cl. err.), the per-region error (average ratio of false labeling of pixels per ground truth mask, abbreviated per-reg. err.), the number of segments that cover each mask (abbreviated over-seg.) and the number of extracted objects (of which 90 % area is correctly segmented, abbreviated extr. obj.).

Table 2. Quantitative segmentation results on PETS S2L2 scenario compared to TSP [11], Greedy [25] and SegTrack [25].

Method	cl. err	per-reg. err	over-seg	extr. obj
TSP	4.03	29.3	**1.17**	5
Greedy	4.13	25.63	**1.17**	7
SegTrack	**3.56**	**24.34**	1.42	7
our	4.48	25.96	1.26	**8**

Table 3. Runtime (in seconds) of the CPLEX solver on an i5 2.6 Ghz, 4 GB RAM.

Scenario	S2L1	S2L2	S2L3	S1L2
Length	50	50	50	50
1 view	7	18	21	7
2 views	12	54	56	13
3 views	29	274	216	-

6.3 Results and Discussion

The qualitative results are shown in Fig. 2. The quantitative tracking results compared to other methods are shown in Table 1. It can be seen that the proposed algorithm outperforms all the previous methods in MOTA (accuracy) and MOTP (precision). In most cases, the introduction of additional cameras improves the overall tracking performance. For example, using two cameras in S2L3 dataset, where many long-term occlusions exist, the tracking accuracy (MOTA) is significantly improved. However, the accuracy goes down when the number of used cameras continues to increase due to the accumulation of calibration errors of cameras as well as the color errors of different cameras. This phenomenon has a greater influence on crowded scenarios and leads to assignment errors.

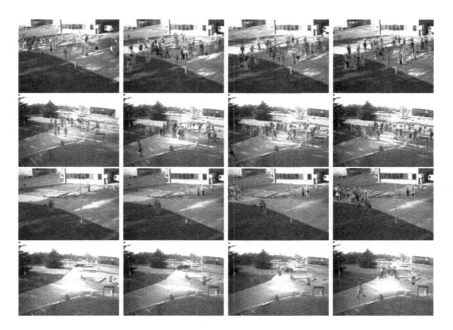

Fig. 2. Qualitative results on PETS 2010 with two cameras; the first and second rows show the results of the first and second views of the S2L2 dataset; The third and forth rows show the results of the first and second views of the S2L3 dataset; solid boxes represent the detected and segmented targets and dotted boxes represent the occluded but reconstructed targets.

The qualitative segmentation evaluation results are summarized in Table 2. Combined video segmentation, reconstruction and tracking in multi-view environment is very challenging. Compared to other three baselines which only manage to segment in a single view, we obtain very close performance, while our task is more complex: segment, track and reconstruct with multiple views.

The runtime of the algorithm on different scenarios and with different numbers of views is shown in Table 3. The computational cost rises with the increasing density of scenario. It can be seen that on the simple scenarios S2L1 and S1L2, the algorithm runs in less time than the scenario length. For other scenarios, the runtime with 2 views is close to the scenario length.

7　Conclusion

In this paper, we have proposed a novel algorithm that for the first time address the problem of joint segmentation, reconstruction and tracking of multiple targets in multi-view video sequences. In contrast to previous works that accomplished either segmentation-tracking or reconstruction-tracking, we accomplish these tasks at the same time using a global optimization framework. We cast the problem into a cost flow graph whose vertices are the superpixels extracted from target detection boxes and whose edges represent the cost of possible associations. We utilized binary integer programming to find the minimum trajectory from source to target of the graph. The obtained optimal superpixel association simultaneously provides segmentation, reconstruction, and tracking of targets. The experimental results confirmed that our algorithm outperforms other algorithms in tracking while segmentation results are comparable to them. Future work should consider some other visual cues such as optical flow into optimization framework to improve the segmentation results by introducing new constraints between superpixels. Furthermore, we currently extract superpixels from detection boxes which could be extended to extracting them from whole images.

References

1. Andriluka, M., Roth, S., Schiele, B.: People-tracking-by-detection and people-detection-by-tracking. In: 2008 IEEE Conference on Computer Vision and Pattern Recognition (CVPR), pp. 1–8 (2008)
2. Andriyenko, A., Roth, S., Schindler, K.: An analytical formulation of global occlusion reasoning for multi-target tracking. In: 2011 IEEE International Conference on Computer Vision (ICCV), pp. 1839–1846 (2011)
3. Andriyenko, A., Schindler, K., Roth, S.: Discrete-continuous optimization for multi-target tracking. In: 2012 IEEE Conference on Computer Vision and Pattern Recognition (CVPR), pp. 1926–1933 (2012)
4. Ben Shitrit, H., Berclaz, J., Fleuret, F., Fua, P.: Tracking multiple people under global appearance constraints. In: 2011 IEEE International Conference on Computer Vision (ICCV), pp. 137–144 (2011)
5. Berclaz, J., Fleuret, F., Fua, P.: Multiple object tracking using flow linear programming. In: 2009 IEEE International Workshop on Performance Evaluation of Tracking and Surveillance (PETS-Winter), pp. 1–8 (2009)
6. Berclaz, J., Fleuret, F., Türetken, E., Fua, P.: Multiple object tracking using k-shortest paths optimization. IEEE Trans. Pattern Anal. Mach. Intell. (PAMI) **33**(9), 1806–1819 (2011)
7. Bernardin, K., Stiefelhagen, R.: Evaluating multiple object tracking performance: the clear mot metrics. EURASIP J. Image Video Process. 2008, 1–10 (2008)
8. Bibby, C., Reid, I.: Real-time tracking of multiple occluding objects using level sets. In: 2010 IEEE Conference on Computer Vision and Pattern Recognition (CVPR) (2010)
9. Brox, T., Malik, J.: Object segmentation by long term analysis of point trajectories. In: Daniilidis, K., Maragos, P., Paragios, N. (eds.) ECCV 2010, Part V. LNCS, vol. 6315, pp. 282–295. Springer, Heidelberg (2010)

10. Butt, A., Collins, R.: Multi-target tracking by lagrangian relaxation to min-cost network flow. In: 2013 IEEE Conference on Computer Vision and Pattern Recognition (CVPR), pp. 1846–1853 (2013)
11. Chang, J., Wei, D., Fisher, J.: A video representation using temporal superpixels. In: 2013 IEEE Conference on Computer Vision and Pattern Recognition (CVPR), pp. 2051–2058 (2013)
12. Dehghan, A., Modiri Assari, S., Shah, M.: Gmmcp tracker: Globally optimal generalized maximum multi clique problem for multiple object tracking. In: 2015 IEEE Conference on Computer Vision and Pattern Recognition (CVPR), pp. 4091–4099 (2015)
13. Ferryman, J., Ellis, A.: Pets 2010: Dataset and challenge. In: 2010 Seventh IEEE International Conference on Advanced Video and Signal Based Surveillance (AVSS), pp. 143–150 (2010)
14. Fragkiadaki, K., Shi, J.: Detection free tracking: Exploiting motion and topology for segmenting and tracking under entanglement. In: 2011 IEEE Conference on Computer Vision and Pattern Recognition (CVPR), pp. 2073–2080 (2011)
15. Fragkiadaki, K., Zhang, W., Zhang, G., Shi, J.: Two-granularity tracking: mediating trajectory and detection graphs for tracking under occlusions. In: Fitzgibbon, A., Lazebnik, S., Perona, P., Sato, Y., Schmid, C. (eds.) ECCV 2012, Part V. LNCS, vol. 7576, pp. 552–565. Springer, Heidelberg (2012)
16. Galasso, F., Keuper, M., Brox, T., Schiele, B.: Spectral graph reduction for efficient image and streaming video segmentation. In: 2014 IEEE Conference on Computer Vision and Pattern Recognition (CVPR), pp. 49–56 (2014)
17. Hofmann, M., Haag, M., Rigoll, G.: Unified hierarchical multi-object tracking using global data association. In: 2013 IEEE International Workshop on Performance Evaluation of Tracking and Surveillance (PETS), pp. 22–28 (2013)
18. Hofmann, M., Wolf, D., Rigoll, G.: Hypergraphs for joint multi-view reconstruction and multi-object tracking. In: 2013 IEEE Conference on Computer Vision and Pattern Recognition (CVPR), pp. 3650–3657 (2013)
19. Horbert, E., Rematas, K., Leibe, B.: Level-set person segmentation and tracking with multi-region appearance models and top-down shape information. In: 2011 IEEE International Conference on Computer Vision (ICCV), pp. 1871–1878 (2011)
20. Jiang, H., Fels, S., Little, J.J.: A linear programming approach for multiple object tracking. In: 2007 IEEE Conference on Computer Vision and Pattern Recognition (CVPR), pp. 1–8 (2007)
21. Leal-Taixé, L., Fenzi, M., Kuznetsova, A., Rosenhahn, B., Savarese, S.: Learning an image-based motion context for multiple people tracking. In: 2014 IEEE Conference on Computer Vision and Pattern Recognition (CVPR), pp. 3542–3549 (2014)
22. Leal-Taixé, L., Pons-Moll, G., Rosenhahn, B.: Branch-and-price global optimization for multi-view multi-target tracking. In: 2012 IEEE Conference on Computer Vision and Pattern Recognition (CVPR), pp. 1987–1994 (2012)
23. Leibe, B., Schindler, K., Van Gool, L.: Coupled detection and trajectory estimation for multi-object tracking. In: 2007 IEEE International Conference on Computer Vision (ICCV), pp. 1–8 (2007)
24. Li, Y., Huang, C., Nevatia, R.: Learning to associate: Hybridboosted multi-target tracker for crowded scene. In: 2009 IEEE Conference on Computer Vision and Pattern Recognition (CVPR), pp. 2953–2960 (2009)
25. Milan, A., Leal-Taixé, L., Schindler, K., Reid, I.: Joint tracking and segmentation of multiple targets. In: 2015 IEEE Conference on Computer Vision and Pattern Recognition (CVPR), pp. 5397–5406 (2015)

26. Milan, A., Roth, S., Schindler, K.: Continuous energy minimization for multitarget tracking. IEEE Trans. Pattern Anal. Mach. Intell. (PAMI) **36**(1), 58–72 (2014)
27. Milan, A., Schindler, K., Roth, S.: Detection-and trajectory-level exclusion in multiple object tracking. In: 2013 IEEE Conference on Computer Vision and Pattern Recognition (CVPR), pp. 3682–3689 (2013)
28. Mitzel, D., Horbert, E., Ess, A., Leibe, B.: Multi-person tracking with sparse detection and continuous segmentation. In: Daniilidis, K., Maragos, P., Paragios, N. (eds.) ECCV 2010, Part I. LNCS, vol. 6311, pp. 397–410. Springer, Heidelberg (2010)
29. Park, C., Woehl, T.J., Evans, J.E., Browning, N.D.: Minimum cost multi-way data association for optimizing multitarget tracking of interacting objects. IEEE Trans. Pattern Anal. Mach. Intell. (PAMI) **37**(3), 611–624 (2015)
30. Perera, A.A., Srinivas, C., Hoogs, A., Brooksby, G., Hu, W.: Multi-object tracking through simultaneous long occlusions and split-merge conditions. In: 2006 IEEE Computer Society Conference on Computer Vision and Pattern Recognition (CVPR), vol. 1, pp. 666–673 (2006)
31. Pirsiavash, H., Ramanan, D., Fowlkes, C.C.: Globally-optimal greedy algorithms for tracking a variable number of objects. In: 2011 IEEE Conference on Computer Vision and Pattern Recognition (CVPR), pp. 1201–1208 (2011)
32. Yang, B., Nevatia, R.: An online learned crf model for multi-target tracking. In: 2012 IEEE Conference on Computer Vision and Pattern Recognition (CVPR), pp. 2034–2041 (2012)
33. Roshan Zamir, A., Dehghan, A., Shah, M.: GMCP-tracker: global multi-object tracking using generalized minimum clique graphs. In: Fitzgibbon, A., Lazebnik, S., Perona, P., Sato, Y., Schmid, C. (eds.) ECCV 2012, Part II. LNCS, vol. 7573, pp. 343–356. Springer, Heidelberg (2012)
34. Zhang, L., Li, Y., Nevatia, R.: Global data association for multi-object tracking using network flows. In: 2008 IEEE Conference on Computer Vision and Pattern Recognition (CVPR), pp. 1–8 (2008)

LCrowdV: Generating Labeled Videos for Simulation-Based Crowd Behavior Learning

Ernest Cheung[1](✉), Tsan Kwong Wong[1], Aniket Bera[1],
Xiaogang Wang[2], and Dinesh Manocha[1]

[1] The University of North Carolina at Chapel Hill, Chapel Hill, USA
{ernestc,ahtsans,ab,dm}@cs.unc.edu
[2] The Chinese University of Hong Kong, Hong Kong, China
xgwang@ee.cuhk.edu.hk
http://gamma.cs.unc.edu/LCrowdV

Abstract. We present a novel procedural framework to generate an arbitrary number of labeled crowd videos (LCrowdV). The resulting crowd video datasets are used to design accurate algorithms or training models for crowded scene understanding. Our overall approach is composed of two components: a procedural simulation framework for generating crowd movements and behaviors, and a procedural rendering framework to generate different videos or images. Each video or image is automatically labeled based on the environment, number of pedestrians, density, behavior (agent personality), flow, lighting conditions, viewpoint, noise, etc. Furthermore, we can increase the realism by combining synthetically-generated behaviors with real-world background videos. We demonstrate the benefits of LCrowdV over prior labeled crowd datasets, by augmenting real dataset with it and improving the accuracy in pedestrian detection. LCrowdV has been made available as an online resource.

Keywords: Crowd analysis · Pedestrian detection · Crowd behaviors · Crowd datasets · Crowd simulation · Crowd rendering

1 Introduction

The accessibility of commodity cameras has lead to wide availability of crowd videos. In particular, videos of crowds consisting of tens or hundreds (or more) of human agents or pedestrians are increasingly becoming available on the internet, e.g. YouTube. One of the main challenges in computer vision and related areas is crowded scene understanding or crowd video analysis. There are a range of sub-problems in crowd understanding and analysis, including crowd behavior analysis, crowd tracking, crowd segmentation, crowd counting, abnormal behavior detection, crowd prediction, etc.

The problems related to crowded scene understanding have been extensively studied. Many solutions for each of these sub-problems have been developed by using crowd video datasets [1–5] along with different techniques for computing robust features or learning the models. However, most of these datasets are

© Springer International Publishing Switzerland 2016
G. Hua and H. Jégou (Eds.): ECCV 2016 Workshops, Part II, LNCS 9914, pp. 709–727, 2016.
DOI: 10.1007/978-3-319-48881-3_50

limited, either in terms of different crowd behavior or scenarios, or the accuracy of the labels.

Machine learning methods, including deep learning, usually require a large set of labeled data to avoid overfitting and to compute accurate results. A large fraction of crowd videos available on the Internet are not labeled or do not have ground truth or accurate information about the features. There are many challenges that arise in terms of using these Internet crowd videos for scene understanding:

- The process of labeling the videos is manual and can be very time consuming.
- There may not be a sufficient number of videos available for certain crowd behaviors (e.g., panic evaluation from a large building or stadium) or for certain cultures (e.g., crowd gatherings in remote villages in the developing world). Most Internet-based videos are limited to popular locations or events.
- The classification process is subject to the socio-cultural background of the human observers and their intrinsic biases. This can result in inconsistent labels for similar behaviors.
- In videos corresponding to medium and high density crowds, it is rather difficult to count the number of pedestrians exactly or classify their behaviors or tracks. This complexity is highlighted in one of the sample images in the UCF Crowd counting dataset [6], shown in Fig. 3. Similar problems can arise in noisy videos or the ones recorded in poor lighting conditions.

In this paper, we present a new approach to procedurally generate a very large number of labeled, synthetic crowd videos for crowded scene understanding. Our approach is motivated by prior use of synthetic datasets in computer vision for different applications, including pedestrian detection [3,7], recognizing articulated objects from a single image [8], multi-view car detection [9,10], 3D indoor scene understanding [11], etc. In some cases, models trained using synthetic datasets can outperform models trained on real scene-specific data, when labeled real-world data is limited.

Main Results: We present a novel procedural framework to generate labeled crowd videos (LCrowdV). Our approach consists of two main components: procedural simulation and procedural rendering. Given a set of parameters or labels, our procedural framework can automatically generate an arbitrary number of crowd videos. These labels correspond to different indoor or outdoor environments, number of pedestrians, pedestrian density, crowd behaviors, lighting conditions, noise, camera location, abnormal behaviors, etc.

Our approach can be used to generate an arbitrary number of crowd videos or images (e.g. millions) by varying these classification parameters. Furthermore, we automatically generate a large number of labels for each image or video. The quality of each video, in terms of noise and resolution, can also be controlled using our procedural renderer. The generation of each video frame only takes a few milliseconds on a single CPU core. And the entire generation process can be easily parallelized on a large number of machines or servers, by running different instance of the framework on different machine.

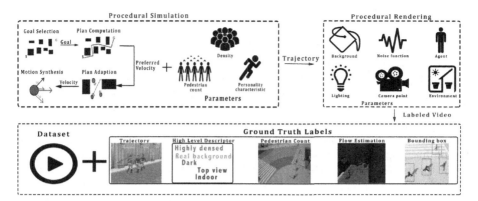

Fig. 1. LCrowdV framework consists of two components: procedural simulation (top left) and procedural renderer (top right). There are several parameters as show in the figure can be adjusted during the Procedural Simulation and Procedural Rendering to produce videos with a range of variety. Each final video/image consists of a number of ground truth labels (bottom). Our approach can automatically generate different videos with accurate labels.

We demonstrate the benefits of LCrowdV over prior labeled crowd video datasets on the following applications:

- **Improved Pedestrian Detection using HOG+SVM:** We demonstrate that combining LCrowdV with a few real world annotated videos can improve the average precision by 3 %. In particular, the variations in the camera angle in the LCrowdV dataset have the maximal impact on the accuracy. Instead of 70 K labeled real-world videos, we only use 1 K annotated real-world videos along with LCrowdV to get improved accuracy.
- **Improved Pedestrian Detection using Faster R-CNN:** We demonstrate that combining LCrowdV with a few real world annotated videos can improve the average precision by 7.3 %. Furthermore, we only use 50 labeled samples from the real-world dataset and combine them with LCrowdV.

The rest of the paper is organized as follows. We give a brief overview of prior work on crowd analysis and crowd datasets in Sect. 2. We describe our procedural framework in Sect. 3 and highlight its benefits for pedestrian detection in Sect. 4.

2   Related Work

The simulation, observation and analysis of crowd behaviors have been extensively studied in computer graphics and animation, social sciences, robotics, computer vision, and pedestrian dynamics [12]. In this section, we give a brief overview of recent work on crowd video analysis, classification, labeling, and prior crowd datasets.

2.1   Crowd Video Analysis

Different models have been proposed to model the crowd behaviors [13–19]. Other methods focus on extracting specific features in crowds, including head counting [2,20–24]. Online trackers tend to use the current, previous or recent frames for tracking each pedestrian in the video at interactive rates [6,25–27]. Tracking the pedestrians to obtain the full trajectories has been extensively studied [1,13,28,29]. There is considerable research on analyzing various crowd behaviors and movements from videos [30]. Most of these methods are designed for offline applications and tend to use a large number of training videos to learn the patterns [1,14,15,31,32]. Different methods have also been proposed to estimate the crowd flow in videos [4,33–35], model activities and interactions in crowded and complicated scenes [16,17,36]. There are also work that compare the performance of simulated data and real videos [37].

Many crowd analysis methods [13–17,33,36,38] tend to be scene specific, which implies that they are trained from a specific scene and haven't been tested in terms of generalizing the results across other scenes. One of the challenges is to find complete crowd datasets that include data samples covering enough scenes and behaviors, and provide labeled ground truth data for learning. Some methods [20,31,34] don't require real data for training, but they are limited by the size of the crowds or specific conditions, including crowd behaviors and color information.

2.2   Crowd Labeling

Crowd behaviors are diverse, and it is a major challenge to model different behaviors. The work described in [31] classified crowd behaviors in five categories in accordance with their dynamical behavior: bottlenecks, fountainheads, lane formation, ring/arch formation and blocking. Besides, the work described in [39] classified crowd behaviors into another five categories based on its dynamics: running, loitering, dispersal(center to edge), dispersal(edge to center) and formation. Interestingly, these two methods cannot cover all behaviors that are observed in crowd videos. Other methods focus on labeling the crowd data that can be described by a predefined set of labels [40–42]. Recently, the work described in [5] uses a model along with manually entered labels to classify crowds based on the location, the subject and the action. Our approach is motivated by these prior works on crowd labeling.

2.3   Crowd Video Datasets

Many crowd video datasets that are available can provide ground truth or estimated labels for analysis or training. the work [1] provides trajectories of the pedestrians, the work [2] describes a database with the number of pedestrians for crowd counting, [3] includes bounding boxes of the detected pedestrians, and the work [4] provides ground truth labels for crowd flow estimation. The work of Shao et al. [5] consists of high-level labels to describe crowd characteristics. Most

Table 1. Benefits of LCrowdV: Not only can we generate a significantly higher (or arbitrary) number of labeled videos, but we can also provide a large set of crowd labels and characteristics for each image and video. We can also control the behavior characteristics, environments, resolution and rendering quality of each video to develop a good training set. Unlike prior methods, we can easily generate accurate labels.

Dataset	CUHK [43]	Collectiveness [44]	Violence [45]	Data Driven [1]	UCF [6]	WWW [5]	CVC07 [46]	LCrowdV
Videos	474	413	246	212	46	10000	N/A	>1 M
Frames	60,384	40,796	22,074	121,626	18,196	> 8 M	2,534	>20 M
Resolution	Varying	670 × 1000	320 × 240	720 × 480	Varying	640 × 360	Varying	Any
Trajectory	×	×	×	✓	×	×	×	✓
Pedestrian count	×	×	×	×	×	×	×	✓
Flow estimation	×	×	×	×	✓	×	×	✓
Attributes	3	1	0	2	0	3	0	7
Bounding box	×	×	×	×	×	×	✓	✓
Generation Method	Manually						Automatically	

of these datasets are generated by labeling the data manually, and this process is time-consuming and error-prone. For example, to allow the deep learning model in [5] to understand the scenes and put appropriate labels, 19 human annotators were involved. Several human operators were needed for determining the number of objects in [2]. On the other hand, LCrowdV compute these labels automatically from the simulation, and therefore is not error-prone and much efficient. Table 1 shows the comparison of existing crowd datasets, as compared to LCrowdV.

2.4   Learning Crowd Behaviors with Simulated Data

The work described in [7] trained a pedestrian detector for a driver assistant system using simulated data. This work focused on the training and testing data from one particular camera angle, which corresponds to the driver's view. The work [3] generated simulated agents on a specific real-world background to enable learning for pedestrian detectors. In contrast with these methods, our work aims at providing a diversified, generic and comprehensive approach for generating different crowd video data for analyzing different crowd behaviors.

3   Synthetic Label Crowd Video Generation

Crowds are observed in different situations in the real-world, including indoor and outdoor scenarios. One of our goals is to develop a procedural framework that is capable of providing all types of crowd videos with appropriate ground truth labels. In this section, we give an overview of our framework and the various parameters used to generate the videos.

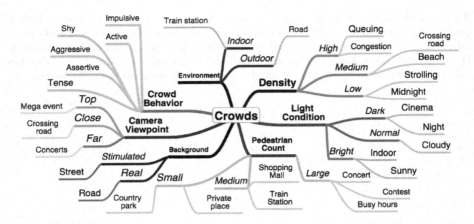

Fig. 2. Hierarchical and parametric classification of crowd behaviors and renderings. Attribute Labels of LCrowdV includes: Background, Crowd Behaviour (Personality), Camera Viewpoint, Density, Environment, Light Condition and Pedestrian Count. We use these labels to classify different characteristics of crowds and use them in our procedural framework. Note that the list above is not exhaustive, as we can further extends attribute like Density to medium-high, medium-low, etc.

3.1 Crowd Generator

Modeling the behavior of large, heterogeneous crowds is important in various domains including psychology, robotics, pedestrian dynamics, and computer graphics. There is more than a century of work in social sciences and psychology on observing and classifying crowds, starting from the pioneering work of Lebon [47]. Other social scientists have classified the crowds in terms of behaviors, size, and distributions [48]. According to *Convergence Theory*, crowd behavior is not a product of the crowd itself; rather it is carried into the crowd by the individuals [49]. These observations have been used to simulate different crowd behaviors and flows [50–52].

Our procedural crowd simulation framework builds on these prior observations in social sciences [53] and on simulation methods [54]. The overall hierarchical classification is shown in Fig. 2. Each of these labels is used to describe some attributes of the crowds or the pedestrians. In addition to the labels that govern the movements or trajectories of each agent or pedestrian, we also use a few labels that control the final rendering (e.g., lighting, camera position, brightness, field of view) of the crowd video by using appropriate techniques from computer graphics. Finally, we can also add some noise (e.g. Gaussian noise) to degrade the final rendered images, so that these images are similar to those captured using video cameras which actually have such type of noise.

Framework Design: Our framework has two major components: procedural simulation and procedural rendering. The procedural simulator takes as input the number of agents or pedestrians, densities, behavior (personality of agent

(a)   (b)   (c)

Fig. 3. (a) Generated using LCrowdV and consists of 858 agents. (c) From UCF dataset [6], it is very hard to accurately count the number of pedestrians or classify other characteristics such as density or behavior in this real-world image (i.e. generate accurate labels). In contrast, our method can automatically generate accurate labels as demonstrated in (b).

groups) and flow characteristics and computes the appropriate trajectories and movements of each agent corresponding to different frames. Given the position of each agent during each frame, the procedural renderer generates the image frames based on the different parameters that control the lighting conditions. Each of these input parameters corresponds to a label of the final video.

Procedural Crowd Simulation: In this section, we give an overview of our procedural crowd simulator. We use the Menge crowd simulation engine [55], which makes it possible to combine state-of-the-art crowd modeling techniques addressed in the previous section. In particular, we have picked ORCA [54] as our navigation algorithm. Given the labels or high-level descriptors, our method can generate crowd movements or behaviors that fit those descriptions. These include the total number of agents or pedestrians in the scene, their density over different parts of the environment or the scene, their global and local movements, and the behavior characteristics.

Global Crowd Characteristics: In the simulation stage, we vary the global parameters, including the personality settings of different agents, density, and the number of agents used to generate different types of trajectories. The number of agents will control how many pedestrians are in the scene, and the density factor decides whether or not the pedestrians would be located very close to each other. It is essential to include different levels of overlapping in the training data set to avoid overfitting. The personality parameters allow the crowd behavior to be more natural-looking.

Crowd Movement and Trajectory Generation: A key component is simulating the crowd or pedestrian movement. We build on prior research in crowd movement simulation [56,57] and use the property that movement specification can be decomposed into three major subproblems: agent goal selection, global plan computation, and local plan adaptation (see Fig. 1). We further elaborate on each of these components and give various possible solutions for each of these subproblems, based on the different crowd behavior classifier.

Goal Selection: In the goal selection module, we specify the high-level goal of each pedestrian. For example, the agent may want to go to a particular location in the scene or just visit a few areas, etc. It is expected that the goal can change across time and is affected by the intrinsic personalities or characteristics of the agents or the environmental factors. There is extensive literature on goal selection methods and we can use these methods in our procedural simulation framework [57,58].

Global Path Planning: Given the goal specification of each agent, we compute a collision-free trajectory to achieve that goal. The path-planning module is a high-level module that computes a preferred velocity or direction for each agent for a given time-step. We use techniques based on potential field methods, roadmaps, navigation meshes, and corridor methods [59–62].

Local Plan Adaptation: Since the path computed in the previous stage usually considers only the static obstacles, we need to adapt the plan to tackle the dynamic obstacles or other agents or pedestrians in the scene. We transform the preferred velocity computed into a feasible velocity that can avoid collisions in real time with multiple agents. Some of the commonly used motion models for local plan adaptation are based on social forces, rule-based methods, and reciprocal velocity obstacles [63–65].

Full Human Motion Computation: The main goal of high degree of freedom human motion computation or motion synthesis is to compute the locomotion or position of each agent in terms of the joint positions, corresponding to the walk cycle as well as to the motion of the head and upper body. We use standard techniques from computer animation based on kinematic, dynamics and control-based methods to generate the exact position of each pedestrian in the scene [66–68].

3.2   Procedural Rendering

After computing the trajectory or movement specification characterized by the global parameters for each pedestrian in the video, we generate an animation and render it using different parameters. We can control the lighting conditions, resolution, viewpoint, and the noise function to lower the image quality, as needed.

Animated Agent Models: We use a set of animated agent models, that include the gender, skin color, clothes and outlook. We randomly assign these models to every agent. Furthermore, we may associate some objects in the scene with each agent or pedestrian. For example, in the case of a shopping mall, a customer may carry items he or she bought in bags; and in a theme park, there may be parents walking along with the children. These attached items could potentially obstruct the agent and change its appearance.

3D Environments and Backgrounds: Our background scenes include both indoor and outdoor environments. Ideally, we can import any scene with a polygonal model representation and/or textures and use that to represent the environment. We can also vary the lighting conditions to model different weather conditions: a sunny day could have a huge difference in appearance compared to a gloomy day. On top of that, we can also add static and dynamic obstacles to model real world situations. For instance, we could add moving vehicles into a city map and animated trees into a countryside map.

Image-space Projection and Noise Functions: In order to render the 3D virtual world and the animated agent model, we render the image using a camera projection model: perspective projection or orthogonal projection. Typically, we render the videos with perspective projections to simulate real world videos. At this stage, we use different parameters to the projection model to obtain the videos captured from different viewpoints. In practice, video and images collected from different camera views could result in significant differences in the appearance. We also add a Gaussian noise filter with varying levels of standard deviation to emulate the digital noise in a video frame.

In our current implementation, we use the Unreal game engine [69] for rendering and generating each video frame. It is an open source engine and we can easily specify the geometric representation, lighting and rendering information, and generate images/videos at any resolution or add noise functions. We can easily adjust the different rendering parameters available in Unreal Engine to control the final crowd rendering.

3.3   Ground Truth Labels

The two main labels related to such datasets are the pedestrian count and the trajectory of each pedestrian. And a single video can provide both kind of labels or even more when the framework is extended in the future. This can be rather challenging for dense crowds, where generating such a labeled dataset is a major challenge. In order to accurately generate such labels, we consider each head of an agent in the video that is not obstructed by other scene objects. We compute the screen-space coordinates during each frame for every agent using the given camera parameters. We can also compute the position of lower body or full body contours. Given these head and lower body information, we can accurately compute the count and the trajectories.

Apart from the trajectories of the head, we also use the bounding boxes for pedestrian detection. Using the same technique mentioned above, we compute the bounding box for each pedestrian, which is centered at the centroid of the model used for each agent. This is more accurate than annotating the bounding boxes manually, especially for high density scenes.

Another major problem in crowd scene analysis is computing the crowd flows. The goal is to estimate the number of pedestrians crossing a particular region in the video. For real videos with dense pedestrian flows, it is difficult and labor intensive to compute such flow measures. This is due to the fact that there may

Labels

Fig. 4. Parameters used in LCrowdV: Samples of images that illustrate the effect of changing different high level parameters in the scene. These parameters are also used as the labels.

be partial occlusion and a human operator needs to review each frame multiple times to obtain this information accurately. On the other hand, we can easily count how many agents are crossing a line or a location in the scene. However, in some of the pedestrian videos, agents could walk around or over the counting line because of collision avoidance. If we can count every agent that crosses the line, this count could increase when an agent is close to the counting line or when an agent repeatedly crosses the line. Therefore, we define an agent as crossing the line only if it has passed a particular tolerance zone or region in the scene.

In addition to these labels corresponding to the tracks, bounding boxes, flows, etc. we also keep track of all the parameters used by the procedural framework, i.e. the seven different high level parameters. As mentioned in the previous section, we have generated the videos using seven different parameters. These parameters can be used to describe the video in a high level manner, as shown in Figs. 2 and 4.

4 Applications and Evaluation

In this section, we highlight the benefits of LCrowdV dataset for improved pedestrian detection.

Crowd Datasets: For our evaluations, we used many real-world datasets: INRIA [70], KITTI [71], ETHZ [72], and Town Center [73]. The INRIA dataset contains 1832 training and 741 testing sample images. We used the object detection dataset in KITTI Vision Benchmark Suite. As annotations are not provided in the test set, we divided the train set into two subsets: 1279 images for training and 500 images for verification. In the ETHZ dataset, trained with BAHNHOF (999 image frames) and JELMOLI (936 image frames) and tested on SUNNY

DAY (354 frames). The Town Center dataset is a 5 min video with 7500 frames annotated, which is divided into 6500 for training and 1000 for testing data for pedestrian detection. We have created a new dataset called Person Search Database (PSDB). This database consists of 18,184 images taken at different angles. Unlike the Town Center dataset, which consists of images at the same viewpoint and scene, the scenes in PSDB are more diverse, including shopping mall, roadside, University, park, etc. For behavior analysis, we evaluated the crowd motion trajectories of the pedestrians, as opposed to the actual appearance. For pedestrian detection, we use selected frames from the dataset.

4.1   Pedestrian Detector Evaluation

In this section, we highlight the benefit of using LCrowdV to train a learning algorithm and apply the results to pedestrian detection in real videos.

Pedestrian Detection using HOG+SVM: We compute the histogram of oriented gradients [70] on both positive and negative pedestrian samples in the training dataset as feature descriptor. We use a support vector machine to learn from these descriptors in order to determine whether or not a new image patch from the training dataset is a pedestrian or not. We refer to this method as HOG+SVM. In particular, our SVM detector is trained with OpenCV GPU HOG module and SVM light [70].

We trained numerous detectors by combining the real world datasets from INRIA [70], Town Center [73] and our synthetic data in LCrowdV. We used 10,000 images from our dataset in this experiment. We observe that the detectors that are trained by combining LCrowdV and the INRIA or Town Center datasets have higher accuracy as compared to only using the real world datasets (i.e. INRIA only or Town Center only). In these cases, LCrowdV improves the average precision by 3 %, though we observe higher accuracy for certain cases. We also evaluated two detectors which are trained using only limited samples: 50/500 positive + 50/500 negative, from the Town Center datasets and combined with LCrowdV. The results of the detectors trained by 500 + 500 samples are shown to be comparable to the results of the detector trained by the entire original dataset. These benchmarks and results demonstrate that one does not have to spend extensive effort in annotating 70 K image samples to train a detector, merely 1,000 annotations are sufficient and can be combined with our synthetic LCrowdV dataset. The results are shown in Fig. 5(a). In this case, the use of LCrowdV labeled data can significant improve detectors' accuracy over prior datasets shown in Table 1.

Varying LCrowdV Parameters: Our LCrowdV framework uses seven main parameters, as described in Figs. 2 and 4. We highlight the effect of using different parameters on the accuracy of our detector. We first train HOG+SVM using a set of synthetic dataset that is generated with variations all seven parameters. Next, we remove the variations in one parameter at a time and repeat the evaluation. The results are shown in Fig. 5(b).

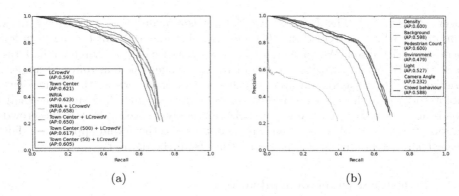

Fig. 5. Results of trained HOG+SVM detectors: (a) Trained using the realworld and augmented synthetic datasets (INRIA+LCrowdV, Town Center(Full)+LCrowdV, Town Center (500)+LCrowdV and Town Center (50)+LCrowdV)). The use of LCrowdV along with the real-world datasets can result in 3 % average precision improvement, as compared to prior results based on only real-world datasets. (b) Different LCrowdV training video datasets obtained by changing each parameter individually. We observe that the variation in the camera angle parameter has maximal impact on improving the accuracy.

Among the seven parameters, we observe that the variations in the camera angle parameter can affect the average precision by 36 %, as compared to the other parameters used in LCrowdV. While it is difficult to capture videos from multiple camera angles in real-world scenarios, it is rather simple to vary these parameters in LCrowdV. These results highlight the benefits of LCrowdV.

Pedestrian Detection using Faster R-CNN: Apart from HOG+SVM, we have also used LCrowdV to train the Faster Region-based Convolutional Network method (Faster R-CNN) [74], one of the state-of-the-art algorithms for object detection based on deep learning. R-CNN [75] is a convolutional neural network that makes use of region classification, and it has strong performance in terms of object detection. A variant, Fast R-CNN [76], combines several ideas to improve the training and testing speed while also increasing detection accuracy. We use a version of the Fast R-CNN algorithm that makes use of Region Proposal Network (RPN) to improve the performance, namely Faster R-CNN. The RPN makes use of a shared set of convolution layers with the Faster R-CNN network to save computation effort. In particular, we use the Simonyan and Zisserman model [77] (VGG-16) that is a very deep detection network and has 13 shareable convolutional layers. We adopt the Approximate joint training solution that makes it possible to merge RPN and Fast R-CNN network efficiently. In our implementation, we make use of the Caffe deep learning network [78], and we iteratively train the model until the performance converges at roughly 10 k to 30 k iterations.

We trained the model with an augmented dataset which combines both a small sample of Town Center dataset and LCrowdV, and then we use the model

to detect pedestrians on the Town Center dataset. The results are shown in
Fig. 6(a). With merely 50 samples annotated in the original Town Center dataset,
adding LCrowdV into the training set results in an average precision of 72 %,
which is 7.3 % better than the model trained with Town Center dataset only. In
addition, we also verify our results by combining LCrowdV with PSDB, KITTI,
ETHZ. For PSDB, the results are shown in Fig. 6(b) where the average precision
improvement of 6.4 % is observed in our combined training set, when comparing
to training with samples from PSDB only. In both experiments, we can observe
that as the sample size of LCrowdV increases, the performance of the model
becomes better.

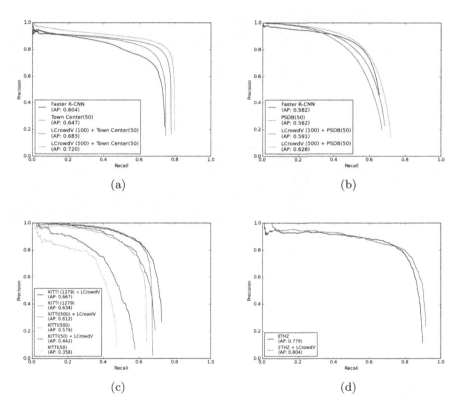

Fig. 6. Results of trained Faster R-CNN model with (a) Town Center dataset, (b)
PSDB, (c) KITTI, and (d) ETHZ, and the augmented version of the aforementioned
datasets using LCrowdV. The model trained with augmented dataset has an improvement in average precision up to 7.3 %, 6.4 %, 3.3 % and 2.5 % comparing to the model
trained with the original dataset for (a), (b), (c), and (d) respectively.

When we evaluate our results on KITTI, we vary the sample size of real
annotations to find out also its impact on the performance. When the number

of images with real annotations is {50, 125, 250, 500, 750, 1000, 1279}, the AP
of KITTI and KITTI+LCrowdV is {35.8, 48.1, 54.9, 57.9, 61.6, 62.0, 63.4}%
and {36.3, 48.9, 55.7, 58.6, 62.7, 64.9, 66.7}%, respectively. The summary of this
result is also shown in Fig. 6(c). We can see the complementary effect of LCrowdV
on the training is consistently beneficial as the sample size of real annotation
varies. We further evaluate the results on a cross-scene scenario using the ETHZ
dataset, the improvement of the model trained with combined data is 2.5 % as
shown in Fig. 6(d). Significant improvements are observed in the detection results
for KITI and ETHZ are also shown in Fig. 7.

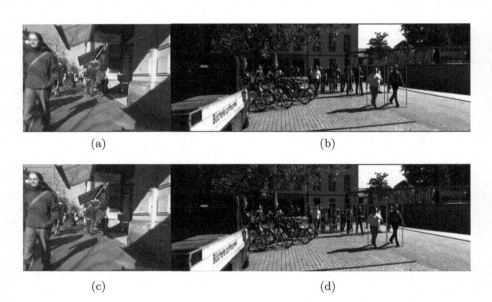

(a)   (b)

(c)   (d)

Fig. 7. Detection results of CNN trained using (a) ETHZ only, (b) KITTI only, (c)
ETHZ+LCrowdV, (d) KITTI+LCrowdV. The alpha channel of the bounding box represents the confidence of the detection.

The results from both techniques for pedestrian detection mentioned above
demonstrate that by combining a small set of samples from the same scene as
the test data with LCrowdV, we can improve the detector/deep model results
significantly.

5   Limitations, Conclusion and Future Work

We have presented a novel approach to generate labeled crowd videos (LCrowdV)
using procedural modeling and rendering techniques. The main benefit of our
parametric approach of procedural crowd simulation is that: our formulation is
general and can be used to include arbitrary numbers of pedestrians, density,

behaviors, flows, rendering conditions, and vary the resolution of the images or video. Compared to prior crowd datasets, our synthetic methods can generate a significantly larger collection of crowd videos with accurate labels or ground truth data in a much easier way. We have demonstrated the benefits of LCrowdV in augmenting real world dataset for pedestrian detections.

Our approach has a few limitations. The current simulation methods may not be able to capture all the details or subtle aspects of human behaviors or movements in certain situations. Our current rendering framework uses the capabilities of Unreal game engine, which may not be able to accurately render many outdoor effects. In particular, we want to improve the trajectory by learning from real videos [19]; and rendering quality using global illumination, data-driven, and full-body animation methods [79]. In terms of future work, we would like to overcome these limitations. We would like to continue investigating how to improve machine learning algorithms in related to crowds, including crowd counting, tracking, abnormal behavior detection, crowd behaviour classification, crowd segmentation and etc. We would also like to include traffic in these videos and generate datasets corresponding to human-vehicle interactions. We also have made the LCrowdV dataset available as an online resource.

Acknowledgements. This work is supported in part by ARO grant W911NF-16-1-0085 and Boeing. We are grateful to Sean Curtis and Andrew Best for their help with Menge and UnReal rendering engine.

References

1. Rodriguez, M., Sivic, J., Laptev, I., Audibert, J.Y.: Data-driven crowd analysis in videos. In: 2011 International Conference on Computer Vision, pp. 1235–1242, November 2011
2. Rabaud, V., Belongie, S.: Counting crowded moving objects. In: 2006 IEEE Computer Society Conference on Computer Vision and Pattern Recognition, vol. 1, pp. 705–711. IEEE (2006)
3. Hattori, H., Boddeti, V.N., Kitani, K., Kanade, T.: Learning scene-specific pedestrian detectors without real data. In: Proceedings of the IEEE Conference on Computer Vision and Pattern Recognition, pp. 3819–3827 (2015)
4. Ozturk, O., Yamasaki, T., Aizawa, K.: Detecting dominant motion flows in unstructured/structured crowd scenes. In: 2010 20th International Conference on Pattern Recognition (ICPR), pp. 3533–3536, August 2010
5. Shao, J., Kang, K., Loy, C.C., Wang, X.: Deeply learned attributes for crowded scene understanding. In: 2015 IEEE Conference on Computer Vision and Pattern Recognition (CVPR), pp. 4657–4666, June 2015
6. Ali, S., Shah, M.: A lagrangian particle dynamics approach for crowd flow segmentation and stability analysis. In: IEEE Conference on Computer Vision and Pattern Recognition, CVPR 2007, pp. 1–6, June 2007
7. Marn, J., Vzquez, D., Gernimo, D., Lpez, A.M.: Learning appearance in virtual scenarios for pedestrian detection. In: 2010 IEEE Conference on Computer Vision and Pattern Recognition (CVPR), pp. 137–144, June 2010
8. Dhome, M., Yassine, A., Lavest, J.M.: Determination of the pose of an articulated object from a single perspective view. In: BMVC, pp. 1–10 (1993)

9. Movshovitz-Attias, Y., Boddeti, V.N., Wei, Z., Sheikh, Y.: 3d pose-by-detection of vehicles via discriminatively reduced ensembles of correlation filters. In: British Machine Vision Conference (2014)

10. Pepik, B., Stark, M., Gehler, P., Schiele, B.: Teaching 3D geometry to deformable part models. In: 2012 IEEE Conference on Computer Vision and Pattern Recognition (CVPR), pp. 3362–3369, June 2012

11. Satkin, S., Lin, J., Hebert, M.: Data-driven scene understanding from 3D models (2012)

12. Ali, S., Nishino, K., Manocha, D., Shah, M.: Modeling, Simulation and Visual Analysis of Crowds: A Multidisciplinary Perspective. Springer, New York (2013)

13. Zhou, B., Wang, X., Tang, X.: Understanding collective crowd behaviors: learning a mixture model of dynamic pedestrian-agents. In: 2012 IEEE Conference on Computer Vision and Pattern Recognition (CVPR), pp. 2871–2878, June 2012

14. Hospedales, T., Gong, S., Xiang, T.: A markov clustering topic model for mining behaviour in video. In: 2009 IEEE 12th International Conference on Computer Vision, pp. 1165–1172. IEEE (2009)

15. Mehran, R., Oyama, A., Shah, M.: Abnormal crowd behavior detection using social force model. In: IEEE Conference on Computer Vision and Pattern Recognition, CVPR 2009, pp. 935–942, June 2009

16. Chan, A., Vasconcelos, N.: Modeling, clustering, and segmenting video with mixtures of dynamic textures. IEEE Trans. Pattern Anal. Mach. Intell. **30**(5), 909–926 (2008)

17. Wang, X., Ma, X., Grimson, W.: Unsupervised activity perception in crowded and complicated scenes using hierarchical bayesian models. IEEE Trans. Pattern Anal. Mach. Intell. **31**(3), 539–555 (2009)

18. Bera, A., Kim, S., Manocha, D.: Realtime anomaly detection using trajectory-level crowd behavior learning. In: Proceedings of the IEEE Conference on Computer Vision and Pattern Recognition Workshops, pp. 50–57 (2016)

19. Kim, S., Bera, A., Manocha, D.: Interactive crowd content generation and analysis using trajectory-level behavior learning. In: IEEE International Symposium on Multimedia (ISM) 2015, pp. 21–26. IEEE (2015)

20. Xu, H., Lv, P., Meng, L.: A people counting system based on head-shoulder detection and tracking in surveillance video. In: 2010 International Conference on Computer Design and Applications (ICCDA), vol. 1, V1-394–V1-398, June 2010

21. Antonini, G., Thiran, J.P.: Counting pedestrians in video sequences using trajectory clustering. IEEE Trans. Circ. Syst. Video Technol. **16**(8), 1008–1020 (2006)

22. Garcia-Bunster, G., Torres-Torriti, M.: A density-based approach for effective pedestrian counting at bus stops. In: IEEE International Conference on Systems, Man and Cybernetics, SMC 2009, pp. 3434–3439. IEEE (2009)

23. Idrees, H., Saleemi, I., Seibert, C., Shah, M.: Multi-source multi-scale counting in extremely dense crowd images. In: 2013 IEEE Conference on Computer Vision and Pattern Recognition (CVPR), pp. 2547–2554, June 2013

24. Zhang, C., Li, H., Wang, X., Yang, X.: Cross-scene crowd counting via deep convolutional neural networks. In: 2015 IEEE Conference on Computer Vision and Pattern Recognition (CVPR), pp. 833–841, June 2015

25. Zhang, K., Zhang, L., Yang, M.-H.: Real-time compressive tracking. In: Fitzgibbon, A., Lazebnik, S., Perona, P., Sato, Y., Schmid, C. (eds.) ECCV 2012, Part III. LNCS, vol. 7574, pp. 864–877. Springer, Heidelberg (2012)

26. Fu, W., Wang, J., Li, Z., Lu, H., Ma, S.: Learning semantic motion patterns for dynamic scenes by improved sparse topical coding. In: IEEE International Conference on Multimedia and Expo (ICME), pp. 296–301 (2012)

27. Song, X., Shao, X., Zhang, Q., Shibasaki, R., Zhao, H., Cui, J., Zha, H.: A fully online and unsupervised system for large and high-density area surveillance: tracking, semantic scene learning and abnormality detection. ACM Trans. Intell. Syst. Technol. **4**(2), 35:1–35:21 (2013). http://dl.acm.org/citation.cfm?id=2438670

28. Ali, S., Shah, M.: Floor fields for tracking in high density crowd scenes. In: Forsyth, D., Torr, P., Zisserman, A. (eds.) ECCV 2008, Part II. LNCS, vol. 5303, pp. 1–14. Springer, Heidelberg (2008)

29. Zhu, F., Wang, X., Yu, N.: Crowd tracking with dynamic evolution of group structures. In: Fleet, D., Pajdla, T., Schiele, B., Tuytelaars, T. (eds.) ECCV 2014, Part VI. LNCS, vol. 8694, pp. 139–154. Springer, Heidelberg (2014)

30. Li, T., Chang, H., Wang, M., Ni, B., Hong, R., Yan, S.: Crowded scene analysis: a survey. IEEE Trans. Circ. Syst. Video Technol. **25**(3), 367–386 (2015)

31. Solmaz, B., Moore, B.E., Shah, M.: Identifying behaviors in crowd scenes using stability analysis for dynamical systems. IEEE Trans. Pattern Anal. Mach. Intell. **34**(10), 2064–2070 (2012)

32. Kratz, L., Nishino, K.: Anomaly detection in extremely crowded scenes using spatio-temporal motion pattern models. In: IEEE Conference on Computer Vision and Pattern Recognition, pp. 1446–1453. IEEE (2009)

33. Srivastava, S., Ng, K., Delp, E.: Crowd flow estimation using multiple visual features for scenes with changing crowd densities. In: 2011 8th IEEE International Conference on Advanced Video and Signal-Based Surveillance (AVSS), pp. 60–65, August 2011

34. Chen, T.H., Chen, T.Y., Chen, Z.X.: An intelligent people-flow counting method for passing through a gate. In: 2006 IEEE Conference on Robotics, Automation and Mechatronics, pp. 1–6. IEEE (2006)

35. Tsuduki, Y., Fujiyoshi, H.: A method for visualizing pedestrian traffic flow using SIFT feature point tracking. In: Wada, T., Huang, F., Lin, S. (eds.) PSIVT 2009. LNCS, vol. 5414, pp. 25–36. Springer, Heidelberg (2009). doi:10.1007/978-3-540-92957-4_3

36. Loy, C.C., Xiang, T., Gong, S.: Multi-camera activity correlation analysis. In: IEEE Conference on Computer Vision and Pattern Recognition, CVPR 2009, pp. 1988–1995, June 2009

37. Guy, S.J., Chhugani, J., Curtis, S., Dubey, P., Lin, M., Manocha, D.: Pledestrians: a least-effort approach to crowd simulation. In: Proceedings of the 2010 ACM SIGGRAPH/Eurographics Symposium on Computer Animation, pp. 119–128. Eurographics Association (2010)

38. Andrade, E., Blunsden, S., Fisher, R.: Modelling crowd scenes for event detection. In: 18th International Conference on Pattern Recognition, ICPR 2006, vol. 1, pp. 175–178 (2006)

39. Dee, H., Caplier, A.: Crowd behaviour analysis using histograms of motion direction. In: 2010 17th IEEE International Conference on Image Processing (ICIP), pp. 1545–1548, September 2010

40. Rodriguez, M.D., Ahmed, J., Shah, M.: Action mach a spatio-temporal maximum average correlation height filter for action recognition. In: IEEE Conference on Computer Vision and Pattern Recognition, CVPR 2008, pp. 1–8, June 2008

41. Reddy, K.K., Shah, M.: Recognizing 50 human action categories of web videos. Mach. Vis. Appl. **24**(5), 971–981 (2013)

42. Soomro, K., Zamir, A.R., Shah, M.: UCF101: a dataset of 101 human actions classes from videos in the wild. CoRR abs/1212.0402 (2012)

726   E. Cheung et al.

43. Shao, J., Loy, C., Wang, X.: Scene-independent group profiling in crowd. In: 2014 IEEE Conference on Computer Vision and Pattern Recognition (CVPR), pp. 2227–2234, June 2014
44. Zhou, B., Tang, X., Zhang, H., Wang, X.: Measuring crowd collectiveness. IEEE Trans. Pattern Anal. Mach. Intell. **36**(8), 1586–1599 (2014)
45. Hassner, T., Itcher, Y., Kliper-Gross, O.: Violent flows: real-time detection of violent crowd behavior. In: 2012 IEEE Computer Society Conference on Computer Vision and Pattern Recognition Workshops (CVPRW), pp. 1–6, June 2012
46. Xu, J., Vazquez, D., López, A.M., Marín, J., Ponsa, D.: Learning a part-based pedestrian detector in virtual world. IEEE Trans. Intell. Transp. Syst. **15**(5), 2121–2131 (2014)
47. Le Bon, G.: The Crowd: A Study of the Popular Mind. Macmillian, New York (1897)
48. James, J.: The distribution of free-forming small group size. Am. Sociol. Rev. **18**, 569–570 (1953)
49. Turner, R.H., Killian, L.M.: Collective behavior, pp. 1–14, 16 (1987)
50. Pervin, L.: The Science of Personality. Oxford University Press, New York (2003)
51. Moussaïd, M., Perozo, N., Garnier, S., Helbing, D., Theraulaz, G.: The walking behaviour of pedestrian social groups and its impact on crowd dynamics (2010)
52. Eysenck, H., Eysenck, M.: Personality and individual differences: a natural science perspective (1985)
53. Guy, S.J., Kim, S., Lin, M.C., Manocha, D.: Simulating heterogeneous crowd behaviors using personality trait theory. In: Proceedings of the 2011 ACM SIGGRAPH/Eurographics Symposium on Computer Animation, pp. 43–52. ACM (2011)
54. Van Den Berg, J., Guy, S.J., Lin, M., Manocha, D.: Reciprocal n-body collision avoidance. In: Pradalier, C., Siegwart, R., Hirzinger, G. (eds.) Robotics research, pp. 3–19. Springer, Heidelberg (2011)
55. Curtis, S., Best, A., Manocha, D.: Menge: a modular framework for simulating crowd movement. Collective Dyn. **1**, 1–40 (2016)
56. Funge, J., Tu, X., Terzopoulos, D.: Cognitive modeling: knowledge, reasoning and planning for intelligent characters. In: Proceedings of the 26th Annual Conference on Computer Graphics and Interactive Techniques, pp. 29–38. ACM Press/Addison-Wesley Publishing Co. (1999)
57. Ulicny, B., Thalmann, D.: Towards interactive real-time crowd behavior simulation. Comput. Graph. Forum **21**, 767–775 (2002). Wiley Online Library
58. Shao, W., Terzopoulos, D.: Autonomous pedestrians. In: Proceedings of the 2005 ACM SIGGRAPH/Eurographics Symposium on Computer Animation, pp. 19–28. ACM (2005)
59. Barraquand, J., Latombe, J.C.: Robot motion planning: a distributed representation approach. Int. J. Robot. Res. **10**(6), 628–649 (1991)
60. Snook, G.: Simplified 3d movement and pathfinding using navigation meshes. In DeLoura, M. (ed.) Game Programming Gems. pp. 288–304. Charles River Media (2000)
61. Lamarche, F., Donikian, S.: Crowd of virtual humans: a new approach for real time navigation in complex and structured environments. Comput. Graph. Forum **23**, 509–518 (2004). Wiley Online Library
62. Geraerts, R., Kamphuis, A., Karamouzas, I., Overmars, M.: Using the corridor map method for path planning for a large number of characters. In: Egges, A., Kamphuis, A., Overmars, M. (eds.) MIG 2008. LNCS, vol. 5277, pp. 11–22. Springer, Heidelberg (2008)

63. Reynolds, C.: Flocks, herds and schools: a distributed behavioral model. In: Proceedings of SIGGRAPH (1987)
64. Helbing, D., Molnar, P.: Social force model for pedestrian dynamics. Phys. Rev. E $51(5)$, 4282–4286 (1995)
65. van den Berg, J., Guy, S.J., Lin, M., Manocha, D.: Reciprocal n-body collision avoidance. In: Pradalier, C., Siegwart, R., Hirzinger, G. (eds.) Robotics Research. STAR, vol. 70, pp. 3–19. Springer, Heidelberg (2011)
66. Bruderlin, A., Calvert, T.W.: Goal-directed, dynamic animation of human walking. In: Proceedings of SIGGRAPH 1989, pp. 233–242 (1989)
67. Lee, K.H., Choi, M.G., Hong, Q., Lee, J.: Group behavior from video: a data-driven approach to crowd simulation. In: Symposium on Computer Animation, pp. 109–118 (2007)
68. van Basten, B.J.H., Stuvel, S.A., Egges, A.: A hybrid interpolation scheme for footprint-driven walking synthesis. In: Graphics Interface, pp. 9–16 (2011)
69. Oliver, P.: Unreal engine 4 elemental. In: ACM SIGGRAPH 2012 Computer Animation Festival, SIGGRAPH 2012, pp. 86–86. ACM, New York (2012)
70. Dalal, N., Triggs, B.: Histograms of oriented gradients for human detection. In: IEEE Computer Society Conference on Computer Vision and Pattern Recognition, CVPR 2005, vol. 1, pp. 886–893, June 2005
71. Geiger, A., Lenz, P., Urtasun, R.: Are we ready for autonomous driving? the kitti vision benchmark suite. In: 2012 IEEE Conference on Computer Vision and Pattern Recognition (CVPR), pp. 3354–3361, June 2012
72. Ess, A., Leibe, B., Schindler, K., Gool, L.V.: A mobile vision system for robust multi-person tracking. In: IEEE Conference on Computer Vision and Pattern Recognition, CVPR 2008, pp. 1–8, June 2008
73. Benfold, B., Reid, I.: Stable multi-target tracking in real-time surveillance video. In: 2011 IEEE Conference on Computer Vision and Pattern Recognition (CVPR), pp. 3457–3464, June 2011
74. Ren, S., He, K., Girshick, R., Sun, J.: Faster R-CNN: Towards real-time object detection with region proposal networks. In: Advances in Neural Information Processing Systems (NIPS) (2015)
75. Girshick, R., Donahue, J., Darrell, T., Malik, J.: Rich feature hierarchies for accurate object detection and semantic segmentation. In: Proceedings of the IEEE Conference on Computer Vision and Pattern Recognition, pp. 580–587 (2014)
76. Girshick, R.: Fast r-cnn. In: 2015 IEEE International Conference on Computer Vision (ICCV), pp. 1440–1448, December 2015
77. Simonyan, K., Zisserman, A.: Very deep convolutional networks for large-scale image recognition. CoRR abs/1409.1556 (2014)
78. Jia, Y., Shelhamer, E., Donahue, J., Karayev, S., Long, J., Girshick, R.B., Guadarrama, S., Darrell, T.: Caffe: convolutional architecture for fast feature embedding. CoRR abs/1408.5093 (2014)
79. Narang, S., Best, A., T.R.A.S., Manocha, D.: Fbcrowd: Interactive multi-agent simulation with coupled collision avoidance and human motion synthesis. Technical report, Department of Computer Science, UNC Chapel Hill (2016)

Anomaly Detection and Activity Perception Using Covariance Descriptor for Trajectories

Hamza Ergezer[1,2]([⊠]) and Kemal Leblebicioğlu[1]

[1] Electrical and Electronics Engineering, METU, Ankara, Turkey
{hamza.ergezer,kleb}@metu.edu.tr
[2] MGEO Division, EO System Design Department, Aselsan Inc., Ankara, Turkey
hergezer@aselsan.com.tr

Abstract. In this work, we study the problems of anomaly detection and activity perception through the trajectories of objects in crowded scenes. For this purpose, we propose a novel representation for trajectories via covariance features. Representing trajectories via feature covariance matrices enables us to calculate the distance between the trajectories of different lengths. After setting this proposed representation and calculation of distances between trajectories, anomaly detection is achieved by sparse representations on nearest neighbors and activity perception is achieved by extracting the dominant motion patterns in the scene through the use of spectral clustering. Conducted experiments show that the proposed method yields results which are outperforming or comparable with state of the art.

Keywords: Covariance features · Trajectory analysis · Anomaly detection · Activity perception

1 Introduction

Improvements in camera technology make the video surveillance systems easily accessible. For this reason, application areas of video surveillance systems are broad. Together with this progress, user expectations have induced new challanges to the field. The biggest challange is that automated handling of some tasks became mandatory for surveillance systems. Activity perception and anomaly detection are among those important tasks for surveillance systems. Many approaches have been proposed in literature for anomaly detection and activity perception in scenes. These approaches generally differ from each other with respect to the visual features they utilize. Despite some difficulties in the extraction stage, especially in crowded scenes, trajectory is still one of the most useful features for an object of interest.

Trajectory is 2D or 3D time series data depending on application. It carries position information of the moving object with respect to time. Other valuable information such as velocity can also be derived from trajectory data. Therefore, trajectory data is crucial for several surveillance applications. In maritime surveillance, trajectory of a vessel is the biggest clue about its behaviour. A hijacked

© Springer International Publishing Switzerland 2016
G. Hua and H. Jégou (Eds.): ECCV 2016 Workshops, Part II, LNCS 9914, pp. 728–742, 2016.
DOI: 10.1007/978-3-319-48881-3_51

plane can be identified from its trajectory in aviation surveillance. For video surveillance, trajectories of the objects in the scene gives information about motion patterns. Also, trajectory of a high speed car will be different from others and can be identified as an anomaly. As can be seen from the examples, trajectories are valuable features of moving objects to handle tasks such as anomaly detection and activity perception.

In this work, a novel descriptor is proposed for trajectories using feature covariance matrices. A feature vector is defined for each point of the trajectory and a feature matrix is obtained by concatenating these vectors. The proposed descriptor is the covariance of the feature matrix. By representing trajectories via feature covariance matrices, essentially, a novel distance measure is introduced for trajectories. This measure is capable of calculating the distance between the trajectories of different lengths. Since covariance matrices lie on Riemannian manifolds, a distance metric which is capable of measuring geodesic distance is utilized while calculating the distance between the trajectories. Another contribution of the work is the achievement of anomaly detection by sparse representations on nearest neighbors. The proposed anomaly detection approach based on sparse representation optimizes the number and weights of the nearest neighbors while setting up an anomaly measure. Spectral clustering is essential block of the activity perception. Distances determined through the covariance matrices are transformed to similarities to build a similarity graph. Activity perception is then treated to extract the dominant motion patterns in the scene through the use of spectral clustering.

Organization of the paper is as follows. A brief literature review is given in Sect. 2. In Sect. 3, the proposed representation for trajectories is introduced. Anomaly detection approach based on sparse representation of nearest neighbors is described in Sect. 4. Activity perception through clustering of trajectories using spectral clustering algorithm is presented in Sect. 5. Experimental results on both synthetic and real datasets are given in Sect. 6. Conclusion is the last section of the paper.

2   Related Work

Feature covariance matrices are first proposed and used as descriptors in [1]. The covariance descriptor basically enables to determine the distance between two instances by representing the instances by their features and their covariance matrix of the feature matrices. After it is proposed in [1] for object detection and classification, covariance descriptor is exploited to solve several computer vision problems such as visual tracking [2], action recognition [3–5], and saliency detection [6]. In all of these works, covariance descriptor is utilized as region descriptor. Some optical flow components are included in the feature vector, however, in none of them, covariance descriptor is used to describe a 2D time series.

Trajectory is a spatiotemporal feature for a moving object and carries information about its journey in the scene. Hence, it is important to get information about the activities and it is used for activity perception in previous works [7–9]. While analyzing trajectories, the critical point is the selection of proper distance measure. Several distance measures [7,10–14] for trajectories have been proposed so far. Two excellent review papers [15,16] compare different distance measures for trajectories.

Anomaly detection and activity perception are two important problems for surveillance systems. In recent years, there are many successful works that handle these problems for realistic scenarios. For anomaly detection, in [17], authors use a mixture of temporal and spatial models to detect the anomalies and in [18], they extend the models to multiple scales to detect anomalies at different spatial and temporal scales. A Gaussian Mixture Model (GMM) based probabilistic model is fit to particle trajectories which is extracted by particle advection in [19]. Trajectories that do not fit to this model are labeled as anomalies. Aside from computer vision community, there are other works focusing on anomaly detection on trajectories. Laxhammar et al. [20] apply their anomaly detector called conformal anomaly detector to the trajectories. In [13], a 1-class Support Vector Machine (SVM) is utilized to detect the anomalous trajectories. The most interesting part of the study is the introduction of a faster solution for SVM training in the presence of outliers. An outlier detection method which is based on the concept of discords is introduced in [21]. Discord for an instance is an another instance that has maximum Euclidean distance to its nearest neighbor.

Nonparametric Bayesian models are widely used for activity perception in recent years. Starting from the pioneer work [22], there are significant works [23,24] in this path. In [22], nonparametric Bayesian models are adapted to activity perception in visual scenes by modeling the motions in the scene as visual words, short video clips as documents and activities as topics. Follow-up works [23,24] adapt Markov models to learn the temporal dependencies between activities.

There is a recent approach [25] that considers the trajectories on Riemannian manifolds. The method is based on a representation called transported square-root vector field (TSRVF) and L2 norm on the space of TSRVFs. Authors have also applied their methods to visual speech recognition problem in [26]. In this method, trajectories are mapped into a tangent space by parametrization via its TSVRF. TSVRF formulation includes the derivative and square root of the derivative of the parametrized version of the trajectory. To conclude, the method has a similar idea with our method; however, in our method feature covariance matrices are exploited to map the trajectories to Riemannian manifolds.

3   Trajectory Representation by Feature Covariance Matrices

Trajectories can be considered as time series of 2D coordinates. For a visual scene, there might be lots of trajectories of different lengths. In order to analyze these trajectories, first, a similarity or a distance function should be defined. In this work, we propose to describe the trajectories with covariance matrices of their features. By doing so, all trajectories are transferred to space of Riemannian manifolds and similarities between them are calculated in this set.

A 2D trajectory can be defined as sequential concatenation of K points or more formally as a Kx2 matrix, $[x_1\ y_1,...,x_K\ y_K]$, as shown in Fig. 1. A point of a trajectory can also be defined by its features

$$f = [x\ y\ v_x\ v_y\ t] \tag{1}$$

where x and y define position, v_x and v_y are velocities in x and y directions respectively and t is the time index. During experiments, several features including cumulative sum, acceleration etc. have been examined to increase the performance. However, the best performance values are obtained with feature set defined in Eq. 1. For the whole trajectory, feature matrix can be defined similarly as

$$F = \begin{bmatrix} x_2\ y_2\ v_{x_2}\ v_{y_2}\ t_2 \\ \cdot \\ \cdot \\ \cdot \\ x_K\ y_K\ v_{x_K}\ v_{y_K}\ t_K \end{bmatrix} \tag{2}$$

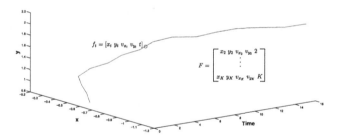

Fig. 1. Representation of trajectories using feature covariance matrices. Trajectory from synthetic dataset [13] is shown as a sample. Length of the trajectories is 16 in the dataset. A feature vector is formed for all points in the trajectory except the first point. For such a case, F matrix will be 15×5 including feature vectors of all trajectories and the resulting covariance matrix will be 5×5.

Feature covariance matrix is determined as

$$C = \frac{1}{K} \sum_{k=1}^{K} (F_k - \mu)(F_k - \mu)^T \tag{3}$$

where μ is the mean vector of all instances in matrix F. At this point, a small multiple of the identity matrix is added to covariance matrices. This regularization is performed to ensure the positive definiteness of the covariance matrix.

Positive definiteness is important for the distance metric which involves a logarithm operation.

It should be noted that for all trajectories of different lengths, we end up with a 5×5 covariance matrix. This enable us to determine the similarity between the trajectories of different lengths. After covariance representation, trajectories are carried onto Riemannian manifolds. The critical point from now on is to calculate the distances between the trajectories on Riemannian manifolds.

A distance measure that approximate the geodesic distance between two points on Riemannian manifolds must be used. For this purpose, as previous works [1–3] that utilize covariance matrices suggested, Euclidean distance metrics must be avoided. We use log-Euclidean metric which was first proposed in [27] between covariance matrices. Compared to other distance metrics [28] and divergence functions [29], the best performance is achieved by using log-Euclidean metric in this study. Log-Euclidean metric is, in principle, based on matrix logarithms. The determination of the log-Euclidean metric starts with the eigenvalue decomposition of covariance matrices.

$$C = VQV^T \tag{4}$$

After this eigenvalue decomposition, matrix logarithm is obtained as

$$log(C) \triangleq V\widetilde{Q}V^T \tag{5}$$

where $\widetilde{Q}$ is a diagonal matrix obtained from Q by replacing Q's diagonal entries by their logarithms. The distance between covariance matrices is calculated via Frobenius norm of the distance matrix logarithms.

$$\rho(C_1, C_2) = \|log(C_1) - log(C_2)\|_F \tag{6}$$

Now, we can calculate all the distances between trajectories via feature covariance matrices. In subsequent sections, anomaly detection and activity perception problems will be based on these distances. Anomaly detection is carried out by a novel approach based on sparse representation of nearest neighbors. Activity perception is achieved by forming a similarity matrix from pairwise distances and utilizing this in spectral clustering.

4   Anomaly Detection on Trajectories

In this work, trajectories are utilized as the feature of objects in the scene. Therefore, to detect the anomalies in the scene, anomalies are determined by detecting anomalous trajectories. An anomalous trajectory can be described as a sample that does not fit to motion patterns in the scene. Based on this definition, the nearest neighbor approach can be considered the simplest solution for anomaly detection. The distance to the nearest neighbor can be a good measure for some cases while deciding anomalies. However, depending on structure of the data and amount of anomalous observations, distance to the nearest neighbor might not be a good alternative. In this work, we propose a method which considers the distances to a set of nearest neighbors and tries to optimize the weights and number of nearest neighbors. A scenario is depicted in Fig. 2 to explain the necessity of the algorithm.

After representation of trajectories via covariance matrices and calculation of distances between trajectories, anomaly detection is carried out by using a measure comprising distances to nearest neighbors. For this purpose, we select nearest neighbors through a sparse representation. In this approach, an anomaly measure is calculated via weighted sum of distances to nearest neighbors for each sample. Our goal is to optimize the number of the neighbors and their weights while deciding if an instance is anomaly or not.

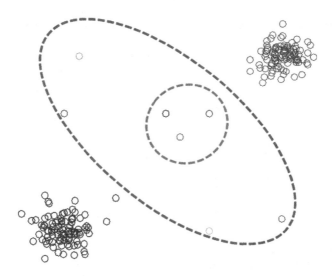

Fig. 2. A scenario to explain the necessity of sparse anomaly detection algorithm. For some anomalies, the nearest neighbor or a weighted sum of nearest neighbors might not be a good anomaly measure. Anomalies are shown inside the red dashed ellipse. For anomalies in the orange circle, the distance to third nearest neighbor should be included in the anomaly measure. (Color figure online)

In sparse anomaly detection approach, the data is assumed to be offline and available to be divided into uniform parts. In particular, we exploit some part of the data for training and derive optimal weights of nearest neighbors from this subset. Same number of data samples are taken into testing process. Anomaly measure is composed of distances to K nearest neighbors for each sample in the training set of M samples.

$$A_i = w_1 s_1 + ... + w_K s_K \qquad (7)$$

where $s_i,...,s_K$ are distances to K nearest neighbors. Equation 7 can be written in a matrix form

$$A_i = \begin{bmatrix} w_1 \ ...w_K \end{bmatrix} \begin{bmatrix} s_1 \\ . \\ s_K \end{bmatrix} = WS_i \tag{8}$$

and finally when all instances are considered

$$A = WS \tag{9}$$

where A is a 1×M vector consisting of anomaly measures for all instances, W is a 1xK vector consisting of weights of K nearest neighbors.

While deciding on anomalies, we can consider a fixed percentage or a fixed number of data points as anomaly. It is also possible that instances whose anomaly measures are above a threshold should be considered as anomalies. For all cases, a nonlinear function, f, is needed to map the anomaly measure to the decision of an anomaly.

$$L = f(A, \mu) \tag{10}$$

where μ represents the parameter of the nonlinear function, threshold value on anomaly measure or percentage on samples. L is the label vector that designates if a sample is an anomaly or not. Besides, since there might be several combinations of weighted neighbors for each instance, a minimum number of neighbors should be used. Therefore, combining with previous observations, the optimization problem can be summarized as

$$w = \underset{w}{\operatorname{argmin}} \{\lambda|w|_0 + |L_{gt} - f(A, \mu)|\} \tag{11}$$

where L_{gt} is the ground truth of label vector in the training set. Since L0 norm is a nonconvex function, L1 norm is a first alternative to L0 norm. However, L2 norm guarantees the positive weights in our problem. Then, the final optimization becomes

$$w = \underset{w}{\operatorname{argmin}} \{\lambda|w|_2 + |L_{gt} - f(A, \mu)|\} \tag{12}$$

In our experiments, we show that anomaly detection with sparse representation gives better results than the single use of nearest neighbors or equally weighted of them.

5   Activity Perception via Trajectories

Activity perception is the second problem for which the proposed representation is exploited. An activity can be considered as a set of similar trajectories. Clustering is the direct solution for the identification of these sets or activities. Therefore, in this work, activity perception is handled with clustering of trajectories.

Describing trajectories through the utilization of feature covariance matrices enables us to construct a similarity matrix between trajectories of different lengths. This similarity matrix can be used to build an undirected graph which allows extracting the motion patterns in the scene. Spectral clustering methods are popular since they are capable of handling non-convex patterns in the data. As in [30], the similarity matrix is built using the distances derived with feature covariance matrices

$$s_{ij} = e^{-d_{ij}^2/2\sigma^2} \tag{13}$$

where d_{ij} is the distance between the trajectories i and j. Spectral clustering is achieved by the clustering of eigenvectors of a matrix called Laplacian. In its unnormalized formulation, Laplacian is the difference of the degree matrix and the similarity matrix.

$$L = D - S \tag{14}$$

where D is a diagonal matrix which contains sum of each row of similarity matrix (or column depending on its symmetry). Laplacian matrix is normalized as in [30] to handle the clusters of different sizes.

$$L = I - D^{-1/2} S D^{-1/2} \tag{15}$$

where L is the normalized Laplacian and D is degree matrix. Clusters are determined by applying k-means algorithm on eigenvectors of normalized Laplacian.

6   Experiments

During experiments, a synthetic dataset and two real datasets are exploited. Synthetic dataset first built in [21] is used. The real datasets are UCSD anomaly detection [17,18] and MIT Parking Lot [8]. It is better to mention about two practical details before experimental results. First, the regularization parameter mentioned after Eq. 3 is selected as 0.005 in all experiments. Secondly, in all real datasets, a size threshold is applied to eliminate small tracks.

There is no ground truth data for anomalies or activities in MIT Parking Lot [8] dataset. In UCSD case [17,18], anomaly ground data are frame based and not appropriate for our approach. Therefore, quantitative results cannot be produced for these datasets.

Anomaly detection on trajectories was carried out on both synthetic and real datasets to evaluate the performance of the proposed representation. For synthetic dataset case, the dataset generated in [13] is exploited and compared with the results acquired in [13,20,21]. This dataset includes 1000 subsets and in each subset, there are 260 trajectories. In each subset, last 10 trajectories are anomalous. Comparative results are given in Table 1 for this dataset and a sample result is shown in Fig. 3. As can be seen in Table 1, the proposed representation has outperformed the state-of-the-art techniques just by utilizing the distance to nearest neighbor only.

Synthetic dataset is also exploited while probing the performance of sparse anomaly detection. Sparse anomaly detection is implemented through running

Table 1. Accuracies of anomaly detection methods for the synthetic dataset built in [13]. The proposed representation outperforms the state-of-the-art techniques with use of anomaly measures, nearest neighbors (NN) and sparse representation (SR). Sparse representation also gives better results compared to single use of nearest neighbor.

Method	Accuracy
1-Class SVM [13]	0.9630
Conformal Anomaly Detector [20]	0.9709
Discords [21]	0.9706
Proposed representation w/NN	0.9805
Proposed representation w/SR	0.9827

of Monte Carlo simulations in synthetic dataset. In each run, we select 100 sets for training from the whole dataset including 1000 sets. The remainder of the dataset is used for testing. Sparse representation or the weights of the nearest neighbors are applied to the testing set. As shown in Table 1, the best results are obtained with the combination of proposed trajectory representation and sparse anomaly detector.

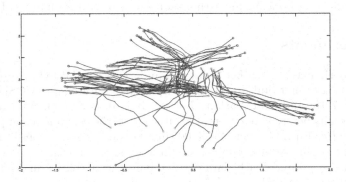

Fig. 3. A sample result for anomaly detection in the synthetic dataset. Ten samples are shown for each cluster of normal trajectories. Anomalous trajectories are indicated with bold magenta lines. (Color figure online)

Synthetic dataset is also utilized for the activity perception part. The previously mentioned 250 non-anomalous trajectories in the dataset belong to five equal size clusters. Similarity matrix shown in Fig. 5 is used to obtain the clustering result shown in Fig. 4. Similarity matrix shown in Fig. 5 also gives an idea about the usefulness of the representation. Correct clustering rate is 0.9055 for whole dataset which contains 1000 subsets of 260 trajectories.

For real dataset case, UCSD anomaly detection [17,18] and MIT Parking Lot [8] datasets are utilized. In UCSD dataset, there are sequences of two scenes.

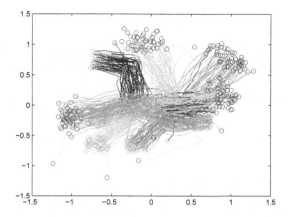

Fig. 4. Clustering result of a set of trajectories in the synthetic dataset. Starting and ending points of the trajectories are indicated by green and red circles, respectively. Correct clustering rate is achieved as 0.9055 for the whole dataset which contains 1000 trajectory sets as in this sample. (Color figure online)

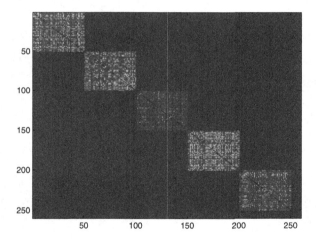

Fig. 5. Similarity matrix of trajectories given in Fig. 4. Five clusters can be observed together with the anomalies which lie in the last rows and columns.

For these scenes, training and test sequences are also provided. Anomalies are motions of non-pedestrian objects such as cars, skaters and bicyclists. A critical issue for UCSD anomaly detection dataset is the extraction of trajectories. For this purpose, KLT tracker used in [31] is exploited to extract the trajectories. After extraction of trajectories for both training and test sequences, a covariance matrix for each trajectory is calculated. Covariance matrix of each trajectory in the test sequences is compared with all covariance matrices of the trajectories in the training set. Training dataset is not sufficiently large to calculate a sparse

Fig. 6. Some examples of anomaly detection results in UCSD dataset. Results lied in the rows are from two different scenes in the dataset. Images in the first two rows indicate the most anomalous trajectories in the folders of Test014, Test019, Test022, Test024 of UCSDped1 scene and the ones in the third and fourth rows are for Test003, Test005, Test006, Test009 of UCSDped2 scene. Starting points are shown with green star and end points with red star, respectively. (Color figure online)

Fig. 7. Some anomalous trajectories from MIT Parking Lot dataset. These anomalous trajectories might be result of problems in extraction stage.

Fig. 8. Trajectory patterns in MIT Parking Lot dataset. Number of clusters is set to eight to get these results in the final k-means step of spectral clustering. Starting and ending points are shown with green and red circles, respectively. (Color figure online)

representation for this dataset. Therefore, a predefined anomaly measure which is the combination of three nearest neighbors are used in experiments. For some test sequences from two scenes of the dataset, the most anomalous trajectories are shown in Fig. 6.

The next dataset utilized is MIT Parking Lot dataset [8]. This dataset comprises trajectories captured from a parking lot containing trajectories of cars and people. There are certain motion patterns in the scene and the dataset is exploited to detect these motion patterns or activities. In this work, the dataset is used for both of anomaly detection and activity perception. Anomaly detection is again based on distance to three nearest neighbors. Anomaly detection results are shown in Fig. 7. Some sharp trajectories which are caused by an error in extraction stage are labeled as anomaly. Activity perception is carried out by a forming a similarity matrix and applying spectral clustering. In the dataset, there are 40453 trajectories and spectral clustering might not be computationally manageable when applied to the whole dataset. However, aforementioned size limit makes the spectral clustering feasible. The activity perception results are given in Fig. 8. The number of clusters is set to eight to achieve these results in the final k-means step of spectral clustering. Obviously, some clusters contain more than one meaningful motion pattern. It is observed that these motion patterns are extracted when the number of clusters are set to a bigger number. A potential improvement lies in this part of the study. A clustering algorithm without specifying the number of clusters and still work on similarity matrices will be a good alternative to spectral clustering.

7   Conclusion

In this work, we propose a novel approach by describing trajectories with feature covariance matrices. We study the problems of anomaly detection and clustering for trajectories in this context. Feature covariance matrices enable us to measure similarity between trajectories of different lengths. Also, conducted experiments show that covariance descriptor for trajectories yields satisfactory results compared to the state of the art.

We have also introduced a sparse anomaly detector to decide the number and the weights of the nearest neighbors that should be used. This sparse representation can be applied to other similar problems. The only requirement is to have a training dataset for which annotated anomaly data is given.

The whole study has been conducted with the assumption that crowd density allows to extract trajectories for each object. In dense crowd scenarios, other approaches such as particle advection used in [19] might be more feasible to obtain trajectories.

There is a possible improvement in activity perception part of this work. Instead of standard spectral clustering approach for which the number of clusters must be given, another clustering approach on distance matrix calculated with the representation can be used.

A representation is proposed for time series of 2D data in this study. A possible extension of this work is shape classification problem. Although there is no time information and invariance on rotation and scale could be problematic, feature covariance matrices can be used to describe 2D shapes.

References

1. Tuzel, O., Porikli, F., Meer, P.: Pedestrian detection via classification on riemannian manifolds. IEEE Trans. Pattern Anal. Mach. Intell. **30**(10), 1713–1727 (2008)
2. Porikli, F., Tuzel, O., Meer, P.: Covariance tracking using model update based on lie algebra. In: CVPR (2006)
3. Guo, K., Ishwar, P., Konrad, J.: Action recognition from video using feature covariance matrices. IEEE Trans. Image Process. **22**(6), 2479–2494 (2013)
4. Bilinski, P., Bremond, F.: Video covariance matrix logarithm for human action recognition in videos. In: IJCAI 2015-24th International Joint Conference on Artificial Intelligence (2015)
5. Wang, H., Yi, Y., Wu, J.: Human action recognition with trajectory based covariance descriptor in unconstrained videos. In: Proceedings of the 23rd ACM International Conference on Multimedia 2015, pp. 1175–1178 (2015)
6. Erdem, E., Erdem, A.: Visual saliency estimation by nonlinearly integrating features using region covariances. J. Vis. **13**(4), 1–20 (2013)
7. Bashir, F.I., Khokhar, A.A., Schonfeld, D.: Object trajectory-based activity classification and recognition using hidden markov models. IEEE Trans. Image Process. **16**(7), 1912–1919 (2007)
8. Wang, X., Ma, K.T., Ng, G.W., Grimson, W.E.L.: Trajectory analysis and semantic region modeling using nonparametric hierarchical bayesian models. Int. J. Comput. Vis. **95**(3), 287–312 (2011)
9. Morris, B.T., Trivedi, M.M.: Trajectory learning for activity understanding: unsupervised, multilevel, and long-term adaptive approach. IEEE Trans. Pattern Anal. Mach. Intell. **33**(11), 2287–2301 (2011)
10. Keogh, E., Pazzani, M.: Scaling up dynamic time warping for datamining applications. In: International Conference on Knowledge Discovery and Data Mining (2000)

11. Hu, W., Xie, D., Fu, Z., Zeng, W., Maybank, S.: Semantic-based surveillance video retrieval. IEEE Trans. Image Process. **16**(4), 1168–1181 (2007)
12. Buzan, D., Sclaroff, S., Kollios, G.: Extraction and clustering of motion trajectories in video. In: Proceedings IEEE International Conference on Pattern Recognition, August 2004
13. Piciarelli, C., Micheloni, C., Foresti, G.: Trajectory-based anomalous event detection. IEEE Trans. Circ. Syst. Video Technol. **18**(11), 1544–1554 (2008)
14. Atev, S., Masoud, O., Papanikolopoulos, N.: Learning traffic patterns at intersections by spectral clustering of motion trajectories. In: IEEE Conference Intelligence Robots and Systems (2006)
15. Morris, B., Trivedi., M.: Learning trajectory patterns by clustering: experimental studies and comparative evaluation. In: CVPR (2009)
16. Zhang, Z., Huang, K., Tan, T.: Comparison of similarity measures for trajectory clustering in outdoor surveillance scenes. In: ICPR (2006)
17. Mahadevan, V., Li, W., Bhalodia, V., Vasconcelos, N.: Anomaly detection in crowded scenes. In: CVPR (2010)
18. Li, W., Mahadevan, V., Vasconcelos, N.: Anomaly detection and localization in crowded scenes. IEEE Trans. Pattern Anal. Mach. Intell. **36**(1), 18–32 (2014)
19. Wu, S., Moore, B.E., Shah, M.: Chaotic invariants of lagrangian particle trajectories for anomaly detection in crowded scenes. In: CVPR (2010)
20. Laxhammar, R., Falkman, G.: Online learning and sequential anomaly detection in trajectories. IEEE Trans. Pattern Anal. Mach. Intell. **36**(6), 1158–1173 (2014)
21. Keogh, E., Lin, J., Fu, A.: Hot sax: efficiently finding the most unusual time series subsequence. In: ICDM (2005)
22. Wang, X., Ma, X., Grimson, W.E.L.: Unsupervised activity perception in crowded and complicated scenes using hierarchical bayesian models. IEEE Trans. Pattern Anal. Mach. Intell. **31**(3), 539–555 (2009)
23. Hospedales, T., Gong, S., Xiang, T.: A markov clustering topic model for mining behaviour in video. In: IEEE 12th International Conference on Computer Vision, pp. 1165–1172 (2009)
24. Kuettel, D., Breitenstein, M.D., Gool, L.V., Ferrari, V.: What's going on? discovering spatio-temporal dependencies in dynamic scenes. In: IEEE Conference on Computer Vision and Pattern Recognition (CVPR), pp. 1951–1958 (2010)
25. Su, J., Kurtek, S., Klassen, E., Srivastava, A.: Statistical analysis of trajectories on riemannian manifolds: bird migration, hurricane tracking and video surveillance. Ann. Appl. Stat. **8**(1), 530–552 (2014)
26. Su, J., Srivastava, A., de Souza, F.D.M., Sarkar, S.: Rate-invariant analysis of trajectories on riemannian manifolds with application in visual speech recognition. In: Proceedings of the IEEE Conference on Computer Vision and Pattern Recognition, pp. 620–627 (2014)
27. Arsigny, V., Fillard, P., Pennec, X., Ayache, N.: Log-euclidean metrics for fast and simple calculus on diffusion tensors. Magn. Reson. Med. **56**(2), 411–421 (2006)
28. Forstner, W., Moonen, B.: A metric for covariance matrices. In: Grafarend, E.W., Krumm, F.W., Schwarze, V.S. (eds.) Geodesy-The Challenge of the 3rd Millennium. Springer, Heidelberg (2003)
29. Chebbi, Z., Moakher, M.: Means of hermitian positive-definite matrices based on the log-determinant alpha-divergence function. Linear Algebra Appl. **436**(7), 1872–1889 (2012)
30. Ng, A.Y., Jordan, M.I., Weiss, Y.: On spectral clustering: analysis and an algorithm. Adv. Neural Inf. Process. Syst. **2**, 849–856 (2002)
31. Zhou, B., Tang, X., Wang, X.: Measuring crowd collectiveness. In: CVPR (2013)

Automatic Calibration of Stationary Surveillance Cameras in the Wild

Guido M.Y.E. Brouwers[1(✉)], Matthijs H. Zwemer[1,2], Rob G.J. Wijnhoven[1],
and Peter H.N. de With[2]

[1] ViNotion B.V., Eindhoven, The Netherlands
{guido.brouwers,rob.wijnhoven}@vinotion.nl
[2] Eindhoven University of Technology, Eindhoven, The Netherlands
{m.zwemer,p.h.n.de.With}@tue.nl

Abstract. We present a fully automatic camera calibration algorithm for monocular stationary surveillance cameras. We exploit only information from pedestrians tracks and generate a full camera calibration matrix based on vanishing-point geometry. This paper presents the first combination of several existing components of calibration systems from literature. The algorithm introduces novel pre- and post-processing stages that improve estimation of the horizon line and the vertical vanishing point. The scale factor is determined using an average body height, enabling extraction of metric information without manual measurement in the scene. Instead of evaluating performance on a limited number of camera configurations (video seq.) as in literature, we have performed extensive simulations of the calibration algorithm for a large range of camera configurations. Simulations reveal that metric information can be extracted with an average error of 1.95 % and the derived focal length is more accurate than the reported systems in literature. Calibration experiments with real-world surveillance datasets in which no restrictions are made on pedestrian movement and position, show that the performance is comparable (max. error 3.7 %) to the simulations, thereby confirming feasibility of the system.

Keywords: Automatic camera calibration · Vanishing points

1 Introduction

The growth of video cameras for surveillance and security implies more automatic analysis using object detection and tracking of moving objects in the scene. To obtain a global understanding of the environment, individual detection results from multiple cameras can be combined. For more accurate global understanding, it is required to convert the pixel-based position information of detected objects in the individual cameras, to a global coordinate system (GPS). To this end, each individual camera needs to be calibrated as a first and crucial step.

The most common model to relate pixel positions to real-world coordinates is the pinhole camera model [5]. In this model, the camera is assumed to make

© Springer International Publishing Switzerland 2016
G. Hua and H. Jégou (Eds.): ECCV 2016 Workshops, Part II, LNCS 9914, pp. 743–759, 2016.
DOI: 10.1007/978-3-319-48881-3_52

a perfect perspective transformation (a matrix), which is described by intrinsic and extrinsic parameters of the camera. The intrinsic parameters are: pixel skew, principal point location, focal length and aspect ratio of the pixels. The extrinsic parameters describe the orientation and position of the camera with respect to a world coordinate system by a rotation and a translation. The process of finding the model parameters that best describe the mapping of scene onto the image plane of the camera is called camera calibration.

The golden standard for camera calibration [5] uses a pre-defined calibration object [19] that is physically placed in the scene. Camera calibration involves finding the corresponding key points of the object in the image plane and describing the mapping of world coordinates to image coordinates. However, in surveillance scenes the camera is typically positioned high above the ground plane, leading to impractically large calibration objects covering a large part of the scene. Other calibration techniques exploit camera motion (Maybank et al. [14], Hartley [6]) or stereo cameras (Faugeras and Toscani et al. [4]), to extract multiple views from the scene. However, because most surveillance cameras are static cameras these techniques cannot be used. Stereo cameras explicitly create multiple views, but require two physical cameras that are typically not available.

A different calibration method uses vanishing points. A vanishing point is a point where parallel lines from the 3D world intersect in the image. These lines can be generated from static objects in the scenes (such as buildings, roads or light poles), or by linking moving objects at different positions over time (such as pedestrians). Static scenes do not always contain structures with parallel lines. In contrast, there are always moving objects in surveillance scenes, which makes this approach attractive. In literature, different proposals use the concept of vanishing points. However, these approaches either require very constrained object motion [7,8,15], require additional manual annotation of orthogonal directions in the scene [12,13], or only calibrate the camera up to a scale factor [8–10,12,13,15]. To our knowledge, there exists no solution that results in an accurate calibration for a large range of camera configurations in uncontrolled surveillance scenes; automatic camera calibration does not work in unconstrained cases.

This paper proposes a fully automatic calibration method for monocular stationary cameras in surveillance scenes based on the concept of vanishing points. These points are extracted from pedestrian tracks, where no constraints are imposed on the movement of pedestrians. We define the camera calibration as a process, which is based as the extraction of the vanishing points with the following determination of the camera parameters. The main contributions to this process are (1) a pre-processing step that improves estimation of the vertical vanishing point, (2) a post-processing step that exploits the height distribution of pedestrians to improve horizon line estimation, (3) determination of the camera height (scale factor) using an average body height and (4) an extensive simulation of the total process, showing that the algorithm obtains an accurate calibration for a large range of camera configurations as used in real-world scenes.

1.1 Related Work

Vanishing points are also extracted from object motion in the scene by Lv *et al.* [12,13] and Kusakunniran *et al.* [9]. Although they proved that moving pedestrians can be used as a calibration object, the accuracy of the algorithms is not sufficient for practical applications. Krahnstoever *et al.* [8] and Micusik *et al.* [15] use the homography between the head and foot plane to estimate the vanishing point and horizon line. Although providing the calibration upto a scale factor, they require a constrained pedestrian movement and location. Liu *et al.* [10] propose to use the predicted relative human height distribution to optimize the camera parameters. Although providing a fully automated calibration method, they exploit only a single vanishing point which is not robust for a large range of camera orientations. Recent work from Huang *et al.* [7] proposes to extract vanishing points from detected locations from pedestrian feet and only calculate the intrinsic camera parameters.

All previously mentioned methods use pixel-based foreground detection to estimate head and feet locations of pedestrians, which makes them impractical for crowded scenes with occlusions. Additionally, these methods require at least one known distance in the scene to be able to translate pixels to real distances. Although in controlled scenes the camera calibration from moving pedestrians is possible, many irregularities occur which complicate the accurate detection of vanishing points. Different types of pedestrian appearances, postures and gait patterns result in noisy point data containing many outliers. To solve the previous issues, we have concentrated particularly on the work of Kusakunniran [9] and Liu [10]. Our strategy is to extend this work such that we can extract camera parameters in uncontrolled surveillance scenes with pedestrians, while omitting background subtraction and avoiding scene irregularity issues.

2 Approach

To calibrate the camera, we propose to use vertical and parallel lines in the scene to detect the vertical vanishing point and the horizon line. These lines are extracted from head and feet positions of tracked pedestrians. Then, a general technique is used to extract camera parameters from the obtained vanishing points. It should be noted that the approach is not limited to tracking pedestrians, but applies to any object class for which two orthogonal vanishing points can be extracted. The overview of the system is shown in Fig. 1. First, we compute vertical lines by connecting head and feet positions of pedestrians. The intersecting point of these lines is the location of the vertical vanishing point. Second, points on the horizon line are extracted by computing parallel lines between head and feet positions at different points in time. The horizon line is then robustly fitted by a line fitting algorithm. Afterwards, the locations of the vertical vanishing point and horizon line are used to compute a full camera calibration. In the post-processing step, the pedestrian height distribution is used to refine the camera parameters. Finally and for distance calibration involving translation of pixel positions to metric locations, a scale factor is computed by

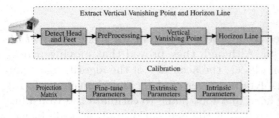

Fig. 1. Block diagram of the proposed calibration system.

Fig. 2. Example head and feet detections.

using the average body height of pedestrians. To retrieve more accurate camera parameters and establish a stable average setting, the complete algorithm is executed multiple times on subsets of the detected pedestrian positions which addresses the noise in the parameters of single cycles.

2.1 Head and Feet Detection

The head and feet positions are detected using two object detectors, which are trained offline using a large training set and are fixed for the experiments. We apply the Histogram of Oriented Gradients (HOG) detector [2] to individually detect head and feet (Fig. 2). The detector for feet is trained with images in which the person feet are visibly positioned as a pair. A vertical line can be found from a pedestrian during walking, at the moment (cross-legged phase) in which the line between head and feet best represents a vertical pole. Head and feet detections are matched by vertically shifting the found head detection of each person downwards and then measuring the overlap with the possible feet position. When the overlap is sufficiently large, the head and feet are matched and used in the calibration algorithm. Due to small localization errors in both head and feet positions and the fact that pedestrians are not in a perfectly upright position, the set of matched detections contains noisy data. This will be filtered in the next step.

2.2 Pre-processing

The matched detections are filtered as a pre-processing step, such that only the best matched detections are used to compute the vanishing points and outliers are omitted. To this end, the matched detections are sorted by the horizontal positions of the feet locations. For each detection, the vertical derivative of the line between head and feet is computed. Because the width of the image is substantially smaller than the distance to the vertical vanishing point, we can linearly approximate the tangential line related to the vertical derivative by a first-order line. After extreme outliers are removed, this line is fitted through the derivatives using a least-squares method. Derivatives that have a distance larger than an empirical threshold are removed from the dataset. Finally, the remaining inliers are used to compute the vertical vanishing point and the horizon line.

2.3 Vertical Vanishing Point and Horizon Line

The vertical vanishing point location is computed using the method from Kusakunniran et al. [9]. Pedestrians are considered vertical poles in the scene and the collinearity of the head, feet and vertical vanishing point of each pedestrian are used to calculate the exact location of the vertical vanishing point.

Parallel lines constructed from key points of pedestrians that are also parallel to the ground plane intersect at a point on the horizon line. We can combine each pair of head and feet detections of the same pedestrian to define such parallel lines and compute the intersection points. Multiple intersection points lead then to the definition of the horizon line. The iterative line-finding algorithm which is used to extract the horizon line is described below.

The horizon line is estimated by a least-squares algorithm. Next, inliers are selected based on a their distance to the found horizon line, which should be smaller than a pre-determined threshold T. These inliers are used to fit a new line by the same least-squares approach so that the process becomes iterative. The iterative process stops when the support of the line in terms of inliers does not further improve. This approach always leads to a satisfactory solution in our experiments. The support of a line has been experimentally defined by a weighted sum W of contributions of the individual points i having an L2-distance D_i to the current estimate of the horizon line. Each contribution is scaled with the threshold to a fraction D_i/T and exponentially weighted. This leads to the least-squares weight W specified by

$$W = \sum_{i=1}^{M} \exp \frac{-D_i^2}{T^2}. \tag{1}$$

The pre-defined threshold T depends on the accuracy of the detections and on the orientation of the camera. If the orientation of the camera is facing down at a certain angle, the intersection points are more sensitive to noise, i.e. the spread of the intersection points will be larger. A normal distribution is fitted on the intersection points. The threshold T is then determined as the standard deviation of that normal distribution.

2.4 Calibration Algorithm

The derived horizon line and the vertical vanishing point are now used to directly determine the camera parameters. As we assume zero skew, square pixels and the principal point being at the center of the image, the focal length is the only intrinsic camera parameter left to be determined.

The focal length represents the distance from the camera center to the principal point. Using the geometric properties described by Orghidan et al. [17], the distance can be computed using only the distance from the vertical vanishing point to the principal point and the distance from the horizon line to the principal point. The orientation of the camera is described by a rotation matrix, which is composed of a rotation around the tilt and the roll angle, thus around the x-axis and z-axis, respectively. The tilt angle θ_t is defined as the angle between the focal line and the z-axis of the world coordinate system. Because any line between the camera center $\mathbf{O_c}$ and the horizon line is horizontal, the tilt angle is computed by

$$\theta_t = 90° + \arctan\left(\frac{\|\mathbf{O_i V_i}\|}{f}\right), \tag{2}$$

where $\mathbf{V_i}$ is the point on the horizon line which is closest to the principal point, $\mathbf{f}$ is the focal length and $\mathbf{O_i}$ is the center of the image. The roll angle is equal to the angle between the line from the vertical vanishing point to the principal point and the vertical line through the principal point. The translation defined in the extrinsic parameters is a vector $\mathbf{t}$ pointing from the camera origin to the world origin. We choose the point on the ground plane that is directly beneath the camera center as the world origin, so that the position of the camera center in world coordinates is described by $P_{cam}(x, y, z) = (0, 0, s)$. This introduces the well-known scale factor s being equal to the camera height. The translation vector $\mathbf{t}$ is computed by

$$\mathbf{t} = -R \cdot P_{cam}, \tag{3}$$

where R is the rotation matrix. If metric information is required, the scale factor s must be determined to relate distances in our world coordinate system to metric distances. The scale factor can be computed if at least one metric distance in the scene is known. Inspired by [3], the average body height of the detected pedestrians is used, as this information is readily available. Because the positions of the feet are on the ground plane, these locations can be determined by

$$s \begin{bmatrix} x \\ y \\ 1 \end{bmatrix} = [P_1, P_2, P_4]^{-1} \begin{bmatrix} u_f \\ v_f \\ 1 \end{bmatrix}, \tag{4}$$

where (u_f, v_f) are the image coordinates of the feet and P_i denotes the ith column of the projection matrix $P = K[R|t]$, where K is the calibration matrix. The world coordinates of the head are situated on the line from the camera center through the image plane at the pixel location of the head, towards infinity. The point on this line that is closest to the vertical line passing through the position of the feet, is defined as the position of the head. The L2-distance between the two points is equal to the body height of the pedestrian. The scale factor is chosen such that the measured average body height of the pedestrians is equal to the a-priori known country-wide average [16]. Note that the standard deviation of the country-wide height distribution has no influence if sufficient samples are available. The worst-case deviation on average height globally is 12 % (1.58–1.80 m), but this never occurs because outliers (airports, children) are averaged.

2.5   Post-processing

Noise present in the head and feet detections of pedestrians affects the locations of the intersection points that determine the location of the vertical vanishing point and the horizon line. When the tilt of the camera is close to horizontal, vertical lines in the scene are almost parallel in the image plane, which makes the intersection points sensitive to noise. As a result, the average position of the intersection points is shifted upwards, which decreases exponentially when the tilt of the camera increases (facing more downwards), see Fig. 4c. The intersection points that determine the horizon line undergo a similar effect when the camera is facing down, see Fig. 4b. As a consequence of these shifting effects, the resulting focal length and camera tilt are estimated at a lower value than they should be. Summarizing, the post-processing compensates the above shifting effect for cameras facing downwards.

This compensation is performed by evaluating the pedestrian height distribution, as motivated by [10]. The pedestrian height is assumed to be a normal distribution, as shown by Millar [16]. The distribution has the smallest variance when the tilt is estimated correctly. The tilt is computed as follows. The pedestrian height distribution is calculated for a range of tilt angles (from -5 to $+15°$ in steps of $0.5°$, relative to the initially estimated tilt angle). We select the angle with the smallest variance as the best angle for the tilt. Figure 7 shows one-over standard deviation of the body height distribution for the range of evaluated tilt angles (for three different cameras with three different true tilt angles). As can be seen in the figure, this optimum value is slightly too high. Therefore, the selected angle is averaged with the initial estimate when starting the pre-processing, leading to the final estimated tilt.

In retrospect, our introduced pre-processing has also solved a special case that introduces a shift in the vertical vanishing point. This occurs when the camera is horizontally looking forward, so that the tilt angle is $90°$. Our pre-processing has corrected this effect.

3   Model Simulation and Its Tolerances

The purpose of model simulation is to evaluate the robustness against model errors which should be controlled for certain camera orientations. Secondly, the accuracy of the detected camera parameters should be evaluated, and the influence of error propagation in the calculation when input parameters are noisy.

The advantage of using simulated data is that the ground truth of every step in the algorithm is known. The first step of creating a simulation is defining a scene and calculating the projection matrix for this scene. Next, the input data for our algorithm is computed by creating a random set of head and feet positions in the 3D-world, where the height of the pedestrian is defined by a normal distribution $\mathcal{N}(\mu, \sigma)$ with $\mu = 1.74\,\mathrm{m}$ and $\sigma = 0.065\,\mathrm{m}$, as in [16]. The pixel positions of the head and feet positions in the image plane are computed using the projection matrix. These image coordinates are used as input for our calibration algorithm. For our experiments, we model the errors as noise sources, so that the robustness of the system can be evaluated with respect to (1) the localization errors, (2) our assumptions about pedestrians walking perfectly vertical and (3) the assumptions on intrinsic parameters of the camera. We first simulate the system to evaluate the camera parameters since this is the main goal. However, we extend our simulation to evaluate also the measured distances in the scene, which are representative for the accuracy of mapping towards a global coordinate system.

3.1 Error Sources of the Model

We define two noise sources in our simulation system. The first source models the localization error of the detector for the head and feet positions in the image plane. The second source is a horizontal offset of the head position in the 3D-world, which originates from the ideal assumption on pedestrians walking perfectly vertical through the scene. This is not true in practice, leading to an error in the horizontal offset as well. All noise sources are assumed to have normal distributions. The localization error of the detector is determined by manually annotating head and feet positions of a real-life data sequence, which serves as ground truth. The head and feet detectors are applied to this dataset and the localization error is determined. We have found that the localization errors can be described by a standard deviation of $\sigma_x = 7\%$ [width of head] and $\sigma_y = 11\%$ in the x- and y-direction for the head detector and a standard deviation of $\sigma_x = 10\%$ and $\sigma_y = 16\%$ for the feet detector.

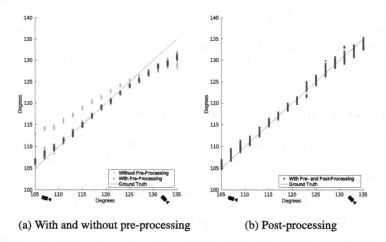

(a) With and without pre-processing   (b) Post-processing

Fig. 3. Accuracy of the camera tilt estimation, the red line shows perfect estimation. (Color figure online)

Estimating the noise level of head positions in the 3D world is not trivial, since ground-truth data is not available. In order to create a coarse estimate of the noise level, manual pedestrian annotations of a calibrated video sequence are used to plot the distributions of the intersection points of the vertical vanishing point and the horizon line. The input noise of the model simulation is adjusted such that the simulated distributions match with the annotated distributions. Input noise originates from two noise sources: errors perpendicular to the walking direction and errors in the walking direction. We have empirically estimated the noise perpendicular to the walking direction to have $\sigma = 0.08$ m and the noise parallel to the walking direction to have $\sigma = 0.10$ m. These values are employed in all further simulation experiments.

3.2 Experiments on Error Propagation in the Model

In our experiments, we aim to optimize the tilt estimation, because the tilt angle has the largest influence on the camera calibration. In order to optimize the estimation of the camera tilt, we need to optimize the location of the vertical vanishing point and horizon line. Below, the dependencies of the tilt on various input parameters are evaluated: pre-processing, the camera orientation and post-processing.

Pre-Processing: To evaluate the effect of the pre-processing on the locations of the intersection points, which determine the vertical vanishing point and the horizon line, the tilt is computed for various camera orientations and 150 times for each orientation. Each time the simulation creates new detection sets using the noise sources. Results of the detected tilt with and without pre-processing are shown in Fig. 3a. The red line depicts the ground-truth value for the camera tilt. The blue points are the estimated camera tilts for the various simulations, with an average error of 3.7°. It can be observed that the pre-processing stage clearly removes outliers such that the estimation of the position of the vertical vanishing point is improved, especially for cameras with a tilt lower than 120°. The average error decreases to 1.3°, giving a 65 % improvement.

Camera Orientation: The position of the vanishing points depends on the detection error in the image plane and on the camera orientation. The influence of the orientation on the error of the vanishing-point locations is evaluated. The simulation environment is used to create datasets for camera tilts ranging from 105 to 135°. For each orientation, 100 datasets are produced and individual vertical vanishing points and horizon lines are computed.

Figure 4 shows the intersection points of the horizon line and vertical vanishing point for a camera tilt of 105° and 130°. The red rectangle represents the image plane, the intersection points are depicted in green and the blue triangular corners represent a set of three orthogonal vanishing points, where the bottom corner is the vertical vanishing point and the two top corners are two vanishing points on the horizon line in orthogonal directions. For a camera tilt of 105°, which is close to horizontal, the intersection points of the horizon line lie close to the ground truth, while intersection points of the vertical vanishing point are widely spread and shifted upwards. For a camera tilt of 130°, the opposite effect

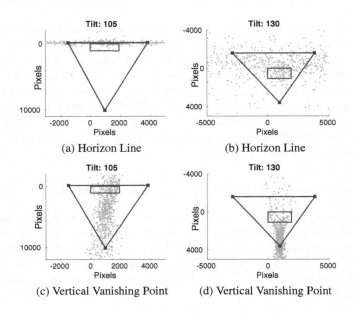

Fig. 4. Shift of the intersection-point blobs for (a, c) 105 and (b, d) 130° tilt. (Color figure online)

is visible. Figure 5 shows the vertical location error of the computed vertical vanishing point and horizon line. It can be seen that when the camera tilt increases, the downwards shift of the horizon line increases exponentially. When the camera tilt decreases, the upwards shift of the vertical vanishing point increases exponentially. The variance of the vertical location error of the horizon line grows when the tilt increases, which means that the calibration algorithm is more sensitive to noise in the head and feet positions. A similar effect is visible in the location error of the vertical vanishing point for decreasing camera tilt.

Post-Processing: Results from the previous experiments show that the detected vanishing point and horizon line have a vertical localization error. The post-processing stage aims at improving the tilt estimation of the calibration algorithm. The effect of the post-processing is evaluated by computing the tilt for simulated scenes with various camera orientations. The results of the calibration algorithm with post-processing are shown in Fig. 3b. It can be observed that the post-processing improves the tilt estimation for camera tilts higher than 120°. The average tilt error is reduced from 1.3° when using only pre-processing, to 0.7° with full processing (an improvement of 46%).

3.3   Monte-Carlo Simulation

The model simulation can be used to derive the error distributions of the camera parameters by performing Monte-Carlo simulation. These error distributions are

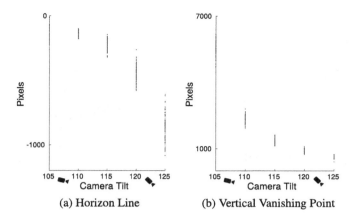

(a) Horizon Line   (b) Vertical Vanishing Point

Fig. 5. Vertical shift of the predicted vanishing points with respect to the ground truth.

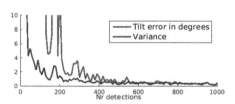

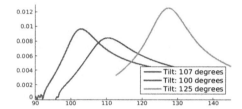

Fig. 6. Accuracy of tilt estimation for increasing number of detections (40 simulation iterations per detection).

Fig. 7. Postprocessing, 1/standard deviation of the body height distribution for several camera tilts.

computed by calibrating 1,000 simulated scenes using typical surveillance camera configurations. For the simulations, the focal length is varied within 1,000–4,000 pixels, the tilt in 110–130°, the roll from −5 to +5° and the camera height within 4–10 m. The error distributions are computed for the focal length, tilt, roll and camera height. Figure 6 shows how the tilt error decreases with respect to the number of input pedestrian locations (from the object detector). Both the absolute error and its variance decrease quickly and converge after a few hundred locations.

Figure 8 shows the error distributions of the previous parameters via Monte-Carlo simulations. The standard deviations of the focal length error, camera tilt and camera roll are 47.1 pixels, 0.41° and 0.21°, respectively. The mean of the camera height distribution is lower than the ground truth. This is due to the fact that when the estimated tilt and focal length are smaller than the actual values, the detected body height of the pedestrian is larger and the scale factor will be smaller giving a lower camera height. The average error of measured distances in

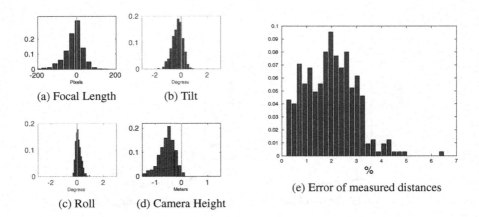

(a) Focal Length   (b) Tilt

(c) Roll   (d) Camera Height

(e) Error of measured distances

Fig. 8. Distribution of the estimated camera parameters from Monte-Carlo simulations.

the scene is 1.95 %, while almost all errors are below 3.2 %. These results show that accurate detection of camera parameters is obtained for various camera orientations.

4   Experimental Results of Complete System

Three public datasets are used to compare the proposed calibration algorithm with the provided ground-truth parameters (tilt, roll, focal length and camera height) of these sequences: Terrace[1] and Indoor/Outdoor[2]. In addition, three novel datasets are created, two of which are fully calibrated (City Center 1 and 2), so that they provide ground-truth information on both intrinsic and extrinsic camera parameters. The intrinsic parameters are calibrated using a checker board and the MATLAB camera calibration toolbox. The true extrinsic parameters are computed by manually extracting parallel lines from the ground plane and computing the vanishing points. In City Center 3, only measured distances are available which will be used for evaluation. Examples of the datasets are shown in Fig. 9, where the red lines represent the manually measured distances.

4.1   Experiment 1: Fully Calibrated Cameras

The first experiment comprises a field test with the two fully calibrated cameras from the City Center 1 and 2 datasets. The head and feet detector is applied to 30 min of video with approximately 2,500 and 200 pedestrians, resulting in 7,120 and 2,569 detections in the first and second dataset, respectively. After

---

[1] Terrace: CVLab EPFL database of the University of Lausanne [1].
[2] Indoor/Outdoor: ICG lab of the Graz University of Technology [18].

(a) City Center 1   (b) City Center 2   (c) City Center 3

(d) Terrace   (e) Indoor   (f) Outdoor

Fig. 9. Examples of the datasets used in the experiments, red lines are manually measured distances in the scene. (Color figure online)

pre-processing, approximately half of the detections remain and are used for the calibration algorithm. Resulting camera parameters are compared with the ground-truth values. The results are shown in Table 1. The tilt estimation is accurate up to 0.43° for both datasets. The estimated roll is less accurate, caused by a horizontal displacement of the principal point from the image center. The focal length and camera height are estimated accurately.

Next, several manually measured distances in the City Center 1–3 datasets are compared with estimated values from our algorithm. Pixel positions of the measured points on the ground plane are manually annotated. These pixel positions are converted back to world coordinates using the predicted projection matrix. For each combination of two points we compare the estimated distance with our manual measurement. The average error over all distances is shown in Table 3. The first two datasets have an error of approximately 2.5 %, while the third dataset has a larger error, which is due to a curved ground plane.

4.2   Experiment 2: Public Datasets

The proposed system is compared to two auto-calibration methods described by Liu *et al.* [10] (2011) and Liu *et al.* [11] (2013). The method described in [10] uses foreground blobs and estimates the vertical vanishing point and maximum-likelihood focal length. Publication [11] concentrates on calibration of multi-camera networks. This method uses the result of [10] to make a coarse estimation of the camera parameters, of which only the focal length can be used for comparison. The resulting estimated focal lengths and the ground truth are presented in Table 4. The proposed algorithm has the highest accuracy. Note that

Table 1. Ground truth and estimated values of camera parameters of the City Center datasets

Sequence		Tilt (deg)	Roll (deg)	f (pixels)	Height (m)
City C 1 1920 × 1080	GT	107.66	−0.92	1693	6.02
	Est	107.88	−1.38	1631	6.16
City C 2 1920 × 1080	GT	107.56	−0.71	1368	4.60
	Est	107.99	2.95	1397	4.37

Table 2. Ground truth and estimated values of camera parameters of the public datasets (No. of detections: 905, 1,958 and 1,665.)

Sequence		Tilt (deg)	Roll (deg)	f (pixels)	Height (m)
Indoor 1280 × 960	GT	104.31	0.07	1048	4.57
	Est	103.98	−0.20	787	3.78
Outdoor 1280 × 960	GT	109.11	0.96	1198	8.78
	Est	108.89	−0.18	1019	8.83
Terrace 360 × 288	GT	108.41	1.19	807	2.45
	Est	105.50	1.82	850	1.93

Table 3. Estimated distances in City Center datasets

Sequence	City Center 1	City C 2	City C 3
Error (%)	2.48	2.62	3.7

Table 4. Estimated focal lengths for the Outdoor dataset

Algorithm	GT	Liu [10]	Liu [11]	Prop. alg
f (pixels)	1,198	1,545	1,427	1019
Error (%)	-	29	19	15

the detected focal length is smaller than the actual value. This is due to the fact that the horizon line is detected slightly below the actual value and the vertical vanishing point is detected above the actual value (discussed later). However, this does not affect the detected camera orientation. Finally, the three public datasets are calibrated using the proposed algorithm, of which the results are presented in Table 2. For all sequences, the parameters are estimated accurately. The roll is detected up to 1.14° accuracy, the focal length up to 179 pixels and the camera height up to 0.53 m. The tilt estimation of the Terrace sequence is less accurate. Because of the low camera height (2.45 m), the detector was not working optimally, resulting in noisy head and feet detections. Moreover, the small focal length combined with the small camera tilt makes the calculation of the tilt sensitive to noise. When the detected focal length is smaller than the actual value, the detected camera height will also be lower than the actual value. However, if other camera parameters are correct, the accuracy of detected distances in the scene will not be influenced. We have found empirically that the errors compensate exactly (zero error) but this is difficult to prove analytically.

Note that the performance of our calibration cannot be fully benchmarked, since insufficient data is available from the algorithms from literature. Moreover, implementations are not available so that a full simulation can also not be performed. Most of the methods that use pedestrians to derive a vanishing point use controlled scenes with restrictions (e.g. numbers, movement etc.), so that the method do often not apply to unconstrained datasets. As indicated above, in some cases the focal length can be used. All possible objective comparisons have been presented.

Comparing our algorithm with [11] when ignoring our pre- and post-processing stages will lead to a similar performance, because both algorithms use the idea of vanishing point and horizon line estimation from pedestrian locations. In our extensive simulation experiments we have shown that our novel pre- and post-processing improve performance. Specifically, pre-processing improves camera tilt estimation from 3.7 to 1.3° error and post-processing further reduces the error to 0.7°. This strongly suggests that our algorithm outperforms [11].

5   Discussion

The proposed camera model is based on assumptions that do not always hold, e.g. zero skew, square pixels and a flat ground plane. This inevitably results in errors in detected camera parameters and measured distances in the scene. Despite these imperfections, the algorithm is capable of detecting distances in the scene with a limited error of only 3.7 %. The camera roll is affected by a horizontal offset of the principal point, whereas the effect on the other camera parameters of the model imperfections is negligible.

In some of the experiments, we observe that the estimated focal length has a significant error (Indoor sequence in Table 2). The estimated focal length and camera height are related and a smaller estimated focal length results in a smaller estimated camera height. Errors in the derived focal length are thus compensated by the detected camera height and have no influence on detected distances in the scene. Consequently, errors in the focal length do not hamper highly accurate determination of position information of moving objects in the scene.

6   Conclusion

We have presented a novel fully automatic camera calibration algorithm for monocular stationary cameras. We focus on surveillance scenes where typically pedestrians move through the camera view, and use only this information as input for the calibration algorithm. The system can also be used for scenes with other moving objects. After collecting location information from several pedestrians, a full camera calibration matrix is generated based on vanishing-point geometry. This matrix can be used to calculate the real-world position of any moving object in the scene.

First, we propose a pre-processing step which improves estimation of the vertical vanishing point, reducing the error in camera tilt estimation from 3.7 to 1.3°. Second, a novel post-processing stage exploits the height distribution of pedestrians to improve horizon line estimation, further reducing the tilt error to 0.7°. As a third contribution, the scale factor is determined using an average body height, enabling extraction of metric information without manual measurement in the scene. Next, we have performed extensive simulations of the total calibration algorithm for a large range of camera configurations. Monte-Carlo simulations have been used to accurately model the error sources and have shown that derived camera parameters are accurate. Even metric information can be extracted with a low average and maximum error of 1.95 % and 3.2 %, respectively. Benchmarking of the algorithm has shown that the estimated focal length of our system is more accurate than the reported systems in literature. Finally, the algorithm is evaluated using several real-world surveillance datasets in which no restrictions are made on pedestrian movement and position. In real datasets, the error figures are largely the same (metric errors of max. 3.7 %) as in the simulations which confirms the feasibility of the solution.

References

1. Berclaz, J., Fleuret, F., Turetken, E., Fua, P.: Multiple object tracking using K-shortest paths pptimization. IEEE Trans. Pattern Anal. Mach. Intell. (2011)
2. Dalal, N., Triggs, B.: Histograms of oriented gradients for human detection. In: IEEE Computer Society Conference on Computer Vision and Pattern Recognition, CVPR 2005, vol. 1, pp. 886–893, June 2005
3. Dubska, M., Herout, A., Sochor, J.: Automatic camera calibration for traffic understanding. In: Proceedings of the British Machine Vision Conference. BMVA Press (2014)
4. Faugeras, O.D., Toscani, G.: The calibration problem for stereo. In: Proceedings of IEEE Computer Society Conference on Computer Vision and Pattern Recognition, CVPR 1986, Miami Beach, FL, 22–26 June 1986, pp. 15–20. IEEE (1986). IEEE Publ. 86CH2290-5
5. Hartley, R.I., Zisserman, A.: Multiple View Geometry in Computer Vision, 2nd edn. Cambridge University Press, Cambridge (2004). ISBN 0521540518
6. Hartley, R.I.: Self-calibration from multiple views with a rotating camera. In: Eklundh, J.-O. (ed.) ECCV 1994. LNCS, vol. 800, pp. 471–478. Springer, Heidelberg (1994). doi:10.1007/3-540-57956-7_52
7. Huang, S., Ying, X., Rong, J., Shang, Z., Zha, H.: Camera calibration from periodic motion of a pedestrian. In: The IEEE Conference on Computer Vision and Pattern Recognition (CVPR), June 2016
8. Krahnstoever, N., Mendonca, P.: Bayesian autocalibration for surveillance. In: Tenth IEEE International Conference on Computer Vision, ICCV 2005, vol. 2, pp. 1858–1865, October 2005
9. Kusakunniran, W., Li, H., Zhang, J.: A direct method to self-calibrate a surveillance camera by observing a walking pedestrian. In: Digital Image Computing: Techniques and Applications, DICTA 2009, pp. 250–255, December 2009
10. Liu, J., Collins, R.T., Liu, Y.: Surveillance camera autocalibration based on pedestrian height distributions. In: British Machine Vision Conference (BMVC) (2011)
11. Liu, J., Collins, R., Liu, Y.: Robust autocalibration for a surveillance camera network. In: 2013 IEEE Workshop on Applications of Computer Vision (WACV), pp. 433–440, January 2013
12. Lv, F., Zhao, T., Nevatia, R.: Self-calibration of a camera from video of a walking human. In: Proceedings of 16th International Conference on Pattern Recognition, 2002, vol. 1, pp. 562–567 (2002)
13. Lv, F., Zhao, T., Nevatia, R.: Camera calibration from video of a walking human. IEEE Trans. Pattern Anal. Mach. Intell. **28**(9), 1513–1518 (2006)

14. Maybank, S.J., Faugeras, O.D.: A theory of self-calibration of a moving camera. Int. J. Comput. Vision **8**(2), 123–151 (1992). http://dx.doi.org/10.1007/BF00127171
15. Micusik, B., Pajdla, T.: Simultaneous surveillance camera calibration and foot-head homology estimation from human detections. In: 2010 IEEE Conference on Computer Vision and Pattern Recognition (CVPR), pp. 1562–1569, June 2010
16. Millar, W.: Distribution of body weight and height: comparison of estimates based on self-reported and observed measures. J. Epidemiol. Community Health **40**(4), 319–323 (1986)
17. Orghidan, R., Salvi, J., Gordan, M., Orza, B.: Camera calibration using two or three vanishing points. In: 2012 Federated Conference on Computer Science and Information Systems (FedCSIS), pp. 123–130, September 2012
18. Possegger, H., Rther, M., Sternig, S., Mauthner, T., Klopschitz, M., Roth, P.M., Bischof, H.: Unsupervised calibration of camera networks and virtual PTZ cameras. In: Proceedings of Computer Vision Winter Workshop (CVWW) (2012). Supplemental Video, Dataset, Code
19. Zhang, Z.: A flexible new technique for camera calibration. IEEE Trans. Pattern Anal. Mach. Intell. **22**(11), 1330–1334 (2000)

Data-Driven Motion Pattern Segmentation in a Crowded Environments

Jana Trojanová[2(✉)], Karel Křehnáč[1], and François Brémond[2]

[1] Neovision, Prague, Czech Republic
[2] STARS, Inria Sophia Antipolis, Sophia Antipolis, France
`jana.trojanova@inria.fr`

Abstract. Motion is a strong clue for unsupervised grouping of individuals in a crowded environment. We show that collective motion in the crowd can be discovered by temporal analysis of points trajectories. First k-NN graph is constructed to represent the topological structure of point trajectories detected in crowd. Then the data-driven graph segmentation and clustering helps to reveal the interaction of individuals even when mixed motion is presented in data. The method was evaluated against the latest state-of-the-art methods and achieved better performance by more than 20 %.

1 Introduction

Understanding crowd dynamics in complex environments remains an open problem in computer vision due to a large number of individuals exhibiting diverse movement. The crowd dynamics evolve depending on each individual's will as well as that of his neighbors. The variety of interactions among individuals is what makes the task of crowd understanding a difficult problem. Some individuals can exhibit an aggregated motion while others can move independently. Figure 1 shows an example of motion pattern segmentation interpreting these interactions. The term *motion pattern* here represents a spatial region with coherent flow in comparison to its neighboring regions.

Prior research in motion pattern segmentation can mostly be classified into two groups: flow field model-based segmentation and similarity model-based clustering. The first one simulates a moving crowd as a time dependent flow field. The flow field consists of regions with quantitatively different dynamics and motion patterns emerge from the spatio-temporal interactions of individuals. They build on optical flow alike features and use methods such as edge-based segmentation, graph-based segmentation or watershed segmentation. These methods can well describe the structured crowd motion and are the most studied in the motion pattern segmentation. However, they are temporally inconsistent over a longer video shot and work only for high crowd density otherwise the video scene would be over-segmented. A nice overview of such methods can be found in [1].

The second group of methods uses the principle of clustering. Once low-level motion features are detected they are grouped based on some similarity

G. Hua and H. Jégou (Eds.): ECCV 2016 Workshops, Part II, LNCS 9914, pp. 760–774, 2016.
DOI: 10.1007/978-3-319-48881-3_53

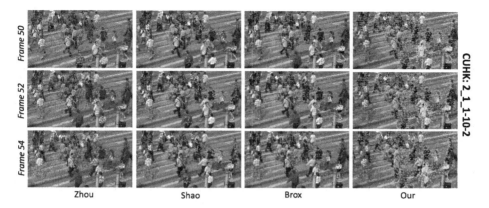

Fig. 1. Segmented motion patterns (or groups segregation) as the crowd evolves in time. The color of point represents the assignment to a group. While groupings are temporally consistent over a set of frames for Brox [2] and Our method. Zhou [3] and Shao [4] fail to maintain consistent groupings between frames. (Color figure online)

measurements or fitted with a probability model. The boom with similarity-based clustering is linked with the success of local motion features such as short point trajectories which can be obtained more easily than the whole trajectory. These points trajectories are more discriminative than local optical flows. The similarity clustering methods can handle structured and unstructured crowds. Representatives of such methods are [5,6]. Recently, probability models showed high potential in discovering semantic regions. Even though the methods can well capture overlapping behaviors and spatial dependencies among them, they require the whole video in advance to learn the probability model [4]. As will be shown in the experiment section the temporal consistency over a longer video shot is not always maintained.

Our framework builds on principles of both groups. No training is required and motion patterns are revealed by temporal analysis of point trajectories detected on a set of 15 frames. First of all an oriented graph is constructed based on k-nearest neighbor of points trajectories. Each node of the graph represents an averaged trajectory. The objective is to keep only the compact neighbor nodes with high collective motion. To do so the graph edges are weighted by correlation among two connected nodes. The graph is segmented by a single threshold to keep nodes with high collective motion. This results in small compact neighbor groups. Clustering is applied to merge compact neighbor groups with similar motion. The propagation of similar motion through neighbors allow us to discover coherent motion in the whole crowded environment. Figure 1 illustrates the capability of our method on crowd data ranging from low to high density.

The automatic motion pattern segmentation in a crowded environment has been an active topic in computer vision for more than one decade. Comparison of the methods is typically done on crowd videos downloaded from the web. The evaluation is done visually on selected videos. Authors often select a set of examples where they have better results than the competing method. Some works annotates the boundary of the crowd and its main direction, but the evaluation only compares the correct direction of the motion patterns. To our knowledge only one public crowd database provides annotation and evaluation respecting motion patterns. The CUHK database [4] has annotation for 300 videos. In each video, a set of 30 frames was selected and detected tracklets were grouped based on the collective motion of individuals. The representation is similar to motion pattern definition, but instead of region only detected tracklets are used to define group segregation.

Moreover, we have found inconsistency and many mistakes in data annotation of the CUHK dataset; see Sect. 3 for more details. The re-annotation we made for the subset of the CUHK database draws the boundary of the motion patterns for a set of frames and captures motion overlaps among motion patterns. The proposed annotation helps to reveal the groupings consistency across a given set of frames. We have benchmarked our results against two state-of-the-art methods and show that in the situation where groups are well segregated (low-motion overlap across set of frames) all state-of-the-art methods provide reliable output. The performance deteriorates with increasing level of mixed motion in the input data.

1.1 Related Work

Segmentation of crowd scenes based on motion has attracted a significant amount of research works. Obtained motion patterns can be used in a wide range of applications like tracking in crowd [7], sink and source seeking [8], or anomaly detection [5]. A recent survey on motion pattern segmentation methods can be found in [1]. Here we concentrate on methods missing from the survey.

The feature extraction is a crucial step and each subsequent task benefits from its clear representation. A high density of people in the crowd performing various irregular motion leads to frequent occlusions. Traditional object detection and tracking algorithms, which are also computationally expensive for a large number of objects, often fail in the case of severe occlusions [1]. The trend is to use pixel-based features, because in high density crowds the local motion features such as point trajectories can be obtained more easily. The generalized KLT tracker [4,6] or Lagrangian framework [5] are quite popular. The provided trajectories capture the actual motion of the crowd and are useful for wide fields of view with low resolution.

Promising results have been shown in [5] where coherent motion is detected based on an analysis of Lagrangian particles. On top of that two-step clustering is applied to construct stable semantic regions from detected time-varying coherent motion. They made a comparison to six state-of-the-art methods on a selected subset of videos. Neither data with annotation or code is provided to the public. Thus we are unable to compare our work to such a promising method.

An interesting characteristic called the crowd collectiveness descriptor has been proposed in [3]. The collectiveness indicates the degree of individual acting as union in collective motion. The descriptor measures the collectiveness in single frame. The grouping consistency between frames is not maintained at all as shown in Fig. 1. Nevertheless the method has a great potential to be extended into temporal domain as shown in [6] and [4].

Collective density clustering was proposed in [6] to recognize local and global coherent motion for varying crowd density. The method was benchmarked against [3] on the Collective Motion Database. The goal was to compare the correct level of collective motion (low, medium, and high). There are only visual examples showing the motion pattern segmentation against state-of-the-art method and one comparison on correct direction detection. The code is not provided therefor we can not compare our work to this method.

In [4] the crowd collectiveness descriptor is used to learn the collective transition priors from a given set of frames. The crowd is analyzed at the group-level where a group is considered as a set of members with a common goal and collective behaviors. The approach provides consistent group segregation in a crowded environment with low motion overlap. Yet the method fails to maintain the consistent groups segregation in complex crowded environment as illustrated in Fig. 1. The groups segregation is equivalent to the motion pattern definition we have. The authors provide a database with annotation and source code. The comparison can be found in our experiments.

We conclude our review with a recent method for object segmentation driven by motion [2]. The graph among each point of a trajectory is formed and minimum cost multicuts function is applied to precisely segment moving object from the scene. The method has incorporated motion, color and spatial distance into the graph to represent the relation between trajectories. The grouping consistency is maintained, but color distance can assign similar individuals with different motion to same group. On top of that it requires extensive training with precisely annotated training data. As the source code is provided we compare our work to this method.

The main contributions of our approach can be concluded as follows:

- We show how to simply extend the crowd collectives descriptor designed for a single frame to the temporal domain by averaging the point trajectories across fixed set of frames. The proposed framework results in temporally consistent groupings of individuals capable of segmenting arbitrary shapes of groups for structured and unstructured crowds with various crowd densities.
- Temporal analysis of point trajectories across a set of frames introduces the problem of overlapping motion patterns. Our framework does not require any training, only one parameter is hardwired. The number of neighbours for k-NN graph construction is set to represent up to four overlapping motion patterns in a particular image area.
- The threshold for graph segmentation is not fixed but it is data-driven and thus better represents the actual motion presented in the crowd. The results on subset of the CUHK dataset show higher accuracy for overlapping motion patterns against the state-of-the-art method.

2   Motion Pattern Segmentation Framework

The idea is that collective motion in the crowd can be discovered by temporal analysis of points trajectories. The analysis of long-term point trajectories has been very popular recently. It played an important role in works related to motion segmentation [2,4,6]. These trajectories are called tracklets, and provide pixel movement in a given set of frames. Nevertheless other optical-flow-based trajectories like large displacement optical flow [9] can be used as input to our framework. Here we stick to dense trajectories presented in [10] since they can filter out movement caused by camera motion. The basic setting is used providing reliable points tracklets for 15 consecutive frames.

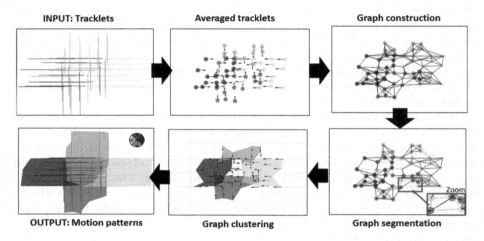

Fig. 2. The framework simplified flowchart. The graph is constructed so that each node (averaged tracklet) is connected by edges to k-NN nodes. During the graph segmentation the edges with low collectiveness are cut-off (red dotted lines). Finally, clustering is applied and connected nodes with similar motion are merged. Best viewed in color. (Color figure online)

We use the similarity graph from the spectral clustering [11] to represent the topological structure of tracklets detected in crowded video scene. We show how to take advantage of the collectiveness descriptor [3] and design criteria for the automatic threshold selection used for the graph segmentation. Figure 2 shows a basic simplified flowchart. The input shows trajectories of four points groups with different directions. Each group of points is starting at different sides of the image and the overlap of their trajectories occurs in the middle of the image. The tracklet of each point is averaged for a given period of time (in this case whole tracklet) and the graph is constructed based on the k-nearest neighbor (k-NN) of averaged tracklets. During graph segmentation with the automated threshold selection, edges with dissimilar motion are cut-off. Only edges with high collective motion remain in the graph. Having obtained a graph connecting nodes with high collective motion, clustering is applied to find coherent motion patterns. The motion patterns can be used in various applications. In this particular work, we concentrate on the overlapping motion pattern segmentation and its evaluation on the CUHK dataset [4]. The individual components of the framework are described next.

2.1 Graph Construction

Interactions of neighbours play an important role in crowded environments. To capture the topological structure of these interactions we construct a similarity graph such that every averaged tracklet is represented by a node v

$$v = (\bar{x}, \bar{y}, \partial x, \partial y) \tag{1}$$

where the first two values are coordinates of the averaged tracklet and the last two represent the average velocity of the tracklet. Every node v is connected via a edge to each of its k-nearest neighbours nodes. Adjacency Matrix A is used to represent the oriented k-NN graph. Matrix rows and columns are labeled with graph nodes $v \in V$. Matrix entries at position (v_i, v_j) are 1 or 0, depending on whether v_i and v_j are connected or not. The matrix A has zero entries on the diagonal, since no tracklet connects to itself.

First we create an adjacency matrix based on k-nearest neighbours of each node. Each line of matrix A (each node with its neighbours) forms a small group of tracklets. In a real scenario noise is present in the data and single distant nodes can connect to the graph. Thus a distance threshold is applied to remove distant nodes from the matrix A with entry 1 as follows

$$A_{Dist}(v_i, v_j) = \begin{cases} 1, & \text{if } A(v_i, v_j) = 1 \ \wedge d(v_i, v_j) < \mu_D + \sigma_D \\ 0, & \text{otherwise} \end{cases} \tag{2}$$

$$\mu_d = \frac{1}{N} \sum_{A(v_i, v_j)=1)} d(v_i, v_j) \tag{3}$$

$$\sigma_d = \sqrt{\sum_{A(v_i, v_j)=1)} \frac{1}{N}(d(v_i, v_j) - \mu_d)^2} \tag{4}$$

where $d(v_i, v_j)$ is the Euclidean distance between two nodes, μ_D and σ_D is the average distance and the distance standard deviation between all nodes in matrix A, N is the sum of entries when matrix $A(v_i, v_j) = 1$.

Figure 3 illustrates the effect of k-NN number selection on graph clustering. In the case when a small number of neighbours is selected the collective motion can not be revealed (first two columns in Fig. 3). Thus we seek the minimum number of neighbors to get precise motion patterns. This number depends on the motion overlap present in the data. For no overlapping movement, $K = 3$ is enough, for partial overlap $K = 5$ is required. For complete overlap $K = 20$

766   J. Trojanová et al.

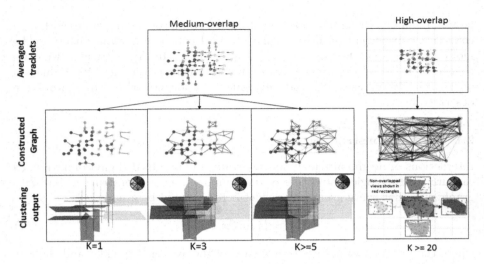

Fig. 3. Visual examples of graph construction for various number of neighbors. First example shows the graph construction for various numbers of k-NN *(first column K = 1 s K = 3, third K = 5)*. The second example shows the constructed graph for high motion overlap. For mixed up motion the minimum number of neighbours is 20.

is required. The lower value of k would result in scattered areas, while a higher number of neighbours would result in the same clustering output. The optimal number of k to reveal up to four mixed motion at a particular segment of the image in 15 consecutive frames is set to $k = 20$ based on empirical evidence. The larger number of neighbours also helps to overcome the noise produced by dense trajectories at a particular area of the image.

2.2   Graph Segmentation

The non-zero entries of adjacency matrix A_{Dist} are weighted based on velocity correlation among a given pair of nodes and forms weighted adjacency matrix

$$W(v_i, v_j) = \begin{cases} corr(v_i, v_j), \text{if } A_{Dist}(v_i, v_j) = 1 \\ 0, \text{otherwise} \end{cases} \quad (5)$$

The matrix W characterizes the behavior consistency among neighbouring individuals in the crowd. The maximum value of matrix W is 1 and it means that nodes have the same direction of velocity vectors. If two connected tracklets move in the same direction and have highly correlated motion we want to preserve the edge, otherwise the edge should be removed from the graph. By applying the threshold T on the matrix W, we ensure that only highly correlated neighbors remain in the graph. The selection of threshold from interval $T \in (0, 1)$ is driven by data. We make use of the collectiveness descriptor from

Fig. 4. The values of collectiveness criteria defined in Eq. 7 can be seen on the right side. On the left side examples for the highest and lowest criteria curve are shown. The top row shows a visual example for curve marked with a when the criteria value is close to 1 for the threshold interval (0,0.98). It is almost an ideal case where the velocity vectors have a similar direction, their correlation variation is not bigger than 2 %. The bottom row shows example for the curve marked with b when the criteria has the lowest value. It shows the hardest example of the CUHK subset. The detail shows that velocity vectors for both directions are mixed. The last column of the figure shows ground truth annotation for selected examples. It can be seen that the criteria value captures the level of motion overlap in input data.

[3] and define individual collectiveness for each node v_i and its neighbours as

$$\phi_{v_i}(T) = \frac{1}{N_i} \sum_{W>T} w(v_i, v_j) \qquad (6)$$

where N_i is number of edges connected to node v_i after applying threshold T and ϕ_{v_i} thus represents the mean correlation value between node v_i and its neighbours v_j higher than threshold T. Each node and his neighbours form a small group. While in Zhou et al. [3] the collectiveness was computed for one fixed threshold, here we change the threshold to evaluate the collectiveness of each group. The $\phi_{v_i}(T)$ measures the individual collectiveness of the group. Now we can define collectiveness criteria for optimal threshold selection as follows

$$T^* = \underset{T \in <0,1>}{argmax}(\frac{N_T}{N_G} \cdot \frac{1}{N_G} \sum_{W>T} \phi_{v_i}) \qquad (7)$$

The criteria measures normalized average collectiveness for all individual groups, N_G is the number of groups, and N_T is the number of groups with individual collectiveness bigger than the threshold. Figure 4 shows the value of the criteria for threshold values in interval $T \in (0,1)$ on a subset of the CUHK dataset. For each video segment we have one criteria curve. The value of the criteria for the minimum threshold $T = 0$ serves as a measure of how much structured motion is present in the video segment. The criteria value for each threshold tell us how big the collectiveness is across all groups formed in the graph.

In the ideal case (top line in Fig. 4) when velocity vectors are highly correlated across the whole sequence, the criteria curve remains the same for a long interval of threshold T. This tell us that graph nodes are well separated no matter which value of T we select and the motion of each group is highly correlated.

The decrease in criteria value is caused by lower correlation between the node and its neighbours which form a group. The threshold value $T = 1$ means that we don't allow any velocity difference between connected nodes. Lowering the threshold means that we allow some difference, but the question is how to define the exact of the velocity variation that is permitted? We seek the optimal balance between the number of groups and their average collectiveness represented by the maximum value of the criteria defined in Eq. 7. The threshold for each video sequence is optimized using the golden section search method. After applying the threshold T^* on matrix W each node preserves the edges with high correlation and cut-off the rest.

2.3   Graph Clustering

Having obtained a segmented graph that forms small compact groups (neighbours around each node) we can proceed with clustering. The existing graph edges maximize average collectiveness across the whole video segment. But the segmented graph tell us only the link between closest nodes. Now we want to cluster the graph nodes to form the motion pattern.

Figure 5 illustrates the clustering on a simple example. The decision whether to merge the neighbour's nodes depends on the correlation between the parent node and its children. The threshold value for graph segmentation defines how big variation is allowed between two nodes. Ideally this value would be set to 1 and only same direction nodes will be connected. In real data the threshold is typically around 0.95 which means 5 % variation between two nodes is allowed. We recursively search through the graph and look if parent/children correlation fits the threshold. If all the children meet the threshold the neighbour node is merged in the same cluster as the parent node. If any of the children violate the correlation threshold the recursive search for the neighbour node is stopped.

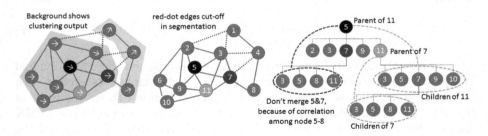

Fig. 5. Visual example of graph clustering through recursive search. Here we start from node 5 and concentrate on neighbour nodes 7 and 11. If the correlation between all of the children nodes and the parent node fits the threshold T the neighbour node 11 is assigned to the same cluster as node 5. Otherwise the recursive search is stopped. Node 7 is eventually assigned to the same cluster through node 11.

The clustering reflects arbitrary shapes appearing in the crowd while allowing varying size of clusters. The proposed framework is capable of segmenting motion patterns for various levels of density, from highly aggregated motion to low density disconnected areas.

3   Experiments on the CUHK Dataset

The proposed framework is evaluated on a challenging subset of the CUHK video dataset [4]. We first describe the details about the dataset and drawbacks of the provided annotation. Then we demonstrate the results obtained for our method versus state-of-the-art [2,4].

The CUHK dataset provides annotation for 300 segments for varying length of video segment ranging from 7 up to 67 frames. Annotation of the data was made for tracklets found by the generalized KLT tracker. The tracklets are grouped based on the criterion that members in the same group have a common goal and form collective movement. Tracklets not belonging to any group are annotated as outliers. Figure 6 show inconsistency and mistakes observed in data annotation. More than 50 % of data have inconsistency in terms of merging distant groups versus splitting neighbours to different groups. Moreover serious mistakes like ignoring the opposite direction of individuals or noise tracklets assigned to the nearest group were discovered. Thus we have decided to re-annotate the database.

Fig. 6. Figure illustrates the annotation inconsistency (first two images in top row) and errors (last two images in top row) in the CUHK database [4] and our re-annotation (bottom row). First image shows merge of the individuals in blue circles who are separated by individual moving in different direction. In contrast let's look at the second image with pedestrians running in a marathon. All pedestrians are running in same direction, there is no obvious reason to separate the groups, thus we keep them as one. The third image shows that the opposite direction was ignored and merged with the main direction. In the fourth image the escalator movement is merged with the main direction (red circles show observed errors). (Color figure online)

The full CUHK dataset contains repeating scenes clipped in separate video segments. From the set of 300 annotated video segments there are actually 140 unique scenes, the rest are the same views for different time window. The database consist of scenes like marathon runners, military marching, protesting pedestrians, escalators, cross walk, public transport stations, shopping malls or people walking in the street.

We have further divided the database to simple and complex scenarios. In simple scenarios the groups of individuals can be easily segregated while in complex scenarios the individuals are mixed in a given set of frames. Mixed individuals means that at a particular part of the image pedestrians move in more than one direction (e.g. cross-walk). Both scenarios typically have a crowd moving in one or two main directions with some individuals moving independently. Two-thirds of the CUHK data contain simple scenarios, the rest is considered as complex scenarios. Some of the complex scenarios are so challenging that annotation of such videos would be very arguable. Thus we selected 25 out of 40 complex scenarios and 25 out of 100 for simple scenarios.

The selected 50 videos spans a wide range of crowded scenes covering different pedestrian size and various crowd densities. Figure 6 compares the original annotation to our new one. The ground truth provides boundary information and main direction of the motion pattern. Two annotators cross-validate their outputs. The boundary is drawn to capture spatial region with coherent flow in a given set of frames. The various speeds (e.g. individuals running on escalators) are ignored. The same starting frame as in [4] was selected for data re-annotation, each re-annotated set last 30 frames. In total 1500 re-annotated frames are used as a benchmark. Our annotation of groups boundaries for a given set of frames helps to reveal the consistency of individuals grouping between frames.

3.1 Results on CUHK Data

In order to evaluate the framework we compare its performance against recent state-of-the-art methods proposed in [4] and [2]. We run available binaries on the subset of the CUHK data comprising 1500 re-annotated images. The obtained results are treated as a clustering problem. To benchmark the performance of the methods we use the Purity and F-measure.

The density of point trajectories between our method and state-of-the-art differs, see Fig. 7. Therefore the computation of the true positives (TP), false positive (FP) and false negatives (FN) is based on overlap between the ground truth area and the area drawn around clustered point trajectories.

The cluster switching between frames is misleading. Building an application for abnormal activity recognition on top of the method with cluster switching between frames would produce an enormous number of false alarms. By using the area overlap and evaluation across the whole sequence of 30 frames we also penalize the clustering inconsistency when clusters switch between frames.

The state-of-the-art method has various parameters that can be change for boosting the performance. For the method in [4] there are 8 parameters. As the available code was tuned for the CUHK dataset we have kept the original setting.

Table 1. Results on the subset of the CUHK database for simple (left) and complex (right) scenarios. We report results for **D**: purity, **P**: average precision, **R**: average recall, **F**: F1-measure. Subscript W represents clusters weighted by their size. The first three rows show unweighted clustering, the last three rows show clustering weighted by the size of the cluster

	Simple scenario				Complex scenario			
	D	P	R	F	D	P	R	F
Our	**81.70 %**	**78.88 %**	**85.92 %**	**81.96 %**	**70.51 %**	**72.16 %**	**81.81 %**	**75.77 %**
Shao et al. [4]	41.37 %	52.77 %	46.06 %	47.43 %	38.04 %	44.68 %	46.70 %	45.08 %
Brox et al. [2]	58.47 %	63.54 %	52.58 %	55.85 %	47.52 %	58.72 %	43.16 %	47.74 %
	D_W	P_W	R_W	F_W	D_W	P_W	R_W	F_W
Our	**91.62 %**	**90.42 %**	**95.26 %**	**92.47 %**	**84.00 %**	**80.55 %**	**91.10 %**	**84.74 %**
Shao et al. [4]	68.10 %	81.28 %	69.16 %	72.27 %	65.11 %	71.86 %	72.52 %	71.27 %
Brox et al. [2]	81.45 %	76.25 %	72.33 %	71.17 %	74.13 %	68.31 %	61.63 %	62.00 %

For the method in [2], we use the available binaries and run the code against the crowd data to see how well the parameters tuned for object segmentation work for crowded environments. Additionally there are two independent parameters: number of frames and threshold. We observe that changing the number of frames from 8 to 15 did not significantly affect the results (change of F-measure was around 0.01 %). Only the threshold influences the final number of clusters in the video. The best results were obtained for threshold 0.5.

Table 1 provides two types of results, unweighted and weighted. For unweighted results the F-measure uses average precision and recall across all the clusters in the given video. For weighted results the precision and recall for each cluster is weighted by the proportional cluster size. For the unweighted F-measure we outperform the state-of-the-art by 30 %. Such a big difference in performance is caused by missed irregular clusters. For instance a single individual walking in a different direction than main clusters, see example in Fig. 7. For the weighted F-measure the performance of state-of-the-art increases by 25 %, since the methods capture the main clusters. Nevertheless we are still 20 % ahead in performance, since our method does not suffer from cluster switching between frames. The methods in [2,4] provide good results for main clusters but lack the capability of detecting the irregular motion of individuals. Moreover, distant individuals are clustered together even if they move in the opposite direction and method in [4] suffers from cluster switching between the frames.

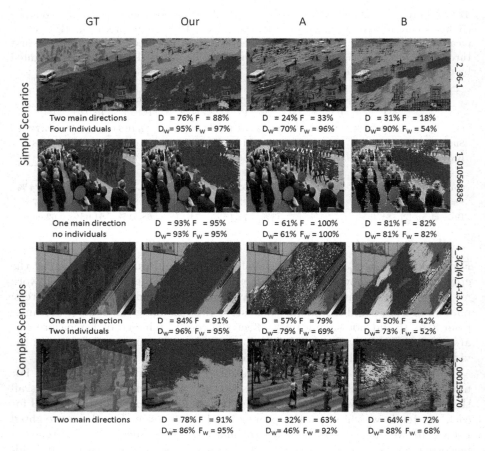

Fig. 7. Results for a simple scenario with easily separable groups and a complex scenario with mixed groups. The first column shows the ground truth, the next three columns show the output of our method, method A [4] and method B [2]. The D, F, D_W, and F_W are defined in Table 1. The first row shows a scene with two main opposite directions and several individuals highlighted by pink, red, yellow and cyan colors. Our method is capable of recognizing all motion patterns, method A can only recognize two main directions and method B incorrectly assigns two opposite direction as one and creates a separate cluster for cars with a different color from pedestrians. The second row shows a scene where a military unit is marching. All methods correctly cluster the scene. The third row shows a scene with escalators. Method A has inconsistent grouping. Pedestrians in the main direction highlighted in blue are assigned to the pink and yellow clusters for some of the frames. Method B merges distant pedestrians to one group highlighted in pink and over-segments the main direction into three clusters highlighted in blue, yellow and cyan. The last row shows a challenging cross walk scene where people mix together. Our method and method A correctly recognize the clusters. Method B over-segments the pedestrians moving down into two clusters and some distant point trajectories in the bottom are merged with the blue cluster although they move in opposite directions. (Color figure online)

4   Conclusion

This paper introduced a framework for motion pattern segmentation in crowded environments. The proposed method is fully unsupervised and uses short tracklets detected by dense trajectories. It reveals the collective motion of individuals independent of the crowd density. Our method can detect different scales of groups with arbitrary shapes and distinguish the big groups and irregular motion of individuals that move otherwise. The resulting grouping of individuals is temporally consistent over the set of frames, a property that requires post-processing in the existing approaches.

We have tested our approach on a subset of the CUHK database. Experimental results show that our approach outperforms existing state-of-the-art method by more than 20 %. However, we note that the annotation of motion patterns is subjective and differs between people. In future work we will evaluate our framework on practical applications like unusual event recognition and tracking in crowded environments.

We will conclude this paper by summarising the framework shortcomings. The average tracklet is computed across 15 frames. This was chosen based on the dense trajectory output and provides satisfying results for the given set of videos. In future this property should be also data driven as the dynamic of the crowd evolves in time. For rapidly moving objects, it might happen that the point trajectories are short. In these cases, we would increase the number of frames for computation of the averaged tracklet.

From our understanding of the framework the graph clustering part is the most weak and offers a real scope for improvement. Clustering of the graph should be done from a bigger perspective than just considering the parent and children of the neighbour node. We plan to apply a multi-resolution approach in order to reduce the over-segmentation of data.

Acknowledgement. This work was partially supported by the People Programme (Marie Curie Actions) of the European Unions Seventh Framework Programme FP7/2007-2013/ under REA grant agreement n[324359].

References

1. Li, T., Chang, H., Wang, M., Ni, B., Hong, R., Yan, S.: Crowded scene analysis: a survey. IEEE Trans. Circ. Syst. Video Technol. **25**(3), 367–386 (2015)
2. Keuper, M., Andres, B., Brox, T.: Motion trajectory segmentation via minimum cost multicuts. In: The IEEE International Conference on Computer Vision (ICCV), December 2015
3. Zhou, B., Tang, X., Wang, X.: Measuring crowd collectiveness. In: Proceedings of the IEEE Conference on Computer Vision and Pattern Recognition, pp. 3049–3056 (2013)
4. Shao, J., Loy, C.C., Wang, X.: Learning scene-independent group descriptors for crowd understanding. In: TCSVT (2016)

5. Wang, W., Lin, W., Chen, Y., Wu, J., Wang, J., Sheng, B.: Finding coherent motions and semantic regions in crowd scenes: a diffusion and clustering approach. In: Fleet, D., Pajdla, T., Schiele, B., Tuytelaars, T. (eds.) ECCV 2014, Part I. LNCS, vol. 8689, pp. 756–771. Springer, Heidelberg (2014)

6. Wu, Y., Ye, Y., Zhao, C.: Coherent motion detection with collective density clustering. In: Proceedings of the 23rd Annual ACM Conference on Multimedia Conference, pp. 361–370. ACM (2015)

7. Rodriguez, M., Sivic, J., Laptev, I., Audibert, J.Y.: Data-driven crowd analysis in videos. In: 2011 IEEE International Conference on Computer Vision (ICCV), pp. 1235–1242. IEEE (2011)

8. Jodoin, P.M., Benezeth, Y., Wang, Y.: Meta-tracking for video scene understanding. In: 2013 10th IEEE International Conference on Advanced Video and Signal Based Surveillance (AVSS), pp. 1–6. IEEE (2013)

9. Weinzaepfel, P., Revaud, J., Harchaoui, Z., Schmid, C.: Deepflow: large displacement optical flow with deep matching. In: Proceedings of the IEEE International Conference on Computer Vision, pp. 1385–1392 (2013)

10. Wang, H., Schmid, C.: Action recognition with improved trajectories. In: IEEE International Conference on Computer Vision, Sydney, Australia (2013)

11. von Luxburg, U.: A tutorial on spectral clustering. Stat. Comput. **17**(4), 395–416 (2007)

W21 - The Visual Object Tracking Challenge Workshop

The Visual Object Tracking VOT2016 Challenge Results

Matej Kristan[1(✉)], Aleš Leonardis[2], Jiři Matas[3], Michael Felsberg[4],
Roman Pflugfelder[5], Luka Čehovin[1], Tomáš Vojíř[3], Gustav Häger[4],
Alan Lukežič[1], Gustavo Fernández[5], Abhinav Gupta[10], Alfredo Petrosino[30],
Alireza Memarmoghadam[36], Alvaro Garcia-Martin[32], Andrés Solís Montero[39],
Andrea Vedaldi[40], Andreas Robinson[4], Andy J. Ma[18], Anton Varfolomieiev[23],
Aydin Alatan[26], Aykut Erdem[16], Bernard Ghanem[22], Bin Liu[45],
Bohyung Han[31], Brais Martinez[38], Chang-Ming Chang[34], Changsheng Xu[11],
Chong Sun[12], Daijin Kim[31], Dapeng Chen[43], Dawei Du[35], Deepak Mishra[21],
Dit-Yan Yeung[19], Erhan Gundogdu[7], Erkut Erdem[16], Fahad Khan[4],
Fatih Porikli[6,9,29], Fei Zhao[11], Filiz Bunyak[37], Francesco Battistone[30],
Gao Zhu[9], Giorgio Roffo[42], Gorthi R.K. Sai Subrahmanyam[21],
Guilherme Bastos[33], Guna Seetharaman[27], Henry Medeiros[25],
Hongdong Li[6,9], Honggang Qi[35], Horst Bischof[15], Horst Possegger[15],
Huchuan Lu[12], Hyemin Lee[31], Hyeonseob Nam[28], Hyung Jin Chang[20],
Isabela Drummond[33], Jack Valmadre[40], Jae-chan Jeong[13], Jae-il Cho[13],
Jae-Yeong Lee[13], Jianke Zhu[44], Jiayi Feng[11], Jin Gao[11], Jin Young Choi[8],
Jingjing Xiao[2], Ji-Wan Kim[13], Jiyeoup Jeong[8], João F. Henriques[40],
Jochen Lang[39], Jongwon Choi[8], Jose M. Martinez[32], Junliang Xing[11],
Junyu Gao[11], Kannappan Palaniappan[37], Karel Lebeda[41], Ke Gao[37],
Krystian Mikolajczyk[20], Lei Qin[11], Lijun Wang[12], Longyin Wen[34],
Luca Bertinetto[40], Madan Kumar Rapuru[21], Mahdieh Poostchi[37],
Mario Maresca[30], Martin Danelljan[4], Matthias Mueller[22], Mengdan Zhang[11],
Michael Arens[14], Michel Valstar[38], Ming Tang[11], Mooyeol Baek[31],
Muhammad Haris Khan[38], Naiyan Wang[19], Nana Fan[17], Noor Al-Shakarji[37],
Ondrej Miksik[40], Osman Akin[16], Payman Moallem[36], Pedro Senna[33],
Philip H.S. Torr[40], Pong C. Yuen[18], Qingming Huang[17,35],
Rafael Martin-Nieto[32], Rengarajan Pelapur[37], Richard Bowden[41],
Robert Laganière[39], Rustam Stolkin[2], Ryan Walsh[25], Sebastian B. Krah[14],
Shengkun Li[34], Shengping Zhang[17], Shizeng Yao[37], Simon Hadfield[41],
Simone Melzi[42], Siwei Lyu[34], Siyi Li[19], Stefan Becker[14], Stuart Golodetz[40],
Sumithra Kakanuru[21], Sunglok Choi[13], Tao Hu[35], Thomas Mauthner[15],
Tianzhu Zhang[11], Tony Pridmore[38], Vincenzo Santopietro[30], Weiming Hu[11],
Wenbo Li[24], Wolfgang Hübner[14], Xiangyuan Lan[18], Xiaomeng Wang[38],
Xin Li[17], Yang Li[44], Yiannis Demiris[20], Yifan Wang[12], Yuankai Qi[17],
Zejian Yuan[43], Zexiong Cai[18], Zhan Xu[44], Zhenyu He[17], and Zhizhen Chi[12]

[1] University of Ljubljana, Ljubljana, Slovenia
`matej.kristan@fri.uni-lj.si`
[2] University of Birmingham, Birmingham, England
[3] Czech Technical University, Praha, Czech Republic

ⓒ Springer International Publishing Switzerland 2016
G. Hua and H. Jégou (Eds.): ECCV 2016 Workshops, Part II, LNCS 9914, pp. 777–823, 2016.
DOI: 10.1007/978-3-319-48881-3_54

[4] Linköping University, Linköping, Sweden
[5] Austrian Institute of Technology, Seibersdorf, Austria
[6] ARC Centre of Excellence for Robotic Vision, Brisbane, Australia
[7] Aselsan Research Center, Ankara, Turkey
[8] ASRI, Seoul, South Korea
[9] Australian National University, Canberra, Australia
[10] Carnegie Mellon University, Pittsburgh, USA
[11] Chinese Academy of Sciences, Beijing, China
[12] Dalian University of Technology, Dalian, China
[13] Electronics and Telecommunications Research Institute, Seoul, South Korea
[14] Fraunhofer IOSB, Karlsruhe, Germany
[15] Graz University of Technology, Graz, Austria
[16] Hacettepe University, Çankaya, Turkey
[17] Harbin Institute of Technology, Harbin, China
[18] Hong Kong Baptist University, Kowloon Tong, China
[19] Hong Kong University of Science and Technology, Hong Kong, China
[20] Imperial College London, London, England
[21] Indian Institute of Space Science and Technology, Thiruvananthapuram, India
[22] KAUST, Thuwal, Saudi Arabia
[23] Kyiv Polytechnic Institute, Kiev, Ukraine
[24] Lehigh University, Bethlehem, USA
[25] Marquette University, Milwaukee, USA
[26] Middle East Technical University, Çankaya, Turkey
[27] Naval Research Lab, Washington, D.C., USA
[28] NAVER Corporation, Seongnam, South Korea
[29] Data61/CSIRO, Eveleigh, Australia
[30] Parthenope University of Naples, Napoli, Italy
[31] POSTECH, Pohang, South Korea
[32] Universidad Autónoma de Madrid, Madrid, Spain
[33] Universidade Federal de Itajubá, Pinheirinho, Brazil
[34] University at Albany, Albany, USA
[35] University of Chinese Academy of Sciences, Beijing, China
[36] University of Isfahan, Isfahan, Iran
[37] University of Missouri, Columbia, USA
[38] University of Nottingham, Nottingham, England
[39] University of Ottawa, Ottawa, Canada
[40] University of Oxford, Oxford, England
[41] University of Surrey, Guildford, England
[42] University of Verona, Verona, Italy
[43] Xi'an Jiaotong University, Xi'an, China
[44] Zhejiang University, Hangzhou, China
[45] Moshanghua Technology Co., Beijing, China

Abstract. The Visual Object Tracking challenge VOT2016 aims at comparing short-term single-object visual trackers that do not apply pre-learned models of object appearance. Results of 70 trackers are presented, with a large number of trackers being published at major computer vision conferences and journals in the recent years. The number of tested state-of-the-art trackers makes the VOT 2016 the largest and most challenging benchmark on short-term tracking to date. For each participating tracker, a short description is provided in the Appendix. The VOT2016 goes beyond its predecessors by (i) introducing a new semi-automatic ground truth bounding box annotation methodology and (ii) extending the evaluation system with the no-reset experiment. The dataset, the evaluation kit as well as the results are publicly available at the challenge website (http://votchallenge.net).

Keywords: Performance   evaluation   ·   Short-term   single-object trackers · VOT

1   Introduction

Visual tracking remains a highly popular research area of computer vision, with the number of motion and tracking papers published at high profile conferences exceeding 40 papers annually. The significant activity in the field over last two decades is reflected in the abundance of review papers [1–9]. In response to the high number of publications, several initiatives emerged to establish a common ground for tracking performance evaluation. The earliest and most influential is the PETS [10], which is the longest lasting initiative that proposed frameworks for performance evaluation in relation to surveillance systems applications. Other frameworks have been presented since with focus on surveillance systems and event detection, (e.g., CAVIAR[1], i-LIDS[2], ETISEO[3]), change detection [11], sports analytics (e.g., CVBASE[4]), faces (e.g. FERET [12,13]), long-term tracking[5] and the multiple target tracking [14,15][6].

In 2013 the Visual object tracking, VOT, initiative was established to address performance evaluation for short-term visual object trackers. The initiative aims at establishing datasets, performance evaluation measures and toolkits as well as creating a platform for discussing evaluation-related issues. Since its emergence in 2013, three workshops and challenges have been carried out in conjunction with the ICCV2013 (VOT2013 [16]), ECCV2014 (VOT2014 [17]) and ICCV2015 (VOT2015 [18]). This paper discusses the VOT2016 challenge, organized in conjunction with the ECCV2016 Visual object tracking workshop, and the results obtained. Like VOT2013, VOT2014 and VOT2015, the VOT2016 challenge considers single-camera, single-target, model-free, causal trackers, applied to short-term tracking. The *model-free* property means that the only training example is provided by the bounding box in the first frame. The *short-term* tracking means that trackers are assumed not to be capable of performing successful re-detection

---

[1] http://homepages.inf.ed.ac.uk/rbf/CAVIARDATA1.
[2] http://www.homeoffice.gov.uk/science-research/hosdb/i-lids.
[3] http://www-sop.inria.fr/orion/ETISEO.
[4] http://vision.fe.uni-lj.si/cvbase06/.
[5] http://www.micc.unifi.it/LTDT2014/.
[6] https://motchallenge.net.

after the target is lost and they are therefore reset after such event. The *causality* means that the tracker does not use any future frames, or frames prior to re-initialization, to infer the object position in the current frame. In the following, we overview the most closely related work and point out the contributions of VOT2016.

1.1 Related Work

Several works that focus on performance evaluation in short-term visual object tracking [16, 17, 19–24] have been published in the last three years. The currently most widely used methodologies for performance evaluation originate from three benchmark papers, in particular the Online tracking benchmark (OTB) [21], the 'Amsterdam Library of Ordinary Videos' (ALOV) [22] and the 'Visual object tracking challenge' (VOT) [16–18].

Performance Measures. The OTB- and ALOV-related methodologies, like [21, 22, 24, 25], evaluate a tracker by initializing it on the first frame and letting it run until the end of the sequence, while the VOT-related methodologies [16–20] reset the tracker once it drifts off the target. Performance is evaluated in all of these approaches by overlaps between the bounding boxes predicted from the tracker with the ground truth bounding boxes. The OTB and ALOV initially considered performance evaluation based on object center estimation as well, but as shown in [26], the center-based measures are highly brittle and overlap-based measures should be preferred. The ALOV measures the tracking performance as the F-measure at 0.5 overlap threshold and a similar measure was proposed by OTB. Recently, it was demonstrated in [19] that such threshold is over-restrictive, since an overlap below 0.5 does not clearly indicate a tracking failure in practice. The OTB introduced a success plot which represents the percentage of frames for which the overlap measure exceeds a threshold, with respect to different thresholds, and developed an ad-hoc performance measure computed as the area under the curve in this plot. This measure remains one of the most widely used measures in tracking papers. It was later analytically proven by [20, 26] that the ad-hoc measure is equivalent to the average overlap (AO), which can be computed directly without intermediate success plots, giving the measure a clear interpretation. An analytical model was recently proposed [19] to study the average overlap measures with and without resets in terms of tracking accuracy estimator. The analysis showed that the no-reset AO measures are biased estimators with large variance while the VOT reset-based average overlap drastically reduces the bias and variance and is not hampered by the varying sequence lengths in the dataset.

Čehovin et al. [20, 26] provided a highly detailed theoretical and experimental analysis of a number of the popular performance measures. Based on that analysis, the VOT2013 [16] selected the average overlap with resets and number of tracking failures as their main performance criteria, measuring geometric accuracy and robustness respectively. The VOT2013 introduced a ranking-based methodology that accounted for statistical significance of the results, which was extended with the tests of practical differences in the VOT2014 [17]. The notion of practical differences is unique to the VOT challenges and relates to the uncertainty of the ground truth annotation. The VOT ranking methodology treats each sequence as a competition among the trackers. Trackers are ranked on each sequence and ranks are averaged over all sequences. This is called the sequence-normalized ranking. An alternative is sequence-pooled ranking [19], which ranks the average performance on all sequences. Accuracy-robustness ranking plots were proposed [16] to visualize the results. A drawback of the AR-rank plots is that they do not show the absolute performance. In VOT2015 [18], the AR-raw plots from [19,20] were adopted to show the absolute average performance. The VOT2013 [16] and VOT2014 [17] selected the winner of the challenge by averaging the accuracy and robustness ranks, meaning that the accuracy and robustness were treated as equivalent "competitions". A high average rank means that a tracker was well-performing in accuracy as well as robustness relative to the other trackers. While ranking converts the accuracy and robustness to equal scales, the averaged rank cannot be interpreted in terms of a concrete tracking application result. To address this, the VOT2015 [18] introduced a new measure called the expected average overlap (EAO) that combines the raw values of per-frame accuracies and failures in a principled manner and has a clear practical interpretation. The EAO measures the expected no-reset overlap of a tracker run on a short-term sequence. In principle, this measure reflects the same property as the AO [21] measure, but, since it is computed from the VOT reset-based experiment, it does not suffer from the large variance and has a clear definition of what the short-term sequence means. VOT2014 [17] pointed out that speed is an important factor in many applications and introduced a speed measure called the equivalent filter operations (EFO) that partially accounts for the speed of computer used for tracker analysis.

The VOT2015 [18] noted that state-of-the-art performance is often misinterpreted as requiring a tracker to *score as number one* on a benchmark, often leading authors to creatively select sequences and experiments and omit related trackers in scientific papers to reach the apparent *top performance*. To expose this misconception, the VOT2015 computed the average performance of the participating trackers that were published at top recent conferences. This value is called the VOT2015 state-of-the-art bound and any tracker exceeding this performance on the VOT2015 benchmark should be considered state-of-the-art according to the VOT standards.

Datasets. The current trend in computer vision datasets construction appears to be focused on increasing the number of sequences in the datasets [22–25,27], but often much less attention is being paid to the quality of its content and annotation. For example, some datasets disproportionally mix grayscale and color sequences and in most datasets the attributes like occlusion and illumination change are annotated only globally even though they may occur only at a small number of frames in a video. The dataset size is commonly assumed to imply quality. In contrast, the VOT2013 [16] argued that large datasets do not necessarily imply diversity or richness in attributes. Over the last three years, the VOT has developed a methodology that automatically constructs a moderately sized dataset from a large pool of sequences. The uniqueness of this methodology is that it explicitly optimizes diversity in visual attributes while focusing on sequences which are difficult to track. In addition, the sequences in the VOT datasets are per-frame annotated by visual attributes, which is in stark contrast to the related datasets that apply global annotation. It was recently shown [19] that performance measures computed from global attribute annotations are significantly biased toward the dominant attributes in the sequences, while the bias is significantly reduced with per-frame annotation, even in presence of misannotations.

Most closely related works to the work described in this paper are the recent VOT2013 [16], VOT2014 [17] and VOT2015 [18] challenges. Several novelties in benchmarking short-term trackers were introduced through these challenges. They provide a cross-platform evaluation kit with tracker-toolkit communication protocol, allowing easy integration with third-party trackers, per-frame annotated datasets and state-of-the-art performance evaluation methodology for in-depth tracker analysis from several performance aspects. The results were published in joint papers [16–18] of which the VOT2015 [18] paper alone exceeded 120 coauthors. The evaluation kit, the dataset, the tracking outputs and the code to reproduce all the results are made freely-available from the VOT initiative homepage[7]. The advances proposed by VOT have also influenced the development of related methodologies and benchmark papers like [23–25].

1.2   The VOT2016 Challenge

VOT2016 follows VOT2015 challenge and considers the same class of trackers. The dataset and evaluation toolkit are provided by the VOT2016 organizers. The evaluation kit records the output bounding boxes from the tracker, and if it detects tracking failure, re-initializes the tracker. The authors participating in the challenge were required to integrate their tracker into the VOT2016 evaluation kit, which automatically performed a standardized experiment. The results were analyzed by the VOT2016 evaluation methodology. In addition to the VOT reset-based experiment, the toolkit conducted the main OTB [21] experiment in which a tracker is initialized in the first frame and left to track until the end of the sequence without resetting. The performance on this experiment is evaluated by the average overlap measure [21].

Participants were expected to submit a single set of results per tracker. Participants who have investigated several trackers submitted a single result per tracker. Changes in the parameters did not constitute a different tracker. The tracker was required to run with fixed parameters on all experiments. The tracking method itself was allowed to internally change specific parameters, but these had to be set automatically by the tracker, e.g., from the image size and the initial size of the bounding box, and were not to be set by detecting a specific

---

[7] http://www.votchallenge.net.

test sequence and then selecting the parameters that were hand-tuned to this sequence. The organizers of VOT2016 were allowed to participate in the challenge, but did not compete for the winner of VOT2016 challenge title. Further details are available from the challenge homepage[8].

The advances of VOT2016 over VOT2013, VOT2014 and VOT2015 are the following: (i) The ground truth bounding boxes in the VOT2015 dataset have been re-annotated. Each frame in the VOT2015 dataset has been manually per-pixel segmented and bounding boxes have been automatically generated from the segmentation masks. (ii) A new methodology was developed for automatic placement of a bounding box by optimizing a well defined cost function on manually per-pixel segmented images. (iii) The evaluation system from VOT2015 [18] is extended and the bounding box overlap estimation is constrained to image region. The toolkit now supports the OTB [21] no-reset experiment and their main performance measures. (iv) The VOT2015 introduced a second sub-challenge VOT-TIR2015 held under the VOT umbrella which deals with tracking in infrared and thermal imagery [28]. Similarly, the VOT2016 is accompanied with VOT-TIR2016, and the challenge and its results are discussed in a separate paper submitted to the VOT2016 workshop [29].

The remainder of this paper is structured as follows. In Sect. 2, the new dataset is introduced. The methodology is outlined in Sect. 3, the main results are discussed in Sect. 4 and conclusions are drawn in Sect. 5.

2   The VOT2016 Dataset

VOT2013 [16] and VOT2014 [17] introduced a semi-automatic sequence selection methodology to construct a dataset rich in visual attributes but small enough to keep the time for performing the experiments reasonably low. In VOT2015 [18], the methodology was extended into a fully automated sequence selection with the selection process focusing on challenging sequences. The methodology was applied in VOT2015 [18] to produce a highly challenging VOT2015 dataset.

Results of VOT2015 showed that the dataset was not saturated and the same sequences were used for VOT2016. The VOT2016 dataset thus contains all 60 sequences from VOT2015, where each sequence is per-frame annotated by the following visual attributes: (i) occlusion, (ii) illumination change, (iii) motion change, (iv) size change, (v) camera motion. In case a particular frame did not correspond to any of the five attributes, we denoted it as (vi) unassigned.

In VOT2015, the rotated bounding boxes have been manually placed in each frame of the sequence by experts and cross checked by several groups for quality control. To enforce a consistency, the annotation rules have been specified. Nevertheless, we have noticed that human annotators have difficulty following the annotation rules, which makes it impossible to guarantee annotation consistency. For this reason, we have developed a novel approach for dataset annotation. The new approach takes a pixel-wise segmentation of the tracked object

---

[8] http://www.votchallenge.net/vot2016/participation.html.

and places a bounding box by optimizing a well-defined cost function. In the following, Sect. 2.1 discusses per-frame segmentation mask construction and the new bounding box generation approach is presented in Sect. 2.2.

2.1 Producing Per-frame Segmentation Masks

The per-frame segmentations were provided for VOT by a research group that applied an interactive annotation tool designed by VOT[9] for manual segmentation mask construction. The tool applies Grabcut [30] object segmentation on each frame. The color model is initialized from the VOT2015 ground truth bounding box (first frame) or propagated from the final segmentation in the previous frame. The user can interactively add foreground or background examples to improve the segmentation. Examples of the object segmentations are illustrated in Fig. 1.

2.2 Automatic Bounding Box Computation

The final ground truth bounding box for VOT2016 was automatically computed on each frame from the corresponding segmentation mask. We have designed the following cost function and constraints to reflect the requirement that the bounding box should capture object pixels with minimal amount of background pixels:

$$\arg\max_{\mathbf{b}}\{C(\mathbf{b}) = \alpha \sum_{\mathbf{x}\notin A(\mathbf{b})} [M(\mathbf{x}) > 0] + \sum_{\mathbf{x}\in A(\mathbf{b})} [M(\mathbf{x}) == 0]\},$$

$$\text{subject to} \quad \frac{1}{M_f} \sum_{\mathbf{x}\notin A(\mathbf{b})} [M(\mathbf{x}) > 0] < \Theta_f, \frac{1}{|A(\mathbf{b})|} \sum_{\mathbf{x}\in A(\mathbf{b})} [M(\mathbf{x}) == 0] < \Theta_b,$$

$$(1)$$

where $\mathbf{b}$ is the vector of bounding box parameters (center, width, height, rotation), $A(\mathbf{b})$ is the corresponding bounding box, M is the segmentation mask which is non-zero for object pixels, $[\cdot]$ is an operator which returns 1 iff the statement in the operator is true and 0 otherwise, M_f is number of object pixels and $|\cdot|$ denotes the cardinality. An intuitive interpretation of the cost function is that we want to find a bounding box which minimizes a weighted sum of the number of object pixels outside of the bounding box and the number of background pixels inside the bounding box, with percentage of excluded object pixels and included background pixels constrained by Θ_f and Θ_b, respectively. The cost (1) was optimized by Interior Point [31] optimization, with three starting points: (i) the VOT2015 ground truth bounding box, (ii) a minimal axis-align bounding box containing all object pixels and (iii) a minimal rotated bounding box containing all object pixels. In case a solution satisfying the constraints was not found, a relaxed unconstrained BFGS Quasi-Newton method [32] was applied. Such cases occurred at highly articulated objects. The bounding box tightness is controlled by parameter α. Several values, i.e., $\alpha = \{1, 4, 7, 10\}$, were tested

---

[9] https://github.com/vojirt/grabcut_annotation_tool.

on randomly chosen sequences and the final value $\alpha = 4$ was selected since its bounding boxes were visually assessed to be the best-fitting. The constraints $\Theta_f = 0.1$ and $\Theta_b = 0.4$ were set to the values defined in previous VOT challenges. Examples of the automatically estimated ground truth bounding boxes are shown in Fig. 1.

All bounding boxes were visually verified to avoid poor fits due to potential segmentation errors. We identified 12 % of such cases and reverted to the VOT2015 ground truth for those. During the challenge, the community identified four frames where the new ground truth is incorrect and those errors were not caught by the verification. In these cases, the bounding box within the image bounds was properly estimated, but extended out of image bounds disproportionally. These errors will be corrected in the next version of the dataset and we checked, during result processing, that it did not significantly influence the challenge results. Table 1 summarizes the comparison of the VOT2016 automatic ground truth with the VOT2015 in terms of portions of object and background pixels inside the bounding boxes. The statistics were computed over the whole dataset excluding the 12 % of frames where the segmentation was marked as incorrect. The VOT2016 ground truth improves in all aspects over the VOT2015. It is interesting to note that the average overlap between VOT2015 and VOT2016 ground truth is 0.74.

Table 1. The first two columns shows the percentage and number of frames annotated by the VOT2016 and VOT2015 methodology, respectively. The *fg-out* and *bg-in* denote the average percentage of object pixels outside and percentage of background pixels inside the GT, respectively. The average overlap with the VOT2015 annotations is denoted by *Avg. overlap*, while the *#opt. failures* denotes the number of frames in which the algorithm switched from constrained to unconstrained optimization.

	%frames	#frames	fg-out	bg-in	Avg. overlap	#opt. failures
Automatic GT	88 %	18875	0.04	0.27	0.74	2597
VOT2015 GT	100 %	21455	0.06	0.37	—	—

2.3   Uncertainty of Optimal Bounding Box Fits

The cost function described in Sect. 2.2 avoids subjectivity of manual bounding box fitting, but does not specify how well constrained the solution is. The level of constraint strength can be expressed in terms of the average overlap of bounding boxes in the vicinity of the cost function (1) optimum, where we define the vicinity as a variation of bounding boxes within a maximum increase of the cost function around the optimum. The relative maximum increase of the cost function, i.e., the increase divided by the optimal value, is related to the annotation uncertainty in the per-pixels segmentation masks and can be estimated by the following rule-of thumb.

Let S_f and S_b denote the number of object and background pixels inside and outside of the bounding box, respectively. According to the central limit theorem, we can assume that S_f and S_b are normally distributed, i.e., $\mathcal{N}(\mu_f, \sigma_f^2)$ and $\mathcal{N}(\mu_b, \sigma_b^2)$, since they are sums of many random variables (per-pixel labels). In this respect, the value of the cost function C in (1) can be treated as a random variable as well and it is easy to show the following relation var$(C) = \sigma_c^2 = \alpha^2 \sigma_f^2 + \sigma_b^2$. The variance of the cost function is implicitly affected by the per-pixel annotation uncertainty through the variances σ_f^2 and σ_b^2. Assume that at most $x\mu_f$ and $x\mu_b$ pixels are incorrectly labeled on average. Since nearly all variation in a Gaussian is captured by three standard deviations, the variances are $\sigma_f^2 = (x\mu_f/3)^2$ and $\sigma_b^2 = (x\mu_b/3)^2$. Applying the three-sigma rule to the variance of the cost C, and using the definition of the foreground and background variances, gives an estimator of the maximal cost function change $\Delta_c = 3\sigma_c = x\sqrt{\alpha^2 \mu_f^2 + \mu_b^2}$. Our goal is to estimate the maximal relative cost function change in the vicinity of its optimum C_{opt}, i.e., $r_{\max} = \frac{\Delta_c}{C_{\text{opt}}}$. Using the definition of the maximal change Δ_c, the rule of thumb for the maximal relative change is

$$
r_{\max} = \frac{x\sqrt{\alpha^2 \mu_f^2 + \mu_b^2}}{\mu_f + \mu_b}. \tag{2}
$$

3   Performance Evaluation Methodology

Since VOT2015 [18], three primary measures are used to analyze tracking performance: accuracy (A), robustness (R) and expected average overlap (AEO). In the following these are briefly overviewed and we refer to [18–20] for further details. The VOT challenges apply a reset-based methodology. Whenever a tracker predicts a bounding box with zero overlap with the ground truth, a failure is detected and the tracker is re-initialized five frames after the failure. Čehovin et al. [20] identified two highly interpretable weakly correlated performance measures to analyze tracking behavior in reset-based experiments: (i) accuracy and (ii) robustness. The accuracy is the average overlap between the predicted and ground truth bounding boxes during successful tracking periods. On the other hand, the robustness measures how many times the tracker loses the target (fails) during tracking. The potential bias due to resets is reduced by ignoring ten frames after re-initialization in the accuracy measure, which is quite a conservative margin [19]. Stochastic trackers are run 15 times on each sequence to obtain reduce the variance of their results. The per-frame accuracy is obtained as an average over these runs. Averaging per-frame accuracies gives per-sequence accuracy, while per-sequence robustness is computed by averaging failure rates over different runs. The third primary measure, called the expected average overlap (EAO), is an estimator of the average overlap a tracker is expected to attain on a large collection of short-term sequences with the same visual properties as the given dataset. This measure addresses the problem of increased variance and bias of AO [21] measure due to variable sequence lengths on practical datasets. Please see [18] for further details on the average expected overlap measure.

We adopt the VOT2015 ranking methodology that accounts for statistical significance and practical differences to rank trackers separately with respect to the accuracy and robustness [18,19]. Apart from accuracy, robustness and expected overlaps, the tracking speed is also an important property that indicates practical usefulness of trackers in particular applications. To reduce the influence of hardware, the VOT2014 [17] introduced a new unit for reporting the tracking speed called equivalent filter operations (EFO) that reports the tracker speed in terms of a predefined filtering operation that the tookit automatically carries out prior to running the experiments. The same tracking speed measure is used in VOT2016.

In addition to the standard reset-based VOT experiment, the VOT2016 toolkit carried out the OTB [21] no-reset experiment. The tracking performance on this experiment was evaluated by the primary OTB measure, average overlap (AO).

4   Analysis and Results

4.1   Practical Difference Estimation

As noted in Sect. 2.3, the variation in the per-pixel segmentation masks introduces the uncertainty of the optimally fitted ground truth bounding boxes. We expressed this uncertainty as the average overlap of the optimal bounding box with the bounding boxes sampled in vicinity of the optimum, which is implicitly defined as the maximal allowed cost increase. Assuming that on average, at most 10 % of pixels might be incorrectly assigned in the object mask, the rule of thumb (2) estimates an increase of cost function by at most 7 %. The average overlap specified in this way was used in the VOT2016 as an estimate of the per-sequence practical differences.

The following approach was thus applied to estimate the practical difference thresholds. Thirty uniformly dispersed frames were selected per sequence. For each frame a set of 3125 ground truth bounding box perturbations were generated by varying the ground truth regions by $\mathbf{\Delta_b} = [\Delta_x, \Delta_y, \Delta_w, \Delta_h, \Delta_\Theta]$, where all Δ are sampled uniformly (5 samples) from ranges ± 5 % of ground truth width (height) for $\Delta_x(\Delta_y)$, ± 10 % of ground truth width (height) for $\Delta_w(\Delta_h)$ and $\pm 4°$ for Δ_Θ. These ranges were chosen such that the cost function is well explored near the optimal solution and the amount of bounding box perturbations can be computed reasonably fast. The examples of bounding boxes generated in this way are shown in Fig. 1. An average overlap was computed between the ground truth bounding box and the bounding boxes that did not exceed the optimal cost value by more than 7 %. The average of the average overlaps computed in thirty frames was taken as the estimate of the practical difference threshold for a given sequence. The boxplots in Fig. 1 visualize the distributions of average overlaps with respect to the sequences.

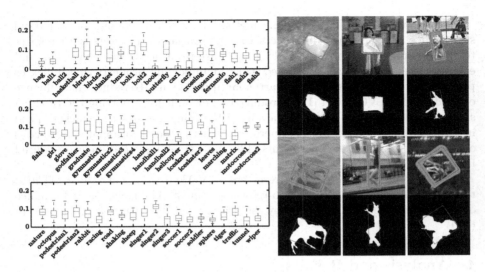

Fig. 1. Box plots of per-sequence overlap dispersion at 7% cost change (left), and examples of such bounding boxes (right). The optimal bounding box is depicted in red, while the 7% cost change bounding boxes are shown in green. (Color figure online)

4.2 Trackers Submitted

Together 48 valid entries have been submitted to the VOT2016 challenge. Each submission included the binaries/source code that was used by the VOT2016 committee for results verification. The VOT2016 committee and associates additionally contributed 22 baseline trackers. For these, the default parameters were selected, or, when not available, were set to reasonable values. Thus in total 70 trackers were tested in the VOT2016 challenge. In the following we briefly overview the entries and provide the references to original papers in the Appendix A where available.

Eight trackers were based on convolutional neural networks architecture for target localization, MLDF (A.19), SiamFC-R (A.23), SiamFC-A (A.25), TCNN (A.44), DNT (A.41), SO-DLT (A.8), MDNet-N (A.46) and SSAT (A.12), where MDNet-N (A.46) and SSAT (A.12) were extensions of the VOT2015 winner MDNet [33]. Thirteen trackers were variations of correlation filters, SRDCF (A.58), SWCF (A.3), FCF (A.7), GCF (A.36), ART-DSST (A.45), DSST2014 (A.50), SMACF (A.14), STC (A.66), DFST (A.39), KCF2014 (A.53), SAMF2014 (A.54), OEST (A.31) and sKCF (A.40). Seven trackers combined correlation filter outputs with color, Staple (A.28), Staple+ (A.22), MvCFT (A.15), NSAMF (A.21), SSKCF (A.27), ACT (A.56) and ColorKCF (A.29), and six trackers applied CNN features in the correlation filters, deepMKCF (A.16), HCF (A.60), DDC (A.17), DeepSRDCF (A.57), C-COT (A.26), RFD-CF2 (A.47). Two trackers were based on structured SVM, Struck2011 (A.55) and EBT (A.2) which applied region proposals as well. Three trackers were based on purely on color, DAT (A.5), SRBT (A.34) and

ASMS (A.49) and one tracker was based on fusion of basic features LoFT-Lite (A.38). One tracker was based on subspace learning, IVT (A.64), one tracker was based on boosting, MIL (A.68), one tracker was based on complex cells approach, CCCT (A.20), one on distributed fields, DFT (A.59), one tracker was based on Gaussian process regressors, TGPR (A.67), and one tracker was the basic normalized cross correlation tracker NCC (A.61). Nineteen submissions can be categorized as part-based trackers, DPCF (A.1), LT-FLO (A.43), SHCT (A.24), GGTv2 (A.18), MatFlow (A.10), Matrioska (A.11), CDTT (A.13), BST (A.30), TRIC-track (A.32), DPT (A.35), SMPR (A.48), CMT (A.70), HT (A.65), LGT (A.62), ANT (A.63), FoT (A.51), FCT (A.37), FT (A.69), and BDF (A.9). Several submissions were based on combination of base trackers, PKLTF (A.4), MAD (A.6), CTF (A.33), SCT (A.42) and HMMTxD (A.52).

4.3   Results

The results are summarized in sequence-pooled and attribute-normalized AR-raw plots in Fig. 2. The sequence-pooled AR-rank plot is obtained by concatenating the results from all sequences and creating a single rank list, while the attribute-normalized AR-rank plot is created by ranking the trackers over each attribute and averaging the rank lists. The AR-raw plots were constructed in similar fashion. The expected average overlap curves and expected average overlap scores are shown in Fig. 3. The raw values for the sequence-pooled results and the average overlap scores are also given in Table 2.

The top ten trackers come from various classes. The TCNN (A.44), SSAT (A.12), MLDF (A.19) and DNT (A.41) are derived from CNNs, the C-COT (A.26), DDC (A.17), Staple (A.28) and Staple+ (A.22) are variations of correlation filters with more or less complex features, the EBT (A.2) is structured SVM edge-feature tracker, while the SRBT (A.34) is a color-based saliency detection tracker. The following five trackers appear either very robust or very accurate: C-COT (A.26), TCNN (A.44), SSAT (A.12), MLDF (A.19) and EBT (A.2). The C-COT (A.26) is a new correlation filter which uses a large variety of state-of-the-art features, i.e., HOG [34], color-names [35] and the vgg-m-2048 CNN features pretrained on Imagenet[10]. The TCNN (A.44) samples target locations and scores them by several CNNs, which are organized into a tree structure for efficiency and are evolved/pruned during tracking. SSAT (A.12) is based on MDNet [33], applies segmentation and scale regression, followed by occlusion detection to prevent training from corrupt samples. The MLDF (A.19) applies a pre-trained VGG network [36] which is followed by another, adaptive, network with Euclidean loss to regress to target position. According to the EAO measure, the top performing tracker was C-COT (A.26) [37], closely followed by the TCNN (A.44). Detailed analysis of the AR-raw plots shows that the TCNN (A.44) produced slightly greater average overlap (0.55) than C-COT (A.26) (0.54), but failed slightly more often (by six failures). The best overlap was achieved by SSAT (A.12) (0.58), which might be attributed to

---

[10] http://www.vlfeat.org/matconvnet/.

the combination of segmentation and scale regression this tracker applies. The smallest number of failures achieved the MLDF (A.19), which outperformed C-COT (A.26) by a single failure, but obtained a much smaller overlap (0.49). Under the VOT strict ranking protocol, the SSAT (A.12) is ranked number one in accuracy, meaning the overlap was clearly higher than for any other tracker. The second-best ranked tracker in accuracy is Staple+ (A.22) and several trackers share third rank SHCT (A.24), deepMKCF (A.16), FCF (A.7), meaning that the null hypothesis of difference between these trackers in accuracy could not be rejected. In terms of robustness, trackers MDNet-N (A.46), C-COT (A.26), MLDF (A.19) and EBT (A.2) share the first place, which means that the null hypothesis of difference in their robustness could not be rejected. The second and third ranks in robustness are occupied by TCNN (A.44) and SSAT (A.12), respectively.

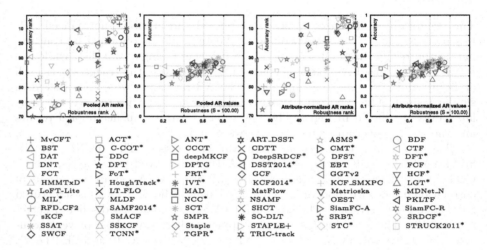

Fig. 2. The AR-rank plots and AR-raw plots generated by sequence pooling (left) and attribute normalization (right).

It is worth pointing out some EAO results appear to contradict AR-raw measures at a first glance. For example, the Staple obtains a higher EAO measure than Staple+, even though the Staple achieves a slightly better average accuracy and in fact improves on Staple by two failures, indicating a greater robustness. The reason is that the failures early on in the sequences globally contribute more to penalty than the failures that occur at the end of the sequence (see [18] for definition of EAO). For example, if a tracker fails once and is re-initialized in the sequence, it generates two sub-sequences for computing the overlap measure at sequence length N. The first sub-sequence ends with the failure and will contribute to any sequence length N since zero overlaps are added after the failure. But the second sub-sequence ends with the sequence end and zeros cannot

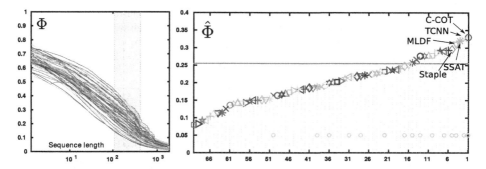

Fig. 3. Expected average overlap curve (left) and expected average overlap graph (right) with trackers ranked from right to left. The right-most tracker is the top-performing according to the VOT2016 expected average overlap values. See Fig. 2 for legend. The dashed horizontal line denotes the average performance of fourteen state-of-the-art trackers published in 2015 and 2016 at major computer vision venues. These trackers are denoted by gray circle in the bottom part of the graph.

be added after that point. Thus the second sub-sequence only contributes to the overlap computations for sequence lengths N smaller than its length. This means that re-inits very close to the sequence end (tens of frames) do not affect the EAO.

Note that the trackers that are usually used as baselines, i.e., MIL (A.68), and IVT (A.64) are positioned at the lower part of the AR-plots and the EAO ranks, which indicates that majority of submitted trackers are considered state-of-the-art. In fact, fourteen tested trackers have been recently (in 2015 and 2016) published at major computer vision conferences and journals. These trackers are indicated in Fig. 3, along with the average state-of-the-art performance computed from the average performance of these trackers, which constitutes a very strict VOT2016 state-of-the-art bound. Approximately 22% of submitted trackers exceed this bound.

The number of failures with respect to the visual attributes are shown in Fig. 4. On camera motion attribute, the tracker that fails least often is the EBT A.2, on illumination change the top position is shared by RFD_CF2 A.47 and SRBT A.34, on motion change the top position is shared by EBT A.2 and MLDF A.19, on occlusion the top position is shared by MDNet_N A.46 and C-COT A.26, on the size change attribute, the tracker MLDF A.19 produces the least failures, while on the unassigned attribute, the TCNN A.44 fails the least often. The overall accuracy and robustness averaged over the attributes is shown in Fig. 2. The attribute-normalized AR plots are similar to the pooled plots, but the top trackers (TCNN A.44, SSAT A.12, MDNet_N A.46 and C-COT A.26) are pulled close together, which is evident from the ranking plots.

We have evaluated the difficulty level of each attribute by computing the median of robustness and accuracy over each attribute. According to the results in Table 3, the most challenging attributes in terms of failures are occlusion, motion change and illumination change, followed by scale change and camera motion.

Table 2. The table shows expected average overlap (EAO), accuracy and robustness raw values (A,R) and ranks (A_{rank}, A_{rank}), the no-reset average overlap AO [21], the speed (in EFO units) and implementation details (M is Matlab, C is C or C++, P is Python). Trackers marked with * have been verified by the VOT2015 committee. A dash "-" indicates the EFO measurements were invalid.

	Tracker	EAO	A	R	A_{rank}	R_{rank}	AO	EFO	Impl.
1.	◯ C-COT*	**0.331**	0.539	*0.238*	12.000	**1.000**	0.469	0.507	D M
2.	✕ TCNN*	*0.325*	0.554	0.268	4.000	*2.000*	*0.485*	1.049	S M
3.	✳ SSAT	0.321	**0.577**	0.291	**1.000**	3.000	**0.515**	0.475	S M
4.	▽ MLDF	0.311	0.490	**0.233**	36.000	**1.000**	0.428	1.483	D M
5.	◇ Staple	0.295	0.544	0.378	5.000	10.000	0.388	11.144	D C
6.	+ DDC	0.293	0.541	0.345	7.000	6.000	0.391	0.198	D M
7.	◁ EBT	0.291	0.465	0.252	43.000	**1.000**	0.370	3.011	D C
8.	☆ SRBT	0.290	0.496	0.350	26.000	10.000	0.333	3.688	D M
9.	▷ STAPLE+	0.286	*0.557*	0.368	*2.000*	9.000	0.392	44.765	D M
10.	☐ DNT	0.278	0.515	0.329	21.000	4.000	0.427	1.127	S M
11.	△ SSKCF	0.277	0.547	0.373	5.000	10.000	0.391	29.153	D C
12.	✩ SiamFC-R	0.277	0.549	0.382	5.000	10.000	0.421	5.444	D C
13.	◯ DeepSRDCF*	0.276	0.528	0.326	16.000	5.000	0.427	0.380	S C
14.	✕ SHCT	0.266	0.547	0.396	3.000	9.000	0.392	0.711	D M
15.	✳ MDNet_N	0.257	0.541	0.337	10.000	**1.000**	0.457	0.534	S M
16.	▽ FCF	0.251	0.554	0.457	3.000	13.000	0.419	1.929	D M
17.	◇ SRDCF*	0.247	0.535	0.419	13.000	9.000	0.397	1.990	S C
18.	+ RFD_CF2	0.241	0.477	0.373	37.000	6.000	0.352	0.896	D M
19.	◁ GGTv2	0.238	0.515	0.471	20.000	21.000	0.433	0.357	S M
20.	☆ DPT	0.236	0.492	0.489	33.000	21.000	0.334	4.111	D M
21.	▷ SiamFC-A	0.235	0.532	0.461	13.000	13.000	0.399	9.213	D C
22.	☐ deepMKCF	0.232	0.543	0.422	3.000	6.000	0.409	1.237	S M
23.	△ HMMTxD*	0.231	0.519	0.531	13.000	33.000	0.369	3.619	D C
24.	✩ NSAMF	0.227	0.502	0.438	24.000	10.000	0.354	9.677	D C
25.	◯ SMACF	0.226	0.503	0.443	22.000	21.000	0.347	91.460	D C
26.	✕ CCCT	0.223	0.442	0.461	54.000	21.000	0.308	9.828	D M
27.	✳ SO-DLT	0.221	0.516	0.499	18.000	14.000	0.372	0.576	S M
28.	▽ HCF*	0.220	0.450	0.396	44.000	6.000	0.374	1.057	D C
29.	◇ GCF	0.218	0.520	0.485	18.000	13.000	0.348	5.904	D M
30.	+ KCF_SMXPC	0.218	0.535	0.499	10.000	10.000	0.367	5.786	D M
31.	◁ DAT	0.217	0.468	0.480	43.000	21.000	0.309	18.983	D M
32.	☆ ASMS*	0.212	0.503	0.522	22.000	29.000	0.330	82.577	D C
33.	▷ ANT*	0.204	0.483	0.513	35.000	21.000	0.303	7.171	D M
34.	☐ MAD	0.202	0.497	0.503	28.000	21.000	0.328	8.954	D C
35.	△ BST	0.200	0.376	0.447	68.000	10.000	0.235	13.608	S C
36.	✩ TRIC-track	0.200	0.443	0.583	51.000	34.000	0.269	0.335	S M
37.	◯ KCF2014*	0.192	0.489	0.569	33.000	21.000	0.301	21.788	D M
38.	✕ OEST	0.188	0.510	0.601	24.000	33.000	0.370	0.170	D M
39.	✳ SCT	0.188	0.462	0.545	46.000	21.000	0.283	11.131	D M
40.	▽ SAMF2014*	0.186	0.507	0.587	22.000	21.000	0.350	4.099	D M

Table 2. (*continued*)

	Tracker	EAO	A	R	A_{rank}	R_{rank}	AO	EFO	Impl.
41.	◇ SWCF	0.185	0.500	0.662	24.000	34.000	0.293	7.722	D M
42.	+ MvCFT	0.182	0.491	0.606	33.000	21.000	0.308	5.194	D M
43.	◁ DSST2014*	0.181	0.533	0.704	11.000	35.000	0.325	12.747	D M
44.	☆ TGPR*	0.181	0.460	0.629	47.000	45.000	0.270	0.318	D M
45.	▷ DPTG	0.179	0.492	0.615	31.000	33.000	0.306	2.669	D M
46.	□ ACT*	0.173	0.446	0.662	51.000	35.000	0.281	9.840	S C
47.	△ LGT*	0.168	0.420	0.605	56.000	34.000	0.271	3.775	S M
48.	✿ ART_DSST	0.167	0.515	0.732	20.000	39.000	0.306	8.451	D M
49.	○ MIL*	0.165	0.407	0.727	62.000	48.000	0.201	7.678	S C
50.	✕ CDTT	0.164	0.409	0.583	58.000	21.000	0.263	13.398	D M
51.	✳ MatFlow	0.155	0.408	0.694	60.000	45.000	0.231	59.640	D C
52.	▽ sKCF	0.153	0.485	0.816	35.000	53.000	0.301	91.061	D C
53.	◇ DFST	0.151	0.483	0.778	40.000	42.000	0.315	3.374	D M
54.	+ HoughTrack*	0.150	0.409	0.771	60.000	51.000	0.198	1.181	S C
55.	◁ PKLTF	0.150	0.437	0.671	51.000	45.000	0.278	33.048	D C
56.	☆ SMPR	0.147	0.455	0.778	48.000	49.000	0.266	8.282	D M
57.	▷ FoT*	0.142	0.377	0.820	65.000	53.000	0.165	105.714	D C
58.	□ STRUCK2011*	0.142	0.458	0.942	46.000	56.000	0.242	14.584	D C
59.	△ FCT	0.141	0.395	0.788	63.000	51.000	0.199	-	D M
60.	☆ DFT*	0.139	0.464	1.002	43.000	61.000	0.209	3.330	D C
61.	○ BDF	0.136	0.375	0.792	69.000	45.000	0.180	138.124	D C
62.	✕ LT_FLO	0.126	0.444	1.164	45.000	63.000	0.207	1.830	S M
63.	✳ IVT*	0.115	0.419	1.109	56.000	61.000	0.181	14.880	D M
64.	▽ Matrioska	0.115	0.430	1.114	56.000	63.000	0.238	25.766	D C
65.	◇ STC*	0.110	0.380	1.007	65.000	60.000	0.152	22.744	D M
66.	+ FRT*	0.104	0.405	1.216	61.000	65.000	0.179	3.867	D C
67.	◁ CTF	0.092	0.497	1.561	29.000	67.000	0.187	3.777	D M
68.	☆ LoFT-Lite	0.092	0.329	1.282	70.000	66.000	0.118	2.174	D M
69.	▷ CMT*	0.083	0.393	1.701	64.000	69.000	0.150	16.196	S P
70.	□ NCC*	0.080	0.490	2.102	33.000	70.000	0.174	**226.891**	D C

Table 3. Tracking difficulty with respect to the following visual attributes: camera motion (cam. mot.), illumination change (ill. ch.), motion change (mot. ch.), occlusion (occl.) and size change (scal. ch.).

	cam. mot.	ill. ch.	mot. ch.	occl.	scal. ch.
Accuracy	0.49	0.53	0.44	0.41	0.42
Robustness	0.71	0.81	1.02	1.11	0.61

In addition to the baseline reset-based VOT experiment, the VOT2016 toolkit also performed the OTB [21] no-reset (OPE) experiment. Figure 5 shows the OPE plots, while the AO overall measure is given in Table 2. According to the

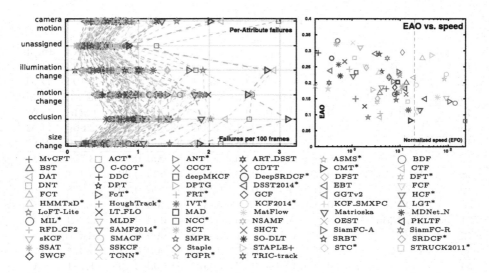

Fig. 4. The expected average overlap with respect to the visual attributes (left). Expected average overlap scores w.r.t. the tracking speed in EFO units (right). The dashed vertical line denotes the estimated real-time performance threshold of 20 EFO units. See Fig. 2 for legend.

AO measure, the three top performing trackers are SSAT (A.12), TCNN (A.44) and C-COT (A.26), which is similar to the EAO ranking, with the main difference that SSAT and C-COT exchange places. The reason for this switch can be deduced from the AR plots (Fig. 2) which show that the C-COT is more robust than the other two trackers, while the SSAT is more accurate. Since the AO measure does not apply resets, it does not enhance the differences among the trackers on difficult sequences, where one tracker might fail more often than the other, whereas the EAO is affected by these. Thus among the trackers with similar accuracy and robustness, the EAO prefers trackers with higher robustness, while the AO prefers more accurate trackers. To establish a visual relation among the EAO and AO rankings, each tracker is shown in a 2D plot in terms of the EAO and AO measures in Fig. 5. Broadly speaking, the measures are correlated and EAO is usually lower than EO, but the local ordering with these measures is different, which is due to the different treatment of failures.

Apart from tracking accuracy, robustness and EAO measure, the tracking speed is also crucial in many realistic tracking applications. We therefore visualize the EAO score with respect to the tracking speed measured in EFO units in Fig. 4. To put EFO units into perspective, a C++ implementation of a NCC tracker provided in the toolkit runs with average 140 frames per second on a laptop with an Intel Core i5-2557M processor, which equals to approximately 200 EFO units. All trackers that scored top EAO performed below realtime, while the top EFO was achieved by NCC (A.61), BDF (A.9) and FoT (A.51). Among the trackers within the VOT2016 realtime bound, the top two trackers in terms of EAO score were Staple+ (A.22) and SSKCF (A.27). The latter is modification

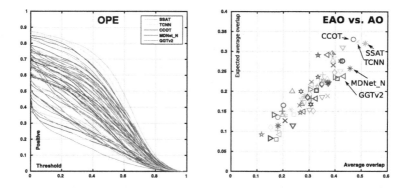

Fig. 5. The OPE no-reset plots (left) and the EAO-AO scatter plot (right).

of the Staple (A.28), while the latter is modification of the Sumshift [38] tracker. Both approaches combine a correlation filter output with color histogram back-projection. According to the AR-raw plot in Fig. 2, the SSKCF (A.27) tracks with a decent average overlap during successful tracking periods (~ 0.55) and produces decently long tracks. For example, the probability of SSKCF still tracking the target after $S = 100$ frames is approximately 0.69. The Staple+ (A.22) tracks with a similar overlap (~ 0.56) and tracks the target after 100 frames with probability 0.70. In the detailed analysis of the results we have found some discrepancies between the reported EFO units and the trackers speed in seconds for the Matlab trackers. The toolkit was not ignoring the Matlab start time, which can significantly vary across different trackers, which is why the EFO units of some Matlab trackers might be significantly underestimated.

5   Conclusion

This paper reviewed the VOT2016 challenge and its results. The challenge contains an annotated dataset of sixty sequences in which targets are denoted by rotated bounding boxes to aid a precise analysis of the tracking results. All the sequences are the same as in the VOT2015 challenge and the per-frame visual attributes are the same as well. A new methodology was developed to automatically place the bounding boxes in each frame by optimizing a well-defined cost function. In addition, a rule-of-thumb approach was developed to estimate the uniqueness of the automatically placed bounding boxes under the expected bound on the per-pixel annotation error. A set of 70 trackers have been evaluated. A large percentage of trackers submitted have been published at recent conferences and top journals, including ICCV, CVPR, TIP and TPAMI, and some trackers have not yet been published (available at arXiv). For example, fourteen trackers alone have been published at major computer vision venues in 2015 and 2016 so far.

The results of VOT2016 indicate that the top performing tracker of the challenge according to the EAO score is the C-COT (A.26) tracker [37]. This is a correlation-filter-based tracker that applies a number of state-of-the-art features. The tracker performed very well in accuracy as well as robustness and trade-off between the two is reflected in the EAO. The C-COT (A.26) tracker is closely followed by TCNN (A.44) and SSAT (A.12) which are close in terms of accuracy, robustness and the EAO. These trackers come from a different class, they are pure CNN trackers based on the winning tracker of VOT2015, the MDNet [33]. It is impossible to conclusively decide whether the improvements of C-COT (A.26) over other top-performing trackers come from the features or the approach. Nevertheless, results of top trackers conclusively show that features play a significant role in the final performance. All trackers that scored the top EAO perform below real-time. Among the realtime trackers, the top performing trackers were Staple+ (A.22) and SSKCF (A.27) that implement a simple combination of the correlation filter output and histogram backprojection.

The main goal of VOT is establishing a community-based common platform for discussion of tracking performance evaluation and contributing to the tracking community with verified annotated datasets, performance measures and evaluation toolkits. The VOT2016 was a fourth attempt toward this, following the very successful VOT2013, VOT2014 and VOT2015. The VOT2016 also introduced a second sub-challenge VOT-TIR2016 that concerns tracking in thermal and infrared imagery. The results of that sub-challenge are described in a separate paper [29] that was presented at the VOT2016 workshop. Our future work will be focused on revising the evaluation kit, dataset, performance measures, and possibly launching other sub-challenges focused to narrow application domains, depending on the feedbacks and interest expressed from the community.

Acknowledgements. This work was supported in part by the following research programs and projects: Slovenian research agency research programs P2-0214, P2-0094, Slovenian research agency projects J2-4284, J2-3607, J2-2221 and European Union seventh framework programme under grant agreement no 257906. Jiří Matas and Tomáš Vojíř were supported by CTU Project SGS13/142/OHK3/2T/13 and by the Technology Agency of the Czech Republic project TE01020415 (V3C – Visual Computing Competence Center). Michael Felsberg and Gustav Häger were supported by the Wallenberg Autonomous Systems Program WASP, the Swedish Foundation for Strategic Research through the project CUAS, and the Swedish Research Council trough the project EMC^2. Gustavo Fernández and Roman Pflugfelder were supported by the research program Mobile Vision with funding from the Austrian Institute of Technology. Some experiments where run on GPUs donated by NVIDIA.

A   Submitted Trackers

In this appendix we provide a short summary of all trackers that were considered in the VOT2016 challenge.

A.1   Deformable Part-Based Tracking by Coupled Global and Local Correlation Filters (DPCF)

O. Akin, E. Erdem, A. Erdem, K. Mikolajczyk
oakin25@gmail.com, {erkut, aykut}@cs.hacettepe.edu.tr,
k.mikolajczyk@imperial.ac.uk

DPCF is a deformable part-based correlation filter tracking approach which depends on coupled interactions between a global filter and several part filters. Specifically, local filters provide an initial estimate, which is then used by the global filter as a reference to determine the final result. Then, the global filter provides a feedback to the part filters regarding their updates and the related deformation parameters. In this way, DPCF handles not only partial occlusion but also scale changes. The reader is referred to [39] for details.

A.2   Edge Box Tracker (EBT)

G. Zhu, F. Porikli, H. Li
{gao.zhu, fatih.porikli, hongdong.li}@anu.edu.au
EBT tracker is not limited to a local search window and has ability to probe efficiently the entire frame. It generates a small number of 'high-quality' proposals by a novel instance-specific objectness measure and evaluates them against the object model that can be adopted from an existing tracking-by-detection approach as a core tracker. During the tracking process, it updates the object model concentrating on hard false-positives supplied by the proposals, which help suppressing distractors caused by difficult background clutters, and learns how to re-rank proposals according to the object model. Since the number of hypotheses the core tracker evaluates is reduced significantly, richer object descriptors and stronger detectors can be used. More details can be found in [40].

A.3   Spatial Windowing for Correlation Filter Based Visual Tracking (SWCF)

E. Gundogdu, A. Alatan
egundogdu@aselsan.com.tr, alatan@eee.metu.edu.tr
SWCF tracker estimates a spatial window for the object observation such that the correlation output of the correlation filter and the windowed observation (i.e. element-wise multiplication of the window and the observation) is improved. Concretely, the window is estimated by reducing a cost function, which penalizes the dissimilarity of the correlation of the recent observation and the filter to the desired peaky shaped signal, with an efficient gradient descent optimization. Then, the estimated window is shifted by pre-calculating the translational motion and circularly shifting the window. Finally, the current observation is multiplied element-wise with the aligned window, and utilized in the localization. The reader is referred to [41] for details.

A.4   Point-Based Kanade Lukas Tomasi Colour-Filter (PKLTF)

R. Martin-Nieto, A. Garcia-Martin, J.M. Martinez
{rafael.martinn, alvaro.garcia, josem.martinez}@uam.es
PKLTF [42] is a single-object long-term tracker that supports high appearance changes in the target, occlusions, and is also capable of recovering a target

lost during the tracking process. PKLTF consists of two phases: The first one uses the Kanade Lukas Tomasi approach (KLT) [43] to choose the object features (using colour and motion coherence), while the second phase is based on mean shift gradient descent [44] to place the bounding box into the position of the object. The object model is based on the RGB colour and the luminance gradient and it consists of a histogram including the quantized values of the colour components, and an edge binary flag. The interested reader is referred to [42] for details.

A.5   Distractor Aware Tracker (DAT)

H. Possegger, T. Mauthner, H. Bischof
{possegger, mauthner, bischof}@icg.tugraz.at

The Distractor Aware Tracker is an appearance-based tracking-by-detection approach. A discriminative model using colour histograms is implemented to distinguish the object from its surrounding region. Additionally, a distractor-aware model term suppresses visually distracting regions whenever they appear within the field-of-view, thus reducing tracker drift. The reader is referred to [45] for details.

A.6   Median Absolute Deviation Tracker (MAD)

S. Becker, S. Krah, W. Hübner, M. Arens
{stefan.becker, sebastian.krah, wolfgang.huebner,
michael.arens}@iosb.fraunhofer.de

The key idea of the MAD tracker [46] is to combine several independent and heterogeneous tracking approaches and to robustly identify an outlier subset based on the Median Absolute Deviation (MAD) measure. The MAD fusion strategy is very generic and it only requires frame-based target bounding boxes as input and thus can work with arbitrary tracking algorithms. The overall median bounding box is calculated from all trackers and the deviation or distance of a sub-tracker to the median bounding box is calculated using the Jaccard-Index. Further, the MAD fusion strategy can also be applied for combining several instances of the same tracker to form a more robust swarm for tracking a single target. For this experiments the MAD tracker is set-up with a swarm of KCF [47] trackers in combination with the DSST [48] scale estimation scheme. The reader is referred to [46] for details.

A.7   Fully-Functional Correlation Filtering-Based Tracker (FCF)

M. Zhang, J. Xing, J. Gao, W. Hu
{mengdan.zhang, jlxing, jin.gao, wmhu}@nlpr.ia.ac.cn

FCF is a fully functional correlation filtering-based tracking algorithm which is able to simultaneously model correlations from a joint scale-displacement space, an orientation space, and the time domain. FCF tracker firstly performs scale-displacement correlation using a novel block-circulant structure to estimate objects position and size in one go. Then, by transferring the target representation from the Cartesian coordinate system to the Log-Polar coordinate system, the circulant structure is well preserved and the object rotation can be evaluated in the same correlation filtering based framework. In the update phase, temporal correlation analysis is introduced together with inference mechanisms which are based on an extended high-order Markov chain.

A.8   Structure Output Deep Learning Tracker (SO-DLT)

N. Wang, S. Li, A. Gupta, D. Yeung
winsty@gmail.com, sliay@cse.ust.hk, abhinavg@cs.cmu.edu,
dyyeung@cse.ust.hk

SO-LDT proposes a structured output CNN which transfers generic object features for online tracking. First, a CNN is trained to distinguish objects from non-objects. The output of the CNN is a pixel-wise map to indicate the probability that each pixel in the input image belongs to the bounding box of an object. Besides, SO-LDT uses two CNNs which use different model update strategies. By making a simple forward pass through the CNN, the probability map for each of the image patches is obtained. The final estimation is then determined by searching for a proper bounding box. If it is necessary, the CNNs are also updated. The reader is referred to [49] for more details.

A.9   Best Displacement Flow (BDF)

M. Maresca, A. Petrosino
mariomaresca@hotmail.it, petrosino@uniparthenope.it

Best Displacement Flow (BDF) is a short-term tracking algorithm based on the same idea of Flock of Trackers [50] in which a set of local tracker responses are robustly combined to track the object. Firstly, BDF performs a clustering to identify the best displacement vector which is used to update the object's bounding box. Secondly, BDF performs a procedure named Consensus-Based Reinitialization used to reinitialize candidates which were previously classified as outliers. Interested readers are referred to [51] for details.

A.10   Matrioska Best Displacement Flow (MatFlow)

M. Maresca, A. Petrosino
mariomaresca@hotmail.it, petrosino@uniparthenope.it

MatFlow enhances the performance of the first version of Matrioska [52] with response given by the short-term tracker BDF (see A.9). By default, MatFlow uses the trajectory given by Matrioska. In the case of a low confidence score estimated by Matrioska, the algorithm corrects the trajectory with the response given by BDF. The Matrioska's confidence score is based on the number of keypoints found inside the object in the initialization. If the object has not a good amount of keypoints (i.e. Matrioska is likely to fail), the algorithm will use the trajectory given by BDF that is not sensitive to low textured objects.

A.11   Matrioska

M. Maresca, A. Petrosino
mariomaresca@hotmail.it, petrosino@uniparthenope.it
Matrioska [52] decomposes tracking into two separate modules: detection and learning. The detection module can use multiple key point-based methods (ORB, FREAK, BRISK, SURF, etc.) inside a fall-back model, to correctly localize the object frame by frame exploiting the strengths of each method. The learning module updates the object model, with a growing and pruning approach, to account for changes in its appearance and extracts negative samples to further improve the detector performance.

A.12   Scale-and-State Aware Tracker (SSAT)

Y. Qi, L. Qin, S. Zhang, Q. Huang
qykshr@gmail.com, qinlei@ict.ac.cn, s.zhang@hit.edu.cn, qmhuang@ucas.ac.cn
SSAT is an extended version of the MDNet tracker [33]. First, a segmentation technique into MDNet is introduced. It works with the scale regression model of MDNet to more accurately estimate the tightest bounding box of the target. Second, a state model is used to infer whether the target is occluded. When the target is occluded, training examples from that frame are not extracted which are used to update the tracker.

A.13   Clustered Decision Tree Based Tracker (CDTT)

J. Xiao, R. Stolkin, A. Leonardis
Shine636363@sina.com, {R.Stolkin, a.leonardis}@cs.bham.ac.uk
CDTT tracker is a modified version of the tracker presented in [53]. The tracker first propagates a set of samples, using the top layer features, to find candidate target regions with different feature modalities. The candidate regions generated by each feature modality are adaptively fused to give an overall target estimation in the global layer. When an 'ambiguous' situation is detected (i.e. inconsistent locations of predicted bounding boxes from different feature modalities), the algorithm will progress to the local part layer for more accurate tracking. Clustered decision trees are used to match target parts to local image regions, which initially attempts to match a part using a single feature (first level on the tree), and then progresses to additional features (deeper levels of the tree). The reader is referred to [53] for details.

A.14   Scale and Motion Adaptive Correlation Filter Tracker (SMACF)

M. Mueller, B. Ghanem
{matthias.mueller.2, Bernard.Ghanem}@kaust.edu.sa

The tracker is based on [47]. Colourname features are added for better representation of the target. Depending on the target size, the cell size for extracting features is changed adaptively to provide sufficient resolution of the object being tracked. A first order motion model is used to improve robustness to camera motion. Searching over a number of different scales allows for more accurate bounding boxes and better localization in consecutive frames. For robustness, scales are weighted using a zero-mean Gaussian distribution centred around the current scale. This ensures that the scale is only changed if it results in a significantly better response.

A.15 A Multi-view Model for Visual Tracking via Correlation Filters (MvCFT)

Z. He, X. Li, N. Fan
zyhe@hitsz.edu.cn, hitlixin@126.com, nanafanhit@gmail.com
The multi-view correlation filter tracker (MvCF tracker) fuses several features and selects the more discriminative features to enhance the robustness. Besides, the correlation filter framework provides fast training and efficient target locating. The combination of the multiple views is conducted by the Kullback-Leibler (KL) divergences. In addition, a simple but effective scale-variation detection mechanism is provided, which strengthens the stability of scale variation tracking.

A.16   Deep Multi-kernelized Correlation Filter (deepMKCF)

J. Feng, F. Zhao, M. Tang
{jiayi.feng, fei.zhao, tangm}@nlpr.ia.ac.cn
deepMKCF tracker is the MKCF [54] with deep features extracted by using VGG-Net [36]. deepMKCF tracker combines the multiple kernel learning and correlation filter techniques and it explores diverse features simultaneously to improve tracking performance. In addition, an optimal search technique is also applied to estimate object scales. The multi-kernel training process of deepMKCF is tailored accordingly to ensure tracking efficiency with deep features. In addition, the net is fine-tuned with a batch of image patches extracted from the initial frame to make VGG-NET-19 more suitable for tracking tasks.

A.17   Discriminative Deep Correlation Tracking (DDC)

J. Gao, T. Zhang, C. Xu, B. Liu
gaojunyu2015@ia.ac.cn, tzzhang10@gmail.com, csxu@nlpr.ia.ac.cn,
liubin@dress-plus.com
The Discriminative Deep Correlation (DDC) tracker is based on the correlation filter framework. The tracker uses foreground and background image patches and it has the following advantages: (i) It effectively exploit image patches from

foreground and background to make full use of their discriminative context information, (ii) deep features are used to gain more robust target object representations, and (iii) an effective scale adaptive scheme and a long-short term model update scheme are utilised.

A.18   Geometric Structure Hyper-Graph Based Tracker Version 2 (GGTv2)

T. Hu, D. Du, L. Wen, W. Li, H. Qi, S. Lyu
{yihouxiang, cvdaviddo, lywen.cv.workbox, wbli.app, honggangqi.cas,
heizi.lyu}@gmail.com

GGTv2 is an improvement of GGT [55] by combining the scale adaptive kernel correlation filter [56] and the geometric structure hyper-graph searching framework to complete the object tracking task. The target object is represented by a geometric structure hyper-graph that encodes the local appearance of the target with higher-order geometric structure correlations among target parts and a bounding box template that represents the global appearance of the target. The tracker use HSV colour histogram and LBP texture to calculate the appearance similarity between associations in the hyper-graph. The templates of correlation filter is calculated by HOG and colour name according to [56].

A.19   Multi-level Deep Feature Tracker (MLDF)

L. Wang, H. Lu, Yi. Wang, C. Sun
{wlj,wyfan523,waynecool}@mail.dlut.edu.cn, lhchuan@dlut.edu.cn

MLDF tracker is based on deep convolutional neural networks (CNNs). The proposed MLDF tracker draws inspiration from [57] by combining low, mid and high-level features from the pre trained VGG networks [36]. A Multi-Level Network (MLN) is designed to take these features as input and online trained to predict the centre location of the target. By jointly considering multi-level deep features, the MLN is capable to distinguish the target from background objects of different categories. While the MLN is used for location prediction, a Scale Prediction Network (SPN) [58] is applied to handle scale variations.

A.20   Colour-Aware Complex Cell Tracker (CCCT)

D. Chen, Z. Yuan
dapengchenxjtu@foxmail.com, yuan.ze.jian@xjtu.edu.cn

The proposed tracker is a variant of CCT proposed in [59]. CCT tracker applies intensity histogram, oriented gradient histogram and colour name features to construct four types of complex cell descriptors. A score normalization strategy is adopted to weight different visual cues as well as different types of complex cell. Besides, occlusion inference and stability analysis are performed over each cell to increase the robustness of tracking. For more details, the reader is referred to [59].

A.21   A New Scale Adaptive and Multiple Feature Based on Kernel Correlation Filter Tracker (NSAMF)

Y. Li, J. Zhu
{liyang89, jkzhu}@zju.edu.cn
NSAMF is an improved version of the previous method SAMF [56]. To further exploit color information, NSAMF employs color probability map, instead of color name, as color based feature to achieve more robust tracking results. In addition, multi-models based on different features are integrated to vote the final position of the tracked target.

A.22   An Improved STAPLE Tracker with Multiple Feature Integration (Staple+)

Z. Xu, Y. Li, J. Zhu
xuzhan2012@whu.edu.cn, {liyang89, jkzhu}@zju.edu.cn
An improved version of STAPLE tracker [60] by integrating multiple features is presented. Besides extracting HOG feature from merely gray-scale image as they do in [60], we also extract HOG feature from color probability map, which can exploit color information better. The final response map is thus a fusion of different features.

A.23   SiameseFC-ResNet (SiamFC-R)

L. Bertinetto, J.F. Henriques, J. Valmadre, P.H.S. Torr, A. Vedaldi
{luca, joao, jvlmdr}@robots.ox.ac.uk,
philip.torr@eng.ox.ac.uk, vedaldi@robots.ox.ac.uk
SiamFC-R is similar to SiamFC-A A.25, except that it uses a ResNet architecture instead of AlexNet for the embedding function. The parameters for this network were initialised by pre-training for the ILSVRC image classification problem, and then fine-tuned for the similarity learning problem in a second offline phase.

A.24   Structure Hyper-graph Based Correlation Filter Tracker (SHCT)

L. Wen, D. Du, S. Li, C.-M. Chang, S. Lyu, Q. Huang
{lywen.cv.workbox, cvdaviddo, shengkunliluo, mingching, heizi.lyu}@gmail.com,
qmhuang@jdl.ac.cn
SHCT tracker constructs a structure hyper-graph model [61] to extract the motion coherence of target parts. The tracker also computes a part confidence map based on the extracted dense subgraphs on the constructed structure hyper-graph, which indicates the confidence score of the part belonging to the target. SHCT uses HSV colour histogram and LBP feature to calculate the appearance similarity between associations in the hyper-graph. Finally, the tracker combines the response maps of correlation filter and structure hyper-graph in a linear way

to find the optimal target state (i.e., target scale and location). The templates of correlation filter are calculated by HOG and colour name according to [56]. The appearance models of correlation filter and structure hyper-graph are updated to ensure the tracking performance.

A.25   SiameseFC-AlexNet (SiamFC-A)

L. Bertinetto, J.F. Henriques, J. Valmadre, P.H.S. Torr, A. Vedaldi
{luca, joao, jvlmdr}@robots.ox.ac.uk,
philip.torr@eng.ox.ac.uk, vedaldi@robots.ox.ac.uk

SiamFC-A [62] applies a fully-convolutional Siamese network [63] trained to locate an exemplar image within a larger search image. The architecture is fully convolutional with respect to the search image: dense and efficient sliding-window evaluation is achieved with a bilinear layer that computes the cross-correlation of two inputs. The deep convnet (namely, a AlexNet [64]) is first trained offline on the large ILSVRC15 [65] video dataset to address a general similarity learning problem, and then this function is evaluated during testing by a simplistic tracker. SiamAN incorporates elementary temporal constraints: the object search is done within a region of approximately four times its previous size, and a cosine window is added to the score map to penalize large displacements. SiamAN also processes several scaled versions of the search image, any change in scale is penalised and damping is applied to the scale factor.

A.26   Continuous Convolution Operator Tracker (C-COT)

M. Danelljan, A. Robinson, F. Shahbaz Khan, M. Felsberg
{martin.danelljan, andreas.robinson, fahad.khan, michael.felsberg}@liu.se

C-COT learns a discriminative continuous convolution operator as its tracking model. C-COT poses the learning problem in the continuous spatial domain. This enables a natural and efficient fusion of multi-resolution feature maps, e.g. when using several convolutional layers from a pre-trained CNN. The continuous formulation also enables highly accurate localization by sub-pixel refinement. The reader is referred to [37] for details.

A.27   SumShift Tracker with Kernelized Correlation Filter (SSKCF)

J.-Y. Lee, S. Choi, J.-C. Jeong, J.-W. Kim, J.-I. Cho
{jylee, sunglok, channij80, giraffe, jicho}@etri.re.kr

SumShiftKCF tracker is an extension of the SumShift tracker [38] by the kernelized correlation filter tracker (KCF) [47]. The SumShiftKCF tracker computes the object likelihood with the weighted sum of the histogram back-projection weights and the correlation response of KCF. Target is then located by the Sum-Shift iteration [38].

A.28   Sum of Template and Pixel-wise LEarners (Staple)

L. Bertinetto, J. Valmadre, S. Golodetz, O. Miksik, P.H.S. Torr
{luca, jvlmdr}@robots.ox.ac.uk, stuart.golodetz@ndcn.ox.ac.uk,
{ondrej.miksik, philip.torr}@eng.ox.ac.uk
Staple is a tracker that combines two image patch representations that are sensitive to complementary factors to learn a model that is inherently robust to both colour changes and deformations. To maintain real-time speed, two independent ridge-regression problems are solved, exploiting the inherent structure of each representation. Staple combines the scores of two models in a dense translation search, enabling greater accuracy. A critical property of the two models is that their scores are similar in magnitude and indicative of their reliability, so that the prediction is dominated by the more confident. For more details, we refer the reader to [60].

A.29   Kalman Filter Ensemble-Based Tracker (ColorKCF)

P. Senna, I. Drummond, G. Bastos
{pedrosennapsc, isadrummond, sousa}@unifei.edu.br
The colourKCF method fuses the result of two out-of-the box trackers, a mean-shift tracker that uses colour histogram (ASMS) [66] and the kernelized correlation filter (KCF) [47] by using a Kalman filter. The tracker works in prediction and correction cycles. First, a simple motion model predicts the target next position, then, the trackers results are fused with the predicted position and the motion model is updated in the correction process. The fused result is the colourKCF output which is used as last position of the tracker in the next frame. The Kalman filter needs a measure to define how reliable each result is during the fusion process. For this, the tracker uses the result confidence and the motion penalization which is proportional to the distance between the tracker result and the predict result. As confidence measure, the Bhattacharyya coefficient between the model and the target histogram is used in case of ASMS tracker, while the correlation result is applied in case of KCF tracker.

A.30   Best Structured Tracker (BST)

F. Battistone, A. Petrosino, V. Santopietro
{battistone.francesco, vinsantopietro}@gmail.com, petrosino@uniparthenope.it
BST is based on the idea of Flock of Trackers [67]: a set of local trackers tracks a little patch of the original target and then the tracker combines their information in order to estimate the resulting bounding box. Each local tracker separately analyzes the features extracted from a set of samples and then classifies them using a structured Support Vector Machine as Struck [67]. Once having predicted local target candidates, an outlier detection process is computed by analyzing the displacements of local trackers. Trackers that have been labeled as outliers are reinitialized. At the end of this process, the new bounding box is calculated using the Convex Hull technique.

A.31   Online Evaluation-Based Self-Correction Tracker (OEST)

Z. Cai, P.C. Yuen, A.J. Ma, X. Lan
{cszxcai, pcyuen, andyjhma, xylan}@comp.hkbu.edu.hk

Online Evaluation-based Self-Correction Tracker aims at improving the tracking performance based on any existing tracker. OEST consists of three steps. Firstly, the long-term correlation tracker (LCT) [68] is employed to determine the bounding box of the target at the current frame. Secondly, an online tracking performance estimator is deployed to evaluate whether the output bounding box provided by the base tracker can correctly locate the target by analyzing the previous tracking results. Comparing existing performance estimators, the time-reverse method [69] achieves the best evaluation performance. Thirdly, if the online tracking performance estimator determines that the base tracker fails to track the target, a re-detection algorithm is performed to correct the output of the tracker. An online SVM detector as in [70] is employed in this re-detection step. Tracker outputs with high confidence determined by the performance estimator are used to update the detector.

A.32   Tracking by Regression with Incrementally Learned Cascades (TRIC-track)

X. Wang, M. Valstar, B. Martinez, M.H. Khan, T. Pridmore
{psxxw, Michel.Valstar, brais.martinez, psxmhk,
tony.pridmore}@nottingham.ac.uk

TRIC-track is a part-based tracker which directly predicts the displacements between the centres of sampled image patches and the target part location using regressors. TRIC-track adopts the Supervised Descent Method (SDM) [71] to perform the cascaded regression for displacement prediction, estimating the target location with increasingly accurate predictions. To adapt to variations in target appearance and shape over time, TRIC-track takes inspiration from the incremental learning of cascaded regression of [72] applying a sequential incremental update. Shape constraints are, however, implicitly encoded by allowing patches sampled around neighbouring parts to vote for a given parts location. TRIC-track also possesses a multiple temporal scale motion model [73] which enables it to fully exert the trackers advantage by providing accurate initial prediction of the target part location every frame. For more details, the interested reader is referred to [74].

A.33   Correlation-Based Tracker Level Fusion (CTF)

M.k. Rapuru, S. Kakanuru, D. Mishra, G.R.K.S. Subrahmanyam
madankumar.r@gmail.com, kakanurusumithra05@gmail.com,
{deepak.mishra, gorthisubrahmanyam}@iist.ac.in

The Correlation based Tracker level Fusion (CTF) method combines two state-of-the-art trackers, which have complementary nature in handling tracking challenges and also in the methodology of tracking. CTF considers the outputs of both trackers Tracking Learning Detection (TLD) [75] tracker and Kernelized Correlation Filters (KCF) tracker [47], and selects the best patch by measuring the correlation correspondence with the stored object model sample patches. An integration of frame level detection strategy of TLD with systematic model update strategy of KCF are used to increase the robustness. Since KCF tracker exploits the circulant structure in the training and testing data, a high frame rate with less overhead is achieved. CTF method can handle scale changes, occlusions and tracking resumption with the virtue of TLD, whereas KCF fails in handling these challenges. The proposed methodology is not limited to integrating just TLD and KCF, it is a generic model where any best tracker can be combined with TLD to leverage the best performance.

A.34   Salient Region Based Tracker (SRBT)

H. Lee, D. Kim
{lhmin, dkim}@postech.ac.kr
    Salient Region Based Tracker separates the exact object region contained in the bounding box - called the salient region - from the background region. It uses the colour model and appearance model to estimate the location and size of the target. During an initialization step, the salient region is set to the ground truth region and is updated for each frame. While estimating the target location and updating the model, only the pixels inside the salient region can participate as contributors. An additional image template as appearance model is used to catch like edges and shape. The colour histogram model is adopted from DAT [45] excluding the distractor-awareness concept.

A.35   Deformable Part Correlation Filter Tracker (DPT)

A. Lukežič, L. Čehovin, M. Kristan
{alan.lukezic, luka.cehovin, matej.kristan}@fri.uni-lj.si
    DPT is a part-based correlation filter composed of a coarse and mid-level target representations. Coarse representation is responsible for approximate target localization and uses HOG as well as colour features. The mid-level representation is a deformable parts correlation filter with fully-connected parts topology and applies a novel formulation that threats geometric and visual properties within a single convex optimization function. The mid level as well as coarse level representations are based on the kernelized correlation filter from [47]. The reader is referred to [76] for details.

A.36   Guided Correlation Filter (GCF)

A. Lukežič, L. Čehovin, M. Kristan
{alan.lukezic, luka.cehovin, matej.kristan}@fri.uni-lj.si
    GCF (guided correlation filter) is a correlation filter based tracker that uses colour segmentation [77] (implementation from [78]) to improve the robustness

of the correlation filter learning process. The segmentation mask is combined with the correlation filter to reduce the impact of the background and the circular correlations effects, which are the most problematic when tracking rotated or non-axis aligned objects. The tracker uses HOG [79] features for target localization and the DSST [48] approach for scale estimation.

A.37   Optical Flow Clustering Tracker (FCT)

A. Varfolomieiev
a.varfolomieiev@kpi.ua

FCT is based on the same idea as the best displacement tracker (BDF) [51]. It uses pyramidal Lucas-Kanade optical flow algorithm to track individual points of an object at several pyramid levels. The results of the point tracking are clustered in the same way as in the BDF [51] to estimate the best object displacement. The initial point locations are generated by the FAST detector [80]. The tracker estimates a scale and an in-plane rotation of the object. These procedures are similar to the scale calculation of the median flow tracker [81], except that the clustering is used instead of median. In case of rotation calculation angles between the respective point pairs are clustered. In contrast to BDF, the FCT does not use consensus-based reinitialization. The current implementation of FCT calculates the optical flow only in the objects region, which is four times larger than the initial bounding box of the object, and thus speeds up the tracker with respect to its previous version [18].

A.38   Likelihood of Features Tracking-Lite (LoFT-Lite)

M. Poostchi, K. Palaniappan, F. Bunyak, G. Seetharaman, R. Pelapur, K. Gao,
S. Yao, N. Al-Shakarji
mpoostchi@mail.missouri.edu, {pal, bunyak}@missouri.edu, guna@ieee.org
{rvpnc4, kg954, syyh4, nmahyd}@missouri.edu,

LoFT (Likelihood of Features Tracking)-Lite [82] is an appearance based single object tracker optimized for aerial video. Target objects are characterized using low level image feature descriptors including intensity, color, shape and edge attributes based on histograms of intensity, color-name space, gradient magnitude and gradient orientation. The feature likelihood maps are computed using fast integral histograms [83] within a sliding window framework that compares histogram descriptors. Intensity and gradient magnitude normalized cross-correlations likelihood maps are also used to incorporate spatial structure information. An informative subset of six features from the collection of eleven features is used that are the most discriminative based on an offline feature subset selection method [84]. LoFT performs feature fusion using a foreground-background model by comparing the current target appearance with the model inside the search region [85]. LOFT-Lite also incorporates an adaptive orientation-based Kalman prediction update to restrict the search region which reduces sensitivity to abrupt motion changes and decreases computational cost [86].

A.39   Dynamic Feature Selection Tracker (DFST)

G. Roffo, S. Melzi
{giorgio.roffo, simone.melzi}@univr.it
DFST proposes an optimized visual tracking algorithm based on the real-time selection of locally and temporally discriminative features. A feature selection mechanism is embedded in the Adaptive colour Names [87] (CN) tracking system that adaptively selects the top-ranked discriminative features for tracking. DFST provides a significant gain in accuracy and precision allowing the use of a dynamic set of features that results in an increased system flexibility. DFST is based on the unsupervised method Inf-FS [88,89], which ranks features according with their 'redundancy' without using class labels. By using a fast online algorithm for learning dictionaries [90] the size of the box is adapted during the processing. At each update, multiple examples at different positions and scales around the target are used. A further improvement of the CN system is given by making micro-shifts at the predicted position according to the best template matching. The interested reader is referred to [89] for details.

A.40   Scalable Kernel Correlation Filter with Sparse Feature Integration (sKCF)

A. Solís Montero, J. Lang, R. Laganière
asolismo@uottawa.ca, {jlang, laganier}@eecs.uottawa.ca
sKCF [91] extends Kernalized Correlation Filter (KCF) framework by introducing an adjustable Gaussian window function and keypoint-based model for scale estimation to deal with the fixed size limitation in the Kernelized Correlation Filter along with some performace enhancements. In the submission, we introduce a model learning strategy to the original sKCF [91] which updates the model only for highly similar KCF responses of the tracked region as to the model. This potentially limits model drift due to temporary disturbances or occlusions. The original sKCF always updates the model in each frame.

A.41   Dual Deep Network Tracker (DNT)

Z. Chi, H. Lu, L. Wang, C. Sun
{zhizhenchi, wlj, waynecool}@mail.dlut.edu.cn, lhchuan@dlut.edu.cn
DNT proposes a dual network for visual tracking. First, the hierarchical features in two different layers of a deep model pre-trained are exploited for object recognition. Features in higher layers encode more semantic contexts while those in lower layers are more effective to discriminative appearance. To highlight geometric contours of the target, the hierarchical feature maps are integrated with an edge detector as the coarse prior maps. To measure the similarities between

the network activation and target appearance, a dual network with a supervised loss function is trained. This dual network is updated online in a unique manner based on the observation that the tracking target in consecutive frames should share more similar feature representations than those in the surrounding background. Using prior maps as guidance, the independent component analysis with reference algorithm is used to extract the exact boundary of a target object, and online tracking is conducted by maximizing the posterior estimate on the feature maps with stochastic and periodic update.

A.42   Structuralist Cognitive Model for Visual Tracking (SCT)

J. Choi, H.J. Chang, J. Jeong, Y. Demiris, J.Y. Choi
jwchoi.pil@gmail.com, hj.chang@imperial.ac.uk, jy.jeong@snu.ac.kr,
y.demiris@imperial.ac.uk, jychoi@snu.ac.kr

SCT [92] is composed of two separate stages: disintegration and integration. In the disintegration stage, the target is divided into a number of small cognitive structural units, which are memorized separately. Each unit includes a specific colour or a distinguishable target shape, and is trained by elementary trackers with different types of kernel. In the integration stage, an adequate combination of the structural units is created and memorized to express the targets appearance. When encountering a target with changing appearance in diverse environments, SCT tracker utilizes all the responses from the cognitive units memorized in the disintegration stage and then recognizes the target through the best combination of cognitive units, referring to the memorized combinations. With respect to the elementary trackers, an attentional feature-based correlation filter (AtCF) is used. The AtCF focuses on the attentional features discriminated from the background. Each AtCF consists of an attentional weight estimator and a kernelized correlation filter (KCF) [47]. In the disintegration stage, multiple AtCFs are updated using various features and kernel types. The integration stage combines the responses of AtCFs by ordering the AtCFs following their performance.

A.43   Long Term Featureless Object Tracker (LT-FLO)

K. Lebeda, S. Hadfield, J. Matas, R. Bowden
{k.lebeda, s.hadfield}@surrey.ac.uk, matas@cmp.felk.cvut.cz,
r.bowden@surrey.ac.uk

The tracker is based on and extends previous work of the authors on tracking of texture-less objects [93]. It significantly decreases reliance on texture by using edge-points instead of point features. LT-FLO uses correspondences of lines tangent to the edges and candidates for a correspondence are all local maxima of gradient magnitude. An estimate of the frame-to-frame transformation similarity is obtained via RANSAC. When the confidence is high, the current state is learnt for future corrections. On the other hand, when a low confidence is achieved, the tracker corrects its position estimate restarting the tracking from previously stored states. LT-FLO tracker also has a mechanism to detect disappearance of the object, based on the stability of the gradient in the area of projected edge-points. The interested reader is referred to [94, 95] for details.

A.44 Tree-structured Convolutional Neural Network Tracker (TCNN)

H. Nam, M. Baek, B. Han
{namhs09, mooyeol, bhhan}@postech.ac.kr

TCNN [96] maintains multiple target appearance models based on CNNs in a tree structure to preserve model consistency and handle appearance multimodality effectively. TCNN tracker consists of two main components, state estimation and model update. When a new frame is given, candidate samples around the target state estimated in the previous frame are drawn, and the likelihood of each sample based on the weighted average of the scores from multiple CNNs is computed. The weight of each CNN is determined by the reliability of the path along which the CNN has been updated in the tree structure. The target state in the current frame is estimated by finding the candidate with the maximum likelihood. After tracking a predefined number of frames, a new CNN is derived from an existing one, which has the highest weight among the contributing CNNs to target state estimation.

A.45 Adaptive Regression Target Discriminative Scale Space Tracking (ART-DSST)

L. Zhang, J. Van de Weijer, M. Mozerov, F. Khan
{lichao, joost, mikhail}@cvc.uab.es, fahad.khan@liu.se

Correlation based tracking optimizes the filter coefficients such that the resulting filter response is an isotropic Gaussian. However, for rectangular shapes the overlap error diminishes anisotropically: faster along the short axes than the long axes of the rectangle. To exploit this observation, ART-DSST proposes the usage of an anisotropic Gaussian regression target which adapts to the shape of the bounding box. The method is general because it can be applied to all regression based trackers.

A.46 Multi-Domain Convolutional Neural Network Tracker (MDNet-N)

H. Nam, M. Baek, B. Han
{namhs09, mooyeol, bhhan}@postech.ac.kr

This algorithm is a variation of MDNet [33], which does not pre-train CNNs with other tracking datasets. The network is initialised using the ImageNet [97]. The new classification layer and the fully connected layers within the shared layers are then fine-tuned online during tracking to adapt to the new domain. The online update is conducted to model long-term and short-term appearance variations of a target for robustness and adaptiveness, respectively, and an effective and efficient hard negative mining technique is incorporated in the learning procedure. This experiment result shows that the online tracking framework scheme of MDNet is still effective without multi-domain training.

A.47 CF2 with Response Information Failure Detection (RFD-CF2)

R. Walsh, H. Medeiros
{ryan.w.walsh, henry.medeiros}@marquette.edu,
RFD-CF2 is a modified version of the Correlation Filters with Convolutional Features tracker (CF2) extended with a failure detection module [98]. Hard occlusions and blurring of the target are detected by extracting features out of the response map. The tracker uses this information to scale the trackers search space and minimize bad updates from occurring.

A.48 Scalable Multiple Part Regressors tracker (SMPR)

A. Memarmoghadam, P. Moallem
{a.memarmoghadam, p_moallem}@eng.ui.ac.ir
SMPR framework applies both global and local correlation filter-based part regressors in object modeling. To follow target appearance changes, importance weights are dynamically assigned to each model part via solving a multi linear ridge regression optimization problem. During model update, a helpful scale estimation technique based on weighted relative movement of pair-wise inlier parts is applied. Without loss of generality, conventional CN tracker [87] is utilized as a sample CFT baseline to expeditiously track each target object part by feeding color-induced attributes into fast CSK tracker [99]. Similar to CN approach [87], low dimensional colour names together with greyscale features are employed to represent each part of the object model.

A.49 Scale Adaptive Mean Shift (ASMS)

Submitted by VOT Committee
The mean-shift tracker optimize the Hellinger distance between template histogram and target candidate in the image. This optimization is done by a gradient descend. The ASMS [100] method address the problem of scale adaptation and present a novel theoretically justified scale estimation mechanism which relies solely on the mean-shift procedure for the Hellinger distance. The ASMS also introduces two improvements of the mean-shift tracker that make the scale estimation more robust in the presence of background clutter - a histogram colour weighting and a forward-backward consistency check.

A.50 Discriminative Scale Space Tracker (DSST2014)

Authors implementation. Submitted by VOT Committee

The Discriminative Scale Space Tracker (DSST) [48] extends the Minimum Output Sum of Squared Errors (MOSSE) tracker [101] with robust scale estimation. The DSST additionally learns a one-dimensional discriminative scale filter, that is used to estimate the target size. For the translation filter, the intensity features employed in the MOSSE tracker is combined with a pixel-dense representation of HOG-features.

A.51   Flock of Trackers (FoT)

Submitted by VOT Committee

The Flock of Trackers (FoT) [67] is a tracking framework where the object motion is estimated from the displacements or, more generally, transformation estimates of a number of local trackers covering the object. Each local tracker is attached to a certain area specified in the object coordinate frame. The local trackers are not robust and assume that the tracked area is visible in all images and that it undergoes a simple motion, e.g. translation. The Flock of Trackers object motion estimate is robust if it is from local tracker motions by a combination which is insensitive to failures.

A.52   HMMTxD

Submitted by VOT Committee

The HMMTxD [102] method fuses observations from complementary out-of-the box trackers and a detector by utilizing a hidden Markov model whose latent states correspond to a binary vector expressing the failure of individual trackers. The Markov model is trained in an unsupervised way, relying on an online learned detector to provide a source of tracker-independent information for a modified Baum-Welch algorithm that updates the model w.r.t. the partially annotated data.

A.53   Kernelized Correlation Filter Tracker (KCF2014)

Modified version of the authors implementation. Submitted by VOT Committee

This tracker is basically a Kernelized Correlation Filter [47] operating on simple HOG features. The KCF tracker is equivalent to a Kernel Ridge Regression trained with thousands of sample patches around the object at different translations. The improvements over the previous version are multi-scale support, sub-cell peak estimation and replacing the model update by linear interpolation with a more robust update scheme.

A.54   A Kernel Correlation Filter Tracker with Scale Adaptive and Feature Integration (SAMF2014)

Authors implementation. Submitted by VOT Committee

SAMF tracker is based on the idea of correlation filter-based trackers with aim to improve the overall tracking capability. To tackle the problem of the fixed template size in kernel correlation filter tracker, an effective scale adaptive scheme is proposed. Moreover, features like HOG and colour naming are integrated together to further boost the overall tracking performance.

A.55 STRUCK (Struck2011)

Submitted by VOT Committee
Struck [103] is a framework for adaptive visual object tracking based on structured output prediction. The method uses a kernelized structured output support vector machine (SVM), which is learned online to provide adaptive tracking.

A.56 Adaptive Color Tracker (ACT)

Authors implementation. Submitted by VOT Committee
The Adaptive Color Tracker (ACT) [104] extends the CSK tracker [99] with colour information. ACT tracker contains three improvements to CSK tracker: (i) A temporally consistent scheme for updating the tracking model is applied instead of training the classifier separately on single samples, (ii) colour attributes are applied for image representation, and (iii) ACT employs a dynamically adaptive scheme for selecting the most important combinations of colours for tracking.

A.57 Spatially Regularized Discriminative Correlation Filter with Deep Features (DeepSRDCF)

Authors implementation. Submitted by VOT Committee
The DeepSRDCF incorporates deep convolutional features in the SRDCF framework proposed in [105]. Instead of the commonly used hand-crafted features, the DeepSRDCF employs convolutional features from a pre-trained network. A Principal Component Analysis is used to reduce the feature dimensionality of the extracted activations. The reader is referred to [105] for details.

A.58 Spatially Regularized Discriminative Correlation Filter Tracker (SRDCF)

Authors implementation. Submitted by VOT Committee
Standard Discriminative Correlation Filter (DCF) based trackers such as [47,48,87] suffer from the inherent periodic assumption when using circular correlation. The resulting periodic boundary effects leads to inaccurate training samples and a restricted search region.

The SRDCF mitigates the problems arising from assumptions of periodicity in learning correlation filters by introducing a spatial regularization function that penalizes filter coefficients residing outside the target region. This allows the size of the training and detection samples to be increased without affecting the effective filter size. By selecting the spatial regularization function to have a sparse Discrete Fourier Spectrum, the filter is efficiently optimized directly in the Fourier domain. Instead of solving for an approximate filter, as in previous DCF based trackers (e.g. [47,48,87]), the SRDCF employs an iterative optimization based on Gauss-Seidel that converges to the exact filter. The detection step employs a sub-grid maximization of the correlation scores to achieve more precise location estimates. In addition to the HOG features used in [105], the submitted variant of SRDCF also employs Colour Names and greyscale features. These features are averaged over the 4×4 HOG cells and then concatenated, giving a 42 dimensional feature vector at each cell. For more details, the reader is referred to [105].

A.59 Distribution Fields Tracking (DFT)

Implementation from authors website. Submitted by VOT Committee
The tacker introduces a method for building an image descriptor using distribution fields (DFs), a representation that allows smoothing the objective function without destroying information about pixel values. DFs enjoy a large basin of attraction around the global optimum compared to related descriptors. DFs also allow the representation of uncertainty about the tracked object. This helps in disregarding outliers during tracking (like occlusions or small missalignments) without modeling them explicitly.

A.60 Hierarchical Convolutional Features for Visual Tracking (HCF)

Submitted by VOT Committee
HCF tracker [106] is a kernelized correlation filter applied to VGG convnet features. The tracker exploits boths spatial details and semantics. While the last convolutional layers encode the semantic information of targets, earlier convolutional layers retain more fine-grained spatial details providing more precise localization. The reader is referred to [106] for details.

A.61 Normalized Cross-Correlation (NCC)

Submitted by VOT Committee
The NCC tracker is a VOT2016 baseline tracker and follows the very basic idea of tracking by searching for the best match between a static grayscale template and the image using normalized cross-correlation.

A.62 Local-Global Tracking Tracker (LGT)

Submitted by VOT Committee
The core element of LGT is a coupled-layer visual model that combines the target global and local appearance by interlacing two layers. By this coupled

constraint paradigm between the adaptation of the global and the local layer, a more robust tracking through significant appearance changes is achieved. The reader is referred to [107] for details.

A.63   Anchor Template Tracker (ANT)

Submitted by VOT Committee

The ANT tracker is a conceptual increment to the idea of multi-layer appearance representation that is first described in [107]. The tracker addresses the problem of self-supervised estimation of a large number of parameters by introducing controlled graduation in estimation of the free parameters. The appearance of the object is decomposed into several sub-models, each describing the target at a different level of detail. The sub models interact during target localization and, depending on the visual uncertainty, serve for cross-sub-model supervised updating. The reader is referred to [108] for details.

A.64   Incremental Learning for Robust Visual Tracking (IVT)

Submitted by VOT Committee

The idea of the IVT tracker [109] is to incrementally learn a low-dimensional sub-space representation, adapting on-line to changes in the appearance of the target. The model update, based on incremental algorithms for principal component analysis, includes two features: a method for correctly updating the sample mean, and a forgetting factor to ensure less modelling power is expended fitting older observations.

A.65   HoughTrack (HT)

Submitted by VOT Committee

HoughTrack is a tracking-by-detection approach based on the Generalized Hough-Transform. The idea of Hough-Forests is extended to the online domain and the center vote based detection and back-projection is coupled with a rough segmentation based on graph-cuts. This is in contrast to standard online learning approaches, where typically bounding-box representations with fixed aspect ratios are employed. The original authors claim that HoughTrack provides a more accurate foreground/background separation and that it can handle highly non-rigid and articulated objects. The reader is referred to [110] for details and to http://lrs.icg.tugraz.at/research/houghtrack/forcode.

A.66   Spatio-temporal Context Tracker (STC)

Submitted by VOT Committee

The STC [111] is a correlation filter based tracker, which uses image intensity features. It formulates the spatio temporal relationships between the object of interest and its locally dense contexts in a Bayesian framework, which models the statistical correlation between features from the target and its surrounding regions. For fast learning and detection the Fast Fourier Transform (FFT) is adopted.

A.67 Transfer Learning Based Visual Tracking with Gaussian Processes Regression (TGPR)

Submitted by VOT Committee

The TGPR tracker [112] models the probability of target appearance using Gaussian Process Regression. The observation model is learned in a semi-supervised fashion using both labeled samples from previous frames and the unlabeled samples that are tracking candidates extracted from current frame.

A.68 Multiple Instance Learning Tracker (MIL)

Submitted by VOT Committee

MIL tracker [113] uses a tracking-by-detection approach, more specifically Multiple Instance Learning instead of traditional supervised learning methods and shows improved robustness to inaccuracies of the tracker and to incorrectly labelled training samples.

A.69 Robust Fragments Based Tracking Using the Integral Histogram - FragTrack (FT)

Submitted by VOT Committee

FragTrack represents the model of the object by multiple image fragments or patches. The patches are arbitrary and are not based on an object model. Every patch votes on the possible positions and scales of the object in the current frame, by comparing its histogram with the corresponding image patch histogram. A robust statistic is minimized in order to combine the vote maps of the multiple patches. The algorithm overcomes several difficulties which cannot be handled by traditional histogram-based algorithms like partial occlusions or pose change.

A.70 Consensus Based Matching and Tracking (CMT)

Submitted by VOT Committee

The CMT tracker is a keypoint-based method in a combined matching-and-tracking framework. To localise the object in every frame, each key point casts votes for the object center. A consensus-based scheme is applied for outlier detection in the voting behaviour. By transforming votes based on the current key point constellation, changes of the object in scale and rotation are considered. The use of fast keypoint detectors and binary descriptors allows the current implementation to run in real-time. The reader is referred to [114] for details.

References

1. Gavrila, D.M.: The visual analysis of human movement: a survey. Comp. Vis. Image Underst. **73**(1), 82–98 (1999)
2. Moeslund, T.B., Granum, E.: A survey of computer vision-based human motion capture. Comp. Vis. Image Underst. **81**(3), 231–268 (2001)
3. Gabriel, P., Verly, J., Piater, J., Genon, A.: The state of the art in multiple object tracking under occlusion in video sequences. In: Proceedings of Advanced Concepts for Intelligent Vision Systems, pp. 166–173 (2003)
4. Hu, W., Tan, T., Wang, L., Maybank, S.: A survey on visual surveillance of object motion and behaviors. IEEE Trans. Syst. Man Cybern. C **34**(30) 334–352 (2004)
5. Moeslund, T.B., Hilton, A., Kruger, V.: A survey of advances in vision-based human motion capture and analysis. Comp. Vis. Image Underst. **103**(2–3), 90–126 (2006)
6. Yilmaz, A., Shah, M.: Object tracking: a survey. J. ACM Comput. Surv. **38**(4), 13 (2006)
7. Yang, H., Shao, L., Zheng, F., Wang, L., Song, Z.: Recent advances and trends in visual tracking: a review. Neurocomputing **74**(18), 3823–3831 (2011)
8. Zhang, S., Yao, H., Sun, X., Lu, X.: Sparse coding based visual tracking: review and experimental comparison. Pattern Recogn. **46**(7), 1772–1788 (2013)
9. Li, X., Hu, W., Shen, C., Zhang, Z., Dick, A.R., Van den Hengel, A.: A survey of appearance models in visual object tracking. arXiv:1303.4803 [cs.CV] (2013)
10. Young, D.P., Ferryman, J.M.: Pets metrics: on-line performance evaluation service. In: ICCCN 2005 Proceedings of the 14th International Conference on Computer Communications and Networks, pp. 317–324 (2005)
11. Goyette, N., Jodoin, P.M., Porikli, F., Konrad, J., Ishwar, P.: Changedetection.net: a new change detection benchmark dataset. In: CVPR Workshops, pp. 1–8. IEEE (2012)
12. Phillips, P.J., Moon, H., Rizvi, S.A., Rauss, P.J.: The feret evaluation methodology for face-recognition algorithms. IEEE Trans. Pattern Anal. Mach. Intell. **22**(10), 1090–1104 (2000)
13. Kasturi, R., Goldgof, D.B., Soundararajan, P., Manohar, V., Garofolo, J.S., Bowers, R., Boonstra, M., Korzhova, V.N., Zhang, J.: Framework for performance evaluation of face, text, and vehicle detection and tracking in video: data, metrics, and protocol. IEEE Trans. Pattern Anal. Mach. Intell. **31**(2), 319–336 (2009)
14. Leal-Taixé, L., Milan, A., Reid, I.D., Roth, S., Schindler, K.: Motchallenge 2015: towards a benchmark for multi-target tracking. CoRR abs/1504.01942 (2015)
15. Solera, F., Calderara, S., Cucchiara, R.: Towards the evaluation of reproducible robustness in tracking-by-detection. In: Advanced Video and Signal Based Surveillance, pp. 1–6 (2015)
16. Kristan, M., Pflugfelder, R., Leonardis, A., Matas, J., Porikli, F., Cehovin, L., Nebehay, G., G., F., Vojir, T., et al.: The visual object tracking vot2013 challenge results. In: ICCV 2013 Workshops, Workshop on Visual Object Tracking Challenge, pp. 98–111 (2013)
17. Kristan, M., Pflugfelder, R., Leonardis, A., Matas, J., Cehovin, L., Nebehay, G., Vojir, T., G., F., et al.: The visual object tracking vot2014 challenge results. In: ECCV 2014 Workshops, Workshop on Visual Object Tracking Challenge (2014)
18. Kristan, M., Matas, J., Leonardis, A., Felsberg, M., et al.: The visual object tracking vot2015 challenge results. In: ICCV 2015 Workshops, Workshop on Visual Object Tracking Challenge (2015)

19. Kristan, M., Matas, J., Leonardis, A., Vojir, T., Pflugfelder, R., Fernandez, G., Nebehay, G., Porikli, F., Čehovin, L.: A novel performance evaluation methodology for single-target trackers. IEEE Trans. Pattern Anal. Mach. Intell. 2016, to appear
20. Čehovin, L., Leonardis, A., Kristan, M.: Visual object tracking performance measures revisited. IEEE Trans. Image Process. **25**(3), 1261–1274 (2015)
21. Wu, Y., Lim, J., Yang, M.H.: Online object tracking: a benchmark. In: Computer Vision and Pattern Recognition, vol. 37(9), pp. 1834–1848 (2013)
22. Smeulders, A.W.M., Chu, D.M., Cucchiara, R., Calderara, S., Dehghan, A., Shah, M.: Visual tracking: an experimental survey. TPAMI **36**(7), 1442–1468 (2013)
23. Wu, Y., Lim, J., Yang, M.H.: Object tracking benchmark. IEEE-PAMI (2015)
24. Li, A., Li, M., Wu, Y., Yang, M.H., Yan, S.: Nus-pro: a new visual tracking challenge. IEEE-PAMI **38**(2), 335–349 (2015)
25. Liang, P., Blasch, E., Ling, H.: Encoding color information for visual tracking: algorithms and benchmark. IEEE Trans. Image Process. **24**(12), 5630–5644 (2015)
26. Čehovin, L., Kristan, M., Leonardis, A.: Is my new tracker really better than yours? In: WACV 2014: IEEE Winter Conference on Applications of Computer Vision (2014)
27. Wu, Y., Lim, J., Yang, M.: Object tracking benchmark. IEEE Trans. Pattern Anal. Mach. Intell. **37**(9), 1834–1848 (2014)
28. Felsberg, M., Berg, A., Häger, G., Ahlberg, J., et al.: The thermal infrared visual object tracking VOT-TIR2015 challenge results. In: ICCV 2015 Workshop Proceedings, VOT 2015 Workshop (2015)
29. Felsberg, M., Kristan, M., Leonardis, A., Matas, J., Pflugfelder, R., et al.: The thermal infrared visual object tracking VOT-TIR2016 challenge results. In: ECCV 2016 Workshop Proceedings, VOT 2016 Workshop (2016)
30. Rother, C., Kolmogorov, V., Blake, A.: "grabcut": interactive foreground extraction using iterated graph cuts. In: ACM SIGGRAPH 2004 Papers, SIGGRAPH 2004, pp. 309–314. ACM, New York (2004)
31. Byrd, H.R., Gilbert, C.J., Nocedal, J.: A trust region method based on interior point techniques for nonlinear programming. Math. Program. **89**(1), 149–185 (2000)
32. Shanno, D.F.: Conditioning of quasi-newton methods for function minimization. Math. Comput. **24**(111), 647–656 (1970)
33. Nam, H., Han, B.: Learning multi-domain convolutional neural networks for visual tracking. CoRR (2015)
34. Felzenszwalb, P.F., Girshick, R.B., McAllester, D., Ramanan, D.: Object detection with discriminatively trained part based models. IEEE Trans. Pattern Anal. Mach. Intell. **32**(9), 1627–1645 (2010)
35. Van de Weijer, J., Schmid, C., Verbeek, J., Larlus, D.: Learning color names for real-world applications. IEEE Trans. Image Process. **18**(7), 1512–1524 (2009)
36. Simonyan, K., Zisserman, A.: Very deep convolutional networks for large-scale image recognition. In: ICLR (2015)
37. Danelljan, M., Robinson, A., Shahbaz Khan, F., Felsberg, M.: Beyond correlation filters: learning continuous convolution operators for visual tracking. In: Leibe, B., Matas, J., Sebe, N., Welling, M., Atadjanov, I.R. (eds.) ECCV 2016. LNCS, vol. 9909, pp. 472–488. Springer, Heidelberg (2016). doi:10.1007/978-3-319-46454-1_29
38. Lee, J.Y., Yu, W.: Visual tracking by partition-based histogram backprojection and maximum support criteria. In: Proceedings of the IEEE International Conference on Robotics and Biomimetic (ROBIO) (2011)

39. Akin, O., Erdem, E., Erdem, A., Mikolajczyk, K.: Deformable part-based tracking by coupled global and local correlation filters. J. Vis. Commun. Image Represent. **38**, 763–774 (2016)
40. Zhu, G., Porikli, F., Li, H.: Beyond local search: Tracking objects everywhere with instance-specific proposals. In: IEEE Conference on Computer Vision and Pattern Recognition (CVPR) (2016)
41. Gundogdu, E., Alatan, A.A.: Spatial windowing for correlation filter based visual tracking. In: ICIP (2016)
42. González, A., Martín-Nieto, R., Bescós, J., Martínez, J.M.: Single object long-term tracker for smart control of a PTZ camera. In: International Conference on Distributed Smart Cameras, pp. 121–126 (2014)
43. Shi, J., Tomasi, C.: Good features to track. In: Computer Vision and Pattern Recognition, pp. 593–600, June 1994
44. Comaniciu, D., Ramesh, V., Meer, P.: Real-time tracking of non-rigid objects using mean shift. Comput. Vis. Pattern Recogn. **2**, 142–149 (2000)
45. Possegger, H., Mauthner, T., Bischof, H.: In defense of color-based model-free tracking. In: Proceedings of the IEEE Conference on Computer Vision and Pattern Recognition (2015)
46. Becker, S., Krah, S.B., Hübner, W., Arens, M.: Mad for visual tracker fusion. SPIE Proceedings Optics and Photonics for Counterterrorism, Crime Fighting, and Defence 9995 (2016, to appear)
47. Henriques, J., Caseiro, R., Martins, P., Batista, J.: High-speed tracking with kernelized correlation filters. IEEE Trans. Pattern Anal. Mach. Intell. **37**(3), 583–596 (2015)
48. Danelljan, M., Häger, G., Khan, F.S., Felsberg, M.: Accurate scale estimation for robust visual tracking. In: Proceedings of the British Machine Vision Conference, BMVC (2014)
49. Wang, N., Li, S., Gupta, A., Yeung, D.Y.: Transferring rich feature hierarchies for robust visual tracking (2015)
50. Vojir, T., Matas, J.: Robustifying the flock of trackers. In: Computer Vision Winter Workshop, pp. 91–97. IEEE (2011)
51. Maresca, M., Petrosino, A.: Clustering local motion estimates for robust and efficient object tracking. In: Proceedings of the Workshop on Visual Object Tracking Challenge, European Conference on Computer Vision (2014)
52. Maresca, M.E., Petrosino, A.: Matrioska: A multi-level approach to fast tracking by learning. In: Proceedings of International Conference on Image Analysis and Processing, pp. 419–428 (2013)
53. Jingjing, X., Stolkin, R., Leonardis, A.: Single target tracking using adaptive clustered decision trees and dynamic multi-level appearance models. In: CVPR (2015)
54. Tang, M., Feng, J.: Multi-kernel correlation filter for visual tracking. In: ICCV (2015)
55. Du, D., Qi, H., Wen, L., Tian, Q., Huang, Q., Lyu, S.: Geometric hypergraph learning for visual tracking. CoRR (2016)
56. Li, Y., Zhu, J.: A scale adaptive kernel correlation filter tracker with feature integration. In: Agapito, L., Bronstein, M.M., Rother, C. (eds.) ECCV 2014. LNCS, vol. 8926, pp. 254–265. Springer, Heidelberg (2015). doi:10.1007/978-3-319-16181-5_18
57. Wang, L., Ouyang, W., Wang, X., Lu, H.: Visual tracking with fully convolutional networks. In: ICCV (2015)

58. Wang, L., Ouyang, W., Wang, X., Lu, H.: Stct: sequentially training convolutional networks for visual tracking. In: CVPR (2016)
59. Chen, D., Yuan, Z., Wu, Y., Zhang, G., Zheng, N.: Constructing adaptive complex cells for robust visual tracking. In: ICCV (2013)
60. Bertinetto, L., Valmadre, J., Golodetz, S., Miksik, O., Torr, P.H.S.: Staple: complementary learners for real-time tracking. In: CVPR (2016)
61. Du, D., Qi, H., Li, W., Wen, L., Huang, Q., Lyu, S.: Online deformable object tracking based on structure-aware hyper-graph. IEEE Trans. Image Process. 25(8), 3572–3584 (2016)
62. Bertinetto, L., Valmadre, J., Henriques, J., Torr, P.H.S., Vedaldi, A.: Fully convolutional siamese networks for object tracking. In: ECCV Workshops (2016)
63. Chopra, S., Hadsell, R., LeCun, Y.: Learning a similarity metric discriminatively, with application to face verification. In: CVPR (2005)
64. He, K., Zhang, X., Ren, S., Sun, J.: Deep residual learning for image recognition. arXiv:1512.03385 [cs.CV] (2015)
65. Russakovsky, O., Deng, J., Su, H., Krause, J., Satheesh, S., Ma, S., Huang, Z., Karpathy, A., Khosla, A., Bernstein, M., Berg, A.C., Fei-Fei, L.: Imagenet large scale visual recognition challenge. IJCV 115, 211–252 (2015)
66. Vojir, T., Noskova, J., Matas, J.: Robust scale-adaptive mean-shift for tracking. In: Kämäräinen, J.-K., Koskela, M. (eds.) SCIA 2013. LNCS, vol. 7944, pp. 652–663. Springer, Heidelberg (2013)
67. Vojíř, T., Matas, J.: The enhanced flock of trackers. In: Cipolla, R., Battiato, S., Farinella, G.M. (eds.) Registration and Recognition in Images and Video. SCI, vol. 532, pp. 111–138. Springer, Heidelberg (2014)
68. Ma, C., Yang, X., Zhang, C., Yang, M.H.: Long-term correlation tracking. In: CVPR (2015)
69. Wu, H., Sankaranarayanan, A.C., Chellappa, R.: Online empirical evaluation of tracking algorithms. IEEE Trans. Pattern Anal. Mach. Intell. 32(8), 1443–1458 (2010)
70. Zhang, J., Ma, S., Sclaroff, S.: Meem: Robust tracking via multiple experts using entropy minimization. In: Computer Vision and Pattern Recognition (2014)
71. Xuehan-Xiong, la Torre, F.D.: Supervised descent method and its application to face alignment. In: Computer Vision and Pattern Recognition (2013)
72. Asthana, A., Zafeiriou, S., Cheng, S., Pantic, M.: Incremental face alignment in the wild. In: Computer Vision and Pattern Recognition (2014)
73. Khan, M.H., Valstar, M.F., Pridmore, T.P.: MTS: a multiple temporal scale tracker handling occlusion and abrupt motion variation. In: Cremers, D., Reid, I., Saito, H., Yang, M.-H. (eds.) ACCV 2014. LNCS, vol. 9007, pp. 476–492. Springer, Heidelberg (2015). doi:10.1007/978-3-319-16814-2_31
74. Wang, X., Valstar, M., Martinez, B., Khan, H., Pridmore, T.: Tracking by regression with incrementally learned cascades. In: International Conference on Computer Vision (2015)
75. Kalal, Z., Mikolajczyk, K., Matas, J.: Tracking-learning-detection. IEEE Trans. Pattern Anal. Mach. Intell. 34(7), 1409–1422 (2012)
76. Lukezic, A., Cehovin, L., Kristan, M.: Deformable parts correlation filters for robust visual tracking. CoRR abs/1605.03720 (2016)
77. Kristan, M., Perš, J., Sulič, V., Kovačič, S.: A graphical model for rapid obstacle image-map estimation from unmanned surface vehicles (2014)
78. Vojir, T.: Fast segmentation of object from background in given bounding box (2015)

79. Dalal, N., Triggs, B.: Histograms of oriented gradients for human detection. Comput. Vis. Pattern Recogn. **1**, 886–893 (2005)
80. Rosten, E., Drummond, T.W.: Machine learning for high-speed corner detection. In: Leonardis, A., Bischof, H., Pinz, A. (eds.) ECCV 2006, Part I. LNCS, vol. 3951, pp. 430–443. Springer, Heidelberg (2006)
81. Kalal, Z., Mikolajczyk, K., Matas, J.: Forward-backward error: automatic detection of tracking failures. In: Computer Vision and Pattern Recognition (2010)
82. Poostchi, M., Aliakbarpour, H., Viguier, R., Bunyak, F., Palaniappan, K., Seetharaman, G.: Semantic depth map fusion for moving vehicle detection in aerial video. In: Proceedings of IEEE Conference on Computer Vision and Pattern Recognition (CVPR) Workshops, pp. 32–40 (2016)
83. Poostchi, M., Palaniappan, K., Bunyak, F., Becchi, M., Seetharaman, G.: Efficient GPU implementation of the integral histogram. In: Park, J.-I., Kim, J. (eds.) ACCV 2012. LNCS, vol. 7728, pp. 266–278. Springer, Heidelberg (2013). doi:10.1007/978-3-642-37410-4_23
84. Poostchi, M., Bunyak, F., Palaniappan, K., Seetharaman, G.: Feature selection for appearance-based vehicle tracking in geospatial video. In: SPIE Defense, Security, and Sensing, International Society for Optics and Photonics (2013)
85. Palaniappan, K., Bunyak, F., Kumar, P., Ersoy, I., Jaeger, S., Ganguli, K., Haridas, A., Fraser, J., Rao, R., Seetharaman, G.: Efficient feature extraction and likelihood fusion for vehicle tracking in low frame rate airborne video. In: IEEE Conference on Information Fusion (FUSION), pp. 1–8 (2010)
86. Pelapur, R., Palaniappan, K., Seetharaman, G.: Robust orientation and appearance adaptation for wide-area large format video object tracking. In: Proceedings of the IEEE Conference on Advanced Video and Signal based Surveillance, pp. 337–342 (2012)
87. Danelljan, M., Khan, F.S., Felsberg, M., Van de Weijer, J.: Adaptive color attributes for real-time visual tracking. In: Computer Vision and Pattern Recognition (2014)
88. Roffo, G., Melzi, S., Cristani, M.: Infinite feature selection. In: ICCV (2015)
89. Roffo, G., Melzi, S.: Online feature selection for visual tracking. In: BMVC (2016)
90. Mairal, J., Bach, F., Ponce, J., Sapiro, G.: Online dictionary learning for sparse coding. In: Proceedings of the 26th Annual International Conference on Machine Learning, ICML, pp. 689–696 (2009)
91. Montero, A.S., Lang, J., Laganiere, R.: Scalable kernel correlation filter with sparse feature integration. In: The IEEE International Conference on Computer Vision (ICCV) Workshops, pp. 24–31, December 2015
92. Choi, J., Chang, H.J., Jeong, J., Demiris, Y., Choi, J.Y.: Visual tracking using attention-modulated disintegration and integration. In: CVPR (2016)
93. Lebeda, K., Matas, J., Bowden, R.: Tracking the untrackable: how to track when your object is featureless. In: Proceedings of ACCV DTCE (2012)
94. Lebeda, K., Hadfield, S., Matas, J., Bowden, R.: Long-term tracking through failure cases. In: Proceedings of ICCV VOT (2013)
95. Lebeda, K., Hadfield, S., Matas, J., Bowden, R.: Texture-independent long-term tracking using virtual corners. IEEE Trans. Image Process. **25**, 359–371 (2016)
96. Nam, H., Baek, M., Han, B.: Modeling and propagating cnns in a tree structure for visual tracking. CoRR abs/1608.07242 (2016)
97. Deng, J., Dong, W., Socher, R., Li, L.J., Li, K., Fei-Fei, L.: Imagenet: a large-scale hierarchical image database a large-scale hierarchical image database. In: CVPR (2009)

98. Ma, C., Huang, J.B., Yang, X., Yang, M.H.: Hierarchical convolutional features for visual tracking. In: ICCV (2016)
99. Henriques, J.F., Caseiro, R., Martins, P., Batista, J.: Exploiting the circulant structure of tracking-by-detection with kernels. In: Fitzgibbon, A., Lazebnik, S., Perona, P., Sato, Y., Schmid, C. (eds.) ECCV 2012, Part IV. LNCS, vol. 7575, pp. 702–715. Springer, Heidelberg (2012)
100. Vojir, T., Noskova, J., Matas, J.: Robust scale-adaptive mean-shift for tracking. Pattern Recogn. Lett. **49**, 250–258 (2014)
101. Bolme, D.S., Beveridge, J.R., Draper, B.A., Lui, Y.M.: Visual object tracking using adaptive correlation filters. In: Proceedings of the IEEE Conference on Computer Vision and Pattern Recognition (2010)
102. Vojir, T., Matas, J., Noskova, J.: Online adaptive hidden markov model for multi-tracker fusion. CoRR abs/1504.06103 (2015)
103. Hare, S., Saffari, A., Torr, P.H.S.: Struck: structured output tracking with kernels. In: Metaxas, D.N., Quan, L., Sanfeliu, A., Gool, L.J.V. (eds.) International Conference on Computer Vision, pp. 263–270. IEEE (2011)
104. Felsberg, M.: Enhanced distribution field tracking using channel representations. In: Visual Object Tracking Challenge VOT 2013, In conjunction with ICCV 2013 (2013)
105. Danelljan, M., Häger, G., Khan, F.S., Felsberg, M.: Learning spatially regularized correlation filters for visual tracking. In: International Conference on Computer Vision (2015)
106. Ma, C., Huang, J.B., Yang, X., Yang, M.H.: Hierarchical convolutional features for visual tracking. In: International Conference on Computer Vision (2015)
107. Čehovin, L., Kristan, M., Leonardis, A.: Robust visual tracking using an adaptive coupled-layer visual model. IEEE Trans. Pattern Anal. Mach. Intell. **35**(4), 941–953 (2013)
108. Čehovin, L., Leonardis, A., Kristan, M.: Robust visual tracking using template anchors. In: WACV. IEEE, March 2016
109. Ross, D.A., Lim, J., Lin, R.S., Yang, M.H.: Incremental learning for robust visual tracking. Int. J. Comput. Vis. **77**(1–3), 125–141 (2008)
110. Godec, M., Roth, P.M., Bischof, H.: Hough-based tracking of non-rigid objects. Comp. Vis. Image Underst. **117**(10), 1245–1256 (2013)
111. Zhang, K., Zhang, L., Liu, Q., Zhang, D., Yang, M.-H.: Fast visual tracking via dense spatio-temporal context learning. In: Fleet, D., Pajdla, T., Schiele, B., Tuytelaars, T. (eds.) ECCV 2014. LNCS, vol. 8693, pp. 127–141. Springer, Heidelberg (2014). doi:10.1007/978-3-319-10602-1_9
112. Gao, J., Ling, H., Hu, W., Xing, J.: Transfer learning based visual tracking with gaussian processes regression. In: Fleet, D., Pajdla, T., Schiele, B., Tuytelaars, T. (eds.) ECCV 2014. LNCS, vol. 8691, pp. 188–203. Springer, Heidelberg (2014). doi:10.1007/978-3-319-10578-9_13
113. Babenko, B., Yang, M.H., Belongie, S.: Robust object tracking with online multiple instance learning. IEEE Trans. Pattern Anal. Mach. Intell. **33**(8), 1619–1632 (2011)
114. Nebehay, G., Pflugfelder, R.: Clustering of static-adaptive correspondences for deformable object tracking. In: Computer Vision and Pattern Recognition (2015)

The Thermal Infrared Visual Object Tracking VOT-TIR2016 Challenge Results

Michael Felsberg[1(✉)], Matej Kristan[2], Jiři Matas[3], Aleš Leonardis[4],
Roman Pflugfelder[5], Gustav Häger[1], Amanda Berg[1,6],
Abdelrahman Eldesokey[1], Jörgen Ahlberg[1,6], Luka Čehovin[2], Tomáš Vojíř[3],
Alan Lukežič[2], Gustavo Fernández[5], Alfredo Petrosino[20],
Alvaro Garcia-Martin[22], Andrés Solís Montero[25], Anton Varfolomieiev[15],
Aykut Erdem[12], Bohyung Han[21], Chang-Ming Chang[23], Dawei Du[9],
Erkut Erdem[12], Fahad Shahbaz Khan[1], Fatih Porikli[7,8,19], Fei Zhao[9],
Filiz Bunyak[24], Francesco Battistone[20], Gao Zhu[8], Guna Seetharaman[17],
Hongdong Li[7,8], Honggang Qi[9], Horst Bischof[11], Horst Possegger[11],
Hyeonseob Nam[18], Jack Valmadre[26], Jianke Zhu[28], Jiayi Feng[9],
Jochen Lang[25], Jose M. Martinez[22], Kannappan Palaniappan[24],
Karel Lebeda[27], Ke Gao[24], Krystian Mikolajczyk[14], Longyin Wen[23],
Luca Bertinetto[26], Mahdieh Poostchi[24], Mario Maresca[20], Martin Danelljan[1],
Michael Arens[10], Ming Tang[9], Mooyeol Baek[21], Nana Fan[13],
Noor Al-Shakarji[24], Ondrej Miksik[26], Osman Akin[12], Philip H.S. Torr[26],
Qingming Huang[9], Rafael Martin-Nieto[22], Rengarajan Pelapur[24],
Richard Bowden[27], Robert Laganière[25], Sebastian B. Krah[10], Shengkun Li[23],
Shizeng Yao[24], Simon Hadfield[27], Siwei Lyu[23], Stefan Becker[10],
Stuart Golodetz[26], Tao Hu[9], Thomas Mauthner[11], Vincenzo Santopietro[20],
Wenbo Li[16], Wolfgang Hübner[10], Xin Li[13], Yang Li[28],
Zhan Xu[28], and Zhenyu He[13]

[1] Linköping University, Linköping, Sweden
michael.felsberg@liu.se
[2] University of Ljubljana, Ljubljana, Slovenia
[3] Czech Technical University, Prague, Czech Republic
[4] University of Birmingham, Birmingham, England
[5] Austrian Institute of Technology, Seibersdorf, Austria
[6] Termisk Systemteknik AB, Linköping, Sweden
[7] ARC Centre of Excellence for Robotic Vision, Canberra, Australia
[8] Australian National University, Canberra, Australia
[9] Chinese Academy of Sciences, Beijing, China
[10] Fraunhofer IOSB, Karlsruhe, Germany
[11] Graz University of Technology, Graz, Austria
[12] Hacettepe University, Ankara, Turkey
[13] Harbin Institute of Technology, Harbin, China
[14] Imperial College London, London, UK
[15] Kyiv Polytechnic Institute, Kiev, Ukraine
[16] Lehigh University, Bethlehem, USA
[17] Naval Research Lab, Washington, D.C., USA
[18] NAVER Corp., Seongnam, South Korea
[19] Data61/CSIRO, Alexandria, Australia

© Springer International Publishing Switzerland 2016
G. Hua and H. Jégou (Eds.): ECCV 2016 Workshops, Part II, LNCS 9914, pp. 824–849, 2016.
DOI: 10.1007/978-3-319-48881-3_55

[20] Parthenope University of Naples, Naples, Italy
[21] POSTECH, Pohang, South Korea
[22] Universidad Autónoma de Madrid, Madrid, Spain
[23] University at Albany, Albany, USA
[24] University of Missouri, Columbia, USA
[25] University of Ottawa, Ottawa, Canada
[26] University of Oxford, Oxford, England
[27] University of Surrey, Guildford, England
[28] Zhejiang University, Hangzhou, China

Abstract. The Thermal Infrared Visual Object Tracking challenge
2016, VOT-TIR2016, aims at comparing short-term single-object visual
trackers that work on thermal infrared (TIR) sequences and do not
apply pre-learned models of object appearance. VOT-TIR2016 is the
second benchmark on short-term tracking in TIR sequences. Results of
24 trackers are presented. For each participating tracker, a short description is provided in the appendix. The VOT-TIR2016 challenge is similar
to the 2015 challenge, the main difference is the introduction of new,
more difficult sequences into the dataset. Furthermore, VOT-TIR2016
evaluation adopted the improvements regarding overlap calculation in
VOT2016. Compared to VOT-TIR2015, a significant general improvement of results has been observed, which partly compensate for the more
difficult sequences. The dataset, the evaluation kit, as well as the results
are publicly available at the challenge website.

Keywords: Performance evaluation · Object tracking · Thermal IR ·
VOT

1 Introduction

Visual tracking is sometimes considered a solved task, but many applied projects
show that robust and accurate object tracking in the visual domain is highly challenging. Thus, tracking has attracted significant attention in review papers from
the past two decades, e.g. [1–3] and is subject of a constantly high number (∼40
papers annually) of accepted papers in high profile conferences, such as ICCV,
ECCV, and CVPR. In recent years, several performance evaluation methodologies have been established in order to assess and understand the advancements
made by this large number (a few hundred) of publications. One of the pioneers
for building a common ground in tracking performance evaluation is PETS [4],
followed-up more recently by the Visual Object Tracking (VOT) challenges [5–7]
and the Object Tracking Benchmarks [8,9].

Thermal cameras have several advantages compared to cameras for the visual
spectrum: They are able to operate in total darkness, they are robust to illumination changes and shadow effects, and they reduce privacy intrusion. Historically,
thermal cameras have delivered low-resolution and noisy images and were mainly

used for tracking point targets or small objects against colder backgrounds. Thus applications had often been restricted to military purposes, whereas today, thermal cameras are commonly used in civilian applications, e.g., cars and surveillance systems. Increasing image quality and decreasing price and size allow exploration of new application areas [10], often requiring methods for tracking of extended dynamic objects, also from moving platforms.

Tracking on thermal infrared (TIR) imagery has thus become an emerging niche and evaluation or comparison of methods is required. This has been addressed by VOT-TIR2015, the first TIR short-term tracking challenge [11]. This challenge resembles the VOT challenge, in the sense that the VOT-TIR challenge considers single-camera, single-target, model-free, and causal trackers, applied to short-term tracking. It has been featured as a sub-challenge to VOT2015, organized in conjunction with ICCV2015.

Since the first challenge attracted a significant number of submissions and due to required improvements of the dataset, a second VOT-TIR challenge has been initiated in conjunction with VOT2016 [12] and ECCV2016: VOT-TIR2016. The present paper summarizes this challenge, the submissions, and the obtained results. The aim of this work is to give guidance for future applications in the TIR domain and to trigger further development of methods, similar to the boosting of visual tracking methods caused by the VOT challenges. Likewise VOT2016, the dataset, the evaluation kit, as well as the results are publicly available at the challenge website http://votchallenge.net.

1.1 Related Work

In contrast to the large number of benchmarks that exist in the area of visual tracking (cf. the VOT2016 results paper [12] for several examples), TIR tracking offers few options for evaluation. For tracking in RGB sequences, the most closely related approach is obviously the VOT2016 challenge [12], as well as those of previous years [5–7].

An evaluation resembling VOT is offered by the online tracking benchmark (OTB) by Wu et al. [8,9], which is however based on different measures of performance. Trackers are compared using a precision score (the percentage of frames where the estimated bounding box is within some fixed distance to the ground truth) and a success score (the area under the curve of number of frames where the overlap is greater than some fixed percentage). This area has been shown to be equivalent to the average overlap [13,14] and is computed without restarting a failed tracker as done in VOT. For further comparisons with the VOT evaluation we refer to [7,12,15].

For TIR sequences, basically two challenges have been organized in the past. Within the series of workshops on Performance Evaluation of Tracking and Surveillance (PETS) [4], thermal infrared challenges have been organized on two occasions, 2005 and 2015. The PETS challenges addressed multiple research areas such as detection, multi-camera/long-term tracking, and behavior (threat) analysis.

In contrast, the VOT-TIR2015 challenge has focused on the problem of short-term tracking only. The challenge has been based on a newly collected dataset (LTIR) [16], as available datasets for evaluation of tracking in thermal infrared had become outdated. The lack of an accepted evaluation dataset leads often to comparisons on proprietary datasets. This and inconsistent performance measures make it difficult to systematically assess the advancement of the field. Thus, VOT-TIR2015 made use of the well-established VOT methodology [11].

The challenge had 20 participating methods and the following observations were made: (i) The relative ranking of methods differed significantly from the visual domain, which justifies a separate TIR challenge. For instance, the EDFT-based ABCD tracker [17] performed very well on VOT-TIR2015, but only moderately on VOT2015 (despite that EDFT [18] was among the top three in VOT2013). (ii) The recent progress of tracking methodology rendered the LTIR dataset being too simple for observing a significant spread of performance: the benchmark was basically saturated, at least for the top-performing methods. Thus, for the VOT-TIR2016 challenge, some of the easiest sequences from LTIR have been removed and new sequences that have been contributed by the community have been added. Furthermore and in parallel to VOT2016, the bounding box overlap estimation is constrained to the image region [12].

1.2   The VOT-TIR2016 Challenge

Similar to VOT-TIR2015, the VOT-TIR2016 challenge targets specific trackers that are required to be: (i) Causal – sequence frames have to be processed in sequential order; (ii) Short-term – trackers are not required to handle reinitialization; (iii) Model-free – pre-built models of object appearances are not allowed.

The performance of participating trackers is measured using the VOT2016 evaluation toolkit[1]. The toolkit runs the experiment in a standardized way and stores the output bounding boxes. If a tracker fails, it is re-initialized and the evaluation is continued after some few frames delay. Tracking results are analyzed using the VOT2015 evaluation methodology [7], but without rotating bounding boxes.

The rules are as always in VOT: Only a single set of results may be submitted per tracker and binaries are required for result verification. User-adjustable parameters need to be constant for all sequences and different sets of parameters do not constitute new trackers. Detecting specific sequences for choosing parameters or training networks on similar, tracking-specific datasets is not allowed. Further details regarding participation rules are available from the challenge homepage[2].

Compared to VOT2016 [12], VOT-TIR2016 is still using a simpler annotation and no fully automatic selection of sequences (as in VOT2014 [6]). The LTIR dataset (the Linköping Thermal IR dataset) [16] has been extended by a public

---

[1] https://github.com/vicoslab/vot-toolkit.
[2] http://www.votchallenge.net/vot2016/participation.html.

call for contributions and replacing simple LTIR sequences with community-provided sequences. A detailed description of the sequences can be found in Sect. 2.

Section 3 briefly summarizes the performance measures and evaluation methodology that resembles VOT2016 [12]. Since top-performing methods showed hardly any failures, no OTB-like no-reset experiments have been performed as done in VOT2016. Instead, a ranking comparison similar to the one in VOT-TIR2015 and a sequence difficulty analysis have been performed.

The results and their analysis are presented in Sect. 4 together with recommendations regarding trackers and a meta analysis of the challenge itself. Finally, conclusions are drawn in Sect. 5. In addition, short descriptions of all evaluated trackers can be found in Appendix A together with references to the original publications.

2   The VOT-TIR2016 Dataset

The dataset used in VOT-TIR2016 is a modification of the LTIR, the Linköping Thermal IR dataset [16], denoted LTIR2016. Sequences contained in the dataset were collected from nine different sources using ten different types of sensors. The included sequences originate from industry, universities, a research institute and two EU projects. The average sequence length is 740 frames and resolutions range from 305×225 to 1920×480 pixels.

Fig. 1. Snapshots from six sequences (*Running_rhino, Quadrocopter, Crowd, Street, Bird, Trees2*) included in the LTIR2016 dataset as used in VOT-TIR2016. The ground truth bounding boxes are shown in yellow. (Color figure online)

Although some sequences in the LTIR dataset are available with 16-bit dynamic range, we only use 8-bit pixel values in the VOT-TIR2016 challenge.

This choice is motivated by the fact that several of the submitted methods cannot deal with 16-bit data. There are sequences recorded outdoors in different weather conditions and sequences recorded indoors with artificial illumination and heat sources.

Example frames from six sequences are shown in Fig. 1. Compared to VOT-TIR2015, the sequences *Crossing*, *Horse*, and *Rhino_behind_tree* have been removed. The newly added sequences are *Bird*, *Boat1*, *Boat2*, *Car2*, *Dog*, *Excavator*, *Ragged*, and *Trees2*.

In contrast to the novel annotation approach in VOT2016 [12], all benchmark annotations have been done manually in accordance with the VOT2013 annotation process [19]. Exactly one object within each sequence is annotated throughout the sequence with a bounding box that encloses the object entirely. The bounding box is allowed to vary in size but not to rotate. In addition to the bounding box annotations, local attributes are annotated frame-wise and global attributes are annotated sequence-wise.

Some attributes from VOT had to be changed or modified for VOT-TIR:

Changed attributes: Dynamics change and *temperature change* have been introduced instead of *illumination change* and *object color change*. Several cameras convert an internal constant 16-bit range into an adaptively changing 8-bit range. *Dynamics change* indicates whether the dynamic range is fixed during the sequence or not. *Temperature change* refers to changes in the thermal signature of the object during the sequence.

Modified attributes: Blur indicates blur due to motion, high humidity, rain or water on the lens instead of defocussing.

Based on the modified attribute set, the following local and global attributes are annotated:

Local attributes: The per-frame annotated local attributes are: *motion change, camera motion, dynamics change, occlusion*, and *size change*. The attributes are used to evaluate the performance of tracking methods on frames with specific attributes. The attributes allow also weighting the evaluation process, e.g., pool by attribute.

Global attributes: The per-sequence global attributes are: *Dynamics change, temperature change, blur, camera motion, object motion, background clutter, size change, aspect ratio change, object deformation*, and *scene complexity*.

3   Performance Measures and Evaluation Methodology

The performance measures as well as evaluation methodology for VOT-TIR2016 are identical to the ones for VOT2016, except for the OTB-like average overlap and the practical difference evaluation. Therefore, only a brief summary is given below and for details the reader is referred to [12].

Similar to VOT2016, the two weakly correlated performance measures, accuracy (A) and robustness (R), are used due to their high level of interpretability [13,14]. The accuracy measurement is computed from the overlap between the predicted bounding box and the ground truth, restricted to the image region, while the robustness measurement counts the number of tracking failures. If tracking has failed, the tracker is re-initialized with a delay of five frames. In order to reduce biased accuracy assessment, the overlap measure is continued with a further delay of ten frames.

The two primary measures A and R are fused in the expected average overlap (EAO), which is an estimator of the expected average overlap of a tracker on a new sequence of typical length. The EAO curve is given by the bounding-box-overlap averaged over a set of sequences of certain length, plotted over the sequence length N_s [7]. The EAO measure is obtained by integrating the EAO curve over an interval of typical sequence lengths of 223 to 509 frames. Overlap calculations, re-initialization, definition of a failure, and the computation of the EAO measure are further explained in [12].

As in VOT-TIR2015, the performance measures are only evaluated in the baseline experiment and we did not consider the region noise experiment for the same reasons as before [11]: Results hardly differed, experiments need more time, and reproducibility of results requires to store the seed.

4   Analysis and Results

4.1   Submitted Trackers

As in VOT-TIR2015 [11], 24 trackers were included in the VOT-TIR2016 challenge. Among them, 21 trackers were submitted to the challenge and 3 trackers were added by the VOT Committee (DSST, the VOT2014 winner, SRDCFir, which achieved the highest EAO score in VOT-TIR2015, and NCC as baseline).

The committee has used the submitted binaries/source code for result verification. All methods are briefly described below and references to the original papers are given in the Appendix A where available. All 24 VOT-TIR2016 participating trackers also participated in the VOT2016 challenge.[3]

One tracker, EBT (A.2), uses object proposals [20] for object position generation or scoring. One tracker is based on a Mean Shift tracker extension [21], PKLTF (A.5). MAD (A.4) and LOFT-Lite (A.16) are fusion based trackers. DAT (A.8) is based on tracking-by-detection learning.

Eight trackers can be classified as part-based trackers: BDF (A.3), BST (A.14), DPCF (A.1), DPT (A.20), FCT (A.15), GGTv2 (A.7), LT-FLO (A.19), and SHCT (A.12).

Seven trackers are based on the method of discriminative correlation filters (DCFs) [22,23] with various sets of image features: DSST2014 (A.22), MvCF

---

[3] Here, we consider SRDCF/SRDCFir and Staple/Staple-TIR being the same, despite the fact that the TIR versions use slightly different feature vectors, see Appendices A.24 and A.13.

(A.6), NSAMF (A.10), sKCF (A.17), SRDCFir (A.24), Staple-TIR (A.13), and STAPLE+ (A.11).

One tracker applies convolutional neural network (CNN) features instead of standard features, deepMKCF (A.9), and two trackers are entirely based on CNNs, TCNN (A.21) and MDNet-N (A.18). Finally, one tracker was the basic normalized cross correlation tracker NCC (A.23).

4.2 Results

The results are collected in AR-rank and AR-raw plots, pooled by sequence and averaged by attribute, c.f. Fig. 2. The sequence-pooled AR-rank plot is obtained by concatenating the results from all sequences and creating a single rank list. The attribute-normalized AR-rank plot is created by ranking the trackers over each attribute and averaging the rank lists.

The AR-raw plots are constructed without ranking. The A-values correspond to the average overlap for the whole dataset (pooled) or the attribute-normalized average overlap. The R-values correspond to the likelihood that on $S = 100$ frames the tracking will not fail (pooled over dataset or attribute-normalized). The raw values and the ranks for the pooled results are given in Table 1.

Three trackers are either very accurate or very robust (closest to the upper or right border of rank/AR plots): NCC (A.23), Staple-TIR (A.13), and EBT (A.2). Three trackers combine good accuracy and good robustness (upper right corner of rank/AR plots): MDNet-N (A.18), SRDCFir (A.24), and TCNN (A.21).

The top accuracy of NCC comes at the cost of a very high failure rate. Due to the frequent re-initializations, the NCC results are very accurate. The excellent robustness of EBT is achieved by a strategy to enlarge the predicted bounding boxes in cases of low tracking confidence. This implies some penalty on the accuracy so that EBT only achieves moderate average overlap.

The three trackers that combine good robustness and accuracy as well as further well-performing trackers are based on CNNs (TCNN, MDNet-N) and DCFs (SRDCFir, Staple-TIR, STAPLE+). SHCT combines DCFs with a part-based model and deepMKCF combines DCFs with deep features. Hence, the top-performing methods are mostly based on deep learning or DCFs.

The robustness ranks with respect to the visual attributes are shown in Fig. 3. The top three trackers of the overall assessment, EBT, SRDCFir, and TCNN, are also mostly among the top robustness ranks for the different visual attributes (exceptions SRDCFir on Dynamics_change & Occlusion and TCNN on Motion_change). The top ranks are sometimes shared with other well-performing methods: Camera_motion FCT; Dynamics_change DPT, MDNet-N, and SHCT; Empty DPT and Staple-TIR; Motion_change SHCT and STAPLE+; Occlusion MDNet-N; Size_change deepMKCF, MDNet-N, SHCT, and Staple-TIR.

The overall criterion *expected average overlap* (EAO), see Fig. 4, confirms the top-performance of SRDCFir, EBT, and TCNN. The EAO curves show that SRDCFir is consistently better than EBT in the range of typical sequence lengths. Hence, SRDCFir gives the best overall performance exactly as in the previous challenge [11]. Still, EBT is the best performing tracker submitted to

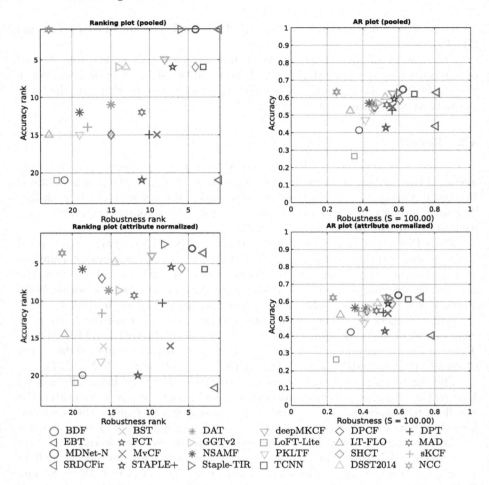

Fig. 2. The AR rank plots and AR raw plots generated by sequence pooling (upper) and by attribute normalization (below).

VOT-TIR2016. Regarding the EAO measure, TCNN is clearly inferior to the two top-ranked methods. The fact that EBT is better than TCNN regarding the EAO measure despite that it is inferior regarding accuracy (c.f. Fig. 2), underpins the importance of robustness for the expected average overlap measure.

Apart from tracking accuracy A, robustness R, and expected average overlap EAO, the tracking speed is also crucial in many realistic tracking applications. We therefore also visualize the EAO values with respect to the tracking speed measured in EFO units in Fig. 4. The vertical dashed line indicates the real-time speed (equivalent to approximately 20fps). Among the three top-performing trackers, SRDCFir comes closest to real-time performance. The top-performing

Table 1. The table shows the expected average overlap (EAO), the accuracy and robustness (S = 100) pooled values (A, R), the ranks for A and R, the tracking speed (EFO), and implementation details (M is Matlab, C is C or C++, M/C means Matlab with mex). Trackers marked with * have been verified by the committee.

	Tracker	EAO	A	R	A_{rank}	R_{rank}	EFO	Impl.
1.	◁ **SRDCFir***	0.364	0.63	0.82	1	1	2.48	D M/C
2.	◁ **EBT***	0.340	0.43	0.81	21	1	1.99	D C
3.	▢ **TCNN***	0.287	0.62	0.69	6	3	0.76	S M/C
4.	▷ **Staple-TIR***	0.264	0.63	0.60	1	6	14.25	D M/C
5.	◇ **SHCT***	0.263	0.59	0.61	6	4	0.91	D M/C
6.	○ **MDNet-N***	0.243	0.65	0.63	1	4	0.61	S M/C
7.	☆ **STAPLE+***	0.241	0.59	0.58	6	7	16.70	D M/C
8.	△ **DSST2014***	0.236	0.60	0.53	6	13	11.29	D M
9.	✕ **MvCF***	0.231	0.55	0.57	15	9	27.83	D M
10.	+ **DPT***	0.219	0.53	0.57	15	10	11.40	D M/C
11.	▽ **deepMKCF**	0.213	0.62	0.57	5	8	2.36	S M/C
12.	☆ **MAD***	0.211	0.56	0.54	12	11	12.54	D C
13.	▷ **GGTv2***	0.197	0.57	0.49	6	14	0.93	S M/C
14.	✳ **NSAMF***	0.192	0.57	0.44	12	19	26.27	D M/C
15.	◇ **DPCF***	0.191	0.54	0.47	15	15	2.73	D M/C
16.	+ **sKCF***	0.188	0.55	0.46	14	18	135.64	D C
17.	☆ **FCT***	0.186	0.43	0.53	21	11	116.33	D C
18.	△ **LT-FLO**	0.163	0.52	0.33	15	23	2.16	S M/C
19.	✳ **DAT***	0.162	0.57	0.46	11	15	15.71	D M
20.	✩ **NCC***	0.160	0.63	0.26	1	23	59.49	D M
21.	○ **BDF***	0.147	0.41	0.38	21	21	189.41	D C
22.	▽ **PKLTF***	0.141	0.47	0.42	15	19	45.99	D C
23.	✕ **BST***	0.140	0.51	0.46	15	15	9.66	S C
24.	▢ **LoFT-Lite***	0.107	0.26	0.36	21	22	1.30	D M/C

tracker in terms of EAO among the trackers that exceed the real-time threshold is MvCF (A.6).

4.3   TIR-Specific Analysis and Results

Likewise VOT-TIR2015, we analyze the effect of the differences between RGB sequences and TIR sequences on the ranking of the trackers [11]. For this purpose, the joint ranking for VOT and VOT-TIR is generated for all VOT-TIR trackers (see Footnote 3), c.f. Fig. 5. The dashed lines are the margin of a rank-change by more than three positions. Any change of rank within this margin is considered insignificant and only eight trackers change their rank by more than three positions.

The most dramatic change occurs for BST (A.14), which ranks 23 in VOT-TIR, but 35 (out of 70) in VOT, corresponding to rank 14 within the set of 24

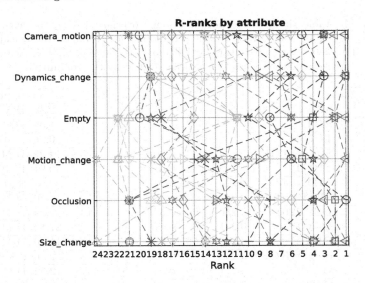

Fig. 3. Robustness plots with respect to the visual attributes. See Fig. 2 for legend.

trackers. Other trackers that perform significantly worse in VOT-TIR are DAT (A.8, 19 vs. 31/12) and GGTv2 (A.7, 13 vs. 19/8).

On the other hand, DSST2014 (A.22, 8 vs. 43/16), MvCF (A.6, 9 vs. 42/15), SRDCF(ir) (A.24, 1 vs. 17/7), LT-FLO (A.19, 18 vs. 62/22), and NCC (A.23, 20 vs. 70/24) perform significantly better on VOT-TIR than on VOT according to the relative ranking.

Similar as for the overall performance, it is difficult to identify a systematic correlation between improvement and type of tracking methods. Tracking methods that do not rely on color (e.g. DSST2014, SRDCFir, NCC) are likely to perform better on TIR sequences than color-based methods (e.g. DAT, GGTv2).

Also the size of targets differ between VOT (larger) and VOT-TIR (smaller) and scale variations need to be modeled (e.g. DSST2014, MvCF, SRDCFir). It is also believed that the tuning of input features is highly relevant for changes of performance. Methods that are highly tuned for VOT2016 and applied to VOT-TIR2016 as they are, are more likely to perform inferior compared to methods that use specific TIR-suited features, e.g. SRDCFir (A.24). In general, HOG features seem to be highly suitable for TIR.

Finally, the dramatic difference in ranking for BST need to be investigated further, as it cannot be explained by previous arguments.

One limitation of VOT-TIR2015 has been the saturation of results: several of the LTIR sequences are so simple to track that hardly any of the participating methods failed on them [11]. Therefore, the three easiest sequences have been removed and eight new sequences have been added, c.f. Sect. 2. In the difficulty analysis 2015, only three sequences were considered challenging and twelve were easy.

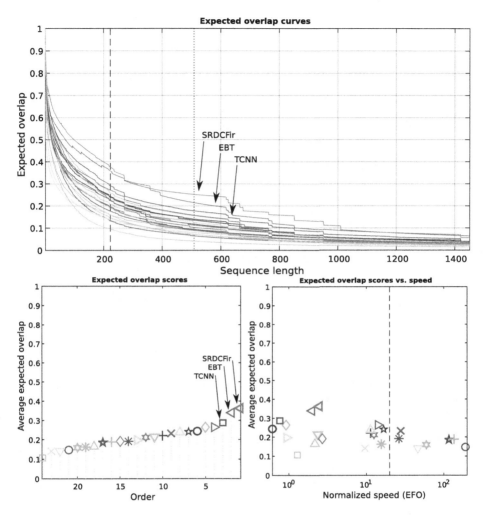

Fig. 4. Expected average overlap curve (above), expected average overlap graph (below left) with trackers ranked from right to left, and expected average overlap scores w.r.t. the tracking speed in EFO units (below right). The right-most tracker in the EAO-graph is the top-performing according to the VOT-TIR2016 expected average overlap values. See Fig. 2 for legend. The vertical lines in the upper plot show the range of typical sequence lengths. The dashed vertical line in the lower right plot denotes the estimated real-time performance threshold of 20 EFO units.

If A_f is the average number of trackers that failed per frame and M_f is the maximum number of trackers that failed at a single frame, sequences with $A_f \leq 0.04$ and $M_f \leq 7$ are considered easy and sequences with $A_f \geq 0.06$ and $M_f \geq 14$ are considered challenging. In the extended dataset, eight sequences are challenging and nine are easy (c.f. Table 2). The average difficulty score

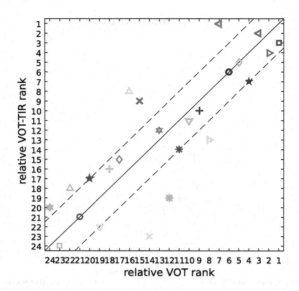

Fig. 5. Comparison of relative ranking of the 24 VOT-TIR trackers in VOT. See Fig. 2 for legend

(1.0 hardest, 5.0 easiest) is reduced from 4.0 (easy) to 3.3 (intermediate), which means that the new dataset is significantly more challenging than LTIR. This also shows in the EAO score of SRDCFir, which has been significantly higher in VOT-TIR2015 (0.70 vs. 0.364) [11].

Table 2. Difficulty analysis of sequences from VOT-TIR2015 and 2016. A score smaller than 3 means *challenging*, a score larger or equal four means *easy*. Mean difficulty VOT-TIR2015: 4.0, VOT-TIR2016: 3.3.

	VOT-TIR	Crowd	Quadrocopter	Quadrocopter2	Garden	Mixed_distractors	Saturated	Selma	Street	Birds	Crouching	Jacket	Hiding	Car	Crossing	Depthwise_crossing	Horse	Rhino_behind_tree	Running_rhino	Soccer	Trees	Bird	Boat1	Boat2	Car2	Dog	Excavator	Ragged	Trees2
2015	2.0	2.5	2.5	3.0	3.0	3.5	3.5	3.5	4.0	4.0	4.0	4.5	5.0	5.0	5.0	5.0	5.0	5.0	5.0	5.0	−	−	−	−	−	−	−	−	−
2016	2.0	2.5	1.5	2.0	3.5	4.5	3.5	3.5	4.5	3.5	4.0	5.0	4.5	−	5.0	−	−	4.5	4.5	3.5	1.5	4.0	3.0	2.0	3.5	3.0	2.5	1.5	

A major limitation of the current evaluation methodology used in VOT-TIR2016 is caused by the criterion of a failure: A failure is reported if the ground truth bounding box and the predicted bounding box do not overlap [5]. As a result, trackers that systematically overestimate the size of the tracked target in case of low confidence, are highly likely to never drop the target at the cost of a low accuracy A, c.f. Fig. 6.

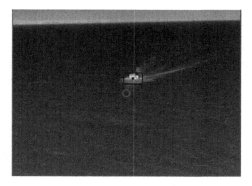

Fig. 6. Example from sequence *Boat2*: A report of failure is avoided by increasing the predicted bounding box to the whole image.

If a tracker succeeds to estimate the confidence for successful tracking well and increases the bounding box only in those cases, a very low failure rate can be obtained at the cost of still acceptable accuracy. The joint measure of EAO score will then be superior to methods that have much better accuracy, but slightly more failures.

In order to limit the effect of arbitrarily large bounding boxes, we suggest to modify the failure test in the following way: We require the overlap to be above the quantization level if we rescale the intersection with the ratio of the bounding boxes. Let A_t^G and A_t^T be the ground truth and predicted bounding boxes, respectively. Let further $|A_t|$ be the size of the bounding box in pixels. The criterion for successful tracking currently used is

$$\frac{|A_t^G \cap A_t^T|}{|A_t^G \cup A_t^T|} > 0 \tag{1}$$

and the suggested new criterion reads

$$|A_t^G \cap A_t^T| \frac{|A_t^G|}{|A_t^T|} > \frac{1}{2} . \tag{2}$$

Since the rules of VOT-TIR2016 cannot be changed retrospectively, we will not provide any results according to the new criterion within VOT-TIR2016.

5   Conclusions

The VOT-TIR2016 challenge has received 21 submissions and compared in total 24 trackers, which is a successful continuation of the first challenge. The extended dataset is significantly more challenging such that the results of the challenge give a better guidance to future research within TIR tracking than VOT-TIR2015.

The best overall performance has been achieved by SRDCFir, followed by EBT, as best performing submitted method, and TCNN. The analysis of results shows that the performance of some trackers differ significantly between VOT2016 and VOT-TIR2016. However, to be top-ranked in VOT-TIR2016 requires a strong result in VOT2016. Modeling of scale-variations and suitable features are necessary to achieve top results. The strongest two tracking methodologies within the benchmark are CNN-based and DCF-based trackers, where several trackers are among the top-performers.

For future challenges, the annotation and evaluation need to be adapted to the current VOT standard: multiple annotations and rotating bounding boxes. The failure criterion might need to be modified as suggested. Also challenges with mixed sequences (RGB and TIR) might be interesting to perform.

Acknowledgments. This work was supported in part by the following research programs and projects: Slovenian research agency research programs P2-0214, P2-0094, Slovenian research agency projects J2-4284, J2-3607, J2-2221 and European Union 7th Framework Programme under grant agreement 257906. J. Matas and T. Vojir were supported by CTU Project SGS13/142/OHK3/2T/13 and by the Technology Agency of the Czech Republic project TE01020415 (V3C – Visual Computing Competence Center). M. Felsberg, G. Häger, and A. Eldesokey were supported by the Wallenberg Autonomous Systems Program WASP, the Swedish Foundation for Strategic Research through the project CUAS, and the Swedish Research Council trough the project EMC^2. J. Ahlberg and A. Berg were supported by the European Union 7th Framework Programme under grant agreement 312784 (P5) and the Swedish Research Council through the contract D0570301. Some experiments where run on GPUs donated by NVIDIA.

A   Submitted Trackers

This appendix contains short descriptions of all trackers from the challenge.

A.1   Deformable Part-based Tracking by Coupled Global and Local Correlation Filters (DPCF)

O. Akin, E. Erdem, A. Erdem, K. Mikolajczyk
oakin25@gmail.com, {erkut, aykut}@cs.hacettepe.edu.tr,
k.mikolajczyk@imperial.ac.uk
DPCF is a deformable part-based correlation filter tracking approach which depends on coupled interactions between a global filter and several part filters. Specifically, local filters provide an initial estimate, which is then used by the global filter as a reference to determine the final result. Then, the global filter provides a feedback to the part filters regarding their updates and the related deformation parameters. In this way, DPCF handles not only partial occlusion but also scale changes. The reader is referred to [24] for details.

A.2   Edge Box Tracker (EBT)

G. Zhu, F. Porikli, H. Li
{gao.zhu, fatih.porikli, hongdong.li}@anu.edu.au

EBT tracker is not limited to a local search window and has ability to probe efficiently the entire frame. It generates a small number of 'high-quality' proposals by a novel instance-specific objectness measure and evaluates them against the object model that can be adopted from an existing tracking-by-detection approach as a core tracker. During the tracking process, it updates the object model concentrating on hard false-positives supplied by the proposals, which help suppressing distractors caused by difficult background clutters, and learns how to re-rank proposals according to the object model. Since the number of hypotheses the core tracker evaluates is reduced significantly, richer object descriptors and stronger detectors can be used. More details can be found in [25].

A.3 Best Displacement Flow (BDF)

M. Maresca, A. Petrosino
mariomaresca@hotmail.it, petrosino@uniparthenope.it
Best Displacement Flow (BDF) is a short-term tracking algorithm based on the same idea of Flock of Trackers [26] in which a set of local tracker responses are robustly combined to track the object. Firstly, BDF performs a clustering to identify the best displacement vector which is used to update the object's bounding box. Secondly, BDF performs a procedure named Consensus-Based Reinitialization used to reinitialize candidates which were previously classified as outliers. Interested readers are referred to [27] for details.

A.4 Median Absolute Deviation Tracker (MAD)

S. Becker, S. Krah, W. Hübner, M. Arens
{stefan.becker, sebastian.krah, wolfgang.huebner, michael.arens}@iosb.fraun hofer.de
The key idea of the MAD tracker [28] is to combine several independent and heterogeneous tracking approaches and to robustly identify an outlier subset based on the Median Absolute Deviation (MAD) measure. The MAD fusion strategy is very generic and it only requires frame-based target bounding boxes as input and thus can work with arbitrary tracking algorithms. The overall median bounding box is calculated from all trackers and the deviation or distance of a sub-tracker to the median bounding box is calculated using the Jaccard-Index. Further, the MAD fusion strategy can also be applied for combining several instances of the same tracker to form a more robust swarm for tracking a single target. For this experiments the MAD tracker is set-up with a swarm of KCF [23] trackers in combination with the DSST [29] scale estimation scheme. The reader is referred to [28] for details.

A.5 Point-Based Kanade Lukas Tomasi Colour-Filter (PKLTF)

R. Martin-Nieto, A. Garcia-Martin, J. M. Martinez
{rafael.martinn, alvaro.garcia, josem.martinez}@uam.es

PKLTF [30] is a single-object long-term tracker that supports high appearance changes in the target, occlusions, and is also capable of recovering a target lost during the tracking process. PKLTF consists of two phases: The first one uses the Kanade Lukas Tomasi approach (KLT) [31] to choose the object features (using colour and motion coherence), while the second phase is based on mean shift gradient descent [32] to place the bounding box into the position of the object. The object model is based on the RGB colour and the luminance gradient and it consists of a histogram including the quantized values of the colour components, and an edge binary flag. The interested reader is referred to [30] for details.

A.6   A multi-view model for visual tracking via correlation filters (MvCF)

Z. He, X. Li, N. Fan
    zyhe@hitsz.edu.cn, hitlixin@126.com, nanafanhit@gmail.com
The multi-view correlation filter tracker (MvCF tracker) fuses several features and selects the more discriminative features to enhance the robustness. More specifically, for the VOT-TIR dataset, the histogram of oriented gradients (HOG) and gray value features play more important roles in tracking than color features. The combination of the multiple views is conducted by the Kullback-Leibler (KL) divergences. In addition, a simple but effective scale-variation detection mechanism is provided, which strengthens the stability of scale variation tracking.

A.7   Geometric Structure Hyper-Graph based Tracker Version 2 (GGTv2)

T. Hu, D. Du, L. Wen, W. Li, H. Qi, S. Lyu
    {yihouxiang, cvdaviddo, lywen.cv.workbox, wbli.app, honggangqi.cas, heizi. lyu}@gmail.com
GGTv2 is an improvement of GGT [33] by combining the scale adaptive kernel correlation filter [34] and the geometric structure hyper-graph searching framework to complete the object tracking task. The target object is represented by a geometric structure hyper-graph that encodes the local appearance of the target with higher-order geometric structure correlations among target parts and a bounding box template that represents the global appearance of the target. The tracker use HSV colour histogram and LBP texture to calculate the appearance similarity between associations in the hyper-graph. The templates of correlation filter is calculated by HOG and colour name according to [34].

A.8   Distractor Aware Tracker (DAT)

H. Possegger, T. Mauthner, H. Bischof
    {possegger, mauthner, bischof}@icg.tugraz.at

The Distractor Aware Tracker is an appearance-based tracking-by-detection approach. To demonstrate its performance on the VOT-TIR dataset, DAT learns a discriminative model from the grey scale image to distinguish the object from its surrounding region. Additionally, a distractor-aware model term suppresses visually distracting regions whenever they appear within the field-of-view, thus reducing tracker drift. The reader is referred to [35] for details.

A.9   Deep Multi-kernelized Correlation Filter (deepMKCF)

J. Feng, F. Zhao, M. Tang
  {jiayi.feng, fei.zhao, tangm}@nlpr.ia.ac.cn
  deepMKCF tracker is the MKCF [36] with deep features extracted by using VGG-Net [37]. deepMKCF tracker combines the multiple kernel learning and correlation filter techniques and it explores diverse features simultaneously to improve tracking performance. In addition, an optimal search technique is also applied to estimate object scales. The multi-kernel training process of deepMKCF is tailored accordingly to ensure tracking efficiency with deep features.

A.10   NSAMF (NSAMF)

Y. Li, J. Zhu
  {liyang89, jkzhu}@zju.edu.cn
  NSAMF is an improved version of the previous method SAMF [34]. To further exploit color information, NSAMF employs color probability map, instead of color name, as color based feature to achieve more robust tracking results. In addition, multi-models based on different features are integrated to vote the final position of the tracked target.

A.11   An Improved STAPLE Tracker with Multiple Feature Integration (STAPLE+)

Z. Xu, Y. Li, J. Zhu
  xuzhan2012@whu.edu.cn, {liyang89, jkzhu}@zju.edu.cn
  An improved version of STAPLE tracker [38] by integrating multiple features is presented. Besides extracting HOG feature from merely gray-scale image, we also extract HOG feature from color probability map, which can exploit color information better. The final response map is thus a fusion of different features.

A.12   Structure Hyper-graph Based Correlation Filter Tracker (SHCT)

L. Wen, D. Du, S. Li, C.-M. Chang, S. Lyu, Q. Huang
  {lywen.cv.workbox, cvdaviddo, shengkunliluo, mingching, heizi.lyu}@gmail. com, qmhuang@jdl.ac.cn

SHCT tracker constructs a structure hyper-graph model similar to [39] to extract the motion coherence of target parts. The tracker also computes a part confidence map based on the extracted dense subgraphs on the constructed structure hyper-graph, which indicates the confidence score of the part belonging to the target. SHCT uses HSV colour histogram and LBP feature to calculate the appearance similarity between associations in the hyper-graph. Finally, the tracker combines the response maps of correlation filter and structure hyper-graph in a linear way to find the optimal target state (i.e., target scale and location). The templates of correlation filter are calculated by HOG and colour name according to [34]. The appearance models of correlation filter and structure hyper-graph are updated to ensure the tracking performance.

A.13   Sum of Template and Pixel-wise LEarners TIR (Staple-TIR)

L. Bertinetto, J. Valmadre, S. Golodetz, O. Miksik, P. H. S. Torr
{*luca, jvlmdr*}@*robots.ox.ac.uk, stuart.golodetz@ndcn.ox.ac.uk,* {*ondrej.miksik, philip.torr*}@*eng.ox.ac.uk*

Staple is a tracker that combines two image patch representations that are sensitive to complementary factors to learn a model that is inherently robust to both intensity changes and deformations. To maintain real-time speed, two independent ridge-regression problems are solved, exploiting the inherent structure of each representation. Staple combines the scores of two models in a dense translation search, enabling greater accuracy. A critical property of the two models is that their scores are similar in magnitude and indicative of their reliability, so that the prediction is dominated by the more confident. Staple-TIR uses one-dimensional instead of three-dimensional histograms and has different hyperparameters as Staple Tracker. For more details, we refer the reader to [40].

A.14   Best Structured Tracker (BST)

F. Battistone, A. Petrosino, V. Santopietro
{*battistone.francesco, vinsantopietro*}@*gmail.com, petrosino@uniparthenope.it*

BST is based on the idea of Flock of Trackers [41]: a set of local trackers tracks a little patch of the original target and then the tracker combines their information in order to estimate the resulting bounding box. Each local tracker separately analyzes the features extracted from a set of samples and then classifies them using a structured Support Vector Machine as Struck [41]. Once having predicted local target candidates, an outlier detection process is computed by analyzing the displacements of local trackers. Trackers that have been labeled as outliers are reinitialized. At the end of this process, the new bounding box is calculated using the Convex Hull technique.

A.15   Optical flow clustering tracker (FCT)

A. Varfolomieiev
        a.varfolomieiev@kpi.ua

FCT is based on the same idea as the best displacement tracker (BDF) [27]. It uses pyramidal Lucas-Kanade optical flow algorithm to track individual points of an object at several pyramid levels. The results of the point tracking are clustered in the same way as in the BDF [27] to estimate the best object displacement. The initial point locations are generated by the FAST detector [42]. The tracker estimates a scale and an in-plane rotation of the object. These procedures are similar to the scale calculation of the median flow tracker [43], except that the clustering is used instead of median. In case of rotation calculation angles between the respective point pairs are clustered. In contrast to BDF, the FCT does not use consensus-based reinitialization. The current implementation of FCT calculates the optical flow only in the objects region, which is four times larger than the initial bounding box of the object, and thus speeds up the tracker with respect to its previous version [7].

A.16 Likelihood of Features Tracking-Lite (LoFT-Lite)

M. Poostchi, K. Palaniappan, F. Bunyak, G. Seetharaman, R. Pelapur, K. Gao, S. Yao, N. Al-Shakarji

mpoostchi@mail.missouri.edu, {pal, bunyak}@missouri.edu, guna@ieee.org {rvpnc4, kg954, syyh4, nmahyd}@missouri.edu,

LoFT (Likelihood of Features Tracking)-Lite [44] is an appearance based single object tracker that employs a rich set of low level image feature descriptors that account for intensity, edge, shape and motion properties of the target. The feature likelihood maps are computed using sliding window search comparing target and reference feature histograms of intensity, gradient magnitude, gradient orientation, and shape information based on the eigenvalues of the Hessian matrix. Intensity and gradient magnitude normalized cross-correlation likelihood maps are also used to incorporate spatial information. Moreover, for stationary cameras LoFT can take advantage of its flux tensor motion module to robustly estimate the location of moving objects [45]. A parts-based target model is added into LoFT to provide a set of patch-based maximum likelihood maps. This increases tracking robustness to partial occlusions and compensates for orderless nature of histogram-based features. The integral histogram method accelerates computation of the parts-based sliding window histograms [46]. LoFT performs feature fusion using a foreground-background model by comparing the current target appearance with the model inside the search region [47]. LOFT-Lite also incorporates an adaptive orientation-based Kalman prediction update to restrict the search region which reduces sensitivity to abrupt motion changes and decreases computational cost [48].

A.17 Scalable Kernel Correlation Filter with Sparse Feature Integration (sKCF)

A. Solís Montero, J. Lang, R. Laganière

asolismo@uottawa.ca, {jlang, laganier}@eecs.uottawa.ca

sKCF [49] extends the Kernalized Correlation Filter (KCF) framework by introducing an adjustable Gaussian window function and keypoint-based model for scale estimation to deal with the fixed size limitation in the Kernelized Correlation Filter along with some performace enhancements. In the submission, a model learning strategy is introduced to the original sKCF [49] which updates the model only for highly similar KCF responses of the tracked region as to the model. This potentially limits model drift due to temporary disturbances or occlusions. The original sKCF always updates the model in each frame.

A.18   Multi-Domain Convolutional Neural Network Tracker (MDNet-N)

H. Nam, M. Baek, B. Han
   {namhs09, mooyeol, bhhan}@postech.ac.kr
This algorithm is a variation of MDNet [50], which does not pre-train CNNs with other tracking datasets. The network is initialised using the ImageNet [51]. The new classification layer and the fully connected layers within the shared layers are then fine-tuned online during tracking to adapt to the new domain. The online update is conducted to model long-term and short-term appearance variations of a target for robustness and adaptiveness, respectively, and an effective and efficient hard negative mining technique is incorporated in the learning procedure. This experiment result shows that the online tracking framework scheme of MDNet is still effective without multi-domain training.

A.19   Long Term Featureless Object Tracker (LT-FLO)

K. Lebeda, S. Hadfield, J. Matas, R. Bowden
   {k.lebeda, s.hadfield}@surrey.ac.uk, matas@cmp.felk.cvut.cz,
r.bowden@surrey.ac.uk
The tracker is based on and extends previous work of the authors on tracking of texture-less objects [52]. It significantly decreases reliance on texture by using edge-points instead of point features. LT-FLO uses correspondences of lines tangent to the edges and candidates for a correspondence are all local maxima of gradient magnitude. An estimate of the frame-to-frame transformation similarity is obtained via RANSAC. When the confidence is high, the current state is learnt for future corrections. On the other hand, when a low confidence is achieved, the tracker corrects its position estimate restarting the tracking from previously stored states. LT-FLO tracker also has a mechanism to detect disappearance of the object, based on the stability of the gradient in the area of projected edge-points. The interested reader is referred to [53] for details.

A.20   Deformable Part Correlation Filter Tracker (DPT)

A. Lukežič, L. Čehovin, M. Kristan
   alan.lukezic@fri.uni-lj.si,   luka.cehovin@fri.uni-lj.si,   matej.kristan@fri.uni-lj.si

DPT is a part-based correlation filter composed of a coarse and mid-level target representations. Coarse representation is responsible for approximate target localization and uses HOG as well as colour features. The mid-level representation is a deformable parts correlation filter with fully-connected parts topology and applies a novel formulation that threats geometric and visual properties within a single convex optimization function. The mid level as well as coarse level representations are based on the kernelized correlation filter from [23]. The reader is referred to [54] for details.

A.21   Tree-Structured Convolutional Neural Network Tracker (TCNN)

H. Nam, M. Baek, B. Han
{namhs09, mooyeol, bhhan}@postech.ac.kr
TCNN maintains multiple target appearance models based on CNNs in a tree structure to preserve model consistency and handle appearance multi-modality effectively. TCNN tracker consists of two main components, state estimation and model update. When a new frame is given, candidate samples around the target state estimated in the previous frame are drawn, and the likelihood of each sample based on the weighted average of the scores from multiple CNNs is computed. The weight of each CNN is determined by the reliability of the path along which the CNN has been updated in the tree structure. The target state in the current frame is estimated by finding the candidate with the maximum likelihood. After tracking a predefined number of frames, a new CNN is derived from an existing one, which has the highest weight among the contributing CNNs to target state estimation. Interested readers are referred to [55] for details.

A.22   Discriminative Scale Space Tracker (DSST2014)

Authors implementation. Submitted by VOT Committee
The Discriminative Scale Space Tracker (DSST) [29] extends the Minimum Output Sum of Squared Errors (MOSSE) tracker [22] with robust scale estimation. The DSST additionally learns a one-dimensional discriminative scale filter, that is used to estimate the target size. For the translation filter, the intensity features employed in the MOSSE tracker is combined with a pixel-dense representation of HOG-features.

A.23   Normalized Cross-Correlation (NCC)

Submitted by VOT Committee
The NCC tracker is a VOT2016 baseline tracker and follows the very basic idea of tracking by searching for the best match between a static grayscale template and the image using normalized cross-correlation.

A.24 Spatially Regularized Discriminative Correlation Filter Tracker for IR (SRDCFir)

Authors implementation. Submitted by VOT Committee

SRDCFir adapts the SRDCF approach proposed in [56] to thermal infrared data. Standard Discriminative Correlation Filter (DCF) based trackers such as [23, 29, 57] suffer from the inherent periodic assumption when using circular correlation. The resulting periodic boundary effects leads to inaccurate training samples and a restricted search region. The SRDCF mitigates these problems by introducing a spatial regularization function that penalizes filter coefficients residing outside the target region. This allows the size of the training and detection samples to be increased without affecting the effective filter size. By selecting the spatial regularization function to have a sparse Discrete Fourier Spectrum, the filter is efficiently optimized directly in the Fourier domain. Instead of solving for an approximate filter, as in previous DCF based trackers (e.g. [23, 29, 57]), the SRDCF employs an iterative optimization based on Gauss-Seidel that converges to the exact filter. The detection step employs a sub-grid location estimation. In addition to the HOG features used in [56], SRDCFir also employs channel coded intensity features. SRDCFir also employs a motion feature channel, computed by thresholding the difference between the current and previous frame. The result is a binary image that indicates if a pixel has changed its value compared to the previous frame. The intensity and motion features are averaged over the 4×4 HOG cells and then concatenated, giving a 43 dimensional feature vector at each cell.

References

1. Gavrila, D.M.: The visual analysis of human movement: a survey. Comp. Vis. Image Underst. **73**(1), 82–98 (1999)
2. Moeslund, T.B., Hilton, A., Kruger, V.: A survey of advances in vision-based human motion capture and analysis. Comp. Vis. Image Underst. **103**(2–3), 90–126 (2006)
3. Li, X., Hu, W., Shen, C., Zhang, Z., Dick, A.R., Van den Hengel, A.: A survey of appearance models in visual object tracking arXiv:1303.4803 [cs.CV] (2013)
4. Young, D.P., Ferryman, J.M.: Pets metrics: On-line performance evaluation service. In: ICCCN 2005 Proceedings of the 14th International Conference on Computer Communications and Networks, pp. 317–324 (2005)
5. Kristan, M., Pflugfelder, R., Leonardis, A., Matas, J., Porikli, F., Cehovin, L., Nebehay, G., Fernández, G., Vojir, T. et al.: The visual object tracking vot2013 challenge results. In: ICCV 2013 Workshops, Workshop on Visual Object Tracking Challenge, pp. 98–111 (2013)
6. Kristan, M., et al.: The visual object tracking vot2014 challenge results. In: Agapito, L., et al. (eds.) ECCV 2014 Workshops. LNCS, vol. 8926, pp. 191–217. Springer, Heidelberg (2014)
7. Kristan, M., Matas, J., Leonardis, A., Felsberg, M., et al.: The visual object tracking vot2015 challenge results. In: ICCV 2015 Workshops, Workshop on Visual Object Tracking Challenge (2015)

8. Wu, Y., Lim, J., Yang, M.H.: Online object tracking: a benchmark. In: IEEE Conference on Computer Vision and Pattern Recognition (CVPR) (2013)
9. Wu, Y., Lim, J., Yang, M.: Object tracking benchmark. IEEE Trans. Pattern Anal. Mach. Intell. **37**(9), 1834–1848 (2015)
10. Gade, R., Moeslund, T.B.: Thermal cameras and applications: a survey. Mach. Vis. Appl. **25**(1), 245–262 (2014)
11. Felsberg, M., Berg, A., Häger, G., Ahlberg, J., et al.: The thermal infrared visual object tracking VOT-TIR2015 challenge results. In: ICCV 2015 Workshop Proceedings, VOT 2015 Workshop (2015)
12. Kristan, M., Leonardis, A., Matas, J., Felsberg, M., Pflugfelder, R., et al.: The visual object tracking VOT2016 challenge results. In: Jegou, H., Hua, G. (eds.) ECCV 2016 Workshops. LNCS, vol. 9914, pp. 777–823. Springer, Heidelberg (2016)
13. Čehovin, L., Kristan, M., Leonardis, A.: Is my new tracker really better than yours? In: WACV 2014: IEEE Winter Conference on Applications of Computer Vision (2014)
14. Čehovin, L., Leonardis, A., Kristan, M.: Visual object tracking performance measures revisited arXiv:1502.05803 [cs.CV] (2013)
15. Kristan, M., Pflugfelder, R., Leonardis, A., Matas, J., Porikli, F., Cehovin, L., Nebehay, G., Fernandez, G., Vojir, T.: The vot2013 challenge: overview and additional results. In: Computer Vision Winter Workshop (2014)
16. Berg, A., Ahlberg, J., Felsberg, M.: A thermal object tracking benchmark. In: 12th IEEE International Conference on Advanced Video- and Signal-based Surveillance, Karlsruhe, Germany, 25–28 August 2015. IEEE (2015)
17. Berg, A., Ahlberg, J., Felsberg, M.: Channel coded distribution field tracking for thermal infrared imagery. In: IEEE International Workshop on Performance Evaluation of Tracking and Surveillance (PETS) (2016)
18. Felsberg, M.: Enhanced distribution field tracking using channel representations. In: Visual Object Tracking Challenge VOT 2013, In conjunction with ICCV 2013 (2013)
19. Kristan, M., Pflugfelder, R., Leonardis, A., Matas, J., Porikli, F., Čehovin, L., Nebehay, G., Fernandez, G., Vojir, T., Gatt, A., Khajenezhad, A., Salahledin, A., Soltani-Farani, A., Zarezade, A., Petrosino, A., Milton, A., Bozorgtabar, B., Li, B., Chan, C.S., Heng, C., Ward, D., Kearney, D., Monekosso, D., Karaimer, H.C., Rabiee, H.R., Zhu, J., Gao, J., Xiao, J., Zhang, J., Xing, J., Huang, K., Lebeda, K., Cao, L., Maresca, M.E., Lim, M.K., Helw, M.E., Felsberg, M., Remagnino, P., Bowden, R., Goecke, R., Stolkin, R., Lim, S.Y., Maher, S., Poullot, S., Wong, S., Satoh, S., Chen, W., Hu, W., Zhang, X., Li, Y., Niu, Z.: The Visual Object Tracking VOT2013 challenge results. In: ICCV Workshops, pp. 98–111 (2013)
20. Zitnick, C.L., Dollár, P.: Edge boxes: locating object proposals from edges. In: Fleet, D., Pajdla, T., Schiele, B., Tuytelaars, T. (eds.) ECCV 2014. LNCS, vol. 8693, pp. 391–405. Springer, Heidelberg (2014). doi:10.1007/978-3-319-10602-1_26
21. Comaniciu, D., Ramesh, V., Meer, P.: Kernel-based object tracking. IEEE Trans. Pattern Anal. Mach. Intell. **25**(5), 564–577 (2003)
22. Bolme, D.S., Beveridge, J.R., Draper, B.A., Lui, Y.M.: Visual object tracking using adaptive correlation filters. In: Proceedings of the IEEE Conference on Computer Vision and Pattern Recognition (2010)
23. Henriques, J., Caseiro, R., Martins, P., Batista, J.: High-speed tracking with kernelized correlation filters. IEEE Trans. Pattern Anal. Mach. Intell. **37**(3), 583–596 (2015)

24. Akin, O., Erdem, E., Erdem, A., Mikolajczyk, K.: Deformable part-based tracking by coupled global and local correlation filters. J. Vis. Commun. Image Represent. **38**, 763–774 (2016)
25. Zhu, G., Porikli, F., Li, H.: Beyond local search: tracking objects everywhere with instance-specific proposals. In: IEEE Conference on Computer Vision and Pattern Recognition (CVPR) (2016)
26. Vojir, T., Matas, J.: Robustifying the flock of trackers. In: Computer Vision Winter Workshop, pp. 91–97. IEEE (2011)
27. Maresca, M., Petrosino, A.: Clustering local motion estimates for robust and efficient object tracking. In: Agapito, L., et al. (eds.) ECCV 2014 Workshops. LNCS, vol. 8926, pp. 244–253. Springer, Heidelberg (2014)
28. Becker, S., Krah, S.B., Hübner, W., Arens, M.: Mad for visual tracker fusion. In: SPIE Proceedings Optics and Photonics for Counterterrorism, Crime Fighting, and Defence 9995 (2016, to appear)
29. Danelljan, M., Häger, G., Khan, F.S., Felsberg, M.: Accurate scale estimation for robust visual tracking. In: Proceedings of the British Machine Vision Conference (2014)
30. González, A., Martín-Nieto, R., Bescós, J., Martínez, J.M.: Single object long-term tracker for smart control of a PTZ camera. In: International Conference on Distributed Smart Cameras, pp. 121–126 (2014)
31. Shi, J., Tomasi, C.: Good features to track. In: Computer Vision and Pattern Recognition, pp. 593–600, June 1994
32. Comaniciu, D., Ramesh, V., Meer, P.: Real-time tracking of non-rigid objects using mean shift. Comp. Vis. Patt. Recogn. **2**, 142–149 (2000)
33. Du, D., Qi, H., Wen, L., Tian, Q., Huang, Q., Lyu, S.: Geometric hypergraph learning for visual tracking. In: CoRR (2016)
34. Li, Y., Zhu, J.: A scale adaptive kernel correlation filter tracker with feature integration. In: Agapito, L., et al. (eds.) ECCV 2014 Workshop. LNCS, vol. 8926, pp. 254–265. Springer, Heidelberg (2014)
35. Possegger, H., Mauthner, T., Bischof, H.: In defense of color-based model-free tracking. In: Proceedings of the IEEE Conference on Computer Vision and Pattern Recognition (2015)
36. Tang, M., Feng, J.: Multi-kernel correlation filter for visual tracking. In: ICCV (2015)
37. Simonyan, K., Zisserman, A.: Very deep convolutional networks for large-scale image recognition. In: ICLR (2015)
38. Bertinetto, L., Valmadre, J., Golodetz, S., Miksik, O., Torr, P.: Staple: Complementary learners for real-time tracking arXiv:1512.01355 [cs.CV] (2015)
39. Du, D., Qi, H., Li, W., Wen, L., Huang, Q., Lyu, S.: Online deformable object tracking based on structure-aware hyper-graph. IEEE Trans. Image Process. **25**(8), 3572–3584 (2016)
40. Bertinetto, L., Valmadre, J., Golodetz, S., Miksik, O., Torr, P.H.S.: Staple: complementary learners for real-time tracking. In: CVPR (2016)
41. Vojíř, T., Matas, J.: The enhanced flock of trackers. In: Cipolla, R., Battiato, S., Farinella, G.M. (eds.) Registration and Recognition in Images and Video. SCI, vol. 532, pp. 111–138. Springer, Heidelberg (2014)
42. Rosten, E., Drummond, T.W.: Machine learning for high-speed corner detection. In: Leonardis, A., Bischof, H., Pinz, A. (eds.) ECCV 2006, Part I. LNCS, vol. 3951, pp. 430–443. Springer, Heidelberg (2006)
43. Kalal, Z., Mikolajczyk, K., Matas, J.: Forward-backward error: Automatic detection of tracking failures. In: Computer Vision and Pattern Recognition (2010)

44. Pelapur, R., Candemir, S., Bunyak, F., Poostchi, M., Seetharaman, G., Palaniappan, K.: Persistent target tracking using likelihood fusion in wide-area and full motion video sequences. In: IEEE Conference on Information Fusion (FUSION), pp. 2420–2427 (2012)
45. Poostchi, M., Aliakbarpour, H., Viguier, R., Bunyak, F., Palaniappan, K., Seetharaman, G.: Semantic depth map fusion for moving vehicle detection in aerial video. In: Proceedings of the IEEE Conference on Computer Vision and Pattern Recognition (CVPR) Workshops, pp. 32–40 (2016)
46. Poostchi, M., Palaniappan, K., Bunyak, F., Becchi, M., Seetharaman, G.: Efficient GPU implementation of the integral histogram. In: Park, J.I., Kim, J. (eds.) ACCV 2012 Workshops. LNCS, vol. 7728, pp. 266–278. Springer, Heidelberg (2012)
47. Palaniappan, K., Bunyak, F., Kumar, P., Ersoy, I., Jaeger, S., Ganguli, K., Haridas, A., Fraser, J., Rao, R., Seetharaman, G.: Efficient feature extraction and likelihood fusion for vehicle tracking in low frame rate airborne video. In: IEEE Conference on Information Fusion (FUSION), pp. 1–8 (2010)
48. Pelapur, R., Palaniappan, K., Seetharaman, G.: Robust orientation and appearance adaptation for wide-area large format video object tracking. In: Proceedings of the IEEE Conference on Advanced Video and Signal based Surveillance, pp. 337–342 (2012)
49. Montero, A.S., Lang, J., Laganiere, R.: Scalable kernel correlation filter with sparse feature integration. In: The IEEE International Conference on Computer Vision (ICCV) Workshops, pp. 24–31, December 2015
50. Nam, H., Han, B.: Learning multi-domain convolutional neural networks for visual tracking. In: CoRR (2015)
51. Deng, J., Dong, W., Socher, R., Li, L.J., Li, K., Fei-Fei, L.: Imagenet: a large-scale hierarchical image database a large-scale hierarchical image database. In: CVPR (2009)
52. Lebeda, K., Matas, J., Bowden, R.: Tracking the untrackable: how to track when your object is featureless. In: Proceedings of ACCV DTCE (2012)
53. Lebeda, K., Hadfield, S., Matas, J., Bowden, R.: Texture-independent long-term tracking using virtual corners. IEEE Trans. Image Process. 25(1), 359–371 (2016)
54. Lukezic, A., Cehovin, L., Kristan, M.: Deformable parts correlation filters for robust visual tracking. CoRR abs/1605.03720 (2016)
55. Nam, H., Baek, M., Han, B.: Modeling and propagating cnns in a tree structure for visual tracking. CoRR abs/1608.07242 (2016)
56. Danelljan, M., Häger, G., Khan, F.S., Felsberg, M.: Learning spatially regularized correlation filters for visual tracking. In: International Conference on Computer Vision (2015)
57. Danelljan, M., Khan, F.S., Felsberg, M., Van de Weijer, J.: Adaptive color attributes for real-time visual tracking. In: Computer Vision Pattern Recognition (2014)

Fully-Convolutional Siamese Networks for Object Tracking

Luca Bertinetto[✉], Jack Valmadre, João F. Henriques, Andrea Vedaldi, and Philip H.S. Torr

Department of Engineering Science, University of Oxford, Oxford, UK
{luca.bertinetto,jack.valmadre,joao.henriques,andrea.vedaldi,
philip.torr}@eng.ox.ac.uk

Abstract. The problem of arbitrary object tracking has traditionally been tackled by learning a model of the object's appearance exclusively online, using as sole training data the video itself. Despite the success of these methods, their online-only approach inherently limits the richness of the model they can learn. Recently, several attempts have been made to exploit the expressive power of deep convolutional networks. However, when the object to track is not known beforehand, it is necessary to perform Stochastic Gradient Descent online to adapt the weights of the network, severely compromising the speed of the system. In this paper we equip a basic tracking algorithm with a novel fully-convolutional Siamese network trained end-to-end on the ILSVRC15 dataset for object detection in video. Our tracker operates at frame-rates beyond real-time and, despite its extreme simplicity, achieves state-of-the-art performance in multiple benchmarks.

Keywords: Object-tracking · Siamese-network · Similarity-learning · Deep-learning

1 Introduction

We consider the problem of tracking an arbitrary object in video, where the object is identified solely by a rectangle in the first frame. Since the algorithm may be requested to track any arbitrary object, it is impossible to have already gathered data and trained a specific detector.

For several years, the most successful paradigm for this scenario has been to learn a model of the object's appearance in an online fashion using examples extracted from the video itself [1]. This owes in large part to the demonstrated ability of methods like TLD [2], Struck [3] and KCF [4]. However, a clear deficiency of using data derived exclusively from the current video is that only comparatively simple models can be learnt. While other problems in computer

---

The first two authors contributed equally, and are listed in alphabetical order.

© Springer International Publishing Switzerland 2016
G. Hua and H. Jégou (Eds.): ECCV 2016 Workshops, Part II, LNCS 9914, pp. 850–865, 2016.
DOI: 10.1007/978-3-319-48881-3_56

vision have seen an increasingly pervasive adoption of deep convolutional networks (conv-nets) trained from large supervised datasets, the scarcity of supervised data and the constraint of real-time operation prevent the naive application of deep learning within this paradigm of learning a detector per video.

Several recent works have aimed to overcome this limitation using a pretrained deep conv-net that was learnt for a different but related task. These approaches either apply "shallow" methods (e.g. correlation filters) using the network's internal representation as features [5,6] or perform SGD (stochastic gradient descent) to fine-tune multiple layers of the network [7–9]. While the use of shallow methods does not take full advantage of the benefits of end-to-end learning, methods that apply SGD during tracking to achieve state-of-the-art results have not been able to operate in real-time.

We advocate an alternative approach in which a deep conv-net is trained to address a more general *similarity learning* problem in an initial offline phase, and then this function is simply evaluated online during tracking. The key contribution of this paper is to demonstrate that this approach achieves very competitive performance in modern tracking benchmarks at speeds that far exceed the frame-rate requirement. Specifically, we train a Siamese network to locate an *exemplar* image within a larger *search* image. A further contribution is a novel Siamese architecture that is *fully-convolutional* with respect to the search image: dense and efficient sliding-window evaluation is achieved with a bilinear layer that computes the cross-correlation of its two inputs.

We posit that the similarity learning approach has gone relatively neglected because the tracking community did not have access to vast labelled datasets. In fact, until recently the available datasets comprised only a few hundred annotated videos. However, we believe that the emergence of the ILSVRC dataset for object detection in video [10] (henceforth ImageNet Video) makes it possible to train such a model. Furthermore, the fairness of training and testing deep models for tracking using videos from the same domain is a point of controversy, as it has been recently prohibited by the VOT committee. We show that our model generalizes from the ImageNet Video domain to the ALOV/OTB/VOT [1,11,12] domain, enabling the videos of tracking benchmarks to be reserved for testing purposes.

2   Deep Similarity Learning for Tracking

Learning to track arbitrary objects can be addressed using similarity learning. We propose to learn a function $f(z, x)$ that compares an exemplar image z to a candidate image x of the same size and returns a high score if the two images depict the same object and a low score otherwise. To find the position of the object in a new image, we can then exhaustively test all possible locations and choose the candidate with the maximum similarity to the past appearance of the object. In experiments, we will simply use the initial appearance of the object as the exemplar. The function f will be learnt from a dataset of videos with labelled object trajectories.

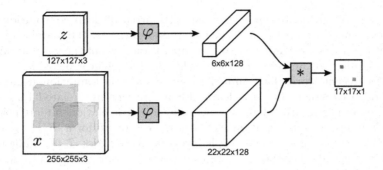

Fig. 1. Fully-convolutional Siamese architecture. Our architecture is fully-convolutional with respect to the search image x. The output is a scalar-valued score map whose dimension depends on the size of the search image. This enables the similarity function to be computed for all translated sub-windows within the search image in one evaluation. In this example, the red and blue pixels in the score map contain the similarities for the corresponding sub-windows. Best viewed in colour (Color figure online)

Given their widespread success in computer vision [13–16], we will use a deep conv-net as the function f. Similarity learning with deep conv-nets is typically addressed using Siamese architectures [17–19]. Siamese networks apply an identical transformation φ to both inputs and then combine their representations using another function g according to $f(z,x) = g(\varphi(z),\varphi(x))$. When the function g is a simple distance or similarity metric, the function φ can be considered an embedding. Deep Siamese conv-nets have previously been applied to tasks such as face verification [14,18,20], keypoint descriptor learning [19,21] and one-shot character recognition [22].

2.1 Fully-Convolutional Siamese Architecture

We propose a Siamese architecture which is *fully-convolutional* with respect to the candidate image x. We say that a function is fully-convolutional if it commutes with translation. To give a more precise definition, introducing L_τ to denote the translation operator $(L_\tau x)[u] = x[u - \tau]$, a function h that maps signals to signals is fully-convolutional with integer stride k if

$$h(L_{k\tau}x) = L_\tau h(x) \tag{1}$$

for any translation τ. (When x is a finite signal, this only need hold for the valid region of the output.)

The advantage of a fully-convolutional network is that, instead of a candidate image of the same size, we can provide as input to the network a much larger *search* image and it will compute the similarity at all translated sub-windows on a dense grid in a single evaluation. To achieve this, we use a convolutional embedding function φ and combine the resulting feature maps using a cross-correlation layer

$$f(z, x) = \varphi(z) * \varphi(x) + b\,\mathbb{1}, \tag{2}$$

where $b\,\mathbb{1}$ denotes a signal which takes value $b \in \mathbb{R}$ in every location. The output of this network is not a single score but rather a score map defined on a finite grid $\mathcal{D} \subset \mathbb{Z}^2$ as illustrated in Fig. 1. Note that the output of the embedding function is a feature map with spatial support as opposed to a plain vector. The same technique has been applied in contemporary work on stereo matching [23].

During tracking, we use a search image centred at the previous position of the target. The position of the maximum score relative to the centre of the score map, multiplied by the stride of the network, gives the displacement of the target from frame to frame. Multiple scales are searched in a single forward-pass by assembling a mini-batch of scaled images.

Combining feature maps using cross-correlation and evaluating the network once on the larger search image is mathematically equivalent to combining feature maps using the inner product and evaluating the network on each translated sub-window independently. However, the cross-correlation layer provides an incredibly simple method to implement this operation efficiently within the framework of existing conv-net libraries. While this is clearly useful during testing, it can also be exploited during training.

2.2   Training with Large Search Images

We employ a discriminative approach, training the network on positive and negative pairs and adopting the logistic loss

$$\ell(y, v) = \log(1 + \exp(-yv)) \tag{3}$$

where v is the real-valued score of a single exemplar-candidate pair and $y \in \{+1, -1\}$ is its ground-truth label. We exploit the fully-convolutional nature of our network during training by using pairs that comprise an exemplar image and a larger search image. This will produce a map of scores $v : \mathcal{D} \to \mathbb{R}$, effectively generating many examples per pair. We define the loss of a score map to be the mean of the individual losses

$$L(y, v) = \frac{1}{|\mathcal{D}|} \sum_{u \in \mathcal{D}} \ell(y[u], v[u]), \tag{4}$$

requiring a true label $y[u] \in \{+1, -1\}$ for each position $u \in \mathcal{D}$ in the score map. The parameters of the conv-net θ are obtained by applying Stochastic Gradient Descent (SGD) to the problem

$$\arg\min_{\theta} \; \underset{(z,x,y)}{\mathbb{E}} \; L(y, f(z, x; \theta)). \tag{5}$$

Pairs are obtained from a dataset of annotated videos by extracting exemplar and search images that are centred on the target, as shown in Fig. 2. The images

Fig. 2. Training pairs extracted from the same video: exemplar image and corresponding search image from same video. When a sub-window extends beyond the extent of the image, the missing portions are filled with the mean RGB value.

are extracted from two frames of a video that both contain the object and are at most T frames apart. The class of the object is ignored during training. The scale of the object within each image is normalized without corrupting the aspect ratio of the image. The elements of the score map are considered to belong to a positive example if they are within radius R of the centre (accounting for the stride k of the network)

$$y[u] = \begin{cases} +1 & \text{if } k\|u - c\| \leq R \\ -1 & \text{otherwise.} \end{cases} \tag{6}$$

The losses of the positive and negative examples in the score map are weighted to eliminate class imbalance.

Since our network is fully-convolutional, there is no risk that it learns a bias for the sub-window at the centre. We believe that it is effective to consider search images centred on the target because it is likely that the most difficult sub-windows, and those which have the most influence on the performance of the tracker, are those adjacent to the target.

Note that since the network is symmetric $f(z,x) = f(x,z)$, it is in fact also fully-convolutional in the exemplar. While this allows us to use different size exemplar images for different objects in theory, we assume uniform sizes because it simplifies the mini-batch implementation. However, this assumption could be relaxed in the future.

2.3   ImageNet Video for Tracking

The 2015 edition of ImageNet Large Scale Visual Recognition Challenge [10] (ILSVRC) introduced the ImageNet Video dataset as part of the new *object detection from video* challenge. Participants are required to classify and locate objects from 30 different classes of animals and vehicles. Training and validation sets together contain almost 4500 videos, with a total of more than one million annotated frames. This number is particularly impressive if compared to the number of labelled sequences in VOT [12], ALOV [1] and OTB [11], which together total less than 500 videos. We believe that this dataset should be of extreme interest to the tracking community not only for its vast size, but also because it depicts scenes and objects different to those found in the canonical tracking benchmarks. For this reason, it can safely be used to train a deep model for tracking without over-fitting to the domain of videos used in these benchmarks.

2.4   Practical Considerations

Dataset Curation. During training, we adopt exemplar images that are 127×127 and search images that are 255×255 pixels. Images are scaled such that the bounding box, plus an added margin for context, has a fixed area. More precisely, if the tight bounding box has size (w, h) and the context margin is p, then the scale factor s is chosen such that the area of the scaled rectangle is equal to a constant

$$s(w + 2p) \times s(h + 2p) = A \ . \tag{7}$$

We use the area of the exemplar images $A = 127^2$ and set the amount of context to be half of the mean dimension $p = (w + h)/4$. Exemplar and search images for every frame are extracted offline to avoid image resizing during training. In a preliminary version of this work, we adopted a few heuristics to limit the number of frames from which to extract the training data. For the experiments of this paper, instead, we have used *all* 4417 videos of ImageNet Video, which account for more than 2 million labelled bounding boxes.

Network Architecture. The architecture that we adopt for the embedding function φ resembles the convolutional stage of the network of Krizhevsky et al. [16]. The dimensions of the parameters and activations are given in Table 1. Max-pooling is employed after the first two convolutional layers. ReLU non-linearities follow every convolutional layer except for conv5, the final layer. During training, batch normalization [24] is inserted immediately after every linear layer. The stride of the final representation is eight. An important aspect of the design is that no padding is introduced within the network. Although this is common practice in image classification, it violates the fully-convolutional property of Eq. 1.

Tracking Algorithm. Since our purpose is to prove the efficacy of our fully-convolutional Siamese network and its generalization capability when trained on ImageNet Video, we use an extremely simplistic algorithm to perform tracking. Unlike more sophisticated trackers, we do not update a model or maintain a

Table 1. Architecture of convolutional embedding function, which is similar to the convolutional stage of the network of Krizhevsky et al. [16]. The channel map property describes the number of output and input channels of each convolutional layer.

Layer	Support	Chan. map	Stride	Activation size		Chans.
				For exemplar	For search	
				127×127	255×255	$\times 3$
conv1	11×11	96×3	2	59×59	123×123	$\times 96$
pool1	3×3		2	29×29	61×61	$\times 96$
conv2	5×5	256×48	1	25×25	57×57	$\times 256$
pool2	3×3		2	12×12	28×28	$\times 256$
conv3	3×3	384×256	1	10×10	26×26	$\times 192$
conv4	3×3	384×192	1	8×8	24×24	$\times 192$
conv5	3×3	256×192	1	6×6	22×22	$\times 128$

memory of past appearances, we do not incorporate additional cues such as optical flow or colour histograms, and we do not refine our prediction with bounding box regression. Yet, despite its simplicity, the tracking algorithm achieves surprisingly good results when equipped with our offline-learnt similarity metric. Online, we do incorporate some elementary temporal constraints: we only search for the object within a region of approximately four times its previous size, and a cosine window is added to the score map to penalize large displacements. Tracking through scale space is achieved by processing several scaled versions of the search image. Any change in scale is penalized and updates of the current scale are damped.

3   Related Work

Several recent works have sought to train Recurrent Neural Networks (RNNs) for the problem of object tracking. Gan et al. [25] train an RNN to predict the absolute position of the target in each frame and Kahou et al. [26] similarly train an RNN for tracking using a differentiable attention mechanism. These methods have not yet demonstrated competitive results on modern benchmarks, however it is certainly a promising avenue for future research. We remark that an interesting parallel can be drawn between this approach and ours, by interpreting a Siamese network as an unrolled RNN that is trained and evaluated on sequences of length two. Siamese networks could therefore serve as strong initialization for a recurrent model.

Denil et al. [27] track objects with a particle filter that uses a learnt distance metric to compare the current appearance to that of the first frame. However, their distance metric is vastly different to ours. Instead of comparing images of the entire object, they compute distances between fixations (foveated glimpses of small regions within the object's bounding box). To learn a distance metric, they train a Restricted Boltzmann Machine (RBM) and then use the Euclidean distance between hidden activations for two fixations. Although RBMs are unsupervised, they suggest training the RBM on random fixations within centred images of the object to detect. This must either be performed online or in an offline phase with knowledge of the object to track. While tracking an object, they learn a stochastic policy for choosing fixations which is specific to that object, using uncertainty as a reward signal. Besides synthetic sequences of MNIST digits, this method has only been demonstrated qualitatively on problems of face and person tracking.

While it is infeasible to train a deep conv-net from scratch for each new video, several works have investigated the feasibility of fine-tuning from pre-trained parameters at test time. SO-DLT [7] and MDNet [9] both train a convolutional network for a similar detection task in an offline phase, then at test-time use SGD to learn a detector with examples extracted from the video itself as in the conventional tracking-as-detector-learning paradigm. These methods cannot operate at frame-rate due to the computational burden of evaluating forward and backward passes on many examples. An alternative way to leverage conv-nets for tracking is to apply traditional shallow methods using the internal representation of a pre-trained convolutional network as features. While trackers in this style such as DeepSRDCF [6], Ma et al. [5] and FCNT [8] have achieved strong results, they have been unable to achieve frame-rate operation due to the relatively high dimension of the conv-net representation.

Concurrently with our own work, some other authors have also proposed using conv-nets for object tracking by learning a function of pairs of images. Held et al. [28] introduce GOTURN, in which a conv-net is trained to regress directly from two images to the location in the second image of the object shown in the first image. Predicting a rectangle instead of a position has the advantage that changes in scale and aspect ratio can be handled without resorting to exhaustive evaluation. However, a disadvantage of their approach is that it does not possess intrinsic invariance to translation of the second image. This means that the network must be shown examples in all positions, which is achieved through considerable dataset augmentation. Chen et al. [29] train a network that maps an exemplar and a larger search region to a response map. However, their method also lacks invariance to translation of the second image since the final layers are fully-connected. Similarly to Held et al., this is inefficient because the training set must represent all translations of all objects. Their method is named YCNN for the Y shape of the network. Unlike our approach, they cannot adjust the size of the search region dynamically after training. Tao et al. [30] propose to train a Siamese network to identify candidate image locations that match the initial object appearance, dubbing their method SINT (Siamese INstance search Tracker). In contrast to our approach, they do not adopt an architecture which is fully-convolutional with respect to the search image. Instead, at test time, they sample bounding boxes uniformly on circles of varying radius as in Struck [3]. Moreover, they incorporate optical flow and bounding box regression to improve the results. In order to improve the computational speed of their system, they employ Region of Interest (RoI) pooling to efficiently examine many overlapping sub-windows. Despite this optimization, at 2 frames per second, the overall system is still far from being real-time.

All of the competitive methods above that train on video sequences (MDNet [9], SINT [30], GOTURN [28]), use training data belonging to the same ALOV/OTB/VOT domain used by the benchmarks. This practice has been forbidden in the VOT challenge due to concerns about over-fitting to the scenes and objects in the benchmark. Thus an important contribution of our work is to demonstrate that a conv-net can be trained for effective object tracking without using videos from the same distribution as the testing set.

4   Experiments

4.1   Implementation Details

Training. The parameters of the embedding function are found by minimizing Eq. 5 with straightforward SGD using MatConvNet [31]. The initial values of the parameters follow a Gaussian distribution, scaled according to the improved Xavier method [32]. Training is performed over 50 epochs, each consisting of 50,000 sampled pairs (according to Sect. 2.2). The gradients for each iteration are estimated using mini-batches of size 8, and the learning rate is annealed geometrically at each epoch from 10^{-2} to 10^{-5}.

Tracking. As mentioned earlier, the online phase is deliberately minimalistic. The embedding $\varphi(z)$ of the initial object appearance is computed once, and is compared convolutionally to sub-windows of the subsequent frames. We found that updating (the feature representation of) the exemplar online through simple strategies, such as linear interpolation, does not gain much performance and thus we keep it fixed. We found that upsampling the score map using bicubic interpolation, from 17×17 to 272×272, results in more accurate localization since the original map is relatively coarse. To handle scale variations, we also search for the object over five scales $1.025^{\{-2,-1,0,1,2\}}$, and update the scale by linear interpolation with a factor of 0.35 to provide damping.

In order to make our experimental results reproducible, we share training and tracking code, together with the curated dataset and the scripts to generate it at www.robots.ox.ac.uk/~luca/siamese-fc.html. On a machine equipped with a single NVIDIA GeForce GTX Titan X and an Intel Core i7-4790K at 4.0 GHz, our full online tracking pipeline operates at 86 and 58 frames-per-second, when searching respectively over 3 and 5 scales.

4.2   Evaluation

We evaluate two variants of our simplistic tracker: SiamFC (Siamese Fully-Convolutional) and SiamFC-3s, which searches over 3 scales instead of 5.

4.3   The OTB-13 Benchmark

The OTB-13 [11] benchmark considers the average per-frame *success rate* at different thresholds: a tracker is successful in a given frame if the intersection-over-union (IoU) between its estimate and the ground-truth is above a certain threshold. Trackers are then compared in terms of area under the curve of success rates for different values of this threshold. In addition to the trackers reported by [11], in Fig. 3 we also compare against seven more recent state-of-the-art trackers presented in the major computer vision conferences and that can run at frame-rate speed: Staple [33], LCT [34], CCT [35], SCT4 [36], DLSSVM_NU [37], DSST [38] and KCFDP [39]. Given the nature of the sequences, for this benchmark only we convert 25 % of the pairs to grayscale during training. All the other hyper-parameters (for training and tracking) are fixed.

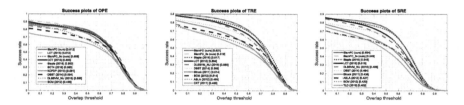

Fig. 3. Success plots for OPE (one pass evaluation), TRE (temporal robustness evaluation) and SRE (spatial robustness evaluation) of the OTB-13 [11] benchmark. The results of CCT, SCT4 and KCFDP were only available for OPE at the time of writing.

4.4   The VOT Benchmarks

For our experiments, we use the latest stable version of the Visual Object Tracking (VOT) toolkit (tag `vot2015-final`), which evaluates trackers on sequences chosen from a pool of 356, selected so that seven different challenging situations are well represented. Many of the sequences were originally presented in other datasets (e.g. ALOV [1] and OTB [11]). Within the benchmark, trackers are automatically re-initialized five frames after failure, which is deemed to have occurred when the IoU between the estimated bounding box and the ground truth becomes zero.

VOT-14 Results. We compare our method SiamFC (and the variant SiamFC-3s) against the best 10 trackers that participated in the 2014 edition of the VOT challenge [40]. We also include Staple [33] and GOTURN [28], two recent real-time trackers presented respectively at CVPR 2016 and ECCV 2016. Trackers are evaluated according to two measures of performance: *accuracy* and *robustness*. The former is calculated as the average IoU, while the latter is expressed in terms of the total number of failures. These give insight into the behaviour of a tracker. Figure 4 shows the Accuracy-Robustness plot, where the best trackers are closer to the top-right corner.

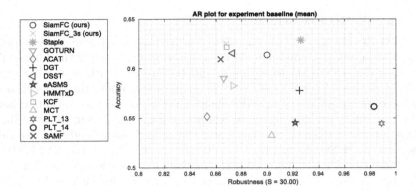

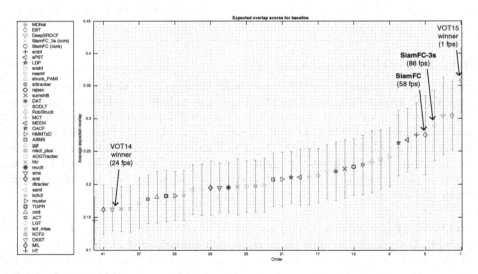

Fig. 4. VOT-14 Accuracy-robustness plot. Best trackers are closer to the top-right corner.

VOT-15 Results. We also compare our method against the 40 best participants in the 2015 edition [12]. In this case, the raw scores of accuracy and number of failures are used to compute the *expected average overlap measure*, which represents the average IoU with no re-initialization following a failure. Figure 5 illustrates the final ranking in terms of expected average overlap, while Table 2 reports scores and speed of the 15 highest ranked trackers of the challenge.

Fig. 5. VOT-15 ranking in terms of expected average overlap. Only the best 40 results have been reported.

Table 2. Raw scores, overlap and reported speed for our proposed method and the best 15 performing trackers of the VOT-15 challenge. Where available, we compare with the speed reported by the authors, otherwise (*) we report the values from the VOT-15 results [12] in EFO units, which roughly correspond to fps (e.g. the speed of the NCC tracker is 140 fps and 160 EFO)

Tracker	Accuracy	# Failures	Overlap	Speed (fps)
MDNet [9]	0.5620	46	0.3575	1
EBT [41]	0.4481	49	0.3042	5
DeepSRDCF [6]	0.5350	60	0.3033	< 1*
SiamFC-3s (ours)	0.5335	84	0.2889	**86**
SiamFC (ours)	0.5240	87	0.2743	58
SRDCF [42]	0.5260	71	0.2743	5
sPST [43]	0.5230	85	0.2668	2
LDP [12]	0.4688	78	0.2625	4*
SC-EBT [44]	0.5171	103	0.2412	–
NSAMF [45]	0.5027	87	0.2376	5*
StruckMK [3]	0.4442	90	0.2341	2
S3Tracker [46]	0.5031	100	0.2292	14*
RAJSSC [12]	0.5301	105	0.2262	2*
SumShift [46]	0.4888	97	0.2233	17*
DAT [47]	0.4705	113	0.2195	15
SO-DLT [7]	0.5233	108	0.2190	5

VOT-16 Results. At the time of writing, the results of the 2016 edition were not available. However, to facilitate an early comparison with our method, we report our scores. For SiamFC and SiamFC-3s we obtain, respectively, an overall expected overlap (average between the *baseline* and *unsupervised* experiments) of 0.3876 and 0.4051. Please note that these results are different from the VOT-16 report, as our entry in the challenge was a preliminary version of this work.

Despite its simplicity, our method improves over recent state-of-the-art real-time trackers (Figs. 3 and 4). Moreover, it outperforms most of the best methods in the challenging VOT-15 benchmark, while being the only one that achieves frame-rate speed (Fig. 5 and Table 2). These results demonstrate that the expressiveness of the similarity metric learnt by our fully-convolutional Siamese network on ImageNet Video *alone* is enough to achieve very strong results, comparable or superior to recent state-of-the-art methods, which often are several orders of magnitude slower. We believe that considerably higher performance could be obtained by augmenting the minimalist online tracking pipeline with the methods often adopted by the tracking community (e.g. model update, bounding-box regression, fine-tuning, memory).

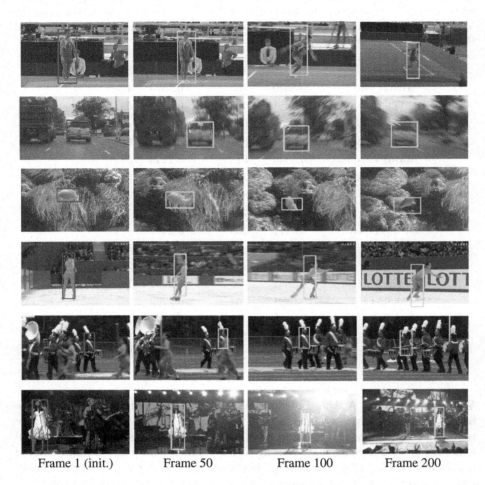

Frame 1 (init.)   Frame 50   Frame 100   Frame 200

Fig. 6. Snapshots of the simple tracker described in Sect. 2.4 equipped with our proposed fully-convolutional Siamese network trained from scratch on ImageNet Video. Our method does not perform any model update, so it uses only the first frame to compute $\varphi(z)$. Nonetheless, it is surprisingly robust to a number of challenging situations like motion blur (row 2), drastic change of appearance (rows 1, 3 and 4), poor illumination (row 6) and scale change (row 6). On the other hand, our method is sensitive to scenes with confusion (row 5), arguably because the model is never updated and thus the cross-correlation gives a high scores for all the windows that are similar to the first appearance of the target. All sequences come from the VOT-15 benchmark: *gymnastics1*, *car1*, *fish3*, *iceskater1*, *marching*, *singer1*. The snapshots have been taken at fixed frames (1, 50, 100 and 200) and the tracker is never re-initialized.

Table 3. Effects of using increasing portions of the ImageNet Video dataset on tracker's performance.

Dataset (%)	# Videos	# Objects	Accuracy	# Failures	Expected avg. overlap
2	88	60 k	0.484	183	0.168
4	177	110 k	0.501	160	0.192
8	353	190 k	0.484	142	0.193
16	707	330 k	0.522	132	0.219
32	1413	650 k	0.521	117	0.234
100	4417	2 m	**0.524**	**87**	**0.274**

4.5   Dataset Size

Table 3 illustrates how the size of the dataset used to train the Siamese network greatly influences the performance. The expected average overlap (measured on VOT-15) steadily improves from 0.168 to 0.274 when increasing the size of the dataset from 5 % to 100 %. This finding suggests that using a larger video dataset could increase the performance even further. In fact, even if 2 million supervised bounding boxes might seem a huge number, it should not be forgotten that they still belong to a relatively moderate number of videos, at least compared to the amount of data normally used to train conv-nets.

5   Conclusion

In this work, we depart from the traditional online learning methodology employed in tracking, and show an alternative approach that focuses on learning strong embeddings in an offline phase. Differently from their use in classification settings, we demonstrate that for tracking applications Siamese fully-convolutional deep networks have the ability to use the available data more efficiently. This is reflected both at test-time, by performing efficient spatial searches, but also at training-time, where every sub-window effectively represents a useful sample with little extra cost. The experiments show that deep embeddings provide a naturally rich source of features for online trackers, and enable simplistic test-time strategies to perform well. We believe that this approach is complementary to more sophisticated online tracking methodologies, and expect future work to explore this relationship more thoroughly.

References

1. Smeulders, A.W.M., Chu, D.M., Cucchiara, R., Calderara, S., Dehghan, A., Shah, M.: Visual tracking: an experimental survey. PAMI **36**(7), 1442–1468 (2014)
2. Kalal, Z., Mikolajczyk, K., Matas, J.: Tracking-learning-detection. PAMI **34**(7), 1409–1422 (2012)

3. Hare, S., Saffari, A., Torr, P.H.S.: Struck: Structured output tracking with kernels. In: ICCV 2011. IEEE (2011)

4. Henriques, J.F., Caseiro, R., Martins, P., Batista, J.: High-speed tracking with kernelized correlation filters. PAMI **37**(3), 583–596 (2015)

5. Ma, C., Huang, J.B., Yang, X., Yang, M.H.: Hierarchical convolutional features for visual tracking. In: ICCV (2015)

6. Danelljan, M., Hager, G., Khan, F., Felsberg, M.: Convolutional features for correlation filter based visual tracking. In: ICCV 2015 Workshop, pp. 58–66 (2015)

7. Wang, N., Li, S., Gupta, A., Yeung, D.Y.: Transferring rich feature hierarchies for robust visual tracking. arXiv CoRR (2015)

8. Wang, L., Ouyang, W., Wang, X., Lu, H.: Visual tracking with fully convolutional networks. In: ICCV (2015)

9. Nam, H., Han, B.: Learning multi-domain convolutional neural networks for visual tracking. arXiv CoRR (2015)

10. Russakovsky, O., Deng, J., Su, H., Krause, J., Satheesh, S., Ma, S., Huang, Z., Karpathy, A., Khosla, A., Bernstein, M., Berg, A.C., Fei-Fei, L.: ImageNet large scale visual recognition challenge. IJCV **115**(3), 211–252 (2015)

11. Wu, Y., Lim, J., Yang, M.H.: Online object tracking: a benchmark. In: CVPR 2013 (2013)

12. Kristan, M., Matas, J., Leonardis, A., Felsberg, M., Cehovin, L., Fernandez, G., Vojir, T., Hager, G., Nebehay, G., Pflugfelder, R.: The visual object tracking VOT2015 challenge results. In: ICCV 2015 Workshop, pp. 1–23 (2015)

13. Razavian, A., Azizpour, H., Sullivan, J., Carlsson, S.: CNN features off-the-shelf: An astounding baseline for recognition. In: CVPR 2014 Workshop (2014)

14. Parkhi, O.M., Vedaldi, A., Zisserman, A.: Deep face recognition. In: BMVC 2015 (2015)

15. Dosovitskiy, A., Fischer, P., Ilg, E., Hausser, P., Hazirbas, C., Golkov, V., van der Smagt, P., Cremers, D., Brox, T.: FlowNet: Learning optical flow with convolutional networks. In: ICCV 2015 (2015)

16. Krizhevsky, A., Sutskever, I., Hinton, G.E.: Imagenet classification with deep convolutional neural networks. In: NIPS 2012 (2012)

17. Bromley, J., Bentz, J.W., Bottou, L., Guyon, I., LeCun, Y., Moore, C., Säckinger, E., Shah, R.: Signature verification using a "Siamese" time delay neural network. Int. J. Pattern Recogn. Artif. Intell. (1993)

18. Taigman, Y., Yang, M., Ranzato, M., Wolf, L.: DeepFace: closing the gap to human-level performance in face verification. CVPR **2014**, 1701–1708 (2014)

19. Zagoruyko, S., Komodakis, N.: Learning to compare image patches via convolutional neural networks. In: CVPR 2015 (2015)

20. Schroff, F., Kalenichenko, D., Philbin, J.: FaceNet: a unified embedding for face recognition and clustering. In: CVPR 2015, pp. 815–823 (2015)

21. Simo-Serra, E., Trulls, E., Ferraz, L., Kokkinos, I., Fua, P., Moreno-Noguer, F.: Discriminative learning of deep convolutional feature point descriptors. ICCV **2015**, 118–126 (2015)

22. Koch, G., Zemel, R., Salakhutdinov, R.: Siamese neural networks for one-shot image recognition. In: ICML 2015 Deep Learning Workshop (2015)

23. Luo, W., Schwing, A.G., Urtasun, R.: Efficient deep learning for stereo matching. In: CVPR 2016, pp. 5695–5703 (2016)

24. Ioffe, S., Szegedy, C.: Batch normalization: accelerating deep network training by reducing internal covariate shift. In: ICML 2015, pp. 448–456 (2015)

25. Gan, Q., Guo, Q., Zhang, Z., Cho, K.: First step toward model-free, anonymous object tracking with recurrent neural networks. arXiv CoRR (2015)

26. Kahou, S.E., Michalski, V., Memisevic, R.: RATM: Recurrent Attentive Tracking Model. arXiv CoRR (2015)
27. Denil, M., Bazzani, L., Larochelle, H., de Freitas, N.: Learning where to attend with deep architectures for image tracking. Neural Computation (2012)
28. Held, D., Thrun, S., Savarese, S.: Learning to track at 100 FPS with deep regression networks. arXiv CoRR (2016)
29. Chen, K., Tao, W.: Once for all: a two-flow convolutional neural network for visual tracking. arXiv CoRR (2016)
30. Tao, R., Gavves, E., Smeulders, A.W.M.: Siamese instance search for tracking. arXiv CoRR (2016)
31. Vedaldi, A., Lenc, K.: MatConvNet – Convolutional Neural Networks for MATLAB (2015)
32. He, K., Zhang, X., Ren, S., Sun, J.: Delving deep into rectifiers: surpassing human-level performance on ImageNet classification. In: ICCV 2015 (2015)
33. Bertinetto, L., Valmadre, J., Golodetz, S., Miksik, O., Torr, P.H.S.: Staple: Complementary learners for real-time tracking. In: CVPR 2016 (2016)
34. Ma, C., Yang, X., Zhang, C., Yang, M.H.: Long-term correlation tracking. In: CVPR 2015 (2015)
35. Zhu, G., Wang, J., Wu, Y., Lu, H.: Collaborative correlation tracking. In: BMVC 2015 (2015)
36. Choi, J., Jin Chang, H., Jeong, J., Demiris, Y., Young Choi, J.: Visual tracking using attention-modulated disintegration and integration. In: CVPR 2016 (2016)
37. Ning, J., Yang, J., Jiang, S., Zhang, L., Yang, M.H.: Object tracking via dual linear structured SVM and explicit feature map. In: CVPR 2016 (2016)
38. Danelljan, M., Häger, G., Khan, F., Felsberg, M.: Accurate scale estimation for robust visual tracking. In: BMVC 2014 (2014)
39. Huang12, D., Luo, L., Wen12, M., Chen12, Z., Zhang12, C.: Enable scale and aspect ratio adaptability in visual tracking with detection proposals
40. Liris, F.: The visual object tracking vot2014 challenge results (2014)
41. Zhu, G., Porikli, F., Li, H.: Tracking randomly moving objects on edge box proposals. arXiv CoRR (2015)
42. Danelljan, M., Hager, G., Shahbaz Khan, F., Felsberg, M.: Learning spatially regularized correlation filters for visual tracking. In: ICCV 2015, pp. 4310–4318 (2015)
43. Hua, Y., Alahari, K., Schmid, C.: Online object tracking with proposal selection. ICCV **2015**, 3092–3100 (2015)
44. Wang, N., Yeung, D.Y.: Ensemble-based tracking: aggregating crowdsourced structured time series data. ICML **2014**, 1107–1115 (2014)
45. Li, Y., Zhu, J.: A scale adaptive kernel correlation filter tracker with feature integration. In: ECCV 2014 Workshops (2014)
46. Li, A., Lin, M., Wu, Y., Yang, M.H., Yan, S.: NUS-PRO: a new visual tracking challenge. PAMI **38**(2), 335–349 (2016)
47. Possegger, H., Mauthner, T., Bischof, H.: In defense of color-based model-free tracking. In: CVPR 2015 (2015)

W23 - Computer Vision for Audio–Visual Media

Speech-Driven Facial Animation Using Manifold Relevance Determination

Samia Dawood[1]([⊠]), Yulia Hicks[1]([⊠]), and David Marshall[2]([⊠])

[1] Cardiff School of Engineering, Cardiff, Wales
{AlbasriSD,HicksYA}@cardiff.ac.uk
[2] Cardiff School of Computer Science and Informatics, Cardiff, Wales
MarshallAD@cardiff.ac.uk

Abstract. In this paper, a new approach to visual speech synthesis using a joint probabilistic model is introduced, namely the Gaussian process latent variable model trimmed with manifold relevance determination model, which explicitly models coarticulation. One talking head dataset is processed (LIPS dataset) by extracting visual and audio features from the sequences. The model can capture the structure of data with extremely high dimensionality. Distinguishable visual features can be inferred directly from the trained model by sampling from the discovered latent points. Statistical evaluation of inferred visual features against ground truth data is obtained and compared with the current state-of-the-art visual speech synthesis approach. The quantitative results demonstrate that the proposed approach outperforms the state-of-the-art technique.

1 Introduction

Visual speech synthesis involves generating synthetic talking heads uttering human speech such that the facial movements and expressions synchronise with the speech. In the last several decades, the rise in popularity of multimedia technologies has led to increased interest in facial animation. Some applications of facial animation techniques include film and television post-production, computer games, surgical planning, education and human-computer interaction (HCI). Parke's [24] pioneering work was the first to build a three-dimensional (3D) geometric model of a human face using a polygon mesh. Facial animation can also be achieved using muscle-based facial modelling. A physically based 3D facial model generated from anatomical models was proposed in [37], this provides high accuracy for facial expression animation. Another pioneering work is the Video Rewrite system [3]. In this work, the speech and video were modelled together by breaking down the recorded video corpus into a group of smaller audio-visual basis units, where each of the units is a triphone segment. To allow an easy mapping from auditory features to visual features, many two-dimensional (2D) visual speech facial animation techniques parameterise the original audio-visual speech. For example, [4,36] used principal component analysis (PCA), while [7,11,17] used active appearance models (AAMs).

© Springer International Publishing Switzerland 2016
G. Hua and H. Jégou (Eds.): ECCV 2016 Workshops, Part II, LNCS 9914, pp. 869–882, 2016.
DOI: 10.1007/978-3-319-48881-3_57

The smallest segment of speech is called the phoneme, and the corresponding visual segment is the viseme. For British English, the British English Pronunciation Dictionary (BEEP) contain 44 phonemes [12]. According to the MPEG-4 standard [29], these phonemes can be grouped into 14 visemes. The phenomenon of coarticulation refers to the way in which the realisation of a speech sound is influenced by its preceding (backward coarticulation) and upcoming segments (forward coarticulation) [19]. Backward coarticulation implies that a speech gesture continues after uttering a particular speech segment, whereas the other gestures needed to create this sound are already completed. In contrast, forward coarticulation occurs when the articulation of a sound unit is affected by other units that are not yet realised.

We focus on data-driven methods using machine learning approaches, as it is necessary to take context into account to model coarticulation. Learning the mapping from audio to visual features have been proposed in some approaches, for instance, [5] used Gaussian-mixture models, [1,23] used an artificial neural network and [18] used regression techniques. However, Deena [10] claimed that the regression approaches, support vector machines and artificial neural networks fail to achieve suitable results because the mapping between speech and facial motion is many-to-one and modelling coarticulation involves taking context into account. Effective approaches that have successfully modelled coarticulation are the hidden Markov models used by [2], switching linear dynamical systems used by [17] and switching shared Gaussian process (GP) dynamical models [11].

Several methods that combine multiple observations because they are tailored to the non-linearities in audio-visual mapping have been recently described in the literature. The most successful approaches are generative models formulated as Gaussian process latent variable models (GPLVMs) [16,28]. However, in these models, a single latent space is assumed to be capable of representing each modality. This implies that the modalities can be fully aligned. The factorised latent variables proposed by [15] solved this problem. In this method, each observation is associated with a private space and a shared space, with the variance that cannot be aligned represented by a private space. Titsias and Lawrence [34] introduced the Bayesian GPLVM, where the latent variables are approximately marginalised out in a variational manner. Following this, Damianou et al. [9] developed this approach by introducing a variational Gaussian process dynamical system (VGPDS). They extended this work and then introduced automatic relevance determination (ARD) priors [25]; this approach is called manifold relevance determination (MRD) or shared variational Gaussian process latent variable model (SVGPLVM).

In our work, we have developed a new framework –a shared variational GPLVM– to learn a factorised latent space representation of audio and visual features. In this approach, a smooth continuous representation is proposed, where a latent point may be more important to the shared space than the private space. We used an MRD framework [8] which is a fully Bayesian latent variable model allowing estimation of both the structure and the dimensionality of the latent space to be done automatically. This approach is used to learn visual speech

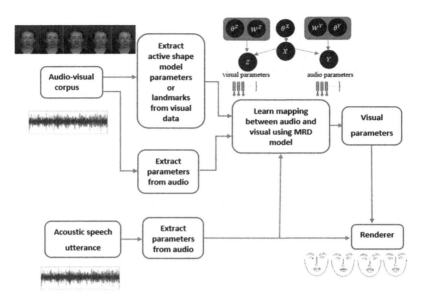

Fig. 1. An overview of the proposed approach for visual speech synthesis. Training is marked by the blue arrows, and synthesis is marked by the orange arrows. (Color figure online)

mapping, and the results are compared with other state-of-the-art techniques. Figure 1 illustrates an overview of our proposed approach. In the next section, a background on the GPLVM is presented. We then describe our new method.

2   Background

In this section, we provide some background on the GPLVM.

2.1   The GPLVM

The GPLVM [21] is an algorithm for dimensionality reduction using GPs. It is a generative model, where observation space $y_n \in \mathbb{R}^D$ is assumed to be generated from a latent space $x_n \in \mathbb{R}^q$ through a mapping f that is corrupted by noise:

$$y_n = f(x_n) + \epsilon \tag{1}$$

where $\epsilon \sim \mathcal{N}(0, \beta^{-1}I)$.

By placing a zero mean GP prior on the mapping f and marginalising it, the likelihood $P(Y|X, \theta)$ is obtained, which is a product of D GPs, while θ represents the hyper parameters of the covariance function

$$P(Y|X, \theta) = \prod_{i=1}^{D} \frac{1}{(2\pi)^{\frac{N}{2}} |\boldsymbol{K}|^{\frac{1}{2}}} exp(-\frac{1}{2} y_{:,i}^T \boldsymbol{K}^{-1} y_{:,i}) \tag{2}$$

where $y_{:,i}$ is the ith column from the data matrix, Y.

Maximising the marginal likelihood in Eq. (2) with respect to both the latent points X and the hyper-parameters θ of the covariance function results in the latent space representation of the GPLVM:

$$\left\{\widehat{X}, \widehat{\theta}\right\} = argmax_{X,\theta} P\left(Y|X,\theta\right) \tag{3}$$

The Back-Constrained GPLVM. A smooth mapping from the latent space X to the data space Y is specified using a smooth covariance function, which means that points close in the latent space will be close in the data space. However, it does not ensure the opposite case. Therefore, an extension to the GPLVM is proposed by using an inverse parametric mapping that maps points from the observation space to the latent space. This constrains points that are close in the data space to be close in the latent space [16]:

$$x_i = g\left(y_i, \boldsymbol{W}\right) \tag{4}$$

where $\boldsymbol{W}$ is the back-constraint kernel function. This is typically computed with a radial basis function (RBF) network or multi-layer perception (MLP). The maximisation in Eq. 3 is then changed from optimisation with respect to the latent points X to optimisation the parameters of the back-constraining mapping $\boldsymbol{W}$:

$$\left\{\widehat{\boldsymbol{W}}, \widehat{\theta}\right\} = argmax_{\boldsymbol{W},\theta} P\left(Y|\boldsymbol{W},\theta\right) \tag{5}$$

Dynamics. An extension of the GPLVM was proposed by Wang [35]; this produces a latent space that preserves sequential relationships between points on the data variables, as well as on the latent variables. This is done by specifying a predictive function over the sequence in latent space, x_t:

$$x_t = h(x_{t-1}) + \epsilon_{dyn} \tag{6}$$

where $\epsilon_{dyn} \sim \mathcal{N}(0, \sigma_{dyn}^{-1} I)$. A GP prior can then be placed over the function $h(x)$, and marginalising this mapping results in a new objective function. By optimising this objective function, the latent points that preserve temporal relationships in the data are obtained. The new objective function is given by:

$$P\left\{\widehat{X}, \widehat{\theta}_Y, \widehat{\theta}_{dyn}\right\} = argmax_{X,\theta_Y,\theta_{dyn}} P\left(Y|X,\theta_Y\right) P\left(X|\theta_{dyn}\right) \tag{7}$$

where θ_{dyn} being the hyper-parameters of the dynamics kernel.

To construct a shared latent structure between two views, $Y \in \mathbb{R}^{N \times D_Y}$ and $Z \in \mathbb{R}^{N \times D_Z}$ with a shared latent space $X \in \mathbb{R}^{N \times Q}$, the GPLVM is modified to learn separate sets of GPs for each of the different observation spaces from a shared latent space. The latent space is given by maximising the joint likelihood of the two observation spaces:

$$P\left(Y, Z|X, \theta_s\right) = P\left(Y|X, \theta_Y\right) P\left(Z|X, \theta_Z\right) \tag{8}$$

where $\theta_s = \{\theta_Y, \theta_Z\}$ is two different sets of hyper-parameters.

In [16], the shared GPLVM (SGPLVM) is used to learn a mapping between silhouette and pose features; the pose ambiguities from the silhouette observations are resolved by considering sequential data. This is done by learning a dynamical model over the latent space to disambiguate ambiguous silhouettes. Deena et al. [10] used the same SGPLVM approach to model coarticulation. First, placing a back constraint with respect to auditory features ensures a smooth mapping from the latent space to the observation space. Second, a dynamical model is placed on the latent space to respect the data's dynamics in the training and inference phases. Canonical correlation analysis (CCA) coupled with linear regression was used in [32] to model the relationship between auditory and visual features; it was also used to predict visual features from the auditory features.

An extension of CCA proposed in [15], called the non-consolidating components analysis (NCCA) model, is used to address the ambiguities in a human motion dataset by decomposing the latent space into subspaces whereby a private latent space for each of the observation spaces is learned in addition to the shared latent space. The NCCA model encodes the variance in the data separately, so that it does not influence the inference procedure; this represents the advantage of using this model compared to other conditional models. An NCCA model is also used for modelling and mapping human facial expression space, represented by facial landmarks, to a robot actuator space [14]. The ambiguity in this case relates to robot poses, with multiple robot poses that are most likely to be the solution to a facial expression in the facial expression space. Figure 2 shows various types of graphical GPLVMs. Recently, Damianou et al. [8] used an MRD framework to predict a 3D human pose from a silhouette in an ambiguous setting. To perform disambiguation, they include latent space priors that incorporate the dynamic nature of the data.

3   Our Proposed Model

Deena [12] introduced a framework that jointly models auditory and visual features using a shared latent points. To cater for the various dynamics involved in speech, they augmented the model with switching states by training a variable-length Markov model (VLMM) [26] on phonetic labels. In this paper, we present a new generative method for speech-driven facial animation using a joint probabilistic model of audio and visual features, which explicitly models coarticulation. The proposed framework to jointly model speech and visual features is based on Bayesian techniques. The latent variable is factorised to represent private and shared information from audio and visual features. To obtain a smooth, continuous representation, a relaxation of the structural factorisation of the model is introduced, where a latent variable might be more important to the shared space than the private space. In contrast to previous methods, using this model allows the dimensionality of the latent space to be estimated automatically. MRD is a powerful and flexible approach to capture structure under very high dimensional spaces [8], it models raw images with many thousands of pixels. In addition, this method has been applied successfully in several multiple-views tasks, such as human pose prediction in an ambiguous setting. The disambiguation is performed by including latent point priors, which combine the dynamic nature of the data. In this section, we describe the model and the variational approximation. We also illustrate the model's ability to re-synthesis audio from visual in Sect. 5.

Two observation spaces of a dataset, $Y \in \mathbb{R}^{N \times D_Y}$ and $Z \in \mathbb{R}^{N \times D_Z}$, are assumed to be generated from a single latent point $X \in \mathbb{R}^{N \times Q}$ through the nonlinear mappings $(f_1^Y, ..., f_{D_Y}^Y)$ and $(f_1^Z, ..., f_{D_Z}^Z)$ $(Q < D)$, giving a low-dimensional representation of the data. The assumption is that the observation is generated from a low-dimensional manifold and corrupted with Gaussian distributed observation noise $\epsilon^{\{Y,Z\}} \sim \mathcal{N}(0, \sigma_\epsilon^{\{Y,Z\}} I)$:

$$y_{nd} = f_d^Y(\mathbf{x}_n) + \epsilon_{nd}^Y \tag{9}$$
$$z_{nd} = f_d^Z(\mathbf{x}_n) + \epsilon_{nd}^Z \tag{10}$$

where nd represents the dimension d of point n. This leads to the joint likelihood under the model, $P(Y, Z|X, \theta)$, where $\theta = \{\theta^Y, \theta^Z\}$, representing two different sets of hyper-parameters of the mapping functions and the noise variances σ_ϵ^Y and σ_ϵ^Z. A GP prior distribution is proposed to place over the mappings [20]; the resulting models are known as Gaussian process latent variable models. In the GPLVM approach, each generative mapping is modeled as a product of D separate GPs parameterised by a covariance function $k^{\{Y,Z\}}$ evaluated over the latent points X:

$$p(F^Y|X, \theta^Y) = \prod_{d=1}^{D_Y} \mathcal{N}(\mathbf{f}_d^Y|0, K^Y) \tag{11}$$

where $F^Y = (f_1^Y, ..., f_{D_Y}^Y)$ with $f_{nd}^Y = f_d^Y(\mathbf{x}_n)$, and the same definitions for F^Z. The nonlinear mapping can be marginalised out analytically, obtaining a joint likelihood:

$$P(Y, Z|X, \theta) = \prod_{\mathcal{K}=\{Y,Z\}} \int P(\mathcal{K}|F^{\mathcal{K}}) P(F^{\mathcal{K}}|X, \theta^{\mathcal{K}}) dF^{\mathcal{K}} \tag{12}$$

To obtain a fully Bayesian treatment, integration over the latent representation X is required. This is intractable, because X appears non-linearly in the inverse of the covariance matrices $\{K^Y, K^Z\}$ of the GP priors over the mapping $\{f^Y, f^Z\}$. By variationally marginalising out X, an approximated Bayesian training and synthesis procedure can be obtained. Afterward, the ARD priors are introduced, such that each observation is allowed to estimate a separate vector of ARD parameters. In this case, the observations are allowed to set the private and shared latent subspaces relevant to them.

3.1 Manifold Relevance Determination (MRD)

Damianou [8] tried to improve factorised latent spaces so that the variance shared (i.e. correlated) between different data spaces can be aligned and disjointed from variance that is private (i.e. independent). In this model, the variance contained in the data space does not need to be governed by geometrically orthogonal subspace, as supposed in [27]. The manifold model has the ability to treat nonlinear mappings within a Bayesian approach. In particular, the latent functions f_d^y that are selected to be separate draws with a zero-mean GP, and ARD covariance function, which is given by:

$$k^Y(\mathbf{x}_i, \mathbf{x}_j) = \left(\sigma_{ard}^Y\right)^2 e^{-\frac{1}{2}\sum_{q=1}^{Q} \mathbf{w}_q^Y (x_{i,q} - x_{i,q})^2} \tag{13}$$

and analogously for f^Z. A common latent space can be learned; however, the two groups of ARD weights $\mathbf{w}^Y = \left\{w_q^Y\right\}_{q=1}^Q$ and $\mathbf{w}^Z = \left\{w_q^Z\right\}_{q=1}^Q$ are allowed to automatically infer the responsibility of every latent dimension to produce points in the Y and Z spaces, respectively. After that, the segmentation of the latent points $X = \left\{X^Y X^s X^Z\right\}$ can be recovered, where X^Y and X^Z are private spaces, $X^s \in \mathbb{R}^{N \times Q_s}$ is a shared space defined by a group of dimensions $q \in [1, ..., Q]$ and $\mathbf{w}_q^Y, \mathbf{w}_q^Z > \delta$ with δ is a number near to zero, $Q_s \leq Q$. If the two sets of weights together are greater than δ and they are different, this allows for softly shared latent points, providing the model with more flexibility. The two subspaces X^Y and X^Z are inferred automatically:

$$X^Y = \{\mathbf{x}_q\}_{q=1}^{Q_Y} \tag{14}$$

$$X^Z = \{\mathbf{x}_q\}_{q=1}^{Q_Z} \tag{15}$$

where Q_Y and Q_Z are the dimensionality of X^Y and X^Z respectively, $\mathbf{x}_q \in X, w_q^Y > \delta, w_q^Z < \delta$. Figure 3 shows the graphical model of MRD. In this figure, the ARD weights $\mathbf{w}^{\{Y,Z\}}$ are separated from the full set of model hyperparameters $\boldsymbol{\theta}^{\{Y,Z\}} = \left\{\sigma_\in^{\{Y,Z\}}, \sigma_{ard}^{\{Y,Z\}}, \boldsymbol{W}^{\{Y,Z\}}\right\}$ to describe the utilisation of ARD covariance functions.

4   Data and Pre-processing

We use a phonetically balanced LIPS corpus [31] consisting of 278 high-quality sequences featuring a female British subject speaking sentences from the Messiah corpus [30]. The sentences were spoken in a neutral speaking style (no expression). The original LIPS corpus consists of images of 50 Hz video stream with 576×720 pixels. Figure 4 shows video frames from the LIPS corpus. In addition, high-quality audio in the form of WAV files and the phonetic annotation for each frame have been made available. Using the BEEP phonetic dictionary, the LIPS dataset has been phonetically aligned.

4.1   Audio Proccessing

Deena et al. [13] performed experiments to determine which speech parameterisation technique out of Linear Predictive Coding (LPC), line spectral frequencies (LSF), Mel-frequency cepstral coefficien (MFCC) and relative spectral-perceptual linear prediction (RASTA-PLP) is better for predicting visual features. They found that RASTA-PLP processed at 25 Hz is a better predictor of

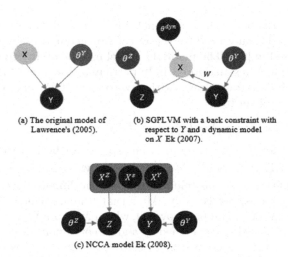

(a) The original model of
Lawrence's (2005).

(b) SGPLVM with a back constraint with
respect to Y and a dynamic model
on X Ek (2007).

(c) NCCA model Ek (2008).

Fig. 2. The structure of different GPLVM models. (a) Lawrence's (2005) original model the observed data Y represented using a single latent variable X. (b) The SGPLVM with a dynamic model on the latent points and with a back constraint with respect to the observation Y proposed by [16]. (c) Private latent spaces introduced by [15] to explain variance specific to one of the observations.

visual features for LIPS, whilst MFCC coefficient downsampled using polyphase quadrature filtering gives the best results for the DEMNOW dataset [17]. In this work, we used RASTA-PLP features, to parameterise speech to represent the acoustic variability within and between the different phonemes. To satisfy the requirement of having a window where the speech signal is stationary, a window size of 25 ms and a hop size of 10 ms is typically used, resulting in an audio processing frequency of 100 Hz. The speech parameters need to be downsampled to match the visual processing rate of 25 fps used for LIPS, so we use an auditory window of 50 ms and a hop window of 40 ms to obtain speech features at 25 Hz. In addition, we use 20 parameters to represent the RASTA-PLP features.

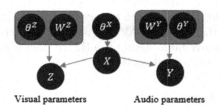

Visual parameters   Audio parameters

Fig. 3. Graphical model of the MRD method.

4.2   Visual Processing

We use an active shape model (ASM) [6] for visual parameterisation, because such models capture the statistical variation in shape and build a generative model to obtain novel shapes. A training set of annotated prototype face images is required. We use 97 landmark points around the face, eyebrows, lips and nose in each of the prototype images. An ASM has been built on the shapes in several steps. First, the shape vectors have been normalised by removing rotations and translations, and then aligned with respect to the mean shape using Procrustes analysis. Following this, PCA has been applied to the normalised shape vectors. After training the PCA model and retaining 95 % of the variance of the shape, ASM parameters can be obtained from novel shapes by projecting the shape vectors to the corresponding retained eigenvectors.

4.3   Training

MRD is learned between Y, represented by the RASTA-PLP feature vector, and Z, represented by the ASM feature vector. The obtained latent space is a nonlinear embedding of both audio and visual features that can generate the two spaces Y and Z. A probabilistic PCA (PPCA) is used as an initialisation of the latent space variational means; this is done by performing PPCA on each dataset separately and then concatenating the two low dimensional representations to initialise X. We perform experiments to compare this method with Deena's SGPLVM approach in Sect. 5.

4.4   Inference

Given a trained model that jointly represents the audio features Y and the ASM parameters Z with a single but factorised input space X, we wish to infer a new set of sequence $Z^* \in \mathbb{R}^{N^* \times D_Z}$ given a set of test points $Y^* \in \mathbb{R}^{N^* \times D_Y}$. The inference procedure is done in three steps; first, the sequence of latent points $X^* \in \mathbb{R}^{N^* \times Q}$ that is most likely to have inferred Y^* is predicted. To infer novel outputs, the recovered information has to propagate. An approximation to the posterior $p(X^*|Y^*, Y)$, which has the same form as for the standard Bayesian GPLVM is used [34]. In order to find a variational distribution $q(X, X^*)$, the variational lower bound on the marginal likelihood $p(Y, Y^*)$ is optimized. Second, the training latent points X_{NN} that are nearest to X^* in the shared latent representation are found. Finally, the output sequence Z from the likelihood $p(Z|X_{NN})$ is determined.

4.5   Computational Complexity

GPLVM training is intractable for large data points and has a time complexity scales and storage of $O\left(N^3\right)$ and $O\left(N^2\right)$ respectively, where N is the number of training variables. Different sparsification approaches have been proposed [22]; however, when the number of training examples exceeds a few thousands, the

Fig. 4. Video frames from the LIPS dataset.

optimisation of the GPLVM likelihood becomes intractable. To overcome this limitation, several approximation approaches have been described in the literature to construct a sparsification dependent on a small set of M inducing points to reduce the typical time complexity from $O\left(N^3\right)$ to $O\left(NM^2\right)$ [33], where N and M are the total numbers of training and inducing variables, respectively. In the MRD model [8], the datasets with very large numbers of features can be modelled because the objective function involves the matrices Y and Z in expressions of the form YY^T and ZZ^T, which illustrates that the model does not rely on the number of features $\{D_Y, D_Z\}$ in the datasets.

5   Results

We trained an MRD model on 50 training sequences, totaling 5332 frames, by taking Y as the RASTA-PLP features and Z as the ASM features; the obtained latent space was represented by six dimensions. In our experiment, we set the inducing points to 100. We then used a validation set of 10 sequences totalling 1234 frames to predict visual parameters from audio parameters. Each visual parameter was represented by a 194-dimensional vector, and each audio feature was represented by a 20-dimensional vector. As illustrated in the inference Subsect. 4.4, given test point y^*, one of the N^* audio tests, the model optimised a variational distribution and found a sequence of K candidate initial training data $\left(x_{NN}^{(1)}, ..., x_{NN}^{(K)}\right)$; these were ordered according to their similarity to x^*, and only the shared dimensions were taken into account. Based on these initial latent points, a sorted series of K novel visual features $(z^1, ..., z^K)$ were found. In assessing the results of this method, we used the average mean squared error (AMSE) between test feature vectors and ground truth, as this is the most commonly used error for multivariate data [13]: this is shown in Eq. 16.

$$AMSE = \frac{1}{K * I} \sum_{k=1}^{K} \sum_{i=1}^{I} (z_{k,i} - \widehat{z}_{k,i})^2 \qquad (16)$$

The AMSE error obtained using the MRD approach for the visual features represented by ASM features was equal to 0.0209, while it was equal to 2.5267×10^{-4} for the representation of landmark visual features. In both experiments, we performed PPCA on each dataset separately and then concatenated the two low-dimensional representations to initialise X. The results of the MRD were compared against the SGPLVM method [10]. Table 1 shows the AMSE for our approach using MRD and Deena's method [10]. The table demonstrates that there was a distinction between the errors obtained using MRD and those using Deena's approach (SGPLVM). In addition, Fig. 5 shows the shape frames obtained from the ground truth, MRD and SGPLVM. The corresponding audio contained a sentence from the LIPS dataset. We found that the shape uttering /b/ from the MRD method showed proper lip synchronisation with the audio and appeared to be the best, whilst SGPLVM gave lip synchronisation with a few jerks in the animation. It can be seen that the difference between the quality of mouth articulation between real and MRD synthetic videos was non-significant. In addition, we observe smooth lip movements compared with the ground truth and SGPLVM methods. Figure 6 shows the results obtained across the ten runs of the experiment. The results show a noteworthy difference between the errors obtained from the MRD and Deena's method. Generally, the errors for MRD are distinctly lower than those for SGPLVM, mostly due to a softly shared latent space.

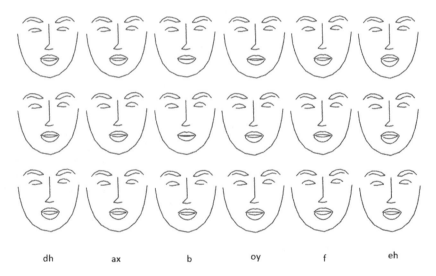

Fig. 5. Example frames of the shapes obtained from the LIPS synthesis results using ground truth (top row), MRD (middle row) and SGPLVM (bottom row). The phonemes correspond to seven different visemes of the words ("the", "boy", "fair") from the test audio sentence (The boy a few yards ahead is the only fair winner).

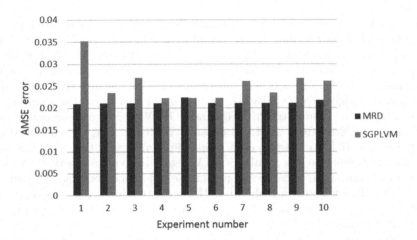

Fig. 6. AMSE errors obtained between ground truth ASM feature vectors and 1- MRD 2- SGPLVM.

Table 1. Quantitative evaluation.

Method	Audio representation	Visual representation	Latent space initialisation method	AMSE
MRD	Continuous	Landmarks	PPCA (separate)	2.5267×10^{-4}
MRD	Continuous	ASM	PPCA (separate)	0.0209
SGPLVM	Continuous	ASM	PPCA (separate)	0.0353

6   Conclusions

In this article, we described a new factorised latent variable model for synthesising visual speech from auditory signals. SVGPLVM was used to represent audio and visual data as a set of factorised latent spaces. A compact and intuitive representation of audio-visual data was learned, represented by the synthesis of novel shapes by sampling from the latent space in a structured manner. We found that using our approach to modelling audio and visual features decreased the AMSE error of the resulting animation compared to the SGPLVM approach. In addition, our approach to the synthesis of facial animation using MRD produced visuals with the correct facial dynamics and proper synchronisation with the auditory signal. In future work, we will use AAM as a representation of visual features. Another possible direction for future work involves extending this method by augmenting the model with switching states represented by the phonetic context to model backward and forward coarticulation. Moreover, experiments will be performed to investigate the degree of correlation between several acoustic subspaces and the corresponding AAM space using MRD.

References

1. Anderson, J.A.: An introduction to neural networks. MIT press, Cambridge (1995)
2. Brand, M.: Voice puppetry. In: Proceedings of the 26th Annual Conference on Computer Graphics and Interactive Techniques, pp. 21–28. ACM Press/Addison-Wesley Publishing Co. (1999)
3. Bregler, C., Covell, M., Slaney, M.: Video rewrite: driving visual speech with audio. In: Proceedings of the 24th Annual Conference on Computer Graphics and Interactive Techniques, pp. 353–360. ACM Press/Addison-Wesley Publishing Co. (1997)
4. Brooke, N.M., Scott, S.D.: Two-and three-dimensional audio-visual speech synthesis. In: AVSP 1998 International Conference on Auditory-Visual Speech Processing (1998)
5. Chen, T.: Audiovisual speech processing. IEEE Signal Process. Mag. **18**(1), 9–21 (2001)
6. Cootes, T.F., Edwards, G.J., Taylor, C.J.: Active appearance models. IEEE Trans. Pattern Anal. Mach. Intell. **6**, 681–685 (2001)
7. Cosker, D., Marshall, D., Rosin, P., Hicks, Y.: Video realistic talking heads using hierarchical non-linear speech-appearance models. In: Mirage, France, 147 (2003)
8. Damianou, A., Ek, C., Titsias, M., Lawrence, N.: Manifold relevance determination. arXiv preprint arXiv:1206.4610 (2012)
9. Damianou, A., Titsias, M.K., Lawrence, N.D.: Variational Gaussian process dynamical systems. In: Advances in Neural Information Processing Systems, pp. 2510–2518 (2011)
10. Deena, S., Galata, A.: Speech-driven facial animation using a shared Gaussian process latent variable model. In: Bebis, G., et al. (eds.) ISVC 2009, Part I. LNCS, vol. 5875, pp. 89–100. Springer, Heidelberg (2009)
11. Deena, S., Hou, S., Galata, A.: Visual speech synthesis by modelling coarticulation dynamics using a non-parametric switching state-space model. In: International Conference on Multimodal Interfaces and the Workshop on Machine Learning for Multimodal Interaction, pp. 1–8. ACM (2010)
12. Deena, S., Hou, S., Galata, A.: Visual speech synthesis using a variable-order switching shared Gaussian process dynamical model. IEEE Trans. Multimedia **15**(8), 1755–1768 (2013)
13. Deena, S.P.: Visual speech synthesis by learning joint probabilistic models of audio and video (2012)
14. Ek, C.H., Jaeckel, P., Campbell, N., Lawrence, N.D., Melhuish, C.: Shared gaussian process latent variable models for handling ambiguous facial expressions. Am. Inst. Phys. Conf. Ser. **1107**, 147–153 (2009)
15. Ek, C.H., Rihan, J., Torr, P.H.S., Rogez, G., Lawrence, N.D.: Ambiguity modeling in latent spaces. In: Popescu-Belis, A., Stiefelhagen, R. (eds.) MLMI 2008. LNCS, vol. 5237, pp. 62–73. Springer, Heidelberg (2008). doi:10.1007/978-3-540-85853-9_6
16. Ek, C.H., Torr, P.H.S., Lawrence, N.D.: Gaussian process latent variable models for human pose estimation. In: Popescu-Belis, A., Renals, S., Bourlard, H. (eds.) MLMI 2007. LNCS, vol. 4892, pp. 132–143. Springer, Heidelberg (2008). doi:10.1007/978-3-540-78155-4_12
17. Englebienne, G.: Animating faces from speech. Ph.D. thesis, Citeseer (2008)
18. Hsieh, C.K., Chen, Y.C.: Partial linear regression for speech-driven talking head application. Signal Proces. Image Commun. **21**(1), 1–12 (2006)
19. Kent, R.D., Minifie, F.D.: Coarticulation in recent speech production models. J. Phonetics **5**(2), 115–133 (1977)

20. Lawrence, N.: Probabilistic non-linear principal component analysis with Gaussian process latent variable models. J. Mach. Learn. Res. **6**, 1783–1816 (2005)
21. Lawrence, N.D.: Gaussian process latent variable models for visualisation of high dimensional data. Adv. Neural Inf. Process. Syst. **16**(3), 329–336 (2004)
22. Lawrence, N.D.: Learning for larger datasets with the Gaussian process latent variable model. In: International Conference on Artificial Intelligence and Statistics, pp. 243–250 (2007)
23. Massaro, D.W., Beskow, J., Cohen, M.M., Fry, C.L., Rodgriguez, T.: Picture my voice: audio to visual speech synthesis using artificial neural networks. In: AVSP 1999-International Conference on Auditory-Visual Speech Processing (1999)
24. Parke, F.I.: A parametric model for human faces. Technical report, DTIC Document (1974)
25. Rasmussen, C.E.: Gaussian processes for machine learning (2006)
26. Ron, D., Singer, Y., Tishby, N.: The power of Amnesia: learning probabilistic automata with variable memory length. Mach. Learn. **25**(2–3), 117–149 (1996)
27. Salzmann, M., Ek, C.H., Urtasun, R., Darrell, T.: Factorized orthogonal latent spaces. In: International Conference on Artificial Intelligence and Statistics, pp. 701–708 (2010)
28. Shon, A., Grochow, K., Hertzmann, A., Rao, R.P.: Learning shared latent structure for image synthesis and robotic imitation. In: Advances in Neural Information Processing Systems, pp. 1233–1240 (2005)
29. Tekalp, A.M., Ostermann, J.: Face and 2-D mesh animation in MPEG-4. Signal Process. Image Commun. **15**(4), 387–421 (2000)
30. Theobald, B.J.: Visual speech synthesis using shape and appearance models. Ph.D. thesis, University of East Anglia (2003)
31. Theobald, B.J., Fagel, S., Bailly, G., Elisei, F.: Lips 2008: visual speech synthesis challenge. In: Interspeech, pp. 2310–2313 (2008)
32. Theobald, B.J., Wilkinson, N.: A real-time speech-driven talking head using active appearance models. In: AVSP, pp. 264–269 (2007)
33. Titsias, M.K.: Variational learning of inducing variables in sparse gaussian processes. In: International Conference on Artificial Intelligence and Statistics, pp. 567–574 (2009)
34. Titsias, M.K., Lawrence, N.D.: Bayesian Gaussian process latent variable model. In: International Conference on Artificial Intelligence and Statistics, pp. 844–851 (2010)
35. Wang, J., Hertzmann, A., Blei, D.M.: Gaussian process dynamical models. In: Advances in neural information processing systems, pp. 1441–1448 (2005)
36. Wang, L., Qian, X., Han, W., Soong, F.K.: Photo-real lips synthesis with trajectory-guided sample selection. In: SSW, pp. 217–222 (2010)
37. Zhang, Y., Prakash, E.C., Sung, E.: A new physical model with multilayer architecture for facial expression animation using dynamic adaptive mesh. IEEE Trans. Visual. Comput. Graphics **10**(3), 339–352 (2004)

GeThR-Net: A Generalized Temporally Hybrid Recurrent Neural Network for Multimodal Information Fusion

Ankit Gandhi[1]([✉]), Arjun Sharma[1], Arijit Biswas[2], and Om Deshmukh[1]

[1] Xerox Research Centre India, Bengaluru, India
ankit.g1290@gmail.com, arjunsharma.iitg@gmail.com, om.deshmukh@xerox.com
[2] Amazon Development Center India, Chennai, India
arijitbiswas87@gmail.com

Abstract. Data generated from real world events are usually temporal and contain multimodal information such as audio, visual, depth, sensor etc. which are required to be intelligently combined for classification tasks. In this paper, we propose a novel generalized deep neural network architecture where temporal streams from multiple modalities are combined. There are total M+1 (M is the number of modalities) components in the proposed network. The first component is a novel temporally hybrid Recurrent Neural Network (RNN) that exploits the complimentary nature of the multimodal temporal information by allowing the network to learn both modality specific temporal dynamics as well as the dynamics in a multimodal feature space. M additional components are added to the network which extract discriminative but non-temporal cues from each modality. Finally, the predictions from all of these components are linearly combined using a set of automatically learned weights. We perform exhaustive experiments on three different datasets spanning four modalities. The proposed network is relatively 3.5%, 5.7% and 2% better than the best performing temporal multimodal baseline for UCF-101, CCV and Multimodal Gesture datasets respectively.

1 Introduction

Humans typically perceive the world through multimodal sensory information [30] such as visual, audio, depth, etc. For example, when a person is running, we recognize the event by looking at how the body posture of the person is changing with time as well by listening to the periodic sound of his/her footsteps. Human brains can seamlessly process multimodal signals and accurately classify an event or an action. However, it is a challenging task for machines to exploit the complimentary nature and optimally combine multimodal information.

Recently, deep neural networks have been extensively used in computer vision, natural language processing and speech processing. LSTM [9], a Recurrent Neural Network (RNN) [35] architecture, has been extremely successful in

---

A. Gandhi and A. Sharma—Equally contributed.

© Springer International Publishing Switzerland 2016
G. Hua and H. Jégou (Eds.): ECCV 2016 Workshops, Part II, LNCS 9914, pp. 883–899, 2016.
DOI: 10.1007/978-3-319-48881-3_58

temporal modelling and classification tasks such as handwriting recognition [8], action recognition [2], image and video captioning [4,31,44] and speech recognition [6,7]. RNNs can also be used to model multimodal information. These methods fall under two broad categories: (a) Early-Fusion: modality specific features are combined to create a feature representation and fed into a LSTM network for classification. (b) Late-Fusion: each modality is modelled using individual LSTM networks and their predictions are combined for classification [40]. Since early-fusion techniques do not learn any modality specific temporal dynamics, they fail to capture the discriminative temporal cues present in each modality. On the other hand, late-fusion methods cannot extract the discriminative temporal cues which might be available in a multimodal feature representation. In this paper, we propose a novel generalized temporally hybrid Recurrent Neural Network architecture called GeThR-Net which models the temporal dynamics of individual modalities (late fusion) as well as the overall temporal dynamics in a multimodal feature space (early fusion).

GeThR-Net has one temporal and M (M is the total number of modalities) non-temporal components. The novel temporal component of GeThR-Net models the long-term temporal information in a multimodal signal whereas the non-temporal components take care of situations where explicit temporal modelling is difficult. The temporal component consists of three layers. The first layer models each modality using individual modality-specific LSTM networks. The second layer combines the hidden representations from these LSTMs to form a multimodal feature representations corresponding to each time step. In the final layer, one multimodal LSTM is trained on the multimodal features obtained from the second layer. The output from the final layer is fed into a softmax layer for category-wise confidence prediction. We observe that in many real world scenarios, the temporal modelling of individual or multimodal information is extremely hard due to the presence of noise or high intra-class temporal variation. We address this issue by introducing additional M components to GeThR-Net which model modality specific non-temporal cues by ignoring the temporal relationship across features extracted from different time-instants. The predictions corresponding to all $M+1$ components in the proposed network are combined using a weighted vector learned from the validation dataset. We note that GeThR-Net can be used with any kind of modality information without any restriction on the number of modalities.

The main contributions of this paper are:

– We propose a generalized deep neural network architecture called GeThR-Net that could intelligently combine multimodal temporal information from any kind and from any number of streams.
– Our objective is to propose a general framework that could work with modalities of any kind. We demonstrate the effectiveness and wide applicability of GeThR-Net by evaluation of classification performance on three different action and gesture classification tasks, UCF-101 [28], Multimodal Gesture [5] and Columbia Consumer videos [13]. Four different modalities such as audio, appearance, short-term motion and skeleton are considered in our experiments.

We find out that GeThR-Net is relatively 3.5 %, 5.7 % and 2 % better than the best temporal multimodal baseline for UCF-101, CCV and Multimodal Gesture datasets respectively.

The full pipeline of the proposed approach is shown in Fig. 1. We discuss the relevant prior work in Sect. 2 followed by the details of GeThR-Net in Sect. 3. The details of experimental results are provided in Sect. 4.

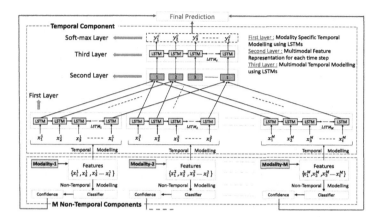

Fig. 1. The overall pipeline of the proposed approach GeThR-Net. The input to the system is a multimodal stream (e.g.: appearance, short-term motion, skeleton and/or audio for action/gesture classification tasks) and output is the class label. The proposed network has total $M + 1$ components (M is the total number of modalities). The first component is a temporally hybrid network that models the modality specific temporal dynamics as well as the temporal dynamics in a multimodal feature space. Corresponding to each of the M modalities, there is also a non-temporal classification component in the network. All of these components in the network are trained in an end-to-end fashion.

2   Related Work

In this section, we describe the relevant prior work on generic multimodal fusion and multimodal fusion using deep learning.

Multimodal Information Fusion: A good survey of different fusion strategies for multimodal information is in [1]. We discuss a few relevant papers here. The authors in [41] provide a general theoretical analysis for multimodal information fusion and implements novel information theoretic tools for multimedia applications. [37] proposes a two-step approach for an optimal multimodal fusion, where in the first step statistically independent modalities are found from raw features and in the second step, super-kernel fusion is used to find the optimal combination of individual modalities. In [10], the authors propose a method for detecting complex events in videos by using a new representation, called bi-modal words, to explore the representative joint audio and visual patterns. [12] proposes a method to extract a novel representation, the Short-term Audio-Visual Atom (S-AVA), for improved semantic concept detection in videos. The authors in [45] propose a rank minimization method to fuse the predicted confidence scores of multiple models based on different kinds of features. Their goal is to find a shared rank-2 pairwise relationship matrix (for the test samples) based on which each original score matrix from individual model can be decomposed into the common rank-2 matrix and sparse deviation errors. [26] proposes an early and a late fusion scheme for audio, visual and textual information fusion for semantic video analysis and demonstrates that the late fusion method works slightly better. In [22], the authors propose a multimodal fusion technique and describe a way to implement a generic framework for multimodal emotion recognition.

Deep Learning for Multimodal Fusion: In [20], the authors propose a deep autoencoder network that is pretrained using sparse Restricted Boltzmann Machines (RBM). The proposed method is used to learn multimodal feature representation for the task of audio-visual speech recognition. The authors in [29], propose a Deep Boltzmann Machine (DBM) for learning a generative model of data that consists of multiple and diverse input modalities. [27], proposes a multimodal representation learning framework that minimizes the variation information between data modalities through shared latent representations. In [38], the authors propose a unified deep neural network, which jointly learns feature relationships and class relationships, and simultaneously carries out video classification within the same framework utilizing the learned relationships. [17, 18] proposes an approach for generating novel image captions given an image. This approach directly models the probability distribution of a word given previous words and an image using a network that consists of a deep RNN for sentences and a deep CNN for images. [36] proposes a novel bi-modal dynamic network for gesture recognition. High level audio and skeletal joints representations, extracted using dynamic Deep Belief Networks (DBN), are combined using a layer of perceptron. However, none of these approaches use RNNs for both multimodal and temporal data fusion and hence cannot learn features which truly represent the complimentary nature of multimodal features along the temporal dimension. The authors in [3], propose a multi-layer RNN for multi-modal emotion recognition. However, the number of layers in the proposed architecture is equal to the number of modalities, which restricts the maximum number of modalities which can be used simultaneously. The authors in [40] propose a hybrid deep learning framework for video classification that can model static spatial information, short-term motion, as well as long-term temporal clues in the videos. The spatial and the short-term motion features extracted from CNNs are combined using a regularized feature fusion network. LSTM is used to model only the modality specific long-term temporal information. However, in the proposed GeThR-Net, the temporally hybrid architecture can automatically combine temporal information from multiple modalities without requiring any explicit feature fusion framework. We also point out that unlike [40], in GeThR-Net, the multimodal fusion is performed at the LSTM network level.

To the best of authors' knowledge, there are no prior approaches where multimodal information fusion is performed at the RNN/LSTM level. GeThR-Net is the first method to use a temporally hybrid RNN which is capable of learning features from modalities of any kind without any upper-bound on the number of modalities.

3   Proposed Approach

In this section, we provide the details of the proposed deep neural network architecture GeThR-Net. First, we discuss how LSTM networks usually work. Next, we provide the descriptions of the temporal and non-temporal components of our network followed by how we combine predictions from all these components.

3.1   Long Short Term Memory Networks

Recently, a type of RNN, called Long Short Term Memory (LSTM) Networks, have been successfully employed to capture long-term temporal patterns and dependencies in videos for tasks such as video description generation, activity recognition etc. RNNs [35] are a special class of artificial neural networks, where cyclic connections are also allowed. These connections allow the networks to maintain a memory of the previous inputs, making them suitable for modelling sequential data. In LSTMs, this memory is maintained with the help of three non-linear multiplicative gates which control the in-flow, out-flow, and accumulation of information over time. We provide a detailed description of RNNs and LSTM networks below.

Given an input sequence $\mathbf{x} = \{x_t\}$ of length T, the fixed length hidden state or memory of an RNN $\mathbf{h}$ is given by

$$h_t = g(x_t, h_{t-1}) \quad t = 1, \ldots, T \tag{1}$$

We use $h_0 = 0$ in this work. Multiple such hidden layers can be stacked on top of each other, with x_t in Eq. 1 replaced with the activation at time t of the previous hidden layer, to obtain a 'deep' recurrent neural network. The output of the RNN at time t is computed using the state of the last hidden layer at t as

$$y_t = \theta(W_{yh}h_t^n + b_y) \tag{2}$$

where θ is a non-linear operation such as sigmoid or hyperbolic tangent for binary classification or softmax for multiclass classification, b_y is the bias term for the output layer and n is the number of hidden layers in the architecture. The output of the RNN at desired time steps can then be used to compute the error and the network weights are updated based on the gradients computed using Back-propagation Through Time (BPTT). In simple RNNs, the function

g is computed as a linear transformation of the input and previous hidden state, followed by an element wise non-linearity.

$$g(x_t, h_{t-1}) = \theta(W_{hx}x_t + W_{hh}h_{t-1} + b_h) \qquad (3)$$

Such simple RNNs, however, suffer from the vanishing and exploding gradient problem [9]. To address this issue, a novel form of recurrent neural networks called the Long Short Term Memory (LSTM) networks were introduced in [9]. The key difference between simple RNNs and LSTMs is in the computation of g, which is done in the latter using a memory block. An LSTM memory block consists of a memory cell c and three multiplicative gates which regulate the state of the cell - forget gate f, input gate i and output gate o. The memory cell encodes the knowledge of the inputs that have been observed up to that time step. The forget gate controls whether the old information should be retained or forgotten. The input gate regulates whether new information should be added to the cell state while the output gate controls which parts of the new cell state to output. Like simple RNNs, LSTM networks can be made deep by stacking memory blocks. The output layer of the LSTM network can then be computed using Eq. 2. We refer the reader to [9] for more technical details on LSTMs.

3.2   Temporal Component of GeThR-Net

In this subsection, we describe the details of the temporal component, which is a temporally hybrid LSTM network that models modality specific temporal dynamics as well as the multimodal temporal dynamics. This network has three layers. The first layer models the modality specific temporal information using individual LSTM layers. Multimodal information do not interact with each other in this layer. In the second layer, the hidden representations from all the modalities are combined using a linear function, followed by sigmoid non-linearity, to create a single multimodal feature representation corresponding to each time step. Finally, in the third layer, a LSTM network is fed with the learned multimodal features from the second layer. The output from the third layer is fed into a softmax layer for estimating the classification confidence scores corresponding to each label. This component is fully trained in an end-to-end manner and does not require any explicit feature fusion modelling.

Now, we describe the technical details of these layers. We assume that there are total M different modalities and total T time-steps. The feature representation for modality m corresponding to time instant t is given by: x_t^m. Now, we describe the mathematical details:

– **First Layer:** The input to this layer is x_t^m for modality m at time instant t. If $LSTM_m$ denotes the LSTM layer for modality m and if h_t^m denotes the corresponding hidden representation at time t, then:

$$h_t^m = LSTM_m(x_t^m)$$

– **Second Layer:** In this layer, the hidden representations are combined using a linear function followed by a sigmoid non-linearity. The objective of using this layer is to combine features from multiple temporal modalities. Let us assume that z_t denotes the concatenated hidden representation from all the modalities at time-step t. W_z (same for all time-step t) denotes the weight matrix which combines the multimodal features and creates a representation p_t at time instant t. b_z denotes a linear bias and σ is the sigmoid function.

$$z_t = (h_t^1, \cdots, h_t^m), \quad p_t = \sigma(W_z z_t + b_z)$$

– **Third Layer:** In this layer, one modality-independent LSTM layer is used to model the overall temporal dynamics of the multimodal feature representation p_t. Suppose, $LSTM_c$ denotes the combined LSTM and h_t^c denotes the hidden representation from this LSTM layer at time t. W_o is the weight matrix that linearly transforms the hidden representation. The output is propagated through a softmax function θ to obtain the final classification confidence values y_t^c at time t. b_o is a linear bias vector.

$$h_t^c = LSTM_c(p_t), \quad y_t^c = \theta(W_o h_t^c + b_o)$$

3.3   Non-temporal Component of GeThR-Net

Although it is important to model the temporal information in multimodal signals for accurate classification or any other tasks, often in real world scenarios multimodal information contains significant amount of noise and large intra-class variation along the temporal dimension. For example, videos of the activity 'cooking' often contain action segments such as 'changing thermostat' or 'drinking water' which are no way related to the actual label of the video. In those cases, modelling only the long-term temporal information in the video could lead to inaccurate results. Hence, it is important that we allow the proposed deep network to learn the non-temporal features too. We analyze videos from multiple datasets and observe that a simple classifier which is trained on 'frame-level' features (definition of frame could vary according to the features) could give a reasonable accuracy, especially when videos contain unrelated temporal segments. Please refer to Sect. 4.5 for more experimental results on this. Since our objective is to propose a generic deep network that could work with any kind of multimodal information, we add additional components to the GeThR-Net, which explicitly model the modality specific non-temporal information.

During training, for each modality m, we train a classifier where the set $\{x_t^m\}$, $\forall t$ is used as the training examples corresponding to the class of the multimodal signal. While testing for a given sequence, the predictions across all the time-steps are averaged to obtain the classifier confidence scores corresponding to all of the classes. In this paper, we have explored four different modalities: appearance, short-term motion, audio (spectrogram and MFCC) and skeleton. For appearance, short-term motion and audio-spectrogram, we use fine-tuned CNNs and for audio-MFCC and skeleton, we use SVMs as the non-temporal classifiers.

3.4 Combination

There are total $M + 1$ components in GeThR-Net, where the first one is the temporally hybrid LSTM network and the rest M are the non-temporal modality specific classifiers corresponding to each modality. Once we independently train these $M + 1$ classifiers, their prediction scores are combined and a single class-label for each multimodal temporal sequence is predicted. We use a validation dataset to determine the relevant weights corresponding to each of the $M + 1$ components.

4   Experiments

Our goal is to demonstrate that the proposed GeThR-Net can be effectively applied to any kind of multimodal fusion. To achieve that, we perform thorough experimental evaluation and provide the details of the experimental results in this section.

4.1 Dataset Details

The dataset details are provided in this subsection.

UCF-101 [28]: UCF-101 is an action recognition dataset containing realistic action videos from YouTube. The dataset has 13,320 videos annotated into 101 different action classes. The average length of the video in this dataset is 6–7 sec. The dataset possess various challenges and diversity in terms of large variations in camera motion, object appearance and pose, cluttered background, illumination, viewpoint, etc. We evaluate the performance on this dataset following the standard protocol [28,40] by reporting the mean classification accuracy across three training and testing splits. We use the appearance and short-term motion modality for this dataset [24,40].

CCV [13]: The Columbia Consumer Videos (CCV) has 9,317 YouTube videos distributed over 20 different semantic categories. The dataset has events like 'baseball', 'parade', 'birthday', 'wedding ceremony', scenes like 'beach', 'playground', etc. and objects like 'cat', 'dog' etc. The average length of the video in this dataset is 80 sec long. For our experiments, we have used 7751 videos (3851 for training and 3900 for testing) as the remaining videos are not available on YouTube presently. In this dataset, the performance is measured by average precision (AP) for each class and the overall measure is given by mAP (mean average precision over 20 categories). In this dataset, we use three different modalities, i.e., appearance, short-term motion and audio.

Multimodal Gesture Dataset [5] (MMG): ChaLearn-2013 multimodal gesture recognition dataset is a large video database of 13,858 gestures from a lexicon of 20 Italian gesture categories. The focus of the dataset is on user independent multiple gesture learning. The dataset has RGB and depth images of the videos, user masks, skeletal model, and the audio information (utterance of the corresponding gesture by the actor), which are synchronous with the gestures performed. The dataset has 393 training, 287 testing, and 276 testing sequences. Each sequence is of duration between 1–2 min and contains 8–20 gestures. Furthermore, the test sequences also have 'distracter' (out of vocabulary) gestures apart from the 20 main gesture categories. For this dataset, we use the audio and skeleton modality for fusion because some of the top-performing methods [5] on this dataset also used these two modalities. The loose temporal boundaries of the gestures in the sequence is available during training and validation phase, however, at the time of testing, the goal is to also predict the correct order of gestures within the sequence along with the gesture labels. The final evaluation is defined in terms of edit distance (insertion, deletion, or substitution) between the ground truth sequence of labels and the predicted sequence of labels. The overall score is the sum of edit distance for all testing videos, divided by the total number of gestures in all the testing videos [5].

4.2 Modality Specific Feature Extraction

In this section, we describe the feature extraction method for different modalities - appearance, short-term motion, audio, and skeleton, which are used in this paper across three different datasets.

- **Appearance Features:** We adopted the VGG-16 [25] architecture to extract the appearance features. In this architecture, we change the number of neurons in fc7 layer from 4096 to 1024 to get a compressed lower dimensional representation of an input. We finetune the final three fully connected layers (fc6, fc7, and fc8) of the network pretrained on ImageNet using the frames of the training videos. The activations of the fc7 layer are taken as the visual representation of the frame provided as an input. While finetuning, we use minibatch stochastic descent with a fixed momentum of 0.9. The input size of the frame to our model is $224 \times 224 \times 3$. Simple data augmentations are also done such as cropping and mirroring [11]. We adopt a dropout ratio of 0.5. The initial learning rate is set to 0.001 for fc6, and 0.01 for fc7 and fc8 layers as the weights of last two layers are learned from scratch. The learning rate is reduced by factor of 10 after every 10,000 iterations.
- **Short-Term Motion Features:** To extract the features, we adopted the method proposed in the recent two-stream CNN paper [24]. This method stacks the optical flows computed between pairs of adjacent frames over a time window and provides it as an input to CNN. We used the same VGG-16 architecture (as above) with 1024 neurons in fc7 layer, and pre-training on ImageNet for the extraction of short-term motion features. However, unlike the previous case (where input to the model was an RGB image comprising of three channels), the input to this network is a 10-frame stacking of optical flow fields (x and y direction), and thus the convolution filters in the first layer are different from those of the appearance network. We adopt a high dropout rate of 0.8 and set the initial learning rate to 0.001 for all the layers. The learning rate is reduced by a factor of 10 after every 10,000 iterations.

- **Audio Features:** We use two different kinds of feature extraction method for audio modality.
  - **Spectrogram Features:** In this method, we extract the spectrogram features from audio signal using a convolutional neural network [21]. We divide the video into multiple overlapping 1 sec clips and then, apply the Short Time Fourier Transformation to convert each one second 1-d audio signal into a 2-D image (namely log-compressed mel-spectrograms with 128 components) with the horizontal axis and vertical axis being time-scale and frequency-scale respectively. The features are extracted from these spectrogram images by providing them as input to a CNN. In this case, we use AlexNet [14] architecture and the network was pre-trained on ImageNet. We finetune the final three layers of network with respect to the spectrogram images of training videos to learn the 'spectrogram-discriminative' CNN features. We also change the number of nodes in fc7 layer to 1024 and use the activations of fc7 layer as the representation of a spectrogram image. The learning rate and dropout parameters are same as mentioned in the appearance feature extraction case.
  - **MFCC Features:** We use MFCC features for the MMG dataset. The spectrogram based CNN features were not used for this dataset as the temporal extent of each gesture was very less (1–2 sec), making it difficult to extract multiple spectrograms along the temporal dimension. In this method, speech signal of a gesture was analyzed using a 20ms Hamming window with a fixed frame rate of 10ms. Our feature consists of 12 Mel Frequency Cepstral Coefficients (MFCCs) along with the log energy ($MFCC_0$) and their first and second order delta values to capture the spectral variation. We concatenated 5 adjacent frames together in order to adhere to the 20 fps of videos in the MMG dataset. Hence, we have a feature of dimension of $39 \times 5 = 195$ for each frame of the video. The data was also normalized such that each of the features (coefficients, energy and derivatives) extracted have zero mean and one variance.
- **Skeleton Features:** We use the skeleton features for the MMG dataset. We employ the feature extraction method proposed in [36,43] to characterize the action information which includes the posture feature, motion feature and offset feature. Out of 20 skeleton joint locations, we use only 9 upper body joints as they are the most discriminative for recognizing gestures.

4.3   Methods Compared

To establish the efficacy of the proposed approach, we compare GeThR-Net with several baselines. The baselines were carefully designed to cover several temporal and non-temporal feature fusion methods. We provide the architectural details of these baselines in Fig. 2 for easy understanding of their differences.

(a) **NonTemporal-M:** In this baseline, we train modality specific non-temporal models and predict label of a temporal sequence based on the average over

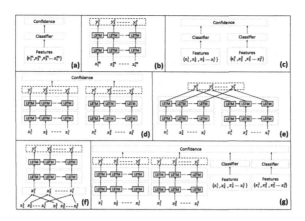

Fig. 2. Different baselines which are compared with GeThR-Net. (a) NonTemporal-M. (b) Temporal-M. (c) NonTemporal-AM (d) Temporal-AM (late fusion) (e) Temporal-EtoE-AM (late fusion) (f) Temporal-AM (early fusion) (g) Temporal-AM+NonTemporal-AM.

all predictions across time. For appearance, short-term motion and audio spectrogram, we use CNN features (Sect. 4.2) followed by a softmax layer for classification. For audio MFCC and Skeleton, we use the features extracted using the methods described in Sect. 4.2 followed by SVM classification. Multimodal fusion is not performed for label prediction in these baselines.

(b) **Temporal-M:** For this baseline, we feed the modality specific features (as described in the last subsection), to LSTM networks for the temporal modelling and label prediction. Here also, features from multiple modalities are not fused for classification.

(c) **NonTemporal-AM (all modality combined):** In this baseline, the outputs from the modality specific non-temporal baselines (CNN/SVM) are linearly combined for classification. The combination weights are automatically learned from validation datasets.

(d) **Temporal-AM (late fusion, all modality combined):** Here also, the outputs from the modality specific temporal baselines (LSTMs) are linearly combined for classification. This is a late fusion approach.

(e) **TemporalEtoE-AM (late fusion, all modality combined):** In this baseline, we add a linear layer on top of the modality specific temporal baselines and use an end-to-end training approach for learning the weights of the combination layer. This is also a late fusion approach.

(f) **Temporal-AM (early fusion, all modality combined):** Features from multiple modalities are linearly combined and then forward propagated through a LSTM for classification. This is an early fusion approach.

(g) **Temporal-AM+NonTemporal-AM (all modality combined):** In this baseline, the outputs from all the modality specific temporal and nontemporal baselines are combined for the final label prediction. Here also, we use a validation dataset for predicting the optimal weights corresponding to each of these components.

(h) **TemporallyHybrid-AM (proposed, all modality combined):** This method uses only the temporally hybrid component of the proposed approach. The non-temporal components' outputs are not used. This network is completely trained in an end-to-end fashion (See the temporal component in Fig. 1).

(i) **GeThR-Net:** This is the proposed approach (See Fig. 1).

4.4   Implementation Details

We used the initial learning rate of 0.0002 for all LSTM networks. It is reduced by a factor of 0.9 for every epoch starting from the 6-th epoch. We set the dropout rate at 0.3. For the baseline methods of temporal modelling, Temporal-M, Temporal-AM and TemporalEtoE-AM, we tried different combinations for the number of hidden layers and the number of units in each layer and chose the one which led to the optimal performance on the validation set. Since, the feature dimension is high (1024) in UCF-101 and CCV dataset, the number of units in each layer is varied from 256 to 768 in the intervals of 32. While in case of MMG, it is varied from 64 to 512 in the same interval. The number of layers in the baselines were varied between 1 and 3 for all of the datasets.

For the proposed temporally hybrid network (TemporallyHybrid-AM) component also, the number of units in the First-layer LSTM corresponding to each modality, the number units in the linear Second-layer and the number of units in Third-layer multimodal LSTM are chosen based upon the performance on the validation dataset. For UCF-101 dataset, the First-layer has 576 units for both the appearance and short-term modality. The Second-layer has 768 units and the Third-layer has 448 units. For CCV dataset, all the three modalities, appearance, short-term motion and audio have 512 units in the First-layer. In CCV, the Second-layer has 896 units and the Third-layer has 640 units. For MMG dataset, the First-layer has 256 units for skeleton modality and 192 units for audio modality. The Second-layer has 384 units and the Third-layer has 256 units. Note that these parameters differ across the datasets due to the variation in the input feature size and the inherent complexity of the datasets.

4.5   Discussion on Results

In this section, we compare GeThR-Net with various baseline methods (Sect. 4.3) and several recent state-of-the-art methods on three different datasets. The results corresponding to all the baselines and the proposed approach are summarized in Table 1. In the first two slabs of the table, results from individual modalities are shown using the temporal and non-temporal components. In the next three slabs, results for different fusion strategies across modalities are shown for both the temporal and non-temporal components. In the final slab of the table, results obtained from the proposed temporally hybrid component and GeThR-Net are shown.

Table 1. Comparison of GeThR-Net with baseline methods on UCF-101, CCV and Multimodal Gesture recognition (MMG) dataset. UCF-101: M1 is appearance, M2 is short-term motion and classification accuracy is reported. CCV: M1 is appearance, M2 is short-term motion, M3 is audio and mean average precision (mAP) is reported. MMG: M1 is audio, M2 is skeleton and normalized edit distance is reported.

Dataset	Modalities Used
UCF -101	Appearance (M1)
	Short term Motion (M2)
CCV	Appearance (M1)
	Short-term Motion (M2)
	Audio (M3)
MMG	Audio (M1)
	Skeleton (M2)

Methods	UCF-101 (Accuracy)	CCV (mAP)	MMG (edit)
NonTemporal-M1	76.3	76.7	0.988
NonTemporal-M2	86.8	57.3	0.782
NonTemporal-M3	-	30.3	-
Temporal-M1	76.6	71.7	0.284
Temporal-M2	85.5	55.1	0.361
Temporal-M3	-	28.5	-
NonTemporal-AM	89.9	78.5	0.776
Temporal-AM (late fusion)	88.0	75.0	0.156
TemporalEtoE-AM (late fusion)	88.4	72.5	0.155
Temporal-AM (early fusion)	86.5	73.1	0.190
Temporal-AM + NonTemporal-AM	90.2	79.2	0.155
TemporallyHybrid-AM	89.0	74.0	**0.152**
GeThR-Net	**91.1**	**79.3**	**0.152**

– **UCF-101 [28]:** For UCF-101, we report the test video classification accuracy. GeThR-Net achieves an absolute improvement of 3.1 %, 2.7 % and 4.6 % over Temporal-AM (late fusion), TemporalEtoE-AM (late fusion) and Temporal-AM (early fusion) baselines respectively. This empirically shows that the proposed approach is significantly better in capturing the complementary temporal aspects of different modalities compared to the late and early fusion based methods. GeThR-Net also gives an absolute improvement of 0.9 % over a strong baseline method of combining temporal and non-temporal aspects of different modalities (Temporal-AM+Non-Temporal-AM). This further establishes the efficacy of the proposed architecture. We also compare the results produced by GeThR-Net with several recent papers which reported results on UCF-101 (see Table 2). Out of the seven approaches we compare, we are better than five of them and comparable to two [34,40] of them. As pointed out earlier, the goal of this paper is to develop a general deep learning framework which can be used for multimodal fusion in different kinds of tasks. The results on UCF-101 clearly shows that GeThR-Net can be effectively used for the short action recognition task (average duration 6–7 seconds).

- **CCV [5]:** We also perform experiments on the CCV dataset to show that GeThR-Net can also be used for longer action recognition (average duration 80 seconds). In this dataset, we report the mean average precision (in a scale of 0–100) for all the algorithms which we compare. In CCV also, GeThR-Net is better than Temporal-AM (late fusion), TemporalEtoE-AM (late fusion) and Temporal-AM (early fusion) baselines by an absolute mAP of 4.3, 6.8 and 6.2 respectively. However, GeThR-Net performs comparable (mAP of 79.3 compared to 79.2) to a strong baseline method of combining temporal and non-temporal aspects of different modalities (Temporal-AM+Non-Temporal-AM). We also wanted to compare GeThR-Net with several recent approaches which also reported results on the CCV dataset. However, a fair comparison was not possible because several videos from CCV were unavailable from youtube. We used only 7,751 videos for training and testing as opposed to 9,317 videos in the original dataset. In spite of that, to get an approximate idea about how GeThR-Net performs compared to these methods, we provide some comparisons. The mAP reported on CCV by some of the recent methods are: 70.6 [39], 64.0 [45], 63.4 [16], 60.3 [42], 68.2 [15], 64.0 [10] and 83.5 [40]. We perform better (mAP of 79.3) than six of these methods.
- **MMG [5]:** In this dataset, we report the normalized edit distance (lower is better) [5] corresponding to each method. The normalized edit distance obtained by GeThR-Net is lower than the other multimodal baselines such as Temporal-AM (late fusion), TemporalEtoE-AM (early fusion), Temporal-AM (late fusion) and Temporal-AM+NonTemporal-AM by 0.004, 0.003, 0.038 and 0.003 respectively. We are also significantly better than modality specific temporal baselines, e.g.: GeThR-Net gives a normalized edit distance of only 0.152 compared to 0.284 and 0.361 produced by Temporal-M1 (audio) and Temporal-M2 (skeleton) respectively. The results on this dataset demonstrates that GeThR-Net performs well in fusing multimodal information from audio-MFCC and skeleton. The edit distance obtained from GeThR-Net is one of the top-three edits distances reported in the Chalearn-2013 multimodal gesture recognition competition [5].

Table 2. Comparison of GeThR-Net with state-of-the-art methods on UCF-101.

IDT + FV [32]	IDT + HSV [23]	Two-stream [24]	LSTM [19]	TDD + FV [33]	Two-stream2 [34]	Fusion [40]	GeThR-Net
85.9	87.9	88.0	88.6	90.3	91.4	91.3	91.1

From the results on these datasets, it is clear that GeThr-Net is effective in fusing different kinds of multimodal information and also applicable to different end-tasks such as short action recognition, long action recognition and gesture recognition. That empirically shows the generalizability of the proposed deep network.

5   Conclusion

In this paper, we propose a novel deep neural network called GeThR-Net for multimodal temporal information fusion. GeThR-Net has a temporally hybrid recurrent neural network component that models modality specific temporal dynamics as well as the temporal dynamics in a multimodal feature space. The other components in the GeThR-Net are used to capture the non-temporal information. We perform experiments on three different action and gesture recognition datasets and show that GeThR-Net performs well for any general multimodal fusion task. The experimental results are performed on four different modalities with maximum three modality fusion at a time. However, GeThR-Net can be used for any kind of modality fusion without any upper bound on the number of modalities that can be combined.

References

1. Atrey, P.K., Hossain, M.A., El Saddik, A., Kankanhalli, M.S.: Multimodal fusion for multimedia analysis: a survey. Multimedia Syst. **16**(6), 345–379 (2010)
2. Baccouche, M., Mamalet, F., Wolf, C., Garcia, C., Baskurt, A.: Sequential deep learning for human action recognition. In: Salah, A.A., Lepri, B. (eds.) HBU 2011. LNCS, vol. 7065, pp. 29–39. Springer, Heidelberg (2011)
3. Chen, S., Jin, Q.: Multi-modal dimensional emotion recognition using recurrent neural networks. In: Proceedings of the 5th International Workshop on Audio/Visual Emotion Challenge, pp. 49–56. ACM (2015)
4. Chen, X., C., L.Z.: Mind's eye: a recurrent visual representation for image caption generation. In: The IEEE Conference on Computer Vision and Pattern Recognition (CVPR), June 2015
5. Escalera, S., Gonzàlez, J., Baró, X., Reyes, M., Lopes, O., Guyon, I., Athitsos, V., Escalante, H.: Multi-modal gesture recognition challenge 2013: dataset and results. In: Proceedings of the 15th ACM on International Conference on Multimodal Interaction, pp. 445–452. ACM (2013)
6. Graves, A., Jaitly, N.: Towards end-to-end speech recognition with recurrent neural networks. In: ICML (2014)
7. Graves, A., Mohamed, A., Hinton, G.: Speech recognition with deep recurrent neural networks. In: ICASSP. IEEE (2013)
8. Graves, A., Schmidhuber, J.: Offline handwriting recognition with multidimensional recurrent neural networks. In: NIPS (2009)
9. Hochreiter, S., Schmidhuber, J.: Long short-term memory. Neural Comput. **9**, 1735–1780 (1997)
10. Jhuo, I.H., Ye, G., Gao, S., Liu, D., Jiang, Y.G., Lee, D.T., Chang, S.F.: Discovering joint audio-visual codewords for video event detection. Mach. Vis. Appl. **25**(1), 33–47 (2014)
11. Jia, Y., Shelhamer, E., Donahue, J., Karayev, S., Long, J., Girshick, R., Guadarrama, S., Darrell, T.: Caffe: convolutional architecture for fast feature embedding. arXiv preprint arXiv:1408.5093 (2014)
12. Jiang, W., Cotton, C., Chang, S.F., Ellis, D., Loui, A.: Short-term audio-visual atoms for generic video concept classification. In: Proceedings of the 17th ACM International Conference on Multimedia, pp. 5–14. ACM (2009)

13. Jiang, Y.G., Ye, G., Chang, S.F., Ellis, D., Loui, A.C.: Consumer video understanding: a benchmark database and an evaluation of human and machine performance. In: Proceedings of the 1st ACM International Conference on Multimedia Retrieval, p. 29. ACM (2011)
14. Krizhevsky, A., Sutskever, I., Hinton, G.E.: Imagenet classification with deep convolutional neural networks. In: Advances in Neural Information Processing Systems (2012)
15. Liu, D., Lai, K.T., Ye, G., Chen, M.S., Chang, S.F.: Sample-specific late fusion for visual category recognition. In: 2013 IEEE Conference on Computer Vision and Pattern Recognition (CVPR) (2013)
16. Ma, A.J., Yuen, P.C.: Reduced analytic dependency modeling: robust fusion for visual recognition. Int. J. Comput. Vis. **109**, 233–251 (2014)
17. Mao, J., Xu, W., Yang, Y., Wang, J., Huang, Z., Yuille, A.: Deep captioning with multimodal recurrent neural networks (m-rnn). In: ICLR (2015)
18. Mao, J., Xu, W., Yang, Y., Wang, J., Yuille, A.L.: Explain images with multimodal recurrent neural networks. arXiv preprint arXiv:1410.1090 (2014)
19. Ng, J.Y., Hausknecht, M.J., Vijayanarasimhan, S., Vinyals, O., Monga, R., Toderici, G.: Beyond short snippets: deep networks for video classification. In: IEEE Conference on Computer Vision and Pattern Recognition, CVPR 2015, Boston, MA, USA, 7–12 June, 2015
20. Ngiam, J., Khosla, A., Kim, M., Nam, J., Lee, H., Ng, A.Y.: Multimodal deep learning. In: Proceedings of the 28th International Conference on Machine Learning (ICML 2011), pp. 689–696 (2011)
21. Van den Oord, A., Dieleman, S., Schrauwen, B.: Deep content-based music recommendation. In: Advances in Neural Information Processing Systems, pp. 2643–2651 (2013)
22. Paleari, M., Lisetti, C.L.: Toward multimodal fusion of affective cues. In: Proceedings of the 1st ACM International Workshop on Human-Centered Multimedia, pp. 99–108. ACM (2006)
23. Peng, X., Wang, L., Wang, X., Qiao, Y.: Bag of visual words and fusion methods for action recognition: comprehensive study and good practice. CoRR (2014)
24. Simonyan, K., Zisserman, A.: Two-stream convolutional networks for action recognition in videos. In: NIPS, pp. 568–576 (2014)
25. Simonyan, K., Zisserman, A.: Very deep convolutional networks for large-scale image recognition. arXiv preprint arXiv:1409.1556 (2014)
26. Snoek, C.G., Worring, M., Smeulders, A.W.: Early versus late fusion in semantic video analysis. In: Proceedings of the 13th Annual ACM International Conference on Multimedia, pp. 399–402. ACM (2005)
27. Sohn, K., Shang, W., Lee, H.: Improved multimodal deep learning with variation of information. In: Advances in Neural Information Processing Systems, pp. 2141–2149 (2014)
28. Soomro, K., Zamir, A.R., Shah, M.: Ucf101: a dataset of 101 human actions classes from videos in the wild. arXiv preprint arXiv:1212.0402 (2012)
29. Srivastava, N., Salakhutdinov, R.R.: Multimodal learning with deep boltzmann machines. In: Advances in Neural Information Processing Systems, pp. 2222–2230 (2012)
30. Stein, B.E., Stanford, T.R., Rowland, B.A.: The neural basis of multisensory integration in the midbrain: its organization and maturation. Hear. Res. **258**(1), 4–15 (2009)
31. Vinyals, O., Toshev, A., Bengio, S., Erhan, D.: Show and tell: a neural image caption generator. In: CVPR (2015)

32. Wang, H., Schmid, C.: Action recognition with improved trajectories. In: The IEEE International Conference on Computer Vision (ICCV), December 2013
33. Wang, L., Qiao, Y., Tang, X.: Action recognition with trajectory-pooled deep-convolutional descriptors. In: CVPR, pp. 4305–4314 (2015)
34. Wang, L., Xiong, Y., Wang, Z., Qiao, Y.: Towards good practices for very deep two-stream convnets. CoRR (2015)
35. Williams, R.J., Zipser, D.: A learning algorithm for continually running fully recurrent neural networks. Neural Comput. **1**, 263–269 (1989)
36. Wu, D., Shao, L.: Multimodal dynamic networks for gesture recognition. In: Proceedings of the ACM International Conference on Multimedia, pp. 945–948. ACM (2014)
37. Wu, Y., Chang, E.Y., Chang, K.C.C., Smith, J.R.: Optimal multimodal fusion for multimedia data analysis. In: Proceedings of the 12th Annual ACM International Conference on Multimedia, pp. 572–579. ACM (2004)
38. Wu, Z., Jiang, Y.G., Wang, J., Pu, J., Xue, X.: Exploring inter-feature and inter-class relationships with deep neural networks for video classification. In: Proceedings of the ACM International Conference on Multimedia, pp. 167–176. ACM (2014)
39. Wu, Z., Jiang, Y.G., Wang, J., Pu, J., Xue, X.: Exploring inter-feature and inter-class relationships with deep neural networks for video classification. In: Proceedings of the 22nd ACM International Conference on Multimedia, MM 2014 (2014)
40. Wu, Z., Wang, X., Jiang, Y.G., Ye, H., Xue, X.: Modeling spatial-temporal clues in a hybrid deep learning framework for video classification. In: Proceedings of the 23rd Annual ACM Conference on Multimedia Conference, pp. 461–470. ACM (2015)
41. Xie, Z., Guan, L.: Multimodal information fusion of audiovisual emotion recognition using novel information theoretic tools. In: 2013 IEEE International Conference on Multimedia and Expo (ICME), pp. 1–6. IEEE (2013)
42. Xu, Z., Yang, Y., Tsang, I., Sebe, N., Hauptmann, A.G.: Feature weighting via optimal thresholding for video analysis. In: 2013 IEEE International Conference on Computer Vision (ICCV) (2013)
43. Yang, X., Tian, Y.: Eigenjoints-based action recognition using naive-bayes-nearest-neighbor. In: 2012 IEEE Computer Society Conference on Computer Vision and Pattern Recognition Workshops (CVPRW), pp. 14–19. IEEE (2012)
44. Yao, L., Torabi, A., Cho, K., Ballas, N., Pal, C., Larochelle, H., Courville, A.: Describing videos by exploiting temporal structure. In: Proceedings of the IEEE International Conference on Computer Vision, pp. 4507–4515 (2015)
45. Ye, G., Liu, D., Jhuo, I.H., Chang, S.F., et al.: Robust late fusion with rank minimization. In: 2012 IEEE Conference on Computer Vision and Pattern Recognition (CVPR), pp. 3021–3028. IEEE (2012)

Suggesting Sounds for Images from Video Collections

Matthias Solèr[1], Jean-Charles Bazin[2(✉)], Oliver Wang[2], Andreas Krause[1], and Alexander Sorkine-Hornung[2]

[1] Computer Science Department, ETH Zurich, Zurich, Switzerland
{msoler,krausea}@ethz.ch
[2] Disney Research, Zurich, Switzerland
{jean-charles.bazin,owang,alex}@disneyresearch.com

Abstract. Given a still image, humans can easily think of a sound associated with this image. For instance, people might associate the picture of a car with the sound of a car engine. In this paper we aim to retrieve sounds corresponding to a query image. To solve this challenging task, our approach exploits the correlation between the audio and visual modalities in video collections. A major difficulty is the high amount of uncorrelated audio in the videos, i.e., audio that does not correspond to the main image content, such as voice-over, background music, added sound effects, or sounds originating off-screen. We present an unsupervised, clustering-based solution that is able to automatically separate correlated sounds from uncorrelated ones. The core algorithm is based on a joint audio-visual feature space, in which we perform iterated mutual kNN clustering in order to effectively filter out uncorrelated sounds. To this end we also introduce a new dataset of correlated audio-visual data, on which we evaluate our approach and compare it to alternative solutions. Experiments show that our approach can successfully deal with a high amount of uncorrelated audio.

Keywords: Sound suggestion · Audio-visual content · Data filtering

1 Introduction

Visual content interpretation is at the core of computer vision. Impressive results have been obtained for visual data over the last years, e.g., for classification and recognition [29,57], segmentation [23], tracking and 3D reconstruction [1,9]. In comparison, learning relationships between audio and visual data is still a largely unexplored area, despite exciting applications on joint audio-video processing [6, 13,17,37].

A fascinating example of joint audio-visual learning occurs daily in our lives. When humans see an object, they can usually imagine a plausible sound that it would make, due to having learned the correlation between visual and audio modalities from numerous examples throughout their life. In this paper, we aim

© Springer International Publishing Switzerland 2016
G. Hua and H. Jégou (Eds.): ECCV 2016 Workshops, Part II, LNCS 9914, pp. 900–917, 2016.
DOI: 10.1007/978-3-319-48881-3_59

to mimic this process, i.e. given an input still image, suggest sounds by interpreting the visual content of this image. Before proceeding further, it worths mentioning that the sounds associated to an image can be highly ambiguous or even inexistent. For example, returning a sound for an image of a flower would not make sense because a flower does not make sound. In the following, we only consider images for which a sound can be associated.

Being able to output a sound for a query image has many practical applications in computer vision and multimedia, for example automatic Foley processing for video production[1] [19], image sonification for the visually impaired [44], and augmenting visual content database with sounds and audio restoration [26].

One approach to generate sound from images is to synthesize audio using physics-based simulation [11,19], however, this is still an open problem for general objects. Instead, we define the sound retrieval task as learning the correlation between audio and visual information collected from a video collection.

Video provides us with a natural and appealing way to learn this correlation: video cameras are equipped with microphones and capture synchronized audio and visual information. In principle, *every* single video frame captured constitutes a possible training example, and the Internet provides us with a virtually inexhaustible amount of training data. However, in practice there exist a number of significant challenges. First and foremost videos often contain a very high amount of *uncorrelated* audio, i.e., audio that does not correspond to the visual content of the video frames. This is due to voice-over (commentaries, speech, etc.), background music, added sound effects, or sounds originating off-screen. This high level of noise in the training samples causes difficulties when employing standard machine learning techniques. An additional challenge is that an object might be naturally associated with different sounds, so we would like to learn and capture a multi-modal solution space. Furthermore, evaluating the quality of suggested sounds is also not trivial due to the difficulty in acquiring ground truth image-sound correspondences.

So, given an image, how can we find a sound that could correspond to this image? As the input to the training phase of our method, we take a collection of unstructured, casually captured videos with corresponding audio recordings. A key observation in our method is that while the input videos may contain a significant amount of uncorrelated data, i.e., images whose audio is uncorrelated (commonly due to added voiceover or music), these uncorrelated examples will not share any common features. On the other hand, the true visual and audio examples will be recurring across multiple videos.

In the rest of this paper, we use the term "correlated" audio-visual examples to refer to pairs of video frames and their associated audio segments whose audio corresponds to the visual content of the video frame. These audio segments are called "clean" since they should correspond to uncorrupted audio segments, i.e., free from background noise, added music or voiceover for example.

Based on this assumption, we develop an unsupervised filtering approach that automatically identifies significant audio-visual clusters via a mutual kNN-based

---

[1] https://en.wikipedia.org/wiki/Foley_%28filmmaking%29.

technique, and then removes the uncorrelated visual-audio examples from the video collection. This filtering is performed offline, once, and results in a clean collection of correlated audio-visual examples that can then be used to retrieve a sound corresponding to the input query image. This approach to output a sound for a query image from a video collection corrupted with uncorrelated data constitutes the main contribution of our work. Given a query image, we can then output a corresponding sound by looking up the most similar visual features in the filtered collection and returning its corresponding audio segment. This retrieval step is conducted online at interactive rates.

2   Related Work

Our paper deals with audio and visual content. We will first review works which are related to either modality, and then works on joint audio-visual content.

2.1   Visual Content

Visual Classification and Recognition. Recent works have demonstrated impressive results for visual classification and object recognition (see review in [57]). A possible approach for our sound retrieval problem would be to classify the query image using one of these classification techniques (e.g., assign it a "phone" label), and then return the sound of this query label from examples in a certain dataset. If a clean sound database with ground truth labels was available, this could be done simply as a lookup problem using query labels derived from image or video classification [7,29,57,61,64]. While such sound databases exist nowadays (e.g., *freesound.org*), the main drawback of this approach is that building and expanding such a database requires a considerable amount of manual and time-consuming work to label and monitor all samples, and moreover, not all types of sounds are available in these databases. In contrast our goal is to develop a fully automatic and unsupervised approach that can mine data from arbitrary unstructured video collections.

Another option would be to identify a video frame from the collection that is visually similar to the input query (e.g., using distance between image appearance descriptors [15,49,58]), and then output the audio segment of that video frame. However, outputting the sound of a video frame selected from visual similarity (obtained via image labels in a classification framework or via image descriptors) might return uncorrelated audio (see our evaluation) since a potentially large amount of audio tracks in the video collection might not be correlated with the observed visual content.

Representative Images. Doersch et al. [20] find visual cues (e.g., patches) representative for some cities by relying on a database of images with ground truth GPS labels. Instead, we aim for an unsupervised approach and our input is a collection of unlabeled videos.

Some other works are dedicated to creating clean image collections. For example, Elor et al. [3] aim to obtain a clean set of images (and their segmentation). In contrast, our work is dedicated to learning image sounds from videos, which requires to consider both visual and audio modalities, in order to reliably retrieve an appropriate sound for a query image.

Another option could be to build on methods that identify canonical images from an image collection [14,60]. However, it is not clear how to extend these methods to multiple modalities in our application scenario.

2.2   Audio Content

Audio Synthesis. An approach to output sound of a given image could be to synthesize the audio corresponding to the image, e.g., using physics-based simulation [10,11,19,54,68,69]. However most of these techniques are dedicated to specific objects (e.g., fire) and cannot be generalized due to the task complexity.

Audio Classification, Recognition and Retrieval. Audio analysis has been studied for a long time [2], and many products are now available on the market, for example Siri and Google Now for speech recognition, or Soundcloud, Spotify, and Shazam for music data. Audio classification techniques [35] could be used to label sounds in a video, but this does not solve our problem since the query image has no sound. One option would be to detect and ignore the frames of the video collection with particular audio, for example tutorial speeches or background music, and then apply the above approach. However it would require the construction of a handcrafted list of heuristics and will not be able to deal with the numerous forms of uncorrelated audio.

2.3   Audio-Visual Content

Audio Source Localization in Images. Some works [4,27,30] use the audio and visual signals of an input video to identify which pixels of the video "sound" by associating changes in audio with visual motion changes. Since these approaches are designed to return pixel locations in videos, it is not clear how they can be extended to learn the sound of an image and output a sound given a still image.

Audio Suggestion from Visual Content. Audio suggestion from visual content is mainly performed in the context of music recommendation (e.g., for a series of pictures [62], picture slideshows [22,36] or videos [38]), and music synthesis [16,42,47,66] for artistic performances. Outputting (or recognizing) speech from videos has been studied in the particular context of lip reading [43,48,67]. Some methods are also dedicated to cross-modal learning [24]. In contrast to these works, we are interested in finding a real-world *sound* (e.g., rather than musical backing) corresponding to a query image. This application requires finer scale retrieval, and notably different datasets. Closely related to our goal is the recent work of Owens et al. [50] which synthesizes impact sounds of objects for silent videos. Our work and theirs were conducted independently and in parallel.

Their method estimates the feature representation of audio given a video using a recursive neural network and selecting the most similar example from their video collection. Their video collection only contains correlated, clean and non-overlapping sounds that were acquired by a user manually hitting the objects with a drumstick. In comparison, we consider an unstructured video collection which in practice contains a high amount of uncorrelated audio. Our proposed approach can process this corrupted collection and returns a clean version, which could be used as an input training set by these methods.

3 Proposed Approach

We first discuss preprocessing steps (visual and audio descriptors, low audio frames), the core filtering step, and finally describe the retrieval step.

3.1 Preprocessing

We first normalize the videos such that they all have the same resolution, frame rate and audio sampling rate. We remove low audio frames and then compute the descriptors of the remaining visual and audio data, as discussed in the following.

Low Audio Pre-Filtering. In practice, only few frames per video actually contain sound related to the visual content. Many of the other frames have a rather low volume or just contain background noise, which we first filter out. This pre-filtering is an effective way to reduce the amount of data to be subsequently processed. To filter out the audio segments of such frames, we use the Root Mean Square (RMS) audio energy computed over short windows [56], and simply keep the audio segments with RMS scores above the median RMS of each video. For reference, on the video collection used in this paper (Sect. 4.1), about 65 % of the frames are filtered out.

Audio Descriptors. To describe audio data, we employ the popular Mel-Frequency Cepstral Coefficients (MFCCs) [45], which are commonly employed descriptors in audio analysis, description and retrieval [39,51,65]. We compute the audio descriptor of a video frame by the MFCC feature over a temporal window centered at that frame. Since sounds might have different durations, we consider multiple temporal windows, and then concatenate these (multi-scale) MFCC features [18]. In practice, we used 5 windows of lengths 1, 3, 5, 7, 9 times of a frame duration (i.e., 40 ms to 360 ms for 25 fps videos).

Visual Descriptors. Recent works showed that reliable visual descriptors for mid to high level image information can be obtained by deep learning [21,28,53,58]. These works also showed that such feature descriptors effectively generalize to different tasks and image classes that they were originally trained on. Based on these impressive results, we compute the visual descriptor of each frame of the video collection by Caffe [28] using a network trained for image classification.

Joint Audio-Visual Features. Every video frame and its associated audio segment from the video collection (after the low audio pre-filtering) constitutes a training sample. We combine both the audio and visual features to create a weighted joint audio-visual feature space. Let s_i be the i-th audio-visual sample and $\mathcal{S} = \{s_1, \ldots, s_n\}$ be the set of n audio-visual samples. Each s_i consists of a pair of corresponding (normalized) visual and audio descriptors, respectively written f_i^V and f_i^A. The distance between two audio-visual samples in the combined space is defined as a weighted sum of both modalities [5]:

$$d(s_i, s_j) = w_V d(f_i^V, f_j^V) + w_A d(f_i^A, f_j^A) \tag{1}$$

where the adjustable weights w_V and w_A allow us to tune the clustering procedure described in the following.

3.2   Clustering of Correlated Audio-Visual Samples

After having a reduced set of frames with audible audio segments, we now aim to identify the correlated pairs of frames and audio segments, and filter out the uncorrelated ones. We achieve this by finding significant clusters of correlated samples in the audio-visual feature space. Straightforward clustering in our joint audio-visual feature space, e.g., using mean-shift or similar techniques, is not practical, as we need to deal with a significant amount of outliers. We instead propose to use mutual kNN, which has been shown to be particularly effective for identifying the most significant clusters [3,40,41].

Contrary to conventional kNN, two nodes of a mutual kNN graph are connected if and only if their k-nearest neighbor relationship is *mutual*, i.e., if they are in each others' k-nearest neighbor set [8]. The clusters are then obtained by computing the connected components of the mutual kNN graph. In our application, we construct a graph where there is a node per audio-visual example, and an edge between two nodes if their feature descriptors are part of the k-nearest neighbors of each other, where the distance is defined at Eq. 1. We ignore small clusters as noisy examples can randomly create small mutual neighbor clusters [40].

The above mentioned weights for the audio and visual features in combination with the mutual kNN procedure allow for an iterative approach to remove uncorrelated samples. Let each mutual kNN cluster $\mathcal{C}_l$ over the set $\mathcal{S}$ be defined as:

$$\mathcal{C}_l = \{\mathcal{S}_l \subseteq \mathcal{S} | s_i \in \mathcal{N}(s_j) \text{ and } s_j \in \mathcal{N}(s_i), \forall (s_i, s_j) \in \mathcal{S}_l\} \tag{2}$$

where $\mathcal{N}(s_i)$ is the set of the k nearest neighbors of s_i according to the feature descriptor distance at Eq. 1. When iteratively exploring the clustering and with dynamic weights, we obtain a set of clusters such that

$$\mathcal{C}_l^t = \{\mathcal{S}_l \subseteq \mathcal{C}_l^{t-1} | s_i \in \mathcal{N}_{w^t}(s_j) \text{ and } s_j \in \mathcal{N}_{w^t}(s_i), \forall (s_i, s_j) \in \mathcal{S}_l\} \tag{3}$$

where $\mathcal{C}_l^t$ is a cluster obtained at iteration t, with $\mathcal{C}_l^0 = \mathcal{S}$ and $1 \leq t \leq T$. To emphasize that the relative weights (w_V and w_A) might evolve along time at

Eq. 1, we write $\mathcal{N}_{w^t}(s_i)$ the set of the k nearest neighbors of s_i obtained with the weights $w^t = (w_V^t, w_A^t)$ at iteration t.

If the influence weights w^t are fixed then the final clustering is obtained after one iteration, i.e., $T = 1$. If the influence weights can evolve, then the clustering at the current iteration is performed on the clusters of the previous iteration in a hierarchical manner. Depending on the weights and number of iterations, Eq. 3 may correspond to one of the following instances:

- $T = 1$ and $w_V = w_A = 1$ represent a one-step mutual-kNN on the joint audio-visual space. It simultaneously considers both visual and audio modalities. We call it "joint". The intuition for this joint space clustering is that it could potentially retrieve multiple sounds for visually similar images (e.g., for a same object), as their different joint audio-visual features will tend to cluster in multiple clusters.
- $T = 2$, with $w_V^1 = 1$ and $w_A^1 = 0$ at the first iteration, and then $w_V^2 = 0$ and $w_A^2 = 1$ at the second iteration. It represents a hierarchical two-step mutual kNN approach where the first step provides visual clusters, and the second step clusters the audio for each visual cluster. We call it "V+A".
- $T = 2$, with $w_V^1 = 0$ and $w_A^1 = 1$ at the first iteration, and then $w_V^2 = 1$ and $w_A^2 = 0$ at the second iteration. It represents the inverse of the above strategy: i.e., first audio clustering, and then clustering the visual features associated to each audio cluster. We call it "A+V". The intuition is to favor objects which are the most common for a given sound, thus is related to the notion of finding objects with unique sounds.

Concretely, the "joint" strategy performs one mutual kNN on the visual and audio descriptors, and returns a set of clusters. Ideally, each computed cluster contains examples that are similar both visually and audio. This is illustrated in Fig. 1b. For clarification of the two-step process, let's consider "V+A". In the first step, we compute visual clusters, and in a second step, for each visual cluster, we compute the clusters on audio features associated to this visual cluster, as illustrated in Fig. 1a. In the first step, we want to find clusters containing similar looking objects or scenes. For this, we apply a first mutual kNN on the visual features. After the first iteration, we obtain clusters containing elements with mostly similar visual features, but varying audio features. Therefore, given a mutual kNN visual cluster, we apply a second mutual kNN to detect the audio features uncorrelated to this visual cluster and remove them.

Interestingly, experiments will show that "joint" is outperformed by the strategies "V+A" or "A+V", each of these strategies "V+A" and "A+V" has its own strengths, and the target application context determines the most relevant strategy.

3.3   Audio Retrieval

The above filtering provides a clean collection of correlated visual-audio examples. Given a query image, we now output a sound for this image by retrieving

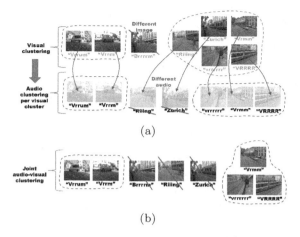

(b)

Fig. 1. Illustration of the filtering step. (a): two-step mutual kNN hierarchical approach on visual and then audio feature space ("V+A"). (b): mutual kNN approach on the joint audio-visual feature space ("joint"). For illustrative purpose and a better understanding, instead of showing the audio signal, we write an onomatopoeia of the sound. In (a), the audio (resp. image) is not used in the visual (resp. audio) clustering step, and thus the sound onomatopeias (resp. the images) are greyed out.

an appropriate sound from this collection. The filtered clean collection allows for an efficient and robust procedure for the retrieval step: we compute the visual feature of the query image, look for the nearest neighbor of this visual feature in the clean collection, and output its corresponding audio segment. In practice, by storing the timestamp and video index of each example of the clean collection, we can access that video at that time, which allows to output its associated sound segment with any preferred duration set by the user.

Depending on the application or context, we might want to return a list of $M > 1$ sounds (rather than a single one). For this, we can return the top M sounds, i.e., the M nearest neighbors, for a user to select the preferred sound via an interactive interface. In case the user wants various sounds, we increase the variety of the sound outputs by retrieving $M' > M$ examples from the filtered collection (i.e., more than the number proposed to the user) and then suggesting a canonical subset of M of these retrieved audio segments via spectral clustering on the audio features [59].

4   Results

Evaluating whether a suggested sound corresponds to the input image is a difficult task. For example, given a door image, we expect to hear a "door" sound, but how can we decide if the suggested sound is indeed a sound of a door or not? The class information is not sufficient due to extra sounds, background noise, etc., as mentioned earlier. Several video datasets exist for various purposes [25, 32, 55, 61] but they either have no sound or do not provide ground truth correlated audio-visual data. Therefore, to evaluate the results, we create a dataset with "clean" sounds and known categories (Sect. 4.1). We analyze different aspects of filtering, and further evaluate our approach with a user study.

We invite the readers to refer to our project website to access our dataset as well as representative results of sound suggestions from query images.

4.1 Dataset

We manually collected several videos with minimal background noise and clean object sounds using a GoPro camera. The key advantage of this collection is that it provides a good estimate of the ground truth and also permits us to automatically measure and compare the accuracy and robustness of our approach.

We recorded videos for 9 different categories of image-sound pairs: *keyboard* typing, *washing* dishes, *door* opening and closing, walking on *stairs*, *vacuum cleaner*, drink *toasting*, using a *binder*, *trams* and *cars*. To reproduce real case scenarios, the videos were acquired from multiple viewpoint perspectives, both indoor and outdoor, with some overlap in visual and audio modalities (e.g., potentially similar appearance of street in *trams* and *cars*). Representative images from the different classes are shown in Fig. 2. Each category contains between 10 and 20 videos, with durations between 15 and 90 s, providing a set of about 150,000 examples of correlated audio segments and video frames.

We split up the samples into training and test sets such that no video has corresponding samples in both sets at the same time, and apply cross-validation over multiple splits. The training and test sets respectively contain around 80 % and 20 % of all the samples.

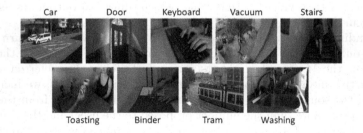

Fig. 2. Representative images of the different categories of the introduced dataset.

4.2 Experiments

Implementation Details. The framework is implemented in Matlab (mutual kNN, etc.) along with VLFeat modules (e.g., for nearest neighbor queries via approximate Nearest Neighbor). The parameters of the filters are set by cross-validation.

Our experiments are conducted on a desktop computer equipped with an Intel Core i7-960 at 3.2 Ghz, 24 GB RAM and a NVidia GTX 980Ti graphics card. Computing the visual descriptors using Caffe [28] takes about 5 s per minute of video. The low audio pre-filtering step (Sect. 3.1) takes about 40 ms per minute of audio. After this step, we have a collection of around 54,000 audio-visual examples. The mutual kNN approaches on this collection take about 15 min. The retrieval step for a query image over the filtered collection takes about 0.1s, which allows interactive use.

In terms of memory consumption, each visual-audio example is described by a 4096-dimension visual descriptor and $5 \times 13 = 65$ dimension multi-scale MFCC audio descriptor. Using single-precision floating-point format (4 bytes), each GB can store about 64,000 visual-audio samples. The additional memory footprint of k-d trees is comparatively small.

Comparison. To evaluate our filtering approach, we compare it to an "unfiltered" approach that outputs audio segments from the video collection without the correlation filtering step (Sect. 3.2), i.e., it returns the sounds of the most visually similar images in the original collection. As a general sanity check, we also apply a random selection of audio segments from the video collection ("random"). For fair comparison, we prefilter out the silent frames for all methods (Sect. 3.1).

Dataset Corruption. To measure the robustness of the methods to uncorrelated data, we corrupt the collection with uncorrelated audio examples. We do this by replacing a certain amount of audio segments by other audio segments randomly selected from a video set. We define the corruption ratio as the percentage of frames from the input video collection whose audio has been corrupted (also called percentage of uncorrelated visual-audio examples).

Evaluation. Figure 3a shows the overall classification rate on our dataset for the different approaches. It is measured as the number of correctly estimated classes over the number of tested frames: the estimated class is obtained by the classes associated to the $m = 5$ output audio segments and then majority vote; in case of tie, then random class.

Note that the aim of this paper is not to categorize images/videos into classes: here, we are using the classification rate to measure whether the retrieved sound corresponds to the input image by checking if the retrieved sound comes from the expected class in a relatively clean dataset.

First, the best classification rate when there is no uncorrelated data is around 70 %. The gap between this rate and the ideal 100 % accuracy is mainly due to similarity in the visual and audio descriptors: some classes share descriptor similarities in audio and/or visual space (e.g., trams and cars in a street environment). The classification rate of the random choice baseline starts at around 11 % as excepted since the dataset contains 9 classes, and its classification rate continues diminishing when the percentage of uncorrelated data increases. "A+V" starts at around 52 % and gives the lowest performance for a small percentage of uncorrelated audio. The performance of the unfiltered baseline starts relatively high at around 68 % but quickly drops down when the percentage of uncorrelated data is higher than 20 %.

The "V+A" strategy provides the best overall performance: it starts at around 70 %, remains relatively stable up to about 50 % of uncorrelated data, and then continues providing the highest performance up to about 65 % of uncorrelated data. This suggests that this strategy is robust to large amounts of uncorrelated audio, and is a relevant method for such application context. For higher amount of data corruption, it is slightly outperformed by "A+V" and the classification rate of the filtered approaches drops to the level of the unfiltered baseline. With such an extreme amount of data corruption, the assumption that the dominant audio-visual correlation is the correct sound might not hold anymore for several classes, i.e., the very numerous uncorrelated examples might lead to another dominant but wrong correlation. For instance, this occurs in the example of the volcano videos with helicopter sounds that is discussed later.

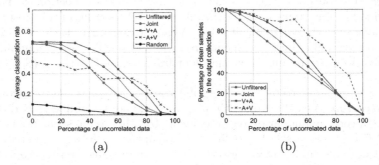

(a)   (b)

Fig. 3. Comparison of methods with respect to the amount of uncorrelated data. It indicates that different weighting strategies are appropriate for different contexts. The "V+A" strategy allows us to retrieve sounds of a query image reliably up to a high degree of corruption (see (a)). In contrast, the "A+V" strategy manages to better filter out noise overall (see (b)).

Filtering Accuracy. In addition, we also measure the quality of the filtered collection, i.e., what is the percentage of clean examples contained in the output filtered collection according to the percentage of uncorrelated data in the input collection. The results are shown in Fig. 3b. The best performance is obtained by the "A+V" strategy. For example even when the input collection contains 70 % of uncorrelated audio (i.e., only 30 % of the audio correlates to the visual signal), it manages to provide a filtered collection with 66 % of correlated audio-visual examples. It shows that it can successfully identify and filter out the uncorrelated examples, and thus can provide a cleaner version of the input collection, even in presence of a high amount of uncorrelated data. "A+V" can then be considered the strategy of choice for the application context of obtaining a clean filtered collection.

It is true that some correlated examples also have been filtered out. We apply a conservative filter approach on purpose in order to increase the probability of obtaining a clean collection, i.e., composed of only (or at least mainly composed of) clean correlated audio. In turns, this allows us to retrieve correct sound for a query image. To further evaluate this, we conducted additional experiments compiled in Fig. 4. Figure 4a suggests that the accuracy of our approach is rather stable with respect to the input collection size, once a certain amount of examples (around 20,000) is available. Figure 4b illustrates that the filtered output collection size grows with respect to the input collection size in a dominant linear manner. On the whole this scalability analysis suggests that our approach can provide a larger (filtered) collection of correlated audio-visual examples from a larger input collection (potentially corrupted by uncorrelated audio data).

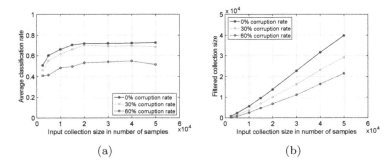

(a)   (b)

Fig. 4. Evaluation of the classification rate (a) and output collection size (b) with respect to the input collection size (i.e., before filtering) with different rates of uncorrelated data. These experiments indicate that the accuracy (classification rate) is stable after a certain collection size (a) and the output collection size increases with the input collection size (b).

User Study. For further evaluation, we also conducted a user study. 15 participants were shown an image and a 2-s audio segment, and then were asked to respond to the statement "This audio segment corresponds to the visual content of this image" by choosing a response from a five-point Likert scale: strongly agree (5), agree (4), neither agree nor disagree (3), disagree (2), or strongly disagree (1). We tested 10 (randomly selected) images per class, over the 9 classes of our dataset, which results in 90 images per participant. For each image, we prepared 3 different possible image-audio pairs for questioning by varying the audio track according to the following three methods: ground truth (i.e., the sound associated to this image in the clean dataset), "V+A" mutual kNN, and the unfiltered version. To mimic practical scenarios, we corrupted 60 % of the audio samples of the training dataset for mutual kNN and the unfiltered version (the ground truth is untouched).

Figure 5 shows that our filter approach is constantly better than the unfiltered approach overall, in agreement with Fig. 3(a). 19 % and 43 % of the responses respectively obtained without and with our filtering step were "agree" or "strongly agree". It suggests that our filtering approach can deal with uncorrelated data and provide a better quality of the suggested sound.

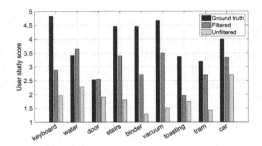

Fig. 5. Evaluation by user study. Overall, our audio-visual filtering approach successfully competes with method retrieving sound from the most visually similar video frames (see "unfiltered").

Limitations and Future Work. As demonstrated by the experiments, our approach is able to handle datasets containing uncorrelated audio and improves on naive classification-based solutions. Our approach can constitute a baseline in follow-up comparisons. Exciting research opportunities exist to further improve the performance for highly uncorrelated data. We assume that sounds that most often co-occur with specific objects are likely caused by the object visible. This assumption holds for many cases, but it can still fail when the majority of videos of an object contain a common uncorrelated sound. For example, when learning the sound of volcanoes, most of the videos we used were recorded from helicopters and contained a continuous helicopter sound in the background. Therefore our method learned to associate volcano images with helicopter sounds. Also, we intentionally applied a conservative approach to increase the probability of obtaining a clean collection. The downside is that it might limit the variety in the output collection and thus in the retrieved audio sets.

We additionally observed some limitations in our descriptors. For example, *trams* and *cars* videos were often confused due to their visual similarity (street scene). While we used existing feature descriptors trained for image classification, learning a descriptor designed for this specific task of audio retrieval could possibly improve result quality. Our visual descriptors are computed globally over the whole image. To deal with objects covering only a small part of the image, different kinds of descriptors should be used and/or in combination with object localization [57] or using saliency information [52]. This would enable, for example, an image to be associated with multiple different sounds, each derived from one or more objects in the scene. The user could also interactively specify which detected objects or which parts of the image to consider.

An extension of our work is to explore how to apply the audio-visual correlation for the converse target problem, that is given an audio segment, suggest pictures or videos. Beyond multimedia entertainment application, it could also be used to augment audio database with visual contents.

Our implementation allows the user to choose the duration of the suggested sounds (Sect. 3.3). Different sounds can have different durations, for example short toasting sound and longer passing car sound. Therefore an interesting research direction is to learn the duration of sounds and automatically output the sound with the appropriate duration.

An exciting direction is to investigate the use of motion descriptors [31,33] in addition to visual appearance descriptors. This would eventually permit to learn and cluster the different "motion sounds" of an object, for example the sounds of a door opening or closing, or the sounds of a car speeding up or slowing down.

Over the course of this work, we often wondered "what is a good sound corresponding to an input image?". In this paper, we used the notion of "significant" sounds [40,41] (i.e., sounds that are the most common for visually similar images) and conducted evaluation on several aspects of applications (Sect. 4.2). However, the answer to this question can be different for other applications. For example, one might rather be interested in finding "discriminative" sounds [20] (e.g., the hoot of an owl which is unique to that animal) or even "stereotype" sounds (e.g., an old creaking door which is potentially not accurately reflecting the daily life reality) [12,34]. These might be valid answers to the question and would require specific approaches to be explored in follow-up work.

5   Conclusion

In this paper, we investigated the problem of suggesting sounds for query images. Our approach takes a single image as input and suggests one or multiple audio segments issued from a video collection. One of the main challenges when solving this problem is the high amount of uncorrelated audio in the video collection. Therefore our main contribution is an approach to filter the data by using both audio and video modalities. The main goal of the filtering step is to filter out the audio segments which do not correlate with the image contents.

We conducted experiments that show that our filtering approach can successfully identify and filter out uncorrelated data, which in turn provides a filtered collection of correlated audio-visual examples. In addition to the application of sound suggestion from query images, this filtered clean collection could also be used as a knowledge prior for various tasks related to video classification or action recognition [7,29,61,64] or to build semantic audio database [46,63].

Moreover the user study results indicate that the sounds retrieved by our approach mainly correspond to the image content. Therefore we believe that our approach opens up new possibilities in the context of audio generation in accordance with visual content.

References

1. Agarwal, S., Snavely, N., Simon, I., Seitz, S.M., Szeliski, R.: Building Rome in a day. In: ICCV (2009)
2. Anusuya, M.A., Katti, S.K.: Speech recognition by machine: a review. Int. J. Comput. Sci. Inf. Sec. (2009)
3. Averbuch-Elor, H., Wang, Y., Qian, Y., Gong, M., Kopf, J., Zhang, H., Cohen-Or, D.: Distilled collections from textual image queries. In: Computer Graphics Forum (EGSR) (2015)
4. Barzelay, Z., Schechner, Y.Y.: Harmony in motion. In: CVPR (2007)
5. Bazin, J.C., Malleson, C., Wang, O., Bradley, D., Beeler, T., Hilton, A., Sorkine-Hornung, A.: FaceDirector: continuous control of facial performance in video. In: ICCV (2015)
6. Berthouzoz, F., Li, W., Agrawala, M.: Tools for placing cuts and transitions in interview video. In: TOG (SIGGRAPH) (2012)
7. Brezeale, D., Cook, D.J.: Automatic video classification: a survey of the literature. IEEE Trans. Syst. Man Cybern. Part C Appl. Rev. **38**(3), 416–430 (2008)
8. Brito, M., Chavez, E., Quiroz, A., Yukich, J.: Connectivity of the mutual k-nearest-neighbor graph in clustering and outlier detection. Statistics & Probability Letters (1997)
9. Cao, C., Bradley, D., Zhou, K., Beeler, T.: Real-time high-fidelity facial performance capture. In: TOG (SIGGRAPH) (2015)
10. Cardle, M., Brooks, S., Bar-Joseph, Z., Robinson, P.: Sound-by-numbers: motion-driven sound synthesis. In: SIGGRAPH/Eurographics Symposium on Computer Animation (SCA) (2003)
11. Chadwick, J.N., James, D.L.: Animating fire with sound. In: TOG (SIGGRAPH) (2011)
12. Chen, H., Gallagher, A.C., Girod, B.: What's in a name? First names as facial attributes. In: CVPR (2013)
13. Chu, W., Chen, J., Wu, J.: Tiling slideshow: an audiovisual presentation method for consumer photos. In: IEEE MultiMedia (2007)
14. Crandall, D.J., Backstrom, L., Huttenlocher, D., Kleinberg, J.: Mapping the world's photos. In: International Conference on World Wide Web (2009)
15. Csurka, G., Bray, C., Dance, C., Fan, L.: Visual categorization with bags of keypoints. In: ECCV Workshop on Statistical Learning in Computer Vision (2004)
16. Dannenberg, R., Neuendorffer, T.: Sound synthesis from real-time video images. In: International Computer Music Conference (ICMC) (2003)
17. Davis, A., Rubinstein, M., Wadhwa, N., Mysore, G.J., Durand, F., Freeman, W.T.: The visual microphone: passive recovery of sound from video. In: TOG (SIGGRAPH) (2014)
18. Dieleman, S., Schrauwen, B.: Multiscale approaches to music audio feature learning. In: International Society for Music Information Retrieval Conference (ISMIR) (2013)
19. van den Doel, K., Kry, P.G., Pai, D.K.: FoleyAutomatic: physically-based sound effects for interactive simulation and animation. In: SIGGRAPH (2001)
20. Doersch, C., Singh, S., Gupta, A., Sivic, J., Efros, A.A.: What makes Paris look like Paris? In: TOG (SIGGRAPH) (2012)

21. Donahue, J., Jia, Y., Vinyals, O., Hoffman, J., Zhang, N., Tzeng, E., Darrell, T.: DeCAF: a deep convolutional activation feature for generic visual recognition. In: International Conference on Machine Learning (ICML) (2014)
22. Dunker, P., Popp, P., Cook, R.: Content-aware auto-soundtracks for personal photo music slideshows. In: ICME (2011)
23. Everingham, M., Eslami, S.M.A., Gool, L.V., Williams, C.K.I., Winn, J.M., Zisserman, A.: The PASCAL visual object classes challenge: a retrospective. IJCV **111**(1), 98–136 (2015)
24. Fried, O., Fiebrink, R.: Cross-modal sound mapping using deep learning. In: International Conference on New Interfaces for Musical Expression (NIME) (2013)
25. Galasso, F., Nagaraja, N.S., Cardenas, T.J., Brox, T., Schiele, B.: A unified video segmentation benchmark: annotation, metrics and analysis. In: ICCV (2013)
26. Godsill, S., Rayner, P., Cappé, O.: Digital audio restoration. In: Kahrs, M., Brandenburg, K. (eds.) Applications of Digital Signal Processing to Audio and Acoustics, vol. 437, pp. 133–194. Springer, New York (2002)
27. Izadinia, H., Saleemi, I., Shah, M.: Multimodal analysis for identification and segmentation of moving-sounding objects. IEEE Trans. Multimedia (2013)
28. Jia, Y., Shelhamer, E., Donahue, J., Karayev, S., Long, J., Girshick, R.B., Guadarrama, S., Darrell, T.: Caffe: convolutional architecture for fast feature embedding. In: ACM International Conference on Multimedia (2014)
29. Karpathy, A., Toderici, G.,Shetty., S., Leung, T., Sukthankar, R., Fei-Fei, L.: Large-scale video classification with convolutional neural networks. In: CVPR (2014)
30. Kidron, E., Schechner, Y.Y., Elad, M.: Pixels that sound. In: CVPR (2005)
31. Kläser, A., Marszałek, M., Schmid, C.: A spatio-temporal descriptor based on 3D-gradients. In: BMVC (2008)
32. Kuehne, H., Jhuang, H., Garrote, E., Poggio, T.A., Serre, T.: HMDB: a large video database for human motion recognition. In: ICCV (2011)
33. Laptev, I.: On space-time interest points. IJCV **64**(2), 107–123 (2005)
34. Lea, M.A., Thomas, R.D., Lamkin, N.A., Bell, A.: Who do you look like? Evidence of facial stereotypes for male names. Psychon. Bull. Rev. **14**(5), 901–907 (2007)
35. Lee, H., Pham, P.T., Largman, Y., Ng, A.Y.: Unsupervised feature learning for audio classification using convolutional deep belief networks. In: NIPS (2009)
36. Li, C., Shan, M.: Emotion-based impressionism slideshow with automatic music accompaniment. In: International Conference on Multimedia (2007)
37. Liao, Z., Yu, Y., Gong, B., Cheng, L.: AudioSynth: music-driven video montage. In: TOG (SIGGRAPH) (2015)
38. Lin, Y.-T., Tsai, T.-H., Hu, M.-C., Cheng, W.-H., Wu, J.-L.: Semantic based background music recommendation for home videos. In: Gurrin, C., Hopfgartner, F., Hurst, W., Johansen, H., Lee, H., O'Connor, N. (eds.) MMM 2014, Part II. LNCS, vol. 8326, pp. 283–290. Springer, Heidelberg (2014)
39. Logan, B.: Mel frequency cepstral coefficients for music modeling. In: International Symposium on Music Information Retrieval (2000)
40. Maier, M., Hein, M., von Luxburg, U.: Optimal construction of k-nearest-neighbor graphs for identifying noisy clusters. Theoretical Computer Science (2009)
41. Maier, M., Hein, M., von Luxburg, U.: Cluster identification in nearest-neighbor graphs. In: Hutter, M., Servedio, R.A., Takimoto, E. (eds.) ALT 2007. LNCS (LNAI), vol. 4754, pp. 196–210. Springer, Heidelberg (2007)

42. Matta, S., Kumar, D., Yu, X., Burry, M.: An approach for image sonification. In: International Symposium on Control, Communications and Signal Processing (2004)
43. Matthews, I., Cootes, T.F., Bangham, J.A., Cox, S.J., Harvey, R.: Extraction of visual features for lipreading. TPAMI (2002)
44. Meijer, P.: An experimental system for auditory image representations. IEEE Trans. Biomed. Eng. **39**(2), 112–121 (1992)
45. Mermelstein, P.: Distance measures for speech recognition: psychological and instrumental. In: Pattern Recognition and Artificial Intelligence (1976)
46. Miotto, R., Lanckriet, G.R.G.: A generative context model for semantic music annotation and retrieval. IEEE Trans. Audio, Speech Lang. Process. (2012)
47. Nayak, M., Srinivasan, S., Kankanhalli, M.: Music synthesis for home videos: an analogy based approach. In: IEEE Pacific Rim Conference on Multimedia (PCM) (2003)
48. Ngiam, J., Khosla, A., Kim, M., Nam, J., Lee, H., Ng, A.Y.: Multimodal deep learning. In: International Conference on Machine Learning (ICML) (2011)
49. Oliva, A., Torralba, A.: Modeling the shape of the scene: A holistic representation of the spatial envelope. IJCV (2001)
50. Owens, A., Isola, P., McDermott, J., Torralba, A., Adels, E.H., Freeman, W.T.: Visually indicated sounds. In: CVPR (2016)
51. Paulus, J., Müller, M., Klapuri, A.: Audio-based music structure analysis. In: International Conference on Music Information Retrieval (2010)
52. Perazzi, F., Krähenbühl, P., Pritch, Y., Hornung, A.: Saliency filters: Contrast based filtering for salient region detection. In: CVPR (2012)
53. Razavian, A.S., Azizpour, H., Sullivan, J., Carlsson, S.: CNN features off-the-shelf: an astounding baseline for recognition. In: CVPR Workshop (2014)
54. Ren, Z., Yeh, H., Lin, M.C.: Example-guided physically based modal sound synthesis. In: TOG (SIGGRAPH) (2013)
55. Rohrbach, A., Rohrbach, M., Tandon, N., Schiele, B.: A dataset for movie description. In: CVPR (2015)
56. Rubin, S., Berthouzoz, F., Mysore, G., Li, W., Agrawala, M.: UnderScore: musical underlays for audio stories. In: ACM UIST (2012)
57. Russakovsky, O., Deng, J., Su, H., Krause, J., Satheesh, S., Ma, S., Huang, Z., Karpathy, A., Khosla, A., Bernstein, M.S., Berg, A.C., Li, F.: ImageNet large scale visual recognition challenge. IJCV (2015)
58. Sermanet, P., Eigen, D., Zhang, X., Mathieu, M., Fergus, R., LeCun, Y.: OverFeat: integrated recognition, localization and detection using convolutional networks. In: International Conference on Learning Representations (2014)
59. Shi, J., Malik, J.: Normalized cuts and image segmentation. TPAMI **22**(8), 888–905 (2000)
60. Simon, I., Snavely, N., Seitz, S.M.: Scene summarization for online image collections. In: ICCV (2007)
61. Soomro, K., Zamir, A.R., Shah, M.: UCF101: a dataset of 101 human actions classes from videos in the wild. In: CRCV-TR-12-01 (2012)
62. Stupar, A., Michel, S.: Picasso - to sing, you must close your eyes and draw. In: International Conference on Research and Development in Information Retrieval (SIGIR) (2011)
63. Turnbull, D., Barrington, L., Torres, D.A., Lanckriet, G.R.G.: Semantic annotation and retrieval of music and sound effects. IEEE Trans. Audio Speech Lang. Process. (2008)

64. Wang, H., Schmid, C.: Action recognition with improved trajectories. In: ICCV (2013)
65. Wenner, S., Bazin, J.C., Sorkine-Hornung, A., Kim, C., Gross, M.: Scalable music: automatic music retargeting and synthesis. In: CGF (Eurographics) (2013)
66. Wu, X., Li, Z.: A study of image-based music composition. In: ICME (2008)
67. Zhao, G., Barnard, M., Pietikäinen, M.: Lipreading with local spatiotemporal descriptors. IEEE Trans. Multimedia (2009)
68. Zheng, C., James, D.L.: Harmonic fluids. In: TOG (SIGGRAPH) (2009)
69. Zheng, C., James, D.L.: Rigid-body fracture sound with precomputed soundbanks. In: TOG (SIGGRAPH) (2010)

Author Index

Printed in the United States
By Bookmasters